WILLIAM BARCLAY
By Juliet Pannett, P.S., F.R.S.A.
Royal Portraitist

WILLIAM BARCLAY
The Authorized Biography

By
CLIVE L. RAWLINS

WILLIAM B. EERDMANS PUBLISHING COMPANY
THE PATERNOSTER PRESS

First published 1984 by
William B. Eerdmans Publishing Company
255 Jefferson Ave. S.E., Grand Rapids, Mich. 49503
and
The Paternoster Press Ltd.
3 Mount Radford Crescent, Exeter, Devon, UK EX2 4JW

Library of Congress Cataloging in Publication Data:

Rawlins, Clive L., 1940—
    William Barclay, the authorized biography.

    Bibliography: p. 715
    Includes index.
    1. Barclay, William, 1907-1978. 2. New Testament
scholars—Scotland—Biography. 3. Church of Scotland—
Clergy—Biography. I. Title.
BS2351.B28R39 1984   285'.23 [B]   84-10194
ISBN 0-8028-3598-8

British Library Cataloguing in Publication Data

Rawlins, Clive
    William Barclay.
    1. Barclay, William, 1907-1978
    2. New Testament scholars—Scotland—Biography
    3. Church of Scotland—Biography
    I. Title
    285'.2'0924   BS2351.B28
    ISBN 0-85364-392-X

Contents

PART TWO: THE COMMENCEMENT

PART THREE: THE FULFILLMENT

CONTENTS

CONTENTS

Preface

THERE are two opposing views of biography. On the one hand there is the view of MacCarthy that a biographer is "an artist on oath"; on the other hand, expressed by Sigmund Freud no less, there is the view that "the intending biographer pledges himself to tell lies, to hush things up, to be hypocritical, to paint things in glowing colours, to even conceal his ability to understand; because biographical truth is unattainable, and were one to attain it, one could not make use of it."[1] There is more truth in this latter statement than many biographers would care to admit, but—while disclaiming any artistic merit—the present writer has sought to fulfill the high demands of an oath conscientiously undertaken.

William Barclay himself laid down the approach any would-be biographer of him should take. Declaring himself to one of his former students to "abominate chatty biographies of alleged public people" (a deliberate stroke against some well-meaning aspirants, as well as a veiled demand, late in life, for the privacy he so much needed), he maintained that the only one he wished published— emphatically postmortem—was one that painted him "warts an' all."[2] To another he expressed his "deep distaste . . . for exalting the person."[3] He has thereby given form and content to the obligation; the discipline of a lifetime is not to be enfeebled by posthumous vainglory. With thousands of people the world over, I confess to a deep admiration for this great Scot, and own with gratitude his influence in many things. But I have sought to depict him with his admonitions in mind, listening to his critics and admirers alike, questioning the image some of his devotees have erected in his honor, scrutinizing his voluminous writings and the records left of him throughout Scotland and far beyond. I have not sought to evaluate his influence—it is still too early for that—but I have sought to indicate where that influence was most felt and how it was shaped by him, despite the many temptations and allurements to do otherwise. In a very real sense he was his own man; but the freedom to be that man came from his being, first and foremost, Christ's man.

In order to fulfill this obligation, at the commencement of my work I placed advertisements in many journals, secular and religious, and the BBC twice broadcast an interview with me that sought to elicit information relevant to the task. I am grateful to the editors for their help in this. Ronnie Barclay, William's son, placed at my disposal such records as remained following the wholesale clearance of his father's study at the time of his death, as well as his own mementos. Among these were two address books and over six hundred letters of sympathy to Mrs. Barclay, Ronnie's late mother; with such a start we were soon launched in the wake of an amazing career and personality. Further, Ronnie gave generously of his time and personal recollections, as did his sister, Jane Wright. To them both I express my gratitude. The commission to write this biography came through the Trustees of the Barclay Estate, of whom Ronnie is one. They are not responsible for the views expressed in this volume; it is the "authorized" life only in the sense that they authorized me to write it and put at my disposal such information as they had.

"The biography of Henry Drummond cannot be a chronicle, it must be a suggestion," wrote John Watson (Ian MacLaren) of one whose influence on William Barclay was incalculable, if indirect. And such we may say of the subject of this book. Nevertheless, sufficient data have been compiled by the present writer for a fairly full suggestion, and even some delineation; after all, a suggestion cannot have warts. If at times this account reads in some parts like a chronicle, that is simply because Willie himself took the real world and its realities more seriously (and consequently the immaterial world less seriously) than did his spiritual forebear of Glasgow. He believed in deep involvement, he was deeply involved, and he regretted his inability to become more involved still. Nevertheless, the old concept of this world being a preparation for the next was never far from his mind. Hence the extraordinary spiritual power of his writings, and the tensions they sometimes manifested. One has to disagree with James Lockhart, who, in writing of Archbishop Lang, said that what makes a life worth reading is "not detail, but revelation of the man's mind, purpose and character"[4]—for the mind, purpose, and character are primarily expressed—even with authors—in the daily detail of life. (Scott's biographer, one may recall, did not spare the detail in his own brilliant portrayal of his father-in-law.) Perhaps the truth of this is more relevant to one writing about a great ecclesiastic like Lang; it is certainly much less true of an avowed nonecclesiastic like Willie, who believed that the Bible should be expounded hand-in-hand with everyday life—with a daily (and serious) newspaper, if not a sword, in hand, Cromwellian style.[5] What mattered to William Barclay was not "what the Bible says" but "what it means for us today"; to understand him outside that framework is seriously to risk misunderstanding him altogether. So much for the mind, and to a large extent, the purpose. As to the character, that is best seen in the pitch and toss of daily life—of which he wrote most carefully, seeking to raise our attitude toward it almost to the level of credal affirmation: "I believe in daily life"! His character is best seen thereby, as he faces joy and sorrow, work and leisure, pain and pleasure, alongside his fellow men and women. He is never more Christian than in the presence of an overwrought housewife who drops coal down her recently vacuumed carpeted stairs in bold exclamation in front of him, or in offering the hand of friendship to a pestilential opponent. If he could talk movingly of heavenly realities, it was because he lived successfully with the earthly ones first. The "detail" is therefore of paramount importance, for it supplies the matrix and the framework out of which arose his telling contribution to twentieth-century Christianity.

I have therefore sought to describe the life and its setting in some detail, as a means of unveiling the mind, the purpose, and the character in their several aspects, with their varying moods and emphases. I have not sought, as some exhorted me to do, to hush things up. Still less have I sought to paint in glowing colors his story, though it is one that is naturally highly colorful, for he was one who loved the springtime of life and lived it fully and enthusiastically. If glow there be, it is his own, and I hope that my account has not diffused it. "Biographical truth" is in the last degree unattainable. Even in the man who endeavors to know himself—and William Barclay was such a man, despite his unconcern over some personal elements—biographical truth is not fully attainable, or even desirable. For what is truth? Is it the concrete facts, however recorded, or the results of those facts, or the intention behind the selection and recording of those facts, or something else? As Simone de Beauvoir observed (well seen, we might stress) in her vast autobiography, "truth is not expressed in any one of its pages but only in their totality."[6] So it is here, with this man of startling opposites.

However we view this—and it is another reason for the detail—no one can deny that William Barclay, despite his apparent simplicity, was a man of immense complexity, living at several levels at once, to some extent suffering from both the undertow of the previous generation and the pull-through of the next, often addressing himself to more than one level at any one time. For example, some of his theological attitudes, and still more his theological statements, mirror not only his immediate concern (academic *and* pastoral) but that which lay behind it in earlier battles with his hugely influential father and with his own conscience as a devotee of the authority of the Word of God. And we must not minimize this aspect. Too many say Barclay was no theologian. He himself said it in self-deprecation far too often. They fail to perceive that he, equally often, in a basic and certain sense, was the best sort of theologian: a theologian of daily life, of the high street, of the home, and of the factory. Nothing epitomizes his attitude better than his story of the man who noticed in a great cathedral window that "Glory to God in the highest" had dropped a letter to read "Glory to God in the high st." Quite so! That was the reality—whatever the experts in conservation and fabric might say. So the question of what the Bible means for us today, when handled by him, is often suffused with earlier questions, answers, and presumptions. The older he got, the more this showed; medical factors exacerbated it. Thus this man of charming if disconcerting opposites allowed to coexist within himself mutually exclusive positions, whereby he sought to safeguard the positive values the extremes encompassed. Like Drummond before him, he believed in "the indivisibility of truth,"[7] that "all truth is God's truth," that truth is "multi-shaped"

xi

and "multi-faceted." He detested "the arrogance of spirit" that pretends to complete knowledge or denies hard-won experience. To him truth was "not static, but dynamic,"[8] and therefore must always be subject to change, to reappraisal. But such was his composure, and such his invincible faith, that he could happily live with opposites, denials, and even contradictions—and war against each side from time to time, as it were Socratically.[9] Engaged himself in a perpetual search for truth, delighting in its kaleidoscopic impressions according to need and situation, he zestfully recommended to others the bold adventure, disconcerting some, alienating others, but winning not a few to a rounder, more complete, more human, more solidly spiritual outlook and lifestyle. For this reason I have tried to keep this account of his life closely geared to his own writings and to those of his friends and enemies, who were in his case not necessarily distinct groups, for he had an extraordinary ability to arouse both admiration and dismay in his hearers and readers.

Following my advertisements of November 1979, an immense correspondence developed, of over five thousand pieces, including the recovery of some fifteen hundred letters from Professor Barclay himself. Not least of this collection (which is to be housed in a special archive kindly made available at the National Library of Scotland, Edinburgh) are the letters to Mrs. Barclay, Ronnie, and Jane from admiring friends saddened by his death. They show the deep affection in which he was held, and above all, his great industry and enormous influence across the entire range of Christian—and even non-Christian—experience, in all denominations throughout the world. (I would be glad to receive any further letters of Professor Barclay that my readers may have, so that they, too, might be deposited in the archive.) Two depositions deserve special mention: twenty-two files of his correspondence were discovered by his former colleague Alistair McIntyre in an understairs cupboard at Trinity College, and over sixty hours of teaching material tape-recorded in the lecture room by Oscar Lutz of Houston in the academic year 1972/73. These, and the precious memorabilia of family, friends, former students, and readers, have been generously made available to me by their owners, keen to perpetuate the memory and work of one of the greatest communicators of the gospel this century. To them all, and not least to those who made themselves available for interview and further correspondence, I express my sincere thanks. I regret that it is not possible to list their names individually; to have done so would have increased unpardonably the size of this already oversize book. But certain helpers should be mentioned: to the librarians of Glasgow University; New College Library, Edinburgh; and Stirling University, I record my thanks for their unstinting helpfulness, as I do to their colleagues in the municipal libraries of Wick, Inverness, Manchester, Motherwell, Renfrew, and Haddington, and to those at the Mitchell Library, Glasgow. Miss Catriona Kidd kindly supplied a complete collection of church magazines for Barclay's thirteen years at Renfrew, and Miss Joy Standen (Editor of the International Bible Reading Association) provided original copies of his early work for the Association which commenced his popular writing career; Mrs. Dingwall, widow of the former General Secretary of the Scottish Sunday School Union, made available back issues of *The Scottish Sunday School Teacher* and the history and minutes of the SSSU which preceded it; the Director of the Church of Scotland's Press and Publicity Department, Bruce Cannon, kindly loaned me his files; Alistair Morton, General Secretary of the Church of Scotland's Department of Education, also offered access to his minutes and records; and Tim Honeyman, Secretary of the Department of Communication, consented to some quotations from his numerous writings in their copyright. No biography of William Barclay could be envisaged without reference to three religious journals whose influence goes well beyond Scotland: *The British Weekly, The Expository Times,* and *Life and Work,* the back issues of which have been a very great help both in reflecting the period covered by this book and in recording some of its subject's literary developments. To Denis Duncan, Dr. C. L. Mitton, and Bob Kernohan, and to their respective proprietors, I record my gratitude. Mr. Arthur Montford and the Head of Administration of Radio Clyde, Norman L. Quirk, kindly gave permission for excerpts from an interview broadcast at the time of Barclay's retirement (shortly to be made available *in toto* to the public); and the BBC generously consented to the use of extracts from another interview, with Stanley Pritchard, broadcast no fewer than three times in 1960. To these both I offer my thanks. And above all I have to thank Messrs. A. R. Mowbray & Co., Ltd., for their kindness in allowing me complete access to their files and for their generosity in permitting numerous citations from the "autobiography" of William Barclay, *Testament of Faith.*

"The child is father to the man" is an expression of indubitable significance for the serious biographer. Carlyle spoke to the point as well when he stated that "the beginning always remains the most notable moment"; I am sure that he was correct, for at the beginning of a life, a venture, lies the full potential and the creative thrust, not yet marred by the passage of time or the assaults of others. Accordingly, I owe a deep debt of gratitude to three local newspapers connected with the Barclay story that captured the atmosphere and the events of the beginnings in Professor Barclay's life, and that made available to me their files: *The John O'Groats Journal, The Motherwell Times,* and *The Renfrew Press.* The latter two added kindness to generosity via J. L. M. Cotter (Managing Director) and Robin Stirling (Editor) of the former, and Henry McNab (Managing Director) of the latter, providing me with comfortable office accommodations for the several weeks of research I spent on their premises. I must also record my thanks to Miss Sheila Archibald, Curator of the West Highland Museum at Fort William; to Alistair Penfold, Curator of the Telford Collection of records at Ironbridge, who assisted in untangling some of the aspects of the developments at the western end of the Caledonian Canal and the fortunes of its builders at Corpach Moss; and to Samuel S. Troy, Director and Editor of *The Coleraine Chronicle,* whose hospitality enabled me to unravel the mystery surrounding Barbara Barclay's tragic death—an event of great consequence for her devastated father.

Some final expressions of gratitude must close this Preface: to the Scottish Arts Council, whose grant covered a tithe of my research and secretarial expenses;

to Mrs. Fiona Lonie who undertook the typing and retyping of my manuscript; and to Miss Juliette Buss who aided Mrs. Lonie from time to time. Professor F. F. Bruce, whose kindness and expertise over many years I am glad to own, read and criticized my first draft, warning me of a number of errors and providing from his own rich store several anecdotes; he must not be held responsible for the consequent work, or the views I state in unfolding the life of his fellow Scot "across the border." To Bill Eerdmans, my publisher, and his highly efficient staff (who are responsible for the Americanization of my manuscript); to my minister, Laurence Twaddle, who kindly helped with the proofreading; to my parents, Mary and Leonard Rawlins, who merit the tribute Willie paid to his own parents in dedicating the first volume of the series that forged his worldwide reputation, I offer my thanks as well. And finally, to my wife, Veronica, and my sons, Stephen and Philip, whose sacrifice and patience over three long years made this book possible, I record my special gratitude.

CLIVE L. RAWLINS
Sycamore Lodge
Belhaven, East Lothian
7 December 1982

List of Illustrations

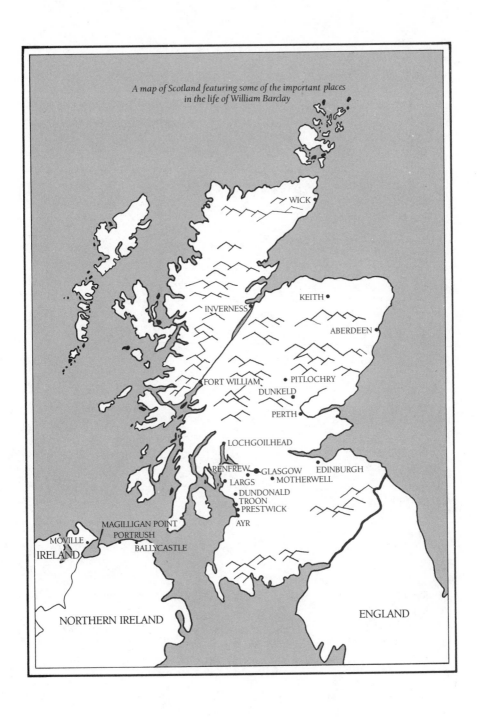

A map of Scotland featuring some of the important places
in the life of William Barclay

PART ONE

The Preparation

CHAPTER ONE

The Background: A Highland Son

A Period of Restless Change

WILLIAM Barclay was born on 5 December 1907, the only child of William Dugald Barclay and Barbara Linton (née McLeish), both then in middle age. They lived at Wick, in Caithness-shire, but were born in Fort William and looked on that one-time garrison town as their true home. To it they regularly returned, and in its peaceful environs they were eventually laid to rest. Willie, however, as their son preferred to be called by his friends, never knew it except for holiday visits. His stay in the far north was of short duration, for they moved south before he was five years old. The industrialized southwest thus became the center from which this talented and energetic child came to maturation, and to which he remained faithful throughout his life.

He was born in an age of transition and growing tension. These tensions were threefold. First, in society generally change was in the air. The Victorian period had closed but four years prior to his birth and the Edwardian, destined to be so short and yet so momentous, had scarcely begun. The new technologies were forcing their attentions on the world and slowly transforming it. Political change was also apparent, and the outcome of the South African War had registered an early warning about the future of the Empire. This had had its effects socially in the birth struggles of socialism and developing sociologies and other movements such as that of the suffragettes, and in the growth of trade union power and efficiency.

Second, in the church there was also marked unrest. The general changes affecting society were impinging dramatically on it, urging greater social involvement and a reconsideration of its attitudes and ancient formulas. In Scotland this was particularly so, for in the aftermath of the union of 1900 between the Free Church and the United Presbyterian Church (which produced the United Free Church of Scotland, to which the Barclays belonged), the nonparticipating party that continued to operate under the name of the Free Church won a successful action in the courts that gave them the property and funds of the former body. A bitter and traumatic struggle developed that rent Scottish Presbyterianism for several years, souring relationships and nullifying much of the work done over the preceding few decades.

The third type of tension was personal to the Barclay family; it also strongly affected the environment into which Willie was born and had a very considerable effect on the development of his parents' characters and attitudes. There had been strong opposition to his parents' marriage from Willie's maternal grandfather, Daniel McLeish. This delayed their plans by several years and added sorrow and that resilience which is born of it to their lives, characteristics that were destined to be marked features of their son. Just why there was such opposition we are not told in detail. In his autobiography Willie gives a strong hint that it was his grandfather's class consciousness that caused the friction.[1] Undoubtedly that formed a part of the problem—the difference between the daughter of the local solicitor–cum–civic dignitary and that of the local joiner's son—but that was not all. There was something about WDB (as we shall call Willie's father) that Daniel McLeish disliked and even resented, and it was this that the young couple had to cope with and conquer.

Daniel McLeish and Family

Barbara's father had arrived in Fort William in the early 1860s, a young man sent (as was the custom in those days) by his solicitor's office in Edinburgh to oversee their interests in the north, and to effect the expansion of the business there. He was neither a graduate nor a qualified lawyer, though he described himself as "writer" on his marriage certificate. There is no trace of him on the records of the Writers to the Signet in Edinburgh; the recognition of writers was then more casual. The son of a Perthshire farmer, he was born at Dunkeld, a cradle of Scots Christianity (but perhaps now more recognizable as the holiday home of Beatrix Potter, who gave the world Peter Rabbit) that lies fifteen miles to the northwest of the city of Perth. He had been indentured as a solicitor's clerk in Edinburgh. Certainly that was the sort of occupation to which middle-class parents like his own aspired for their sons. He made good progress and soon earned the respect and trust of his employers. In his mid twenties he was sent to Fort William, primarily to act in their name as factor for the estates of Mrs. Cameron Campbell of Monzie, recently widowed. It was a good move for him in every way. Professionally, it could not have been better, for he now had the entrée into the cream of society, overseeing their commercial interests. A man of some distinction, both mentally and physically, he had from an early age the bearing of the lieutenant colonel he later became—he held himself upright even when relaxing. Heavily bearded after the manner of those days, he had as well a voice that was decisive and commanding, reflecting the clear mind of the commander.

His application was rewarded with the increasing responsibilities that devolved upon him not only for Mrs. Campbell's estate, but more widely in the community. In the census returns of 1871 we find him (at age thirty-six) described as the "Managing Law Clerk" in his firm's local office and the "Depute Clerk of the Peace" for the town. He had been appointed Senior Magistrate following the enactment of the General Police (Scotland) Act of 1862; the police commission appointed under this Act comprised nine members, of which Daniel was the head. Moreover, he was housed in the very fashionable Parade Cottage, a large residence of some eight rooms just off the old parade square that stood above the recently demolished fort. His neighbors at Parade House were the town doctor, Duncan McIntyre, his assistant and household. This house, which was destined to be the McLeishes' one day, boasted some prestige historically: it was the former residence of the governor, a position that lapsed in 1854, despite which fact it still retained some of the former dignity and deference due it. By mid century the fort was doomed to make way for the railway company, then seeking to establish itself throughout the area and thus open up the Inverness–Fort William route, which did not materialize beyond Fort William itself. Norman McLeod sardonically speaks of the governor commanding "all the dignity of a man who—with a dozen rusty guns and half as many soldiers—was supposed to guard the great southern land against the outbreaks and incursions of the wild Highland clans now long dead."[2] That, of course, is the remark of one who resented the intrusion of the southerners and regretted the lost cause of the Stuarts:

> No more we'll see such deeds again;
> Deserted is the Highland glen,
> Who fought and died for Charlie.

McLeish, who could trace his Highland ancestry back far beyond that of the Barclays, was justly proud of this heritage and background, and sought to uphold the traditions amid the change and movement of the times.[3] Fluent in Gaelic (unlike WDB), he played no small part in preserving the traditions of his people, and even gathered some of the folklore into written form. He would have seconded Osgood MacKenzie's comment that "life for me . . . would not have been worth living without Gaelic."[4] It was not just the language but the historical overtones, the culture, and the spirituality of which it is the proper expression that he revered. The School of Scottish Studies now preserves four of McLeish's folktales in their archives. They were given to the School by Willie's cousin I. M. Mackintosh of Troon and are held in the Tale Archive. I list them with their classifications, as follows:

1. Lochiel's Fairies (Supernatural)
2. Gormshuil, the Witch of Moy (Historical Tradition)
3. Ticonderoga, the ghost of Inverawe (-do-)
4. Mary of Callart (-do-)

Another example of this interest lies in a blackthorn stick he acquired that had been carried into battle in the Rising of 1745 by Macdonald of Kinlochmoidart at the Raising of the Standard for Prince Charles at Glenfinnan; it was one of the

A statue of Sir Donald Cameron of Lochiel in Fort William. Behind and to the right stands Parade Cottage (as marked). The photo on the right is a close-up of the Blackthorn Stick used in the uprising of 1745, seen resting against the base of the statue.

few artifacts to have survived the deliberate destruction of all pertaining to that lost cause. In 1926 the stick was passed on to the West Highland Museum via McLeish's sister Isabella, who in making the deposition gave her address as Bank House, Motherwell—the second home of the Barclays. We need not doubt that the recommendation to place it on formal display came from WDB himself, who was a very enthusiastic Gaelophile and presumably undertook the necessary paperwork for his wife's aged and infirm aunt (she died in their care in 1932, and WDB ensured that her remains were laid to rest in the family plot, looking appropriately westward toward Glenfinnan).

Daniel married in July 1862 "according to the Free Church form." His bride was the daughter of James Linton of Coruannan, a farm adjoining the Cameron Campbell estates at Onich. Like Daniel, Linton was an immigrant to the area, hailing from Broughton in Peebles-shire; but, unlike him, he was a Lowlander. Mr. I. Mackintosh, a cousin of Willie, informs me that the family originally worked the very farm where the Black Dwarf of Sir Walter Scott lived. Doubtless from this and similar associations Willie's own love of literature originated.

We need have no doubts that both Linton and McLeish were delighted at the wild and sublime countryside to which they had lately come; they gladly made their home there, amid "scenery unequalled for picturesque beauty in any part of the Highlands."[5] McLeish may well have controverted Joseph Mitchell's description in the light of his native Perthshire countryside (Dunkeld is, after all,

6

"the scenic jewel of Perthshire"), but it is very beautiful and he clearly reveled in it. From Loch Leven the land rises into a rocky hillside dotted with pines and mountain ash and elms, interspersed with the cottages, once whitewashed, with their patches of garden decorous with fern and flower. In the summer boats can be seen plying across the loch, and the grandeur of the surrounding mountains adds depth and awe. It is an ideal place for romance to flourish, and it was a happy couple that committed themselves to each other that year.

Daniel found additional security in marrying into this now well-established family, and with his wife could look forward to his success and growing eminence in the area. Alas, their mutual joys were to be short-lived, for having provided him with a son and three daughters, she died in 1870. He had used his good offices to acquire a superb site for his parents-in-law's grave on the second highest knoll in the Fort William cemetery overlooking Loch Linnhe, a little way from Glen Nevis. The Black Watch had been given the most prominent point, but his father-in-law's stele commanded the view from the north. Alongside it the forlorn widower placed the earthly remains of his wife, Jane Scott Linton. Fortunately for Daniel, his sister-in-law Barbara Linton temporarily, and then his own sister Isabella permanently, were able to step into the breach and care for the family amidst the busy father's activities. It was a splendid sacrifice for "Bella" to make, involving as it did the breaking of her own engagement and henceforth a life of spinsterhood in the cause of her brother, nieces, and nephew. From now on, Aunt Bella would be the mother figure in the family; contact between her and "the three graces," as McLeish's daughters were called, remained strong and affectionate till the end of her life. So it was that James William (age six), Jane Scott (five), Margaret Ellen (three), and Barbara Linton (two) were put in the safekeeping of their maiden aunt of twenty-five years of age. There was also a general domestic, Margaret Hogarth of Aberfoyle in Perthshire, who looked after the more menial aspects of their lives.

Thus the family continued for some years, eventually moving from Parade Cottage to Bank House, High Street, Fort William, when Daniel was made agent for the Bank of Scotland. This did not terminate his other business activities, however; bank agents frequently—and at their own risk—undertook the affairs of a bank almost as a subsidiary branch of it. In point of fact, the Bank of Scotland has no trace of McLeish on its staff registers, though there is ample proof of his work for it in this capacity from other quarters. His senior accountant will have been in charge of the day-to-day duties, under whom will have been the tellers and clerks. By this time McLeish had become a person of some authority and had extended his services to suit his clients' requirements; chief among these were those of Sir Donald Cameron of Lochiel.

By 1881, the McLeish household had enlarged, and comprised Daniel, its head; his sister Isabella, housekeeper; the four McLeish children (ages seventeen, sixteen, fourteen, and thirteen respectively), all at school; Janet P. Mellie, governess; Hannah Cameron, housemaid; and Isabella McKenzie, cook; eight in all.[6] He had made it to the top and now enjoyed its fruits fully. Gaelic literature and lore apart, McLeish's hobby was collecting antique watches and militaria, which he proudly showed in a special glass case.

Miss Mellie, the governess, had particular responsibilities, being in charge of the children's education. At first this was done privately at Fort William, but then they were transferred to a school in Edinburgh (possibly the famous Queen Street School, whence Miss Mellie had come), as the custom of the times dictated for the children of the wealthy. They were all well-educated, receiving in addition to the elementary subjects instruction in music, painting, and deportment. Mr. I. M. Mackintosh adds that his mother, Barbara's sister "Jean" (Jane Scott) also became proficient at wood carving. We can see from Willie's own upbringing that music and literature featured very highly in the house, from which Daniel's passion for Gaelic literature and folklore must not be omitted.

The happiness of the family was soon to be blighted again, for his only son, James William, was lost in his mid thirties, unmarried, in November 1894. He was exactly the same age as WDB, both being born in 1864. The tone of the household may be judged from the nickname given to the three sisters—"the three graces"—a treasured asset to their father, who continued to make his way upward in the life and influence of the community and beyond it. It was in fact a highly religious family: Daniel was a Session Clerk (Church Secretary) to the local Free Church, and the family, including the cook and maids, always knelt in prayer before meals.

The sisters separated in time. Jean became housekeeper to her uncle, Dr. Andrew Linton of Bishopbriggs, where she met and married Dr. H. J. Mackintosh. Margaret became a nurse in the army, caught up in the enthusiasm for such work that Florence Nightingale generated in her tempestuous campaigns for nursing standards and dedication. She served in the Boer War, and was actually at Kimberley when it was relieved by Lord Roberts—"Bobs" in her terminology.[7] She was befriended by Miss Nightingale, and certainly shared "the mystical devotion" to the British Army that her mentor manifested.[8] This she learned from her father. She was one of the many who visited "the lady of the lamp" at home in her final years and, like Cecil Woodham Smith, was greatly impressed with its "whiteness, order and light."[9] Those impressions were doubtless recounted to her sister Barbara, along with her many and daring exploits, and were not to fall on deaf ears. They were reproduced not only in the somewhat similar work her sister was shortly to do among the fisher-girls of Wick and then at Motherwell, but chiefly in the deep compassion and humanity she passed on to her only son, a compassion that fed all his work and attitudes and helped to make him the fine pastor he became.

As the youngest daughter, Barbara seems naturally to have spent much more time at home than her sisters. It will have been a very busy life socially. Her father was now not only the senior banker in town, factor of several large estates, and a one-time Sheriff Substitute, but was also involved in the affairs of the town at a semipolitical level. To all of this he added close commitment to the affairs of the Free Church and subsequently those of the United Free Church. His pride in

8

the Highlands took another form that was also conspicuous. It was the custom of those days for junior bank employees to join one or another of the "volunteer" regiments which then proliferated throughout Scotland. McLeish, brought up on the exploits of the Cameronians (albeit a Lowland regiment opposed to the Highland soldiering of James II), enrolled and pursued his involvement with the Inverness-shire Highlanders with such energy that he was eventually appointed Colonel of the Regiment, whereupon he could on parade days be found attired in the full splendor of those blood-stirring uniforms, with their large cairngorm brooches, dirks, and all the rest. (His uniform was eventually passed on to his son-in-law, C. M. Hipwood, now resident in America.)

His daughter Barbara, "tall, fair, blue-eyed, gracious, beautiful, every inch an aristocrat," to use her son's glowing description of her,[10] could only accentuate the excellence of his appearance, and it is not unexpected that she turned the heart, and perhaps temporarily the head, of WDB. Daniel McLeish was not amused.

The Barclays

No details have been preserved as to when WDB and Barbara first met. Most probably it took place at the Free Church of which they were both members and

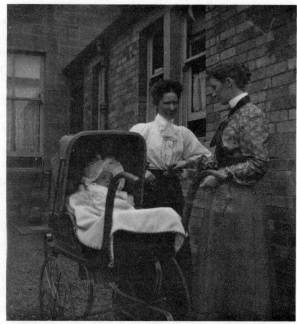

The McLeish women: on the left, Isabella McLeish, Willie's great-aunt, circa 1910; on the right, his mother, Barbara, with her sister Jean and the infant I. M. Mackintosh

which provided them with the most likely opportunity to get to know each other: young people together in the cause of Christ. But her father's bank will also have given another opportunity for them to do so, putting WDB and Daniel McLeish to some embarrassment: it was a classic case of the junior employee falling in love with the boss's daughter.

When Willie refers to his father as "the son of the village joiner,"[11] he is being somewhat unjust. Samuel Barclay (great-grandfather of Willie) was a tailor according to the census returns for 1841, by all accounts very successful and accustomed to living well. His origins in Scotland lay in Lochgoilhead, where the family resided in the prestigious Dramsynnie House, which stands at the head of the loch in a very commanding position.

The background of the family is somewhat obscure, but so far as it is traceable, it is as follows: Willie's great-grandfather was born in Manchester in 1781. He moved north (against the population flow) for reasons no longer apparent, but perhaps connected with the fact that many English merchants in the early nineteenth century came by sea to Fort William to buy and sell there. Samuel Barclay will have been interested in the sales of wool and cloths for which the market at Fort William had become famous. Perhaps a local laird, knowing of his craftsmanship, secured his services for personal reasons, or perhaps it was simply the beauty of Loch Goil and its surrounding countryside that won his heart. There he met and married his wife, Jean, and there the family took root and grew. Two children survived: William, born in 1823, and Joseph, who was born seven years later. That the Dramsynnie House was too large for them is obvious, for there were two other families who shared the building with them: Neil and Agnes Brodie, agricultural laborers, and their three children; and Donald and Lilian Campbell and their household of eight (including domestics).

The Barclay boys were educated at one of the local schools (there were no fewer than eight of them in 1841, for a population of 1,018), and given that basic but highly reputed schooling that is much admired throughout the world—of reading, writing, and "reckoning" (arithmetic), along with a sound drumming in the Shorter Catechism (then the backbone of religious education). They seem to have taken well to it, and Samuel seems to have established himself well in both the area and in Highland Presbyterianism, for its strong evangelical/Calvinist form became the family's way of life.

The family attended the small church dedicated to "the three holy brethren"—though which three brothers these were remains something of a mystery. There are two contenders for the privilege. First there are the three sons of Nissen, who formed part of the early Drummond *Calendar of Saints* and whose festival falls on the Ides of March—perhaps appropriately, for the festival has now lapsed, and there remains little to distinguish them in the Catholic calendar. A second possibility—the less likely of the two—is that the three brethren were the three men of the book of Daniel, Ananias, Azarias, and Misael (more popularly, Shadrach, Meshach, and Abednego). They were not brothers, except in the loose ethnic sense, and there is no obvious connection with Lochgoilhead. The dedication reflects the early, Catholic origins of the church, which became

Presbyterian at the time of the Reformation, but as was common in so many other parts of the Highlands, held clandestinely onto its Roman Catholicism.[12] This will have meant little to the parvenu family now making its way and fortunes in Argyllshire whose own roots lay in the county of Lancashire and, centuries before that, of Gloucestershire. (It was from the Berkeley family of Berkeley in Gloucestershire that they were descended, John son of Roger de Berchelai being their progenitor.)

It is William, Samuel's son, who provides us with the most early information as to the Barclays' settlement in Scotland. Following his schooling he was made an apprentice joiner, though with whom we do not know. It may have been locally, but it is more likely that he was sent to Glasgow. (There was a very regular boat service between Glasgow and Lochgoilhead that Mitchell graphically describes.) It seems that some family connection remained in Glasgow for many years, and to the "capital" of the southwest the family was eventually to return, as we shall see.

For the Free Church 1847 was a sad year, as it mourned the death of its great leader Thomas Chalmers. It was a sad time all round, in fact. The famine created by the blight of the potato crop was felt throughout Great Britain, but it was particularly sore in Ireland and on the west coast of Scotland. It was also the time of the railway crash, which affected thousands of large and small speculators, ruining many. At the climax of railway investment enthusiasm there were no fewer than 620 registered companies, many of them four times oversubscribed, enjoying "a frenzy of speculation." The wealthy and the not-so-wealthy alike lost their capital, and the workers lost their means of employment. Europe generally, to quote Keir Hardie, was "a seething mass of revolutionary enthusiasm."[13]

In that year Willie's grandfather William Barclay married Sarah MacVicar in Glasgow. Five children were born of their union, of whom the youngest, William Dugald Barclay, was to be the father of Willie. (There was a *Dugald* MacVicar at Fort William in the 1861 census returns who was probably Sarah's father, but we have no precise information on this; there is certainly no other "Dugald" connection in the Barclay family, and it was in any case normal to name the first son after both fathers.) The family soon returned to the north, though to Fort William rather than Lochgoilhead. Soon after this, Samuel Barclay passed on, leaving his widow Jean in the safekeeping of their son Joseph, then age thirty-two, unmarried, and now living in a small cottage at Glashait. By 1871 Jean too had passed on, and Joseph (whose career was very checkered, passing from joinery to agricultural labor) married and disappeared from the records.

The family left two memorials in Lochgoilhead. The first, which remained for many years and gave great service to the community, was "Barclay's Jetty," to which Willie occasionally referred. Curiously, Willie knew nothing of this edifice until late in his life when he visited the village along with his much-loved Trinity College Choir. It was then, and much to his surprise, that Mr. and Mrs. Mac-Dougall apprised him of his family connections in the area and pointed out to him the just-visible "jetty" in the center of the lake. It shows that his grandfather not only had joinery abilities but also those of a stonemason, for the structure was of an immense size, L-shaped, running out from the west side of the loch into its center to a sufficient depth of water to allow oceangoing ships transporting fish and coal to moor alongside it. Further, it needed to stand the strains of tidal movements, some of which were very strong during the winter months. At this very structure Joseph Mitchell the road builder and Highland engineer will have arrived on his diaried journey.[14] It adds another string to his grandfather Barclay's professional bow, which must have received recognition at a high level, the whole community being dependent on the loch as the sole inlet for its supplies.

It may well have been this expertise that produced the reason for this consequent move to Fort William, for there was a continuing need for engineers and craftsmen of his sort, not merely for the general needs of the much larger community (twenty times larger than that of Lochgoilhead then), but for the recently reopened Caledonian Canal. First declared open in 1822, the Canal had been a constant headache to its maintenance engineers due both to the immense amount of water it had to channel and to the simple fact that ships' captains seemed not to understand the need for a careful approach to the loch-gates and walls at the loch's western end (dubbed "Neptune's Staircase"), which raised the level of water by over twenty meters through nine locks. Following the reopening of the Canal (closed for major repairs from 1843 to 1847), a timber jetty was built in 1848 on the northwest wing wall of the sea loch (on the Corpach side), and a ferry pier was built at Bona. From now on permanent maintenance was the rule, and this was exactly the sort of work William Barclay, Sr., was expert in.

The second memorial left at Lochgoilhead is the Barclay tombstone, which lies close to the north wall of the parish church there, its prominence reflecting the position the family earned during its time there. It is essentially the record of a migratory family, not one of the great clan-linked groups of traditional Scottish life. It sadly records the little family's tale:

1854
Sacred
to the memory
of
SAMUEL BARCLAY
who died on the 2nd Feby. 1852
aged 77 years. And of his son
Samuel, who died, on the 10th May
1848, aged 22 yrs. And of Dund.
who died, on the 28th January 1857,
aged 13 years, And of Betsy,
who died, on the 8th September, 1818, aged
3 yrs. And of Catherine, who
died, on 14th May 1818, aged 19 months.

This stone is placed here by
his only surviving sons, William
and Joseph, as a tribute
of dutiful affection.

The churchyard of the Three Holy Brethren, Lochgoilhead. The Barclay grave is marked by the small headstone second from the right.

We find the first mention of the Barclays at Fort William in the census returns for 1861, by which time William Barclay, Sr. (age thirty-nine), is already established with Sarah (age thirty-six) at 9 Low Street. With them are their three daughters, Catherine (eleven), Jane (nine), and Mary (one), and their son Samuel (five). They also have a servant-girl by the name of Catherine Cameron (age seventeen). Grandfather Barclay is now described as a carpenter. One of the features of his professional life is the vacillation between "carpenter"—that is, general artificer of wood and at times of stone—and "joiner," which was a more refined and domestic application of his skills. Undoubtedly the scarcity of work was its cause; the completion of major public works was having grievous effects on family life in the slack periods. An interesting light on the day-to-day problems of this period is given by Osgood Mackenzie, who speaks of the difficulty of getting timber, and of coffin planking and nails in particular. (As a "joiner," William Barclay, Sr., will have made many of the coffins now interred in this area.) Catherine was destined to become a milliner; Jane was to marry early; and Samuel, at the early age of fifteen, became an assistant teacher attached to the local school. His is the sole early example of academic interest in the Barclay family. One of his duties will have been catechizing, which provides a link between the artisan and the religious enthusiast that we shall see emerging from time to time in WDB's and Willie's own work.

13

On 7 July 1864 an additional member of the family appeared: William Dugald Barclay, the youngest son, soon entrusted to the care of his sisters Jane and Mary, the domestic help having departed (the chief reason for which may well have been the size of the house rather than any pecuniary disadvantage, for by 1881 we find WDB's father employing two men and describing himself as "joiner" *tout simple;* he is so listed, along with three competitors, in the Inverness County Directory for 1887). By the census returns of 1891, the house at 9 Low Street is occupied by WDB, now listed as its "head," age thirty-six, and his unmarried sister Catherine, age forty-one.[15]

CHAPTER TWO

William Dugald Barclay: A Highland Father

From Clerk to Agent

W$_{DB}$ had grown up as the youngest of five children. His brother, Samuel, who went off to be a teacher, was nine years his senior and therefore somewhat distanced from his young brother by adolescence. In fact he was beginning to make his way in the world by the time WDB commenced school. (This gap in ages may well explain the curious fact that Willie was never given much information about his father's family; he never once refers to any of them except his own father and mother, not even to his son. WDB had apparently virtually lost contact with them by his mid manhood.) The fact that the elder children had found gainful employment for themselves by the time WDB was entering school served to remove some of the financial burden from the shoulders of the parents after the family's recent fall in fortune. Only Mary, but four years WDB's senior, was still at school.

Alexander Whyte tells us that at the sort of Free Church school to which WDB went (Kilmallie Academy, now long since destroyed, alas) there will have been a vigorous concentration on the essentials—reading, writing, and reckoning, to which was added the Shorter Catechism and games. The costs will have been in the order of one shilling and sixpence per quarter for reading, plus four shillings and sixpence per quarter for the rest of the subjects.[1] It was the consuming ambition of the sons of all working folk in Scotland to get as much education as possible in order to enter one of the learned professions, away from the irregularity and the susceptibility to failure to which their fathers' employment lay at risk.[2] In light of this, and with the family's background of better times plus the counsels of an elder teacher-brother, we need have no misunderstanding as to the application and success to which WDB gave himself. He is characteristically one of the self-made men for which Scotland is so well reputed, men who are hard-working, loyal, honest, and responsible.

WDB's early years were spent under the ministry of Thomas Davidson and Arnold Clerk, Disruption ministers both of them, the latter being a great Gaelic scholar who first-infused WDB with an interest and love for the language. (It was this Arnold Clerk who produced the translation of the Bible into Gaelic after the

Revised Version was introduced in 1881 and 1885.) The Barclays, being immigrants, would not have had any use for the Gaelic at home; it was not till the 1920s that WDB found time to study it in any depth, as we shall see. WDB was a member of the Subscription Library at Fort William, which commenced in 1819; its most prized possession was a twenty-six-volume set of Sir Walter Scott, all handsomely bound and lettered in gold leaf, donated by the author himself. The bookman that WDB later became had his literary baptism among such volumes as these.

In the mid nineteenth century, Scotland shared the boom-time conditions that Britain then enjoyed at the head of the Empire. Banking was considered one of the brightest opportunities open to a young man, even if he did not have the advantages of university education (which WDB did not), and many families were very desirous of getting their sons established in this secure profession. It was a period of rapid growth for the banks, and of rapid change too.[3]

In 1845 there were no fewer than seventeen banks in Scotland; by 1878, nearly two years before WDB was apprenticed to the Bank of Scotland, there were but ten. The banking centers had been reduced from five to three: Edinburgh, Glasgow, and Aberdeen (Dundee and Perth having lost two banks each). For everyone associated with Scottish banking, 1878 was an unforgettable year. The City of Glasgow Bank failed, with hard repercussions on many throughout the west of Scotland and beyond. It had pursued an aggressive, expansionist policy, which produced over 130 branches throughout the land, but its expansion was too fast, too adventurous, and without adequate controls. Thus, largely due to an unhappy commitment to speculation in American railway development, it overextended itself and paid the ultimate price. Of its 1,800 or so shareholders, fewer than 250 remained solvent after its affairs were wound up, and over 2,000 families were reduced to poverty and ruin. It had an unusually large clientele among Free Church families, which fact *The Glasgow Herald,* no friend to the Free Churches in those days, reported gleefully.

It provided a powerful lesson for any prospective bank trainee, and helped to accentuate the mandarin character of the managers and agents, whose sternness became even more awesome. Severity and aloofness were part of their stock-in-trade, and it is against this background that we need to see the developing affection of WDB for Daniel McLeish's daughter Barbara. Bankers were urged to keep themselves somewhat aloof from their clients in the cause of business propriety—they might have mercantile or other schemes requiring funding! The agent's job was to provide that, of course, but not too adventurously. The banks preferred them to act as procurers of investment rather than as its disseminators. Thus they kept themselves a little remote from normal society; within it, involved, but nevertheless distant. The photograph of Daniel McLeish (on p. 17), one of their number, reflects this exactly: participating in the life of the town, but apart from it. Their dress was very conventional (and likewise set them apart from others), a business uniform: severely black with cut-away frock coats, pinstripes, and "lum" hats, gold watches and cufflinks, and gold- or silver-headed walking sticks. They were men who earned and nurtured their respect.

Many of the agents were former "lads o' pairts"[4]—talented youth from poor backgrounds who dragged themselves up like many others by hard work and sheer native ability to be successful businessmen, doctors, or ministers. They were usually quite religious, and did not forget their origins or the help they received from ministers, schoolmasters, and the like. They were elders, Sabbath-school teachers, and Bible Class leaders, and could be relied on to aid younger men coming up. Perhaps one of the greatest examples of a "lad o' pairts" is Samuel Smiles, formerly of Haddington. He wrote a number of self-help books, with such titles as *Self-Help, Character, Duty,* and *Thrift,* as well as some first-rate biography. By the time WDB was making his mark in the bank, these "improving" books had achieved phenomenal sales and were required reading for anyone with ambitions. We can be sure WDB mastered them and passed their Victorian ethic on to his son.

By the time WDB was ready to take up his career, clerks and apprentices were a clearly identifiable group within the banking system.[5] The banks tended to take on far more than they required, knowing that their overseas interests would take up the slack thus created. The dominions were peopled with such, Scotland being in the van of banking method and efficiency. The banks were also very prominent in the army volunteer movement—McLeish's rise in the

The opening of the West Highland Railway, Fort William, 1894. Second from the left at front is Willie's maternal grandfather, Daniel McLeish. To the right of the church in the background stands Parade Cottage. [Photo courtesy of The Aberdeen Press and Journal]

17

Inverness-shire Highlanders is a classical example of what ambitious and talented men could do. These part-time soldiers were often used for civic occasions and later in the armed conflicts in the Crimea and South Africa and in the Great War. Thus military discipline was wedded to business method, conduct, and civic pride, which created the background for the present system. All parents knew that their sons, if possessed of any talent at all, could fall prey to such entice-ments. But the security and training could not go amiss, and the rewards would be great, though slow of development because of the numbers involved.

The Barclays were one such family impressed by the opportunities, and thus WDB was indentured in 1879, following his fifteenth birthday. Physical as well as educational acceptability was demanded, and we know that he passed in both areas, being naturally bright, healthy, and keen of sports (football, cricket, golf, and especially his beloved shinty). Excellence of character was also required, and WDB was well-mannered and well-spoken. Prior to being taken on, appren-tices were examined in writing, dictation, and arithmetic. To pass, especially in the Bank of Scotland's examinations (it is the only bank ever to have been incorporated by act of a Scottish Parliament, and the only surviving body thus created) was no mean achievement. We can well imagine his elation, and that of his parents and family, on hearing that he had done so. The training was to last for three years, during which period the apprentices would be paid a pittance of from two to four shillings per week (i.e., ten to twenty new pence). A personal bond against their defalcation was required of the parents or some other person of substance in the community. The records no longer survive, but we may be sure that his father was only too pleased to put up this money for WDB.

Banking, according to the standard textbook on the subject (H. G. Rae's *The Country Banker,* which WDB will have used in one of its early editions), was not then "an exact science or branch of economics or law, but a business in which a primary requirement was a close knowledge of man: motives, prejudices and weaknesses. A good judge of men is of fundamental importance."[6] The requirements, such as they were, naturally fitted WDB for what would become the two consuming activities of his life: his professional and pastoral work. Unaware of it at the time, he was already being prepared for an almost unique service, and one which—via his son—would be of inestimable value throughout the world.

But the outlook was not an easy one. There were over six thousand bank employees engaged at the time of WDB's commencement, five thousand of them clerks. They were divided into three classes, and there were no trade unions to defend their rights. They were entirely at the mercy of their employers and could be instantly dismissed whenever those employers were so minded. Increases of remuneration were irregular, not to say arbitrary. More often than not a bonus was offered instead, which had no continuing effect on their income and thus gave little promise for the future. But once they were raised from senior clerk to teller they were much better off. They could enjoy more security and share the respect of their juniors as well as the trust of their managers and the bank's customers. Promotion came only through zeal and fidelity, and against very strong competition. Male employees were not allowed to marry before the age of twenty-six, and could hardly afford to do so even then. Despite its security, Checkland commented that "banking in Scotland was popularly regarded as the most dismal of respectable professions."[7] Little wonder Daniel McLeish was not amused at the thought of his daughter's romance with WDB!

W. G. Riddell, a senior engineer on Clydeside at the very time WDB was making his advances, preserves an amusing reaction of his own upon learning of his daughter's involvement with one of their number:

"What kind of young man?" says I.

"Oh! He's a very well-doing young man," says the wife. "He's a clerk in an office. . . ."

"A clerk?" says I.

"No, No! I'm not proud, Mister, as you know, but the line must be drawn somewhere."[8]

Daniel McLeish, in opposing the affections of WDB and Barbara for each other, also sought to draw the line, permanently.

But the one thing that bank clerks had over other workers was time and leisure: they did have great opportunity to better themselves in "extramural" activities acceptable to their employers and were expected to make good use of it. In this WDB was to exceed even his own ambitions, for not only did he fulfill his time very acceptably, but English literature became an especial delight to him. His application caught the eye of his manager, who perhaps had other motives than merely the professional development of his young charge, and so WDB was promoted to Pitlochry in Perthshire. Away from his family and friends, away from the charms of McLeish's youngest daughter, he now had more leisure time than he could handle. It was both an opportunity and a danger. It was the turning point in his life. Brought up in the religious life of the Free Church, though apparently without any special interest in it, he now passed through a conversion experience. The date would be 1882/83. It was the period following the evangelistic meetings in Scotland of Moody and Sankey, when much religious excitement was about and the realities of and the demand for the "new birth" were well promoted.

For reasons now lost, WDB found himself at a meeting organized by the forebears of the Church of the Nazarene (a Methodist holiness group not unlike A. S. Peake's Primitive Methodism—which may account in part for WDB's later devotion to Peake's writings). Here he became aware of his sinfulness before God, his need of a Savior. Here he gave his life to God, determining to be a true disciple of Christ. Here he laid the foundation for his life, on which he was to build magnificently over the next forty years or so. It was the year the Young Men's Guild of the Church of Scotland was founded, and others copied that organization with similar success. The Guild's textbooks were to have extraordinary influence throughout the land, beyond the boundaries of the Church of

Scotland, and were in fact to provide the pattern for WDB's son's early books, as we shall see.

A little further north from Pitlochry, in the valley of the Tummel at Bonskeid, resided Alexander Whyte's in-laws, the Barbours. G. F. Barbour, father of R. W., was himself a former Manchester merchant (he died in 1887). Like many wealthy folk from Edinburgh, they divided their time between the capital in the winter months and the beauty of the Perthshire hills in the summer. The area was a well-known watering place, where preachers of Whyte's ilk were in great demand.[9] Thus it was that WDB came under Whyte's influence at the time he most needed spiritual direction; and through him he came to know some of the best preachers in the land. From this time dates WDB's power and renown as a sermon taster. Whyte himself was now very much in fashion as a preacher (the newly founded newspaper *The British Weekly* began to publish his evening sermons in 1888). We need not doubt that WDB reveled in his preaching and teaching. He was certainly there during the period when Whyte was particularly under the influence of William Law's mysticism and the historical writings of Macaulay.[10]

One of the friends Whyte had taken along to Bonskeid was Henry Drummond, every young man's idol at the time, and a visitor to the lively Young Men's Association at Pitlochry (of which WDB was now a member) since 1877.[11] We may well date WDB's extraordinary religious interest and commitment from this time; much of it was due directly to the influence of Henry Drummond. Drummond had been drawn early into Moody and Sankey's evangelistic campaigns and was one of the main reasons for their continued success among students. He gave them intellectual stature and he provided continuity when the evangelists were elsewhere. Moody was at times concerned over his protégé's theology. I am grateful to Professor Bruce for supplying a remark of Whyte's that drives at the very center of this concern: said Whyte of Drummond, "The trouble with Henery is that he disna' ken onything aboot sin."[12] Drummond was himself a man of singular power and persuasion, some said with almost hypnotic qualities of voice and gaze. As with many lads of his own age, theological students included, WDB came under his influence and sought to emulate his ways. As a teacher, Drummond was utterly free from convention, ardent and enthusiastic, and quite fearless of facts. He was loyal to the intellectual methods of the age, and, having been raised in the Highland traditions, he possessed an unshakable belief in God and the reality of spiritual experience.[13] His unusual path to fame had a special attraction for men like WDB who had enjoyed no university education.

Drummond had left off his theological studies in order to take up his mission work and extend his love of natural science. Since 1859, when Darwin published his *Origin of Species,* the book had been attracting the energies of many men's minds. Drummond's natural love for nature, along with the disputations all around him, distracted him from the classics-oriented course that he had undertaken at New College. He seems to have realized earlier than many that such an orientation was no longer valid in the modern world, that a practical, science-related course, as opposed to a "pure," classical one, was required, and in the absence of this at his alma mater he simply followed his own inclinations.[14] At first Moody and Sankey were quite unknown in Scotland, but on their arrival they spotted Drummond and brought him into their work, with astonishing results. This led to work all over the United Kingdom, from the northeast of Scotland to London, via Sunderland, Liverpool, Manchester, and Dublin, affecting "nearly every town of the country" according to his biographer.[15] He completed his theological studies, but he was a changed man. The system could no longer enchain him; evangelizing and geologizing were now his constraining interests. His peripatetic work continued to the end of 1876, when he accepted an invitation to assist the minister at the Barclay (!) Church in Edinburgh. But in this he felt cramped—"like a squirrel in a cage"; thus, following "the most miserable time of my life," he found vacant the Lectureship in Natural Science at Free Church College, Glasgow, applied for it, and was appointed. His work there provided a base for all his future activities and exploits.

Between 1884 and 1890 Drummond was at the height of his fame and usefulness; WDB was then an enthusiastic and impressionable young man of twenty to twenty-six. To such Henry Drummond was almost an idol: suave, humble, learned, keen, intensely devout, yet scientific in outlook and at ease with the discipline's more disturbing conclusions. Drummond's humor was no small help in winning the confidence of young men, and they delighted in his response to the Robertson Smith troubles that were continuing to agitate many. (*The Old Testament and the Jewish Church,* Robertson Smith's popular reply to the General Assembly's adverse judgment, was published in 1881 and went through several reprints before a second edition appeared in 1892.) Drummond postulated, for example, Moses' annoyance at meeting Smith's denigrators, saying, "How dare you say I wrote the Pentateuch!" and suggested a tract along these lines should be written.[16]

Drummond has had a bad press, in many cases an unfair and one-sided press, but it cannot be denied that the atmosphere created by him and extended by his students was one of the chief influences of the period, and of WDB in particular. It has been said that the work of A. S. Peake prevented a conservative/liberal split in Britain such as that which rent the USA in the 1920s;[17] we should not forget the earlier work such as that done by Henry Drummond and others was also strongly influential.

Slowly, WDB developed his skills and abilities, at first commercial, then in Bible Class and Young Men's work, thence to preaching and teaching on a broad front. This defied all denominational and theological barriers and made of him a rare example of lay leadership, the influence of which is still remembered today in north and south Scotland.

In 1891 he returned to Fort William as a teller, now thirty years of age, and clearly a man with a future. The census returns for that year show him as head of the old family home at 9 Low Street, where he now resided with his spinster sister Mary (then age forty-one). His stay there was not of long duration—perhaps reflecting McLeish's continuing unease—and so to Glasgow he went as senior teller at the Anderston branch of the bank. It was a developing area of the city, attracting the attentions of many and being swiftly urbanized. It brought WDB into contact with big business, its special needs and attitudes, an experience that was to stand him in good stead in his later appointments. Perhaps more importantly, it again brought him into contact with the very best pulpit traditions and a form of Christianity now largely weaned from the Highland Calvinism in which he had been brought up. It gave him unrestricted opportunity to explore and exploit his own gifts in his leisure hours, not least in the relaxed environment of the YMCA to which he was now as committed as he was to his own church. For nine long years this continued, and during that time his love for Barbara remained true, as did hers for him. It was a cruel state of affairs, but he was determined to prove false the doubts and misapprehensions of her father. They kept contact by a secret correspondence, finding enjoyment in the adventure of it as much as in each other's love.

On 25 July 1905 his moment arrived; he was appointed agent (manager) at Wick.[18] His goal had been reached. Alas, his own parents were no longer alive to savor the success, but Barbara was there, and they wasted no time in planning their future together. On 26 July 1906, almost a year to the day following his establishment at Wick, they were married "according to the Free Church form" at the Alexander Hotel, Glasgow, by the Reverend John McIntosh of Fort William, apparently in the absence of Barbara's now aged father. The marriage was witnessed by two of WDB's friends, Alexander G. Miller and J. McLuckie. WDB was forty-one years of age; Barbara was thirty-eight.

Fulfillment: The Gift of a Son

It was in very good heart that WDB took up his appointment at Wick, confident in himself and enjoying all the prestige of a young professional. By now his mode of entry into banking was fully established and recognized. That very year George Anderson was knighted—the first of the bank apprentices to be so honored; it was a guarantee that the sky was now the limit in their chosen career. Banking systems were still being refined in those days. There was very little mechanization, and even less cohesion within personnel structures; checks were beginning to make their dramatic transformation, though they would not be in general use till 1914. In 1908, the banks demonstrated their civic pride upon being chosen to provide the Guard of Honour from among the many ranks of soldier volunteers on their staffs at the Scottish National Exhibition. When WDB was apprenticed, careerist agents formed only a quarter or so of all agents, the rest being independent businessmen and, more typically, lawyers (as with McLeish). Now they were leading the field, totally committed to the professionalization of banking, a real force of expertise to be reckoned with.

Wick (Old Norse *vík,* meaning "little bay"), to which WDB was now sent, had established itself as the busiest fishing port in the far north of Scotland.

Ancient rocks, sparse resources, scant population, and remoteness are the things that come to mind when one considers the County of Caithness, the most northerly county of the Scottish mainland, so dependent on the primary industries of farming and fishing. Henry Rees speaks of "the granite intrusions of Caithness,"[19] and it is a felicitous phrase. But it is not only the granite masses that intrude. There is an insularity about it that is almost tangible. Caithness has managed to preserve its independence and its cultural identity to such an extent as to constitute a distinctive region. Perhaps the chief surprise one has on moving through the mountainous Highlands to it is the sudden expanse of sky and the different light one *feels* there. Caithness is virtually a coastal plain, and has about it a dawn-light effect.

By this time the former "herring metropolis of the world"[20] had lost much of its trade and the related occupations. The stocks of herring had been run down to perilously low levels, forcing contraction of the fishing fleet. In the year of WDB's birth it boasted over eleven hundred vessels filling the harbor area with activity and commercial power; forty years later its numbers were reduced to double figures and were still declining. The mobile workers—sorters, dressers, curers, and the like—had gone away for the last time, many of them to quite different occupations, some of them to ruin. WDB had attained his much-dreamed-of appointment, but in a backwater. He now had plenty of time and opportunity to make good his professional claims, to build his home life after his long bachelor-hood existence, and to reflect on the enormous changes, theological and denominational, that had taken place. Lord Kelvin once remarked that "when you're up against an impossibility, you're on the edge of a discovery"; WDB's discovery lay in his realization of Paul's own experience, that God's power is enhanced in those who recognize their own weakness. Forced to rely on divine help over a long period when nothing seemed to happen, he was now able to call upon the training that had been continuing through these long years, putting it to good effect in home and church.

The Barclays' first home was directly above the bank, a three-storied building with very spacious and pleasing accommodations, though little garden. But what they missed in that regard, they made up for in the adjacent river walks and the countryside around them. But ten minutes' walk away lay the harbor and the sea. Many were the hours they shared in strolling about this picturesque town, and many were the hours in which they indulged their mutual delight in literature and music and sacred contemplation.

Their joy was greatly increased on 5 December 1907, when their own son was born, to be baptized William Barclay. As with the Israelites of old, they were only too pleased to dedicate him to the service of God, not realizing then that the little one entrusted to them relatively late in life would one day be world-famous, fulfilling a ministry far beyond their wildest imaginings. Their second Christmas together was thus blessed as no Christmas before had been, the registration certificate (dated 24 December) being the nicest Christmas card Barbara could have wished for.

Bank House, Wick, where Willie was born

No fewer than eighty-eight William Barclays were registered that year, but none was more welcome, more loved or cosseted than that of the little Barclay family of Wick. Nor were any parents more zealous in committing their child to the Lord for his blessing. For WDB and Barbara it was a dream come true, a prayer answered:

> Unto us a son is born.
> Unto us a son is given. . . .

It was noted earlier that it was the custom in Scotland for a family's first son to take the first names of his grandfathers. Alas, Daniel McLeish's opposition to the union of Willie's parents does not seem to have been set right even by the birth of his latest grandson: his name was not given to the child. It has sometimes been said that Willie's godfather was none other than Cameron of Lochiel. Willie himself was prone to mention this, but there is no evidence that this was the case. For one thing, the couple had been living in Wick during this period,

24

nearly two hundred miles from Fort William; for another, Sir Donald Cameron died in 1905, and the son who succeeded him, a young officer in the Grenadier Guards, had no connection with the family; still less had they any claim on his interests (unlike that with his father, for whom McLeish had worked).

In the biographical sketch of Paul Tillich by Rollo May, the author records a very interesting and significant comment of the philosopher-theologian: "My belonging to the privileged class early aroused in me that consciousness of social guilt which later was to become of such decisive importance for my work and the course of my life."[21] It was a privilege similar to Tillich's that Willie was to enjoy as the only child of gifted and reasonably well-off parents who enjoyed a certain amount of prestige in town and community and in their other world, the church. From now on WDB was to receive well-earned respect and attention; he was to be aided by the presence of a wife of quite unusual quality, grace, and intelligence; and his son, who early showed high responsiveness and vigor, was to enjoy its benefits to the full.

These experiences were to make of Willie what he later became, but he was to show at various times a confusion of response that suggests that while he was abundantly grateful for everything he so richly enjoyed, he was very mindful of his privileges and of the want of them in others. Commented Lord Moran of Churchill, one of Willie's heroes, "To understand Winston you must go back to his childhood"; it is no less important with Willie. The ambience of Willie's life as an infant and throughout the formative early years was to be genuine (if irregular and indirect) involvement on at least the fringe of the minor aristocracy of Scotland; regular and increasing intimacy with those who held the reins of society—municipal, business, and so on; a grandfather who exemplified the very best of the self-made traditions, resplendent in his uniform as Colonel of the Inverness-shire Highlanders, occupying the dignity of Parade House, Fort William; a father who was possessed of unusual sympathy for the ordinary man but with the knowledge that he was no social upstart, but a successful man enjoying the fruits of his success; and a mother whose manner betokened a particularly privileged childhood and who was elevated above the ordinary by talent, beauty, and many skills, social and domestic. Household help was undoubtedly present, though records of it are no longer available. (It was so in Motherwell, when Rebecca came to share their lives, remaining with WDB after Mrs. Barclay's death.) Willie enjoyed and was enriched by all the advantages his position gave him.

H. Cecil Pawson, Willie's friend in later life over many years, quoted James M. Barrie, also a solid favorite of the Barclay family, as having said that "the God to whom a little boy says his prayers has a face very like that of his mother."[22] There is a wealth of reality in that statement, and of unrecognized theology as well! Undoubtedly, the essence of Willie's religion, and therefore of his theology, was created in that happy and privileged home, the home of two middle-aged, intelligent, and contented people. A. T. Guttery reflects it when he remarks that "It was the Christ incarnate in my mother that made me desire to be a Christian.

25

It was the passion of my father's prayers that made me long to preach."[23] In a chapter title in his autobiography that echoes the title of his hero John Buchan's book of favorite personalities, "This for Remembrance,"[24] Willie expresses his admiration and gratitude to his parents:

> Whatever I have done in life, it is because "I have stood on the shoulders of my parents." . . . [Chesterton's] father had unlocked for him so many doors to wonderful things—and I too can say that of my father. My mother . . . she *was* a saint. . . . She could write, she could paint, she could play the piano, but above all she was kind . . . my mother, lovely in body and spirit, good all through. . . .[25]

There speaks the real man, the subject of this biography: a happy man.

A Passion for Literature

Within a few months of arriving at Wick, WDB began to make his presence felt not merely through his business connections and the local United Free Church to which he devoted many hours and much labor, but also culturally. The love for English literature he shared with Barbara now found opportunity to express itself publicly. The ravages of time have eclipsed the memory of many of his leisure-time pursuits, but in the Local History Department of the Carnegie

Carnegie Public Library, Wick, where WDB shared some literary delights with other members of the Wick Literary Society

Library at Wick I came across a forgotten and insignificant (except to us) Minute Book of the Wick Literary Society, which has preserved one of the central pleasures of the Barclay's home life.

As early as November 1906 we find WDB, an already established member of the Literary Society, nominating one Donald Sutherland for membership. The following month he is at it again, this time proposing two names: G. M. Smitten and D. W. Rose. The December entry is particularly interesting, for it records a paper read before the Society by WDB on Tennyson's *Idylls of the King*. The minutes refer to it as "a most interesting paper" and offer a very significant description, not only for the light it sheds on his method and interests, but also for the indication it gives of traits that he clearly passed on to his son: "In a masterly fashion he first dealt with the general plan of the tales and with their *spiritual significances,* and proceeded to give a comprehensive sketch of each of the twelve stories, *dwelling upon the characters and their allegorical meanings.*"[26] The italicized phrases offer an insight into his mind and attitudes: his literary appreciation was subservient to the gospel even in a literary society. Perhaps it would be as accurate to say that it was motivated by his religious interests, too. We shall note repeatedly that there is much in his makeup that suggests the minister *manqué.* Thirty years later, though he had not dealt with Tennyson in his arts course, his son Willie takes this work of Tennyson's and does a very similar thing with it for his congregation at Renfrew Trinity. Like father, like son. . . .

Tennyson, of course, was a great favorite in those days. David Cairns spoke of him and Robert Browning as "our divinities" at about the time WDB presented his paper.[27] Tennyson possessed a great hold on his contemporaries. Having assimilated the ideas of his age thoroughly, he was able to express them in limpid and melodious verse which attracted a huge following. The brevity of the entry in the Minutes Book rules out any further word of the "higher critical" type, though we shall not be far wrong in assuming that much of WDB's love for Tennyson was probably learned at the feet of the highly influential editor of *The British Weekly,* William Robertson Nicoll. This newspaper, "a journal of social and Christian progress," to cite its subtitle, had an unequalled effect on its generation. Perhaps no man has been made for his job as much as W. R. Nicoll. To his newspaper he brought not merely a spiritual sensitivity and nose for newsworthiness hard to find elsewhere in such balance, but also a sure literary touch that was recognized by all. And his output was prolific. His third book (his first "secular" work) was published pseudonymously, under the name of Walter E. Wace, in 1881; its title was *Alfred Lord Tennyson: His Life and Works.* Nicoll's biographer comments that it brought together "by far the fullest collections of personal facts regarding Mr. [*sic*] Tennyson and his works"[28]—material that was soon recognized as superior in quality to anything previously written on the poet (it was used, for example, in Palgrave's article on Tennyson in *Chambers's Encyclopaedia*). Nicoll shared this love for the poet with his own father,[29] and WDB was soon to pass it on to his only son.

27

The mark WDB made on the Society was substantial, and it was given recognition early in 1907, when he was elected to act as a substitute for its Chairman, Sheriff Stuart. It was his first recorded public recognition outside his profession and church work. In this capacity, at the February meeting he proposed a vote of thanks to the speaker who had taken "Some Local Stories" as his theme. The stories were of Highland tales much beloved to the Barclays, including "the evil eye, old sayings, dreams, death warnings, old saws and superstitions," and they held the members enthralled.[30] The next month WDB was elected to be one of the six Vice Presidents of the Society, being made a member of the committee in the process. At the very first meeting following this he was asked to take the chair, and on that occasion they decided to erect a plaque to another of his favorite authors (and of Willie too): Robert Louis Stevenson. The plaque is still to be seen today, on Harbour Brae; it reads as follows:

Robert Louis Stevenson
lived here
in Autumn 1868
Erected by the Wick Literary Society, 1907

In all truth it was a short stay, RLS being there for only six weeks. He stayed near the harbor, at the New Harbour Hotel in Pulteney Town, Wick. There is no suggestion that WDB ever sought to share in Stevenson's "thrilling experience" of going under the sea in diver's gear. Such things as the plaque erection help to underscore Willie's contention in his autobiography that "there are places in Scotland where I am still my father's son—and I am glad that it is so."[31]

The pattern was now set for WDB's close involvement with, not to say management of, the Literary Society. In October, again in the Chair, he gave a vote of thanks following a paper on Wordsworth at Grasmere and Burns at Ayr; in November he replied to two papers on the life of Thackeray and on his *Vanity Fair*. In January 1908 he filled the same role, this time responding to various papers on the Covenanters (as portrayed in Scott's *Old Mortality*, and in Samuel Crockett's novel about the Covenanters). The following month, February, he presented another paper himself, on Browning's *Paracelsus*; the Secretary commented that it was

> treated in a most exhaustive and painstaking manner. After giving a short account of the Paracelsus of history and of legend, he proceeded to deal with each of the five divisions of Browning's dramatic poem and showed the Paracelsus of the poet in all his ambitious aspirations after limitless knowledge. The paraphrase of the poem was interspersed with fine quotations from its pages, and we listened with great attention.

The entries concerning WDB's offerings to the Society are always longer and more detailed than those for others, which suggests something of the impact he made on his contemporaries. It is a great pity that this essay on Browning was not printed, for, to quote W. R. Nicoll, "no poet of our race had so strong a hold of the evangelical ideas as Browning had,"[32] and it would have been helpful to see in detail this aspect of Willie's background. Significantly, one of Willie's early contributions to *The Expository Times* was on the general question of poetry.[33]

Service in the United Free Church

The Committee meetings of the Literary Society were held in the Free Church manse, the minister of which was Robson Mackay, who had been there since 1902. It may well have been at Mr. Ross's suggestion that WDB joined, for unquestionably the church was his first love.

The United Free Church's lot in those days was not a happy one. The springtime of reunion had flowered into a late summer in October 1900, when the longed-for union between the Free Church of Scotland and the United Presbyterian Church took place. But the warmth of those months was soon dispersed as a decidedly frosty snap set in when the nonuniting part of the Free Church, composed mainly of Highlanders ardent for a rigid Calvinism, took the matter to court. Their argument was clear, simple, and astonishing. They recognized only themselves as the guardians of Free Church tradition. Because the unionists had moved away from this base laid in the Disruption of 1843, notably in the Declaratory Act of 1892, it was claimed they had forfeited all rights to their Free Church inheritance. This included all trusts, endowments, properties, and so on. The "Wee Frees," as the rump element was called, were alone the true descendants of Chalmers; they alone were loyal to the faith of their fathers. The thinking behind this claim is well demonstrated in Professor Collins's comment that the United Free Church "*arrogates* to herself the right to determine from time to time 'what points fall within this description,' and leaves herself without fundamentals, without essentials and without discipline."[34] James Denney drew his contemporaries' attention to the strange fact that those who opposed any shift in theological emphasis or ecclesiastical position actually urged more for their position than did natural justice, which recognized that you cannot bind one's descendants beyond the second generation.[35]

Their response to the reunion was diametrically opposed to the scriptural injunction to avoid taking one's brother to court. For those who genuinely believe in biblical authority rather than merely pretending to, Paul's words are final here: "The very fact that you have lawsuits among you means you have been defeated already." But biblical authority is of little importance when cherished dogma is at stake, and so to court they went. And to everyone's surprise, they won. The continuing Free Church body, which could claim fewer than thirty ministers, and only twenty-seven members of the legally constituted General Assembly,[36] were now given legal possession of an organization they had no hope of containing, let alone running successfully. The Scottish courts had recognized the absurdity of this, and had actually confirmed the powers of the United Free Church, but the battle was lost on appeal to the House of Lords in 1904.

Both parties agreed that the matter be remitted to a Royal Commission to partition the properties and endowments justly. The Commission reported in April 1905, and it resulted in the Churches (Scotland) Act in June of that year. This called for the appointment of an Executive Commission to oversee the partition, but even this was subjected to successive interruptions and delays, and it only progressed with its work after the Free Church element had withdrawn in high dudgeon. The work of the Commission was to continue till 1909, when the final apportionment was made. A year before this the Church of Scotland had made new overtures to the United Free Church with a view to full union, a move that all those with an outward, forward-looking disposition welcomed as a sign of divine grace and activity. Little did they realize that the talks and discussions would continue for twenty years, being interrupted in turn by the Great War and the sniping of the Free Church, not to speak of some within the United Free Church itself, close to WDB, who had real misgivings as to its propriety.

I have made this brief foray into Scottish church history because it is such an important aspect of the environment in which WDB and his wife served and worshiped, and in which Willie was brought up—an environment that was by no means ideal to Christian expansion and nurturing one's only child satisfactorily in the faith, but one in which they strove to keep themselves from being distracted from their commitment. It was a long haul from the revival and evangelistic meetings of the 1860s, '70s, and '80s, and many longed for those good old days to return, with an urgency that was only heightened when news of the Welsh revival filtered through in 1904.

WDB himself had come through "the naughty nineties" on fire for God and the gospel, his zeal unabated. One of the reasons for this was his fixed rule of a "family altar" at which daily prayers were said, along with the Bible reading for the day. (WDB was ever a member of the Daily Bible Readings scheme of the Bible Societies, an adherence to which he passed on to his son with literally worldwide repercussions). He early became an elder in his church, in which he soon built up a successful Bible class and became leader of the local Brotherhood Movement. He also added another string to his bow by commencing to preach. Work at Pitlochry, Fort William, and Glasgow among young people had prepared him for this well, and it was not long before his supply services were sought after. Living above his bank, he had plenty of time for these and other activities, and soon acquired a reputation as a speaker and preacher of note.

The Brotherhood Movement was his special delight. (Mrs. Barclay occupied herself with the Sisterhood to some degree, though she did not get the same sort of publicity that her husband did.) It was an organization Henry Drummond had helped to popularize, having been started a little while after the campaigns of the '80s, usually under the somewhat precious name of the "Pleasant Sunday Afternoon" (PSA). Drummond found time for them even in his last illness,[37] out of a dedication much in line with WDB's own. Another of WDB's favorite preacher-authors involved with the movement was Alexander Whyte, who helped found the Edinburgh branch in 1893. His biographer tells us that it was against some opposition that it commenced. No doubt the ministers and elders felt that it could challenge the normal pattern of church activity and Christian fellowship—which it undoubtedly did on occasion. Whyte's involvement is especially interesting to us inasmuch as he helped to get the Book Club side of the movement going, and this was a great incentive to WDB's own book-collecting habits. The figures for Wick have not been preserved, but we have Willie's testimony to the fact that "he had the best library I have ever seen in the possession of a layman,"[38] and that was the cause, along with his wife's keen interest, of that passion for books and literature which is so notable a feature of their son. We shall see that WDB was soon to express this interest to the broader enjoyment of the public at Motherwell when he was appointed to the Library Sub-Committee.

Another person strongly associated with the Brotherhood Movement who affected Willie via his father is Arthur Samuel Peake. As a layman, he had special attractions for WDB. It was in 1904 that Peake delivered his Hartley Lectures on "The Problem of Suffering in the Old Testament," which were published a year later under that same title. It was to be the most widely read of all Peake's books (its last reprint took place as late as 1952) and was perhaps the most influential; it certainly brought Peake's name before a broad constituency, including the far north of Scotland. In 1908 his *Christianity, Its Nature and Its Truth* was published, and such was the enthusiasm for Peake that the Brotherhood Movement had a special edition published for its members. This gave Peake particular delight, for he was now very concerned (as were many denominational leaders) that the cozy atmosphere of the PSAs was in danger of swamping the systematic teaching and doctrine of Christianity. It was the time when the "new theology" was at its height, and credal affirmation was under fierce assault. Peake's involvement with the Movement reached its zenith when he wrote the volume *Brotherhood in the Old Testament* "to express," as he puts it, "my sympathy with the aims of the Brotherhood Movement." Typically, and despite its title, it carries a chapter on brotherhood in the New Testament that is in effect a stirring appeal to take the Fatherhood of God seriously; Peake was stealing the clothing of liberalism and using it in the cause of his own passionate evangelicalism.

Everything that WDB set his hand to (with the exception of the Literary Society) carried the hallmark of success. By 1911 we find *The John O'Groats Journal* reporting a special celebration of the Wick Brotherhood, of which WDB was President, when its membership reached six hundred (the town's population was then only nine thousand). At this meeting they set a new membership target of eight hundred! The local minister, Alfred Coutts, presented them with a special banner. The meeting was also attended by the Sisterhood of the town, for which WDB proposed a vote of thanks.

His energies were unbounded, and almost every issue of the local paper contains some reference to his activities. In the April 7 issue he is named first of five conveners of the United Free Church who reported favorably on all organizations and finances. On the same day it is reported that he chaired the meeting of the Band of Hope, to the principles of which he was staunchly committed. It was their last meeting of the winter session, and WDB is referred to as founder and leader. The paper reported on its wide range of activities, some of which were highly imaginative. His leadership was clearly marked not only by an ebullience of manner, but by real style; people enjoyed themselves under his leadership. A week later he gave a lantern lecture (one of his favorite forms of address) on "The Doctor's Fee" and "Jessica's First Prayer." Mrs. Barclay, meanwhile, is reported as being the delegated member due to report on the Ladies' Auxiliary at the General Assembly in May. She was there without her husband's company, he being found taking the general salute alongside the Senior Scouts' Commissioner for Scotland and Ex-Provost Nicholson at the Annual Inspection and Drill Display.

The summer months gave them time to relax and to enjoy the spectacle of the launching of Wick's first motorboat, gleefully reported in the press. We are not told where they took their holidays, but Willie speaks of their habit of returning to Fort William, so one presumes that some sort of conciliation between WDB and his father-in-law had by now been effected.

The Transfer from Wick

It was now mid May 1912, and the session was beginning to wind down for the summer. The congregation, too, was being depleted. It was to be the last session at Wick for the Barclays. On the 30th of August there appeared a report in *The John O'Groats Journal* that voiced local appreciation of the indefatigable interests of both Mr. and Mrs. Barclay. The piece created such an impression in Motherwell that *The Motherwell Times* reprinted it *in toto* on 6 September 1912. The *Journal* also carried a special request from WDB to members of the Bible class to meet him at 8 P.M. in Zion Hall to say goodbye; it is typical of his thoughtfulness, yet another trait he would pass on to his son.

The next issue of the paper reported fully on this meeting, showing the extent of respect and affection given the Barclays in Wick. A number of speeches were made, and WDB was presented with a silver inkstand as a token of their esteem. He left to take up his appointment on the 1st of September, but returned to the town on the Friday following (the 5th) for a specially convened meeting of the Sisterhood. At this Mrs. Barclay was given a solid silver tea service "in recognition of her service to the organization." WDB was also given "a silver sovereign purse," and "Master William," achieving his first public mention since his birth, was also given a gift of a silver chain. During the course of these proceedings a telegram was read out from the Reverend Alfred C. Coutts sympathizing with the Sisterhood in their great loss. Mrs. Barclay had rendered "invaluable service to the movement since its inception, especially in visiting the sick and the sorrowing." Concluding, Miss Georgeson commented that "in their guest they had ever found a kind friend and counsellor, unassuming, yet capable to a degree, ever considerate of the wants and wishes of others and to them all a true sister whose name and loving ministry would be enshrined in their hearts while life should last."[39] The only actual words from Mrs. Barclay left on record are given by this newspaper, and highly appropriate and significant they are, too, showing where their son acquired his unfailing courtesy and readiness to show gratitude to others. They are simple, yet profound: "I thank you very much for your beautiful gifts." It was enough.

CHAPTER THREE

Motherwell Claims Them

I⊤ was as a five-year-old, his hair fair and tinged with auburn, that Willie arrived in the town of Motherwell, Scotland's largest steel town. It was an appointment of some prestige for his father, in which the son was to share. For the next seventeen years, through adolescence to early manhood, this was to be his base, and he never ceased to refer to it as his hometown. The area became, with nearby Glasgow and Renfrew, both the domestic and work centers for the rest of his life, and into this industrial southwest corner of Scotland he sank a deep taproot that was to nurture his life, color his attitudes, and bring to fruition his international and transdenominational activity.

A Home of Distinction

Bank House, Motherwell, could hardly have been more different from Bank House, Wick. Both were situated in the center of the towns, but there the similarities ended. The crisp, dawn-light atmosphere of rural Caithness had gone; in its place was the damper, sootier, noisier atmosphere of an important coal and steel town. Instead of the soft waters of the Wick River, they now had the harsh commotion of the Great Western Railway—within three hundred yards of their doorstep, with marshalling yards nearby. In place of the dreamy clip-clop of horses' hooves on the cobbles, there was now the unremitting clanking of the trams. The unhurried flow of Highland life, with gentle manners and courtesies to match, was now exchanged for that of the madding crowd, albeit a friendly and warm-hearted one.

The atmospheric conditions were the chief change, however. Almost over-night Willie became a sickly child. Unprepared through early childhood, ever guarded and cossetted by his watchful parents, he now fell a prey to every militant microbe that chanced his way. Quite apart from the usual coughs and colds and outbreaks of flu, he was subjected to seven major children's diseases in five years, as he recalls in *Testament of Faith.*[1] Public health, especially in the Glasgow area, was then in a very poor condition. This very year, 1912, Glasgow

34

had opened its first school clinic, reporting at the end of the session the very sorry state of its children, eighty percent of whom had defective teeth, thirty percent of whom suffered from "vermin," and ten percent of whom were subject to rickets.[2] The less crowded city of Motherwell was superior to Glasgow in this respect, but the Barclays had much to concern them as they saw their only child totter from one indisposition to another, experiencing a disruption of his schooling, an impoverishment of his slender reserves, and a real threat to the consecration of his birth. In two aspects at least this change of fortunes had definite and deleterious effects on Willie's health that lasted for the rest of his life and that imperiled his work and ministry. The most evident effect was the deafness that early on consigned him to deepening that solitary existence which is often the hallmark of the only child. It resulted from an attack of scarlet fever in 1913, and became progressively worse until in the late '30s he had become virtually stone-deaf. The second effect unquestionably reduced his influence and opportunities and led to some cruel comment by those who should have known better. I refer to his harsh voice. It is not sufficiently realized that this, too, was part of the steel

Bank House, Motherwell, the influential home of Willie's youth

35

town's legacy to him, contracted during one of his periodic bouts of illness (the red, almost beery face was a companion symptom, as Doctors Black, Jackson, and Holti have pointed out).[3] Unlike his deafness this could have been ameliorated had it been recognized, but it was not attended to. Indeed, help for it was not brought to his notice till he was nearly sixty, by which time it was too late. The very things that an informed health care would have excluded from his diet—smoking and alcohol and other vasodilators—he partook of as a means of relaxing the tension imposed by the symptoms; such is the human condition! The voice, as developed in puberty, was a matter of consternation to his parents, who were both possessed of melodious and winsome voices that were a delight to listen to. Willie grew up self-consciously overcoming these deficiencies commenced in Motherwell, the direct offshoot of industrial pollution.

But it so often happens that the things in life that are temptations and pitfalls become strengths and even means of grace in the hands of God, and so it was with Willie. Had he remained in Wick, had he been free of health hazards (if that can ever be the case), had he developed without disability among his high-minded Highland ancestors, who knows what sort of man he might have been? Who could risk asserting that his ministry would have been anything like what it became after having been tempered by these fretful disabilities? Who can doubt that through their soreness, and in the working-class world into which he was now plunged, he learned lessons the hard way and thus became the great servant of God, the caring and sympathetic pastor we all know? "No discipline seems pleasant at the moment," he wrote in translating Hebrews 12:11; "it is always painful. But afterwards it repays those who were trained by it with the happy harvest of a good life." We shall see that that harvest was rich indeed, and the happiness of it was enjoyed in full measure. But we will misunderstand William Barclay if we fail to see that throughout his life suffering never failed to raise its ugly head; and we will misinterpret his ministry if we fail to see that it was directed primarily at those whom he was glad to own as his fellow sufferers.

Curiously for a man with a hearing disability of his magnitude, one of his recollections of the things he most missed when he went on holiday to the Highlands with his parents was the noise of Motherwell. "I still remember," he wrote in 1962, "not being able to sleep at night for the silence. I missed the rattle of the tramcars, the sound of the railway-engines, and the noise of the traffic."[4] He may well have missed it then, but it was not long before "a majestic silence" was to fall on his entire world that could not be penetrated except by an act of will, and always at personal cost. This silence we find throughout his writings, most clearly in the complete absence of auditory memory or imagery. He speaks of the beauties of nature, but it is very rare for him to mention its sounds (birds, bees, brooks, etc.), though paradoxically he was passionately fond of music.

His age was still a prewar, Edwardian age, proud of its Victorian inheritance and still glorying in the idea of an unlimited potential for human progress and accomplishment. Indeed, his life and thinking is incomprehensible without the assertion of its Edwardian influences, both as to their old-world charm and courtesies, and as to their over-sanguine optimism. He grew up at the very heart of man's confident achievements, surrounded by expressions of goodwill (at church and at his father's bank), and in the comforting assurances of familial love, neighborly esteem, and material plenty. It was a very different age from our own, as he once reflected:

> I remember the time when an aeroplane was an incredible sight
> I remember when motor cars were rarities
> I remember the first wireless sets . . .
> I remember when people could not have proper medical attention
> because they could not pay for it . . .
> I remember children with rickets and diphtheria.[5]

It was at this time that a young woman by the name of Rebecca became part of the Barclay household after the manner of the Edwardian pattern of house-maids. A local girl (as much responsible for Willie's Motherwellian accent—and it was Motherwellian, *not* Glaswegian—as anyone), she was able to acquaint the Barclays with the area, its customs, habits, and *mores,* and provide Mrs. Barclay with the leisure time to pursue her wonted interests and role as hostess for WDB.

Even in the relaxed standards of the Edwardian era, their home life reflected very much the somewhat austere and mannered pattern to which Mrs. Barclay had been accustomed at Parade House, Fort William. To first-time visitors, formality was the most impressive characteristic; Rebecca was never seen without her "uniform" of black touched off with white lace collar and cuffs. She soon acquired a matronly disposition that was not far from autocratic at times and thereby ensured the smooth running of the household. This was exactly accord-ing to her employers' wishes—WDB had not waited all those years in order to provide for his wife in less than a fitting manner—and it was all second nature to Mrs. Barclay.

WDB always wore the accustomed morning suit (he never gave up his frock coat), with wing collar, his "gold Albert" adorning his waistcoat, and his bowler; and Mrs. Barclay dressed to match, ever demure and perfectly *soignée*. They were not ostentatious in their standards, but quality and excellence were their watch-words in a quiet way, and they were strictly adhered to. Willie's cousin Harold Barclay was to relate the impressions created by them when he visited Motherwell with his father, a senior insurance agent who shared business contacts with WDB. Unlike his own father's household, that of Uncle Willie and Aunt Barbara made a deliberate point of elevated standards of the outward sort that could be stiff and starchy at times and even risked alienating more sensitive spirits. But once befriended, these relatives provided nothing but warmth and friendship, serving as a receptive audience for WDB's unlimited range of anecdotes and stories—full of fun and even self-deprecatory when in full swing. Not a few of them found their way into Willie's collection and pulpit.

The serious side of life was never far from the conversations and thoughts of the Barclays. "Improving" tales dear to the Victorians were given their full emphasis (becoming a direct and very influential aspect of Willie's ethical forma-tion), as were the standard authors of the time: Jane Austen, Walter Scott, Emer-son, Thackeray, Lamb, Carlyle, Dickens, Macaulay, George Eliot, the Brontë sisters, Ruskin, Trollope, Shakespeare, Tennyson, Browning, Milton, and so on. The "Kailyard" authors—Ian MacLaren, J. M. Barrie, S. R. Crockett, and Annie S. Swan—were never far away. Commented Willie one day to his father, in that innocent cruelty of the young child, "Daddy, when you're dead all these books will belong to me." The things of the spirit (in the French connotation) were taken very seriously, "high-mindedness and simple living" being two of the great Highland inheritances they both enjoyed. There was undoubtedly deference to Willie's boyish needs (Beatrix Potter's link with Mrs. Barclay's forbears at Dunkeld will not have been overlooked), though we may be sure that it was not long before he was introduced to Bunyan, Defoe, Swift, and Scott—though not in that order! It was a musical family as well as a literate family, and Willie was introduced to his first piano lesson at an early age at the side of his accomplished mother. We shall see both literature and music developing in influence through-out Willie's life, both of them becoming essential characteristics of the mature adult. Indeed, it might well be argued that the geographical triangle formed by Motherwell, Glasgow, and Renfrew in which his life and work was framed, was set off by a congruent cultural triangle of literature, music, and the Bible—again, not in that order.

Outside the home, and apart from the Dalziel Sisterhood meetings, we have very little preserved concerning Mrs. Barclay. By this time both her sisters were firmly rooted in the Lowlands, and so she was able to see them more frequently than before. Her aging father, still at Fort William, was visited from time to time, not least during Willie's holidays, when he was able to enjoy to the full the "football matches" his father and he played together on the Highland hillside[6]— no mean feat for a stocky bank manager approaching his half-century. But for the rest Mrs. Barclay's activities have claimed the accolade of silence. Like her son, she seems to have been content to maintain friendship at a deep level with very few, though, less like him, does not appear to have had a similarly wide circle of acquaintances. Perhaps we have here the basis for Willie's undoubted need for solitude, which was fed by his deafness and the burden of his literary commitments. At any rate, her background and spare-time interests released her from the need for a multitude of friendships, and what time she rescued from her husband's whirlwind activities, her son claimed by his voracious appetite for their reading and playing the piano together. He grew up through those early years dominated by the figures of his parents, not least his mother. It may well be that he suffered as well as gained from the closeness of the relationship, even as Janet Adam Smith has argued that John Buchan was stifled by his relationship with his mother (it is paradoxical that the very relationship that was to be of such sterling value to Buchan, providing security and stability, as well as opening his eyes to a broad view of life, was nevertheless to breed inhibitions in his development and attitudes, not least toward other females).[7]

The nineteenth century, of which the Barclays (Willie included) were so much a part, did not really give way till the outbreak of the First World War in 1914. But already features that were to loom large in the new century and that would be very different from those of its predecessor were becoming apparent. Some of them were quite unlike those in which the Barclays were raised, and which they sought to select for their personal and professional lives. Most notable was the growing tension in society: 1912 was a year of strikes and the militant activity of suffragettes, "the Irish rebels," and other groups, all flexing their political muscle in the name of change. The miners were in pursuit of five shillings (old coinage) per hour, and two shillings for the boy workers. The dockers were creating havoc in their campaign for decent pay and conditions in London, Liverpool, and Glasgow. Some of their number (Tom Mann and Guy Bowman, for example) were to find themselves imprisoned for advising soldiers not to shoot their fellow workers for striking. And hundreds of women sought publicity for their cause by numerous well-known activities, for which imprisonment was by no means the exception, and in which the horrors of forced feeding were an additional outrage.

Meanwhile, the Cabinet was split over the third Home Rule Bill for Ireland amid growing civil unrest and disobedience that bordered on civil war. The Socialists sought to make political capital out of this situation despite the ever-present specter of Marxist Communism being suggested by their detractors. They were aided by the additional strength of the Fabians, who now joined with the International Labour Party in a move to eradicate poverty. (It was at this time that Sir Oliver Lodge contributed to the Socialist thrust by allowing one of his pieces to be used as a Fabian tract, despite the fact that till then, and unlike G. K. Chesterton, he had never heard of the Fabians!)[8] On another front, the churches engaged in a rare display of united action when no fewer than sixteen denominations declared in favor of the Scottish Temperance Bill.

As if in marked contrast to this gloom, 1912 was also the year the tango was introduced, and although that was of no consequence whatever to our two redoubtable Highlanders, their son was shortly to find it of consuming interest and attraction—much to their regret. It was in this year, too, that the first Royal Command Performance was ordered (this also failed to win approval from the Highlanders). As if by way of symbolic gesture, the greatest triumph of man's engineering ability to date—the *Titanic*—was launched with much boasting of man's subjection of the natural order. Alas, it sank amid the ice floes off Canada with great loss of life and wealth: nature, after all, declared her resilience.[9] Not many of WDB's generation could fail to recall a similar incident in the Tay Bridge disaster of 1879.[10]

WDB's Public Life

Willie's father lost no time in seeking to make his presence felt in Motherwell. Within five weeks of arriving in the town, in a story on a school board meeting of the 4th of October, *The Motherwell Times* was reporting his application for the recently vacated post of Treasurer (at £50 per annum). Undoubtedly his predecessor had put him up to this, and we may take for granted that he had the encouragement of the Chairman, the Reverend Thomas Marshall, who just happened to be WDB's new minister at Dalziel United Free Church. But there was more to it than that, on both sides. For WDB it was an opportunity to express his hard-won belief in Christian involvement in society, quite apart from the not unwelcome extra income; but for the minister and other Presbyterian hard-liners locally, it was a matter of no mean importance. "The case of Miss J. M. Marshall" (no relation to the minister) was then receiving full exploitation in the press following her suspension from a teaching post after her conversion to Roman Catholicism, a suspension that shortly developed into an outright dismissal. Soon *The Scotsman* and the teaching union (via a public demonstration in Edinburgh) were to take up the cause. The debate was long, bitter, and very public. That WDB was prepared to become involved in such an outcry shows the sort of stuff he was made of, not a little of which was passed on to his son. We should not, however, draw the conclusion that WDB shared the grotesque intolerance of some of his colleagues, any more than we may draw that conclusion of Willie himself. The vote, however, was lost; WDB placed second out of eleven applicants. Thirteen years were to elapse before he again became involved with the school—in a very different capacity, as we shall see.

If his civic aspirations were thus disappointed, not so his other interests, for we now enter a period of five years in which WDB cast himself into a ceaseless round of activities that was arrested only by poor health, and that but temporarily. His son grew up in the shadow of this activity, positively influenced—not to say awestruck—by his father's activist manner, and aware that he was playing a notable part at the very center of the commercial, social, and religious life of the town and district. It was an influence that was not to be wasted, and we find the same pattern emerging in Willie himself. For all this activity, "he never took a penny piece," Willie declared in his autobiography.[11] He was to follow his father's example to the benefit of countless churches and charities.

There is a curious link between Motherwell and the town of WDB's upbringing that must often have occurred to him. The town that grew up around the garrison community at Fort William after General Mackay of Scourie rebuilt it after the '45 was named after King William II's wife, Mary—hence Maryburgh, a mark of respect much appreciated by the Court. In truth the citizens preferred it to stand for the mother of our Lord, but they did not see why the ambiguity should not serve their purposes and defend them against further anti-Catholic pressures. There was no such ambiguity with Motherwell, which from the very beginning had marked Catholic origins, the name being derived from "mother" and *wella* (Old English for "pool" or "eddy").[12] It is characteristic of primitive religion to be associated with such natural phenomena, rivers, pools, and wells being particularly prone to it, and it was normal for Christianized communities simply to transfer the former religious significances and allegiances to their newfound faith and deity. So it was at Motherwell. The Barclays will not have pursued too strongly the Catholic aspects, but will certainly have enjoyed the link between their former and their present homes. We need have little doubt that the topographical significance of the well will have found its way into some of WDB's sermons, linked with such texts as Genesis 21:19, Numbers 21:17, 2 Samuel 23:15, and Isaiah 12:3.

The year the Barclays arrived in the south was an important one in the history of church reunion in Scotland, for in it "a definite milestone was reached"[13] that "provoked a winter of discontent in the Church of Scotland"[14] and led to the historic *Articles Declaratory of the Church of Scotland in Matters Spiritual* (they are printed in full as an appendix to Muir's biography of John White, who was very largely their author).[15] There was consternation on both sides of the ecclesiastical divide at this time, but it is beyond doubt that reunion would have come sooner, and less painfully, had not the Great War intervened. Because of this, eight years were to elapse before the *Articles* were passed into law, and the rearguard action against union was meanwhile much strengthened. All that we know of WDB from this time suggests that he was solid for it, despite his growing friendship with the arch-antiunionist James Barr (later M.P. for Motherwell and grandfather of the present Professor James Barr, late of Manchester and now of Oxford).

As if to reinforce the blinkered pietism that now threatened the evangelical churches, the campaigns of Chapman and Alexander distracted Scotland from the issues raised by these and other writers and reinforced the old viewpoints through the winter of 1913/14. Like Moody and Sankey in their earlier campaigns, Chapman and Alexander offered a blend of evangelism and sacred music, evangelistic zeal and gospel preaching, that was difficult for those affected by their nineteenth-century counterparts to resist; mass evangelism, like theological liberalism, was taking on a classic framework that was quite different from the traditional teaching and preaching of the gospel. Alexander Whyte, despite his learning and age, was to admit that he simply could not stay away from the meetings, such were their spiritual and emotional constraint.[16] Into this atmosphere Willie was baptized, and we shall see its influences breaking out during his career and ministry. He was an ardent evangelical long before he came to understand and own the fruits of liberal thought. The deep impressions of these and similar meetings were made at an emotional level and would later obtrude themselves from time to time, giving rise to the charge of inconsistency by some, and perplexing others as to his true standing. What Chapman and Alexander pioneered in Willie's early years was soon established by the very similar ministry of Gypsy Pat Smith, ever a welcome visitor to the Barclays' home, whose endeavors WDB supported materially as well as by regularly chairing his meetings when they were held in Lanarkshire. Sadly, experience came to be valued more than doctrine in Smith's ministry and faith was reduced to an easy "believism" of facile formulas and stereotyped phrases.

WDB was now on an emotional and spiritual high, if one may use so trendy a term to explain the state of mind in which he found himself. It propelled him into an astonishing lay ministry that brought his name to the fore in the churches of Motherwell and Lanarkshire and beyond. By the time this five-year period was over, he had indeed preached in thirteen out of the fourteen churches of Motherwell to which his son refers in *Testament of Faith*. This was the period described by James Denney as being marked by "an immense dearth of preachers" in the Glasgow area;[17] the opportunities for a man of WDB's energy and talent were unlimited. Willie's schooldays' friend John Smith recalls as many as fifteen hundred men gathering to hear WDB preach in Motherwell. Fortunate the minister with such a collaborator and helper in his congregation!

The first reported sermon of WDB took place on 17 November 1912 at the Brotherhood meeting of his new church; clearly, the recommendations from Wick had made their mark. He preached on "A More Excellent Way," using as a text 1 Corinthians 12:31 (A.V.), which introduces the necessity for love over and above the possession of even the best talents. His great model had been Henry Drummond, who said of this passage, "To love abundantly is to live abundantly";[18] that was WDB's way, both more excellent than that of flashy gift, and more lasting. Mrs. Barclay herself was not much slower in commencing a similar role; we find her addressing the sisterhood meeting on the 23rd of January. Public speaking was not her forte and this is the only time a reference is made to her doing so. Her husband, however, now came to the fore, and very many of his engagements were for the various Sisterhood meetings of the district. *The Motherwell Times* reports over forty such engagements during the next twelve months (there were certainly others that went unreported), which gives an indication of the pace he set himself. By April 1916 the paper carried a notice that he was unable to preside at the Brotherhood Meeting's "Patriotic Concert"—he appears to have become President very soon after their settlement in the town (in August 1913, in fact)—"through ill-health."

It was not only adults who enjoyed his services and sermons; the children also held him to be a great favorite. He was full of stories ("they just tripped out of him" commented his nephew, sixty years later), and the local newspaper commented that he was "a gifted speaker to children." I have not found a similar commendation for any other speaker in its pages over many years, which shows the impact he made. One of his regular engagements was at the Hallelujah Mission in Motherwell (also a Methodist holiness group), where they went so far as to label him "the local evangelist."[19] Evidently he had not lost the Moody touch! But it was his message rather than his method that evoked this description, for in that he was purely evangelical. Withal he had "the common touch": he spoke their language and knew the things that motivated them and distressed them and led them to the Source of help and happiness. In his church there was a branch of the Christian Workers' Association, largely a lay organization that existed to promote fellowship and evangelism at "the shop-floor level." It is wholly characteristic of WDB's style that they should find him a very acceptable speaker, admiring particularly the courage of this senior banker who was not ashamed to nail his colors to the industrial mast.

With all this going on in Willie's formative years, it is not surprising that he formed an impressive picture of his father in his mind, as Willie's psychologist friend observed.[20] WDB was a *very* impressive man, whether judged by his sporting interests and activities (cricket, shinty, golf, rowing, and football), by his business accomplishments, by his home life (not least the daily prayers at which all gathered, without fail), by his church work (elder and lay preacher of particular note, despite Willie's mistaken denial of it),[21] or socially, local literary and musical associations finding in him an intelligent and articulate supporter. But this list by no means exhausts his interests and responsibilities. In addition to all this he served as treasurer of the Motherwell Auxiliary of the National Bible Society of Scotland from 1912 to 1916, as treasurer of the Lanarkshire Christian Union from 1913 to 1929, and in various other capacities for other groups involved in the industrial and civic life of the town.

Another aspect of WDB's service, connected with his being an elder of the church but taken a good deal more seriously than is often the case, was the visiting that he so conscientiously and methodically saw to. I am put in mind of a deacon in a church I once served as minister who refused the task of visitation precisely because he *was* the local bank manager; not so with WDB, who refused to partition his life into airtight compartments. In March 1914 his duties were extended even further when he became the treasurer of the Dalziel United Free Church. *The Motherwell Times* commented that it was "a dreich, dreich job,"[22] but no job undertaken for Christ and his church would be so described by WDB.

During this time WDB's YMCA interests were not allowed to perish. From the first he showed himself willing to serve the local branch in any way he could—by helping from time to time in its supervision, taking on occasional fellowship meetings and administration duties, and so on. By the end of 1916, despite his illness, he was appointed to its governing body and was found actively promoting (if not actually siring) its first "At Home" gathering. Other positions in it had been picked up on the way—for example, in 1914 he had been made honorary Vice President of the recently established Golf Club of the YMCA, happily uniting two of his many interests.

There are two other quite extraordinary aspects of WDB's activities that are worthy of note. One of the regrets WDB carried was that he, a proud Highlander, son-in-law to a Highlander of Highlanders who not only spoke the national language but actually sought to perpetuate its literature, was not familiar with Gaelic himself. Undoubtedly, he had sought from time to time to remedy this, but fitfully and without any success. Learning the language in earnest became his leisure-time pursuit at the age of fifty-five. Aided presumably by his wife, who had been fluent in the language since childhood, he now enrolled at his son's school and eventually became so proficient in the language that he was frequently selected to preside over the local Highlanders' Association and asked to read to them from the Gaelic New Testament.

The second extraordinary activity carries over from his Wick (and former) days in literary societies. In January 1917 he delivered a paper at the Literary and Debating Society of the YMCA on Tennyson's *Idylls of the King,* which the paper described as "a realistic and beautiful exposition." Because it mirrors the atmosphere in which Willie grew up, as well as portraying the influences under which he came, I excerpt from the long report:

> Mr Barclay traced the growth of the Arthurian legend from its frail historic basis of a Welsh King who ruled about 500 AD and a band of doughty knights who formed his retinue. He referred to the numerous attempts made by writers and poets to immortalise the story, but Tennyson, he said, had raised it to rank with the classics of literature. . . . Mr Barclay was of opinion that they were most significant as allegorical expositions of the poet's outlook upon life. In this sense the motif of the whole poem was the great moral struggle between good and evil—the low against the high, the animal against the spiritual. He went on to show how the moral issue worked out in the poem; how the unhallowed love of Lancelot for Guinevere the Queen, affected the whole order; and how, notwithstanding the purity and high-mindedness of King Arthur, and the lofty ideals to which his knights were sworn, this defection of Lancelot from the path of virtue brought about the final break up of the "table round" and the passing hence of Arthur himself into the great unknown.

Manifestly, it follows the line he took when he read a similar paper at the Wick Literary Society. Its most prominent point is his instinctive application of such matters to life and faith.[23] That it did not gratify everyone may be seen when Dr. James Knight took the same subject a few months after this, interpreting the *Idylls* quite differently, reversing some of WDB's conclusions, and arguing for a Central Scotland provenance for the legend. What WDB made of that we are not told, but one suspects that, having delivered himself of the ethical value of the piece, and having enjoyed "the intellectual sneeze" of giving the lecture, he was quite content to listen to controversial viewpoints with a satisfied chuckle; in that his son certainly emulated him later!

These were not carefree days. On 4 August 1914 war was declared, taking both government and nation by surprise. Scotland did not fare so badly as England at this time, particularly in the matter of food shortages, as Annie S. Swan (one of WDB's favorite authors) has pointed out,[24] but the issues relating to the hostilities were tremendous. Scotland more than England had taken German culture and scientific progress very seriously: her ministers were much more frequently trained there than the English, and this overturned the predominating attitudes. WDB was not caught up in the theological interchange that went on except at a distance, still less in the philosophical exchanges (or, more accurately, borrowings), but the shock waves were nevertheless acute and lasting. By the spring of 1916, the Kaiser's men had left their visiting card in Scotland in the form of the first zeppelin raid, and the grim reality of war and its convincing negation of civilization's most cherished beliefs had been made. Too old to fight, WDB sought to play his part in stirring up interest in "the righteous cause," and by making provision for the easing of the troops' conditions with gifts of money and tobacco (e.g., to the fund established by Captain Kidd of Motherwell)[25] and by making contributions for the aid of those overrun by "the German menace" (e.g., to the Belgian Relief Funds). He followed the progress of the war assiduously and was even found seeking to heighten morale by giving lectures on "The Present War" and similar topics. One of the key meetings took place in 1915, when he chaired a meeting that was attended by all civic dignitaries and ministers (that fact itself demonstrates the respect in which he was held by the community) and at which Alderman Wilkins of Derby (a former mayor with important industrial connections with Motherwell) spoke on the subject "On the Tracks of the German"—a hopeful title, as at that time the allies were in retreat. Nothing mattered more to WDB than his Brotherhood cause; it was never in greater danger.

School for Willie, Public Recognition for WDB

On the personal side of things, life continued for the Barclays through a period of sadness and infirmity (quite apart from WDB's own indispositions). In 1914 Daniel McLeish died, just short of his eightieth birthday. It was a particularly harsh blow for his youngest daughter, who had lived with and cared for her father over so many years. The blow fell heavily on Isabella McLeish too, she being now an aged lady whose latter strength had largely been consumed in looking after her failing brother. She was to become a regular and honored guest of Bank House, often staying for long periods, and beguiling young Willie (then only a boy of seven) with tales of Highland daring and mischief. (When she was not with them she would be found at the homes of Mrs. Barclay's two sisters, the three of them ensuring for her a happy and carefree time in the twilight of her life.) As we noticed earlier, it was from here that Miss McLeish donated the blackthorn stick of '45 fame to the West Highlands Museum, WDB himself making the necessary arrangements. Just to hold that unprepossessing piece of history is to feel the ancient arguments and exploits in a personal way! Doubtless Willie felt so too, though at an age when its meaning will not have been fully appreciable to him.

Despite the problems of the past, WDB ensured that his father-in-law was suitably laid to rest, and in full honor. Through the proud gates of the former military cemetery they passed (erected with McLeish's blessing some eighteen years earlier, when the last remains of the fort were taken over by the railway company), past the knoll soon to manifest the triumphs and glories of the Black Watch, and on to that reserved for the Lintons and the McLeishes, which looked westward across Loch Linnhe and northeastward to Glen Nevis and its mighty neighbor. The Linton memorial, standing four meters high in grey marble, is an effective symbol of the worthiness of the family at Coruannan. The McLeish monument, slightly smaller (appropriately smaller for immigrants, one may infer) and made of red marble, already declared the sad tale of McLeish's misfortunes—of both wife and only son William. Had Willie been older, he might well have recalled Cicero, one of his favorite Greek authors, by the mouth of the Elder Cato describing the sad inversion of the order of nature when a father is called to bury his son, as they looked at the comments memorializing James Williams's early demise.

On a happier note, and doubtless with much prayer for another Willie's health and safety, they returned to the steel town to further their son's academic development. With the majority of Edwardian parents, the Barclays were charged with a great desire for social and intellectual brilliance and were hopeful that their son would do well. They were not to be disappointed. Of the elementary years we know nothing at all, but we do have information concerning his secondary schooling from Willie himself, and from the records of Dalziel High (DHS in popular parlance). Thanks to the capital reporting of *The Motherwell Times* we are able to compile Willie's school record. There is no mention of him at the end of the 1913 session, though Irene Tyrell, whose abilities were to challenge Willie's right through the nine-year period they shared together, already made her mark by sharing the top prize in her year. Perhaps Willie was enduring one of his bouts of poor health. Certainly this was the year in which his main work seems to have been done at home and from his sickbed, when he "learned more miscellaneous knowledge than school could ever have taught me."[26]

Dalziel High School had no special claims to make; it was not even the best-rated school in the area (Hutcheson's Grammar School took that honor). The sons of the gentry and of the *nouveaux riches* were sent to the well-known schools in Glasgow or Edinburgh. But DHS did have a great reputation for solid, broadly based work, along with a good sporting tradition.[27] We should see Willie's enrollment there as much a political decision as academic, for his father would not have considered sending his boy to a school of special privilege, though financially it could easily have been done. What Mrs. Barclay thought of this, from her position of privilege and prestige, we are not informed; but to Dalziel High School Willie went. Founded in 1898, in Aibles Street, the school had been opened by Lord Haldane in September of that year. It moved to its present site in 1914, but, being requisitioned by the War Office, it was not open to pupils till August 1918, just after Willie's commencement as a junior. As will be seen from the photograph on page 47, it has a most handsome appearance (*The Motherwell Times* described it as "the most attractive school building in the country") and is more like a university college than a school in an industrial town. The Duchess of Hamilton Park opposite lends to this appearance. Its compactness generates a certain intimacy, which in turn begets the friendliness for which it is noted.

When Willie first attended DHS, the rector was David Grieg, a dignified, frock-coated, austere man of whom it was often said that "his laugh certainly did

Dalziel High School, "the most attractive school building in the country"

not echo along the corridors." His forbidding manner matched the dignity of the main corridor of the school, with its vaulted ceiling, tessellated floor, and large pillars. But it seems to have had no effect on the sometimes irresponsible Willie, whose usual reserve was wont to break down from time to time in boisterous laughter and high jinks. By now Grieg was approaching retirement and unwell, with the result that both the academic pitch and the general discipline of the school were slipping somewhat. It changed, as we shall see, in the autumn of 1923 when David Anderson, M.C., M.A., F.E.I.S., became Rector. And how it changed!

By the time the results were publicized for the next session, Willie had begun to make his mark, taking first place in the boys' section of his class though slightly disadvantaged by age, his birthday falling in December. Irene Tyrell, yet again, was placed first: their "rivalry" had commenced. The session ended on a jolly note, with an exhibition of drill and dancing in the Town Hall, a call for "three cheers for the holidays" (adequately sustained), and the national anthem.[28]

The next session's results went unreported owing to wartime conditions, but *The Motherwell Times* did dwell at some length on the scarlet fever epidemic that raged during that winter, reporting that "nothing like it has been seen for years."[29] It was almost certainly this epidemic that resulted in Willie's deafness (he often referred to it as its cause in later years), and it is sad to reflect that he was not the only "ecclesiastical" casualty of it: in nearby Glasgow the great John White's daughter succumbed to it, too, as did very many children in that city. That epidemic was followed by another, in March 1917, of German measles, to which Willie also fell prey.[30] At the next School Board meeting it was reported, amid dark laughter, that "that is another grievance we have against the Germans."[31] Even the small comic relief that comment afforded was soon lost when it was later reported that of the children who went down with the malady no fewer than ninety-three had lost their fathers in armed conflict. The sorrow that was never far from Willie's experience of life thus impinged early upon him, not least in the sadness that permeated the whole school at such times. As if to impress the problems of such conflicts, A. D. Robertson, Willie's favorite teacher of a later time, went off to serve the colors, happily to return in good shape and with even a deeper appreciation of his beloved English literature and "the magic of words" that certainly never lost its grip on Willie.[32]

The war was not to end without one further—and savage—blow to the Barclay family. On 18 October 1918, just days before the armistice was declared, *The Motherwell Times* carried a report of the sinking of the *S.S. Leinster*, torpedoed off the British coast while on its way back home with several thousand soldiers returning for leave. "Ah Dieu! que la guerre est jolie!" cried the cavalier Guillaume Apollinaire, with sickening misapprehension. Among those many who died at sea was one Samuel Dugald Barclay, son of Robert and nephew of WDB. It was a broken uncle that Willie now saw coming to visit his parents with aunt and cousins stunned by the appalling waste and wantonness of the action. Lieutenant Barclay, of the Scottish Rifles (part of the famed Cameronians, whose exploits as the only rifle regiment in Scotland had won great honor for them in the troubles of South Africa in 1877 to 1879 and at Ladysmith in 1899 to 1902) had himself served with distinction, only to lose his life unarmed, unprepared, and on the eve of the peace. The tragedy was followed by an epidemic of influenza that raged through the schools of the area, closing many of them and actually doubling the mortality rate for the period. Troubled, anxious days!

The whole of Europe was suffering, of course, not just one family of one community—"suffering from shell-shock" in W. R. Nicoll's vivid phrase[33]— which led to "the menacing ground-swell which followed the storm of the great war."[34] The menace touched all aspects of life—social, economic, physical, psychological (who will deny that war—the word is derived from the old High German word *werre*, "confusion"—is but a form of madness?), and religious. The men who returned were very different from the men who went out, and those who failed to return, or only half-returned, left lasting gaps in the memories of many and in society as a whole. From such times Willie early imbibed from his parents (still very Brotherhood-conscious) a horror and a hatred for conflict, particularly armed conflict.

One of the first duties incumbent upon society after settlement had been reached and a return to "civvy" life was under way was to record the heroisms and list appropriately those whose lives had been lost. WDB was in the forefront of aiding special assistance funds of various sorts, organizing memorial funds—civic, banking, and ecclesiastical. In the midst of this postwar recovery, the world was shocked by horrific tales emanating from postrevolutionary Russia; WDB was presently appointed Honorary Treasurer of the Russian Famine Relief Committee, though whether from political or merely humanitarian reasons we cannot now say. To this post he added that of local treasurer to the Royal Infirmary, which brought his treasurerships to six, no less. Mrs. Barclay was not left out of this work. She found herself appointed to the War Pensions' Committee for the County of Lanark, which used to meet in the public library at Motherwell. It was continued for many years, and was an appropriate way to end her public service, which had commenced with auxiliary nursing work before the start of the century.

On a different level the quest for peace was disrupted by the ongoing strife over "the Irish problem." Some respite was achieved in the Anglo-Irish Treaty of 1921, but it was a superficial pact and only temporarily distracted public attention from the real problems in that unhappy land. A better hope was raised when the League of Nations was founded with much speech-making and naive optimism. WDB was now firmly committed to peace: the new organization found a very ready supporter and helper at Bank House, Motherwell.

One of the by-products of the War was an increasing dependence on machinery; the public sector experienced a considerable mechanization in subsequent years as well. At his bank WDB had now to cope not merely with writers and copyists, clerks and accountants, but with such strange devices as typewriters, adding machines, telephones, teleprinters, and even carbon paper. The innovations were greatly to facilitate commercial activity, but their introductory phase did nothing to alleviate the pressures on an already overworked, undermanned manager. Banks were still very much a male preserve, and the rewards were not overgenerous. The standard remuneration for bank clerks was a mere £247 per annum at the time, even after twenty years' service. Returning servicemen, now well used to dealing with officers and officialdom on less autocratic terms than some old-fashioned bank mandarins, became more assertive and reliant on the good offices of the Bank Officers' Guild. It did little to lessen WDB's pressures, which were made considerably worse in 1922, when his senior teller was transferred to his old branch at Anderston, Glasgow. It was the year in which the Barclays celebrated their tenth anniversary at Motherwell, but, typically, he chose to do it by adding yet more responsibilities to himself, in the form of the suboffice at Newarthill, the oversight of which he now undertook.

By this time WDB's position locally was both strong and influential. His bank was looked on as one of the firm's most important branches, and WDB enjoyed the personal friendship of the Secretary of the Bank of Scotland, Arthur Rose. They had both been apprenticed in the early 1880s and had much in common, not least the pursuit of stronger handicaps on Hamilton's and other golf courses. Unlike many of his colleagues, WDB did not conclude his business meetings and arrangements "wi' a dram o' the hard stuff," a forebearance that was counted for special righteousness in those temperance-sensitive days.

His public recognition reached its apogee in May 1925 when *The Motherwell Times* announced his appointment to the bench as a Justice of the Peace for the County of Lanark.[35] In a spirited article the paper pointed out that from now on he was to be known as "Mr. Justice Barclay," reminding its readers that his friends had often chaffed him with the comment that one day he would find "in his morning budget" a call to the kirk. The state had beaten the kirk to the draw, but

> knowing Mr Barclay as we do, and appreciating his fitness for either church or bench, it comes as no suprise to find him called to the high and responsible office of a Justice; and assuredly he will "wag his heid" on the bench with the same facility and friendliness of disposition as hitherto he has wagged it in the pulpit while fulfilling the pulpit for one or other of the local ministers.

The Editor goes on to express on behalf of the community the hope that "the new duties may be light and the territories free from serious crime and trouble." In the light of these comments we may wryly reflect on the goings-on twelve months hence in the vicinity, when the calamity of the General Strike convulsed the region, and when the courts were full of crime and trouble. However that may be, the readers were at this juncture reminded that the usual duty of a Justice "is to sign certificates for lost pawn tickets, and applications for relief in some form or other"—duties WDB was very glad to perform in pursuit of righteousness, menial though they be.

Final Schooldays and Accomplishments

All this did not go unnoticed by Willie. Even had his father not taken a keen interest in Willie's out-of-school passion, the local YMCA (by now WDB was on the governing body permanently and regularly installed as one of the Vice Presidents), it could not be otherwise. He was himself going through that "complex stage of adolescence, with its gleams of blinding light, its pitiful falls, its loneliness, its wistfulness, its perplexities"—words that Willie is said to have written scarcely a dozen years after the experience, and that are highly suggestive of his conflicting moods and feelings.[36] Not least does it express the peculiar difficulties of an only child of successful and publicly appreciated parents, greatly loved by them to be sure, but perhaps not quite understood because of the huge gap (not merely of age) that separated them. We shall see that something of this tension remained with him throughout his life, finding expression in home and habit and work. Despite the rock-like outward appearance, there was a sensitivity, a vulnerability even, which is an essential characteristic of the man. Not that he was a Peter Pan figure, especially in the Barrie-esque sense of personal and ethical immaturity, but he never found complete self-dependence nor did he escape from the need to have support and encouragement.

Like many young men at this age, Willie developed acne, which proved to be of a persistent and troublesome sort and left him with a rough complexion that was to characterize his features henceforth. It may well have been another cause of his equivocal relationships with women and his preference for male company which many have remarked on. This should not be overemphasized, however; his physical appearance was not the only cause. Consider this description by Sir John Colville, of one of Willie's great heroes of our time: "Having no sisters, and a mother whom he placed on a plane above the ordinary mortals, Churchill was slow in learning to understand the other sex, much as he admired female beauty."[37] It was so with Willie too, though not to the same extent; church and school provided opportunities to redress the balance. And the balance was redressed by his friendship with a veritable *entourage* of mainly younger girls—known in the school as Barclay's harem! It was quite unexceptionable, particularly in light of contemporary standards of school behavior; their one laxity lay in the girls procuring for Willie cigarettes, which he smoked in places well-known to school children the world over. With special daring, he even smoked some at home during his parents' absences, blowing the smoke up the chimney to hide the deed.

We know little of his spiritual development at this time. He attended his parents' church with them Sunday by Sunday, was a member of the Sabbath school, learned well his catechism and many passages of scriptures, read "improving" books, and was especially fond of the tales of the Covenanters and the adventures of missionaries as they opened up the dark continents of India and China and Africa with the gospel, as became a member of the Boys' Brigade. Thomas Marshall prepared him for his first communion, that "entrance on manhood," to use Alexander Whyte's phrase.[38] His involvement in the Boys' Brigade built on the foundation the other activities laid, in physical as in moral and spiritual terms.

Willie's interests were by no means all religious in tone. Happily, WDB never lost his love of sport, and so athletics—swimming, tennis, football, golf, and cricket—were woven into the texture of his outdoor life, with table-tennis, billiards, and dancing (the latter much to his parents' concern) woven into that of his indoor life. During these years, he was later to recall when writing to W. J. Noble, they holidayed in Largs, staying at a hotel called The Silverne. Rebecca's presence ensured that he was not completely lonely. One suspects that it was as much her influence as anyone else's that preserved in him a love for the common things of life. Nothing vulgar was ever allowed, but her much more relaxed attitude toward ordinary things and people, indeed her appreciation of them, was noticed by Willie and made his own. It contrasted sharply with his mother's high-mindedness and regal presence.

Scholastically, things were now going very well for Willie. The unhealthy start he made at Dalziel High School was now a thing of the past, and his parents were delighted at the manifest aptitudes he displayed. He now took the top position on the boys' side of the school, just as regularly as Irene Tyrell took it on the girls'. In 1920 he was placed first in English, History, Geography, Maths, Science, French, and Latin (though unplaced in German, at which he never excelled: anti-German feelings were still high at this time, and may well account for his failure—now and throughout his life—to appreciate their language and literature; whenever he felt the need for a Continental viewpoint, it was usually to French that he went, as the library records show). It was a year of triumph, for he was made *Dux* of the Intermediate School, the highest place achievable, the first sweet taste of real success.[39] Additionally, he was awarded a Special Prize (of "light literature") for the best essay on Temperance in the twelve-to-fourteen age group.[40] On this occasion he was paraded before the local M.P. (R. F. W. R. Nelson), the Governing Board of the school, and the usual gathering of parents, teachers, and friends. Not least among these last were Captain and Mrs. John Colville, owners of the great steelyard nearby and important clients of WDB; more importantly, they were closely involved in the work of the Lanarkshire Christian Union which lay so near to WDB's heart.

It was during this summer of 1920 that Willie resolved to become a minister. Ever shy of speaking of his own spiritual experiences (his father's excessive partiality for "testimony meetings" may well have been a factor in this, for Willie attended a number of them when he accompanied his father to various churches), he only once writes of the origins of the decision. It occurred, appropriately, at Fort William, while he was on holiday with his parents; it followed a sermon (presumably by Reverend John Mackintosh, whose ministry lasted for over thirty years, and who is still talked of today).[41] After this service Willie took a solitary walk along the High Street, at the end of which he dedicated himself to the service of God at a stone that many years after he could look upon as his private Bethel. His decision brought nothing but sheer joy to his parents; it was a fulfillment of their hopes and prayers and of their friends' prayers and blessings over so many years. WDB's joy was completed when he heard that he had been appointed Commissioner to the General Assembly of the United Free Church on their return from holiday.

The excellent results obtained in 1920 were not quite continued the following year, but were nevertheless very satisfactory. Willie was placed first in English (his favorite subject at this time) and in History and Geography, and came second in Latin. By now the immediate postwar boom conditions were deteriorating sharply, not least in Motherwell, where the local paper refers to the "collapse in the steel trade."[42] The paper also speaks of "the moral slump" in society in connection with which it includes political agitation—notably the miners' activities, now of many weeks' duration; the Irish problem (a Sinn Fein arsenal had been found at nearby Wishaw),[43] and the aggressive activities of the Orange Order, led locally by Ephraim Connor, the Ian Paisley of his day.[44] Some growth in industry (especially engineering, chemicals, and the motor trade) was being made, but already signs of the thin-faced '30s were evident and causing much apprehension.

The academic year of 1922 closed with Willie touching the lowest point of his entire school career, obtaining only a first in English and a second in History. We need have no doubts that WDB did not let the matter go uncommented upon! But the year following the effect of his timely exhortation bore fruit: Willie gained first place in his beloved English as well as in History (which he shared with Irene Tyrell) and Greek. It ought not to be supposed that WDB's exhortation was solely responsible, nor that Willie was entirely to blame for the lapse, however; the poor health of David Grieg in this his final year at the school led to a general loosening of academic standards throughout the institution.

On the arrival of David Anderson from the nearby Hutcheson's Boys' Grammar School, where he had been head of the maths department, a new tone was introduced along with new ways and attitudes. Tall, elegant, and military in dress and bearing, he brought to the school a discipline and sharpness quite unknown hitherto. Fear arrived with David Anderson: the fear of a single word of reproof, of the lash of the tawse, and like punishments. Silence pervaded the corridors as pupils and staff went about their business in serried ranks and superorderly conduct. It brought new meaning to the idea of manliness. A former Guardsman, with military distinctions of no common sort, Anderson was respected as well as feared; he was admired as an ideal example for impressionable youth. Lazy work or careless dress brought its proper response, and soon Motherwell was humming with the transformation being made. He gets no mention in *Testament of Faith*—a Freudian omission?—but we know that on at least one occasion Willie and his friends crossed his path and were hauled before him for an explanation. The incident took place after an examination, when the pupils treated themselves to a walk around the park opposite in celebration of their finished ordeal—without permission! And Willie could remember the results with pangs of conscience over thirty years later.[45]

It was not only the discipline that Anderson transformed. He made the classes coeducational (thus greatly freeing Willie from the reserve he showed toward the opposite sex) and he introduced rugger, a cricket club (in the process, talking the civic authorities into allowing them to use the park for this), hockey (for the girls), swimming, badminton, a literary society, and a school magazine, *The Dalzielian*. A new "House" system was provided to put the discipline on a basis of competition between pupils rather than staff, and "At Home" meetings, at which parents could come and see for themselves what life at Dalziel High School was all about, were also introduced.

A Log Book records these and many other matters that concerned the new Rector, such as the new timetable based on eight equal periods per day that he introduced. There was "much dilatoriness on the part of the pupils coming into school" he wrote on the 23rd of August, and "prayers are still not to my liking" he noted on the 4th of October. That same day he reports "the clocks very erratic; new batteries to be installed," and three weeks later he ominously comments that he had "dealt with 'the ice-cream problem.'" Little wonder the Inspecting Clerk to the Authority, R. C. T. Maer, commented that "the new

Head-master has thrown himself into the work of the school with much enthusiasm and energy and is doing everything possible to enhance the reputation of the school and to foster a good school spirit. . . . The general tone and discipline are excellent."

Inevitably, academic standards throughout the school rose, though the inspector commented adversely on the fact that "none of the candidates in Higher Latin reached a high standard in the written tests" (they did so in the vocal tests), a view that conflicts with Willie's unstinting praise for "Geordie" Robertson. Despite his "glorious voice," as Duncan Black recalls it, "like Harry Lauder's,"[46] he was ill-equipped to teach beyond the third grade, and was retired early in consequence. Maer favorably reported on the newly established Greek classes, "good progress" having been made under "Monkey Brand" Paterson. As we learn from *Testament of Faith,* it was in the tower of Dalziel High School that Willie bathed his soul in Homer's delectable verses.[47] Whatever emphasis he later placed on his sporting interests (I shall show that it was a somewhat inexact emphasis), he was now willing to put that aside to further his academic potential—as was Jimmy Paterson, his conscientious teacher. The situation between them was rather like that which obtained between C. S. Lewis and William T. Kirkpatrick, who tutored the young Lewis, also destined to become a classicist and lover of English literature, and not least a great apologist for Christian faith and thought.[48] This was the year that Dalziel High School made the Schools' Football Cup Final, but Willie was not chosen to play. "Bun" Barclay, as he was called, was not entirely cut out for such events. As *The Dalzielian* was to report, "William Barclay is whole-hearted and fast; can cross a nice ball, but his ball-control is weak."[49] On another occasion, when they were beaten by Bellshill Academy, it commented that the match "proved that Shaw was not a forward, nor Barclay a half-back."[50] Despite this, he was selected to play for Saint Andrew's Guild against Larkhall in the YMCA league, which they won by a score of one to nothing. Willie played center-half (those were the days of traditional placings and formal play) but he failed to attract the eye of the reporter—not for the last time, as we shall see.[51]

But if his sporting accomplishments did not reach the highest levels, his literary talents had caught the eye of the Rector, resulting in his appointment to his first editorial post: a place on the editorial committee of *The Dalzielian* (composed of teachers A. Sommerville and R. A. Cormack, and pupils S. Anderson, Walter Henderson, A. R. Paterson, Irene Tyrell, and Willie). Willie (under Sommerville and Cormack's watchful eyes) was editor, though it was a very cooperative undertaking between Willie and his fellow pupils.

The first issue of *The Dalzielian* appeared at Christmas 1923, unpriced. It was an excellent effort of twenty-eight pages, with ten pages of advertisements from local traders (it should have been eleven, but the last page is blank except for the appeal "Support our Advertisers" and two blocks "To Let"). The proofreading was not quite as good as it might have been, Julian Huxley's name being misspelled, but it carried a broad range of articles and comments, not a few of

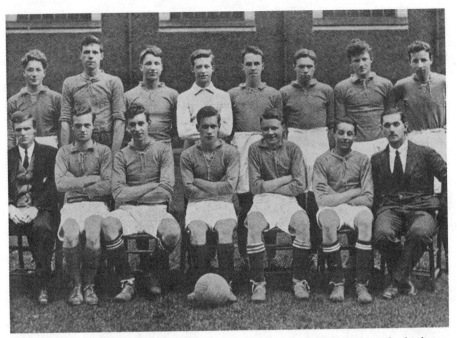

The 1923 Dalziel High School football team. Willie stands third from the right, back row.
[Photo courtesy of *The Dalzielian*]

The 1925 Dalziel High School Magazine Committee. Willie sits first on the left, front row.
[Photo courtesy of *The Dalzielian*]

which betray Willie's puckish sense of humor and "the seriousness of immaturity." One article, for example, is on the School Hymnary, and carries suggestions for the various occasions:

Morning Praise:	"Come Children, Join to Sing"
Lunch Bell:	"We Have Heard a Joyful Sound"
Lunch:	"We Could Not Do without Thee"
Examinations:	"Oh, Dark and Dreary Day"
Critical Lessons:	"Courage, Brother, Do Not Stumble"
English Lessons:	"Sleep on Beloved, Sleep"
French Lessons:	"Here We Suffer Grief and Pain"
The Magazine Contributors:	"How Bright These Glorious Spirits Shine"

The second issue of the magazine continued the good work, providing a lively insight into school and community. Sadly, it also offered an obituary to David Grieg, their late Rector. In this issue the first published piece definitely from Willie (signed simply "B") appeared, a poem entitled *Ave Atque Vale* ("Hail and Farewell"). It is notable not only for demonstrating his powers as a schoolboy poet, but for providing a real insight into both his general attitude and his thoughts on individual subjects.

> Within these four gray walls for twelve long years
>   The even tenor of my way has lain.
>   I have been bound, in youth, by learning's chain
> To tread instruction's tortuous paths with fears;
> And in my conquests I have laughed, and tears
>   Have been my only mead, when I would fain
>   Have sent my cheerless tasks to Pluto's reign.
> But now the hour to quit thee, school, appears.
> I sport no more in careless joy of heart.
>   To learning's business must I turn, from play,
>   From youthful joy to manhood's sterner day.
> Alas! I find it wondrous hard to part.
>   I never saw thy pleasures till they fade away,
> Thy days are unappreciated while they stay.
>
> The stony ways of Maths. I've trod with fear;
>   At French's tasks I've labour'd late at night
>   That I might gain upon its myst'ries, light;
> Amongst the whirling eddies did I steer
> Of thy forgotten tongue, oh! Latin, dear
>   To pedants, with thy tales of blood and might.
>   No less I've journey'd through Greek's Stygian night,
> Until with Xenophon, I seem'd to cheer.
> The sea! The sea! With poets I have soared
>   To Elysian fields, in fancy's highest flight,
>   Whilst over wrong, the victory of right,
> As all day long the crash of cannon roared,

The Book of History to me has shown
As I approached the steps of learning's throne.

The dawn of schooldays was to me a pain,
Their sometimes weary course I did disdain;
But now I ask thee to prolong, in vain,
The way which I alas! did often stain
    With hours of idleness and wasted time.
    But now the final bell's last ring doth chime;
    The curtain's down; and this the youthful mime
    Is finished, and I tell in faltering rhyme
My last regrets, my many hopes, my fears
For times that are gone by, and future years.

He was to contribute two more poetic pieces to the magazine. The first was a short and somber piece entitled "Regret," which may well have made WDB anxious, inasmuch as it offers very little understanding of a life revitalized by the life of Christ.

Regret, thou grimmest phantom of our life!
    Crouched o'er the ashes of the silent past,
    Too late we realise that what is cast
Returns not, knowing failure in the strife.
Brooding Regret! Thy thrice envenom'd knife
    Cuts to our inmost souls, e'er to the vast
    Abyss of slumb'rous death we sink, aghast
At the close swish of Time's unfailing scythe . . .

The second, entitled "From Catullus," is much more a school exercise, and closes on the same note as his first piece. This latter piece appeared in December 1924, when his mind was on the final two laps before school days were ended. In that same issue he included two more articles of his own, which probably indicates a lack of response to appeals for material from his fellow pupils rather than an early symptom of writer's itch. We may well infer the pressure he was putting on his friends and acquaintances from an editorial in which he quotes the verse of "one of our younger poets" who wrote "not long after we took over our duties":

Oh, Dalzielians! Oh, Dalzielians!
    Whose inky bards have often sung.
The lunatic staff is still at large,
    The Editor is still unhung.

The other articles by Willie in this issue consisted of a spirited piece on the pitfalls of teatime (produced in full below) and a review of a third-form challenge to the school magazine. "It is usually with feelings far from pleasant," wrote Willie, "that an Editor views the production of a periodical as a rival to the child of his own genius."[52] However, he was *not* like the average editor, and therefore welcomed the newcomer "in spite of the somewhat bitter and violent threats expressed against us." He applauds "the delightful freedom" that pervades the magazine (and is expressed by its pained reaction to French and Latin), and even greets with equanimity "its last inspired outburst against the unfortunate Editor of *The Dalzielian*": forgiveness was offered! He especially likes the cartooning (he always had time for this underestimated art form, as we shall see), but wished "that the artist responsible for these pictures would lend his talent to the aid of the school magazine and not, so to speak, blush unseen and waste his ability on the desert air." *Deuce!* Nevertheless, he emphasized that his aim was not to discourage but to encourage, and in congratulating the producers, and wishing them good success, he characteristically greeted their effort "not as a rival but as a supplement and companion." This is vintage Barclay: he was never more himself than in the magnanimous expression of encouragement and succor.

The magazine offered quotations of great authors selected by the pupils, much in the way *The Reader's Digest* offers "Quotable Quotes" today. An early one came from Byron and is easily identified as the Editor's own:

> 'Tis pleasant, sure, to see one's name in print;
> A book's a book altho' there's nothing in't.

Four were explicitly offered as Willie's selection and carry his name. They are as interesting for their observations on life as they are for the indications they provide of the sort of authors he now found pleasure in:

> And tho' that he was worthy, he was wise,
> And of his part as meek as is a mayde.
> —Chaucer

One suggests a thought—and a temptation—that may well have been congenial to him:

> Blest with each talent and each art to please,
> And born to write, converse and live with ease.
> —Pope

And one he was soon enough to discover, once his real vocation had been realized:

> The devil can cite Scripture for his [own] purpose.
> —Shakespeare

The last one shows how early he had developed humbleness of mind, and what it was based on:

> Like Cato gives his little senate laws,
> And sits attentive to his own applause.
> —Pope

His last word in this regard must be the one he chose for the whole school, and dedicated to it. It comes from an old Scottish toast and exemplifies the irrepressibility of spirit that characterized his whole life, though not without an element of self-criticism:

Here's tae us!
Wha's like us!

Who indeed?

And now to that prose piece, the only one we have from this time, which displays his style, humor, and, incidentally, the sort of behavior he could imagine of himself at some of the drawing-room occasions he endured when his mother and her sisters and friends met.

On Taking Tea

THERE are two sets of circumstances under which a man may take tea. In the first place he may partake of the delightful beverage in the seclusion of his own home and in the company of his own family, in which case there can be no more pleasant occupation. But the second method is a dreadful nightmare. It happens when you are ushered into a drawing room of ladies, among whom you are the only man.

There follows the interchange of small-talk, accompanied, on your part, by sickly smiles and inane giggles. Now, however brilliant a conversationalist you may normally be, unless you have the nerves of a big game hunter and the self-assurance of a quack doctor, you can never be successful in a ladies' drawing-room. If you are lucky the conversation only lasts for about three minutes, which, stretched by the elasticity of uncomfortableness, feel like three hours; and into these three minutes you contrive to pack enough spoonerisms, stutterings and stammerings to supply a careful humourist with material for a dozen books.

Your hostess, whom you know to be a malignant spirit disguised as a distressingly beautiful young lady, begs you to accept a cup of tea. Not knowing what else to do you accept the offer. You are handed a cup, as highly coloured with paint as the surrounding female society, as thin as an egg-shell, and as small as a thimble.

You try to balance it on your knee, and, not being a conjurer, your early efforts do not meet with success. You at last succeed after spilling half the contents in your saucer. Then comes the crisis. You want to drink your tea—presuming that is why you got it—but you want to drink it GRACEFULLY! You grasp the handle of your cup with your thumb and forefinger and raise it to your lips with a spasmodic jerk, which, of course, is not conducive to the stability of its contents. You know you will gurgle fearfully as you swallow, and, as you are contemplating this contingency, your cup slips from the perpendicular and deposits the contents in your lap.

Immediately you jump up, and incidentally send your cookie on an aviation trip to the opposite end of the room. In your confusion you make a half-turn and switch a plateful of meringues on to the floor. Just to swell the wreckage you kick out with your heel for some insane reason and—down goes the cake-stand! Quite confounded at all this devastation, you flop down on a chair and, in doing so, inadvertently sit down on a specially juicy apple-tart. With marvellous alacrity you spring up, clawing the seat of your trousers, and dash from the room.

'En route', of course, it is up to you to break enough ornaments and little mirrors to keep a large family in bad luck for a hundred years.

At the door you meet the maid with a tea-pot. Ruthlessly you take her in your stride and she and the tea-pot describe a neat parabola in mid-air. Muttering what you shouldn't you at last make your exit, after tramping on the kitten and falling down stairs, and, needless to say, you crown it all by taking the wrong hat.

A. D. Robertson was his English teacher, and he must have found great satisfaction in the way Willie was preparing himself for the future. He it was who taught him not only "the magic of words," but the much more important "love for the beautiful." It extended the deep influence of his parents' home and lives, where Philippians 4:8 reigned supreme ("whatsoever things are true . . . honorable . . . just . . . pure . . . lovely . . . gracious"). As Duncan Black has pointed out, "A. D. Robertson merits all the praise which Bun can give. He let us see the beauty of words and language and, more than anyone else, taught us to think."[53] By such Willie was preserved from the austerity and dourness of Presbyterian life that influenced so many Scots; he was already appreciative of the absolutes of truth, goodness, and beauty he had tasted in the classical authors. Such things even now formed the domestic backdrop of his life in many ways.

It is at this point that the concept of *loveliness* (a Barclayan keyword) began to come to the fore, amid Motherwell's smoke and noise. It was a concept with which he had lived since birth, it being so obviously an essential part of his mother's life, but now he came to grasp it intellectually, and it provoked a deep internal response. Willie began to think of order, rightness, and propriety (all wholly characteristic of Daniel McLeish) as being integral to the sense of *wholeness* that was becoming basic to him. "Loveliness" had little to do with "beauty" as understood by beauticians; it was not cosmetic but real, and the search for it was to be a life-long pursuit for him. Amusingly, one of his lunchtime meetings in later life in Glasgow was interrupted by a cosmetic exhibition in an adjoining room. Willie's response was curt and devastating: he had no time for such superficialities (perhaps the emphasis many have made concerning his alleged indifference to women and his preference for male company touches reality at this point). He stressed the inner reality of beauty, "the idea of loveliness, of attractiveness, of graciousness, of that which delights the heart and gives pleasure to the eyes," as he interprets *kalos;*[54] sound, we may assert, is absent once more.

Mention of the good things, of the wholeness of life, reminds us of the place the YMCA had in his life at this time. Ignoring his father's influence for the moment, and it was very great, we might note that he often made light of his membership, waggishly suggesting that it was the dancing and the billiards that attracted him. Undoubtedly they did, but there was a far deeper and more lasting attraction, one that kept father and son involved with the movement for over eighty years between them.

Harold Begbie has suggested that the "Y," as it is known to its members, is essentially "an empire of *Christian manhood.*"[55] Clyde Binfield has suggested that it is dominated by "a muscular and evangelical faith." Nothing could have been better designed to attract Willie than this, as forty years earlier it had attracted his father. Moreover, Binfield claims that the YMCA "was among the last fruits of the Evangelical Revival," and this influence was not yet lost on its leaders and members. (Moody, it will be recalled, had his origins in the movement and introduced Drummond early to it—yet another strand in the close-knit Barclay tapestry).

Its motto, as Willie pointed out after his first visit to the London "Y," is *ut omnes unum sint:* "that they all may be one" (John 17:21).[56] And unity is one of the most crucial aspects of Willie's personality; it is the interpretative key to his thinking and, indeed, to his life, not merely in church unity (on which he possessed a particular viewpoint),[57] but more importantly in a comprehensive attitude toward reality in all its forms and expressions. The aim of the YMCA was "to win young men for Jesus Christ by uniting them in fellowship through activities designed to develop their powers of body, mind, and spirit, and to enable them to serve God and their fellows"[58]—body, soul, and spirit: the traditional tripartite structure of man's nature, which Willie strove in his teaching and preaching, his writing and broadcasting, to keep conjoined. The material and the spiritual, the physical and the incorporeal, the things of God and the things of man: he saw all these in their differing modes as essentially indivisible, different sides of the same coin, variable aspects of the same underlying reality. His world was truly one, and it was essentially—not contingently—sacramental, as we shall see.

It is precisely this aspect that produced in him a great admiration for the Boys' Brigade (which Henry Drummond always saw as the link between Sunday School, the YMCA, and the church),[59] as Willie emphasized when he wrote *God's Men, God's Church, and God's Life* (1952/53); its object is, he says, "The advancement of Christ's kingdom among boys, and the promotion of habits of Obedience, Reverence, Discipline, Self-respect and all that tends towards *true Christian manliness.*"[60] Both the YMCA and the Boys' Brigade sought to promote a healthy and balanced life-style, one that was appreciative of the best in man and in nature, wherein God revealed himself. Moffatt translates the "gracious" things of Philippians 4:8 as "high-toned," and while Willie was not yet aware of Moffatt's translation—WDB insisted upon the Authorized Version, using it only in their daily prayers—that was exactly the ideal he had been brought up to cherish, the one he sought to attain in his own life.

It is interesting that both organizations should mention Christian manliness at the time of expressing their respective objects, objects that hold together the material and the spiritual worlds of experience. It is another key trait of Willie's, one which used to get a great deal more emphasis than it does at present. John Caird preached a memorable and much-publicized sermon before the University of Glasgow on this very subject in 1871, seeking to show to his students that the true and full life was one of comprehensiveness, though his own understanding of Christian faith was deficient in some important aspects.[61]

On 4 July 1924, the staff and students, parents and distinguished guests of Dalziel High School gathered for the annual prize-giving in the Town Hall. It was an occasion of special interest as the Rector was to give his first sessional report. Notable changes, he explained, had taken place throughout the school. Enrollment was up by ten percent (there were now 570 pupils, reflecting the baby boom of the war years), an agreeable improvement to Anderson's mind. But unhappily, fewer than half of those eligible for higher education chose to avail themselves of it; he found this all the more curious in the face of the deepening depression. Some had even left their courses to go into mundane and unskilled work. The Rector was not happy, for he was now introducing a sixth form and clearly did not get the enrollment he had anticipated. Attendance at school was excellent, averaging ninety-four percent, no doubt a reflection of the introduction of stiffer discipline. Extramural activities were sustaining more interest as well, including the clubs for hockey, swimming, and cricket—this last "yet very much in its infancy." He was especially glad to report the founding of *The Dalzielian*. Mr. Anderson warned that those now obtaining their school-leaving certificates (Willie among them) were those "who had suffered through want of educational facilities in the war" (thus averting any undue criticism of his predecessor).

Competition, Mrs. Elizabeth Lumsden recalls, was very keen among the top classes, which included several quite brilliant pupils. James Longmuir became Moderator of the General Assembly in 1968; Andrew Bonar became a surgeon at Glasgow's Royal Infirmary; Kenneth Grant also became a surgeon; William McWhinnie became Procurator Fiscal at Aidrie; Walter Henderson became Headmaster at Bothwell, Glasgow; and Irene Tyrell became Headmistress of the nearby Hutchinson's Grammar School.[62] The *Dux* was in fact Irene Tyrell, Willie's archcompetitor over twelve years, who now claimed "the highest honor the school can bestow." She had excelled in both the academic and the sports spheres. *Proxime accessit* was Edward Houston. Willie came third. He sportingly states in his autobiography (though it is not entirely true of his school career), "True to form, I was . . . runner-up."[63] Lord Hamilton of Dalziel presented the prizes and made an appropriate speech. In it he sought to remind his hearers that "character is the one thing that helps us more than anything in life"; Willie was learning its lesson as a roar of cheers went up for the *Dux*. His lordship referred to two great features of the Scottish character that history has demonstrated: independence and a fine natural courtesy. Both of them were very readily seen in Willie, who returned home with his parents tucking his (shared) Watson History Prize under his arm, along with his school certificate, a somewhat minor accomplishment. The subjects enumerated on this were English, Maths, Latin, and French at Higher Grade, and Greek at Lower Grade. This latter result must have disappointed him, as it was by now his favorite subject. We should note that he took more subjects than even the *Dux* herself, so his "lesser" achievments may simply be a sign that he undertook too much, something he was to do on more than one occasion in the years to come.

There was much to talk about that year, for in February Ramsay Macdonald had become the first Socialist Prime Minister in the history of the country. True, he was still dependent on the votes of the Liberals to stay in power, but nevertheless it was a great talking-point for aware people, not least in the Barclay household. Willie's school came into contact with some of the related social problems in the winter, when the Rector introduced a Home Training Class for the unemployed girls of Motherwell. Twenty registered for it, which produced delighted comment in the Press and satisfaction in the School Log.

In the General Election of October an old friend of WDB's was elected Labour Member for the Motherwell and Wishaw constituency and gave cause for much comment. No doubt James Barr had much to say when he came to the Barclay house, as he was wont to do from time to time, and Willie must have listened to this unusual United Free minister with attention well above the average. Barr was a convinced pacifist, a passionate devotee of Keir Hardie (who was well known in this area, not least for his involvement with the Evangelical Union; he was, in fact, a convert of the post-Moody campaigns of the '80s). *The Motherwell Times* announced Barr's success over the other candidate as "a blow for war and militarism and all that they stand for." It gave Willie, despite the comment of a number who thought Barr had now forsaken his ordination vows (particularly as he had been doing good work as Home Mission Secretary of the United Free Church), a wider purview of what can be done for God in the service of the gospel if one is determined enough and unblinkered by stereotyped thinking. The unity between sacred and secular was again forcing its reality upon him. Willie, meanwhile, was back at DHS, the sixth year having been established.

A little time after returning to DHS (the sixth form having been established), another innovation occurred that was to be very influential on Willie, though in a quieter way. Dalziel High School, after a great deal of painstaking preparation, put on its first performance of *HMS Pinafore*. A daring move by the new Rector (that was not made without some opposition), it was met with great success, and Anderson was proclaimed "a pioneer in the educational aspects of Gilbert and Sullivan." The School Log carries two entries for the first and second performances respectively. Anderson noted the good attendance at the first, adding that the second act went particularly well, and commenting that the whole scheme was "a great success." The Rector did not overrate the operas—he referred to them actually as second-class—but he recognized their art as extremely important and expressed the view that "all true education is a search for beauty," which reinforced the lesson Willie was learning from A. D. Robertson. Everything had been done by the pupils themselves—set-making, costumes, rehearsals, and so on. One professional theater critic from Glasgow declared it "the start of things to come" and prophesied good success for the school. There is no record of Willie having played a part in it (almost certainly he did not), but it clearly had a great effect on him. Referring to the wide education Dalziel High School provided—"more than just book-learning"—he wrote, "and . . . best of all . . . every year the school produced a Gilbert and Sullivan opera. In the unlikely event of the operas getting lost I can supply them all—words and music—from memory. It was magnificent schooling."[64] Willie's memory is a little at fault in this: the operas were, in fact, *not* performed every year in his day (*HMS Pinafore* was the first one, and he had gone on to the university before the second was put on). Professor John Ferguson, former Dean of the Open University, had occasion to write to Willie in May 1971 playfully admonishing him for a *faute de mémoire* in this very area. Replied Willie, suitably contrite,

> Thank you very much for your letter . . . and for your comments. This is distinctly a case of "pride going before a fall." I frequently claim that if the Gilbert and Sullivan operas got lost I could replace the whole of them from memory. I shall now do penance in dust and ashes.[65]

He wrote that shortly before he took a lavish lunch in the university club, so we can presume that his penance was appropriately Gilbertian. Doubtless he took great pleasure from the fact that he who had given him such pleasure in "secular" music also composed the immortal tune traditionally sung to Sabine Baring-Gould's "Onward Christian Soldiers," which as much expressed Willie's vigorous and "muscular" Christianity as the operas expressed his full-blooded life-style: things, both of them, "true, honorable, just, pure, and lovely"—if not always entirely high-toned.

And so the academic year passed to its conclusion, with Willie busy at his Classics—Cicero, Virgil, Catullus, Terence, Livy, and Horace on the Latin side, and Homer, Thucydides, Sophocles, and Plato on the Greek. "Eng. Lit."[66] added breadth, and History depth, and he filled in what time he had left with preparations for the Glasgow Bursary Competition he was to enter during the summer vacation. In March a fresh temptation threatened when the school's own tennis courts were laid and Willie found yet another outlet for his energies.

Preceding the annual speech-day events in his final year was the school sports day, which was to be a time of particular merit for Willie. It took place (according to the Rector's log) "in a deluge of rain." Willie placed first in the 100-yard and 220-yard races, achieving times of 11.2 and 26.2 seconds respectively (good times in the '20s). He placed third in the cricket-ball throwing competition, the winner casting his ball only half a meter further than Willie. A few days after this he ran at a sports meeting at Fir Park to which some of the schools had been invited, but only managed to take second place; as he mentioned to Arthur Montford on Clyde Radio in 1976, he knew he was roundly beaten, and he never attempted to run again (in fact, he lost the race to R. Tennant by just one-sixteenth of a second).

The view is often propounded that Willie was Scottish Schoolboys' Champion, the latest occasion being in the Introduction Professor Allan Galloway has supplied to Willie's posthumous book on the Psalms, *The Lord is My Shepherd*.[67] I have found no confirmation whatever that this was the case, nor any reason for the legend to have grown. It may have developed from Willie's own comment in *Testament of Faith* that he "played well enough to share the sports' championship of the school,"[68] but, whatever the reason, the fact remains that he participated only in school sports (apart from the Fir Park incident, which was wholly exceptional), and he only *shared* in the championship. It is by no means the case that "he distinguished himself even more [than academically] as an athlete."[69] It is questionable whether he could have done so; his strength and sportsmanship at this time are best viewed in the context of the broad range of his interests rather than in terms of isolated attainments. More significant of his accomplishments in this regard is the fact that he was made the Sports Captain of the school, as well as Captain of Avon House.

And so the school days drew to their proper conclusion. The results were again published in *The Motherwell Times*, from which we see that Miss Tyrell was again made *Dux*, collecting other prizes in passing. Willie placed first in English and History, but only second in Latin, though this time he had the satisfaction of being made *proxime accessit*. The annual prize-giving took place with WDB and his wife as part of the platform party. Following this, WDB offered his own prize for excellence in English, which became a regular feature of the prize lists till his death. (It is said that he had wanted to do this earlier, but thought it would be embarrassing should his son win it.[70] It marked a fine conclusion to his own passionate enjoyment of the subject.)

The 1925 Dalziel High School Joint Sports Champions: Willie (right), Peter Bonomoy (standing), and Duncan Black (left)

·HIGHER·EDUCATION·SCOTLAND·
·LEAVING·CERTIFICATE·
1924.
THE LORDS OF THE COMMITTEE OF THE PRIVY
COUNCIL ON EDUCATION IN SCOTLAND
HEREBY CERTIFY THAT *William Barclay*
A Pupil in the *Dalziel High School, Motherwell*
having completed a Course of Secondary Education according
to a Curriculum approved for the purpose by Their Lordships,
and having satisfied, in respect of General Proficiency, both the Authorities
of the School and the Examiners appointed by Their Lordships, is entitled
to receive a LEAVING CERTIFICATE. The following subjects were
included in the Curriculum, and the Standard of Proficiency shown in
them was such as to warrant their entry on this Certificate :—

English Latin
History Greek
Mathematics French

Head Master.

Secretary to the
Scottish Education Department.

Willie's Leaving Certificate from Dalziel High School, bearing the signature of headmaster Anderson

Willie's school days were now over, and there remained but one more hurdle before he commenced his higher education. This was encountered not in the local confines of his own school, but on the basis of an all-Scotland examination at which over five hundred sat. It took place on 3 July 1925.

Dalziel High School had just cause to congratulate itself on the results, for three of its pupils were placed in the first twenty, and six in the first one hundred places, results that gave it placing equal to that of Hamilton Academy (with which it had broken many a lance in the local tournaments); it was bettered only by the schools at Dumbarton and Allan Glen, altogether "probably the best representation from any school in the west of Scotland," as the paper reported.[71]

Willie placed second in honors from Dalziel High School, Laura Bowyer taking the first place; Irene Tyrell came six places below Willie in the overall positions—sweet victory for him at long last! "This lad distinguished himself," *The Motherwell Times* commented on his excellent thirteenth position, and reminded its readers of his abilities in sporting events and his work on the Magazine Committee. The bursary results meant that Willie had gained the Biggart Memorial Bursary, worth £25 per annum, the precursor of many awards and prizes he was to receive.

CHAPTER FOUR

Glasgow Revisited: Humanity and Happiness

THERE is a world of difference between the callow youth who matriculated in October 1925 and the broad-browed, intelligent young man of winning personality who graduated M.A. (Hons.) in 1929, B.D. (Distinction) in 1932. During that time Willie's world changed, and he changed with it; he grew up physically, matured spiritually, found his intellectual feet, and—with it all—found his real vocation.

It was natural for a lad from the West of Scotland to look toward Glasgow to continue his education. There was not then the same adventurousness among pupils; they usually went to the university nearest to them, the ones attended by their fathers whenever possible. Willie could not thus follow his father—in this, at least, he led the way—but his parent was happy in the knowledge of his commitment, with the ministry as its goal.

The University of Glasgow

It was a great university to which he went, and it is not claiming too much to say that he was to enhance that greatness, if not immediately, then eventually. Glasgow is one of the very few British universities that can trace its history beyond the great divide of the Reformation that separates medieval from modern Europe (a distinction it shares with the Universities of Aberdeen and St. Andrews). Founded in 1451 by Bishop William Turnbull and established by the papal bull of Nicholas V, a great humanist and one of the founders of the Vatican Library, it was placed on the same footing as the pope's own university of Bologna, which was democratic, at least in theory.[1] Untroubled by the crosscurrents of the Renaissance and the Reformation, it continued to expand, all the while asserting "a sturdy independence common to all Scottish universities, but conspicuously absent abroad." By the last quarter of the sixteenth century, the University had created Chairs in Divinity, Medicine, Law, Hebrew, Church History, Astronomy, and Anatomy. The "inspiring genius" behind these developments, and others of an administrative nature (for example, the creation of the post of Principal, whose function it was to oversee all departments and cohere all activities) was Andrew Melville, later of Saint Andrews, a name found frequently in Willie's writings. A key to the University's successful growth was its ability to attract the respect and interest of the townspeople, so that no artificial barrier between "town and gown" was created, a tradition it has zealously sought to continue, and one highly congenial to Willie. By the time Willie came to matriculate, the institution had an enrollment of over three thousand students, and the number was rising rapidly.

Undergraduate of the Faculty of Arts

Willie registered for his first-term courses on 5 October 1925, a week before classes were due to begin; he was not yet eighteen. A copy of his matriculation certificate shows the handwriting of a confident and careful student and, despite his pretences to the contrary, it is admirable for its neatness, legibility, boldness, and character, all features that characterized his father's life and business methods, as they would Willie's own.[2]

Willie spent the following week acquiring his books, notebooks, and other effects. He had to travel each day from Motherwell to Glasgow, a distance of just thirteen miles, the pattern being broken only when his father retired, in July 1929. His high school friend Duncan Black always traveled with him, enjoying the prestige accorded his friend by the other youthful passengers. Willie was the natural leader of their group, manifesting a particular maturity of attitude and some flamboyance; they hung on his words and were often dazzled by his ability in comment and epigram. Having matriculated, their first action together was to join the Liberal Club—the only organization Willie associated himself with at the University. At home, they founded (with Willie Bishop, now of the USA) the Twenty-five Club, which met in Fraser's Tearoom in Muir Street; it survived for nearly five years (significantly, until Willie exchanged secular subjects for theological ones). Both prior to and following the day's work in the lecture halls, the library, and the nearby coffee shop in Eldon Street (a favorite haunt of the student), he looked forward to his journeys to and fro as only an ardent train spotter can. They had pleasures above the ordinary for him, being on the main London-Glasgow line. Already his world was becoming cosmopolitan.

His registration for the first year was in the Latin and Greek classes of the Faculty of Arts. The Faculty covered a very broad foundation and was then divided into four departments: Language and Literature, Mental Philosophy, Science (which covered Mathematics, "Natural Philosophy," Astronomy, Chemistry, Zoology, Geology, and Geography), and History. Whatever thoughts Willie may have had from time to time about specializing in English Literature, it is clear by now that the Classics, the traditional entrée for divinity studies, had taken precedence.

His first subject, Latin—or "Humanity," as it was more descriptively called— was of very ancient foundation in the University, and reached back before the appearance of the first Professor of Humanity in 1637. Since 1906 John Swinnerton Phillimore had been the incumbent of its prestigious chair, filling it with grace, learning, and, above all, a profound humanity. He was to make an impression on Willie that would be recalled vividly fifty years later in his autobiography. Phillimore had been appointed to follow in the Chair of Greek the venerated Gilbert Murray, whose stamp on classical learning is still rightly prized. Willie was indeed fortunate to commence when he did. Phillimore was then at the height of his powers, with an immense reputation in Europe and beyond, especially in Terence and Plautus. He has been described as "the don who had never said or done a donnish thing, who was a poet, and a poet of great excellence, in his own language, while he interpreted, with the subtlest discernment, the poets of other tongues."[3] He firmly believed that the unpardonable sin of any professor was to give his students a distaste for the authors they were reading. He also believed that a professor's duty was to leave nothing undone that can command or make the subject matter more attractive to his students' minds. Hence his private room was ever open to those who wished to see him for his assistance. That meant an enormous amount of extra work for the Professor, in addition to his many extramural activities. His Ordinary Humanity Class was always large, young, and difficult to manage—young men and women in the first blush of success, sharpening their wits on each other and ever seeking to demonstrate their developing powers. Willie characteristically emphasizes the fun and boisterous nature of these classes: nearly three hundred voices singing "Ye Mariners of England,"[4] "Rolling Home by the Light of the Silvery Moon," and their own version of "There Is a Better World Above."[5] He was a teacher of incomparable ability and style—and there is not a little J. S. Phillimore in the later Professor William Barclay. He was the perfect demonstration of profound knowledge and dexterous delivery. The essayist Walter Raleigh said of him, "of all the scholars I know, in cask or in bottle, none has the vintage of John Phillimore."[6]

Phillimore's influence on Willie is all the more surprising in that Willie sat under his teaching for only one academic year, which in those days was even shorter than it is today. Sadly, Phillimore had contracted a terminal illness and was forced to take a leave of absence in the next session, characteristically offering to mark his students' papers from his sickbed (from which he never rose). On 16 November 1926 he died, bringing grief to the academic world and to many in the west of Scotland, not least to Willie.

Willie so gave himself to this teacher's work and demands that despite the size of the class, he won the first class prize and was consequently invited to Phillimore's room (on the day prior to the Professor's last journey to hospital) to choose his book. "Surely," comments Willie wistfully, "there was unparalleled courtesy in the heart of the man who gave all of himself to a student an hour before he was to go out to die."[7] The comment may well be melodramatic—Willie's Highland background was ever prone to appear in such circumstances—

John Swinnerton Phillimore: "a teacher of incomparable ability and style"

but this was his first contact with cancer. Doubtless his recollections of Phillimore's premature demise were in later years colored by the yet more painful memories of his mother's subsequent defeat by the disease. Such strong reactions on Willie's part to calamities of this sort stand as partial evidence of his steadfast refusal to accept them as part of God's purposeful activity.

70

Essential Preparation: Latin, Greek, and English

His first year was very busy indeed, for Willie was embarked on the honors course. The prospectus warned that "in all classes the students prepare work prescribed, and are liable to be examined orally every day." This was the year he set to work in earnest, drinking deeply of Terence's *Andria* and *Adelphoe*, Cicero's *Pro Caelio*, and Catullus's and Horace's *Odes*, along with the history of the literature, Roman antiquities, and essays of various sorts.

Willie's second subject was Greek, under the spell of which he had fallen thanks to Jimmy Paterson's timely arrival at Dalziel High School. His professor was the renowned Gilbert Austen Davies, also elected in 1906, "the most fastidious and meticulous scholar"[8] Willie had ever met. He was ably assisted by William Rennie, who became Professor of Greek and Dean of Faculties following a short period as Phillimore's successor. It was Davies who gave Willie that love for the nuances of words and grammar that is such a strong feature of his later work, and that he ably demonstrates in the comparatively few scholarly contributions he chose to make.

These heady days developed Willie's personality; he was at once boisterous and modest; a fast talker; opinionated, but never conceited; in deadly earnest about his career and learning, yet relaxed, fun-loving, and given to pinpricking of the kindlier sort. His fellow student William Barclay of Troon recalls his avid note-taking and the small notebook that he never failed to carry with him as an aide-mémoire. He took great pains with his set-work and was highly conscientious in preparing his essays (none of which unfortunately has survived). He combined single-minded commitment with great awareness of the problems other students faced, helping some of them in an elder-brotherly way, though he was actually younger than many of them. From the start he showed that he was out to do well—but alongside his associates, not over them.

Peter Alexander, who succeeded Professor MacNeile Dixon in the Chair of English Language and Literature,[9] was fond of recalling Willie's year as one which displayed particular talent and ability—the sort of eagerness for knowledge that stretches and contents academics, justifying and making worthwhile their routine. It was under MacNeile Dixon, professor for no fewer than thirty-one years (1904–35), that Willie's writing skills and style flourished. They studied in turn Chaucer, Spenser, Shakespeare, and the Elizabethan drama school; Milton, Dryden, and Johnson; Wordsworth and his contemporaries; the Renaissance writers; Willie's great compatriot, Walter Scott; and Palgrave. Walpole also became a firm favorite at this time, and Willie soon had a fine collection of first editions of his works (sign of his freedom from financial anxiety) that was the envy of staff and students alike. (Duncan Black recalls Willie's study, a luxury in itself in those depressed days in the west of Scotland. In it Willie sported a reading lamp—a real status symbol—as well as other things that marked him as specially privileged, many of them clearly the benefits of his father's enthusiasm for innovations.) Willie also learned the secret of popular writing from this brilliant and amiable Irishman—a tall, gaunt, and gracious man, with a playful sense of humor. It was his Gifford Lectures (established to promote the cause of Natural Theology among "all classes and among the whole popula-tion of Scotland") that became a best-seller under the title *The Human Situation* in 1937. Drummond and Bulloch sourly comment that it "contains much wit but not one solid conviction from cover to cover,"[10] a minority view of the work, to be sure. Dixon wrote other books that were also well received in their day, but perhaps his chief value to Willie was the way in which he enforced (after the manner of WDB) the importance of enthusiasm and dedication. In the frontis-piece to his fine book on tragedy, he quotes John Keats in this respect: "The excellence of art is its intensity, capable of making all disagreeables evaporate from its being in close relationship with beauty and truth."[11]

I emphasize the question of intensity for the moment, though we have seen elsewhere that beauty and truth were also very important to Willie. This intensity now consumed him, and was to do so even more once he had realized his vocation. He saw it expressed in MacNeile Dixon not merely as an expression of personality, nor even of professional conduct, but acutely, as a matter of *art*—the way things are done. It was an asset that another favorite writer of Willie's, the Roman Catholic, Fabian writer G. K. Chesterton, expressed when he said that "when we want any art to be tolerably brisk and bold, we have to go to the doctrinaries." Certainty and intensity were two elements of Willie's armory that he acquired early and never relinquished.

Hard work was rewarded: the session closed with prizes for Willie in Humanity and English—prizes, as he was later to recall using the words of his Eng. Lit. hero Robert Louis Stevenson, that were infinitely worthwhile "when I see my mother's face."[12] Of course he still had considerable work of a preparatory nature to do; he was as yet only a beginner at University. In his second year he deepened and broadened his classical understanding as he buried himself once more in the *Iliad* of Homer, Pindar's *Olympians,* Plato's *Republic,* Aristophanes's *Acharnians,* and Demosthenes's *Aristocrates* and *Timocrates,* while also delving into Roman history, Virgil, and Horace. Duncan Black can testify to the zeal with which Willie pursued his classical studies: he recalls his friend cycling past him early one Saturday morning and calling out happily (and not without some self-satisfaction), "Fifty lines of Ovid this morning!" It was a typical expression of his enthusiasm for, and enjoyment in, his work—enthusiasm that served to spur a dedication that earned him yet more prizes at the conclusion of his second year.

His third year brought continued Latin and Greek studies for his honors degree. Sitting next to William Barclay of Troon, Willie also read Moral Philoso-phy under Professor Archibald Allan Bowman. Appointed Professor in 1927 in succession to Hector Hetherington (later to be one of Scotland's most distin-guished and able university Principals), Bowman held his Chair for only two years before death claimed him. But that was sufficient time in which to inculcate

in Willie an interest that would continue to captivate him throughout his professional career, a concern to which, as we shall see, he returned with great enthusiasm in his retirement. Interestingly, Professor Black thinks Bowman "spoiled"
Willie by overcomplimenting him for his work, by stimulating him to greater
things (by recommending further reading and reflection), and by making occasional gifts of books. Andrew Herron also remarks on Bowman's encouragements.[13]

The purpose of Bowman's course was "to consider the main problems and
theories of the philosophical interpretation of the moral life . . . with reference to
the psychological, social and metaphysical aspects of their theories, and to their
bearings on the problems of contemporary civilisation"—a daunting prospect
for any serious nineteen-year-old! But under Bowman's sure touch, held as he
was "by the gloom of Glasgow" despite the temptation and inducements of
Princeton University, he remained lecturing to huge classes and receiving warm-
hearted responses. It was from Bowman that Willie gained a deep respect for
Bishop (later Archbishop) William Temple's writings. Temple's emphasis on a
"sacramental universe"[14] struck chords of deep understanding in Willie, struggling as he was to see not a division between the sacred and secular, but a unity.
Like Temple, Willie found himself more and more antagonized by "other-
worldliness," more and more drawn to that comprehension of life that owns
God's love for and activity in his whole creation. He came to be more and more
at odds with his father, who was concerned at the lowering of the barriers of
orthodoxy and the dangers this exposed Willie to. It is from this time that we
should date "the explosive rackets" between himself and his father.[15]

The summer's preparatory reading for this course was Plato's *Republic* and
John Stuart Mill's *Utilitarianism* and *Essay on Liberty*. Mill, like his father James
Mill before him, had learned much of Jeremy Bentham's philosophical and
radical doctrines, from which socialism began. But at this moment in time it was
Bentham's "greatest happiness principle" (as expounded by J. S. Mill) that
chiefly occupied Willie's mind. It did not do so in a vacuum. His summer
reading took place just a few months after the shattering event of the General
Strike of 1926, culminating in the horrors described by Willie Gallacher in
Glasgow's George Square,[16] as well as similar doings elsewhere. Students were
used for "National Work"—a hollow euphemism for strikebreaking, which raised
the grievances to the level of civil disorder. Willie's sensitive conscience felt the
dilemma of this to the full. He knew, despite the privilege and protection of his
upbringing, that working men and women were scandalously treated and suffered
abominably in consequence. There is more than a suggestion in his writings that
he was drawn to a "Christianized" concept of utilitarianism, and he certainly
responded positively to the socialist (if not the radical) elements that it contained.
He had much to ponder and discuss with his father during these days, and it is
not surprising to hear that some of those discussions could be described as
"blazing guns"—requiring the irenical intervention of his mother, who was ever
"the buffer and the peace-maker."[17]

But there was one area in which WDB could not be involved, in which he was merely the proud and joyful onlooker, and that was in the honors Latin and Greek courses Willie was now following. The previously listed authors and works were extended by studies in Plautus, Juvenal, Martial, and Quintilian, to which were added the history of Latin lexicography and its lectionary. And on the Greek side there were Aeschylus, Aristotle, and Aristophanes, plus prose composition, criticism, and work on the history of Greece and Greek literature. In this Herodotus and Plutarch were to the fore, and a much-loved and influential volume of Hicks and Hill—*Greek Historical Inscriptions*—supplemented this work and provided a bridge between the present classical and his later biblical work.

These courses were pursued in his next and last session, in 1928/29, Willie now working from the new Glasgow base his parents had taken at 198 Wilton Street, after his father's retirement. It was a spacious apartment in a three-story house (rented), which they shared with four other tenants. Its choice illustrates WDB's "pilgrim" emphasis. Rebecca, ever faithful to their needs, accompanied them.

Master of Arts, First Class

During the first two weeks of June, Willie sat his most important examination to date: his finals for the arts degree. Not that anyone expected him to fail—the very opposite was the case—but there was the question of grading, for his career depended on these results. Happily, the expectations of tutors and parents were fully rewarded, and with them the justification of Willie's school ambitions and hopes. *The Motherwell Times* was not slow to recognize his success, commenting that this was "the first time in the History of Dalziel High School that a former pupil has gained this distinction."[18] His position in the first class amply made up for past disappointments. In the very prime of young manhood, he had finally claimed his victory over those schoolgirl competitors!

But we misunderstand him if we think of him as in any sense purely a "swot." His love of sports, games, and music continued from his school days at university. From his first long vacation, we find him "tramping and cycling" with his friends of the YMCA. It was one of his special pleasures to take trips on the Glasgow steamers up the Clyde, feasting on the stunning beauty of its banks and reveling in the late-evening activities—the singing and dancing in fervent Scots style. These were the days when forty or more steamers plied the estuary, bearing such evocative names as *S.S. Lord of the Isles, S.S. Ivanhoe,* and the still serviceable *P.S. Waverle.* For many families during these straitened times, a single trip "doon the watter" had to suffice as the sum total of their annual holidays. These little jaunts of Willie's were not altogether well received by WDB, though we may assume his mother had not the same sharp reaction to "worldly pleasures" as her conservative, vocal, twice-born husband. At such times the peacemaker role was critically important—that being, as Willie states in his commentary, "not the passive acceptance of things because we are afraid of the trouble of doing anything about them, but the active facing of things, and the *making* of peace, even when the way to peace is through struggle . . . a god-like work."[19] And Barbara Linton Barclay was a god-like woman.

Nor was Willie a prude. He enjoyed Dean Inge's irreverent ditty, which went the rounds of the University following a visit by the far-from-gloomy gentleman:

> I love the little daisies
> I love all nature's ways;
> I love the nice white laces
> On Grandmama's new stays!

One of the interesting aspects of his undergraduate life is his lack of involvement in any of the religious societies—denominational, SCM, or CSF. Addressing the conference of YMCA Secretaries in 1961, he points out that it was far from fashionable to be religious at university in the mid '29's: "religion was laughed at as being something quite useless,"[20] a state of affairs that he saw change quite dramatically (though not universally) in his own time, in no small part due to his own influence.

A pertinent feature in this lack of respect for religion was the apparent dearth of rationality and scholarship which then obtained in some Christian circles. The Scopes trial in America, for example, was having a wide press in Britain in 1925, reawakening Huxley's derision of the previous century. In WDB's younger days, Darwin was "the scare of the religious school," to use Alexander Whyte's phrase,[21] and the battle was far from over in Willie's time. Moreover, the rejection of biblical criticism by the most vocal, defensive, and at times hysterical party in the church merely highlighted their recognition of "Saint Obscurantismos." The sixteen hundredth anniversary of the Council of Nicea was being celebrated at this time, which did nothing to alleviate matters, awakening as it did new arguments as to credal relevancy. This debate had been going on almost permanently, of course, since the last quarter of the nineteenth century, but such "celebrations" made the matter public, as had the "New Theology" debate and the publication of *Foundations* shortly thereafter. The controversy over "fundamentals" poured more fuel on the flames, which reached their height in the early '20s, as Robertson Nicoll's biographer points out.[22] Such matters were not taken lying down in the "tumultuous west" of Scotland.

But to undergraduates, Willie among them, the saddest spectacle was the public rift between the SCM and CSF, then at its worst in Glasgow. G. A. F. Knight, who later became Overseas Secretary of the Glasgow SCM, has given an account of the unhappy state of affairs in his autobiography, *What Next?* It concerned the Religion and Life campaign that took place in February 1926, which featured William Temple as one of the many speakers. As Professor Knight puts it,

> There was one jarring note that underlined for me still further my belief that certain forms of "evangelicalism" are really sub-Christian. As Secretary I had to

write to the Evangelical Union [i.e., the Christian Students Fellowship] inviting them to share in this mission to the university, but received no reply to three successive letters of invitation. Finally, the Evangelical Union ran a rival mission the week preceding ours. Never more than twenty persons attended its meetings, while our mission attracted several hundred students daily.[23]

Having perused carefully the minutes of the Glasgow University Christian Students Fellowship, kindly lent me by Dr. Oliver Barclay, a former General Secretary of the UCCF, I can only endorse Professor Knight's sorrowful indignation. There never was any hope that the CSF could bring off a campaign to compete with the united strength of the SCM (then strongly mission- and evangelism-minded) and the affiliated denominational bodies, even if it had been desirable. Their minutes for 23 November 1925 record their concern over the small and decreasing attendance at their meetings. Minutes of the next meeting state that they discussed Knight's invitation, debating whether it would be "proper" to participate, and finally postponing the decision till the Annual General Meeting (at which time they simply ignored the entire matter). Instead, they arranged a picnic, revised their membership roll, and planned a spring conference (a Keswick Conference house party), and some "drawing-room meetings"—presumably at a safe distance from where the real spiritual conflict was taking place. The next year they did reconsider the matter, rejecting participation: "owing to a different point of view, it would be difficult for *our* speakers to work with others."[24] Not, of course, that their speakers were asked! Their whole attitude was introspective, self-indulgent, and proudly humble. The *Glasgow University Magazine* caught the spirit exactly when it published its "Ballad of the SCM; or, How to Be Rebuked by a Non-believer,"[25] which went a long way toward nullifying the valiant efforts made by the SCM and the students' chaplains:

> Twixt CSF and SCM
> Interminable split is
> Although we learn in each of them
> Anthropomorphic ditties,
> How wrong the Jesuit is,
> And Biblical Who's Who,
> —But 'tis a hundred pities
> We've nothing else to do. . . .

It continues, "There is a flooding tide to stem . . . ," but introversion obscured that challenging fact.

There is an "oral tradition" that Willie was a member of the Christian Union, but this rests on a misunderstanding.[26] It was William Barclay of Troon, Willie's bench-mate in the Moral Philosophy classes of Professor Bowman, who joined the group, though not till 1927. And there was also a William J. Barclay of Springburn who was a member. Moreover, Willie himself has complicated the account: Dr. John Laird, a leading light in the CSF of those days, has published a letter he received from Willie confirming that he was a founding member of the Glasgow group! This is simply incorrect, part of a pattern that Willie embroidered in his retirement in order to imply a more extensive association with conservative groups than was in fact the case.

Willie certainly attended the Religion and Life campaigns, but his main religious outlet aside from Dalziel North United Free Church was the YMCA branch at Motherwell, of which he had been a member since 1923. By now he was playing a leading part in running the local associations; for example, in early February 1927 he was a member of the Organizing Committee for the local infirmary's flag day. It was in this group that he built on the foundation laid by his father's example and exhortations, and became—as did some of his friends from Dalziel High School—a public speaker. He recounts some of the details in *Testament of Faith.*[27] His first episode lacks the positiveness and distinction of his later involvements: in it he merely attacks the hapless, though better-informed speaker who had recommended dropping the comma from the Messianic description of Isaiah 9:6 between the words "Wonderful" and "Counselor," thus making it a four-fold prophecy of the child. Willie, clearly, was as ignorant of the Revised Version's alternate reading as he was one of the many scholars who had suggested this rendering of the text for some decades, not excluding A. S. Peake, as is clear from some of his own recent comments.[28] "I was so conservative in my attitude to scripture," he confessed fifty years later, "that the removal of a comma seemed to me nothing short of a sin."

In any case, a start had been made, and by June 1927 *The Motherwell Times* was reporting his first preaching engagement in the nearby Baptist church, following many such occasions on which his father had occupied its pulpit. It was the commencement of a great ministry, significantly begun outside his own denomination. Fifteen years had elapsed since his avowal at Fort William; he was now on the way to its fulfillment.

Political Economist: Humanity Completed

The Barclays moved to Glasgow on 1 July 1929, WDB having completed an almost unique fifty years' service at the Bank of Scotland and retired on the 29th of June. For WDB it was the completion of a circle that he had begun in 1895 (a year that saw the celebrations of the Queen-Empress for having reigned longer than any former British sovereign) when he went to Anderston as teller for his bank. Typically, the parents stayed in Glasgow—despite the temptations of Fort William—in order to facilitate Willie's studies at Glasgow. Their hopes of moving later were shortly to be destroyed by death.

Willie's mind by this time had been made known to his closest friend of the period, Duncan Black, typically between billiard shots in the Students' Union. His choice of vocation "was a possibility that had not previously been mentioned," Black recalls. "The news came as a complete surprise, and I never subsequently adapted to looking at him as a minister of the Scottish Church."[29]

WDB on his retirement after nearly fifty years of service to the Bank of Scotland, 29 June 1929 [Photo courtesy of *The Motherwell Times*]

He also recalls Willie's vigorous ambition, more sustained than that of any other student known to him. At the time, Black says, he felt let down. "It seemed to me that the one genius whom I knew was abandoning his genius for the sake of gain." It was Black's opinion at the time that Willie simply wanted to get to the top and knew he could do so more easily in the church than in secular society. "I could not understand it," he has sadly recalled. It throws an interesting light on Willie, on the complexity of his character and of his relationships, and on his complete disinterest concerning what others—even his closest friend—thought about him. Professor Black went on to change his views, to accept this alteration of course as something other than an "abandoning of his genius for gain; on the contrary, his genius used Bun for its own ends," adding—a point to which we must return later—that "in the course of time [that genius] destroyed him." The deeper, private side of Willie had determined his course. He had put his hand to the plough, and could not turn back. In October 1929, when the Presbyterian Church in Scotland was facing the difficulties arising from the greatest union of churches since the Reformation, Willie again presented himself at the Registrar's offices. "William Barclay, M.A. (Classics Hons.)" now registered for a course quite unlike any he had taken in the previous four years. His fifth year was to be spent in the Faculty of Arts studying Political Economy, in accordance with a recommendation laid down by the Church of Scotland. The thinking behind this recommendation was first-rate, and well in advance of the time compared with other denominations. The Church was well aware that its ministers could be disconcertingly innumerate and lacking in commercial knowledge, and therefore proposed this extra course as a remedy. It was one that naturally lay very close to the heart of Willie, whose whole life had been based at the Bank Houses of Wick and Motherwell. Having watched his father prepare various organizations' accounts from his earliest recollections, he was of no two minds concerning the necessity and usefulness of the preparations. Moreover, it allowed him a relatively quiet year in which to consolidate his studies, and spend some of his free time on pretheological tasks (notably Hebrew).

There was another reason that Political Economy should rank so highly in Scotland: Adam Smith, Kirkcaldy's most honored son, had founded the modern science of "PE" with the publication of his historic and brilliant book *The Wealth of the Nations*. The "division of labor" was but one part of Smith's doctrine, though perhaps the best known (in 1950 Willie was to use the phrase in a spiritual sense—of the gifts God had given to the church—in his first Boys' Brigade handbook, *God's Plan for Man*);[30] another aspect, much appreciated by WDB and his like, was that the man who actively pursues his private responsibilites and interests is a public benefactor. From such roots as this grew Willie's acceptance of the importance of the ordinary things of life—of daily work, the common task. It became, not least in this year of PE, an inseparable part of his ethic, locked into the duty of daily life—itself counted as service for God. (Adam Smith was also the author of an ethic that expressed the feeling of human sympathy which may not have bypassed Willie's notice, but is not well-known today.) The man under whom Willie was to learn so much was in fact the Adam Smith Professor, William Robert Scott, who held his Chair for twenty-five years. Appropriately, the chair had as patrons the University Court, a representative of the Merchants' House of Glasgow (one from the city's Trades Houses), and a representative of the Glasgow Chamber of Commerce. The unity between town and gown was beyond doubt in this subject. It was in this year that Willie's social awareness really developed, and in which he grasped the principle of efficiency that would characterize his work as a minister and, thereafter, his work as Trinity College representative to the University Court and as Dean of Faculty.

In enrolling for this course Willie was well ahead of his time—almost uniquely so. I have not been able to locate anyone who had similarly spent a complete year in an already extensive training program. It occupied at least seven years: four in the arts, and three in theology. (The church did allow English or History to be substituted for PE, and most seem to have opted for this.) That he was willing to follow the church's recommendations is surely a sign of WDB's influence on him, and of the influence of second-hand memories of his father's long and perhaps trying experiences with ministers grappling with balance sheets. He may well have already perceived, as Bishop Newbigin and others were to assert fearlessly in later years, that economics is an integral part of ethics; Willie was not to be one of these who took refuge from the real world under the pretext of a rejection of the social gospel.

The course on which he was now embarked had, besides the usual introductory matter (of definitions and the evolution of the subject), three particular areas of study: the questions of Value, the Agents of Production, and Distribution and Exchange. The lectures were to be partly analytical and partly historical, but with broad references to contemporary conditions and problems—no mean or irrelevant objective at the commencement of "the thin-faced '30s"! It was not just matters of pure economics that were to be addressed, as the course title shows. Adam Smith's doctrine rested on the changes that followed in the wake of the Industrial Revolution, of which such topics as the division of labor, supply and demand (freed from all prohibitions), and the elevation of competition into a principle of economic life are the main components.

By the time WDB had come to commercial maturity, the gilt had worn off the principles. Adam Smith's doctrine was an estimable contribution, but the Victorians had reduced it to economic chaos. Authors such as Sidney Webb deeply resented this and its concomitant social evils. These in turn gave rise to Marxism, the many forms of left-wing liberalism, and socialism. The boundary between this aspect of economics (true "political economy") and politics is virtually indistinguishable. Willie was alive to much of it, but because of the traditional "discretion" of ministers of religion in matters relating to party politics, it is difficult to follow the development of his political understanding. Nevertheless, he obviously did hold some clearly defined political convictions, traces of which are discernible throughout his public statements on certain matters, as we shall see.

Perhaps there is no better expression of Willie's overall view than that expressed by James Keir Hardie, that "Socialism means fraternity founded on justice."[31] We should not understand his socialism—if we may call it that—as being a matter of a political party of any kind; to him it was primarily a *moral* thing, the fulfilling of the royal law of brotherly love which, as the story of the Good Samaritan asserts, is nothing more than attending to one's neighbor's needs at the proper time. Its roots were in the prophetic imperatives of the Old Testament, wherein the primary call is "to do justice, to love mercy, and to walk humbly with your God." We shall later see that his admiration for the service-oriented denominations such as the Quakers and the Salvation Army never waned; indeed, the reverse is true.[32]

Willie's love of Burns provided a significant stimulus in Hardie's direction (Hardie had himself been influenced by Burns). That Willie's commitment was not complete can be seen from his politically naive admiration of his father's favorite writers: Dickens, Thackeray, Tennyson, and Browning. In all of these, as Beatrice Potter points out, following Sidney Webb, there is no real social (i.e.,

80

civic) awareness.[33] Man is described by these authors as lover, husband, father, friend—but never as citizen; the political dimension is entirely wanting. But in this Willie was a man of his times, not behind them, and he enjoyed the authors for the rich appreciation of life they did possess.

Mention of Sidney Webb and his fiancée Beatrice Potter brings us to one who influenced them enormously, and who influenced Willie too, though to what extent we are now unable to judge completely. He was Alfred Marshall, Professor of Political Economy at Cambridge University. Willie's set books for the 1929/30 session were Marshall's *Elements of the Economics of Industry* and *Money, Credit and Commerce,* and Smart's *Theory of Value* and *The Distribution of Income*—dull stuff to someone fresh from the *Iliad* or Herodotus's *History* perhaps, but we have no reason to believe his response accorded with Potter's, who found PE à la Marshall as "hateful, most hateful *drudgery*."[34] Rather, his response was nearer to that produced by David Cairns, who noted that Marshall had posited religious and economic factors as "the two greatest forces in the forming of human character."[35] Cairns had supplemented his own (private) studies in PE with Burnmouth's volume, which accentuated the importance of the economic factor in human affairs. There is no evidence that Willie ever read Burnmouth, but the lessons he learned in this "secular" session were potent enough in themselves to tide him through much of the theological ferment of the seething '60s, itself substantially a matter of simple secularization: he was not unduly alarmed by the furor and was thus saved from the overreaction that spoiled some of his colleagues' work.

"The course of social evolution is making us all socialists against our will," Marshall wrote to Beatrice Potter (soon to be Webb) in 1889, a year before his *Principles* were published.[36] That may well have been true of Willie too, raised as he was in the liberalism of Scotland that dominated his father's early years, and that began to wane in the early 1920s, when the twitter became a thin peep, and then an angry roar.

The purpose of Willie's Classics course was to impart to him a deep humanity, of which the renaissance was but a fine flowering. Through this he became a *humanist,* not in the stereotyped and jaded sense that word now connotes, but more after the definition of John Watson of Manchester, who was such a great influence on his father and who said of it that it was "the love of the beautiful, both in literature and in art, together with the culture of one's mind and the unrestrained joy of living, and the fulfilment of one's nature."[37] Willie learned this deeply, and it permeated his whole life; to it he added a social conscience of considerable depth, which we shall find expressed, whether in religious or civic or familial contexts, simply as "service." Service was for him the highest form of existence; the noblest men and women were those who served best. As he said in one of his journalistic pieces, "true royalty is service."[38] James Martin, in his essay "Barclay's Humanity and Humility,"[39] rightly emphasizes his compassion, but overlooks the deeper—and richer—backdrop of his classical scholarship.

It cannot be stressed too much that Willie had by this point in his life become a very complex individual, with deep currents that crossed and recrossed each other in a network of considerable complexity. His down-to-earthness was a part of this, but a somewhat superficial part. It developed as a result of his earnest attempt to understand his fellow men (and served incidentally to facilitate his enjoyment of their company), and it came to be itself a realization of life, the acceptance of a valid life-style in which snobbery and class had no place. There is far more in Willie than can be discerned in the shallow portraitures of Martin and many other journalists, as we shall see in greater detail later.

Academically, we hear nothing more of PE from Willie but that which his graduation certificate records—that he was awarded a pass mark (without special mention) in May 1930 as a postgraduate student, which registration cost him a guinea. It had been a five-year period of immense happiness for Willie in which his humanity truly came of age, thus preparing him for life: a life of self-sacrifice and service.

CHAPTER FIVE

The Disciplining of Faith

THE matriculation form of October 1930 is in Willie's writing, which had notably deteriorated in the scramble of his five years of incessant note-taking. Still it is unmistakably Willie's hand on the form registering him for the course in theology based in Trinity College that leads to the degree of Bachelor of Divinity. Curiously, he makes two mistakes of fact on his form: first, he gives his age as twenty-three (not so till December), and second, he states that it is his fifth year of studies, when in fact it was his sixth. Clearly his PE course had not made his arithmetic infallible! We shall see that from time to time he could be remarkably unaffected by the academic demand of strict accuracy; the inner reality of a thing always mattered more to him than its outward form, even if that outward form should be expressed in mathematical certainty: he already *felt* twenty-three, and he was so enjoying his studies that it only seemed like five years! (In *Testament of Faith* there is a similar lapse when he gives the year he started at Trinity College as 1929.[1] He probably confused that date with the great Union that finally unified the major part of Scottish presbyterianism, a watershed in everyone's experience at the time.)

The course was to be funded by two awards: the Stevenson Scholarship (worth £32 per annum, tenable for two years, and awarded to "a *distinguished* graduate of the University of Glasgow preparing for the ministry") and the Ainslie Bursary (worth £25 per annum and administered by the Deacon's Court of Fort William—thus preserving a link with his parents' hometown, to their great delight).

WDB's Conservatism Confronted

A piece of verse published in the handbook of the Students' Union well illustrates what some thought of those who did theology at Trinity College in those days:

> There was an old fellow of Trinity,
> A Doctor, well versed in Divinity.
> But he took to free-thinking,

And then to deep drinking,
And so had to leave the vicinity!

In the view of men like WDB, theological college was a danger as well as an opportunity; he coveted the opportunity, but regretted the temptations to which his so carefully groomed son was to be exposed. Willie, a seasoned student with preparatory learning and high honors under his belt, had no such fears. Indeed, his mind was now broadening in its sympathies and deepening in its penetration not only of human nature—and theology is, after all, the human response to God's record and dealings with man—but also of the development and growth and risks to which ancient literature is exposed.

Two aspects of Willie's development now joined to increase "the explosive rackets" between himself and his father of which he writes in his autobiography.[2] It is from this time that the two of them "fought to the end of the day" (i.e., to his father's death): "we fought—for my theology was if anything even more to be suspected than my dancing." To the "worldliness" that Willie had contracted first in the local YMCA's billiard hall (to which snooker was added after 1927) and then on its dancing floor, he now added a disconcerting preference for "liberal" thinking and belief. WDB was never more worried. His son not only spent too much time up the Clyde—the trip to Rothesay on its pleasure steamers with the bad language and fun-loving, sometimes half-inebriated crowds with their wild singing and raucous laughter—but he now threatened, or appeared to threaten, all their hopes by allowing his spiritual preparation and commitment to weaken. Never more fiercely did Willie feel the heat of his father's "explosive temper,"[3] and never more welcome were his mother's peace-making interventions.

We should, however, be careful not to exaggerate these theological conflicts with his father—as Willie tended to do, retrospectively. They had much more to do with biblical criticism than the overthrow of orthodox doctrine, with matters regarding the textual history of the Bible, the provenance and date of its individual parts, and the human factors involved in the transmission of the sacred text. WDB's faith rested on a monochromatic view of biblical revelation that found no place for an understanding of Scripture other than that supplied by a mechanical view of inspiration the authority of which rested on the literal understanding of the text, and he supposed his son to be in real danger of forfeiting "the deposit of faith" transmitted to him. We should not conclude that Willie's doctrine was other than orthodox. In fact it was the very model of orthodoxy, being rigidly biblical in emphasis and stressing the historical facts of the gospel story (including the miracles) and, notably, the physical resurrection of Jesus. His doctrine of the person of Christ—in both his deity and his full humanity—was impeccable, as was his doctrine of the Holy Spirit. What WDB saw, and feared, was the opening of the door to free appraisal—as opposed to the primary commitment to orthodox belief from the outset—a fear that his son would aggravate in his doctrine as he had done in his humanity.

What was at stake alongside this was not "worldliness" so much as humanity, not the throwing aside of his religious upbringing, but its interpenetration with life. There were many virtues apparent in his life, virtues that led F. F. Bruce, a former associate and friend of many years not entirely on Willie's side theologically, to express himself thus when he heard that I was embarked on his biography: "You will find yourself in spiritual touch with a man who had some of the essential qualities of sainthood."[4] And that was written by a foremost member of the Brethren, who do not believe in "sainthood" except in the New Testament usage of the form.

Among Willie's virtues was what Disraeli's biographer called his "muscular Christianity." It was the element of *manliness* that Willie stressed, not thereby obliterating other, quieter aspects of character and life, but expressing it as an essential part of them. It found consummate expression in the objective of the Boys' Brigade, as we have seen. Significantly, it was this that excited Henry Drummond's interest in the Boys' Brigade as well: "true Christian manliness" perfectly expresses Drummond's character and predispositions. At Dalziel North United Free Church, the "4th Company, Motherwell" enjoyed not only the usual routine of Boys' Brigade activities—drill, games and sports of all sorts, camps, inspections, and so on—but it also had its own jazz band, occasionally to the annoyance of other groups in the church. This "muscular Christianity" was all the rage in the latter part of the nineteenth century, as we have seen. WDB was no stranger to some of its aspects himself; Willie exemplified and extended its reality.

It was this more than anything else that evoked Willie's admiration and work for the YMCA. Historically, the movement grew to meet "the mental, then the social, and lastly . . . the physical needs of young men."[5] By Willie's time there was a near-perfect blend of activities that did indeed minister to the complete man. Their avowed intention was to provide the various agencies young men needed for *"symmetrical development"* (the words *symmetry* and *equilibrium* were in vogue at the time, having been taken from the jargon of economics in which Willie had recently immersed himself; in the light of the gloomy conditions then prevailing, one wag suggested that the greatest point of equilibrium, the point at which supply and demand balanced precisely, was in the state of death).

It is typical of Willie that he should turn a matter of ordinary life into a religious principle. Like Drummond in his *Natural Law,* Willie recognized the organic connection between the physical and spiritual world; and, like Wesley and Karl Barth, he was to preoccupy himself (actively, if not intellectually) with this connection, applying it to the development of a relationship between the world of the Bible and that of the newspaper.

Another of the lasting influences on Willie (also via WDB) was the figure of W. R. Nicoll, whose editorials, books, and papers found their way week by week into the Barclay home. Nicoll's love of life (and the literature of life with which his books are replete) comes out well in his reflections on "the loss of the living presence, the hearty laughter, the brisk, conscious, vigorous life of congenial companionship," a perspective he shares with C. S. Lewis—another popular Christian writer whose love for hearty, "manly" company is so similar to Willie's own.

And so he made his way to Trinity reflecting, if not actually repeating, the words of Molière: "Oh! I may be devout, but I am human all the same." His

Trinity College Football Team of 1931 at Lesser Hampden Football Field. Willie stands in the back row, fourth from the right.

Trinity College photograph. Willie's picture is immediately to the right of Principal W. M. Macgregor's in the center row.

life was to be spent in a pursuit of the balance that does justice to both. The University was making a uni-verse of his own world and experiences. WDB was well aware of this, and he shared in its objectives, but he nevertheless felt that Willie's view was too broad, too open to misuse, too exposed to subtle temptations. Their clash continued and deepened. But so did their love.

Trinity College

Willie was fortunate in his tutors, enjoying the intellectual mastery of W. D. Niven, who specialized in both New Testament and Church History (like Moffatt before him) founded on a broad and penetrating philosophical concern. His Croall lectures, *Reformation Principles after Four Centuries* (1953), show his ability to combine historical and biblical learning in an appeal for theological integrity that is still called for today. Spare in words, they epitomize true Protestantism, boldly recalling their readers to the first principles of biblical authority and justification by faith alone.

In Old Testament studies Willie worked under John Edgar M'Fadyen, a Hebraist of no mean standing and a meticulous scholar. M'Fadyen followed George Adam Smith to the Chair of Old Testament Languages and Literature in 1910 and was a great favorite among the students even in those days, when distance between professor and student was the norm. He had married a girl from Marburg, which appears to have been the main reason why Willie, at the end of his theological course, spent a semester in that great university town, the seat of Protestant learning in Germany. M'Fadyen preached in Motherwell on many occasions prior to Willie's attending his classes, and seems to have made friends with WDB, perhaps as a result of the deep sympathies for the Brotherhood movement evidenced in his Chalmers Lectures (1931).

We shall see that a great influence on the development of Willie's own theology at the time was exerted by William Adams Brown of the Union Theological Seminary in New York, who had studied under Adolf Harnack, foremost exponent of Protestant Liberalism (which highlighted so strongly the fatherhood of God, the brotherhood of man, and the supreme worth of the individual). Interestingly enough, Brown's own background was conservative-evangelical (he was a convert of the Moody campaigns in America), and he knew all about the tension between fundamentalist and liberal viewpoints. As John H. Leith points out, he became an outstanding representative of "evangelical liberalism" and sought to shake off the old scholastic language of dogma in favor of "the pure English of common experience—ever centred in Christ."[6] The line of Harnack-Brown-M'Fadyen established a definite channel for the development of Willie's own theology and its application. I myself have M'Fadyen's copy of Brown's *Christian Theology in Outline* (which he bought in July 1907, four months before Willie's birth), and it is interesting to see the neat markings by which he indicated the salient points of his friend's argumentation; he passed them on in turn to Willie, who similarly annotated his own books. (It should be added that Adams Brown's *Outline* was one of no fewer than thirty-four textbooks suggested by Macaulay for his Apologetics course.)

The famous tower (in which Willie later had his study room) at Trinity College, Glasgow

Yet another significant influence on Willie came from Professor A. B. Macaulay. Solidly theological in his approach, Macaulay was Alexander Whyte's assistant at Free Saint George's, Edinburgh. (Whyte had set up a theological literature prize in 1896, and Macaulay had been the first one to win it, with an elaborate essay on Augustine's writings.) But the temperament that had made him such a sensitive theologian (he followed D. W. Forrest in James Orr's Chair of Dogmatics and Apologetics in 1919) overcame him, and he had to relinquish his post in 1933. Willie confessed that his indecipherable handwriting caused Macaulay to ask him to read his examination papers to him,[7] but even though it was then in decline, his writing was not by any means indecipherable; Macaulay's request would appear to be more a sign of tenseness and scrupulous desire to understand his student more closely than of his inability to read the actual script. It was Macaulay who warned Willie to get rid of his "Glasgow accent" or he would "never get anywhere in the Church"! Prophecy was clearly not his forte. It is interesting to note that this is the sole example of negative comment that Willie made of any of his tutors from Dalziel High School to Trinity College, covering his entire educative process. It seems likely that the quibble is more a reflection of Willie's own sensitivity on the matter than of Macaulay's. His self-consciousness about his voice was exaggerated in the light of his parents' beautiful Highland enunciation; but on the other hand we should not undervalue this as one of the crosses he had to bear, especially since, as we have seen, it was the result of a genuine physiological disorder.

And then there were W. M. Macgregor and A. J. Gossip. It is difficult to know how to rank these two in Willie's experience. Willie himself states that the former "had more influence on me than anyone outside my home."[8] Macgregor was Professor of New Testament Language and Literature and undoubtedly helped to rescue Willie from the crippling conservatism of his upbringing. As he poetically expressed it, using Macgregor's expression of his own tutor A. B. Bruce, "He cut the cables and gave us a glimpse of the blue waters."[9] But curiously, in Willie's magnum opus The Daily Study Bible he never once cites his great mentor in seventeen volumes of New Testament commentary, nor does he do so in his more academic tour de force, the two-volume work The Gospels and Acts. The editor of The British Weekly, doubtless from "inside knowledge," made public a comment of Macgregor's that Willie was "the best New Testament student that passed through my hands [in seventeen years]"; it was his recommendation that provided the impetus to Willie's academic career via the Bruce Lectures (in 1937).

New Testament enlightenment apart, Macgregor's dour personality seems to have had a significant impact on Willie, contrasting as it did so pointedly with Willie's sunny, outgoing, extrovert disposition. Willie has described him as "a man of terrible silences, a man with a tongue dipped in vitriol."[10] And yet despite that, he was "amazingly kind," and deeply religious, with a depth and breadth that was pure liberation for Willie. It was this spirituality that captured the young student, that soared over the artificial barriers of denominationalism and the pettiness that so sadly marks some aspects of Scottish ecclesiastical history. In the churches' Reunion Address of 1900, Macgregor generously acknowledges the great contribution that D. L. Moody made to the Free Church—"no force so powerful or so wholesome"—adding that "he came upon us like a breath of God's air from outside." A few years later he preached a memorable sermon at a New College retreat on repentance that typified his humble walk before God. He abhorred any delusions of grandeur, and was especially emphatic on the principle of ministerial equality. Despite an apparently frosty exterior, he was held high in the esteem and affection of his students, who referred to him, as Andrew Herron reminds us, as "Williemac."

I have no doubt of the importance of Macgregor's influence on Willie, and it would be foolish indeed, in the absence of more concrete proof, to argue against Willie's own statement. But close reflection on his career and a detailed study of his writings lead me to question whether his influence was in fact greater than that of Arthur John Gossip. It is not merely that Willie regularly quotes Gossip, whereas he seldom cites Macgregor, but rather that there is a deeper kinship of temperament, especially of devotion and of religious expression, that constantly challenges the assertion that he owed more to the latter than to the former. Even in describing the spectacular powers of Macgregor's memory Willie uses a remark of Gossip's.[11] The question of influence apart, there can be no doubt that a tie of close personal friendship existed between Professor Gossip and his enthusiastic student that grew over the years till Gossip's lamented death in 1954. Perhaps Gossip's influence was so pervasive, so wholesale, and felt over such an extended period that Willie came to take it for granted and failed to recognize it in himself. Perhaps the fact that it was of a piece with WDB's influence rendered it more transparent to him.

The seeds for the friendship had commenced as far back as the early '20s, when Willie was but a boy, just a few months after his resolve to enter the ministry. The staff and students of the Glasgow College had organized the Hamilton Campaign in 1920, when most of the congregations in the area were invited to join together "to bring the evangel into practical touch with modern life and the problems of a large industrial community." Gossip was one of the leaders (A. B. Macaulay was another) preparing himself, though all unbeknown to him, for his work in practical training. The campaign provided a welcome relief from the wearisome church union debate then being pressed hard on the local congregations. WDB made his own small contribution directly by preaching at Hamilton Primitive Methodist's Sisterhood, and indirectly by becoming involved on the Board of the Lanarkshire Christian Union, which was closely involved in the campaign. Apart from a short break when Gossip went to Aberdeen, he was to become an increasingly conspicuous and popular figure in the area, particularly appreciated for his personal piety and his powerful preaching (Willie called him "one of the world's supreme preachers"). We shall see that Gossip was directly instrumental in furthering Willie's career in at least two aspects, ministerial and literary, the two central aspects of his life's work. He owed very much to Arthur John Gossip.

There were other tutors, too. His first year was the one following the great Union of 1929, when churchmen on both sides, according to D. S. Cairns, "hardly knew where [they were]. It is as if some greater Power has inveigled us into it."[12] The church had two of everything, including theological colleges and lecturers. Willie now came directly under those on "the other side," although there was still a great gulf between both students and staff members, as we shall see. Nevertheless, the presence—if not the influence—of such men as William Fulton and W. B. Stevenson and Archibald Main must be recognized.

The reunification of mainline Presbyterianism was only one of four separate but interpenetrating factors that combined to produce the unique environment in which Willie was coming to theological understanding and maturity. In addition to the turmoil caused by the Union of 1929, the ongoing debate over biblical criticism, the beginnings of a decline in the still considerable influence of theological liberalism, and the first motions toward ascendancy of reformed theology served to generate the excited and exciting times in which Willie pursued his education.

Theolog and Fellow Student

The university regulations required that "candidates for the BD must attend classes during two sessions in each of the four departments of study . . . and a special course of study in one selected department during a third session." Since ordination was his next step, the student was also expected to attend classes in public reading and speaking, pastoral theology, and homiletics. Willie's PE year counted for his special session (in which he also did Preparatory Hebrew and Biblical Knowledge for his Scriptural Examination).

He was now no longer his own man as at university, but under the direction of the Presbytery of Glasgow. Having satisfied it as to both his character and motives for entering the ministry, and having produced a certificate signed by his minister verifying full communion with the church, he had gone on to receive formal nomination by presbytery to commence his studies in their Glasgow College. This was secured by means of a postgraduate Entrance Examination that took place on Wednesday and Thursday, 25–26 September 1930. The cost was 2/6d, perhaps the best half-crown purchase of his whole career!

The examination covered five subjects, four of them compulsory (Scripture Knowledge, Hebrew, Greek, and Moral Philosophy); the fifth subject was to be selected from among a list of eight possibilities: English, Latin, French, German, Mathematics (pure or applied), Economics, and Gaelic. Willie remained faithful to his first love and chose English. The Church of Scotland Handbook for 1930 has preserved the actual texts in which he was examined, in demonstration of the remarkable emphasis the church places on a learned ministry and its desire to produce students who are "trained sufficiently and suitably," a training they were careful to emphasize is to be "not only in Theology, but in Literature, in Philosophy, and even in Science."

The scriptural knowledge in which candidates were examined was based on the English text of Genesis, Exodus, Isaiah 1–39, Matthew, and 1 and 2 Corinthians—nearly two hundred pages of text in the Authorized Version. In studying Hebrew, Willie had been brought into contact with some of the great names of Scottish biblical learning, such as A. B. Davidson, author of *Hebrew Grammar,* and J. E. M'Fadyen, who had revised Davidson's work. He had studied the first thirty sections of this text during the year of his PE course; anyone who combines Economics with Hebrew has special qualities, and Willie's results underscore the fact. For the Greek examination he used Rutherford's *Greek Grammar* and the first sixteen chapters of Acts for Greek text, plus Xenophon's *Memorabilia 1* (the only text requiring revision from his arts course). In Moral Philosophy he was put to work on Mackenzie's *Manual of Ethics,* parts I and II. From all this, a return to his much-loved English was pure relaxation; the examination in this area covered Macaulay's *State of England* (volume 1, chapter three), Strachey's *Eminent Victorians,* and Shakespeare's *Julius Caesar* (which undoubtedly recalled "the sheer delight"[13] of McNeile Dixon's classes). The regulations state that on the successful completion of these examinations, the results would be "regularized as part of his theological course." Willie, having passed, was thus admitted to Trinity College.

As we noted, it was a training to be carried out under the watchful eye of the presbytery, which was obligated to confer with the students at least once per session and to set five "exercises" in addition to the B.D. work required by the University. These exercises were to take the form of two essays in Apologetics, Historical Theology, or Dogmatic Theology; an essay in both New Testament and Old Testament Exegesis; and "a popular sermon."

The late James L. Dow has given us his own humorous recollections of this work, which shows well Willie's surpassing ability and, more importantly, his generous spirit:

> In the last year, students had to prepare a New Testament exegesis, which is a full analysis and interpretation of a passage of Scripture. He is supposed to look up all the available manuscripts, and make his own translation of the Greek. He then writes down all the variants, which are the textual differences between one and the other. Having completed this useful and, no doubt, necessary task, he then examines carefully the background of the book, the authorship and the rest, and finishes with a homiletic expansion which, in plain language, is a sermon.
>
> The idea is that after you qualify, you do this every week, twice. In college they gave you a year to do it once. Willie Macgregor handed out the passages one morning, and after class Willie Barclay asked me what I had got in the draw. I told him I'd got the second chapter of the Epistle to the Hebrews. There may have been a trace of gloom on my face. For next day my friend handed me a foolscap sheet with all the variants written on it. He said it hadn't taken him as long as it would have taken me. I wonder how he knew. I did not question the accuracy of them. He didn't make that kind of mistake.
>
> Knowing that my exegesis had at least a good start, however it finished, I worked hard at it, trying to live up to the variants. There would be about a hundred pages of writing in it. And in due season I handed it in.
>
> Some months later a friend and I were having coffee in the common room when Willie Macgregor entered, bearing in his hand a manuscript. I recognized it and told George so out of the corner of my mouth. He looked as anxious as he would have looked had it been his own. Macgregor came with slow deliberate step and stood behind us, like a High Court judge returning to pass sentence after going out to find his black cap. The only sound was the tapping of the manuscript on his hand. There was no sound of heavy breathing. George and I were not breathing at all.[14]

This actually took place in 1931. Dow has overlooked some of the aspects of this set work, but the main point is clear enough. He was not the only person Willie helped in this way, though few have chosen such a public vehicle for their gratitude. Shortly after Willie's death, for instance, Harry Cummings told his widow of an occasion on which he had been delayed by illness en route to the examination hall for one of the final B.D. papers. Arriving on a subsequent bus, he was surprised to find Willie *outside* the hall, pacing up and down in great concern: he had been waiting to comfort his friend, and went into the examination late with him.

That Willie was academically ambitious his associates and fellow students of the time do not deny. But the spirit in which this ambition was then realized—and which typified his later work—was wholly different from that of many students. It is in this sense that we should understand such statements as "when I was a student, I never attended lectures," which he made at the time of the 1968 College Dinner. Though strongly competitive and single-minded, Willie was always kind and helpful. He was never conceited, always gregarious. Merricks Arnot, his desk-mate at Trinity, recalls how part of their friendship was founded on Arnot's drawing ability, which Willie clearly admired. He also admired his socialism (in the wake of H. G. Wells, Bernard Shaw, Fosdick, and Sayer, all of whom were influences on Willie), though his own political commitment "swithered about" (in Arnot's phrase), checked, no doubt, by his father's moderate views and his own studies of the previous year. Even then, his deafness was beginning to impinge on his work and attitudes, and his stentorian voice was frequently heard well above the rest, above all sixty-seven of them in fact. This disability did not prevent him singing duets with George Boyd, as Stanley Pritchard (of a later time at college than Willie's) recalls. And very musical and entertaining they were, too, their songs being not always on strictly religious themes!

It was a time not only of academic seriousness, but of social competitiveness too, made more interesting by the continuing rivalry in a sort of sweet-and-sour way between the Auld Kirk students and the "Uffies" (UFC). Sometimes the rivalry even showed between the professors themselves, as when a small group of Uffies was caught "cutting" an Auld Kirk professor's lecture. Approaching their tea table in Craig's Tea Room, Professor Niven asked why they were out and about at such an hour. The students guiltily replied that it was so-and-so's lecture. "Ah!" replied the polymath knowingly and, forgetting his accustomed reserve on such matters, ordered another pot of tea for them. The Uffies also defiantly founded the British Israel Original Succession group, wittily based on the acrostic *bios* (Greek for "life"), a deliberate tilt against their stuffier colleagues.

A Moral Censor was appointed annually, whose job it was to oversee the demeanor and habits of students, and bring them back into line where necessary. In reality it was a ruse to stimulate the students to public speaking, which it did in a serious and amusing manner. Arnot recalls one student, George Fraser, who was reprimanded by the said official for brightening the dreich classroom with a colorful pullover. His answer was that it was socially desirable, for the student-body should be well-knit.[15]

These were the days, despite the more pietistic attitude of the Uffie students, when Willie was to be found in the University Union, playing billiards with the best, or rampaging at the piano with one of his favorite Music Hall ditties, his voice echoing round the room.

> You may have Rose,
> With the upturned nose,
> But you won't have Lulu!

Much to his father's consternation, Willie was no stranger to the music halls of the area, the Metropole, the Pavilion, and the Princess. He especially enjoyed the comedians, following their movements and often repeating their less risqué stories. He was fascinated by the way they built up their rapport with their audiences, and later would speak in much esteem of the professional techniques of such men as Lex Mclean and Rikki Fulton. Despite the seriousness of his background and his clear-sighted convictions, he was no prude; he respected the common things of life and reveled in wit, gaiety, and repartee. This aspect of his character is reflected in the two highly significant "farewell texts" given to Willie on leaving the college, which were culled from Swinburne and Gay respectively:

> He is Master and Lord of his brethren
> Who is worthier and wiser than they.

and

> Life is a jest and all things show it;
> I thought so once, now I know it.

His more high-spirited activities did not endear him to some of the Auld Kirk students, who were more restrained and genteel in their behavior; their sense of communal life was less developed than that of the Uffies too, and their professors were more distant and inclined to stand on their dignity. Whereas "Johnnie" M'Fadyen would often appear among the congregation of some hapless student on preaching duty, only to reward him with an encouraging word in the vestry afterward, men like Stevenson held court aloofly, sometimes inviting the students to musical soirées at which his wife played and sang classical and improving verses, much to the unexpressed boredom of their guests.

WDB also sought to sanctify his son in this aspect, not only by direct confrontation in season and out, but by influencing his friends with "wholesome literature," some of it of a distinctly onerous kind. John Smith, for example, was given A. S. Peake's *Outline of Christianity* in five volumes—almost two thousand pages of condensed history and theology! There is more than a hint of post-retirement blues about his father at this time, which heightened the clashes between them.

Not least of the influences on Willie during this course was the communal life of the students and of the excellent library facilities of Trinity College. The library was particularly important in that it provided an environment in which the love and respect for books with which Willie had grown up was nurtured and encouraged to develop to new heights. In this sacred hall was a collection of some forty thousand volumes, which of course dwarfed Willie's own library, despite the fact that that private collection was a large one by normal standards. (John Smith was to recall, fifty years later, how books were to be found everywhere throughout WDB's apartments in Motherwell and Wilton Street, Glasgow, being by far the most visible indications of interests within the home, Mrs. Barclay's piano notwithstanding.) Merricks Arnot recollects a feature of Willie's book usage that rather surprised him, but that reflects the range and speed of Willie's reading: Willie placed great reliance (perhaps not altogether wisely given the inconsistency of many books) on the use of indexes to get to the heart of the subject immediately, bypassing the author's argumentation. Even great classics were not immune from this literary ravishment. He read quickly, omnivorously, devouring in this way everything that might be relevant.

In all this lecturing and study Willie thrived, enjoying the enrichment of mind and soul that accompanied the strenuous tasks to which he had set his hand. He was now marked out for distinguished results, though they were not to come to him without pressures of a very different sort. In February 1932, just a few weeks before her son's all-important finals, Mrs. Barclay was taken ill with what turned out to be a carcinoma of the spine. Study, games, and all other pleasures fled from Willie's mind in the shock of this news. His final preparations were disrupted by an agony of suspense as he attended to her in daily visits to the hospital.

He passed with distinction (honors classes not then being applicable), adding a number of prizes, including the Dykes Prize for Practical Training and the Dods Prize for New Testament Exegesis, but he found it difficult to rejoice in the triumph, for his mother died but six weeks after the commencement of her illness, early in the morning of 21 March 1932; she had not lived to make worthwhile (in R. L. Stevenson's manner) the industry of her son. He thereafter rarely spoke of it, but whenever he did, even forty years afterward, his voice was charged with emotion. The experience tore at the very vitals of his faith. Just as he was taking his first steps in his vocation, he was confronted with the loss of one of the greatest and tenderest joys of his life—and more, one of the greatest influences on his faith. As his mentor A. J. Gossip stated in the frontispiece to *The Galilean Accent,* "Christianity is within a man . . . associated with your mother's chair, and with the first remembered tones of her blessed voice." Like Gossip, Willie could also recall his mother's face—"in whose face I saw God's." Remarked his father through his own distress and grief, "You'll have a new note in your preaching now";[16] he had, and it hurt.

> Thou shouldst have longer lived, and to the grave
> Have peacefully gone down in full old age.[17]

PART TWO

The Commencement

THE REVEREND WILLIAM BARCLAY, M.A., B.D.
The official ordination photograph

CHAPTER SIX

Ordination and Early Days

Call and Ordination: A Pledged Life

H<small>IS</small> training now completed, two opportunities presented themselves to Willie. The first was Saint Andrew's Church, Kirkintilloch, within the Presbytery of Glasgow, situated to the northeast of Glasgow on the Forth and Clyde Canal, near the site of the old Antonine wall. The church had a membership of 460, with 13 elders, a Bible class of 15, and a Sunday School of 80. Many considered this to be an ideal charge for a new man. It was within his own presbytery, where he was known and loved, not far from his father's retirement lodgings in Wilton Street; moreover, there was another feature of the community that would have recommended it to WDB: since the '20s, and by repeated popular vote, the town had been "dry"—and to his father's way of thinking, abstention from alcohol on such a scale was a sure sign of Christianity in action.

The other possibility was Trinity Church, Renfrew, within the Presbytery of Paisley. It was located on the other side of town, to the southeast six miles from the city's center on the Clyde, "which made Glasgow." The membership of Trinity Church stood at 1,053, with 22 elders, a Bible class of 112, and a Sunday School of 258. Not a few considered this too big a challenge for a first charge, particularly in light of the church's reputation as "the fechtin' kirk." At the very time the elders were considering the question of the new minister, their session minutes (later scored out!) record an unpleasant contretemps between two senior church officers, one of whom demanded that the other be unchurched for having allegedly insulted him. No minister had stayed for more than four years since 1919; it would clearly stretch any man, let alone a probationer, to serve such a congregation. Despite that, it was an extremely zealous church, with great traditions and an enviable group of workers. Willie could not resist the challenge.

We have already seen that Willie radiated confidence and trustworthiness. He was no stranger to what Wallace Williamson has called "the tumultuous west" of Scotland, though he was seldom ruffled himself; there was about him a quiet sense of power, even in the early days, which betokened success. One of the sayings he cherished at the time came from W. S. Landor: "When God has told you what you ought to do, he has already told you what you can." This was the real source of his strength, which was clearly visible to those around him. Impressed by this, as by his winsomeness and sheer ability, all soon became convinced that he was the man for the job. Professor Gossip was foremost in advocating him for the vacancy. Thus it was that on Sunday, 9 January 1933, he made his first appearance in the pulpit of Trinity Church as Sole Nominee. The local newspaper, *The Renfrew Press,* which was to have so much influence on his career, stated that "he made a most favourable impression."

The following evening a "well attended and fully representative meeting" was held in the church, and a report on Willie was submitted by the vacancy committee. It was agreed "without a single dissenting vote to present a unanimous call to him to be minister of our church." The paper listed some of his accomplishments under a very becoming photograph; it spoke of his

> distinguished academic record, [noting] that he was a native of Wick, resident in Glasgow, educated at Dalziel High School, Motherwell, and Glasgow University [and] that he was a prizeman in English, Latin and Political Economy, graduated MA with First-Class Honours in the Classics, and had been awarded the Maxwell Forsyth Fellowship as "the most distinguished student of the year," that he had won the Dods Prize in the Senior New Testament class, and was the joint holder of the Dykes Prize for Practical Training. He had graduated BD with distinction in New Testament Language and Literature, and had recently returned from a spell in Germany, having studied at the University of Marburg.[1]

Not surprisingly, it made a great impression on both town and church, adding to the respect gained when he preached from their pulpit. The newspaper congratulated the church "on securing such a man." They were making the challenge good.

The Church of Scotland, apart from having one of the best educated ministries of any church in the world, also had a high conception of the ministry and the minister's role in the church. This is what Principal J. H. S. Burleigh wrote of it:

> Those who hold ministerial office are still within the church. Before they enter on their office, they are proved by the church as to character and attainment. They are chosen by it in a carefully regulated manner as befits the importance of the office they are to hold. They are solemnly set apart for the service they are to render to their brethren, but even in office they are not elevated above the judgement of their fellow members.[2]

Having been "proved" in the accredited manner, Willie was now ready for the final act: his ordination. The formalities for this were undertaken by the Presbytery of Paisley, in whose jurisdiction he was to be placed. A pleasant touch to the presbytery's minutes of 24 January states, in the clipped manner of such chronicles, that "Mr W D Barclay, ruling elder of Stevenson Memorial Church and Parish, of the Presbytery of Glasgow, father of the Probationer under call to Renfrew Trinity, was associated with the Presbytery." Whatever help Willie had received from others, it was the moment of his father's greatest pleasure and fulfillment, and he was there supporting his son and enjoying every minute of it, which lessened the deep hurt created by Mrs. Barclay's absence—of which not a word was spoken by either of them.

The "form of call" was signed by 594 members and 64 adherents—a wonderful encouragement to the young minister. It was laid before presbytery, along with a letter from Willie (now sadly lost) that intimated his willingness to accept the call, plus his Extract of Licence and Presbyterial certificate. Signing themselves in support of the call were the Moderator *ad interim* of the church, the Reverend J. Mackinnon, Messrs. Copland, Ferguson, Ramsay, Sutherland, and Miss Bain. A report on Willie was submitted by the Students' and Ministers' Committee of the General Assembly, which stated that it "was highly satisfied with the exercises submitted on trial for ordination." And so the call was placed in Willie's hands. Mr. Sutherland seconded the resolution, and the matter was carried unanimously. "Mr Barclay," we are told, "suitably replied." A special meeting of presbytery was arranged to take place four weeks later at Trinity Church, Renfrew, for "his ordination and admission to the pastoral charge of the church and parish."

On the evening of Wednesday, 22 February 1933, William Barclay became a minister of the Church of Scotland, a servant of the people of God. He was never to forget the occasion, and never to surrender the task then undertaken.

The edicts having been read and attested on the two Sundays preceding the ceremony, and presbytery having examined them in formal session, the gathering moved to the sanctuary of the church, where "devotional exercises" were conducted and "a discourse suitable to the occasion" was delivered by the most recently inducted minister of the presbytery, the Reverend A. G. Fortune of Saint George's East, Paisley. This was a well-established custom, known as "preaching in" a minister, which had the dual advantage of making known to the presbytery the new minister, and offering to the new incumbent a word of encouragement from one who was himself but recently inducted. The church was packed to capacity. Commented Willie to Mrs. Gray (née Campbell), "Do they aye turn out like this?"

Mr. Fortune based his sermon on Ephesians 4:13, "Till we all come into the unity of the faith, and of the knowledge of the Son of God, unto a perfect man, unto the stature of the fulness of Christ." The Authorized Version then held undisputed sway, as it would for nearly two decades more, but even given the complexity of its rendering, it was a most apposite choice of text and gave a prophetic note to the occasion and direction to Willie's vocation. The preacher began by reminding the gathering of the criticisms to which the church was subjected by society at large. He emphasized that men had a right to know what the church stood for, what message it had to deliver, and whether that message was worth delivering. "These questions," he cautioned, "demand a decided answer." The challenge was thrown down, and the new minister was not the sort of man to let it pass unheeded; the next forty-five years were spent in seeking to

101

Renfrew Trinity Church—on a dull day!

give that "decided answer"—not to soft-nosed questions of faith and life, but to difficult ones, for which candor and honesty and total integrity alone suffice.

Mr. Fortune himself described the nature of the message as "distinct . . . a message for the times, and for all times and for all people." The gospel was the knowledge of the Son of God, and the church's task was to draw men to Christ; it had to proclaim his truth, thereby to reach both heart and conscience—on Christ's fullness should they ever insist. Moreover, unity of the faith meant cooperation in the service of Christ. All had to employ their distinct gifts. This cooperation was itself part of the fulfillment of the task entrusted to them. This second aspect likewise presaged Willie's ministry, in which the centrality of Christ would be the most outstanding feature, presented as a universal message, ever aware of—and willing to cooperate with—God's people of whatever hue.

The service of ordination now reached its climax. The Preamble was read, underscoring the presbytery's authority "to ordain in the name of Jesus Christ, the Head of the church, and as part of the universal church." The doctrines to be affirmed by the ordained are "according to the Word of God, the supreme rule of faith and life," and accord to the Westminster Confession of Faith, the church's "subordinate standard," which recognizes

> liberty of opinion on such points as do not enter the substance of the Faith, and claiming the right, in dependence on the promised guidance of the Holy Spirit, to formulate, interpret, or modify its subordinate standards; always in agreement with the Word of God and the fundamental doctrines of the Christian Faith contained in the said Confession—of which agreement the church itself shall be sole judge.

From Willie's background, already described, and the confirming attitudes and statements made following this solemn avowal, we need have no suspicions concerning the total and conscientious commitment with which he affirmed his fitness for this sacred office. Following this avowal, the signing of the Formula took place. Kneeling, William Barclay, M.A., B.D., was ordained to the ministry of the Church of Scotland by prayer, with the laying on of hands of the Moderator and the other ministers present, and with these words:

> I now declare you to have been ordained to the office of the Holy Ministry, and in the name of the Lord Jesus Christ, the King and Head of the Church, and by the authority of the Presbytery, I induct you to this charge: and in token thereof we give you the right hand of fellowship.

Regrettably, we do not have any firsthand account of what passed through Willie's mind at that time; he never recorded the thoughts or emotions that were then his. Ordination is a unique experience both in nature and objective; it is both a fulfilling and a commissioning, a climax and a commencement. Thoughts personal and professional, undoubtedly shadowed by the fact that his beloved mother had so recently been denied through death this great occasion, must have crowded in upon him. For twenty-one years he had contemplated this event. Perhaps his mind went back to that holiday at Fort William when, in the

High Street as a lad of twelve years of age, with his foot resting on the boulder that ever marked his private Bethel, he decided to be a minister. Or perhaps he recalled the much longer period during which his parents had watched over their only child, beginning the day of his birth, when, already in advanced years, they gratefully and freely offered him in service to God.

It was not only a time of dedication for the new minister. The congregation, too, had its share in the proceedings, and was challenged to play its part:

> Do you, the members and adherents of this congregation, receive William Barclay, whom you have called to be your Minister, promising him all due honour and support in the Lord, and will give of your means, as the Lord shall prosper you, for the maintenance of the Christian ministry and the furtherance of the Gospel?

Their affirmative response was to be tested and confirmed over the coming years in ways that none of them could then have conceived, and was to help shape his views and his style of ministry, and make of them a singular instrument in the cause of God's love.

The Reverend John Muir of High Church, Paisley, delivered the charges to both pastor and people. The minister was reminded of his calling, "which demanded consecrated and devoted service," of how he could only deliver the message he himself had received and had therefore ever to keep himself "in touch with the realities of religion—the deep things of God," and of how his life must be consistent with that message. He closed with a cordial note of welcome to Willie on behalf of the Presbytery of Paisley and the promise of their prayers that his work be crowned with divine blessing. To the congregation Mr. Muir underscored the need for their consecration "in the fellowship and service of Christ." They were the ones who would make the ministry successful in the best sense of the word: by their sympathy, regular attendance, and prayers as well as by their gifts. They could support and uphold the ministry inaugurated that evening: he called on them so to do.

The service came to an end with prayer and with the congregation welcoming its new minister into their midst. WDB returned to the loneliness of his flat very well content, his greatest ambition realized, his many prayers answered.

One of Trinity Church's outstanding characteristics was its ability to put on church socials. These were so well done that they were virtually of professional standard. Willie's initiation into them started the very next day, at his first congregational meeting. Many years later, in 1975, he was to write to David Anderson about the social life of American churches. His comments betray his early conservative, overserious background: "At one time I was critical of the social life of churches, but not now." It also reflects his earlier tendency to compartmentalize his interests and activities, for we have seen how much he enjoyed the atmosphere of the theater and music halls. But in these early years, he clearly found himself surprised at Trinity's relaxed and close integration of the serious and pleasurable, although he quickly learned to respect the attitude and enjoy the festivities. Tea, itself a rare performance in those austere days of Depression, was served in the large hall. It had just been renovated, and was in fine condition. The choir, under the baton of Mr. Hamilton Kerr, rendered a number of popular anthems; "By Babylon's Waters," "In Silent Night," "Annie Laurie," and Robertson's "The Islands of Mull" were among those presented. Trinity found no difficulty, or incongruity, in blending the secular (particularly "Auld Scotch Sangs") with the sacred. And the congregation believed in showing its response to what was done. The communal singing of "The Second Paraphrase" followed, with prayer by the Reverend A. W. Sawyer of Old Parish Church, Inchinnan.

John Mackinnon chaired the meeting, expressing his gratification at "the very large number" of people present, believing it augured well for the future, as truly it did. In a short search for a successor to the former pastor, Mr. Robertson, that "scoured the whole of Scotland," he said the vacancy committee had sought for "nothing less than the best for Trinity Church, and they had secured the right man." The proceedings had been undertaken with great cordiality and utter honesty on both sides, and this too was indicative of that which was to follow. He read out messages of greeting, including one from the Reverend Robertson, now of Aberdeen, which were well received.

Miss Bowie, in a short but moving speech on behalf of the ladies of Trinity Church, presented the minister with his first set of pulpit robes, which had been made by Mrs. Crosbie, now in her ninetieth year. She had made all the robes for Trinity's ministers since the church was founded seventy-two years before.

Willie then took the chair for the first time, speaking with style, humor, and great personal warmth. Characteristically, his first words were ones of gratitude:

The Renfrew Trinity Induction Social (1933). The group includes Willie and Merricks Arnot (first and third on the left, respectively), and Mitchell Ramsay, A. M. Ferguson, and WDB (first, second, and third on the right, respectively).

to the ladies of the church for their generosity, and to Miss Bowie for "her gracious welcome and good wishes." "It is," he said, "the greatest night of my life; at least it is one of them." All the knowledge he had gained at school, university, and college, and all the home training and influences—"and no man ever had a finer home training than I"—together with the high ideals he cherished were all to be put to the test in the business of daily living and in service for Trinity Church. He acknowledged that they were both taking immense risks: the church in calling a probationer, and he in hoping that his untried abilities would, in some measure, prove equal to the great task that lay before him. He needed all their sympathy and support, their prayers and friendship and, given them, he was assured that "the greatest days for Trinity Church are ahead." This last comment was not a sign of undue confidence on his part, but the expression of one of his essential traits: an unshakable belief that "the best is yet to be." It recurs endlessly throughout his career, like a refrain in a great anthem. The training being concluded, he was now setting out in his life's work. He was aware of that succession of "foremost preachers" who had gone before him. He was equally aware of the very great traditions of the church, and would endeavor to become a humble follower of them, trusting the members for their help and assistance. And of course, "back of all," he affirmed, "is God himself." Without *his* sustaining powers all their endeavors would be to no avail. It was on this basis that he relied for the future. He wanted to be a friend of every member, and he promised to serve them as he had opportunity and ability (this drew great applause, especially when he committed himself to early visits in their homes).

Returning to the note of gratitude, he offered his thanks to Mr. Mackinnon and the officebearers of the church who had "extended so much friendship to him over the past few weeks. . . ." He valued very highly their assistance and appreciated their kindness.

Such occasions are always heightened by the presence of fellow ministers and colleagues, and Willie's genius for friendship ensured a good turnout for this one. The first to speak was the Reverend Merricks Arnot, who had been Willie's desk-mate at college. They had been through many scrapes together, and Willie had participated in Arnot's induction at Saint Michael's, Dumfries. Now it was Arnot's turn to reciprocate the honor. He began by congratulating the church for making "a wise decision" in calling his friend. William Barclay, he remarked, was a man as well as a student and a minister—they would soon discover that! He spoke to them of his great capacity for hard work, and he warned them that he was not afraid to speak out against what he considered evil and wrong in every form. Gifted as a preacher, he would bring them week by week a message that was fresh and clear, to which would be added a note of intense enthusiasm. "The need of the pulpit today," Mr. Arnot continued, "is very great. Old truths require to be presented in fresh form, so that the appeal to the heart of the hearer might be stronger. It is such a message that William Barclay will bring." The speaker had clearly touched a responsive chord in his hearers' minds in reiterating Mr. Fortune's comments: applause broke out again. Interrupting it, he added that he had not the least doubt that the ministry inaugurated that evening would be blessed by God.

The '30s were rigorous years, not least in the demands they made on church-goers' stamina and patience. The reporter covering the evening's events notes that "no fewer than ten ministers delivered speeches," darkly adding "of greater or lesser length." No fewer than fifty-six column inches were given to the occasion. The *locum tenens,* the Reverend J. L. Craig of Queen's Park, added his contribution, pointing out that Trinity was a congregation of workers and helpers, and that anyone who could not preach in its pulpit could not preach at all, a comment that provoked some laughter and more applause. He was certain that Mr. Barclay would present his message to them "in striking fashion," just as he was certain that they had found the right man. David Young, minister of Old Parish Church, Renfrew, the "senior" church in the locality, followed. He could speak personally of knowledge and respect for WDB and was sure that his son would show the same gifts. He had attended many socials at Trinity, and not a few induction socials, so he hoped that the new incumbent's ministry would be a long one. And so the speeches wore on: Mr. Ramsay, Session Clerk; Mr. Mackinnon; Mr. Ferguson, Preses; and more of Willie's college colleagues. A high spot was reached when Professor Gossip rose to speak, he who could turn a lecture hall into a sanctuary, a lectern into an Ark of the Covenant. It was entirely character-istic of him to say that of all the young minister's contributions, the outstanding one would be his gift to the members of Trinity Church of a fresh vision of God. This was the urgent need of the time, and William Barclay's message would stir them to fresh interest and endeavor. It was clear that this was a church, a congregation now hungry for God, and on that platform Willie was to build. The proceedings were eventually concluded on behalf of the Presbytery of Paisley by the Reverend Lewis Sutherland, who offered Willie every help and encourage-ment they could muster. He had known Willie personally from his early Mother-well days and could commend him unreservedly to them.

And so a very happy and lively occasion was brought to its end. The church had opened a new chapter in its history, and the new minister had been brought to the outset of his work for God: it was in the light of that commitment that they set out together to serve him and their community.

The Royal Burgh of Renfrew and Its Church

The move to Renfrew gave Willie his fourth opportunity to put down roots. From the "latent unrealised baby-days" at Wick, through his boyhood and maturing manhood at Motherwell and Wilton Street, Glasgow, he had come to the outset of his career at Renfrew.

The town itself is situated in West Renfrewshire, which had once ranked greater than Paisley. By the time Willie arrived, it possessed great self-awareness and independence, and boasted of its royal connections. We shall see that royalty still made its way to the town from time to time. The title "Baron

Renfrew" presently adorns the Prince of Wales, and to this day visitors are reminded of this when they pass the proud sign at the entrance to the town: "The Royal Burgh of Renfrew, Cradle of the Stuarts"—those "implacable enemies of Presbyterianism" whose encroachments form such a dark background to the history of the Scottish Church.

Renfrew does not possess the magic of the lochs or the Highlands, or the panoramic beauty of those towns further south on the Firth of Clyde and the west coast; indeed, the Clyde at this point is almost hidden from view behind its docks and termini. Nevertheless, it is an attractive place, with a pleasant town hall and parish church, and nearby the famous Argyle Stone and the Blythswood Testimonial School. The airport (built over the old golf course, scene of Willie's many sporting endeavors) gives it added distinction.

Positioned on the country's western slopes, it was at first disadvantaged relative to the more important eastern coastal plain, then under the dominance of European commerce and contacts. But as the commercial center of gravity shifted with the development of American trade, the west's importance grew, and Glasgow grew with it. Its proximity to Lanarkshire's coal and iron fields, with their related industries, made Renfrew an obvious choice for development. At one time half the country's shipbuilding tonnage was constructed on the Clyde, and some of the world's best dredgers (formerly a specialty of Renfrew) had their origins on its banks. Manufacturing, shipbuilding, and agriculture constituted the chief sources of wealth, providing its citizens with employment, and its quiet rural charm tempted Glasgow's artisans from their homes. It is essentially a working-class area, and is dominated by the meaner dwellings that typify such places—tenement blocks and the like.

The town has claims to greatness apart from those stemming from the Industrial Revolution, however. Here and there are still to be seen signs of the Roman occupation, as at Oakshawhead, Castlehead, and Woodside. Willie will have found this especially interesting, and will have recalled his second year as an undergraduate, when he studied the Roman occupation of Britain under Stuart Miller. He may well have remembered the plantations of fruit trees the Romans established, and resolved to sow different, and more lasting, fruit in their place. Cotterall suggests that there may once have been a series of Roman forts and fortlets along the Renfrewshire coast, but there is no evidence that Willie ever sought to pursue the studies undertaken at Glasgow in this direction. In the post-Roman era the settlement was known as Strathgryffe, and formed part of the Kingdom of Strathclyde, which stretched from Cumberland in the south to beyond the Clyde, with its capital on Dumbarton Rock. Under the ancient kings of Scotland it was a regal burgh, but in the hands of the Stuarts it became a burgh of barony, designated the Barony of Renfrew. It was one Walter, made steward (hence "Stuart") of the King's household, who was responsible for elevating his family to royalty. By loyal service, military and otherwise, the family obtained royal approval that culminated in Walter's great-grandson gaining the hand of Robert the Bruce's daughter in marriage, and thus access to the crown. It was made a shire in 1404.

Of this there was little left when Willie came to Renfrew except a proud memory and an independent spirit. The castle has now gone, though a house named Castlehill stood close to its original site; other names, such as Orchard Street and Meadowside Street preserved the connection, but feebly. But if the town bore witness to a declining recognition, it was otherwise with Trinity Church, the story of which was one of growth from obscurity to full vigor, the zenith of which was about to be reached.

In the Union of 1929 Willie became with many others a member of the Church of Scotland. In any such union (or reunion, as some would prefer to call it), quite disparate elements are brought together for the greater good. We noted something of the uneasy relationship that existed between students and staff members during his theological training. That was not surprising, nor did it create any major problems. Happily for Willie the church that now called him was of almost identical persuasion to his own, both backgrounds being "Free Church" with a fine evangelical emphasis. Trinity Church, Renfrew, had been in the United Presbyterian (UP) tradition, which stressed, unlike the old Free Church, the separation of church and state; it was thus in the tradition of the "voluntaries," who owned no duty except to fulfill the law of love to God and man responsibly. They were more like the English nonconformists in attitudes toward the state and, like them, were more visible in the cities and towns than in the thinly populated rural areas.

UP government was solidly presbyterian, and its doctrine was emphatically Reformed (in the Genevan mold). The dichotomy expressed in its clear-cut division between church and state was carried over to the internal aspects of church government, inasmuch as they rigidly preserved the distinction between the spiritual and the business aspects of church life and order: elders were responsible for the former, managers for the latter. The leader of the elders was the minister, as a "first among equals"; that of the managers was the preses, who could wield great power, even over the minister. The person who arranged the minutes and other formalities in the session was the session clerk, who acted as the minister's right-hand man. At the annual business meeting, the minister presided over the first ("sessional") part, dealing with the spiritual affairs of the church, and the preses presided over the second ("business") part, dealing with everything related to the finances, buildings, and similar aspects of church life. In essence this twin system of government split the church's leadership, leaving no serviceable mechanism for proper liaison between the two halves except that of personal rapport between minister, session clerk, and preses. This could easily have been a recipe for disaster—indeed, the contretemps between the Trinity Church officebearers that immediately preceded Willie's arrival there arose out of just such a question of jurisdiction—and yet Willie managed to overcome such difficulties in due time.

The question of authority is a perennial one, however, and Willie sought after the best division of labor to accomplish the many tasks of his new church.

His own responsibilities and prerogatives were a matter of special interest to him of course, and he was to some extent of two minds concerning them. On the one hand, he was wont to criticize himself for his failure to delegate responsibility—a fault for which his friends often chided him as well. On the other hand, on 4 July 1939 he preached a sermon entitled "The Mistake of Leaving Things to Others" in consideration of the opposite temptation. Happily, the UP system of government, with its careful delineation of officers' duties, was designed to guard against either extreme, a fact that pleased Willie considerably. "That's the place to go," he once said to the Reverend J. G. Lees on hearing of the offer to his friend of a UP call. He staunchly maintained the advisability of keeping administrative functions separate from ministerial functions, the latter of which clearly call for the minister's training (specifically as a "teaching elder"—which does not entail just public utterances).

The Prevailing Climate

By the time Willie came to Renfrew, much of the wealth and affluence of the area had been consumed by the painful days of the Depression; "the Devil's Decade" was under way. One of the great symbols of the period in the west of Scotland was the rusting, half-built hull of the Q.T.S.S. *Queen Mary,* which lay just opposite Renfrew in John Brown's shipyard on Clydebank.

The population of the town in 1931 was 40,814 with a "working population" of 11,500.[3] But there was no work. A third of British seamen were unemployed, nor was it any better in Scotland than south of the border—and considerably worse in some industries. Local unemployment stood at 13.59 percent (30.66 percent if one includes those working on reduced hours). Industry was stagnant and morale very low. It was a time of brutal inhumanity, the ultimate degradation of men and women being cast off like early summer apple-drop. Survival was now their concern, and many failed to survive. Harry Stevenson, former General Secretary of the YMCA, and a long-standing friend of Willie, actually recalls seeing unburied corpses in the streets of Glasgow.[4]

In face of this there was little the town council could do. Some work was found for the privileged few; sports for the unemployed were arranged in the local parks; plots of land were offered free of rent to alleviate boredom and famine. It was an age of anger. Since the early '20s the anger had grown, peaking in the General Strike of 1926 and its aftermath, but with little to show for it. The population was powerless to act effectively and had to stand by as the world's money markets crashed and confidence in industry evaporated in the fierce winds of change. That anger flashed throughout society, not only among classes but among individuals as they grimly held on to what they possessed. In Renfrew violent outbursts by local merchants against the itinerant traders were reported. They were dealt with by the urgent action of the town council, which "solved" the problem by banning street traders. The tensions were also apparent in the growing "rowdyism" of the period, as the younger members (and many of the

110

not-so-young members) of society vented their feelings on whatever, or whom-ever, stood in their way. Such disturbances were curiously prevalent on Sundays, as if the anger were being directed against God himself.

The churches sought to play their part not only by objecting to the "sabbath breaking," but in more meaningful ways, with works of mercy and help. The YMCA and the Salvation Army were conspicuous in this, greatly impressing Willie and reinforcing the admiration he had for them, learned from his father. No fewer than seventeen of his twenty-six elders were out of work and knew firsthand the heartbreak it caused.[5] Entertainments and "resting facilities" were provided, notably by Trinity Church, the Players of which were foremost in the town in putting on plays and shows; the sets (which the unemployed talent of the area was thoughtfully hired to construct) were marvels of care and ingenuity.

Willie was not merely an observer, but a participant in the suffering of the period, and he worked to alleviate it as best he could with the mean resources at his disposal. General conditions abetted him in this task: the worst was over by the time he came to Trinity, as the area unemployment statistics for the period indicate:

	Unemployed	Not Wholly Employed
December 1932	1,563	3,527
December 1933	1,427	3,067
October 1934	889	1,851
October 1935	653	1,358
October 1936	499	1,034
October 1937	367	761

No one could have foreseen such dramatic improvement in so short a time (the 1937 figure places unemployment at just three percent of the work force—an enviable rate in any era); just as difficult to foresee, however, was whether the calamitous conditions might not as swiftly return. Shaken by their recent ill fortune, people were haunted by a sense of foreboding—through which cloud of gloom the light of Willie's natural optimism pierced again and again.

Despite his optimism, however, Willie did have some reservations about the overall merits of the recovery on account of the social and political events that had brought it about. It was "the devil's decade" not merely because of the economic horrors and degradation throughout the Western world and the reac-tion this had on life and culture and politics (a reaction that caused A. L. Rouse to describe the '30s as "the heyday of the second-rate"), but because of another, more dreadful menace, a menace that was creeping forward like some malignant organism—the growth of Hitlerian Nazism.

In the very month in which Willie was selected as sole nominee for Renfrew Trinity, Adolf Hitler became Chancellor of Germany. Few saw anything terrible in this, certainly few in the churches. As R. D. Kernohan laconically records, in reviewing the reporting of the Church of Scotland's magazine *Life and Work* during the period, "Hitler passed, it seems, unnoticed. But he was to thrust himself on the notice of everyone soon enough"[6]—and with what hideous, what unspeakable consequences! The imposition was to intensify throughout the next eighteen months, with the abolition of political parties and the imprisonment of opponents, till it climaxed on 30 June 1934—"the night of the long knives"—when Hitler achieved supreme political power in Germany. Within a decade over six million Jews would be annihilated, millions maimed and slaughtered on the fields of battle, and millions more lost in the wholesale devastation of towns and cities.

Willie did not foresee this either, but whatever the benefits arising out of the conquest of the Depression through the growth of the armaments program, nothing in his opinion could justify it. However cordially he greeted the news that poverty and want, unemployment and waste, were on the downturn, he quickly perceived the superficiality of its effect, and its dangers. His response to the threat to society was to be one of his major concerns and was to remain unaltered throughout his life and influence his teaching considerably. Because of it, as we shall see, even his Christianity was to be called into question.

Introductions and Settlement, "In Good Set Earnest"

The excitement of Willie's ordination and induction was followed by a time of taking stock, personally and in the church. He had many letters of thanks to write (he was ever an assiduous letter writer and never failed to express his appreciation for any help or encouragement received, no matter how small). And the final preparations before taking over the manse—now being renovated for him—had to be made. Chief adviser in this, to be sure, was his fiancée Kate, who had the surer touch in such matters.

A pleasant and typically thoughtful tradition of Trinity Church took place in the vestry immediately following his induction. The church treasurer, Mr. William Knight (himself the son of a former treasurer of the church) placed in his hands his first quarter's stipend: the first money ever earned by this twenty-six-year-old, and a real milestone in his life. Not that money meant much to him. In that respect, as in others, he was an unworldly character. But in receiving his first stipendiary allowance he was on the road to professionalism, to fulfilling his calling; at long last he was a breadwinner. It meant independence from WDB, and would help to keep on the road the motorcar he now owned—a gift from his proud father.

Sunday, 26 February 1933, saw him ensconced in his pulpit. In the morning he led the worship, and the Very Reverend W. M. Macgregor preached. Dr. Macgregor was pleased to introduce Willie not only as the son of a loyal servant of the church, known throughout the region, but as his former and distinguished student, now a trusted fellow worker in the cause of the gospel. The weather was not as welcoming as the people were, being boisterous and stormy, but this did not prevent the people turning out in large numbers at both morning and evening services.

112

Dr. Macgregor, whom Willie once described as "the princeliest soul I ever met,"[7] was said to have been at his very best, delivering "a striking discourse" on the mission and purpose of the church. He reminded the church of the new chapter in its history now opening before it, and encouraged the individual members to support the new minister in his task. "The Christian message," he concluded, "is never more required than it is in these days," thus emphasizing again what was to become Willie's main task in life.

Although the titles of virtually all of Willie's Trinity sermons have survived him (see Appendix I), the sermon notes themselves have, alas, all been destroyed. At regular intervals of two or three years he discarded unwanted manuscripts, not considering them to be of any value. His records of illustrations were kept for a time, though regrettably these too were later thrown away. Only a small booklet of Children's Talks has survived. He believed in the virtues of the "WPB," as he was later to write:

> A waste paper basket is an essential part of life's equipment. There is an art, and a necessary art, of throwing things away. I suppose that the word *discard* must be connected with those card games in which the presence of certain cards in your hand constitutes a handicap and a danger, and in which the aim is to get rid of them as quickly as possible. . . . In life there are certain things for which the waste paper basket is the only right destination.[8]

He preached his first sermon as minister that evening. It was based on the Old Testament passage, Numbers 21:11, that describes the journeying of the children of Israel toward the promised land: "And they journeyed towards the sun-rising." The choir, we are told, brought the service to a conclusion with the singing of Mendelssohn's "How Lovely Are the Messengers." The local paper summed up everybody's feelings when it said that "the entire service was helpful and attractive."

His next appearance was in the role of Chairman at a function put on by the church's Junior Choir under the efficient leadership of Mr. Mitchell. It marked the twenty-fifth year of its leader's work, and was celebrated with a fine performance of *Rob Roy*. The minister commented on how pleased he was that his "first public appearance as minister of Trinity Church should be under the auspices of the Junior Choir, which had gained a reputation for its productions." It had indeed, and the minister was specially pleased that two of his own loves, music and young people, should be brought together at this time.

The third undertaking was very different, and took place under the auspices of the Presbytery of Paisley. The new minister, having been warmly welcomed yet again to the presbytery, was particularly gratified to receive at that meeting confirmation of a grant from the Home Mission Committee for £327, which meant that his church was now entirely free from debt. Presbytery also completed plans on its Mission of the Kingdom Week (March 26 to April 2). This was part of the Forward Movement then taking place throughout Scotland and beyond, involvement in which clearly found a place in the new minister's interests. He devoted all four sermons of that week to its ends: "A Personal Religion?" and "What Is a Christian?" on March 26, and "What Is the Gospel?" and "What Is Happiness?" on April 2. We shall see later that these were to make a great impression on the community and were, in fact, to precipitate him into a writing career for which *The Renfrew Press* must take first credit.

A milestone in any minister's career is his first communion. To understand Willie's response to this, it is necessary to reflect on its place in the Church of Scotland. The "preaching of the Word" is *the* characteristic expression of the Presbyterian minister's work. Cox, the official authority for all matters legal and procedural in that church, defines the function of the minister thus: "The ministry of the word, the conduct of public worship, the dispensing of the sacraments, and the instruction of the young belong to the Minister, subject to the control and direction of the Presbytery."[9] The order of the aspects of ministry is significant: communion takes third place, after preaching and the ordering of public worship.

His first communion took place in mid March. The elders were encouraged to visit the people of their districts, and the minister reminded his members of the importance of the occasion of the Sunday following their visits. At the preparation service, on Friday, the 10th of March, the Reverend J. W. Macphail preached, and Willie conducted the worship. On Communion Sunday the minister took the morning and afternoon services, and his future father-in-law, the Reverend J. H. Gillespie, preached at the evening service (the numbers turning out for communion necessitated the provision of the extra service).

It was at this communion that church officers and members alike began to realize the spiritual depth of their minister. Dignified and reverent, with a businesslike movement devoid of superfluous word or action, he brought them to the table of the Lord. A sacred relationship was struck, to which the congregation responded enthusiastically. The singing, always good, became thrilling; the prayers, never short, became rich and uplifting; and the sermon opened to them the reality of the divine love and empowerment demonstrated in the cross. Together they worshiped. The elders were so moved that a special notation was made in the session minutes that "the session places on record its devout thanks to God for the strength given to our Minister that enabled him to carry through his first Communion Service so successfully." The church magazine later wrote of "the fine achievement" made. Numbers attending the services stood at 633—a record, the first of many to be established by Willie.

His next public duty was very different—a service of infant baptism the following week. The subject on this auspicious occasion was one Colin Campbell *Barclay* McMaster. The name is interesting, for, as the church magazine points out, "It being the first christening by Mr Barclay, the child was given his name." Quite apart from the religious significance of the occasion, such actions have an enormous effect on both church and family.

In March his first pastoral letter appeared, which I reproduce in full. It bears the familiar characteristics of his writings: gratitude, friendliness, warmth of

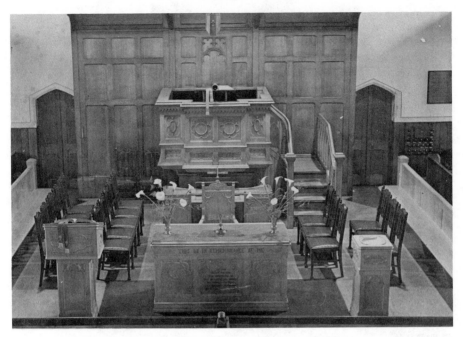

The interior of Renfrew Trinity, featuring Willie's pulpit of thirteen years

expression, a somewhat luxuriant use of adjectives, some hyperbole, apposite use of quotations and felicitous illustration, a strong emphasis on duty and obligation ("privilege and responsibility," ever going hand in hand), hopefulness and optimism, and the ever-present (though never ostentatious) note of reliance upon God:

My dear friends,

By the time that you read this letter the excitement of the Induction and Ordination time will be past and we will be on the way to settling down to our work in good set earnest. In this, my first letter to you, I cannot begin otherwise than by offering to you my heart-felt thanks for all that you have done for me. No congregation throughout the length and breadth of Scotland could have done more to make their Minister welcome and to ensure his happiness in his first charge. No one is more aware than I am of my own youth and of the size of the task whereto I have set my hand. It is only by sympathetic co-operation between us and by the mutual desire to help each other that we shall win through to success. But if we do our work as it comes, and if "we expect great things from God," He will certainly not fail us.

It will take me a long time to get to know you all, and to visit you all in your homes will take many months. As soon as the Manse is ready for me I will be amongst you, and it is my earnest hope that you will never hesitate to come and see me and ask for anything that you would wish me to do. My time will always be yours, and it will be my privilege and my honour to serve you at all times in every way I can. You have chosen me to be your Minister, and now I want you all to make me your friend. It was said of one of Scotland's great preachers that he "fell in love with his first congregation." I have done that, and because it is so, all my duties will become pleasures and all my work a privilege.

Once the great Saint Augustine met a man who did nothing but groan and tremble over his own sins and insufficiencies. "Look away from yourself," said Augustine; "look away from yourself and look to God." "Look at God," let us make that our motto in the days to come, and with His help we shall find that the greatest days of Trinity Church, Renfrew, are yet to come.

With every best wish to every one of you,

I am, very sincerely yours,
WILLIAM BARCLAY

It was a good start to his time at Renfrew and placed him firmly in his members' affections.

Early Industry—a Foreshadowing of Greatness

In many ways February was an ideal time to be inducted. It was in the middle of the church year; the annual meeting and assessments had just taken place, and Willie was able to observe how things were going without the immediate necessity of planning.

The Trinity Players presented their first play (A. A. Milne's *Dover Road*) with the new minister present in early March, which was followed by a special soirée for the outgoing conductor, Mr. Mitchell, after twenty-five years' valued service. The Brownies went off to their regional competitions in Glasgow and returned triumphant, winning a "notable success" according to the local paper. And at the end of March the Sunday School teachers met with the parents, and Willie (in the Chair) was able to see with what enthusiasm the work among young people was done. Event followed event in swift succession, and it was not unusual for minister and church to get—unlike any other church in the area—four mentions on one page in *The Renfrew Press*. Fortunately, the minister enjoyed what Gibbon has called "the insolence of health" and was able (and willing) to be plunged into a wide range of quite different activities in addition to his ministerial duties.

As noted, the presbytery encouraged the churches to become involved in the Forward Movement of the Church of Scotland, which found ready acceptance in the outgoing mind of the new minister. His activities in this regard caught the eye of *The Renfrew Press*, which produced a seven-column-inch report, under the heading "What is a Christian?"—the title of his second sermon in the series. In it Willie's essential and exuberant Christianity finds its full expression. There are many possible lines of approach to answering the question. The one he selected was based on an expression of Galatians 2:20—"I am crucified with Christ; nevertheless I live, yet not I but Christ liveth in me." This text might well be cited as the *locus classicus* of Pauline mystical theology, and it is significant that Willie should choose it to answer the question. (As we shall see, his theology, like his personal religion, but unlike his life-style, leaned very heavily to the mystical side, though always with great practical awareness.) We outline Willie's explication of his text as given by the newspaper; typically it had a three-tier structure:

A Christian, firstly, was one "whose ideals were those of the Master; the whole life was shaped and directed by an intense love for Christ"; one's faculties were "inspired by a great desire to eliminate self and to be done with every inferior motive or ambition." Secondly, the life of a Christian was a life of love, this being "its compelling power and inspiration. Love is the greatest power known, a power which has led men and women to do great heroic deeds to help their fellows." Thirdly, it was a "life of sacrifice. The Christian ceased to live for self: his aim was to give himself for others. The spirit of sacrifice has made men go to the dark and ignorant places of the world to make known the good news of salvation through Christ. The Christian was not only one who made a profession of faith in Christ; he was one who *did* things for the Master. . . . Christ himself came not to be ministered unto but to minister; like Christ, the Christian was a servant seeking to minister to others in whatever way was possible."

If he has not given us the mechanics of the mystical relationship with Christ, if he has ignored the way in which the doctrine is experienced, it cannot be denied that he has explained clearly and challengingly the effects of the relationship, and their realization in self-sacrificing service. And that surely is the crux of the matter. At any rate those present now knew their responsibilities and the source of strength to fulfill them. And they were shown how to fulfill them as they watched the pattern of service provided by their young minister.

His practical concerns (*doing* things) showed themselves during the following week, when he was called on to chair a meeting of the League of Nations in the Town Hall. The international situation was deteriorating. Questions were being asked about the viability of the Disarmament Conference (Hitler was to walk out of it in October), and not even the British Prime Minister's bold intervention with his Draft Convention seemed to offer much hope. As Chairman, there was not a great deal of opportunity for Willie to speak his own mind on the subject, but he declared his commitment to peacemaking and left the explanation of what precisely that meant to another occasion; it was the opening salvo in the local battle.

This meeting was overshadowed by the sudden death of David Young, minister of Renfrew Old Church, the "senior" church of the area. For Willie himself it was a personal blow. Mr. Young, in conjunction with Arthur Gossip, had originally proposed him for Trinity Church and done much to prepare the way for his coming. He had played a key role in the induction service and the social that followed, and Willie was ever welcome at his manse. It was therefore with some emotion that Willie paid tribute to his friend at this meeting of the League of Nations: "his were the hands stretched out to me, and his speech at my ordination was filled with kindly counsel and gracious charm." He proposed an epitaph for him: "He did a good day's work, and had many souls to his hire." Gratitude and duty—the one offered, the other fulfilled—were the twin marks of Willie Barclay.

The second Sunday of the Forward Movement saw him extending its thrust. If the first two sermons were leveled at the disciples of Christ, what they were and how they evidenced their faith, then the last two were directed to the would-be Christian, the man in the street who looks for serious answers to his doubts. In "What Is the Gospel?" and "What Is Happiness?" the minister sought to supply those answers. His sermons provoked an even greater interest than those of the previous week and led directly to his first literary article (since his school magazine), an article in *The Renfrew Press* printed just a few weeks later under the title "On the Secret of Happiness." It is printed in full at the conclusion of this chapter. It is an interesting piece, not least because in it we see his approach to people outside the church.

A treat lay in store for him following the Easter services. That year the RAF celebrated its twenty-first anniversary. (The Royal Air Corps, as it was first called, was actually founded the year the Barclay family moved from Wick to Motherwell.) One of the imaginative ways the town council had found extra work for the unemployed was in the extension and renovation of Moorpark Airport, which lay just behind the manse. In it there was a much-publicized display by the Marquis of Douglas and Clyde, recently returned from an historic flight over Mount Everest. "Every variety of aircraft is represented," the paper commented, "from the big liners to tiny aircraft."[10] From now on Willie was to visit the airfield regularly, and soon became a mine of information on aircraft, their design, ranges, and payloads; later, when his deafness made a hearing aid necessary, he even found a bonus in using it to tune in to the instructions given to the pilots by the control tower!

But the political realities ever intruded themselves. At this very pageant the notorious "Red Shirts" of Glasgow made an antiwar demonstration. Although Willie shared in the antiwar viewpoint, he certainly did not share in their mode of its expression. Peace, he firmly believed (as had his father), could only be attained by peaceable means.

In May WDB occupied his pulpit, a matter the local press heralded with some pleasure, commenting on his long association with the area in three aspects of his life: commerce, his duty on the magistrates' bench, and his service in religious causes. On the 13th of May the Scottish Sunday School Union was inaugurated at Paisley, appropriately the center of the oldest Sunday School Union in Scotland, in this the largest town of Scotland. Willie did not know it at the time, but association with this movement was to open up his career and provide him with a nationwide platform from which he was to move on to secure even greater opportunities. For the present, it made him determined to ensure that adequate training and preparation took place among his band of teachers, matters he took directly under his own control.

A month after this he was found at the side of his preses, A. M. Ferguson, taking the salute at the colorful annual scout parade. He addressed the gathering, presenting the story of Saint Christopher in vivid terms. The talk was reported as being "the most successful yet heard" at such an occasion, the lads being held spellbound by his power of storytelling.[11] He was making his mark on the community.

Activities were now drawing to a close at the end of the church year, but other things were pressing in on Willie's mind—the planning of the coming session, the possibilities of extending the church's work in new groups and activities, and, by no means least, his marriage to Catherine Mary Gillespie.

On the Secret of Happiness: Taking Life as We Find It

—by the Rev. William Barclay

IN one of his essays Mr. Hilaire Belloc spoke of "the habit of despair" which had gained such a grip on the folk of these modern days. It is a phrase which rings unfortunately and accusingly true. It is no part of any true man's duty to bewail the times that are, and to long for the days that have gone by. Nor would it be doing anyone the slightest service to shut our eyes to the clouds which encompass us and the difficulties which rise so unsurmountably before us. And yet to fall a victim to that frame of mind which can imagine no dawn to follow the night, and no gleam of sunshine to pierce the dark, is to court defeat and to become something less than a man.

A Desired Cheerfulness

It is not a cheap optimism which is required; the cheerfulness so much to be desired is not the blind cheerfulness which shuts its eyes to the things that exist. The only optimism which is any use is that which, in Plato's phrase, "sees things steady and sees them whole," and yet refuses to despair. The only cheerfulness which can tear things out of the rut of defeat is that which has seen all the evil that is to be seen and is yet, in spite of it all, convinced that there is good cause for hope.

There is a curious and widespread mistake abroad in all ages in all whose thinking is shallow and without depth. It is the common error of all who but skate along the surface of things to think that somehow man was sent into this world to enjoy himself. The facts are not so. It is the truth of life, and of religion, writ in capital letters across the universe, that man must take life as he finds it and make the best and noblest thing that he can out of the seeming muddle and chaos. He must take into his hands such talents and such gifts as life has given to him, and in the circumstances in which he finds himself and with the tools nature and training have given to him he must seek to shape them into the fairest whole he can. Most likely he will never "enjoy himself" but if he makes the attempt he will be happy. There is a wealth of deep philosophy and a touch that goes close to the heart of things in the whimsical sentence of one of W. L. George's characters, "What I say is, life ain't all you want, but it's all you 'ave; so 'ave it; stick it like a geranium in yer 'at, an' be 'appy "

A Great Epitaph

It was exactly that that Abraham Lincoln meant when he coveted for himself the greatest of epitaphs: "Die when I may, I want it said of me by those who know me best,

119

that I always plucked a thistle and planted a flower where I thought a flower would grow." A man who could honestly claim that epitaph as his own would have honestly satisfied the necessity of being happy. And when all is said and done, most of us have vastly fewer grounds for complaint and tears than we think. It is one of the strangely true and strangely rebuking facts of life that it is those whose pain is greatest and whose sorrow is deepest and who have the greatest grounds for mourning who are always the happiest and who put the rest of us to shame by their cheerfulness. It was Hartley Coleridge who wrote of Charles Lamb that he always took things "by the better handle." And it is a way of taking things that all might copy. As old Jeremy Taylor put it as he bade men reckon up the things they have and forget the things they have not. "I sleep, I eat and drink, I walk in my neighbour's pleasant fields, and see the varieties of natural beauties, and delight in all in which God delights—that is in virtue and wisdom, in the whole creation, and in God himself. And he that hath so many causes of joy, and so great, is very much in love with sorrow and peevishness who loses all these pleasures and chooses to sit down upon his little handful of thorns." There are a deal of folk who neglect all the rest to sit down upon their own little handful of thorns.

Valuable Happiness

There is no virtue in being happy when all is going well. It is when things are dark and everything seems to be as bad as it can be that the man who can still be happy is really valuable. And in these dark days it is such folk who will in the end set things to rights again. And the folk who insist in pointing out all the black spots with never a word for what is right and fine in the world are the enemies of mankind.

There is a Chinese proverb which very wisely says, "You cannot prevent the birds of sadness from flying over your head, but you can prevent them from building nests in your hair." None of us can prevent sorrow from coming upon us, but we need never hug it to our breast and forget the necessity of being happy.

We should not expect too much divinity in a piece written for a secular newspaper, and there is an almost secular air about this that highlights Willie's ability and flexibility. It is what we might term "threshold evangelism"—an attempt to gain the ear and awaken deep-seated needs in the minds of one's readers. Happiness is one of the most cherished of human aspirations, one that Willie early identified and built on—though not, of course, as an end in itself. This article shows how utilitarian his attitude toward it was, in keeping with his service role. Henry Drummond defined it as "a great love and much serving," and Willie exemplified this totally. As the proverb has it, "If you want to harvest a crop of happiness, the surest way is to plant a field of good deeds." But Willie's approach was more than mere good works. One of his favorite passages of Scripture—soon to be preached on, written about, and broadcast to countless millions—was the Sermon of the Mount, and in particular, the Beatitudes. For the *blessed* of the Authorized Version Willie preferred the more exact translation, *happy,* or *blissful.* His point in doing so was that the man who is serious about his own frame of mind and that of others around him will not be long in discovering its spiritual basis and its spiritual dimension. There is something about the pursuit of happiness that is an inalienable right of mankind, a "necessity" (to use Willie's word) in the human condition. For this reason, though "secular" in tone, it was a clever piece of writing, and it was received with much appreciation in Renfrew and beyond.

We should also note that there are certain aspects of it, very similar to those that we noted (biblical material apart) in regard to his first pastoral letter and first sermon: it is very direct in style and expression—even challengingly so; it is rich in statement, description, and numeration (note how often "all" appears); its quotations are full and apposite, at once gaining the eye of the reader and thrusting the point home to his mind; it is "coldly optimistic"—not blindly, not mindlessly, but thoughtfully and courageously so, as of one who is prepared to risk all for his beliefs. And there are other traits that are as characteristic of the man himself as of his writing: the need to live with an eye to the future, not trapped by the past; the motif of manliness (lost if one falls victim to hopelessness); the need to "take life as we find it" and not to hug misfortune or sorrow to our breast; and, towering above this high-minded and strenuous level of endeavor, the need to "make the best and noblest thing he can out of the seeming muddle and chaos" of life—in short, to pluck a thistle and plant a flower.

CHAPTER SEVEN

Marriage and Family Life

Kate Gillespie and Her Family

By the time the Dinner Convener met the cook, the name of Gillespie was known and respected throughout the west of Scotland. James Hogg Gillespie, father of Catherine and shortly to be father-in-law to Willie, hailed from the Dennistown district of Glasgow, on the eastern side of the inner city. His family worshiped at the fashionable Barony Church, which had a unique and fascinating history in the story of the Scottish Church. Its minister in his early days was the venerated Marshall Lang, the father of a future Primate of All England, who rebuilt his Glasgow church in pure Gothic style and introduced attitudes and customs that some, despite his "liberal evangelicalism," feared were too "high" for safety. Nevertheless, he was one of the very few to have been given a standing ovation by the General Assembly (following a report on the religious conditions of Scotland of the time); Willie, following John White, was to be only the third minister so honored.

It is one of the quirks of human affairs that Lang's manse was situated in Dundonald Road, as if to point young Gillespie in the direction of his long and fruitful ministry. Not that that was in his mind when he first used to visit it. His father was an accomplished engineer, and James was destined to follow in his steps. From an early age he showed a great talent for all things mechanical and scientific, which his father spoke of with pride and keen anticipation. His mother, however, had other ideas—as mothers are wont to do. She possessed a more artistic and idealistic temperament than her husband, and this surfaced in their son's growing interest in the humanities. By the time he had graduated Master of Arts in Classics at Glasgow University, it was already admitted that his greater love was for that side of things, and his father released him from his own ambitions. James went on to graduate Bachelor in Divinity, and thence to become assistant to the minister at Dundonald Parish Church in 1900. By 1902 he had succeeded the man he was assisting as minister of the parish.

He brought to his work the emphases he had received from both his parents, both idealist and practical. Unlike many students, he did not jettison his love for the classics once his studies were completed. They were ever kept fresh by him, nurturing and stimulating his pastoral work and providing insight and depth to his biblical exposition. His attitude toward the philosopher was very similar to that of John Ruskin: "I must do my Plato. I'm never well without that." What he would have made of Willie's confession, some forty years or more later to Allan J. Bowers of Walsall, that he had never read *The Republic* straight through, we can only guess.[1] It would certainly not have been overcomplimentary, for Gillespie was raised in the old school of scholarly thoroughness and had little respect for such timesaving habits as dipping and scanning. (In 1927, when Gillespie's silver jubilee was celebrated, he was to surprise his kirk session by asking for the two-volume edition of Plato as a token of their appreciation; to him it was more valuable than the silver mementos that usually mark such occasions.) Relief from pastoral and mental preoccupations he found in indulging his passion for wood carving, an interest he shared with his talented wife.

Mary Muir Gillespie, whom he married in 1902, could trace her family back to a very honorable connection.[2] Her father, Joseph A. Ferguson, was Registrar of Glasgow City and came of one Allan Muir, a master plumber and brass founder. But the family had a more auspicious connection than that implied. It was of the house of Rowallan, which had become connected with the royal house of Stuarts (of Renfrew, no less!) when Robert II took as his wife Elizabeth More, a woman "of excellent buetie and rare vertues," qualities that her descendants shared. They could also lay claim to a direct descent from the Covenanter John Paton,

The Reverend and Mrs. Gillespie with daughters Mary and Alisa (standing) and Mrs. Gillespie's home help (seated, holding dog)

123

who eventually died a martyr's death in the Grassmarket behind Edinburgh's famous castle. Mary, Kate's mother, was actually his great-great-great-great-great-great-granddaughter. It was said of Captain Paton that "he lived a hero and died a martyr,"[3] and this indomitable courage and unswerving loyalty are ingrained deeply in Scottish character, the Muirs and Gillespies included. Loyalty and courage were to be characteristics of Willie's wife, too, by which his work was sustained and furthered.

Clearly the Gillespies had made an excellent marriage and rapidly gained the respect and affection of their small community. We need to remind ourselves that it was still the Victorian age in all but name, the age of the horse and cart, when life was so much slower than it is today. An almost feudal system predominated in the parish, with the wealthy supporting the life and welfare of the village. The minister himself was dependent on the heritors (i.e., the landowners) for his stipend, which was calculated on the performance of the barley and related crops market. Although some ministers of the Auld Kirk had rich livings, times could be very precarious for many of their brethren, and on more than one occasion it was only the astute handling of the finances by Mrs. Gillespie (who of the two had the better head for business in the partnership) that kept the family on the right side of want. On at least one occasion gambling debts held up his stipend. Natural carefulness and homespun inventiveness were elevated to chief virtues in such a situation and saved not only the minister's family but many of the parishioners' too.

Not that the minister was seen to be in need. There was a squirelike quality about manse life that raised such ministers well above the common lot, as we know from the descriptions of Angus Macvicar and others.[4] James Gillespie ran a pony and trap, and for special occasions an ancient phaeton was brought out of storage. The boys and girls of the village would respectfully bow and curtsy as he drove by. Halcyon days! The horses were kept in the stables, at the rear of the manse—a roomy, rambling residence, once the glory of pastoral charges, but now the misery of struggling incumbents. Adjoining the stables was a series of buildings that would have graced any farm: barn, hay shed, and dairy house (byre). There was also the hen house for Mrs. Gillespie's beloved chickens. (In the cold days of winter it was not unusual to find her nursing the sickly ones in her armpits, supplying them with doses of sustaining milk and brandy.) Together with the pig house, these buildings were situated in a lovely glebe surrounded by woods and set off with hedging, trees, and lawns. It provided the setting in which their five daughters grew up.

Merricks Arnot related to me a conversation that took place in those early days which showed that Willie, despite his great zeal and evangelical upbringing, had a much less enthusiastic approach than his father (who was labeled a ranter in the Gillespie home). Arnot was remonstrating with him over what he considered to be overinvolvement by the younger minister ("doing everything himself") when Willie let fall the very non-Uffie comment, "I will give them what they want to hear."[5] Nothing could be further from the prophetic role of the minister, and there is more than a little evidence to show that Willie's statement to his friend did not correspond to his pulpit attitudes. He was never a men-pleaser. But it was remembered precisely because it was so unexpected and uncharacteristic, and in it we see something of his low-key approach. It is an attitude of mind that allows a style of "threshold evangelism" to be born, that listens as well as speaks.

In this he had a reliable and safe guide in his future father-in-law, with whom he had many conversations away from the noise and banter of the manse. Listen to this statement of Willie's, made in 1965, but suggestive of that teamwork that they enjoyed especially in the early years of ministry at Renfrew, in which he is commenting on the Jewish belief (with which he agrees) that a good wife is "the greatest blessing in life":

> I would not want it to be thought that I have a doting wife—I haven't. My wife is my most severe critic and most constant critic. Actually she will read this before it goes off to the Editor! The rest of the page she will not read, because after all in the rest of the page I am expounding the Bible or praying with people—and I can't go so very far wrong there. But in this part of the page I am just, so to speak, talking all by myself, and I need a critic in case I say something silly.
>
> My wife knows far better than I do what I can't do—and she will not let me try to do it. She knows far better than I what I ought to be doing, and she sees that I do it. . . . Certainly God's greatest blessing to any man is a good wife.[6]

This commonsense attitude Kate learned from her parents and sisters. She learned it particularly at the side of her competitive sisters and mother, whose accomplishments were a realization of the ideal of Proverbs 31:10ff., an exhortation in praise of the worthy wife. Mrs. Gillespie's practical and business abilities were commensurate with her artistic predilections—a rare combination! Kate learned well from the sheer organizing ability of her mother, from her man-management (decades before that phrase achieved recognition) and from her respect for, but dominance over, the forces of nature in the glebe: she wrested such wonderful harvests from the soil and livestock that her larder shelves positively groaned under the weight of jams and cheeses, vegetables and fruits, flours and grains and meats. And she learned from her, too, a love of literature (not least of Dickens and Shakespeare) and of life—after the manner of the very best of the "Moderate" tradition in Scotland, which saw all things as the bounty of God, and never let pleasure overpower a refined sense of *duty,* always preserving a certain distance which kept sentimentality at bay—a "fault" with which Willie was frequently to be charged in later life! If Mr. Gillespie was the philosophical dreamer (a thesis that ought not be overstressed), Mrs. Gillespie was the one who built the "pastoral republic" of his dreams in the parish of Dundonald. Kate learned all this at the very same time that Willie was learning his own, somewhat different lessons in Motherwell.

The Gillespie daughters were schooled under the tuition of Mr. Hugh Gibb at the elementary level; for more advanced education they had to go into nearby

Mrs. Gillespie with her five daughters. Kate stands to the left of her mother with her hand resting on her knee.

Troon (once within the parish of Dundonald). But Kate did not follow this path. She was schooled privately, first at Milngavie, then at Troon High Grade School, and thence to Glasgow where she lived with her uncle James Muir, a noted Professor of Mathematics, and his unmarried sister.

From Dundonald to Renfrew

Kate more than fulfilled her parents' expectations academically. In 1921 she gained the Intermediate Certificate ("Lowers") as a pupil of Troon High Grade Public School in English, Maths, Science, French, and Drawing—an accomplishment her former teacher Mr. Robert Houston was able to recall with pleasure long afterward, at ninety-three years of age.[7] In 1923 she obtained her Leaving Certificate ("Highers") at the High School for Girls, Glasgow, in English, History,

Maths, Latin, and French. This was no mean achievement; it is interesting to compare her results with Willie's at Dalziel High School.

Following the successful completion of a course in Home Economics at the famous Dow School in Glasgow (now part of Queen's College), she went into professional catering. Always a superb and conscientious cook, she was, not surprisingly, somewhat less than satisfied in her first two appointments—at the Erskine Hospital for the limbless (just a few miles from Renfrew), and at the Western Infirmary in Glasgow. Large institutions of this sort do not offer much opportunity for the demonstration of an artistic temperament, and her sensitive and high-strung nature must have found the atmosphere of a mid-'20s hospital very disagreeable. As she occupied the position of assistant cook, her duties will have been fairly menial; she was brought into contact with drudgery, heavy work, and the sort of people whom she will only have seen from a distance until now. By 1925 she had seen enough of it, and left. Her next post was highly congenial, as the "nanny" to the sons of Sir Charles MacAndrew, M.P., Ronald and Colin. In this she travelled *en famille* between Sir Charles's two homes, at Newfield and Westminster, looking after the two boys until they were ready to go to preparatory school. Ronald, after whom Kate named her firstborn, was to go on to distinguished service in the Air Force, but his career was grievously cut short by a shooting accident; Colin succeeded his father to become Lord MacAndrew.

In 1928 Kate was appointed to another major position, which not only changed her life, but Willie's too. In that year she became cook at Trinity College, Glasgow. It would appear she had kept in contact with her former college (as was her wont, out of a sense of loyalty that found ready expression in her letters), for the appointment came via the Domestic Science College itself working with the College Committee. It was ratified on 11 October 1929, when she was appointed— on a strictly probationary basis, for three months, at the unenviable rate of £2 per week.[8] (The Committee included the Principal, Professors Macaulay and Niven, Mrs. Macgregor and Miss Buchanan; she was to get to know the latter two ladies very well, as they were appointed to supervise the weekly dinner accounts.) There were some on the college staff who felt it was a little risky putting a young woman in charge of such a place, but she acquitted herself well and was soon very popular with staff and students. It was not easy sailing at first. Students were charged thirty-five shillings (£1.75 new pence) per term, and visitors were charged fifteen new pence, which provided small sums indeed for the task at hand; she needed all her careful training at college and the upbringing in the manse to do a satisfactory job within the strictures of the penny-pinching committee. Moreover, the equipment in the kitchens was not exactly *cordon bleu* standard, though she soon talked the authorities into bringing it at least up to date.

It was not her first contact with the members of the United Free Church. Dundonald had its own United Free Congregation, which at one time had had a former Professor of the college, James Moffatt, as its minister. Relationships between the rival churches were "not always very religious," to quote Mrs. Livingstone, one of Kate's sisters, but in such a small community they learned to get on with and appreciate each other. Numbered among her friends were some committed to the United Free Church persuasion, including some baptized by the great Dr. Moffatt.

The United Free students of the time found her cooking highly acceptable, and more than one was overcome by her cheerful, outgoing personality and good looks. In the irreverent, sporting manner of theological students, a guessing game began to be played as to who the lucky fellow to secure her hand would be; the fact that she would acquire a husband from their number seems to have been taken for granted, which reflects perhaps something of her amiable disposition and lively attitudes in those "twittering '20s."

It was shortly after her arrival at Trinity that Willie's friendship with Kate began. Already making his mark at the college in sports, in the classrooms, and in general, he had been given the post of Dinner Convener. This involved oversight of the students, ensuring that they performed their tasks properly, and also entailed his maintaining a liaison with the catering staff in a variety of ways. Duty turned into deepening friendship and then romance in that kitchen. As Professor Allan Galloway commented, "What is more natural than that the Cook and the Dinner Convener should strike up a partnership?" Their affection for each other found in that place of service was soon to be extended into a life of service beyond all telling.

For both of them friendship with the opposite sex was not a new thing. They were in their middle twenties (Kate a year older than Willie), and both were looking seriously for their partners. "The only truly happy man," Willie wrote forty years later, "is the man who seeks and finds the other half of himself."[9] This view—like some of his others—was based on Platonic myth, but he clearly held to its reality. In Kate he found "the person whom he must really and truly love, because . . . she is the other half of ourself." To some of Willie's friends the match occasioned some surprise. But Willie, well-built and athletic, with brown wavy hair falling across his broad brow and framing an open, determined face, answered exactly to Kate's dreams. And she, much lighter in complexion, as WDB might have expressed it in Gaelic mood, a *bhantighearna meadh* (an auburn—mead-colored—lady), vivacious and petite, her aquiline features radiating an infectious spirit of fun and gaiety, incessantly talking, stole his heart forever. Still, it was a surprising romance: Willie broad and solid, Kate slim and fussing; Willie deeply committed to academic distinction, Kate preoccupied with the mundane things of life; Kate a daughter of an Auld Kirk manse that teemed with people, Willie the lone apple of his parents' eye, a protective net ever threatening to envelope him, somewhat molleycoddled, and an "Uffie" protagonist. But they had found each other, and in so doing, themselves.

But we have progressed too rapidly. The seriousness of their attachment necessarily produced the usual student wisecracks and practical jokes. Willie, privileged in his capacity as Dinner Convener, and known to love his food—a *bon viveur* in the making—was much chaffed. And if it was truly a case of "love at first bite," their friendship was looked on as a smart move by his friends, inasmuch as it guaranteed Willie at least one aspect of his future happiness! The Reverend A. C. Dow preserves a vivid picture of Willie and Kate, standing together in the dining room, serving the food and chatting happily. Roars of protest went up if it was noticed that he had *peas* in his pea soup. "Favoritism!" they exclaimed.[10] And who would deny it? No matter how demanding the weekend activities, in preaching or in traveling, Willie would always be found in the kitchen early on Monday mornings talking to Kate about his activities and listening to hers, as Dr. Brock Doyle recollects.[11]

Soon they were introduced to each other's family, and with different responses. From the very first Kate seems not to have got on well with her future father-in-law. There was in all truth something a little pompous, not quite relaxed, about WDB's manner. He had shown his own attitude toward marriage in not asking for Miss Linton's hand until he was over thirty, and then only when in an established position professionally, when he was able to keep her in her accustomed style. After all, the biblical injunction was clear enough, "Make the field ready for thyself, and afterwards build thy house"! And he simply did that, unswervingly.

At the very time when Willie was within sight of great accomplishments, this slight, seemingly flighty, and decidedly extrovert female had won his heart, posing a threat to his career and his commitment. WDB in his turn was not amused. Kate did not meet his expectations of what his daughter-in-law ought to be, perhaps because those expectations were too much influenced by his perceptions of his own perfect spouse. We may be sure that Mrs. Barclay was more welcoming and less doubtful of Kate. She was more like Kate's own mother in grace and charm, though more formal. Kate had no reason to apologize for herself, and had no intention of doing so. An accomplished young woman, with a commonsense perception somewhat masked by her spirited exterior, she found WDB's attitudes opinionated, and his religious zeal and language cloying; he was, to her taste, too much the minister *manqué,* and of the wrong sort, quite unlike her own "moderate" father. Even physically she found him unattractive. His portliness, with a face like a bottle of port, contrasted sharply with her own father's lean, almost ascetic figure. Older than her father, WDB had a florid, almost beery complexion, despite his lifelong abstinence from strong drink. And he could not see Willie's weaknesses! The chemistry between them simply was not of the right kind. Nor does WDB seem to have learned very much from the strained relationship that he had had with his own father-in-law. Willie did his best just trying to ensure that the sparks flew between them as little as possible, aided by his wise and sympathetic mother, who was ever the buffer in such situations.

Willie was better received in the Dundonald manse. Kate's father, a cautious man, clearly admired him for his academic record and saw in him a promising servant of the church. They had much to talk about: the problems of belief and action in those difficult times, of the ministry and the integration of the two churches, and of the incredible activities in the Gillespie household and parish.

They both shared an historical bent, and both were admirers of Plato. Mr. Gillespie was glad to take Willie into his study, away from all that girls' talk which ever threatened his solitude. Mrs. Gillespie, however, seems to have been a little more concerned over the match. She quickly perceived the strength of dedication in Willie and knew something of the cost required to fulfill it. She was aware of Kate's vulnerability as well as her strengths, and knew well the demands parish life would make on her. No doubt her daughter's reactions to WDB had been well-voiced, and the mother will have had more than a little concern over Willie's likeness to his father in determination.

The courtship continued for two years, ripening into a deep affection both between the two young people and between Willie and his future father-in-law. There were outings to concerts, theaters, and sports meetings. Kate was soon to realize that part of Willie had been left behind in the move to Glasgow from Motherwell: his devotion to the varying fortunes of the football team of the former in the Scottish League could not be eradicated. It never left him throughout his long career; delegates from the club would be found wishing him well more than forty years later at his retirement, as we shall see.

Meanwhile, life at the Dundonald manse attracted him enormously, though he could never have accepted a country charge. He was to confess that he could not sleep in the quiet of the countryside after having become used to his Motherwell bedroom overlooking the main street, with its noisy trams and trains constantly rumbling by. He was no countryman, and enjoyed nature only in small doses. But there was no doubting the way the Gillespie family influenced the community, the way they were at the center of everything, and this appealed to Willie enormously, becoming his own pattern for church life and activity.

Much was to be done before he would be ready to take his first charge—studies and examinations, licensing, a student assistantship, and post-graduate work at Marburg—but he found time to spend some at least of his weekends at Dundonald, delighting in the friendly company of Kate and her sisters—even if the talking was unbearable at times! They would travel there by bus from Glasgow, or sometimes by train, walking the mile and a half from Drybridge Station to Dundonald, spend their time around the village, visit nearby Troon, enjoy a local concert or picture show, and be returned on Saturday night by Mr. Gillespie in his car.

Eventually the great day of their wedding arrived: 30 June 1933. We can imagine the excitement at the Dundonald manse, as mother and daughters got themselves ready and as father prepared to take the service. They had been through it before (Marjorie had married in 1931), but that could not detract from the occasion. Kate's unmarried sisters, Mary, Elspeth, and Alison, were to be bridesmaids, and it was a great occasion for them and indeed for the whole village. The church was prepared carefully and decked out with flowers from the manse gardens.

Willie was escorted by his former school friend John Smith, who was best man. He was carefully groomed by the ever-faithful Rebecca, and the two of them set off in John's car. On the way down they fortified their spirits with tea at a small wayside cafe, causing a small sensation as the Morris Cowley drew up and revealed those two overdressed young men, one in a clerical collar. Doubtless the fortunes of their football team were among the many things discussed on the way down—and the grievous fact that Willie would be missing that match![12]

The wedding went off without a hitch; the vows were made and the formalities witnessed by Mrs. Gillespie and John Smith. Following the celebration meal, the couple set off for their honeymoon in Bournemouth. Their life together had commenced.

"A Bit of God's Work for Him"

Parish life and their responsibilities were reentered in the comparative quiet of July. Mrs. Cameron, who had looked after Willie as housekeeper prior to his marriage, had departed, and Kate was free to organize the manse according to her own ideas. The things they had gathered together over the years, along with their wedding presents (including a lovely oak gate-leg table from the church and a study chair from the Sunday School) were arranged to their taste, and very quickly this accomplished daughter of the manse was impressing everyone, not least Willie, with her talents and abilities.

Willie resumed pulpit duties on the evening of August 6, preaching a sermon entitled "The Sunless Stretch," presumably not a reference to the honeymoon weather they had enjoyed. It is clear that his pulpit reputation was increasing rapidly, for his sermons were the only ones in the town to get regular newspaper comment. It was at this time that the Renfrew branch of the YMCA placed him on their list of speakers at the weekly fellowship meetings. This was a homecoming for Willie that he much appreciated. In one sense the "Y" was more his home than church itself, and he ever delighted to be in its atmosphere. There he found his true self, without restrictions of the ecclesiastical kind, and in male company with its rugged ways and its banter. He had preached his first sermon under its auspices, and one of his last preaching engagements, four decades on, would be to its international secretaries.

Toward the end of August, he preached on the theme that is central to his thinking and acting in all spheres, an axiom of life for him: "Onwards, Not Backwards." He had introduced it as early as his induction speech, when he somewhat audaciously said "the greatest days for Trinity Church are yet to be," and he repeated it at the end of his first pastoral letter. Now he took it up again, as he sought to muster his workers for the coming winter session. It was to be repeated in his September letter to them, and would recur endlessly throughout his life. He had learned its lesson at the hand of his father, who long ago sloughed off the shackles of Highland tradition (though never his love for the Highlands), and it found its biblical base in the one who is the same yesterday, today, and forever. It was precisely because he located his faith in the unchanging

131

Christ that he was able to risk new methods, rephrase old beliefs, and face without qualms the changing scenes of life.

Two special, even unique, meetings took place on Tuesday and Thursday, the 29th and 31st of August 1933. "Welcome" meetings were held in the hall, in order for Willie to introduce Kate to the church. It was Willie's idea, and the session expressed great appreciation for it.

Two events took place shortly after this which show that Willie was finding his place outside his parish. Prince George, brother of the Prince of Wales, visited Glasgow for the celebration of the Jubilee of the Boys' Brigade, and Willie had his first taste of involvement in such official occasions as minister. And at presbytery he found himself appointed to the committee that looked after the interests of foreign and Jewish missions and Colonial and Continental affairs. It was the continuation of an interest he learned from his parents, which he never lost, though his presbyterial record of attendance did not prove to be entirely con-scientious. Behind this was his activist attitude and a somewhat anticommittee bias, both of which soon became very apparent. The work and mental attitudes of committees were never his cup of tea; they affected his appreciation of some of his brother ministers who were never happier than when sitting on a committee. He summed this up succinctly in 1975 when he wrote, "I take no delight in saying so—I am ashamed to say so—there is in me a strain of anti-clericalism."[13]

Harvest Thanksgiving came and went, Willie preaching on "The Garden of God" and "God's World." Another special service took place in early October in which his past touched his present. He organized a "Sankey Night," emphasizing the evangelical roots of both church and minister in an extravaganza of songs and hymn singing. The campaigns of D. L. Moody and Ira D. Sankey had made a tremendous impression on British Free-Church Christianity, and *The Sankey Hymnbook* was one of its enduring contributions. It was in fact a best-seller, second only to the Bible, following their campaign. WDB himself loved these services, and his appreciation of them was one of the great influences on his son, which now surfaced and would reappear on an almost monthly basis. At first individual hymn sheets were supplied, but soon they decided to use *The Sankey Hymnbook* itself. No doubt the fervor of the congregation and "swing" of the tunes meant as much as the words, not all of which could boast theological integrity. But what matter if they were inexact in theology, or sentimental in tune? In this regard Willie believed that the end justified the means, and the end was clearly visible in the sheer enjoyment of the congregation, its swelling numbers, and the growing reputation of the church.

But he did have a deeper understanding of their popularity, which recalls Charles Raven's "conversion" experience in Liverpool, in which a somewhat conceited product of Cambridge came to find among the plain men and women

Above: *Willie and Kate on their wedding day, 30 June 1933, at the Dundonald manse.*
Below: *The newlyweds on honeymoon at Bournemouth, books a-ready.*

of Liverpool an unsuspected reality in their hymns of "desolating Protestantism." He recorded the matter in his autobiography: "beneath the cant phrases and the old-fashioned if unintelligent testimony to the influence of Jesus Christ . . . it gave me, what hitherto I had had no chance of learning, an unbounded belief in God."[14] Willie, too, had learned this, but he learned it before he embarked on his professional life; what he was learning now was how to put it forcefully into practice. *The Renfrew Press* called attention to his success in doing so: "There is considerable interest and enthusiasm evinced in all the varied societies and organisations under the direction of the Reverend William Barclay."[15] He was determined to break down the old tag of ministers being "invisible all the week, and incomprehensible on Sundays," and he was succeeding.

On October 15 we find him commencing a vital feature of his ministry: his first sermon series, which was given the title "The Seven Churches of Asia." It was based on chapters two and three of Revelation. This passage, along with the Lord's Prayer and the Beatitudes, was to form the basis for many such series in the future; the day would come when he would produce articles, broadcasts, and entire books based on all three passages.[16] In a manner of speaking they could be said to form the basis of his understanding of Christianity, important alike for what they contain and omit. But they were not inflicted on his people in a way that might have been off-putting to this "working-class" congregation. The series was spread over several weeks, on a fortnightly basis, the first four sermons being presented toward the end of 1933, and the remainder in February, March, and April of the next year.

There was no minimizing the spiritual force of his pronouncements at this time. The opening chapters of Revelation have a peculiarly incisive edge, and this was applied with vigor and dexterity by the young minister. "Even in Pergamos," he was to write, "men held fast to the name of Jesus Christ, and refused to deny their faith in him."[17] It was the simplicity of such passages and the fixation on Jesus which they foster that he liked. (Amusingly, the local paper found these place names too much to handle, the church at "Parjamas" appearing in the report. We may be sure that there was nothing soporific about the exposition of his text and its clarion call to discipleship.) The series was so well-received that by mid November he was encouraged to embark on another: "Studies in the Life of Jesus"; it received the same response. "The Sunday evening lectures are proving popular," the paper again commented. He was clearly taking the Presbyterian designation of a minister as "a teaching elder" very seriously. He had discovered his real vocation.

It was not only the need to produce well-informed church members and leaders that stimulated him to take up these series. Para-Christian sects were beginning to make headway in the country at this time, and he was aware that only by the exposition of true Christian doctrine—no matter how he might dress it up with eye-catching titles—could progress be made and the faithful kept on course. At the very weekend his first series commenced there was massive publicity in Renfrew and throughout the country for the relay broadcasts of Judge

134

Rutherford, leader of the Jehovah's Witness sect. They were to present an unrelenting challenge to mainstream Christianity during the whole of Barclay's ministry and to constitute part of the background of his teaching and writing.

He did not take them on in a frontal attack: he was too skilled a man for that. His method of defense lay in the promulgation of truth, not the unraveling of error; we shall see how he repeatedly turned his back on controversy and the opportunities that presented themselves through other men's pronouncements and weaknesses. The decision to do this was formed of two other equally important convictions (apart from his natural courtesy): one, a total commitment to freedom of belief and its expression, and, two, an awareness of the reactionary response that usually accompanies purely negative approaches. Later, in bequeathing his *Testament of Faith,* he was to call this unwillingness to do battle into question,[18] but for the greater part of his life it was an inviolable principle with him.

In early November, with the echo of the appreciative comments that followed his first published newspaper article still ringing in their ears, Willie had published in *The Renfrew Press* his second article, under the title "The Art of Forgetting."[19] Like "The Secret of Happiness," it was written with the nonchurchgoing public in mind and supplies another useful example of his method. In it he employs the same sort of telling quotations, clear and punchy argument, concentration on the future ("the task that is given to man is not to think of what is gone, but to get up and work in the present"), and a recurrent call to "make use of time."

In the presbytery meeting in December, a question of vital significance that was to remain in the forefront of church affairs for several decades came up for discussion: the role of women in the church. The report handled by presbytery had been sent down by the General Assembly, the ultimate decision-making body of the Church of Scotland. The place of women in the church was related to two aspects of leadership: their eligibility to the diaconate (presbytery found that "there is no barrier to their appointment" in this regard), and the much more contentious problem of their eligibility to the eldership. On appointment, elders are *ordained* "to join with the minister in the government of the church," and this ordination carries responsibilities of a pastoral sort—hence the problem. We are not informed of Willie's position in this debate, though presbytery found in favor of their admittance "in a certain proportion"—that is, so as not to crowd out the men—which was a fairly advanced position for the time. It is probable that Willie was among the minority against admittance, since that would be in line with his generally conservative views of the time; indeed, that was the position he took when the matter came up ten years later.[20]

We do not have Kate's view of this chauvinism (albeit then theologically respectable), but we can be sure she had a view! However, she seems to have been more than content with her own role, which was the traditional one of a healthy "subservience" to her husband's interests and work. She found her activities as minister's wife and President of the Woman's Guild to be quite enough, and we find her and Willie working harmoniously together in their respective areas. Some were to say that her only and passionate interest at Trinity was the Woman's Guild, but that is too harsh. The life and activity at the manse was well above the average at Trinity, Renfrew. Kate told Jean Haggard, for example, of one occasion on which she answered the telephone no fewer than twenty-two times between 10 A.M. and 12 noon—once every six minutes. Little wonder Willie preferred to write his sermons in the vestry! By shouldering a wide range of duties, domestic and secretarial, she freed Willie for other work, and still found time to play a leader's role in the work of the Woman's Guild. This very month, December 1933, for instance, she organized a baking competition for the Guild sponsored by the catering firm Brown and Polson, which was a great success. In such matters she was a natural champion and provided a first-rate example, especially to the younger women of the parish. In 1962, at the centenary celebrations of the church, Willie was to write of "the surging energy of the Woman's Guild,"[21] which was inspired and harnessed by Kate during these busy months. The membership figures reflect this: within a year she had increased their numbers from 180 to 262. Also in December of 1933, we find Kate chairing the Guild and Willie speaking on "Impressions of Germany," which was very well received though regrettably not described anywhere in full. It was the first of many such occasions, and gave the church a pleasant unity of spirit as they saw husband and wife leading them forward. These "secular" addresses were always well received by the untraveled people of Renfrew, and the next month Willie showed his powers of description and imagination by giving his impressions of a country he had not stayed in personally—Italy—when he gave the illustrated talk "By Sea to Venice." He subsequently gave similar presentations on various other foreign locales, not least among which being the Holy Land.

Things were changing so quickly in Germany that the impressions he received while living there would have been somewhat out of date in any case by this time. The staggering unemployment problem (up to six million jobless when he studied under Bultmann—or at least attended his lectures and soirées) had given way under their new Chancellor to an amazing program of rebuilding and reemployment. The political parties that had been vital in 1932 were now being bulldozed out of existence, and violence and attendant chaos were on the increase. By March of 1933 Hitler's party had gained 288 seats in Parliament, and the imprisonment of opposing party leaders was under way. The first German concentration camp, at Dachau, was opened toward the end of April, basically for agitators against Hitler. Following Hindenburg's death in August, Hitler became Führer, and the country was well on the road to assuming his dream of its being "the master race." By the winter of 1933/34, Hitler's "bully boys"—the notorious SA—had been increased to four million members, but their victory was to be short-lived. Within six months or so the infamous Night of the Long Knives had taken place, and the leaders of the SA were slaughtered, thus making way for the SS. Interestingly enough, one of the most percipient and critical figures of this development hailed from the University of Marburg; von Papen, its Chancellor, was the first to warn of the dangers his people faced if they continued to take the road of belligerence. It was such statements that brought Hitler's wrath on the universities, which led to the removal of men of the stature of Paul Tillich (the first to be dismissed by Hitler), Karl Barth, and many others. The "catastrophe of barbarism" had begun.

In September there had been a fearful reminder of the darker side of things when the film *All Quiet on the Western Front,* released in 1928, was shown in Paisley. A little later Willie attended another meeting of the League of Nations Union, in which the fears provoked by the disarmament talks were well to the fore. Inexorably the shadows were darkening. A week prior to Remembrance Sunday, a terrible account of the plight of the refugees was published under the title "Not Only a Jewish Problem." In it, Commander Kenworthy, RN, detailed the awful situation: "Today in Germany, perhaps tomorrow in Austria, it is a crime to be a pacifist, a communist, a socialist or even a liberal." The "German terror" had begun. No one knew how many were fleeing it, but in France alone there were sixty thousand refugees.

The editor of the church magazine surely spoke no untruth when he remarked, "Our minister is having the year 1933 stamped deeply on his mind."

Willie's "Most Difficult and Exhausting Work"

Willie kept no diaries and most of his papers were destroyed at his death, so what follows is of necessity a description of his activities shaped by a dearth of hard information and the demands of economy. But in this and the next section I trace the unfolding of his ministry during 1934 to show the variety of his tasks and how he went about them in a single year. Two things stand out in this period, as they do of the whole of his life: his religious zeal and his extraordinary busyness. Ever careful to heed Quarles' injunction to "make use of time," he flung himself into a range of activities that would have threatened the health of most men. "He has done the work of ten men all his life," Kate was to write somewhat despairingly forty years on, when she realized that he was determined to die in harness rather than "rust out"—which was the fate he feared most of all.

There was nothing frenetic about his manner of working. It was simply that he packed more into his days than most men by the careful guarding of his time, and by sleeping less. "Nearly all the great men," he wrote in 1966, "have been haunted by the sense of the shortness of time—and the uncertainty of time."[22] He calculated that in an average lifetime of seventy years, one spends three years (fifteen days each year) eating, twenty-four years sleeping, and only one hundred and seventy-three days of each year actually working! Willie's conscientious use of time (which has its biblical roots in such passages as Ephesians 5:16 and Psalm 39:4) expressed itself in a variety of ways. In the kirk session in January he brought to the attention of the elders the lack of cohesion among the church's activities: leaders tended to go their own ways and make their own arrangements without consulting the session. This was a waste of energy and effort, as much as other habits were a waste of time and opportunity. In similar vein his son Ronnie recalls an obsession his father had for turning out lights and switching off appliances: he abhorred waste of any kind. His training in political economy had produced a *principle* of economy in him that influenced him in every way, as we shall see. In him the Protestant work ethic reached its apogee.

These were days of unremitting application: in the mornings, in study ("fencing in the morning hours," to use Henry Drummond's impressive phrase), writing sermons (usually in the vestry of his church), reading, preparing addresses, and dealing with correspondence. The afternoons, when there were not meetings, were spent in visiting the sick, the elderly, the unemployed, and anyone who *needed* a visit. He visited a different hospital every weekday. It did not come easily to him, this visiting, but he was acutely aware of the fact that "a house-going minister means a church-going people." As he tells us in *Testament of Faith*, the responsibility of visiting weighed heavily upon him.[23] He was not there for social calls, nor could he risk making an ordeal of his visit to those he attended, since real work had to be done; for this reason he "dreaded pastoral visitation." Every family received a visit from him at least once a year. Some of this was done in the evenings, when there were not meetings or other claims on his time. These visits had to do with baptisms, weddings, deaths—the critical points of intervention for the gospel in parish work. He never had any objections to weddings, or even baptism, taking place in members' homes. He looked on them (the latter surprisingly) as "sacraments of the home," as he admitted to David Anderson forty years later. And there were the times of simply "rounding up the sheep," perhaps harrying them a little, but always pointing them toward Christ, in as natural and unforced way as possible. There were the young to befriend and teach, sometimes to prepare, sometimes to amuse, always to inspire. And there were their seniors with their own fears and worries, their discontents, and sometimes their warring. And there were the shipwrecked, the old and the infirm. With a circle of over a thousand homes to visit, and more than twenty organizations attached to his church, he was besieged with work; and he loved it.

The new year commenced with the festivities of Christmas (which was not popular in Scotland at this time) and Hogmanay (which was unfailingly popular!). In an annual pictorial review in *The Renfrew Press,* a photograph appeared of Trinity's "new minister," but little else gave hope. The Disarmament Conference was in its death throes, and there was a report of the Bishop of Ripon's statements against dictatorship which elicited from the editor regrets that not more clergy would speak out strongly for justice. It would not be correct to speak of anticlericalism in the newspaper, but it is clear it had little time for the milksop Christianity, the pussyfooting and the cant that was so much in evidence. Renfrew was an area of red-blooded humanity, and Willie's vigorous approach evidently caught the sympathy and the commendation of the editor. The question of whether there would be another war was now openly discussed, provoking an ostrich-like response from the authorities. The Disarmament Conference was reconvened, but without any hope in the face of Germany's intransigence. Literary men took up the cause of freedom in syndicated articles: Bertrand Russell wrote on "The Sphere of Liberty in the Modern World," and one of Willie's favorite authors, G. K. Chesterton, expounded his views on "A New and Neglected Liberty." Domestic problems were highlighted yet again by the editor of the paper, who appealed for a greater sensitivity towards the unemployed, whom he felt were being treated as statistics and trends, rather than as persons. There were continued signs of a thaw in the economy, but it was too slow for comfort—especially in the light of the inflation rate which showed "an alarming increase" of three percent.

In early January the paper reported on the diamond jubilee of R. R. Robertson, Trinity's former minister, whom it said "was succeeded by the present *popular* minister, the Reverend William Barclay."[24]

His father was no less welcome than Willie, and gave "a most inspiring address" to the church in February, a lantern lecture on "The Church of the Isles." WDB was a member of the Highlands and Islands Committee of the General Assembly, and his retirement passion was to advance the cause of his homeland. Kate was learning the hidden depths in her father-in-law, and he, clearly, was appreciating her much better by this time. Willie had never been happier. WDB still refused to come and live with them, even though Rebecca had now found full-time employment in a hospital management post. His faith and the memories of the last years with Mrs. Barclay kept him company, and he realized that close involvement in his son's home and work would not work out well. So he gave himself to what work he could manage (he was now very nearly seventy), eagerly anticipating his son's telephone calls each evening. ("Oh, those telephone bills," Willie was to exclaim on more than one occasion.)

In March Willie shared the local Baptist pulpit and joined in a church social in honor of James Duff's second anniversary in Renfrew. The two men new to the town had found they had much in common, and Willie's Motherwell days had made him appreciative of the wider church. Willie also took part in a *conversazione* (a nineteenth-century feature of church life that was still very popular) at Rutherford Memorial Church. A sale of work by Trinity's Woman's Guild followed, raising £40 for church funds, and a second Sunday School teachers' and parents' night was held. After this Willie was found presenting the prizes and giving a short speech at the Men's Club, concluding the very lively proceedings with the usual "Auld Lang Syne." It was a busy month, full of incidents and meetings, and Willie's name often made it into the weekly editions of the local paper.

Among all the activities then taking place the most important was the Seventy-second Annual Congregational Meeting of the church, when the books were opened for inspection, reports were compiled and given, and the pulse of the church was checked and recorded. Willie had no need to be anxious. Trinity was in great shape, functioning with a good heart, and the meetings (both sessional and business) were all well-attended and operating smoothly. The editor of the church magazine added another slant to Willie's reputation as a first-class Chairman by remarking, "Mr Barclay is to be congratulated upon his first Annual Congregational Meeting being finished in record time, by nine o'clock." He was to be complimented on his efficiency and punctuality through-out his life, not least when he functioned as Dean of Faculty. A somewhat anticlimactic note was added when the church magazine recorded that "the most exciting event was the cup of tea served at the interval." We are not told of the minister's comment on this observation.

In April it was announced that the minister was to take "Modern Problems" as the subject of a new series at the evening services. A reference to the list of sermons in Appendix 1 will show that they were not modern problems in the present-day sense of the term (i.e., topics such as euthanasia, racism, abortion, etc.), but *religious* aspects of man's unchanging condition. They were delivered between May 7 and June 7, and may better be described as a short series in "soul care." (A supplementary series of three sermons that followed these was nearer to our concept of modern problems: on Jesus and money, on pleasure, and—so characteristic of Willie's whole approach—on the common things of life.) It is difficult for those who have been introduced to Willie through the iconoclastic image the press gave him in the late '60s and '70s to realize his spiritual intent and power. Some of those who knew him in his early days and had read his earlier books could even speak of his "resiling the faith," a comment I shall later challenge. Merely to read the sermon headings is to remind ourselves of what he considered, even in those dark days of fear and want, to be the *real* questions in life: "Temptation, the Attack on the Soul"; "Prayer, the Defence of the Soul"; "Conversion, the Turning of the Soul"; "Sin, the Disease of the Soul"; "Repen-tance, Forgiveness, and God's Love for the Soul." It is in this last phrase concern-ing God's love that we have the vibrant core of his theology and the mainspring of his activity, the expression and elucidation of which was to be his life's work, fulfilled in unwearying service over forty-five years.

April was no less busy than March, as the church year moved toward its completion. He presided at a meeting of cubs and parents at this time, affirming that "the cubs is one of the most important branches of the church. . . . They will become the leading men in Trinity Church in later years." They did, and not only in Trinity. In mid April Willie presented an illustrated lecture, the first of many, on "Negro Spirituals." For his listeners it was a great exposition of a genre of music not often dealt with in church, and it provides us with yet another side to his character and interests.

The quinquennial visitation of the church took place that month, the dele-gates from presbytery remarking in the low-key manner proper to such reports that the work was being done satisfactorily. They did complain that fireproof safes were not always available; it was a fault shared with other churches that was regrettably not taken to heart early enough: part of the records were lost a few months later.

Willie almost never wrote letters to the editor, and certainly never when his

140

own interests and reputation were at stake, but an incident took place at this time concerning the letting of the church halls that presents us with a rare specimen of this sort of thing from his pen and throws some extra light on a different aspect of church and minister:

Sir,

There has been distributed throughout the town during the week a somewhat misleading handbill. The handbill stated that "An evening's entertainment kindly provided by Messrs W D and H O Wills, comprising a programme of talking pictures will be shown on Friday May 25th at 7 P.M., at the Trinity Church Hall."

The facts of the matter are as follows. The Church of Scotland Social Club, which has its headquarters in Fulbar Street, applied to the Kirk Session of Trinity Church for the use of a hall to be used for an entertainment provided for them by Messrs Wills. The Kirk Session are always glad to help that club in any way possible, and it is under the auspices of that club that this entertainment is being given. There is, however, no mention whatsoever of the Church of Scotland Social Club on the handbill. We therefore wish it clearly to be understood that it was to that club that the use of the hall was granted by Trinity Church Session, and not to Messrs Wills or to their representatives.

We hope that this makes the matter clear.

Yours, etc.,

WILLIAM BARCLAY
Minister of Trinity Church

MITCHELL RAMSAY
Session Clerk

A M FERGUSON, JUN.
Preses, Trinity Church

W T SMITH
Assistant Secretary,
Church of Scotland Social Club

In May Willie presided at the Brownies concert, attended the ninety-first birthday party of Mrs. Crosbie (the robe maker), and accompanied Kate to her first Woman's Guild Annual General Meeting, at which "a large and enthusiastic attendance of members" was present. There were by now just short of three hundred members, and Kate paid a generous tribute to her committee and all who had helped make the first year of her presidency such a success. Then they were off to East Kilbride on the annual Sunday School outing, which gave the athletic minister a chance to demonstrate his interest and skills in a wide range of activities, to the amusement and admiration of the onlookers. Mrs. Haggard recalls the consternation he caused among some of the older members when he took off his collar, studs, and tie at such events. Ministers without their clerical collars were bad enough—and rare enough—but ministers without any collars at all!

Parish work is the most variegated, the most demanding professional occupation there is, and it did not then generate the sort of identity crises that came to beset ministers in the '60s. For the conscientious minister it could be a twenty-four-hour, seven-day-a-week commitment, and so it was for William Barclay. Listen to him pugnaciously affirming this toward the end of his life:

> The minister has to be always on call, whenever trouble may strike a home in his congregation. That is why there can never be a part-time ministry. If a minister is sent for, he cannot arrange that a message be sent back: "I'll come when I get back from work at six o'clock." By that time it may well be too late. . . . I once said these things in print, and a minister wrote in and said that he had trained his congregation never to call on his services on a Monday. I suppose he must have had an arrangement with God that no one in his congregation died on a Monday, that no home was stricken with some tragedy, that no one needed God. There are some things which will not wait; if they are not done now they cannot be done at all.[25]

On another occasion he referred to the decision W. E. Sangster took with his wife at the outset of their ministry. Sangster knew there had to be a choice: family life or church? He chose the latter, and became one of the greatest minister-preachers of the twentieth century.[26] Kate and Willie also made that decision, as witness these powerful and disturbing words: "As I come near to the end of my days, the one thing that haunts me more than anything else is that I have been so unsatisfactory a husband and a father."[27] We shall later see the accounts his wife, son, and daughter gave of it; but for the moment we record it as characteristic of this period as it was of every other: it was a life of denial for himself and for his family. The few hours they did take for themselves were used to steal into Glasgow to listen to their beloved Scottish National Orchestra or, more seldom, to go to the theater or visit friends or relatives; and there were also times when Willie slipped away to recharge his batteries in solitude in the country.

The session ended on a happy note, one that marked Willie's public recognition as an exceptional preacher: his name was advertised as "Special Summer Preacher" for the fashionable Rutherford Memorial Church in August, alongside such masters of the pulpit as James S. Stewart, then of Aberdeen, and J. Reid Christie of London. His ministry was expanding.

A Worker and a Family Man

Holidays over, Willie again plunged deeply into his work. The reputation for preaching that led to his invitation to Rutherford Memorial Church came to light in other ways. The local churches decided to hold an open-air service on June 24 in the nearby Robertson Park, and Willie was chosen to be the speaker. "A large and representative gathering" met, attended by all the local ministers and featuring the combined choirs of the churches and the Renfrew Burgh band. His next public engagement took place at Renfrew High School, where he awarded the academic prizes, no doubt enjoying pleasurable memories of his own schooldays; after the ceremony he proposed a vote of thanks to the headmistress.

In mid August, away from the honor of being Special Preacher at Rutherford

Memorial church, he was again in the open air, this time speaking at the Ferry Green Mission service. Like his father, he took every opportunity that came to him to preach the gospel, realizing not only the importance of his commission to do so, but also the helpful fellowship thus provided. He never became an "ecumaniac," but he felt that this form of church unity was surely more productive than dozens of hours spent in committees, and he spent a great deal of his time nurturing it. At his own church he recommenced his sermon series on the life of Jesus, which the newspaper reported to be very popular, and for which excellent crowds (unusual for the summer months) were observed; there were, for example, more than three hundred in attendance on the evening of August 12, when he preached a sermon entitled "A Strange Contrast."

Great excitement erupted in the town in the days leading up to September 25. After years of anxious idleness in the Clydeside docks opposite, the great *S.S. Queen Mary* was launched. The King and Queen, escorted by the Baron of Renfrew (the Prince of Wales), performed the ceremony, symbolically launching the area back on a steadier economic course. From now on the story of the locality was to be one of rising employment (within twelve months the unemployment figures were to be reduced by more than half); order books were to be filled, and even the street vendors, once the bane of the shopkeepers' lives, were to be back unmolested on the streets. The National Party of Scotland, also showing its increased self-confidence, prevailed on the town council to raise the Scottish flag on Wallace Day.

The optimistic mood was reflected in the church magazine, and in the leisure activities of the church itself. The editor made an amusing comment about the session at Trinity having "descended from the pinnacle of solemnity on which it is believed to stand—or sit—in order that a photograph of it be taken." The result was good, and it hung in the Session House for many months. "Stooping even lower," the magazine continued, "the Session challenged the Men's Club to a bowls match competition," and "the results may be published as the Session won." It is a good example of the splendid spirit that obtained during his time there.

The phrase "to launch a book" now became popular. One of the books thus launched, and joyfully taken up by Willie, was H. V. Morton's *In the Steps of the Master,* which he now began to mention in his sermons and, later, in his books. Another much more important series of publications was that of the papyri finds (discovered from the 1880s onward in Egypt's accommodating sands), which after 1930 began to make their impact on New Testament studies, and on Willie himself. A particularly exciting discovery, in 1935, was that of the earliest scrap of New Testament papyrus to date (five verses from chapter eighteen of John's gospel), which overturned much speculation on the late dating of that book.

But good fun such as the bowls match was not to interfere with the business of the hour; in his "Prayer for Busy People," which Willie had printed at the head of his fourth pastoral letter, he called them to spiritual warfare and religious awareness using the words Sir Jacob Astley had uttered before he went into battle:

> O Lord, Thou knowest how busy I must be this day;
> If I forget Thee, do not Thou forget me.

It was a prayer much on Willie's own lips in those busy days, and the pastoral letter continued its theme, recalling the motto of one of the old Scots families: "Saved to Serve." This should be their watchword too, Willie told them. They should manifest it in closer friendship with Jesus and thereby with one another. Little differences should be forgotten that others might be drawn into their circle—a circle of friendship, love, and service.

For his own part, Willie continued to work at providing his own special service in a considerable variety of ways, and the church continually made its appreciation known, which greatly encouraged him. And he needed encouragement: "There is nothing in this world which will pull the best out of a man as encouragement will," he wrote in 1967. "To feel that someone is willing you on to achievement is one of the greatest things in life. . . ." As an only son, he had never lacked encouragement at home, and Kate supplied it in her own way now. The friends and colleagues at Trinity never failed him, no matter how he might need to battle on in session. In later life, when things got very rough at times, we shall see how gratefully he responded to the encouragers, and never failed to encourage others also.

In September he was reappointed to the presbytery committee on foreign affairs. At the end of the month he went off with the Sunday School teachers to the ninth annual convention of the Scottish Sunday School Union for Christian Education. (In April he had obtained the session's agreement to affiliate his Sunday School with the Scottish Sunday School Union.) This was one of the most important aspects of his ministry, one in which he took very close personal concern, running *two* training classes per week in order to ensure that the teachers had the materials and the preparation to do their jobs satisfactorily. As with his venture into writing, it was to issue in a wholly unexpected opportunity, to pave the way directly to no less than a world ministry: "Faithfulness in little things produces opportunity in great things."

Kate did not accompany him to the convention: she had other things on her mind. Four days after Willie's return, their first-born arrived. Mrs. Palethorpe-May was on duty as nursing sister at the time, and vividly recalls Willie emerging triumphant from seeing his new son, "as if walking on air"! The baby was to be named William James Ronald in good Scottish tradition (William after his father's side of the family, James after his mother's, and Ronald after the deceased son of Sir Charles and Lady MacAndrew, whose photograph still adorned their wall in the manse). He was to be known as Ronnie. There is another aspect to his being so called, which was not of primary significance, but which cannot have been far from Willie's and certainly WDB's minds at this time: the Clan Ranald hailed from Lochaber district and was reminiscent of heroic days gone by; they had joined with the Macdonalds, "the Gentle Lochiel," and Prince Charlie in the Rising of '45.

> No more we'll see such deeds again
> Deserted is the Highland Glen
> And mossy cairns are o'er the men
> Who fought and died for Charlie.

Whether the link was deliberate or not, it cannot have failed to remind WDB of the land and romance of his youth, of his wife and her proud connections, and of the blackthorn stick now proudly exhibited in his home town.

The church magazine greeted the arrival with enthusiasm, though a little tardily, since Ronnie arrived just after the October issue had already gone to press. It commented on Willie's well-known preference for a secretary, rather than an assistant-minister (he had neither), adding that "a small assistant has come—Barclay Tertius—and before long the little fellow will no doubt make his presence felt among books and papers." Barclay primus—WDB—could not have been more content. Kate had finally conquered.

In November Willie strengthened his reputation as an expert on popular songs by giving an illustrated lecture (in words and song, the songs being provided by the ladies of the group, some of whom had almost professional qualities) at the Woman's Guild. The title of the lecture was "Lady Nairne and

Kate Barclay with her mother and son Ronnie

145

Her Songs," and it produced such a response that he was asked to repeat it at the Men's Club early in 1935. In a very different mood, he reported to the session his talks with the Young People's Society concerning the question of their use of jazz bands at their socials. Complaints about these had been received, and Willie was happy to be able to say that he had "persuaded them to dispense with the bands forthwith." It was a reversal, under pressure, of his own youth and early manhood preferences, which reemerged thirty years later, when he became a fan of the Beatles. Also in November, he acted as local organizer for the Western Infirmary Flag-day Appeal, in which capacity his second letter in *The Renfrew Press* appeared, an appeal for collectors. This was followed a fortnight later by a letter of thanks from him for help received, stating that £11.18.1¾d (£11.90 new pence) had been collected—good going for those days.

WDB was a regular visitor to the manse now, as were the Gillespies. In November WDB gave an address at the Woman's Guild on "The Three Homes: Animal, Church and Heaven." The "animal" home was the natural home of man, and was as much an example of the datedness of his language as the latter was an example of the center of his thoughts in old age.

An important innovation took place that month, following the "At Home" meetings Willie and his father had enjoyed at the Motherwell YMCA. Willie now introduced the idea to Trinity Church. Based on elders' districts, they were an instant success and contributed in no small way to the life and fellowship of the church, and to the community at large, for all were welcome: house groups long in advance of their time. The only requirements, the advertisements said, were their presence and their slippers; the church paid for everything else. Another innovation was the launching of the church's Badminton Club, with Willie as President and chief organizer. Soon the monthly tournaments were a great feature in the church, the minister showing that he had not lost his touch with the onset of ministerial and fatherly duties.

At the end of November the church opened its doors to a quasi-civic occasion (the Old Parish Church was the official venue for such things), and introduced yet another innovation. This was pure Barclay: an invitation to local councilors Mitchell and Somerville to debate the question of democracy before a packed meeting of the Men's Club. It was of such vigor and excellence that sixteen column inches in *The Renfrew Press* were given to reporting it. The timing was as masterly as the need for it was great. Serious discontent was brewing in the town; members of the Communist party, always strong in that part of Scotland, were very active in the cause of Marx and Engels's dialectical materialism; fascism was rapidly becoming popular (bus drivers and other workers, it was reported, gave each other the Hitlerian salute); and much alarm was expressed. Moreover, at the nearby airport another presence was obtruding itself onto their consciousness: the 602 Bomber Squadron had recently set up shop. The menace of armed conflict was at their door.

Another sort of conflict was apparent which was by no means new to the church, but of troublesome proportions. It concerned the touchy issue of credal

146

definition. Willie approached it somewhat cautiously—though not so cautiously that he did not arouse some criticism against himself in the process (though the worst of that still lay in the future). Theological restatement was to be one of the chief preoccupations of the church during his time, and to it he applied himself, not as a theologian but as a man biblically trained and seeking the truth as he saw it in Jesus.

The discussion was triggered by presbytery, the General Assembly having sent down for discussion *The Brief Statement of the Church's Faith*. Willie was not present for this discussion. (He only managed three appearances at presbytery this year, as against ten in 1933; and his attendance record was to get worse, as we shall see, though this did not prevent him from writing to Hamish MacColl in May 1974 in most endearing terms of Hamilton Presbytery, and saying how he loved "every minute of it." Perhaps it was the very scarcity of those minutes spent with that body that made it all the more appealing in retrospect!) A good deal of dissatisfaction was expressed with the report, especially Articles III and IX, and so it was sent back for further consideration. Willie became directly involved with it in its revised form on behalf of the Scottish Sunday School Union, as we shall see in a later chapter.

In December a plethora of meetings took his time, some of them relaxing, such as the Men's Club Christmas party in which the minister played a lively part, and some of them rather more serious, such as his chairmanship of the local meeting of the Scottish Reformation Society. With a name and upbringing in the west of Scotland like his, we should expect loyalty to the Protestant beliefs of his spiritual forebear William of Orange, and indeed he gave it, though he never actually became an Orangeman. On this occasion there were two speakers, both converts from the Roman Catholic church, with strong family commitments to that church. It was a time for parading the worst of religious excesses on both sides—religion then had some of the qualities of a blood sport—and Willie does not seem to have offered any restraining influences on the proceedings. Very different would be his action forty years on, when the most repugnant form of protests could be made in the Christian name, and Willie, ever more tolerant himself, would lambaste them, and would find his writings recommended by one of the most powerful archbishops of the Roman Catholic church.

Another meeting he attended took place on December 12, at Houston West Church, where he returned the honor paid to him when Reverend A. G. Fortune "preached him in." On this occasion Willie preached in J. W. Girvan, basing his sermon on 1 Corinthians 2:2, "for I determined not to know anything among you, save Jesus Christ, and him crucified"—a fine motto text to give any new incumbent and one that increasingly characterized Willie's own studies and ministry. The next day saw the first of three annual socials at Trinity, followed on the 15th of December by their Toy Service, when Willie preached on "The Passion for Novelty." That was not a passion that he needed to confess to himself—we shall see that he actually opposed some of the more advanced ideas—but the church

147

was getting used to records being broken and to an invigorating freshness being used in its minister's approach to old ideas.

By this time his personal prestige had grown to embarrassing levels, and on December 7 there appeared in *The Renfrew Press* a précis of a report carried by the influential *British Weekly* on him.[28] The profile was signed "AG" and was undoubtedly the work of his friend and mentor, Professor A. J. Gossip. It reviewed his career to date, spoke very highly of his gifts and accomplishments, mentioned the honor in which he had been held by both staff and students alike, and pointed out that "preaching is in his blood." It referred to his voice "of more than usual strength" ("like an Ayrshire farmer," J. G. Lees was to describe it later)[29] which never failed to be heard, though the author added a caution that greater variety of tone was necessary. To all this *The Renfrew Press* added its own appreciation, recalling the risk the church had taken in calling an untried man to such a demanding congregation. No regrets, the writer stressed, were entertained by church officers or people. A pleasanter end to any year is hard to imagine. He was now an established minister and family man. He was moving forward.

CHAPTER EIGHT

The Prewar Years

The End of an Era

By the end of 1934 Willie was confidently settled at Trinity Church. The honeymoon period was over; he had now established himself in church and community, fulfilling his role with a rare combination of humility and panache. He showed no sign of strain from his many tasks, the pace of things being clearly to his liking. The church, for its part, showed no sign of strain either: the congregation liked its minister and his ways, and said so. As the editor of the church magazine commented at his second anniversary, "the more we see and hear him, and the more we get to know him, the better we like him."[1]

The year 1935 began with the usual profusion of events and socials. Three major ones took place in almost as many weeks. The membership was now of such strength that it was decided to break with tradition by holding the church's annual social gathering in three groups based on the elders' districts and following the lines taken in the highly successful "At Home" meetings. By the time the last such meeting was over, in late January, more than six hundred people had enjoyed themselves in this way.

The fellowship was broadening and deepening and, because of this, more telling in its impact on the town. As Mrs. Gray, a former church member now living in New Zealand, was to tell me, it was becoming *the* place to go; strangers coming into town naturally made their way there—and they could be sure of a welcome.[2] (Willie had recently taken to task his managers and elders over their failure to appoint someone to greet people at the door of the church, which led to a minor quarrel as to whose job it was, both parties claiming the honor!) One visitor to Renfrew, standing in a front-room window in Paisley Road, in which the church stands, asked what the commotion was one Sunday morning; people were thronging the pavement. "Oh," said his guilty host, "they are going to Mr. Barclay's church." Going to Trinity on Communion Sundays was "like going to the pictures," according to Miss Campbell (another former member and onetime scholar in his Sunday School), such was the size of the congregation. Early arrival was necessary to ensure getting a seat. It was not uncommon to have

149

people standing during the services, and on many occasions pressure of numbers caused even the pulpit steps to be requisitioned for the purpose.

But Willie never let the numbers get in the way of his performing his duties. Such were the minister's powers of observation and memory that he could spot an absentee in a congregation of seven hundred—and he would be after them during the week following. (A few years later, having preached in the roomy and well-packed Bloomsbury Chapel, his friend William Braidwood met him in the vestry, asking if he had seen him in the congregation. "Yes," replied Willie, "and you were sitting in your usual place."[3] They had not then seen each other for some years.) He also encouraged members to use the collection plates as a "post box" for notes to him concerning the old and the infirm.

Evangelism was ever in Willie's thoughts, with the result that his church played, through its multifarious activities, its proper part, as his pastoral letter at the beginning of 1935 suggests:

> My Dear Friends,
>
> By the time you read this letter you will already have started out upon another new year. The New Year is always the time for making resolutions. What resolution shall we make this time before we start out again? I think that we ought to resolve that we will make of life a wider, a bigger, and a more spacious thing than we have done hitherto; that we will remember we are the citizens of eternity besides being dwellers and workers in this world of space and time. Somewhere I have read of one who went to call on a cobbler whose shop was on the shores of the Moray Firth. The shop was very small; there was hardly room to work. The visitor said to the man, "Do you not feel stifled and smothered in this little confined shop of yours with hardly room to breathe?" The old man said "No. Whenever I feel like that I just open my door for a moment and look out." So saying he crossed the little room and opened the door and there was disclosed a glorious view of the sea and open sky which made one forget the littleness of the cramped room. So when we feel stifled and breathless and confined in this narrow life we can open the door and look out on the larger life that is ours because we are Christ's folk, and the view of that great spiritual life into which we can enter will surely refresh us.
>
> It is all just another example of the great truth that there are always two ways of looking at things. As a poet put it,
>
> > Two men looked out from the prison bars;
> > The one saw mud, the other saw stars.
>
> There will always be mud to be seen and there will always be stars; and it depends entirely upon ourselves to choose which we shall look at. . . .

His Christianity, as with his life-style, was that "wider, bigger, more spacious thing" that he wrote of and exemplified before them. In February this was demonstrated when he repeated his illustrated lecture on "Lady Nairne and Her Songs" to the Men's Club, which went down extremely well, no doubt the presence of the ladies rendering the songs adding to the occasion. No one saw any inconsistency between this and a series of sermons, his fourth, on "Men of the Bible," which had already been running for some weeks. He was keeping in balance the sacred and secular, seriousness and leisure, the demands of the gospel and its joyfulness.

A singular honor now befell him: he was able to announce at the end of February to his delighted kirk session that he had been invited to give the Bruce Lectures for 1936–37. The lectureship was founded in 1900 (the year his father-in-law went to Dundonald) in honor of the memory of Alexander Balmain Bruce, who occupied the Chair of New Testament Language and Literature at Trinity College from 1875 to 1899. We shall see that Bruce and Barclay had a great deal in common. For the moment we merely record the pleasure that Willie enjoyed and shared with his delighted father that he was to officiate in the lectureship that commemorated so great a man, a bold thinker in what was then the comparatively new field of New Testament criticism, and one of the few Scottish theologians to have delivered the prestigious Gifford Lectures. "His glory," says Stewart Mechie of Bruce, "is that he so profoundly affected Christian thinking in his generation that ideas which once were original with him seem almost commonplace to us now."[4] The session clerk expressed the pleasure of the session in the minutes: "knowing our Moderator and the earnestness with which he prepares all his work for the ministry, we are certain that the honour will not have been misplaced."[5]

The seventy-third anniversary of the church was celebrated on Valentine's Day that year, and once again *The Renfrew Press* gave much space to the proceedings of the annual congregational meeting, speaking particularly of the big turnout of members who were "keenly interested in the affairs of the church." The minister conducted the first (sessional) part of the meeting, and Mr. Ferguson took the second part as preses. Mr. Ferguson's words summed up the feelings of those present when he reported the church to be in "a very satisfactory state of affairs." Little wonder that they finished an hour later than the preceding year (at 10 P.M.), since, apart from the minister's comments and those of his session clerk and the preses, there were reports by the Sabbath School, Senior Bible Class, Choir, Musical Association, Girl Guides, Brownies, Boy Scouts, Rover Scouts, Wolf Pack, Woman's Guild, Women's Foreign Missions, Men's Social Club, Badminton Club, and Trinity's Players Club, among other groups. Willie was following the excellent advice of John White of the Barony ("Keep them busy!") not only as a way of avoiding trouble, but as the proper and true way of fulfilling their mutual calling and commitment. The reports were approved, and God was thanked for his sustaining help and grace.

At the session meeting that dealt with these matters a short speech was offered by the minister:

> I am deeply thankful to my people for their loyalty and their devotion to the Church and its services, a loyalty which has made [me] very happy during the year that has just closed. [I am] looking forward with confidence and hope that the year we are just beginning [will] be crowned with God's blessing. I am deeply

grateful to the Kirk Session and Managers for all the valuable help [I have] received from them in the work of the congregation.

There may be truth in the assertion that he tended to fail to delegate, but he never failed to express his appreciation and gratitude when such work as he did delegate was completed. Following this, the annual social of the Senior Bible class was held, in which Willie was able to repair the damage done to their relationship by his veto of their jazz sessions.

But while the local situation gave cause for such contentment, the international one did not. *The Renfrew Press* carried the headline "Hitler's Dramatic Pronouncement."[6] It heralded the return of conscription in Germany, which the paper reported being "greeted with wild enthusiasm on the streets of Berlin." It was the most ominous breach of the Treaty of Versailles to date. The Chancellor of Germany, in defense, spoke of the breeches of the Treaty by other European states in this regard (though not by Britain). Another step away from peace had been taken, and rearmament and military training programs were given a further boost.

The clouds darkened swiftly and devastatingly for Willie in May, for after a very short illness WDB died. Despite a difference of forty-one years, and the great cultural changes that had arisen between the birth of a proud Victorian and our young Edwardian, they were very close, and the loss left a deep void in Willie's affections. It marked the closing of another chapter in his development, the sundering of another tie with his old life and associations. It may well be that this lessening of ties with the old conservative evangelicalism of his father, of Dalziel High School and the Motherwell YMCA, and Thomas Marshall at Dalziel North Church also stimulated his "liberal" tendencies. Certainly his new associates (by virtue of his imminent lectureship) were more aligned to that side than that of his childhood and early manhood, though the needs of pulpit and pew kept the fire of devotion brightly burning.

His dependence on Kate and the family at Dundonald increased, and church and friends gathered round him in support. Commented the church magazine,

> Very deep regret was felt by all members of the congregation on the death of our Minister's esteemed father, Mr W D Barclay, J.P. . . .
>
> As a token of their esteem the office-bearers sent a floral tribute to accompany the cortege and be laid on the grave at Fort William.
>
> The main interest of father and son was the same—the church. One therefore realises how much our Minister will miss his beloved parent.[7]

The Motherwell Times also recalled WDB's tremendous contribution to his adopted town, remarking that he was "a fine type of north country gentleman, possessing special sagacity, perseverance and native ability. . . . His name became a household word amongst us.[8]

WDB's refound love for Glasgow was not overlooked by *The Glasgow Herald*, which carried a small obituary mentioning that he had completed fifty years' service with the Bank of Scotland at the time of his retirement and that he had been an active worker in the Brotherhood Movement and Chairman of its Motherwell Branch for sixteen years. The paper also carried a second notice, clearly from Willie's hand, stating that the funeral service would be held in the Stevenson Memorial Church, Belmont Street, on Saturday, and in the Mackintosh Memorial Church, Fort William, on Monday, with interment at Kilmallie Cemetery. "Friends," implored Willie, "please accept this as the intimation and invitation."[9]

In his *Testament of Faith* Willie quotes William Soutar's words: "If I have been privileged to catch a more comprehensive glimpse of life than many other men, it is because I have stood on the shoulders of my parents." Commented Willie, "I have to make the acknowledgement without making the claim. . . . Whatever I have done in life, it is because 'I have stood on the shoulders of my parents,' and to this day there are places in Scotland where I am still my father's son—and I am glad that it is so."[10] Considering the life and witness of WDB, we can see that Willie's "filial piety" was well justified.

There was a tremendous bond between them, fused of the loving atmosphere in which he was reared and of a proper respect he showed for this highly active and successful businessman–cum–lay preacher, a respect that Willie saw was shared by all who met him, perhaps at times a little fearfully. He knew the speed of his father's mind, the sharpness of his tongue, and his consummate ability to assume command of any situation. But he knew the other side, too: the deep devotion to Mrs. Barclay, their mutual love of literature and the things of the spirit, the music and the calm gaiety of their home life, and above all its godliness. If it were true that WDB battled and fought with men and knew through his intimate understanding of human nature their strengths and weaknesses and follies, it was also abundantly true that he was possessed of a real pastoral heart: he felt for men, suffered with them, shared with them, and was ever generous with his time and money. Willie's very human poet, Rabbie Burns, expressed the matter beautifully in his *Epitaph on my Father,* the first verse of which concludes "The tender father, and the generous friend," a description entirely appropriate for this truly outstanding man; the last verse is similarly evocative of WDB's true character:

> The pitying heart that felt for human woe;
> The dauntless heart that fear'd no human pride;
> The friend of man, to vice alone a foe;
> For ev'n his failings lean'd to virtue's side.

One might think that with their background and success the Barclays senior would have been well off. The truth is they could have been, but were not. The stewardship of WDB was foremost in all his activities, and when he died, though rich in spirit, he left little (relative to his position and long service) apart from some furniture, some clothing, and what Willie described as "the best library I have ever seen in the possession of a layman." He had laid up his treasures elsewhere, not in Bank House, Motherwell, or in his shared digs in Wilton Street, Glasgow.[11]

Those treasures are seen, even today, in the lives WDB affected for the Kingdom of God, most notably in, through, and beyond Willie's own life. In this he deposited heavily, and the world has reaped the interest, year after year unfailingly. It is astonishing that so much of WDB rubbed off on his son, both physically and spiritually. Even the leisure-time activities (dancing and the Glasgow holiday row-de-dows excluded) were passed on, gladly taken up and furthered: work among young people in such groups as Sunday Schools, the Boys' Brigade, the YMCA, and the temperance movement; the enjoyment of literature and of theological writings (even of the same authors, such as A. S. Peake, David Smith, Alfred Edersheim, and Alexander Whyte, to name just a few). Together they played football and preserved Motherwell Football Club's cause with delight and passion; they strode the golf courses together (Willie's account of his play in *Testament of Faith*[12] should be taken with a pinch or two of salt: he once played off a handicap of four); they loved cricket and journeyed to London together to watch the great Jack Hobbs and others in subduing form. And how they shared the love for Christ and his church! That they had different ways of expressing it no one need deny, but it was ever a shared love, and Willie's work in it and for it, like his academic successes, reached the peak of pleasure when he saw the delight on his parent's face.

In his autobiography Willie recounts the question of a psychologist friend asking him when he first discovered that his father was not infallible. His reaction was that he had never considered him to be so. But the incident is worth noting. Clearly his friend had seen something of the depths and intricacy of their relationship; perhaps he felt that Willie was a bit too much influenced by the forceful Highlander's character. Perhaps even Willie himself felt that from time to time. Whatever the truth of this, it is clearly the case that Willie maintained an unfailing devotion to his parents as is evidenced in these words he wrote in 1967, more than thirty years after their deaths:

> It is long since my father and mother died, and there are times when I forget them, and even when I think of them the days seem very far away when they were here. But, if I go and stand behind a certain grave in a little highland cemetery, I feel that, if I stretch out my hand, I will touch them.[13]

These words are found in his discussion of the meaning of the Lord's Supper for today, at a point where he is seeking to draw out the point of Christ's presence in the sacrament. He goes on to say that "Memory always has a purpose and, even if it has no purpose, it certainly has an effect." A sentimentalist does not have the same need for physical evocations as others—and Willie was a great sentimentalist—but on the few occasions when he did return to the little Highland cemetery of Kilmallie (in which lay members of the Cameron Clan and other worthies of Lochaber, not least among which was Mary MacKeller, "the sweet singer of Loch Eil"), he could vividly recall the times when he and his parents sat on that hillside at Corpach and looked away from the little church in which his father was reared, across Loch Eil to Loch Linnhe, with the mystery and menace of Ben Nevis towering in the distance, awesome and grand. And he could almost touch them, for they were with him still, a realized presence beneath the shadow of that conspicuous Celtic Cross with its engraved harp at its base, asleep in "God's Acre" as some were wont to call it.

There is one further aspect of the relationship over which we cannot pass. One of Willie's favorite children's addresses concerns G. K. Chesterton's story of the man with the golden key, a character in that author's toy theater, the actual point of which Chesterton admits he could no longer recall. But he always associated that man with the golden key with his father, because his father had unlocked for him so many doors to wonderful things. "And I," says Willie in wistful gratitude, "can say that of my father."

No doubt he reflected on all this as he made the long and lonely journey to Fort William (the women remained at home at such times in Scotland), perhaps considering the quasi-superstitious lore of the Highlanders concerning their loved ones. Norman MacLeod recalls this well, adding the example of one of their number who was brought back to Kintail from the Hebrides escorted by twelve strong men sixty miles back to the old churchyard.

The mood of the occasion was disrupted by an unpleasant experience on the return journey to Glasgow, as he was to recount later in one of his journalistic pieces.[14] Still wearing his "vocational badge," the clerical collar (which he donned only for "official" functions and occasions), he had to share the carriage with a navvy, "an alarming character" who used the leather window strap to sharpen his open razor, somewhat threateningly to Willie's way of thinking. Happily, nothing came of the incident, but his Highland imagination worked at full stretch for an hour or two! Occurring at a time when surrealism was at its height, the incident adds a little extravagant color to the state of Willie's mind.

Another journey was undertaken in June, when the Men's Club, feeling especially adventurous that year, chartered a bus to take them to North Berwick. With an enthusiastic anticipation of the pleasures they were to enjoy that serves to underscore the distinction between the prevailing mentality of the residents of the west and east coasts of Scotland (even Alexander Whyte was wont to refer to Edinburgh as "the fastidious city" and to its occupants as being "chillingly intellectual"), the church magazine announced that:

> this trip across Scotland [it was only fifty miles or so] to the *rendez-vous* of elite society will be a very attractive outing. To partner a cabinet minister or a retired colonel at golf on the famous links may not appeal to workers from the west. We might feel at ease in the bathing pool, for there stripped of outer coverings we would be "a' Jock Tamson's bairns." But if in July the temperature of the water of the east coast is a few degrees above freezing point, what will it be like in June? No, we'll just enjoy the sights.[15]

They did, alongside their minister, who was fast becoming their friend.

155

Kilmallie Cemetery, Corpach, Fort William, where WDB and his wife Barbara are buried. In the distance stands Ben Nevis.

A close-up of the Barclay memorial

A notable sermon series, this time on a more contemporary set of "modern problems," followed the series on the men of the Bible. "Christianity and . . ." dealt with such subjects as citizenship, industry, war, and "you." The words and phrases of those sermons, so carefully worked and illustrated—for he never forgot Gossip's warning that when sermon preparation became easy it was time to examine one's conduct to see what ruts one had fallen into—have now all gone, but the spirit of these occasions has not.

Many still recall vividly his emerging hurriedly (he was incapable of doing anything slowly!) from the vestry in those days, in the dignified wake of his beadle, his gown flapping, members of the choir waiting to see whether it would catch on the corner of his pulpit as he swept by and took the pulpit steps two at a time (it never did). He recounts in his autobiography that preaching was "literally a terrifying experience" to him, though the people who observed it never dreamed of the terrors the young minister felt. He felt the need for company before preaching, unlike some men whose preference is for solitude and quiet. He carried from vestry to pulpit but a single sheet of paper: the intimations, made up to include last-minute information of the sick and suffering for whom he never failed to pray by name in the long intercessions. The rest of his paperwork (order of service, prayers, sermon notes) had all been laid out by the beadle well in advance, for Willie could not then, nor did he ever, like the "idleness" of last-minute preparations in the vestry. The sermon itself was always written by Thursday, at least till the outbreak of war, after which the fire-watchers would sometimes find him hard at it on Friday nights or in the early hours of Saturday mornings.

And so the services started: a call to worship made in earnest supplication of the divine presence and blessing, and a hymn of worship to which the choir gave firm and tuneful lead and the congregation added its own lusty contribution. It is common for those of the south, especially the Welsh, to criticize Scottish singing, but no such criticism was valid at Renfrew Trinity: they *sang*, mercifully drowning out the minister's gravelly voice, which ever threatened to be heard. It was not unknown for the minister to wink in friendship or encouragement at this or that member of the congregation. And there were the prayers. Long prayers. Detailed prayers. Prayers that defied the conventions of public praying in their complexity and personal references. But what praying! Not a few former members, some of whom were then quite young and therefore normally thought to be unable to support such long utterances, have said that they were the best thing about his ministry, great preacher though they recognized him to be. The sick, the aged, the infirm, the weak, the strong, the lonely, the heartbroken, the adventurous, the uncaring: all were brought before God, and for all his blessing and grace were sought. In them the congregation was made aware of God; it was indeed his house they sat in, not some artificial shrine dedicated to some far-off deity, but the dwelling of God the Father of our Lord Jesus Christ, and their Father as well. The sermons following these prayers were never long, always interesting, replete with quotations, illustrations, and anecdotes, and not infrequently based on "strange texts"—another hangover from early influences, but one that helped to keep curiosity alive. Mrs. Julian, then a teenager, vividly remembers how she and her friends were held "spellbound" by his sermons, always full of humor, and yet so deeply challenging.[16] Later on she was to marry a Roman Catholic, discovering in the process Willie's ability to center on the things that matter most in a young couple's attachments to each other, and his tolerance—even in those days—of the views of others. And after his services, at the door, there was a friendly handshake and an encouraging word. Not for him the escape into the vestry in Highland tradition "to lick his wounds": he was there to meet his people, talk to them, and lead them. And they gladly followed.

The summer of 1935 brought the development of friction between Italy and Abyssinia, in the face of which the League of Nations was characteristically ineffectual. Willie, on the other hand, was characteristically vigorous, calling his own troops to battle in the autumn pastoral letter, a call to arms that exceeded both in length and strength any that had preceded it, and that betrayed the pressure he was feeling with its unusual lack of style. In his sermons he resumed his series on men of the Bible. To this was added a rare treat for minister and congregation alike when, on the 4th of October, Professor A. J. Gossip supplied pulpit for him.

The busyness of the year Willie alluded to in the pastoral letter included the extra duty of preparing his script of "The Use of the New Testament in the Apologists" for the Bruce Lectures, which brought two paramount interests of his together: New Testament and early church history. Another pulpit series (his seventh) commenced at this time and attracted much attention: "Lessons from Famous Books." He delivered two of the series' sermons before the end of the year: an assessment of Walpole's *Fortitudes* and a reflection on Masefield's *The Everlasting Mercy*. This series, a short one of only four sermons (Kipling and Browning were the other authors treated), was followed by two more before his Bruce Lectures were concluded: "The Emotions of Jesus," given in May–June 1936, and the "Eight Modern Characters," from January to June 1937. Following this a period of over six months elapsed before he commenced another very short series—an indication of the way these lectures sapped his strength in every way; he did not return to the practice before war broke out.

Barclay Tertius was now giving great pleasure and was the cause of much thanksgiving. Kate, ever busy with her beloved Woman's Guild, had to call in the services of two members for help—Miss Dougal (later to be Ronnie's school-mistress) and Marie Campbell, whose friendship with Willie over forty years developed into a very supportive alliance for them both.

Looking back over the year to date, Willie found three accomplishments to be of particular importance. The first was that he had persuaded the session to allow an introit to be included in the services, thus introducing a better spirit of worship into them at the very start. Second, he had commemorated the importance of the eldership with a special service of thanksgiving for four long-serving elders. The session minutes carry a seven-page tribute by the minister to the work of Messrs. A. Mitchell, M. Ramsay, C. Craig, and A. Bradley, who together had provided the church with 121 years of service. The first two gentlemen had rendered special service in leading the Junior Sunday School and Church Choir, and each had been a Session Clerk. Willie, in regretfully accepting their resignations, made full use of his rhetorical eloquence in expressing his sense of gratitude. Listen to his comments, which are a striking example of the young minister's response to his colleagues and their work:

> Sometimes, as I stand in the pulpit and hear that wave of sound come up to meet me as the people sing, I am more deeply moved, even to tears, than at any other time. That fervour and that excellence of singing is largely due to the teaching that Mr Mitchell has given to generations of young people. . . . To see him with the children is a delight, and as he goes on his way he radiates a happy eager young spirit that does us all good. . . . He has been to many people a father in the faith. . . . [And of Mr Ramsay,] inevitably a Session Clerk is in a peculiar relationship to his minister. He is either the rock on which the Minister splits; or he is the rock to which the minister goes for shelter and support in times of difficulty. Mr Ramsay has been to me a tower of strength, a mine of counsel, and a great and wise counsellor in everything. Today we delight to do him honour.[17]

Lovely is the concluding statement, "Afterwards the elders individually shook hands with, and congratulated, the four honoured fellow members. It was a most impressive meeting and one that will long remain in the memory of those privileged to take part."

Willie's third major accomplishment that year was of a different sort, having to do with the services of communion. In May 1933 the church had appointed Willie its liaison officer with the Scottish Temperance Alliance, one of the sworn objectives of which was to remove fermented wine from communion and replace it with the nonfermented alternative. Willie's well-known friendship with John Barleycorn had not yet developed—he was still the advocate of that form of "temperance" that brooks nothing less than total abstinence, and so he had no difficulty in commending this change to his church, which consented to it in due course. Reverent worship, public gratitude, and integrity of action were hallmarks, all of them, of William Barclay's ministry at Renfrew.

The new year, 1936, had scarcely commenced when the nation, and "Royal Renfrew" in particular, were called to mourn the loss of one of the city's most honored visitors, King George V. It marked the end of an era that had commenced on 6 May 1910, when Willie was but a toddler at Wick. At this time a wall-card was widely sold, framed in black in honor of the late sovereign, that listed the six maxims that had most inspired his life. They were typical of the age, when "gentlemanliness" was admired, and good sportsmanship inculcated; they praised the ability to distinguish between sentiment and sentimentality, warned of the dangers of cheap praise, and celebrated the virtues of contentment and forgetfulness of things now done that could not be undone; lastly, His Majesty resolved that "If I am called to suffer, let it be like a well-bred beast that goes away to suffer in silence." Willie had suffered much during these last four years

On a Sunday School outing (ca. 1938). From left to right: J. B. Kidd, Mr. Williams (Sunday School secretary), Willie, and Alexander Mitchell.

The Renfrew Trinity minister with the kirk session (ca. 1934)

(and much more was in store for him, alas), but it was in a regal and Christian spirit that he bore it, and he sought to encourage others to shoulder their misfortunes and difficulties in a similar manner. His attitude was one of acceptance, but others took a very different line. In some respects, the new age that was opening before him was symbolized by the unwillingness of the Heir Apparent to serve his people and by the resolute refusal of the people to allow him to serve on his own conditions. Crises other than constitutional ones were to follow. From now on it was to be an age of rejection, of the breaking down of traditions, of widespread insecurity, of national and international schizophrenia, and of the destruction beyond all imagination of life and property.

It was against this background, the loss of a sovereign (who symbolized the integrity of the state), and before that the loss of his father (who symbolized the dependability of his home life), that William Barclay was to discover the calling within his calling, penetrate to the heart of the gospel, and learn to hone its presentation till it resembled for him a trusty blade with which he might do great work. An era had ended; another commenced.

Activities Multiply, Willie Discovers a Secret

The new year of 1936 opened with a vigorous call by Trinity's minister to take seriously the opportunity it gave to make good resolutions. In his pastoral letter he took the risk of repeating himself *ad nauseam,* urging them to forget what lay behind: "the first sign that a man is growing old is that he begins to look back instead of forward." He reminded them of the permanence of their actions: "let us resolve to remember the importance of words and deeds that cannot be got back." He exhorted them to fix their attention on the Master who led them on: "let us all resolve to be such copies of our Master that by our very lives we shall make him known." He stressed the importance of doing more and talking less, of doing without, and of preparing themselves for that day when "everyone shall give account for the things he has done. . . . All of us should live in the remembrance of eternity and, as ever, in our great Task-master's eye."

His third anniversary at the church was not allowed to go unnoticed, and once more highly appreciative comments were made of him. (In countless hours of research and interviewing, I have not unearthed a single adverse criticism of this period of his ministry.) The celebration of the anniversary included a visit from James Barr, stalwart defender of the United Free Church and its traditions, onetime M.P. for Motherwell, and, as we have seen, a regular visitor to the Barclay, Sr., household, to lecture to the Woman's Guild. He did so in February, presenting a lantern lecture on "Scotland in Story and Song," which was a great success. It is one of the regrets of this biographer that he could not listen in to the conversation that took place as this experienced and indomitable campaigner chatted with the son of his former friend at Motherwell. One surmises that some comments may have disconcerted presbytery even more than Willie's poor attendance, for Barr had not given up fighting for the United Free Church cause.

161

Just recently he had published his book *The United Free Church,* which pulls no punches ecumenically or doctrinally, and carries as its Foreword the words of Christ used by George C. Hutton, the Moderator of the General Assembly of the United Free Church of Scotland in the year of Willie's birth: "hold fast that which thou hast, that no man take thy crown"!

At the annual business meeting of the church, everything was found to be in fine fettle, and *The Renfrew Press* once more showed its close interest by devoting an unprecedented three complete columns to reporting it. The most conspicuous decision emerging from the discussions was the church's readiness to renovate its buildings despite the high costs involved. Willie's optimism was clearly winning, though some did express concern at doing it on the basis of a bank overdraft. The "yours today, five years to pay" motto then used by banks and credit houses evidently held no fears or concern for the minister.

But the year was to be lived within earshot of sabre rattling on all sides. Not that war was yet talked about as an inevitability, but the great issues of armed conflict were now being aired as never before, heightened by the Italian-Abyssinian conflict now in full swing and the illegal entry of German troops into the Rhineland. Further, two Renfrew men on holiday in Spain were drawn into the Spanish Civil War, thereby bringing the European furor home to Scotland. The League of Nations spluttered on, causing headaches for its defenders and evoking acid comments from its detractors as to its usefulness and viability. Glasgow's civic authorities alarmed many by encouraging public consideration of the construction of an airport of their own, separate from that of Renfrew. Perhaps the Barclays were not themselves too concerned—after all, they had the things flying low directly over their manse—but there were commercial and economic effects that could not be dismissed.

In September, the church was reopened in pristine condition, and again the local paper declared its admiration for the style and vigor it projected. A total of £1,200 had been spent on the renovations (worth more than ten times that amount today). A new lighting system had been introduced, the organ had been overhauled, the seats were revarnished, and the driveway had been relaid. The exterior had been repainted to give the building "a bright and most attractive" appearance, and at the rear the hall had been refloored and the walls repaneled. Delighted, the minister nevertheless downplayed the ultimate significance of such cosmetic changes in his next pastoral letter.

Gratitude, remembrance of (but not concentration on) things past, fresh consecration: these were Willie's principles for future advancement and blessing. But above all was loyalty to God. The secret was spelled out more clearly in a new series of addresses which was given to his Senior Bible Class. Under his personal control and leadership, it now had seventy-nine members, the forty-four boys outnumbering the girls by nine. The theme of the series was "Self, Self-will, Selfishness and Self-denial," which gives some indication of the sterling character and challenge of his message.

He had now pierced to the core of the Christian message, and himself lived at its heart. He is much more confident in his statements, more Christ-centered, more demanding of the call to discipleship by this point in his career. From his early years of borrowed ideas and thinking (not that they were false to him, but simply that they were neither tested nor wrought by his own efforts), he had now progressed to his own understanding. Using his own studies and experiences he could now speak as one who *knew*, who had seen and heard, and who could therefore speak. This was the basis for everything that followed, the secret of his success in speaking, preaching, writing, and broadcasting. Like David of old, he took off the untried armor that belonged to others—be it his father's or his mentors'—to fight with his own weapons. And we shall see that, like David's opponents, there were those who belittled his weapons, who derided his actions, and who became curiously silent when success was attained.

Perhaps the most significant thing about this newfound knowledge and power was that he remained essentially the same: positive, constructive, optimistic, fun-loving, and completely human—a man's man. And yet he remained vulnerable: he recognized his weaknesses, and knew the Source of strength through which they could be overcome and turned into goodness:

> Let me no more my comfort draw
> From my frail hold on Thee,
> In this alone rejoice with awe,
> Thy mighty grasp on me.

Through the devotions of his home life, the ministry of Thomas Marshall at Motherwell, and the instructions of his college tutors (most notably that of A. J. Gossip), he had risen to a deep religious awareness. Perhaps the real turning point came at the death of his father, when the last human prop was removed and he stood alone; perhaps it was then that the presence and promise of Christ became most real. But, whatever the specific juncture, he had by now clearly passed on to a greater spiritual maturity both in his life and in his teaching.

This cannot be said of Kate, who, though unswervingly loyal to Willie and his commitments, understood the religious life differently, less mystically, more institutionally. She was ever more worldly (and certainly more worldly-wise) than Willie and would pull his leg—and sometimes chide him—for his "softness" and unwillingness to see things in the cold light of reality. But she also admired him for these qualities, and passed her admiration on to others. As Stewart Borthwick informed me, nearly half a century later, Kate regarded Willie as the most outstanding man she had ever met.[18] He never brought his worries home with him, nor ever retaliated when abused. His religious experiences produced the man he became; his reliance on Christ flowered in a serenity and winsomeness that few could resist. He was Christ's man, and sought to bring him to others. It is the very essence of sainthood.

Willie himself was an incurable and unrepentant optimist, by nature and faith. He often reminded his hearers of the difference between an optimist and a pessimist in the old story of two drinking men: one remarked his glass was half empty, the other that his was half full; his glass was ever half full. He was not reckless in his optimism; he never forgot the wise counsel of Lord Oxford and Asquith: "it is an excellent thing to have an optimist at the front provided there is a pessimist at the rear." Willie, needing encouragement himself, never failed to supply it to others by kindly word and personal note. One of his unfailing habits was to drop a letter of thanks to his helpers after important functions—a special service, an anniversary, a party, or whatever. He was essentially a man of action, of ideas; life was for living, for getting things done. His newfound secret was to be woven into the fine tapestry of his life and work.

Fresh insight invariably precedes further responsibility, and to his pastoral work at Renfrew and the careful safeguarding of the Sunday School he undertook by way of special training classes for his teachers, he now added a series of monthly lectures for the Renfrew District of the Scottish Sunday School Union. This marked a decisive step in his career, as we shall see, but the knowledge and experience he gained thereby also produced its own problem: it perpetuated the devotion he had learned from his father and reawakened the tensions between the "evangelical" and "liberal" understanding of the faith. On the level of the spirit, he was totally for the former, having seen it in his family and having felt its power within himself. But on the level of the mind, especially when confronted by the difficulties and doubts of others, he was not doctrinaire; he was prepared to be tolerant and willing to concede dogma for the living Christ of his own certain experience. This is the root of the dichotomy in his character that we shall see opening up from time to time. Its resolution was always evangelistic or pastoral.

The annual congregational meeting of 1937 marked the church's seventy-fifth anniversary, and the report of it produced over thirty column inches in *The Renfrew Press*. The membership now stood at 1,108, an all-time record. Another broken record concerned the minister himself: Willie had exceeded the four-year "term" of ministry that had repeatedly interrupted the church's life since 1919. He did not allow the point to go unnoticed: "As for myself," he wrote, "I look forward with hope and expectation to still another year's service among the people whom I have come to love and look on as my own folk." And the editor of the church magazine commented, "Mr Barclay has all but completed that year which Trinity has from past experience come to look on as fatal—his fourth. . . . We must admit he is far from being idle." There had been rumors of changes, and more than rumors. The local paper, relying on a finely tuned ear that was not often wrong, stated that "it was not that the opportunity to leave had not come to Mr Barclay. He had determined to abide by his first love, and the Kirk Session and the congregation were deeply grateful for this decision."

His phrase "another year's service" was significant. That he had academic hopes—if not actual ambitions—is beyond dispute. Some of his fellow students believed they were apparent even in his college days. Now two different temptations were making themselves sharply felt: calls from larger and more prestigious churches than Renfrew Trinity, and the lure of academe.

Meanwhile the usual reports of the organizations were presented: numbers in the Sunday School stood at 265, and a high average attendance was recorded, no fewer than 68 teachers guaranteeing that. (And in the background was a group of young people all waiting to be called to the task of teaching.) The Senior Bible Class counted 83 on its roll and they were also in good heart, as were the many other organizations. Two extra ones had been added to their ranks: a stamp club and a football team. The former ("this relic of boyhood" in Drummond's phrase) was doubtless Willie's idea: philately remained a favorite hobby of his to the end. This club had arranged some open lectures and an exhibition, and by October had contributed eighteen thousand stamps to the nearby Deaconess Hospital. The football team soon became part of the Scottish Football Association (entering it via the Paisley YMCA League, another of the minister's interests). They played on a pitch on the adjacent Blythswood Estate, mustering two teams and a coach, and they acquitted themselves well, frequently being urged on in a less-than-ministerial way by the touch-line minister whose vocal training had been at Motherwell FC.

For Willie and Kate these were idyllic days, with their happy family life. In June a sister to Ronnie, Barbara Mary—after both grandmothers—had arrived, completing their family unit. And they were at the appreciative center of a youthful community that was often the talk of the town. They were not well off, but neither were they poor; unlike some of their ministerial colleagues, they had a car to transport them about when necessary. Prior to his coming to Trinity, the church managers had *reduced* the minister's salary by £50 per annum—a reduction of ten percent from £500 (plus a manse) to £450. The question of a raise in the stipend was discussed, but Willie refused it on the grounds of the church's overdraft. Their pleasures were simple ones, but they were deeply enjoyed: an occasional visit to Kate's parents at Dundonald, a walk or a drive in the countryside, or regular walks round the popular Robertson Park in Renfrew itself—which had led one budding poet to write

How fickle is the mind of man
    When he is bent on pleasure,
Yet still above all others can
    The park be, Renfrew's treasure.

It brings all beauty to our door,
    It gives us room to breathe in,
And makes us grieve for Glasgow's poor,
    And the foul streets they seethe in![19]

Kate herself was enjoying life as never before. To the satisfaction of being a much-appreciated wife and mother, she had added the public success of her presidency of the Woman's Guild. As *The Renfrew Press* noted in March, its meetings "have recently been brightened by the introduction of several novel schemes." It went on to give twenty column inches to the latest of these, an

"Exercise in Thanksgiving," which was very characteristic of their mood at this time, both Trinity's and the Barclays'.

This "Exercise in Thanksgiving" was a sort of domestic market research on members, who were asked to nominate the thing for which they were most thankful in life, and make a thank-offering for it. Out of 113 replies, the following responses were made:

33 votes for good health
11 votes each for home and domestic harmony, for life and its good things
 9 votes for the Guild and its fellowship
 8 votes each for sufficiency of material things, for friendship and family ties, and for a good husband
 4 votes each for sufficient work and for small mercies
 3 votes each for the church, for God's guidance, for children, and for recovery from illness
 2 votes for long life
 1 vote each for good books, for a contented mind, and for country.

"There was someone," said Willie after reviewing the results, "who said that everything in this life has two handles, one of gold and one of base metal, and according to the handle by which you picked it up, so was the thing, and to exercise oneself in thanksgiving is to look for the golden handle of things. . . . In almost every case," he concluded, "the things which called for the greatest gratitude were the 'common things of life.' . . . There can be no heart in the world in which some echo of assent does not quiver when it is said to us 'Let us Praise God.'"

To these simple things the Barclays added their trips to Glasgow, seething streets or no, to hear their beloved Scottish National Orchestra, which Willie always held was the best way of spending the Saturday evening before preaching. And the summer of that year saw festivities of a wholly different order when the coronation was celebrated. Flags and bunting decorated the streets, and there were special sports meetings and displays, fireworks, and souvenirs of all sorts. Willie was not one of them, but to those lucky enough to own one of the newfangled television sets, the event could be seen live in their homes, as another invention made its way onto the market, and another first was achieved in the progress of man.

But real progress was defied, for the international situation was visibly worsening. The Franco-Turkish dispute had broken out at the beginning of the year, to which was added Mussolini's expanding belligerency. Elsewhere Hitler's machinations were causing great alarm, and armed conflict seemed to be at the threshold. As early as May the local firemaster was warning that Renfrew had no protection in the event of an air raid, and the arguments about pacifism were growing in strength.

The new session was opened by the minister with his pastoral letter, delayed a month by pressures professional and domestic. In it he counseled his people to face "the new adventure" adventurously.

The Phony Peace

The excellence of Trinity's seasonal parties and festivities could not camouflage the grim realities of the times. The thin-faced '30s had fleshed out, but on the wrong basis; prosperity was now sought in the rearmament program. False prophets were crying peace when there was no peace, and the politicians and captains of industry were only too glad to see a slackening of the constraints and anxieties of the Depression. Despite this, appeasement was now becoming an obsession, soon to be exposed as a lie, but not soon enough. And Beaverbrook's policy, often interpreted as appeasement, but in reality a morally indefensible form of isolationism, was making its shrill cries heard among the corridors of power and deadening the public's suspicions that all was far from well.

Willie, writing in the January edition of the church magazine, could exhort his members to give thanks for the lifting of the blight of depression, but he did not try to cover up the underlying threat or the true source of their security:

> No man may look at the future with other than a wonder what its days shall bring to him. It is in the providence of God that we do not know what is coming to us, but only that whatever comes we shall meet it with him.

Ever the optimist, even in this situation, he could speak of the year as "a time of new beginnings" in which he encouraged them with a twofold call: "to put first things first" and "to put ourselves last." He was not going to let the central lesson of his newfound secret go lost. He used the old acronym JOY to drive home the point, as had been done countless times before by his father:

> Someone once said that the secret of joy lies in the very letters of the word: J stands for Jesus, O stands for Others, and Y stands for Yourself. Let us resolve to live life on that principle and then we shall render God a more perfect service, and we shall find ourselves a more perfect joy.

The minister reflected both this joy and this service in a new sermon series, when he again took as his texts various Negro spirituals. An "identity competition" was organized by the stamp club, followed by a lecture from Willie entitled "Here and There in the Stamp Album," the first of several such lectures. It was in such times as these that his parables-of-life approach began to make a dramatic affect on his style. Names, mottos, colors, designs—every little detail was to become a suggestion, from which he would make a sermon or an illustration. A visit to a concert with his young people would be followed by a sermon in which several commonplace things would weave their own lesson, giving warning or cause for thankfulness. His religious life was truly at one with his everyday responsibilities, and this unity of thought and action grounded his theology and shaped his "plain man's" religion.

At the end of that month we find him involved with the Woman's Guild in a "Scotch Night." "Of course," the local reporter drily commented, "there had to be a new idea from Trinity."[20] Yes, of course! The paper went on to report "a feast of dramatic entertainment from Trinity," this time the body responsible for it being the Men's Club. In this the minister was deeply involved, bringing the occasion to an appropriate end by a hearty rendering of "Auld Lang Syne." This was followed by an outing to the largest industrial complex of the area, Messrs. Babcock and Wilcox, to whose Literary and Debating Society Willie delivered a captivating lecture on "The Life and Work of Sir James Barrie" in the tradition of his father, but with his own special powers of analysis and description. (There was a hidden reason for this involvement: William Braidwood had recently moved into the area, and was employed by them in a senior management role. It was not long before he was drawn to the reputation of Trinity's Church and its extraordinarily active minister. He was to move on after the war, but happily for us their friendship ripened into regular correspondence, which has been preserved and is one of the best personal sources of Willie's thinking in the immediate postwar years.)

Notwithstanding the international climate, it was in many ways Willie's year. Certainly it seems that seeds of the Barclay legend began to grow from this time. The boundless energy, the innovative ideas, the sparkling wit, and his sheer managerial ability—all came together and were fused in a transparent love for God and his fellow men.

On the 4th of March the front page of the *The Renfrew Press* carried a banner headline, as if of an event of international significance: "TRINITY CHURCH STEP: SEAT ALLOCATIONS ABOLISHED." Trinity was no longer to charge pew rents! While it was an important step for the church and minister (expressive as it was of deeper things), it was no innovation. In fact Trinity lagged well behind other churches in getting around to the matter; the Barony Church, for example, had done so in the last quarter of the nineteenth century. The problem was essentially one of numbers: over 1,200 church members, and a mere 690 seats to provide for their comfort. The paper spoke of "the ever-increasing numbers of the congregation"; "standing room only" was a literal problem for latecomers.

The step had been taken at the annual congregational meeting of the church, and was passed by "an overwhelming majority." The minister, it was stated, pressed for it "in the future interests of the church." But more than numbers was involved. To Willie it was a principle: God's house could not be "let out" in the way pew rents suggested: all may come and have their choice of seat. However, the paper was wrong in attributing this move solely to the forward-looking minister. It had been originated by the church managers, and Willie was at first a restraining influence on the idea, urging caution and a fact-finding process to ascertain the mind of the church. Whatever else he may be, he was no hotheaded revolutionary attempting to sweep his congregation along with him.

But there was more. Page four of the newspaper carried headlines nearly as large as those on page one: "TRINITY CHURCH AFFAIRS: THREE RECORDS BROKEN: AN EPIC YEAR FOR TRINITY CHURCH." The newspaper was in danger of running out of superlatives. The records broken were those of church membership, of communion attendance, and of "congregational liberality" (its collections). It was put down to the energies of the minister. "No man," remarked

the session clerk, "could have put more into these five years than Mr Barclay."
But, said the minister, placing the emphasis elsewhere, and revealing the Source
of his strength and convictions:

> Somewhere Marcus Aurelius advised men to live "as if they lived on the moun-
> tainside." What he meant was that life should be always an upward progress
> towards some peak or goal. It is a thought and an ideal fit and very suitable to the
> beginning of another year in the existence of our church. Here in these reports
> we have the record of the year that is past. It is a record of which we do well to be
> proud; it is a record which may well make us say, "Hitherto hath the Lord helped
> us." And yet it must ever be true that we must never think of the past except to
> think how we may better it. . . . The beginning of the new year in our congregation
> life is not only an occasion for a reviewing of the past, it is also an opportunity to
> set down and make clear our ideals and aims for the future. . . . So, remembering
> above all Him Whose we are and Whom we serve, it is our honour to serve, to go
> forward to another year. . . .

In that spirit they did serve; in that spirit they went forward.

Trinity's standing was now such that when the church officer's post was
advertised, no fewer than 120 applications were received for it—and that despite
the fact that the post must have been one of the hardest-worked positions in the
area. By now Willie had been ordained for six busy and successful years. "Success" is always a difficult word to define in spiritual matters; it can mean—
classically, it *does* mean—unrecognition, a martyr's blood (real or metaphorical);
or it can mean, as with Willie, a full church that is religiously serious, outward-
looking, active, and influential. Six years—the same point at which F. W. Robertson of Brighton (himself a founding Christian Socialist of the Maurice-cum-
Kingsley type, who influenced Willie not least with regard to that aspect of the
gospel, and whose psychological penetration in pen and pulpit portraits were to
deepen the contact) completed his ministry at the early age of thirty-seven and
died. It would be too much to urge too close a parallel, but Willie's mark had
been made, and he was shortly to reenter the tension when rival claims and
opportunities were to disrupt the placid calm of the parishes of Renfrew.

But outside his church and town appreciations were growing, and being
expressed. The "life of academe" was made concrete in an invitation to him to
apply for the Chair of Divinity and Biblical Criticism at Aberdeen University. Few
things are more convincing of the appreciation in which Willie was held by his
mentors than the testimonials written for him in April 1938 on his application
for this Chair. Commented W. M. Macgregor, Principal of Trinity College,

> I have no hesitation in saying that, with the exception of one man who
> preceded him in College by several years and is no longer working in New
> Testament fields, the Rev. WILLIAM BARCLAY is the ablest student in my
> Department who passed through my hands. He came with a First Class Honours
> Degree in Classics, but he did not content himself with a mere linguistic mastery:
> he pressed through to essential meanings. Whilst still at College, he acquainted
> himself with the range of Early Christian Literature, and used it for the illustration

and interpretation of New Testament texts. Since leaving College he has resolutely pursued his studies and in the winter of 1936 he delivered in Trinity College an important course of Lectures ("The Bruce Lectures") on "The Use of the New Testament in the Early Apologists," in which both his mastery of the subject and his power of lucid exposition were apparent.

It is not without importance to add, in regard to one wishing to teach in a Theological Faculty, that for five years he has effectively served a large working class congregation, with all its demands for human understanding and friendship.

His former professor in practical training and ethics, Arthur J. Gossip, sent this recommendation from his retirement home in Kingussie (but fifty miles away from the old Barclay home at Fort William):

Mr WILLIAM BARCLAY stands out as the most brilliant student who has ever passed through my classes. Even at College he was not only a man of quite unusual width of reading but also as one with a strikingly mature way of using stores of knowledge. For example, he came to Trinity with a 1st class in Classics, and his knowledge of the Classics had become part of his own being, on which he drew with an aptness no other student of mine has ever approached. And that was characteristic. No other man in my time—now a lengthening period—has had anything like his knowledge of English Literature and especially of the poets; and here again the thing had been absorbed into himself with the happiest results. A man of remarkable application, he mastered any subject set him with a kind or fierce zest and then set it down with an originality of mind and statement that made each essay or answer a bit of literary work of interest and value.

Mr Barclay is a man of a most likeable nature—modest, and in college, generous to a degree in helping other students. I feel sure his students would take to him and find him an eager friend.

Mr Barclay is an admirable preacher; and has, moreover, pursued his studies with avidity since leaving college. Some of his results were given to an interested audience in Trinity in his Bruce Lectures.

And A. B. Macaulay, also in retirement (in Correnie Drive, Edinburgh), wrote,

A glimpse at the splendid library of the Rev WILLIAM BARCLAY, BD, Trinity Church, Renfrew, would instantly reveal the fact that he was a scholar. He was outstanding among a group of remarkable contemporaries in Trinity College, Glasgow. His work in Systematic Theology was so excellent that, had his attainments in Classics not been so distinguished, as they were, I would have urged him to devote his life to the study of the Philosophy of Religion and Christian Dogmatics. But the New Testament was conspicuously his province. And his rare gifts so eminently fitted him for future service as a teacher of that subject that I reluctantly abstained from trying to influence him in another direction. That he would adorn the Chair of Divinity and Biblical Criticism in the University of Aberdeen, and win the admiration and affection of his students, is my sincere belief.

Professor G. H. C. Macgregor's comments, though less fulsome (and not without some inaccuracy, surprising as it may be), added this interesting comment to the sparsely documented Bruce Lectures of 1936:

170

I had the privilege recently of presiding at a course of "Bruce Lectures" delivered in Trinity College, Glasgow by the Rev. William Barclay. His subject was "The New Testament and the Fathers," and the lectures both in matter and manner were wholly admirable. The treatment indicated skill in methods of research and a profound knowledge of the field, while the lecturer's vigorous and attractive delivery held the interest of the students to the end.

Others added their own estimates of his aptitudes. Robert M. Buchanan, Librarian and Depute Clerk of Trinity College, spoke of his "fine qualifications in scholarship and in character," adding that he was "the ablest New Testament scholar I have known in seventeen years, and one of the ablest all-round students." Buchanan listed Willie's various accomplishments and prizes, which culminated in his Bruce Lectures—"a course which was recognised as most scholarly." Duncan Blair, his "bishop" of 1932, wrote of his "outstanding capabilities as a teacher and expositor of New Testament Literature," which was specially evidenced in his senior youth classes, wherein "he commended himself so highly to the general esteem and intelligence that his influence as a leader still abides." Mr. Blair spoke of "his singular aptitude for gaining the ear of the thinking youth of today by the liveliness of his mind, the thoroughness of his work, and the winsomeness and modesty of his personality." He was ranked "as easily the most influential and successful assistant I have had," to which was added the view that "those who are capable of judging [his work] in this congregation have always predicted a sphere of usefulness for him in our church such as this Chair would supply." Finally, the senior minister in Renfrew, John F. Marshall, drew attention to two things in particular that impressed him:

> The first is his undoubted ability to turn his high scholarship and intellectual powers to good account. . . . This has been proved not only in his preaching, but also more particularly in the training class [for teachers] . . . which he has conducted at the request of the local union. The second is his unusual capacity for interesting and influencing young men.

It was not to be, however. The warm collective paean to the accomplishments and capacities of Willie was not successful in securing the Chair for him. And so he returned his attention to the task at hand, renewing his commitment to his people at Renfrew.

The political deterioration was evident all over; the necessity of training air wardens was announced, and the shadow of conscription had fallen. The government, like its predecessor in the Great War, was to prevaricate on this for months, adding to the uncertainty of the times. The fate of Czechoslovakia provoked concern as to Hitler's designs on central and southeast Europe. He entered Austria in March. News of the Spanish Civil War continued to alarm many, alerting them to the threat of fascism and inspiring some to arms. Air-Raid Precautions (ARP) regulations were now being disseminated around the town, and the paper ran an article entitled "Women and the ARP." Actual military

171

activity took place in Renfrew and elsewhere, and the real state of things was symbolized by the launching from the nearby shipyards of *H.M.S. Forth,* a mother ship to eleven submarines, which was followed in quick succession by the destroyer *H.M.S. Jackal* and the cruisers *H.M.S. Kenya* and *H.M.S. Duke of York.*

By September the paper was referring to the summer situation as one in which "the world tottered on the brink of the abyss."[21] The euphoria that followed Chamberlain's third visit to the German Chancellor and his acquisition of the Munich Agreement was pure romance, celebrated locally in verse by "Auld Monk," who frequently contributed to the pages of *The Renfrew Press:*

> Bravo, brave Chamberlain, thy name
>> And fame throughout the years will be sung;
> Posterity will own thy claim,
>> For thee chiming bells will be rung.

"There is no such eventuality as the inevitability of war," declared the editor, but sought to safeguard his reputation by appending the qualification that "1939 will be a critical year in our history." The year was to have seen celebration of the Silver Jubilee of peace, but it offered something very different indeed. Austria was now sucked into the German expansion, and the unspeakable acts against the Jews—who had already been deprived of civic and religious rights, expelled from the professions, and forced to suffer humiliating and practically impossible trading conditions (including the confiscation of their capital and property)—was under way. Even Burns's pungent phrase "man's inhumanity to man" would fail to convey the tragedy, the horror, the historic enormity to be unleashed on the world.

In the light of all this it is almost indecent to describe the day-to-day events of a small church in the west of Scotland. But we should not forget that they were not favored—or burdened—with our knowledge. There were many rumors and stories, and some highly disconcerting facts concerning events on the Continent, but there were also attempts by government, by some members of the media, and by some church leaders to minimize the realities, to discount the rumors and the stories, and to play down their implications out of a pure failure of nerve: the reality, in the light of their past twenty-five years of suffering, was simply too awful to contemplate or act upon decisively.

So the presbytery organized a "Recall to Religion" campaign, which soon involved the minister of Renfrew Trinity along with the other ministers of the area. It seems that an attempt was made at this time by presbytery to draw Willie more fully into its activities. In September he was appointed to the Publications Committee and reappointed to the Life and Work and Public Questions Committee. He now attended presbytery for the first time since 1936—but a year was to elapse before he reappeared. One wonders to what extent presbytery's tendency to be consumed with trivia in the face of world-shaking events engendered this careless attitude. The questions the Life and Work Committee dealt with when he last attended related to Sunday trading and Sunday observance. Willie was by no means indifferent to such matters, but he may be excused for considering them to be of secondary importance in the face of conditions that threatened to disrupt society at a far more fundamental level.

Because of the need for maximum output by industry, the churches were beginning to suffer a manpower crisis: the ministers were reduced to distributing their own handbills and galvanizing support directly for the campaign. Special addresses were delivered on a monthly basis throughout the winter session, and other activities were commenced to strengthen the Recall. For his part, Willie presented a series of addresses at his midweek meetings, which were short and well-attended, and he exchanged pulpits with the other ministers of the area. The public do not seem to have been overimpressed by this. A carping letter was published challenging the church's right to describe itself as "the church militant": its activities, in the face of the real militancy of the time, seemed somewhat unconvincing. The habit of the church to set up a committee or propose another meeting was bitterly attacked. Society, in Mr. Fortune's words of five years prior, was calling for a "decided answer" to the questions it was asking. It by no means perceived that it was getting them. There was a concentration on the things of the spirit, the moods of the hour, instead of a bold intervention in the metal-and-concrete problems that were rankling. The world cried out for justice; the politicians preached peace; the church offered "grace." Men and women demanded work; the politicians supplied an armament program; the ministers spoke of "mercy." Humanity cried for life; parliament offered materials rewards; the church sang of trust and heavenly hope. The holocaust inched nearer.

Even the cries from the Continental churches, sometimes suppressed by denominational leaders, went unattended. The Church/State confrontation in Germany which issued in the struggle of the "Confessing Church" and which had so recently occupied the minds of the Scottish church (though for different reasons) was regarded almost academically. This is especially strange in the light of Scotland's involvement with Continental theology (as against traditional English isolationism) and the widespread influence of Karl Barth. One might justifiably wonder whether the fêting of Dietrich Bonhoeffer that took place in the '60s and early '70s was not a sort of conscience money paid to one of the most illustrious and winsome figures of the Confessing Church struggle by those who misunderstood or refused to lend help when it was needed. Even the Barmen Declaration, perhaps the greatest thing (in view of its christological emphasis) to emerge from the German struggle, was passed over in silence and finds little comment, and still less support, today.

It was at this time that Willie commenced what was to become a lifelong service to his fellow ministers quite literally the world over—and not for ministers alone, but for educators, theologians, and students of religion of all descriptions. Largely through the recommendations of A. J. Gossip, already well known for his column in *The Expository Times,* that monthly magazine now invited Willie to join the ranks of its contributors. Its editors were Dr. Edward Hastings and Miss Ann Hastings, who, like Gossip and Willie, were ex-members of the United Free

Church. The pair was blessed with considerable editorial acumen, not least in finding potential authors of note. Thus there appeared in the August issue an article by Willie under the title "Church and State in the Apologists." It was the first of a series of more than 350 pieces, which continued to appear even after his death. The very title of the article is indicative of his broad range of interests: church and state, religious and secular, theological and ethical, past and present-day concerns.

Whatever the menace might be in the world situation, Willie's own situation was showing signs of distinct promise; he was on the point of achieving significant recognition and influence. It was a very pleasing sequel to the successful completion of his Bruce Lectures on "The New Testament in the Apologists," which, while more specialized, were in the same area of interest—early church history.

An important visitor came to Renfrew in October in the person of Andrew McCosh. Ordained in 1932, a year before Willie, McCosh had a distinguished academic career in Scotland and America behind him, and was, to quote the newspaper, "one of the brilliant young men of the church." Willie, as President of the YMCA branch that had invited him to address the fellowship meeting, was clearly responsible for getting him to Renfrew. No doubt they enjoyed some good talks on the way things were going at home and elsewhere, but neither of them could have foreseen that the outcome of their friendship was to have literally worldwide repercussions. Nevertheless, it was specifically through their friendship, vision, and tenacity that Willie was to find not merely an international platform for his work, but the means to introduce the Bible to firesides the world over, to establish an influence, and to make a contribution that is beyond assessment, as we shall see.

Writing in the October issue of the church magazine, the minister reminded his members of the dual function of the church member: to receive from and to give to his church. He deplored the "complications" of modern life: he ever remained an Edwardian at heart, with the virtues and the mentality of the Edwardians. He regretted the loss of former simplicity, an essential trait both in his life-style and in his ethics. He urged them to seek afresh "some echoes of the voice of God"—a curiously indirect comment from this man who knew the power of the secret place, who was strong in prayer. He exhorted them to share their burdens, and their dedication to the centrality of Jesus and that forward thrust that is characteristic of the gospel: "As we go forward . . . we must always remember . . . who we are working for, we are working for God. . . ." Despite the round of activities that befell him, despite the innumerable pressures under which he worked, and despite all that was to come his way in the future, he never left that central affirmation, for him the fulcrum of Christianity. It was the Welsh Anglican theologian Griffith Thomas who coined the phrase "Christianity is Christ," but William Barclay lived it, preached it, taught and exhorted it, and, at the end of his life, when bequeathing his *Testament of Faith,* simply stated that "I believe in Jesus, for me Jesus is the centre and soul of the whole matter." It would not be untrue to say that this biography is essentially the story of the unfolding of that belief, from the ABC of Sunday School confessions, through theological training, to close and detailed linguistic and New Testament study on a platform that became worldwide. He never moved from the center at which he started. His faith was centrifugal: everything was determined by the force that operated from that center; and it was centripetal: everything was made to move back toward that center. Everything was judged by its relationship—we might say by its faithfulness—to that center. Just how he interpreted Jesus, and the actual doctrines concerning his person and work, we must leave to more detailed consideration at a later point. Suffice it to say now (it would be a libel to say otherwise) that his religious understanding and experience were rooted in the historical Jesus, who was the subject and content of his teaching and work.

But this emphasis did not obscure other things. Within days of urging this "Christological concentration" on his members, he was found leading his Men's Club on a visit to Walker's sugar refinery, which was followed by an absorbing lecture recital (with a double quartette) on "The Songs of Robert Burns." The balance is preserved!

The annual riot of socials, parties, speeches, and suppers was upon them again when festivities multiplied, and Burns would indeed be in spate. Willie's pastoral letter maintained its optimistic, encouraging note. "It is," he wrote at the start of the year that ushered in the holocaust, "in the goodness of God that we cannot see what lies ahead." He outlined what could be done, things that are wholly characteristic of him: the future could be met "in the right way"—that is, cheerfully, in hopeful anticipation and trust.

That January the church suffered a great loss when the father of the preses, A. M. Ferguson, died. A joiner by trade, and therefore related to some of Willie's family interests at Lochgoilhead and Fort William, he was "one of the few remaining links with the age of real craftsmanship," as the minister put it in his obituary.[22] The church suffered another loss at this time. The ancient iron pot that had always been used in the traditional "burning of the tatties" was lost, perhaps the victim of the renovations. In their very different ways, these incidents were further indications of the era that was now passing, when the foundations were being shaken and things were being unmade.

Meetings proliferated in the usual way of things for Trinity and its minister, with Kate ever holding the fort in the background and being both mother and father to their children. She was also busy organizing and producing a play for the Woman's Guild: Andrew Wilson's *The Jumble Sale,* a happy choice in view of Trinity's penchant for such things. By March Willie was at it again, launching yet another new venture, this time the fourth choir in Trinity—that of the Woman's Guild.

At the seventy-seventh annual congregational meeting, satisfactory reports were once more presented and approved. The church took particular pleasure in hearing that there had been an increase of over three hundred members since their minister arrived.

Others, too, had seen the extraordinary abilities of Renfrew's minister, and sought again to tempt him away from the area. Celebrating his sixth anniversary, the church magazine spoke of these attempts: "a tug of war has been going on recently, but the prize is still ours." The editor further commented that "It is our hope that we may have Mr Barclay as our minister for many years; we congratulate him on the success of his work, and extend to our minister and his wife our sincere good wishes." Another temptation had been overcome. Such offers were real temptations, not only because they came from churches more in the public eye than Renfrew Trinity—in Glasgow and elsewhere—but because the possibilities of academic work continued to appeal. Despite the affection Trinity maintained for its minister, it was still "the fechtin' church," and its session meetings ever threatened to erupt into strong debate. From these meetings Willie would wearily make his way home, more open to those inducements than ever, only to receive a cheerful telephone call from one of this most vociferous opponents remarking "that was a rare discussion tonight, Mr. Barclay!" And Willie then knew that all was well, despite the contentions.

The pleasure of those words of appreciation expressed by the editor was diluted by the war clouds that now hung everywhere. Still firmly against conscription in the early part of the year, the government was making preparations for defense in earnest. Searchlights were installed and there was much talk of "sound-locating machines" being tested at nearby Glasgow University. In a spirited article, Dr. Henderson argued that if only the Prime Minister had read *Mein Kampf* (published in 1924) he would not have embarked upon his appeasement policy. It was unthinkable that the economic recovery program of Germany, based on rearmament, could now simply unwind.[23] At the dockside, companies of Sherwood Foresters were already on guard, and the airfield was now in the hands of the RAF (946) Balloon Squadron.

An open-air service of a sort very different from those at which Willie excelled was now held. Organized by the civic authorities, it was a "teach-in" on war responses, and civilian procedures in the event of air attack were outlined, as were other ominous matters—the dedication of the tennis hut as a municipal first-aid headquarters, for example. Nearby, in Glasgow's Hampden Park, "unprecedented scenes" were observed when a National Service rally was staged; according to the Lord Provost, it was "the most unique demonstration of defence ever." And there was a great procession that included the RNVR, the Saint Andrew Ambulance workers, the British Red Cross, the Women's Auxiliary Services, Fire-fighters, Rescue Squads, and Decontamination Squads, all led by a thousand-strong contingent of the Glasgow police force. It was a schoolboy's dream, but the grim reality was not masked from the general public; within two weeks of this display, gas masks had been distributed throughout the area (even horses had them, carrying them on their noses in little rolls). This was followed by the long-delayed and inevitable Military Training Bill. Willie thus found himself lining up on registration day, 3 June 1939, with the rest of the males in his age group, offering himself for king and country, but not as a combatant—

though in any case his increasing deafness would likely preclude his being called into service. By now he was obliged to wear a hearing aid, and the only type available to him in those prewar days came with an unbecoming headband and a large portable battery. His deafness became more profound throughout the war, until he was virtually stone-deaf, and the batteries increased commensurately (in weight and conspicuousness); he was learning suffering of a different sort through this disability.

Amid this deadly seriousness, a different note was struck on the 12th of June, when the Glasgow Police challenged the local clergy in a football match. Glasgow presbytery seems to have been short of players, for Willie was brought in to play alongside some of his former college friends in the famous jerseys of the Rangers Football Club. He played at left back, as he had done alongside John Smith at Dalziel High School. This time his teammates were the Reverends W. G. Snow, W. V. MacDonald, D. MacPherson, A. A. Smith, R. S. Cairns, J. L. Cotter (whose family owned *The Motherwell Times*), T. F. Neill, G. Nicholson, J. C. Grant, and Father Coulon (whose presence served to demonstrate that if the churches did not score very well in the ecumenical league, it had no worries when the collars were reversed and the leather was brown, not black). It would be pleasant to report that the upholders of the moral and spiritual order beat these who upheld the power of the magistrate, but this was not the case. Playing on a day more suited to cricket than football, in blazing sunshine and a dead calm, the police gave the clergy a lesson in teamwork and ball control that garnered six goals to their three by the time the final whistle was blown. It was by all accounts a hard game, and the clergy did well to keep the score as low as it did. In the second half MacPherson retired hurt, and as there was no substitute available, the clergy had a rough battle against their taller, fitter competitors. Willie's name, alas, does not appear in the reports at all; apparently he failed to distinguish himself. Perhaps the years of ceaseless activity were already beginning to make their mark, and certainly the effects of Kate's cooking were evident in his broadening shadow. But it was good fun, and the match took their minds off the problems of the day for an hour or two.

The next month, July, Willie recorded another first in his growing influence when he led the Bible studies at Mayfield House, Dundee, that year's venue for the Scottish Sunday School Union. It was the first of very many such engagements, and naturally followed from his having been chosen by the Union to give monthly lectures to its Renfrew District (begun in October 1936). It provided a wider circle for his influence, which was now extending beyond the west of Scotland. The combination of educational awareness, detailed New Testament expertise, and a high spiritual approach (not to mention earthy sanity) were just right to inspire the Sunday School teachers in their work, and his friendly disposition was ideal for house-party leadership. The "vocation within the vocation" he had found earlier was now strengthened by this opening; he was on the road to great things—ever looking forward, not backward.

On returning to Renfrew, he attended a function that should have given great joy to him but that turned out to be an embarrassment to everyone. Because of the large numbers of troops now stationed in the town, the YMCA decided to put on an evening's entertainment for them at the Town Hall. Willie was Vice President, and so was closely involved in the proceedings. Unfortunately, it was marred by too much "speechifying"—a fact that the newspaper did not hesitate to criticize. Despite his own embarrassment, Willie wrote to the town council giving his thanks for the availability of the hall. In September, the YMCA was once more in the news, but for quite different reasons: this time it was found registering a strong protest to the authorities because its buildings were being commandeered. It went unheeded, for the hour of maximum danger had struck, and Renfrew Trinity's halls had to be pressed into even greater service. No longer having a YMCA building to offer hospitality to the troops, it was left to Willie to offer his own church halls, which he did with alacrity, and with astonishing success. The minister was now to put on yet another new cap—that of catering manager. It fit perfectly!

It was at this time that *The Daily Express* in a classic *faux pas* carried the headline "THERE WILL BE NO WAR." But within days war was declared, the worst fears of the populace were realized, and the phony peace was finally and completely exposed. Not a few felt, in Enoch Powell's gloomy words, that "all was up with the Empire."

The announcement was made on Sunday morning, September 3, while Renfrew Trinity was at worship. A church officer was seen making his way up the steps of the pulpit while Willie was in full flight (appropriately, he was preaching that morning a sermon entitled "There Is No Going Back"). He paused, read the note passed on to him, and then simply announced, "I am sorry to have to tell you that war has now been declared between Great Britain and Germany. Let us pray." And with that prayer he peremptorily closed the service. There was indeed "no going back."

CHAPTER NINE

In Part Summary: Views and Method

W<small>E</small> have seen that soon after commencing his work at Renfrew, Willie received calls from various quarters to preside, speak, and preach. In this he was extending his father's principle of serving at every opportunity, whatever the group or denomination. He was also extending the reputation that he had earned as "the most popular student-preacher of his year" as he traveled all over the southwest of Scotland and sometimes further afield. We therefore pause briefly to review some of the traits of his preaching and beliefs at this significant stage in his story.

Characteristics of His Preaching

Good minister though he was, it was his preaching that set Willie to the fore in the area. Merely to peruse his sermon titles is to get an idea of his broad, human, but essentially evangelical approach, in which devotion to Christ through costly discipleship, issuing in a life of practical goodness, was the aim. There may be a significant absence of great doctrinal subjects, but the large and difficult subjects of everyday life were constantly passed under review, and the growth of the church as well as its welcoming influences are proof enough of the successfulness of his ministry at this halfway point.

The components of this ministry were fivefold. First, there was his biblical orientation. It cannot be too strongly stated that William Barclay was first and foremost a *biblical* preacher. The training he received at his home, at Motherwell's Young Men's Guild, and at the YMCA fellowship meetings, in which a conservative biblical understanding of his text was uppermost, never left him. He stated this, as part of his testament of faith, in 1976: "I am quite sure that the best background a student can have is a conservative attitude to Scripture, in which he knows and loves his Bible, and in which he is prepared to learn and to mature and to use and to benefit from the riches that scholarship and learning can bring to him."[1] We should note the broad emphasis of this statement, encompassing as it does knowing, loving, wanting to learn, maturing, and using and benefiting from scholarship's riches. We should note, too, his statement that "for me scholarship and discovering made the Bible a far greater book than ever it had been before." And to that earlier training the rich stores of scholarship (notably through W. M. Macgregor) were opened to him as he became an omnivorous and assiduous student.

This broad biblical sensitivity enriched both his pulpit and study approach. As he stated elsewhere in *Testament of Faith,* "preaching ought to be biblically and credally centred."[2] As Sir Walter Scott put it, there was "but one book" for the true Scot.[3] All others, and all other viewpoints, were subservient to it. It follows, therefore, that his thinking and his teaching must be in that sense derivative—"as a man under authority"—and that in the search to benefit from its riches, the views of scholars must be continually sought, tested, and appropriated. He took this so seriously, early and late, that he was quite willing to espouse a view that some held to be discomfitingly close to that of the Roman Catholic Church, a view that rejected the validity of private interpretation. "The second rule for the study of Scripture," he asserted (the first being an attitude of prayerful reverence), "is that it is best done within the fellowship of the Church."[4] And he quotes Peter the apostle, whom he held to be the rock on which the church was founded, to prove it: "no prophecy of Scripture is a matter of one's own interpretation." Furthermore, "it is an obvious fact that all learning begins in a fellowship of learning, and Christian learning should begin in the Christian Church." It is interesting to note that both of these emphases, regarding Peter and the church, he had also learned from W. M. Macgregor—part, no doubt, of the masterful influence he owed to his former principal and tutor.

The second component of Willie's preaching was its eloquence: his great facility with words put him in the front line of extempore speakers—though in these early years he consistently resisted the temptation to indulge in off-the-cuff discourse, favoring instead studious preparation. "I never wrote a sermon after Thursday," he confessed in *Testament of Faith.*[5] Of the early period of his ministry this was undoubtedly true, though later in his career he was not always able to maintain such an admirable habit. The very fact that he, almost uniquely among Renfrew's ministers, was able to publicize the titles of his sermons in *The Renfrew Press* week by week is a good example of his self-management here. And it is indicative of his assiduous application and forethought. He was never one of those preachers found in a dither at the weekend as to what he should preach on. Sermon series helped him in this, relieving him of potential anxiety as well as providing a directional view for his congregation: they knew what he was up to, where he was taking them. Early preparation, moreover, had another advantage: he could, at his leisure, add to his script last-minute illustrations and anecdotes that were telling just because they were freshly minted. Not unusually his Saturday evening "dose" (to use his own expression) of classical music at the Scottish National Orchestra would bring a small fund of such illustrations.

The third component of Willie's preaching was an extraordinary richness of detail drawn from his astoundingly tenacious memory, about which there was something almost superhuman. Kate stood in awe of it and on one occasion tested it. Early one evening she handed him a copy of *The Glasgow Herald* in which there was a four-column article about a complex civic matter. He read it quickly (he always read with great dispatch, long before speed-reading became popular), made one or two comments about it, and returned to other matters. Late that evening, after supper, she quizzed him on the article using a list of questions she had prepared without his knowing. Not only did he get every one right, but he was able to quote large sections of the piece verbatim. Walter Henderson recalls Willie saying on one occasion that he only need read a page of *The Glasgow Herald* twice to have its entire contents firmly engraved in his mind. With books, he deliberately worked at storing their contents in his memory by marking the text and producing his own index sheets of comment, as his salvaged notes testify.

The fourth component of his preaching was its logical accessibility and orderliness. Willie worked to organize his material, to shape and present it in an easily assimilable form. We shall see this more clearly when we examine his editorship of *The Scottish Sunday School Teacher,* but suffice it to say that he invariably used a threefold structure: an interesting introduction (he never forgot the importance of the "attack" of the musical hall artist), a lively middle section (itself usually in three parts), and a purposeful (i.e., practical) conclusion. Speaking as he was wont to do for fifteen to eighteen minutes, and sometimes for only twelve, the different sections of his message were presented in short and punchy bursts of just a few minutes each. As with his written work later, he usually commenced with a clear statement of the aim and subject that conveyed the thrust of his sermons memorably. This was later used to even greater effect in his Sunday School lesson notes, the first heading of which was as unmistakable in its directness ("AIM OF LESSON") as it was commendable in its method.

And, fifthly, his sermons reflected his fine devotional spirit, which inspired the congregation he addressed as much as it motivated the preacher. It was made up of two related aspects: reverence and love for God, which overflowed in a deep respect and love for man his creature. Many preachers have the first— some have it to such a degree that they become unaware of their congregations and, worse, of their congregations' need—but far too few have the second, which is not to be equated with a sentimental or paternalistic "caring." Willie *respected* his hearers; he was willing (like Ezekiel of old) to "sit where they sat," to understand their needs and the things necessary to speak to their needs. Like John Wesley, he was not too proud to call in the help of "a common domestic" to help him with his sermons, and on other occasions used a roadside navvy to ensure that his addresses were intelligible to those to whom he preached. Jesus himself was marked by this same dual emphasis—of love for God and for his fellowmen. Together, these features constituted that humility that ever characterized William Barclay, that humanized his work and energized his every activity, especially his preaching.

The central emphasis on Jesus that Willie maintained in his theology he maintained in his approach to men, too. He did what his Master did—he who ate and talked, laughed and drank with some of the shadiest of characters. Willie too *shared* their lives, unselfconsciously. He did not stand off from them, figuratively beating his breast and thanking God that he was not like other men or, worse still, pretending to like and respect them but never associating with them—keeping himself "unsullied from the world" by turning his back on it. People mattered to him; there was no such thing as a second-class person. The common people were the real people, those whom he sought to serve. To misunderstand this is to misunderstand William Barclay.

A most important aspect of Willie's care for the common man was the special care he took to communicate with him from the pulpit. On more than one occasion he explained the reason for his concern on this score by citing the somewhat apocryphal story of one of his visits to a bedridden parishioner: she declared that she understood him perfectly in her own home, but that she had trouble catching his meaning as soon as he mounted the pulpit. It was Willie's bemused contention that, having been chastened in this manner, he made a sincere effort to alter his preaching style in order to make his sermons more accessible. Ronnie Falconer gave the anecdote uncritical acceptance in 1977,[6] and since then it has gained considerable currency, but, like many of Willie's stories, it ought to be taken with a grain of salt with respect to its literal accuracy. I spoke to the daughter of the invalid who made the "complaint," and she assures me that Willie's sermons were as well-crafted and cogent before his visit to her mother as after. It was simply another case of Willie's self-deprecating sense of humor—and of his impish delight in crediting an aged working-class lady with having made him the "prince of communicators." On the other hand, he doubtless did pay attention to this small reminder that he was not without room for improvement in the area of his communication skills, that his pulpit pronouncements did in fact go over the heads of some members of his congregation. But the reproof he received did not so much "open his eyes to the nature of Christian communication" as it rather strengthened his resolve to communicate yet more effectively than he already did.

Willie's communication skills were in part inherited: one need only consider his father's preaching, which was remarkable for its simplicity and acceptability among the Free Churchmen of Wick, Motherwell, and elsewhere. It had little to do with the "literary essay" style that characterized many sermons of the day. We should not forget WDB's reputation as a preacher and sermon-taster of note here. He knew what men needed and knew how to put it across. His sermons had little theology, well-read though he was; they offered nothing at all to those whose predilections lay in the realm of abstract ideas and highfalutin philosophy. Mr. I. M. Mackintosh could not at first bring himself to refer to WDB's "sermons" without encasing the word in quotation marks; they were rather "several appropriate, interesting and amusing stories strung together, which captivated his congregations."[7] This reminds us of the description offered by others who heard WDB's preaching—that he was "a ranter," that being a term used to characterize the Primitive Methodists at the very time WDB was growing up and beginning his early ministry, a group under the influence of which he undoubtedly came. (A. S. Peake, it will be recalled, was among their number and did such sterling work to raise the standards of preaching and ministry at Hartley College and Manchester University. WDB was no doubt glad to see A. B. Macaulay among others recommending Peake's books in Willie's courses.) Clearly, in his preaching as in his temperance work, WDB shared much with the Primitive Methodists and other holiness groups. He did tend, in that largely precritical age, to speak "textually" (i.e., using texts as pretexts without much concern for contexts), as well as biographically and anecdotally. Not to WDB can Burns's ironic words of the preacher be applied:

> Learning, with his Greekish face,
> Grunts out some Latin ditty;
> And Common-sense is gaun.

And we must not overlook the fact that WDB's preaching was very well received, and much sought after; it filled the churches, captivated the attention of children and young people alike, and kept his Brotherhood Meetings at a high pitch of activity. In short, it worked.

And, of course, Willie by this time had many years of experience and success under his belt, his career as a preacher having begun "somewhere about 1925,"[8] almost certainly before he went to university. As we have seen, it was at the Motherwell Young Men's Guild that he first preached (though, interestingly enough, it seems that at no time before his pastoral work began did he conduct a Sunday School class). This opportunity progressed to his being appointed President of the local YMCA, a position that he maintained till his father's retirement in 1929, when they moved to Glasgow and Willie commenced his theological studies. All the evidence of this period points in the direction of his chairing and preaching ability being even then of a high caliber, much along the lines of his father. In addition to inheriting a conservatism of outlook, he also borrowed his father's practice of banging the pulpit to emphasize this or that point. (A number of his church members did not care for this and suggested he stop; he did so, forthwith!) By the time we come to his student ministry period, we find him enjoying a fine reputation, which Professor Gossip was glad to extend by personal encouragement and recommendation.

It was his preaching ability as much as anything else that convinced the elders and members of Renfrew Trinity that he was the man for the job. They "scoured Scotland" we were told, looking for a replacement for Mr. Robertson; Willie's was the name they favored. At his induction social, Willie remarked on "the succession of foremost preachers" who had preceded him, and Mr. Craig remarked on the fact that Trinity's pulpit was one of the easiest to preach in, that is, it had a receptive and appreciative congregation. The filled pews corroborated his judgment. Natural ability, the model and encouragement of a successful and godly father, and his own experience were all developed and brought to a fine pitch at Trinity.

But how did he go about pulpit work? We shall see that later he would inveigh severely against those who dare to appear before their congregation unprepared. For the minister who was "invisible all week, and incomprehensible on Sunday" Willie had no time.

In his occasional pieces gathered together by Denis Duncan in *Through the Year with William Barclay,* he refers to the notebooks that he kept as a young minister. Fortunately for us one of these survived the clear-outs, and it throws interesting light on his style and habits of work. It is a simple fifty-four-page exercise book entitled *Children's Talks.* Under this title on the cover appears a list of the contents:

1. Difficulties: J. L. Baird
2. Our Part and the Church
3. The Church at Work
4. The Magpie's Nest

Inside, in his impressive but almost illegible handwriting (in green ink), he details the outline of his talks on alternative pages, so as to allow for entry of additional material or comment. It is typical that four talks appear on the cover, whereas there are actually twelve in the book itself! The others are "For a Promotion Service," "Light," "Trouble-makers," "Sacraments," "Play the Game," "Our Good Queen: Address for a Children's Service," "Shaving," and "The Hard Way."

Every word was written out and the outlines were entered in the record, to be used or altered as the need determined. Having made himself thoroughly familiar with his material, into the pulpit he would go, his astonishing memory facilitating his delivery. He would deliver his talk as if speaking impromptu, but behind it stood hard work, careful thinking, and choice expression—and the written notes.

If Falconer was wrong in accepting too easily Willie's explanation of the origin of his communicative powers, he is not wrong when he refers to it as "a quest": it was indeed a lifelong attempt to make ever more acceptable the content and manner of his speaking, even as he sought continuously to refine and develop its ends.

We turn now to five pieces he produced in this early period—some written, some reported—that set forth his views on various quite different matters, show the range and color of his thinking, and indicate the lines along which his writing and thinking were developing in these "apprentice years."

The Immortal Memory

On the 25th of January each year, Scotland is given over to the celebration of its national bard, Rabbie Burns, on whom more orations have been delivered than on any other poet in the United Kingdom, perhaps the world. More than seven hundred editions of his works have been published, and there is no sign that interest in him is diminishing. It is all part of Willie's full-blooded humanity that he was a devotee (as well as a critic) of Burns, and a ready champion of his work, as Renfrew learned early in his ministry. He remained for many years one of its best-known toasters to "the immortal memory." This is somewhat curious in that WDB seems not to have spared much time for Burns; his grandfather would scarcely have understood him, and there is little in his son's or grandson's lives to suggest interest of this sort either. It may be an influence more from Willie's mother's side, though the godly Daniel McLeish must have been made to feel more than a little uncomfortable at some of the poet's extravagances, and some of his sallies against the *unco guid* mentality. We may be nearer the mark in seeing this enjoyment of Burns as one of his youthful rebellions, one that rang bells for his "common touch" ideology. In dealing with Burns's humanity, we are very near the core of Willie's own, his affection for the classics notwithstanding.

The first full reports of his exploits in this area come from 1935, when he so impressed the local paper that it reported his address almost verbatim, to the tune of a two-and-a-half-column report. The headlines declared "THERE WAS A LAD: MEMORABLE EVENING IN TRINITY CHURCH HALL,"[9] and the article applauded the "inspiring address" Willie had delivered. First, he gave his assessment of the place of the poet in the affections of his countrymen:

> Never was a poet better loved than Burns, and never one more truly the poet of his country and his people. For it can be said of him what can be said of no other book except the Bible itself, that were every line of his poetry lost, and every copy of his works destroyed, we should yet be able to recover every syllable that he wrote from the memories of those who treasure and remember his lightest word. So truly is he the heritage of his nation, so truly the poet of his fellow-countryman, that there is no one however poor and unlettered who cannot repeat a line of what he wrote, and does not remember some story that he told and some counsel that he gave.

We might feel today that such Celtic effusion is overwrought, but we cannot deny the magnificence of his zeal for the bard, nor need we doubt the rapturous welcome the appraisal received. It is significant that the first characteristic that Willie highlighted was Burns's charm, which was then as much a quality of Willie as of his hero. He describes this charm in terms of Burns's delight in simple things—in "the common things of life." It was in "the sacredness and the holiness of the things which lie on the doorstep of every man" that he excelled; he saw "the beating heart in every blade of grass." The address, like many others, fairly bristles with telling quotations, apposite allusions and insights. He reminds his hearers of Burns's love for the little, ordinary things of life by citing his treatment of the humblest flower of the field, the daisy; by referring to the field mouse's home; by mentioning the louse on the lady's bonnet; and by his "Address to the Toothache." Space forbids the amount of citation that *The*

Renfrew Press afforded, but we pause to sample an early ecological consciousness that delighted Willie:

> I'm truly sorry man's dominion
> Has broken Nature's social union,
> An' justifies that ill opinion
>   Which makes thee startle
> At me, thy poor earth-born companion,
>   An' fellow mortal!

Willie's feelings for common humanity were so heartfelt that he too, like the bard, could describe even a common rodent as a "fellow mortal." Kate's views were more down-to-earth. To be sure, there is much in the poem to a mouse who has lost her nest that Willie in a sober theological mood would not have accepted: the bard's pessimism and his fear of the future fly in the face of all that Willie stood for and believed; but it is idle to take these into account. It is poetry—to be felt, not thought—and that which failed to stir the blood or move the emotions was scarcely real to Willie.

But there was moral depth in Burns, too, which "gave him thoughts that go out beyond the world," as when he quotes the reflections on the louse on the lady's bonnet and draws the moral, "O' wad some po'er the giftie gi'e us/ To see oursel's as ithers see us." It was, says Willie, "with a certain hand" that Burns drew the lessons from life; indeed "everything turned out to him a song, and before it was done, he made it a sermon." And herein spoke the avid disciple, who was careful to repeat the lessons with telling power in his own work. The lesson did not go unnoticed, for we see it in equal power in Willie's remarkable ability to produce his own "parables of life." These were also low-key examples, drawn with a hand like that of the poet from everyday subjects, with which Willie enticed the imagination of his hearers before leading them to a deeper dimension.

Burns was no sentimental rhymer; he commented on life. Other qualities lifted him into the ranks of the immortals, which Willie went on to describe and illustrate: his scorn and hatred of hypocrisy and his abomination of sinning in secret, "which turned his stomach" ("Holy Willie's Prayer" is cited). "Cant, hypocrisy, long prayers at the street corner, solemn, bland, smug, self-satisfied respectability were repugnant to Rabbie Burns, as they are to all who inherit his warm heart and impulsive nature." He and Willie had much in common: a despising of the *unco guid,* the smug, and the self-satisfied—and those who more often than not "had the east wind in their voices" (that being one of the few terms of opprobrium in Willie's vocabulary).

Another quality Willie found congenial was Burns's love of independence; "there is none so proud and independent as the Scottish peasant at his best," he explains. He also admired the bard's "wide sympathy and understanding," his freedom from the narrowness of a censorious mind, and the "gentleness of touch upon human frailty that his own great heart must have taught him." We might well comment that these are subjective judgments, and that in one sense they are more an unconscious self-portrait of Willie than a straightforward portrayal of Burns himself. It is a feature not uncommon throughout Willie's work, a product of his inclination to find the good and the positive wherever possible and to defend them even in the meanest of creatures and human conditions. He would, like Abraham Lincoln of old, ever prefer to plant flowers than pluck weeds. He who insisted upon spending the day with the hated tax collector Zacchaeus, he who censured the Pharisees and refused to condemn the adulteress, he who went out of his way to find the five-times-married woman even then "living in sin" to make of her a prize for the church cannot be displeased with this modern-day exemplification of that same spirit.

"The highest things in life," Willie continued, "are not wanting either, despite his wayward conduct." He believed there is more real theology in Burns's "The Cotter's Saturday Night" than in anything else produced by him, and reminded the audience of the need to fulfill—as Burns unhappily did not—such excellent counsel as the following:

> And O! be sure to fear the Lord alway,
> And mind your duty, duly, morn and night!
> Lest in temptation's path ye gang astray,
> Implore his counsel and assisting might,
> They never sought in vain that sought the Lord aright.

Nor did he forget to mention the poet's self-awareness in personal failing:

> Fain would I say,
>   Forgive my foul offence
> Fain promise never more to disobey
>   But should mine author health again dispense
> Again I might desert fair virtue's sway;
> Again in folly's path might go astray;
> Again exalt the brute and sink the man
> Then how should I for heavenly mercy pray
> Who act so counter heavenly mercy's plan,
> Who sin so often have mourned, yet to temptation ran?

And again he prays:

> Where weakness has come short,
> Of frailty stepped aside,
> Do thou all good—for such thou art—
> In shades of darkness hide.

> Where with intention I have erred,
> No other plea I have,
> But thou art good and goodness still
> Delighteth to forgive.

In the spirit of that vision of goodness—the high-toned elements of Philippians 4:8 and of planting flowers rather than plucking weeds—Willie then described the song "which will be sung so long as there are two Scots to join hands and to think of home and friends that are away and are gone" in a passage that demonstrates to us his power of writing sound and stirring prose:

> It was the twilight of an autumn evening when the shadows are falling and Burns was sitting alone in the parlour of Poosie Nancy's Inn in the town of Mauchline. And Burns's thoughts were long and sad, for he had trysted to meet there Maclaren, his life-long friend, for the last time. The friend of his life was leaving Scotland to go to Carolina, and in these days there was little hope of ever seeing him again or even hearing of him. Darker and darker the shadows fell, till Nancy herself came ben.
>
> "Will I give you a light, Rab? Its getting dark."
>
> But Burns preferred to be alone with his thoughts. And just then there passed the window an old and blind fiddling beggar-man, playing an old Scotch tune. At this point the strains of "Auld Lang Syne" were heard, becoming louder, and then fainter as they passed away. And then there came the sound of horses' hoofs and Maclaren was in the room.
>
> "Ah, Rab," he said, "this is terrible! Here is an end of all our ploys and tricks and times together, and I go away, and you will forget."
>
> And so "Auld Lang Syne" came into being.

"I ask you," concluded the speaker triumphantly, "to charge your glasses and to drink with me the immortal memory of Rabbie Burns." The men of Trinity Church Men's Club so drank, triumphantly.

There can be no denying the pure entertainment of such an address, even when it comes to us second- or third-hand today. The entertainment was made the instrument of deeper things: another example of his "threshold evangelism." (In 1937, and again in 1941 and 1942, Willie returned to the theme in an evening sermon, "Robert Burns: The Glory and the Shame.")

The Possibility of Impossibilities

The Burns Supper address was given to those he knew, and among whom he was known. A very different case presented itself in the occasional articles he published in *The Renfrew Press*. We have already seen what an impact he made in the community when "The Secret of Happiness" was published in 1933. Shortly after he had delivered the Burns address Willie wrote another article for the paper that also elicited a marked response.[10] By both the spoken and the written word he was making good his calling, honing the instrument of communication which one day would be employed phenomenally.

It was his second "secular" piece, reflecting all the techniques of his "threshold evangelism" style, not least his optimism, but this time applying the truth of the gospel in conclusion. Moreover, it is one of the most self-reflective pieces that he ever wrote, albeit unselfconsciously. Apart from its ebullient optimism, we should note its jibe at the Oxford intellectual (we may well ask ourselves if history is in fact merely "the experience of mankind at large") as well as his appreciation of the indomitable will of the dynamic, hurrying man in general and Robert Moffat in particular. The emphasis on manliness is strong, and its opposite is denigrated. This is not to say that he celebrates mindless man, all brawn and bullying; rather he promotes the idea of the spiritual man, the practical visionary whose imagination is sanctified and fired and directed by "a man who was also God." Such a man was Willie's real hero and model, and such he strove to become. I reproduce it in full here, retaining the headings inserted by the editor.

Man, Plus an Idea: Possibilities and Impossibilities

—by the Rev. Wm. Barclay

THERE is a strange streak of unteachableness in the nature of man. From his own experience a man does learn something simply because he must. A man with a bad digestion soon learns by force that there are some things which he will do well not to eat. But from the experience of mankind at large, which is called history, he will not learn, because it requires some effort of mind and intellect to do so, and so a man who is a pessimist seems incapable of learning the lesson that history declares to him, that he ought by all the facts to become an optimist.

Men are strangely slow to learn and to believe that the phrase "nothing is impossible" is not merely a preacher's tag and an orator's exaggeration, but a cold statement of indisputable fact. Somewhere Boreham reminds us of Alice in Wonderland when she was pursuing the White Rabbit—"For, you see, so many out-of-the-way things had happened to her that Alice had begun to think that very few things indeed were really impossible." And so many "out-of-the-way things" have happened to the world that by this time we ought to be at least beginning to learn that very few things are impossible.

It is strange how history seems to echo with a sort of sardonic laughter at the men who talked of things as impossible. C. L. Hodgson in a recent book tells us that there was a certain eminent Oxford mathematician once, a Doctor Lardner, who published a treatise to prove that no steamship could ever cross the Atlantic Ocean; and by a hilarious jest of fortune, the steamer Sirius a few weeks later, actually took the first copies of the treatise across the Atlantic to America. And this same prophet of the impossible also "staked his reputation as a man of science" before the House of Commons, on his statement that no railway train could ever go faster than ten miles an hour, and the slightest curve would immediately throw it off the track. How the fates must have chuckled with laughter at such prophecies!

Again Boreham tells us what happened to Robert Moffat, the missionary, when he set out for Namaqualand. The people of the Cape lamented over his certain destruction. "The great Chief, Africaner, will tear you to pieces," they said. "He will strip off your skin and make a drum of it to dance to," said one. "He will make a drinking cup of your skull," said another. Yet, in a few weeks Moffat and Africaner were friends and comrades in Christian service. Again the fates must have laughed at the prophets of impossibility.

1. Mistakes in Thinking

All this deluded talk of impossibilities comes of the fact that we make certain radical mistakes in our thinking. For instance, because we have never seen a thing done, we call that thing impossible. I suppose that if you had told Columbus that someone would sail to America in about four days in a ship over a thousand feet long, he would have said, "Impossible." Or I suppose that if you had told Captain Cook that someone would one day fly to Australia in less than a week, he, too, would have said, "Impossible." If you had told our great-grandfathers that you could send telegrams along wires they would have laughed at you; and if you had told our grandfathers that you could send telegrams without wires they would have been for locking you up in some safe place. They had not seen these things done, and therefore they declared them impossible.

Again we tend to call things impossible simply because they take a very long time to do. It is characteristic of man that he wants things done in a hurry, that he wants actually to see them being done, and when they cannot be done that way he is apt to say, that they are impossible. To take a very slight instance: a man finds a knot on a bit of string. He says after a moment's effort, "It's impossible to unravel this," and so he takes a knife and cuts it. It was not impossible at all; it simply would have taken a considerable time. As someone long ago succinctly put it, "The only difference between the difficult and the impossible is that the impossible takes a little time longer."

Now all this is not to say that the impossible is the easy thing and that it will fall gently into our laps if we wait on it coming. Far from it. The achievement of the impossible demands certain definite conditions for its fulfilment.

For one thing "it demands a man." And a man in the full sense of the term is a unique and an extraordinary phenomenon. It demands a man who is not content simply to be like other men and to do what other men do. Somewhere R. L. Stevenson once wrote something to the effect that to stop saying "Amen" to all that the world says is the only way to keep your soul alive. And the man who also refuses tamely to acquiesce in everything which satisfies his more lethargic fellow mortals is also the man who will perform the impossibilities. Edison is once reported to have said that he never attempted possible things and that impossibilities were the only things that were worth trying. For the achievement of the impossible it is necessary that there should be a man like that, a man who is in the fullest sense of the term a man, and not just one of the mass produced, machine-made articles, which all conform to the same pattern with a dull lack of initiative and originality.

2. A Vision Essential

And for another thing, "the man must be a man plus an idea." Before a man can attempt to achieve the impossible he must have a vision. At some time in his life he must have been raised and lifted out of the common way of things and been granted a flash of insight and vision of the things which may be. And that is just to say that he will be a man in whose soul there dwells a want and a discontent. So long as a man is satisfied with things as they are he will never make things as they ought to be. To achieve the impossible he must have an idea born of a vision which was cradled in dissatisfaction with things as they are.

And for a third thing, not only a man and a man plus an idea is required to produce the impossible, "but the man with the idea must be as certain, as he is that night follows day, that there is a way towards his idea." It is no use to have an idea and then to be ignorant of the path that leads to its realisation. He must know the way. To most of us the way to impossibilities is an utter black darkness without a way, but just as to the skilled sailor a black night is nothing of any consequence because he knows the way, so to the man who will achieve the impossible the darkness is a little thing because he knows the way through.

3. Finding the Way

Somewhere H. M. Tomlinson in one of his books tells of a man who was making a voyage in a little boat from Singapore to a little place on the way to Bangkok called Tampat. The voyager was with the Captain on the bridge one pitch-black night. "I can't make out, Captain," he said, "how you find your way in a darkness like this." "Find my way?" said the Captain, "this darkness is nothing. It is a fine night. I know my course. There is the compass. The darkness is nothing. I keep my course. Tomorrow we shall be off Tampat. I know where I am."

We have talked much of impossibilities in these troubled post-war [i.e., post-World War I] days. We have talked of the impossibility of a world without crime, without war, without evil. We have talked of the impossibility of a nation without an army and battleships and aeroplanes and weapons of destruction.

Are they impossibilities? There was a man who was also God who lived nearly two thousand years ago and He talked impossible things about making men new all over again, about turning cowards into rocks of heroism, of making mud-stained sinners shine with a wondrous purity, *and He made His impossibilities come true*. It is in His following, in the Christ-spirit that the impossibilities become facts. A man, a man plus an idea, a man plus an idea who knows the way, and a man with the spirit of Christ in his heart will in truth achieve the impossible. And the world only awaits such men.

There are some lines by Edgar A. Guest:

> Some said that it couldn't be done,
>   But he with a chuckle replied
> That maybe it couldn't, but he would be one
> Who wouldn't say so till he tried.
>
> So he buckled right on with the trace of a grin
> On his face. If he worried he hid it.
> He started to sing as he tackled the thing
> That couldn't be done—and he did it!

"Remember these lines," Willie concluded, his gaze resting unwaveringly on the impossible situation in which they lived. Willie's Professor Macaulay had warned that with his accent "it couldn't be done," but Willie did it—not only with a chuckle, but with a flourish and a prayer, and if not actually with a grin then certainly with a knowing gleam in his eye!

What Shall We Do with Sunday?

For decades now there had been misgiving in Scotland over the use of "the Sabbath" (a designation of the Christian Sunday Willie was to deny firmly). As early as 8 April 1934, he had preached a sermon entitled "What Shall We Do with Sunday?"

In 1936, with newfound wealth but not the leisure time to use it, the subject of Sunday usage had spurred heated discussion in the locality. One minor battle concerned the low-flying aircraft at Moorpark, which considerably disrupted services on Sunday mornings. In this the churches scored a complete victory: flying was prohibited in this area from 11.00 to 12.30 hours. There had been consternation as well aroused by the Glasgow crowds that tended to invade Renfrew in the summer months to get to the steamers (MacBrayne's sea and loch tours were almost as popular as London's Green Line bus tours at this time) and to enjoy the parks and countryside. The "breaking of the Sabbath" reached heinous proportions when vandalism was added to it, for material ownership has a peculiar way of making a religious principle its own.

The problem came to a head when it touched a vital nerve in every Scot—the question of his Sunday golf. So *The Renfrew Press* organized a plebiscite to ascertain the mind of the people; and in order to give the churches a fairer chance of winning the argument, it called on local ministers to offer their views in a series of articles. Willie, by now well-known as an innovative minister, an upholder of traditional views, and a reputed golfer, was a natural choice. His answer, presumably an expansion of his earlier sermon on the topic, was not to be his last word on the subject, but it does provide some interesting insights into his early, somewhat ambivalent stance on the issue at this point in his career.

What Shall We Do with Sunday?

—by the Rev. Wm. Barclay

WE of the twentieth century have travelled a very long way from those days in which John Ruskin could say that he looked forward with dread to the coming of the Sunday. We have travelled far from those days in which Sunday was a day of drawn blinds and funereal drabness; when every book except the Bible was banished; when the Sunday was a day of compulsory attendance at services of wearisome length; and when everything that legitimately might be done on a Monday was forbidden on a Sunday. We have indeed travelled far from these days. But to-day the question arises, "Are we in danger of travelling too far?" "Is there not a line at which to call a halt?" "Was there not some grain of truth buried, however deeply, in the older and the stricter ways?" In any discussion of the place of Sunday we may start with a point upon which all alike will be agreed.

It is a fact beyond dispute that one day of rest in the seven is not merely something desirable, it is essential, for physical and for mental reasons if for nothing else. It is significant that in the days of the French Revolution they tried to banish the Sunday along with the old order of things; but they found that they had to bring it back because the health of the people was suffering from the lack of rest. It is noteworthy that Cobden spoke in Parliament of the Sunday, "which seems to have been particularly adapted to the needs of mankind." It is to be remembered that Lord Macaulay in a most eloquent and notable passage stated his conviction that of the day when things were at a standstill, when the stock exchange was silent and the workshop at rest and the market place empty, there was a process just as important and just as essential going on, for on that day, man, like a clock, was being wound up to return with redoubled vigour to his work on the Monday. The day of rest was not a thing to make a nation poorer but richer by far. On the necessity of a day of rest there will be no difference of opinion.

1. What Is Rest?

The point is, what do we mean by rest and how shall we use this day of rest? It may be said that the best rest is not to do nothing; but that the best rest is change of scene and change of occupation. That admittedly is so. But here we have a guiding principle. If Sunday is a day of rest it must be a day of rest for everyone and we have no right to make others work for our pleasure and for our enjoyment. That is one of the condemnations of Sunday excursions by train or bus or steamer, of Sunday theatres, and Sunday restaurants and the like. To demand such things is to demand that engineers and drivers, waiters, porters, cooks, attendants of all kinds should have to work for other people's pleasure on the day that ought to be the day of rest.

That is not to say that all such services should be suspended. There must be some means of transit and some place where the traveller may have shelter and food; there must be some work under the conditions of modern industry. But such work should be limited to such as is essential and no one should be forced to work simply that others should enjoy themselves on what should be a day of rest for all alike. Now, so far as we have gone, we have spoken only of the physical side of the matter. No machine can be driven relentlessly all the time without rest. A man's body and still more a man's mind is the most delicate of all machines, and less than any can it do without its period of rest. But, besides having a body, a man has also a soul. And it is with the needs of the soul that the spiritual side of the Sunday deals.

2. The Soul Forgotten?

In the days of the week, amidst the press of business and amidst the many calls upon his time and attention, a man is very apt to forget that he has a soul. Further, the days of the week bring with them a constant stream of temptations and difficulties which try the strength of a man's soul. It is, therefore, very necessary that on that one day of the week a man should remember that he has a soul, that there is a God, and that he should see to the developing and the strengthening of the sinews of his soul. That is to say that on that one day, a man should make some attempt to meet God; and where will he be more likely to come into contact with God than in God's House and amidst God's people?

It is easy to say that a man may meet God better in the open air and in the countryside and amongst the hills. And it is true to say so of some few people; but it is sheer nonsense to say that the vast majority of Sunday hikers, cyclists and excursionists go into the country to commune with God. They do not; and for the great part of men corporate worship is the way to God. But it is possible for someone to say, as indeed many do say, "May I not go to Church and worship in the morning and then take my golf clubs and go to the golf links in the afternoon?" That indeed is the question that is at stake.

We have already dealt with the fact that to do so would make others work for our pleasure on what ought to be a universal day of rest. That is the physical side; but there is a spiritual side too. And the point is this; there are some things which will not mix. Suppose you decide to go to church in the morning and to golf in the afternoon. Man is so constituted that to get any good out of anything he must concentrate and think of one thing at a time. If he decides to mix up his golf and his Church attendance either he thinks so much of the coming golf at the church service that he gets no good out of the Church or else during the golf he thinks so much of what he heard at the service that he plays a bad game. The two things cannot be mixed: to get the maximum good out of each they have to be kept separate.

3. Sabbath Made for Man

The whole of a Christian community's duty in the matter of Sunday observance can be summed up in the saying of Jesus, "The Sabbath was made for man and not man for the Sabbath." Although the Sabbath and the Sunday are not the same the principle applies alike to both. And the principle means that whatever else Sunday may be, it must never be a tyranny. A religion of tyranny and a worship by compulsion is a bondage to men and an abomination to God.

The words of Jesus mean that whenever the Sunday is being used to the ultimate good of men it is being used well. It will so be used when it is used as a day of rest and when men do not force other men to work that they may enjoy themselves; and above all it will be used when every act in it is ordered by the remembrance that it is the day to think of the soul and of its strengthening and renewing. We do not want to go back to the days when the Sunday was a weariness to the flesh; but neither do we want to go on to a day when selfish pleasure rules supreme, or when men try the impossible in mixing the material and the spiritual in such a way that they benefit by neither.

Interesting as it is as a document showing Willie's thinking and writing, this article cannot claim (especially at the end of section two) to present the most cogent argumentation on the subject. It shows that he was wont merely to string comments together rather than to engage in genuine argumentation in the deeper sense of logical development and reasoning. He has scarcely made an airtight case; for this subject there is none. I fear he was conscious of the weakness of his case, though concerned to deny it through an emotional appeal to tradition. To suggest that "man is so constituted that to get any good out of anything he must concentrate and think of one thing at a time" and to conclude from that that he ought not to "mix up his golf and his Church attendance" is surely special pleading of the worst sort.

No one, certainly not Willie, thought that the whole of Sunday was to be given over exclusively to thoughts of the church and related things; nevertheless, he could not at this point bring himself to say so, since he feared that to do so would open the door to exactly what many then wanted: freedom of action. He is caught in the classic dilemma of admiring the principle of freedom but doubting that man can be trusted to use it properly. We shall see how his thinking changes in this regard (within two decades), and how it came to affect even groups within his own church. For the moment he remains a traditionalist, impaled on the horns of a discomfiting dilemma.

Willie and War

It is not surprising that anyone brought up in a home where the father, strong-minded and dominant and a vociferous leader in the cause of peace, who (unlike Colonel McLeish, his father-in-law) had never taken to arms, should point his son in that direction. Through his involvement in the International Brotherhood Movement, and his work on behalf of local branches of the League of Nations, WDB showed how that cause could be served—how, indeed, it *must* be served, as a corollary of the gospel. And in doing so, he gave Willie an example of loyalty to the ideal that (unlike his views on Sunday) never left him.

Willie had learned of the terrors of war not only by way of the literature and cinema of the period, but more pointedly and personally: at the impressionable age of eleven, as we have seen, his revered cousin (and no one can be more looked up to in the mind of an only child than a cousin who takes to the colors, wins an early commission, and does battle on the fields of France) was killed in most despairing circumstances. WDB never failed to drive home the waste of his nephew's life to Willie and others. And what Willie had learned at home was reinforced in college, when both sides of the question were dealt with, Principal W. M. Macgregor making the point his cousin and successor G. H. C. Macgregor was soon to make on a worldwide platform for the Fellowship of Reconciliation. (Macgregor did not take up his post at Trinity College till 1934, after Willie had left; their really fruitful relationship commenced in 1946, though he and Willie did rub shoulders in the meantime, most notably when Willie delivered his Bruce Lectures in 1937.) By December 1936, Macgregor's book *The New Testament Basis of Pacifism* was launched with considerable publicity and excellent reviews.

It was in November 1936 in Renfrew that Willie first declared himself publicly to be a pacifist. On 21 June 1935 he had preached before his own congregation on the subject of "Christianity and War" (though this attracted little attention), and he had also chaired meetings for the League of Nations before this, so his views were not unknown. But this occasion was different: he was now fighting for a deeply held principle which he felt—and we must not minimize this—threatened a most vital aspect of Christian faith and life itself. The speech in which he made the announcement cannot have been lengthy, since three films were also shown at the meeting he addressed (one of the films featured Professor Joad; the second, a German film entitled *Kameradschaft*—"Fellowship"—told the story of France; and the third dealt with the frontier problems of Germany following the Great War).

Willie was in no mood to pull punches, living up to Merricks Arnot's description of his fearlessness in speaking out against "what he considered to be evil and wrong in every form." "War," Willie bluntly stated, "is mass murder."[11] He pointed out that every man had to face the problem and resolve it for himself; he condemned both the church and the League: the one for failing to take a definite moral stand, the other for its failure to act effectively. He spoke of the seriousness of the armament buildup, which created distrust and acted as a standing invitation to make war. He noted that during the past thousand years, a year of war had been waged for every year of peace, urging his audience to take that fact more seriously. Moreover (a telling comment, if not exactly true), he suggested that theirs was the *first* generation ever to make the stand for peace, the *first* to make of the problem a moral principle:

> The greatest men of the churches have stood for war in the days gone by. Statesmen and leaders of the churches believed in the rightness and inevitability of war. We have now broken away from that idea.

This sense of innovation, of making progress in the history of ideas, was very important for Willie: Forward, not backward! It is a fact of history that the church to this time had accepted the need for war and soldiery, had allowed for such in its creeds and confessions. Even Willie's beloved Bunyan had been a soldier in the Parliamentary Army. Only in the dominical and apostolic periods had total pacifism been maintained, though even that may be disputed. Willie was thus recalling the church and society to that standard. He further called society to denounce "the romance of war" on which children are brought up, to expose and acknowledge it as a lie. He knew that antiwar speeches involved their adherents in trouble. Wisely, he was not attacking those who had fought in the last war, but he was appealing to them to prevent a fresh outbreak. The war to end all wars had not done so; they must now do so by other means, he argued: by a decisive rejection of the war principle.

As a first step toward such a goal, he continued, the stockpiling of arms had to be halted. They were no guarantee of protection; they were, to the contrary, an incitement to violence. "We must pull down the barriers between nations," he declared, "not build them." He referred to "the pitiably small contribution" to this building task the League had made; the Germans and the Americans were not even members of it! And he again warned the church of its failures to inspire peace and peacemaking. He quoted Earl Haig's comment to the churches—"Your business is to make my business impossible"—disregarded then as now.

It was at this juncture that Willie began to develop a strikingly new perspective: the church had failed, and the League had failed, he argued, and therefore "we must not leave this to any organisation *or church*," but, as responsible individuals, act upon it ourselves. "It is *our* duty to make war unthinkable in any part of the world," he concluded. The significance of this argument lies, of course, in his call to transfer power from the authorities to the individual, not anarchistically, but nonetheless definitely. It was a direct appeal to the electorate, the populace. We shall come to see that this inclination pervades his career and work. He was a "popularizer" not because he enjoyed the exposure, the thrill of the platform, the ecstasy of the media, but because he believed in the populace: the common men and women. He loved the saying of Abraham Lincoln that God must love the common people, because he made so many of them. He was against elitism in any form. He despised committees for being obstructive, self-perpetuating, and inefficient, and he steadfastly declined the invitations of the various bureaucracies that sought to ingest him. He had little respect for them, except and insofar as they acted courageously. Self-important functionaries, careerists, and timeservers were collectively an abomination to him. He only took power in order to effect his work, and then he used it not by pulling rank—that least effective and most juvenile mode of leadership—but by convincing argumentation, by example, by encouragement, and by friendly inducement. One of his favorite sayings was that of Cromwell—"I beseech you, by the bowels of Christ, to think it possible that you may be mistaken." That was Willie's way: the way of entreatment, the way of trust, the way of tolerance—the way of Christ.

The subtitle the newspaper gave to this address was "A Stirring Appeal for Peace," but unhappily it stirred some in different ways. The Auld Kirk minister at Inchinnan objected to Willie's criticisms of the League and to his descriptions of the horrors of war (it was an age when the details of automobile accidents and the like were described unsparingly, and Willie's powers of description were always effectively evocative). Willie's ecclesiastical antagonist appealed to the townspeople to join the League of Nations and to take it more seriously. He urged them to commence a local branch and make it effective.

Mr. Sawyer's censures did not serve to alter Willie's stand, however, for he returned to the subject at a YMCA fellowship meeting some weeks later, speaking on "War and Peace."[12] It has to be confessed that he said little concerning peace, and how it may be achieved. Perhaps he realized it was a futile dream. War was now his bogey. If anything, he pressed further in describing its horrors, adding details from the wars in Abyssinia, Spain, and China. He put great emphasis on the sheer waste of war (his economic sensitivities were finely tuned in those deprived days), and he dealt in turn with the brutal destruction of human life and dignity, the wanton spoiling of artistic creations (one of his relaxations was found in architecture—always the first to suffer in armed conflict), and the elimination of civilization's finest gains. He feared that another war would mean the collapse of Western civilization, returning them to the dark ages. He pointed out that the cost of one battleship was equivalent to that of fifteen thousand houses, that one tenth of Britain's annual armament expenditures would relieve British hospitals of all pressing needs for the next five hundred years. (The reforms in national health and social security were as yet unfulfilled.)

Why did not men prefer, he asked, the way of sanity and peace? He did not offer his own answers, but discussed instead the idea of the history of the race being essentially the history of the individual and made this the basis of his appeal. Once more we see a return to his principle of going directly to the public over the heads of the powers that be. It is also typical of him not to become personally embroiled in party politics. His denunciation of war was one thing, a clear-cut moral issue, but actual proposals for peace or appeasement he left to others. It was ever his approach, reflecting the regular position of the ministers of the Church of Scotland who were involved so far as moral issues were concerned and in line with the doctrine of the church being "the conscience of the people," to stay aloof, or at least apart, from party issues.[13] He asserted that humanity's salvation lay not in the League of Nations (despite its valuable work), nor in the church (for its present constitution inhibited that—a curious remark to which

197

we must return), but in Christianity solely, as if that was generally perceived to be different from the church! "Only the loving Spirit of Christ would bring all the nations into a single brotherhood. But we, individually, must each contribute towards the consummation of the ideal."

We have running together now two aspects of his thinking: his pacifism, which addressed the social and political realities of the day head-on (though not without sharp criticism of the general attitudes which obtained), and an essentially Free-Church attitude that sought to divorce religion from the affairs of state, to separate the Kingdom of God from the kingdom of the world. This latter view is not strictly an "antiestablishment" line; he does not reach the point at which he actually denies the validity of the establishment, but he does criticize it very strongly, at a time when others were seeking to strengthen it. He even suggests that humanity's future, its "salvation" no less, lies elsewhere. It would be interesting to hear what presbytery made of this, but we have no record of any comments its members may have made, and in any case Willie was now more or less a stranger to its counsels—he had attended but one of its gatherings in 1935, one in the following year, none this year (1937), and he would attend only one in 1938. Busy beyond telling in the affairs of parish, the Scottish Sunday School Union (SSSU), and university, he had no intention of expending more labor in mere committee work, at least one step removed from what he felt to be his real work and opportunity. In this he was unrepentant.

November each year provided the perfect opportunity to reflect on the cost of armed conflict, in the Remembrance Day services (then called Armistice Day). Willie's outspokenness had caused sufficient interest, not to say irritation, to warrant the editor to invite him to present another article on the issues now being hotly controverted. Only three weeks had elapsed since the last installment; the next was to achieve banner headlines: "PACIFISM: THE ONLY WAY."[14] He had firmly nailed his colors to the mast; there could be no withdrawing now. War on war had been declared.

It was Dean Inge who once commented that "no one can govern who cannot afford to be unpopular." Unpopularity mattered little to Willie, the arch-popularizer. Psychologically it was a bad time to launch an attack on militarism or to attempt to demonstrate its uselessness and unreasonableness.[15] Willie, always an empathetic pastor, well knew that many hearts would be especially sore at this time as they recalled loved ones now dead in the cause of the war, and that his message would be even less popular among those who led injury-diminished lives, who would unavoidably interpret his criticisms as a full frontal attack on what they had stood for and suffered. It was thus he approached his church, which was ever appreciative of "a bonnie fechter," to assume a position in which he was outnumbered on every side, with almost no back-up support.

Willie astutely commenced his Remembrance Day campaign by emphasizing the importance of showing gratitude (one of his foremost virtues, after all) to those who had suffered and fought in the Great War. But the very enormity of their sacrifice, he neatly urged his readers, was the most potent argument for ensuring that it must not happen again: "there are none who do not pray that there shall never be a recurrence of the grim happenings of 1914–18." He reiterated points he had already made in the preceding months: the breakdown of civilization, the horrors of combat, the "proficiency of killing which has now reached such a pitch of diabolical perfection," the prospect of the "miniature gas-mask which will soon be part of every child's school bag," and the economic aspects—"a curiously unproductive form of national expenditure." Returning to his criticism of the League of Nations, he acknowledged that it had done good work "stopping famines and the like," but he argued that the point of "the League was not to stop famines, but fights." It was not enough for it to be a forum for debate, he insisted; it must have teeth. The only way to enable it to fulfill its real function was "to give it the biggest force of all"—which would only be a kind of "reduction to absurdity" (he pointedly translated the Latin phrase into English, as was his practice) of an institution pledged to the securing of peace; and yet, failing this there was no way it could guarantee security.

On the positive side, he asserted that the only kind of pacifism that could work was Christian pacifism, a pacifism that accepts the Christian way: "It is no exaggeration to say that the future of the world lies in the hands of the Christian faith. . . . It is the lesson of the history of Christianity itself that the way to ultimate and lasting victory is the way of non-resistance and of pacifism."[16] He recalls John Milton's phrase "the irresistible might of weakness" to urge nonresistance, pure and simple, to which he adds the moral argument against killing: "If there is any sense in Christian teaching at all, it surely teaches that there is no case in which I am justified in taking another man's life. No man was ever commanded to kill in Christ's name." That, for Willie Barclay, clinched the matter—the biblical (i.e., the New Testament) record and injunction. The struggle, he therefore argued, was "between Christian and non-Christian forces," and "it can only be won as it was won before—by those who profess the faith," who "have courage enough to follow their convictions to the logical conclusion." He knew what that conviction might mean: "It may mean a sacrifice that would astonish the world; and it may mean that in order to save others a man must be content not to save himself."

The application of his beliefs here—at once theological and ethical—is as naked as a needle, and just as sharp. There have been few public men willing to state their case as baldly as this, which does not stop short of putting everything on the line in the cause of a minority principle, even loved ones and life itself. The article precipitated a lively discussion, not to say a howl of protest, in the town. Objections were soon being printed by the editor, foremost of which, in venomous judgment, was that from the pen of the Reverend W. G. Snow, who peremptorily brought the discussion to an end by bluntly declaring that "a true Christian cannot be a pacifist." The voice of the establishment had spoken, not that of a New Testament–oriented prophet. The challenge issued by Willie was not answered; as with all prophets true to themselves, it was merely cast aside: "It is better that one man should die than that the whole nation should suffer."

Public opinion grew in favor of Snow's contention, and thus the cause of pacifism was routed in Renfrew, as it had been in the country at large.

He who had fought as hard as he knew how against the threat and the evils of war now put his hand to the work that was possible to him. Not that he gave up fighting for pacifism—he would never do that (he returned to the theme on 7 May 1939, when he preached a sermon entitled "A Christian and War," and he would preach again on the subject even during the war itself). But the time for dialectic was now over, at least for a time. There was a job to do, and in doing it wholeheartedly (the only way Willie knew to do anything) he not only put his church at the center of the map but outdistanced everyone else in the area, including those who had most vocally opposed him. He had lost the battle for peace; he now sought to help win the war.

A Faith for the Times

We have now reviewed a number of major statements that reveal Willie's thinking in this early period and gotten some sense of his homiletic concerns. But what of his theology? What was his doctrinal position during this first half of his parish ministry? How had the early beliefs of his immaturity weathered first the storm of academic discipline and then the searching pastoral needs of "a decided answer" for society's questions?

Happily, we are given a resumé of his beliefs in a series of articles he was asked to write for *The Scottish Sunday School Teacher* at the outbreak of the hostilities. Published in eight monthly installments beginning in January 1940, they were slanted "to assist in particular those who feel perplexed by the religious problems presented by the war."[17] The articles were based on a booklet entitled *What We Believe*, which was published by the Church of Scotland Youth Committee, and this booklet was itself based on Professor J. G. Riddell's book of the same title, which had been specifically produced as a companion to *A Short Statement of the Church's Faith*, a key document published by the Church of Scotland in 1935. The Convenor of the Committee that had drawn up this prewar confession was H. R. Mackintosh of Edinburgh, himself one of the most influential British interpreters of theological development in this century. Mackintosh had hoped to write the volume, but was prevented from so doing by poor health.

Thus it was that in this series of articles Willie found himself thrust into the very center of the most crucial debate of his ministerial period, found himself called on to expound some at least of "the decided answers" the Church of Scotland had formulated. It is the first doctrinal statement he ever wrote. Ten years were to elapse before he returned to the debate, and twenty-five years were to elapse before he could give it anything like a full treatment. Although very much shorter than *The Plain Man Looks at the Apostles' Creed* (1964)—sixteen pages compared with nearly four hundred—it is an important bridge between the young and the mature man, between the conservative and the (alleged) liberal. The volume was designed for the use of the teaching staff of the Scottish Sunday School Union, thirty-seven thousand members strong at the time, all of them in positions of great influence on Scottish youth (the Church of Scotland alone had over three thousand Sunday schools); that such an imposing task was entrusted to Willie shows the growing weight of his reputation and influence.[18]

We have seen that Willie was born and nurtured in a period of ecclesiastical and theological ferment. Doctrinally, the '20s did not so much twitter as rumble and roar. Such things as Lambeth's *Appeal to All Christian People*, the outpourings of the Anglican Evangelical Group, Dunkerley's *Unwritten Sayings of Jesus*, the alleged discovery of Noah's Ark on Mount Nebo, the Revised Prayer Book debate, and *The Basis and Plan for Union*, contributed to the general unrest—to which was added the agnostic, and not infrequently the atheistic, polemic of men of the stature of Bertrand Russell and the Huxley brothers. Individuals such as Whyte, Peake, William Temple, Fosdick, Streeter, Cairns, Gore, John Baillie, Inge, Barth, Bultmann, T. W. Manson, C. H. Dodd, and the Niebuhr brothers argued for a modern approach to traditional beliefs, which affected every aspect of Christian faith and order. Much of the work was conservative; indeed, the majority was. In the wake of Nunn's *What is Modernism?* even the ultraconservative faction sought to overcome the defensiveness of the past and produce solid work for the future. It too was beginning to look forward not backward, coming to the realization that "all truth is God's truth," that it had nothing to fear from vigorous scrutiny no matter how clinical or detached. In 1938, for example, senior members of the Inter-Varsity Fellowship met "to consider how best the reproach of obscurantism and anti-intellectual prejudice might be removed from evangelical Christianity."[19] This meeting had far-reaching results, to which Willie was to respond directly and joyfully in the early '50s.

Quite apart from economic and international concerns, it was a time for affirmation, and thus Willie wrote these "general articles" on "the faith of a Christian." The *Short Statement of the Church's Faith* on which he based his material—popularizing (not for the last time) a popular document—consisted of thirteen articles summing up the broad perspective of Christian belief as traditionally understood. It maintained that the actuality, the essence, of the Church's faith is "the unchanging Gospel of God's love made manifest in Jesus Christ."[20] Nothing could approximate more closely Willie's own central viewpoint, as we shall see.

Willie's contributions contained no preamble—such prefatory matter being too dilatory for Willie's dynamic attitudes! He went straight to the heart of the matter—the doctrine of God—and dealt with his subject in bold, telling strokes, while yet making room for his normal use of quotation and anecdote. It has to be admitted that he treats his basic text in something of a cavalier fashion—that being perhaps characteristic of his doctrinal, though not his biblical, attitudes. It was meant to be "assistance for the perplexed," not detailed commentary and apologetic for the strong. We should bear in mind that we do not have Maxwell Blair's briefing letter, and it is inconceivable that Willie should have gone ahead without first ascertaining the mind of this influential editor. Moreover, there were ecumenical constraints imposed on him in treating a Church of Scotland document for an all-Scotland (i.e., Protestant) body. Willie knew the susceptibilities of the minority groups very well indeed; it would not be overstating the case to say he shared some of them.

The *Short Statement* is a model of succinctness and clarity, resting on the twin pillars of Scripture and the historic creeds. He could have proceeded by emphasizing either scriptural proof texts and detailed exegesis or an exposition of the history and background to the ancient formularies (especially the Apostles' and the Nicene Creeds and the Westminster Confession of Faith)—or both, as Professor Riddell had. It is typical that whereas these elements were not wholly absent in Willie's treatment (especially the biblical aspect), he chose to offer his own essentially homiletic approach. Every article is presented with a threefold sectioning, and two of them have two groups of three each. Professor Riddell entitled each article "What we believe about. . . ." Willie, in line with his homiletical approach, made it more personal, more demanding: "I believe in. . . ." We shall see that this approach produced doctrinal problems for him, from which he emerged only "after a blinding flash of illumination." But that is to anticipate. This is what he now offered:

1. *I Believe in God.* His essential emphasis here, always present in his writings, is that God's existence is axiomatic: "it was the one certain fact with which the biblical writers started and *from* which they started. God for them was not only the supreme reality; he was the only reality in life and history." He acknowledges that this contrasts with modern thought, which reacts in different ways— sometimes hostilely, as with Swinburne's "supreme evil-God"; sometimes in denial, as with Hardy's cynical failure to find him; and sometimes complacently, as when people assent intellectually but not morally to his existence. Real belief, Willie always insisted, affects conduct; this attitude was for him the reason for all belief, and therefore the basis of all conduct.

He lists three characteristics of God that should produce appropriate responses in our lives: because God is wisdom, we must respond with trust; because God is purpose, we must respond in submission to him; because God is the loving Father, we must respond as obedient children. He strongly denies any sense of fate in our lives, laying stress on destiny instead: we are not automatons, but instigators of moral responses that either fulfill or obstruct God's purposes. It is the Christian's *duty* (a Barclayian keyword) to submit "and daily strive to make himself an obedient son."

As an exposition of the full Christian doctrine of God, this first article in the series is not entirely adequate (in contrast to the more substantial *Short Statement*): Willie fails to introduce such concepts as God's eternal being, his omnipotence, his role as creator, or his judgment of the world in holiness and righteousness. On the other hand, in stressing God's wisdom, purposefulness, and fatherly care, Willie has provided an intelligible anchor for those for whom the articles were meant—the perplexed in time of war. That was Willie's essential pastoral thrust, as well as his essential belief.

2. *I Believe in Jesus Christ.* "The essence of Christianity," Willie emphatically affirms, "is that it is not belief in a creed or a set of statements, but belief in a *Person*." In seeking to answer who and what Jesus was, he gives a double answer. First, "he was in a unique sense the Son of God." In evidence of this, he catalogues the texts in which Jesus makes plain his own unique relationship with the Father (Matt. 21:33–46, 27:63–64; John 4:6, 9:37, 10:30, 14:9). He also lists those who knew him best, who also made the uniqueness plain (John the Baptist, Peter, Martha of Bethany, and even the Roman centurion at his cross). He does not define this uniqueness further, nor does he seek to expound any ontological relationship between Jesus and God, but neither does he propound anything other than an orthodox understanding of Jesus. Second, Willie states that Jesus "was also in the truest sense a man; he was perfectly man," for which contention he also supplies a list of Jesus' feelings and emotions as proof. His perfect humanity is a necessary part of our salvation. It was ever so in Willie's theology.

He further proceeds to show that there are three aspects of Jesus' life from which we should take our regard of him. The first is his teaching, which has permanent value and is "marked by a note of authority; it is not derivative. . . . He speaks as God would speak to men." The second is his deeds. In this Willie tackles head-on the question of Jesus' miracles, asserting their historicity with perfect confidence, arguing from the trustworthiness of the Gospels of Luke and Mark. In light of the testimony from those living when the latter Gospel was written and circulated, he concludes that "the evidence for the miracles is too strong for one to do anything else than to admit that they *did* happen." The third outstanding thing about Jesus' life, he affirms, is his essential nature, his sinlessness. Only by false evidence could his detractors bring anything against him. In the cross and resurrection we see the full measure of his life: on the human side it shows the lengths to which evil can go, and on the divine side it shows "the length to which the love of God can go in that it would make so bitter a sacrifice to win the hearts of men." It was "a bearing of the sin of the world to open the way for men to God." Jesus' sinlessness, his sacrifice, his bearing man's sin "in his body on the tree" are elements, all of them, in a traditional understanding of the vicarious atonement, which Willie here expounds.

The cross, he continues, was not the end of Jesus: "after the agony of the Cross, there followed the triumph of the Resurrection. . . . The Resurrection is the foundation stone of the Christian faith. . . . It was the fact of the Resurrection which changed [the disciples'] despair into joy, and which gave them a gospel to preach." He stops short of speaking of a bodily resurrection and an empty grave, but it is clear that these are tacit concomitants of his doctrine rather than matters he questions, still less denies. In these quite orthodox respects, he affirmed "I believe in Jesus Christ."

3. *I Believe in the Holy Spirit.* Acknowledging that this belief is "our most

vague and shadowy and unreal," he nevertheless affirms that "without the Holy Spirit, Christian doctrine would be a dead body without a living soul. . . . The day of Pentecost was the most important date in the history of Christianity."

The Holy Spirit was sent not so much to "comfort" as to bring "the power of Christ which strengthens us and encourages us and enables us to meet the circumstance of life." In this sense he is the Paraclete, "someone who is called in to help and assist," sent in fulfillment of Jesus' promise. Jesus, Willie adds, made certain definite statements about the Holy Spirit: (a) he would teach his disciples all things; Jesus' teachings being ever illuminated by the Holy Spirit, "our understanding of the truth is becoming ever clearer, and our application of it ever wider"; (b) he would bring to the disciples' remembrance whatever Jesus had said to them, not only acting "as a kind of conscience" to them, but shedding new light on the truths, turning them from intellectual matters to living reality in their experience; (c) and, more than anything else, the Holy Spirit would be a power and a transforming influence in the disciples' lives, bringing them to "a likeness to Christ, which is the goal of Christianity." "The final aim" of the Christian, Willie says, "must be to be so surrendered to and so controlled by this Spirit of God that it may be true of us, as it was of Saint Paul, that it is no longer we who live but Christ who lives in us." Once again we find total orthodoxy of understanding, this time in relation to both the personality and the work of the Holy Spirit.

4. *I Believe in the Christian Hope.* At first it might seem strange that Willie makes Christian hope his fourth article—since the *Short Statement* has made it the last (i.e., the thirteenth) article, in keeping with the traditional "scheme of salvation." Since it deals with death, the last enemy, hope is usually made the final element in expressions of Christian faith. But Willie was never inhibited by traditional forms of belief and expression! And in deliberately altering the time-honored order he is asserting a spiritual logic that flows directly from Jesus' message, even though he does not quote it: "If a man keep my word, he shall never see death" (John 8:51); ethics and eschatology, discipleship and hope, are inextricably related. Willie recognized and applied the force of that logic.

To many who then read those words, sudden death would be an actuality: many were the departing hands he shook in those days, his Godspeed literally accompanying them into eternity. The conviviality of his canteen concerts never once detracted from the serious religious effort he made, for they always concluded with an epilogue, no matter how briefly. He had good reason to highlight this as a central message for the times, as men went out to die at the hands of the enemy. Perhaps in no other place in these eight articles of Christian faith are we so near to his deepest, most unshakable belief.

In order to confirm his readers in the validity of Christian hope, Willie shows how "belief in immortality is *not* one of the dominant notes of the Old Testament"; it was rather in Jesus that the fullness of that belief came, through the *Christian* intimations of immortality. These intimations he finds (a) in the nature of man—through his being made in the likeness of God, there is something of God in every man "which is bound to be preserved" (this is not a biblical argument in the strict sense in which he applies it); (b) in the nature of God, who is love and justice, and who will therefore judge accordingly—"there must be another life where 'the broken arcs shall become the perfect round'"; and (c) "the fact and the voice of Jesus," the promise of Jesus, and above all the resurrection of Jesus constitute "our guarantee of a life beyond death."

It is clear that the doctrine he had learned from his earliest days, the one that he clung to when first his mother and then his father were laid to rest in Kilmallie, the one by which he lived through the diverse experiences of a pastor close to his people, had through his study and proclamation now deeply permeated his thinking. This hope had stirred and comforted his congregation during seven years; it now gave strength to those growing up surrounded by brutality and destruction, and even to some who would face death as their daily companion. It was a sure and certain word for the day, issuing naturally from his doctrine of God, of Christ, of the Holy Spirit—a word of particular and necessary emphasis declared above other issues, a faith, indeed, for the times.

Not that it commended itself to everyone. Willie refers to a conversation he had at this time with a lady who said after one of his extramural lectures that the one thing she feared was immortality: she was tired, and the thought of a life to which there was no end was intolerable.[21] Willie answered this by pointing out that eternal life is essentially a quality, not a duration—"it is foolishness, resulting in idle speculation, to ask for details of what the future life will be like." He maintained that eternal life, best described "in the words of the apostle: 'to be with Christ'" (Phil. 1:23), was a great gift: he sustained hope despite the opposition and even the depths of suffering into which he and Kate were later plunged.

He omitted treatment of the doctrine of the holy Trinity—article five of the *Short Statement,* which says that "the Church, knowing God through Jesus Christ His Son, and through the working of His Spirit in the world and in the lives of believers, confesses and adores one God—Father, Son and Holy Spirit." The doctrine itself, which finds no explicit expression per se in the New Testament, he clearly found to be less than important (i.e., useful) at this particular juncture, with his very limited space and *practical* intent. That he personally held to it at this time is beyond doubt, and we may see that elsewhere he could give it full and orthodox expression.[22]

5. I Believe in the Holy Scriptures. Willie's treatment of this article demands a more extended consideration on our part than do the other articles—not because he himself gave the material a lengthier treatment, but because this document is so crucial to his developing views on the nature of Scripture. His statement here formed the basis for his future work on the topic, work that has not infrequently been misunderstood—sometimes deliberately misunderstood and misrepresented—and so a little extra care in evaluation is called for.

We ought first to note that Willie does not deal with the first part of the *Short Statement,* on natural revelation, but isolates the biblical data and deals with it alone. This must have been another decision forced upon him by the constraints of space, for he was strong on natural revelation, giving more emphasis to it than some deemed justifiable, as we shall see.

The *Short Statement* makes four points on Scripture that bear repetition: (a) "the Scriptures of the Old and New Testaments *contain* the Word of God"; (b) that Word was "given by inspiration"; (c) "the Church welcomes every aid provided by linguistic, literary and historical research"; and (d) "the authority of Scripture depends on their effectual truth being made sure to faith by the Holy Spirit, not on their scientific or historical accuracy or their verbal inerrancy."

These four points are crucial to a contemporary understanding of the Bible. They go beyond the orthodox definitions of the church in its great councils and Reformation confessions by reasserting and enriching them. Nor did they contain anything that Willie found objectionable—including the so-called "Barthianism" of the first point (though Willie was never a Barthian and almost never quotes him; he is at his most anti-Barthian when he asserts the propriety and usefulness of "natural theology," on which hinges his "threshold evangelism" and his "parables of life" method). We must not forget that the phrase "the word of God as contained in Holy Scripture" was in regular and authorized usage by the Church of Scotland. He tackles the subject in his own way, first giving pride of place to defining "inspiration," then showing the relationship between and the necessity of the Old and New Testaments, and finally giving his view on "development."

His first point regarding inspiration is the assertion that the Bible is inspired in a way that no other book is inspired, his intent not being to minimize the timeless quality of great books, but to highlight the uniqueness of the Bible. He rejects any form of "mechanical inspiration": the "dictation theory" (though he does not use the phrase) is ruled out. He maintains that God's servants were willing and full partners in the discernment and transmission of his word, and that God himself was dependent on the awareness of his servants "to catch his thoughts and to understand his requirements." This, he admits, is only "one factor in the situation," but "it is not possible either to disregard or eliminate the human elements," so he urges what he describes as *the cooperative view of inspiration*—"as the human mind reached up, the Spirit of God reached down and met it." The men involved in this work were prepared men whose lives, whose constant search for truth and reality, and whose love "had placed themselves in such a relationship to God that they could hear His voice and understand His counsels and interpret His message to men to a supreme degree." It has to be admitted that in his attempt to emphasize the human element he has all but obscured the divine element—God's purpose and planning, his initiative in revelation—again, not because these aspects had no place in his thinking, but because they were already well emphasized, part of the general understanding of inspiration that Willie could express elsewhere but felt entitled to leave unexplained here. But the resultant material, he is at pains to own, is *God's* word, not man's, and it is the ground of faith and the rule of life.

This statement does not represent the fullness of Willie's doctrine of inspiration at this time or later, but it does offer very large clues to the way he worked theologically: piecemeal, noncomprehensively, with his practical concern (and sometimes his emotions) outweighing the intellectual considerations. If we wish to, we can find enough material elsewhere to offset this imbalance, but to do so would run the risk, to Willie's way of thinking, of undermining the human aspect, something he was not prepared to do. Wherein lay this unwillingness to lessen this aspect? Was it just that the older theories, mechanical or otherwise, had made such an impact that he was determined to stress only the human side? Or was it because God was so very large in and so very real to his thinking that the divine dimension was left as an implicit datum? Or was it that this doctrine had an exaggerated importance for Willie because it had been forged in the "explosive rackets" that took place between himself and his father in earlier years? Elsewhere he admits his ongoing sensitivity to the conservatism of his youth, which even held the punctuation points of the Authorized Version to be beyond challenge. One suspects that the memory of those contretemps and the slow and painful process by which he came to a greater historical and literary awareness so impressed itself upon him that he tended to fight his own internal battles again when he came to write of these issues, and thus presented the side of the doctrine that had once called for full-scale expression, leaving other aspects merely tacit. Be that as it may, we must note that the divine element is not denied: the "principle of cooperation" demands it. And he remained ever assertive, combative even, that it was primarily and authoritatively *God's* Word, not man's.

He subsequently dealt with the two broad divisions of the Bible—of the Old and New Testaments—which highlight our need of the whole Bible for "the purpose of faith." It is not certain how this last phrase is to be construed: faith as doctrine, or as personal trust. Perhaps the ambiguity is deliberate. The Old Testament, he writes, "deals with certain permanent human emotions which can never be out of date." And "we shall never be able to do without the record of how human souls found God, and how God found them." The relationship to God of the men of old remains "of permanent value for those who are seeking to enter into the same relationship." But of further importance—we might say greater—is the way the Old Testament provides "the background without which the life and teaching of Jesus cannot be understood. . . . Jesus was not an intrusion into history but the culmination of a long process wherein God more and more revealed Himself to man. . . . [Jesus' coming] was not an afterthought of God . . . but the peak of centuries of definite preparation undergone by a nation." Only a little thought will prove how wrong his detractors are when they assert that his views were merely "humanist" ones: no matter how strong and explicit his emphasis on the human angle (i.e., men seeking and finding God), the working of God in history, in providence, which "peaks" in Jesus, supplies a balancing emphasis. Nothing could be further from mindless evolution than this understanding of man's history and the assertion of the purposes of God within it, which at a stroke denies fatalism, doctrines of chance, and other schools of thought that suggest God's absence from his creation. It is the firm foundation on which all concepts of God rest, and these peak in Jesus precisely because he is the word and mind—the *logos*—of God, as he later repeatedly emphasizes (following John 1:14). Nor has he concluded his argument for the indispensability of the Old Testament; we need it finally, he says, because Jesus himself needed it, as is demonstrated in his refutation of the Adversary with the Old Testament. George Adam Smith's comment is conclusive: "What was indispensable for the Redeemer must always be indispensable for the redeemed."

"Even more we need the New Testament," Willie asserts trenchantly. In substantiation of this he asserts that "Christianity is an historical religion, whose Founder was Jesus Christ; and in the New Testament alone we have the account of His life, His deeds and His words. Without it we have no solid basis for our faith; because it tells of him, it is the foundation of our belief." If we find his explanation of inspiration in the confined areas of these articles indicative of his manner, rather than of his matter, it is perhaps more so—tantalizingly so—here: in this two-sentence advocacy of our need of the New Testament we again have statement rather than argument, belief rather than reasoning, commitment rather than advocacy. It was ever Willie's way. It is the mark of the preacher rather than of the teacher of the Christian faith; he sought to convey rather than explain, to illustrate rather than define. We need to look elsewhere to see why and how it should be a historical religion, what the nature and extent of the historicity of Jesus is, and how we may build on it. But Willie is totally clear as to what—or rather *who*—"the solid basis" and "the foundation" is. And he describes a large deposit from which we may draw: the life, the acts ("deeds"), and the teaching of Jesus Christ. He was to spend the rest of his life expounding and illustrating him, though even here we shall see that his preference is to seek and highlight the relevance rather than the fact, the meaning for people rather than the historical details.

But if he is muted on some questions and arguments of faith, he is perfectly plain when it comes to *how* we should understand the Bible. "Two things," he asserts, "must always be remembered in thinking of the Bible." First, "we must expect to find in it development. God could reveal to men only as much of the truth as they could grasp. . . . There is steady development towards a fuller knowledge of God." (He give such examples of this as Genesis 11:5 and Psalm 139, which portray both a localization and a universality of God's presence among men.) Second, "we must remember that that development is not finished. It is folly to think that God stopped speaking nineteen hundred years ago; it is little short of blasphemy to think that God put all he had to say between the covers of one book. We worship not a dead book but a living Savior. The Holy Spirit still speaks to us, seeking to lead us deeper and deeper into the Kingdom of God." Development and an increasing knowledge, forward not backward, were ever his true orientation.

Once again in these matters we can see Willie's tendency (heightened here by the limited space available) to present crucial ideas with only partial exposition or argument. But the point he is making about revelation is paramount in his thinking, and it eclipses other issues he might have discussed in a fuller fashion had he sufficient space. Willie of all people, especially at this time, did not accept or follow "open-ended doctrine," beliefs that are indulged in by fancy or personal whim. He did accept and maintain the primacy of the Word of God, and that comprehensively—the Word of God in all its parts and emphases, not just in the much-read sections of most people's Bibles. He found place for the Sermon on the Mount as well as the Prodigal Son (he would prefer to term the latter the Loving Father), for the cross and for the resurrection. He maintained the need for Jesus, and Paul, and Peter, and James. He asserted this primacy and this comprehensiveness even against the historic creeds and confessions. Nor did he ever move from that attitude, as witness the occasion, forty-five years later when, as renowned biblical exponent, with over seventy books to his credit, and despite his phenomenal memory and power of recall, he rereads the whole of the New Testament and a good deal of the Old in order to prepare adequately (i.e., biblically) for his lectures on the ethics of the New Testament: that is biblical integrity, and that was the essence of William Barclay's style and method.

In closing this section he states that "we know that the Bible is the Word of God because, as we read it, it brings its own evidence in the effect which it has upon our hearts." In this connection he makes the point yet again that we must "give ourselves up to the guidance of the Holy Spirit who speaks to us from its pages, [so] we shall find each day that he is bringing us nearer to the perfect Kingdom of God." Experience, the ongoing work of the enlightening Spirit, is thus his final emphasis. It was in that Spirit he lived, in that Spirit he worked, and in that Spirit he served the worldwide church over many years.

He omits references in the *Short Statement* to the three composite articles of Creation and Providence, Man and Sin, and Salvation in Christ. Space again is the key factor in his choice here, and not a weak hold on—still less a rejection of—the elements omitted, as we shall see elsewhere. Once more he selects what he feels to be the more important aspect, namely article six, his belief in the church.

6. *I Believe in the Church*. His approach to this commences with a rejection of the solitary religious life. He uses Wesley's example to show that "the highest form of Christian activity" is within the church. That is a very significant comment, going beyond many Protestant and Presbyterian emphases. Did he really mean it? Is the church the highest form of Christian life or activity? Or is this simply verbal looseness? Certainly verbal loosenesses do occur in his writings, most often in the form of exaggeration (for example, superlatives abound at this time, as does his isolation of "unique" occasions and usages in New Testament expressions and doctrines; we shall return to these later). But the comment nevertheless serves to explain his moderation relative to Roman Catholicism and certain Protestant denominational bodies. Wherever Christ is owned as Lord, he is saying, there is real belief, real Christianity; and wherever believers meet, there

the church finds its necessary, duty-bound expression. Willie indubitably did have a "high" view of the church, but not a high view of a high church. He was at pains to assert the corporate and social demands of worship and mutual action; at Trinity he orchestrated activities so as to ensure that the church operated at the center of communal life, in witness and service (understood in both a religious and a secular way). But this church was essentially a company of believing, love-constrained individuals, not an ecclesiastical body, by law established—be it of church councils or those of state intervention. Willie's view comprehended two realms—that of King Jesus and that of the secular Crown—so we should see that he had at once a high and a low view of the church at this time. It was "high" in the sense that he recognized the importance of fellowship, mutual worship, witness, and work (we may detect the YMCA influence here), but "low" in the sense that he lacked enthusiasm for the organized church and its institutions (again, YMCA and Free-Church influences were at work). We shall see a similar ambivalence emerging in his views on church union in the '60s and '70s.

He saw the necessity of church involvement in three ways: first, as a human necessity, stemming from our need for one another; second, as historical necessity, deriving from "certain historical facts" on which it is founded, and for which it has acted over many centuries as "teacher and guardian of the truth"; and third, as a divine necessity, the church being "the agent of God in the world" for achieving his purposes, his feet to run upon his errands, his hands to work for him—a very Barclayan emphasis.

This naturally leads to two questions, which he proceeds to answer: "Why should I join the church?" and "What must I believe in order to be a member of the church?" In answer to the first question he reminds his readers of the house-group nature of early Christianity. If one joins such a group his knowledge of Jesus can be refined and perfected, and he can thus become involved in a "continuation" of discipleship. Further, his meeting together with others is an act of witness; by so joining, he shows "which side he is on": it is a declaration of loyalty that Willie considers to be "an affair of honour." The second question, concerning what one must believe, he answers by reminding us that the earliest creed was one "of only four words, but those four words included everything essential": Jesus Christ is Lord. To assert this is to assert that "Jesus is a unique Person, that He commands a unique devotion, that He deserves a unique obedience, that His words have a unique wisdom for the human mind, and His Person a unique appeal to the human heart."

He has now expended three quarters of his allotted space, and he has not yet begun to address the issues of the sacraments, repentance and faith, or the Christian life. The first two he simply ignores. After all, one who can believe so earnestly in Jesus as Lord, Savior, and Messiah is not likely to be wanting overmuch in such matters, but he may well need guidance in the way of life commensurate with such theological heights. To this Willie now turns, "unbalancing" his treatment by giving twenty-five percent of his total allotted space to the penultimate article, which occupies but one-thirteenth of the *Short Statement*. In so doing he declares his belief in the necessity of one's life matching one's belief, in the importance of the practice matching the preaching. He was ever pragmatically concerned.

7. *The Life of a Christian: As an Individual.* "The experience by which a man enters the Christian faith," Willie declares, "is commonly called Conversion." He warns against the dangers of stereotyping the conversion experience. It is a fact of life that not everyone has a Damascus road experience; indeed, he thinks that most people (and it is clear that he includes himself) do not. On the reality and meaning of the experience, however, he does not equivocate: it is when "the reality of God and of the importance of His place in life" become apparent. This has to take place "through Jesus Christ." Paul recognized it when he asserted a multiform expression of his ministry: "I am made all things to all men, that I might by all means save some"—a characteristic Willie would exhibit in his own way. So, concludes Willie, does God use different approaches to different hearts—for both the suddenly converted ("twice born") and the "once born"—*"provided each has made a definite decision to follow Christ."* Whether one grows into the decision, or discovers it in a flash of light, it must come as a decisive act of the will—that is, it must have a moral base.

Conversion, he explains, literally means a turning round. So what are the characteristics of the life turned round? He finds them to be threefold. First, one must turn from rebellion to submission before God: God must become the supreme reality in life, and Christ the motivating force. Second, one must turn from fear to faith, to the safety of the hands of God in a hostile universe. Third, one must turn from earth to heaven, from men to God. This does not issue in escapism, but an earthly reality, the proper fulfillment of man's life before God. If this be so, then "one essential practice" results: prayer becomes a fact of life. In prayer the Christian speaks to God, "Who is now so real and precious to him"; in prayer "he will learn what is the will of God for him." In such a life the spirit of prayer is continually maintained and, in Tennyson's words, the vision is experienced that

> The whole round earth is every way
> Bound by gold chains about the feet of God.

8. *The Life of a Christian: As a Member of a Community.* In this article Willie contends (via a quotation from his favorite author, G. K. Chesterton) that we are all members of a community from the very beginning, in our home life, which is a "microcosm of the world in general": "Christianity, like charity, must begin at home." He thus raises home life to the status of a theological article (we shall find him still emphasizing its importance forty-five years later, when he issues his testament of faith). In doing so, Willie has gone beyond the document he is expounding; the *Short Statement* gives no space to the home, a deficiency Willie could not tolerate.

The second community to which he draws attention is that of the church, in a discussion of three Christian duties: first, the duty to those outside the church, ensuring that we do not cause offense to them, but rather win them to the Master; second, the duty to those within the church, for the church is a community of special relationships, a brotherhood in Christ the unity of which must be translated into proper behavior; and third, the duty to the church as a whole, which requires our support by our giving and by our presence.

He concludes this article, and the series itself, with a reference to a third community in which the Christian functions—that of his common humanity. It is in the world that we serve God—God's world. As such, the Christian's life is one of principle, of total self-giving and dedication to Christ. We may recall that his favorite hymn was "When I Survey the Wondrous Cross," which concludes

> Were the whole realm of nature mine,
> That were an offering far too small!
> Love so amazing, so divine,
> Demands my soul, my life, my all.

Such a life, motivated by and geared to such a principle, is naturally a life of service "to be lived not for our own sake, but for the sake of others. We have been sent here not to get but to give. All our actions are to be directed towards the service of our fellow-men. . . . It is the Christian's duty to live with generosity and with service towards the men for whom his Master so generously lived—so sacrificially died." It was Willie's belief, even as it was his way.

CHAPTER TEN

The War Years: An Extended Ministry

The Opening Salvos

"IF you desire peace," says the old Roman proverb, "prepare for war." The tragedy for Britain and the free world was that Britain had at this time, despite its position at the head of the greatest empire ever known, a prime minister who desired peace at any price, who underestimated his nation's and its allies' enemies, and who therefore failed to make the necessary preparations for the awful eventuality.

The world was by then in a sorry mess, with tension and strife dominating economic and political life. Hitler himself was not yet ready for full-scale war, still less his Italian partner in belligerence, Benito Mussolini. America was intent on staying neutral, and urged appeasement on a British government it despised for weakness and back-room wheedling. In 1938 Duncan Sandys had threatened to expose in Parliament the complete inadequacy of the country's defenses, and they were not much further advanced by September 1939. The British Expeditionary Forces were scandalously unprepared for war, in spirit as well as in armaments and manpower. Not a few believed Germany could win, that all was up with the Empire and life as they knew and loved it. Through all this despondency a ray of hope was expressed, in a Signal issued by the Admiralty within hours of the declaration of war. It simply read, "Winston is back." For Churchill the "wilderness years" (1929–1939) were over; he was invited to rejoin the government, and he accepted the post of First Lord of the Admiralty. The passion for bold design and extravagant color that characterized his paintings during his period out of office was now infused into military strategy and general public life. At least this was a comfort.

In Renfrew, already a garrison fort with all three armed services very much in view throughout the town and the surrounding countryside, the war impinged still further. It was declared a neutral area, much to the surprise of the civic authorities, whose first battle was with the government to get it reclassified as a sending area, to permit them to evacuate the children and take other preparatory decisions. "Once more war is raging," commented the Editor of *The Renfrew Press* sorrowfully, as he reported the sinking of the aircraft carrier *H.M.S. Courageous* with the horrific loss of twelve hundred men.[1]

The 29th of September was Registration Day in the town, a preliminary to the issue of identity cards and ration books. Other activities emphasized the reality of the situation: lectures on the proper response to poison gas attacks were given by the ARP, and public buildings (such as cinemas and churches) were roped off to facilitate speedy emptying. It was found that Trinity Church could be emptied in two and a half minutes, and all worshipers could be in the safety of their shelters and basements within ten minutes—something of a jolt to those who were used to the long and friendly talk that normally followed the end of a service. Afternoon services were introduced in fulfillment of black-out requirements, and these speedily proved even more popular than the evening services. Soon a Know Your Warden campaign was under way, and the community began to feel more prepared for the opening of the hostilities.

Scotland had its first taste of air raids in the middle of October when the Rosyth and Forth bridges were bombed and an air battle took place over Fife and the Lothians. No one heard the air-raid warnings! In Glasgow, the population was put on a stand-by warning, but nothing came of it. It was the lull before the storm, when the war of nerves was more disruptive than the exchange of fire itself to life and activity. The reports of appalling brutalities in the Nazi concentration camps aroused much comment in early November; this "descent into barbarism" added to the fears of many and inspired others to greater resolution and effort. Britons were particularly disappointed to read of Hitler's escape from a time-bomb on November 17, the work, it was said, of a discontented faction within his own government rather than of British or French intelligence agents. In March there was a similar reaction to the reported refusal of the ship's complement of the *Graf Spee* to sail under Captain Langdorft. "This is Rat Week," the paper commented acidly.

It was at this time that Willie published his fourth article in *The Renfrew Press,* one of the earliest ones to be included in a new morale-boosting feature of the paper called "The Press Pulpit." It was not his first venture into print following the declaration of war. The church magazine had that honor, though his September pastoral letter was actually written before war broke out. In this letter he had seen that war was now inevitable—only Chamberlain and his cohorts seemed not to have recognized that in the late summer of 1939—and therefore Willie wrote to steady his members' resolve for "another winter's work" and to point them to the Source of "all the help and strength that religion and faith can bring to us." He quoted R. L. Stevenson's prayer that God should make them "constant in danger, steadfast in affliction, and unmurmuring in tribulation." The great characteristic of the Christian religion, he said, is that it makes men ready for anything; they had to learn to take one step at a time, one day at a time. He reminded them that their church "has two main objects, one in relation to God, and one in relation to our fellow-man," and that preparation for both was required: they had to come in a spirit of worship, possessing "the spirit of concentration upon the highest." Moreover, they had to prepare themselves "to practice those virtues and that way of life which our Master taught" before their friends, family, and neighbors.

The article Willie published in the local newspaper was very different from this. War had now been declared, the threat of invasion hung over the nation, and barbarities were now frequently reported. He sought to provide a much-needed Christian voice and counsel.

A Calm Spirit in Troubled Days[2]

—by the Rev. Wm. Barclay

SOMEWHERE in the works of Robert Louis Stevenson there is an illuminating sentence. "Quiet minds," he wrote, "cannot be perplexed or frightened, but go on in fortune or misfortune at their own private pace like a clock during a thunderstorm."

Irrespective of the weather the clock pursues its even course and irrespective of the storms of life the quiet mind preserves its undisturbed calm. That is what Paul meant when he wrote to the Corinthians: "We are troubled on every side, yet not distressed; we are perplexed, but not in despair."

Now in these days the aim which most people have is how to obtain this quiet mind; how in days of danger to acquire a calm confidence; how in days of suspense and tension to acquire a peaceful spirit; how in days when things threaten our peace and our happiness to go on without fear.

Every man can obtain that quiet spirit if he is prepared to do certain things and to live life in a certain way. For one thing he must learn to live one day at a time. That is one of the hardest of all things to do. Almost alone of the creatures, man has the power of foresight, and yet he must learn to live one day at a time. Principal Rainy once said: "To-day I must attend a committee meeting; to-morrow I must preach; some day I must die. Then let us do each duty as it comes as best we can." The man who has schooled himself to take each thing as it comes, to live each day as it comes, is well on the way to the attainment of the quiet mind.

Wasted Effort

For another thing he must teach himself to believe that worry never did anyone any good. Most people have an inveterate habit of crossing bridges before they come to them. Worry is wasted effort. The fact is that worry, so far from helping a man to face anything, actually impairs his efficiency to cope with the thing when it does come. It is a solemn and yet at the same time a calming thought that if a thing is going to happen it will happen and that nothing that we can do will stop it happening.

It is on record that the Emperor Napoleon was standing close to a young soldier during a battle. A cannon ball passed overhead and the young soldier instinctively ducked his head. "Young man," said Napoleon, "it is no use, if that cannon ball had been meant for you, if you had burrowed a hundred feet in the ground it would still have got you."

In a world which is ruled by God there can be no such thing as chance. It is true that a man by the free power of his will can make of any event what he chooses; he can make of his tragedies triumphs and he can make of his loss his glory, and equally he can make of his success his ruin and of his victory his shame. But the fact remains that we cannot stop things happening, and therefore to worry about them is not only useless; it is only to make them worse and to dissipate our power to meet them when they do come.

Strength of Cause

And for still another thing the man who would have the quiet mind must remember that there is a God. It is told that on the death of Abraham Lincoln, the friend of the black people and the slaves, two negroes met; the one was weeping bitterly and could only keep on saying: "Massa Lincoln is dead." "That is true," said the other, "but God is not dead."

In *Saint Joan*, George Bernard Shaw puts certain words into the mouth of Joan of Arc. She is leaving the council chamber to be burned, abandoned by all who should have supported her. She turns to those who have betrayed her. "Do not think," she says, "that you can frighten me by telling me that I am alone. It is better to be alone with God; His friendship will not fail me, nor His counsel, nor His love. In His strength I will dare and dare until I die." Anyone who is quite, quite sure that he is right, and who has the verdict of his conscience on his side, must be sure that soon or late, in this world or in some other world, God will vindicate His cause.

In threatening and in uncertain days each man must find his own calmness and preserve, as best he can, a quiet mind. He will do it by living one day at a time, by seeing the futility of worry, and by remembering that there is a God. So he also may be "troubled on every side, yet not distressed; perplexed but not in despair."

The article reflects Willie's style and state of mind, which had not altered since he last wrote for *The Renfrew Press*. The illustrations and authors quoted are typically Barclayan: R. L. Stevenson, Principal Rainy, Napoleon, Abraham Lincoln, G. B. Shaw, and, above all, Paul. The inutility of worry is characteristically Willie's, linked as it is to his principle of efficiency. His denial of chance in human affairs is also typical—though having denied it, he seems to allow something like a doctrine of fate: "the fact remains that we cannot stop things happening."

It would not be an exaggeration to say that man's lot—the human situation (to remind ourselves of his English tutor's best-seller)—and the providential governing of it by God are the basic motifs of Willie's faith. At times it was on the problems of human life, of evil and destruction, that he concentrated (a curious tendency, perhaps, in one who was on the whole so optimistic and joyful), and at other times he would indicate an almost Churchillian (or should we not rather say Jeremiac or Pauline?) comprehension of special personal calling. WDB certainly believed him to be a gift of God in late life (i.e., at forty!) and constantly reminded Willie of both his dedication at birth and his Highlander's blessing in childhood. But whatever the personal consciousness, the motifs regularly find expression in his sermons and written work.

The religious element looms larger in this piece than in its predecessors, but only in a very broad sense—recalling people's attentions to God, but not offering the inner realities of his fatherhood, still less the revelation of his Son. It is a long way off from the full Christian understanding of God's providence, and it conflicts with statements he made elsewhere at this time. Once again we are in the area of "threshold evangelism"—he is speaking to the public at large, encouraging them to take the first step of faith (the recognition of God in their lives), rather than exhorting church members to trust in God's fatherly care or rely on him to set the pattern for their lives.

There is another element that should not be overlooked in this regard, for it is central to Willie's religious understanding. It is the area of man's responsibility, of his duty to think and to act. We shall see that this eventually developed into a full ethic of "reciprocal obligation" in the associated relationships of God to man, man to God, and man to man. We have already seen how he discovered the secret of reliance on Christ's strength and resources not only in the pursuit of his everyday life—his *doing*—but also in the more personal aspect of his character and habits—his *being*. Willie never lost his, but he always kept it in balance with the idea of man's own responsibility and power of action. It is sometimes said that Willie's position was Pelagian, but such a judgment is not fair either to Scripture itself, which stresses man's freedom of action and responsibility to decide and act for himself (and its consequences, if neglected), or to Willie's own doctrine, which also sought to keep free will and God's sustaining help in balance. In such an article as this, at such a time as this, it is natural that he should remind his readers of their responsibilities and exhort them to exercise for good the opportunities that present themselves, rejecting in the process a defeatist attitude by remembering God's friendship, counsel, and love. Willie delighted in the American proverb that says if you are in need of a helping hand you should never forget that there is one at the end of your arm. At the same time he knew and relied on "the higher help" that never leaves man entirely alone, never leaves the seeking mind to its own devices, never abandons the trusting life to its own fates.

Willie was very much concerned that his work would truly be that of a *parish* minister, that he would serve all the people within his parish (and often beyond it), and not just those who attended his services. We shall shortly see that the breakdown of parish structures was one of the chief postwar preoccupations of the church, necessarily so in larger civic units (as opposed to country parishes), where the members of society interacted with one another across parish boundaries. Willie was only too well aware that his own dynamic attitudes created problems for some of his colleagues, but sadly was denied the opportunity to study the issue. His church was ever the focal point of that care and service, and he sought in many ways to ensure that it stayed that way. Already we have seen this intention applied to all ages and social groups, and was effected in the new clubs and societies he formed; all of them centered on Trinity Church.

The requisitioning of the YMCA building in Renfrew opened another opportunity which was to be quite spectacular and was to consume Willie's energies consistently during the next four years. It was via Kate's beloved Woman's Guild that first notice was made of this, when the newspaper reported in late October that "the Woman's Guild is making garments for war work," and that it needed

217

materials and help.³ Within a month of this it further reported that "the Reverend William Barclay has been doing a considerable amount of welfare work for the army, chiefly arranging concerts it would appear, and now he is doing the same work for the Church of Scotland Canteen Scheme for soldiers established in his Church."⁴ On the 30th of November "a big gathering of men" was recorded at a special concert, and it was announced that there would be weekly concerts for soldiers from then on. The undergraduate life-style that so concerned his father now reached its own fulfillment and was greatly appreciated by both town and military authorities. A public appeal was also made for "comfortable" furniture and "readable" books. The church magazine spelled out the activities more carefully: games—darts, carpet bowls, and so forth—might be played, tables and writing materials were provided free of charge, and a collection of books and magazines ("readable ones, *not* ancient commentaries") was being assembled. It is probable that WDB's and Willie's own fine collection of nontheological books was partly broken up at this time. Certainly most of the volumes were gone by shortly after the end of the war—a real sacrifice in the service of his fellow men, for many of them were prized first editions. Easy chairs and couches were installed, and a piano was given to "contribute towards home comforts."⁵ They do not seem to have had access to recorded music, despite the fact that jukeboxes had already made their appearance elsewhere. Tea—an essential prerequisite of the "comforts" they sought to offer—was continually available. The soldiers were delighted to find, from time to time, the minister himself at the piano, and they were even more delighted to discover his repertoire was not narrowly religious.

A small army of helpers, mostly housewives, helped him in this work, but predictably it was not long before trouble developed. Breaking his own rule never to respond to anonymous letters, he wrote to the Editor of *The Renfrew Press* in explanation:

> Sir,
>
> In your issue of 15th December I note that there is a letter headed "Married Women Only" and signed, "Evil to Him Who Evil Thinks." It is not my custom to answer anonymous letters, but, lest a totally incorrect impression should gain currency, this letter demands an answer. The letter states that "seemingly one must be a married woman before one can be trusted to serve in the Church of Scotland Canteen." That is definitely not the case. Any lady, married or unmarried, who has a genuine desire to help will be made most heartily welcome. In the four weeks in which the canteen has been open a number of unmarried ladies have given invaluable assistance. There are no qualifications for helpers save the desire and ability to help. If the person who wrote the letter will approach me I will most certainly see to it that his or her services are made use of in the canteen.
>
> WILLIAM BARCLAY,
> Convener of Local Committee

This was not the first problem he had to face due to war conditions. On the 6th of December an elder had raised in the kirk session the question of rescinding agreed procedures in order to facilitate the church's wartime work. It raised a nice constitutional point and sent the Moderator away to study his *Book of Procedures*—the only time on record he resorted to it. It also throws more light on his determination to keep things shipshape, orderly, and efficient.

The year was now drawing to a close. For many it had been a shattering year, when their worst fears were realized, with no sign of an early end to hostilities. Indeed things seemed to be accelerating toward calamity. For Willie, ever preserving that "calm spirit in troubled days," there was simply the multifarious day-to-day work to be done—as parish minister, Sunday School Superintendent, Bible Class Leader, and family man. He was particularly active in seeking to strengthen the work of his beloved YMCA: he preached at the Association's annual United Church Service on the 3rd of December and at the Fellowship Meeting on the 17th—the latter sermon (significantly on providence) causing the paper to say "his powerful address threw fresh light for many on the mystery and power of God."[6] In this sermon he spoke of the moral influence that the acknowledgment of God's existence produces. Clearly the lack of this, presumably in the soldiers attending his canteen and services, was provoking a good deal of soul-searching for him at this time. He argued that such acknowledgment, when sincere, penetrates every thought and aspect of our lives; it is part of God's work within us, and its end is to produce triumph and peace.

He presided over the Y's annual At Home service on the 22nd of December, for which the paper promised that "a very special surprise which will create a precedent may be expected." A reputation for innovation was clearly not going to be allowed to die quietly! Again under YMCA auspices he preached on the 26th, on "Christ and Our Possessions." It followed the historic broadcast of King George VI, who closed his "Call to the Nation" with words which Willie was often to use in the months and years which lay ahead: "I said to the man who stood at the gate of the year, 'Give me a light that I may tread safely into the unknown.' And he replied, 'Go out into the darkness and put your hand into the hand of God. That shall be to you better than light and safer than a known way.'"[7] It was a most suitable call, preceding as it did "the year of disaster," 1940.

But it was enjoyment, not disaster, that was in Willie's mind on the 28th of December, when he—together with 150 soldiers, the Provost, and Mrs. Mechie—sat down to a late Christmas Dinner. It was so successful that it was repeated a week later (in the form of a New Year Dinner, on the 4th of January). The Editor of *The Renfrew Press* described these meals in a way that shows that Trinity's social abilities had not diminished even with the onset of war. Even rationing was somehow circumvented: steak pie, potatoes, vegetables, and dumplings were served, followed by fruit and custard, tea and cakes. Musical entertainment followed this: three female and two male vocalists were accompanied by Hamilton Kerr, and there were also acts by "various airmen and soldiers." To the latter part of the evening's pleasures civilians were admitted, being allowed to sit in the side seats. The place was packed, and the overall view was that they were "grand concerts and the audiences most enthusiastic and appreciative." Special thanks were made to the members of the Woman's Guild, who, "like the Genie of the Lamp, can produce anything from a play to a haggis." Those not attending, especially the men of the district absent on service, were not forgotten: forty-one were sent assorted parcels of socks, scarves, writing materials, cigarettes, chocolate, and toffee.

By this time his helpers were getting used to their minister's unwillingness to allow any opportunity to be missed, and in any case his own New Year Call, expressed in his pastoral letter, was still reverberating in their ears:

By Dear Friends,

Many things have happened since in September I wrote my last letter to the congregation. In those days the clouds of war were gathering; the signs were ominous; but we hoped against hope that some way might be found out of our threatening situation. But that was not to be; and we find ourselves facing a new year in which no man can tell what will happen.

These are the days which test and try our faith and our Christianity. It is easy to have a serene and an unmoved faith in God when things go well. To-day on every side we will hear of the "failure of Christianity"; to-day there are many people who are threatened with the collapse of their faith. Nothing is worth anything if it collapses at the first stress and strain. Once G. K. Chesterton said that a man is not a man until he has passed the breaking point and has not broken and that a faith is not a real faith until it has passed through a situation in which all the grounds of belief were swept away and yet still insisted on believing. You remember Job when he said, "Though he slay me yet will I trust Him." In face of anything he would retain his faith in God. There was a stage in the career of Jesus when it became increasingly clear that He was to end not in triumph but in a cross, and John in his gospel tells us, "From that time many of his disciples went back and walked no more with Him." They left him when things went hard. Let us see to it that however dark and inexplicable things may be our faith is not eclipsed.

But also, these are the days which show us the worth of the faith we hold. The beauty of a home is that we can go into it after the struggle and the stress of the world and find a time of rest and refreshment that we may go again less weary to the battle of living. That is what our faith does for us in these days. It gives us, as it were, a quiet room where we can for a little stay in the company of God that we may be the better able to face the world and its uncertainties and its anxieties. I think that in these days we have found out as we rarely did in calm days the preciousness of prayer. To those of us who have friends or loved ones absent on the country's business or in the vital interests of the nation, prayer has become something which is not a formal offering of words to God, but a lifting up to Him of our very hearts and souls that He may keep them safe. There is this at least to be said—that at a time like this it is our faith which alone makes life tolerable to live.

In the days to come there are two things in our Church life which stand out. The one thing is that OUR CHURCH WILL NEED US. Upon our time, even upon Sundays, there are the increasing claims of work and of national service and of many other things, until the worship of the Lord's day is in danger of being crowded out. Upon our resources there are increasing calls until we must all be tempted to forget our obligations to our Church. If the Church is to bear the witness she ought; if she is to do the work she ought; and if she is to be the force in the life of the community she ought to be, she will need increasingly our presence and our support in the days to come.

The other thing is this, that, in the days to come WE WILL NEED OUR CHURCH. The danger of a time like this is that when we are assessing things we leave God out of the reckoning. We think in these days of the prospects of victory and of defeat, of what will happen to us if ever our worst fears and expectations are realised. And we are apt to think altogether in terms of material things, material defences and material advantages. Napoleon once said, "God is always on the side of the big battalions." But that is not true. Any nation, any community, which in its time of stress reckons up only its material resources, and leaves the things of the spirit and God out of the reckoning, has left out the most powerful force of all. Increasingly we shall require some place to which we may come that we may be reminded that behind all things and at the back of all things there is a God.

So, far from viewing the present situation with gloom or with despair, let us view it as a challenge to our faith and a challenge to show what the Church can do for men and women and for a world in days of darkness.

To each one of you I wish all good things in the New Year; I pray constantly that we and our loved ones may be kept safe through all its days; may God bless this people and may He answer our prayers that peace may speedily return; and in days of darkness may He keep us loyal, keep us loving and keep us true.

I am,

Always very sincerely yours,
WILLIAM BARCLAY.

The concerts continued week by week, producing great relaxation and merriment for the troops, and much hard work for the helpers. Sometimes the contacts resulted in romance; on several occasions Willie was called in to officiate at weddings between his younger parishioners and service lads, many of them from south of the border. Later on it would be his joy to baptize their children, and several remained in touch with him over many years. Sometimes the problems were of a different sort, though they had not yet reached the threefold malady ascribed to American soldiers—that of being "overpaid, oversexed, and over here." But the basic problems were there, and sometimes they were very basic; Willie was unperturbed and simply got on with the job. Some soldiers turned up the worse for drink and had to be escorted (i.e., carried) by the young minister back to their barracks and the all-too-sobering response of the authorities.

The demand for Willie to provide the "special functions" of a minister (baptisms, funerals, and marriages) rose from 62 requests in 1939, to 93 in 1940 (it was to peak in 1941 at 127), all of which demanded various sorts of visits and counseling. He never underrated these times, but used them as levers with which to prize the pearls of the gospel from their hiding places. The "Y" continued to claim his (presidential) interest, and he preached a sermon entitled "I Believe in Jesus Christ, the Son of God" on the 19th of January to much acclaim. Reported *The Renfrew Press,* which went out of its way to highlight the stress the minister made on Jesus' divinity, the sermon was described as showing clearly "how we must look upon Jesus as the Son of God, speaking with divine truth and not as fallible man. Proof that he is indeed the Son can be found in Jesus' own words, in his friends' words and the words of even his enemies."[8] J. W. D. Smith was later to challenge Willie on this emphasis on Christ's divine sonship, and argue—with some real success—for the importance of his messianic role in the context of Judaism (as belonging to the lineage of God's anointed kings),[9] but at the time Willie seems to have understood Jesus' unique sonship only in terms of his divinity.

In February the good work of the Christmas parcels was extended when two hundred similar parcels were sorted, packed, and posted on behalf of the local paper. Containing sultana cake, chocolate, Oxo cubes, cigarettes, copies of *The Renfrew Press,* and greeting cards, the packages represented a contribution of over £65—a magnificent response to the newspaper's appeal that came from all quarters of society, not excluding "the swears, lies, and mornings late box" of local factories! In celebration of this the Woman's Guild held another concert (it was a repeat of the February 9 performance) with standing room only available at its commencement; its choir of twenty-six voices was conducted by Willie himself. Commented the church magazine, undoubtedly without the approval of the Woman's Guild, "It was once said of a promising musician that he was able to knock music out of a lamp-post. . . . Mr Barclay produced music from a source thought at one time to be unpromising." With it went a play produced by Kate. Perhaps the criticism that followed this in *The Renfrew Press* of March 22 is not unexpected: the writer, the Interim Welfare Officer for the troops, expressed disquiet over the lavishness of the proceedings. "What was suggested," he wrote, "was not elaborate entertainments, but invitations to spend an hour or two with the household [of a local citizen], say in the evenings or on Sunday afternoons." But Willie and Trinity Church knew better, and so the concerts continued, to the relief of the troops. By April 26 Willie was reporting "a very successful season" and assuring everyone that a good cash balance would take them through till September. Kate, as President of the Woman's Guild, meanwhile, was reporting "a splendid year" to her members.

Things were not otherwise with Willie's church. On the 22nd of February Willie completed his seventh year at Trinity. As the magazine Editor (John Kidd) commented in heralding the event,

> Seven years ago we did not think anyone could achieve such a record—we had become so accustomed to the maximum of four years. We congratulate Mr Barclay on his success; no minister ever put more work into his first seven years than he has done. We congratulate ourselves on having been able to hold him; and in spite of war-time difficulties we are determined to do all we can to encourage him in his work.[10]

222

It was not the only mark of appreciation he received at the time. Another came to him in the form of a note of gratitude for the work he undertook on behalf of *The Renfrew Press's* War Fund. Its author, a member of Willie's church and afterward his lifelong friend "Gunner" Archibald Maynard, wrote,

> I would like to thank you very much indeed for the fine parcel sent to me by the Renfrew Press. I can say without any hesitation whatever that it was the finest parcel I received from any of the newspapers. Trusting you will have every success in your appeal for funds for your parcels for the troops.[11]

Because of the restrictions on paper usage, it was decided not to produce the Annual Report in its usual extended form. The annual meeting took place on Monday, the 26th of February (*The Paisley and Renfrew Gazette* commented that "owing to present conditions, the meeting was on a smaller scale than is usual"),[12] and encouraging results were intimated for the year now ended. Despite the fact that income was down as a whole throughout the presbytery, it was up at Trinity by almost twenty-five percent (from £1,134 to £1,410), and the church's expenditures were actually down by nearly fifteen percent (the amount payable to presbytery being the only increase, it having been raised by twelve and a half percent). This gave great heart to managers and members alike, and emphasizes yet again how efficient Trinity Church was under its dynamic leaders. Other gauges of the church's vitality more important than its financial health were also positive: despite the loss of several young men, membership was up by 24 (to 1,224); the Junior Choir had been restarted; the scouts were again functioning at full strength; the Woman's Guild was in good heart; and the Sunday Schools (the plural is justified) were lively and outgoing, organizing a special collection "for the sick of Renfrew" that culminated in Easter eggs all round, "enough to fill several baskets."

The text for the month that followed, March, was culled from the life of George Fox, the Quaker. It could not have more aptly described Willie: "He was completely master of himself because he was completely a servant of God." It was enough.

A Career Checked

Willie's friends the Galls (he was to baptize their child in June) were troubled to hear his view that seven years was the longest a minister should stay in his first charge. Remembering the rumors and struggles of former times (in 1937, 1938, and 1939), this was indeed gravely disquieting. They knew that larger churches were "interested," and Willie spoke of hints from Glasgow University that there might be a vacancy shortly. He assured them, however, that a move was out of the question so long as the war continued—a position he sustained not merely till the cessation of hostilities, but till all of his members had returned from the military to civilian life. He was determined *not* to enjoy advantages himself while others were disadvantaged.

There can be no doubt that such a decision definitely checked his career. He expressed disappointment that it should be so, but he was resolute, and the well-meaning counsel of friends—and potential colleagues—was firmly denied. But there was another consideration involved: he was not certain that he really wanted the life of a don. He was fulfilled enough, and excited enough, by his pastoral work, and he looked on scholarship's alleged glories with some deep misgivings. Six years were to pass before he really grappled with the move, and we shall find that the misgivings were still with him then, if anything more strongly.

But while he refused outside calls and offers, he did accept some extramural work gladly and enthusiastically, finding in it even greater fulfillment. The first offer came early in 1940: he was appointed Reserve Chairman on the Appeal Tribunal to adjudicate on billeting orders. In view of his strong denunciation of war and the part he played in appealing the requisition of the Renfrew YMCA buildings, the appointment may seem surprising. But his wisdom was now well recognized—in many ways he was wise beyond his years—and there could be no doubting his willingness to serve his country in any way available to him except by the use of armed force. No details of this work have come to light, but the pleasure of this thirty-three-year-old must have been great in so responsible a task, and it will have been multiplied by the remembrance that his own mother did similar work in Motherwell twenty years previously.

The second offer was even more fulfilling than the tribunal work, and lay at the heart of his whole commitment. On February 24 the Scottish Sunday School Union's Annual Business Meeting took place. This august body had been meeting its goal of providing solid religious education to the youth of Scotland since 1797, when the Society for Erecting and Supporting Sabbath Schools in Paisley was founded.[13] Willie was now invited to a co-opted position on both its Executive and its General Council—high recognition indeed for one who had no particular training in education, and whose church was not listed among the prestigious churches of the day (although he was fairly well known by this time, having taken a number of Summer School Conferences, and many evening lectures on the SSSU's behalf). His name now appears in the minutes of the Scottish Sunday School Union for the first time, and it marks the formal opening of an association that brought him into full view of the religious and ecclesiastical establishment and paved the way for the enlargement of his preaching, teaching, and writing ministries. For the next fifteen years its increasing demands were to be an outstanding part of his work routine, and he was to influence tens of thousands of children and more than thirty thousand Sunday School teachers and workers.

At this Annual General Meeting Willie himself moved the adoption of the reports and the election of the Union's officebearers,[14] a distinct honor for one of his years and relative inexperience with the affairs of the Union. Further, he delivered the Annual Address at the plenary session. It created so favorable an impression and inspired so many people that it is worth printing in full.

I count it an honour and a privilege to be allowed to speak here to-day; and even more I count it a responsibility. I speak to those whose task is the education of the young in the knowledge and in the principles of Christianity. Now it must be clear to any thinking man that this work of educating the young in the Christian faith was never so important as it is to-day. It is one of the clear facts of the present situation that the only remaining hope for the world is Christianity; and that if ever a generation grows up which has left Christianity behind there can be nothing but inevitable chaos ahead. Therefore, it is most important—indeed, it is imperative—that the teaching of Christ be instilled into the hearts of the young people of to-day who are to be the men and women of to-morrow.

That being so, a great and a personal responsibility rests upon those whose duty it is to take part in this teaching. No man can teach anything if he does not know it himself: no man can lead another along paths which he himself has not explored: no man can open to others truths which he himself does not understand. We talk much of new methods of teaching; new orders of service; new ways of doing things; but what is supremely wanted is men and women with new hearts.

The more one considers the church and the more one looks at the average member and the average official of the church, the more one is forced to the conviction that the clamant need of the church to-day is for men and women who will take their Christianity seriously. The great characteristic of Christianity is that it is all or nothing. Dr. Hutton once said that unless a man finds Christianity a necessity, he will find it a nuisance. You cannot hope to make Christianity a hobby or an appendage of life; it must be made the business of life. And it is just that seriousness of outlook towards Christianity which is lacking and which must be supplied.

Pope the poet tells of a conversation that was once carried on between Tillotson, the then Archbishop of Canterbury, and Betterton, a famous London actor of the day. The two were very good friends. One day Betterton visited Tillotson who said wistfully to him: "How is it that after I have made the most moving discourse that I can, a discourse which touches myself most deeply and which I speak as feelingly as I can, I am not able to move the people in church as much as you do on the stage?" "I think," said Betterton, "that is easily accounted for; you are only telling them stories while I am showing them facts." So long as Christianity remains merely a story, a man can neither understand it, teach it, nor live it.

One of the notable characteristics of men who have achieved things worthwhile has always been the seriousness with which they have taken themselves and their self-chosen task. Gibbon, the historian, for instance, frankly and openly declared that he was about to write the greatest history ever written. Milton, when he was a young man, declared flatly, "I am going to write something which men will not willingly let die." When Virgil began the Aeneid he deliberately set out to write a poem which would be the epic of Rome and which would embody the spirit and the traditions of that Empire. Jerome K. Jerome in *Paul Kelver*, which is a novel, but which is none the less his own biography, quotes the words of his mother, "The gift of being able to write is given to anyone in trust; an author should never forget that he is God's servant." You see the seriousness with which these people took both themselves and their task; they magnified and glorified their work. It was not something which was to be dismissed with a deprecating smile; they knew they were engaged on something great—not something to be done in a happy-go-lucky way, but a matter of the utmost seriousness.

Think of the prophets of the Old Testament. There is not one of them but was conscious of a direct call from God. You remember Isaiah—"Whom shall I send and who will go for us? Then said I, Here am I; send me" (vi. 8). His commission came straight from God; he took it as seriously as that. You remember Amos—"I was no prophet's son; but I was an herdsman and a gatherer of sycomore fruit; and the Lord took me as I followed the flock" (vii. 14/15). Note how these men saw God in it all; they took themselves and their message so seriously that they were sure that they were none other than instruments in the hands of God. It was the same with Jesus. You recall how again and again He mentions His work, His task; He was as a man absorbed in some tremendously important piece of work. "I must work the works of Him that sent me while it is day" (John ix. 4). Then at the end, "I have finished the work which thou gavest me to do" (John xvii. 4). You see how serious, how desperately in earnest He was about his task.

If only men and women would take their call to Christianity as seriously as the writers I have spoken of took their call to literature; take it as seriously as the prophets; take it as seriously as the Master; what a difference it would make. Somehow one gets the feeling again and again that people take Christianity so lifelessly and so calmly; there is so little of that intensity of purpose; that singleness of aim; that sense of the seriousness of the whole business. And here the crux of the matter appears. People, above all young people, children, know when a speaker is sincere. They have an instinct that is almost uncanny which tells them when a teacher is not speaking out of a seriousness and a sincerity of conviction. A man who is sincere demands and commands the respect and the attention of every one who hears him.

There is a famous and an often quoted story of Martineau and Spurgeon. Martineau was a Unitarian, that is to say he held a faith which had no place for the Deity of Jesus Christ. Spurgeon, on the other hand, believed with intensity in our Lord's divinity. Martineau used on occasion to go to hear Spurgeon preach. Someone said to him one day, "Why do you go to hear Spurgeon? You do not believe what he says." "No," replied Martineau, "but he does." Martineau could tell the note of sincerity straight away, and that note of sincerity commanded his respect. An utterance that comes straight from a man's heart will always achieve its purpose.

You remember Carlyle on the publication of his masterpiece—*The French Revolution*. His friends were wondering what kind of reception it would have. "Let them do what they like with it," said Carlyle, "they never had a book that came more directly from the heart of any man." What is wanted is that teaching of and that belief in Christianity which comes direct from our hearts to the hearts of those who listen to us and who see us.

You remember Pilate's question to Jesus, "Art thou the king of the Jews?" And you remember the answer of Jesus that goes straight and sure to the core of the matter—"Sayest thou this of thyself or did another tell thee?" So much of our Christian life and our Christian teaching is a kind of second-hand story; we are repeating only what we have heard; not what we have worked out for ourselves and what we have laid hold upon with our whole hearts. Was not the first demand of Jesus—Thou shalt love the Lord thy God with all thy heart and soul and mind and strength? That is to say that a man was to take Christianity with such seriousness that it penetrated every fibre of his being.

What is needed to-day to enable us to build up a generation, which will remake and refashion this world, is that we ourselves should rediscover the infinite wonder of Christianity. I have no doubt that we all know what Christianity is; I have no doubt that we all know the facts of life of Christ and the history of God's dealings with men as the Bible tells them to us; I have no doubt that we have all a working knowledge of the doctrines of the faith, and that we give to them a placid and an almost unquestioning acceptance. More, however, than that is needed. Somewhere Richter once said, "A man may for twenty years believe in the immortality of the soul, and in the one and twentieth at some great moment he may for the first time discover with amazement the rich meaning of that belief." It is that new awakening and that new discovery that is wanted.

It has been said, and most wisely said, that all education is the transmission of life to the living by the living; that is to say that, when we teach, we are not so much trying to teach facts as we are trying to give life to those whom we teach. True, we have to work with facts, and we have to build upon a foundation of facts; but a man might be able to pass a very complete examination on the doctrines and the history of Christianity and yet be far from a Christian man. Beyond and above the facts, there is a spirit without which the structure of Christian doctrine is only a dead body without a soul; and it is that spirit which we try to teach to others. We cannot teach it unless we have it; we cannot have it unless we take our Christianity seriously; unless, like Paul, we can say and say honestly—"This one thing I do"; unless we can declare as he did—"For me to live is Christ."

It would be a good thing if we made our gathering to-day not only a business meeting, but an act of rededication, so that when we go back to our tasks we will take them more seriously than ever we did. Then, not by our words, but by the real sincerity of our hearts and the real seriousness of our purpose, we would accomplish more than ever we have done to spread the knowledge of our Lord.[15]

How very different is this from those articles printed in *The Renfrew Press!* How clearly did he understand the needs of the general public and of the Sunday School teachers and leaders! He spoke, and wrote as he lived—with discernment, understanding the times, the needs, and the aptitudes of the people, serving them, not lording it over them.

The most notable aspect of his approach in the piece is the seriousness with which he committed himself (and called for his hearers' commitment) to this work. It represented a "clamant need"; it required "an intensity of purpose"; it must "penetrate every fibre of [one's] being": the real business at hand was the rededication of the delegates to this consuming task. He was aware that churches, unlike places of learning, industry, and entertainment, were exempt from fire regulations—people simply did not expect them to catch fire! He had "the gift of enthusiasm," which he was later to term "the one essential quality," typically adding that "the man who matters most of all" is the fanatic.[16] In any case, he did manage to spark a fire among his listeners; they went away with fresh enthusiasm and determination. In this respect it is untrue to say that he was obsessed by his work. He was much keener than that! He felt the urgency expressed by one of this contemporary heroes, General Montgomery, in his D-Day Address: "every officer and every man must be enthusiastic for the fight, and have the light of battle in his eyes."[17] As Browning put it, "religion's all or nothing."

Following this annual meeting, a fine Sunday School Week was organized by the Scottish Sunday School Union and held in Glasgow. It was a big affair, planned and executed with some panache, despite the wartime conditions. Lasting four days, it opened with a civic welcome (on Tuesday, April 16), in which there was an abundance of goodwill shown to those in the movement by the city fathers. Remarkably, two thousand attended, drawn to see the exhibitions (the epidiascope was one of the main attractions) and to attend the group conferences, missionary talks, and various addresses.

Willie himself participated on the first day, speaking on "The Challenge of the Present Situation to the Teacher" at the opening lecture of the gathering. "Challenge" was ever one of his keywords, and he exploited its meaning and thrust to the full. The Editor of *The Scottish Primary Quarterly* reported that "Mr Barclay spoke to us as teachers and insisted, with pithy sayings, that we should face the situation as it was. He emphasised the crucial importance for future history of the generations now in our Sunday Schools."[18] I do not know of another place in his writings or recorded broadcasts where the phrase "future history" is used, but the paradox is entirely Willie's: he whose writings ring with the call "Forward, not backward" could do no other. It reminds one of the brutal Russian proverb quoted to Churchill by Stalin not long after this time, that "A man's eyes should be torn out if he can only see in the past." Brutal, yes; overstated, perhaps; but infinitely better than an entanglement with that which lies behind, that which enervates and stultifies and blinds one to present opportunities. Willie's attitude, like Paul's, was ever one of "stretching forward to that which lies ahead." As he once exclaimed to his church, it was a time for "hats off to the past, and coats off to the future." It was the simple and sufficient reason for his involvement in children's and young people's work, and it never left him, not even in illness or old age. Little wonder that no fewer than forty area delegations indicated their intention to organize their own Sunday School Weeks: twenty actually did so immediately.

It is a feature of Willie's life that some of his finest work was done against a difficult and depressing background. We saw it first when he produced brilliant results in his B.D. examinations at the time of his mother's terminal illness. He was to do so again during this period with his wartime church and Sunday School work, although his fortitude and perseverance were taxed as they never had been before. The international situation was deteriorating precipitously. And then on 10 May 1940, a memorable day in the history of the Western world, the

Right Honorable Winston Churchill, P.C., M.P., became First Minister of His Majesty's Government. On that appointment turned not only the war effort in Great Britain, but the very life of Western civilization, culture, and freedom.

By this time things had come to a very sorry pass indeed. The British forces in Norway had been beaten by the German war machine; France was collapsing (by a slow and painful process that would be completed by the end of June); Holland was about to be overwhelmed; and the Belgians would shortly capitulate. The end of the phony war had come. The King's command was issued, and the First Lord of the Admiralty, aged sixty-five, made his way to the palace to fulfill his sovereign's pleasure. Commented Churchill at this time, "all my past life has been but a preparation for this hour and this trial." Willie might have made the same statement. Sir John Colville speaks of Churchill's admission to office as echoing the poet's description of the Assyrian invasion of long ago: he "came down to his new abode, like a wolf on the fold."[19] As is well known, he promised Parliament, and through it the people, "nothing . . . but blood, toil, tears and sweat." His policy was merely "to wage war by sea, land, and air, with all our might and with all the strength that God can give us; to wage war against a monstrous tyranny, never surpassed in the dark, lamentable catalogue of human crime." It was an auspicious moment to realize his life's ambition; no one was better fitted to galvanize the nation. And "militant" Willie thoroughly admired this tireless, imaginative, and enthusiastic leader.

The church magazine for June speaks of "the alarming development of the fighting in France," but before it was distributed, "Operation Dynamo"—the relief and evacuation from Dunkirk—was under way. It presaged a very dark outcome. Within a week the Germans were almost at Paris, and within a further fortnight they overran France. As *The Renfrew Press* expressed it, "the baying of the jackal now heard across Europe is 'one people, one Reich, one Führer.'" The events culminated in Churchill's astonishing suggestion to Le Premier Ministre Reynaud that Britain and France should be combined in an European Union, which was rejected. More positively, his growing friendship with President Roosevelt resulted in the "loan" of fifty destroyers, the establishment of the U.S. Lend-Lease Act, which funded Britain's war effort, and the inauguration of the Atlantic Charter.

Willie sought to alleviate fears in personal contacts and pulpit pronouncements, but the hearts and minds of his parishioners were very weighed down. A special series of midweek services was arranged, but they achieved very poor attendances. Perhaps his choice of title offered little inducement for once: "The Disease and Cure of the Soul." It does not sound quite relevant, though we are assured that "Mr. Barclay . . . was at his best thoughout; such was the opinion expressed by all who were privileged to hear him."[20] Within a year Willie was to refer to the evacuation of the British Expeditionary Force from Dunkirk as a very special sign of God's providence over his people, and many in the country echoed that feeling. Others, more concerned at the lack of practical help in the area, wrote to the *Press* to air their ideas. It produced a swift reply[21] from Willie, piqued that the sedulous work of his helpers went unnoticed:

Sir,

There appeared in your columns last week a letter headed "Concessions to Soldiers." The writer of it pressed for measures to be taken for the social welfare of the troops at present in the burgh and asked: "What are we doing and what could we do?"

I should be grieved to feel that the letter gave the impression that nothing at all was being done for these strangers in our midst. I should like to draw the attention of the writer and of the general public to the work that is being done for the troops in the Church of Scotland Canteen in Trinity Church Hall. The Canteen is open from 6.30 to 10.15 each evening. Billiards, carpet bowls, darts, draughts, dominoes and other games are supplied without charge. Writing paper and envelopes are supplied free. Refreshments—tea, coffee, etc.—are supplied at very cheap prices. During the last week approximately 1600 teas were served. On Thursday evenings a free tea and a free concert are provided, and the hall is scarcely able to contain the number of men who wish to attend.

From this sketch of the programme of the Canteen it will be seen that good work is being done. But this winter we who run it are faced with a grave difficulty. Last winter we ran these Thursday evening concerts and admitted the public at a small charge. It was the income from that source which largely financed the Canteen. This winter, due to the number of men in the burgh, it will not be possible to admit the public to the concerts which we shall continue to run for the troops. Therefore our main source of revenue is gone. I feel sure that there must be many who sympathise with the work that we are doing, and I appeal to them to send to myself practical expression of their good-will.

There is room for still more to be done; but so long as the work of the Church of Scotland Canteen goes on I do not think that it can fairly be said or implied that nothing is being done.

Yours, etc.

WILLIAM BARCLAY,
Convener

Those who minimize Willie's commercial know-how should note that he even numbered the teas served in any given week: 1,600 in the one now past—that is, more than 260 a day, six days a week—over 80,000 in a full year!

He was not to rest content with this activity, however. He had plans for the coming winter session that would surpass those of the last few months. In early August he presented an inquiry to the civic authorities concerning the use of the Town Hall each Thursday for the foreseeable future, for the purpose of some Soldiers' Nights. Enter William Barclay, Impresario! His application was sent to the Property Committee of the Renfrew County Council on August 5, confirmed in Letter 308 of August 14, duly signed by the town clerk "for the purpose of entertaining the members of HM Forces in the district," and, best news of all, granted free of charge. Willie wrote on August 22, thanking them for their help—a week after *The Renfrew Press* had advertised the new weekly concerts, which meant the paper was notified on the same day the authorities issued Letter 308: a matter of a few hours before final advertising copy was agreed! Nothing is more typical of Willie's manner of working than this.

Alongside the letter reprinted above, in the same issue of the paper, there appeared another letter from Willie under the heading "Show Them Scotland." It is a rare example of his positive and direct attitude toward civic authority. It drew attention to the new concert season, and offered yet another suggestion:

Sir,

May I again beg the courtesy of your columns to make first of all an acknowledgement, and second, an appeal.

Since I last wrote to you about the work done for the troops in the Church of Scotland Canteen much practical help has been forthcoming, and to all who gave or sent me gifts I would offer sincere thanks. But in particular I would like to place on record one outstanding benefaction. Our own hall was rapidly becoming completely inadequate to house the men who wished to attend our concerts, and the Town Council have stepped in and have granted to the Canteen Committee the use of the Town Hall every Thursday evening, without charge.

A Town Council is in the position of being a body who cannot very well defend themselves in the press against ill-founded attacks, and who cannot very well proclaim their good deeds through the newspapers, but I feel that the public ought to know of this generous gesture—and it is only one among many—which the Town Council have made for the benefit of the men stationed in Renfrew.

As for the appeal. It has been repeatedly suggested to me that we as Scots should show something of the beauties of our native land to Englishmen stationed in Scotland for the first and perhaps the only time. In particular, it has been suggested to me that it would be a fine thing if we could arrange to take some bus loads of men round the famous Three Lochs Tour. Now, you cannot very well ask a man who is left with 7/- a week to pay 3/- or 4/- for a bus run, much as he would desire to do so. But if by public subscription we could reduce the cost to 1/-, or 1/6, the thing could be done.

I hesitate to ask again the kindness of the public, but I feel that a "Show them Scotland" movement must surely touch the sympathy of the community, and if any of your readers could see their way to help, I will most gratefully receive and most carefully acknowledge all donations.

Yours, etc.
WILLIAM BARCLAY

It is also one of the rare occasions when Willie allows himself expression of his love of his homeland; typically, he does so in order to share it. By August 30 the *Press* was reporting that to date one hundred soldiers had made the Three Lochs Tour.

Appropriately, an anonymous letter to the Editor was published at the conclusion of the first year of war that said "all honour to the Reverend William Barclay for the good work he is doing among the troops," and was signed "Last War."[22] Clearly, it was not only the young who were appreciative of his strong-willed commitments. He was proving that a pacifist could be a good Christian, a good minister, a good catering manager, and an excellent impresario: "all things to all men," that he may win some. . . . His career may have been checked, but in his ministry he found ever more fruitful means of fulfillment, of service.

The Background of War

It is often said that it was Churchill's speeches that won the war. But although they were of tremendous influence, it was surely his military intuition and speedy action during the first months of the war that laid the foundation for later success. Had he not ordered the troops at Calais to stand firm whatever the cost, thus tying up the enemy troops in an inessential action, it is unlikely that the evacuation from Dunkirk would have been possible. There would have been no troops to continue the war, from which now developed the "formidable army." By the evening of June 6, "one of the most fertile days of my life" in Churchill's own words, the rescue was complete.[23] And the counteroffensive was launched.

Britain was now transformed into a huge armed camp. Lorries roared in all directions as everyone feverishly prepared for the coming onslaught. It was clear that Hitler had to defeat the British Army, which was regrouping in preparation for a counterattack. Gun emplacements, tank traps, and aerial and sea defenses were constructed with whatever materials lay at hand. Within months a Home Guard of one million men was assembled, some of them armed literally with pitchforks. And Churchill's decisive voice reverberated throughout the land: "the Battle of France is over . . . the Battle of Britain is about to begin." By mid August the first great offensive had been launched, and staved off—but only just: "Never in the field of human conflict was so much owed by so many to so few." It was touch-and-go indeed, with every available plane committed to the ferocious attack, every nerve and fiber taut in concentration. By mid September it was clear that the worst of that opening battle was over; the enemy had been subdued temporarily. On the 17th of September Operation Sea-Lion (Hitler's invasion plan for the Channel ports) was called off. The country was saved, and King and people, not least Willie, gave thanks.

Indiscriminate bombing was now to be the horrendous tactic the country would have to endure. It reached its climax on October 15 in a devastating attack on London, when tens of thousands were made homeless, killed outright, or wounded. But there were many other peaks in a rough terrain of sustained physical and mental onslaughts—for example, the infamous November 14 "Moonlight Sonata" blitz on the Midlands, when Coventry was laid flat and the industrial heartland of Britain was all but destroyed. It was at this time that the BBC introduced the one minute of silence, at 9 P.M., when the nation reflected in prayer on their plight, their hopes, and their determination. It was against this background that Willie now worked.

Britain did, indeed, stand alone. The Netherlands had fallen, as had Norway and North Africa. Belgium and France capitulated, Italy and Spain made deals, and vast tracts of Eastern Europe were simply eaten up. The map of Europe had been transformed beyond all recognition. By early October Japan had signed a pact with Germany and Italy, which was further warning to America to keep out of the war. It was nevertheless Willie's responsibility in Renfrew Trinity to show that they did not actually stand alone. Repugnant as war was to him, no one could say he was not deeply involved in urging others on in their own commitments and responsibilities, be they parishioners or troops.

In September, a cake "baked by a well-known lady expert" was made the subject of a lottery, the proceeds of which went to the Soldiers' Canteen Fund (in the end, Kate's handiwork went to a couple celebrating their golden wedding anniversary).[24] The Canteen was now in full swing, enjoying a popularity that was outrunning the meager resources available. Fresh appeals were therefore made for donations of money, food, tea dishes, and "especially plates." "It is our duty," said a writer in the church magazine, "to make life as pleasant for the soldiers as possible." In extension of this appeal, a special concert was given on Friday, October 11; Fred Stuart presented "The Sparklites" and the Scottish Command Welfare Officer set up an Entertainment Fund.

Willie now organized the showing of "talkies" in the area in addition to the Thursday evening concerts. The films were mainly of a religious character, unlike his concerts, but very popular despite that. The Committee on Church and Nation of the Church of Scotland had notified the press as well as the churches and presbyteries of its concern that some of "the entertainment and social amenities" were too secular in tone. This was especially true of what was offered on Sundays. Said the encyclical, "The important thing to remember is that in all that we do on Sunday evenings for our men and women in service, their spiritual welfare must be our constant aim."[25] Willie's outreach often consisted of little more than a "threshold approach"—seeking to gain their ear and their confidence—though no one could contest the spiritual elevation of his sermons and addresses.

The war involvement was continued in early November when *The Renfrew Press* noted that "the Reverend William Barclay struck an unusual note in his sermon . . . when he spoke on the life of Winston Churchill." It was not only the homeless of London who could say "he cares—he's crying," but the equally sensitive and responsive minister in Renfrew. Willie, like many others at this time, was specially drawn to this incredible statesman, with whom he shared not a little in the way of leadership qualities: both were men of action; neither expressed interest in the world of ideas or "vain speculation"; both were masters of the spoken and written word, with great powers to inspire and encourage; both were able to determine the essentials in debate and in decision-making, albeit intuitively, not abstractedly; both were fired by the qualities of kindness, moral courage, magnanimity; and both had great powers of memory and imagination. Clemenceau's characterization of Churchill as giving "the impression of a terrific engine of mental and physical power, burning and throbbing" was applicable to Willie too. Both the men were in their very different ways spiritual forces, prophets even, in the Old Testament mold.

Willie gave some evidence of these leadership qualities when he came to terms with the grim realities in his autumn pastoral letter, displaying there his determination to keep things in balance, the essential things of life taking priority:

My Dear Friends,

In the work of this winter there will of necessity be a difference. There are many difficulties which will conspire to make the carrying on of our work very much harder than usual. There are restrictions in the use of our halls; there are food restrictions which will make our valued social meetings more difficult to carry on; there is the problem of darkened streets; there are the calls of national service and of increased work; there is in life a new element of actual danger; there is in short *the background of war* to all our activities. But the plain fact is that a man and a Church prove themselves by the way they meet their problems. Anyone can make some sort of success out of a situation which is easy and trouble free. It takes someone and something worth while to make something out of a situation which is set with difficulties. Therefore let us look on the present situation not as something hopeless but rather as a challenge to show that the Church can function with distinction even when she has many problems to solve.

Any time of emergency is a time of discarding things. Slowly but surely the non-essentials have to go and only the essentials can be kept. The one thing that we must not discard is our Church and our duty to our Church. This is a time when all luxuries are being given up; but the Church is not a luxury; it is an essential in the life of the community and the individual.

Let us be faithful in our Church attendance for our own sakes. It is well that there should be some oasis of peace in a desert of war. It is well that there should be some place where we remember, as Luther had it, that "God is not dead." It is well that there should be some source which will give us light for the day and strength for the burden.

Further, let us be faithful to the Church for the sake of those we love. Some of us in these days have learned what it means to pray. So let us see to it that, if for no other reason, we come to God's house each Sunday to commend our loved ones to God's keeping.

And above all let us, leaders and members of organisations alike, remember that things cannot be just the same as they used to be; that there must be restrictions; that everyone will have to sacrifice something that the good of the whole may be served and that grumbling and complaints about it all will not help but only hinder. Let us go into this winter with but one thought, that we will show the community in this town that even in time of war a Church can carry on.

May God's blessing be upon this congregation and on every member of it and may God's protection be on those who in these days are absent from us on their country's business.

Ever very sincerely yours,
WILLIAM BARCLAY

The normal work of the church went ahead, week by week, with pastor and people overcoming the problems as best they could. Willie was still busy with his work for the Scottish Sunday School Union, lecturing and addressing various groups in the area, always with a careful eye to his very limited petrol ration. He participated in the Sunday School Week at Greenock—the center of John Paterson Struther's ministry between 1882 and 1914, which was such a great influence on Willie's own ministry, not least for Struthers's godly bearing and close friendship with James Denney. (WDB had long been under Struther's spell, despite his absences from the area.) The theme of this conference was "The Mastership of Christ," a preeminent concern of Willie's too.

Harvest Thanksgiving came and went, this year with less fresh and more packaged foodstuffs on display—a sign of the changing conditions. Hospital Sunday was celebrated in usual style at Trinity. As the editor of the church magazine said, in a somewhat exaggerated fashion, "While crowned heads fall and states disappear, the Junior Choir keeps moving steadily on, unperturbed by the events of history." Mr. Mitchell had now resumed leadership of the choir and brought back *Rob Roy*, which reminded Willie of his first week in the church. Willie celebrated this remembrance by forming a Bible Class choir, and immediately planned to give two concerts in its first session! The year closed with the usual range of Christmas parties and festivities, and a special dinner and concert for the troops, 150 of whom were entertained before the Provost and town councilors. They went on to send, via the Woman's Guild, parcels "consisting of woollen garments and other useful articles," plus postal orders for five shillings each to sixty-seven men serving in the army, navy, and air force. Like Elijah's pot, the deeper they dipped into their meager resources the greater seemed to be their continuance.

It had been a year of mixed fortunes for the Barclay household, witnessing the evacuation of their children to Dundonald in the summer, and the sad loss of Kate's mother, Mrs. Gillespie, just before Christmas. They needed the exhortation Willie—reliant, as ever, on poets great and small—caused to be printed at the head of the church magazine, in its last issue for the year:

> There is no noble height thou canst not climb.
> All triumphs will be thine in time's futurity,
> If, whatsoe'er thy faults, thou dost not faint nor halt
> But lean upon the staff of God's security.[26]

The new year, 1942, opened with a special comment in the church magazine regarding their "indefatigable minister." Under the heading of "Versatility," the editor wrote that

> Some churches have singing ministers; some are proud of their play-acting minister; but our minister can do almost anything. He can play centre-forward when called upon, best members of his Kirk Session on the golf course, talk with philatelists, play the piano and organ, train and conduct choirs—even ladies' choirs—and lecture on any subject one cares to select. In addition to the many duties that come to him from a congregation over twelve hundred, he has found time to attend to the welfare of the soldiers stationed in the district and for this he has been thought worthy of being selected as an Army Chaplain.

The chaplaincy was not a "noble height" he had ever aspired to, this convinced and militant pacifist, but he knew duty when he saw it, nor was he halt or fainthearted in meeting its exigencies; he knew well the Staff whereupon he had constantly to lean. He was, in fact, appointed not Army Chaplain, but Officiating Chaplain of the Royal Air Force in Renfrew, thus extending the enjoyment he obtained from aircraft into solid service for his country and fellow man. He found no incongruity in turning up for rehearsals of the Woman's Guild Choir in his siren-suit outfit à la Churchill and was shortly made master of ceremonies in their annual concert, presenting a veritable cornucopia of items old and new: solos, duets, and quartettes, plus the full choir rendering various choruses and anthems. Other special attractions were a local ATS member from Northern Ireland who sang haunting Gaelic songs, and a play specially written for the occasion (probably by Kate and Willie) entitled "Small Talk." The concert followed one given by the Bible Class, whose choirs Willie also conducted.

It was a splendid introduction to the celebration of his eighth year at Trinity (the church's seventy-ninth), which was surveyed at the end of February in the annual business meeting. Once again the membership was found to have been increased, this year by forty-one members no less; income was held more or less static (it actually declined by seven pounds), and their expenditures had increased by just over twenty pounds. As if to symbolize the session's commitment to austerity, no tea was served. They were now almost at the end of the five-year plan Willie and the managers had introduced in 1936 when the church was refurbished. All but £406 had been cleared—an outstanding feat considering the economic and military conditions. The various organizations reported good success, and there was already a sign that the pessimism of the previous June had begun to lift; they were preparing to scale afresh the noble heights.

The day before this annual meeting, a very somber action was taken by the authorities when fire-watching was introduced for all public buildings. It was no idle innovation of the government. Seventy thousand incendiary bombs had been dropped on London alone on one night in October, and since then high-explosive and incendiary devices had rained down over Great Britain perpetually, bringing appalling death and destruction to their recipients. From now on five people (three men, two women) were to guard carefully their beloved church and halls every night for the next two years. In the first week they only just managed to scrape together sufficient numbers to fill the rota, but soon a list of 140 watchers was compiled, which necessitated one duty night every four weeks for those listed. Their enthusiasm did not last long, unhappily, and soon appeals were being publicly made for greater commitment to this arduous task. When the church celebrated its centenary in 1962, a special memorial volume, *A History of Trinity Church, Renfrew: 1862-1962*, was published; among the detailed appendices of church workers, one page was properly reserved for the Fire-Watchers—seventy-six persons (forty men and thirty-six women, twenty-seven of whom were unmarried young ladies), many of whose names are recognizable as former Sunday School teachers, Bible Class members, and founders of the Young People's Society.

The Fire-Watchers began at 10 P.M., kept watch till breakfast time, and then went to their daily work—a gruelling routine month in month out for already hard-pressed, underfed, overworked people. A regular visitor to their stations was Willie himself, though rarely before midnight. He would enjoy a cup of tea with them, recount a few amusing anecdotes drawn from his long and varied day, and then disappear back to the manse when he was not actually on duty himself, for he had insisted on being listed despite his many jobs. He was frequently found writing his Sunday sermons while on duty—an excellent example perhaps of how best to fulfill the dominical injunction "to watch and pray." When not so occupied, he engaged in "mental hikes" with those who had not yet succumbed to sleep, not least with William Braidwood and friends. Many were the vigorous discussions that took place on the outcome of the war and the need for reconstruction (which included the role the Socialists might play in the new society).

March saw the sorriest nights of the war for Clydeside as they received heavy bombardment, the 13th and 14th being by far their worst. Wave after wave of bombers delivered their messages of hate, resulting in enormous damage and great bloodshed. Over twenty thousand incendiary bombs were dropped, and the noise and fires could be seen and heard for miles around. The paper reminded the victims that London and the south coast had endured a thousand such raids, and the ARP and emergency services did heroic work among the wreckage. Renfrew had its moments as well; two bombs narrowly missed the manse itself, causing some structural damage to the walls and part of the roof. All over the area churches and halls and private accommodations were ruined. One of those who lost everything at this time was Mrs. Jean Haggard, who had been the youngest church member (at fourteen) when Willie came to Renfrew. He had married the Haggards six months earlier in the manse, but was now called upon to console them in their desolation. Willie spoke of the deep regret he felt that such beautiful work (that of the bridegroom's own furniture, carved in handsome mahogany) should be destroyed; a joiner's grandson may be expected to sympa- thize and dwell on that. Little did he then realize that in two years he would be back to the devastated young widow after her husband was killed in Abadan, this time offering consolation not so much by his words and his prayers as by his presence: "in all their affliction, he was afflicted," true shepherd that he was.

Mrs. Wilson, who later emigrated to New Zealand but was then postwoman for the area, recalls two Polish army officers being killed just outside the manse air-raid shelter.[27] Willie had invited them in, but they insisted on watching the events, to their great cost. It was this same lady to whom Willie used to offer tea and scones when she delivered the post—Willie typically urging her to eat, saying he had made them himself specially for her! The only direct casualty of Trinity Church at this time was Alexander Ross, a young man of fifteen years; his death served to bring the war's savage wastage grimly home to them all.

The situation was very grave. On the 14th of April Willie preached a sermon on "The Present Situation" which extended the theme of a special pastoral letter in the church magazine for that month. The letter read as follows:

My Dear Friends,

It is not my custom to write monthly letters to the Supplement [the church magazine was actually circulated as an inset to the Church of Scotland's magazine *Life and Work,* often referred to as "the Supplement"], but only to say something to the congregation on what might be called special occasions. It seems to me that such an occasion has arisen in these days. We in this town were for long spared the full realisation of what war meant. Life for us proceeded normally enough with but few interruptions, with but minor discomforts and with no real threat of danger at all. But when our testing did come it came in no uncertain fashion and from now on we face a future always uncertain, assuredly difficult and probably dangerous. In two things we have great cause for devout thanksgiving. The one is that the loss of life in our town has been small; and the other is a matter more personal to us; I mean the fact that our Church, whose every stone is dear to us, has suffered no damage that really affects it. For these things we are grateful to God.

These happenings of the past ought to have certain repercussions upon our Church-life. For one thing they ought to draw us closer together than ever we were before. In times of danger barriers break down. People meet not as strangers but as comrades in a common peril. Differences among men depart when they are under fire. We ought in these days to be one united body, sharing a common danger with a common fortitude and in a fellowship of peril which joins us all together.

For another thing our religion must have become a thing that is more intense and more real to us. There were nights when we learned to pray again. It is a strange thing that times of ease and prosperity have never been great ages in the Christian Church. It was when they were in danger and in adversity that men were thrown back on God. In these days we must slowly learn to be able to say, "God is our refuge and our strength; therefore will not we fear."

But these days have also brought to us a new duty. Difficult times face this congregation. Many of our members have evacuated themselves to safer areas; some have left the district for good; parents have removed children to less dangerous places. Now all this means that those of us who have elected to stay here must with the more earnestness support our Church. Those of us who are left must seek by our presence and by our liberality and by our prayers to see to it that the Church's work goes on undiminished although her numbers are temporarily fewer. We are left to carry on and we must see to it that we hold the standard as high as ever it was held.

Our nation in this time is standing for the greatest principles in the world. Let us unwaveringly stand by the Church and Christianity and Christ; for only Christianity can save and keep secure these very principles for which we struggle.

"Into thy hands we commend our spirits." With that prayer of our Master let us go on.

Ever very sincerely yours,
WILLIAM BARCLAY

It is interesting that in his penultimate paragraph, he comes very near to abandoning his pacifist position, apparently acknowledging the need to fight against evil. As far as we can now judge, he never returned to the Gandhian position of nonresistance that he urged before the outbreak of war—but neither did he ever actually abandon his pacifism.

The war was taking its toll, though signs of a British offensive (for example in Greece and Crete, which unhappily ended in disaster) were present. In May, Parliament itself was damaged by bombs, and the next month—on June 22— Hitler broke faith with the Russians by attacking them in defiance of their treaty, an eventuality the Russians had expected, having broken the German intelligence system. In North Africa, Rommel's troops had reached the very frontiers of Egypt, and *H.M.S. Hood,* so proudly launched from Clydeside in 1935, went down in the Atlantic, a victim of the deadly U-boat campaign.

It was essentially a year of defeat, not least in the Far East, where the Japanese flag was raised over territory after conquered territory. With the attacks on Russia, Hitler's military might turned aside from Great Britain and so some respite from the blitz was found. Curiously, perhaps, Willie now preached a sermon (on the evening of June 13) under the title "Is the World Getting Better or Worse?" One would have thought the answer was obvious, but Willie's natural exuberant optimism was not so sure: he was looking at the stars, not the mud, destruction, and grief. He found time for the annual prize giving at the local school, attended the outing of the Sunday School (reduced to forty percent of its normal numbers due to evacuation) at the local King George V playing fields, and preached at a Flower Service at Trinity. To top it all, he preached on "The Infinite Possibilities of Human Life" at the end of June, just before he and Kate took some holiday at Dundonald.

September saw the commencement of a new campaign on behalf of the government: "Work for Victory, and Shorten the War." It also saw the compulsory registration of the eighteen- to sixty-year-olds for civil defense. Some good news of the war began to emerge: it was soon reported that the Russians had scored some notable victories and could "prove to be [Hitler's] undoing" yet.[28] The threat of invasion was therefore receding, and thoughts were turning toward a real counterattack. This good news naturally inspired Willie's confidence to do more, and so we find him in September "confiding" to *The Renfrew Press* (which promptly published the fact to the world) that he was considering the establishment of a Youth Fellowship to be held each Friday evening during the winter months, the purpose of which would be to hold debates and discussions on life's problems. Willie had already secured some local professional people to lead a series of meetings under the title "Looking at Life." The series would complement his Senior Bible Class, though in fact it represents a break with Bible Class tradition, a "secularizing" of it before its time, and a significant development in Willie's thinking. In a very real sense it was yet another application of his threshold evangelism technique, applied to church life.

His autumn pastoral letter, which went to press in August, does not yet reflect any awareness of an improvement in Britain's wartime fortunes:

My Dear Friends.

It has always been my custom to write a short letter to this issue of our monthly supplement as a kind of introduction to the work of the winter months which lie ahead. Even in normal times every winter brought its own quota of problems, of tasks and of perplexities; and of this winter we can only say one thing with certainty—that the Church's life will become more difficult than ever it was, and at the same time more necessary.

There are certain difficulties that are inherent in the present situation. It is inevitable that the claims of Sunday work should lessen our congregation. The conditions during the black-out at night and, still more, our knowledge of what is liable to happen during the hours of darkness, make it almost impossible for us to hold regular services in the evening this winter. As a congregation we depended much on our mid-week activities. They, too, will be gravely interrupted. There are so many who have loved ones separated from them, many of them in danger and in peril. And in the minds of all of us there is a general anxiety and unrest. All this makes for an atmosphere of unsettlement and of tension which is hard to bear.

Now it is well to state and to face our difficulties, but it is not well to brood over them. One thing I ask of those of you who, in these days for any reason, find it impossible to attend Church. I ask that you will remember the Church. Church-going is a habit; a habit once broken is difficult to re-make. Will those of you who at present cannot come to Church please try not to lose all touch with the Church, so that even when you can you have forgotten the desire to come? Will you try to keep alive the memory of God's House and the desire to worship in it so that when normal times come back there will be none who have strayed away and lost touch altogether.

To all of us I would say this. It seems to me that this is a time when we cannot do other than live in the present. It is no good looking back. The mistakes have been made; we reap the fruits of them, but we cannot unmake them. It is little good looking forward; never at any time could we tell what a day would bring forth, least of all now. Our duty lies in the present.

When Sir Richard Grenville, the famous English sailor, was dying after a struggle against tremendous odds, he said:—

"Here dies I, Richard Grenville, with a joyful and a quiet mind, for that I have ended my life as a true soldier ought to do that hath fought for his country, Queen, religion and honour. Whereby my soul most joyfully departeth out of this body, and shall always leave behind it an everlasting fame of a valiant and true soldier that hath done his duty as he was bound to do."

He found his peace in doing his duty. Let us think all the time not of yesterday's mistakes and not of to-morrow's, but of to-day's duties. Our duty may be to serve in His Majesty's Forces; our duty may be to stay at our post and work with redoubled energy; our duty may be in civil defence; our duty may be to see that a home is a haven of peace and comfort in troubled days; our duty may be to see that a family is cared for in a way that will shield it from this hard world; our duty may be—hardest of all—to wait and watch and pray. Whatever it is let us

240

not be found wanting; in the doing of it we shall find happiness even in trouble and peace of mind even in war.

It does not matter what the situation is, we cannot do without our Church, because we cannot do without God. In the days to come stand by your Church. We shall need its support now; and we shall need its guidance when, after the storm, we re-make the world.

May God's blessing be upon us all and night and day may He keep us in our going out and our coming in and may He hasten the day when we and our loved ones will meet—please God—in an unbroken circle in a world at peace.

Always very sincerely yours,
WILLIAM BARCLAY

Forward, not backward—but never without a word for the present.

Meanwhile, presbytery, aware that it was not attracting the attention, still less the energy, of Renfrew Trinity's minister, nominated him in his absence to three different committees: the Life and Work and Public Questions Committee, the Publications Committee (on which he had previously served, though only nominally, due to his other exertions), and—with more than a touch of irony—the Ceremonials Committee. Presumably he was considered to be a negative wire for this committee, for it would be difficult to find anyone less interested in ceremonials per se than Willie. He knew how to dress, of course, and his services were models of orderly, reverent, and well-planned meetings. But not ceremonies! Never ceremonies! Rather, meeting places for men and women, boys and girls and young people, with each other and with God, places where emotion and feeling were definitely given their place, where people could relax, laugh, cry, enjoy, and pledge themselves for serious work. Little wonder presbytery saw nothing of him the next fourteen months; it had totally misjudged its man. Between September 1940 and January 1942 Willie did not put in a single appearance at presbytery.

It did not take this action (not a deliberate snub) lying down, but appointed him in December—again in his absence—to the Renfrew group of presbytery dealing with the so-called Baillie Report, otherwise known under the cumbersome title "Interpreting God's Will in the Present Crisis." Willie's group was to deal with Sections 1–13, but there is no record of their meetings, still less of their conclusions. When presbytery met in November 1942 to take stock of the viewpoints so gathered and expressed, Willie was again absent; nor were any "apologies for absence" received from him. He had simply ignored them. This is not to say that Willie had no interest in the Report itself. In fact he had, for the Report sought to give fresh emphasis to the importance of the parish as a unit in the church. This was very definitely in line with Willie's thinking, and the fact that John White was made Convener of the General Assembly Committee entrusted to study it can only have added to his interest. What did not interest Willie, however, were the endless meetings, the pitch-and-putt of unending debate, the bureaucratic approach. That he could (and did) forget, unceremoniously.

Meanwhile, he was at it again, founding an Old Men's Club in October. At the first meeting, *The Renfrew Press* reported that he spoke to them "in a racy and appropriate manner"[29]—asking for his name to be included on their roll by virtue of his presence if not by age (he was but thirty-three at the time). They were given the freedom of his church hall (between 10:00 A.M. and 5:00 P.M.) every day except Tuesday, and had access to all games and facilities. That, like his canteen work, was his interpretation of God's will for the present crisis, along with the other activities in which he was immersed. It had been possible to offer the halls for such extended periods because the Canteen's usage had dropped off through the winter following the deployment of the troops elsewhere. But having offered the hall to the men, Willie now found a new detachment of troops in town and a renewed demand for the Canteen facilities. Commented the editor of the church magazine,

> Keeping up the march of an army of trained men when there is no action in prospect must be very difficult and must give the officers in charge some concern. If the church can do anything to make things pleasant for the men who have had to leave their homes and their dear ones it is surely worth while. A brass band has been formed by some of the local soldiers; it is not a large band; it consists only of ten or twelve, but it gives the players something to do, they say, and it helps to cheer the other fellows.

And, he continued, "the staff of assistants are hard pressed at times to cope with their numerous customers."[30]

Later that month Willie had the pleasure of being included in Renfrew's civic reception for a special visit of the Moderator, the Very Reverend J. Hutchinson Cockburn of Dunblane Cathedral. Doctor Cockburn was there to help launch Scotland's Churches' Week of Witness, which was to take place from November 30 to December 7, emphasizing the missionary role of the world church. The symbol chosen for the event was a Celtic cross over a bombed building, illustrative of the new hope they sought to raise in men's hearts. Five hundred gathered to hear the Moderator, whose theme was "When a Man Dethrones God, He Enthrones Himself." Willie opened the gathering with one of his memorable prayers, and the whole gathering found the evening "an uplifting experience." In Glasgow, similar proceedings were opened by the veteran missionary William Paton, and the speaker was the General Secretary of the British and Foreign Bible Society, A. M. Chirgwin. The latter was of considerable influence on Willie, who was later to use many of his stories about the power of the Bible to illustrate his own teaching and writing.

On 7 December 1941, the Japanese navy attacked Pearl Harbor without warning or the declaration of war. It marked the turning point in the war. From now on America and the British Empire were allies indeed.

The Turning Tide: Makers of a New World

Christmas 1941 was a troubled time, with increased financial burdens on the congregation due to blackout, ARP, Fire-Watching Regulations, and War Risk

Insurance. For individuals the restrictions of various government departments, notably the Food Controller, imposed special limitations and even deprivations. The teachers of the Sunday School (under Willie's leadership) were determined not to disappoint their children, and "a local purveyor [promised to] make everything attractive as possible."[31] Kate did so, even if the buns had no icing, and the currants were sparer than usual. They still had their Toy Service, making a good collection of toys available for the Sick Children's Hospital, and Willie managed to raise £36 for "his boys" in the forces, 110 of whom received postal orders when such goodies were in very short supply.

America's direct intervention was regarded as a decisive turning point in the war, and Willie promoted that spirit in his New Year pastoral letter. Endurance, contentment, optimism, and trust were rekindled in good order:

My Dear Friends,

Whatever else we may say about 1942 it is true to say that it is a year when the most momentous issues will be settled. We are in these days living in great times and it seems to me that our first endeavour and our first prayer must be that we should show ourselves great enough worthily to play our part in them.

Now if we are to be great enough to be worthy of the times in which we live there are certain qualities we shall need in the days of this new Year.

1. We shall need the quality of endurance.

There come times in every great and prolonged struggle when there remains nothing to do but to hold on. When two great forces are opposed against each other there comes a time when one or other must crack; and it is to those who can hold on longest that the final triumph comes. You remember the famous lines of Kipling when he says that the test of a man is

> If you can force your heart and nerve and sinew
> To serve your turn long after they are gone,
> And so hold on, when there is nothing in you
> Except the will, that says to you, "Hold on!"

It is nearly always true and it is truer than ever to-day that he who endureth to the end shall be saved. There is nothing very romantic and colourful about this quality of endurance but it is a quality upon which life must be built in these days, and Christ's people, as they have often done in every age and generation, must once again show the world how they can endure.

2. We shall need the uncomplaining spirit.

No one likes to have to make sacrifices; no one likes to have life grow narrower, more filled with restrictions, more crowded with limitations, more emptied of the comforts and the luxuries that meant so much. It is human nature under such circumstances to want to complain and to allow ourselves to grumble and to murmur. There is one thing that we must in such a case remember. No man, said Paul, liveth to himself and no man dieth to himself. Neither does any age live or die or suffer and endure entirely to itself. The sufferings and the sacrifices of one generation win the privileges and the freedom of the next. Were our trials endured only for our own sake they might daunt us; but in these days the life and the world of future generations depend on us. We are therefore to be upheld by the thought that all that is called for from us is for the sake of the times to be. If we think of ourselves as the makers of a new world we will not complain.

3. We shall need the quality of hope.

When things are easy and when there are no clouds on the horizon and when the future is set fair there is no virtue in hope. But there are times in life and in history when hope becomes the greatest of the Christian virtues. When we grow hopeless we might as well give up at once. So long as hope remains everything is possible. You remember how Browning describes the heroic man—

> One who never turned his back but marched breast forward,
>   Never doubted clouds would break,
> Never dreamed though right were worsted wrong would triumph,
> Held we fall to rise, are baffled to fight better,
>   Sleep to wake.

With the certainty that in the end God's kingdom must and will come we need never abandon hope.

4. We shall need the quality of trust.

In the end the only kind of peace that matters is the peace of mind which can honestly say, "My times are in thy hand," and leave it at that. We can be sure that a father's hand will never cause his child a needless tear. We can be sure that the God who spared not his only son will with him freely give us all things. We can be sure that the Lord of Hosts is with us and the God of Jacob is our refuge. We can be sure of the everlasting arms underneath and about us. And in that certainty we can be content. To have perfect trust is to have perfect peace and to know no fear. In these days we must learn to seek and to find a trust like that.

I wish you well in the days of this New Year. It is my hope and my prayer that the Church and the fellowship of the Church and the services of the Church may do much to bring us and to help us through the difficult days that lie ahead. May God bless each member of this congregation and may He strengthen and uphold us all to meet whatever the future may bring. God's blessing be upon us and upon our Church.

Ever very sincerely yours,
WILLIAM BARCLAY

But if hope burned brightly, reality was ever to obtrude itself, and it did so brutally in those opening months. In the Far East, Malaya and Singapore were overrun by the Japanese army (the latter being "the worst disaster and the largest capitulation in British History" according to Churchill,[32] which loss cost him much esteem and support at home). The Dutch East Indies went the same way in early March. Rangoon also fell, and the drive into Burma was on, all too soon to be successful. In Europe indecision predominated. Worried by the dangers of a collapse of Russian morale (they held on with unbelievable courage at Stalingrad), the Americans contended strongly for a landing in Europe; Churchill and

Montgomery stood firm, a militarily correct step, but divisive. Operation Torch— the action in North Africa—eventually won through, with the Americans entering the war theater via French Northwest Africa, but not before Tobruk fell (in June), putting the whole of North Africa at risk, and largely in the power of the Axis armies.

A very notable event took place on 1 January 1942, when the Declaration of the United Nations was signed by twenty-six states, its object being to lay the foundations of an international peace organization (the charter was eventually drafted and signed in June 1945). Thus it was that the hope for the world was built on not merely a military strategy, but on international cooperation: a brave new world was at last in sight. As if to celebrate this, another Sunday School Week was held in Glasgow, with the theme "The Sunday School and the New Order." In Trinity's fire-watching sessions, a sort of pastoral think tank, they were coming to grips with the issues—ecclesiastical and national, but especially moral.

The austerity campaign was well under way at Trinity, as can be seen in the annual budget, which showed an expected increase in expenditures of only three hundred pounds. Income for 1941 was down by forty pounds and declining, as the shortages continued to force prices up. The church was clearly determined to continue vigorously, even if a deficit was reached by October. In the February issue of the church magazine, Willie expressed his concern over finance with an updated version of the story of the widow's mite.

Of Such is the Kingdom of Heaven

I have already related in Church an incident which recently happened to me; but I desire to set it down in print that there may be a more permanent record of it and that the story of it may reach even more people. I ask you not to enquire or to speculate or to guess at the identity of the person concerned, for that, I think, would hurt her, but for all that I believe her deed should be held in memory. There is in this congregation a widow whose material resources are very, very small indeed. Further, she has had much of sorrow and a great deal of suffering in her life; more than once I have seen her at death's door. She lives entirely alone. For long she came to the Church when it was really beyond her strength to come; but now, at least for a time, she is not able to come any more.

It had always been almost impossible to prevail upon her to accept the assistance which the Church would have been honoured to give her, but I had a pledge from her that if ever she needed it she would ask me for it. Some time ago a letter from her was handed in at my house. I thought that perhaps now she needed the help that I could give. I opened the letter. Inside it there was a little bag carefully sewn up and a note asking me to accept what was in the bag and to use it as I thought best for the good of the Church. Inside there was a letter which will remain much more precious to me than the other contents of the little bag, notes to the sum of almost £20. It was a careful savings of years handed over to the Church she loved. Twenty pence would have been from her a great gift; £20 must have been more like a king's ransom. I was unwilling to accept so great a gift, but when I went and saw her she refused to take any of it back.

I believe that some permanent record of a gift like that should remain; so with a little of the money I have arranged for a pulpit copy of the Anthem Book to be bought—that is the only book which the pulpit set lacks—and on that book there will be inscribed the record of this lovely deed; the rest of the money I have handed over to the Church Treasurer. Such a thing is enough to uplift anyone's heart at the thought of such love and devotion to God and to the Church of God. It may be that the setting down of this extraordinary gift may touch the hearts of others to a greater generosity and perhaps even a little sacrifice for the house of God.

You remember—"And Jesus called unto Him His disciples and saith unto them, Verily I say unto you, that this poor widow hath cast more in, than all they which have cast into the treasury; for all they did cast in of their abundance; but she of her want did cast in all that she had, even all her living."

A lovely deed has been written in the Book of Life.

The Church did not allow February 22 to pass without calling attention to its being the commencement of Willie's tenth year as their minister. The special preacher for the anniversary services was Professor John Mauchline of Trinity College, a former minister of Motherwell. He also spoke very highly of Willie's development as a young man, of his promising undergraduate days, and of the clear success he was making of his work at Renfrew. He reminded the congregation of Willie's late father and the family tradition in which he had been nurtured. The vigor of his ministry had made the nine years now past seem "more like months than years," to quote one breathless record; moreover, "they have been very happy days within our Church, and the good fellowship that exists must be credited to our leader's personality; he understands men (and women) and knows how to get the best out of them."

And now appears the first indication of some personal trouble: "It is our earnest prayer that his health may improve . . ."; severe dental disorder was the difficulty noted in the session minutes.[33] Willie's affliction necessitated a leave of absence for two months from all pulpit duties and the lessening of others. (From this time dates his pulpit habit of tapping his teeth before he commenced preaching, one of the idiosyncrasies of his pulpit style; another was tapping his hearing aid to ensure that it was on.) One result of this indisposition was Willie's inability to attend the meeting for the National Day of Prayer. H. L. Adamson, a former missionary in Poona who was now, like Willie, a chaplain to His Majesty's Forces, supplied pulpit for him. While in the pulpit, Mr. Adamson conveyed the appreciation to the Scottish Command for the war effort made by Trinity through its Canteen, and particularly that of its minister-manager.

Willie's treatments did not stop him, in the wake of the usual spate of parties and concerts that took place in the first quarter of the year, from putting on his Young People's Concert, which was deemed to be "very courageous," particularly as the date set for it was March 13! Before this the Woman's Guild had held its own concerts, at which Willie complimented some of its choir members for having attained perfect attendance over four difficult years. Trinity was like that. As Addison wrote:

'Tis not in mortals to command success,
But we'll do more, Sempronius, we'll deserve it.

A very practical aspect of this Young People' Concert was made public after its full-house performances. The profit amounted to fourteen pounds, which was immediately earmarked for the purchase of new seating for the church hall. Some managers expressed concern over this; the church was still nearly three hundred pounds in debt, the repayment of which was now exceeding the five-year limit. Willie's answer was entirely characteristic, and it kept at bay the church managers, who had no responsibility for this group and its separate finances: "The debt is steadily being reduced, and the Young People wish to achieve a definite objective." So they deposited their money, and planned a Whist Drive and a social for the 1st of May—an appropriate day to have a social, but one not presently overemphasized by Willie. They also announced that during the next winter they would run a special event every month. The Woman's Guild was delighted (they, too, enjoyed a certain independence from the Manager's Court) and sent a contribution. As Marie Campbell, Secretary to the Young People's group, recorded, "There is no jealousy between Mr Barclay's choirs": choir conducting by Willie had now become one of the leg-pulls of his ministry, despite its serious intent, and at the end of this month he was found leading the Young People's choir at the evening service, which was followed a week later by his Woman's Guild Choir doing the same duty. There was no jealousy, certainly, but a sure and certain diplomacy was called for nonetheless. "Now we have choirs to suit all ages," exclaimed the editor of the church magazine, perhaps wondering from which group the next one might emerge.

There was nothing introspective about the departments or the work of Trinity Renfrew. Its responsibilities to presbytery, to the church-extension, missionary, and evangelistic aims of the church were never lost sight of, as the accounts for consecutive years show. Some of these extramural interests were financed by the various organizations of the church, notably the Woman's Guild. There was also a system of "Missionary Collectors" who were responsible for direct giving. Overall, the amount the church spent on external organizations beyond its presbyterial allocation amounted to an average of twelve to fifteen percent of its income. Moreover, it was always ready to give to special appeals, sometimes with a comment or two by way of recommendation or suggestion for the furtherance of the particular venture at stake.

Despite the trouble with his health, Willie initiated another series of midweek meetings that ran from April to the end of May. The church magazine somewhat bluntly reported that "they were a failure from an attendance stand-point." Willie was nevertheless thanked for a very fine series of addresses on "The Wisdom That Is from Above," based on James 3:17: "The wisdom that is from above is first pure, then peaceable, gentle, easy to be entreated, full of mercy and good fruits, without partiality, without hypocrisy"—a passage that recalls Philippians 4:8, the "motto" of WDB's household. Willie never failed to stress the significance of eternal life and the hope it inspired, but he was much more concerned with its qualitative aspects than with the more quantitative one of duration, as is the New Testament itself, of course.

Willie had scarcely resumed his preaching duties when he heard that one of his elders had been ordered to rest. Unconcerned over his own health, he immediately took over his precommunion visiting and other duties, much to Kate's concern. His attitude toward his health reminds one of Lord Moran's comment about Churchill's attitude to health—that "a fine desregard for common sense has marked his earthly pilgrimage."[34] His inclination to self-sacrifice can also be seen in an incident that William Johnstone, Renfrew's main funeral director, once brought to my attention. One of his drivers was taken ill, and Mr. Johnstone was in a fix over fulfilling his promises. Willie's eagle eye spotted his discomfiture, and he asked what the trouble was. On being told, he assured the funeral director there would be no problem: he would himself drive the hearse following a funeral service he had to conduct on that same day. He did so, covering his clerical collar with a suitably tied scarf, though one or two of the funeral party were surprised to see a familiar face in such an unfamiliar setting!

The war machine, meanwhile, rumbled on. Sometimes it caused deep distress, sometimes fanciful elation. To Willie it was a diabolical waste of men and means, an abhorrent intrusion into their lives, a disruptive parenthesis. As early as 1940 he had begun to speak of doing things "when the war is over"; he did not accommodate well the disorderliness, the chaos, of war. Not that it was unreal to him, but its reality was of the wrong sort, a tangled thread in the tapestry of life. There was, however, some good news of the defeat of the U-boats, and some comforting reports concerning Renfrew's prisoners of war at Stalag VIIIB Camp provided some light in the darkness. But then, in August, the British forces (still constituting the largest portion of the Allied forces) were trounced in an abortive raid at Dieppe under Louis Mountbatten, and in the autumn the long-expected invasion of North Africa took place: Churchill's "two most anxious months of the war" had begun. A National Day of Prayer was arranged for September 3, Willie participating with his fellow ministers at a United Churches Service in the Town Hall. A gradual change in the fortunes of war now took place, and with it came a rise in morale and hope. On the 9th of September Allied troops landed at Salerno, in the toe of Italy, in an attempt to outflank the Axis troops. They met ferocious opposition, but the symbolic victory of their arrival was more important in any case than the military event itself, and the free world took fresh courage. This had increased to such an extent by September 1943 that, to give but one example, when the management of the Clyde's shipbuilders asked their men to work two Sundays out of four, they responded by offering to work three!

By late October Montgomery had smashed through Rommel's fortifications at El Alamein, and on November 8 the biggest amphibious operation of all time took place when the huge fleet of the Allies (assembled in secret in the Atlantic) swooped down on Morocco and Algeria. Within days the German forces were swept out of Egypt and across Cyrenaica. If it was not the beginning of the end, it was, in Churchill's memorable words, the end of the beginning. Through all this the work of the Canteen went on, Willie all the while conscious of the ultimate sacrifice many of the men relaxing before him would pay in the cause of right, and making much of their work in his epilogues, which ever preserved the YMCA's pattern of being "brief, bright and brotherly."

Willie faced new mundane problems along with his congregation under the heading "Fuel Economy: Forewarned, Forearmed" in the church magazine. New heating regulations were to be part of the congregation's contribution to the new war effort, and this meant no extra heating before the 1st of November—a sacrifice he was sure they would accept gladly "even if we have to appear in Church like walking wardrobes." But Willie's sermons did not get shorter, still less his prayers. As a minister, and as a chaplain to His Majesty's Forces, Willie never forgot the inner reality of faith, or the duty he had to expound it effectively. While the Allies were mopping up in North Africa, Willie turned his mind to deeper things in a letter to *The Renfrew Press*,[35] in which he helped to promote the Week of Witness cause:

Sir,

The week from the 29th of November to the 6th of December will be observed throughout the churches of the town as the Week of Witness. Now this week has certain very definite objects in view.

For one thing, a witness is a person who is prepared to say of certain things and certain facts, "These things are true and I know it." Therefore the week of witness is, in the very first place, a time when the church reaffirms its faith in God. It is a time when the church states again its beliefs, and its conviction that these beliefs are the only principles upon which a good and a happy life can be founded.

Further, the week of witness is a time when the church acknowledges again its obligation to bring as many people as possible in every country, both here and throughout the world, to its own way of belief and of life. No man has a right to keep truth to himself. Anyone who really believes in anything wants everyone to believe in it too. And in the week of witness the church publicly affirms that it recognises its duty, not only to its own members and adherents, but to all men everywhere.

Further, the week of witness is meant to be a demonstration of the essential unity of the church. It is in no doubt that those who call themselves Christians are inwardly united on the great truths of the Christian religion. But there is also no doubt that there has been far too little outward and visible sign of that inward unity. We have to acknowledge with regret and indeed with shame, that the different denominations and communions of the church have too often treated each other as strangers and sometimes even as enemies. Throughout the Week of Witness all the Protestant denominations and communions will share a common platform and will deliver a common message. It is a sign and a guarantee that, whatever the superficial differences, Protestant Christianity presents to the community a united front.

There is still one other thing to be added. The Week of Witness will present opportunities for discussion. For once people will not only have to sit and listen; they will have the right to speak and to express their own views. Different people have different views, different outlooks and different methods. And it cannot be doubted that when these views, outlooks and methods are laid in a common pool of experience all will benefit and all will receive a new inspiration for their task.

Throughout the Week of Witness all the churches invite all their members to present a united front to the community which will bear witness to the principles for which they stand and to their sense of obligation to make these principles known to all the world. And they invite all who are not inside the church to come and, at least, to examine the church's position. The Week of Witness is not only for church members; it is for all who are interested in Christianity and in the future of mankind.

I am, etc.,
(Rev.) WILLIAM BARCLAY

Some may well grumble that Willie underrated the differences between the churches—calling them "superficial differences"—as he was wont to do. But in the light of the field of battle, in his daily rubbing of shoulders with the unchurched masses from all over the country, he had little respect and still less time for the theological niceties of a less anxious, less involved, and—to his way of thinking—less enlightened approach.

It is frequently stated that the finest cuts of salmon are from the middle. Willie had now reached the midpoint in his life, and his photographs give some indication of the sort of man he had become: a sportsman somewhat run to seed, a brilliant undergraduate evincing the wisdom of alert postgraduate years, the enthusiast now turned a model of discretion—yet still full of energy and ideas. Vintage Barclay, if not yet in print, was nevertheless apparent, and well on its way to recognition. His attitudes were expressed in the pastoral letter (though written with less style than was his custom) with which he began the new year of 1943:

My Dear Friends,

Strange as it may seem to say so in times like these, it must be true that the main feeling in our hearts at the end of this year is a feeling of great gratitude and of devout thanksgiving. As a nation in a way that can be called nothing other than miraculous, we came through a time when it seemed that all was lost. As a community we have in the past year enjoyed a time of peace and of safety from danger which none of us could have dared to hope for or to expect. And as a Church, so far from falling back, we have, at least in certain directions, been able to advance in our work. We may well say, "Hitherto hath the Lord helped us."

As for the future, we may well steel our hearts to do and to endure. The burden of work grows no lighter, and the hours of work no shorter. Many of us have to work with no day of rest at all, and inevitably there are many who are tired. But it is a man's part, as G. K. Chesterton always insisted, somehow or other to pass the breaking point and yet not to break. Further, I do not think that, as far as this situation is concerned, we can feel otherwise than that, while the best is yet to be, the worst is still to come. It is a Christian's duty to be ready for anything. There is, as Carlyle had it, an eternal duty to be brave. And there is a grace that is sufficient for all things.

But along with this duty to endure there comes another and an equally binding duty. There is the duty to prepare ourselves to play our proper part in the reconstruction of the world, of the nation, of Society, of the Church in the days to come. At this of all times, we should be searching out the will of God for us. At this, of all times, we should be saying, "Lord, what wilt thou have me to do?" Clear in our minds we should have a plan and a purpose for the new world to come; and whatever our plan it must be one which gives the first place to God.

I would ask you, therefore, not to forget the House of God and the worship of God. I know that for many of you anything like regular attendance is not possible. But I would say to you, when it is possible, even if it means some inconvenience and some sacrifice of hard earned leisure, be there. For only in the presence of God will we get the strength to endure and the light to lead us on that we so much need.

It is our earnest hope and prayer that when we greet the next new year we shall be greeting it in happier circumstances and in a world where the lights have come back again and in a community where we shall have regained the fellowship of our dear ones who are scattered throughout the world to-day. I pray for God's blessing on every one of us and especially on all our absent dear ones who are serving their country in any part of the world or in any branch of the Forces. May God bless and keep us, and may He bless and keep them in the unknown pathway of the new year that lies ahead.

I am,

Always yours very sincerely,
WILLIAM BARCLAY

The tide was turning, and he was all enthusiasm to ensure it was taken at the flood.

Several months after this pastoral letter appeared the actual celebration of his tenth year at the church took place. The session clerk recorded that "those ten years have proved beyond all doubt we had made a wise decision," and once again the way he presided at communion services was emphasized. Willie expressed his thanks and appreciation for the trust in him so evidenced, and pressed on. The celebrations did not in fact take place till June 11, when at a special meeting of the Woman's Guild Willie was presented with a new set of robes (doubtless the wear on his first set had been noted by some sharp-eyed matrons), and a new hood was given him by his Young People. Kate's own work was not overlooked; she was presented with a handbag. In this giving of the robes there lies a lovely story, so typical of the fellowship at the church. Having decided on the gift of a set of new robes and placed the order for them, it was found that they did not have sufficient clothing coupons to cover the purchase.

251

Panic! Then Mrs. Duncan thought of her bedridden mother's allowance, and with characteristic generosity the problem was solved. A special word of gratitude was called for in that regard, and so Willie, who was unaccustomed to being seen outside his pulpit in robes, paid a special visit to the old lady in full dress to show the result of her sacrifices; she was greatly delighted by the thoughtful gesture. By now he had developed something of a reputation for his clothing, provoking such comments from the Woman's Guild as "The Meenister disna wear a hat. No' very reverent, eh?"[36] To Willie, unconscious of such things, reverence was of a different order than the mere external appearance.

In April–May they had launched themselves enthusiastically into a Book Drive, which resulted in over eight thousand books being "rescued" for the war effort (three thousand went to the troops, nearly nine hundred went into library service, and the remainder were salvaged). This was work very close to Willie's heart—and pocket—as yet more of his beloved tomes made their way out through the front door—to Kate's gleeful relief. And while they were dispatching volumes of all descriptions, thus participating in their own way in the war effort, the Air Forces commenced their first thousand bomber raids over Germany: the Great Retaliation was under way.

In July 1942 Willie had married William W. Braidwood and his fiancée Mary Smith, staunch supporters both of them of the church and the Young People's group. In less than a year Braidwood's war work took him far away to a key industrial appointment. On behalf of the recently founded Young People's Society, Willie conveyed to him greetings and a book token signed "From the Friday-night Firewatchers." (It would appear that the conversations of the fire-watching nights directly paved the way for the Young People's Society being formed, Willie discovering in those talks the power of dialogue as opposed to ministerial monologue.) The book token pictured, appropriately, a tulip growing out of a bomb site; it was headed "Can Spring be far behind?"

It was not long after this that Willie received the most tempting offer yet, from the vacancy committee of Springburn Parish Church, Glasgow, a church three times the size of Renfrew Trinity, and with traditions to match. Willie was tempted to go. Recently, as he confided in a letter to Braidwood, he had made "my threat to pack up and go," which had had the effect of stimulating management and membership splendidly at the beginning of the new session; as he put it, it had "given things a push on." The matter had leaked out in Renfrew, and following Willie's preaching at Springburn, members of Trinity put great pressures on him to stay. They managed to resolve his early doubts. By the eighth of the fourteen days Springburn had given him to decide, his mind was made up: as he explained to Braidwood, he could not conscientiously leave his people; in particular, he did not wish the servicemen to find a new man in the pulpit when they eventually returned home. "The balloon then proceeded to go up," he added, for further pressing (and tempting) offers were made by the Glasgow church, but on Sunday, October 10, "I burned my boats completely, and told the congregation at the evening service that I was staying."[37]

The convener of the vacancy committee was Professor J. G. Riddell, of Trinity College, well known in Sunday School and Young People's circles for his keen interest in youth, and author of the much-publicized book *What We Believe* referred to earlier. Destined to be a colleague of Willie, he was as much impressed by Willie's response to the call as he had been by his growing reputation. Thus another peg dropped into place that would one day reshape his career. At the same time Willie was prevented making a move that would have made his later response to his real calling very difficult, if not impossible.

At the end of October the fourth anniversary of the Canteen was duly celebrated and recorded by the ever-present reporter of the local paper. The long report properly commented on the work outside Renfrew (e.g., direct gifts to soldiers and airmen and surprising grants to headquarters).

THE canteen has been greatly benefitted by having no local expenses at all except a nominal charge of 2/6d a night for cleaning, lighting and heating paid by Trinity Church. Because of this the canteen has been able to send up a sum of £200 over the four years of its existence to the Church of Scotland Huts Committee in Edinburgh for the support of canteen work in other places. The canteen has always been greatly indebted to the kindness of local firms and of local people who have ever been generous with their help.

Activities

It is estimated that since the canteen opened [over] one hundred and fifty thousand teas have been served to soldiers. A cup of tea can be got for half a penny [old coinage] and a sandwich for one penny. Notepaper and envelopes are supplied free to all men asking for them. The canteen comes under the government scheme which supplies cigarettes to men at pre-budget prices. The canteen possesses darts, dominoes, drafts and also a billiard table, all of which are used by the men free of charge.

Every Thursday night ever since its opening the canteen has supplied all who care to come with a tea free of charge. On the first of these Thursday nights there were eight men present; but there have been times when there were as many as five hundred and fifty and there are rarely fewer than one hundred and fifty.

There have been many notable dates in the history of the canteen. Many will remember the famous Thursday night concerts first in the canteen itself and later in the Town Hall in the early days of the war. And many will remember the tours organized for men round the Three Lochs when the local people decided to show their visitors the beauty of Scotland.

To mark the fourth anniversary this Thursday night the canteen is distributing to all men who come to the usual free tea, a packet of cigarettes and a bar of chocolate without charge.

There can be no doubt that the canteen has been a great blessing to service men and women stationed in Renfrew and there are many all over the country and abroad who today have happy memories of Renfrew because of the Church of Scotland Canteen.

Every Sunday evening just before the wireless news bulletin at 8:45 P.M. a short ten-minute service is held and that too has been very greatly appreciated and men of all religions and all communions have worshipped and sung and prayed together.

Convener's Thanks

The convener, Reverend William Barclay, desires to render thanks to all in the community—and they are very many—who by their kindness helped the canteen. Without gifts of furniture and money and food and books and games and many other things the canteen could never have been made the comfortable place it is.

Of all people the ladies who gave such faithful service, week in week out at the tables, at the counter and in the kitchen deserve most thanks. Helpers have come and gone and staffs have changed but since the very beginning of the canteen Miss Baxter of 3 Inchinnan Road, Renfrew, has held the office of treasurer and—what is considerably more important—catering manager. Her service in dealing with the food supplies and the many forms involved has been invaluable.

We all hope that the days when a canteen is necessary will soon be gone and that peace will soon return, but Renfrew can well be proud of the happiness and the friendship and the welcome that the Church of Scotland Canteen has brought to many a sojourner in the royal and ancient burgh.[38]

The gratitude of the community to its Convener is well stated, and it was followed a fortnight later by a letter from one of the senior officers of the Royal Army Service Corps.[39] Once again Willie was given a "prophetic" D.D.:

> Dear Sir,
>
> Rather belatedly, I want to thank you, your committee, and the voluntary helpers in the Canteen, on behalf of the Unit, for your great kindness to us during our stay in Renfrew.
>
> I do not know how much you realize what a boon the Canteen was. I know how much we appreciated it, and the fact that there is no comparable institution here makes its loss the greater.
>
> I know that, despite the fact that we were predominantly an English Unit, many of us were loath to leave Renfrew, and I personally feel that this was in no small degree due to the warm welcome we received at the Canteen.
>
> Major, R.A.S.C.

But gratitude, important as it was (especially for his fellow workers and helpers), and looking back, is not enough. In his next New Year pastoral letter, he called the church and parish to look ahead to new resolutions, though not omitting the word of encouragement that was ever his hallmark:

> My Dear Friends,
>
> The year that has just closed has brought to many people many different things. To some of us it has brought sorrow and it has brought loss and has left life lonelier and emptier than it was. To most of us it has brought an ever increasing amount of work, of responsibility and of care, a burden that grows progressively heavier all the time. To many of us it has brought partings and separations that have left sore hearts. To some of us it has brought joy, for there

are joys which remain in any time of conflict, however hard. But it seems to me that the year that has closed has brought one thing to everyone, and that one thing is anxiety. It is of the very essence of a time of war that we are ever waiting for news and ever wondering what is to happen next. When we look back on these years through which we have lived and through which we are living, I think we must see that the dominating feeling of them is anxiety.

Now, that being so, there are certain things we must keep aiming at all the time. Hard as it is, *we must try to live one day at a time.* A great man once bade his friends to cultivate the habit "of not looking round the corner." When Jesus taught us to pray He said, "Give us this day our daily bread." And in so doing He taught us that we could leave to-morrow till to-morrow came. He said, "Sufficient unto the day is the evil thereof." He meant us to deal with each day's problems and troubles as it came and to deal valiantly and faithfully with them and to leave the unknown to-morrow to itself. It is the hardest lesson we will ever have to learn, but there is peace once it is learned.

And further, *hard as it is we must try to cultivate the quality of serenity.* In these days we are all tired and the natural accompaniment of tiredness is irritability. Things chafe and fret us that in easier times we could throw off. In days like this life is made up not only of great sacrifices but of a host of little restrictions and little inconveniences; and somehow we are better at hearing the soul-shaking demands of life than we are at facing up to the annoyances of every day. It would be well for us even now if daily we were to sit down and count our blessings. We might be astonished at what we have left and a little more ready to do without what has been taken away.

And still further, *it is essential these days that we should keep in touch with God.* A saint once demanded of his followers, "Make time for God." Many of us cannot now worship in God's House on God's day. It is, then, all the more essential that every day we should find a moment or two where we seek the presence of God for ourselves. If we do that we shall find His peace stealing around our cares and around our restlessness His rest.

No one knows what a day may bring forth just now, still less a year. But we do know this, that no man is tried above what he is able to bear. We do not face the new year alone; we face it with God, and He can make us able to meet whatever comes with steady and unflinchable eyes.

May God bless you all; and may God bless and keep safe all these absent ones who are ever in our thoughts and ever in our prayers. And may God grant that when we greet another New Year we may be greeting a happier world and happier times.

Ever yours very sincerely,
WILLIAM BARCLAY

It was to be the most decisive year of the war that Willie now faced, decisively and serenely.

The Final Phase

The first event of any interest at Trinity reported by the local paper in this decisive year was a debate by Willie's Young People's Society on the topic

"Should there be equality of the sexes?" In the light of the past gains made by women toward "liberation," especially in the war effort, one would have thought the matter clear-cut. But the outcome was equally split: for the affirmative forty-three votes, and for the negative forty-two votes. It is not certain that their President used his vote in the cause of modernity; in fact, judging from later statements and attitudes, it is highly unlikely. Willie was possessed of an old-fashioned chivalry toward "the weaker sex." He got on with the many women he had to deal with admirably, but he never showed much enthusiasm for the changing conditions, still less for encouraging them himself. But what did it mean, this liberation and this equality? Particularly, what did it mean to William Barclay? We shall return to this in due course, for the matter was one that would regularly challenge his mind for the next thirty years, without many signs of a liberated position having been attained.

The Young People's Society, however, with over eighty subscribed members and many others who attended with varying regularity, took up a great deal of his time and energy. His heart lay in this organization more than in any other in his church: he was building for the new day. He had grown up professionally with its members, who were members of his Junior Sunday School when he first came to Trinity; the thought that he could guide them into adult life thrilled and energized him. He had raised the possibility of commencing the society, against hostility from some elders, in the kirk session back in February 1942, and it was only after the delay of a month for reflection and a tough debate that the elders had consented to the idea. Willie's view was that it was crucial to get the young people discussing secular topics "under the influence of the church."[40] Now he took this a stage further and got the session to agree to his separating Senior Bible Class (which he still ran) from the Young People's Society functions, the latter "not being suitable for Bible teaching."[41] We can see the broad seriousness of his intent if we look at some aspects of the Constitution of the Society, which was formally ratified by the church courts:

> The object of the Society shall be to cater for the religious, the educational, the cultural and the social welfare of its members. Membership cards will only be issued to young people of over 16 years of age who show genuine interest in all the activities of the Society. There shall be an annual membership subscription of 1/-.

> The society shall meet on Sunday evenings after the evening service, and otherwise as the members may decide.

> It shall be the duty of each member to contribute all that he or she can to the success of the Society, and to place at the disposal of the Society such special knowledge and such special talents as he or she possesses.

This was one of first signs of his reforming postwar spirit, though others were not far below the surface. The collections, for example, had shown an increase relative to those of 1942; Sunday School attendance was up; and the reintroduction of Burns Night Suppers marked the revival of the sort of all-round planning and gaiety for which Trinity was well known. In March a joint concert of the Woman's Guild and Young People's Society choirs was held with Willie conducting them both. A few weeks later the first "postwar" meeting of the Stamp Club was held, after which it was announced that the Young People's Society Seating Fund for the halls had now topped one hundred pounds and was still growing.

The Annual Business Meeting took place and showed a drop in both income and expenditures for 1943; they had managed to retain a balance in hand of over £250 with which to face the future. The renovation debt was now fully paid off, and the church showed its resolution and gratitude by raising the minister's stipend by a magnificent £100 per annum, to £600. (It budgeted for only £520, but nevertheless met the full twenty percent increase—the first increase Willie had received, despite spiraling costs, since 1937.)

In March A. M. Ferguson resigned from the Manager's Court after twenty-one years of splendid service, apparently after a slight argument between the preses and his minister, the latter having contended that for the remainder of the war joint meetings should be held between the session and the managers. Naturally, Willie would take the chair, and so Ferguson felt displaced. It was also a move against the very heart of the church's constitution. What lay behind this move at this particular time we do not know, but Willie certainly achieved his aim. The rebuff was sufficiently strong to take the whole Ferguson family out of the fellowship of the church, and they only returned after Willie's own departure. It was a sad and unique episode in Willie's ministry, and serves to give us a rare glimpse of his steely determination, if not the iron fist of leadership. Willie drew notice of the members to it formally in an article in the church magazine (for which he had gained the approval of the session).

Tribute to Our Former Preses
—Mr A. M. Ferguson

ON behalf of the Kirk Session and very specially on my own behalf I desire to pay tribute to Mr Ferguson on his retiral from the office of Preses of this congregation.

Seldom can any single individual be equipped with so many gifts as he, and still more seldom can anyone have laid them so unreservedly at the service of his church. He was a leader of the work amongst the young. The Sunday School and the Scouts will long bear the impress of his influence and his direction. He was the main-spring of the Players' Club which, it is to be hoped, will soon be functioning with all its brilliance again. But it was on the Managers' Court that he made his greatest contribution to the life and work of the congregation. Perhaps it may fitly be said that the new halls are his best testimony for they were built under his convenership and under his guidance and direction. It is further to be remembered that in my own time the redecoration of the church and halls and the wise and far-seeing step of abolishing sittings and seat rents in the church very probably would not have been carried through but for his leadership and enthusiasm.

If I may insert one personal word, Mrs Barclay and I will never forget his

RAF Padre Barclay (standing third from left) with some local dignitaries (ca. 1942)

The minister and his kirk session (1942)

kindness and his helpfulness to us both when we first came to Renfrew and when extensive alterations were being carried out at the manse.

For twenty-one years he guided and directed the policy of the Managers' Court and presided over the material affairs of the congregation, and we had begun to look upon him as a permanency. In a time like that it could not be otherwise than that he should leave his mark upon the life of the congregation. Of one thing we are assured—everything he did, he did in a firm belief that it was for the ultimate good of the congregation. It is typical of him that he neither desires nor will accept any reward we might seek to give him. Through all these years he worked for the joy of the working and thought only of how he might serve this people without any reward and without any desire either for thanks or praise.

The congregation and I personally owe him a very great debt. We rejoice that his work has been passed on to hands worthy and able to carry it on, but his passing from the office of Preses will leave a blank on the Managers' Court and in the life of the congregation which will be hard to fill. We offer him our thanks and we assure him that we shall not soon forget his work for Trinity Church.

WILLIAM BARCLAY

It was a magnanimous letter, and shows Willie's skill in averting unwanted publicity and criticism.

Another aspect of Willie's dominance appeared in May, when he raised the question of elders' dress at communion.[42] He argued that black ties were much more suitable than white ones; they agreed, and the change was effected! This may fall surprisingly on some ears, who have been conditioned to hear adverse comments about his dress and personal appearance. He could at times, usually when relaxing, appear to have been dressed by a committee (to use Bob Martin's phrase), but he was essentially careful to do the right thing at the right time. In 1958, for example, he is found writing letters of inquiry to Doctor Scobbie, Rector of his old school, Dalziel High School, as to how he should be dressed at their prize-giving ceremony. It had to be *right;* it must not be slovenly, and it must not be antiquated (as here in the old manner of communal white ties). We shall see later that he could be devastating to the point of mockery on the effects the Moderator's robes (which reflect seventeenth-century court dress with its tricorn hat, silks, breeches, and all) produced on people.

The first half of the year closed with two events of special appeal to Willie. The first was a tea honoring Mitchell Ramsay, the retiring session clerk, that was given after the adjournment of the May 31 session meeting. Kate and her helpers prepared the food, and thirty-two members of session sat down to fête this devoted servant of the church. Gifts in honor of the occasion included Willie's own personal presentation of H. V. Morton's *In the Steps of Saint Paul*, a favorite volume, which he often referred to in his preaching. The second event was a luncheon organized by Babcock and Wilcox (to whose literary and debating society Willie was no stranger) as a part of the Salute the Soldier campaign that was launched that day, June 3. Thus, within the space of four days, he saluted loyalty and discipline of two very different kinds in which he was deeply involved as minister and forces' chaplain.

The Salute the Soldier campaign could not have been better timed. Since the beginning of the year the Allies had been straining every nerve and muscle to prepare for the invasion of Europe with the horrific saturation bombing of Germany and the training and equipping of their armies. Greece was soon liberated from its four years of Nazi occupation; Churchill's personal and opportune action prevented it being entrapped in the Communist web. The Normandy landings—Operation Overlord ("a majestic plan")—now took place: a million troops of the British Empire and a million troops from the United States battling side by side in an offensive that had been planned and prepared over three long years. The German forces replied with their flying bombs and rockets, but it was too late, and with the might of the United States and the British Empire from the west and the armed forces of Russia from the east, the writing was on the wall for Hitler's dreams of world domination. Soon the enemy was being routed in France and Poland, and by September 5 rumors were reaching London of Hitler's private suit for peace. Unconditional surrender was the only term now acceptable to the Allies, now being led (as of the 1st of September) by General Eisenhower.

A grim reminder of the tragic cost of such offensives appeared week by week in the local newspaper under the heading "Killed in Action." But the elation of certain victory helped overcome the sorrow of personal loss. It was not all grimness, however. One of the inspiring experiences of the time came to Willie in a letter from one of his soldiers dated 2 March 1945, which he kept for over thirty years. It read:

> During the last few weeks I have thought much. God and Christ I have sincerely believed in, but the Church has always stumped me. I looked for faults and saw only faults. Now I can honestly say I look on the Church in a different light. . . . I must admit there are still many points I can't see eye to eye with, but they are of little importance. Next Sunday I shall take the oath, stating that I believe in God and Christ, and that I shall strive to uphold his Church with all my power. I pray to God that I shan't fail.[43]

As Willie said, "it is something to get a letter like that from a boy whose daily business was to face death, and to know that the Sunday School and the Bible Class did not go for nothing." At least in one case, he had the satisfaction of providing "decided answers" for this young man's troubles.

In October Willie celebrated the expected victory in a new series of sermons under the heading "Men of Destiny." There could only be one choice for the first of these—Winston Churchill, whose resolution and genius he was wont to praise highly. Others quickly followed: Franklin Roosevelt, the treatment of whom was "most enlightening" (although Churchill was "the most popular") according to the church magazine. Chiang Kai-shek followed, whom Lord Moran described as "a formidable-looking ruffian, with a square jaw, carelessly shaven, dressed in a black robe like a monk."[44] We do not have Willie's view of him, though we can be sure the former atheist's conversion to Christianity and subsequent courageous witness were stressed. He did pass his description of Joseph Stalin on to Braidwood—"a blood-thirsty ruffian and a most unscrupulous character."[45] He was very outspoken about the Communist leader and expressed concern that "after Stalin, all the Communists are gunning for me." Willie very rarely opened his soul but in this letter to Braidwood he confesses, "I devoutly prayed that no such régime as obtains in communist Russia would ever descend on this country." It is one of the very few pieces of direct political comment we have; we shall not hear its like till after his retirement, when once more he risks "party political comment," though again privately. Consideration of Gandhi and General Smuts, whose devotion to the Greek New Testament equalled Willie's own, was to follow.

In his 1944 autumn pastoral letter, Willie had once more found cause to give voice to his perpetual optimism:

My Dear Friends,

Always at this time of the year, when the winter work of the congregation is about to begin, it has been my custom to write this foreword. Surely it must be true to say that the feelings in our hearts as we look forward to this winter are very different from our feelings at this time in the last few years. Had anyone told us last winter that by October 1944 victory would be almost within our grasp, we would have believed it, but we would have wondered how it could possibly be. God indeed has done great things for us; in Him we have trusted and we have not been confounded.

I think that at this time we can say three things about ourselves. For one thing we are all very tired. After five years of war it could not be otherwise. Both in mind and in body we have felt the strain of things, and yet at the same time we are very thankful. Some of us have suffered the sorest of sore losses; all of us have had in some way trials and anxieties to bear, yet when we make a balance of things there can be nothing but a humble gratitude to God within our hearts. For still another thing there is, I think, in the hearts of us all[,] a determination that we will not fail, and we will not falter on the last lap of our race.

This is always a time when we look ahead; and at this time it is doubly so; there is laid on us in these days a great and a serious duty. Please God, before so very long, we shall be welcoming back many of our friends, and our dear ones to our homes and to our Church. We must see to it now that we have our house in order. We must also see that we have a Church to offer them which will not only give them a welcome, but which will be a place *throbbing and vibrating with life*. Every organisation must be ready with plans laid for action; it may be that we shall have to set up new organisations, but everything must be ready to welcome and support those to whom we owe so much. More than that, there will be problems after the war—social problems and international problems—and we must see to it that we have a Church which will not be afraid to speak for God; a Church which is ready to play its part in the re-making of the world; a Church whose support will never be wanting in word and in action, in support of every good cause.

We dream of the day and we pray for the day when God's kingdom will come. It is our duty to make that kingdom come in this sphere in which God has set us to live and to work. Mr Baldwin—as he then was—when he was Prime Minister once said, "If I did not feel that our work was done in faith and the hope that at some day, it may be a million years hence, the kingdom of God would spread over the whole world, I could have no hope, I could do no work, and I would give my office over this morning to anyone who would take it."

We may well say "Amen" to that. Fundamentally and essentially our task is to make God's kingdom come within this place. Every bit of honest work we do, every helping hand we give the Church, every generous action, every act of service helps on that kingdom. Anything that brings bitterness, anything that divides us, anything that exalts self, any meanness and pettiness, any strife and jealousy among the brethren hinders that kingdom. Once I heard a great preacher demand of a congregation, "Are you on the way, or are you in the way?" That is the question! Let us as a people determine to be ever on the way.

May God bless you all. May He very specially bless and protect all those from whom we are separated in these days. May He bring us and them together very soon now. God's blessing go with every one of you in your homes, in your work and in our Church this winter time, and by the end of it, may it so be that we have done something together to make His Kingdom a little nearer its coming.

With every good wish to you all,

Ever very sincerely yours,
William Barclay

Willie was now all set for Reconstruction. In August there had been a change of editorship on the church magazine, Mr. John Kidd retiring and being replaced by Mr. Alexander. In that same month a new committee was formed that brought together all youth and children's organizations under Willie's chairmanship in an endeavor to ensure that the ultimate objectives of the church were truly served by these organizations, and to ensure that their varied activities were properly coordinated. There was also proposed a complete visitation of the district for the first attempt at parish outreach of the church since hostilities began. Willie's members were not going to be allowed to rest on their laurels! One of their first concrete arrangements for the following month was a series of "At Homes" similar to those of the YMCA. In early September, in response to a directive from presbytery, he had proposed to the session that a Service of Thanksgiving be announced on hearing of the cessation of hostilities. They clearly expected a quick conclusion to the war, though it was not to take place for another eight months. In October he proposed forming a Young Men's Guild, but the session resisted, contending that his work with the Senior Bible Class, the Young People's Society, and the YMCA was quite sufficient an outreach to the youth. He conceded. (The Young Men's Guild had had a notable effect on both Willie and his father, and its Handbooks were still a force to be reckoned with—hence Willie's keenness; but his continued interest in the movement shows Willie's lack of awareness that the gulf separating young men and women had been bridged.) The Scottish Temperance Alliance, fearing the worst excesses following victory, contacted the churches and schools at this time, suggesting the formation of a Blue Bonnet Association at Renfrew and elsewhere. Willie and his elders declined to encourage it, feeling that the arguments for abstinence (and it was *abstinence* that the Scottish Temperance Association wanted, not *temperance*) were already receiving sufficient discussion; they did, however, promise to rejuvenate Temperance Sunday.

Two distinguished preachers were invited to Trinity's pulpit in October and November. The first was George Johnston Jeffrey, a close friend and mentor of Willie's in the Scottish Sunday School Union movement; the second was G. T. Bellhouse who was known countrywide for his books and preaching. It was the commencement of a winter scheme of special monthly preachers that culminated in March, when Willie's "bishop," Duncan Blair of Newlands South Church, Glasgow, preached. "A more lovable character than Mr Blair," declared Willie in memory of those student days, "it would be impossible to find."

On December 24 a token return to normality was made when restrictions on headlights and other general lighting usages were lifted. Trinity was glad to fall in line, and celebrated next day in a special way the occasion when "the light which lightens every man" came into the world. Willie was now a mature thirty-seven years of age—Lord Beaconsfield's "fatal age." It was not proving fatal to Willie, but rather fulfilling and fruitful—more like Neville Cardus's "the noon of man's years, the thirties"—and even fascinating, as he developed his powers and turned them into action in Renfrew and beyond.

Kate had lost her mother, to whom she was deeply attached, some months earlier, and now both she and Willie were surprised to hear from Mr. Gillespie that he was to remarry. Two years prior to this he had been at Willie's Young People's meeting, speaking of his experiences over fifty years as a parish minister, to Willie's great delight. His bride-to-be was Jean, elder daughter of William Campbell of Kilmarnock. "Gad!" said Willie gleefully, quoting Doctor Linton's comment, "He's got a big heart."

It was at about this time that some members of the congregation began to wonder about Kate's commitment to the work at Trinity. She rarely appeared there apart from the morning service any more, except for the Woman's Guild activities. Two growing children made their own special requirements felt, and Kate was nothing if not the most conscientious and attentive of mothers. Ronnie was now a lively ten-year-old, not infrequently found on the roof of the manse kitchen in pursuit of his football. At church he was regularly installed in his father's pulpit—the only way found to keep his energies subdued during the services! He relied on Kate for help with his homework and was deeply attached to her. In January "he wept and howled consistently for a week,"[45] in his father's brutal phrasing, over his change of school (from Moorpark Juniors to Paisley Grammar School; Barbara continued at Moorpark), but it was quite usual for him to go off to Hampden Park to watch Glasgow Rangers Football Club by himself, and there were by now many other signs of sturdy independence. Barbara, now a lovely seven-year-old, was showing signs of special intellectual and social vitality, a little nurse in her own right, beloved of congregation and neighbors alike. Many have been the indications of her warmth and helpfulness: "like a big sister to me," commented Mrs. Young later.

Some members of his Young People's Society noted an increasing absence of Willie from home, a willingness to stay out at all hours. As with many other ministers, the relentless, unforgiving call of different aspects of his work was taking its toll. We should not forget that this work was undertaken at real cost to both Kate and Willie. Annie S. Swan, comforter of tens of thousands in days gone by and a central figure in the Scottish "Kailyard" literary tradition, once spoke of "the acid tests of marriage" in terms of exasperation and excessive boredom. Some might well think that life with Willie could never be boring, certainly not excessively so, till one recalls his constant and long absences from home; he was always at work either in his study or his vestry in the mornings, always away in the afternoons, and very rarely at home in the evenings. It is true he usually returned between 10:00 and 11:00 P.M., but by then Kate—ever living on her nerves, and in her own way as active as Willie during the day—was exhausted and needed her rest. The drain on her made by the daily routine in this eleventh year of their work at Trinity was exacerbated by the recent death of her mother and the impending remarriage of her father. Exasperation, a twin sister of impatience, can easily strike at such a one, especially if she be neglected and taken for granted: Mrs. Swan notes that she "heard the wife of a distinguished divine once say, 'It is possible to love your husband dearly, and yet wish, quite often, to throw him out of the window.'"[46] Kate, too, felt like that; it only made it worse for her that Willie understood so well!

Annie Swan's close friend and editor, W. R. Nicoll, refuted "the false doctrine" that a domestic woman is a woman like a domestic. And Kate was even now troubled by the tendency to be so regarded. Cut off from the independence of her former professional life, unable to utilize significantly the education she attained with such distinction at school and college, she now had to watch her sister Marjorie pursue with great success her medical career. It was truly exasperating to be hemmed in by Willie's work and by her domestic responsibilities, with no hope of release. Bridling at such constriction, she began to pursue the prerogatives of self-expression to which she knew she was entitled.

Willie described his typical Sunday at this time (not his busiest day even if it was his most public) to his friend William Braidwood: "My normal Sunday is 11.15 Church; 2.30 Sunday School; 3.45 Bible Class; 6.30 Church; 7.45 Young People's Society, which is quite enough." Indeed it was! But he fails to mention that the last activity never concluded before 10:00 P.M., and frequently after 11:00 P.M. if we include the informal conversations—in church, in his car, or over a "cuppa" in someone's home. He added that in addition to his Sunday duties he "was now running two training classes for Sunday School teachers—one on Mondays (for Seniors) and one on Tuesdays (for Juniors), and a large range of other activities, plus a Scottish Sunday School Union training session at least once a week, with a Girls' Association and a Men's Club about to restart." And "outside the church," he concluded, "I am trying to do a hundred and one things," which he proceeded to list. The Abot de Rabbi Nathan said "A man can die if he has nothing to do," but Willie's problem (and therefore Kate's) was the exact opposite. He was never found in bed before 3:00 A.M. at this time, and was always about before 8:00 A.M. *The Renfrew Press* emphasized this incessant round of activities when it reported on Willie's speech after the Burns Night celebrations, in which he once more proposed the toast to the Immortal Memory. Commented the chairman, "they were indeed fortunate in securing the services of the Reverend William Barclay, who was in such great demand at social services everywhere."[47]

We have already reviewed one of his Burns addresses, but it is worth looking at this one as well, for it helps us hold in balance both Willie's love of work and his works of love in addition to demonstrating how he himself held in balance the emphasis on things sacred and secular. This night he dealt particularly with Burns's love songs, reminding his audience that Fletcher of Saltoun had once remarked that he would rather write all the songs of a country than its laws. Willie pointed out that "the common people had a better liking and a fuller knowledge of the book of Psalms . . . whereas they knew little or nothing about the book of laws, viz. Leviticus." He peremptorily dismissed the notion then enjoying something of a vogue that Burns was a teetotaller and never looked at a woman: "This Burns would not have liked. He would have preferred being painted as he was." He lived, genius that he was, at a higher rate and saw things more vividly than the ordinary person, and thus was capable "of producing the most marvellous poetry from simple occurrences." He was "utterly passionate in his sincerity." "Holy Willie's Prayer," in which the poet satirized William Fisher's hypocrisy (his excessive drinking and womanizing, not to speak of his ecclesiastical embezzlements), was "the most savage piece that Burns ever wrote."

Willie went on to suggest that Burns "was probably the first out-and-out Socialist that Scotland ever had," backing up his contention by noting Burns's preference for Washington over Pitt. Returning to his theme of Burns's love songs, Willie noted that "A Red, Red Rose" was the first such poem that his favorite bard had written. (He also took advantage of the occasion to refer them to Arthur Gossip's latest book, just published—a canny plug for his mentor, and a good example of his "threshold" approach in religious matters—in which Gossip cites this same love song in remembrance of his wife who had died twenty years earlier.) Willie concluded that Burns owed his enormous popularity "to the fact that he could say the things that we wanted to say but could not." This may be an explanation of the one thing that perplexed his friend Merricks Arnot: Willie's willingness to give the people of Trinity "what they wanted to hear." He was already well down the road to understanding the craft that was to be his own true vocation—not a matter of merely giving the people what they wanted, but of giving them what they needed, and much more!

Willie's was no daydream existence remote from reality; still less was it constructed of the effusions of an intellectual cloistered in the unreal world of some ivory tower or the untainted experience of some holy Joe—as an amusing incident recounted by one of his female church members, whose bedridden mother Willie regularly visited, will testify. He was used to letting himself into the house without knocking, and did so one day just as a piece of coal fell out of the scuttle and bounced all the way down the stairs. "Damn!" exclaimed the overworked housekeeper in the privacy of her own home, only to find the minister picking up the offending coal behind her. Seeing the acute embarrassment his presence caused, Willie smiled and said how good it was to get such feelings out of one's system. Life, real life—that which according to the songwriter Tom Lehrer "is like a sewer," and which, according to Charlie Chaplin, "is a tragedy when seen in close-up, but a comedy in long-shot"—was for Willie the real theater in which he worked. And work he did. "I have plans," he remarked at this time to Braidwood; "I want more halls and I want them badly." The same indomitable, unrelenting drive comes through his pastoral letter greeting the New Year:

My Dear Friends,

I am writing this at the very end of 1944. Perhaps earlier in the year we all had the hope that the foreword of 1945's supplement might be greeting the return of peace. It is clear now that in these optimistic days we allowed ourselves to hope for too much, but we must on no account let our emotions swing to the opposite extreme, and we must not fall into pessimism and gloom. If we will only look at it honestly and in proportion, 1944 has been a year of wonders, and almost of miracles of God's grace to us as a people. Who could ever have thought in 1939 and 1940 that we should stand where we stand today? The note within our hearts today should not be gloom but thanksgiving, because the end of it [though] not here is none the less clearly in sight and God has done great things for us.

We are, in these days, on the last lap of our race, and just because that is so, there are certain things laid upon us. For one thing, in our ordinary life and work, tired and exhausted, and near to breaking point as we may be, we must gird ourselves for one last effort. The last lap is always the worst. A famous Victorian Statesman refused absolutely to have his biography written while he was still alive. "Wait," he said, "until I am dead and my life is finished. I have known too many men who have fallen out in the last lap of the race. We must see to it that we do not fall out in the last lap." There is only one key word today and that key word is DUTY. There is little romance and glamour about that; but it is the one thing that matters. Mr Jeffrey points out in one of his sermons that the soldier in the trenches is not asked, "Do you feel like going over the top today?" It is not his wish and his preference that is the dominating thing; it is his DUTY. In these days it is not what we want to do, but what we have to do that counts, and we must bend every energy we possess for the hard and the final struggle of the last lap. It will be hard, but after toil there comes in the end rest, and rest is never so precious as when we have earned it and know that we have earned it.

For another thing in our Church life this must be a time of preparation. Let us remember this—that those who went from us to work and serve in every branch of National Service left us this Church of ours as a sacred trust. If they come back and find that we are not ready to receive them, then we have failed them. Of all times this is the time to rally round the Church. Home Guard activities have ceased; Sunday work is not quite so demanding. I appeal, not in my own name, but in the name of those who will one day return, let all who can come now to God's house and God's service, that the work and life of the Church may reach a new peak and a new standard. We have much for which we ought to be thankful, and much in which we can take a just and a legitimate pride, but a Church was never so good that it cannot be made a great deal better; and such an effort should be put forth now so that in the year 1945 this congregation of ours should become a very outpost of the kingdom of God.

Always our thoughts at this time go out to our absent friends. They are never absent from our hearts and from our prayers. May the angel of God's presence stand guard upon their bodies and their souls, and by the end of another year may they be sharing our homes and our church again.

May God bless each one of you and may God keep you and strengthen and protect you and those you love, and may 1945 in the mercy of God see the dawn of that day of peace for which we have longed and prayed.

Ever very sincerely yours,
WILLIAM BARCLAY

"A new peak and a new standard": forward, not backward.

The "year of victory" was one of victory in war and defeat in peace. The capture of Berlin in May following the mass surrender of Italy, and that of Japan in August, were only symbols of a changing reality—welcome, wondrous, and liberating symbols, to be sure—but the ongoing reality was to be one of gloom and danger for the free world, and continuing struggle for the British people. Even as for Dietrich Bonhoeffer, the martyr and the seer of the new age and the new religious awareness, "the beginning of life" was not to be newfound life and freedom, but a hangman's noose, in the obscurity and indecency of the Flossenburg woods. The dream of Churchill and others of a united Europe was but a chimera, an old man's dream, morning mist floating across the tide of history. The hopes of the Yalta Conference in February soon evaporated; the Soviet armies overran Eastern Europe, dug in, and took root; the Chinese Communist party seized that vast people; the world convulsed at the horrors of atomic power and devastation at Hiroshima and Nagasaki; and the realities of demobilization, unemployment, rationing—starvation even—thrust themselves on a world drunk with gladness that six years of hostility were at an end.

But how to proceed? Roosevelt died in April, Churchill was ejected from office, and an icy grip took hold of international and domestic affairs. Had Churchill stayed in power, and had Roosevelt lived, an economic union of the English-speaking world (and perhaps even of common citizenship) might well have materialized. As the title of Churchill's final volume suggests, the end of the war was both a triumph and a tragedy. Britain, the sole European victor of the war, proceeded apace to lose the peace. There was deep gloom concerning Britain's finances, despair over the state of industry, a dreadful housing situation, strife brewing over the question of a mixed economy versus nationalization, concern over education and health. Not a few Britons were simply too tired to face the challenge; the zest had gone out of life.

Renfrew's Joe Kidd, long held a prisoner of war, came home to tell of his release at the hands of General Paton—pearl-handled revolver and all; and Willie became embroiled in a bitter debate as to how the Victory Fund should be spent. Once more he fell afoul of "the worst labour type and the communist element." They had wanted to raise £20,000 and disburse it equally, £12 to each man. Willie objected: first, because he knew they could never raise that amount in Renfrew; second, because "it is far too much like giving a tip, and you can't give a tip to soldiers and sailors and airmen"; and third, because it would be so impermanent—it would be blown in a couple of nights. Willie's view, strongly presented and urged, was that a community center should be built; better, *two* should be built, one for Renfrew and one for Moorpark. "But the powers that be won't budge and they hate me for opposing them," he admitted. Their opposition was strong, but Willie claimed to have the view of the forces' personnel, among whom he was still working. The debate and the strife rumbled on, as it was to do in the country at large once the victory celebrations were over and the bunting was packed away.

It would be a mistake to look on these early postwar days simply as a time of anticlimax, though there was a real element of that abroad. War-weariness was rampant. Churchill himself, as Lord Moran has so ably demonstrated, was too languid to respond to the new situation.[49] His broadcasts now lacked sparkle, and he had no heart for the bread-and-butter issues of domestic economy and industrial rejuvenation. Postmortems galore flourished. Trinity's Young People's Society debated anew such topics as "Were we right to use the A-bomb?" and so on. Willie himself preached sermons with such titles as "The New Day," "Cities from Ruins," "Our Share in the Task," "Privilege and Responsibility," and "The Christian and the State." As early as March, Willie had organized an "Open Door" day conference, inviting the town councilors to attend to help plan together the new age; four councilors did attend, but the outcome was indecisive.

Along these lines, Willie himself, just returned from preaching at a United Churches' Service in Denniston, Glasgow, made a rare admission to Braidwood: "I am physically and mentally weary."[50] Other invitations were coming in: normal preaching engagements here and there and special invitations to preach with a view to a call being made at Lansdowne Church in Glasgow and at Saint John's, Dunoon (which two opportunities presented him with "no attractions what-soever").[51] The Aberdeen Chair of New Testament, recently declared vacant, was still not filled, and now came more exciting prospects: Gossip's Chair at Glasgow was about to be vacated, for which Willie confessed, "I would give my eyes."[52] This latter Chair was at the very heart of the present discussions, offering unparalleled opportunities to study and pursue new ideas, to think and live forward not backward. And Willie was sorely tempted. A new chapter in the new world was beckoning. What would it offer? And could he take up that offer?

CHAPTER ELEVEN

The Joy of Achievement

Working for the Future

WE have seen how Willie was deepening, in various ways at this time, his involvement in the leadership of young people's work—with his own Young People's Society and Sunday School, with the YMCA at a local level, with the Boys' Brigade and Scout opportunities of an irregular sort, and in a growing penetration of the Scottish Sunday School Union at local and national levels in conferences, lectures, summer schools, and so on. And he was doing all this in addition to a very busy ministry which still included his RAF chaplaincy work, itself largely among young men.

Ever since his academic hopes had been checked by the outbreak of war, friends had been seeking to acquire for him a vehicle for the expression of his gifts either academically or in alternative parish work. In the forefront of this encouragement were men of the caliber of A. J. Gossip, W. M. Macgregor, Duncan and J. Maxwell Blair, J. G. Riddell, and G. J. Jeffrey. Not a few regarded him as excellent ministerial training material—academically distinguished, but with a powerful practical understanding that held in due proportion the conflicting demands of pastoral care and duty. His appointment to the Students and Ministry Committee in September 1942, and his consequent reappointment to it in following years (1943, 1944, and 1945) kept this matter near the surface of his mind.

His was a record that offered total justification for the "risks" taken when he was introduced to Trinity, Renfrew. It was widely recognized as a post of considerable difficulty, but his work had resulted in an increase by more than a third in the church's membership (from 1,074 to 1,418 members), a growth of over forty percent in the Sunday School (284 to 396 scholars), and a similar growth in the number of elders (from 28 to 40), plus a local reputation for good work well done in several areas. There was but one blot on his copy book: his poor attendance at presbytery. But although this lapse was serious, no one could fault him for not having the needs of the broader church in view; his record put the lie to any such accusation.

From very early in the war, the Church of Scotland had taken a long view of things (with the single exception of ministerial training and needs), and was now seeking to meet the needs of the postwar situation. At the General Assembly in 1941 John White had already called attention to the decline in membership figures generally, noting that one of its causes was "the migration of Church communicants from the centre of large towns to new housing areas."[1] This had long been apparent, but had accelerated with the great population and service shifts of the war. It was to challenge the thinking of church leaders continuously in postwar days. In late 1942, in the context of the Week of Witness, Neil Davidson had made an attempt to get the church involved more deeply in social matters. What was required, he insisted, was "a new departure, in striking contrast to its age-old attitudes."[2] A year later reports were circulating about the church's concern over ministerial applications, and it was revealed that preparations were in hand "to counter the serious shortage of ministerial students after the war," although the actual need was significantly misjudged (and the results of the miscalculation were to have a definite effect on Willie's future). The understandable depletion of the theological colleges gravely worried those responsible for ministerial training, and a special committee was set up to precipitate service candidates through selection procedures.[3] This was the year (1943) in which the General Assembly produced its report *The Church Faces the Future,* which did not get the attention it deserved in the postwar period.

The reawakened interest in working for the future soon became widespread. Scott Latourette's views of the variegated nineteenth-century developments are well known, but the doyen of church historians was also in the van of such rethinking movements. In 1943 he published on both sides of the Atlantic *The Unquenchable Light,* the last chapter of which, "The Outlook for Christianity," foresaw the breakdown of organized religious life (in extension of that which had already been taking place in the twenties and thirties): "It seems probable that, in the age into which we are entering, the Church will be less a community institution (i.e., national) and more an organised minority. . . ." Interestingly enough, he saw this breakdown occurring more relentlessly in those communities in which church and state were closely intertwined than elsewhere. He held that the alienation of "the two kingdoms" would proceed from a pair of causes: a generalized dislike of the organized church on the one hand, and hostility from various alternative religious groups either favored by or not aligned with the state on the other hand. Willie was never to theorize in this way, but we shall see his mind moving constantly in this direction within a decade or two of his full emancipation from the world view in which his father and his training had molded him.

Meanwhile, early in 1944 *The British Weekly* commented on the call to the presbyteries to examine the parochial system, which it said was in danger of breaking down.[4] It was at least clear that while the system had held together in the rural areas, it had notably failed in the towns, especially in large industrial conurbations. Further, the shortening duration of some ministries, detectable before the war, was exacerbating the critical problem of increased population movement. Ministers, once one of the most stable elements of civic leadership, were now themselves as much on the move as others, thereby robbing both congregations and parishes of much-needed continuity. Moreover, the question of church extension—the rebuilding (and frequently the resiting) of churches— was also a major factor in church planning. It would be necessary to build 105 new churches within ten years, Willie declared in April 1944,[5] aligning himself with John White's great task. As long ago as 1932 the General Assembly had considered plans for church extension, but the economic conditions and the subsequent war demands forced their suspension. The need for this work may well have come home early to Willie via both Principal Macgregor, a generous personal subscriber to the Church Extension Fund, and WDB, an enthusiast for church extension who was also a member of White's Highland Committee and ever deeply conscious of the economic factors at work. Willie's interest in this project was strengthened when he met White at a special meeting of presbytery in September 1944 to debate the issue.

Following his absence of fourteen months prior to September 1943, Willie seems to have purposed to attend the meetings of presbytery more regularly thereafter. He was serving on the Life and Work Public Questions Committee, the Ceremonials Committee, and Students and Ministry Committee, and had happily been appointed to the Youth Committee as well. Whether it was this latter appointment that triggered his newfound enthusiasm for presbyterial work or whether it was a private wigging or friendly counsel, we cannot tell, but from now on his attendance at presbytery becomes exemplary: The October, November, and December meetings all saw him firmly in his place, as did those in the new year.

The October meeting was particularly important inasmuch as it brought before presbytery the report of a special Conference on Youth the outlines of which had been presented to the General Assembly; soundings of its merits were now being widely canvassed. In passing, it is amusing to see the disparate reaction this sort of thing could provoke in people. For example, Archibald King in July 1943 could say "juvenile delinquency is rampant . . . due largely to the general slackness among parents and guardians."[6] A month later the editor of the *SSST* would speak of "much that is interesting and encouraging"[7]—one saw mud, the other saw stars. We shall see that Willie's view, as ever, was hopeful and constructive. Because Willie was deeply involved in the controversy (he took over the convenership of the committee the year following), I print the summary of the agreed plan of action as reported by presbytery.[8] It may be regarded as a plan of action, according to which Willie now directed his church and other responsibilities:

> i. The Home. Closer co-operation between the Church and the Home was unanimously desired, with more frequent and purposeful visitation of the homes by the Kirk Session in conjunction with Sunday School Teachers, Bible Class

Leaders, and Leaders of Youth Organisations. Instructive literature dealing with the Church's Youth Programme should be placed in every home.

ii. Sunday School and Bible Class. New schemes of lessons are asked for, especially for senior scholars. Improvements are desired in the co-ordination of the various methods of conducting Sunday Schools, and greater scope afforded for utilising modern methods in expression work, and more opportunity given for self-expression and leadership in the senior classes and Bible Classes.

iii. Teacher and Leader Training. A strong desire is expressed for centralised courses in Teacher Training, including preparation classes, and for training in Leadership.

iv. Congregational Youth Department. Wherever possible, Congregational Youth Departments should be instituted, and Youth Councils formed in congregations.

v. Church and Youth Clubs. The formation of Youth Clubs, including branches of the Girls' Association, where not already existing, should be encouraged by Kirk Sessions. Such might be started within a congregation or with neighbouring congregations.

vi. Voluntary Organisations. It is suggested that Kirk Sessions might manifest a deeper interest in the work of the voluntary organisations whether attached to their own congregations or constituted on an area basis.

It will be noticed that a number of the findings have definite links with Willie's innovations at Trinity: the At Home meetings of parents of Sunday School scholars; changes in the Bible Class/Young People's Society work; greater emphasis on teacher training; formation of a Girls' Association (and the aborted Young Men's Guild); strengthening of links between the YMCA and church; and, not least, the emphasis on home life. The call "for a new scheme of lessons" led directly to his being invited to join the Senior Lessons Panel of the Scottish Sunday School Union, which helped to transform his career.

In December, it was recommended to presbytery that kirk sessions should be enlarged to enable elders to designate a Youth Executive. Trinity's response to this, as we saw, was to introduce a liaison group of youth organizations and to conjoin the activities of elders and the managers' court. Further endless discussion followed—the sort Willie hated—when ideas were shunted back and forth between the Youth Committee and presbytery.

In March 1944 he was appointed one of ten presbytery representatives to the Paisley and District Sunday School Union, which further strengthened his ties with the work of the Scottish Sunday School Union. Following the resignation of Youth Convener Wilson in September, Willie was appointed in his place and moved the following deliverance, which was fully approved.[9] It is his first such involvement, and for that reason worth recording.

1. The Presbytery appoints the Reverend Colin Campbell to be a member of the Youth Committee, and agrees to the co-option of Mr John Smith, B.Sc., Miss Jessie Rodger, Miss N. Elliott, representing the Girls' Association; and of one

member to be chosen by and to represent the Paisley and District Sunday School Union.

2. The Presbytery welcomes the New Training Plan for Sunday School Teachers, and instructs the Youth Committee, in co-operation with the Paisley and District Sunday School Union, to take all necessary steps to put the plan into operation within the bounds of the Presbytery.

3. The Presbytery agrees that the guarantee of £60 formerly granted to guarantee the expenses of its own committee's Teacher Training Scheme, and not drawn upon, should be transferred to guarantee the expenses of this scheme.

4. The Presbytery authorises the Youth Committee to call a meeting of all super-intendents and leaders of Sunday Schools within the bounds that the New Plan may be explained to them, their interest aroused, and their support enlisted.

This convenership had a side effect that deepened Willie's understanding of presbyterial procedures and responsibilities: he was made an *ex officio* member of the Business Subcommittee. Already astute in the affairs of his church and several of the independent organizations attached to it, Willie was further prepared for greater responsibility in college and university courts. He made good use of this base, and shortly delivered a blistering attack on the General Assembly's attitude toward youth as reflected in what he called the "unjust" apportioning of its funds to its work. It had a marked effect on presbytery, and was well-publicized in the press. The remainder of Willie's work as convener is fairly routine stuff: the arrangement of Youth Weeks, joint conferences with Bible Class leaders, attendance at interdenominational meetings to arrange the appointment of County Youth Councils, the extension of the "Open Door Experiment" that had been pursued in nearby Glasgow (and was now being planned by Willie and his colleagues for Renfrew). In May 1946 he defended the existence of Young People's Societies in addition to Senior Bible Classes, though with the provision that the former should never replace the latter: there could be no substitute for regular schemes of biblical study, ever an axiom of his view of teaching and ministry. "Threshold evangelism" must always lead to deeper things.

At the time of his appointment to the Youth Convenership Willie was also appointed to a special subcommittee of the Life and Work and Public Questions Committee. If a university chair in this area was to be denied him, at least he could employ his intellect at a more mundane level! This subcommittee was instructed to come to grips with a report of a General Assembly Special Committee on Returning Service Men and Women. A great deal of work had to be done with regard to this matter: there was a real risk that normal church life (excepting Renfrew Trinity's!) would be found too staid, too formal for the returning veterans. Their special needs in making the transition from wartime to peacetime environments were complex. A sense of camaraderie had to be sustained, changes in worship considered, meetings and interviews with them arranged at the earliest possible opportunity, letters of welcome prepared and sent, new organizations (such as Men's Clubs) set up, and an attempt had to be made not merely to bring them into the fellowship of the church, but to enlist their talents in its vital church work.

It was suggested that advisory councils be established in each congregation, and a scheme of key ministers for each population area was drawn up. Willie was appointed to handle the affairs of Renfrew and Inchinnan. It is one of the ironies of his story that Inchinnan should be added to his responsibilities, for it was Inchinnan's minister who had been Willie's most vociferous opponent in the pacifist row of the late '30s, denying Willie's right even to call himself a Christian. Now Willie was in charge of arguably the most important aspect of postwar work in that district!

The letter of welcome, which Willie had a hand in drafting, read as follows:

The Presbytery of Paisley extends to you a very warm welcome on your return to civil life.

You will find yourself in a world of great changes. It is a world in which many plans for a new order of society will be laid before you. It is nevertheless our conviction that there can never be a lasting peace between nations, nor a real security within nations, until men acquire a new outlook based on the principles and the spirit of Christ, the achievement of which is the aim of the Christian Church.

The Church will have much to offer you within herself. It is our aim that within each congregation you should find such organisations as a Men's Club, a Girls' Association, a Youth Fellowship, ready and willing to welcome you. You will get every chance to express your own views, and you will find us very willing to listen and to learn. Within the Church, we are certain, you will find the friendship of men and the fellowship of God. There are many things in which the Church can give you guidance, and there are many in which she will be willing to accept guidance from you.

We would like to say that we believe that the Church is not only willing and eager to help you within herself, but also within the world. There are great problems waiting to be solved. We believe that we can assure you that you will find the Church alive to the importance of such matters as social security, better working conditions, improved housing, and a more equitable distribution of the world's goods, and that you will find her voice and her influence behind you in every crusade for a better world. That is not to say that the Church will lend herself to any particular party or programme. It is to say that the Church realises her function to be a conscience to the world, and that she will leave no evil uncondemned and no good unsupported.

The Church is ready to receive and to welcome you. She is still striving to bring in the Kingdom of God among men. Her crusade will be, first, to win men for God and, second, to win for men the life God meant them to live. And to fulfil that crusade, she needs you.

We wish to assure you that the Church of Scotland in your area extends to you a most cordial invitation to enter into her fellowship.

Note should be taken of the closing twofold aim of the church: to win men for God, and to win for them the life God meant them to live. Willie's views on "threshold evangelism," the maintenance (and promotion even) of natural activities alongside the religious ones, were thus given official recognition. It was not new to the church, of course, but Willie's emphasis on it was fresh and necessary.

The correspondence he now undertook in this cause should not be minimized. Each month a fresh batch of names was received that demanded individual attention and not infrequently special visiting, phone calls, and other arrangements. It fully justified Willie's earlier decision not to move from Renfrew until "his boys" were back and he had provided them with a solid and dependable psychological framework on which to build their future lives. It was not "public" work, but who can tell of its importance and lasting influence for good?

During these months Willie was also extending himself in his work for the Scottish Sunday School Union. The prewar popularity of his lectures (at Summer Schools and in special training sessions) continued to grow. A special rally, for example, was held at the Christian Institute, Glasgow, from the 14th to the 16th of April 1943, and Willie was among the lecturers, speaking on "The Living Word," presumably a practical exposition of his favorite text, John 1:14. In April 1944 he was chief speaker at a Sunday School Teachers' Rally, speaking on "The Sunday School and the Christian Way." And at the Saint Andrews Summer School that year he was appointed Chairman and Morning Speaker, occupying at thirty-seven years of age a position often reserved for the more venerable members of the Union. In his morning addresses, he spoke on the problems confronting the church today in its fellowship, worship, message, and mission. It made a considerable impact on the School and elicited this characteristic response from one of the members, which the editor of Trinity's church magazine printed:

> Our warmest thanks to the congregation of Trinity Church for "lending" Mr. Barclay to us as Chairman of the School. We appreciate the fact that in spite of his duties he has managed to give us his wonderful guidance and encouragement, and above all his friendship. It is in no small way due to his presence that the School has been such a great success.

Following this Summer School he now added a further very demanding task to his busy schedule when he accepted the invitation to take charge of a correspondence course on behalf of the Scottish Sunday School Union, replacing George S. Stewart, who had to relinquish the job due to the pressures of his other work. Founded in 1933, these courses were not intended to be academic or literary in any deep way; anyone could take them so long as they fulfilled the condition of working at them for half an hour a day, or for a full afternoon or evening per week. Willie's subject was "What We Teach Our Children," which followed naturally from his successful article series in the SSST in 1940 entitled "Our Faith Today." Each month he sent copies of his notes to the course members, along with four questions designed to test how well they had assimilated the material. On receipt of their answers, he marked them and offered advice according to the needs of each member. For this they paid half a crown (twelve and a half new pence). Just how much work this involved him in may be guessed from the fact that 77 enrolled for the course, necessitating at least 924 letters in that first year, involving no fewer than 1,848 questions and answers. Little wonder he got behind in his personal correspondence! This is how he wrote to his friend Braidwood four months after the commencement of the course:[10]

> My Dear WWB,
>
> Yesterday was the last Sunday of the year and in one of the prayers in the church I was praying for forgiveness for all the things that we had meant to do and had never done. Even as I spoke the words a vision of your accusing face rose up before me; true it did not quite silence me, but it did make me make one resolution which I keep when I write this letter.
>
> I am not going to make excuses; I stand before you in the white sheet of the penitent. Bit by bit as the letter goes on the fact that I have been fairly busy will emerge. . . .

It did so, over seven pages of packed information, humorous, detailed, and highly readable, concerning family matters, the Young People's Society Choir, Babcock and Wilcox (Braidwood's old firm), and the progress of the war. Regarding the correspondence-course work he notes that although it was wreaking havoc with his schedule, "I like it; the finest answer I have got so far was one sentence: 'I just cannot imagine any answer to this question'!" Dull student or searching question? Continued Willie, "I very nearly gave that student full marks!" He went on to say that he had been given the job of lecturing at Sunday School Unions "at least once per week" through April. And on 18 January 1945, he was scheduled to start lecturing once per week for the School of Study and Training in Glasgow. But that was not all—it could not be, could it? He had "another big job on." It is this which he now confided to Braidwood:

> The church—not Trinity, but the Church of Scotland—is running a New Training Plan for Teachers. It proposes to give Sunday School Teachers the chance to take a two-year course of study with a Diploma in Teaching at the end of it. There are nine subjects, each with a handbook on the New Testament course. It will be a slight thing—to publish at a shilling or so—but it will be my first incursion into print.

"The rest of the time," he added wryly, "is absolutely my own."

Like all fond dreams, this was to die almost immediately. From the 10th to the 12th of April he spent his time empaneled with eighteen members of the Scottish Sunday School Union Lessons Committee at 70 Bothwell Street, Glasgow. It was their annual Lessons Conference and Willie is listed as having attended with George Mills (Convener), G. M. Allison, James Greig, C. A. Smith, and the Misses Hill and Ireland on the Senior Panel. No documentation exists as to who invited him, although presumably it was the Reverend R. L. Findlater, Convener of the Conference, supported by Mills, who had worked alongside him at rallies and Summer Schools.

It was his first such conference. This needs to be stressed, as a number of people are of the opinion that his Lesson Notes date back to the early '30s. It is true that two lessons, those of the 23rd and 30th of December 1934, are marked with his initials ("WB") in the General Secretary's own copy of bound Lesson Notes, and the fact that he contributed others from time to time is equally certain, but no record of these has survived, and it seems safer to omit guesswork altogether. A careful study of all the Notes from 1933 to 1945 reveals a number that could be from his pen, but the reliability of higher (i.e., literary and theological) critical methods is not certain without corroborative evidence, which we do not possess. We have to bear in mind that all lessons were commissioned and confirmed by the Lessons Committee, and all Notes submitted to them were passed through the sieve of their mutual consideration before being published. This, together with the stereotyped framework imposed on the lessons, and the fact that Willie could write perfectly to order, makes very difficult any totally assured authorship claim. This is so even when typical Barclay keywords and sentence structures are present, along with reference to his favorite authors—on which he had no monopoly, of course. His name certainly does not occur in the Lessons Committee's minutes at all prior to April 1944.

In the minutes of that Lessons Conference we do find, however, that Willie was asked to provide specimen notes (which imposition would also be unlikely if he had been a seasoned writer of the Notes) for January–June 1947 on "Thou Art the Christ . . . a Series of Lessons in Historical Sequence, Running for Six Months without a Break," and to include Easter and Whitsunday lessons as appropriate. They also asked him, willing horse that he was, to stand by in case they needed him for the September–December period, when the Ten Commandments were to be dealt with, plus a Christmas lesson. As it happened, their first choice for this second period, Miss Ewan, was unable to write for them, and Willie generously found time to write both sets of Notes. It was an auspicious commencement, and led to his preparing the Senior Notes virtually single-handedly from 1947 to 1953. Even after this date, when other duties precluded his further involvement, they recycled some of his older Notes. It was an unparalleled record in the history of the Scottish Sunday School Union.

I list here the subjects expounded by Willie during his stint as Notes writer, when he carved out a niche in the system peculiar to himself. In all, he provided enough new material to cover over four and a half years' continuous instruction—that is, 237 lessons, which included introductory, background, and expositional matter; worship aids, prayers, and illustrations; and devotional material for the teachers. It will be noted that once again his preference for series and sustained exposition is apparent, along with his ability to organize and project his material.

SSSU Senior Lesson Notes, 1948-1952

Titles	No. of Pts.	Dates
Life at Its Best (I): Jesus, the Pioneer of Life	6	Jan. 1948
Life at Its Best (II): Followers of Jesus	7	Feb.–Mar. 1948
Power to Live Right (I)	7	Apr.–May 1948
The Four Gospels	4	June 1948
Parables of Jesus	4	Sept. 1948
The World in Which We Live (I)	5	Oct. 1948
The Christian Fellowship (I)	8	Nov.–Dec. 1948
Life at Its Best (III): Jesus and Life	16	Jan.–Apr. 1949
Power to Live Right (II)	8	May–June 1949
God the Creator	5	July 1949
Jesus Our Friend	4	Aug. 1949
The World in Which We Live (II)	5	Sept. 1949
The Life of Jesus According to St. Luke	25	Oct. 1949–Apr. 1950
The Christian Fellowship (II)	4	May 1950
The Worship of God	4	June 1950
Faithful Servants of God	9	July–Aug. 1950
Old Testament Stories	4	Sept. 1950
The God in Whom We Believe	12	Oct.–Dec. 1950
Jesus Reveals God	12	Jan.–Mar. 1951
God Worketh in Us	6	Apr.–May 1951
The Church of God	6	May–June 1951
The Lord's Prayer	5	July 1951
The Apostle Paul	4	Aug. 1951
The Four Gospels	5	Sept. 1951
God Makes Himself Known	11	Oct.–Dec. 1951
We Would See Jesus	13	Jan.–Apr. 1952
Ye Shall Be Witnesses	7	Apr.–May 1952
The Christian Fellowship (III)	4	June 1952
Jesus Shows What God Is Like	5	July 1952
Parables of Jesus*	4	Aug. 1952
The World in Which We Live (II)†	5	Sept. 1952
The Life of Jesus According to St. Luke‡	13	Oct.–Dec. 1952

*Repeat of Sept. 1948 Lesson Notes
†Repeat of Sept. 1949 Lesson Notes
‡Partial repeat of Oct. 1941–Apr. 1950 Lesson Notes

"A Law of Costly Service"

On 17 April 1945, while the final offensives were being launched in Europe, Willie addressed another teachers rally under the auspices of the Scottish Sunday School Union. The theme of the conference, which lasted three days, was "A New Day Dawns for the Sunday Schools." Hopes for victory had by now been flickering on and off for many months in Willie and in others. This is well illustrated by three contradictory letters he wrote to Braidwood. In the first, dated

11 October 1943, he wrote "I don't think the war in the west will be long now. Flying Fortresses all day and Lancasters all night must be just too much for any people to endure for very long." In a letter of 1 January 1945, however, he was taking an opposite view: "I am afraid that I was never one of the optimists who saw victory at Christmas"; and six months later he was expressing surprise at the speed at which peace did eventually come—"far sooner than we had any right or reason to expect." But these are just examples of the way many felt as the changing fortunes of the war dipped and rallied.

What was not in doubt during this time was the need for sound policies and planning. The liberalism of the '20s had failed, the conservatism of the '30s nearly cost the country its liberty, and the wartime government was too engrossed in waging effective war to plan for peace. Lord Beveridge sought to give the lead in various ways, as in his social security concepts of 1942 and the full employment schemes of 1944. Churchill followed this up in his own inimitable style by broadcasting talks on postwar reconstruction that paved the way for the influential Oxford pamphlets on Home Affairs. We should not forget that these were days of considerable hardship, with petrol and clothing rationing, and a real scarcity of food and other common necessities. The churches and denominational newspapers offered what ideas they could. For example, a series in *The Expository Times* on "the new era" provoked admiring comment from *The British Weekly,* but the majority realized that there was little point in such attempts till the war was won. It was not a time for idealism, and the minority who had the insight to understand the reality of the situation knew that the postwar situation was going to be very grave economically, industrially, and socially.

It is not surprising to find that Willie's "New Day" address was more religious than political, as became an address to the Scottish Sunday School Union. In it he sought to arouse the moral qualities that would be called for in the new situation. Because of paper rationing, the speech was not printed in full (something Maxwell Blair, then the *SSST* Editor, regretted, for he discerned its importance). Alas, it was preserved by no one. We do, however, learn from the Editor that Willie's primary point was that "the precise challenge of the hour is that we have a world, a country, a generation, crying out for God."[11] In these days he saw everything through the lens of God's activity, holding that man's primary responsibility was to come to terms with that activity. He asked, "What will it mean for the future of the world that not simply statesmen, but likewise individual citizens like ourselves should be fully surrendered to the guidance and the power of the Holy Spirit?" In his Daily Study Bible he gives the illustration of the little boy who could not complete his jigsaw puzzle: the map of the world that was its subject was too complicated. And so the parent points out that on the reverse side of the picture is a more recognizable guide, a man's face: "Get the man right, and the world will right itself." It was a firm principle of Willie's approach, long before the Daily Study Bible was penned, and he frequently reiterated it in these years of reconstruction and planning.

He concluded his address with a double appeal. On the one hand he appealed to his listeners personally: in the light of the grave difficulties they faced, he emphasized their need of energy, courage, better training to fulfill their tasks, "and especially the sense of the possible." On the other hand he appealed to their consciences as teachers: "There is one law for Sunday School teaching," he affirmed, "and that law is summed up in David's question, 'Shall I render unto God that which cost me nothing?'" This was an aspect of his life that was by no means new to those who knew him; indeed, it was one of the most distinguished features of his whole approach. He ended his peroration by adding, "We shall keep *that law of costly service* as we have a new vision of him who loved us and gave himself for us."

In early July Willie again wrote to Braidwood, informing him that he had just returned from "a week's lecturing at Aberdeen"[12]—yet another conference under the auspices of the Scottish Sunday School Union, which more and more claimed his time and energies. In this letter he mentions he was just about to send "The New Testament Handbook" to the press—in hopes of seeing it published by September! He reported having had "a great time" at the conference; he "doubly enjoyed it because I had Isabel Lewis and Kitty Maynard and Muriel Ovenstone up with me," all three of them keen members of his teaching team and Young People's Society at Trinity. Doubtless others would have been taken had Willie had more room in his car. The cost of teaching he had exhorted the Glasgow people to assume in his April address he here reflected in his own experience: "These schools always leave me spiritually and mentally uplifted but physically exhausted."

Other things were now in the offing. It is the lesson of Willie's life that responsibility breeds further responsibility, that good work, well done, was rewarded by more work, better done, and yet more work. And so it proved to be in this case. Referring to his recently completed manuscript *New Testament Studies,* he mentions to Braidwood that "I have in this connection acquired another job." The minutes of the Presbytery of Paisley for 11 September 1945 are as succinct: "The congratulations of the Presbytery were extended to Mr. Barclay [on his] appointment as Editor of *The Teachers' Magazine*." In less than eighteen months he had reached the top position.

It is astonishing that in all the obituaries and memorials that were eventually printed of him around the world, not one referred to this aspect of his ministry, nor has there been given due recognition for the striking service he rendered to the Scottish Sunday School Union, and thereby to all the Protestant Sunday Schools of Scotland, the influence of which is still being felt, albeit usually unconsciously. Willie himself recognized it as "a sizeable job," and he was loath to make such quantitative judgments of any of the work he undertook. We should remember that the 1944 Education Act of R. A. Butler had but recently made religious education compulsory south of the border. Scotland retained its traditional position that such education was the direct responsibility of the churches, but state schools were nevertheless expected "to strengthen their efforts to transmit the traditional pattern of Christian belief and conduct."[13] In the face of these equivocal signals concerning religious education, Willie felt a need to get involved to ensure that it did not somehow fall between the cracks of the church/state bureaucratic jurisdictions.

Next to Gossip's activities in ethics and practical training, religious education became *the* vital issue in his life, receiving his unreserved commitment. He had outgrown parish work and was clearly looking for an academic niche. The editorship offered him the opportunity to fill one in a particularly significant way. With a monthly circulation of twenty-three thousand at this time, the publication reached virtually the whole of Scottish youth who had any religious attachment at all (excepting Roman Catholics). His appointment signified as great an act of trust in Willie on a national scale as the call to Trinity Church in 1933 had been on a local scale.

Not that those responsible for appointing him felt they were taking risks: "None has been more willing than he to further the work of Christian education through the Sunday School, and the demands made upon him for this work are evidence of the distinctive value of his services," the Convener of the Committee wrote in introducing him. He pointed out that Willie was one of the correspondence course tutors, and that "the number of enrolments for his Course has been increasing steadily—indeed, alarmingly, when one realises the amount of work that has to be done in reading and correcting papers."[14] The appointment had been made by the Executive Council of the Scottish Sunday School Union "with the utmost unanimity," and they were "confident that through the magazine he will render most helpful service to a still greater number of Sunday School workers." It added (and we cannot be surprised to hear it) that "he is already making plans to introduce new features." He did so immediately, by introducing a Motto of the Month and a Prayer—and sometimes a Thought or Poem for the Month, as he had done with the church magazine at Trinity. It was not till 1947 that *SSST* was given a comprehensive new look, after the lifting of paper restrictions.

Willie's first editorial undertaking was to write to his twenty-three thousand fellow teachers a "personal" letter that contained greetings and a characteristic appeal:

My Dear Fellow Teachers,
     I am very conscious of the honour of being chosen to edit this magazine. But, conscious as I am of the honour, I am still more conscious of the responsibility of the task. It is a grave responsibility to direct, in however small a way, the policy of the magazine which is read by Sunday School Teachers throughout the length and the breadth of the land. Thackeray, one of the master novelists, once prayed a prayer for himself as a writer, in which he asked God "That he might never write a word inconsistent with the love of God, or the love of man; that he might never propagate his own prejudices or pander to those of others; that he might always speak the truth with his pen; and that he might never be actuated by a love of greed." It was a high request and a high ambition, and it is a prayer that I would take and make my own.

This magazine goes out to a public of Sunday School Teachers. No body of people in the country does a more important task. During the last war Dr Halliday Sutherland was a ship's surgeon in the Navy, and in one of his books he tells of his feelings before going into action for the first time. He tells of the fear which every man has of a violent death; he tells of his professional determination as a doctor to help. And then he says, "There is an emotion which in such a time sustains the mind—that it is a privilege in however humble a capacity to exercise the power of England." The Sunday School Teacher must ever be sustained by the feeling that he is, in however humble a capacity, exercising the power of Jesus Christ.

This at least will be true, and this will dictate the policy of this magazine—that I come to this task not as one who speaks from theory, and not as one detached from the practical problems of Sunday School teaching, but as one who, Sunday by Sunday, is actively engaged in the task.

Before we think of the future and of plans, one thing must be said. In the interim period between the death of Reverend J. Maxwell Blair and my own appointment as Editor, the whole work of this magazine has fallen on the shoulders of Reverend G. A. Mills. He shouldered the task of editing and of producing the magazine, and I am happy to know that his wise guidance will always be available and will always be willingly given in the future.

As for the plans for the future, at present there can be no change and no development in the magazine. The paper shortage still continues acutely. The one thing in the magazine that cannot be cut down and that must have first place in importance is the Lesson Notes. In the old days there were a number of pages available for general articles and for topics of interest. Now that space is severely limited. And until the paper shortage comes to an end the form of the magazine must remain unaltered.

All of us who read this magazine must have been more than delighted when Glasgow University conferred the degree of Doctor of Divinity on Reverend George Johnstone Jeffrey. Never was an honour more deserved, and never did an honour given to one man bring pleasure to so many. I know the great help that Dr Jeffrey's "Quiet Hour" articles with their wealth of spiritual power bring to many of you, and these articles will continue until the end of the year.

In the new year a new series of articles will begin. They will be on the practical aspect of Sunday School work. They will include such topics as Worship in the Sunday School, Music in the Sunday School, Drama in the Sunday School, The Bible in the Sunday School, The Teachers' Book Shelf, and other such subjects. Already experts in these subjects have promised their help.

One thing I would like to say. Will you please write to me and make any suggestions and make any criticisms which you think ought to be made? Although we cannot have changes just now, these suggestions and these criticisms will be considered and will be remembered, and will be acted upon as soon as possible and as soon as circumstances permit. We want to make this magazine of real vital help for the teacher, and we will be greatly helped if the teachers will tell us how we can best achieve that object.

Many of your schools will be springing into life and activity this month. May God's blessing be on you all and on your work in the busy days that lie ahead.

With every good wish to you all.

Ever yours very sincerely,
WILLIAM BARCLAY

In this appointment Willie's career reached a new climax, and he was made aware of a new direction for his talents and energies. Preparation and commencement had given way to achievement; great was his joy and his enthusiasm. But great, too, was his consternation, for at the very time his mind was set to proceed along the vitally important road of religious education, another quite different opportunity obtruded itself. It was at this time he received two requests from the Nomination Board of the Presbytery of Glasgow to apply for two different academic positions. The one was for Professor Robertson's Chair of New Testament at Aberdeen, and the other for Professor Gossip's Chair of Christian Ethics and Practical Theology at Glasgow. The Board was not actually offering the jobs, but merely asking him if he wished to submit his name for consideration. It would be interesting to learn who was behind this move, but the documentation is no longer extant. *The British Weekly* later reported that A. M. Hunter and Matthew Black were among the candidates for the Aberdeen Chair. Willie's response (expressed in a letter to his friend William Braidwood) is brief and characteristic, and very surprising for those who have only known him in his New Testament role: "I don't want the New Testament one. I don't want to teach technical Greek. It is too soul-less and I have worked too long in the warm intimate contacts of a congregation."[15] Soul-less, indeed, and limited, compared with the thousands to whom he now sent his monthly magazine, and the tens of thousands he would reach through them! But crucially important! (Willie could always overlook things which were not at the center of his concentration, to the chagrin of his colleagues.)

His attitude reminds one of Dean Inge's earlier negative reaction to the request that he contribute the volume on John's Gospel in the prestigious *International Critical Commentary* series. Inge said he "rather despised the breed"[16] (i.e., of technical commentators) and felt he was cut out for other things. It would be wrong to say that Willie ever looked down on any man, let alone a servant of the Word of God, but we should not forget that during more than eight years at university he had watched academics at work and had been reintroduced to their life-style when he delivered his Bruce Lectures in 1937. He clearly had no wish to exchange their detached, impersonal life-style (as he saw it) for the warm, intimate contacts of lively congregations. The life of pure subject specialization, of pure research, held few attractions and was not, he judged, for him. This perspective, as we shall see, survived long after his appointment to an academic post. Indeed, it is doubtful that he ever surrendered it; certainly he had not done so before he was elected Professor in 1963—twenty years after this confession to Braidwood.

It was not that he did not wish for any academic post. "To be honest," he confided in that same letter to Braidwood, "I would give my eyes for the Practical Training job. It means practical training for the ministry." He had watched Gossip, distinguished among his academic colleagues for his practicality and ever deeply involved in the ongoing life of the church and individual parishes, discharge his responsibilities in this area, and he had greatly admired him.

Willie had known what it was to be inspired to the great task of ministry, and he had enjoyed inspiring others—in parish life, but more especially in Sunday School and Youth work. He now *coveted* A. J. Gossip's role, and the whole thing left him with "a mentally unsettled life"—a unique confession of doubt and uncertainty. Not the smallest part of that problem was the thought of leaving Trinity Church, in the happy fellowship of which he had come to professional maturity and in the respect and love of which he rested contentedly. "I am filled with horror at the thought of leaving my church," he wrote, and for once he wavered in his commitment to his perennial forward-looking vision.

As if to underline this frame of mind, he wrote to Braidwood but a week later (a rare event, indeed). Once more he reflected adversely on a New Testament post: "It is—thank goodness—very unlikely that I will go to Aberdeen. I did not want [the change of tense is indicative of a mind already resolved] to abandon all that I have here to teach less than a dozen students the inhuman things necessary for them to gain a BD degree. . . ."[17] And, he continued, "it is with my entire good wishes" that someone else will get the appointment. (A. M. Hunter did, and filled it with distinction for thirty years.) But Gossip's *practical* Chair was something different! And he scarcely hid his anticipation: "I would give my ears to get it. Although an entirely unsatisfactory minister myself I think I could tell other people how to do the job." So both eyes and ears were laid on the altar of sacrifice. And there they remained, for the matter was no longer within his control. Presbytery and higher church authorities were reconsidering the appointment, not merely as to which candidate they might choose, but as to the actual nature and role of the job itself. On that reconsideration William Barclay's life and ministry, fame and fortune, now turned.

There was nothing of this uncertainty reflected in his autumn pastoral letter. By mid August (and with some well-earned rest behind him) he was once more encouraging his people to face the new season. Its tone is heavy with emotion of various kinds as he reminds them of the realities of life; he again appears to accept some of the main arguments for a "righteous war."

> My Dear Friends,
>
> I never thought that when I came to write the letter to the September Supplement that I would be writing it in a world to which peace had come. Far sooner than we expected—far sooner than we had any right or reason to expect—victory has been granted to us; and for this we humbly and gratefully thank Almighty God.
>
> I cannot begin in any other way than by expressing our deep and sincere sympathy to those who lost dear ones in the days of this war. It is the tragedy of war that victory and peace always come too late for some people. Those who went out from us never to come back laid down their lives in a great cause. We will not forget them; they have left us a memory which makes us sad but which makes us proud.
>
> To many of us the end of war must have given a feeling and an emotion of unspeakable relief. Our fears were not for ourselves. Still less were they for the

stringencies and the shortages and the limitations which the days of war brought. Our fears were for our loved ones and for our friends. Even when the war in Europe was over we could not forget that many of them were likely to have to face a yet more bitter war and yet more cruel enemy on the other side of the world. But now we give thanks to God that they are spared that and that they are safe. And there are those who, for so long now, have had all the anxiety of knowing that some of their own people were prisoners of war in the Far East under the most terrible conditions. Now the days of their waiting are almost over and soon they will be welcoming back those for whom they have waited so long. We share in their relief and in their joy.

And now we turn to the future. It is true that the war has ended. But we have to face the fact that the end of war cannot bring with it any relief to the material hardships and trials through which we have been passing. There may have been those who thought that with the return of peace there would be an almost immediate return to the old ease and the comfort and the old plenty which used to be characteristic of life. But far from that there are still hard days ahead. After the last war Dorothy Thompson the famous American writer said, "War has become a greater menace than any enemy can possibly be, and the first call upon our patriotism is to defend ourselves against war itself—if I had children I would tell them just one thing about the last war and I would tell it to them over and over again; no nation won it. Everyone lost it. And from now on all great wars will always be lost by all the combatants." That is not altogether true. The victory God gave us preserved for us inviolate the freedom and the heritage that are ours and that are beyond price; it saved us and saved the world from a way of life that is worse than death. But in one sense it is true; because war leaves us with a shattered world which will not be fully rebuilt in our life time. It is to that rebuilding that we have to address ourselves. And that is why we have still to accept all the hard things that lie before us and to accept them in no grumbling spirit but with a good grace. It is a strange thing to take a quotation from a nazi publication: but the official organ of the nazi storm-troopers for 14th May, 1942 had this sentence, "Henceforth nobody has rights and everybody has only duties." However much we would like our rights and however much we would like to get back to ease and plenty and prosperity we have to remember that there is laid on our generation the tremendous task of rebuilding a broken world and we have to face the disciplines and the sacrifices that the task of peace no less than the struggle of war involves. Let there be no grumbling and no discouragement and no pessimism if things move slowly and if life is still a narrow thing and if sacrifices still have to be made: but let there be a willing shouldering of our task.

As for our church—in a few weeks' time we will be entering upon another winter's work. First and foremost in our church life there must come the public worship of God at our Sunday services. I hope that you will be faithful in your attendance thereat. Charles Kingsley in his own church at Eversley used to lean over his pulpit on a Sunday morning and say to his people [a habit Willie had learned from WDB and A. J. Gossip], "Here we are again to talk about what is really going on in your soul and in mine." That is what we do on Sundays. Let us not forget the duty of bearing our witness to God by our attendance at the House of God.

All through the week there will be the many activities of our organisations. I hope that young and old will take full advantage of them. It is true to say that our fellowship through the week serves as great a purpose as our worship on the Sunday because therein we find the friendship and the comradeship which enriches life.

I hope that very soon all our absent friends will be coming back again. I hope with all my heart that when they return to civilian life and to civilian work they will also return to the church to which they used to come. I can assure them that we are ready to welcome them, to help them as we can, and in many things to learn from them.

May God bless you all and may He soon re-unite us all within our homes and within our church and may He give us good success in that whereto we lay our hands in this winter session of our church's work.

With every good wish to every one of you,

Very sincerely yours,
WILLIAM BARCLAY

Thus, the "new day" was not going to be allowed to break without their first giving recognition of the one that now passed. And none of the new day's activities was more reminiscent of that antecedent work and service, its relaxation and its seriousness, than his Canteen. On the 15th of October a closing social of some two hundred people was held, at which Provost Lang and others attended, representing the town council. There was a special presentation to Willie's aide-de-camp Miss Annie Baxter, who had worked so hard as Treasurer and Caterer. (She was Kate's lieutenant, too, in the affairs of the Woman's Guild, which now numbered 320 on its membership role.) Willie, appropriately, received a fountain pen as a mark of civic gratitude for his own contributions. The festivities—and such they were—concluded with the singing of "Auld Lang Syne."

The autumn was not free from domestic anxiety for the Barclays. It had started off well enough with their son Ronnie moving from cubs to scouts, and from junior to senior school. Within twelve months he would be as proud as a peacock over being selected to play for the school's sixth XV—but at rugger!— much to his father's regret. "He has turned traitor" Willie sadly informed Braidwood. In December, following a particularly bad bout of asthma, Ronnie was whisked away into hospital to endure a tonsillectomy; it took a month for him to recover, itself an indication of postwar conditions and wartime conditioning. Meanwhile, Barbara was having her own health problems. Now an attractive and highly intelligent nine-year-old (she had taken second prize at school in July), she was taken ill in October with what was thought to be diphtheria, but this was later disproved. Unfortunately, the large dose of medication given to her affected her heart, leaving her confined to bed for six weeks. Kate herself, by no means immune to disease, was simply worn out after the many years of all-out exertion. Willie's letters to Braidwood now catalogue a series of her health problems that compounded themselves as the years went by. We shall never know the full story, but from now on we need to keep in mind an unending and worsening health pattern for Kate (and consider, too, the effects this must have had on Willie and his work). She bore it stoically, at least for those early postwar years, and Willie himself was all sympathy, though he never reduced his workload. At this time it was a bad carbuncle on her arm (doubtless another result of wartime deprivations, accentuated by her natural generosity to others and her passionate devotion to her children and Willie), to which was added "a fearful cough which will not let either herself or anyone else sleep."[18] As regards Willie, he himself professed that "I being still indestructible have survived, although I can only be said to be hanging together at the moment."

The church magazine carried as its Thought for the Month the anonymous quotation, "God give me hills to climb, and strength for climbing." Evidence of the answer to that prayer was found when Willie's literary firstborn, *New Testament Studies,* appeared in December. He had conquered his first peak, and from it he viewed the possibilities and satisfactions authorship offered. Within four years we shall find him plunged into the making of yet more books, and finding great satisfaction in it. In many ways this first volume is typical of wartime publications, having a make-do appearance that suggests why Willie was glad to forget all about it afterward. It contains no foreword, dedication, or acknowledgments. These latter he had to attend to in his correspondence, as when he acknowledged his need for help in a letter to Braidwood, saying "I only wish that you had been here so that I could have discussed it line by line with you as it was written. It could do with being submitted to your clear and analytical mind." To another member of his church and Sunday School (the sister of the Gunner Maynard mentioned earlier) he wrote,

> To Kitty Maynard
> whose unfailing interest and
> encouragement helped to
> write this book.
>
> With every good wish.
> (WB. II. xii. '45).

It is a small book (eighty-two pages in length) covering five chapters: "The Gospel Portraits of Jesus," "The Four Gospels," "The Teaching of Jesus," "The Works of Jesus," and "The Expansion of Christianity." *New Testament Studies* is clearly a somewhat pretentious title for so slight a book, though we must not forget that for "untutored" Sunday School workers it would be serviceable in setting targets for careful study in keeping with the Church of Scotland's ninefold scheme. Nevertheless, it regrettably bears all the marks of the author's pressures and habits of hasty writing. Its organization is weak, for example—the introduction to the gospels comes after the portraits of Jesus contained in them—and the overall emphasis is very conservative, both doctrinally and critically. All biblical quotations are taken from the Authorized Version; it accepts the miracles as literal, historical events; it is strong on the physical resurrection of Jesus; and it maintains the "perfect identity" between Jesus and God—"He was in fact God come down to earth." Like David of old, the book "served its generation and fell asleep," a temporary book for a temporary situation.

One of Willie's amazing traits was his ability to keep several quite pressing things going together, like a juggler who not only juggles several balls, but also balances the brim of his hat on his forehead, rocks the baby with his foot, and smokes a pipe. Two further literary exertions had been taxing him during the past few months. The first was the New Testament section of the New Syllabus for day-schools for 1945, the preparation of which was a responsible and fulfilling task that significantly brought him to the attention of the secular educational community. It was so successful that he was invited to write for the two subsequent volumes in 1947 and 1949. The second literary venture was more homespun, but nevertheless completely challenging. His Bible Class, "a flourishing institution"[18] that now boasted an enrollment of forty, presented a series of plays entitled *Scotland for Christ* to the Parents' Night in February 1946, and Willie was both writer and producer! Alas, no copy of the plays has been preserved. *The Renfrew Press* admiringly reported on the performances in March; among the actors it commended was one Barbara Barclay. This is the only time Willie's name is connected directly with the dramatist's art, though he continued to attend plays from time to time, and avidly read James Agate, the drama critic of the prestigious *Manchester Guardian,* who was one of his favorite journalists.

During these weeks a discussion of some personal interest to Willie had been carried on in his kirk session, in the form of a suggestion that he be provided with an assistant. In October it was decided that a motion to that end ought to be proposed at the next meeting after the normal manner for "large and vigorous churches." It was moved in November by Mr. W. Alexander, with Mr. Macfee seconding, but the suggestion was then made that it should be held until the original proposer (Mr. Ramsay) had recovered from a bout of illness. It was thus taken up again in December. Mr. Ramsay pointed out that members and adherents now made a congregation of over nineteen hundred people—too many for any one man to cope with, especially a man with the many extra responsibilities Willie now shouldered. The view was put that such a request should normally be initiated by the minister, who replied by stating that he was not sure that he wanted an assistant! He did, however, ask for the elders' cooperation in acquainting him with any sickness or other need for which his company might be required.[19] The matter of an assistant was dropped.

For Willie 1946 was to be a decisive year. It opened with his call to the church "to dare to look forward." We can see that his pastoral letter, like most of what he wrote during this period, exhibits more a preaching style than a literary one:

My Dear Friends.

Once again we have come to the New Year and, as Charles Lamb once said, "No one ever regarded the New Year with complete indifference." New Year is always a time when we are compelled to stop and to take stock of ourselves and of our work and of our life.

There is one great difference this New Year; it is the fact that war is over and we are at peace. In one way it would be true to say that this Christmas and this New Year are not the first Christmas and New Year of the peace; they are rather the Christmas and the New Year between the war and the peace. We are still living amidst shortages and restrictions and discomforts and controls but bit by bit these will pass away.

All the time in these days we will have need of at least two things. We will have need of patience. We often wish that we could get back more quickly to something like the old ease and comfort and plenty but that must of necessity be a slow process. A long and a serious illness is always followed by a lengthy and sometimes a wearisome convalescence; and we must have patience until things slowly come back to normal again. And further we will have need all the time to teach ourselves to take a long view of things. It may well be necessary still to make sacrifices and still to endure a certain narrowness in life with a good grace in order that we may reap still greater benefits later on.

But this at least is true—that this New Year we do dare to look forward. In the days of the war we scarcely dared to do that. It was too uncertain and it was too frightening. We did not dare to think what might happen to ourselves and to our loved ones. But now for most of them the dangers are past; some of them we have already had the pleasure of welcoming home; as the days go by still more and more of them will be coming back amongst us and it is a great joy to see them. And yet at the same time as others are coming back still more of our young people are going out from us to take their share of their country's service. Our good wishes go with them and we will not forget them.

I would like us all to remember one thing in the year to come and that one thing is that the church needs YOU. The church needs every one of you, and I would like you to remember that. Field Marshal Montgomery was never tired of saying, "One man can lose me a battle." Victory required every man to be pulling his weight. An old Greek General said to his men before an engagement, "Now, my men, every one of you must so act as to feel that his own will be the chief contribution to victory." We must always have this feeling that the church needs each one of us. Will you remember that on a Sunday—that the church needs YOU at its services, that it makes a difference if YOU stay away. Will you remember it in your prayers—that the church needs YOUR prayers. Will you remember it always—that the church needs YOUR help and YOUR support. It will only be when every individual member gets this feeling of individual personal responsibility for a personal loyalty to the church that the church will be all that it could be.

I hope that before the end of this year things will be a great deal better and easier than they are. I hope that by that time by far the most of our own folk will be back in their homes. I hope and pray that our church will add to its high record and its high achievement. I pray that God may bless you and give you all good things in the New Year. May you and all your loved ones wherever they are have every prosperity and every blessing in the year to come.

With every good wish,

Ever very sincerely yours,
WILLIAM BARCLAY

It was not long before his own looking forward and expectations were realized. In April he conveyed to his session the sudden request of the university that he take over "a lectureship in one of the University classes formed for demobilised men intending to enter the ministry."[20] The classes were to be held Mondays, Wednesdays, and Fridays, from 2:00 to 3:00 P.M., and would run for the duration of the summer term. The ready consent of the elders was given, and Willie's first professional step on the academic ladder was thus taken. The post was not one of pure academic fulfillment, but rather one of pastoral—and ministerial—urgency, and he was thereby helped over his former reluctance to teach the New Testament and other "soul-less" things. His great ambition for practical training still remained, and Gossip's Chair was still being held in abeyance.

Willie described the teaching job as "very interesting."[21] Once again we see his ability and willingness to change course and settle down to what befell him, not fatalistically, but as "one under authority," as a servant of God, rendering costly service indeed. This trait had been most noticeable when war was declared and he, an ardent pacifist, sought to make easy the condition of the local troops and then went on to become a part-time R.A.F. chaplain. It now appears as he lays down (perhaps only temporarily) his hopes to teach and explore practical training and devote himself to New Testament responsibilities. The course itself was in the nature of a "trial run" for intending theologs: "if they got through that class they were to be allowed to start the course in October." It also had the effect of keeping returning servicemen, some of whom had wives and families (one was even training for the ministry alongside his own son), in touch with the church. Arriving back after Christmas, there was a real risk that some of them might find temporary jobs developing into permanencies if something was not found quickly for them to do.

With so much else going on, it was for Willie an exhausting period. He spoke of the soldier-students' potential; they were "splendid stuff," the youngest being twenty-eight and the oldest forty-six. Despite the pressures on him, he found time to spend with the students over coffee in the refectory. During these breaks he would chat with them about their weekend work, opine authoritatively on football matters and every aspect of their everyday lives, and then remember he had unfinished work to attend to and make his excuses. They were amused to see him move to a small table in the refectory itself, unplug his hearing aid, and commence work amid the noise and banter. He was, to quote John Graham (one of their number at this time), "far and away the most interesting lecturer" in college,[22] his lectures being lively, easy to listen to, and filled with pastoral asides and practical suggestions. His first series of lectures was on the parables of Jesus.

But the way ahead was still very uncertain. Among his motivations to leave Renfrew were problems with Kate's health that could not be adequately dealt with there. She did submit to surgery in a local hospital, and then at the end of one week Willie was asked to remove her because of bed shortages, a circumstance that he confessed "infuriated" him; the loss of his normal equability was itself a sign of his own exhaustion. It was becoming clearer by the week that change he must: and change forward, not backward.

Two opportunities, both appealing, now arose. The fact that he found them appealing shows how willing he was to be led by circumstances (a point he was to make many times over in the coming years to those seeking vocational guidance), and how adaptable, too: the "inhuman things" necessary for a B.D. were again beginning to capture his mind. (He had also heard that the authorities were to suppress the Chair of Ethics and Practical Theology.) The first opportunity was his nomination for the Chair of New Testament at Edinburgh—"the plum of all the chairs"—for which he said he expected to be "runner up."[23] The second opportunity, which he clearly hoped to get, was a lectureship in the largest teacher-training college in Scotland—at Jordanhill, Glasgow. The lectureship was to be in Religious Education, and seems to have arisen directly out of his work for the Scottish Sunday School Union and the syllabus work just published. We shall see that his future enthusiasm for teaching Religious Education in day schools was thus based on personal hopes as well as personal experience. But it was not to be. He got neither post. The mills of God grind slowly, as do those of a great church headquarters, and exceeding small.

Not a Real Professor

One cannot avoid the feeling that Willie must have been living with a constant sense of tension from anticipation during the year following the end of the war. His career had been checked more than once; surely it could not happen again? Besides the very natural release of tensions at the cessation of hostilities, he was experiencing a greater willingness to consider new opportunities, even ones he had criticized previously, and with this there went the feeling that his work at Trinity—now that his boys were more or less home—was completed. But his call to the church "to dare to look forward" was heeded adequately enough. In January 1946 he took up an occasional sermon series commenced earlier on modern apostles such as Dick Sheppard, Eric Liddell, C. T. Studd, and Grenfell of Labrador; he also commenced a new series on "The Story and the Lesson of Famous Hymns," including "Just As I Am," "Abide with Me," and "Lead Kindly Light" (the latter being especially appropriate to this year of decision). In April another two series were commenced, on the Lord's Prayer, and life in Palestine in Jesus' time.

The Young People's Society was now back to full strength with lively meetings and challenging subjects, all of which were well reported by the press. In May a special Welcome Home social was held for ex-P.O.W.s Joe Kidd and Bill Jessiman, and several other servicemen (many still in uniform) who had not lost their freedom during wartime. Willie also continued his part-time lecturing at Glasgow and sampled the conditions and challenge of a don's life. But, normal fatigue apart, there seems to have been an undeniable (and uncharacteristic) element of lassitude about him during this period. In June he wrote to Braidwood about how "things are rather unsettling" and about how he hoped that "everything will be settled by the end of August. . . . I can't go on indefinitely doing my own job and doing odd-jobs at the university as well."[24] By the time he wrote his autumn pastoral letter things were no further on, though he betrayed very little of his disaffection:

My Dear Friends,

It is always the custom at this time of year that a Pastoral Letter should appear in the supplement. With the coming of this month plans are being laid and preparations are being made for the winter's work of the congregation. Each of us has our own share in this work and each has his or her part to play; and yet we will do our own share and play our own part best and most efficiently when we have a clear idea of the aim and object towards which all our work and all our activity is moving.

The Church, it seems to me, exists for three main purposes. First it exists for *instruction*. It is within the circle of the Church that we are helped to train our children and our young people in the knowledge, the love and the fear of God; and it is within the Church that we ourselves come to a deeper and a fuller knowledge of what the Christian faith means and demands. Within this congregation we are doubly fortunate. We have a very large number of children in our schools and of young people in our Bible Classes and societies; and furthermore we are blessed with a staff of teachers and leaders whose work and whose devotion is beyond praise. Let us as parents and as members of the Church give all the support we can to this work of instruction. Only so shall we train and raise up a body of men and women who in the future will maintain and add fresh lustre to the Church. And further let us ourselves be ever learning. The danger which ever confronts every Church is the danger of the shut mind. Christianity is not something which is finished and static; it is something which moves steadily onwards towards a deeper appreciation of the unsearchable riches of Christ. Therefore let us walk, not looking backwards to days however great, but forward to new ways and things under the guidance of God.

The second thing for which the Church exists is *fellowship*. No one who is a Church member need ever be friendless. Wherever a Church member goes he has in every town a ready-made, waiting circle into which he may enter. There have been times when a Church has been more noted for the divisions which separated its members than for the bonds which united them.

Behold how good a thing it is,
And how becoming well,
Together such as brethren are
In unity to dwell.

Let us remember that. It is at times not easy. It means courtesy in every situation; it means constant consideration of others; it means a willingness to listen to others' points of view; it means an ability sometimes to sink our own likes and dislikes and personal preferences; it means that if we do not get our own way we have with a good grace to fall into what others have decided. It means above all a

292

constant memory that all things are done in the presence of Christ and in His spirit of love.

The third thing for which the Church exists, and it is the supreme thing which includes all the others, is *worship*. It is the great aim of the Church that through its instruction, through its fellowship, through its services, we should find contact with God. It is true that the days of war are over; but the days of peace are no less difficult. We need guidance; we need strength; we need grace; we need sometimes comfort; we need encouragement. And only in the presence of God do we receive these things. Will you remember the public worship of God? Will you set aside that brief time each week for Him? And will you come not dully and unexpectantly but, in very truth, waiting upon God? If we do that all other things will take their proper place, and we will build up a congregation which is a colony of the kingdom of Heaven.

It has been a great delight to welcome so many of our members and friends back home, and to see so many families together again. Bit by bit we hope that all those who have returned will take their place within the life of the congregation again. There are still those who are away and still those who are being called out on their country's service. Our thoughts are with them and we do not forget them.

May God bless you all and all who are dear to you and may He keep us and our loved ones safe within His power and within His love.

With every good wish,

Very sincerely yours,
WILLIAM BARCLAY

The first hard news of the long-awaited change in Willie's future is recorded in the session minutes of the 13th of October. It is the shortest, most poignant entry in the book:

Today, after the morning service, Mr Barclay intimated to the congregation that he had been appointed Lecturer in New Testament Language and Literature in Glasgow University and that he would be relinquishing his charge as minister of Trinity Church at the beginning of the new year.

By the 25th of October *The Renfrew Press* had got hold of the story and issued it under the headline "Burgh Minister's Notable Appointment." It describes Willie's academic achievements (adding what is nowhere else recorded, that he was a prizeman in Political Economy as well as English, the Classics, and Divinity) and states that the Church of Scotland's Board of Nominations for Church Chairs had unanimously nominated him to the newly appointed post. The church magazine carried the news the following month with this entry:

Resignation of Rev. Wm. Barclay, B.D.

THE announcement made by Mr Barclay, on Sunday 13th October, that he had been appointed Lecturer in Glasgow University on New Testament Language and Literature, did not come as a surprise to many of us. His lectures throughout the country during the past few years, particularly in connection with the Youth Movement, brought him very much into prominence, and the appointment which he has accepted is just the sequel to the enthusiasm and energy he has put into that work. We have not realised, perhaps, the value set on Mr Barclay as a lecturer and author, but those prominent in Church affairs are unstinted in their praise of him and of his work.

His appointment is unfortunate from our point of view, but we rejoice to know that such an honour has been conferred on him, and we extend to him and Mrs Barclay our heartiest congratulations. Our hope is that he will be as happy in his new sphere as he has been in Trinity, and that he will impart that enthusiasm, which is characteristic of him, to the students in his classroom, so that they in turn will pass out from the Divinity Hall zealous preachers of the Gospel of Christ.

For nearly fourteen years Mr Barclay has been our minister, sharing with us our joys and our sorrows—the period of unemployment, the six years of war and the days of final victory. The Session and Managers feel that they would like Mr Barclay to take away with him a token of their esteem, and it is the expressed wish of many in the congregation that they also should have an opportunity of showing their appreciation.

It has been decided to hold a congregational meeting of a social nature in the Church on Friday, 27th December, which will take the form of a Concert and Presentation. Because of the large attendance anticipated, the possible B.U. difficulty between Christmas and New Year and the "China" problem, it has been deemed inadvisable to attempt to serve tea. For the event souvenir admission programmes, price One Shilling, will be on sale early in December, and it is hoped the congregation will respond heartily and give Mr and Mrs Barclay a good send-off.

Subscriptions towards a parting gift may be put in envelopes addressed to Mr Gibson or to Mr Inglis, and dropped into the collection box any Sunday during November; or they may be handed to any member of the Committee. For this purpose also representatives of the Committee will be in attendance in the old Session House on Tuesday, 12th, Wednesday, 13th, Tuesday, 19th and Wednesday, 20th November, between 7.30 and 9 P.M.

J. B. Kidd,
Session Clerk

Willie's thoughts were very divided. To Braidwood, ever his confidant, though now at a distance, he wrote, "To tell you the truth, I feel I need sympathy as much as anything else. It is going to be a tremendous wrench to go away from Renfrew after fourteen years of almost unbroken happiness."[25] But his eyes were already focusing on the task, and while the emotions—never far below the surface, though perfectly restrained—were moving in one direction, the tiller of his mind was already set on a different course. He thus continued in this same letter,

There is a job to be done up there. There are fifty-five students in the first year and most of them demobilised men. Up till now there were two professors of New Testament. One died; they have not enough money to fill his chair with a real professor so they are giving me his work to do but calling me a lecturer and paying me as such. But it is the kind of job that will almost inevitably lead to something else.

We need to take seriously this comment. It is not just that Willie was excusing himself for not making it to the top in one bound (as A. M. Hunter and J. S. Stewart had done). He had himself been asked to apply for both posts (and we may well detect Williemac's encouragement here). He had been led to believe he was professorial material, and the Jordanhill College appointment (leadership of the department) could be equated with that position. We shall soon see him fulfilling professorial functions, at times actually running the New Testament department at the university in the absence of his chief, G. H. C. Macgregor. But *seventeen* years were to pass before his anticipated rank was attained formally, during which time he arguably did his best work. His readinesses to accept a junior post (and that only for a provisional five-year term) and the patience and fortitude shown by him are themselves indications of the spiritual stature of the man. He courageously hid the disappointment he felt, although it was to emerge implicitly in some of his early writings, in which he speaks of the need for reliable "second lieutenants," of "men who played the second part," and we might deduce that the harsh criticism he makes of John Mark for having left his uncle Barnabas and the apostle Paul devolve from his recognition of the need for such subservience in the call of duty. But it did hurt him. Note this comment, written in the early '50s, when the memory was still strong: "There is nothing more hurting than to be passed over. There is nothing more difficult than to take the second place when you once held the first place, or when you are expecting to get the first place."[26]

To get at the political reality behind Willie's appointment as something less than "a real professor," we need to remind ourselves of the problems both university and church were facing, problems that had grown out of the temporizing decisions made at the time of the Union of 1929, in which two separate divinity training schemes—those of the Church of Scotland and of the United Free Church of Scotland—had been brought together, though not completely amalgamated. It was not possible to amalgamate them fully without serious disruption and inconvenience to both students and staff, and so change by gentle phasing was sought. Unfortunately, financial complexities (and instabilities) and the international turbulence rendered this impossible in the short term, with the result that some functions continued to overlap and some that should have been kept separate were combined with others. A. J. Gossip's Chair was one of the latter. There was enormous potential for both Ethics and Practical Training at this time, but the exigencies of the hour disallowed adequate exploitation. Some changes were made, however. In 1935 three chairs (of Old Testament, New Testament, and Systematic Theology) were transferred from Trinity College to the university, though the Church of Scotland undertook to remunerate their incumbents. The Chair of Ecclesiastical History was then suppressed, and Gossip's Chair was also transferred to the university. As we saw earlier, this was suppressed in 1945, as was the Chair of New Testament itself, and in their place two Lectureships—of New Testament and Ecclesiastical History—were proposed. The church undertook to pay for the stipends of these new posts.

Principal Macgregor retired in 1938 and was succeeded as Principal by Professor William Fulton. In June 1944, amid the general planning for "the new day," Sir Hector Hetherington, Principal of the university, asked Principal Fulton if he was happy about the B.D. degree, now under the university's control.[27] Sir Hector clearly was not, and it was basically this concern that geared the present changes and appointments. In particular, and with a true sense of the changing postwar situation, he felt the B.D. to be "overweight linguistically" and doubted whether its construction offered "the maximum educational experience to the ordinary good candidate . . . still less the best kind of preparation for the practical experience of a Christian Ministry." He would like to see changes, he added cautiously.

Indeed, he needed to proceed cautiously, for he was not treading so much on holy ground as volcanic. The problem was not merely a twofold relationship of university and church facing a radically changing world, but a threefold relation of university, church, and Trinity College, each of which had its unique background, traditions, and outlook. When Willie later spoke of Sir Hector's brilliant administrative talents, it was exactly this situation he had in mind. As a casualty of the reorganization himself, he knew only too well the sense of upset, disappointment, and anxiety that could be provoked by such bold moves. But real issues were at stake as well as personal feelings. Sir Hector was suggesting a new approach to theological training, largely ahead of its time—a less linguistic and a more broadly educational and practical approach, a very daring action in the face of Glasgow's proud leadership of Free-Church and biblical traditions in Scotland. And it should be remembered that Hetherington was a former classics man himself; he knew the worth of a linguistic approach, but still felt the B.D. course was improperly balanced, too heavily oriented toward linguistics for the modern world. We shall shortly see Willie coming to terms with this challenge, though he himself was not prepared to weaken the emphasis for many years. In any case the practical result of all the politics was that his hopes for Gossip's Chair were dashed (Professor Pitt-Watson was soon appointed to a newly created Chair of Practical Theology); he was persuaded to undertake the "inhuman work" of New Testament Language and Literature instead. Although there is not direct evidence to support such a supposition, it may well be the case that Hetherington's concern was passed on to Willie and that he accepted the lesser post in order to be able to offer "the maximum educational experience" to his students, albeit within a strictly New Testament sphere.

Thus the checkered career of 1939 became the half-fulfilled career of 1946. Under G. H. C. Macgregor, Professor of Divinity and Biblical Criticism, Willie became "a natural second" all over again, clearly in the hope that it would "lead to something else." It eventually did, but via a route as tortuous as any man was ever asked to travel. The law of costly service could not be evaded; the gold could be refined only in the crucible of life if it was to be refined at all—and that meant the death of all Willie's personal hopes, dreams, and ambitions. In a new and sharp way he was learning the lesson of Paul: "not I but Christ."

His appointment found formal expression in the minutes of the Presbytery of Paisley for 3 December 1946 under the heading "Demission of Mr William Barclay":

There was laid on the table an extract minute of the General Assembly of date 20th November, bearing that the Commission of Assembly resolved to confirm the nomination of the Reverend William Barclay to the Lectureship in New Testament Language and Literature in the University of Glasgow, loosed Mr Barclay from the charge of Renfrew Trinity as from 31st December, 1946, subject to the confirmation of his appointment by the University, and instructed the Presbytery of Paisley to declare the charge vacant.

A more personal comment was made by Willie himself in a farewell letter to his congregation at Renfrew,[28] in which he bared his soul as never before:

My Dear Friends,
    I think you will understand and realize at least some of the feelings in my heart as I sit down to write this letter to you all. Somewhere Dr Johnson said that if you have done a thing many, many times, even if you heartily disliked it, to do it for the last time always brought a pang of regret. This is the last time that I shall write a pastoral letter to you as your minister, and so far from disliking my work, I have literally loved it, and you can understand my thoughts and feelings in my heart as I come near the day when I must lay it down.
    It can have been granted by God to few ministers to have fourteen years of such unbroken happiness as I have had in Renfrew. It would be utterly impossible for me to set down what I owe to this congregation. I came to Renfrew straight from college with little or no experience. I did not fully realise it then fourteen years ago, but now I stand amazed at the risk this congregation took in calling me, and the almost reckless way in which I responded to that call. One thing is true—this congregation taught me my job, and whatever I am or whatever I will be I owe to Trinity.
    Paul once wrote to one of his churches, "I thank my God upon every remembrance of you." I can only echo that. Never was a minister blessed with so loyal and understanding a band of office-bearers who so lovingly and wisely upheld his hands. Never had a minister such a band of young people around him who opened their hearts to him and who so generously gave him their friendship and made him one of themselves. Especially dear to me was the work amongst the boys and girls. It is one of the great joys of a fairly long ministry to see them grow up and to be given their confidence and sometimes to have the real joy of being treated by them not as a minister or as a Sunday School Superintendent, but as one of themselves. And never had a minister a more loyal congregation. What I shall miss most of all is the feeling that around me there was a circle of homes, hundreds of them, into any of which I could go and find a welcome. And never was there such a congregation to preach to. Of late years my work has taken me to many places, but there was none like my own pulpit, no congregation in which there was such an uplift of expectancy, no congregation which so helped, nay compelled a man to preach with all his might and all his heart.
    And yet as I look back I am conscious of so many things undone, and so

many things that might have been done better. I wish that I could have been oftener in your homes, but latterly our membership had grown so great that visitation had become an almost impossible task. And now as I look back I wonder and marvel at the forbearance of this people in the many shortcomings of my work here. The work of Trinity Church is a demanding and often an overwhelming task, yet in no congregation can a minister have been so repaid for anything he did, so constantly encouraged and so constantly uplifted by the understanding kindness of his people.

I think I can honestly say that so long as strength for the work here remained to me I would never have left you for any other congregation. The years had thirled me too closely to you for that. But there has come to me an appointment which it was not possible for me to refuse. Although I go to the University to teach the Language and the Literature of the New Testament it always remains true that no man can teach any subject in a theological college without having some share in training students, not in academic subjects, but for the work of the ministry. And I would wish to say this in all sincerity, if it shall be granted to me to do something to fit a man for the work of the ministry and to teach him something about it, it was from you and from this congregation that I learned that work myself. Anything of value that I can teach or say was learned in Trinity Church.

No matter where I go and no matter how long I may be spared to live I shall never forget this congregation. It lies too close to my heart for that. Here I have made friendships which I do not think any time will dull or any distance sever. From here I will take memories that will never fade and at least a bit of my heart will ever be left in Trinity.

I envy with all my heart the man who will succeed me. May God so guide this congregation that it will go from strength to strength and from triumph to triumph for Him. I hope that sometimes I may be allowed to come back to you and once again to stand in the pulpit which is so dear to me. I shall be thinking of you and watching what happens and remembering you in my prayers wherever I may go. God bless you all.

With every good wish to each one of you,

Ever and always very sincerely yours,
WILLIAM BARCLAY

"Unbroken happiness" (the same phrase used when he wrote to Braidwood); his undying gratitude to Trinity which had taught him his job; his special enjoyment of his youth work; the love and loyalty of the congregation that ever opened its homes to him and that "compelled a man to preach with all his might and all his heart"; and the deep and lasting friendships that were indeed kept unbroken till the end of his life: these were the prizes he was to take away from Renfrew Trinity. And much else that lay unexpressed: a community the better and the more unified than hitherto; an immeasurably stronger church; marriages founded on love for God as well as that of the individual partners; children blessed, baptized, cherished by their minister, and brought—by a multitude of paths—into the fellowship of the church; weak hearts made strong in faith; sad hearts made independent and courageous; bereaved made to feel wanted and sustained; and so much more. From these fourteen selfless years Willie and Kate reaped a huge return and a huge correspondence that was devotedly kept up year by year. On the 26th of December, at Willie's last meeting with the kirk session, a motion was put forward by Mr. Ramsay "and unanimously accepted by the Session [which] instructed that it be recorded in the minutes of the Session our deep appreciation of our Moderator and of his conduct of the meetings of the Session which throughout the past fourteen years had been a pleasure to attend and had resulted in unbroken fellowship among the members of the Session."

For its part, the church organized—what else—another concert, and a presentation, which took place on the 27th of December. The performers invited were Miss Helen Logan and Miss Chrys Taylor, along with the Church Choir and the Session Glee Party (how better could Willie and Kate be sent off than by a Glee Party!), all accompanied by Mr. Hamilton Kerr and Miss Betty McCullum. The chairman, appropriately enough, was the Reverend A. G. Fortune, who had spoken so perceptively at Willie's Induction Meeting in 1933, and who had helped point him in the direction of providing those "decided answers" to the difficult questions society was asking of the church. There were other addresses besides the chairman's—from Donald Swanson of Old Renfrew Old Church, Professor J. G. Riddell of Trinity College, Willie's college friend Stanley Munro, and Alexander Mitchell, the senior elder, on behalf of the kirk session and managers. John Kidd made presentations on behalf of the congregation, to which Willie replied, and the proceedings concluded with an address by the preses, George Munro. Kate's father, James H. Gillespie, was to have spoken, but illness and poor weather prevented his attending. Fittingly for one who could recall vividly his own Bethel experience so long ago at Fort William, they all sang "O God of Bethel, by Whose Hand" in conclusion.

The Renfrew Press publicized the affair to the extent of a three-column report, occupying over thirty column inches. The event was described as having drawn "the largest congregation ever to assemble in the Trinity Church."[29] Willie was complimented for having sustained the large church and its vigorous organizations so admirably and for having thrived on hard work while still finding time to pursue his studies. D. M. Swanson commented that for all his good points, Willie was nevertheless "a problem minister": he worked too fast, he had gone through too many motor cars (which comment provoked a good deal of knowing laughter), and he exceeded the capacity of even Trinity's virile life-style to exploit his gifts and energies to the full. (He also added, but privately, that he was not the only minister in Renfrew to breathe a sigh of relief that this unstoppable colleague was going: at least he and his brother ministers could now fulfill their own ministries without being constantly compared with the headline-maker of Trinity Church!) Professor Riddell was high in praise both of Willie's academic attainments and practical accomplishments. He had been especially impressed by his Bruce Lectures on the use of the New Testament in the Apologists in 1937 and by his lectures to the returning servicemen of the previous summer term, adding that many of these men had given ample proof "of their deep appreciation of his services." It was the unusual combination of informed comment, persuasive presentation, and practicality that the Church of Scotland's Board of Nominations had found so convincing, and therefore "there was no question as to who was the man for the post." Stanley Munro spoke of Willie's highly successful university record and his similar results in the pastorate, noting that he expected him to be "one of the leaders of the church of tomorrow." He also gallantly spoke of Kate's special gifts and personality—"one of the most bright and gracious ladies" of the times.

Mr. Mitchell talked of Willie's work as being specially interesting and broad-minded. It is not every minister who can be said to have increased the range and raised the horizons of his church, he said, especially when that church was already alive and responsive to the complex range of demands a parish such as Renfrew Trinity makes. John Kidd, the session clerk, let fall a secret when he reminded them that Willie had been expressly advised not to come to Trinity, as it was considered to be "a battlefield" in which even experienced ministers had become casualties. Nevertheless he came, and worked, and flourished. The elders and managers presented a specially framed photograph of the two groups, the congregation gave a radiogram and a wallet of notes containing fifty pounds, and his Young People's Society presented him with a radio and a chair for his study—gifts of love, all of them.

Willie, who had difficulty in finding his words for once, replied in a suitable vein. He wished, he said, to express his thanks to his predecessors, for he had entered upon their work. He thanked the congregation for their splendid support, and he was especially appreciative that his wife's name had been coupled with his own on the inscriptions, for "All the good things that you have said about her are not half good enough. She was the one person to whom I could go home and explosively unburden myself." He was "extremely thankful I disregarded the warning not to come to Trinity": their liveliness, their cheerfulness, their frank yet supportive (if exacting) ways had made him what he was. He urged them to support his as-yet-unnamed successor. And he concluded decisively, "when you shut the gate, shut it. There will still be the previous friendship between you and me which nothing will turn over." It was typical of his attitude and style: forward, not backward, and on to further costly service.

PART THREE

The Fulfillment

The Reverend William Barclay, B.D., at the outset of his academic career (1946)

CHAPTER TWELVE

The Aftermath of War

A New Year, a New Job, and a New Base

Dᴙʟᴀɴ Thomas wrote of Glasgow that it was "a lovely, ugly town," and such it is, though it would be more correct today to describe it less critically, thanks to the city planners' efforts and the march of progress. This was much less true when the Welsh poet saw it and when Willie came to take up his new job in January 1947. The ravages of time, of social deprivation and war, had made their mark. Nevertheless, nothing even then could nullify its vibrant life, the friendliness of its people, and its rich humanity. Thirty-six years previously, when the Barclays were still living at Wick in Caithness, John White had returned with relish to a Glasgow parish from Leith, Edinburgh. He ever looked on the metropolis as "the centre of the country's vitality,"¹ ever glad "to share again in the pulsating life of the great city."² And Willie did so, too.

The return to Glasgow was a homecoming for Willie, and that in two ways. First, it had been his home after his father's retirement in July 1929. And second, he had been nominated to the ministry by the Presbytery of Glasgow in 1932, under whose auspices he had been trained. "All roads lead to Glasgow"; at least the best ones do in the west of Scotland, and Willie was glad once more to feel about him the vitality of the third city of Great Britain. Behind all this lay the deeper associations of the Barclay family, of his father at the end of the nineteenth century, and of his cousins and perhaps even his great-great-grandfather, Samuel Barclay, the Manchester merchant-cum-tailor. In making his home at 87 Vardor Road, Clarkston, on the southern edge of the city, he placed himself in a church (Williamwood) that had long associations with the old Presbytery of Hamilton, in which he had grown up. Both connections were now happily preserved; the latter would never be broken by him.

Willie once described Clarkston as "a Glasgow suburb where people buy their homes, but not in the expensive bracket."³ To William Braidwood he had expressed concern about his domestic arrangements, which were very severe for a man moving out of a tied-home (the manse) into home ownership at forty years of age: "I, too, am faced with the problem of getting a house. There are plenty of houses here in Scotland but their owners seem to think that they are made of pure gold judging by what they want for them."[4] Fortunately, a small bequest from Kate's Aunt Bessie and Trinity's monetary gift of £50 (which he described as "a lot of money") helped.

They had hoped to settle in Paisley—but a stone's throw from Renfrew, which had provided them with so much happiness, musical and otherwise—but it was not to be. So they moved ("flitted" in the Scottish phrase) on December 23–24 and began "the slow process" of settling down. It was not easy. For one thing it was "a much smaller house than the manse." Kate and Willie both had "the feeling that if you stretch you will knock the place down."[5] And they both felt deeply the loss of former friends and neighbors.

It is said that "a man's history is often to be traced in his addresses." Like WDB, Willie nurtured few worldly possessions; and, like his hero Winston Churchill, he left little mark on the houses he inhabited. A three-bedroom terraced dwelling, the Vardor Road house had a very small front garden and no drive or garage. It had been built just before the war, in 1939, and was very easily cleaned and maintained. Because of its compactness, it was "a godsend for Mrs Barclay," who was completely exhausted physically and mentally, and still not quite recovered from being "worried sick" over Barbara's recent bouts of poor health and hospitalization. (Her throat and heart complications had been followed by a painful cranial abscess that took several weeks to resolve.) The farewells had exacerbated things, despite the great generosity and the many expressions of affection they had received from Trinity Church. The final Sunday was "pretty terrible," to quote Willie, who was ever reluctant to expose himself publicly to emotionally charged atmospheres and partings.

Ronnie, now as tall as Willie and as sportive as his father had been at that age, had to move to Eastwood School. Situated "about one minute from our door," it gave him no problems of travel, and, as the school had seven of its scholars in the first hundred of the Bursary List, they were pleased to have him settled there. Barbara settled in even more quickly at Clarkston Junior School, "and loves it."

We have little information as to what Willie did with his large library. Having no room of his own at Trinity, we can be sure his collection dominated "the best and the biggest room in the house"[6]—one of the causes of matrimonial friction in the ministry, he believed, and for those just out of it. In a letter to his friend and fellow author Rita Snowden he presently remarked, "I have had to clear out my already over-size library. . . . I have put out all the non-technical stuff."[7] Nevertheless, it still occupied three walls, from floor to ceiling, of their lounge. But they were content—"I live surrounded by gifts from Renfrew," he commented; he had the challenging opportunity of his new job, and Kate had a real chance to regain her wonted strength and equilibrium.

"There is a job to be done up there," Willie wrote in November 1946,[8] and so there was, even if it was deprived of professorial status. Battle-experienced and widely traveled men could not be trained as former students had been; the

Ronnie and Barbara (1947)

courses were shortened and a (temporary) accommodation to their lack of linguistic attainments was made. One of the reasons for the great impression Willie made on those early theologs was his ability to understand their needs, to speak for them, and for the needs of the parish in the postwar era, as well as the obvious fact that he alone of the faculty staff was of their age and broadly shared their aspirations. His lectures to them, the same men whom he had taught during the "emergency" summer term, soon broke down any remaining barriers. They were quick to realize that his four years' experience as an RAF Chaplain had given him deep insight into their minds, and trust and affection were established.

Willie could not but agree with the vigorous words of John White of early 1944, and sought to establish their reality in his students' thinking: "the salvage heap is the place for many a sermon that does not take into account the deep needs of a generation that has passed through five years of fierce and human strife."[9] White, whose authority and influence on the Church of Scotland defy measurement—as architect of the church in its united form and as twice-nominated Moderator of its General Assembly—was leading the cause of the new-era thinking and reform at the age of seventy-eight. Before the General Assembly of May 1944 he asked, "Has the Church a definite, relevant message for those who will come back with victory from the jaws of death . . . ? There has been unsettlement, deep questionings. Have we in the church that will to attract and hold them—something that will meet their needs?"[10] An ex–Trinity College man himself, he admitted envy of their task and opportunity: "Perhaps, if I could, I would put back the hands of the clock and get alongside you now to face the future."[11] But he could not put back the hands of the clock, and his venerability precluded too close an association with the students. Such was not the case with Willie, however: he was unable to see himself as a pure academic, had no heart for the total demands and strict specialization of academe, but never wavered in making practical use of his New Testament course. Further, "the deep needs of a generation" echoed through his pastoral and evangelistic concern, and the need for "a definite, relevant message" had goaded him since Fortune preached him in in 1933—and before that, for we ought not to forget W. M. Macgregor's and A. J. Gossip's similar admonitions and examples.

Partly consumed by concern over militant Communism's encroachments and blandishments (since Churchill had sent his "Iron Curtain" telegram of 12 May 1945, the Western world had become hypnotized by Communism as "the great beast" with which it had to do battle), White was now in a lather over the need for the church to meet the atheistic and materialistic challenges of Communism boldly and adequately. To the students of Trinity College he stated,

> The mass atheism that is an integral part of Communism will never be stemmed by your preaching to a few folk in a church. You must grapple with it, by personal touch, with the many in their homes. You must get alongside them in their occupation. There must be something positive in the appeal and the challenge. . . .[12]

And for Willie it was fuel to a fire that had been burning ever more brightly as opportunities to teach and preach (mainly through his Scottish Sunday School Union work) increased, and took him all over the country. But he was at Trinity to do a particular job, to teach New Testament Language and Literature. It was this task that now consumed his main energies, and to its cause he devoted himself.

The General Course provided three areas of study. First was a general introduction based on F. B. Clogg's classical—if dull—New Testament introduction, a fairly conservative book representing the position that then largely obtained in Britain as to the authorship, provenance, and chronology of the New Testament documents (the other two general introductions available, by McNeile and Dods, were considered too detailed and too scanty, respectively, for this course); to this were added lectures on the text and canon of the New Testament (following Lake, Souter, and Kenyon). The second area of study covered prescribed books of the New Testament: Matthew 5-10, Acts 1-9, John 1-4 and 12-14, and Galatians; for these, no fewer than ten commentaries were recommended. The third area concerned a much more detailed approach to the Synoptic Gospels (Matthew, Mark, and Luke) and the Catholic Epistles (James, Peter, John, and Jude); three further textbooks were recommended for these. With all his other encumbrances, Willie had his work cut out preparing and writing lectures to cover such a broad spectrum of studies.

Moreover, the special course for honors students offered different prescribed texts of the Greek New Testament and a deeper penetration of the four Gospels, John's epistles, and the Apocalypse (Revelation); for this a further ten textbooks were listed. In addition there was a choice of either The Hellenistic Background to the New Testament or Aramaic, the former being a subject Willie was to make his own specialty. A part of this work he published as his first "academic" book—*Educational Ideas in the Ancient World* (1959)—which never found its true market, partly because the Judaic background became more popular than the Hellenistic after the discoveries of the Dead Sea Scrolls, and partly because of the essential narrowness of its purview. The texts laid down for the special subject were Macgregor and Purdy's *Tutors unto Christ* and Levinson's *Jewish Background of Christianity*. The alternate subject was a course in Aramaic following Dalman's *Aramaische Lesestücke* and Merx's *Chrestomathia Targumica*. In this latter choice Willie had no involvement, nor did he at any time offer Aramaic to his students. Not a few felt it was a weakness in his scholarly equipment that he stressed mainly the Greek side of his subject and not the Semitic.

I have given details of these courses and textbooks because we shall see these same areas of study appearing frequently in Willie's work and interests. For example, the General Course prescribed Matthew 5–10 (following the expositions of Swete, Rawlinson, and Branscombe). Willie had already made this passage—which includes the Sermon on the Mount—his own at Renfrew. From now on it would feature very largely in his public ministry and would become a prime source for his views (theological and ethical) and for his publications. Other examples we shall note later. It is a common thing for anyone having to give lectures to make that same material the base for his extracurricular work, but with Willie it was not so much a choice as an imperative. Even as he had striven to keep pulpit in touch with pew at Renfrew, so now he strove to keep the larger world of his varied tasks in touch with that of his lectures at the University.

He wasted no time in settling down to his work, and G. H. C. Macgregor, cousin of W. M., had no intention of allowing grass to grow under his assistant's feet either. By January 1947 (having taken no time off for special preparation), Willie was writing to his friend Braidwood that he was already lecturing for five hours each week, which included two hours of lectures to postgraduates. He expressed both surprise and gratification at this, "since as a lecturer I am totally untried." He was not really totally untried of course: his Bruce Lectures, his work (at a lower level, to be sure) for the Scottish Sunday School Union around the country, and his recent summer-term lectures all disproved this. But it was a new undertaking, and a severe test of his energy and ability, for ex-servicemen are sharply perceptive—and vocal—when it comes to being hard-pressed with work. An indication of Willie's aggressive attack on his newfound duties may be seen from the shelf register at Trinity College Library. During 1947 thirty-one books were lent to Willie on general background, textual, and literary criticism, especially on the Gospels, and on the parables of Jesus (another subject he especially enjoyed expounding) and the Pauline literature. These were books he did not have in his own excellent library, and by no means exhaust the range of his reading in other directions—official papers and reports, secular and religious papers, books for review, and, be they never omitted, his daily diet of fiction and poetry.

The five hours Macgregor had assigned to him represented almost half of the New Testament lectures offered at Trinity College (eleven hours altogether). And how Willie enjoyed that trust!

> Better yet my chief tells me that he intends that one of us should do the work of the department in the summer term alone. That would mean that every second year one would have to work like a black doing the whole department alone but that in the alternate years one would have no set lecturing between 20 April and 20 October or thereby. That would leave one of us free to go to America or Germany every second year. It sounds good. How all this works out I will let you know.[13]

How it all worked out we also shall presently see, and it was not to Willie's advantage. Macgregor, never wholly well, soon fell prey to two quite separate things: first, attacks on the condition mortal, which often kept him bedridden for weeks at a time—"a martyr to asthma" in Willie's phrase[14] (and Willie knew its ravages, as he had suffered from a form of it himself in his youth). The second assault is less defensible for the head of a department in a college with 110 men in "emergency" training for the ministry, 55 of them in their first year (we should not forget that one of the excellencies of the Scottish tradition was for the professor himself to take certain courses with the first-year men): "He has been attacked by wanderlust in his old age," Willie commented at the beginning of 1949. He goes on to describe Macgregor spending six months in America the previous year (almost within a year of Willie's commencement), and adds "and then [he] went away for weeks to London and Cambridge and all over the show."[15] We are not here concerned with anything other than Willie's own work, but must note that this time was to be one of awesome responsibility and application, when Willie—no stranger to the midnight hour, as we have seen— learned to squeeze a quart into a pint pot, if not more. The record needs to emphasize that over the course of many years this "Junior Lecturer" played more than a junior's role, quietly, uncomplainingly, and with great educational and "pastoral" success. No doubt this experience as well as his professional appoint- ment itself colored his appreciation of "men who played the second part," a theme that recurs in some of his earlier books, as when he wrote, "It takes a really big man to be passed over for the first place which he might legitimately have expected, and cheerfully and uncomplainingly serve in the second place; and the world needs a man like that."[16] If Macgregor was laid low as a martyr to asthma, Willie soared as a martyr to work. He loved it, and abandoned himself to it in all its aspects. And this a man in his fortieth year, without the advantages of postgraduate biblical study: his biblical studies were postgraduate only in the sense that he proceeded to them after his Classics degree, his work at Marburg having been very superficial and of a short duration. Moreover, it was the work of a man who had filled "each unforgiving minute, with sixty seconds of distance run" in a pastorate of unusual dynamism over fourteen strenuous years, a man who commenced his lecturing without a holiday, without a refresher course or time for real preparation.

Neil Alexander, who studied under Willie from 1947 to 1948 and returned to become a faculty colleague in 1964, wrote a portrait of him as "a scholar and colleague."[17] After first surveying his academic equipment ("impeccable linguistics"—Aramaic apart—and "an immense background knowledge of ancient literature and culture"), Alexander observed Willie's "passionate love of teaching," his "sheer love of teaching." Professor Allan Galloway, later Principal of Trinity College, talked similarly of Willie's "charisma for teaching."[18] The word *charisma* is now hackneyed, debased through overuse, but it is an exact word in this situation. When one considers the splendid background and upbringing of William Barclay, his deep devotion and responsible discipleship, his great spiritual power and success, who can say of him that he was not specially "anointed" to do this task?

There is an interesting and significant contrast between Sir William Ramsay and his admiring reader William Barclay. We should not allow Willie's detractors to cause us to forget that his scholarship was not the dismissive sort that Ward Gasque rightly bewails in his short biography of the Glaswegian archaeologist.[19] This was another thing Willie had learned from W. M. Macgregor, who greatly admired Ramsay's application and interpretations. He was willing to seek information out, no matter how ignored or underrated his sources might generally be. Willie was never one for jumping on popular bandwagons. "The idea was simmering unconsciously in my mind," wrote Ramsay of his university days, "that scholarship was the life for me; not the life of teaching, which was repellent, but the life of discovery."[20] Willie, too, loved discovery, the adventurous mind. Ramsay recalls William Robertson Nicoll's father, who, unlike Willie, had "no didactic instinct" and was "by choice rather a student than a teacher"—whom Willie significantly assails (somewhat unfairly) for putting books and book learning above home and the practical duties of fatherhood.

We shall need to return to the characteristics that made Willie such a superlative teacher again, and more comprehensively. But for the moment this enthusiasm and love for his job must retain our attention. It energized his long hours of study and preparation, allowing him to inspire his students as no other lecturer inspired them. He believed what he taught; he was endlessly thrilled by it, even after years of repetition, and to its fulfillment he gave himself unreservedly. He magnified his office, but the task never overtook the content, the subject never became the object. He once quoted Heraclitus: "Education is a second sun to its possessors";[21] while Willie's material never dislodged his students from their primary loyalty to Christ, he was at pains to promote a healthy love and respect for biblical knowledge per se. There was much of the ancient teacher in William Barclay, and he managed in himself to promote all three aspects of the Greek teacher he thought important: the *grammatistēs,* who was responsible for the rudimentary things (the three R's, if you will); the *kitharistēs*, who was responsible for nurturing the more cultured aspects, such as music and song, in his not always willing pupils; and the *paidotribēs*, who looked after the physical development of his young charges. It was this breadth of perspective, along with his deep understanding of their minds and the notable reputation he had already made by his parish work and service for the SSSU, that caused such admiration of and devotion to him in his students. They not only preserved, even in these early days, his lectures in full, but even excerpted the practical matter in the form of "Gleanings from William Barclay." He held steadily to his immediate subject in his classes, but he never forgot the wider purview, and ever sought to ensure that his students kept a balanced personal life and a unified world view as their goal: faith and life, pulpit and pew.

W. M. Macgregor had counseled this to his students in 1938 when he said, inducting William Fulton to the principalship,

> nothing could be imagined more maimed or more futile than a scheme of theological instruction which takes no account of personal character. . . . [We have no use for ministers who are] content to be mere mechanics—tiresomely busy creatures, whose whole life is in committees and guilds and organisations, and without any touch of the Eternal. . . . If a minister lacks book learning he can study and acquire it; if he lacks grace he can pray and God will give it; but if he lacks sense neither earth nor heaven can help him. In large measure the same is true of the endowment of humanity, the unforced interest in the men and women about us, without which no minister can ever do his work aright.[22]

He must have been highly gratified in seeing Willie reflecting that attitude to his students.

Willie's mind was nearer to the Roman than the Greek, however. It did not lend itself to speculation, and while his "worldliness" was held firmly in check, it was nevertheless a marked counterpoint to his otherwise strong and "un-worldly" religious emphasis. Stewart Borthwick has provided an interesting window into Willie's attitude at this time.[23] Borthwick was himself one of the men brought into Trinity College direct from the armed forces. Prior to the war he had been with the Glasgow Criminal Investigation Department, and was therefore a man of wide experience who knew men, a man of the world. Such things were ever of special interest to Willie—manliness reasserted, of course. Willie sought out Borthwick on this occasion as to his views on the use of alcohol. It would appear that his own views were changing, that the temperance (i.e., the total abstinence from strong drink) of his earlier years was now being exchanged for a convivial dram with his students. That the change was under-taken with real heart-searching, and against the colossal influence of his father's strong views, is indicated by this incident and others discussed elsewhere. He was to speak that evening at a women's group, and was clearly concerned as to the impression he would make by his views. (We shall dwell on the importance of this later, but for the moment it is his openness and "balance" that are our concern.) Borthwick, surprised at his tutor's reliance on him, took the line that total abstinence was not a ready pass into the kingdom of heaven; Willie was

310

clearly pleased to hear it. No doubt it comforted him before making such views known to a faction of the church that often takes a different (and considerably tougher) line. His lectures, Borthwick adds, were "always bristling with anecdotes and experiences of the parish ministry," and he welcomed and warmly reciprocated the friendship Willie offered.

Never lost for a word or two, Willie had no difficulty in lecturing for a full period from a single sheet of paper, though his lectures were usually written out fully. The same ability to organize his material that we see in his sermons and *Scottish Sunday School Teacher* "Lesson Notes" now characterized his lectures. They followed a clearly defined course, and each was prefaced by its aim and content. He spoke as he read—very fast—and not all students could keep up with his rapid delivery. He was especially sensitive to those who had difficulty in their courses, though he respected and encouraged the high-fliers wherever possible. Without advanced degrees himself, he was keen to promote postgraduate research, though his own mind was directed toward a different goal. At this point in time, in the deprived, "first aid" days of short-term courses following the war, he entered fervently into the spirit of things, aware of his students' deficiencies in background and training. John Burns, one of his early students, objected to Willie's lowering his standards in such cases, finding (naturally enough for a talented honors graduate) the transliteration from the Greek that Willie constantly made on the blackboard irksome and demeaning. Willie, an easy and brilliant linguist himself, usually ignored him. "Och, John," he exclaimed on one such occasion, with that befriending but steely glint in his eye, "you know everything!"[24] Daniel Jenkins recalls an opening prayer of Willie's in Bloomsbury Baptist Church that epitomizes his approach to his students as well as to his general hearers: "Bless those who don't know, and those who do not wish to know"; he would convert and enlighten them if humanly possible. His attitude is well-expressed in one of his *British Weekly* articles: "Learn! Learn! Learn!"[25] Forward, not backward.

His new job created a new experience for Willie in that he was for the first time a junior colleague in a faculty of accomplished and experienced men. We have already mentioned his immediate chief, Professor G. H. C. Macgregor, who was publishing learned articles on the fourth Gospel (his particular area of specialty) in *The Expositor* a dozen years before Willie even matriculated. Readers of *Testament of Faith* will remember that Macgregor learned his love of the Gospel of John from Professor H. A. A. Kennedy of New College, who lectured his admiring students on the Gospel for three months, four days per week, at the end of which he had only reached "the first half of the second verse of the first chapter!"[26] But Macgregor was much more than just a competent exegete and expositor. Like Denney, and sharing with him the Scottish expositional tradition, he never forgot the real world of which theology is but the servant and guide. It was at this point that Willie's and his chief's mutual interests and commitments touched their most public aspect, for they both shared a convinced pacifist ideal.

In 1936 Macgregor published *The New Testament Basis of Pacifism* (it was reprinted with Willie's blessings as late as 1971), which centered the debate on its real Christian basis—the scriptures—and not that of personal idealism or national or denominational tradition. His friendship with Charles E. Raven, and their mutual involvement in the work of the Fellowship of Reconciliation, increased Willie's admiration for such transdenominational activity, though Willie himself did not join the Fellowship till the late '60s. Raven, of course, was a distinguished Anglican with sympathies that readily responded to the Iona Community of George Macleod.[27] At the time of "the year of disaster," Macgregor was doubly daring in both bringing out a sharp challenge to Reinhold Niebuhr's trenchant book *Why the Christian Church Is Not Pacifist,* and in risking the displeasure of the authorities when he published his wartime book *The Relevance of the Impossible.* The young man who wrote an article on "possibilities and impossibilities" was bound to find the author of such a title as this, which Willie called his "manifesto and credo,"[28] more than a little worthy of his respect and affection.

"Throughout the years I came to love him," commented Willie, musing on their seventeen years of work together in the faculty; he recalled how the old and dying man had held his hand, saying, "Willie, when I die they'll find your name written on my heart."[29] Thus we cannot really be surprised that Garth Macgregor was the only colleague from the theology faculty that Willie chose to name in *Testament of Faith.* One wonders if he was not some sort of surrogate father at Trinity College, even as Mitchell Ramsay and John Kidd had been at Renfrew Trinity. Willie, ever a man's man, showed a willingness and a gratitude for being directed by others. Even as he said of his book writing, "I never chose to write one single one of them,"[30] so he was content to be directed by others in his professional life. In 1965, as the last act of friendship and respect toward Macgregor, he edited with Hugh Anderson what was to have been a festschrift, but was sadly transformed into a memorial by Macgregor's sudden death: *The New Testament in Historical and Contemporary Perspective: New Testament Essays in Honour of Professor Macgregor.* Principal Mauchline's obituary was carried in place of a foreword to the book, and reflects Macgregor's approach to his work (which Willie himself also strongly reflected):

> How do G H C Macgregor's friends and former students remember him? As an orator? No. As a master of the finely turned sentence or the memorable phrase? Not notably. As a fine classicist and New Testament exegete? Yes, very much so. But he was much more than that. He put so much of himself into his teaching, and the grace of his personality commended so much of what he said. A cold intellectualism was foreign to his nature; in him heart and mind did not co-exist in mutual isolation, they were in deep harmony. The fact that he so often spoke of the ministry of reconciliation showed how greatly he longed to see a like deep harmony in others.[31]

Those were things for which Trinity College firmly stood, Willie not least so. He was pleased to be back.

Postwar Reconstruction

Willie's sparse involvement with committee work at presbytery and the poor reputation he had made for himself thereby were not continued at the University. His first faculty meeting duly saw him in his place and warmly welcomed by Professor Riddell, then Acting Dean. It was not otherwise at his first meeting of Trinity College staff, though its minutes fail to record the event, perhaps due to the previous term's collaboration.

It was not only the special needs of the servicemen's training that had to be implemented. The whole college had been disrupted—virtually closed—during the war, and much had to be done to put the place back on the academic and ecclesiastical map. Not the least of their concerns was a suitable memorial to the fifteen of its alumni who had paid the ultimate price in the cause of freedom.

On the outbreak of war it had been decided to hold all classes on the university's premises, and by the end of 1940 all of Trinity College's buildings (with the exception of the Library Hall, the chapel, and the janitor's house) were under military requisition. Shortly after this even the Library Hall fell prey to the demands of army bureaucracy. The books were piled into cases and boxes— irreplaceable bequests and collections of Principal Fairbairn (totalling four thousand volumes), incunabula of various sorts (some dating from the fifteenth century), the famous Tischendorf Collection (over three thousand volumes), and many smaller, though not necessarily lesser, gifts of ministers and teachers who represent part of the glories of Scottish church life and history. They were mainly stacked behind a huge screen at one end of the hall, and many a student during the next five years fervently prayed that no incendiary bombs would fall near this priceless and largely unprotected collection. It was not till the spring of 1946 that the Royal Army Pay Corps derequisitioned the college, and its students— including Willie, as "emergency" New Testament lecturer—found their way back inside. Many alterations and repairs had to be effected during the first months of its being reopened, and staff and students worked in decidedly siege-like conditions. In point of fact it was five years, as Mechie states,[32] before the problems were fully overcome. One of the most important aspects of the college—its communal life—had been seriously disrupted: gone were the common dinners and the other functions that strengthened the esprit de corps. Many felt the college could never be the same again. But the world was changing too. It was not a time for looking back.

The librarian during the war was R. M. Buchanan, who had been appointed to his post in 1920. He was related to A. S. Peake's friend and colleague J. Gray Buchanan, himself a victim of a U-boat attack while returning to this country in 1944. He retired at the end of the war and was succeeded by James Mackintosh, a trained lawyer and former Church of Scotland missionary to India (where he worked as Professor of English Literature at Wilson College, Bombay). He was also deeply involved in general book work in the Church of Scotland, and was a leading light in the postwar scheme to get "a library in every parish," along with adult education ventures of various sorts. He and Willie had much in common, having, like all former Free Church men, the evangelical/missionary cause so deeply at heart, not to speak of Eng. Lit., Peake, and a shared passion for books. The huge collection of books boxed and stowed behind screens (some even in the gymnasium) had to be sorted, collated, indexed, and reshelved. While it is surprising to find Willie having the energy for any further infringements on his time, it is entirely in character that he alone of the college staff should find some time for this work. He was formally made Mackintosh's assistant in December 1947.[33] Enter William Barclay, librarian! By February 1948, they had between them transferred over three and a half thousand volumes to their appointed shelves, having checked the indexing and cataloguing and made alterations where necessary. No doubt his delight in books drew him to this practical task: he had to help free their resources for others.

He and Mackintosh soon became firm friends—"one of my closest friends" was how Willie described him in his obituary, "Mac, Keeper of Books."[34] Willie, himself a lover of knowledge with a specially retentive memory for the curious and the unusual, greatly respected Mackintosh, whom he called "the most erudite man I ever met." Willie once said he could not have written any of his books without him, and if we disregard the exaggeration for the generous compliment it was meant to be, we should at least retain a high regard for this modest, unassuming friend, who was content to be not only "keeper of books" but also errand boy, finder of quotations, guide, and counselor: a true second lieutenant. Moreover, recalled Willie, "He lived close to learning; he lived close to nature; and he lived close to God." That was the sort of man whom Willie chose to befriend at a deep level, and there were not many of them. As he commented in 1975, "there are few, very few, people with whom I am really friends."[35]

Later, and for over two years, they traveled to college together, Willie typically offering to collect the older man on his way in from Clarkston. But in the early postwar period Willie had to make the journey by train, as the Petrol Controller severely restricted his petrol coupons once he had left pastoral work. In 1954 he dedicated his book on Mark's Gospel to "all librarians and keepers of books, without whose help no author could ever hope to write a book and in particular to J M to whom I have caused endless trouble and from whom I have received endless kindness."[36] And in 1958 Willie dedicated the latest of his books—his daily readings of James and Peter—to Mackintosh, "On whose staff it is my privilege to serve, in gratitude for help and guidance so often and so graciously given."[37]

This was the time when he was, to use former student Richard Baxter's phrase, "a lecturer without a side-room."[38] He was, like the books he so cherished, positioned behind a wooden screen where "he battered his typewriter, cheerfully oblivious of the noise, since he had removed his deaf-aid." He was indeed heavy-handed on the keyboard, and failed to realize that his typing made the library an impossible place to read in! Like Neville Cardus, whom he admired, Willie also could say "the typewriter was never conquered by me."[39] Working it hard with two fingers, and chiefly from the elbow, he produced sheets well populated with mistakes and strikeovers.

Richard Baxter recalls Willie's lecturing style, which did not change through the ensuing years and became one of his television attractions: his slightly hunched stance; his face wrinkled in concentration, yet ever liable to break into that generous, gleeful smile; his voice heavily accented and husky, and very rapid of delivery. As in his preaching—and this is part of his huge success as a teacher—he made his points decisively, numerating his argument step by step, a style much admired by the ex-servicemen in his classes who were used to a laconic method. Now and then he would pause from his pacing of the rostrum to inscribe key words on the blackboard, his gown becoming chalky-white in the process. Not a minute of the fifty-five minutes allocated was lost. He was ever ready to answer questions, but he did not really favor the seminar method. His lectures were a pure and uninterrupted outflow of information, facts, viewpoints, theories. Each was dispassionately described, leaving the students not always sure which "line" Willie himself preferred, he being generous to a fault with the views of others. It was hard work for his students, who were expected to take down what he gave out. Jack Stuart and others formed a lecture-note pool, from which a fair copy of the lecture was made and circulated. Some of these notes are still extant, and show well his orderly and informed approach to the problems then besetting New Testament studies. His lectures, unlike Professor Riddell's "disorganized" approach, were assiduously prepared—hence the battering his series of replacement typewriters received. But at least they were much clearer than if handwritten, for his writing now defied the normal laws of calligraphy; he was a man in a hurry, and his fingers simply could not keep up with his cerebral impulses.

He was very conscientious as to the content of his lectures. Every lecture had to count toward the completion of his course. This did not mean that his lectures were pure exercises of the intellect, however; as we have repeatedly seen, Willie was constitutionally incapable of separating "pure" from "applied" aspects: life was *one*. He was too practiced a speaker not to seize every available opportunity (and sometimes create them) to make practicable his views, be it by way of illustrating a biblical point or early church problem, or even a Greek conjugation. Many, therefore, were the pastoral asides subjoined to his expositions, even outdoing W. D. Niven's own tendency to do this.

His practical and personal approach differed markedly from that of Ian Henderson, who joined the staff twelve months after Willie, occupying the Chair of Systematic Theology with distinction, unafraid to make waves publicly for certain cherished political aims. Henderson did not hesitate to publish in areas beyond his own academic discipline (he was more naturally responsive to German theology and historiography than Willie, and was deeply sensitive to the sociopolitical dimensions of theology; he produced a very useful introduction to *Myth in the New Testament* in 1952). This was particularly apt in Scotland, where

Presbyterianism is the "established" form of religion, rooted in and linked to many functions of civic life as the expression of the state church ideal. Willie, of course, was anything but thrilled by this dimension in its technical aspects. While a loyal son of the church, and glad to make use of any "handle" the church/state relationship offered him to evangelize, he was still essentially a Free Churchman in his approach and views. It was not just in intensity and earnestness that he reflected this trait. Henderson knew and understood power, and sought to use it; Willie was but an observer, wary then of the dangers such wholesale involvement set, and preferring to continue the tradition of distance from party politics. Three years younger than Willie, Henderson's professorial rank gave him greater authority around the University, which was confirmed by a more radical and scholarly attitude toward his subject despite his boyish face and exuberance. In 1967 Henderson published *Power without Glory,* which created a great disturbance north of the border, falling, if not exactly like a bomb on the playground of the theologians, at least like an incendiary that lit up brightly the issues that churchmen take seriously. By this time Willie's own views were even more open to the secularizing process, and Henderson—along with Ronald Gregor Smith—must take some credit for this influence.

The other members of the faculty—Principal William Fulton and Professors John Mauchline, W. D. Niven, and James Pitt-Watson—fostered a more measured, almost patriarchal approach to their subjects, to their students, and to ministerial training itself. Mauchline was even known as "Yahweh"—not out of any calculated irreverence, but because of his aloof style, and out of a determination to weaken the hold *Jehovah* had on the English Bible versions. Niven was affectionately referred to as "Daddy Niven," and was as much respected by the students in those days as he had been in Willie's own college days. Besides his immense erudition, he was notorious for his asides, although his actual course material was, unlike Willie's, considered dull by some of the older men. Pitt-Watson was considered "the most impracticable practical professor," too philosophical for many of these war-experienced, impatient men of action. They felt keenly his unbending attitude to life and were not impressed by his intellectual penetration of the subject and its related matters. Willie naturally evoked a warmer response, despite his still strongly pacifist line—over which he clashed with Pitt-Watson in public debate, to the delight of the students. Willie, ever the peacemaker, did not often provide them with material for this particular amusement, though it did not take great powers of observation to see where differences existed. In one of their debates they clashed over the problem of the language of worship for today. Willie was now discovering the modern approach, and making it his own by careful and rigorous self-discipline. (It is a gross mistake, however, to say that he always took the modern line in prayer, *pace* James Martin's contention that "Willie Barclay never used the traditional 'thee' and 'thou' when addressing the Almighty in prayer.")[40] Not that he was yet willing to go modern publicly. His prayers for the Scottish Sunday School Union and for the Boys' Brigade both use the archaic familiar form in addressing God, as does *The Plain Man's Book of*

Prayers, which was published as late as 1959. But with the students he was progressive, and he became highly critical of long, involved prayers. The language of prayer must be that of ordinary people, he would insist; not elevated, still less stilted; not "ecclesiastical," and never parsonic. The language of prayer must be dignified, and beautiful when possible, but its essence as conversation with a Father-God must be kept as the goal in our praying, be it personal or public. This point of view led to strong clashes with the evangelical section among the students, who felt Willie's common touch—after the later manner of Michel Quoist—lacked reverence, deference, and "godliness"; it was too worldly for them. The clash even involved the question of posture in prayer—whether sitting was a tolerable and worthy attitude. Willie, whose prayer life was that of one who walked with God rather than one who beheld and contemplated the deity from a stationary position, found this an unreal and artificial pose, and he said so bluntly.

We cannot leave this early review of Willie as lecturer, of his style and his practical outlook, without stressing his closeness to the student body. Indeed, it would be true to say that he first taught his students and then his subject, the old liberal idea of the worth of the individual ever charging and fashioning his attitude toward people. His teaching was also shaped by his essential optimism; he could always see cause for hope and eventual success. Even in these early days he ran a choir for the college, which was organized as a means to reach out to the churches, to make known the needs of the college, and to engender interest in ministerial training. But it was by no means a purely religious thing. Two of the music sheets that Willie retained from this time have been preserved and are good guides to their repertoire. There is, first, "The tickling trio"—and what better way to express his sense of enjoyment, naturalness, and general bonhomie than this piece? And his datedness, too! It is difficult to imagine present-day theologs being willing to sing its fuddy-duddy lines:

> Don't tickle me, I pray,
> Come let me alone, I say.
> You'll make me laugh that way.
> Ha ha ha, ha ha ha, ha ha,
> You'll make me laugh that way.

But if any then thought so, they did not make known their views, and in any case the churches were evidently enjoying this fresh, relaxed approach. The spirit of Renfrew Trinity was spreading. The second piece, "Loch Lomond," captures a crucial aspect of the choir's presentation, and of Willie's own personality too, proud Highlander that he was; even if they sang it to Vaughan Williams's (the Welsh composer's) "Scottish Air"! Shades of "Ye Mariners of England" here. But Willie was never provincial in his outlook, and the rightful pride and haunting melodies of such fine Scottish sentiment paved the way for the more religious songs, chief among which was the conductor's favorite, never omitted, "When I Survey the Wondrous Cross." A strange trio of songs, perhaps, but if it did not mirror the normal view of dour Presbyterianism (too much emphasized, and not wholly accurate), it did mirror perfectly the naturalness of the One who was a true observer of nature, a friend of publicans and sinners, whose choice of friends and appreciation of beauty flowed into insurpassable teaching and counsel. To follow such a one, to mirror such a life, was Willie's chief aim. He also found time to run the college football team, and, while his own broadening girth restricted his playing, he was still a vigorous and energetic supporter—and a vociferous one, too, who was not known for sparing the referee's blushes when throwing light on his myopic propensities.

Engaging, informed, persuasive lecturer with a finely pitched spiritual tone; conscientious keeper—and promoter—of books; choirmaster of many moods with a Mozartian touch of freedom and joy; and sportsman—these diverse roles did not exhaust the Barclay contribution to college life at this and subsequent times. Commented Neil Alexander, having mentioned that like so many other students he knew Willie better than any other tutor at the time, "Mr Barclay had—towards all the students—a forthcomingness and positive friendliness that marked a new departure in staff-student relations."[41] It is not certain whether his students' attachments to him were any deeper or richer than his own attachment to Arthur Gossip, but that genius for friendship (if I may use a phrase coined to describe A. S. Peake)[42] was nevertheless a marked aspect of his involvement with his students. This note of friendship is struck in virtually every letter of sympathy sent to Mrs. Barclay after her husband's death (and there are over six hundred of them); the many former students I have interviewed have been at pains to stress it as well. His approachability, facilitated by his habit of sitting with them in the Library Hall, albeit behind a screen, was consummate. He *showed* he was interested in their viewpoints, their problems. Facile of learning himself, and never lost for the right word in self-expression, he could, nevertheless, understand the student whose memory was like a sieve, and patiently encouraged the one who struggled to convey his convictions from a spent imagination and a wordless pen.

And he was kind and generous, too. Though not having suffered in this way himself, he knew the deep anxiety caused by the penniless pocket, and the incalculable sacrifices some parents and students—and wives—made in order to fulfill the highest calling. In later days he would be able to offer liberal support and relief to such, but even in those austere days he would at least share what he did have. (As a junior lecturer he was on virtually the same pay as he had got at his church, but he no longer enjoyed the free accommodation and many expenses he had had there.) Many (and hilarious) were the suppers he and Kate put on for his students, in which she displayed brilliantly her culinary abilities, not least in the ever-popular whisky cake. But Willie was not generous to an unlimited degree, which made some doubt his generosity. And he could be tough and unyielding on points of principle. Woe betide the student caught cheating in his examinations! One poor fellow so caught was back in secular life before he could catch his breath, Willie himself having triggered the mechanism through college, university court, and presbytery, for he clearly thought that this betrayed the truthfulness that lies at the heart of the gospel: truthfulness toward oneself and one's fellows.

Another aspect of the seriousness with which he discharged his functions is reflected in *Testament of Faith*. At the end of his first academic year of teaching, he went to his favorite secondhand theological bookshop near the University to rummage along its shelves. To his dismay, he found deposited there the key textbooks from his students' courses, all with their late owners' names inscribed on them. We should remember the harsh economic conditions of the time, and that these men were going to empty or half-filled manses after several years of penurious studying. Willie was aware of that, too, but he was nevertheless "daunted"—a strong psychological reaction (the word earlier had to do with the hard pressing down of herrings at Wick and elsewhere into already overfull barrels). It was betrayal! It was rejection! "It was," he explained, "as if . . . farewell to college meant farewell to study."[43] He who could give away rare first editions, limited editions, and special bindings without a second thought for the amusement of troops could not understand this lack of professional integrity, a shortcoming Willie was always at pains to attack, even as he ever pursued his vendetta against "the closed mind."[44]

To those who came to him with such closed minds he gave particular attention. Raised conservatively, he knew the particular handicaps under which they wrestled. Ever tolerant, he preferred to follow the Quaker line—surely the way of Christ?—that the best way to deal with an enemy is to make of him one's friend. And he met with real success. "I have had students come to me after their first month of classes and apologise," he wrote in his retirement, "and when I asked them what they were apologising about, they have said that, before they came up, they had been warned against me."[45] That, of course, was written from the vantage point of the '60s and '70s rather than that of the '40s and '50s, but his attitude was ever thus—the pacifist's, the peacemaker's way.

W. M. Macgregor, in a memorial address at the unveiling of a plaque to honor James Denney at Trinity College, said, "A Professor of Theology who has not been a working minister is scarcely half-prepared for his task."[46] And so it was for Willie. But it was "Forward, not backward" that rang in his ears, not "Well done, you've made it." His eyes were on the future. Reconstruction was his goal. As with David Livingstone of old, he was willing to go anywhere, so long as it was forward. This can be seen in the earliest broadcast interview of him, conducted by Stanley Pritchard. (Pritchard and Willie were no strangers to each other. As early as August 1936 the former had as a probationer supplied pulpit for Willie; he went on to be minister of Stevenson Memorial Church, WDB's postretirement church.) In the *This Is My Job* series,[47] Willie stated that soon after being appointed to his lectureship he was beset by the problem of the direction in which his new work should be pointed. The hopes of direct practical training per se being denied him, it was not long before he perceived another opportunity, which became his *parergon*—his second job—and which rapidly outgrew this real one in influence: "My years in Renfrew . . . were a training in *the obligation of intelligibility,"* he stated. (We should note the sense of duty, of imposition, and of realization that the career checked was in fact the career prepared.) Those years behind him, he now had to put his lessons into effect. He was aware of the varied temptations that beset the university teacher, which were

> to become a slave to the examination system, and to evaluate the success of my teaching by the height of the percentage a student achieved in class and degree examinations . . . to regard my duty as the obligation to insert into students a series of predigested and rather disconnected facts rather than to try to enable them to think for themselves . . . to retire into the ivory tower of the academic life and to become remote from ordinary life and living . . . to become a specialist and to pursue a course of study which would issue in knowing more and more about less and less . . . and—I am sure this is the greatest of all academic temptations—to think of nothing but what other academic teachers and experts would think of it, for in the academic world there is almost a phobia against writing anything that is "popular."

He admits that he had not seen all this with the same force and clarity in 1947; indeed, he could hardly have done so on the threshold of an academic career. We shall see presently that he was careful to establish his work in a deliberately academic direction till at least the early 1950s and even beyond that, until his other works, the *parerga,* which had such a different orientation, were thrust upon him. Nevertheless, the seeds had been sown—not just in these opening months, but during his whole time at Renfrew, when the relentless needs of his "working-class parish" and work among troops goaded him into considering the reality and the effect of his ministry and work. He was becoming uncomfortably conscious, he said, of "the wide gap between the knowledge and the work of the theological experts and the men in the street"; he was aware that "the work that was done in the colleges and the Universities never seemed *in any sense* [his emphasis reveals a characteristic imbalance] to penetrate to the pew"; there seemed to be "no connection at all between the work of the theological scholars and experts and the ordinary church member." Not that he doubted, be it emphasized, that their work was not of "the utmost importance." What troubled him was that "somehow or other they were saying the right things to each other and saying them in the class-room, but not saying them to ordinary laymen and laywomen." He explained this comment by stating the perception that changed his life: *"The problem of communication began to be the problem which first came in my thoughts."*[48] Religious language—"the language of Canaan," conventional and long-established phrases, frequently a form of code language to those on the inside—began to worry him. It was not just that, as in Chesterton's day, the fault lay with the outsiders, with whom Christianity had not been tried and found wanting, for it had simply not been tried; what now worried Willie—the verb is consciously repeated—was that it was not being tried because it was not being understood. It was not apathy but ignorance—and the church was responsible for it. The gap between its language and that of modern man had widened too much. Willie's whole concern thus became such as to ensure that ordinary men and women could read the Bible with understanding if not with agreement or commitment. He was working at this problem long before John Robinson made it public, long before the various –ologies of the seething '60s, and even before that magnificently human pope (John XXIII) had proclaimed the farsighted Second Vatican Council, which introduced the process of *aggiornamento*—"bringing up to date"—to an astonished world.

We need to discriminate between two things here, since Willie was very conscious of the discrimination himself. There are two aspects to theological work. First, there is the intrinsic demand of the subject as a science, ever seeking a greater self-understanding, applying to itself the ever-increasing knowledge of language and history, of the secular sciences and the world views that predominate. Second, there is the need for dissemination, the act of theological writing, lecturing, and publishing, when the writer or broadcaster is acting as a purveyor of theology rather than seeking to broaden its boundaries or lift its horizons (except to the masses). It was of this latter area that Willie was wont to express himself adversely on scholarship, criticizing the use of often unexplained technical terms, scorning highfalutin attitudes, and even calling into question the very right of this work to be called true theology. We must leave till later the question of whether Willie was successful in the second aspect, and whether, in it, he was true to the first. But we should at least note here his willingness to agree—and stress—the validity of the first. Nevertheless "communication" was overtaking "content" in his mind; he was becoming absorbed in the method, not the matter, of theology. We shall see that the process that the radio interview highlighted was concluded by the advent of television, an involvement with which he long resisted, but to which he eventually added his own distinctive contribution.

We need to remind ourselves that these were the days before Bible translation really got under way. The Authorized Version held undisputed sway (some even felt that if that version was good enough for Paul, it should be good enough for us!). The Revised Version was only admired by a coterie, as were Weymouth's and Moffatt's versions, and still more so those of J. N. Darby and Robert Young. *The Twentieth Century New Testament*, G. W. Wade's *Documents of the New Testament* (1934), *The Basic English Bible* (which might have been more influential had it not been published at a time of national calamity),[49] and *The New Testament in the Language of the People* (of C. K. Williams) all provoked the need, rather than satisfied the demand, for clear, intelligible, unambiguous translations from the underlying and respective Hebrew, Aramaic, and Greek texts. It was becoming the time of agitation toward that end, but there was still much complacent satisfaction with the old version and much opposition to the new ones, especially in churches—the only public places where the Bible was read communally.

In 1946 the Revised Standard Version appeared, "a thorough-going revision of the American Standard Version" of 1901. Professor Bruce, whom I have just quoted,[50] used the approving words of his predecessor at Manchester University,

T. W. Manson, which are not without particular meaning vis-à-vis Willie's own attitude and quest: "I like the Revised Standard Version; and I like it because it is readable and because it speaks directly to the man in the pew in language he can reasonably be expected to understand." But it was Willie's own church, the Church of Scotland, that in May 1946 set pulses going, and perhaps Willie's fastest of all. In that year the General Assembly received and eagerly agreed to implement an overture from the Presbytery of Dunblane that a completely new translation of the Bible be made into English, based on the best and most recent work done in textual and related disciplines. Nothing is more powerful than an idea in its own time, and the timing of this idea was perfect. By October of that same year every major Protestant denomination had expressed its approval and its readiness to help in whatever way possible. Having led the way in the cause of church union seventeen years previously, the Church of Scotland was now doing so again, and thereby taking one of the greatest steps of the century toward "modernizing" Christianity. By the following year, 1947, a joint committee of the churches and of the Bible publishers who were at that time the most experienced in the world—the university presses of Oxford and Cambridge— were united in conference; the work was under way. By March 1949 the main lines of approach had been determined. As a mark of gratitude to the Church of Scotland, its own nomenclature was kept, and so the doyen of New Testament scholarship, C. H. Dodd (A. S. Peake's successor at Manchester, and T. W. Manson's immediate predecessor), was appointed "Convenor" of the New Testament Panel, and T. H. Robinson was appointed Convener of the Old Testament Panel (he was succeeded by Sir Godfrey Driver in 1957). Some of the most prestigious names in biblical scholarship are listed in the various translation panels. Among them, though nominated a little later, was one William Barclay, who was appointed to work on the Apocrypha Panel under the Convenorship of his friend Professor W. D. McHardy.

Matters of moment were running through Willie's mind during these months of expectation, fulfillment, and reconstruction. The challenges of the induction speeches at Trinity—to find "decided answers" to society's questionings—and the similar calls of the General Assembly and of his own presbytery and faculty colleagues, challenged repeatedly this sensitive, responsible, equable man. Was he fulfilling his ordination vows? Was he fulfilling them not just by going through the motions—attending the meetings and occupying pulpits, giving lectures and filling uncountable sheets of paper—but by *really* discharging "the duties of [his] ministry, seeking in all things the advancement of the Kingdom of God"?[51] In moving from parish to college he had not opted out of these vows, but extended them. Now he began to shape them to his own personality and strengths. As he explained to Pritchard in that same interview,

> Something else became clear to me. I began to see that I never could be a great technical scholar, and I knew that I had no power to be an original thinker. But I *began* to think that I might become a theological middleman, to take the results of scholarship, to take the things done in the classroom, to take the great books the

scholars have written and to restate this in ordinary nontechnical language which ordinary people could understand. But how?

As he said in another context, "To be given a task is to be obliged to find a method to carry it out."[52] Willie went on to describe how he sought to fulfill that task, but we need to remind ourselves that the chronological sequence has become somewhat disengaged. He is speaking in 1960, having completed his magnum opus[53] and a dozen other books, with the advantages of afterthought— and perhaps some feeling of self-defense already in his mind. But it is important to understand that in 1947 the essential problem was only being formed, as was its resolution, as he faced his ex-serviceman theologs, as he heard the rumble of fundamental attitudes in church and society being pressured, and as he sought before God to fulfill his ministry. He was indeed moving forward, but slowly.

Some Extramural Activities and a Sermon

They were therefore momentous days through which he was living, not less so for the vital work he was doing beyond Trinity College. When he left his church at Renfrew, he had promised to help them in any way that he could, and this he was able to do almost immediately. Thus we find him addressing the Young People's Society on three separate occasions during the first quarter of 1947: on January 19 he gave a general talk; on January 26 he took the Epilogue; and March 16 he offered a very characteristic talk on "The Life and Music of Grieg." But while personal friendships were to be closely nurtured, these were sadly to be his last public associations with the church for many years.

But other opportunities were abundant, and Willie's diaries were full of engagements for his pulpit services and Saturday and weeknight lectures. These diaries have been destroyed, but in any case it would have been somewhat tedious even to list them, let alone (were it possible) to trace his subjects and comments. He spared neither himself nor his growing family. He confessed to Braidwood that he only had two Sundays off from preaching this year, and had weeknight and Saturday appointments to fulfill besides. His commitment to Williamwood Church, now his home church, was restricted, his main ministry being at Trinity College, supplemented by a peripatetic ministry on weekends and during the holidays.

It was about this time that Willie and Percy Strachan first met. Strachan was running a local church mission at Keith in Banffshire.[54] (The William Barclay who published the well-known local history book *Banffshire*—in the Cambridge County Geographies—is not the subject of this biography, nor related to Willie in any way.) The mission was conducted under the auspices of the Presbytery of Strathbogie, and great care was taken with the planning. Preparatory to the mission's being started, it was decided to hold a retreat for the ministers and lay people involved. It is a sign of Willie's widely recognized spiritual maturity that he should have been invited to conduct this—though we must understand that his idea of a retreat was ever a sharp call to advance! Thirty-four years later Mr. Strachan was still able to "recall vividly his warm, kindly personality and the enthusiasm he put into helping us in our small venture, and—as you would expect—his stimulating interpretations of the scriptures."[55] He explains that this latter characteristic was the impressive thing about him at the time—

> the way he was able to combine real scholarship with a deep understanding of the way in which ordinary people can be helped to see the relevance of the Christian faith. Already he had "the common touch" to a very high degree, and he challenged us to make our message equally simple and penetrating. And perhaps best of all, he kindled in us a spirit of warm affection both for himself and each other, making us realise that this was the real *sine qua non* of any effort in making the gospel known and winning people for the Master.

Plus ça change, plus c'est la même chose! His battle for intelligibility was already being won, and its condition lay at the center of things: love. To be able to do this is a mark of special grace and talent, and Willie was ever conscious of the great *responsibility*[56] such work imposed upon him.

Another, but more consequential event took place in February 1947, while Willie was fulfilling one of his speaking engagements at the Paisley YMCA fellowship meeting. It was one of those incidental meetings that resulted in great opportunities, emphasizing once again how Willie's faithfulness and care in little things led to greater ones. Harry Stevenson was in charge of the local branch of the YMCA, and a ripe friendship between the two men was soon established. He regularly called on Willie to address various types of meetings held under the auspices of the "Y." By this means Willie's name gained weight in the wider circle of YMCA Secretaries, and with it arose splendid opportunities for service and influence, much of which was to the nonchurchgoing youth of the '50s and '60s. This local friendship continued for ten years, and then in 1957 Harry Stevenson was appointed to manage the London "Y," and thus Willie was not only introduced to the national and international circles of the movement, but found a home-from-home in the capital the importance of which for his ministry was incalculable (and the description of which we must leave till a later chapter).

What was his preaching like during these days? What was it about this man that was so compelling? Below there is reprinted one of his sermons, first preached as early as 1945 but repeated on various occasions after this. If we ask ourselves why of all his early sermons this one alone survived (and there would from time to time be several dozen of these), one can only surmise that it was specially important to him. The typescript is very badly done, as is its punctuation and even its style, but its message is plain, and its spirit is a lovely expression of his preaching and pastoral caring. Even through its hasty deficiencies one can feel the real man speaking, his typical turns of phrase and range of illustrations. It was simply headed "A Morning Sermon, Written for 18 February, 1945." Reference to Appendix I shows it was originally entitled "On Coming to Terms with the Inevitable," which reflects an important aspect of his faith and theology, the centerpiece of which is simple trust. As it has some broad similarities with his first published article, we might entitle it "The Secret of Life." Certainly it expresses the secret of Willie's life, of his strength and his success. It reflects something of his attitude toward the personal disappointments he was then facing over the uneven development of his career and work as well.

On Coming to Terms with the Inevitable

2 Corinthians xii: 8,9: (A.V.) For this thing I besought the Lord thrice that it might depart from me; and he said unto me, "My grace is sufficient for thee; for my strength is made perfect in weakness." Most gladly therefore will I rather glory in my infirmities that the power of Christ may rest upon me.

One of the staggering facts about the life of Paul is that all his life he lived in pain. He might well have been justified and he might well have been pardoned if he had lived the protected and the sheltered and the secluded life of an invalid. But instead—pain or no pain—he was the greatest traveller the world has ever seen. If you read the book of Acts you find that Paul made four missionary journeys and if you add up the distances that he travelled you find that in these journeys Paul travelled just a little less than nine thousand miles. Now remember in these days it was no question of boarding a train or taking a bus or driving along a road; for far the greater part it was a question of walking and yet this man suffering this continual pain, with his recurring spasms of illness which left him helpless, covered this colossal distance for the sake and for the name of Jesus Christ.

Now Paul in this chapter of Second Corinthians tells us how he felt about this affliction which had him in its grip. What the affliction was we do not for certain know. Some people have thought that Paul was a subject to epilepsy. He tells the Galatians in his letter that when he came to them in his illness they did not reject him. The Greek word he uses literally means that they did not spit at him; and in the Greek world it was customary to spit when you saw an epileptic because by doing so you were supposed to avert the evil demon that dwelt within the sufferer. Basing on that it has been supposed that Paul was an epileptic. Others have thought that his suffering had something to do with his eyes. He tells the Galatians that they were so kind to him that they would if it had been possible have given him their eyes themselves. Basing on that there are those who have guessed that Paul suffered from some trouble of the eyes. All through Christian history there has been a tradition that what was the matter with Paul was that he suffered from chronic and from constant prostrating headaches. Modern scholars think that what he suffered from was a particular violent type of malaria which was prevalent in Asia Minor and which was accompanied by headaches which are described by sufferers as like a stake turning round inside your head. However it may be, all his life Paul suffered from this agonising thing. Now he tells us that there was a time when he besought God, when in a very wrestling in prayer he battered at the gates of heaven that this thing might be taken from him. But it was not to be; and finally Paul came to accept this thorn in his flesh not as a burden and a cross but as something through which there came to him the grace of God itself. Paul had learned to accept the thing that hurt him most.

Now it must always be true that everyone of us has our troubles and our pains and our sorrows and our disappointments, and it seems to me that the great [secret] of living is to accept these things in the right way.

Samuel Horton tells of an old Negro in America. He had had in his long life a good deal more than what you might call his fair share of trouble and yet somehow he was a very happy and a very radiant person indeed. No one ever heard him whining or grumbling or complaining. So one day someone asked him, How do you manage in spite of all your troubles to remain so cheerful and so calm? Whereupon the old man answered. Well sir I'll tell you; I've just learned to co-operate with the inevitable.

Now that is the lesson that everyone of us got to learn and the sooner we learn it the better for us. If we can learn to come to terms with life; if we can learn to co-operate with the inevitable it will save us a great deal of heart-burning and heart-breaking, and it will make life a happier and a more peaceful thing. Now if we are to co-operate with the inevitable we will need to learn certain things.

1. We will need to learn that there are certain things which are just not for us.

One of the fundamental facts about life is that all life is lived under certain limitations; and he is a wise man who learns and abides by the limitations which life has set him.

No matter what material a man is working with he does not expect and he does not demand that that material should do more than it is capable of doing. If a man is building a bridge or a machine or anything else he knows the stresses and the strains that the metals and the woods that he is using can bear. And he only asks them to do their work within these limits.

Now it is so with human life. We all have our dreams but bit by bit we come to see that there are certain of these dreams that will not and cannot come true. We all have our ambitions but bit by bit we come to see that some of these ambitions will never be fulfilled. And, if we are wise, we accept that limitation and instead of bemoaning the things that are not for us we set to, to do the best with what we have. And there is always something which every man is meant to do and can do supremely well.

You remember the old fable in which the mountain was looking down with contempt in all its greatness and its strength on the squirrel in all its littleness and its weakness. Whereat the squirrel said, "it is true that I cannot bear forests on my back but it is also true that you cannot crack a nut." Now there is a great deal of fundamental truth in that. And the truth is that your gift may not be my gift and my gift may not be your gift but all of us have some gift.

If we realise this necessary limitation of life it will rid us at one stroke of envy and of jealousy. For we would know that there is neither any need for jealousy and envy, nor yet any reason for them.

These two sins are perhaps the commonest of all sins and yet they are the sign always of a little and a petty mind. Really big men were above these things.

I came across the other day one of the finest letters ever written. In Cambridge University one of the greatest scholars in the world last century was H. M. Gwatkin. He was the world's greatest authority on Church History. Now it so happened that for long there was no professorship of Church History at Cambridge, it was only a Lectureship. The authorities prepared to appoint a full professor of Church History and everyone expected that Gwatkin would unquestionably receive the position. Somehow or other he did not; a man name Mandell Creighton was appointed. Now you might have expected Gwatkin to feel a bit disappointed, even soured and frankly jealous of the lesser man who had stepped over him. But Gwatkin wrote to Creighton.

> For twelve years I have taught Church History almost alone in Cambridge. I have worked faithfully and to the utmost of my power hitherto and I trust not without success; and now that my work is taken up by stronger hands than mine I pray the Lord of all history before whom we both are standing to give you health and strength and abundant blessing to carry on far better than myself the high and arduous task entrusted to your charge. For myself I am ready to work under you and to support you loyally in all that falls to me to do. So far as I know my own heart no jealousy shall rise to mar the harmony and friendship in which I ask and hope to live with the first professor of Church History, in Cambridge.

There is no jealousy there, only the humility of a man who had willingly said good-bye to that which was not for him.

If we would only realise that we have our limitations but that also we have our own gifts jealousy would die.

But if we realised this it would also be the end of discontent. Discontentment comes of wanting to have what we have not got and to be what we are not. But if we simply accepted the fact that there are things not meant [and] not possible for us this discontentment would go.

Horton tells us how once a girl rescued a throstle [song thrush] from a cat, but its wing was broken. There was no way to mend the broken wing so she got a big cage and kept the bird there. For a long time it was frightened and bewildered and silent. Then one day she took the cage out and hung it in the garden. And a strange thing happened; all of a sudden the captive bird began to sing, pouring forth his little heart in melody; and at the sound of the captive throstle's song suddenly every bird in the garden took up the chorus and the whole garden was like a choir of birds all singing together. And always afterwards every sunny day it was the same. The bird you see had discovered how to sing within a cage. And it seems to me therein is life. In some sense every one of us lives within a cage; within bars and bounds which we cannot overpass. But you remember Paul, "I have learned in whatsoever state I am therewith to be content."

When we remember that we have our limitations and when we remember that God made us and made us so for his good purpose, that as we are we might do something for him, then there comes that sweet content.

2. And further we must remember this—that there is in life a kind of complete finality.

There is no way of undoing a thing once it is done. There is no way of altering a fact. In life there is a kind of finality against which there is no way out and against which it is useless to batter your head.

There are many things in life that we cannot and will not ever understand. Once there was a lad forever asking 'why?' and never content with any answer he was given. One day his father said to him gently,

> Laddie you must remember to allow God to know some things he isn't going to tell you.

Always life must remain encompassed with mystery because we are men and God is God.

And once again the secret of life lies in accepting these things that can neither be changed nor undone. Something really hurting or even shattering happens to us. Well then we can wriggle and wrestle and moan under it. If so it hurts all the more. Or we can in humility accept it and sometimes the thing that hurt so much becomes our glory.

Do you remember George Mathieson? He was a young man preaching down there in Inellan and he was already known as one of Scotland's greatest preachers. Suddenly he realised that his eye-sight was failing and that in a short time he would be blind. He was engaged to be married. He went to the girl whom he loved with all his heart. He did the only thing he could do; he said that he could not hold her to her pledge: that he could not ask her to marry a blind man; and he offered her—doubtless hoping that she would take it—her freedom. But she [did], she took her freedom and Mathieson whose preaching had so often brought comfort to others was faced with this shattering blow. He went back to Inellan. He went out to the hillside; he had a pencil and paper in his hand and he began to write, and you remember what he wrote:

> O love that wilt not let me go,
> I rest my weary soul in thee;
> I give thee back the life I owe,
> That in thine ocean depths its flow
> May richer, fuller be.

Out of the failure of human love he had found the love of God and out of his own heartbreak he had made something to men[d] the hearts of others for many a day.

If you accept these buffets of life you get the most staggering wonders from them.

There is an old parable. There was a girl who was alone at home. Her father and mother were away on holiday and were to return that night. She was preparing for them; and there came an old woman to the door and told her that her father and mother were dead and would return no more. The girl sank down dumb and overcome with grief. When she looked the old woman, a repulsive hag, was still there taking off her coat and bonnet.

The girl said, "I will give you food and then you will go."

"No," said the old woman, "I will not go; I will stay and keep you company."

"I will not have you here," said the girl, sickened by the ugliness of the old crone.

"You will have to," said the old woman, "for I will not go."

She even tried to escape the old woman. She fled to other places, the old woman followed; she even went to other countries, [but] she could never shake her off. Then one day she even crossed to another continent to escape but when she got there the old woman was waiting for her. The girl fainted and when she came to the old woman said,

"You cannot fly from me; others have tried but they cannot do it."

"What is your name?" said the girl.

"They call me," said the woman, "'Mother sorrow,' and sooner or later I come to stay with men. Let us go home."

So they went home; and the girl no longer tried to escape and in a wondrous way the old woman became less ugly and more beautiful each day and her presence became a thing most sweet. Then one day Mother Sorrow disappeared. Everywhere the girl searched, for she loved her now. And when she returned from her searching she found a lovely child. And the child said,

"Mother Sorrow left thee and left her blessing, for she can stay no longer, but she has sent me, one of her children, to bear thee company."

And, said the girl, "What do they call you?"

And the child answered, "They call me 'Sympathy,' and sorrow is my mother."

Into our lives there come these inevitable things that none escape. If we twist and chafe beneath them we do but hurt ourselves; if we accept this finality of life into our lives there comes for ourselves peace and for others blessing and we know what it means to say that we have beauty for our ashes.

That is what Paul found. He found that in his trouble and his tribulation he found God and that with God somehow all things were sweet. And it will be so with us. If we learn to accept things we will know that in spite of our limitations and in spite of our wounds, our Father never causes his child a needless tear; that his strength is made perfect in our weakness; that his grace is sufficient for all things and that its splendour clothes the grey of life in heaven's glory.

This was the spirit in which Willie himself lived at this time, and this was part of the content of his preaching, tested over long years of personal and pastoral experience.

"Inestimable Service": His Work for the SSSU

General opportunities in many churches and denominational affiliations and a broadening scope through his beloved YMCA were by no means the end of his extramural activities of this time. It is arguable that the most important one has been left till last: the continuing, the continually increasing work of the Scottish Sunday School Union for Christian Education, and the educative part was clearly the aspect of the work that most appealed to Willie—as he would demonstrate by expending so much labor on it.

The phrase "inestimable service" comes from a Deliverance made by the Youth Committee to the General Assembly of the Church of Scotland,[57] and was specifically directed to Willie's accomplishments and those of his colleagues in the Sunday School movement. It was the highest recognition of his work to date, and represented an appreciation of an otherwise grossly underestimated piece of service. Willie's involvements in this work had been fourfold: he conducted teacher-training courses at least once a week, and sometimes as many as four times per week; he attended to the correspondence courses attached to the newly introduced diploma (for which his first book, New Testament Studies, continued to play a prominent part); he wrote the Senior Lesson Notes, which reached literally tens of thousands of young people; and he served as editor of The Scottish Sunday School Teacher magazine.

During the war he had been his own Sunday School superintendent (ostensibly due to the shortage of staff) and had from the first instituted training classes for his teachers "to ensure efficiency among the staff," as one teacher expressed his resolve to me.[58] It resulted in "a very happy Sunday School"—not only happy, one might conclude, but proficient too. And a "heavyweight Sunday School" to boot, if we may use his own description of those schools with over four hundred children on their registers.[59] It now became his responsibility to give the lead on a national and transdenominational scale. We find him punctilious in the committee involvements, especially the Lessons Committee. Well, at first, anyway!

In April 1946 his lesson schemes for January–June and September–December 1948 were approved. Mrs. Dingwall, widow of a former General Secretary of the Scottish Sunday School Union, who was on the committee at this time, recalls that they rarely found a single thing to question. A year later the Committee gave approval to his next batch of Lesson Notes, Willie this time being responsible for the whole year (1949). In June 1947 they again met and Willie was asked to do the Notes for the next academic year (1950/51). In March 1950 a rare complaint was recorded, apropos Willie's comment that the instruction in Luke 8:55—to give the "resurrected" young woman something to eat—was unique. (It also occurs in Mark 5:43, as his observant critic was quick to point out.) He extended the 1950/51 Notes onward through 1951/52. (An analysis of the individual lessons and cycles appears in Appendix II.) No one else had undertaken such a prolonged stint of lesson writing, and it was by no means completed even yet, for the Lessons Committee commenced to recycle his Notes following his resignation—which was necessitated by "other editorial pressures." This reuse of his Notes caused his influence to extend over a complete decade. And even after his withdrawal his approach was preserved; for example, when the themes and lessons were discussed at the planning meeting of 14 September 1950 (for the period 1953–56), it was decided that "the essential character of recent lesson Schemes should be preserved," which shows how widely acceptable his work had been.

We saw the high commendation of the General Secretary when he was welcomed to his editor's chair in September 1945, and Willie's consequent activities and travel merely underscored this. In February 1947 the same individual, George A. Mills, penned further complimentary words under the headline "The Editor Honoured," on Willie's appointment to his lectureship. But chief among the many comments made was one of collective relief: "It is gratifying that, whatever demands his new work may make upon him, he is resolved to continue his services to the Sunday Schools of Scotland."[60] The Editor's reply to this expression of appreciation was typical and stark: "God needs our work these days," he announced, adding that a quarter of a million children and thirty thousand Sunday School teachers established that claim in a challenging reality. "These figures," he continued, "should be to us an inspiration"; and further, "these figures are the proof that if our work is well done, we cannot do other than leave a deep and lasting impress on the life and the faith of the country where we live."[61] He was thus not only providing leadership of a high quality, not only

330

producing training notes and schemes—generally written, but individually marked through his correspondence courses (he wrote and supervised six of these: see Appendix III)—but he was also providing resource material for the teachers to use in their lessons.

He properly distinguished between the various "phases of understanding" a growing child passes through, thus anticipating the approach to religious education that was soon to become axiomatic, in line with the day schools' and armed forces' educational techniques. (This was not done in detail, nor yet scientifically, the work of such men as Ronald Goldman, also of Manchester, not having yet been concluded.) We should, as a partial demonstration of this move toward experience-centered teaching, note how much he used and recommended the question method. One sample lesson, printed below, includes no fewer than twenty-three questions. He never weakened on the matter of memory work, and even reintroduced a restrained use of The Shorter Catechism (though one suspects that this represents the Committee's concern, as Willie never integrated the Catechism in the actual Notes, still less advocated a catechetical method). It is true that he did not reach the point of many of the "new syllabuses" that began to appear in the mid '60s—his approach was always geared to biblical themes and passages not actually centered in the child's experience—but it was an "experimental" approach, and it reflected, as Douglas Hubery was at pains to show,[62] the same approach Jesus used when his lessons began. "Consider the lilies of the valley. . . ."

As in his other involvements, Willie's chief qualifications were interest, enthusiasm, and a sensitive willingness to learn. He admitted as such in his first editorial letter: "I came to this task, not as one who speaks from theory . . . but as one who, Sunday by Sunday, is actively engaged in the task."[63] We can rest assured that he read everything available to him on "the new learning." But we should not forget that religious education was then—like general educational techniques—"still in its infancy" (to quote J. W. D. Smith, sometime colleague of Willie, who wrote an important book at this time, *Introduction to Scripture Teaching* [1948]). As far back as 1931, the Board of Education had called for a new approach to curricular preparation, one that went beyond the application of merely intellectual aspects, arguing for the introduction of activity and experience as opposed to just knowledge and memory work. These were matters that came naturally to Willie, for although he had the rare gift of a photographic memory himself, with amazing powers of recall, he could sympathize with those who had no such powers. Moreover, he knew there was much more in life than just mental power and dexterity. His approach made demands, called for decision making, offered opportunities, and was serious and funny: it was for living rather than learning. Good storyteller that he was, he naturally incorporated a dramatic element into his teaching, and because this was always highly charged with apt illustration and anecdote, it was never far from life and daily experience; application was rooted in both.

Between the wars the earlier unsettlement caused through biblical criticism gathered steam, and was intensified by the breakdown of the moral and religious framework of society. This produced some gains for religious education, but also led to a loss of the original clarity of purpose and content. Thus the Education Act of 1944 had much ground, and somewhat different ground from hitherto, to cover. It sought to do so by emphasizing the importance of introducing values into education, and by including the fundamental elements of instinct, emotion, and community. Character, and not merely factual or examinational attainments, was emphasized, and experience-centered endeavors (such as scriptural projects, drama, and classroom worship) were encouraged. Rote methods were disapproved, and thus the Shorter Catechism approached its demise. The full potential of the child was sought, not merely the provision of adult skills and knowledge. This was an exciting advance.

I do not intend to list chronologically Willie's varied activities for the Scottish Sunday School Union. While we should not forget that he was extremely active at its formal meetings—he was on the Executive Committee as a co-opted member (having no longer a link through his own Sunday School), and the regular if less frequent meetings of the Lessons Committee also required his presence—other duties on its behalf were very pressing: lectures, addresses, and Summer School involvements. For example, the Summer School at Aberdeen in September 1947 had 360 delegates, an immense opportunity for training, fellowship, and influence. The one held at Woodlands, Galashiels, was somewhat smaller and saw Willie in action as the Morning Lecturer. His subject was "The Development of Man's Religious Ideas, and the Preparation for Christ in the Old Testament." He gave five lectures under the heading "Learn about Me," which dealt with learning about God, ourselves, others, forgiveness, and life after death. They were the backbone of the conference, the delegates dividing into groups after the opening session each day to discuss his points.

But important as such engagements were, the really important and influential part he played concerned his Lesson Notes and the work of his editorial desk, the lamp of which burned ever later and more brightly. This work added sixty pounds per annum to Willie's meager salary, plus one pound for each lesson, and twelve shillings and sixpence per page for general articles—a very welcome augmentation of income as he struggled to provide for his young family in their new home.

He contended for good business order, too. For example, in October 1947 he publicly took the General Secretary to task for having circulated letters appertaining to the appointment of an Assistant General Secretary before obtaining the authority of the Executive Committee. His motion expressing disapproval clearly surprised some committee members and found no seconder, but it reveals his attention to matters of form and regulation. Again, in February 1948 he proposed two resolutions—one dealing with free accommodations for the said Assistant, and the other inquiring after the usefulness of the Scripture Examinations. The latter got enthusiastic support, and Willie got another job!—being nominated Convenor of a Subcommittee to explore the situation. They reported in March—

he was not noted for getting on with the job in hand for nothing!—with a sevenfold set of recommendations (arguing the continuance of the examinations), which were approved. The recommendations were brought into force in September 1949, but they proved to be out of step with the movement as a whole and were discontinued in February 1951.

In March of that year the Executive Committee dealt with the recent proposal of the government to allow cinemas to open on Sundays. Once more the fiery debate over the irreligious "Continental Sunday" exploded. Willie, more temperate and more farsighted than many, argued that something deeper than "mere protest" was necessary. It marks a definite shift in his attitudes toward "the Sabbath," a term he rejected on biblical and historical grounds. They should be taking steps to ensure that only the best of films were seen, he argued, not trying to stem an unstoppable tide of secularity. By May the cause was lost; the cinemas were to be opened on Sundays "for an experimental period." A letter from the Scottish Sunday School Union was sent, asking for the license not to be renewed—a forlorn hope indeed. The real opportunity, surely, lay in Willie's own proposal. Many would have been willing to back a restrained use of films— not necessarily "religious"—during the trial period. But, as usual, the all-or-nothing demand offered no room for maneuvering, and the churches' influence was eclipsed by its negativism. The Committee did, however, reject a suggestion from the Lord's Day Observance Society to affiliate with it in its starkly negative "witness" to Sunday usage, thus enabling the members to keep a more independent and slightly more positive view of the developing situation.

The work Willie was doing did not go unnoticed. Commented the Deliverance of the Youth Committee to the General Assembly of the Church of Scotland in May 1948,[64]

> The General Assembly warmly approves the close and fruitful co-operation between the Committee and the Scottish Sunday School Union for Christian Education, which is rendering inestimable service to the Scottish churches through its Lesson Schemes and Teachers' Magazines. . . , and records its thanks to . . . the Editor of *The Scottish Sunday School Teacher.*

The influence continued to grow, and the present session (1948/49) saw the Presbyterian Church of Ireland adopt the Lesson Schemes, bringing about a very encouraging rise in distribution levels, in consequence of which the Editor's honorarium was happily raised to eighty pounds.

In April 1948 Willie had been elected Vice President of the prestigious and influential Glasgow Provincial Sunday School Union, arguably the most important in Scotland; it was certainly the largest. Willie's stature was thereby raised yet further, and more publicly, as was the recognition of his work and influence. His first function in that capacity took place a few weeks later, when he was prize giver and guest speaker at the Glasgow North-West District Sunday School Union Annual Meeting. It was the first such service in the new area for twenty-five years, and it was well attended. The aspect he most enjoyed was presenting the long service diplomas to forty-one teachers, whose cumulative teaching record amounted to an astonishing 1,189 years—an average of twenty-nine years each. Willie warmly congratulated them, urging them to continue the good work, but especially to give the benefit of their experience to the schools and churches, not least by inspiring the younger teachers by their example.

He was still fully occupied with the writing of his Correspondence Courses, and the private tuition which this produced, a six-year stint. In May 1947 the Executive Committee, aware of its exigencies, had discussed the burdensome nature of the work and come up with some useful (and work-reducing) recommendations: that each tutor be restricted to not more than forty students; that the Scottish Sunday School Union secretariat itself send out the monthly lessons and letters; that the students use exercise books for written work; that the courses be brought into line with the lessons of *The Scottish Sunday School Teacher* and *The Scottish Primary Quarterly;* and that the fees be raised to five shillings per course. But the diminution of this work only facilitated the expedition of another, such was Willie's commitment.

During this period of service for the Scottish Sunday School Union he wrote over 250 lessons. Each lesson occupied about three and a quarter pages of *The Scottish Sunday School Teacher* (in small print). Put together, they would make a book of more than eight hundred pages, amounting to almost half a million words. If we add the editorial matter he contributed, plus the occasional articles, obituaries, and book reviews, an extra fifty or so pages would be required. Every lesson was given a one-sentence aim, a general introduction, explanatory notes and suggestions for teachers, and a meditation for the teacher's own use (Willie never forgot the importance of teacher preparation in such work, one of his chief contributions to Summer Schools and similar conventions); prayers were also provided. The lesson itself, which could have been simply passed on intact to the child, was fully written. An order of service was also included, with hymn (and even tune) suggestions. That is what Willie meant when he said that service, and its law—to him, and to his family—was costly indeed.

It is very difficult to assess these lessons from a contemporary perspective, but if we do so from the standpoint of what was then recognized to be the best standards—as the officers and teachers of the Scottish Sunday School Union did (and not a few of these were professional teachers)—we will find near unanimity of judgment entirely in Willie's favor. No one else had been found to unite the various qualities of heart and mind and conscience or to effect the writing of the lessons in such a balanced way over so long a period. It is the simple truth that no one else was found to do the job so well.

Rather than discuss them individually (Appendix II lists them all and demonstrates their range), we might take a single example to demonstrate his approach and style. One of the first to be written by him, probably in the first quarter of 1947 (when he was in the thick of his New Testament work at the University, preparing and giving his lectures virtually simultaneously), was a lesson accepted by the Lessons Panel at its spring conference, which met from the 15th to the 17th of April.[65] It formed part of the theme "Life at Its Best," which was commenced in January 1948, reached a part-climax at Easter that year, and was concluded under the same title at the end of March 1949.

I have chosen this lesson for two reasons. First, as *The British Weekly* pointed out,[66] Easter was then being observed increasingly in Scotland, along with Christmas and Whitsunday, and Willie soon latched on to these and other aspects of the Christian calendar as useful tools with which to teach the gospel. This "teaching the gospel" was essentially Willie's way, contrasting sharply with the mass-evangelism techniques that were beginning to make their impact. C. H. Dodd's famous division of 1935, between preaching and teaching, is not reflected in Willie's early work. But in any case his cohesive viewpoint, conjoining faith and life, doctrine and action, could not admit of any such separation. To believe was to do, to think was to act, to confess was to work; for in believing one acted and in confession one wrought, the end of which—more valuable than mere affirmation—was that one showed the fruits of one's beliefs: that was the real test.

The second reason for choosing this sample lesson lies in its usefulness as an example of his orthodox doctrine and in his commitment to an historical understanding of the events of which he wrote. Commenting on this matter in *God's Plan for Man* (the third book antedating *Ambassador for Christ*, which he regarded as his literary firstborn!) after having strenuously argued the case of the physical resurrection, he says, "We need never have any hesitation about believing that Jesus rose from the dead. No other explanation will anything like fill the facts and no other explanation will explain the new-found faith and courage of the disciples."[67] The practical aspect was always vigorously stressed: "The great meaning of it is that Jesus is not a figure in a book. He is not someone who lived and died and whose history we can read. It means that Jesus is alive, and that He is with us always wherever we are and wherever we go." It might even be argued that the practical aspect was for him paramount, as it certainly came to be later. But here he asserts the full facticity of the gospel story; he strives to emphasize that it happened in order to produce specific results, that it was the means to an end, great and glorious though the means certainly were, and that, consequently, the question "What does it mean for us?" ranks higher than "When and how did it happen?" In fact, Willie never put it quite this way—perhaps rightly so, since there is an element of high presumption in emphasizing the one above the other: they are both part of the purpose of God in salvation, and, like the interminable problems of divine sovereignty and human free will, they do not allow of a neat formula by way of resolution. But we should note that wherever there was an apparent collision between the divine and the human factors, be it in revelation itself or in the practical application of God's will, Willie tended to stress the latter—hence his (somewhat undeserved) reputation as a Pelagian. If we take into account all his statements, and not just the deliberate provocations offered for homiletical effect (his gadfly technique), we find a quite orthodox and balanced presentation of biblical truth—which is not necessarily the same as Calvinist or evangelical dogma! Likewise, it is not that he did not accept the

335

full historicity of the Gospels at this time, but rather that his mind was dominated by an overpowering awareness that the concrete experience of today is the theater of God's activity for us, and therefore the human, the now, takes precedence over the supernatural, the historic. The resurrection of Jesus was unquestionably the vibrant center of his religious life as well as of his theology; it was, like the miracles themselves at this time, the mainspring from which all else developed and by which all else was empowered. Jesus, to William Barclay, was not a figure in a book; he was the living, ever-present reality.

The foregoing may seem to be an unwarranted digression, a theological intrusion into the more mundane matters of his Sunday School work. But that, in fact, is exactly the point: precisely because of his practical turn of mind, precisely because his work grounds and frames his beliefs, this detour is most significant. When the General Assembly praised his work as "inestimable service," it was affirming very much more than efficiently planned and expeditiously presented material, however much it informed and inspired Sunday Schools the length and breadth of Scotland; it was giving its august recognition to a work of God at once theological and practical, doctrinal and educational. And Willie was its architect and mainstay.

In April 1949, having a half page at the end of the magazine to spare, he inserted a causerie on teaching method.[68] In many ways it represents his last word on the subject of teaching in Sunday Schools, as well as reflecting his style (he used a lectionary approach, with due regard for memory work), for pressure of other work now forced him to hand in his resignation, which was made public at the start of the new academic year, in September.[69] The Executive Committee's minute of 9 May 1949 records the reception of the letter from Willie intimating his desire to be relieved of the editorship he had held since September 1945. Curiously, it was said to have been forced on him due to his "having agreed to undertake other important editorial duties." There is no clue as to what these other editorial duties may have been; it is likely that he meant to say "writing duties" rather than editorial duties. Be that as it may, the Committee "learned with regret this decision of Mr Barclay and authorised the Secretary to write to him expressing their appreciation of the valuable services he had rendered as Editor of the Magazine." He also retired from the correspondence-course activity, and attended his final committee meeting with the Scottish Sunday School Union on November 17. His period of direct "inestimable service" for the Scottish Sunday School Union was over; a new phase of ministry was now beginning.[70]

A Sample Lesson: More Views and Method

April 17 [1949]
LIFE AT ITS BEST

Teaching aim of the section: To help the scholars to realise that Jesus Christ is their Saviour and Lord.

JESUS AND LIFE
EASTER

Lesson Passage: Matthew 28:1–10
Motto Text: Matthew 28:19–20
Shorter Catechism: Question 36

I. For the Teacher of the Preparation Class

Devotional

Prayer: O Lord Jesus, who hast promised that thou wilt be with me always, be with me at my work that I may work so well that I may be a workman who has no need to be ashamed. Be with me in my pleasure that I may never find delight in anything that will bring regret. Be with me in my temptations that I may be strengthened to overcome them and to do the right. Be with me in the daytime that when I move throughout the world and along the streets of men I may ever walk with Thee. Be with me in the night time that I may rest in peace. Hear this my prayer; for Thy love's sake. Amen.

BIBLE READING: Matthew 28:1–10

MEDITATION: At Easter time our thoughts inevitably turn to the life that is beyond death and to the glory that is beyond the grave. The eternal question which is ever in the heart of men is, "If a man die shall he live again?" Can we help ourselves to answer that question, with a triumphant certainty?

1. We live in a world of Resurrections. Every day the sun sets and every morning it rises again. Every winter the earth dies and every springtime it springs to newness of life again. There is nothing in this world which dies finally; there is newness of life in everything. Is it possible to believe that in this world of resurrections man is the only creature over whom death triumphs with finality?

2. The very nature of man requires a life beyond the grave. All life is a development. Man grows from helplessness to strength. Man grows from ignorance to knowledge. Even when bodily strength grows less the vigour of the searching mind continues. Is it reasonable to think that all this development and all this growth leads to nothing but extinction?

3. The very nature of God necessitates a life beyond the grave. God is justice. In this world it is far from true that goodness has its reward and evil its punishment. It is far from true that all men have the chances that they should have. The very justice of God demands another life in which the inequalities and the injustices of this life will be righted. God is love. Could He have put the immortal longings into men's hearts only to disappoint them? Could He urge us upwards and onwards only to obliterate us? If God be love, then life beyond death is a certainty. And there is one argument which the Christian can and must use. It is the fact that Jesus said, "Because I live ye shall live also." When a man is really one with Christ then neither life nor death, nor time nor eternity, can separate him from Him who was dead and who is alive for evermore.

The Preparation of the Lesson

1. *The Resurrection Narratives.* The narratives about the empty tomb should be studied in their parallel accounts in all four gospels. The accounts will be found in Matthew

28:1-8; Mark 16:1-8; Luke 24:1-12; John 20:1-18. The differences between the narratives are very revealing. Even in this short passage Matthew reveals quite clearly his characteristics. One of these characteristics is that he loves the thought of angels. No fewer than nineteen times are angels mentioned in his gospel as against only five in Mark's gospel. And in this story he begins with the angel.

It is interesting to study the changes in the four gospels regarding the Messenger who gave the news, "the Lord (is) risen." In Mark (16:5) he is a young man sitting on the right side clothed in a long white robe. In Luke (24:4) it is two men who stand by in shining garments. In Matthew (28:2) it is the angel of the Lord who descended from heaven. In John (20:11) it is two angels in white who appear. It is plain to see that in this there is a development of the supernatural. In Mark, the earliest gospel, there is no mention of angels: in John, the latest gospel, the one young man has become two angels. However that may be we can see and understand what had happened. The Resurrection is the unique fact of history, a fact of such consummate splendour that the wonder of men saw the events of it with a kind of sheen of unearthly glory.

2. *The Sepulchre and the Visit to it.* The tomb itself was a rock cavern. The body was rolled in long linen strips like bandages and then laid on one of the shelves within it. Across the front of it there ran a groove and in the groove a stone as big as a cart wheel. In the case of Jesus that stone was rolled across the front of the cavern and then sealed (Matthew 27:66) to make assurance doubly sure. When a person died in Palestine it was the custom to pay frequent visits to the tomb for the three days after burial to see if by any chance the spirit of life had returned to the departed one. That explains the visit of the women. After the three days had passed the fact of death was accepted as final.

3. *Belief in the Resurrection.* No one need hesitate to believe implicitly in the Resurrection. It is one of the best attested facts in history. Many attempts have been made to explain it away.

i. It has been suggested that Jesus only fainted on the Cross; that in the tomb He revived and somehow escaped away. The theory has only to be stated to be disproved. How could He escape from the sealed tomb? How could He, weak and helpless, disentangle Himself from the grave wrappings? How could He after the experiences of the Cross appear a radiant figure to His followers unless indeed He had been raised to glorified life?

ii. It is suggested that the whole thing was a hallucination. *First,* it is quite obvious that the disciples never expected the Resurrection. When it happened they at first refused to believe in it. An hallucination does not come to men in a frame of mind like that. *Second,* most of His appearances were made to more than one person at a time. A band of people do not all at once undergo the same hallucination.

iii. It is suggested that the Jews stole His body away lest it be reburied and lest He be glorified as a martyr. If they had done so they would later have only been too forward to say so in order that they might disprove the Resurrection which was the centre of early Christian preaching.

4. *Apart from anything else two things guarantee the Resurrection:*

i. The Christian Church itself. There is no means of explaining the change in the disciples from hopeless, broken, defeated despair to utter radiant certainty and courage than by the fact of the Resurrection. Had there been no Resurrection there would have been no Christian Church.

ii. The fact of Christian experience. To the non-Christian this is not only to learn something about the Resurrection, not only to pass the fact of it on to the scholars, but to experience again in our own lives the power and the presence of the Risen and Ever-Living Lord.

Aim of the Lesson
To help the scholars to realise that the Resurrection means that Jesus is always with us.

II. For the Scholars

1. *Two Scenes from the one Life.* Turn up your Bibles at Luke 22:54-62. (Either get the scholars to read it quietly to themselves or else get a good reader to read through the passage.) Who is that story about? What did Peter do? What was Peter on that occasion? (A coward and a traitor). What feeling was uppermost in Peter's mind then? (Fear). Turn to Acts 4:13-20. Have it read in the same way. What was it that surprised the rulers about Peter and John? (Their boldness). What was the feeling uppermost in Peter's mind this time? (Courage). Can you tell me how long there was between these two incidents? Let us try to work it out. At what Feast of the Jews was Jesus crucified? (The Passover—Acts 2:1). Will you tell me the name of another feast of the Jews. What is it? (Pentecost). Pentecost means "the fiftieth." It was so called because it fell on the fiftieth day after the Passover. Can you tell now how long there was between these two incidents in Peter's life? (Just over seven weeks).

2. *The Great thing Between.* Now in between these two events in Peter's life two things happened to Jesus. One of them looked like a tragedy and a disaster. What was it? (The Crucifixion). The other was a triumph and a victory. What was it? (The Resurrection). Why was Peter so afraid and so cowardly just before Jesus was crucified? (Because He thought that Jesus was being taken from him for good and all). Why was Peter so brave after the Resurrection? (Because he knew that now Jesus was always with him and always beside him).

3. *Jesus is with a great Follower.* Look up and read a very great thing that Paul once said. Read Romans 8:38, 39. It was part of our worship service today. What does Paul say there? (That nothing can separate us from the love of God). Who told us about God's love? Who was God's love come down to earth? (Jesus). So this really means that nothing can separate us from Jesus. Now look up Acts 18:9. Read it. Who spoke to Paul in a vision that night? (The Lord; that means Jesus). Where was Paul when this happened? (Acts 18:1 will tell you). Corinth was believed to be the worst city in the Greek world. When Paul was facing a very very hard task Jesus was there to help and encourage him. That was about twenty years after the Resurrection. Now look up Acts 23:11. Read it. Who appeared to Paul again? (The Lord). Where was Paul when this happened? (Jerusalem). At the moment he was a prisoner on trial and he was going to go ultimately to Rome to be tried by the cruel and wicked emperor Nero. Once again when Paul was up against it Jesus was with him to help him. This was all of thirty years after the Resurrection.

4. *David Livingstone.* Now let us take a big jump down the centuries. David Livingstone was once in a very tight corner in Africa. It was so dangerous to go forward that for once he thought about turning back. He took his New Testament. It fell open at the last chapter of Matthew's gospel. His eye was caught by verses 19, 20, "Lo, I am with you alway, even unto the end of the world." "It is the word," he said, "of

339

a gentleman of the most strict and sacred honour. I will go on." He did go on and no harm came to him. Jesus was still with His follower in his hour of difficulty.

5. *Jesus with us.* It is still the same to-day. We must not ever think of Jesus as just a figure in a book. We must not think of Him as someone who lived and died and about whom we read and about whom we hear. He is still alive and still with us to help us. When you are tempted to do wrong and when you are just about to do it, can you do it without any trouble or is there something which says to you, "You must not do that?" Sometimes we call that the voice of conscience; but that is Jesus still speaking to us. Sometimes we feel that we would like to do something fine and worthwhile. The voice that tells us to do it is the voice of Jesus. Over and over again people who have had something very difficult to do tell us that they have been able to do things they never dreamed that they could do. That was Jesus helping them. You cannot actually see Jesus, but there are a great many things that you cannot see that are very real for all that. You cannot see the heat of the fire but you feel it. You cannot see the cold on a cold day but you can feel it. You cannot see the wind but you can feel it. You may not be able to see Jesus, but you can hear Him speak and feel Him help.

Your Text
Please say your Motto Text. (Matthew 28:19, 20). We must remember that text. If we remember it we will find that it enables us to do things we never thought we could do and that it keeps us from doing things that we should not do.

Notebook Work
Question:—Of what does Easter remind us?

Answer:—Easter reminds us that Jesus rose from the dead and that He is with us always.

Local Examination Question
What turned Peter, the coward, into Peter, the hero?

III. Suggestions for Worship

Invocation:

"I am He that liveth and was dead, and behold I am alive for evermore."

> Jesus stand among us
> In Thy risen power;
> Let this time of worship
> Be a hallowed hour.

Even so, Lord Jesus, come Thou amidst us in Thy risen power this Easter Sunday: for Thy love's sake. Amen.

Praise: Paraphrase Psalm 48:5–9. (Tune: *St. Magnus*).

Prayer

Thanksgiving:

> O Lord Jesus, who didst rise again on the first Easter Day, hear us this day
> as we lift up our hearts in gratitude and praise unto Thee.
> O God, our Father, we give Thee thanks for all Thy good gifts unto us
> and especially to-day we give Thee thanks for Jesus, our Lord:

For His Life,
For His words of wisdom and His deeds of healing;
For His kindness and His gentleness and His love;
    We give Thee thanks, O God.
For His Death,
That He loved us and gave Himself for us;
That having loved His own He loved them to the end;
That He was obedient unto death, even the death of the Cross, for us;
    We give Thee thanks, O God.
For His Resurrection,
That He conquered death and rose from the grave;
That He is alive for evermore;
That He is with us alway even unto the end of the world;
    We give Thee thanks, O God.
Help us ever to remember that nothing can separate us from Him;
    for His love's sake we make our prayers. Amen.

Praise: Hymn 119, "Jesus Christ is risen to-day" (R.C.H.)

Lesson: Romans 8:31–39.

The Offering and the Dedication:

O God, our Father, accept these offerings which now we bring to Thee, and help us to offer Thee our whole lives in service and in love; through Jesus Christ our Lord. Amen.

Praise: Hymn 116, "Blest Morning, Whose First Dawning Rays" (R.C.H.)

The Lesson

Prayer

Petition:

O Lord Jesus, help us to remember that Thou art ever with us. When we are afraid make us think of Thy presence that with Thee beside us we may be brave.

When we are tempted help us to remember that Thou art there to help and to strengthen us to do the right.

When we have some hard task to do help us to remember that Thou art helping us to do it.

Help us to remember that we are never alone for Thou art always with us.

Intercession:

O Lord Jesus, who art everywhere present among men, be with all sick people and heal them; be with all sad people and comfort them. Bless all those who, we know, especially need Thy blessing and Thy presence. Hear us as in the silence we name them unto Thee.

A silence:

Bless Thy Church here in this place and all over the world.

Bless all our absent friends and when we are anxious about them teach us that though they are absent from us they are present with Thee. Bless us all and help us to walk in Thy presence until we see Thee face to face; for Thy love's sake. Amen.

Praise: Hymn, "Golden Harps Are Sounding"

The Blessing

We should note that Willie's belief in the resurrection does not rest on the citation of proof texts, but on empirical argument based on the evidence of nature, the essential character of God, and the trustworthiness of the New Testament record. From this data he builds his belief, and on its conclusions he rests his case. We should note especially the emphasis on *experience.* There is more in this emphasis than meets the eye. The Reformers, in seeking to weaken the power of the papacy and the teaching authority (the *magisterium*) of the church, not only attached great importance to the Bible as *the* canon of doctrine (the *sola scriptura* principle), but also to individual conscience. But this latter was never—must never be, Willie would emphasize—exercised individually, still less individualistically, but only as the reader is enlightened, prompted, and constrained by the Holy Spirit, and that within the sphere of the church. (If Willie was "Barthian" in any of his affirmations and emphases, it was here: the church is constituted by, and follower of, Jesus—which is different from saying it is constituted by this or that body of followers of Jesus. The Holy Spirit is the source of power; his is the essential authority for matters of faith and life. The internal witness of the Holy Spirit (the *testimonium internum Spiritus*) is of immense importance; some have argued that it is equal to that of the scriptures themselves, and Willie's view—though implicit—is not very different. Clear-cut answers to "decided questions" stand or fall at this point: cogency and relevance are the proof of his message and of his faith's claim on its listeners and readers.

We should note that the empirical arguments, like those on the afterlife, were expounded to the teachers and not propounded to the children. He was ever careful to offer what could be understood and appropriated by those to whom he spoke. He was not merely covering a blank sheet of paper or filling in a twenty-minute gap before the benediction, but communicating with a view to a decision being reached, the aim of the lesson being a set objective. It is a further stage in his "threshold evangelism" approach, resting as ever on the spiritual needs of the recipient for his message, not on the sometimes ego-serving interests of the teacher or on any sense of obligation to cover any given amount of this creed or that confession. He believed in teaching "the whole counsel of God," but not all at once, in one fell swoop; rather, "line upon line, precept upon precept."

We need to review more carefully some of the things that characterized his lesson writing. These aspects fall into five categories. The foremost was *his childlike faith and enthusiasm* (the latter a typical Celtic trait). There are not many sexagenarian theologians who would be content to quote a hymn from the primary section of the hymnbook to make his point, but Willie could, and did, in his autobiography nearly thirty years later: "Glad that I live am I; / That the sky is blue . . ." (and so on—he quoted all three verses of the hymn!).[71] It sums up his trusting, contented, grateful, and enthusiastic attitude toward life: "I have enjoyed living," he adds—words of a man who saw the stars, who saw potential and opportunity, not mud, setbacks, and difficulties. As he said in one of his occasional pieces (under the significant heading "Fire!"),[72] "There can be no great preaching without warmth, nor can there be any real teaching without warmth." His beloved author Robert Louis Stevenson once remarked, with pardonable exaggeration, "Acts can be forgiven, but not even God can forgive the hanger-back." Willie enjoyed his life, enjoyed his job and threw himself into it devotedly, and encouraged others to do so too, not least in their teaching. He was a success in his lessons because he was able to preserve the interests of the child and not burden him with the experiences of age and maturity. Unlike Robert Lee, who did much for biblical exegesis in Scotland at the end of the precritical age, Willie enthusiastically intensified his work and made it more appropriate.

The second aspect of his lesson writing that we ought to consider concerns *the range of information* he offered: linguistic, historical, and cultural. Sometimes this was culled from the biblical period itself, and sometimes from some other point in time; sometimes by way of a direct explanation, and sometimes obliquely, by way of application. Scottish history and topography were not totally absent, but Willie used them much less than did many of his compatriot writers at that time, and his use of Scotticisms was negligible. His citation of authors is also typical, but I leave the detail of this third aspect to later, when it will be dealt with in connection with his other written work.

Thirdly, his own *language* is easily recognizable. In the lessons his stylistic idiosyncrasies were less marked than in the sermon on pages 325–29 (its deficiencies apart), but they were nevertheless present, as in his use of double and triple nouns, adjectives, and clauses: "glory, radiance and joy"; "hate, suspicion and the red ash of national prejudice"; "the readiest welcome, the strangest support, and the most eager help"; "full of joy and song and poetry"; "wet through and through"; "many and many a time"; and so on. The Barclay keywords (duty, privilege, responsibility, lovely, big) constantly appear, and there is a marked zest for life in their selection and usage, a high-toned quality that is never divorced from real life in its down-to-earthness. Already our author is demonstrating a relish for words that is almost poetic in nature, and he is not afraid to repeat phrases or words for emphasis after the manner of the old rhetoricians.

Fourthly, the *devotional content* is never absent. It remains the goal of his teaching: to introduce the children to God their Father, and Jesus his Son as their hero, friend, and Savior (in that order!). We should note his care in this, and the sequence of those essential traits of Jesus. It owed as much to the deep understanding of the child's (particularly the boy's) needs, as it did of his loyalty to New Testament teaching. The child who found his admiration in Jesus the hero (we may recall that Isaiah 9:6 may best be translated "Hero-God"), who went on

343

to discover Jesus' friendship, early discovered his need of a Savior. It was ever Willie's way, the way of threshold evangelism: from friendly contact to deeper insight. He did not like stereotyped imagery that had lost its power to attract and inform, that all too often hid the teacher's paucity of training and of faith. He took seriously the senior child's love of novelty and change and the practicality of his mind. Willie wrote to mold him gently into the ways of Christ, leading rather than directing, and he frequently expressed himself strongly on the dangers of not respecting the intellectual level, the will, or the feelings of the individual. Moreover, the essence of good teaching, he strongly held, was the conveyance of truth through personality, and he therefore placed much emphasis on the teacher's preparation—not of his lesson material only, but of his heart and life; it was indeed "the essential prelude to every act of public teaching." In February 1949, the magazine commenced with an article entitled "The Quiet Hour," indicative of Willie's strong emphasis on prayer. He who was to write nine books and many articles and broadcasts on prayer early found a public willing to read and use his prayers. As his congregation at Renfrew had found, this was one of the most moving and notable parts of his ministry; none is more demanding.

It is interesting in this regard to recall Alfred North Whitehead's definition of religion—what a man does in his solitariness—and compare it with Willie's understanding (a self-understanding, surely) of "the solitary existence of the only child." Despite his love of company, and of spiritual company at that, he was in many ways a solitary man, by inclination and by his disabling deafness. He pretended to use this as a reason for his solitary behavior, but this should not conceal from us his great need for quietude. Willie's favorite cricket and music critic, Neville Cardus, once said he himself needed six hours alone each day to retain his pensive, poised (not posed!) attitude to life, and Willie was very like that. At such times he prayed, and that prayer life was the secret of his triumph and success. He may frequently have wrestled with doubt (though this was not obvious at this time to those who knew him), but he ever walked with God.

Fifthly, the *practicality* of these lessons is never omitted. It is the essential concomitant of the life that recognized God; goodness is its unselfconscious objective. Willie was never negative in his approach, save that he was against prudery. He did not seek to make goody-goodies of his children, but real boys and girls, red-blooded and joyful like himself, not followers of Swinburne's "pale Galilean." The influence of the YMCA and the Boys' Brigade all pointed toward complete and balanced childhood and manhood. And that was the aim of his teaching—through the "manly" virtues of honesty, kindness, and purity, to which were added the need for perseverance and courage. He repeatedly takes note of the heroic deeds and stature of Jesus and his predecessors and followers, not least the great adventurers of the recent past—whether missionaries, explorers, discoverers, or sportsmen. The texture of his own life was tough and resilient, despite a real strain of artistic sensitivity.

344

CHAPTER THIRTEEN

He Extends His Base

Life Begins Again

W_{ILLIE} celebrated his fortieth birthday in December 1947, almost exactly one year after having relinquished his pastoral work at Renfrew. Life for him, settled and contented in his new job, had certainly begun again.

They were curiously mixed and difficult days, composites of hope and despair, triumph and defeat. On the one hand (and of particular interest to Willie) Chuck Yeager broke the sound barrier, and the world was alive with talk of man's sovereignty over nature and new conquests yet to be. Television sets were becoming popular; the "new day" was dawning and offering amazing possibilities. Princess Elizabeth married Prince Philip, and the nation rejoiced once again in its Royal House, which had given such an admirable lead and example to the country.

On the other hand, in Glasgow a report was published revealing that over eighty percent of its houses were still one- or two-roomed; the repulsive shadow of the war trials at Nuremburg fell across the Western world; and fears of Communist atrocities and ambition numbed a people already sick of strife and bloodshed. The Russian army was still not demobilized, and fears as to their intentions proliferated. In America, anti-Communist purges were to break out in ways that terrified the open-minded and tolerant (Willie included) from 1949 on, as McCarthyism entrenched itself as a principle of formidable and wounding power. The ethics relating to the atom bomb were still being discussed, and those relating to the use of bacteriological warfare began to stir minds and consciences. Another disruptive element of the body politic was shortly to explode on the public, when the National Government of South Africa came to power in 1948 and apartheid became a leading principle of its actions and domestic institutions. It was a long way from the recently displaced Jan Smuts, a devotee of the Greek New Testament, whom Willie used to hold up to his Young People's Society and congregation as an example of moral and even military rectitude. There were also strange sightings of Unidentified Flying Objects, and five American aircraft went missing in inexplicable circumstances. The period of "managerial politics" was ushered in, and the nationalization of energy and other resources became a reality. Electricity was the first to be nationalized, on All Fools' Day 1948.

The first generation of colored immigrants arrived at this time from Barbados, having been offered five hundred spare bunks on a returning troopship. Basil Matthews, one of Willie's favorite authors in the early days of Renfrew Trinity and in his writing for *The Scottish Sunday School Teacher,* had expressed himself this way when he published his perceptive, not to say prophetic, book *The Clash of Colour:* "The challenge of Mount Everest and that of the Race Problem are clearly parallel." Alas, the latter was to prove more intractable than the former, and was to disfigure the human situation for the rest of Willie's life and ministry. In 1949, NATO was founded and offered hope at a different level, though there were not a few who wondered if this would not simply be a resurrected, and equally incompetent, League of Nations.

In the religious sphere, signs of resurgence of interest in general matters appeared. *The British Weekly* had spoken of an "ecclesiastical spring-time," and foresaw "a renascence in theology."[1] Theological colleges were full of eager war-experienced young men, and the churches had returned to them from active service their former ministers and priests. In November 1946 Archbishop Fisher made his famous call for "full communion" between Episcopalian and other churches. John White, seeing the reluctance of the Anglicans to recognize the validity of his church's ministry, expressed disapproval for this attitude, and sorrow that Lang's broader proposals had been rejected.[2] (Lang, being a Scot, had more carefully tuned sensitivities, and was much more accommodating than the former headmaster of Rugby School.) But despite this disagreement, it was now broadly accepted that church reunion was "the first and fundamental problem which underlay all other problems." The World Council of Churches was still in process of formation.[3] As long ago as 11 August 1937 the principle of a World Council had been accepted at the Edinburgh Conference,[4] but implementation had been proceeding less than smoothly with the interruptions of war and its attendant social ferment. The Provisional Committee during these "Ten Formative Years" (1938–1948), to use the title of one of Stephen Neill's books, did sterling work despite the international situation. In February 1946 it proposed that the first Assembly should take place in August 1948.[5] So the first, tentative steps toward ecumenism were taken. Significantly, apart from the "internal" problems of its member churches, the first real issues it studied were those of religious liberty (especially regarding Russia and Spain) and race, matters that are still with us today and that Willie himself addressed from time to time.[6]

In the biblical studies sphere, Matthew Black's *An Aramaic Approach to the Gospels and Acts* was published. It aroused tremendous interest and established an Aramaic source behind the Gospels that had far-reaching consequences. Black was critical of C. C. Torrey's excessive enthusiasm (Torrey had published a similar, though less restrained work in 1924) and contended that the Gospels of Mark and John were based on an Aramaic document known as "Q" (that being the first letter in the German word for *source*) that also stood behind the teaching tradition common to Matthew and Luke. More popularly, Dodd's *The Bible Today* was published (in early 1947) and confirmed the success of his broadcast talks with huge sales. It prefigured the growth of "popular" religious publishing, even as Penguin Books did so in the secular sphere. Bishop Wand published a revised edition of his *New Testament Letters* and signaled thereby the importance new versions would have in the postwar era. Indeed, his translation was eclipsed by the sensational sales J. B. Phillips achieved with his *Letters to Young Churches*. Soon the rest of the New Testament followed, and a veritable springtime for the publishing of biblical material dawned.

The door to Continental scholarship was now cautiously reopened, and the public began to learn of Rudolf Bultmann's program of demythologization, which sent tremors throughout Christendom. The question of his being subjected to ecclesiastical discipline for heresy was raised, but not even such stalwart opponents as Karl Barth—a significantly changed Barth—were willing for this to take place.[7] The Basel theologian knew only too well, as many did not, that the only effective way to oppose bad theology was by the statement of good theology, not by attempting to demean or silence the perpetrators personally. And in any case, Barth was much too preoccupied with the eradication of the "evils of an existential framework for theology" in his own work.

In August 1949 an astonished world woke up to read sensational news of the discovery of Hebrew texts at Khirbet Qumran in West Jordan. For the next twenty years the Dead Sea Scrolls were to be, with the revival of evangelical theology (not least through the "new" methods of mass evangelism, its sharp conflict with "broad" theology, and the questioning of "God-talk"),[8] at the very center of the theological debate. This latter was increasingly to impinge on Willie's own thinking and position. A marked shift in opinion was taking place generally, and in him personally. The brilliant researches of men like B. H. Streeter, C. H. Dodd, T. W. Manson, and Vincent Taylor, to name but a few, were now beyond the stage of initial reaction, and solid work was being built on the foundations they had laid. The older evangelicals, aware of the ground they had already lost, became defensive, more denunciatory, even shrill. The younger ones were forced to tread warily, very conscious of the dangers of being ostracized and even silenced if they stepped over the line of traditional understanding. Only those in secular educational appointments such as F. F. Bruce held were really safe, and even then it was not uncommon for bannings to take place on the grounds of their alleged "unsoundness."

Interesting things were happening for Willie much nearer home. Richard Niebuhr delivered his course of Warrack Lectures on Preaching at Glasgow in early 1947. We can imagine that his militarily activist views were not overlooked by the Professor of Divinity and Biblical Criticism and his energetic assistant. Charles Duthie was appointed Principal of the Scottish Congregational College, and thus was brought to the public gaze one whose path would constantly cross with Willie's, especially as fellow journalist for *The British Weekly*. A little later, in

1949, another telling appointment took place when Andrew McCosh was appointed Publications Manager to the Church of Scotland's Department of Publicity and Publications. This was to have a direct influence on Willie's career as author, as we shall see. McCosh had been unhappy with ministerial work for some time, and in 1947 had tried to become a research student alongside Willie (who had supported his application) at the University. But this had been refused because of his unwillingness to forsake completely his pastoral work at Cambuslang, a former scene of evangelical work in the revival days.

In April 1947 a special meeting of the faculty regarding the question of teaching biblical studies had been convened. It was clearly attracting a large number of young men and women who had no intention of becoming ministers. Religious education in the schools was increasing in importance as a subject in its own right, and so they met to discuss the ways of utilizing their offices in its cause. J. W. D. Smith, whom we briefly encountered in regard to the Scottish Sunday School Union, was co-opted to advise them.[9] His chief contribution stressed their slow response to the situation compared with what the English universities were doing. This was perhaps a little unfair, as the Principal of the University had long been aware of this, but moves to improve things were hampered by the tripartite system of university, college, and church. At the very time this matter was being discussed in Glasgow, Willie's coeditor of later years F. F. Bruce was being interviewed for the new post of Head of Biblical Studies in the University of Sheffield.[10] And at Leeds a similar move was also being made, which resulted in Matthew Black's appointment to the new post of New Testament Lecturer (Bruce himself being a member of the panel who appointed Black). D. M. G. Stalker at Edinburgh and William Neil at Aberdeen were also appointed to similar posts in biblical studies. The renascence of biblical studies was accelerating, and Scots were again in the van of a significant movement.

This concern was followed up in two important ways in the autumn. In the first, a "School of Study" was set up to aid those not able to follow a full-time course in the University. Based at Trinity College, the first lectures (at two shillings and sixpence for the course) were to be given by the indefatigable Willie on "The Teaching of Jesus." The second, confirmed in the faculty minutes of December 3, was for A. C. Craig to begin a lectureship on Biblical Studies after 1 January 1948. Craig was already well known at the University, where he had been a distinguished Student Chaplain for many years; he was to provide another fruitful friendship for Willie. It is pleasant to learn that the pecuniary aspects were not overlooked, both men being awarded an extra fifty pounds per annum for these additional responsibilities. About this time, the Annual Reunion of Trinity College Students took place, when Willie was able to meet his former fellow students in his new role, under the presidency of Duncan Blair, his former "bishop" at Newlands South Church.

In 1948 a rare treat lay in store for the Faculty of Theology. Emil Brunner, the famed Swiss theologian and one-time colleague of Karl Barth, arrived to deliver the Alexander Robertson Lectures. The aim of the lectureship was "the defence of the Christian Religion," and Brunner fulfilled that aim by addressing himself to "The scandal of Christianity." Shortly after this, approval was given by the Church of Scotland for the University to take over the nomination and supplementation of the former "Church Chairs." It was a decisive move, and did not fail to draw strong objections from some quarters. It now meant (though changes were not made to existing appointments) that these posts—in theory at least—would not be subject to religious or theological tests, a move taken five decades earlier in England, when fierce disputation over doctrine precluded such action in Scotland.

In this same year Willie was elected—a great honor, he told Braidwood—to be a member of the prestigious Society for the Study of the New Testament (Studiorum Novi Testamenti Societas).[11] In many ways his membership was significant of his relationship with the scholarly world, for while formally a part of it, he was not deeply involved with it. He regularly attended its meetings in the immediate postwar years, but when in 1963 he at last became Professor, the appointment curiously squeezed such particularly scholarly interests out of his timetable. C. L. Mitton—himself a scholar of some note, a former editor of *The Expository Times,* and Willie's editor for several years—remembers that while attending most of the formal meetings, at which technical papers were read and discussed, Willie never billeted with the society members who were usually ensconced in university halls or similar places.[12] This independent action was misunderstood, and occasionally gave rise to ungallant comments as to its reason. It is not only doctrinal matters that make up the *odium theologicum,* even as theological matters alone do not constitute the reason for church disunity; psychological and personal as well as traditional features also play their mischievous part. For thirty years Willie remained a member of this august body, but not once did he read a paper to it or show any interest in serving on its various bodies or committees; nor did he ever travel outside the United Kingdom under its auspices. He was glad to be kept in touch with scholarship via its journal, its occasional papers, and its meetings, but he never felt obliged to extend its activities personally. One of its charity appeals sent to him, along with the booking form for the 1973 annual conference at Southampton, was accidentally preserved among his papers. There is no copy of the reply appended to the paperwork. His secretary had merely written "Refused" at the top of the invitation. His thoughts and the direction of his life's work were essentially elsewhere; Willie had no intention of strengthening the walls or increasing the height of his ivory tower.

In February, a proposal was put forward by Professor Porteous that the students pursuing New Testament Greek and Elementary Hebrew courses should be allowed to sit the entrance examinations at the conclusion of their first year and not at the beginning. It is an odd approach, for the whole point of the entrance examination was to test the candidates' ability to cope with and sustain advanced work at these subjects, not to reward them for having done so. But Porteous was presciently making a point that was to gain increasing currency throughout the whole of Willie's academic life, and with which he had scant sympathy—namely, the suggestion that such linguistic expertise is not essential to the average parish ministry, many of the applicants for which presented themselves with no linguistic background and little understanding of its importance. The suggestion was unanimously defeated. Willie was present and certainly among those whose voices were raised against the suggestion. For one thing, it flew in the face of Scottish ministerial tradition, which highly prized the status of a "learned ministry" for its incumbents. For another, Willie was himself a great natural linguist, one who had found no difficulty in mastering Latin, Greek, and Hebrew (though he never worked to keep up the latter language and does not ever appear to have effected any great facility in it). We shall see that his views on this question began to alter when mature professional men commenced to apply for training in the '70s.

We cannot here pause to discuss Willie's convinced view (and a valuable interpretative key to his thinking) that "theology is grammar."[13] But we must note that the linguistic approach was wholly characteristic of him, from which position he never moved far. He would certainly have agreed with A. B. Davidson, through whose influential grammar he studied Hebrew, when Davidson asserted that "any exposition now to be valuable or even bearable must base itself immovably on Grammar, for Grammar is the foundation of Analysis, Analysis of Exegesis, Exegesis of Biblical Theology, and Biblical Theology of Dogmatic."[14] No clearer statement of Willie's approach could be found; no better defense of his essential method is possible. It was for this reason that his expositions reflected little of the preliterary forms and compositions that increasingly characterized postwar work. The scriptures as we have them form the basis of our doctrinal font. It is part of his legacy to us, and he was content to remain a spadeworker for the "higher" disciplines, though more often than not popularizing the spadework of his colleagues in New Testament exegesis—"a theological middleman," as he called himself. He would have agreed with Peake that one has to beware of what Phillip, a great exegete, called "grammatical terrorism,"[15] and would have strongly dissociated himself from Drummond and Bulloch's demeaning of such research as "grubbing in the empirical ditch."[16] He had highly commendatory things to say about Arndt-Gingrich's *Greek-English Lexicon of the New Testament and Other Early Christian Literature,* and he enthusiastically reviewed it for two different journals.[17] But in one of these he warned that this work was not just a lexicon, but supplied interpretation also, adding characteristically that that needed watching! He significantly described himself as "a dictionary, not a theologian,"[18] and he always maintained that without the dictionary—which is to say, without adherence to biblical data—real theology is not possible.

He was committed to doing some of this work himself, the only true way to achieve a "balanced" theology (i.e., of Paul *and* James, Jesus *and* John, the Synoptic Gospels *and* the fourth). When it came to close linguistic usage—as opposed to literary traditions, sources, and forms—whether in the old Greek writers, the narrower fields of Hellenistic and New Testament usage, or that of the early Church Fathers (Greek or Latin), there were few to equal him, though once again his work was more descriptive than analytic. Professor Galloway recalled an instance of this that amazed him and led to his speaking of "Willie's erudition of gargantuan proportions."[19] He had asked of Willie about a rare Greek word that he came across in one of the Greek Fathers. Willie's reply was immediate. He knew the word (and expatiated upon it), and went on quite off the cuff to cite the four other places in the Fathers' writings where it occurred, giving references, background information, and further explanations of it.

Willie had his own views about scholarship and certain attitudes of some scholars, but we misunderstand him if we think he was opposed to it *simpliciter*. As for ministers not possessing Greek—*phi* upon the outrage! As he tartly remarked to one of his intending students when the idea of non-Hebrew and non-Greek B.D.'s was all the rage, "You don't really know the New Testament unless you know it in Greek."[20] He was once asked by one of his friends, Johnston McKay, how his son (who was then one of Willie's first-year men) was doing. Willie's enthusiasm for language work is seen in the response he made, that he and his freshmen were "Discovering first declension Greek nouns together"—almost the first lesson in Greek! Like William Ramsay of old, learning for Willie was discovery, but never more so than when in the company of eager, open-minded young people with whom he, too, could learn.

By early 1949, the School of Study had petered out. Why it did so is not recorded, for Willie elsewhere was continually attracting large numbers to his addresses and sermons. It may well have been due to his inability to continue to support it, for by this time (as we shall see) crushing demands were being made on him. In December 1948 the Senate had sent down a remit to the faculties concerning its wish to expand such courses, which was discussed in the Divinity Department with some care. Its intentions were related to those of the Home Board of the Church of Scotland, which had set up an Evangelism Committee to investigate "experimental work in adult religious education." Therefore, Professor Mauchline (then Dean of the Faculty) and Willie were nominated to serve on the Committee—Willie's first such post since he had laid down his committee work at the Presbytery of Paisley outside his SSSU involvements. It reminds one of his earlier hopes to get the post at the Jordanhill teacher-training college. He clearly saw the immense possibilities in Religious Education that were there for the seizing. Had he been given the Chair of Practical Training and not this junior lectureship, he might well have pioneered in a branch of religious education well in advance of the time. Now, alas, he simply had not the time, and so their investigations and deliberations were kept at a general (and unimaginative) level.

It was at this time, Willie noted in a letter to Braidwood, that G. H. C. Macgregor was "attacked by the wanderlust in his old age."[21] Willie himself, ever prone to make light of life's difficulties, saw this as a source of contentment and challenge. Continued he,

I have been exceptionally lucky in my chief. . . . He has never at any time treated me as a subordinate, as I am, but has let me have a free hand. . . . For quite long times I was left alone to do the work of the department. It was hard work and meant double shifts, but it was grand experience and I enjoyed it very much indeed.

Hard work and double shifts it was, indeed. It was only his second full year at his post, and he was now all but running the department "for quite long times" (i.e., for six months, while Macgregor was in America) single-handedly. This entailed at least eleven hours lecturing a week, plus related preparation, the marking of papers, and the setting of homework tasks—at both ordinary and honors levels. In College there were now 140 students, most of whom "were something else before they decided to enter the ministry." They were a good deal older than the average student, too. Ex-servicemen were continuing to be the chief "problem" of theological training, and its chief challenge. How he thrived on such challenge!

Some External Involvements, Mainly Literary

It will be understood that only a fraction of these involvements can be given for reason of space. But I choose a few that took place in 1949 to give the flavor and extent of his work.

At Easter he delivered a series of addresses at the popular Morningside Church, Edinburgh, whose minister had been James S. Stewart. (It was this Stewart who had just beaten Willie to the appointment of the Chair of Biblical Criticism at Edinburgh, and in so doing had perhaps fulfilled in part Macaulay's warning.) Neither man was the sort to harbor personal thoughts against the other, and it is very pleasant to see Willie happily stepping into Stewart's former pulpit and sphere of influence. It was to be no easy matter, however, for "Stewart of Morningside" had established his pulpit reputation in high Scottish tradition, and his people were very able to discern between good and indifferent sermons. Commented *The British Weekly,* "Mr Barclay has only recently been discovered in Edinburgh. He preached with great acceptance at Palmerston Place in March . . . and conducted a week of Easter services at Saint Matthew's, Morningside, when the congregation increased each night until the church was quite full."[22] The reporter went on to talk about Willie's "outstanding pulpit gifts," which had long been known in the west of Scotland, as being "greatly in demand everywhere for special services." Betraying perhaps a stereotyped attitude to what constitutes acceptable preaching, he added, "his style is essentially his own, but he often reminds one of the sheer preaching power and intensity of Professor James Stewart."

Capital cities are not unknown for their ability to underrate provincial preachers, even those from the third city of the kingdom, and there is some veiled competition and humor in this report. In point of fact, Willie's preaching powers had reached even the Home Counties before this time, for he had already preached on at least two occasions in London (at the Scots' Church, Saint

Columba's, in Crown Court, London, and at Saint James' Presbyterian Church, Dulwich, in 1946).

In May he preached at Jack Gunn's church in Perth, which was particularly pleasant for him as Mrs. Isabel Gunn (née Lewis) had been a prominent member of his Young People's Society. In September he took the Youth Leaders dedication service at Victoria Tollcross for James Lees. This was the start of a ten-year relationship with this church for Willie; from now on he would conduct a service there every other year. As we shall see, he liked nothing more than being able to do consecutive work of this sort, amazing everyone by his grasp of their affairs and his ability to recall small details of their personal lives. He and Lees found sympathetic strains in each other's company, expressed each Wednesday evening over supper (placed before them by Kate before she went to bed). Mr. Lees used to come between 10:00 and 11:00 P.M., thus giving Willie a much appreciated break from his writing, which was continued when his friend left at midnight. Following a standing ovation Willie received at the end of the General Assembly twenty-five years later, with everyone keen to make known his own appreciation and good wishes for his retirement, he spied across the large entrance hall Mr. Lees, whom he had not seen for fifteen years. "How are your boys doing?" he asked of his old friend, mentioning their names and some earlier details of their lives—as if it were yesterday when he had met them. In *Testament of Faith* Willie applauds W. M. Macgregor's "prodigious and Christ-like memory"[23]—a phrase Gossip had used of the late Principal—and discreetly omits that his own memory was not less prodigious and certainly not less Christlike in its interest and kindliness.

To Lees he displayed another of his unselfconscious qualities, his natural Highland consideration. Lees had attempted to thank him for one of his services and sermons but was interrupted by Willie. He had overrun his allotted time by two minutes, and so interrupted Lees's word of thanks to offer an apology for doing so. The minister said he had not even noticed the overrun, nor did he think anyone else would have noticed it. Willie rejoined (doubtless with memories of Trinity Church in his mind) that the ladies preparing the tea would have noticed it. They prided themselves on having it freshly made, and just right, and their service was as important as anyone else's—including his own and the minister's![24]

Mr. Lees was then the secretary for recruitment for foreign missions in the west of Scotland, and he had a deep, practical approach to things. One of the reasons he and Willie got on well together was that they shared this approach. Just how practical Willie's approach was may be gathered from another of his engagements undertaken for Lees during this period—preaching at Strathaven Church in his old County of Lanarkshire, in late November. He did so with wonted exuberance, drawing a vivid picture of the missionary task and the whole church's responsibility to fulfill it. He preached a *ten*-point sermon on giving, and the collection amounted to £115, a record for those deprived postwar times.

In the middle of the year Willie was asked by the Western Committee of the National Bible Society of Scotland to serve on its Board of Directors. This gave him particular pleasure, for his love of literature was ever Bible-centered, and his father had been a passionate advocate of the Society's work as well as one of its distinguished branch treasurers. On July 13 Willie took his place at the first meeting following his election to its membership. Alas, he was now exceptionally busy, and had no heart for merely keeping warm a committee seat, even with an organization as great as that of the National Bible Society of Scotland. He next attended in July 1954, and then again, for the last time, a year later. The contact could not have been more propitious, and yet again we shall see how, in the hands of God, a large oak from a little acorn grows.

His job at Trinity College, now a full-fledged university post tenable for five years, he ever held to be his main work; it was to remain such till his retirement. Week by week he made his way there, nothing preventing the execution of his duties save illness, and that not for many years yet (and even then very infrequently). He was to do a great deal more than teach the "inhuman" and "soulless" things of the B.D. course—not that he really considered them so to be now that he was discovering afresh their delights with his students. The lectern, the classroom, the blackboard, and his chalky gown were the most prominent features of his life, along with his ubiquitous typewriter. Allan Galloway makes this point emphatically in the obituary notice he wrote in 1978 for *The College Courant* (Trinity College's magazine). I repeat it here because it was as true of the beginning of his academic life as it was of its end, and it is crucial to understand that Willie's *primary* commitment was that which the Church of Scotland committed him to when it nominated him for the post, and from which he retired only when forced out by poor health. Galloway referred to Willie's "extensive popularity as a writer and broadcaster," which brought "an ever-increasing body of mail to his desk." And, he continued,

> every enquiry, every request, received a courteous and painstaking reply. Yet this massive public involvement never tempted him to give short measure to the domestic affairs of the Faculty. He did his stint as Dean with flair, panache and evident enjoyment. He never stinted his availability to students.[25]

It was a rigid commitment which refused all external inducements—even highly prized opportunities in America and elsewhere. Having seen the effect of his chief's absences, he was determined not to go down the same road himself.

Yet despite this attitude, his extracurricular output in these early years at the University is astonishing. Quite apart from his *Scottish Sunday School Teacher* responsibilities (which continued to the end of 1949), he now found time to produce the complete New Testament section of the second-year syllabus of *Religious Education for Secondary Day Schools* (1947) and, two years later, the third-year syllabus of the same. Thus, between 1945 and 1949 (and subsequent years for those who wished to rework the material, and many did) he influenced every day school in Scotland offering courses in religious instruction. This amazing contribution has never been adequately recognized, though in the nature of things—as with his Senior Lesson Notes—it was perhaps inevitable, since both these organs of education were published without personal names attached: they were deliberately anonymous, representing the "authorized" teaching of the bodies that published them. In assessing Willie's work we must bear in mind not only the thirty thousand Sunday School teachers he reached via *The Scottish Sunday School Teacher,* but the thousands of day school teachers he reached with his syllabi. Beyond them lie the countless tens of thousands of children, all of them at the most impressionable age religiously speaking.

In 1946 a new opportunity arose of which Willie gladly availed himself, and which hence became a monthly commitment for him. It came in the form of an invitation from *The Expository Times* (Willie never wrote to publish except by invitation) to contribute to its well-known column for ministers, "In the Study." For those less trained or less naturally skilled for pulpit work, this section has ever been an inestimable boon. Willie's contributions to it were both an extension of his training work at Trinity College and a promise of a far larger ministry of that type yet to come. If we take some space to review this, it is only because therein he most typically expressed himself. It was a direct fulfillment of the ministerial training hopes that had been checked when he failed to secure the Chair of Practical Training.

His first piece appeared for "the fourth Sunday after Epiphany" (yet another indication of his preparedness to use the books the Christian calendar provided). Entitled "Fearfulness," it is based on the story of the storm on the lake recorded in Matthew 8:26, a passage and a theme that was to become his own in years ahead. Because it is quite short, and because it handles a subject for which he was to be roughly treated later, it is worth printing in full. Moreover, it brilliantly recaptures the fearfulness of the postwar years, and the strength and center of Willie's own faith, which was to change specifically.

Fearfulness

PAUL Tabori in a book called *Epitaph for Europe* described the spirit of his countrymen in the days immediately before the war. "They have lost two things," he wrote, "the courage of the heart and the laughter of the unafraid. They laugh at the wrong thing and their courage is that of a man whistling in the dark—it may vanish suddenly leaving him with his knees turned to water." There have been certain ages in history which have had a placid, easy, comfortable sense that all was well; and there have been others when there has been an atmosphere of nervous and fearful apprehension. The first age to which Christianity ever spoke was a fearful age which, as someone has put it, was seeking everywhere "a ring wall to defend it against the chaos of the world"; and in that, history is repeating itself to-day.

In the story of the storm on the lake there is given to us an insight both into the causes and the cure of fearfulness. For one thing, the disciples were afraid because they were caught up in a situation with which they were quite unable to cope. It is perhaps the worst of all fears to feel our own utter weakness and our own utter

355

powerlessness and our own utter inadequacy to deal with the situation in which we find ourselves. So long as there is something to which we can hold, things are at least tolerable. But when it seems that there is nothing to which we may hold and that there is no way of coping with things in general then there comes fear. Conrad tells of sailing the sea in the midst of a terrific storm. He had come close to the boatswain from the sheer need of human companionship. Through the wind he shouted to the man, "Blows very hard, boatswain." His answer was, "Ay, and if it blows only a little harder things will begin to go. I don't mind as long as everything holds, but when things begin to go it's bad." When things began to go there would be nothing left but to drift helplessly before the elements. Just so when a man gets caught up in a situation which he feels himself powerless to deal with and to cope with then comes fear. It was precisely that that the disciples felt in the storm on the lake and it is precisely that that many people feel to-day.

But this fear goes deeper than that in these times. There is in many human minds and hearts not only the feeling that we are incapable of dealing with the situation but that the situation is out of control. The basic fear is not so much that we cannot control things but that God has lost control of things. There are those who have a feeling that God's world has, as it were, broken loose and is running amok and that even God is powerless to deal with things. Some one tells of a child on a night when a violent gale was blowing. "Daddy," said the child, "God has lost hold of the wind to-night." So there are those who in troubled times find it hard to believe either in the love or in the power of God. Zoroastrianism had as its fundamental doctrine the belief that in the universe there is going on a ceaseless struggle between the power of light and the power of darkness; and at the root of the fear in many a heart is the thought that the power of light has lost the struggle and that the power of darkness is closing in.

So then the first cure for fear is quite simply belief in Almighty God. What is needed is the kind of belief that the writer of the forty-sixth Psalm had. "Therefore will not we fear, though the earth be removed, and though the mountains be carried into the midst of the sea." It is a kind of belief that the forty-fifth chapter of Isaiah lays down. Cyrus might never have heard of Jehovah and Cyrus might seem to be running amok; yet the fact remained that Cyrus, quite unwittingly and quite unconsciously, was in the control of the purposes of God and was working out the plan of God.

One of the great answers of history was given by Luther to the Cardinal Legate at Augsburg. The Pope had sent the Cardinal to compel Luther by any means to recant. Everything—bribes and entreaties and threats—had been tried and had been tried in vain. The Cardinal was amazed that any one should so withstand the command and the might of the Pope. "Do you think the Pope cares for the opinion of a German boor?" demanded the Cardinal. "The Pope's little finger is stronger than all Germany. Do you expect your princes to take up arms to defend you? I tell you, no! And where will you be then?" "Then as now," said Luther, "in the hands of Almighty God."

Again and again we glibly take this phrase, Almighty God, upon our lips without fully realising what it means. If it means anything it means that things cannot slip out of God's control. It means that God in His own way is working His own purpose out. As Froude laid it down, "One lesson and only one history may be said to repeat with distinctness; that the world is built somehow on moral foundations; that in the long run it is well with the good; in the long run it is ill with the wicked. But this is no science; it is no more than the old doctrine taught long ago by the Hebrew prophets."

356

To cure our fears we need to lay hold again on the certainty of the power of God. We need to sing with a new kind of belief Faber's lines:

> For right is right, since God is God;
> And right the day must win;
> To doubt would be disloyalty,
> To falter would be sin.

But further, to gain the real cure for fear we must not only believe in the almightiness of God but we must believe that that power of God can come and dwell within a man in such a way that it will make him master of all things. When Peter and John were brought before the Council to answer for their deeds and for their words the rulers were astonished at their boldness. Here were men with no kind of learning, with no kind of influence, and with no kind of backing. They were facing the wisest and most influential and the most powerful people of their country. And yet these ignorant and unlettered men, in face of all that, were obviously masters of the situation and obviously without fear. Wherein lay their secret? There can have been no more terrorizing age for Christians than the age of which the Book of Acts relates the history; and in that book there is one article of the faith which recurs again and again. It is the centre and the core of early Christian preaching. It is the Resurrection of Christ. These men had discovered something. They had discovered by personal experience that Jesus Christ was not one who had lived and died and passed on. He was not a figure of the past however heroic and however great. He was not a great character in past history. He was not a figure to be remembered. He was a powerful present reality. He was with them as really as any one could ever be with them; and in that presence and that power there was an end of fear.

Let those who live in an atmosphere of fearfulness rediscover the fact of the power of Almighty God. Let them rediscover not only the fact of the power of God but the experience of the presence of the living Christ, and in that power and in that presence fear will turn to faith and faith will abolish fearfulness in a new-found confidence.

It is, however, one thing to state a remedy and to recommend a cure. It is another thing to say where that remedy and where that cure is to be found. How are we to make this rediscovery of God's power and how are we to gain this new experience of the presence of the living Christ? It is here that there is a lesson which our own age finds it hard to learn. We live in a time which believes above all things in action. We must be doing something. But in life there must be kept a place and a time for receiving, for waiting, and for communing with God. "Be still," said the Psalmist, "and know that I am God." "They that wait upon the Lord," said the Prophet, "shall renew their strength." When in life we learn to depend less on our own almost frenzied effort and to spend more time in the practice of the presence of God we shall gain more strength and more confidence. A man can only face life fearlessly in action when he emerges from the stillness of waiting wherein he has laid hold on God and companied with Christ.

For over thirty years he wrote his column, an impressive and influential contribution for ministers. In 1978 I was privileged to edit a number of reviews that Willie had contributed to *The Expository Times*, in a volume entitled *Men and Affairs*.[26] The College of Preachers caught their spirit exactly when it reviewed the book: "light enough for leisurely armchair after-dinner reading, and yet containing so much of value that no busy preacher need feel guilty for having spent a relaxed half-hour enjoying all this very unusual volume has to offer."[27]

Preachers are seldom given to influence other preachers. We should note that Willie was not only a preacher's preacher, but he could indeed captivate, relax, inform, and make enjoyable this aspect of church life. And how his ministry was universally esteemed! The day was not long distant when one of the best-known Roman Catholic publishing companies would be glad to include his name on their lists. And at the other end of the ecumenical spectrum, *The Officer* (the journal of the Salvation Army's leadership) commented, "It is safe to say that any book written by Professor William Barclay is welcome to Salvationists."[28] Happy the man with such a ministry opening before him, and happy his grateful students and lay readers!

I include this first piece both for the sake of its historical value—it is his first homiletic piece in a highly influential journal—and for its indication of the sorts of things that moved and inspired him. Worth specific consideration are the following six features: (1) a recognition of man's inadequacy, here described in terms of his essential fear;[29] (2) an unwavering trust in God's almighty power, which in this piece he found epitomized in the life and work of Jesus; (3) an absolute declaration that the world and its history are under God's control, bound by inherent and unchallengeable laws of existence and procession (a crucial element in both his theology and his ethics); (4) an emphasis on the resurrection of Jesus—"the centre and core of all early Christian preaching"; (5) the continuous need for an "experience of the presence of the living Christ"—of Christ as a powerful contemporary reality, and not as merely a figure of the past; and (6) the conjoining of courage and laughter: armed with the presence of the living Christ, men would have "the courage and the laughter of the unafraid." How significant! And how like William Barclay! It reminds one of his delight over Hobbes's definition of laughter as "sudden glory."[30]

It was not only sermons that were published in his twenty-five *Expository Times* pieces published between 1946 and 1950; he also wrote an article entitled "Modern Autobiography"[31] and reviewed several books on poetry (ever a favorite source of relaxation to him), one of which was in fact the first of his pieces to go into the "Entre Nous" column of the journal (its title was later changed to the more popular "Men and Affairs," under pressure from the editor, not Willie). In addition, he published an impressive article on "Worship and the Child,"[32] in which he called attention to the importance of the "preliminaries" of a service—hymns, lessons, and prayers, which were all "an even greater thing" than the address—and in which he laid down six principles of worship for the child (they characterized his approach to adults, too), describing them as "particularly necessary and essential":

1. Worship must be intelligible. "The language of prayer should be carefully chosen so that it does not contain words or ideas which are not within the child's comprehension." Dignity and sheer beauty are not sufficient by themselves, and

colloquialisms are too trivial, although beauty of language is a thing to be sought after and learned.

2. Worship must be relevant. Any subjective aspects must be curtailed. It is the public's needs not the preacher's that are paramount, and it is the child's needs not the adult's that are the priority. He recommends a form of "market research" to ascertain what those needs are. His quest for intelligibility was rooted in hard reality, the real world experienced by the congregations ministered to by the preachers he was addressing.

3. Prayers must be definite. We should not say, he suggests (following Luther), "I am a dreadful sinner" to God in prayers, but "I am a liar," "I am a procrastinator" (a significant Freudian slip this), "I am lazy," and so forth. It is in this that many of the great prayers and collects of the church fail: they are too vague, too general.

4. Children should be helped to share in the worship. And for this to be true sharing they must understand what is going on; the service must be explained to them. Short explanatory talks on its various aspects must be given. Moreover, children must be involved in the worship, play some part in it, either by spoken or silent prayer.

5. When one does not know what to say, one should be able to recall from memory the great prayers and hymns that are the possession of every generation. Printed sheets might also be used, and he recommends the use of the *Sarum Primer* ("God be in my head," etc.) of Saint Anselm, or Ignatius Loyola's prayers, or those of Richard of Chichester.

6. Finally, prayers must never be repeated; they must be *prayed*.

All of this was thrust home in his inimitable style, with anecdotes and quotations—from Edward Seager, Elinor Mordaunt, the Anglican *Book of Common Prayer*, the Authorized Version's better renderings, F. W. Robertson, Martin Luther, Dr. Johnson and Mrs. Thrale, Tom Thumb, Wordsworth, and Tennyson.

He had clearly found his part-time métier as a reviewer, and was soon introducing and assessing a wide range of works and authors for his readers: the Jesuit poet Gerard Manley Hopkins, Miller's *Book of Common Order*, Burnet's *Teaching the Old Testament in Sunday School*, Marchmont's *What Life Has Taught Me*, Zander's *The Theology of Dostoevsky*, Stanley Jones's *The Way*, Sampson's anthology *The Englishman's Religions*, A. M. Hunter's *Saint Mark*, and many others. He also contributed more sermons—on Temptation, Church Unity, Patience, Palm Sunday, the Way of Joy. And, especially interesting, he wrote another article on the preacher's task and techniques, significantly entitled "Prophet and Craftsman." There could be no doubting the value and the enjoyment of such work as this.

From time to time he reviewed for his own journal, *The Scottish Sunday School Teacher*, and also for its sister journal *The Scottish Primary Quarterly*. In the latter magazine there appeared a full-page review entitled "Modern Translations of the New Testament,"[33] in which the most important translations of the Bible then available were discussed. These he considered to be Weymouth, Moffatt, the American Revised Standard Version, and the Roman Catholic New Testament in English of Ronnie Knox—"one of the best of all translations . . . with its simplicity, its naturalness and its beauty." He had found his second vocation a fruitful *parergon;* its hallmark once more was service.

We should not lose sight of the wider constituency he was influencing in *The Expository Times.* By this he preserved his toehold in the world of "applied scholarship"—by popularizing among ministers and teachers the various trends, viewpoints, and contributions of others. We look at this endeavor in detail not only because it is an area of work of great importance in itself, but also because it provides us with some informal aspects of Willie's mind, a genus of table talk, even though the table be occupied by his incessantly rattling typewriter.

Between 1950 and 1954, Willie published no fewer than fifty-eight pieces for *The Expository Times;* there were only ten issues in five years in which his name did not appear. We might say that what James Agate was to the theater, and what Neville Cardus was to cricket, and then to music, Willie was to many ministers. Three of these pieces were sermons (or rather sermon aids), one was a prefatory article to "an important new series," and the remainder were reviews or review articles. The sermons were on subjects of consuming interest to Willie, and show how well the Hastings (editors of the journal since 1924) knew their man: "Sympathy," "Prayer," and an exposition of Romans 12:18 significantly entitled "The Problems of Living Together."

"No man," Willie once declared, "has the right to comfort other people unless he has lost his mother." And the depth and fragrance resulting from his own heartbreak of twenty years previous is unmistakable in his piece on "Sympathy," into which were also infused his classical training and his appreciations from a still earlier period. "It was Christianity which taught the world what sympathy really is," he argued,[34] and demonstrated this by contrasting his faith with the ancient Greek religion, marked by the indifference of its Olympian gods to the plight of humanity, and also with the relative harshness of thought in pre-Christian Jewish circles. Arguing from his textual base in Hebrews 4:15, he stresses that the characteristic quality of Jesus was compassion—to the sick, the hungry, the heartbroken, whether children or adults or those in the full bloom of youthful energy. "Jesus taught men to care for each other," but "more than anything else" Jesus taught men that *God* cares. "The fundamental truth about the Incarnation," he baldly states, "is that it is the greatest act of sympathy in all the universe"; he expands his theme by expounding Philippians 2:6–11. For one who was soon to explore (albeit tentatively) the Adoptionist position, this exposition is a tour de force of orthodox Christology: Jesus gave up his equality with God "and became an ordinary man"; "the Christian conception of God is that of a God who sympathizes in the most literal sense, *who suffers with men.*"

In his sermon "Prayer," based on Luke 11:13, he touches the very nerve center of his life, without which he admitted he could not live.[35] His exposition of the text (and its "conflicting" parallel passage in Matthew) is well known, so it need not detain us here. But in "The Problem of Living Together" his peaceable intent (not necessarily noncombative!) is asserted. "If possible," declares the apostle, "so far as it depends upon you, live peaceably with all men." Willie's life was very largely a commentary on that text. As we shall see, the controversies into which he was plunged from time to time always developed out of reactions to what he had said or done, never out of his own initiative or criticism of the views or actions of others. He was the attacked, not the attacker. In this sermon he throws down the supreme challenge of the postwar years to both church and society. He was to find himself embroiled soon enough in their rejection of the way of peace as "an unrealistic position." It was always better that one man should die—however morally correct his position—than that the whole nation suffer. . . .

In "The Religious Education of the Child," which was designed to be "a general preface to the whole series" on the principles and methods of Religious Education,[36] Willie draws on his experience as a Sunday School leader and SSSU Lesson Notes writer rather than theories of formal teacher training. An echo of his recent *Boys' Brigade Gazette* article is found in the ubiquitous three-fold division of his subject along the lines of giving the child something to *feel,* to *remember,* and to *do.* And it also echoes the essential man: "Detachment," he declares, "will not make a teacher." The teacher must be on fire, impassioned. He firmly believed—and demonstrated—that "a lesson should almost always be reducible to a sentence"; "every lesson should finish with a question and answer in which the substance of it all is summed up." Methodology and approach to religious education were now changing fundamentally; the experiential approach was to transform the scene, and Willie, despite preserving a high place for experience-related teaching, was out of touch with its extreme forms. Not for him the understanding of religious education as "sensitising the child to the spiritual values of life." He stood fast for "declaring, always at their level, and their level of interest and absorption, the whole counsel of God."

His chief contribution to *The Expository Times* lay in a different direction than these sermons or articles, however. It is primarily as a reviewer, as a stimulator of interest, thought, and action that he should be remembered. How many readers of that prestigious publication turned first of all to "the Barclay page"—whether under its old title of "Entre Nous" or the more recent, and plainer, "Men and Affairs"! The following classification of the sorts of books he reviewed domonstrates the considerable range (and quantity) of the pieces he contributed at this time:

Biography	11
General (usually quasi-theological)	10
Preaching	8
Bible Introduction	8
Poetry	7
Church History	6
Education and Method	4
	54

They are not merely reviews but spirited causeries, ideally suited to inspire weary ministers to revive from postweekend lassitude. And what a galaxy of stars he described: the versatile and prolific John Buchan; the lonely, preeminent T. S. Eliot; the courageous Booker T. Washington; the notable preacher A. T. Cadoux; saintly Father Andrew (who saw "loveliness in common things," a double reflection of Willie himself); the innovative General Booth; the wise W. E. Sangster; the capable leader Bishop Newbigin; the influential Florence Allshorn; and so many more. Sometimes Willie took a single book, sometimes a whole cluster; but the effect is the same, and the method is unfailingly fruitful. First he found something good to say about the book or author in order to claim the reader's attention, then he described it, offering a bird's-eye view, and finally he drew the moral or lesson. Despite the fact that his early writings show an undeveloped style—some tautology, a rich use of adjectives, and above all repetition—Willie had the master's eye for excellence in others' works.

He is never more the teacher *manqué* of English Literature than in these pieces, and he rises like a trout to catch the finest, freshest, and fastest morsel. He gloried in "the echo of a great soul" Pseudo-Longinus spoke of, which he found in the books he reviewed. He thrived on the taut economy of T. S. Eliot, and wherever "a Tennysonian delight in words" is expressed, this friendly and sympathetic critic is all agog. His datedness is seen in his response to some aspects of modern poetry, in which he finds "irritating things," as well as in his penchant for the classical poets. Two things in particular are "apt to repel" him, and they are related and totally characteristic of him: "the cult of unintelligibility" and "a distressing intellectual snobbery."[37] He is quick to spot the true artist, whose artistry is unselfconscious. He is scholar enough to enjoy those whose work exhibits "mastery of detail" and man enough to own both frailty and strength in human endeavor. He especially enjoyed strength in a writer (even wrongheaded strength) and praises R. E. McIntyre's "pleasant pugnaciousness," by which phrase he also unconsciously revealed himself. He describes McIntyre's work as being "as peppered with imperatives as the Epistle of James," though he cannot let him get away with such "jesuitical comment": "an interpretation may be evangelically sound even though it is based on a doubtful exegesis." Och no!

He loved human history. Reviews of biographies were bound to top the list, and he always rose to praise an author's lack of expediency, the besetting sin of clerics and committees. He enjoyed a mental romp, and especially commended those who sent him to his dictionary (a very infrequent excursion, thanks to his linguistic sensitivity and prodigious memory). But he sharply turned on those authors who sprinkled their pages with too many loan words from other languages: "a habit which does not impress the scholar and which ruins the book for the man without the necessary linguistic equipment to understand it."[38] His own writings often betray—as did his very first piece in *The Renfrew Press*—a conscious translation of Latin or Greek or French tags, even when the original is universally recognized; but he can still drop a few himself when he wishes to make a point! One of his favorites, the subject of several causeries throughout his life, is *parergon,* which he almost always left unitalicized. *Parerga* were now built into his life, as we have seen; and, unlike his model A. S. Peake, he required not merely two desks for his different tasks, but a chain of them.

A man of action, in Willie's view, has a right to speak out, and he therefore welcomed the descriptions—and the confessions—of those who lived adventurously. His is a Germanico-Lutheran enjoyment of life, not Franco-Calvinist—big, bold, and even brassy at times. But alongside this there is often found a subtlety and delicacy that is French in tone. It is interesting that his preference in modern languages, almost his only skill therein, was in French, which he had learned from Miss Shedden of Dalziel High School and never forgot. Part of his complexity lies in the rugged nestling close to the fine, but the former tended to show more clearly, thanks to his close relationship with the people.

He loved boyish pranks and *jeux d'esprit,* and found it hard to believe in people who were motivated by principle rather than humane considerations. For example, he delighted in the significant elements in Leyton Richards's life—he of Carrs Lane, Birmingham, of Free-Church disposition and a Quaker conscience, a public supporter of unpopular causes and a relentless and uncompromising advocate of pacifism (for which he was heavily fined), a member (later Secretary) of the Fellowship of Reconciliation, a popular preacher and arduous worker, and so much more. But from Richards's biography, Willie sadly reflected, there emerged in the last analysis the picture of a man who loved causes more than he loved people, and who therefore in the end "missed greatness."[39]

It was not only an informed, artistic, delicate human approach that evoked Willie's admiration, but also the mental equivalent of a fullback's shoulder charge when his own goal is threatened. He admits elsewhere that he is a natural believer,[40] and so he was. Faith for him was axiomatic, and it always possessed a recognizable (if developing) structure. But he was a "natural unbeliever" too, and felt deeply the paradoxes of faith that he encountered. His refusal to accept paradox as a defensible thought-form accentuated the problems of faith, of course, sometimes leading him to denial, and sometimes to oversimplification. But it was (paradoxically!) accepted by him elsewhere—as, for example, in *The Mind of Jesus* and other books. He therefore respected doubt, sympathized with incredulity, and associated himself with the expression of thoughtful reassessment. Karl Barth wrote a great book on Anselm's theology under the title of *Faith Seeking Reason (Fides Quaerens Intellectum).* It is a true reflection of William Barclay's attitude, too. His open, adventurous mind eagerly devoured what arguments for or against his position came his way, and always found extra sympathy for those who could not follow a fully charged doctrinal system.

In 1950 A. T. Cadoux, rightly venerated by succeeding generations of Bible students, produced a small book of poems, *Songs of Self and God,* the two foremost notes of which were a personal encounter with Jesus Christ and a questioning mind which could not live on borrowed capital. In his review of the volume, Willie selected these two elements from a rich store in a way that was significantly subjective. First a prayer:

> Give me a sceptic faith, a mind
> To think and think until I find . . .

And then a confession:

> I lived on borrowings of belief;
> Only the arguments were mine—
> An unremunerative brief,
> And hard, defending the divine.

> Then Jesus stood before my mind;
> I was arrested, held by Him;
> And in astonishment I found
> Belief in God no longer dim.

He may, as he did, fault Cadoux for his monotonous short-line quatrains of double rhythm, but he bowed in worship and rededication at the newfound and deeply real experience of Christ to which Cadoux led. This, to Willie, was true faith. And we find ourselves once more at the living center of his faith, but more—of his daily life, too—thereby demonstrating yet again that there is more in books than bookishness, and more in religion than theology.

But while he felt a profound respect for Cadoux's questioning faith, he also registered a respect if anything yet more profound for the very different sort of faith evidenced by the Salvation Army. Indeed, for no other human institution does Willie find the space and quality of admiration as he found for that Christianly militant organization. And it was a genuine sorrow to him to feel distanced from such a practical, self-abnegating body of workers over matters of faith. "It is strange," he reflects in reviewing the second volume of Sandall's *History of the Salvation Army,* "that those who never shrink from novelty of method refuse the greater adventure of thought"[41] (a thought Willie was to reencounter in 1970, when Major Fred Brown was dismissed from his commission for writing "a magnificent confession of real faith").[42] In that phrase "the adventure of thought," a landscape window into Willie's mind is opened before us. It is the expression of the whole man, confident in his faith, resolute in his decision, open in his attitudes and sympathies, seeking truth and—above all—God, wherever they may be found. He was unable to pass the Bible through the prism of this or that confessional body, be it Nicaea, Geneva, Westminster, or whichever. And in so reading the Word of God with untinted spectacles, he found the world of his upbringing and early doctrines increasingly being challenged. Some of the books that now came his way for review, demanding close and uninhibited attention, brought him into even deeper touch with the acids of modernity; he was not the sort of man to buck at these. His perspective was once more broadened, taking us into his fourth phase of development beyond the previous three of home, university, and pastoral experiences.

One of the books that influenced him in this way was J. V. Langmead Casserley's *No Faith of My Own,* written by a man brought up in complete isolation from the Christian faith, in a family committed to the principles of the rationalistic Press Association. No greater contrast could be conceived from Willie's own background, and it is therefore especially interesting to see him responding to this book.[43] Doctor Casserley became fascinated by the Christian faith, decided to investigate it, and ended by being captivated by it. Like C. S. Lewis, he was yet another example of a "reluctant convert." So, Willie comments, "it was bound to be an interesting book." He was himself fascinated by the author's open mind (which, he emphasized in *Testament of Faith,* is not the same as a mind open at both ends); he applauds Casserley's "adventurous mind" and, ever a word lover, delights in "the vivid, stimulating sentences" that are scattered throughout the book. The incarnation, he reports, was "a thrilling adventure of which God is the hero, crossing infinite spiritual distances . . . a spiritual romance in which God is the lover clamouring passionately at the gateways of the human heart." Prayer is "a great adventure, a launching out into the uncharted spiritual spaces which separate God and man." He uses the word *adventure* three times in fewer than four hundred words in this piece; it is clear that Willie needed the excitement of fresh appreciations and imagery and saw it as part of his role to reflect and extend that spirit of adventure wherever possible, not by way of riding another's coattails, but as a joyous way of preserving God's sovereign ways with men. The new age was calling for new ways and new expressions: forward, not backward. Willie indignantly faults Casserley for "the bizarre notion that Jesus contemplated and founded the Episcopal Churches but not, for instance, the Presbyterian Churches." The author's tendentious claim for apostolic succession (at a time when the Anglicans were making no secret of their demand on other churches to absorb prelacy) was of little import to Willie: "It is a pity that a man who . . . has said so many wise things could say such a foolish thing."

Yet despite that rejection, his admiration for Bishop Lesslie Newbigin, a Presbyterian minister raised to the bishopric in the recently united Church of South India, was total.[44] He particularly appreciated the Bishop's warnings about being immersed in administration, about being swung aside from the real work of God's family and the apostles' teaching by social service. The way union was achieved impressed Willie both in spirit and in method. Confronted with difficulties over treading an unknown ecumenical path, the Bishop said, "I put a large Bible on the table and pointed out that our constitution was already there, and we were only making local rules." Little wonder that the reviewer found "there is not a page of this book without interest. . . . We get again the authentic thrill of the Acts of the Apostles. When one has finished this book one does not want to criticize it; one wants to get to one's knees and pray. . . ." Willie was that sort of reviewer, that sort of man.

Another book that influenced him was Georgina Harkness's *The Modern Rival of Christian Faith,* a penetrating study of secularism.[45] We have already seen that Willie was not unacquainted with the rising problem of secularism, but so far as I can trace this book was his first encounter with "the rival" in a formal sense. He begins by congratulating Professor Harkness for "absolute fairness of mind," for her "extraordinary power of lucid analysis," and for "a unique gift for producing definitions which are helpful and stimulating." These were elements in his own aspirations as a teacher, of course, so it is natural that he should find the author's approach congenial. And we should also note how willingly he placed himself at the feet of this gifted woman. Mrs. Harkness defined secularism as "the ordering of life as if God did not exist," in the light of which scientism, democracy, racism, and fascism are all judged and found wanting. "Essential Christianity"—Willie's Christianity—is characterized by four things: an act of commitment to Jesus Christ, a real attempt to live by the example and teaching of Jesus (as understood directly from the New Testament), belief in God the Father and the divinity of Jesus, and membership of the church universal. "There are few better books on the modern situation than this," comments the grateful reviewer, his eagle eye noting "a shattering misprint" (*immorality* for *immortality*), and a single Greek sentence "wrongly spelled, wrongly accented and wrongly printed."

We mentioned Willie's need for exciting books, but it was a need ever kept in check. In reviewing George A. Buttrick's *Faith and Education,* he dealt with an area of absorbing interest beyond the merely professional. He comments that it is "not so much exciting as . . . excited."[46] Buttrick's criticism of modern scholastic life is that the universities have become "bustling cafeterias of information" rather than "homes of wisdom." He contends that when modern education ignores God it "evades the central fact of the whole situation"; academic detachment does not necessarily imply suspended belief. For all the secularizing influences on the reviewer at this time (and they were to accumulate over the next decade or so and directly influence his work and teaching), Willie was very far from suspending his own belief; indeed, it was deepening and hardening at its base and in its essential outline. If some things were being subjected to rigorous reassessment, others were embedding themselves yet more deeply into his faith and actions: forward still, but not without pain.

The Birth of a Bible Commentator

In one sense this is a misleading heading. Willie's Bible commentary began as far back as 1924, when he sought to expound (albeit reactively) Isaiah 9:6.[47] His theological training soon reinforced the lessons of his youth and childhood and, following his father's lay example, he sought to make the Bible his textbook. His sermons, addresses, and SSSU Lesson Notes were all an extension of that principle, in fulfillment of Reformed teaching practice.

In January 1948 a new series of articles began to appear in *Life and Work.* Its title was "Beginning Again," a title that is as significant of its author's position as it is of the transmutation of religion from Judaism into Christianity with which it dealt—and, as we saw earlier, significant of the reawakening in interest in and usage of the Bible at that time. The title of the series was explained by an editorial comment accompanying it: "A Page for those who are wishing to find their way into Bible Reading, and to relate it to their lives." The editor was so enthusiastic for this awakening and so committed to its exploitation that he wrote an article further highlighting the present mood. This preceded the new series and was titled "The Bible Is Regaining Its Place."[48] In it Jack Stevenson called attention to "Three Important Signs from 1947": the introduction of new lectureships (Neil, Craig, and others) and their courses of biblical training; a national recognition by the state of the Bible, seen in its recognition of the need for proper training in scripture teaching; and new developments in school chaplaincies.

This new series was a popular exposition of Mark's Gospel, and Willie was its author, making his first contribution (at forty years of age) to his church's magazine. The editor, who took up his post about the time Willie came to Glasgow, deserves great credit for this commission, which has never been rightfully accorded. Even Stevenson's present-day successor, who has high regard for Stevenson's skills, surprisingly passed off the event with a perfunctory two-line comment in his book *Scotland's Life and Work*, which celebrated the centenary of the periodical.[49] Stevenson recommended the new series "as a small contribution towards the revival of Bible reading." It ran for eight months.

If Stevenson did not exactly discover William Barclay for popular biblical exposition (Willie, for all his work for the *SSST*, himself attributed this to Aubrey Smith, the Assistant General Secretary of the International Bible Reading Association),[50] he certainly set him on the right road and gave him a telling opportunity. Just after the outbreak of the Second World War, the *Scottish Sunday School Teacher* included a lesson on Paul and Barnabas. Commented the anonymous lesson writer on Barnabas, "he brought together a great man and a great task."[51] And that is exactly what Stevenson did, and in so doing put a large proportion of the Christian world in his debt. This was the unheralded commencement of Willie's magnum opus—if we understand by that phrase not the most solid or original piece of work he did, but the most influential, and perhaps the most lasting. For directly from this small beginning came the Daily Bible Readings, from which developed his world-famous Daily Study Bible.

The following is Willie's first short contribution to the "Beginning Again" series.

The Gospel According to St. Mark

READ Chapter 1 in sections and as a whole this month. Try to answer the questions honestly.

1. A Declaration of the Faith

Note how the very first verse of the Gospel is a declaration of Mark's faith—the Gospel of Jesus Christ, *the Son of God*. It is sometimes demanded that we should give a detached, unprejudiced account of the life of Jesus; but it has been said that a biographer can only produce a notable biography if he either loves or hates his subject. Mark was not ashamed to show at the outset that he was "prejudiced" in favour of Jesus. Are we too much concerned in religion to keep all the arguments in balance, and too much ashamed of our convictions, when we are not ashamed of strong convictions elsewhere—e.g. in politics? Do we who are Christian sometimes *argue* too much and *witness* too little?

2. *The Preparation*

Verses 2–9 indicate to us that God had been steadily throughout the ages preparing the world to receive Jesus Christ. As God leads and guides men into truth, he gives them just as much as they can at any stage understand and is always preparing them for another stage. *Are there any signs of this happening in our own lives just now?* What seems to be the next thing God is trying to teach us? What does it mean to take upon ourselves full allegiance to Jesus Christ? Are we helping to prepare others to take that step?

3. *The Kingdom*

Verses 14 and 15 tell us the message with which Jesus came to men. Jesus came to preach the good news of *the Kingdom*. What is the Kingdom of God? In His prayer Jesus taught us to pray: "Thy kingdom come; Thy will be done in earth as it is in heaven." The second phrase explains the first. The Kingdom is a society in which both for the individual and for the society as a whole the will of God is the only law. Do we talk too much of *political* necessities and *economic* necessities and *social* necessities and too little of the *divine* necessities which should be our real law? What differences might it make in our country if we were concerned first about what God thinks necessary? And in our own lives—what, in His view, is most urgently necessary?

4. *What Jesus Did*

In this chapter, right at the beginning of His ministry, Jesus is shown engaged in two activities: (1) He is engaged in a *teaching activity*. Verse 21 tells that He went into the synagogue *and taught*. Verses 38 and 39 show Him setting out on a tour of the synagogues to preach and teach, and declaring that that was the very object of His coming. He came to tell men the truth about God and about themselves. *Are we putting ourselves in the position to be taught what He has to tell us?* If His teaching work is to go on He needs voices to speak for Him. Are you doing your part within the Church, for example in the Sunday School, to help Christ in this task? Is the Church as a whole accepting its task of *teaching,* not only its members but the whole world, the Christian truth? (2) He is engaged in a *healing activity*. Verses 23–26, 30–34, 40–42 show Jesus engaged in healing. Clearly Jesus is showing that the Kingdom of God not only involved that men's *minds* should be instructed but that their *bodies* should be healthy and strong. The work that goes on in the hospital ward or the doctor's surgery is a sacred work. Isn't that a challenge to our usual way of dividing life into compartments? What does that say to us, to the Church, to the State? Should there be a closer alliance between the Church and the work of healing? Does the Church face as it should the social task which it must face if it is to assist in bringing in the kingdom?

5. *Jesus' Source of Power*

This chapter shows Jesus from the very beginning of His Ministry strengthening Himself from two sources of power: (1) Verse 10 tells of "the Spirit" descending upon Him. Read through the book of Acts and note how every great decision was taken in guidance of the Spirit. The Spirit cannot be *won;* it must be *asked for and received.* Is there enough asking and waiting upon God in our lives? (2) Verse 35 shows us Jesus at Prayer. Do we really believe that "more things are wrought by prayer than this world dreams of?" At the back of our feverish activity is there this central determination to keep in living touch with God for guidance and correction?

Read this chapter again. Think now what "The Kingdom of God" means, and what is the method of its coming.

It was a small contribution to the great task of the extension of Bible reading, and for those used to Willie's maturer approach (and even those used to his *Scottish Sunday School Teacher* lessons) it is very light on exegesis, as it is on exposition. The style is easy but not loose, relaxed but not chatty, light but not trivial. The most notable feature is a heightened use of the question technique: in the first article no fewer than nineteen questions are asked in a mere ninety lines of text, covering over half the space at his disposal. We need to bear this in mind, for one of the major aspects of Willie's literary success was his ability to keep in mind his readers' needs and levels of understanding, and this questioning method is an example of that, a sign of the master teacher working "from the known to the unknown."

Another notable feature of the series is the change of approach at the second article. The first piece was offered as a monthly installment ("Read Chapter 1 in sections and as a whole this month . . ."), but the subsequent seven pieces were decidedly *weekly* in structure and they were presented in like manner thereafter. We thus can trace the development of the Daily Bible Readings to a weekly forebear, which actually commenced on a monthly basis. The daily need was not forgotten even in this less frequent cycle, for in the first weekly piece Willie asked, "Have you a time set aside in daily life when you look and speak (even in slender faith) to him?"[52] And this attitude is repeated and recommended later: "life must be a daily increasing submission to His will."[53]

Robertson Nicoll, one of the all-time great Christian editors and journalists, once commented that there are four essential features of a successful periodical (which he brilliantly fulfilled in his own highly successful journal, *The British Weekly*): Thrills, News, Sense, and Pastimes. It is not too much to say that this all-round balance was a feature of Willie's Bible-commentating success too, as it had been a feature of his pastoral ministry. It was certainly characteristic of his journalistic pieces even when expositional. (Shortly after this time he became a member of the Scottish Institute of Journalists.) We have already seen how his resolve to be "intelligible" had been taking shape in his mind and, Bible lover that he was, when it came to expounding the scriptures, his mind could not but put these things into practice. He was able to keep interest alive by apt citation of his favorite authors—Shakespeare, Matthew Arnold, Hilaire Belloc, Francis Thompson, Augustine, Gossip, Wesley, Carey, Scott (all of whom are cited in this series).

Even this short piece shows how he sought to move his readers by the wonder ("thrills") of the gospel story. Awe and wonder, reverence and joy, were marks of his own devotional spirit and found regular expression in his preaching and writing. They are proof of not only a lively mind, but a lively ongoing religious experience—the experience of the risen Christ.

But, like the scribe of old (see Matt. 13:52), he is ever seeking to distribute things new and old from his store. And in the most literal sense, Willie's expositions were "news," expounding the passage before him by drawing on the universal and historic heritage of the church, whatever the denomination or provenance of his sources—and not only of the church! Free Churchman that he originally was, it is natural that he found good exposition useful whatever the source. To those who read his articles it was news in the strictly biblical sense, too, an exposition of the *euangelion*—the good news of Jesus Christ.

All of this was put forward without betraying his balanced and commonsense approach to life. There were never any flights of fancy in his periods, never any loss of contact with hard reality. To speak of his commonsense approach is to raise again Willie's bold humanity, his appreciation and enjoyment of "the common things of life." He did not hanker after unnecessary refinement or highbrow things, though he could, and did, appreciate things that were refined in themselves and often regarded as highbrow (e.g., the classics, great literature, music, drama, and so on). Such things he took naturally, and kept them in close touch with everyday reality and the ordinary experiences of people's lives. "Jesus," he said uncompromisingly, in commenting on Mark 8:1–9 and 22–26, "taught men to see God in common things";[54] he went on approvingly to quote Wordsworth, who regarded the world as "the garment of the living God." It was this "natural theology" element (a phrase that carried a broader meaning for Willie than it does in common usage, applying not only to the physical world, but also to the evolution of man and of human history) that kept him anchored to life, always without bathos.

It was thus part of his "sensible" approach that justified the vigorous rehearsal of his own pastimes and allowed him to recognize their validity in others' lives and use them as apt vehicles for getting at higher meaning and truth. If they "lowered the tone" of an exposition by making it homely, they also vastly increased its range and usefulness. I well remember the sense of shock I had when, in the course of interviewing one of Scotland's best-known philosophical theologians about Willie's role, he mentioned that he and his colleagues regarded Willie "as the Annie S. Swan of theology." It was a highly demeaning comment. Mrs. Swan, after all, was not theologically enlightened; she was a novelist, and only came to contribute to the religious scene of Scotland by way of her secular writings, through which she became one of the earliest "agony aunts" in the history of journalism. (The wife of a doctor, she stayed, despite her great success, close to the people of whom and for whom she wrote.) Willie's contributions were infinitely higher than those of Mrs. Swan, and broader, and longer lasting. But if he learned anything at all from such members of the Kailyard School, it was that he knew the people for whom he wrote, understood and responded to their common humanity, moods, defeats, and aspirations, and was unwilling to serve merely their intellectual or religious needs. Like Thomas Chalmers, Willie had "a passion for intellectual generalisations" and could spot and fasten on to the main point, applying it acutely to daily behavior. He appreciated the needs of the whole man (pastimes and all), and served the needs of the spirit, of the heart and the soul, and only indirectly of the intellect.

His first contributions to *Life and Work* were commissioned sometime during the late summer or autumn of 1947. Not long after this (perhaps because of the response it aroused) the Publications Committee of the Church of Scotland decided to take up a scheme for which the International Bible Reading Association was famous, which had been relaunched in the autumn of 1945 under the title *Daily Bible Studies*. Within three months of this relaunching, *The British Weekly* was reporting the immense success of this scheme, commenting that "people of all ages" were using the booklets provided.[55] Not that daily readings schemes were new to Scotland, of course; they had often been tried in the past. Thomas Chalmers, for example, wrote three volumes of daily scripture readings. But the most successful author of them was Alexander Whyte, whose "Welfare of Youth Scheme" had, by 1892, over a hundred affiliated societies that enthusiastically encouraged its twenty-five thousand members to use his *Daily Bible Reading Programme*. By 1894 over forty thousand were doing so, thus confirming Sir Walter Scott's opinion of Scotland being a people of one book. Most of the handbooks commissioned by both the Youth and the Publications Committees carried daily reading in the text, as did Willie's, as we shall see.

Behind all this activity and interest lay the influence of the National Bible Society of Scotland, whose recent survey of biblical guides had shown the scarcity of the right sort of material. Consequently, Jack Stevenson had been in touch with the International Bible Reading Association (IBRA) and it would appear that Willie's series was a trial run of a new scheme written to test its possibilities. It was decided not to use the material of the British organization (despite its international name and appeal), but to produce a uniquely Scottish system, though the IBRA would be responsible for the actual printing and binding. Aubrey G. Smith, a former General Secretary of the IBRA, recalled the occasion:

> The International Bible Reading Association received an approach from Reverend J W Stevenson . . . as a result of which I travelled to Edinburgh for discussions which resulted in our agreeing to launch special editions of daily Bible reading notes for the Church of Scotland, carrying their name. . . . Jack Stevenson supplied names of Church of Scotland ministers and lay people whom he suggested should be invited to contribute material to the new booklets; one of the first was William Barclay. I remember visiting him in Glasgow to discuss the work he was undertaking for us. We travelled, I recall, on top of a double-decker bus through the Glasgow streets, and sat in my hotel room considering a scheme I had drawn up.[56]

And Willie recalled it too: "It was just then," he said, "that a chance to do something came to me out of the blue."[57] As if he were not already doing something!

And so it was that he became a Bible commentator at an international level, via *Life and Work* and the good offices of the IBRA, which extended his influence beyond Scotland through joint productions with the Church of Scotland. The IBRA immediately detected the skills of this new writer, finding space for his expositions in their international editions within three months of the appearance of the Scottish edition and encouraging him to continue to write for them after the Church of Scotland's scheme had folded up.

Accordingly, toward the end of September 1948, a small (four-by-five-inch) booklet of thirty-two pages came into the shops, Book Rooms, and vestries under the significant title *Life and Work Daily Bible Studies: The Foundation of Christian Faith, The Gospel according to Saint Luke.* It was designed for the last quarter of that year and was published "in conjunction with the International Bible Reading Association." Appropriately, Jack Stevenson supplied a preface to the Scottish edition entitled "Ask!"; Robert Denholm, then the Honorary Secretary of the IBRA, supplied one for the international edition. To help launch the idea, Stevenson wisely prevailed on Willie to write another short (three-part) series for *Life and Work;* he did, and the series was published in the September, October, and November 1948 issues under the title "The world's most beautiful book." The three parts comprised a general introduction to the Gospel of Luke, its character-istics, and its universal appeal, respectively.

And so the Readings were launched, at eight pence a copy (only sixpence if the purchaser bought ten or more copies). It met with instant and quite breath-taking success. By October the editor was reporting dramatic sales. Innovative marketing techniques were used throughout the land. For example, a Fife church placed copies in the pews and invited members to take them and pay via the collection plates (230 copies were thus sold), and in Aberdeenshire specimen copies were distributed to *every* home in one parish. It shows that Jack Stevenson was not only a great editor (at once in touch with the contemporary situation, and the needs of his readers), but possessed great powers of commercial exploi-tation too. By December he was reporting that stocks (of eight thousand) were completely exhausted.

Willie recalled the event to his friend Braidwood at the beginning of 1949, and we should note especially the astonishing (total) circulation being achieved, which Willie himself seems to have difficulty in believing:

> Outside the College I have been busy with my pen. I have been doing daily bible readings with three hundred words of comment on each day's reading for the Church [of Scotland] and for the International Bible Reading Association. It does not sound difficult to turn out three hundred words per day but it is a big task when you take it by the year. They have been selling up to about fifty thousand copies a time.[58]

It is significant that Willie should have been the pilot author of the scheme; we shall shortly see him continuing the work, albeit in a different form, after others had been dropped off. Mention was made that Stevenson had recom-mended several Church of Scotland ministers to do this work. Their contributions soon followed: G. J. Jeffrey and B. Burnet provided the Notes for the next quarter, January to March of 1949, and J. Alexander Findlay, Frederick Greeves, and Willie did so for those of April to June. Willie covered the whole of April. His contributions were based on miscellaneous passages of scripture gathered round the theme "Easter Meditations." They were later excerpted in *Life and Work* under the title "Gleanings from William Barclay." The period from July to September saw Willie at it again, this time writing alongside G. W. Anderson, expounding Ephesians and Philippians. They continued to collaborate in the final quarter of the year, Willie expounding 1 and 2 Corinthians.

But there was some evidence already of the difficulty the sponsors found in finding the right men to do the job, and this was confirmed on the back page of the last booklet. It had been intended expressly to be "an all-Scottish course"— perhaps unwisely. The editor admitted that as yet no writer had been found to handle "The Beginnings of the Church in the New Testament," the subject chosen for the following year. One need not think long to guess who would be found to fill the gap at short notice. He who had done so when the correspondence course of the Scottish Sunday School Union ran into difficulties and who had sacrificially written the SSSU Lesson Notes for several years was but a telephone call away. And he could not allow any opportunity to go by unseized.

The difficulties encountered were sadly of the planners' own making—not only because of their insistence on an all-Scottish edition, which also had the sad effect of increasing the booklet's costs (collaboration on an international edition would have decreased them), but also because of their immoderate ambition. Encouraged by the early success of the Daily Readings, they quickly launched a similar scheme for children in January 1950 under the name *The Sword*, the first two quarters of which (on the Gospel of Mark and "The Last Days" of Jesus) were also written by Willie. It failed to make the sort of impact its predecessor enjoyed, and was reduced from four three-month booklets to two six-month booklets in 1951, after which it expired altogether. Yet another new series, called "Series B," was produced for readers older than those for whom *The Sword* was designed, but "less advanced" than the audience for the normal Readings. Once again Willie was found ready and able to fulfill the Committee's requests. He contributed Notes on a wide range of biblical passages and themes: James, Philippians (this being a specially "downgraded" reworking of what he had written for the Notes of July to September 1949), "Stories Jesus Told," "The Hymns of Israel" (various Psalms), "God and Myself" (i.e., the Fatherhood of God), Genesis 27–50, and "The King and the Kingdom" (readings for Christmas). James Reid wrote the Notes for 1951. But again the new scheme was proving too ambitious and the final edition of the year carried an editorial note informing its readers of the Committee's intention to amalgamate "Series B" with "Series A" for 1952. The scheme had gone full circle, and not without cost.

The normal Notes for the first half of 1951 were written by Willie, T. Ralph Morton, and G. B. Hewitt; a whole galaxy of ministers—Edwin S. Towill, G. B. Hewitt, James Wright, and T. P. Strachan (the latter Willie had met at his Keith

Mission it will be recalled)—contributed to the second part of the year. The same approach was adopted for 1952, in which no fewer than twelve different themes were treated by eight different authors—one of whom was Willie, who wrote on the books of Ezra and Nehemiah, Joshua and Judges, and Proverbs, and on the theme "Christian Hope amid the World's Despair" (based on Revelation). It is an outstanding example of the destructive powers of a committee in a field where more personal skills are required. Once again Stevenson commented on the need for reducing the series, his explanation that it was due to "the steep rise in printing and paper costs" being but a half-truth. The real problem was the reduction of the market into too many component parts and a consequent loss in the normal economies of scale. It was not helped by the decision to use many hands in Note writing (all of them far less practiced than Willie)—always a beguiling temptation in a church that prides itself on a learned ministry. The seeds of disaster were sprouting.

Meanwhile, the IBRA had latched onto Willie's great success by commissioning him to write the Notes for the whole of 1950. These covered John; Ezra and Nehemiah; Joshua; The Lord's Prayer (Willie's first published series on this favorite of passages); selections from Amos, Isaiah, Jeremiah, and Hosea; "The Works of Jesus"; "Paul the Dauntless"; "The Risen Christ and the Power of Darkness"; "The Wisdom of Israel"; and Christmas and end-of-year readings. Willie's notes on Luke were reprinted in their January–March 1949 Daily Bible Studies, and those on Easter and the books of Ephesians, Philippians, and 1 and 2 Corinthians followed in 1951. He also wrote their complete Notes for all of 1952.

The IBRA had undertaken all the production work for the Church of Scotland. When Willie wrote his autobiography, he was at pains to exempt the Association and the various contributors from responsibility for the failure: "Through no fault of the association or of the writers, the series did not sell, and the association . . . was forced to discontinue them."

As their Honorary Secretary commented in the preface to the 1951 edition, it was a new system they were offering. Willie had continued the much-loved habit he had established in his parish magazine and in *The Scottish Sunday School Teacher* of providing "Thoughts for the Day" and prayers. They were looking forward, the jubilant organizers of the IBRA commented, to "great things" from their new "skilled expositor." Just how great these expectations were may be judged by the fact that the international edition was then being produced in no fewer than twenty-eight languages, and plans were afoot to increase this by adding translations into the Efik and Ibo dialects of Nigeria and resuming translation halted by the war into Polish and other languages. Enter William Barclay, international commentator. It was a good start to the IBRA's sixty-eighth year, and Willie was glad to share in it. Not least did he share the reality of the IBRA hymn:

> Thy Word is Truth—the Truth that burns,
> And breaks, and binds, and sets men free.

Now let Thy Truth sweep through the World
And bring its wayward heart to Thee.

A False Start: Orthodoxy Reconsidered

But even this aspect of Willie's involvements does not exhaust his interests and energies, challenged as he was now with a dual responsibility: meeting both the needs and hard-nosed questionings of his theological students, and the quite different needs of his daily readers. The one group sought truth, oftentimes through doubting statements and conflicting theories; the other sought sustenance. The needs of both groups came together, as Willie knew instinctively and by hard-won profession, in Jesus. But who was this Jesus? What was he? And how can he fill the needs of both at this point in the twentieth century? Willie's essential emphasis, after all, was not that "of a figure in a book," but someone who "is with us always wherever we are and wherever we go."

Writing to this friend Braidwood on New Year's Day 1949, Willie commented "I have been busy with my pen. . . ." He had been indeed: the Daily Bible Readings schemes, *Ambassador for Christ*, three handbooks for the Boys' Brigade (of which more later) and, most interesting of all, he states,

> In my spare time [!] . . . I am at work on a book on New Testament Christology. It will be years before it emerges; my only object in writing a book which no one will ever read is to prove that I too can write unintelligibly when I want to. I have also been preaching every Sunday.

We should note the purport of this final sentence. His written work was ever done in a framework of practical church life.

But what of this book? And what of his curious motives (even given his incorrigible sense of humor) in so preparing to write it? This book never appeared—it was never more than a private essay—but it is wholly characteristic of Willie's theology that the only writing he ever undertook without an invitation from a publisher was an essay on Christology. He was a man of two impulses: Christ and his people; his faith and actions oscillated between, and for, the two. And although he soon found that he had no need to prove himself, at least other than in academic circles, he did outgrow the challenge to write "unintelligibly." It is a significant circumstance, for had he published this piece, his career might well have taken a very different turn indeed, inasmuch as the views expressed therein mark a point of departure in his theology.

It expresses radically different views from those of his upbringing, of his ordination faith, of his brief commentary on the *Short Statement of the Church's Faith* of 1940, and even of the more recent works listed above. The viewpoint is old hat now, but in the pre-Bonhoeffer, pre–J. A. T. Robinson era, it was strong stuff, and would have produced a reaction on a far broader scale than his pacifist pronouncements in Renfrew had ten years earlier. There can be no doubt that it would have brought to an abrupt end his involvement with the Scottish Sunday

School Union, the Boys' Brigade, and most probably with the Church of Scotland Youth Committee, too. Not that he did not already have his critics, most of whom were brother ministers. Mrs. Rita Perry, a Sunday School teacher of the time, has recounted one such criticism made of him at a refresher course for missionaries at which he and Robert Menzies were the main speakers.[59] She overheard, much to her dismay, one of the listeners remark, "Of course, everyone knows that Barclay is no theologian"—a statement his old tutor A. B. Macaulay, would have keenly contested. It reminds one of the comment of a member who left Trinity Church, Renfrew, toward the end of Willie's ministry there because he found his theology unacceptable—though in respect to his understanding of Willie's doctrine of sin, not regarding his teachings concerning Christ.[60] Those who have read carefully Willie's statements about evil, not least in his word studies and expositions, may be surprised to hear of such a censure. But it again highlights his manner, rather than his matter—his passion for "intelligibility," the intelligibility of the Gospels, of the law of love, and his ability to emphasize one issue over others, to omit certain lines of argument or evidence in order to highlight others.

In any case, this is what he wrote; despite its being long and sketchy, it is worth producing in full.

1. *The Necessity of Christology.* It is perfectly possible to regard certain doctrines and certain parts of Christian Theology as things which are "indifferent." No great harm will result if in regard to them we preserve an attitude of suspended judgement or even of reverent agnosticism. But to whatever parts of doctrine that attitude may legitimately apply it cannot and must not apply to Christology. If it is true to say that "Christianity is Christ," and it is true so to say, then we must be clear as to who[m] and as to what we believe Jesus Christ to be.

2. *Theology and Temperament.* The difficulty of giving any one answer to that question springs from the fact that there is not any one answer. I do not think that the part that temperament plays in theology has ever been sufficiently realised and appreciated. Undoubtedly a man's temperament will play at least some part in the theology in which he finally comes to rest.

a) *The Mystic.* In regard to Christology the differing temperaments will send a man to differing solutions. The Mystic will not require any theological doctrine at all. He will not think his way to the truth; he will feel his way to the truth. He will not try to understand so much as to be alone with the alone and to lose himself in Christ. In a way he will be right because, as has been well said, "We admire people for reasons; but we love people without reasons." Love is not in essence a reasoning or a reasonable thing, and love is the basis of mysticism.

b) *The Authoritarian.* The Authoritarian on the other hand will be more than willing, he will be eager to accept. That the thing passes comprehension will be nothing to him. There is a certain type of mind which can still echo Tertullian's "credo quia impossibile" ["I believe because it is impossible"]. There is indeed a certain type of mind to which nothing is great unless it is unintelligible and which will insist on repeating over and over again that Christian theology is in the end bound to be unintelligible anyway, that the very nature of the infinity of God makes it so.

It may be said that that is far more a pagan than a Christian outlook. The Christian conception of God is that God is a self-revealing God; and if God be a self-revealing God then, as some one has audaciously said, the mind of man has a right to demand that God should stand and deliver. It is no part of Christian theology to take the intellectually cowardly resting place of the impenetrability of God.

c) *The Searcher.* The third kind of temperament is that which for a better name we can only call that of the thinker or the searcher. To give that name to the third temperament is not to disparage the other two or to look at them with any kind of conscious superiority. But there are those who have a passion to understand. Athenaeus in that gastronomic and intellectual banquet of his, *The Deipnosophistae,* says amidst all the physical food, "We feed on questions." There is a type of mind which must have its questions answered or perish.

To this type of mind there is one kind of theological outlook which is completely inadequate—that is the outlook, by no means uncommon, which insists that the Christian faith is a series of paradoxes, which must be set side by side before the truth can be arrived at and that, if one arm of the paradoxes is unduly stressed, then heresy immediately arrives upon the scene. Chesterton declared that Christian faith is like a man walking along a narrow knife-edged precipice. One step to the right, or one to the left, and disaster follows. Now, at least for some people, perhaps for most people, it is impossible to find final rest for the mind in a paradox. How after all could a man ever know rest and peace if he spent his intellectual life tightrope-walking on the edge of a mental precipice? In the last analysis surely it must be true that a man can only find satisfaction and rest for his mind and his heart and his spirit in something of which he can say, "This is true, because it satisfies my heart and my mind, my feelings and my intellect."

And that is the reason why over and over again a man is under the necessity of trying to work out some Christology which is his own. That he will almost certainly finish up a heretic does not greatly matter, because, as T. R. Glover, quoting Dean Inge, used to love to say, "The genius of Christianity is to be recognised chiefly in its heretics."

3. *The Two Christologies.* Broadly speaking in the early Church there were two types of Christology. Both regarded Jesus Christ as divine in the fullest sense of the term. But they approached the matter from opposite sides. The one regarded Jesus Christ as a pre-existent divine being who had become human. That Christology found its centre in Ephesus. The other regarded Jesus Christ as a human being who had been taken up into divinity. That Christology was largely connected with Rome and with Antioch. It happened in the history of Christian thought that the first type of Christology became the Christology of the Church and triumphed at Nicaea and Chalcedon; while the second kind of Christology became branded as a heresy and is the basic thought of Adoptionism. It never wholly died out, but it never ceased to be greeted with cries of horror whenever and wherever it raised its head.

4. *Adoptionism.* I do not propose to deal in detail with the history of Adoptionism. Suffice it to say that I think that it can be proved that there is a strong strain of Adoptionism in New Testament thought and that it occurs not only in the primitive Christology of the very early Church, but even in the thought of Paul; that it reappears in full strength in *The Shepherd* of Hermas; that its real intellectual father is Paul of Samosata; that it is again at the basis of Nestorianism; and that it came to its full

fruition in the 9th century in the persons of Elipandus of Toledo and Felix of Urgel against whom Alcuin campaigned, and campaigned successfully. It is to be noted that it is only the ninth century manifestation to which theologians technically give the name of Adoptionism.

Although it really much oversimplifies it, we may define Adoptionism by saying that Adoptionism believes that Jesus was a man into whom God came.

What we shall proceed to do now is to look at the New Testament to see whether or not it gives us any justification for this view of Jesus; then to glance very briefly at some of its post–New Testament manifestations; and then to look at certain of its repercussions and, finally, to ask if there be anything of value in it.

5. *Adoptionism in the New Testament.* If we are looking for Adoptionism in the New Testament it is clear that we must begin by looking for something which must of necessity precede Adoptionism. The predecessor of Adoptionism must be Subordinationism. There is not the slightest difficulty in discovering Subordinationism in the New Testament, because it is there. Over and over again in all the gospels, both Synoptic and Johannine, Jesus repeatedly refers to "Him that sent me":

a) The Synoptic Gospels.
Luke 4:18: "He hath sent me to heal the broken-hearted."
Luke 9:48: "Whosoever receiveth me receiveth him that sent me."
Luke 10:16: "He that despiseth me despiseth him that sent me."

There are things that are not known to him but known only to the father:
Mark 13:32: "But of that day and that hour knoweth no man. No, not the angels which are in heaven, neither the Son but the Father."
Matt. 31:33ff.: Again the point comes out in the very significant parable of the Wicked Husbandman. Again in that parable the son, who can only be Jesus Himself, is sent.

Now it might be held that that is not so very surprising in the Synoptic gospels; but what is far more surprising is that this Subordinationism is even more apparent in the Fourth Gospel, high as the Christology of the Fourth Gospel may be.

b) *The Fourth Gospel.*
John 4:34: "My meat is to do the will of him that sent me and to finish his work."
John 5:19: "The Son can do nothing of himself but what He seeth the Father do."
John 6:38: "I came down from heaven not to do my own will but the will of him that sent me."
John 9:4: "I must work the works of him that sent me while it is day."

c) *Acts.* For the moment regarding the Book of Acts we will notice only one thing—that the Resurrection is the centre of early faith and belief, and that the Resurrection is always looked on as the work of God the Father. There is not the slightest suggestion that the Resurrection was as it were a triumphant victory achieved by Jesus; always the Resurrection is a vindication of Jesus by the exercise of the power of God.

d) *Paul.* Just as in Acts, so in the Pauline epistles. The Resurrection is entirely the work of God:
1 Cor. 6:14: "*God* hath raised up the Lord."
2 Cor. 13:4: "He liveth by the power *of God.*"
Philippians 2:9: "*God* also hath highly exalted him." (On this passage the whole background of thought is that the Resurrection is a *reward;* a signal mark of favour).
Romans 4:24: "*Him* that raised up the Lord Jesus Christ."

So in Paul the coming of Christ into the world is the result of the will of God:
Romans 3:25: "Whom *God* hath set forth to be a propitiation."
Romans 8:3: "*God* sent his Son in the likeness of sinful flesh."
Ephesians 1:17: "the *God* of our Lord Jesus Christ."

In Paul, there are not wanting indications even more definite than this of a Subordinationist view in the Pauline Epistles.
1 Cor. 11:3: "The head of every man is Christ and the head of Christ is God."
1 Cor. 15:28: This speaks of the final victory of Christ and then goes on to say, "And when all things shall be subdued unto him then shall the Son also himself be subject unto him that put all things under him, that God may be all in all."

e) The Apocalypse. It is sufficient regarding the Apocalypse to point out that in it the glorified Christ is made to address God as *his* God.

All through the New Testament there runs this strong Subordinationist strain of thought. In point of fact it could not be otherwise. The New Testament is a Jewish book and the Jewish faith was stubbornly and consistently monotheistic. It is the natural outcome of this that nothing is allowed to interfere with, or to lessen the supreme authority of, God.

f) Certain Special Passages. It is therefore clear that on the general grounds of Subordinationism there is no insuperable barrier to the Adoptionist conception.

But is there any definite evidence for the existence of a distinctively Adoptionist Christology in the early Church?

We must begin with the most suggestive and significant of all passages—Acts 2:22.

[Two numbered sheets of the original manuscript have been removed from this section, alas, which deprive us of twenty percent of his argumentation, which had to deal with the biblical proofs of this "Subordinationist" section.]

6. *Hermas.* Going beyond the New Testament we come to Hermas. In the case of Hermas there is no doubt at all; there is positive Adoptionist teaching. He tells a parable about a servant who was sent to work in a vineyard and who did his work in a supremely obedient and a supremely excellent way. Then the master adopted him unto his own mastership; and he gives the explanation:

> The Holy Spirit which is pre-existent, which created all creation, did God make to dwell in the flesh he willed. Therefore this flesh in which the Holy Spirit dwelled, served the Spirit well, walking in holiness and purity, and did not in any way defile the spirit. When therefore it had lived nobly and purely, and had laboured with the spirit, and worked with it in every deed, behaving with power and bravery, he chose it as companion with the Holy Spirit; for the conduct of this flesh pleased Him, because it was not defiled while it was bearing the Holy Spirit upon earth . . . (Therefore he decided that) this flesh also having served the Spirit blamelessly should have some place of sojourn and not seem to have lost the reward of its service.

It is a difficult passage and comes in a difficult section, but the only possible meaning of it is that the man Jesus served God so well that he was finally adopted into the very life and being of God.

We must glance very briefly at two names, names of men who are not reckoned

379

Adoptionists, and who yet definitely have a place in the lineage of the Adoptionist Christology.

7. Paul of Samosata. The first is Paul of Samosata, who flourished about 265 A.D. He started with two main ideas: First, he refused to allow the logos any personal existence, but insisted that Jesus, who was born of Mary, was entirely a human figure; but into him the logos came. But the logos was only present in him as an indwelling spirit as wisdom was in the prophets. What makes Jesus different from others was the logos [that] dwelt in him in a unique degree; he was, as Mackintosh puts it, "a temple for the higher presence." With such an endowment of the logos Jesus kept himself in a relationship of perfect love and of perfect obedience to God. In virtue of this perfection of love and obedience Jesus acquired such transcendent merit that he became in the realest sense the son of God. Apparently he fixed the entry of Jesus into son-ship at his baptism and held that his Resurrection was the final consummation of it.

Here then we have the same basic thought, the thought of a human person who so entered into and was so united with the mind of God that he became God, and so can be truly called the Son of God.

8. Nestorius. The other name which must be briefly glanced at is Nestorius; very briefly, Nestorius held that in the person of Jesus there were two natures. Jesus is fully man; but God is present in him in complete fulness as He was partially in the prophets of old. But this presence of God is by grace and by favour and not as it were in essence. What unites the two natures is a moral bond. Here again is this same ever-recurring thought—that it was the perfect loving unity between the mind of God and the mind of Jesus that made Him in the unique sense son.

9. Elipandus. The position of the later Adoptionists was more complicated. They held that the son in his divinity was divine by nature and by race; but that in his humanity, in the person of the man Jesus, the son was *adopted* into the sonship of God.

10. The Unity between God and Jesus. We are now pressed back on the great question, "Wherein does the unity between God and Jesus Christ consist?" It was characteristic of Greek thought that it sought that unity in metaphysical and essential terms; but let us turn to the New Testament.

11. The Unity of Mind. That which ultimately makes a man what he is comes from his mind; that part of him which can and does dominate the body and control the emotions. The essential man is in the mind.

Now in the Synoptic gospels we get a very significant parallel passage:
Mark 1:38 reads, "Let us go into the next towns, that I may preach there also, *for therefore came I forth.*"
Luke 4:43 is the parallel and it reads, "I must preach the kingdom of God to other cities also, *for therefore am I sent.*"

Now there you have the same thing stated twice, but it is stated with a very significant difference. In the first instance it is actively stated, *"for therefore I came forth."* In the second instance it is passively stated, *"for therefore was I sent."* To Jesus it was one and the same thing to speak actively of doing a thing and to speak passively of being sent by God to do it. So completely was his will one with God's will that to speak of doing a thing was to him exactly the same thing as to speak of being sent to do it.

There is an echo of this in Galatians 1:4 where Paul speaks of Jesus, "who gave *himself* for us that he might deliver us from this present evil world, *according to the will of God.*"

The action of Christ was active: He gave himself; it was also passive: it was according to the will of God. But so identical was the will of Christ with the will of God that the active and the passive expression mean one and the same thing.

Now herein is just the point where we must take care. Pressed to its logical conclusion this might issue in Apollinarianism; it might be taken to mean that the logos or the spirit of God was indeed the mind and will of Christ, dwelling within him.

12. *The Development (of Jesus).* But that is not the case; and it is in fact here that we come across one of the great values of this Adoptionist line of thought.

One of the puzzles of any orthodox Christology is the question, "How could Jesus develop at all? If he was in essence the son of God where is the room for any kind of development?" And on any orthodox Christology how are you going to think of the child in the manger and the growing boy and the young man without a perfectly monstrous picture? W. M. Macgregor quotes (in *Jesus Christ, the son of God,* p. 113, 114) with his own incredulous scorn, a passage from A. B. Davidson,

> Did it ever strike you that Christ never was a child? . . . You do not fancy him a child like your children, gay and free of concern; he was grave, retired, and sad. He moved about with a weight upon him. It is not anywhere recorded of him that he smiled . . . You can hardly fancy that he ever looked young.

Beyond a doubt you cannot think otherwise of Jesus in terms of ordinary Christology, because ordinary Christology leaves no room for development because at all times this person Jesus was perfectly God. Whatever else Adoptionism does, it avoids that monstrous inhuman picture of a child who was no child. Either Jesus was never in any sense a man; or at some time he became conscious of a certain relationship to God; and once you have said that you are not far from Adoptionism.

But the Adoptionist line of thought leaves room for this development in the personal life of Jesus. For he who holds the Adoptionist position, or something like it, must go on to say this—that the unity of the will of God and the will of Christ was not something which was automatic, it was not an attribute; it was an acquirement; and it was the outcome of a constant struggle. Here we have facts on our side. What is the story of the Temptations but the story of a struggle, a choice between two ways, the way of man and the way of God?

Why was Jesus almost violent to Peter at Caesarea Philippi? Was it not because that which Peter suggested was precisely that against which he was struggling? If the struggle in Gethsemane was not a real struggle then words mean nothing. That at least was not play-acting. And in every case the effort was to keep His will in this complete identity with God's will.

The more I think of this the more I am convinced that therein is the unity between Jesus Christ and God. If there could be any one who identified his will with God, then that person would speak with the very voice of God; that person would act with the very action of God; that person would live the very life of God within the limits of humanity; that person would acquire the very power of God in a way that no one else could . . . and that is precisely what Jesus did.

We may think of the thing this way—God's purpose of salvation was an eternal purpose; God always acts through men; He had to find someone who would completely identify His will with God's will, and through that man God acted and God took that man into Himself.

13. *The "when?" of the Adoption.* When did that adoption take place? Many answers have been given to that. It might be answered as early as the visit to the temple when Jesus was twelve. More often it [is] answered that it took place at the Baptism when Jesus made his decision, when the spirit descended upon him, and when he heard God's voice. It could be argued that it happened at whatever happened on the Mount of Transfiguration; it could be argued that it happened in Gethsemane; and it is often argued that it was completed at the Resurrection. But happen it did.

14. *Adoptionism and the Atonement.* It has often been objected that one of the gravest difficulties about Adoptionism is that it leaves no room for any doctrine of the Atonement. But that is not wholly true. It will still be true that God was in Christ reconciling the world unto himself. Only one in whom dwelt the mind of God could bring to men the message of God's love for man and God's hatred of sin; only one in whom dwelt the mind of God could show men what God was like. In the most real sense such a one can be called the Son of God and is kin to God.

Even the sacrificial element in the Atonement is safeguarded and it is doubly safe-guarded. It is a sacrifice on the part of God that this person who had become his Son should be so condemned to suffer. And there is something else—suppose we take into consideration the idea of Christ being the representative of humanity. Then he, just because he was perfect, brought to God a perfect life and a perfect sacrifice for all men.

15. *The Objections.* One of the great objections which has always been [made], was [made] from the very first to Adoptionism, is the risk of it from the point of view of God. It is objected that if anything like Adoptionism is true then everything depended on the action and the life of Jesus. Had he failed, then all God's plan failed and God's salvation was hindered. Is not that the case in any view of Jesus? Surely no Christology would conceive of Jesus as in the grip of a completely unavoidable fate which drove him inescapably and inevitably to the Cross. Do we not see clearly from the gospel narrative that Jesus could time and time again have chosen a different way? Is not that the case in the wilderness? And is it not the case in Gethsemane? Is there any reasonable view of the work of Christ which takes away this risk? This is just what is meant by the statement that Jesus is the pivot of all history. It was literally true that everything depended on him—and that is precisely what Adoptionism says, with more force than any other Christology.

16. *Conclusion.* Adoptionism is a curiously neglected conception. Even one so unnoted for orthodoxy as Kirsopp Lake can say,

> Adoptionism seems to me to have no part or lot in any intelligent modern theology.

Yet unquestionably there is something to be said for it. It conserves, as few Christologies do, the real unequivocal manhood of Christ; it expresses, as few Christologies do, the relationship of Jesus to God in a way that is intelligible.

Vincent Taylor once said that a theology to be a good theology must be reducible to a tract. Certainly a man might preach the great truths that lie in the Adoptionist position. For not only do they give a living vital picture of Christ, even in spite of their inadequacies, but more, they offer to all men the highest of all destinies—they tell a man that he may take the same way as Christ took and that, by the grace of Christ, he may become as Christ.

It is not within the province of the biographer "to expound in detail, still less to criticise, the writings of the man whose life he is portraying."[61] But one is committed by Willie's own injunction as well as by the canon of good biography to be open, to describe him "warts an' all." And here, by any standard, we are confronted with an outsize theological excrescence. Except he did not see his theological position here as an *ex*-crescence (something that grows out of the real thing), but the restatement of the reality itself, the return to a biblical conception, a true "Christological" understanding of Jesus.

In the light of this there are certain things that we should bear in mind. The first and most important is that *he never allowed this paper to be published.* Some may well think his biographer at fault in allowing it to see the light of day over thirty years after its author penned it. I do so because I believe it throws great light on a crucial aspect of his theologizing—the way he did theology, his approach to theology. As such, it would be misleading to omit it.

The second point follows on from the first: *it was never finished: it remained tentative and explorative.* As he said to his friend Braidwood, "it will be years before it is published." Moreover, the reverse side of his final sheet is covered with penciled notes, offering more than two dozen additions to the actual typescript, many of them regrettably unreadable. This accounts for its uneven style—so unlike his normal style in parts—in which he did quite literally write "unintelligibly"! And it probably accounts for the missing two pages between items 5f and 6, which may well have been taken up into other lecture notes, leaving his Christological reconstruction to lie dormant, wakening from time to time in this or that book or interview or broadcast—usually to provoke discussion and thought.

Accordingly, my third point: we should understand that *he must be criticized by what he published,* not by that about which he evidently had second thoughts, and still less by what some people have *thought* he said. Christian theology, like Christian morality, depends on truth, integrity, sincerity. To misrepresent anyone is to betray truth, integrity, and sincerity. Alas, Willie has suffered at the hands of critics and would-be commentators who do not follow the rules, who are willing to denigrate rather than describe and evaluate justly. Some of these have simply turned their backs on the data and used their imaginations (if not their evil intentions) to subvert his reputation and undermine his authority.

We have already seen how during the nineteenth century the church was again learning to differentiate (as had the Reformers of old) between the primary and the subordinate standards, how it sought to bring dogma into line with biblical statement, and even some biblical emphases into line with "that which urges Christ"[62] and his truth. Willie was doing so no less, and he did so unfailingly. He would have been outraged—alike for its morality, as its theology— at the retort of one minister at the public examination for heresy of McLeod Campbell. Campbell was arguing fearlessly for an appeal to the Bible over the Westminster Confession. Retorted one of his examiners, "We are far from appeal- ing to the Word of God on this ground; it is by the Confession of faith we must stand; by it we hold our living."[63] Willie emphatically believed the Reformation principle of *sola scriptura*. And if he found, or thought he found, inconsistencies between Scripture and creed, if his own understanding of the biblical data did not confirm this or that aspect of creed or confession or conform to what he believed to be their essential and relevant thrust (*essential* and *relevant* are both keywords of his), he believed he had a duty to argue the case, to say so.

And so my fourth point is that *we must acknowledge his lack of fear or inhibitions in facing what he believed to be the full thrust of the biblical witness,* regardless of cherished doctrines: Jesus *and* Paul, James *and* John, Acts *and* Hebrews. It may be that he failed to interpret Scripture "correctly," it may be that we can fault him with "unorthodox theology," but at least we should credit him with having clearly seen in, and earnestly sought to claim for, the Bible what every self-respecting Protestant and Reformed Christian understands to be his birthright—namely, that "the Word of God, which is *contained in* [*nota bene!*] the Scriptures of the Old and New Testaments, is the only rule to direct us how we may glorify and enjoy [God]."[64] We would also do well to remind ourselves of the vows he made when he replied to the "Solemn Questions" during his ordination to the ministry of the Church of Scotland—that he did "most firmly believe the Word of God, which is contained in the Scriptures of the Old and New Testaments, to be the supreme rule of faith and life." "Contained in" is significantly the specific wording in both documents: Willie was well aware of the truth of the poet's perception (and poetry may well prove to be a better vehicle for such things than philosophical or credal modes) that

> Our little systems have their day;
>> They have their day and cease to be,
>> They are but broken lights of Thee.
> And thou, O Lord, art more than they.

As he forcefully, if briefly, stated at the time of writing this tentative essay in a popular ("intelligible") handbook, "the Bible is the text-book of the Christian."[65] And it will be recalled that it was on that basis that Mr. Fortune challenged him to frame "the decided answers" to the real, hard-nosed questions society was asking. Chiefest among such questions (and recent events and publications show that it still sustains its interest and its challenge) was the question "Who is Jesus?" or "What is Jesus?" And we may recall Jesus' own question to the disciples, "Whom do you say I am?" This is what Willie now sought to answer, albeit privately, in this essay.

As we have already seen, when we talk of Jesus in the theology of William Barclay we are at the very center of his thinking. Jesus, for William Barclay, is the fulcrum point, the pivot, the kernel, around which everything else turns, for as Willie never tired of emphasizing (using the words of Jesus in a key and favorite passage), "He who has seen me, has seen the Father."[66] That was the central affirmation in his faith, his foremost "decided answer." That, of course, is how the essay—and such it was, in the French sense of that word (i.e., a trial, an experiment)—commenced, following Griffith Thomas's brilliantly accurate epigram: "Christianity is Christ." That was not only Willie's most central theological affirmation; it was the truth after which he searched through his lifelong ministry, the end and the meaning of his life.

There are several further aspects which we may note about this Christological essay:

1. His willingness to concede that there are some doctrines over which one may be "indifferent." We shall presently see his agreeing with Donald Soper's and (before Soper) Heinrich Vogel's concept of "iron rations" in Christian truth[67]—that is, aspects that are *essential*. We shall need to delineate what they are, and to understand why Willie regarded other aspects as unnecessary shibboleths foisted "unlawfully" on people.

2. He ever preserved a place in his thinking (despite owning himself to be "a natural believer") for a form of "reverent agnosticism"—for suspending judgment on certain matters. We shall later see how he advocated *certitude* in the religious life, but not as an absolute covering all aspects of theology. He was honest enough to concede difficulties for what they were, be it a dubious point of Greek or Hebrew interpretation, a manuscript or papyrus uncertainty, a contradiction of evidence (e.g., between different Gospel accounts of the resurrection), a moral ambiguity, or whatever. No man, he would say, has the right of total certainty in all things; God has not chosen to make his mind known in total revelation.

3. His assertion that temperament, in addition to revelation and tradition, plays an important part in theological definition is a key aspect of his theological understanding. (We may note that he does not explain the temperament causation necessary to Adoptionism.) We shall see that it was ever a trait of his theologizing to set things side by side without drawing the connection explicitly—and perhaps permitting himself in so doing to overlook the fact that there was not always a logical progression between his points.

He does not say which he preferred among the three "types of theology" he delineates—the mystical, the authoritarian, and the searcher's. We shall soon see that there is a good deal of both the first (the mystic) and the third (the searcher) in Willie Barclay. And we shall see him inveigh again and again against the second type, the authoritarian, which he would insist negates the path of the mystic and nullifies the search of the honest enquirer, not least because it takes the things of the spirit—things that elsewhere he would claim are best expressed poetically—and reduces them to an inflexible code, often "unintelligibly."

We cannot pause here to ask whether a type of theology is *necessarily* unintelligible, nor whether it is fair to lump with this type Tertullian's exaggerated and overwrought exclamation. (Never was a perception more nearly an apperception than when Tertullian declaimed, "I believe because it is impossible!") But we are entitled to see in this essay a fulfillment of the earlier challenges to Willie's faith (not least to the orthodoxy he inherited from his father) and a promise of a purposeful, undeterred pursuit of integrity and truth according to his own lights. To such, a "God of the gaps" approach was a sign of intellectual cowardice, and was self-defeating in the long run. Theological doubt, on the other hand, he never regarded as being in any way unethical, weak, or unspiritual; it was part of the structure of thought and understanding itself—a junction on the way to a clearer comprehension. God could not be limited. Willie's view was ever the long view; "forward, not backward." His sympathies extended toward those who, like the searcher, possessed "a passion to understand," who, like Athenaeus of old, "fed on questions." In so doing he baldly rejected the principle of paradox, a principle he elsewhere found meaningful, and even essential.

4. He speaks of the need for working out one's own Christology. Is this merely a form of individualism, a species of old-time Protestantism that sniffed at the great creeds and the great councils of the church? Or is it not rather a profounder understanding that colors one's whole religious appreciation of the very essence of Christianity, a realization that unless one faces in a personal, responsible way the challenge of the living Christ of the Gospels, unless one steps out of the security and repetition of the historic formulas of the past, one risks a view of (and therefore a response to) Jesus that is hopelessly formal, staid, and unadventurous, that is essentially unreal? It is wholly in keeping with Willie's own inner security that he was unaffected by the need for domestic security, by being called names. He was careless, in fact, of being taken less than seriously by his colleagues, and may even be charged with sometimes being too insensitive to others' views. To such a man, being called a heretic "does not greatly matter"—which view carried the imprimatur of the Anglican Inge via the Baptist layman T. R. Glover! It was the recognition that whatever the claims of earthly authority (a present-day Solomon) or whatever the claims of divine symbol (a new ecclesiastical temple), a greater than Solomon, than the Temple, was here. . . . And Willie was in search of that other greatness of Jesus. Relentlessly.

5. Willie was not afraid to think adventurously, even as far back as before the '60s, at a time when there was a lull on the theological battlefields. This private essay presents us with an interesting insight into his contemporary view of doctrinal authority and credal affirmation: he can look with equal regard, apparently, at the conflicting biblical voices of Ephesus, Rome, and Antioch, and at the postbiblical creeds of Nicaea, Chalcedon, and elsewhere (even of Geneva and Westminster). And he can look on the emergent opinions as "a triumph," the one over the other, with almost the detachment he applied to one of his beloved football scores. He argued that mainline Adoptionism[68] developed after the ninth

century—a view that may be controverted—as if that made more acceptable the position that preceding generations had found wanting.

6. He turns to the biblical evidence as the real source of doctrinal verity (ignoring in the process the question of the virgin birth of Jesus and what it has long been held to imply, and other things in the New Testament besides Subordinationism), and looks for evidence of the reality beyond the great creeds and councils. And his present theology reflects change when compared with his former views. Gone now is the former assertion that Jesus is "God come down to this earth";[69] as he stated in an article in *The Renfrew Press,* "there was a man who was also God."[70] Jesus is now "a man into whom God came," a view he clearly finds justified in the New Testament and in "post–New Testament manifestations."

In passing, it should be noted that there was a disparity between his definition of Adoptionism in his third point ("Jesus Christ as a human being who had been taken up into divinity") and in that of his fourth point ("Jesus was a man into whom God came"), even if we bear in mind his explanation of the New Testament data being active and passive aspects of the one substance. It is another example of the unfinished nature of the piece, and does not affect its purport. A similar disparity exists between his call for clear thinking in point one—on the necessity of a defined Christology—and his bland acceptance that "there is not any one answer" in point two. (If that were really the case when he denies the validity of suspending judgment in Christology, then unclearness of thought may be yet another term for paradox—which he also denies.)

7. He finds the grounds of his doctrine of Adoptionism in Subordinationism. Jesus' complete obedience to the Father's will he interprets as proving the "pure humanity" in Jesus. (His comment at point ten that "the essential man is in the mind" affronts the normal doctrine of man as a tripartite unity of body, mind, and soul/spirit.) This definition of pure humanity necessitates a rejection of the doctrines of "Jesus' pre-existence, of the incarnation, of the virgin birth, as historically understood; of the dual nature of Jesus, of the *essential* deity of Jesus, of the tri-une God, and of the historic formulas of the Christian Church." It also necessitates a reassessment of some texts, such as John 1:14, a favorite text of Willie's the meaning of which he was later, and frequently, to argue in the traditional sense of the incarnation, namely, of God becoming man. Or we may take from the same Gospel Thomas's confession, "My Lord and my God." Incidentally, it is widely accepted that this Gospel was written in or near Ephesus—one of the centers, according to Willie's own argument, of the Subordinationist position, where the thinking and influence of Rome and Antioch were lightly regarded.

Willie rightly argues that New Testament Judaism was "stubbornly and consistently monotheistic" (though he could not be more wrong than when, in the same sentence, he says baldly that the New Testament "is a Jewish book"), but he fails to see that that is precisely the enigma, the paradox of the New Testament.

8. We should note some of the "Certain Special Passages" Willie does *not* deal with: Philippians 2:6–11 (Willie was faulted by H. Dean in *The Expository Times* in 1961 for "not drawing the significant conclusion" of this passage),[71] Colossians 1:15–18, the so-called trinitarian formula of Matthew 28:19–20, and Hebrews 2:3, to mention but a few. Willie is surely right to argue the dangers of proof texts, but that awareness can never be used to avoid statements that run counter to his preferences, that demand careful exegesis and theological integration. If such are avoided, one is entitled to shout "Foul!" Why did he not deal with these passages and several others like them not instanced? Why, for example, in rightly asserting that much of the New Testament ascribes the resurrection of Jesus to God's intervention and power, did he not come more carefully to terms with the Gospel of John, which speaks very differently, asserting Jesus' own power and nature—he who was the resurrection, who declared of his own life, "I have power to lay it down and have power to take it again"? We might also add from that same Gospel the *ego eimi* sayings of Jesus, the purport of which is very different from the purely human figure Willie described. Was it a realization of this incompleteness that caused him to leave unprinted his essay? During this period he held to the fourth Gospel in a curiously inequable way. No one can doubt his love for it, or the beauty of his conservative expositions of it, but despite his being aware that it was not then good form to use it too seriously as a history of Jesus' life (in *The Mind of Jesus* [1960] he expressly denied that he made this sort of use of it),[72] he frequently did so.

9. We need to remind ourselves of his method and approach in this essay: he progressed from the New Testament passages, through post–New Testament manifestations to repercussions, and then to assessments. His key New Testament material is gathered under the heading of Jesus' Subordinationism, and we need to remind ourselves that traditional theology (albeit under the umbrella of a paradox) has never wished to assert anything other than the total truth of this. Paul expressed it perfectly in Philippians, which Willie later splendidly translated as follows:

> He shared the very being of God,
> but he did not regard his equality to God
> as a thing to be clutched to himself.
>
> So far from that, he emptied himself,
> and really and truly became a servant,
> and was made for a time exactly like men.[73]

There is nothing incompatible between this Subordinationism and traditional Christian doctrine; indeed, the Subordinationism is a vital element of it. But it is going beyond the evidence to assert that it offers sufficient evidence to argue a "purely human Jesus" when the whole framework of the New Testament, the whole "scandal" of Jesus' descriptions of himself, and those of the early Christian preachers, argue otherwise. Incarnation and glorification, not filial adoption and deification, are surely the real emphases of the New Testament, the firm foundation on which all Christological belief are built.

10. In gathering together his post–New Testament data, one has to admit that Willie's choice of material is weak and one-sided. There is much more to weigh than *The Shepherd* of Hermas, Paul of Samosata, Nestorius, and Elipandus. Even accepting his attempt to redress the balance (as he would have seen it), it is not good argument to ignore so much traditional theology and historical development. And it is somewhat unnerving to be told so little about the particular authorities he chooses to cite. For example, although Hermas was read in churches in the postapostolic period and was sometimes quoted authoritatively in doctrinal disputations, *The Shepherd* was nevertheless an allegory, and was widely regarded as such when so used. Its point of reference was, therefore, illustrative, for edification, not as a solid source of doctrine. It has not the epistolary form (like the works of Clement, Polycarp, Ignatius, and others), and from the start—despite sometimes being classified by some as scripture—was meant to be understood differently: as devotional literature and religious romance. Hermas's relationship to the fathers is similar to that between the Book of Revelation and the rest of the New Testament, though it differs in many ways from the Apocalypse. The author hailed from Rome (he was almost certainly not the Hermas of Romans 16:14). Many consider the work to have been written with a Judaizing aim, representing the last struggle between Judaic and Hellenic Christianity.[74] Its influence waned quickly and decidedly.

11. The parable Willie selects from *The Shepherd* to further his Adoptionist emphasis occurs in the Fifth Similitude of Hermas, "Concerning the Vineyard and the Faithful Servant." "Positive Adoptionist teaching" it may be, but this must be viewed in the light of the minor position that *The Shepherd* held in the early church, a position that has declined still further since then. The book is emphatically sub-Christian in that it does not convey a full Christian understanding of New Testament (especially Pauline) teaching; its framework is essentially legalistic, stressing the fulfilling of laws rather than the building of lives on love through a loving response to God as Father. Moreover, Willie's translation is somewhat misleading. Hermas is not writing of the Holy Spirit as traditionally understood, but (according to Hoole) of "the holy pre-existent spirit which created the whole creation, [which] God hath made to dwell in the flesh which he chose"—a curious omission for one well-known for strongly differentiating between the doctrine of the Holy Spirit in Judaism and in Post-Pentecost Christianity. Christ is presented in an entirely different light than that conveyed by Paul in, for example, Philippians 2:6–11. He is portrayed not as lovingly and willingly responding to the Father's will, but as one "[made] to dwell" with the Spirit, who "laboured with the Spirit, and worked with it in every deed," who was chosen to be a "companion" with it, "bearing the Holy Spirit upon the earth," and so on. It is for this reason, among others, that men of the stature of Eusebius, Athanasius, Jerome, Gelasius, and many others since chose to exclude it from the canon, classing it with the spurious books of the church. Jesus here is no more than a

man indwelt by God's Spirit, as were the prophets of old, as were the kings of Israel (who were also called "sons of God"). It is indeed positive Adoptionism—and positively out of touch with the main thrust of the New Testament, which owns Jesus as *Lord,* prays to and serves him as God himself, as Jesus himself taught.

12. His cataloguing of the similar teachings of Paul of Samosata, Nestorius, and Elipandus is not more compelling than this. And it is curious that Willie, who in his Bruce Lectures professed some expertise in the Early Fathers, should have this penchant for those regarded as heretics (Hermas informally so), and not infrequently rich heretics! Most surprising of all is his omission of any reference to the heresiarch Arius, after whom the doctrine Willie appears to favor is named. Had he dealt with Arius directly, he would have been thrown into the heart of the Christological controversy and forced to come to terms with the teaching of Athanasius (whom he ignored here, but cited on other matters from time to time), Eusebius of Caesarea, and the deliberations of the Council of Nicaea itself on the doctrine of the mutual "substance" (*homoousion*) that Jesus shared with the Father. Willie makes no reference to the solid body of teaching that has been argued and expounded repeatedly since Nicaea first declared itself. (The *Acta* of the Council itself have been lost, though its Creed, Synodal Letter, and twenty Canons have survived. Arianism was specifically anathematized by the Council.)

13. Willie rightly calls attention to "the great question, 'Wherein does the unity between God and Jesus Christ consist?'"; in doing so, however, he makes a jump of logic. Admitting that Greek thought found its answer in "metaphysical and essential terms," he proceeds, "But let us turn to the New Testament," thereby ignoring the fact that the New Testament itself is not unconscious of such aspects of Jesus' dual nature.

14. He only thinly argues the unity between God and Jesus (which rests solely on a moral basis—of will, not of essence) and goes on to the question of the human development of Jesus. How could development be possible at all in the sort of person offered by traditional theology, Willie asks. Traditional belief has for generations provided a picture of this which, while not without problems, has nevertheless rarely produced "a monstrous picture"; indeed, it has earned a worldwide devotion and respect. It is not evasion to emphasize that here we are in the area of mystery and wonder. Willie was never one to pretend the gospel was anything other than one of mystery and wonder, despite this attempt to make it "intelligible." (We may note a different understanding of intelligibility between that which we saw earlier and now: the previous understanding was that intelligibility was an attempt to make it plain in language and argument, to omit jargon; now he seeks to rid it of its mystery and transcendental reality. In the process he oversimplifies it by omission and distortion. Faith is no longer seeking understanding; understanding is seeking faith—and laying down preconditions.)

It is not correct to assert that "ordinary Christology leaves no room for development because at all times this person Jesus was perfectly God." In quoting Macgregor, Willie fails to note that his old Professor utterly refuted the "liberal" picture of Jesus as formal slander, as had Davidson before him. In any case, the citation is from a sermon on "The Geniality of Jesus," not a Christological statement on the dual nature of Christ. The non sequitur is as obvious as the miscomprehension is plain. "Ordinary Christology" has ever sought to reflect comprehensively the unsystematic statements of Jesus recorded by the New Testament—that is, to make plain the teaching that at Jesus' birth God became man, and through his infancy, childhood, and manhood developed naturally. Astonishingly, Willie ignores the whole problem of *kenosis*—the "self-emptying" of Jesus—which was being debated in a lively way in the immediate postwar decades.

Elsewhere Willie himself gives very adequate expression to two factors that he ignores here. First, Jesus was a *unique* person, for in him dwelt, without restraint, the Spirit of God. What other men failed to avail themselves of, Jesus perfectly possessed, and thus he became perfect in obedience and in legal standing before his Father. Second, Jesus' sinlessness gave him unequalled insight, authority, and power. One must not argue from the unique to the general. Willie complains that the older doctrine failed to provide a full and perfect humanity; he fails to note that precisely *because* Jesus' humanity was perfect, we need to rearrange in its light our all-too-human definitions. Nothing in all the old Christology weakens the force of the temptations or misguided attempts of his disciples to reroute Jesus. (Elsewhere, Willie himself was at pains to heighten their intensity.) The only way "God takes man into himself"—an unbiblical concept—is by spiritual rebirth; there is no evidence of or need for it in Jesus.

15. The "when" of adoption Willie leaves open. He ignores the possibility of its taking place at his birth, when "Immanuel" was announced, perhaps because he recognizes that Adoptionism is based on Jesus' "earning" his place with God, whereas traditional doctrine always asserted it of him as of right. Such an omission is logically correct, for his doctrine of adoption rests largely on the basis of reward, the resurrection being the ultimate reward, as he stated. (Contradictorily, he rejects the idea that adoption might have taken place at the resurrection by asserting the sacrificial nature of Jesus' self-sacrifice on the cross.) But if succeeding generations of Christian thinkers are correct (and Willie elsewhere regularly aligns himself with their views), then "the saving event" has to be understood as part of the whole story of Jesus, and not just as its climax in crucifixion and resurrection; it is a matter of his life as well as of his death. As John's Epistle emphasizes repeatedly, those who enjoy the life of the world to come are those who believe that he came "by water and by blood": his coming is as important as his final work and witness. It is with his whole person that we have to deal, and the wonder of it is that though fully a man (and John is especially at pains to stress Jesus' humanity), he is more than a man—not by adoptive right or reward, but in essence.

391

16. It is not necessary to consider the question of the relation of Adoptionism to atonement, though it will generally be admitted that Willie's argument has serious weaknesses, both in its use of New Testament evidence and on purely logical grounds. We should note, however, that the atonement doctrine he wishes to preserve is *sacrificial;* and it is surprising that the obstacle of a finite sacrifice (in the face of an infinite problem) never touched him here. It shows that Willie has lost contact with the Old Testament basis of sacrifice and the morality on which it is based, by which the world was prepared for the coming of Jesus, things that he is elsewhere at pains to assert.

He feels it necessary to strengthen the atonement doctrine in the light of his Christology. We have seen that simple Adoptionist doctrine is inadequate and has always been held to be so by the Christian Church; perhaps Willie himself came to feel so, too. He never allowed this essay to go to publication. He rightly preferred his "unintelligible" statement to stay unintelligible. But, as we shall see, he was constantly troubled by the issues he dealt with in this unpublished piece, issues that ever remained to him enigmatic, paradoxical, and a source of worshiping wonder. The important conclusion we must draw from this is that whatever his reaction to the "hard questions" asked of this doctrine, he always loved, followed, and obeyed Jesus. And that is the ultimate test. As Professor Bruce recalled, Howard Mudditt, proprietor of The Paternoster Press, once commented "impatiently" of those who criticized his "liberalism," "Yes, I know, but he loves the Lord." Whatever the faults of this essay, at least he has preserved one aspect of incalculable significance: that Jesus is, whatever we may make of him, the center of God's plan and working, "the pivot of history"; and that fact is certainly reducible to a tract. If he only temporarily shouldered the theological method, he never abandoned the Christological task. In 1951, writing to the leaders of the Boys' Brigade, he spoke of the importance of the Christocentric task (he used that phrase). A little later, in reviewing Stauffer's great book *New Testament Theology,* he states that "any book of theology stands or falls by its Christology."[75] And when he came to produce his trilogy on Jesus, but ten years on, it was a very different view he expounded.

CHAPTER FOURTEEN

The Battery Hen Years

He Builds His Nest

THE midpoint of the twentieth century was reached jerkily and without acclaim; it was an undistinguished period in national and international life in which were sown the seeds of the seething '60s.

Winston Churchill bemoaned "the dreadful degradation of standards"[1] that then obtained and were widespread in all aspects of life. The Labour government was seen to be tottering; even the premature dissolution of Parliament before the Budget nearly failed to stave off its defeat. The opposition had little to offer, however, and so Clement Attlee was returned, with a reduced majority of six votes. It struggled on for a further eighteen months, only to fall in October 1951. State interventionism was high, and costly. The pound was worth about half its prewar value (ten shillings and ninepence, actually). Taxes were heavy, production low, and the industrial and social outlook bleak. Trade union power was negligible, but the fuses of discontent were even now being lit. It was the time of "Butskellism" (to use a description coined by *The Economist* to refer to R. A. Butler and H. Gaitskell's economic politics). The Labour Party was shortly to be rent by furious arguments between the Bevanites and Attlee's supporters, a split that put the party out of office for more than a decade.

The return of Winston Churchill was hardly historic. His majority was but eighteen, and neither he (now in his seventy-eighth year) nor the country was able to rediscover the vigor of the war years. Churchill was, moreover, essentially out of touch with the era and with the people he led. He relied on the immense reputation his former victories had gained, but was unable to lead effectively. He no longer had heart for mere party politics. He was appalled to find that despite all the hardships of the postwar recession, a billion pounds had been spent by his Socialist predecessor on atomic research without the consent of Parliament. The standards degraded still further. The key issues of the day were three: finance, food, and housing. These matters touched the very quick of the nation, and anxiety and agitation were great. Even the hope engendered by the New Towns and Boom Cities (e.g., Coventry) could not overcome the general feeling.

Moreover, the West felt the chill east winds of Russian imperialism about its ears as the cold war intensified. This mood was shortly to catapult politicians and others into the H-Bomb era, when "the danger of world suicide" (to quote a WCC phrase of the time) was anxiously debated. It looked as if Huxley's atheistic comment "In the beginning was—Hydrogen" was about to have its logical conclusion. By October 1952 Churchill was warning his aides that war with Russia was a real possibility. Egypt was also a source of concern, with the threats it posed to passage through the Suez Canal.

Britain's role in the world was changing. The Empire was shrinking and her influence waning. Formerly the king's title had been "King of Great Britain beyond the Seas"; now it was "King of all the British Dominions beyond the Seas"—a subtle, yet highly significant change, which symbolized Britain's loss of status. The King himself now attracted growing attention as visible signs of his poor health showed. His end came early in February of 1952—"a perfect ending," according to his Prime Minister: after a period of recreation at one of his favorite shoots and dinner with family and friends, he passed away in his sleep. He who had stood at the gate and led the way in the nation's darkest hour now went out himself into that very individual experience of darkness, still clasping the hand that is safer than a known path. "The King is dead! Long live the Queen!" echoed round the country, and the nation stirred as the young queen recalled to mind the first Elizabeth, who had lifted her subjects from despondency to triumph. Not possessing a television set of their own, the Barclays watched the inspiring coronation ceremony at the home of the MacCalmans round the corner, in Mearns Road, Cathcart. It was also the year the first passenger jet flew, and the story of the Comet airliners (like the Comet steam packet on Loch Lomond) was one of both hope and disillusionment: a symbol of the age, of man himself.

Willie was an interested, if somewhat silent observer to all this. His work was highly congenial to him, but totally demanding; in it he was becoming somewhat cut off from day-to-day affairs. Had he moved to Practical Training and not New Testament, his response would have been very different—involved and constructive. He would have answered John Reith's public question at this time, when commercial television was being debated in Parliament and beyond—"Need we be ashamed of moral values or intellectual and ethical objectives?"—with a bold "No!" Given the chance, Willie would once more have plunged himself into concrete reality, seizing the opportunity to promulgate "decided answers" in the cause of the gospel. But, closeted as he was by his subject, he proceeded to do what he could for as large a constituency as possible, within the limits of his discipline.

This is not to imply that he was restricted in his endeavors, however. Indeed, his work now offered more opportunities than he could manage, and he was thrilled and delighted to feel so busy and needed. He served as co-opted member of the SSSU's Executive and General Councils as well as the Convener of its Scripture Examination Committee (and President of the Glasgow Provincial

Union of the SSSU); his face and gifts were also becoming recognized on the wider ecumenical scene as a regular attender of the Scottish Advisory Group of the United Society for Christian Literature (USCL), and as a member of the Home Committee of the National Bible Society of Scotland (on which he served for ten years). His own church was making an increasing ecumenical contribution. In 1951, for example, it laid down no conditions for intercommunion or the mutual exchange of pulpits, a generous step forward, highly congenial to Willie's welcoming attitudes. But these were times of increasing anxiety for the church despite such elements of promise. At the General Assembly that agreed to this move, it was reported that over 750 churches had no Bible Class. Soon the Boys' Brigade and youth club movements would be reporting similar losses; the challenge was irresistible to William Barclay.

On 17 August 1950 *The British Weekly* published a three-column report by Alexander Gammie entitled "A Rising Scottish Preacher: A New Note in a Great Tradition." It referred to Willie's recent address to the National Sunday School Union of England, in what Gammie mistakenly judged to be Willie's debut in London. He spoke of Willie's "great and growing reputation" and of his being one of Scotland's "most promising preachers." We should remember that these were still days of pulpit veneration, when preaching was valued more highly than it is today. The reporter went on to say how fortunate Willie's students were: "He has come to be regarded as one of the most vital forces in the famous Divinity Hall today, influencing the students alike by his sheer skill as a teacher and by the charm of his unobtrusive but warm-hearted personality." Gammie also spoke of how Willie's job at that time freed him for service to the church at large—and how widespread that service was. Further, and somewhat unusually, it was noted that Willie had recently been invited back to the Scottish capital for the second year in succession as one of its special summer preachers; "his driving power is now pronounced," Gammie observed, perhaps remembering the old adage that if American preachers go to heaven by way of Paris, those from Scotland go by way of Edinburgh. The report continued:

> There are several elements in his pulpit power. His preaching is always palpitatingly alive. He holds his hearers by the freshness of his thought and language, and he comes close to life and its problems. Out of his wide reading he brings a wealth of apt illustrations without ever over-doing them. And he had a fine easy flow of natural eloquence. Above all there is an intensity in Mr Barclay's preaching that is irresistible. . . . Yet his style is emphatically his own, and he brings a *new* note to the Scottish pulpit of which more will be heard in the coming days.

Billy Graham had made his first appearance in Britain a few months earlier, and it is tempting to think that had not American mass evangelism come to this country, Willie's ministry might well have developed differently. How delighted his father would have been, and his mother too! As *The Perthshire Advertiser* commented, following highly successful services at both the Annual General Meeting of the Sunday School Parent-Teachers' Association and at Wilson

A rare family photograph: Ronnie and Barbara, Willie and Kate (ca. 1955)

Church, Perth, "he is one of the first preachers in the Church of Scotland."[2] Later he was Special Guest Speaker at a conjoint meeting of Lowland Boys' Brigade leaders, following which he gave a series of lectures at Manchester's Northern Baptist College in scintillating style. Among those entranced by his skills was Alec Gilmore, himself to be a distinguished communicator and General Secretary of the USCL. Entranced as he was, Gilmore was nevertheless concerned to see one so relatively young (at forty-three) looking like "an old man";[3] the toil was taking its toll. In October Willie returned to his boyhood town of Motherwell, giving yet another course of lectures in extramural classes organized by his university—lectures that proved to be so popular that new premises had to be found for them.

His family gave him great support and joy, a solid, restful base from which he went forth like a man commissioned. Kate's health was better than it had been for some years, and she enjoyed it to the full, and would do so until early 1956, when fibrositis struck as if by way of portent. If there were any worries at all, it was on account of her children—the natural anxiety of a caring mother over two delightful children, the apples of her eye. As vivacious as ever, a charming hostess, one who could set a supper table well enough (even in those difficult days) to make students' eyes water, she was now the perfect "help" for Willie's arduous life-style. "You helped him reach his peak," commented Mrs. Rutland from New Zealand,[4] and so she did. Willie never failed to express his gratitude for the lifeline she was to him and their family.

Barbara was by now a young teenager and Kate's constant companion, providing an almost sisterly friendship in the long hours of Willie's absence from home—and those absences when he was at home but locked away in his study. They were inseparable, Kate and Barbara; together they helped the neighbors and their children, did Barbara's (and Ronnie's) homework, listened to music, played the piano, and gardened. Barbara's interest in her aunt's medical profession also gave cause for joy and proud hope, though it was not to last. They were often helped by Kate's friend Isobel MacCalman, who assisted in all the heavy work, such as choosing and fitting linoleum, laying cement, identifying forgotten plants, and so on. Willie's "handless reputation" was already, but not quite justly, being formed. Ronnie was by this time as tall as his father and "quite out of my control," as Willie expressed his son's sturdy independence to Braidwood. The delightful ways and shapes of the opposite sex had not gone unnoticed, and his father's sporting interests had also been fully reflected in his son, and more so. Nothing delighted Willie more than to hear of his being made captain of his school football team (thankfully back at football!), with invitations for trials at both Glasgow and Edinburgh.[5] His parents' intellectual powers were also reflected in him, his penchant being for modern languages. (He actually excelled in Latin, French, and German.) By June 1952 his place at his father's university was secured and the whole family celebrated appropriately. Willie was well content.

Willie himself was known to the neighbor's children as "Daddy Barclay," as Mrs. Young recalls.[6] He loved to join in a game of football on his way up the street, though he was not reputed for having the straightest shot in the neighborhood! Their house was always full of young people, Barbara and Ronnie both being completely free to invite home whomever they wished; they did so generously. At such times Willie (when at home) would get them all arguing, employing his gifts as a "Socratic stirrer" to the full. It was all very reminiscent of the fast and furious days of Renfrew Trinity, which were never far from his thoughts, though sadly its pulpit remained closed to him. A typical example of the continuing relationship he had with many of his former church's individuals can be found in the following letter, which he wrote to Miss Kidd, daughter of the former session clerk and church magazine editor. It provides an interesting window into Willie's mind:

My Dear Catriona,
Thank you so much for your letter. It was indeed kind of you to write and I can assure you that I appreciate it very much indeed. It uplifts a preacher's heart to get a letter like yours. To tell the truth I was feeling a bit depressed about the Dunfermline week-end. I had just got back from Oxford on Thursday; I had been

at the Annual Meeting of the West Lowland Boys' Brigade on the Saturday afternoon; and I had been preaching in Airdrie on the Sunday morning; the result was that I was a bit weary; and further, I always feel slightly lost in Abbeys! So you can see that a letter like yours is a cheering thing.

You say that you like to think that you took your vows of Church membership with me. I would like to return the compliment; not exactly to you but to your family. The greatest good fortune I had in all my ministry was to have your father as session clerk—and I mean that literally. You can have no idea of the number of mistakes his wisdom and judgment saved me from. I used to take schemes to him and test them on him and if he did not approve I knew there must be something wrong. I owe him a debt that I can never fully repay; so, you see, it is a double pleasure to get a letter like yours from his daughter![7]

Despite his relentless work he was in the rudest of health. Apart from his dental trouble of 1944 he had suffered only a black eye (the result of a fall during a wartime blackout, perhaps running where he should have walked!) and a burst blood vessel, also in his eye, in twenty years of vigorous activity. His vigor was to last for almost another twenty years, broken only by a bout of flu in 1956 and golfer's shoulder (not hip, as is usual) a little later.

Willie's attendance at Faculty and Trinity College meetings was nearly a model of perfection. In June 1949 he had been nominated a member of the Senate of the University (delegated by the Faculty of Theology), and this nomination was continued in subsequent years. Thus from a fairly early point in his academic career he was involved at a high level in the affairs of the University. Sometimes they dealt with trivial things affecting the day-to-day ordering of the place and sometimes they had to do with historic and long-term planning the effects of which are still with us. In January 1950, for example, he participated in a discussion about the size of the classrooms and the need for increased accommodation. In October 1952 he was involved in the planning celebrations for the fifth-centenial celebrations, when it was agreed to publish a celebration volume. (The Faculty of Theology also planned to produce its own volume of essays, Dean Mullo Weir being appointed editor, but nothing seems to have come of this.) His first interuniversity appointment took place at this time, when he was appointed (for three years) External Examiner at the University of Edinburgh. A year later he was appointed to a similar position at the University of Saint Andrews. He was also appointed Chairman of the Scottish Universities Missionary Association about this time, missions being an aspect of Christian work he had long enthusiastically supported, as is evident in special lessons he wrote from time to time in *The Scottish Sunday School Teacher*.

A don's life is necessarily a quiet one, and Willie's fit the pattern; during his tenure as don, there was little that rippled the surface of the waters save his studying, lecturing, setting and marking of private work and examination papers, and some faculty involvement. To all of these Willie attended with singular devotion—it was his primary task—alongside his chief for seventeen years, G. H. C. Macgregor.

A Trinity College photograph. Willie sits second from the left in the front row.

In October 1950 Macgregor's great friend and collaborator in the cause of peace, Canon Charles Raven, became the Honorary President of the Theological Society and adorned some of its meetings with his presence and provocative addresses. It extended their Fellowship of Reconciliation ties, but even this did not propel Willie into joining the Fellowship or make of him an agitator in its cause. In early 1951 Stuart Mechie was welcomed to the faculty as Lecturer in Ecclesiastical History, thus bringing to completion the reorganization of the early and mid '40s. At this time Willie's friend Andrew McCosh, the Publications Manager for the Church of Scotland, made a formal visit to the College in the interest of the literary work of the church, which contact was soon to issue in the opening of another, more dramatic sphere for Willie personally. In February Martin Buber arrived to give his lectures (open to the public) on Psalm 73—"A Study of Good and Evil." To be exposed to one of the profoundest minds of the twentieth century, that of a Jew who stood before them in all the horror and profundity of the recent Jewish experience, and hear him speak of such things was a moving and stimulating experience. It was not lost on Willie. This took place at the time that Professor Joseph Hromadka had been scheduled to deliver the Robertson Lectures. He was not able to appear because at the last minute he was refused permission for an exit visa: the cold war's influence impinged still further. Subsequently, following a visitation of the Education for the Ministry Committee, a "regency" system of tutorial guidance was set up at Trinity College, each staff member having his own group of students; the new system served to tie Willie still more closely to his students' needs and interests. A month later the faculty, and indeed the University, rejoiced in Macgregor's being elected Doctor of Divinity of Cambridge University. In May the planning for Trinity College's approaching centenary in 1956 took place. It was finally agreed that a volume recounting the life and contributions of the College would be written by Mechie, the church historian. The volume was published to coincide with the celebrations.[8]

Willie's own position was placed under review, his having been appointed for a temporary period only (of five years) that was due to expire at the end of December 1952. He had no need of concern, however, for if the "emergency" nature of the postwar years was now over, it was clear that a job remained to be done—and it was equally clear that he was fulfilling his role beyond all expectations, with panache and inspiration. In particular, his linguistic brilliance was well recognized and was asserting itself in and beyond the department. The Classics Department of the Faculty of Arts appointed him Lecturer in Hellenistic Greek in addition to his New Testament Lectureship. This necessitated an extra four hours' lecturing per week, often to a small handful of students, and had repercussions beyond the University itself. Among the few actual lecture notes of his that remain, a number relate to this work in the classics and show the effort and care he put into his translation of works from the later Greek period. In the early '60s he was approached by Miss Moira McCulloch, a retired headmistress who wished to study Greek. Willie outlined the syllabus enthusiastically—

Milligan's *Selections from the Greek Papyri,* Theophrastus's *Characters, The Didache,* Pseudo-Longinus's *On the Sublime,* Paul's letter to the Philippians, and the Apocalypse. There was no one else to do this job, as usual, and he expressed enjoyment of his position of lonely eminence: "I am monarch of all I survey!" he exclaimed![9] This work was to result in a formal letter of appreciation on behalf of the Greek government at his death. The nest he was building was one of substance and breadth, firmly rooted in the real world.

He Moves up the Pecking Order

Just how well he was building his literary reputation is indicated in a letter he sent to Braidwood describing the fruit that was soon to come before the public. Writing in early 1949, he said, "besides [the Bible notes] I am at work on a Bible Class Handbook on Paul for the Church of Scotland, and three Boys' Brigade Bible Class Handbooks. . . . It will be 1950 before these things appear, but they have to be done early."

One of Willie's colleagues on the Lessons Committee of the Scottish Sunday School Union latterly was John Howat of the Youth Department of the Church of Scotland. They had met earlier in meetings pertaining to youth planning when Willie officiated as Convenor of the Youth Committee of the Presbytery of Paisley. Out of this relationship (strengthened by the enthusiastic support of the Secretary of the Committee at that time, W. M. Wightman, whom Howat succeeded as Director of Education in 1948) grew Willie's first "real" book, *Ambassador for Christ: The Life and Teaching of Paul.* One of the first things Howat did on taking over was to institute a new four-year course for youth training, and Willie's book for him was to stand in succession to such introductory classics as A. C. Welch's *The Preparation for Christ in the Old Testament,* J. S. Stewart's *The Life and Teaching of Jesus Christ,* and, to a lesser extent, J. G. Riddell's *What We Believe.* The commission was highly fortuitous for Willie and the Church of Scotland—and for tens of thousands outside the Church.

The origin of the book needs to be emphasized. *Ambassador for Christ* was commissioned for the particular purpose of serving the needs of the *Junior* Bible Class courses arranged by the Church in its youth training program, as the first edition clearly states. This accounts for its particular internal divisions—twenty-seven chapters covering just two hundred subsections, one chapter for each of the weeks in the half-year over which the course was to run. We should also note that, as with Willie's *Life and Work* articles of 1948, the daily element of the reader's spiritual diet was not neglected. Each chapter was prefaced by a lectionary, which gave appropriate Bible readings for each day; thus the conscientious teacher (for whom the book was written) was prepared "devotionally" prior to passing the lesson on, as were those Junior Bible Class members who chose to follow the course personally.

In so writing, Willie was ostensibly lowering the level of his material from senior to junior. At the same time he was producing this book, he was also writing B.D. (and some honors B.D.) lectures for his students, daily Bible reading notes for over seventy thousand adults from all walks of life and many denominations and nationalities, similar readings and notes for younger people of his own church, and three handbooks for the Boys' Brigade! It was inevitable that the modest origins of the book would be overlooked when it was transformed by public demand from a class handbook to that of a "formal" introduction to the life and teaching of Paul, but any fair assessment must take them into account and not, for example, compare it *tout simplement* with such works as C. H. Dodd's brilliant essay on a similar subject.

The response to the book fully justified the commission, despite a brown paper cover scarcely designed to attract the would-be purchaser. Offered at three shillings and sixpence, it was an instant success and raised Willie's standing in the estimation of many to new heights. Commented *The Scottish Sunday School Teacher,* "it is packed with scholarly and fascinating detail . . . and illuminated with many a modern parallel. . . ." *The Scottish Primary Quarterly* said it was "worthy to be a companion of J S Stewart's *Life and Teaching of Jesus Christ . . .* [the reviewer being] amazed at the wealth of knowledge and scholarship in so small a book." The years of preparation, training, and conscientious execution were reaping their own reward; "vintage Barclay" was being encasked.

If we ask more specifically for whom it was written, we find one answer on the dedication page of its many editions:

> To
> Barbara Barclay and Ronnie Barclay
> for whom and such as whom
> this book was written.
> And to
> Kate Barclay
> without whose patience
> it could never have been written.

Willie, supremely the family man (albeit too often *in absentia*), could not fail to demonstrate his love and gratitude in this his proper literary firstborn.[10] Ronnie and Barbara were seventeen and fifteen years of age respectively—somewhat older than the Junior Bible Class members for whom the volume, according to the title page, was intended. But that was beside the point!

The review in *The Scottish Sunday School Teacher* refers to it as "this characteristic piece of work."[11] It was indeed wholly characteristic of Willie to commence his account of Paul's life with a chapter entitled "This Was a *Man.*" Writing for young people, he was as careful to stress the heroic aspect of Paul's life, his dauntless courage, the sheer manliness of it, as he was to demonstrate the need for his young contemporaries' adventurous thinking—virtues, both of them, entirely at the center of the author's consciousness and valuable in attracting and sustaining the attention of young people.

The book is presented in three parts: the first twelve chapters expound a chronological development of the apostle's life and ministry, in which Willie's innate conservatism finds clear expressions, as much in its dependence on the traditional understanding of the framework of Acts as in his acceptance of a conservative provenance of the New Testament documents (for example, that 2 Timothy was written by Paul, that John of Ephesus was the author of Revelation, etc.). The second part is topographical in approach; he develops his exposition of Paul's life and ministry around the great centers in which Paul worked: Philippi, Thessalonica, Athens, Corinth, Ephesus, and so on. This approach has the advantage of linking Paul's letters to his life at a time when Roland Allen's great book on Pauline missionary strategy was receiving fresh emphasis. The third and concluding part, chapters 23–27, covers what Willie judged to be the key theological issues that Paul deals with.

It is a great pity that the revised edition, in dispensing with the six-month framework of the handbook, does not bring this aim and structure out more clearly, because the aim supplies an adequate reason for both the alleged theological weakness of the book and the brevity with which Willie treats some important developments in the church that directly affected Paul's work (e.g., Stephen's Hellenism and the Council of Jerusalem). This is not to say that Willie does not deal with some important Pauline ideas in the first section—he does—but, as was his wont, he deals with them historically and expositionally rather than systematically. Thus, he deals with Paul and the Law in the fifth chapter, and baptism (surprisingly offering a view of believer's baptism) in the seventh chapter, to give but two examples. In writing a handbook, even for young people, Willie's lack of dogmatic concern is revealed; his approach is homiletic and practical, related to life, devoid of jargon, lucid and simple. His language and style are clearly recognizable, though not idiosyncratic. As in all his books, his writing is stylish, but not trendy. Nor was he afraid of polysyllabic words, believing an educative element to be part of his responsibility.

The book reveals Willie's typical illustrative sources: from the classics, Julius Caesar, Seneca, Alexander the Great, Pliny, Heraclitus, and others; and from church history, his favorite (and oft-quoted) *Acts of Paul and Thecla,* Dunkerly's *Unwritten Sayings of Jesus,* and selections from Jerome, Muretus, Augustine, and others. His range of modern authors is also predictable: Milton, Matthew Arnold, Kipling, Bunyan, Studdert Kennedy, Frances Barclay, Charles Lamb, and selections from the faith's adventurers—John Wesley, David Livingstone, Dick Sheppard, the Quakers, Hugh Redwood. Only one New Testament scholar is cited throughout the whole book, the American translator and commentator E. J. Goodspeed—and his work does not appear among the sixty-six volumes recommended in the bibliography! This bibliography (unhappily omitted in the revised edition, rather than modernized) is well above the heads of even a Senior Bible Class, let alone one for juniors. It shows all the symptoms of having been an afterthought, perhaps requested by the publisher after the volume was completed. Many of the volumes in the bibliography were also on Willie's lists of recommended books for the Glasgow B.D.

Another significant aspect of his style and approach is the "evangelical" language he uses, a clear indication of the author's milieu. As with his prayers and theology, and in keeping with the YMCA usages of his youth, he is quite traditional in this, speaking of people "witnessing for Christ," arguing "the claims of Christ," urging the need "to win the world for Christ," speaking of the apostolic band as "men with a message" who "preached Christ," and so ·on. Some of these phrases are echoes of the biblical text, and were soon to be made doctrinal shibboleths following the mass evangelism campaigns of the '50s. We shall see Willie disengaging himself from such usages quite consciously later, as the "back to the Bible" call and "the Bible says" method degenerated into a literalism and proof-text method that he considered to be uncongenial to a deep biblical understanding.

At the commencement of his second section he speaks of "the wander-lust . . . in Paul's blood"—"we have a sense of some great power driving Paul relentlessly on."[12] It might well have been said of Willie himself. Professor Macgregor's own wanderlust activities were soon to be passed on to his equally relentless assistant (though never at the expense of his students), as he pursued his own ambassadorial role for the church generally and the Church of Scotland in particular. But the abiding importance of Paul, at least in the Reformed tradition, lies not so much in what he did but in what he said, in his doctrine, and it is perhaps regrettable that Willie should have relegated his analysis of Pauline doctrine to a section that occupies less than a fifth of the whole book—regrettable, but perhaps inevitable, given the parameters of the course and his immediate reader's capacity. He finds the key doctrine of Paul in the classical doctrine of justification by faith, but Paul's bold teaching about the Holy Spirit, his breathtaking perception of the church universal, and his "mystical" under-standing of union with Christ find virtually no comment.

The pure Jewishness of Paul's background is strongly portrayed (importantly so in view of the racially prejudiced atmosphere of the time, with its still-sharp memories of the recent Holocaust, details of which were then continuing to emerge). Paul's rabbinic training is well demonstrated, though Willie goes beyond the evidence to describe his subject as "one of the greatest scholars of his day" (20). Paul, a member of "the shock-troops and the spearhead of the Jewish religion," the *apostolos* of the Sanhedrin, becomes an apostle of Jesus through the transforming experience of spiritual rebirth on the way of Damascus. This was not Paul's first encounter with "the Jesus of history" according to Willie, who accepted the view that Paul had known Jesus at Jerusalem in the days of his flesh, a point he makes twice (on pp. 53 and 174). Contrasted with this vigorous assertion of physical encounter is Willie's understanding of Paul's con-version as one of "heavenly *vision*," perhaps heightened (he suggests) by a clap of thunder for which the locality is noted. Paul, accordingly, "capitulated." It is not surprising that Willie, who had spent nearly fourteen years in a little-known parish, should find significant Paul's "desert experience," as he did those of Jesus and Saint Francis. Listening to God was ever an essential element in

404

Willie's devotional teaching, though anything less like a desert experience than industrialized Renfrew and busy-busy Trinity Church is hard to imagine! Barnabas the encourager, we may note, is described in ways strangely reminiscent of Willie's grandfather Daniel McLeish: tall, handsome, impressive, a man who commanded respect and, despite his wealth and prestige, served Christ preeminently by serving his people. From all this Paul emerged to serve with an intensity and zeal unparalleled, the true "slave of Christ."

The revised edition weakens Willie's special emphasis on brotherhood in the section treating the relationship between Paul and Ananias.[13] This emphasis was another hangover from Willie's past (as the only son of a leader of the Brotherhood Movement), but it became an abiding and central element of his theology. A similar change affects Willie's understanding of the church as a "gathered" community and his view of the wider world of mankind. "God's family was the world," Willie asserts in the first edition, which some understood to threaten the Pauline emphasis on conversion and rebirth. We shall return to this later, for God's Fatherhood of all men was a key aspect of Willie's developed theology, a part of his "liberal" possession. (Curiously, he finds no room here to develop God's Fatherhood regarding the Aramaic original *Abba,* which term received fresh light from Jeremias in 1949.) It involved a certain contradiction to claim in this light that "the Christian community"—as opposed to "the fellow men" among whom we live—"is the Church." We come very close to the real heart of Willie's theology at this point, and of Paul's too, for Willie believed that "the greatest leap of originality that Paul made was his conception of all men being one in Christ Jesus" (178). He lays special emphasis on the repetition of the words *every* and *all* in Colossians 1:27–28 (a crucial text), but we should note that what we have here is not yet *universalism* (he did not arrive at that for many years, as we shall see), but the *universality* of the gospel: "Paul wanted every man of every nation of every class and of every condition for Jesus Christ" (178). "The only common brotherhood," he goes on to explain, "is to be found in the discovery that all men are sons of God"—only achievable through a preaching and an espousal of Christianity.

Willie also demonstrates other contributions Paul made to the progress of ideas, such as the concept of "the independence of the Christian from the state and all earthly powers," not in a revolutionary or anarchic sense, but in owning the Lordship of Jesus—"the center of the Christian religion" (another particular emphasis of his). He thus preserves the genius of Scottish Presbyterianism as demonstrated by Andrew Melville, one of Willie's great heroes, reflective of his Free-Church roots. "That principle," Willie enjoins (i.e., Melville's principle of the two kingdoms, of the earthly crown and of Christ), "we owe to Paul, and that principle we must maintain" (182). He can speak of it (another qualification of too strong an emphasis on the brotherhood of all men) as "the great truth of the independence of Christ's Church," with which he brings his book to its close. Other dominant concepts in Paul's theology that find expression include the idea that the world is not only "the garment of the living God" but the stage on which the divine drama is played out: it was to a world *prepared* that Jesus came, Willie points out in what is significantly the longest chapter in the book—it was a central aspect of Willie's theology as well. And he always preserved a prominent place for a lively sense of history: "The New Testament and the Christian faith is not concerned with the length of time but with the plan of time" (81), and Jesus was "the Culmination of History." He sharply rejects any notion of "the sheer senselessness of history." Paul's arrival at Thessalonica was "one of the hinges of history" (99), and thus its whole expression is understood within a divinely controlled framework; as he forcefully puts it in the conclusion of his chapter on the work of Jesus, "All [is] of God" (171).

A viewpoint that encompasses the unity of all men in Christ is bound to be strong on Christian unity, and this Willie points to in both the principle and the practice of Paul's life (the latter being evident in the collection for Jerusalem that Paul organized [124]). Willie's doctrine was pragmatic and mission-oriented, not denominational; it was ever unity of spirit and work, not uniformity of polity or method. This also develops out of the YMCA (and the Student Volunteer Movement) of his father's day, when "unity in diversity" was frequently stressed. It was a part of Moody's understanding, too, and rested (in Scotland) on Chalmer's early tag of "co-operation without incorporation."[14] This practical orientation is seen in other ways too, notably in the sheer demand that the gospel stays at the center of life: "Religion is the most important thing in the world" (110),[15] and "real Christianity"—the essence of religion for Willie—"is a *disturbing* thing" (102). Thus the ardent pacifist sought to maintain the prophetic role of the church, in keeping with the Church of Scotland's tradition of being the conscience of the nation.

A year after *Ambassador for Christ* was published, the Youth Committee of the Church of Scotland published his next book, *And Jesus Said: A Handbook on the Parables of Jesus.* Again John Howat was behind the adventure, and is suitably thanked in the dedication—as much for his criticisms as for his encouragements. The new book is more substantial (forty-five pages longer) than *Ambassador for Christ,* not least because "it has been my duty and privilege [twin pillars of Willie's ethical awareness] now for some years to lecture on the Parables,"[16] much of the material of which he now confesses to reproduce in this permanent form. For this reason he asks pardon for not always owning his literary and other debts. John Graham, a student of Willie's at this time, has preserved a remarkably detailed set of lecture notes that bear this out, not only as to viewpoint and interpretation (which are light on historico-critical aspects), but as to illustration and application also.

Unlike *Ambassador for Christ,* there was no attempt to make of *And Jesus Said* a book explicitly for weekly usage, though it is still specifically written for Bible class courses. It is much more a book than a handbook in the old sense, and although the structure is uncomplicated and the contents somewhat dated (of the twenty-six recommended in the bibliography, only C. H. Dodd's can still be said to have contemporary value), it remains a useful introduction to the parabolic teaching of Jesus. As with the majority of Willie's books, it is a mistake to approach it too analytically. It was not written purely for the mind (despite his tirades against shut minds), but for the heart and soul. Nothing is more characteristic than his fourfold exhortation to appreciate "the necessity of prayer and of quietness and of devotion and of study":[17] "the main interest of life" must not be neglected. For the furthering of that interest he specifically wrote.

As we saw earlier, Willie's gospel, like Paul's, was nothing if not all-embracing, and its universality is made especially plain in this book. He makes no reference to the Scofield Reference Bible of his father's influence, which dodges the challenge of the parables of Jesus by shunting them onto the sidings of "dispensational truth," but reaction to its influence may well have been under the surface. Willie is at pains to emphasize "the wide welcome of Jesus" (40), "the all-embracing invitation of Christ" (45, 48), and to condemn (as "judaic") exclusions of every kind as well as the false spirituality that flees from contact with evil men in the name of preserving righteousness. Willie, like Burns before him, is never more incisive than when faced with the *unco guid* mentality of "respectable" churchmen, an attitude he condemns uncompromisingly as "the *sin* of exclusiveness and of contempt" (48).

We should note this well, for it is one of the really important lessons of the life of William Barclay, raised as he was in a hothouse of spirituality at his parents' home in Motherwell, under an influence that owed much to the holiness movement of the early YMCA days, sharing much with the Northfield (USA) and Keswick (England) emphases—of A. T. Pierson, D. L. Moody, the Studd brothers, and Henry Drummond. Influenced as he was by the classic authorities of Puritan and evangelical spirituality—Bunyan, Milton, Jeremy Taylor, C. H. Spurgeon, and many others—he early came to a different appreciation of the spiritual life, much to his father's regret. It found particular expression in this book on the parables and lies at the base of all his future understanding and action. His view takes its root, in fact, in the classic definition of a parable—an earthly story with a heavenly meaning—"that is to say," Willie offers in explanation, "Jesus used earthly things to lead men's minds to heavenly things" (12), and then extends it to reflect his own essentially sacramental understanding of the world "as the garment of God." This, he adds, recalling a long-forgotten source, "*is no mere analogy but an inward affinity between the natural and the spiritual order.*"[18] Willie had no qualms about using the old definition; but he was determined that its use would not blind his readers as to the reality of the physical world. Elsewhere he defines a sacrament as "an ordinary thing which has in it a meaning far beyond itself"[19] and develops the definition in the context of the presence of Christ in the Lord's Supper. By the time he came to expound John 6 for his Daily Study Bible, the "secular" aspect was fully developed.[20] It reminds one of Malraux's comments that the art galleries, the libraries, and the conference centers are to modern man what the cathedrals were to his forebears. They were becoming such to William Barclay, whose journeyings at this time were often broken to take in their delights. He goes on to quote John Keble's great hymn of the common life, "The trivial round, the common task / Will furnish all we need to ask." He could not forego this "earthy" aspect, and went on to stress its message in a number of different ways, social and political. The seeds of one issue in his later clashes with evangelicals, who are only now relearning this crucial truth, were thereby sown. Willie was unrepentant, and continued to condemn withdrawn "Puritan" attitudes toward the world "as the precise opposite of the point of view of Jesus."

Not that Willie went in for condemnation. Tolerance for him was a besetting virtue. To Peter Cowe in October 1973 he said the first two "demands" he would make of any "good Bible student" were first concern, and second tolerance! We should note he refuses the usual identification of the Good Samaritan in Luke 10:25–36 as "a racial Samaritan," preferring the attacked man's helper to be simply one under "the gravest suspicion, distrust and dislike by the orthodox and good people of the day," a characteristic he amplifies with references to heretics and "loose livers" further on (82, 84).[21] He was nonjudgmental (if one may use such jargon of one who so carefully eschewed it) in his attitudes, believing that "what really matters is not so much where a man is as the direction in which he is facing" (50), "forward, not backward" being his constraint in moral matters as well as administratively and strategically.

But the disturbing aspect of Christianity, "the sheer adventure of Christianity" as he put it in *Ambassador for Christ,* now finds fresh expression. It is not only a disturbing thing, but an unsettling and upsetting thing. It is in fact "revolutionary" in three ways: morally, socially, and economically (62–63). This is as near to political involvement as Willie gets; perhaps if his task had been directly in his aspired Ethics and Practical Training we might have seen it vigorously developed. Yet he still asserts that "it is not the primary function of Christianity to make new conditions, but to make new men and new women" (65). His doctrine of the two kingdoms is kept intact. As New Testament Lecturer he remained faithful to the primary task—regrettably perhaps, since this deeply human and sympathetic observer might otherwise have extended the "revolutionary" aspects in bold and imaginative ways.

Reviews of *And Jesus Said* (for example, in *Life and Work* and *The Expository Times*) were enthusiastic, but none more so than Willie's old magazine *The Scottish Sunday School Teacher,* which noted that

> thousands of Sunday School teachers regard him as their special property. . . . [The book presents] a clear, scholarly explanation of the parables. . . . There is a type of scholarship which is so deep a shadow of learned abstraction that the ordinary man or woman is mystified; but there is another kind whose clarity lights up the whole scene. This book helps to make clearer the pathway along which Christians must walk.[22]

Just because it emanated from his previous sphere of service, this comment was very gratifying to Willie, but its greater significance may lie in the fact that it marks one of the earliest instances in which he is set apart from the world of scholarship, in which he is specifically recognized as "the plain man's apostle." It is both unfair and dangerous to emphasize this overmuch: it is unfair both to Willie, whose scholarship was by this time attracting wider attention, and to the world of scholarship at large, in which many other scholars were also very ably serving their fellow men; and it is dangerous, insofar as it overlooks the fact that scholarship *qua* scholarship was an imperative that Willie was keen to preserve and from which he gratefully learned. Nevertheless, he also agreed with Neville Cardus about the dangers of forgetting the things which really matter:

> He who would study organic existence,
> First drives out the soul with rigid persistence;
> Then the parts in his hand he may hold and class,
> But the spiritual link is lost, alas![23]

In this exposition of the parables, working from an intimate knowledge of the original Greek, hand in hand with some of the best scholarship to date, at least in English (we should note the bibliography for this book develops out of his exposition and is no mere appendage, as it is in *Ambassador for Christ*), he delineates a pathway of Christian truth along which any man may walk in safety—yet adventurously—as Willie himself did.

The introduction (Chapter One) explains what a parable is and does and what effect it has in the life of a man—good seed variably sown. He then treats of the central theme of the Kingdom of God, through which God's dominion and kingship is expressed. The rest of the book is an expansion of this, expounding the parables in close touch with the biblical text in highly practical (if not always critical) detail. As such, it is indeed a handbook of Christian theology in its widest sense, applied with a fascinating range of illustrative material covering nearly every facet of life, living, and literature. Over one hundred different authors are cited, from black American poets to Oxford professors; from women aviators to Greek philosophers. If we include biblical citation, it works out at the rate of nearly four illustrations per page—a feast of good things, through which "the spiritual link" is never lost and from which the meaning and "the organic existence" are unfolded.

In contrast to "the false start" of his private essay, Willie's doctrine is undeniably orthodox; we should perhaps note especially that both the preexistence and the deity of Jesus feature: "As we have seen again and again, after sending His Son to this world, after entering the world Himself in the person of Jesus, God can do nothing more. . . . Jesus is . . . the touchstone of God, and by our reaction to Him we are finally judged."[24] There is more here than a mere "unity of will" with the Father: there is a unity of essence and being.

The heart of the gospel he rightly sees in "the life, death, resurrection and ascension of Jesus" (54), understood in the contemporary expression "the Kingdom of God," that is, the church (45). Uniformity is not to be expected, but there is a deep "fellowship in difference," which is itself a virtue and a blessing

(58–59). A minor key sounded throughout the book is the old one of needing to go "forward, not backward": "We owe the good in the world to our forefathers; we live on their spiritual capital; but it is the plain duty to maintain that heritage and not simply to live on it." It was still the hallmark of Willie's life; he was advancing yet.

In December 1952 *The Scottish Sunday School Teacher* suggested sixteen books it considered a useful start in a Christian (and especially a Christian worker's) library. We may judge Willie's growing influence in Scotland—and beyond—by the fact that of fourteen well-known names, his is the only one to get more than a single mention, and actually gets three of his books recommended: *New Testament Studies, Ambassador for Christ,* and *And Jesus Said.* Not only advancing, but securing, too!

Expositor of "True Christian Manliness"

No one hailing from Glasgow and interested in boys work could avoid the immense reputation of the Boys' Brigade, and Willie was no exception. In the last book he wrote for the organization he proudly refers to it as "the institution in which I was brought up."[25] Moreover, as is so often the case with this highly complex man, there is more than merely a Glasgow (or Motherwell or Henry Drummond) dimension. The founder, William A. Smith, a self-made businessman, came from Caithness, Willie's county of birth. He was himself a model of Christian rectitude and service whom WDB must have found extremely impressive in those demanding, exciting days of youth and early manhood, and although he could not have met him while in the far north, he may well have done so during his nine years at Anderston when the Boys' Brigade was proving itself to be a dynamic means of capturing the imagination and loyalty of boys. Clearly he had much to do with his son's early involvement in the organization, which drew Willie into its circle for life. We have seen how Willie, a former corporal in the movement, was included in some of the activities of the Boys' Brigade from time to time at Renfrew. Like the Scottish Sunday School Union and the YMCA, it was an interdenominational body.

In 1947 Dr. J. Martin Strang became Vice President of the movement, and it would appear that Willie's literary work for the movement began at that time. For many years the Boys' Brigade selected each year a "text book" on which its teaching centered. This was either a book already available (such as Adam Welch's *The Preparation for Christ in the Old Testament* or J. S. Stewart's *The Life and Teaching of Jesus Christ*) or a book especially commissioned by the Brigade's Bible Class Committee. Because of the particular aims of the Boys' Brigade, a marked preference for producing its own handbooks was now accelerating under Strang's purposeful leadership.

Willie was commissioned in early 1949 to write one such book for use in the 1950/51 session. Its title was *God's Plan for Man.* It was no less a success than his earlier work, selling just short of a record-breaking five thousand copies. The average sales of the textbooks over the previous eighteen years (since Willie's ordination) were just below two thousand, and even if the adverse effect on usage in the war years be taken into account, it can still be seen to be a considerable increase. The textbook that came nearest to Willie's in sales was G. M. Dryburgh's *Right Ways of Living*, of 1947/48, but it still fell below the sales of *God's Plan for Man* by over thirteen hundred copies. Even J. S. Stewart's great book, used in two courses, only managed cumulative sales of 4,718 copies. Doctor Strang had found a winner!

The actual book was, like *New Testament Studies* and wartime furniture, strictly utilitarian, fulfilling no aesthetic demands with its wire-stitched binding and plain blue cover. It commences with a three-page general introduction by Willie which explains the course and the objectives of the book. The book is composed, the author declares, of "two inseparable ideas [which] are closely woven and closely intertwined,"[26] those being (1) "the idea that God has a purpose and a plan for the world . . . that history is no merely haphazard affair of chance and unrelated events but . . . the arena in which God's purpose has been working itself out," and (2) "the great idea that the plan of God needs men to carry it out." That this latter emphasis involves the problem of free will did not deter him from pursuing the idea. Man's freedom of action—"to help or to hinder God"— was central to Willie's convictions, as we have already seen and as we shall see repeatedly. To take one's part "in the true life and work of the world"—that being a fair definition of *duty*, so important an element in his ethical system—was an essential, a "natural" concomitant of his plan, to which duty Willie unfailingly called. The great aim of the book therefore is "a practical aim," as befits one designed for boys in their teens.

Interestingly, the book has a format almost identical to that of the original edition of *Ambassador for Christ*. Designed to cover the six-month cycle of lessons common to Scottish Sunday Schools of the day, it offers twenty-four chapters (in addition to the introduction) that encompass the two "inseparable ideas" just mentioned. The first ten chapters treat of the Old Testament, expounding and illustrating the unfolding purpose of God through Israel's call and history, and the men (Abraham, Moses, etc.) God chose to accomplish it. The following fourteen chapters fulfill the same function for the New Testament, preeminently with the coming of Christ, but also via the establishment of the Kingdom of God and the men used to extend it throughout the world. As with the early Church of Scotland handbooks, a lectionary for daily reading was provided (in this volume by Doctor Strang).

Willie did not have a completely free hand in writing this or the subsequent handbooks. Doctor Strang was a vigorous leader of industry and of his local Free Church. His conservatism was of a different, less enlightened sort than Willie's, owing to his not having enjoyed the advantage of biblical and linguistic training. But their real differences lay at a somewhat deeper level and affected the question of basic approach and method in Bible-class work.[27] Long free of the theological incubus of his father, Willie must often have been reminded during the discussions with Strang of those "explosions" at his Motherwell and Glasgow home, and that by a man who must have recalled WDB in several ways, being successful at business, a keen churchman, a teetotaller, and a lay preacher of some excellence dedicated to working among young men. There were two areas in particular over which they crossed swords. The first involved Strang's habit of commissioning books individually rather than with any sort of integrated overarching strategy. Willie's view, based on a carefully wrought pastoral and preaching experience (he being fresh from the reapplication of that experience to Sunday School lessons covering three-year cycles), was of a different order than Strang's, and he argued its merits with the authority for which he was recognized.

The second area of dispute between Willie and Strang concerned the Old Testament and its place in the Christian church and in the canon. Willie felt that Strang was wrong in his attitude toward the Old Testament: he deferred to it as the Word of God, but failed (to Willie's way of thinking) to understand dynamically its place in God's purpose for the world as an unfolding ("evolving") revelation. There was no disruptive confrontation between the two men, however, though the subject is a minefield, as the conservative/liberal divide over the last few decades has shown. Their relationship, despite such basic differences, was nonetheless one of mutual esteem and trust; and Willie was ever willing "to work to order,"[28] a thing he could do here with clear conscience, having so broad a canvas to work on and the need being essentially practical. He did not win Strang to his Old Testament views, nor did he really change the way in which the handbooks were commissioned, but his work provoked widespread admiration and success; he was commissioned to write for the Brigade over five successive years (a record in its history) and in so doing was able to build his themes and lessons more acceptably to his own way of thinking—that is, cohesively.

As with the International Bible Reading Association, the Boys' Brigade, having found its man, stuck with him, exploited (in the best possible sense) his talents, and thereby opened for him a sphere of very great potential. So it was that *One Lord, One Faith, One Life* (1951/52), *God's Men, God's Church, and God's Life* (1952/53), *The King and the Kingdom* (1953/54), and *God's Law, God's Servants, and God's Men* (1954/55) came to be published, and reprinted in subsequent years. In fact, from 1950 to 1981, Willie's books were used in no fewer than twenty-two of the thirty-two annual sessions: two years out of every three. This is a splendid record by any standard, and it is made even more impressive when one considers that his influence was extended by the Brigade's taking up his recommendation to use two of his former students, Donald M. McFarlan and A. Douglas Scrimgeour, as writers; their books served the Boys' Brigade for another five years. William (later Sir William) Smith founded and set the Brigade on its characteristic course, but Willie had an immense share in shaping the moral and religious framework in the postwar years, by his own and his students' books.

We must not minimize this service, which was particularly strong in the

Church of Scotland and the Free Churches. (The Boys' Brigade has had little influence in the Anglican Church and almost none in the Roman Catholic Church.) During these years the Boys' Brigade comprised tens of thousands of boys and their officers. Each book sold could affect, therefore, not merely the purchaser, but his family and a whole company of boys and officers. I myself recall their influence in the early '50s with particular gratitude, despite the deficiencies (in method and style) of the Bible teaching of those days—many of the lessons simply being read to the company. (Willie had foreseen this would happen, as with his *SSST* lessons, and wrote them with that in mind.) The Boys' Brigade insisted on adhering to them, and the matter was stressed to be of serious import: no band rehearsals or games till learned!

In 1950, Willie was invited to attend a national planning meeting of the Boys' Brigade Council, which was held in the Queen's Hotel, Birmingham (at which Henry Drummond stayed at the height of the Moody and Sankey campaign).[29] Willie met his fellow travelers before departing from Glasgow Central, apologizing that he would not be traveling in the same compartment with them as he had some work to do, but promising to join them for lunch. His colleagues, unable to suppress their curiosity, peeked at him from time to time as he wallowed in the delights of his beloved Greek, hearing aid unplugged. Little wonder one of these books carried a paragraph about "Stealing Time,"[30] in which Willie warned his readers to guard against its sly dangers. He had by now reduced his life-style to a fine principle of controlled activity; *minutes* were counted (and accounted for), not just hours, and he, a ceaseless working, writing machine, was ever conscientious of and penitent over the wasted minute. Time, he said, is one of "the most valuable things in the world."[31] One of the stories he liked to tell concerned Dr. Chalmers's reproof before the General Assembly of the Church of Scotland. The matter for which he was reproved took place in "the days of his ignorance," when Chalmers held an appointment at Saint Andrews University alongside his pastoral charge. He paid scant attention to pulpit preparation and used to say that one day a week was ample for discharging the duties of a country parish. When reproved for this, he confessed his failing to the fathers and brethren and asked, "What is the object of mathematical science? Magnitude and proportions of magnitudes. But then, sir, I had forgotten two magnitudes. I thought not of the littleness of time, I recklessly thought not of the greatness of eternity."[32] Willie knew that one of "the essential things" was not to forget time; and he did not.

His next book, *One Lord, One Faith, One Life* (1951/52), has a deliberately "Christocentric" objective (Willie specifically uses the word in the introduction): to establish that "Jesus Christ is the centre of the Christian faith. . . . He is the source of all its truth and its power." It is a development of the basic theme of his first handbook—from preparation to fulfillment. He quotes Griffith Thomas's great dictum, "Christianity is Christ"; this might remind us of his "false start" (see Chapter 13), but there is nothing in it to suggest that the Adoptionist position is being infiltrated here. He begins with "the birth of Jesus and the entry

413

of the Son of God into the world";[33] "He was God himself come down into this world"(9); and Willie could speak pointedly of the time when "God entered the world." The consciousness of Jesus' destiny "dawned upon him" in the temple at the age of twelve. That was "the Great Discovery," when Jesus "very gently, but very definitely, took the name father from Joseph and gave it to God," when "Jesus made the great discovery that in a special sense God was His Father" (9). The manhood of Jesus is naturally well-emphasized: "Whatever else He was, he was a man among men" (16); but in the discussion of his baptism his uniqueness is clearly evinced: "God said to Him, 'You were not wrong in thinking of yourself as My Son as no one else can ever be; you are My Son'" (20). And so, following a full discussion of "Man and Sin" that explores the fivefold nature of sin denoted by the five Greek words for it used in the New Testament (*hamartía* = missing the mark; *parábasis* = trespass; *anomía* = lawlessness; *paráptōma* = slip; and *opheílēma* = debt), the stage is set for "the Remedy of Sin" to be expounded. This took place after "the Divine Approval" was given (in the transfiguration), when Jesus took "His last decisive step" (72) on the way to Calvary. In such a book one could not expect to see any theory of atonement argued, but some may feel that even given his readers' limitations it is somewhat inadequate to speak of the cross as "a demonstration of forgiveness" (118–19). The office of the Savior-hood of Christ is boldly stated: it was a duty "laid upon Him" (17). Nevertheless, Willie is equally clear in asserting that the Son of God "died for all men" (117), that "Christ died for sinners," a death undertaken in obedience to his Father's will, and that he died "with the victor's shout of triumph on his lips" (116). That victory was supremely demonstrated in the resurrection, the fact and significance of which Willie argues for in Chapter 22 from the viewpoint of the empty tomb. Jesus' resurrection, he says, supplies the basis for the hope of "the life to come" (120, 126)—ever one of Willie's fundamental beliefs.

It will not have escaped the careful reader's attention that the title of this second textbook—the most comprehensive statement of Willie's doctrine to date, much fuller than that of his *Scottish Sunday School Teacher* articles of 1948—is a quotation from Paul in Ephesians 4:5—but not exactly! Paul's phrase is "one Lord, one faith, one baptism"; the last element (baptism) was felt by the Brigade to be inexpedient in a publication intended for interconfessional use. With this Willie agreed, for although committed to the doctrine of the Church of Scotland on baptism (and having long practiced it), he was nevertheless an adherent of a narrower position in his exposition of the New Testament, as we have seen. The tripartite nature of the title suggests the three elements that make up the book, which were interwoven with each other to maintain interest: (1) the life and work of Jesus—ever his chief element, (2) a series of chapters on "what we believe," and (3) "a series on the Christian life." The first topic covers the greatest part of the book, fulfilling Willie's objective to be "Christocentric," over no fewer than sixteen of the book's twenty-five chapters. The second topic occupies five chapters, and covers belief in God, man and sin, the Holy Spirit, the life to come, and the church. The last topic is surprisingly short, comprising just four chapters on "the Christian and . . ." theme, well-practiced at Renfrew Trinity; here he deals with the community, pleasure, possessions, and work, in each case stressing his balanced position, which shrank from creating a divide between sacred and secular, religious and common. He expressly makes this point—ten years and more before the great secularization debate really got under way: "Religion has to be lived out in everyday life. We make a great mistake when we divide life into two compartments and label one *sacred* and the other *secular*." He quotes Brother Lawrence's high view of common things, and speaks of the desire of Jesus to "show God to men in the common work and the common problems of life and living" (73–74).

His third Boys' Brigade book, *God's Men, God's Church, and God's Life*, follows a pattern similar to that of the first, with Old and New Testament sections on the developing purpose of God in the nation of Israel and the church and with an additional section (on Christian ethics) interleaved. In this latter section we see the main elements, if not the actual "system," of Willie's ethic and life-style being asserted. The first chapter, "The Making of a Man," expounds the object of the Boys' Brigade: to teach obedience, reverence, discipline, self-respect, "and all that tends towards a true Christian Manliness."[34] Subsequent chapters deal individually with the virtues of fortitude, prudence, self-restraint (typically subtitled "Everything in Proportion"), justice, hope, charity (i.e., love—"the badge of the Christian" [115]), faith, and temperance. The chapters "The Making of Man" and "Temperance" were included by special request; the former apparently arose out of one of his talks to Boys' Brigade companies for which he had become well-known at the grass-roots level of the movement, and the latter was included because it was felt that the subject had not been sufficiently emphasized—shades, no doubt, of Dr. Strang's influence.

The chapter on Temperance is of special interest inasmuch as it illustrates Willie's willingness to accept the task of "writing to order." He had already covered the territory in Chapter 10, "Self-Restraint: Everything in Proportion," which outlines his real position. The first section of that chapter addresses the issue of temperance, and his view is undeniably one of moderation, not abstinence: "If life is to be right all the things which go to make up life must be present in exactly the right proportion, neither too little of it nor too much" (57). "Temperance," he goes on to assert, "means having all the ingredients of life in their correct proportion. . . . And we will only achieve this temperance when we test all things by the presence of Jesus" (62). This clearly did not satisfy Doctor Strang, whom Willie thanks in the preface for the daily readings included in the book and for being "in part responsible for the arrangement of the chapters"— though clearly not only arrangement, but also inclusion of certain things was involved. And so a full chapter, significantly subtitled "For the Sake of Others," is included on this theme that was of such particular concern to the leaders of Glasgow's youth. Willie, under great pressure, seems to have simply stood his view (but not his practice) on its head: "It might indeed be better and more honest if we dropped the word Temperance and bluntly pled for and advocated, and consistently practised Total Abstinence" (144). We should note he says "might be," not "should" or "will." He goes on to argue the benefits of the total-abstinence case on the grounds of the "unknown danger" of alcohol to the health of the individual, the financial cost ("at least ten shillings per week"), the physical danger (as pointed out by international athletes), the moral danger ("the characteristic of alcohol is that it loosens self-control. . . . It is too much of a risk to indulge in alcoholic liquor" [147]), and supremely, following the biblical principle, for the sake of others: "If not for our own sakes, at least for the sakes of others, our faces should be set against all indulgence in strong drink" (148).

He wrote perfectly to order, but clearly he did not really believe what he was asked to write. It reminds one of what he said to his friend Merricks Arnot just before his ordination, causing much concern to his student friend: "I shall give them what they want to hear." And it raises a disturbing question: If he can do so on practical and ethical issues, what of the doctrinal and theological? Is he there also "writing to order," setting down what he believed his commissioning editors and readers wanted to see? The answer to that question will have to wait, but we may recall that Paul conducted himself in a not dissimilar fashion—he spoke of his being "all things to all men." Just two years after Willie had written to order about temperance, he wrote about Paul's method of accommodation—with some vigor:

> This is not a case of being hypocritically two-faced and of being one thing to one man and another to another. It is a case of being able to get alongside anyone. The man who can never see anything but his own point of view, who is completely intolerant, who totally lacks the gift of sympathy, who never makes any attempt to understand the mind and heart of others, will never make a pastor or an evangelist or even a friend. . . . Paul, the master missionary, . . . saw how utterly essential it was to become all things to all men.[35]

That, too, was Willie's way, that he might win some; in so doing he won thousands. His skills were principally in being able to cast a broad net, not in maneuvering a single rod. We might here recall the experience of the sainted Norman Macleod of the Barony Church, Glasgow. He was appointed editor of *Good Words,* and caused much irritation to some enthusiastic Christians by including things thought unseemly in an evangelical journal. Nevertheless, he explained,

> I have a purpose—a serious, solemn purpose. I wish in this peculiar department of my ministerial work . . . "to become all things to all men, that I might by all means gain some." . . . I may be wrong in my ideas . . . but I have a purpose which I believe to be right . . . [and I] firmly go ahead, whatever the religious world may say.[36]

The King and the Kingdom, Willie's fourth Boys' Brigade book, appeared for the 1953/54 session. "A closely integrated whole"[37] Willie called it; and it followed the usual plan of the evolving purpose of God (which does not preclude special interventions) in the Old and New Testaments. He selected the theme of Leadership to organize the material. The only real king of Israel was God Himself, and in the coming of Jesus that kingship was fully embodied and expressed. The work extends over thirty chapters (too much detail for normal Bible class usage, Willie stresses; he urges the leaders to study and select it carefully, having appended a summary to each lesson for this purpose). The same threefold elements are also apparent. In many ways the subject justifies his claim of close integrity of purpose; nothing more practical than obedience to God's reign could be envisaged. And his doctrine is fully orthodox, whether regarding the incarnation—"In Jesus God came down to this world" (176)—or the atonement, both the sacrificial and vicarious aspect of Jesus' death being asserted (182): it was essentially, Willie said, "A Death for Us. . . . Jesus on the Cross bore the punishment that should have fallen on us" (186–87).

The following year, in *God's Law, God's Servants, and God's Men,* the ethical element is supreme, handled from the standpoint of the Ten Commandments and the New Testament descriptions of the believing man as soldier, pilgrim, light, fellow laborer, salt, and witness. Sandwiched between these is a six-part series treating "Men Who Played the Second Part" to great leaders. The mixture is wholly characteristic of Willie's conception of dutiful service.

It was not his final word to the Boys' Brigade, except in the sense of being his most heartfelt understanding of Christian work. Willie himself happily continued to serve under G. H. C. Macgregor, himself playing the second part with unselfconscious abandon and ensuring the peaceful running of the department through rapidly changing postwar conditions. Ten years hence, by which time the foregoing books had all been reissued with some minor revisions here and there, he returned to write for the Brigade, but for the moment he felt that he had done enough. As he stated in the Introduction, "With this handbook I say, at least for the time being, goodbye to Bible Class Leaders. This is the fifth handbook that I have written and it is time that another mind and another hand were brought to this task. No guest should ever outstay his welcome. . . ."[38] It was not quite his last book for the time being, however! While he was writing these handbooks, John McNaughton, then Convener of the Glasgow Battalion's Bible Class Committee, had asked him to prepare "a book of prayers suitable for use at camp." Despite the extraordinary demands on his time at this juncture, the Convener recalls that "He not only readily agreed, but offered to include a five-minute talk to accompany each prayer." The privately circulated result, hailed by the Boys' Brigade headquarters as "an outstanding success,"[39] made its way into book form in 1958 under the title *Camp Prayers and Services,* and was to be a substantial guide (not to say crutch) for camp leaders and chaplains all over the country for many years.

This influential and useful work, now not easily accessible, contained the following materials: a selection of "Graces, Hymns and Praise" (three pages); groups of morning and evening services (twenty and eighteen pages' worth, respectively), each including "Lessons, Praise and Prayer"; a selection of morning and evening prayers (sixteen pages); a group of twenty-five "Short Talks for Camp Services" (thirty pages' worth; several of the talks were taken from his Children's Addresses notebooks—sadly, his only children's addresses to see print); and finally a series of fourteen talks on "The Beatitudes of the New Testament" (twenty pages).

To say that Willie's was a great contribution to the movement is to risk gross understatement. It was a worthy sequel both to his ministry at Trinity and to his unparalleled work for the Sunday Schools of Scotland—and arguably more influential, for the handbooks were not only used throughout Great Britain, but internationally as well. But this is not to say that he was without criticism. One of the most frequent comments made against his writing was his practice of repetition (the distinction was not drawn between stylistic repetition and redundancy). In *God's Men, God's Church, and God's Law* he deals with the criticism directly, stating—in repetitive style—that such repetition is inevitable:

> It is inevitable on personal grounds, for every man's mind has favourable pictures and passages and favourite lines of thought. But it is also inevitable on much higher grounds than personal grounds. There are certain basic things which have to be learned over and over again; and there are certain foundation things which have to be said over and over again; and for the repetition of them no apology is necessary. (viii)

His critics got none.

In *The King and the Kingdom* he reveals that "much of the criticism has been kindly and some of it violent" (vii; regrettably, this apologetic was omitted from the revised edition). Specifically—and it is of special interest to us in view of his "false start"—he was charged (by persons unknown) with having presented "an inadequate view of Christianity and of Jesus Christ." His answer to this is crucial: "I have always tried to present, not necessarily an adult view of Christianity, but a view which is relevant and intelligible *to the Boy.*" He speaks of the harm done to young people by trying to foist "an adult religious experience and an adult view of religion on them"—the most harmful of all misdirected religious education in his view. He argues that normal boys (and we may be sure he included himself in this category) should not have "a deep or terrible sense of sin as Paul had"; to deal with them as wretched or miserable sinners, he says, "is quite wrong." Such things do become more relevant later, in maturer life, amidst "the failures, the defeats, the frustrations and tragedies of life," but they are out of place in young manhood. "The presentation of Jesus Christ as Saviour," Willie defiantly argues, "has not a supreme relevance. To the Boy Jesus is Hero, Master, Friend," and he quotes in support Frank Fletcher's hymn "O Son of Man, Our Hero Strong and Tender." He is content in, and insistent upon, leaving the other things "to life and God and the Holy Spirit of God . . . and God's good time." It did not stop the criticism, nor was it expected to. But we should note that frequently behind his writings was such definite method, an approach that sought to understand and draw alongside those to whom he ministered, another example of being "all things to all men," by which approach he won not a few. Not the least important aspect of his approach was his willingness to let God do his own work in his own way.

Let Willie's own words be his last word on the subject of how to fulfill such a ministry to young men. Printed in *The Boys' Brigade Gazette* of December 1950, the following is a resume of the address he gave at the Council meeting already mentioned. It carried the editorial comment that "it is impossible for the printed word to convey fully the inspiration and *glow* of the Reverend William Barclay's memorable address. . . ."[40] We might note, too, that it is a very clear statement of his whole approach to communication with both spoken and written word; this is especially true of the five techniques he suggests.

The Company Bible Class

THE Company Bible Class is the most important activity in The Boys' Brigade. It is indeed almost a terrifying business, for here we are working with the most valuable material in the world—the Boy. The story is told of a young boy visiting a diamond factory where he was almost overwhelmed by the beauty and brilliance of the diamonds. While watching an operator skilfully polishing one worth thousands of pounds he asked, "What happens if you spoil a diamond?" To which the operator replied, "Laddie, you daren't!" Still less dare we spoil a Boy, dare we in our Bible Class spoil a Boy's idea of God. Permanent damage may be done if we are not wise—and unlike a diamond, a Boy cannot be replaced.

Just what are we trying to do in our Bible Class? It is essential to know our objective. As indeed in all teaching there are three things we must aim to do:—

(1) We must give the Boy something to feel, something that will arouse his emotions and kindle his heart. We all know how a congregation can listen unmoved, placid and almost asleep, to a recital of the most staggering truths. But the Boy is not deadened thus and something new and alive will make its impression. The newness of Christianity to the Boy can make a wonderful impact. But there is only one way in which this can be done. We cannot transfer to the Boy what is not in our own heart. A friend looking at an artist's portrait of Christ said, "You don't love Him, or else you would have painted it better." In our teaching we must be men who know Christ more than at second-hand.

(2) We must give the Boy something to remember. To-day we are up against an appalling ignorance of Christianity. So it is essential that:

(a) We must never abandon systematic teaching and this should be done by one suitable person—it is far too dangerous, in Christian instruction, to leave it to anyone.

(b) We must respect the Boy—It is not our duty to compel the Boy to think exactly as we do; rather must we encourage him to think for himself. It is far better for a Boy to think himself into a heretic than to accept calmly all we say. To illustrate this point there is a story of the Agatha Christie characters Hercule Poirot and Hastings. Poirot admired Hastings and remarked one day that he would like to be the same as Hastings, to which the latter replied, "I do not want you to be a second class Hastings but a first class Poirot."

(c) We must have technique [which techniques he outlines]:

(i) We must be interesting—otherwise the Boy will not listen as it is so easy for him to withdraw into himself. The first paragraph of our lesson is, therefore, supremely important. If we start with something local, recent and known, we can "get" the Boy at the outset and hold his interest for the whole time.

(ii) We should address our lesson to one Boy—without him knowing, of course. We must speak to him rather than at him and keep our eyes on him. If we notice that he is getting bored, we must change our tactics! We should not be tied to a manuscript but should look the class in the face.

(iii) We must arrange that our lessons can be summed up in one or two sentences. Let us remember that there are two ways of shooting—with a shot gun, when we aim in the general direction and hope that one of the whole volley of pellets may hit something; or with a rifle, when we aim at a particular point.

(iv) We should give the Boys some memory work—even though it may not be fully understood at the time. The learning of the great passages of scripture is well worth while—many will testify how in after life, in times of trial and stress, passages learnt in youth, have helpfully come back to mind.

(v) It is a good plan to ask the senior Boys to keep a notebook in which, after each lesson, they record one question and the answer to it.

(3) We must give the Boy something to do. So many folk today have got the idea that Christianity is something to do with the Church or Church Hall, but fail to see that it makes any impact on everyday life. They think there is no place for it in the office or at the bench. Every lesson or sermon should therefore lead to the question "What about it, chum?" There is a story told of a preacher who, looking at a stained glass window at the back of the church, noticed that the sun's rays were playing a peculiar trick. A shadow had blotted out one of the letters of the inscription and, instead of "Glory to God in the Highest," it read "Glory to God in the High St"! That is what and where our religion should be. A famous referee once said that when he was refereeing a game in which Tommy Walker, the Chelsea Soccer star—a real Christian—was playing, he had to watch only twenty-one men—not twenty-two!

We will not get quick results—do not let us be impatient in our Bible Class work. Imagine a glass bowl filled with clean water. From a small bottle a single drop of dye is dropped into the water which still remains clear. Another drop of dye and the water still remains clear. This process is continued until finally one drop added to that already there is enough to change the colour of the water.

There is the story of the man who had been imprisoned many times, and was really down and out. He had a little daughter whom he loved very dearly. One day she died, and he was stricken with grief, for the only thing that he lived for had been taken from him. Making his way to a bridge he was intending to commit suicide, but as he climbed up on to the parapet he heard ringing in his ears the words he had repeated so often as a young fellow at Church. "I believe in God, the Father Almighty. . ." Thus he was spared from a watery grave.

Let us concentrate on getting to know our Bible and keeping in close communion with God. Our best example is the great Teacher of whom it has been truly said, "First he listened to God—then he spoke to man."

A Race against Time

You will recall problems had been developing for the *Life and Work* Daily Bible Readings almost from the beginning. By the summer of 1952 the decision was made to jettison the scheme. But if failure greeted the Committee at one point, it was clear that the fertile idea of Jack Stevenson had produced a marked response at another. To build on that response was now their objective. They did so in a temporizing fashion. A committed readership had been gathered over the last two or three years; the Committee was duty-bound to provide something for them for the new year (1953). Apparently use of the International Bible Reading Association's own notes, now thriving under Willie's contributions, was out of the question. (He continued to serve the IBRA directly in this and other ways—for example, by becoming a member of its editorial panel, which post he held for several years, though it was a somewhat nominal role, after his usual committee manner.) And so Andrew McCosh, Publications Manager for the Church of Scotland and Stevenson's colleague, made his suggestions. Why not produce a more substantial commentary for daily readings? And could they not prevail on William Barclay to write it for them—in three months?

Willie himself, as we have seen so frequently, was also duty-bound. It was not so much that he could not say No as that he could not let a fruitful opportunity to serve pass ungrasped. We saw that he made his second contribution to *The Scottish Sunday School Teacher* Lesson Notes when others were "too busy." He, with the forbidding tasks of church and presbytery and Scottish Sunday School Union involvements (at a time when he answered as many as 247 letters in one week), found time. That was his way, however great the personal and familial cost. Willie recounted the invitation from McCosh (not quite accurately—he played down the unsound judgments and indecision of the Publications Committee) in *Testament of Faith*:

> The then Publications Manager of the Church of Scotland came to me and said very bluntly: "Would you be prepared to do us a volume of daily bible readings as a stopgap until we get some one decent to do them for us?" I immediately agreed. When the first volume was coming to an end they still had not got "some one decent." So I did a second, and so on and on until the whole New Testament had been covered.[41]

And so he found time yet again—time to study the best available commentaries of Acts, the book chosen to fill the gap, a book that had recently been placed (in July 1952) at the center of the biblical map by the publication of F. F. Bruce's *Acts of the Apostles*. Willie's sources for this work were already in his library and were well known to him, and he undoubtedly reverted to the sermon notes made for his Bible Class at Renfrew when, in 1945, he provided them with "a serial story on Acts . . . on the principle of the old continued serial pictures in the cinemas in the old days,"[42] a description of telling significance, as we shall see. The university and library records show that he did not borrow a single book on Acts for this hurried job. He was particularly reliant on *The Beginnings of Christianity* by Foakes Jackson and Kirsopp Lake—"that amazing commentary on Acts and store-house of information."[43] But Bruce's commentary on the Greek text (its companion volume on the English text of Acts was not published till 1954), and "the unjustly forgotten commentary" of T. M. Lindsay—one of the old (1885) Church of Scotland *Handbooks for Bible Classes* used by his father and presumably passed on to Willie in 1935, which he considered to be still "the best commentary for the non-technical *student* of Acts"—were also stalwart guides, as was G. H. C. Macgregor's as yet unpublished commentary,[44] which Willie read in manuscript form.

One of the deficiencies of the International Bible Reading Association notes was their lack of biblical text (in days of paper shortage, it was also a strength). Interested readers had to carry both Bible and notes for maximum usefulness. In the new style of daily readings proposed by McCosh that deficiency was to be overcome. A new translation of Acts was provided, and Willie's preoccupation with it was to result in his first published piece of New Testament translation. The book still owed much to the original Daily Bible Readings, in title and format. The first edition was dated "Thursday 1st January to Thursday 13th April," and the commentary is best understood on the basis of such daily usage—"keeping the morning watch," in the old YMCA phraseology. It was essentially a devotional commentary, written to draw out the main "lesson" of the passage (as the writer saw it) and apply it in a personal way. In this sense it is wrong to regard it simply as a commentary on Acts. The translation of the text was provided to make whole passages plain; it was never envisaged to be a verse-by-verse, much less a sentence-by-sentence, treatment of the whole book. (In subsequent volumes this attitude shifted somewhat, and for many years Willie entertained the idea of rewriting this first volume, but when the opportunity arose he had outgrown and outlived the concept, as we shall see.) As he stated in the foreword to the first edition, "it aims, all the time, at making these events [in the lives of Jesus and the apostles] relevant for to-day." His commentary followed his division of the text regardless of other considerations, which led to some unevenness. Thus, for example, Sunday, January 4, 1953, offered nine verses— Acts 1:12–20—with just under three pages of commentary, whereas Tuesday, January 6, offered fourteen—Acts 2:1–13—and nearly six pages of commentary. Willie was not one for weakening the discipline aspect of discipleship! Similarly, there is no recognition of the Christian calendar—no special readings for Lent, Easter, or whatever—a significant break with the IBRA method, and against the trend toward such recognition that was beginning to make itself felt in Scotland.

Willie had debts to much more than "mere" book learning, and they were acknowledged in the dedication:

> In grateful memory of
> WDB and BLB
> from whose lips I first heard
> the name of Jesus
> and in whose lives
> I first saw him

The dedication to his parents (regrettably, the initials of his mother have been consistently misprinted since the second edition) was a fine thought, and in a sense closes this first period of his ministry while opening the second and more influential one. "Whatever I have done," he wrote in 1975 quoting William Soutar, "it is because I have stood on the shoulders of my parents."[45] He was glad to own that debt now.

Characteristic of both author and approach are the *six* prayers that preface the commentary. The doyen of British scholarship of the last century, B. F. Westcott, is cited to praise the providence by which the scriptures were written and preserved, and to offer prayer for "grace to study them this and every day with patience and love." George Adam Smith of Glasgow and Aberdeen asks that "our study may not be made vain by the callousness and carelessness of our hearts"; *The Book of Common Prayer* is quoted to remind us of the need to "hear, mark, learn and inwardly digest" in order to "embrace and ever hold fast the blessed hope of everlasting life": the very selection is both a demonstration and an illustration of the author's breadth. Willie himself accentuates the dependency on God necessary to understand his Word, using a prayer that frequently prefaced his lectures at this time as he sought to complete the promise of relevance in his foreword:

> Grant, O God, that that which I have read with my eyes and understood with my mind and received into my memory, I may now go out to show forth in my life. Grant that what I have learned by Thy grace I may use to Thy glory; through Jesus Christ my Lord. Amen. (iv)

We should not only note the spirit in which he approached and fulfilled his Bible study, but the marked personal attitude of it—the personal pronouns *I* and *my* are used in the brief prayer no fewer than nine times; the "secret" he learned early in his pastoral ministry was not to be forfeited in the new sphere in which it was now extended; indeed, it was to be explored and relied on increasingly.

The pressures to complete the book quickly are evident in his exposition of his text, and account for some of his emphases—or lack of them. On the average, one page of commentary treats of just over four verses of text, but there is great variation of treatment within this average. Sometimes he will carefully expound a small section, not by way of exegesis—word for word, in minute detail of textual and critico-linguistic usage—but paragraph for paragraph, capturing the point Luke is making in the whole section, be it only two verses (as when he explains the meaning of the early disciples' arrival at Antioch—"one of the greatest events in history" [92–94]). Sometimes he will condense his treatment of large blocks of text into a single page (as with the important Jerusalem Decree of Acts 15 [126], or the unmasking of the plot against Paul in 23:11–24 [181], or the section on the "Unsympathetic Jews" of 28:16–29 [210]; all three passages comprise fourteen verses of text but are given only one page each of commentary).

If we take his six-fold structure of Acts (which followed C. H. Turner) it will be seen that the pressures to finish quickly built up his commentary in an upward spiral till the last section, though too much reliance on statistical features can be misleading:

Section	Passage	Verses per page
i.	1:1 — 6:7	3.7
ii.	6:8 — 9:31	4.9
iii.	9:32 — 12:25	4.9
iv.	13:1 — 16:5	5.0
v.	16:6 — 19:20	5.1
vi.	19:21 — 28:31	4.1

Acts he considered to be "in one sense the most important book in the New Testament" (v);[46] the "one sense" there intimated is the historical, ever of critical importance to Willie (we shall see others presently). Acts is not a late rewriting of the events and experiences of the early church, but a faithful portrayal of the acts of God. Willie took pains to make this point as a necessary corrective to what was elsewhere being retailed. For example, Bishop Barnes caused a furor in 1948 when he published *The Rise of Christianity,* which overturned the normal view of biblical chronology and gospel origins and had the distinction of provoking more acutely aware historians (C. H. Dodd and F. F. Bruce chiefly) into publishing suitable replies. "Luke," Willie bluntly states, at once declaring his belief in the traditional authorship of the book and in the reliability of his sources, "was an historian." And the history of which he wrote was "not a haphazard conglomeration of chance events which are going nowhere," but part of God's purpose: "the world is going somewhere" (6–7). Once more the historical basis is emphasized and once more the real world of man's experience is asserted. For Willie the two hang together, inseparable entities in God's plan; they are part of Willie's understanding of "the essential teaching of Christianity."

But we should note that his view was not only historical, as if to assert that once the record is well grounded the end of the matter is reached. For that sort of history Willie had little time. Of the life and death and resurrection of Jesus he asserted (and the assertion was an axiom of his teaching), "these historical facts were not the sum total of everything. Jesus was to them not someone about whom they read or to the story of whom they listened; He was someone whom they met and knew and experienced. He was not a figure in a book, one who lived and died; He was a living presence, alive for evermore" (78). The "secret" was his source of power, because it was his daily experience. We need to take this terribly seriously if we are to understand William Barclay's teaching. He asserts the *facticity* of Jesus. He said nothing to weaken the facts, though he may place them in a new light according to the evidence—linguistic, archaeological, topographical, or whatever. But he does seek to raise them from their lifeless historical matrix and make them *relevant* for his readers. What point a risen Christ if his presence and power and victory (over sin and death, troubles and grief) are not experienced? None, in Willie's view. He rose for us; he lives for us; we live in him.

And it is precisely at this point that we must note the mystical strain in Willie. Not that he would have been too careful to have done so himself! He was only too aware of the problems of asserting such a thing. A reliance on mysticism as a way of knowing God beyond the services and sacraments of the church, much less of scripture, was not his way. His view of mysticism, though more positive than the well-known outburst of Denney, owed not a little to that great leader's this-worldly stance. As with Principal Rainy, *relevance* was a quality high on his list of virtues. He shared the viewpoint of some Highlanders who were uneasy over the pietism of Keswick and looked for greater solidity, balance, and especially involvement. Willie's mysticism was of the Pauline sort, the beginnings of which we saw taking place early in his ministry as he sought to come to terms with Galatians 2:20—"I have been crucified with Christ; it is no longer I who live, but Christ who lives in me." An interesting and characteristic commentary on Willie's understanding of this text is found in his Sunday School lesson for 31 December 1950, "For Me to Live Is Christ." The "mechanics" are once more ignored, but the scripture lesson chosen to expound that text is 1 John 4:7-21— the apostle's exhortation to brotherly love, by which one verifies one's religious experience. This is how he now describes the original disciples' experience, a dozen or so years after his first sermon on this great theme and after having discovered his "secret":

> The early preachers always stressed the power of the Risen Lord. They never regarded themselves as the sources of power but only as channels of power. They were well aware of the limitations of what they could do. They were also aware that there was no limitation to what the Risen Christ could do through them and with them. *Therein lies the secret of the Christian life.* The Christian knows that so long as he thinks of what *I* can do and what *I* can be, there can be nothing but failure and frustration and fear; but when he thinks of "not I, but Christ in me" there can be nothing but peace and power. (30-31)

Acts he found to be the immediate and bold, if embryonic, expression of that experience; hence its importance. We have indeed reached the heart of Willie's own experience, of his doctrine, of the reason he was such a great public prayer and writer of prayers—and how he came to do so much, too.

Einstein said that "the most beautiful and most profound emotion we can experience is the sensation of the mystical. It is the sower of all true science. He to whom this emotion is a stranger, who can no longer wonder and stand wrapped in awe, is as good as dead." Willie thus enjoyed God, and sowed fertile seeds of religious experience in many ways. As he had written in *God's Plan for Man* a few month's earlier (a very characteristic attitude of his), "the highest form of prayer is just leaning back without any words in the presence of God." That was his way of prayer, not infrequently in the open with the glories of nature about him and work on his knee. Again and again he was to be found, not on his knees (at least physically), but, hearing aid switched off, meditating—at Logan's Well, on Bonnyton Moor, at Denure near Ayr, or on the foreshore between Granton and Cramond at Edinburgh. More often than not he would have his binoculars with him, spotting a distant knoll, a greedy shag, or a gently bending tree, all of them markers of the unseen, demonstrations of divine power whose resources are ever available to believing, obedient man. Lord Rosebery said of Oliver

Cromwell that "he was a practical mystic; the most formidable of all combinations." Cromwell's intolerance and megalomaniacal approach to life were completely different from Willie's, but Willie shared his "formidable combination" of practical mysticism—not isolated from life, not cosseted, but involved, with chalk dust and printer's ink on his hands.

And Jesus was central: he was "the hinge of all history, with His coming, eternity had invaded time and God had entered the human arena. . . . With the coming of Jesus something crucial, unrepeatable, all-effecting had emerged" (18). The centrality of the person of Jesus builds on the historicity of the records and is sustained by them—not as a book figure, but as a living reality. That is Willie's message to those who would read him. He will go on to say and explain many things, but nothing will detract from this twofold asseveration.

Such purposes do not detract from the human element in the record. Luke the doctor, sometime companion of Paul the apostle, writes "to commend Christianity to the Roman government" (in the person of the Most Excellent Theophilus, which Willie takes to be a pseudonym perhaps for a highly placed official of the court); it was also his aim "to show that Christianity was a universal religion for all men of every country." But these are "merely secondary aims." Luke's "great aim was to show how that religion which began in a little corner of Palestine had in little more than thirty years reached Rome," "to set before men the well-nigh miraculous spread of the Gospel, and he laid down his pen when he had shown Christianity established in the capital of the world" (xv–xviii). Willie held that in constructing this record, he used two sets of sources: first, the records of local churches, many of which were oral (chief among which were those of the church of Jerusalem, along with those of Caesarea and Antioch), and second, the "cycles" of stories built around the great figures of the early church, as contained in *The Acts of Peter* and those of John, Philip, Stephen, and Paul himself. (We should not confuse these "Acts" with the later books of the same name, largely Gnostic in tone and aim, some of which have survived. But we should note that Willie himself put some store by these early accounts; the *Acts of Thecla and Paul* he acknowledged for its reliable if unimpressive physical portrayal of Paul.)

There was a further source of Luke's writing, which is implicit in the text of Acts 16–28 itself. Of much of this section, Willie asserts, "Luke had personal first-hand knowledge" (xix). These are the well-known (and now much more widely recognized) "We" passages, in Acts 16:10–17; 20:5–16; 21:1–18; and 27:1–28:16. From this close acquaintance with Paul and that of every other great figure in the story of the early church, Luke penned his story of the expansion of Christianity. Thus, with typical exaggeration, Willie writes, "When we read Acts we may be quite sure that no historian ever had better sources and no historian ever used his sources more accurately and more honestly." And from that essential position he never moved.[47] He can even argue that Luke, a Gentile, can mistake the meaning of his sources—as when he "confused speaking with tongues [at Pentecost] with speaking with foreign languages" (16). We may or may not agree with Willie here, but the reason for his speaking this way rests on his bold recognition of the human element alongside the divine in scripture, a recognition that called for the use of the best technical equipment he could muster and a humble seeking after truth through spectacles untinted by creed, confession, or denominational pressure of any kind.

We were looking at Willie's conception of Jesus as the hinge of history, which achieved fresh emphasis in this book, and we should note how orthodox his doctrines are: Jesus' preexistence; his coming into this world ("in Jesus, God in person arrived on the scene of human history"); his returning to the Father ("the Ascension—understood as a physical event—was absolutely necessary," though "one of the most difficult conceptions in the New Testament" [28]); the bodily resurrection; the facticity of Jesus' miracles (18); and the doctrine of God as "eternally Father, Son and Holy Spirit" (4, 42). He owns in Acts especially, but also throughout the New Testament, that "it is very difficult to draw a line between the work of the Spirit and the work of the Risen Christ" (2). He could not be clearer, however, on the actuality and the effect of the doctrine: "if ever a doctrine needed to be rediscovered it is the doctrine of the Holy Spirit" (11–12)—justly so in light of the more than forty references to the Holy Spirit in Acts. He offers a clear explication of the Second Coming of Christ, the chief effect of which is to remind us "that God has a plan for man and the world . . . a summons to strive for the coming of that day." And, predictably, he emphasizes afresh that "in Jesus alone is salvation."

But the chief significance of his exposition of the book is its view that the church continues the mission Jesus commenced by his coming, which God vindicated by raising him from the dead. The resurrection is the base on which all that followed was built: Jesus "is not the one who *was;* He is the one who *is* and His life still goes on" (2). He later illustrates this in his treatment of the storm on the lake, concluding "the point and the fact is that Jesus *is* here; and the real Christian, the real apostle, is the man who still lives all his life with Christ" (11). Thus, "in one sense it is the whole lesson of the Book of Acts that that life of Jesus goes on *in His Church.*" And in that simple statement, we once more arrive at his doctrine (for such it was) of cooperation: God is sovereign—his purposes are immutable and will be fulfilled—but "he needs men" and has chosen to work through them to achieve his will. Man's personal freedom is ever protected, as is the need of personal discipline and moral effort. Nevertheless, we would be wrong to construe this emphasis as Pelagianism, despite the strength of Willie's statements (e.g., "It is the universal fact that God does not do for men what man can do for himself" [29]); we have, after all, just seen ample evidence of his orthodoxy. His intent in this regard is simply to stress that "failure to use our talents is a sin against God." It is from making the choice to use our talents to serve God's will, from accepting that privilege ("not the privilege of honour; it is the privilege of service" [38]), that there flows the supreme reality of *the sacredness of the common life,* the "religious" reality of daily work: "Everything, however humble it may be, that contributes to the health, the happiness and the welfare of mankind is work done for God" (43).

In order for the early church (mainly Jewish, of course) to expand, a lesson in "common sanctity" had to be learned. They had to be weaned from the elementary attitude that regarded special things and special people as being particularly holy; they had to come to terms with God's broader purpose, with his love for the whole creation. And so, of Acts 10:9–11:18 Willie writes that "Peter learns a lesson" that takes him to "the heart of the gospel" (83–92). It is clear that Peter had already begun to learn that lesson, for we find him staying with Simon the tanner with a clear conscience (in Jewish tradition Simon was a perpetually "unclean" man because he worked with dead animals). At this home Peter fell into a trance, and through his vision of the many animals and birds of creation God provided for him, he learned of the cleanness, the common sanctity, of all creation: "In the trance of moments Peter has to unlearn the habits of a lifetime" (85). That Willie himself had learned this thoroughly has been indicated many times, perhaps nowhere more starkly expressed than in his sermon titles, such as "There Is Nothing That Does Not Matter" (27 April 1941), which was followed by "When We Understand." Through this experience Peter's mind was liberated, and he went willingly to the house of the Gentile Cornelius. "The barriers are beginning to come down," notes Willie, as is "typical of the work of Christ" (86). Perhaps momentarily forgetting Luke's dependence on the story cycles of his sources, Willie suggests that "the importance that Luke attached to this incident is shown by the amount of space that he devoted to it," adding that despite the constraints of space Luke made it a point to recount this incident "in full, twice"; he "sees it as a notable mile-stone on the road along which the Church was groping its way to the conception of the world for Christ" (90).

Our purpose here is to understand Willie's treatment of Acts, accidentally but significantly the first of the commentaries for which he achieved world fame and by which he served the cause of the gospel (and continues to serve it) on five continents and in many languages: his magnum opus. But we must bear in mind that at this time materialism (in the wake of the postwar economic revival) and secularism (in the wake of renewed optimism as to man's own powers) were beginning to make a decided impression on the church and on theology itself. For example, in August 1953 Doctor John Highet, a notable Christian sociologist of Glasgow University, spoke of "the retreat from Christianity" that he saw taking place in two quite different directions: (a) into irreligion and pure secularism, and (b) into new (usually Eastern) forms of religion.[48] Another example of the tendency is seen in the publication, in November of that same year, of Dietrich Bonhoeffer's *Letters and Papers from Prison,* which rapidly accelerated talk on secularism and popularized the concept of "religionless Christianity." Willie rarely quoted Bonhoeffer—he never really cared to understand his ambiguous teaching—but from his days at Marburg he had kept a distant interest in the struggles of the German church which was being confronted with issues of even greater importance than those his own church had faced in an earlier period. At the end of the war (on 2 December 1945) he preached a powerful sermon entitled "Stephen Grund: The Pastor Who Defied the Nazis" and thereafter never hesitated to speak of the heroism of the leaders of the confessing church, as for example when he reviewed Emil Fuchs's *Christ in Catastrophe.*[49] By such influences as these, Willie was himself being led on to a broader, fuller, richer understanding of the world and of the "unsearchable riches of Christ," whose Lordship was over all. For him, too, the barriers were coming down, little by little, though he never made of such "new light" a principle of all-out commitment, as some of his colleagues did.

And so, in three hectic months, his translation and commentary were completed, edited, and passed on for printing. At the very time it arrived in the office of the Publications Manager, the Editor of *Life and Work* was advising his readers that "the International Bible Reading Association are unable to continue the printing of this special series [The Daily Bible Readings] owing to the rise of costs,"[50] and informing them that the Publications Committee had decided to replace the Readings with an entirely new project that would cover four months, not six, and would begin by dealing with the book of Acts. For this a new translation and commentary were being prepared by William Barclay, whom the Editor described as one who "combines scholarship and popular appeal to a remarkable degree." A full-page advertisement (a rare thing in those paper- and price-conscious days) was provided, and the forthcoming book was described as measuring six by four inches, of two hundred and twenty pages, with a map (curiously omitted in later editions), and priced at two shillings.

It was "partly in hope and partly in trepidation" that Willie "sent out this little book."[51] The trepidation was caused mainly by the lack of adequate time to prepare himself or his material: "The circumstances of the case demanded that it should be written much more quickly than it should have been." Nevertheless, his hope was that "with all its faults, it may be used by God to awaken interest in His Word and to lead those who use it"—he enjoined them to carry it wherever they went—"to a better understanding of it." And indeed, the volume met with as encouraging a response as had been received by the editions of the earlier Readings. The first printing was soon exhausted, and a reprint was ordered. Andrew McCosh was in no doubt as to what to do next, and the *Daily Bible Readings: The Gospel according to Luke* was got under way. Willie did not then know it, but he had entered the "battery hen years." (*The Methodist Recorder* first characterized this period of his career in this fashion in 1974, likening the pressures under which he worked to those of the process of forced poultry raising known as "battery hen" production.) For the next six years his every waking moment was to be consumed in fulfilling a variety of commitments.

Because the new series was essentially an internal affair of the Church of Scotland, review copies were not circulated. In one sense, then, this new series was regarded less as a commentary than as a devotional book, the likes of which were not often reviewed at that time. Even *Life and Work* did not review it formally. Biblical scholarship per se was now seeking to make up for lost time, as were the publishers of religious books, and "more important" books claimed the limited space at the disposal of the review editors. Willie, as we saw, had himself found a niche as a reviewer of such material in *The Expository Times*. But even in this work his interest was markedly practical. Following the publication of his book on Acts he castigated H. F. D. Sparks's *The Formation of the New Testament* and C. H. Dodd's important work *According to the Scriptures* as "products of the study rather than the battlefield of life"[52]—which criticism earned him a broad-side from H. Cunliffe-Jones. But although Cunliffe-Jones was right to call attention to the rich value of these books, his criticism of Willie violated somewhat the importance of his pastoral emphasis. Willie was in the business of baking bread, not refining flour.

We should not suppose that in those early days Willie—as his colleagues—foresaw what was to happen. He had been diverted by church authority from his real aspiration (the Chair in Practical Training and Ethics) and had come more or less accidentally, as it appeared on the surface, into biblical work via his "emergency" lectures to returning servicemen in early 1946. His immense repu-tation as lecturer, lesson writer, and editor for the Scottish Sunday School Union had naturally heightened his Renfrew Trinity skills as a popular teacher, which paved the way for daily reading notes after the IBRA tradition. He thought this new opening never more than a temporary task, to which he set his hand with his usual dispatch. Like so many aspects of his life and ministry, it was a duty undertaken willingly; he was simply doing his job as a servant of Jesus Christ. Because of this the commentary is thoughtful, but not contemplative; practical, not exegetical; designed for the heart and life, not the head or study; it broke no new ground academically, nor was its translation particularly polished. When R. P. Morris of Illinois came to classify it for the Theological Education Fund (using the later edition published by the Westminster Press in 1958) it was correctly entered in his "simple books" category and described as having "popu-lar, exegetical value" for the user. His were essentially lessons, not studies. But it was, as its sales demonstrated, exactly what was required. As David H. C. Read noted in an article in *Life and Work*, the times called for a "transition from argument to demonstration," and here Willie is found—as Billy Graham had been in another sphere—asserting the primacy of "Thus saith the Lord." As he boldly asserted at the Youth Rally of the General Assembly for 1952, contradicting those who called for a return to the preaching of first-century Christianity, "what is needed is a forward-looking twentieth century Christianity."[53] Forward! as ever.

Untypical Catechist

We have seen how extraordinarily busy he was during the early '50s, the first part of the so-called battery hen years, which continued till the end of 1958. But this canvas needs to be broadened even further, as other interests and opportunities were still being undertaken despite the burden of the Daily Bible Readings scheme and the menacing international situation.

The times had generally continued their forbidding developments, foremost of which was the escalation of the cold war on the international front. In March

1953 Stalin died, which event was followed by the post-Stalin purges. In June Churchill suffered a near-fatal stroke, which delayed from June to December the Three-Power Conference (of America, Great Britain, and France) concerning the upkeep of military forces in northwest Europe. Fears had never run higher concerning the possibilities of a new worldwide conflict, and it was not just confined to the Western alliance. Soon Egypt declared itself a republic following the abdication of King Farouk, and a new chapter of Middle East uncertainty opened. In 1954 France lost control of Indo-China, and a vicious war of attrition was undertaken by the United States, the consequences of which were to develop into a frenzy of political agitation that, in turn, would reshape democracy in the 1960s. The Domino Theory of Communist expansionism became an integral element in international affairs. In Britain concern over the cost of living continued to dominate the domestic scene, leading to the dismantling of the "overlord" system of ministerial supervision (which had linked together such ministries as food and agriculture, fuel and power, scientific resources and atomic power). Within a year of America's exploding its first H-bomb in November 1952, the Soviet Union had produced one of its own; thermonuclear test blasts were soon heating up the cold war. Moreover, the area of personal morality was again subjected to liberalizing attitudes, some of which made even the twittering '20s look conservative. This was the age of Hollywood's worship of the superstar, sex-bombs, and many similar extravagances; not least in this was the spreading acceptance of homosexual behavior. A "confusion of morals" was reported, and the churches were called to take action. In a different area, but not less disconcerting for some evangelicals, the ecclesiastical historian James Bulloch wrote of the growth of Roman Catholicism in Scotland—it now claimed fifteen percent of the population among its adherents.

On 22 February 1953 Willie celebrated the twentieth anniversary of his ordination. This was the year in which the first postwar reunion of students of Marburg University was held, but Willie was not in attendance to hear Ernst Käsemann's review of the theological situation. He was far too busy at home—on the councils of the Scottish Sunday School Union and at its conferences at the University's faculty and senate meetings, as External Examiner in New Testament at Leeds University, and above all in his prolific writings. He was still finding time to attend home matches of the Motherwell Football Club and occasional concerts of the Scottish National Orchestra, and preaching every Sunday remained an inescapable duty and pleasure. A series of "Bible Weeks" was held throughout Scotland in honor of the sesquicentennial of the British and Foreign Bible Society. Willie, with his family roots deep in the movement, played his part in evening and weekend lectures. He had been appointed Alternate to the General Secretary of the National Bible Society of Scotland in 1953, and his duties in that post now took him to various places for work on the New English Bible. (It was later that he was empaneled under Professor McHardy's convenership at Oxford on the Apocrypha.) All this did not exclude him from regularly attending the Glasgow Park Head Ministers' Fraternal, at which, to quote Malcolm

Furness, he "sounded the authentic prophetic note."[54] Mr. Furness does not overlook the personal sacrifice entailed, mentioning particularly Willie's "very cumbersome hearing aid—earphone, headstrap and heavy valve amplifier in black square box with carrying handle, [which] whistled noisily" and which required a table to rest on. Two members of the Fraternal, James N. Alexander (father of Neil, a subsequent colleague of Willie's at Trinity College) and Willie, wore these hearing aids, each whistling in its own key—to the amusement of their colleagues. "James or Willie?" was the good-humored question of the host minister of distinguished name, R. L. Stevenson, as the whistling grew louder down the passage leading to the vestry.

In December Willie celebrated his forty-sixth birthday without following the advice of one of his literary heroes, Samuel Johnson, who laid it down that at this time in life Sunday must be used to examine oneself to see whether one has gained any virtues and to rid oneself of any old faults. Still, such personal stock taking appealed greatly to Willie, though never morbidly, much less publicly. He had already recommended such habits in his Sunday School lessons: "On Sunday we ought to examine ourselves and to measure up our progress or lack of progress in the spiritual life." Willie's ideas of religious assiduity were never negative, mean, or judgmental—forms of discipleship with which he strongly disagreed.

Even if Sunday was becoming less quiet for him, with less time for such things, he was not losing sight of his need for them. Nor was he alone in this. Throughout Great Britain a reviving spirit had been at work as the churches and affiliated organizations took stock of their diminishing numbers and effectiveness. Not the least part of this awakening were the preparatory meetings and evangelistic campaigns of Billy Graham, whose work at once unified and polarized Christian concern over "the unchurched masses." In Scotland he led meetings in connection with the "Tell Scotland" campaign, and there were very few who did not feel something of their virility and power. Over twenty thousand attended the North Glasgow mission services, and the church papers were full of reports, assessments, and appreciations. In May 1954 the first profile of the American evangelist was published; his work in Scotland began with the Kelvin Hall campaign of 1955.

Early in 1954 the Presbytery of Glasgow instituted its Standing Order X.2.d, which barred all ministers who had not attended at least five of its meetings from representing it at the General Assembly. Not a few were excluded by this ruling— including the Moderator-Elect himself, E. D. Jarvis! Willie not unexpectedly was also of their number, though he did attend the General Assembly that year by virtue of being the specially invited speaker of the Woman's Guild. He had stirring and controversial things to say, this time declaring himself on the subject of the decline in the number of ministers and ministerial students. By now his view of women and the church had changed, and we find him forecasting that women ministers would be ordained in the Church of Scotland—"in accordance with

New Testament teaching"—but laying it down, from which view he never moved, that should the women so ordained marry they should resign their charge.

His status as "a teaching elder" of extraordinary power and authority in his church was by this time widely recognized. Notwithstanding the labors of his books, he found time to become involved in one of the major issues of the day: the perplexing question of doctrinal redefinition and teaching. In February a meeting of the Senior Lesson Panel of the Scottish Sunday School Union and the Doctrinal Sub-Committee of the Church of Scotland Youth Committee met with representatives of the other member churches to discuss the Draft Catechism of the Church of Scotland. A move had been made to integrate the Draft Catechism into the lessons schemes of the SSSU, but this was dropped in favor of making separate expository material available. The subcommittee recommended this to the SSSU's Executive Committee; it was approved on March 8, and a circular to all interested parties was sent out for comment. This was collated by autumn, the upshot being that Willie was commissioned to write a series of articles on it for *The Scottish Sunday School Teacher*. Once again the willing—and able—horse was found, and he proceeded with accustomed style and speed. The Draft Catechism was indeed only a draft, designed to serve a two-year trial period. He wrote thirteen expositions of its doctrinal aspects (the practical section, Questions 40–60, was omitted in order to give more space and consideration to what were thought to be weightier matters). It was virtually Willie's swan song for *The Scottish Sunday School Teacher,* and a highly appropriate one at that. It is appropriate that we briefly survey the aspects of the scheme he chose to set before the Scottish Sunday School Union teachers.

There were not a few who felt that the catechizing method suggested by the drafters was long outdated. Willie was among their number, though he never rejected the need for some form of memory work. But it is characteristic of him nevertheless to agree to expound this not by emphasizing the method, but by "making plain" (Willie's significant rewording of the Draft Catechism's "setting forth") the truth of Christianity, which he was at pains to show is the truth of Jesus himself. George Dryburgh, on behalf of the Youth Committee, had already published in full the Draft Catechism with expositional notes; Willie, after the manner of one being "all things to all men," now did likewise for the far broader constituency of *The Scottish Sunday School Teacher*. Another aspect of this work appealed to the one whose motto was ever "Forward, not backward": it was essentially an experimental catechism. While Willie was not persuaded that the method was right *simpliciter,* he was ever willing to try things out, no matter what the criticism or opposition.

As we should expect from a church standing foursquare in the Reformed tradition, the doctrine of the Draft Catechism was faithful to the theological position of the Westminster Confession. And so was Willie's exposition. There is nothing in these thirteen articles that raises a single doubt as to his own doctrinal understanding or commitment; the infrastructure of his beliefs is still that of his early days, of his parish ministry and of the books now widely circulating through the Boys' Brigade, the Youth Committee, and the Publications Department of the Church of Scotland. It may be argued that the Draft Catechism itself is silent on the deity of Jesus per se, but that omission is not attributable to Willie, nor may we fairly criticize him for following his text faithfully. Indeed, in discussing Questions 6 and 7, concerning how God made himself known, he actually departs from his text boldly to assert that the meaning of the incarnation is "God on earth in human form. . . . In [Jesus] we see the mind of God. In Him we see what God is like fully and perfectly."[55]

The exposition is vintage Barclay—whether we think in terms of style, doctrine, emphasis, illustrations, or quotations. And what is fundamental to Willie's approach and theology, which is partly obscured by his expositions of the New Testament books, is the method we saw him using in his pastoral work, particularly in his "threshold evangelism" articles in *The Renfrew Press*—that is, of asserting both natural and special revelation (if we may be permitted to use such technical terms of one who consciously avoided them). That, too, is vintage—and essential—Barclay. His appreciation and enjoyment of the present world as the valid theater of God's actions held even more strongly. He would brook no denial of this, whether in faith or life, belief or work. To some extent he found this approach already in his text, and it is clear from the expositions that a movement from the natural order to the spiritual, from the external world to the internal, from the earthly and human to the heavenly and the divine was not only satisfying to him personally, but was spiritually and logically requisite and theologically sound, warranted by the testimony of science, history, and man's experience. If we may risk a presumptuous comparison, while Barth was seeking to define belief within the sphere of the church, Willie (albeit "nontheologically") was seeking to define it as contiguous with the world, as a concomitant factor of it, rather than as something extraneous to it. This approach, known well to all who have sought to understand the "experiential method" of Bible teaching, is conspicuous in the format of the Draft Catechism itself, the first section of which deals with the scriptural "Teaching about Man" prefatory to its "Teaching about God." But Willie's primary source was ever the Bible itself; he was anchored to its world view, unprepared to deal in purely intellectual ideas or convictions, however plausible. What took him to the Bible was the reasoning process of man face to face with the world of experience: a world that ever directs thinking, lonely man to God. We can thus see that "threshold evangelism" is but another, if incipient, yet plainer name for "natural revelation," an aspect he three times emphasizes in his exposition of the Draft Catechism. The world is "a great, wonderful machine," whose "perfect order" implies the divine mind at work, thus excluding all forms of chance, fatalistic development, or progress.[56] God, he asserts plainly, makes himself known by means of this world ("a world of beauty, wealth and bounty") in a fourfold way: by its sheer power, by its orderliness, by its detail, and by its bounty. Likewise, God makes himself known in history and in conscience.

But it is through the Bible, chiefly in Jesus, that our knowledge of God is brought to maturity. In the Bible we read of those who lived closest to God and could therefore speak of him authoritatively. (We shall see that this remained a key plank in the structure of Willie's understanding of biblical inspiration and authority.) But if we really want to know what God is like, we must see him in Jesus—"the perfect expression of the thought of God"[57]—who, with the Holy Spirit, constitutes the "difficult" doctrine of the trinity, which, Willie always emphasized, was better understood experientially than abstractly. (He was ever careful not to teach the individual members of the trinity as a progressive self-realization of God in different "modalist" forms, a heresy that troubled the church from time to time, as in the Monarchian doctrines of Sabellius.) Willie presented the orthodox conception of the trinity as three separate persons, perfect in goodness, wisdom, love, and power, who are one in an eternal union, exercising their attributes concertedly and harmoniously, the wisdom and love "controlling" the goodness and power, and so on.

Outflowing from this revelation is the doctrine of the Fatherhood of God—he whose providential control may be unreservedly trusted—which should never be sentimentalized, since he is ever holy and just. The Son—"really and truly and fully a man"[58]—comes to us as both Savior and Lord, rescuing us from our sin and failure, and marking out for us a new direction and purpose in life. Willie is careful to emphasize that man is incapable of this by himself (a factor in his teaching too easily overlooked by those who mark him down as a Pelagian); such power is given by the Spirit—"God active in our lives"—whose five-fold functioning (of comforting or en-couraging; of revealing and interpreting; of perpetually reminding us; of discovering new truth to us, which he draws from the infinitude of God and the unsearchable riches of Christ; and of daily directing us) fully meets our needs.

The third section of the Draft Catechism deals with sin and salvation, and again the movement from the common things of life to spiritual things is well brought out. Willie could have approached this topic from the side of law and its transgression, but he chose instead to deal with it in its obvious effects in society at large. His gospel was ever social in the sense of never forgetting man's place in the world as established by God or the effects on society that individual behavior produces. Sin ruins peacefulness and raises barriers between men (which point allows him to stress its international as well as its racial reality, the sole "political" applications he made in this series) as well as disrupting the personal relationship between man and God. At the root of all such disharmony and conflict lies "the exaltation of self,"[59] the very opposite of love (to God and man), which is the apex of the divine command. The consequence of sin is injury to ourselves—and to each other, bound up as we are in the one entity of human life. This injury renders us still less able to do God's will, thereby hindering fellowship (with God and each other), a thing grievous to God. Consciences, Willie asserts, are "the moral traffic lights" in our behavior, the Holy Spirit speaking within us. His subsequent exposition, ideally written for the young people who were the object of the exercise, could have graced any evangelistic platform and would have delighted D. L. Moody (of whom the Editor presently wrote, in preparation for Billy Graham's campaigns). The consequences of sin in entrapping man and feeding his guilt were emphasized, to which was added mention of the need for repentance (a turning from, as well as sorrow for, sin). Faith in Christ, trust placed in him with reliance on his word, is necessary, and inevitably issues in action consonant with that trust; moreover, it results in a restored relationship with God, and a life and conduct appropriate to it.

The fourth section of the Draft Catechism dealt with the church, which Willie interpreted in noninstitutional terms. The church, he insists, is not a building, but a community whose common possession is Jesus Christ—the Lord and master, the king and head of his people (his thinking was bound to revert to this fulcrum point). The church—one universal, historical, indestructible church of his commitment—is composed of "men and women who believe in Christ and know and love God."[60] His vision of the church is ecumenical as ever, a gathered community of believers, a believing (and practicing) company of those indwelt by the Holy Spirit. In expounding Question 22, he defines still further their activities. They worship God, thereby seeking his forgiveness, thanking him, receiving fresh power from him, and asking for his blessing for others. "Real worship," Willie declares, "is anything which brings us close to God, and makes us aware of the presence of God" (a concept, as we shall see, that allows of universal definition and practice).[61] But believers are those who tell others about the Christian faith and seek to help them live the Christian life, and who, moreover, seek to tell all men: they are (in typical emphasis) Jesus' legs, hands, feet, and voice.

Willie's attitude in these things was essentially individualistic, which emphasis conducted him naturally to expound the means of grace, the fifth section of his text. The Bible and prayer are foremost here. He characteristically describes the Bible as "our route map" in the way of life,[62] and prayer as both a speaking and a listening process. In keeping with the traditional understanding of scripture, he points out our need to find God's word "in the scriptures of the Old and New Testaments," a process that requires openness of heart, mind, and conscience. It is in this spirit that the Bible must be studied, remembered, and practiced, in which things the Holy Spirit's help predominates.

The question of the sacraments takes him once more to the heart of his theological method and understanding, for there is a sense in which "ordinary things acquire meaning beyond themselves,"[63] a statement of historical fact. "Most people think in pictures and not in abstract ideas," he explains, adding his former professor McNeile Dixon's view that "It is by imagination that men have lived. Imagination rules all our lives. The human mind is not, as philosophers would have you think, a debating hall but a picture gallery."

He argues that the verb to baptize "does not mean to sprinkle; it actually means to dip."[64] Baptism therefore symbolizes the heavenly origins of new life in Christ and the cleansing and purifying thereby received. Through baptism, he holds, God's love is conveyed to us, becoming an effective force in our lives; and it is "the door by which we enter the church." He states that it may be administered to both adults and children—the former because the early church started from a position of adult response to Jesus' message; the latter, because believing parents actually seek for their children the blessings of the gospel. He expounds certain specific duties of the church regarding the sacrament (though curiously he says nothing about parental responsibility): it must help the newly baptized both to know and to know *about* Jesus; it must help them to love Jesus; and, especially, it must make them responsible church members.

The Lord's Supper, Willie states, is, after the pattern of Old Testament prophetic dramatic symbolism, "a memorial of Jesus,"[65] but "far more than that." This extra dimension is not a matter of intrinsic meaning, but of what the sacrament *does,* and particularly what it does for the individual who thus confesses his allegiance: it brings one into contact with Jesus; it assures one of forgiveness; it provides sustaining power to follow him; and it makes one feel part of God's family. Willie notes that certain things are necessary if the believer is to be the partaker of these benefits: self-examination, penitence, the renewal of one's personal allegiance, and an understanding of the sacrament's significance— "discerning the body of Christ," in Paul's language—itself a "social" activity. A long section on prayer (Questions 35–39) follows, which includes an exposition of the main themes of the Lord's Prayer, all in typical style.

As noted earlier, Willie did not handle the section "Teaching on Conduct" (Questions 40–60) because of space pressures, though the tone of the whole exposition was acutely practical, as was his way. Questions 61–63 deal with the vitally important aspect of the Kingdom of God. The Draft Catechism rightly sees this as involving "the reign of God's love and righteousness in the realm of eternity, within the lives of men, and in the affairs of the world"—a rich definition, considering the wide range of problems confronting the church of the mid '50s! It has to be admitted that Willie's exposition of this section is somewhat disappointing, though entirely in line with the lack of social conscience in the evangelical wing of the church at that time. He is strong on asserting the Kingdom in personal terms—not geographically, but ethically, as became one who had but recently hoped to fill Gossip's Chair of Ethics and Practical Theology. We shall need to watch how this element reasserted itself as he became disentangled from the claims of the Daily Bible Readings scheme. What emphasis he does give in dealing with how we advance God's Kingdom, he supplies by way of almost pietistic generalizations about loving God and man, about offering words and deeds.

The Kingdom of God is traditionally wrapped up with the things of the end times, and Questions 64–68 follow that strategy. They start with a definition of eternal life, in which Willie characteristically affirms the quality, rather than the duration of that life, though he does acknowledge that longevity is also part of it. Our responsibilities to God, by whom we shall be judged "at the end of the day," are of tremendous significance, and are two in number: to use the gifts given us and, a thing reminiscent of his second literary piece from his Renfrew days, to fulfill our "possibilities." The judgment will also be made on a twofold basis: our response to Jesus and our attitude toward our fellow men.

There remain but two of the catechism's questions to deal with. Question 67 involves the Christian attitude toward life and death, in answer to which Willie's probationary view of life (after Browning and others—"life is a training-class for the higher class-work is to come") finds full and emphatic expression. The final question raises the issue of the consequences of neglecting the Christian way: in natural life unused gifts and faculties, like muscles, will atrophy and disappear if they are not used; so it is, Willie holds, with spiritual gifts: it is possible to lose them altogether. This is not the view of the later universalist, but of one who takes seriously the dire warnings he has elsewhere been expounding. Damnation is not, he explains in conclusion, punishment, but a self-inflicted wound: the love of God is ever ready to welcome and bless those who heed it.

It is interesting to compare this exposition with the one he made fifteen years earlier (to the same Scottish Sunday School Union constituency). The first, it will be remembered, was a word of encouragement to a people in the shadow of war in 1940. The second presents constructive doctrine to a postwar people now highly confident of its ability to rebuild society and replenish the national coffers. Merely to state that shows how little new thinking had been attempted, even though the seeds of such reconstruction were present in the Draft Cate-chism, as we saw vis-à-vis the Kingdom of God question. But having said that, one must emphasize that the objective of the Draft Catechism was to provide material for the training of youth already attached to the church, to deepen its spiritual awareness, and to motivate it afresh for evangelistic activity rather than to redirect the church's mission. Other thinkers saw it differently, but while Willie preserved a lively sense of "this-worldliness," he was not yet of their number.

It is not surprising in an age given over to spiritual introversion—if we may so describe evangelistic campaigns designed to "catch" men rather than equip the church for "socializing" the gospel—that such an emphasis should be made. And who would suggest that it was not correct? Greater authority in belief and in its expression is undoubtedly present, rightly so from this foremost trainer-of-men for the ministry and communicator of the gospel. Behind that authority lies the preparation and the maturity of the war years and subsequent work and experience throughout the land. It is a mistake to look for differences of doctrine between the Short Statement of the Church's Faith and the Draft Catechism. Both of them belong to his "conservative" years, the former being the affir-mation of a leader under pressure and the latter being those of a scholar now well-versed in his source documents but on the threshold of new ideas and emphases. The effects of that pressure and of rapidly changing social conditions were to harden his belief in some ways and soften it in others, but they would affect the basic "I believe . . . I pledge" that held them and all subsequent statements together.

Translating "The Sheen of Heaven"

In the same way that Willie's career was checked by the onset of war, so now the expansion of his ideas into a challenging, workable ethic for the postwar situation was also checked by his involvement in the Daily Bible Readings scheme of his church. It is clear from the appeal to him by Andrew McCosh that nothing more than a stopgap between the IBRA's style of reading notes and the popular Bible commentaries suggested by the National Bible Society of Scotland was envisaged. The need was recognized, a decision was made to fulfill it, and Willie was once more found to be the man for the job. He was delighted to be involved in "a big task," but did not dwell on either its potential or its consequences.

And so the enterprise was born, piecemeal and falteringly. To his little blue-jacketed "commentary" on Acts he added a red-jacketed volume on the Gospel of Luke written in almost as short a time: 340 pages of introduction, analysis, and commentary that fed its grateful readers from 1 September 1953 to 15 January 1954. As in the volume on Acts, the daily readings schedule was printed and bound into the front of the Luke work in its first edition. The "little red commentaries" of worldwide fame were thereby born. His statement of dissatisfaction with the book (omitted from later editions) is interesting: "again I am conscious that this book has been written with too much haste."[66] He regrets that his commentary has gone beyond (by fifteen days) the space allotted to him: "Before I began the book I divided the gospel into sections which lasted for exactly four months; but as I wrote and explored I found that some of the sections were too long and that they had to be divided." He excuses himself from not making any attempt to provide equal portions of text and commentary for each day—"I do not believe that the words of the Bible can be measured out in equal portions as one might measure yards of cloth"—and he admits to using material he wrote in other books. The reason for that duplication is his hope "that this book will reach a different and a wider public." But his real aim, the now consuming passion of his life, is "to make the life and words of Jesus live against their contemporary background and, above all, to make them relevant for today," to which objective he adds the prayer of Richard of Chichester, which may be called the signature tune of the whole enterprise (used here for the first time): "to know Jesus Christ more clearly, to love Him more dearly, and to follow Him more nearly." The resultant work must be judged in that light.

It was inevitable that he should choose to expound Luke's Gospel, for he ever regarded Luke and Acts as two parts of the one work, in line with the majority of British commentators. Moreover, as we saw with his *Life and Work* articles on the Gospel, the sheer humanity of it was exhilarating to him, as were its rich spirituality and "modern," emancipated outlook. "Dr. Luke" was very definitely a man after Willie's own heart, as he had been after his mother's too. It was, he declared, "the Gospel of women," "the Gospel for the Gentiles," "the Gospel of Prayer," and, despite its outstanding characteristic of universality, notably "the Gospel of Praise." As Willie puts it, "There is a radiance in Luke's gospel which is a lovely thing, as if the sheen of heaven had touched the things of earth."

He owns, amid gratitude to his publishers for entrusting to him the task of writing this second volume, his debts to the Revised Standard Version of the New Testament, claiming in passing "no special merit" for his own translation. He owns, too, the debts owed to other commentators who had gone before: Alfred Plummer (1896), J. M. Creed (1942), H. Balmforth (1930), and William Manson (1930). Merely to cite these names and the dates of their commentaries is to remind ourselves how dated his source material was and what changes have taken place in New Testament studies. For example, the phrase "form criticism" does not once occur in this or any of the subsequent fifteen volumes of the series. This is not to say that the application or relevancy remains dated! But it is important to recall that he was writing only shortly after the end of the war, when the nation was still struggling to get back on its feet and when biblical scholarship, and religious publishing generally, still bore the essential traits of the recessed prewar era. Willie, if not in the van of academic work per se, was nevertheless setting standards and goals, as well as making and breaking records in his own way. He was not alone in this work. At the very time the volume on Luke went on sale to the public, D. M. G. Stalker was putting the final touches to his Daily Bible Readings volume on Genesis, and others were to follow.

It is invidious to compare the work of such men, whether in devotional tone or academic excellence. The very nature of the commissions put all the contributors under pressure, and the times themselves were pressured. But what no one, least of all Willie's friends, can discount is the sheer energy and relentless drive of this man Barclay. Like his beloved *Royal Scot,* which many a time thrilled him between Glasgow and London during these and earlier years, he powered along in an apparently tireless and effortless way, never giving the appearance of haste, but never wasting time either. He always found time to listen to this student's problems or supply for this or that minister's help, anniversary, or special occasion.

And yet this inhuman pace was already telling on him physically. He was beginning to show some signs of premature aging. Perhaps most significantly, despite his mobile features in preaching, teaching, and conversation, in his unguarded moments he was beginning to display what Lord Moran called "the expressionless mask of a deaf man,"[67] of a man who had *slaved* these past twenty years (his hard work did not begin at ordination), of a man disabled by deafness, whose hearing aid was "hammering away all the time"[68] (anything less than maximum power was useless). And if that harmed and weakened its wearer, which it undoubtedly did, the effect on those in his company was not always less marked. Deafness is a curiously ostracizing disability, and its sufferers are all too often the victims of unsociable and unsympathetic behavior by those who are irritated by the general helplessness of the hearing-disabled and the shrieks and whistles of their hearing aids. Willie was learning yet another great lesson on the road to sainthood—that "My grace is sufficient." It was never an easy lesson.

This time the response to the commentary was more widespread. If the praise received by the volume on Acts came from all Protestant denominations throughout Scotland, an international dimension was added for the volume on Luke. It would not be long before its distribution was applauded worldwide, especially throughout the overseas missionary world. One copy, for example, made its way into the hands of the Chief Justice of the Supreme Court of Ghana, Quashie Idun, and was gratefully accepted.[69]

Space forbids any detailed description of Willie's exposition of Luke or the other books he expounded, but his attitude toward the Gospel is worth keeping in mind, as it is greatly reflective of Willie's own personality. He agreed that it is "the loveliest book in the world."[70] It works to support worthwhile tradition (e.g., the early church imagery of the gospel as a calf, an ancient sign of sacrifice), but more importantly Luke the Gentile (the only Gentile, Willie reminded his readers, to have contributed to Holy Writ) stresses how the traditional barriers are broken down by Jesus: barriers between God and man, Jew and Gentile, slave and free, saint and sinner, between society and children, and especially in the liberation of women. Its gospel is universal, for all mankind, and thus the book—"an exceedingly careful bit of work" in which the Greek is "notably good"—is set on a secular worldwide stage. Willie characteristically highlights the elements of prayer and praise in the Gospel, seeing them as particularly important elements of the Christian life in both personal and corporate situations. Above all else it is a demonstration of the truth of Faber's great hymn, that "the love of God is broader / Than the measure of man's mind"—to which breadth Willie ever felt drawn, and to which he ceaselessly drew others' attentions. The universality of the gospel was becoming a principle of Willie's mature theology, an essential dimension of his understanding of the encompassing love of God. The lessons of the past, not least of his soldiers' canteens, were showing; the shibboleths were being questioned, found wanting against this wider background, and rejected. "Forward, not backward"—he was now moving, even in these still-conservative days, away from the administrative and pastoral orientation of the past, to matters of the mind, of faith and doctrine and practice. Opening salvos against the shut mind—ever his bête noire—were being resolutely fired; they were soon to become unceasing, and would alienate him from his natural constituency of "Bible-centered" conservative people. Thus originated the dichotomy in Willie's thinking and influence—rejected by both conservatives and liberals, truly at home with neither.

It was not only to the Publications Committee and his academic forebears that Willie felt indebted. The dedication to the Luke commentary underpins the gratitude expressed in his book *And He Had Compassion on Them*: "To the Kirk Session of Trinity Church, Renfrew, over whom God called me to preside from 1933 to 1946, and in particular to M R [Mitchell Ramsay] and J B K [John Kidd]: men of God." In the same way he had signaled the termination of the early period in dedicating the Commentary on Acts to his parents, so now he marked a symbolic farewell to the chief men of his parish days, the elders of the church that he claimed "made me." The unfolding of dedications in these commentaries is one of widening debt from home to national church life, a moving tale of influence and gratitude.

By May 1954 he had produced another minor miracle. His third volume to the series treated Galatians, 1 and 2 Thessalonians, and 1 and 2 Corinthians. He provided his own translation from the Greek for each of the epistles, along with eighteen pages of introductory matter (with Paul's correspondence there are issues of particular complexity, as we shall see), the whole amounting to 403 pages of exposition. The element of indebtedness in his preparation for such work is not overlooked; George A. Mills, General Secretary of the Scottish Sunday School Union for Christian Education, was the subject of the grateful dedication: "To me a Father in God who first gave me the Opportunity to write a Book, Whose Encouragement has often compelled me to go on when otherwise I would have given up, Whose Guidance has saved me from many a mistake, and Whose Wisdom has saved me from many a heresy, and to whom I owe more than I can ever repay." His parents, the church, and the Scottish Sunday School Union itself were also suitably thanked.

The trepidation with which he sent out the book on Acts was again present here: "I send out this volume with a question in my mind as to how it will be received."[71] His handling of the complexity of Paul's relationship with his churches and his correspondence was chiefly to blame for this: "It is true to say of Paul's letters that they will not give the man who studies them a meal unless he is prepared to break mental sweat." The trepidation this time is not for himself (George Mills, perhaps with his challenge to orthodoxy in mind, had seen to that). It is for his readers he is anxious: "I wonder how many people in our Church, and outside it, are prepared to make the effort to study Paul?" We need to take this question seriously today as well. Willie's career, his success and his fame, were founded on a pastoral realism and an understanding of discipleship that never omitted the element of discipline. Whatever else we may make of the postwar church, we should at least give it this credit: it did take Paul seriously; it did seek to make that effort, abundantly so, as the proliferation of postwar biblical and religious undertakings show. Willie was loved and honored precisely because he was recognized as one who was such a disciple, one worth following.

Moreover, what kept him going in all this effort and labor was the new sense of exploration he felt. He was not merely repeating old lessons, but discovering anew the continuously fresh old truths. He described this work as "one of the most enriching experiences which has ever come to me." Like J. B. Phillips in the south (whose *Letters to Young Churches* was ever at Willie's side), he was also finding the New Testament a thrilling book, constantly being shocked and delighted and awed as the divine truth penetrated his being. He was a man aflame, lit by God himself.

He again named the particular guides on the exegetical side: on Galatians, Martin Luther (1517, "one of his greatest commentaries"), J. B. Lightfoot (1890, "can never be superseded"), E. de Witt Burton (1921, "a monument of patient scholarship"), and G. S. Duncan (1934, "the best English commentary"); on Thessalonians, J. E. Frame and George Milligan (1912 and 1908, respectively, "two very great commentaries . . . the greatest of all English New Testament Commentaries"), William Neil (1950, "excellent") and Leon Morris (1956, "helpful and illuminating"); on Corinthians, T. C. Edwards (1897), A. Robertson and Alfred Plummer (1911), and A. Menzies (1912, "supremely valuable"). Yet again the Revised Standard Version had been a constant source of help in translating. As to his critical standing, he was restrained in the treatment of such matters as the identity of the Galatians (in dealing with "the North or South theories") and the Judaizers, though we should note that his placement of Galatians first in his sequence of expositions is indicative of his view that Paul did indeed write it before he wrote the other epistles. He expands more readily on the history of the Thessalonians, and retains the accepted chronological relationship of the two letters to each other. This latter point allows him to put the blame for the Thessalonians' excitement over the Second Coming of Jesus on their misunderstanding of Paul rather than on any significant change in Paul's thinking and theology. It is notable that he does not emphasize much internal comparative theology, preferring to exegete the text before him, and particularly individual words of his text, as it were under a microscope rather than panoramically. (It is different when he deals with the Synoptic Gospels, for there his eye is ever on the differences between the parallel accounts, not infrequently making the most of *both* traditions for practical ends, rather than adjudicating between the readings.) As he deals with Thessalonica, so he deals with Corinth, providing a substantial historical description of the city, its features, and the habits of its citizens. But as to the sequence of the Corinthian correspondence, he was only too ready to recognize that it is "out of order," adding that Paul's correspondence was not collated till A.D. 90. He follows the now traditional tabulation of the correspondence as follows:

1. The *Previous Letter* ("possibly" 2 Corinthians 6:14–7:1)
2. *1 Corinthians*, written in reply to Chloe's people's visit
3. The *Severe Letter*, sent after Paul paid the Corinthians his unhappy visit. (The *Severe Letter* is "almost certainly" contained in 2 Corinthians 10–13.)
4. The *Letter of Reconciliation* (2 Corinthians 1–9), written after Titus informed Paul that all was now well

I outline this because it shows his preparedness to ask his general readers to handle difficult "technical" issues and it serves to balance what was said above about his concentration on the text as it is presently disposed. Such a popular airing of the problems was guaranteed to give trouble, appearing as it did when many conservative souls were feeling embattled over many views that were considerably more "liberal" than Willie's here. This is not to say that conservative scholars did not broadly share his viewpoint; many did, but chose not to make their viewpoint widely known, especially to the rank and file of their denomination's membership. Sadly, some of the less hardy of their number (and the less generous) chose to make a fight over such things, unaware that the integrity of the word of God was not at stake in such things, still less the inspiration or authority of the Bible. It was from such strictures as these that the criticism that he was "unsound" began to circulate; each of his alleged failures to expatiate on every item of the whole creed (regardless of its relevance to the biblical text under discussion) was regarded as an attack upon it by him, a "resiling" (to use the word *The Monthly Record of the Free Church of Scotland* preferred) by him of the Christian faith. Sadly, the "battle for the Bible" was on—"sadly" in the sense that the enormous public response to Willie's writing shows that a real breakthrough was achieved. Popular biblical exposition was possible—profitable in fact—and enthusiastically received.

By rights any approach to the foundations of Christianity (and of the life of Jesus in particular) should be made through Mark's Gospel, for although it is not the earliest New Testament document, it does have chronological priority over the other Gospels.[72] Moreover, Willie was convinced of the reliability of Papias's tradition of Mark as being Peter's "interpreter" (the Greek is *hermēneutēs,* from which we get our word *hermeneutics,* the science of biblical interpretation). In Mark we have therefore a source of great trustworthiness, one written close to the commencement of the Christian church. It is, Willie baldly says, "a report of Jesus' life."[73] To this Gospel Willie now turned, the resultant volume of commentary being published for reading in the September–December 1954 period.

His commentary on Mark ran to over four hundred pages and treated very fully this, "the most important book in the New Testament." But once again, despite the historical importance of the book, he asserts that "My one aim has been to make the picture of Jesus live again." Immediacy and relevance were twin motives in his explorations. Despite that, he had in preparation studied carefully the works of such available exegetical masters as A. W. F. Blunt (1929), A. E. J. Rawlinson (1949, "one of the best commentaries in the English language"), B. H. Branscomb (1937), R. H. Lightfoot (1950), Austin Farrer (1954), H. B. Swete (1927, "still indestructible"), and Vincent Taylor (1953, "a monument of scholarship . . . fit to rank with the great commentaries of all time"). He is fully conversant with the main literary theories of the Gospel (though quiet about some new work then being undertaken, for example in form criticism, for which we may well blame the speed with which he was working, though his intention was always to treat of the text as we have it rather than how it came to us). He supports the standard accounts of Gospel criticism which see Mark being used as a primary source for Matthew and Luke. We might note in passing that he has very little to say of the "Q" tradition, and nowhere seeks to build on or expand its particular emphases after the manner of T. W. Manson in the early '30s. His biblical stance was definitely conservative, even though he had moved well away from his teenage understanding of an infallible English text and punctuation.

Mark's Gospel, he affirmed, is "the essential gospel," the preaching of Peter himself, and as such merits study "with loving care." He apologizes for the repetition of some points already dealt with in his commentary on Luke, explaining that a failure to repeat them would leave Mark somewhat depleted. As we saw with his Boys' Brigade handbooks, he was never particularly penitent about this sort of duplication, and never felt obliged to expound peripheral matter in order to avoid it. Perhaps, like Kierkegaard, he believed that only robbers and gypsies must never return where they have once been. Few would deny it to be good educational technique; just such loving care and emphasis made William Barclay the fine expositor and preacher he was now widely recognized to be.

No one raised in the Reformed tradition (of which the Church of Scotland is a notable expression) can deal with the New Testament without early coming to Paul's letter to the Romans. And so it was that Willie expounded it in the series that by now had all but taken his own name. It was his fifth volume, and ran for 244 pages, plus 31 pages of introduction and analysis. Its chief attraction for Willie, however, was the simple fact that it "contains more of the quintessence of the mind of Paul," to which Willie would be shortly directing the minds of the readers of his *British Weekly* articles[74]—and not only of the *mind* of Paul, but of his *heart* too, for Willie never omitted the applications of the gospel to the whole man—his emotions as well as his intellect. To judge by the number of times he referred to the legendary *Acts of Paul and Thecla,* which purports to describe Paul physically, we may see how important the body was in his thinking.

He acknowledges the rich wealth of commentaries on this letter, especially those of Sanday and Headlam (1895, "one of the great commentaries") and of C. H. Dodd (1932, "one of the two first commentaries in that series"). He also used works by E. H. Gifford (1886, "full of help"), K. E. Kirk (1937, "excellent in every way"), and James Denney (1900, "one of the best things Denney every [sic] wrote").[75] He also notes the revolutionary character of Barth's commentary (1919, "marked the beginning of an epoch")—though without once referring to him in his text—and greets Anders Nygren's work, recently translated into English (1952, "one of the greatest of all modern commentaries"). Appropriately, this "chiefest of the epistles" is dedicated to Willie's own chief, G. H. C. Macgregor, "whom it is my honour to call my Chief, and my privilege to call my friend."

Willie states that the letter is of "fundamental" importance (xxi), *fundamental* being a word he rarely used, but which he chose here to demonstrate the central role Romans occupies in a true Christian theology. His usual preference was for *essential* over *fundamental:* he clearly believed that getting to the essence of a thing was more useful and relevant than getting at its fundamental character- istic—which implies, perhaps, a greater attachment to fruits rather than roots. His sense of the immediacy of things—almost a Kierkegaardian passion with him—overrode at times his sense of historical propriety. If we may use the language of the experts, he preferred the *Geschichte* to the *Historie.* He does not dispute the Pauline authorship of the epistle, for there is very little challenge to its apostolic origins even by the old liberals of the Tübingen tradition. Nor is there any problem over its consignees, though Willie does recognize the problems asso- ciated with the doxology of Romans 16:25–27, which occurs at 14:23, 15:33, and

16:24 in some manuscripts. This problem leads him to assert an early dissemination beyond Rome of the principal bloc of the epistle in the form of an apostolic encyclical, which also emphasizes the importance of the letter. He is not overimpressed by Dodd's theory that chapter 16 was once an independent unit written to commend Phoebe, Aquila, and Prisca. Characteristically, he is drawn to this latter couple, who are preeminently those of "the open door, the open hand, and the open heart" (229).

But if the letter deals with fundamental things and demonstrates the quintessence of Paul's mind, Willie does not hesitate to emphasize as well the "occasional" character it possesses: it shows Paul "grappling with the problems of the Early Church," not those of the twentieth century. In doing so, Paul was naturally using concepts Willie believed to be outmoded in the modern world. For example, Willie suggests that the validity of Paul's steadfast assertion of the solidarity of mankind in Adam is open to question, despite his acceptance of the social consequences of sin; he is not thereby degrading Paul's teaching, but seeking its relevance for today, ever his task and objective. This cannot be done before the original situation is reconstructed, which Willie sees devolving on us as a continuous necessity (xvi). His evaluation of this issue offers no surprises, following the intimations Paul himself gives (in Romans 15:25, 28, etc.). The most dominant characteristics of the letter, Willie believes, are its testamentary and prophylactic elements: testamentary in the sense of "distilling the very essence of the last word of his faith and belief," and prophylactic in the sense of building up "a true word of Christian doctrine [as] a powerful and effective defence . . . against the infection of false teaching," the effective agent being "the analysis of truth" (xxi–xxii).

He analyzes the letter in terms of its four classical parts: chapters 1–8 ("the problem of righteousness"), 9–11 ("the problem of the Jews"), 12–15 ("practical questions of life and living"), and 16 (Phoebe's letter of introduction). His understanding of Paul's gospel is one that no follower of the Reformed tradition need be ashamed of, not least because, like John Robinson of old, Willie was ever certain that "the Lord hath yet more light to shed upon his sacred word." He was more trustful than many to whom that task was given. He emphasizes a recognition of sin's enormity and of the rightness of God's wrath against it, but at the same time he recognizes the *organic* nature of early man's rebellion and of its consequences in nature and history. He appears to accept, moreover, "the Jewish argument" of man's solidarity in Adam, by which man's moral power was broken and through which death pervaded all mankind. But, true to his mission to make relevant and intelligible a two-thousand-year-old principle, he also sees its "one great flaw" in the difference between his relationship to Adam and that with Christ: in the former it is involuntary; in the latter, entirely voluntary. Some may well distance themselves from Willie here, but the concluding assertion— entirely orthodox in Reformed theology—remains the backbone of his own theology: "Whatever else we may say about Paul's argument, it is completely true that man was ruined by sin and rescued by Christ" (82).

Merely to list some of his sectional headings is to be reminded where he stood doctrinally: "God's Fidelity and Man's Infidelity" (3:1–8), "All Is of Grace" (4:13–17), "Ruin and Rescue" (5:12–21), "The Exceeding Sinfulness of Sin" (7:7–13), "The Glorious Hope" (8:18–25), "The Love from Which Nothing Can Separate Us" (8:31–39). His practical aspect also clearly surfaces: "The Responsibility of Privilege" (2:1–11), "The Practice of the Faith" (6:12–14), "The Christian Life in Everyday Action" (12:9–13), "Tolerance for Another's Point of View" (14:2–4), and so much more. The epistle ends where it should—"The end is praise"; that, too, as we saw in his work on Luke, was Willie's way.

Having dealt with the primary Gospel, it was natural that his thoughts should turn to John's Gospel. There is very much about it that was especially congenial to Willie, the mystical and the more broadly Hellenic background being chief among several favored characteristics. It was therefore particularly appropriate that this Gospel, symbolized by the eagle (whose ability to gaze directly into the sun's light ever provoked Willie's imagination), should be dedicated to George Johnston Jeffrey, "Preacher of the Word, Prince of the Church, Writer of Books, Whose friendship has enriched my life, Whose encouragement has strengthened my effort, And in whose presence I have been nearer to God than at any other time" (a comment later challenged by what he said of A. J. Gossip in 1974—that he "lived closer to God than any man I have ever known").[76] We do not have to look far to see what particular debt Willie was owning in this dedication. In many ways Jeffrey (like Gossip) consolidated in himself the interests that had molded Willie. He was blessed with an immense pastoral and preaching ability, not least among young people, and was a man of the closet whose "Quiet Hour" pieces in *The Scottish Sunday School Teacher* had created a new atmosphere and set new standards for teachers and scholars alike. Since 1953, when his church bestowed upon him the high honor of the Moderatorship of its General Assembly, Jeffrey's influence had indeed grown to that of a veritable "Prince of the Church."

Willie's fondness for the deeper things of the spirit, which his bold human exterior sometimes masked, is significantly revealed in the significantly more extended treatment that he gives the Gospel of John compared to his previous works in the series. In the foreword to the first edition Willie takes note of this increase in the amount of exposition relative to the biblical text:

> I would like to point out one new feature in the setting of these Daily Bible Studies. None of the sections for each day has been allowed to become too long. In former volumes I put everything I wished to say about any passage into the reading for one day. In this volume, if there was a great deal to be said about any passage, I have asked the reader to spend two or even more days studying the passage with me.

In so writing, he not only explains the "new feature"—a very welcome one, which standardized (more or less) his readers' daily diet—but he also dropped two highly suggestive clues as to his own approach. The first is that the volumes are not commentaries in the accepted sense, namely, that they exegete, expound, and apply every aspect and the resultant whole of the biblical text; rather, the works present things that the author "wished to say about any passage." This must not be overpressed, however. William Barclay was a man of integrity who sought to uphold the integrity of scripture in both his translating and his commentating. Nevertheless, there was a personal element—of emphasis, selection, preference, or whatever—that hit the author and powered his writing. We need to bear this in mind as we judge both him and the successive volumes of his daily Bible study. It is what elsewhere might be termed a prophetic consciousness, as his exploring, pondering mind felt the power of the Word, perceived the reality of "Thus saith the Lord" emerging through it, and wrote, "I heard, and therefore did I speak." It has long been held that real preaching is "truth through personality"; it is the dual secret of Willie's writing success—a worldwide, transdenominational success—even as it was the secret of his preaching from pulpit and lectern nationwide.

The second clue to his approach rests in the final phrase of the passage quoted from his foreword: "studying the passage *with me.*" It will be remembered that in another context the father of one of his students was told that his son was doing well in his first year of theological studies: he and his fellow students, along with their revered tutor, were "discovering First Declension Greek nouns together." Willie's work and writing was never mere communication, the simple conveyance of information. He was not repeating things ad nauseam till the things were learned. They were discovering truth together: teacher and pupil. It was ever that way. He may use the same phrases, the same linguistic key, the very same (and sometimes very dated) illustrations, but he is doing so freshly, not repetitively; he is entering into his reader's mind and his feelings (a very important Barclay keyword), himself feeling the truth once more. Never did he teach by way of "authority," nor did he seek to impress his readers with his erudition; they learned together. And thus it was that countless thousands around the world who had never met him counted themselves as his friends, felt they knew well their guide and mentor; his own feelings and approaches reflected theirs—whether in joy or in sorrow, in strength or in weakness, in success or in failure. It is the mark of the supreme pastor.

In grappling with John's Gospel we tread on sacred ground. And in looking at Willie's exposition we feel we tread on ground especially sacred to its author. Never one to speak much about his personal devotional life, being aware that some were deeply embarrassed to read of such things (though he himself was perfectly natural in speaking of prayer and friendship with Jesus and many related issues), we cannot but feel that there is much here that is quasi-autobiographical in his exposition—immediacy revisited. Many, he well knew, regarded John as "the most precious book in the Bible."[77] We may note the superlatives: Acts is the most important, Luke the most beautiful, Mark the most important—how he loves and duplicates these superlatives! But John is the most *precious,* a thing of costly value. Its preciousness stems out of no sentimental attachment, but, like all Willie's sentimentality, out of symbolic meaning (as is elsewhere the case with his attachment to the Kailyard stories for their witness to home life and manhood, and in his treasuring of the sermon case that his dying mother had given him, which he used for over forty years,[78] the symbol of her lovely life, and so on). Further, John is "precious" because it is "an amazing book. . . . The more we study John the more wealth arises out of it. . . . Every verse is overflowing with riches." A lifetime, he holds, will not exhaust the Gospel's greatness.

And so the first of two volumes was born, albeit tardily. He pleads with his readers to "understand . . . that the task of producing three or four of these volumes per year, in addition to much other work, is no light one" (viii). If they did not, then certainly his family and neighbors could, for they could hear his typewriter banging away into the small hours and throughout the weekends, even as his students could hear it coming from behind his inadequate screen in the library of Trinity College. Never was work nearer to worship, never was worship more expressed as work, than in the presentation of these expositions.

The first edition of the first volume carried thirty-nine pages of introductory matter, for which length Willie offers an apology: "There is no book which gains so much from being set against the background from which it emerged," he states. And few would challenge the comment, especially at a time when the implications of the Dead Sea Scrolls, then in course of translation and publication, were still largely unrecognized. Again he owns the chief debts—always a moral duty to him rather than mere literary custom: to G. H. C. Macgregor's commentary (1928, "no volume so good"), B. F. Westcott's two commentaries on John's Gospel and epistles respectively (1887, 1892, "magnificent"), the dual volumes of J. H. Bernard (1928) and those of Marcus Dods (1907, "full of illumination"), Godet (1899, "outstanding"), works of general interest by E. F. Scott (1908), R. H. Strachan (1941), W. F. Howard (1943), and C. H. Dodd (1953), and, lastly, Basil Redlich's "small but excellent introduction" (1939) and William Temple's devotional commentary (1943). He regrets that C. K. Barrett's long-awaited commentary was not available to him (it appeared in 1956, too late for inclusion here): "it is not too much to say that that is a volume which the whole world of New Testament scholarship awaits with expectation"—one of his few theological forecasts that proved to be understatement.

Space forbids any discursive treatment of Willie's introduction and exposition here. Suffice it to say that he was bound to regard it as "the gospel of the Eagle's Eye" (xiii), the whole delight of which was to gaze and to explore "the sun of righteousness." In describing its differences when compared with the Synoptic Gospels, he comments that

> It omits so many things that they include. . . . [There is] no account of the Birth of Jesus, of His Baptism, of His Temptations; it tells nothing of the Last Supper, nothing of Gethsemane, and nothing of the Ascension. It has no word of the healing of any people possessed by devils and evil spirits. And, perhaps most

surprising of all, it has no parables . . . so priceless a part of the other three gospels. (xiv)

Other differences are also dealt with. Willie's is a masterly account of the Gospel's chief characteristics; one cannot but recognize the author's own confession when he asserts that "there are many people who find themselves closer to God and to Jesus Christ in John than in any other book in the world." It is undeniable that his essential theology—his iron rations, if you will—like his preferred style of devotion (lying on Jesus' breast, saying little) had much in common with those of John, and Johannine theology generally.

As to who this John was, Willie is certain of one thing: "beyond doubt the authority of John [the Apostle] lies behind the gospel" (xxix), though he owns the final penmanship to be another's, for he states categorically that "the penman" was actually John the Elder (xxxii). That the actual writing and authorship is inessential, though interesting, he does not doubt:

> John is not so much *The Gospel according to Saint John;* it is rather *The Gospel according to the Holy Spirit.* It was not John of Ephesus who wrote the Fourth Gospel; it was the Holy Spirit who wrote it through John. . . . Behind this gospel there is the whole Church at Ephesus, the whole company of the saints, the last of the apostles, the Holy Spirit, the Risen Christ Himself. (xxxviii, xxxix)

It was in that light he expounded its sacred text, in that light he theologized.

Recognizing the deliberate anonymity of the Gospel, he calls attention to the problem of the identity of the beloved disciple, and he fully accepts as beyond doubt that this enigmatic figure is John himself. Two final aspects need to be stressed concerning the 641 pages of exposition and application that he provides in this two-volume commentary. The first is its Christological concentration. In this Gospel "a curious double emphasis" (xxvii) is maintained: "On the one hand, there is no gospel which so uncompromisingly stresses the real manhood and the real humanity of Jesus"—and Willie demonstrates that decisively through his commentary. "But on the other hand, there is no gospel which sets before us such a view of the deity and the godhead of Jesus" (xxviii)—which Willie also, and equally forcefully, demonstrates. The first is demonstrated by a statement of "facts"—Jesus' anger, his tiredness, his hunger, his sympathy, his weeping and, supremely, his agony at the cross. The second is declared by the bold statement of inferences: his preexistence, his omniscience, his sovereign acts and attitudes. Willie conclusively states that "Jesus had a divine independence from all human influence. He was self-moved and self-determined" (xxix). The second aspect requiring our attention develops from this unity of the dual nature of Jesus, who is "the Creator of all things" (17) and who comprehends, sustains, and controls all things, be they what we might call sacred or mundane. This emphasis lies at the heart of Willie's world view, of his life-style, of his churchmanship, and of all his acts and attitudes. We have already encountered it expressed in his appreciation, veneration even, of "the common things," and it finds consummate expression here. He never sought, as did the post-Bonhoefferian theologians, to work his

secularity out systematically—he was far too unashamed of the word "religion"
for that—but we do now find a striking secularization of what many feel to be
the most sacred aspect of Christian worship: the Lord's Supper.

We noted earlier his view that there was no Last Supper in this Gospel. He
does not take this to mean that there was no Lord's Supper. "Quite certainly," he
writes apropos 6:50–59, "John was thinking of the Lord's Supper" (232).[80] But
now note the effect of his exposition, which internalizes or spiritualizes the
experience. Because of this, the outward form, the mode of presentation, the
occasion, the liturgy is secondary to the reality:

> There is no doubt what John is saying—he is saying that for the true Christian
> every meal has become a sacrament . . . every meal, in the humblest home, in the
> richest palace, beneath the canopy of the sky with only the grass for a carpet, is a
> sacrament. John refused to limit the presence of Christ to an ecclesiastical
> environment and a correctly liturgical service. . . . It is the wondrous thought of
> John that the communion table, and the dinner table, and the picnic on the
> seashore or the hillside are all alike in that at all of them we can taste and touch
> and handle the bread and the wine which bring us to Christ. Christianity would
> be a poor thing if Christ were confined to the Churches. (232-33)

In that statement the molding influence of his Free-Church upbringing and of
his beloved YMCA (essentially a lay Christian organization), and his long-
standing respect for the Salvation Army (which denies that the sacraments are an
essential part of worship and action) and the Quakers (whose emphasis on the
inner light took spirituality to its internal zenith) all reached a theological
conclusion: "It is John's belief that we can find Christ anywhere in a Christ-filled
world." A Christ-filled world! How different from this world view of Willie's is
that of the ascetic, the separatist (whether Exclusive Brother or obmutescent
monk), or even of the ancient Greek (or contemporary journalist!) who loathes
his body, his physical environment. There was no sense of shock over the friend
of publicans and sinners in this Clydebank, crowd-loving follower, there was only
a profound, and disconcerting, understanding of the reality of the incarnation.

Willie is at pains to ensure that the sacrament is not belittled. Anyone who
worshiped with him there would know with what awe and reverence, what joyful
wonder and thanksgiving, he would participate in it. But he was strenuously
against those who were "making too much of the Sacrament *within the Church*, . . .
making a fetish and a magic of the Sacrament, . . . saying or implying that the
Sacrament is the one place where we might find and meet and enjoy the rest in
the *nearer presence* of the Risen Christ." He has thus secularized the Supper; he
has returned it to the place where it began: in the homes and on the hillsides of
Galilee and Jerusalem. It was an essential part—sometimes an unheeded part,
sometimes a contemptuously dismissed part—of Willie's prophetic role.[81] We
shall see that he would recommend even more daring attitudes later, but for the
moment the insight is simply stated—and sadly, all but lost in the welter of work
in which he thrived.

We do not know the principle on which he selected for commentary the books of the New Testament. Acts we know to have been selected for him by the Committee, but the rest seem to have developed according to Willie's own preference, always with a view to stimulating further interest and study, his own as much as his readers'. The next volume, on Hebrews, however, he dedicated to "D A, for all his many kindnesses to me and especially because it was at his request that I wrote this book." We do not know who this "D A" is, but this dedication does show that he was not only content to study *with* his readers, but *for* them too. In the foreword to this volume he thanks "all these many people who have written to me so graciously. . . . Their letters have been a great encouragement."[82]

The textbooks on which he relied in preparing the work on Hebrews present us with a familiar, if somewhat dated picture of his day: B. F. Westcott (1899, "still unsurpassed"), J. Moffatt (1924, "a monument of scholarship"), F. D. V. Narborough (1930, "small, but very suggestive and illuminating"), T. H. Robinson (1933), E. C. Wickham (1910, "in every way first-class"), E. F. Scott (1922, "especially good"), and A. Nairne (1917). He finds, as ever, W. H. Griffith Thomas's writings helpful, this time recommending his *Let Us Go On: The Secret of Christian Progress in the Epistle to the Hebrews* (1923). But the most outstanding aid he found to be A. B. Bruce's commentary of 1899 ("stands supreme"). There remained but one further debt to acknowledge, and it is highly typical of the writer, not least in his proneness to overstate his debts:

> The first man whom I ever heard lecture on Hebrews was the late W M Macgregor, my teacher when I was a student at Trinity College. These lectures I will never forget. To me they were the high water-mark of the work of him who was the greatest interpreter of the New Testament I ever met. If this present book has anything of good in it, it remains due to the inspiration of W M Macgregor.

As he conceded in his autobiography, referring to Macgregor's indebtedness to his own teacher, A. B. Bruce, "I too could say that I had learned some few things from W M Macgregor that I wanted to pass on."[83] Whatever traditions other New Testament men stood in (in these postwar days some were actually *making* the traditions), Willie's was that of Bruce and Macgregor. Sadly, Macgregor has left very little published work for posterity, but if we are denied his own work, we are at least able to see its reflection in Willie's efforts to uphold his tradition in his lectures to his own students during these last seven years, and in the fruit of that study now distilled in this eighth volume of the Daily Bible Readings series, which became public property in March 1955, a book of twenty pages of introduction and 231 pages of exposition.

Willie was aware of the extraordinary difficulty this treatise (he actually calls it a letter) presents to the average reader, and claims that it was written "by a scholar for a little group of scholars" (vii). But he suggests that the effort to understand it is entirely worthwhile. Once more resorting to a superlative, he says, "I believe that there is no book in the New Testament which is more worth the effort to understand." The particular reward of such effort is to see "a glorious picture of Jesus Christ in all the splendour of His manhood and in all the majesty of His deity." Having warned his readers of the difficulties (of thought, language, and tradition) the treatise presents, he acutely selects the means by which their interest may be awakened by asking the question "In the final analysis, what is religion?" His answer suggests that religion means different things to different men. To the writer of Hebrews it meant primarily *access to God*. The text around which the epistle is built, therefore, is the call "let us draw near" (10:22)—a call that resounds throughout Willie's exposition.

But the writer of Hebrews is treating of his theme from a double background: the Greek, and especially the Platonic world of perfect forms and patterns, an ideal of which this world is but a very imperfect semblance. But into this the writer infused his Jewish background, formed of God's transcendent reality and the alienating principles of law, wrath, animal sacrifice, and priestly administration. Bridging the gap between man and God were the promise and the gifts of the covenant that God made with his chosen people, the enjoyment of which depended on obedience to God's commands. Men failed; even the appointed priests and sacrifices failed, for they (through man's failure) were not adequate for sin's enormity. And worse, they could not provide men with the power to live according to God's will. The "glorious picture of Jesus Christ" that this treatise presents is glorious not only because of the inherent glory of its subject, but also because of the work he efficaciously performs. He does triumphantly what the Jewish religious system failed to do slavishly. He is the perfect fulfillment of all that God intended: the perfect law, the perfect priest, the perfect sacrifice, and the perfectly adequate power by which men may live and have total access to (and enjoyment of) the presence of God.

Critics may note that, as with much of his exposition elsewhere, his treatment is essentially from the Greek side, despite the ostensible Jewishness of his subject matter (after all, "Hebrews is written with the best Greek in the New Testament" [xx]). They may also note that he does not latch onto the theme of preparation quite so solidly as he had hitherto, as in his Boys' Brigade handbooks, or even when he dealt with the Jew-Gentile problem in his commentary on Romans. And he does not wrestle with the implications of the failure of God's covenant with Moses. But no one can deny the depth of spirituality in his treatment of this letter, a compound of awe and wonder, grace and gratitude, that is profoundly uplifting, presenting a moral challenge and a practical appeal that cut into the deepest fibers of one's being.

Willie preserves an open mind on questions of authorship, dating, and initial recipients. Whoever the writer was (and Willie agreed with Origen that only God knows the answer to that problem), he is convinced it was penned by someone with at least the stature and background of a Barnabas or an Apollos, somewhere between A.D. 64 and 85, probably to an Italian colony or college of men destined to be teachers in the Christian church. Interestingly, he does not say that they were formerly of the Jewish faith, though clearly they were well acquainted with the Old Testament, as many Hellenists were.

His commentary on Ephesians closely followed that on Hebrews. It was appropriate to treat a book in which the thought and teaching of Paul concerning the church is paramount close on the heels of a book that (in his view) addresses a group of people in training for leadership in the early church. His dedication, "to all the students of Trinity College whom it has been my privilege to teach," was correspondingly appropriate. There is a definite internal logic at work in the selection of these books for commentary, to which the need for interest born of change supplied a counterbalance. He had underpinned his exploration of the founding and expansion of the early Christian witness and community recorded in Acts by studying the life of Jesus according to Luke, of which Acts is the final part. He then went on to see how that community was consolidated in his commentary on Galatians, Thessalonians, and Corinthians— all of them, in different ways, "problem churches"—following which he again returned to Christian beginnings in Mark's Gospel. Thence he came to terms in Romans, expressing as it does "the quintessence of Paul's mind," not only with the weighty matters of law and righteousness, justification and the practical outcome in daily behavior that follows, but with the equally practical yet historical problem of the relationship of Jew and Gentile and God's purpose through them both. Deepening his penetration, he came to terms with John's Gospel, reflecting on the life of Jesus as it transcends history. The historical framework he does not deny—indeed, he strengthens it—but he argues that John was written for "evangelical" and "theological" ends (that we may believe and have eternal life), and it is these ends with which he prefers to grapple: relevance rather than mere facticity. And so to Hebrews, not so distant from John in approach as might at first be thought, and thence, as if in climax, to its literary neighbor, Ephesians, "the Queen of the Epistles," "the divinest composition of man."[84]

The volume was first published on its own—159 pages of pure delight, a spiritual feast that carried its first readers through Lent of 1956. (It should have been published for January, but Willie was late with his manuscript.) He again lists the names of those on whose work he has deliberated, albeit at speed: J. Armitage Robinson (1904), B. F. Westcott (1889), T. K. Abbott (1899), E. F. Scott (1930), H. C. G. Moule (1908, "old now, but still of very great value"), and, by no means least, *God's Order* by John A. Mackay (1953, "most excellent").

It is impossible to resist the thought that Willie reached the peak of his own explorations in this volume, which also represents the halfway stage in his monumental undertaking; and it is a great pity that the volume is now placed second to (and following) his work on Galatians—a strange and off-putting letter for many would-be students of Paul. It is as if one were seeking to hide a beautiful mountaintop in scrubland, for although Galatians is of vital importance, it is in a different league than Ephesians. You cannot compare a workhorse and a Rolls Royce. Of Ephesians Willie roundly declares, clearly including himself, "There are many who would hold that it is indeed the highest reach of New Testament thought." And surely we do not err in finding in his exposition of this letter the high point of Willie's own achievements as a biblical commentator, in

March 1956, at the age of forty-nine. He will go on to write many things after this, to be sure, important and impressive things, bold and adventurous things, but nowhere else does he handle such sacred and awesome things so sympathetically, nor yet so devotedly. From the earthly holy of holies of Hebrews he moves gladly into the truly heavenly places of Ephesians.

He deals with the usual problem associated with the letter, but first he insists on dealing with "the certainties" (xiii)—a very Barclayan method. The upshot of these certainties (space forbids us listing them) is that he firmly held to the Pauline authorship of the letter, which he believes was penned toward the close of Paul's life, when he was in chains for the cause of the gospel. The chief problem of the letter for Willie, therefore, was not (as it has been for many who have studied the document) a matter of who wrote it, but of whom was it written to. He reminds his readers that ancient postal custom did not require the use of external addresses, so the titles are not original to the letters; this was especially so in the case of the letter to the Ephesians. Indeed, "we find that it is in fact in the last degree unlikely that it was written to the Church at Ephesus" (xiii). He gives four lines of argument in defense of his contention: (1) the letter is written to Gentiles (though he admits that this proves nothing!); (2) it is the most impersonal of Paul's letters; (3) all the indications are that Paul and the recipients did not know each other; and, most importantly, (4) none of the early Greek manuscripts contain the words "in Ephesus" at 1:1. Arguing from Paul's direction to the Colossians to read his letter to the Laodiceans (Col. 4:16), he concludes that our book of Ephesians is the "lost" letter to Laodicea, thus following the heretic Marcion, the first to state this argument in a written form. (Willie, we might note, was never afraid to use sources unsympathetic to him if they held or suggested truth, even as he had followed the argument of certain Adoptionists earlier.)

He is aware, of course, that some who reject the Pauline authorship of Ephesians do so on the strong basis of the viewpoint expressed in the letter. He recognizes that such arguments are impressive, involving as they do the difference in vocabulary between this and Paul's other letters (there are over seventy words peculiar to Ephesians), the difference of attitude in Paul's thinking (we shall return to this aspect), and a certain difference of style, which itself rests on the different circumstances and objectives of the letter. Willie's natural ebullience was not quite kept in restraint in handling such issues, a thing over which some of his academic colleagues would gently—and sometimes ungently—chide him. He regarded it as "ridiculous" that such a mind as Paul's should be so circumscribed; the force of his conviction here is indicated by his use of so strong—and for Willie, so unusual—a word. And the Eng. Lit. teacher *manqué* returns to his beloved Shakespeare to prove that great writers can write very differently, according to their themes and aims. (It is characteristic of Willie that in so arguing from Shakespeare to Paul he makes no mention of, let alone gives credence to, the theories of multiple authorship that have been forwarded about the body of work typically attributed to the English bard—theories of which he was similarly dismissive.) Ever generous, expansive, and positive, he holds that the difference between Ephesians and the other (especially the "cardinal") letters does much more to extend and deepen Paul's greatness than it does to support suppositions concerning an anonymous, unhistorical figure whose understanding of the gospel rises over the thought of Paul as his beloved Ben Nevis rises over Corpach Moss.

But what is the particular contribution of Ephesians? And what does Willie make of it? How did it affect, if at all, his own views? This is not the place to answer these things extensively (I hope to do that elsewhere), but we must pause to see what he finds so impressive about this, "the Queen of the epistles." He explains this by returning to an earlier letter of Paul—a good example of chronological inversion in the service of theological emphasis: "The great central thought of Colossians," he claims by way of introduction, "is the all-sufficiency of Jesus Christ." And he adds emphatically, "the thought of Ephesians is a development of that conception" (xvi). It is development in a startling way, especially startling to one brought up in the zealously monotheistic faith of Judaism, as Paul had been:

> The key thought of Ephesians is the gathering together of all things in Christ. Christ is the centre in whom all things unite, and the bond who unites all things. . . . The central thought of Ephesians is the realisation of disunity in nature, disunity in man, disunity in time, disunity in eternity, disunity between God and man, and the conviction that all that disunity can only become unity when all men and all powers are united in Christ. (xvii–xviii)[85]

There are many beautiful, moving, and elevating things elsewhere in the New Testament, and we see Willie repeatedly responding to and rising with them, but never so much as here. It is not only the peak of New Testament teaching and experience, but the nerve center of Willie's knowledge and experience, too. All his early background, especially that pertaining to WDB and the old evangelicalism of the eighteenth- and nineteenth-century revivalists and evangelists, was fashioned around this concept. And throughout his ministry at Renfrew and beyond he had sought to come to terms with it—not abstractly, or in any academic or withdrawn way, but concretely, as a man of words *and* action, belief *and* work. In seeking out his own uni-verse, this is where he found its linking mechanism, its linchpin, its fulcrum point. He could go no higher, he could climb no further; the secret was now trebly his: borne of faith and study and application. As he said of the great apostle who discovered its truth for the church, "all Paul's thinking and experience would lead him precisely to that" (xviii). It was no less true of Willie himself.

He divided the letter into halves, according to what he called its "double thesis," adding a practical peroration. The first three chapters deal with a "conception of the unity in Christ," and the second three deal with the place the church has in God's plan to bring that unity about. It is a very great pity that this structure is not brought out in either the first or the revised editions in tabling the contents of the letter in the introduction, for it would have strengthened his analysis and aided readers, many of whom pass over the introductory and quasi-academic comments at the beginning, which in this volume take note of the crucial fact that it is in seeking to outline and demonstrate these great truths that "Paul strikes out one of his greatest phrases. The Church is the *Body of Christ*. The Church is to be hands to do Christ's work, feet to run upon His errands, a mouth to speak for Him, an instrument, a body through which He can work" (xix).

The double thesis is strengthened by the arguments that, first, Christ is God's instrument of reconciliation, and second, the church is Christ's instrument of reconciliation. Once again the cooperative principle is stressed: God has chosen to work through men, which work requires their glad and obedient surrender. This is not merely the peak of Paul's understanding of Christ, of God's will for the world (and even beyond), but of the church itself: "it is *the Church* who must preach the Christ in whom unity alone is possible, and it is within the Church that this unity must be achieved and realised." Because it was Paul's conviction, and because Willie grasped it completely, it became Willie's too. He became, as he had heretofore striven to be, God's slave. From now on everything he wrote and did is commentary on this double thesis. His work stands or falls in relation to it. Ephesians is the queen of letters because in it God's eternal, universal purpose is set forth, anchored in Christ. How delighted Willie's father would have been in this apprehension, and how delighted WDB's own mentors, not least the too lightly dismissed Henry Drummond, who considered such an emphasis to be so wholesome.

Perhaps the greatest pity of Willie's career is that he never saw the need to systematize his general outlook, his theology. He was not by nature or constraint a theological thinker in the accepted sense, still less a systematic theologian. I do not mean, of course, that he was not always theologically engaged; he was. A man of the Word, a man of God (marvellously so, indeed), he was also a tireless, ceaseless activist, claiming every opportunity to serve that came his way, scrupulous in his use of time and energy. But such heroic attitudes and commitment afforded little time for reflection, and none for the building of a system.

Scarcely had he taken from his typewriter the last sheet of his commentary on Ephesians when he was inserting another for his commentary on the pastoral epistles, 1 and 2 Timothy and Titus. With them his gaze was diverted from the majestic heights to mundane things of the common life, and the less elevating things of pastoral activity. He had found the pearl of greatest price, but was diverted to sweep out the shop floor. Not that he would have so regarded it! Again we see a natural progression of thought at work, grounding, as it were, the high voltage of Ephesians. He wrote of the pastoral epistles that "no letters in the New Testament give such a vivid picture of the growing Church. In them we see a little island of Christianity in a sea of paganism; and in them we see as nowhere else the first beginnings of the ministry of the church."[86] He was not pleased with the efforts of some scholars to reduce their importance and their relevance by dismissing them as "second-generation Christianity," subapostolic material, matter that falls below that of other letters. And he who never quite came to terms with the institutionalization of the church, who came to seek space for a secularity of outlook within the church and its sacraments, stated that "just because they were written when the church was becoming an institution, they speak most directly to our situation and condition" (vii).

Unlike other sections of the New Testament, he notes, "the Pastoral Epistles have been most unfortunate in their commentaries." He goes on to list some exceptions, his particular debts: Walter Lock (1924, "a monument of sound and sober scholarship"), Sir Robert Falconer (1937, "full of illumination, compressed"), E. K. Simpson (1954, "written with verve and with a mastery of Hellenistic Greek words which will ensure it a place among the great commentaries"), P. N. Harrison's detailed examination of the language of the letters (1921, "unsurpassable"), A. E. Humphrey's "old commentary" (1895, "very far from negligible"), B. S. Easton (1948, "excellent," especially on the meaning of words), E. F. Brown ("unique," not least because he brings the wisdom of many years in "the younger churches" of India to his expositions), and E. F. Scott (1936, "consistently useful"). Among his debts he does not fail to mention such colleagues in committee as the convener, R. G. Macdonald (to whom Willie dedicated the volume, "a great encourager"), and Andrew McCosh, the Publications Manager. He concludes his introduction autobiographically: "To myself, the Pastoral Epistles were at least to some extent a new discovery": forward, not backward, even if he had just scaled the Everest of theological insight.

Emphasizing the personal and intimate nature of the pastorals, he shows unconcern at using sources and attitudes inimical (it may be thought) to the Free Church traditions of his upbringing. His attitude, as we saw earlier, was nothing if not tolerant of others' views, not merely out of courtesy, nor yet of idealism (i.e., a concern for freedom of speech), but out of genuine humility. The *odium theologicum* is never more odious than when propelled by credal *hubris,* but Willie was not smitten by either. His line in this, it is often conveniently forgotten, followed on the one side that of Alexander Whyte, who found time to study such works as John Henry Newman's *Essay on the Development of Christian Doctrine* and, on the other side, Norman Macleod. Accordingly, Willie accepted the early designation of "Pontifical Letters," adding the explanation that "the description is drawn from *pontifex,* the priest, the controller of the church" (xv).[87] One aspect in particular is underscored in this introductory section, which paved the way for his future universalistic beliefs, that being the emphasis in the pastorals on the gospel's efficacy for all men. "There are times when the Pastoral Epistles stress the word *all* in a most significant way," he notes (xix). We should also bear in mind the effect produced by his logical development of the theme of the unity of Christ already so admirably expounded in his commentary on Ephesians. With views fixed on the mainstay of God's love, he was already looking on that love as all-triumphant, as brooking no failure or rejection. It is appropriate that we should bring the kindly tolerance of Norman Macleod together with the universalism of Macleod Campbell, for Willie's theology has some real indebtedness to these two cousins' great, if different, influence on Scottish theology.[88]

There are indications in his exordium that he had not overcome the conservatism of his youth, at least in matters introductory. In describing the difficulties that beset acceptance of Pauline authorship, he accepts the view that the church had by the time the letter was written effectively grown beyond the infant prodigy of apostolic days, a view that has often been overpressed. We may argue that this stance is simply part of his open-minded approach, ever ready as it was to examine afresh old problems and lines of argumentation. But sometimes there are definite signs (especially in this period) of an oscillation between the traditional and the modern, the conservative and the liberal viewpoints, a tendency that colleagues such as Johnstone McKay used to twit him about. Still, he could not be neatly pigeonholed: he was neither liberal nor conservative, but an amalgam—sometimes a contradictory amalgam—of the two.

He outlines the central issues taken up in the epistles without attempting to lessen the force of the problems involved by conservative counterargument. The issues at hand involved a developed organization of church leadership, salaried officials, orders of widows, credal attitudes more self-conscious of "orthodoxy" (paratheke, a word that, unfortunately, he never attempted to define in his wordbooks or articles), and the "dangerous heresy" of incipient Gnosticism, which he describes as a proud, speculative intellectualism with Jewish legalistic undertones that expressed itself both ascetically and licentiously, denying the resurrection of the body in particular (xxiff.). In Willie's view the most significant of all the difficulties is the language of the pastorals. Thirty-six percent of the words used (306 out of 848, if we exclude proper names) are found nowhere else in Pauline usage, and 175 of them are found nowhere else in the New Testament. Moreover, typical Pauline emphases and words find no expression here; 112 particles of speech—enclitics, pronouns, and prepositions—that Paul uses in his other epistles no fewer than 932 times are completely absent. Finally, Willie tackles the problem concerning Paul's stated activities, which find no verification from other sources, although Willie recognized "a stream of tradition which held that Paul journeyed to Spain" (xxviii). Paul's mission to Crete and his wintering in Nicopolis may have taken place in postimprisonment work there and in the far west, but on the whole Willie is unconvinced, especially as there are no valid traditions relating to Paul from those areas. Nevertheless the view resulting from his appraisal of the difficulties preserves the integrity of the great apostle's influence: "we are still hearing the voice of Paul, and often hearing it speak with a unique personal intimacy" (xxix). But equally, he recognizes the hand of a collator, editor, and even an amplifier working over the fragments of Paul's personal correspondence and devotedly putting them together for posterity.

The first volume of Willie's commentary on Matthew appeared in September 1956. The pressure of the completion date is hinted at in the dedication, but more important is the note of sincere thanks, richly deserved by its recipient;

surely it struck a responsive chord in the hearts of the hundreds of thousands of readers of these commentaries:

To
Andrew McCosh
always my friend
and sometimes my task-master
without whose help and encouragement
this book would never have been written.

We must never forget that alongside the tireless industries of William Barclay, his friend and task-master was also hard at work, supplying whatever help was required (and Willie's manuscripts required a lot of editing, a task not made more pleasant by the disconcerting smell of the newly discovered carbonized paper on which he typed!) as well as performing the more technical and professional tasks. McCosh was, during these hectic years, the great encourager, supplying the emotional fuel that kept the human writing machine almost perpetually at work, parrying the insults, laughing at the criticisms, blocking the objections from this and that committee member concerning the scale and the costs of the exercise. By the time the commentary on Matthew was completed, there were fourteen volumes in the series totalling almost 4,200 pages of translation, introduction, and commentary, all written and produced in less than four years—an incredible accomplishment for a church committee, especially one that worked without the usual backing of trained personnel in the varied fields of publishing expertise.

The Matthew readings, like the John readings before them, were published in three volumes to begin with (volume one: 1:1–7:29; volume two: 8:1–13:58; volume three: 14:1–28:20). Despite his having scaled the higher reaches of thought in Ephesians, the space he gives to the Sermon on the Mount shows that Willie's feet were firmly anchored in day-to-day reality. He explains his concentration on it thus:

> The volume may seem to have taken a great deal of space to cover a short section of the gospel. But it must be remembered that in this volume we study the Sermon on the Mount, [which] is so central to the Christian faith and life that it often has to be taken sentence by sentence, and even word by word.[89]

He regrets that commentaries on Matthew had not been very laudable on the whole to that point, although he had been glad to make use of A. B. Bruce (1907), W. C. Allen (1907), A. H. McNeile (1915), Alfred Plummer (1920), T. H. Robinson (1928), and the general introductory work *The Synoptic Gospels* by C. G. Montefiore (1927).

It is in this commentary of Matthew that vintage Barclay really comes into its own. Here the full range of Willie's considerable learning, his wide and eclectic reading, and the enlightening background information (linguistic, historical, and religious) form a compressed entity, to which he adds spiritual fervor and the incisiveness of his moral imperative. His method and style reach new heights, aided by the natural appeal of the Gospel itself. It is, he explains, a Gospel founded on "two great characteristics"—that of the teacher ("for in no other gospel is the teaching of Jesus so systematically assembled and gathered together"), and that of the Kingship of Jesus ("it is pre-eminently the gospel which is concerned to show us Jesus as the man born to be King").

Space forbids a detailed description of his exposition. We might note, however, that of the 829 pages of commentary covering the twenty-eight chapters of the Gospel itself, over one quarter are given to the Sermon on the Mount (he elsewhere calls it "the new law"),[90] which occupies only three chapters (i.e., approximately ten percent) of the text of the Gospel. Surely this emphasis is very indicative of Willie's whole understanding of Christianity: the mysticism (if we may use the word) of Paul must be counterbalanced by the practical demands— at once religious and ethical—of the common things of life. He may soar to the heights in *Ephesians,* but such flights will always be matched and harnessed by the simple demands of everyday life. Indeed, those demands, and the challenge of the changing postwar world, became more and more important to him. One cannot separate devotion from obligation, life from work. "All are agreed," he said of his expositional forebears in typical triple-emphatic style, "that in the Sermon on the Mount we have the core and the essence and the distillation of the teaching of Jesus to the inner circle of His chosen men."

The second and third volumes were published in early and mid 1957, respectively, by which time Willie's and Kate's domestic bliss had been convulsed by the agony of the death of their lovely daughter Barbara (of which more later). The stern, unremitting calls to discipleship of this Gospel, sensitively heard and lovingly obeyed and transmitted, were not made in some quiet, blissful backwater. The bliss of the brokenhearted (see Matthew 5:4—"the strongest word for mourning in the Greek language") was learned firsthand, in grief and sore tears, and in a devastated household. "You'll have a new note in your preaching now," commented his grief-stricken father at the time of Mrs. Barclay's death in 1932 as Willie approached the glittering goal of his early years of preparation, the dream of their lifetime and retirement hopes shattered. It was so here, too, as high honors and worldwide acclaim rained upon him. It was ever Willie's lot to walk hand in hand with suffering and sorrow.

The subsequent volume in the series, treating Philippians, Colossians, and Philemon, was finished in July 1957. It bore all the marks of the traumatic ordeal through which the author and his family had so recently passed. His commentary on Philippians, "the epistle of joy," was written out of a "well-nigh crushed heart and spirit"; that he was able to produce a work that is itself alive with an innate joyfulness is one of the surpassing signs of his own thoroughbred faith.

The volume is dedicated to "J K" and "H C M," "whose sympathy and kindness we will not forget." Willie also stresses once again Andrew McCosh's role when he states in the foreword, "I owe more and more for his constant encouragement and never-failing sympathy and help." Nor was McCosh the only helper through this trauma: "I do not think that I could have carried this series this length without the constant encouragement of many friends at home and abroad, known and unknown, and to all those who have written or spoken to me with gracious kindness I offer my most sincere and cordial thanks." Any lingering doubts as to his readiness to work with others, such as may be provoked by his confessed failure to delegate, or the denial early in his ministry of the usefulness of an assistant (made emphatic in 1946) are surely dispelled by such statements. "Forward" it may well be, but it was always "Forward *together.*"

Philippians is not one of the critically difficult letters, and Willie clearly found it one of the most charming. He again acknowledges the reliance he had been able to place on previous commentators: M. R. Vincent (1897, "of first-rate importance"), H. G. C. Moule (also 1897), J. H. Michael (1928), and above all J. B. Lightfoot (1878, "among the supreme commentaries in any age and in any language"). For his work on Colossians Willie also referred to Lightfoot (1879), as well as C. F. D. Moule (1957, "invaluable"), E. F. Scott (1930, "all that writer's customary lucidity and helpfulness"), and C. J. Ellicott (1888). E. J. Goodspeed was found to be his best support for Philemon.

Philippians, being largely without critical problems, he accepted as "undoubtedly an authentic and genuine letter of Paul";[91] one of its chief virtues is in directing the student's mind to Paul's strategy. Willie was ever appreciative of that which *did* things, a characteristic evidenced in his appreciation of Philippi, a city with "three great claims"—its commercial vitality, its historic worthiness, and its undisputed loyalty to the Roman empire. Another of his penchant attitudes comes across in his introduction, in which he approvingly notes that the Philippian church (founded on Paul's second missionary journey, "about AD 52") encompassed all humanity, regardless of class, condition or status: "The whole Empire was being gathered together into the Christian Church" (5). He was ever glad to assert the leveling nature of God's love and grace. The one critical problem he does find space for is the "extraordinary break in the letter" at 3:2. Everything till then is "serenity"; then follows "this stern warning." The word *finally* occurs twice, which strengthens the view—which Willie finds "perfectly possible" (8)—that two letters to Philippi are here amalgamated (Polycarp, in fact, speaks of the letters Paul wrote to them), the first one (3:2–4:3) being a letter of thanks and warning sent after the arrival of Epaphroditus, and the second (1:1–3:1 and 4:4–23) being sent "a good deal later," when Epaphroditus had recovered and been sent back home. It was a "perfectly possible" interpretation of the letter's composition perhaps, but Willie nevertheless wrote that "it seems to us that there is no good reason for splitting this letter into two." He believes two other explanations are equally reasonable: the break occurs either because Paul is interrupted by bad news from Philippi, or because of a sudden change of thought that can occur in letter writing. Whatever the outcome of such problems, Philippians is, using another of his keywords, "the lovely letter"—the "Epistle of excellent things," the "epistle of joy."

In introducing Colossians, the letter written to "the unimportant town" (Willie, like Paul the master strategist, had an eye for such things), he shows that he has to come to terms more fully with the heresy that ever threatened the early church. He acknowledges it as "one of the great problems of New Testament scholarship" (115), one that threatened to turn Christianity into a philosophy or a theosophy rather than a way of life. That is the importance of this letter, and Willie's finely tuned pragmatism receives and transmits the message plainly. In dealing with this subject again (we saw him outlining it in his commentaries on Ephesians and the pastorals) he is motivated afresh by things that changed his own life and work; he was ever on the attack against things that would divert the would-be disciple from his main consideration. Willie was always especially fired when such things made Christianity less than intelligible, and he scorned the "pseudo-intellectualism" of such attempts.

His treatment of the text of Colossians overturns the judgment he made of Ephesians as the peak of Paul's writing. "No Pauline letter has such a lofty view of Jesus Christ, and such an insistence on His completeness and His finality" (115). Other aspects of Jesus described here include his work as creator of the physical world and his real humanity: "For all His deity Jesus Christ was really and truly human flesh and blood." Various matters that undermine the Gnostic views include a rejection of the power of the rudimentary spirits of the world (personalized into demonic and spiritual forces by the ancients) and a rejection of speculative and vain philosophy (as opposed to "the simplicities of the gospel"—on which Willie remained strong), especially when tainted with "something which can only be called spiritual and intellectual snobbery" (118). Any suggestion of a spiritual or intellectual aristocracy, like a social or industrial one, is anathema to him because it denies "the wide welcome of the Christian faith"; and he rejects all ritualistic and ascetic practices—Paul's gospel stands foursquare in favor of freedom from legalistic ordinances, rules, regulations, festivals, and sabbaths, though of course never condoning license or libertinism.

Colossians is not accepted by all scholars as a work of Paul, because of its language, because it makes references to Gnosticism (which some believe to have been strictly a second-century phenomenon), and because some hold that the thought of the letter is far in advance of Paul's thinking. Willie agrees that the language is individualistic—"but that does not prove anything" (121), since Paul had "new things to say and found new ways to say them." He agrees that the great Gnostic systems (of Basilides and Valentinus, for example) came later than Paul, but he contends that what we have here is incipient Gnosticism, "ideas which are deeply woven into both Jewish and Greek thought," not to mention the Persian influence of Zoroastrianism. As to its being far in advance of Paul's thought, he rejects this on the ground that Paul's doctrine did not remain static; in discovering "the unsearchable riches of Christ," Paul had discovered an unplumbable well from which he drew increasingly fresh draughts to meet new and developing situations. He holds, as Coleridge had, that Colossians is "the overflow of Ephesians, not a new source of truth and reality." "New implications of Christ" were here being thought out and, changing the imagery, he suggests that "the seed [of 1 Corinthians 8:6] was there in Paul's mind, ready to blossom when a new climate and new circumstances called it into growth." Thus Paul attains "the highest reach of his thought" in this letter.

It is not quite exact to describe Philemon as "the only *private* letter of Paul which we possess" (213), but it is a unique expression of Paul's mind and heart. In accepting the condition of slavery (with which the letter does not directly concern itself), Paul is merely reflecting, as a man of his time, the status quo. The apostle chiefly emphasizes the new relationship of men to each other that has come via Christ—a not uncostly relationship. It may not, therefore, be a social document of marked revolutionary importance in terms of *emancipation*—which word, Willie recalls Lightfoot's saying, "seems to tremble on Paul's lips, but he never utters it." It is nevertheless of supreme value in demonstrating the power of that new relationship within the Christian church that has meaningful, even revolutionary, things to say about the fabric of society. And that mattered tremendously to Willie Barclay: "When a relationship like that enters into life, social grades and castes cease to matter. The very names, master and slave, become irrelevant" (216). We shall soon see Willie refusing to attend a communion service at one of his summer schools because this attitude was not carried into the ecclesiastical arena, which had caused an ecumenical row. There are certain things that tolerance cannot overlook, and the question of relationships is high among them—incontrovertibly so, to Willie's way of thinking.

The assertion of this principle he places before a small but significant critical point, which, if taken, overturns the view that the letter is a private one and makes it (against the view he espoused when dealing with Ephesians) the lost letter to the Laodiceans, in which Paul "mobilises church opinion in Onesimus' favour" (217–18). Whatever we may make of this (and we should not overlook his identification of Ephesians as the lost Laodicean letter), Willie was drawn to the fact that Onesimus went on to be "bishop" of Ephesus (where the Pauline corpus was almost certainly collated), and thus we find not only personal justification, but the ecclesiastical confirmation of what Christ can do despite human divisions, classes, and grades. "A lovely story," Willie concludes, adding characteristically, "we hope that it is true" (220)!

The pace notably quickened in the writing of these later volumes. Only two months elapsed between the publication of the commentary on James and Peter (February 1958) and that on John and Jude (April 1958). Behind this torrential outflow we must see the broken heart of a devoted father whose only consolation lay in his work, through which the sorrow (not to speak of the turbulent testing of his faith) was eased of its persistent throbbing. James Little has conveyed to me the gist of a conversation Willie had at the time with his friend and Daily Bible Readings colleague Hugh Anderson in which he admitted that he almost lost faith through this tragic experience. Only by throwing himself wholesale into feverish activity and thus escaping the full blight of disconsolation did he survive. Added Little, "I sensed that in Willie myself. . . . It was as if he was papering a bit over the cracks that *might* be there underneath, as if by repetition and enthusiasm he could avoid facing doubts that he never resolved."[92] We will return to the effect this had on him later, but for the moment we might just note the toil now sacrificially expended, remembering Pericles's contention that "an Athenian's true holiday is the day on which he serves his country best."

From the high plateaus of Paul's thinking Willie found no difficulty in returning to the less exalted plains of "the daily round, the common task" in his next consignment. "The longer I companied with James the greater this short letter became to me," he comments.[93] And he agrees with Marty's declaration that "the Epistle is a masterpiece of virile and reverent simplicity." On such simplicity he thrived, nor was he alone in doing so. To guide him through the epistle he found useful a whole galaxy of commentaries—of J. B. Mayor (1913, "one of the best commentaries in the English language"), J. H. Ropes (1916, "a model of judicious and meticulous scholarship"), W. O. E. Oesterley (1910, "very helpful . . . specially illuminating on the Jewish thought and belief behind the letter"), A. Carr (1896), James Moffatt (1928, "useful, but rather slight"), R. V. G. Tasker (1956, "conservative scholarship at its best"), E. C. Blackman (1957, "one of the outstanding volumes in that [the Torch Bible Commentary] series"), and B. S. Easton (1957, "stimulative and suggestive"). It is notable that, as paper restrictions and other war effects fell away, so the pulse of religious publishing quickened, and Willie was able to take notice of more recent scholarship in these concluding volumes. There was also a similarly marked difference in his lecture notes material; the SSSU material (on the Lord's Prayer, the Sermon on the Mount, etc.) had given way to genuine study and reflection and maturity of viewpoint. He might still be criticized for his conclusions, but he could no longer be faulted for his groundwork.

He found James to be yet another "new discovery" (8) and hoped his readers would discover it, too. His discoveries were quite basic, both in matters introductory and expositional. The problems confronting the reader of the letter are chiefly fourfold. First, the early church was reluctant to admit its canonicity (usually because of its absence from the early writings, an argument from silence and inference). Second, this reluctance was greatly strengthened by Luther's strictures—not to say derision—which were based purely on a theological principle of "that which urges Christ" (anything that does not do so in the evangelical sense Luther had discovered for himself he rated as subapostolic). The third problem concerns the identity of James himself (briefly, which James of the five people who bear that name in the New Testament wrote this letter?). The fourth difficulty is intimately linked to the third, and concerns the date the letter was written. In all these things Willie found the lines of argument extremely well balanced, and although he had his own strong views in the matter, he did not, as usual, state them dogmatically. His introductory matter extends to thirty-nine pages, the longest introduction in any of his books and out of all proportion to the 108 verses of the letter (the epistles of Peter, dealt with in the same volume as James, receive but thirty-one pages of introduction).

What is more important than such matters for Willie is the treatment of the text of the letter, the teaching itself. To understand this, he explains the method of teaching in the ancient world—the communication aspect, which ever excited his attention. The aim of these early preachers and writers was "to confront men with the good life in the midst of the looseness of their living and their forgetfulness of the gods" (33). In passing we might note this use of "the good life," another feature of his understanding of gospel realities that, as it were, secularizes them. Those who followed Willie's exposition found him to be completely faithful to his text and, despite his tolerant attitudes, inflexible in the application of the moral imperative. This is another example of his preoccupation with the *fruit* of the gospel, as opposed to its *root*.

In dealing with the letters of Peter, the second and third of the catholic or general letters, he came to terms with an aspect of New Testament study that was particularly congenial to him. He believed that 1 Peter "is the best known and loved, and most read" (164). He agreed that its "distinctive characteristic" is its warmth, a significant statement for one who found the spirit of fellow churchmen who had "the east wind in their voices" alien to the gospel of love and wide welcome. The letter was written "out of the love of a pastor's heart to help people who were going through it and on whom worse things were still to come"; he who had the pastor's heart par excellence and had been "going through it" himself of late knew and expounded it feelingly.

He owned his debts to the works of C. Bigg (1901, "the product of sound, if conservative, scholarship"), C. H. Plumptre (1879, "old, but still full of wise illumination"), James Moffatt (1928, "an outstanding commentary"), E. G. Selwyn (1946, "has already taken its place among the great commentaries in the English language"), F. W. Beare (1947, "much more radical in its conclusions but . . . of the first importance"), A. M. Hunter (1959, "characteristically helpful"), G. W. Blentin (1914, "a scholarly and helpful volume"), and most especially to C. E. B. Cranfield (1950, "a masterpiece of brief but lucid and illuminating exposition"). As we saw earlier, particular gratitude was shown to the librarian of Trinity College, James Mackintosh, for "help and guidance" given over the whole period of writing these commentaries.

It had been but recently, he observes, that doubts had been entertained about the authenticity of 1 Peter; but Willie, while candidly describing the reason for these doubts, "unhesitatingly accepts" the traditional view (165). There are three aspects of the letter that substantiate an early date and that commended themselves to Willie's understanding of the Christian message at that time: the emphasis on the Second Coming of Christ, the organizational simplicity of the church, and the undeveloped theology reflected in the letter. In this the character of Acts (with which these readings had begun five years earlier) and 1 Peter concur. It is summed up in a word recently made popular by C. H. Dodd: *kerygma*. "These are the fundamental ideas which the Church in its first days heralded forth," Willie states bluntly (167). He might well strongly object, as he did before the General Assembly of his church, to the backward-looking attempt to repeat the first-century gospel, but while he constantly sought for the message for his own time, he never strayed from those fundamental ideas of the early church—the ideas of Jesus and Paul, John and Peter, Hebrew and Jude. The five aspects of the early *kerygma*, he says, "are the five main planks in the edifice of early Christian preaching" (168). Further, he does not allow the correspondence between 1 Peter and "the Queen of the epistles," be it verbal, doctrinal, or ethical, to go by unobserved. And he is not a little drawn to the idea that the latter may well have used the former, thus reversing the flow of the "stream of tradition."

Willie's commentary on the epistles of John and Jude followed closely on the heels of the volume on the epistles of Peter and James, and brings us near the end of this magnificent, unique undertaking. He had read widely and written abundantly, but there are still few signs of fatigue. He applied himself to these new letters with the same dispatch that he employed when he began Acts. Indeed, it can be argued that he was now applying even greater care, deeper sensitivity, and a fuller understanding than he had in 1952. His explorations were still proceeding, but the greater maturity of viewpoint and the quiet confidence of expression are all too plain. The literary and expositional debts that adorn his pages are of the very best: A. E. Brooke (1912, "a mine of information"), B. F. Westcott (1892, "distinguished by Westcott's almost unique combination of exactly [*sic*] scholarship and warm devotion"), Alfred Plummer (1883, "still a most useful and excellent volume"), and C. H. Dodd (1946, "the outstanding volume of these letters . . . without question one of the best commentaries in the English language"). Of the Welshman he further wrote, "It would have been tedious to detail every one of my debts to C H Dodd; I can only say here and now that there is hardly a page in this book which does not contain its debt to him."[94]

He was concerned that the letters of John are not among the most widely read of the New Testament books because they are "of the greatest importance for the light they shed on the thought and on the theology of the New Testament, and for the information they supply on the administration of the growing church." It was in that light that he explored them, but always with a view to distilling their relevance for the present.

If he found 1 Peter warm and pastorally concerned, it is not less so with this "loving and anxious sermon written by a pastor who loved his people" (3). The letter— or rather, the homily, to give it a truer description—he believed to have been written about A.D. 100, like 1 Peter, near Ephesus, to guide the early believers from the danger of falling away in those postapostolic days, when Christianity had lost its "initial glow." At such a time the difficulty of maintaining high personal moral standards was a burden, and therefore the sharpness of the call to discipleship had to be sounded afresh. New standards of moral purity, of kindness, continuing service, and forgiveness had to be inculcated if Christians were to maintain true sainthood and not conform to society's standards. (We should infer here Willie's deeper understanding of worldliness, which was worlds apart from a superficial condemnation of football matches, dancing, or in those days cigarette smoking, whatever "old man Barclay" may have said.) Moreover, their courage had to be strengthened against renewed violence and persecution as well against those who corrupted believers from within with lax and relaxing standards. Once again Willie sees the Gnostics at work, with their particularly dangerous denial of Jesus' messiahship, incarnation, and resurrection.

When he comes to Jude, via the fine commentaries of Charles Bigg (1901), James Moffatt (1928), J. B. Mayor (1907), and M. R. James (1912), he acknowledges that this slight letter is unjustly neglected, though his usual style of commendation is missing here. (Curiously, his perfunctory comments on the sources used merely outline the series in which the respective commentaries appear and the other letters with which they are associated, but offer no help to the reader as to worthiness or reliability; at most he notes that Mayor's work is "the most massive commentary on it.")

There are few New Testament books, he cautions, that demonstrate more vividly than Jude (despite its peculiar thought and imagery) "the dangers which threaten the early church from false doctrine and from misguided ethical teaching" (x). The dangers to those to whom Jude is directed came not from speculators floating willy-nilly in a world of pure thought, but those whose insistence on the use of the body was misdirected. Willie was never of their number; he preserved a respect born of a healthy understanding of the creatorial and incarnational doctrines of Christ for man's God-given nature and functions. The Antinomians (such as those Paul refutes in Romans 6) denied the importance of bodily functions and allowed sexual looseness, as did the Gnostics. "There is always abounding grace to forgive such indulgence" is a cry heard throughout church history; it would rear its head in new forms just after this time at which Willie wrote, rousing him to opposition. Doctrine ever goes hand in hand with practice, and the doctrine lying behind Antinomianism Willie recognized as being in essence a denial of God and Jesus Christ. And so it is here that this supremely practical letter has the companionable edge of doctrinal regularity.

In December 1958, just after Willie celebrated his fifty-first birthday, the first of his three volumes on Revelation appeared. Commented the author, "With the publication of this volume our task is very near at an end, for with it we have reached the last book of the New Testament."[95] He added that when he wrote Acts he "never meant to go beyond that volume." He was particularly grateful, therefore, "to the many people who throughout these years have written to me . . . grateful alike for their thanks and for their criticism from which I have always benefited." These "years of study . . . have been an experience the value of which is beyond words to tell." He acknowledges (Kate would have been only too willing to agree) that it was "a heavy task," but his chief word of thanks goes, according to the dedication of this final volume, to those

> who began with me
> at the beginning of this series
> and who have persevered with me
> to this the end.

To be sure, they were not the only ones thanked. The new Convenor of the committee, W. M. Campbell, and "the committee's manager [sic]" were also thanked "for constant help and encouragement, without which this task would never have been completed." And the expositors who had helped him to understand "this notoriously difficult book" were also gratefully acknowledged. It was "a magnificent assembly of commentaries" from which he was able to draw, among them some of the "great commentaries of the world": R. H. Charles (1920, "completely indispensable"), H. B. Swete (1907, "combines scholarship and devotion"), I. T. Beckwith (1919, "of first-rate importance"), F. J. A. Hort (1908, "precious," despite the fact that it was unfinished), James Moffatt (1910, "still valuable"); W. H. Simcox (1890), Martin Kiddle (1940), E. F. Scott (1940, "not a commentary, but . . . a lucid and illuminating exposition"), R. C. Trench (1863, "has all the author's usual width of learning and spirit of devotion"), M. R. Newbolt ("well worth reading"), Austin Farrer (1949, "sometimes as difficult as the Revelation itself"!), and finally, the "best of all commentaries for the English reader," that of T. S. Kepler (1958).

Three times in the Introduction he admits that Revelation is "notoriously the most difficult book in the New Testament," unique both in method and message. Its style does not suit all would-be readers; it "either finds a man or leaves him mad," and has long been "the playground of religious eccentrics" who tend to use it "for mapping out celestial time-tables of the future." It was by no means popular among the early Reformers, a few of whom (like their modern-day counterparts) would have liked to exclude it from the New Testament altogether. Nevertheless, in a statement that is revealing and typical of Willie's broad and inclusive approach, he points out that it is "the only masterpiece of pure art in the New Testament" (xvi).[96] Behind the appreciation of the art lay the appreciation of truth, and the excavation and delineation of that truth was Willie's goal in expounding this book: "The centre and essence of [the] creed," he again asserted, having described the dangers of Caesar worship, which was the basic issue against which the original author contended, is the fact that "Jesus Christ, and Jesus Christ alone is Lord" (xxxiv). It is appropriate to recall that his first sermon series at Trinity Church, Renfrew, was based on the first three chapters of Revelation. Twenty-five years later, through personal, national, and international experience the like of which were enough to shake to its roots any man's faith, Willie's central message is still the same: "Jesus Christ, the same yesterday, today, and forever." For those who would listen, it was never anything other than that.

To release this kernel from its difficult shell, Willie offered thirty-nine pages of condensed introductory matter in which what he calls "the unintelligibility of the Revelation," by way of emphasizing again his explicitly shouldered task, is made plain. He was outstandingly successful in this, as tens of thousands of readers may testify, because his attitude is one of ground-level common sense. Once you recognize the literature for what it really is, he says, you have the key to its cryptic language and art.

Revelation may be unique in the New Testament writings, he says, ignoring what he has said in an earlier volume about Matthew's "specially strong apocalyptic interest"[97] and other similar passages, but it belongs to a well-known genre of Jewish writings that has its roots deep in the prophetic literature of the Old Testament. Indeed, he can even quote with appreciation Jülicher's comment that "Apocalyptic is prophecy turned senile" (xxi), though we should not allow that savage judgment to divert us from the very positive teaching Willie's commentary upholds. Apocalyptic literature asserts important truths—pillars of God's revelations to man, elements actually fulfilling that plan, and thus of crucial importance for us today. He lists five points relating to this literature that ought to be borne in mind:

1. The Jews are God's Special People, whose leader (King-Messiah) will overturn the misfortunes of their history and restore their preeminence.

2. The doctrine of the Two Ages resulting from the messianic intervention in history (the present age of misfortune and defeat, and the Golden Age of restoration and peace) is thus central to the whole.

3. The hinge of the Two Ages is "the Day of the Lord," a time of terror and judgment that will shatter the old age and usher in the new.

4. Apocalyptic literature describes and interprets these events by means of dreams and visions. It is "continually attempting to describe the indescribable, to say the unsayable, to paint the unpaintable." It is "necessarily cryptic," having to rely on symbols and pictures. ("Picture," we should note, is another Barclayan word of some significance; it camouflages a profounder understanding of theology than many give him credit for. For example, twenty years later he uses it in volume one of his *The Gospels & Acts* no fewer than eight times in a single paragraph denouncing some New Testament writer's "flight from history"; there it is used as a synonym for *contents,* though *definition* would also capture his meaning, as would *disclosure,* a term made important at that time by the arrival of linguistic analysis, a department of theology many would not associate with Willie's work.)

5. It came into its own at times of persecution and oppression, when the crypticism of its apparatus, well-known and understood by its adherents, would both encourage and defend them (by virtue of its very obtuseness and complexity).

And that is precisely why Willie's exposition was so successful. Once his fifth point is taken seriously, once we have grasped the "standard apparatus" (xix, xxi ff.) with which writer and reader were familiar, we have already embarked on decoding the cryptograph that Revelation actually is. It is not a "celestial timetable of the future," but a word for its day (i.e., two thousand years ago)—and, by decoded extension, a word for today, a word of relevance, of encouragement, a word "infinitely worth studying, for it contains the blazing faith of the Christian Church in the days when life was an agony" (xxxviii). Such days Willie had himself known (it bears repeating), and therefore he could write with insight and feeling. The first volume ends at 5:13–14—"The Song of all

470

Creation"—and the final volume ends extolling the grace of God. That, too, was Willie's way.

By the time Willie had asserted this "symbolic" and "fitting" primacy of grace, *twenty* volumes of commentary were circulating in ever-increasing numbers throughout the world, and steps had already been taken to adjust them to their present (but hopefully not their permanent) state of seventeen volumes. The response had fully justified the bold move, and provided a major advance to the International Bible Reading Association's daily notes that had been their prototype. It was a notable forward movement for biblical interest.

Appreciations now rained down upon both author and committee, from private and collective sources. Space can only be afforded for a few examples of these comments, but first I produce one of the earliest, which is equally appropriate to these later volumes, published by *Life and Work:* "No one could follow through the readings and notes for the year without having a more vivid sense of what Christian faith really is, and the extraordinary drama and poetry and sheer knowledge of life which is wrapped up in the Old and New Testaments."[98] *The British Weekly* was not long in recommending them as "the best Bible Readings in print."[99] This was followed a few weeks later with another *Life and Work* reader's comment that they were "the first Bible-reading notes I have ever used," and that they were so good that "I could not wait until the next day, but read the volume right through."[100] And another stated that they were "a perfect mine of expository sermon material."[101] The latter comment adumbrated what was to become a key function of the series, though it was not originally designed with that in view at all—namely, its usefulness to ministers who required predigested sermon material. Willie took special delight being able to offer such material, even as he had enjoyed helping his former college colleagues and his present students.

"We are making up the leeway in our teaching of the faith"[102] was the comment made a year later by Jack Stevenson when he reported that the early volumes were having to be reprinted through demand. Willie himself referred to this demand in a letter to Rita Snowden, and in so doing gave the reasons that lay behind the bottleneck in supply that had prevented the commentaries from reaching New Zealand: "The trouble was we were subsidising them. We printed ten thousand of each and when they sold could not be reprinted; and they sold very quickly. . . . Bit by bit the whole series will emerge. . . . I sometimes wonder what I will do when I do come to the end."[103] The "we" referred to here was essentially the Publications Committee. The IBRA had subsidised the earlier notes (by twenty-five percent), but this had ceased with the failure of the diverse Scottish editions. The new format was therefore undertaken at the risk of the Church of Scotland alone; and expenses now included a royalty payment to Willie. He expressed a different view of them in writing to the editor of *The Expository Times,* C. L. Mitton: "I know that they are full of faults because they have been produced at such a speed, and it is a great encouragement to me to know that you think well of them."[104]

It was inevitable that the publicity should awaken memories in places where he had formerly been known. Robin Stirling, editor of *The Motherwell Times*, was soon hot on the scent of a story of unusual interest. On being asked to be the subject of an early profile, Willie, ever available and ready to please (and incidentally revealing yet another string to his bow), replied, "If you think it will do the 'Times' any good, I'll be very happy to do anything you wish. After all, I'm a member of the National Institute of Journalists myself, and I'll be very happy to do anything to help."[105] The result was a full-length profile, his first to date. It is interesting to note the editor's response to his writing, the comments of a trained professional journalist on this latecomer to the profession: "The present-day reader of any of Dr Barclay's books must surely be struck by the simplicity of the exposition and by the easy, acceptable style of the writing." Indeed, "simplicity" and "easy style" very nearly sum up the requirements for intelligibility. The editor was also impressed by the "voluminous" quality of his writings, rightly believing the Daily Bible Readings (now called the Daily Study Bible) to be "the greatest example" of them. He pointed out that to date 320,000 copies had been sold, and moves were afoot to get a special edition published in the United States of America. He continued, "This is truly phenomenal when it is remembered that Dr Barclay was asked originally to write a volume on Acts simply because another series issued by the Church of Scotland had come to an end."

Willie was shown a copy of Stirling's article prior to publication, and he diplomatically requested two alterations in this "remarkably well done" piece. Stirling had picked out the popularizing principle that activated Willie's writing successes, a principle he rightly saw brought to full maturity at Renfrew when Willie was "talking to artisans and working class people." Willie had clearly been somewhat forthright in speaking of some of his colleagues' attitudes in this regard, and asked for this criticism to be reduced; the need, he said by way of explanation, "just compelled you to express religion in the terms of ordinary people who were not theologians," adding, "That sounds less patronising." (It was the effectiveness of Willie's use of the popularizing principle that later led Professor George Knight, writing in *The Outlook* in faraway New Zealand, to say, "he always expounded the New Testament *as if he were addressing his senior Bible Class.*"[106] The second alteration Willie requested had to do with the consequences of Barbara's death (a matter we shall return to later).

Toward the end of 1959 *The British Weekly* carried the editorial headline "DR WILLIAM BARCLAY HONOURED." A banquet marked the completion of the series and its production in seventeen volumes: the Publications Committee fêted both Willie and Kate (Mrs. Barclay was presented with a specially bound set of the series—perhaps a somewhat ill-considered gift in light of her antipathies to Willie's single-minded concentration on it) and themselves. The event was also reported by *The Glasgow Herald*, though less dramatically.[107] It was indeed a time for celebrations. Andrew McCosh toasted to Willie's health, and speeches of congratulations rained upon them both from R. H. W. Shepherd, Moderator of the General Assembly on behalf of the Church of Scotland; from

Professor James Stewart (with whom Willie was presently in close touch over his Croall Lectures) on behalf of the academic fraternity; and from Frank Doubleday of the Epworth (Methodist) Press, on behalf of the ecumenical community.

What was it that Willie had done during these battery hen years, when commentary followed commentary, and readers and scholars alike paused in admiration of the sheer scale and immensity of the expositions? A brief look at some of the statistics is helpful here, for by the time he had completed the series he had translated the whole New Testament, in the process beating even J. B. Phillips, who was then working full-time in the project. Moreover, he had minutely studied no fewer than 123 full-scale commentaries and scores of other reference books—linguistic, historical, topographical, and so forth—thus fully justifying his gratitude to his overworked librarian friend, James Mackintosh. Records show that he borrowed all of 243 books from the libraries of Trinity College and Glasgow University during this time, not to speak of many unofficial borrowings and his continual use of his own extensive library. And, of course, the commentaries are peppered with references to a characteristically wide range of illustrative authors and subjects drawn from very many aspects of life, litera-ture, the arts, sports, and history. In all, no fewer than 7,509 personal names are cited in these volumes, and there are 488 allusions to the classics involving, overall, commentary on no fewer than 11,188 subjects and places and the exposi-tion of 1,909 foreign (mainly Greek) words, terms, and phrases.

Within this plethoric abundance there is a vital element that must not be minimized, underpinning as it does all his work and attitudes, providing them with direction, power, and authority. I speak of his use of biblical material to interpret, illustrate, and expand the text in hand. Exempting the references of close proximity (i.e., of adjacent texts), there are no fewer than 8,557 references to the Bible within the 5,109 pages of the seventeen-volume set (the revised edition of 1976–78 reduced this, mainly by flattening his style, by 567 pages).[108] Almost six thousand of these references relate to the citation of New Testament passages, and just over two and a half thousand are from the Old Testament.

December 1958 marked the completion of this great work, as well as Willie's fifty-first birthday. Its steadily increasing circulation proves it to be his magnum opus, as we shall see.

Journalist Extraordinary

There can be little doubt that Willie was by this time well affected by "scribbler's itch," but in an extrovert, serving capacity, not selfishly or egotistically. The exertions of the sports field, the golf course, and the more voluble demands of the football terraces had now given way to the not less demanding ones (for one so serious about his powers of communication) of typewriters, desks, and librar-ies. We have already noted that Willie prized the literary traditions of his parents (not least those of William Robertson Nicoll, certainly the greatest Christian journalist of the century)—so much so, indeed, that he very nearly made of them his own career. Perhaps we should rate more highly the undergraduate influence of his old mentor in Eng. Lit., MacNeile Dixon, whose direct influence on Willie prior to his ministerial training of 1930–37 was replaced by the indirect influence of his best-selling book *The Human Situation* of 1937—at the very time Willie was becoming unsettled as to his career. And we should not forget that he found a place for his English professor in *Testament of Faith* when other, equally prominent influences (e.g., David Anderson, the rector, and Miss Sheddon, his French teacher) were omitted.

Whether or not we accept the importance of this influence, it is incontestable that by this time he had made up his mind—or had had it made up for him by external pressures—to devote himself to the plain man's need. As MacNeile Dixon himself stated in his Gifford Lectures, "if I could not be so profound as my predecessors, I might for that reason be more easily followed."[109] His responsibility, the Irishman acknowledged in giving these lectures, was to deliver "popular discourses," presentations "within the compass of the plain man's understanding" (a concept the generality of Gifford Lectures notably exhibit, whatever the brilliance and intellectual penetration displayed). He further noted his intent "to employ familiar words, the words of our daily speech, and to use them in the sense to which we are all accustomed."[110] Such had become Willie's main purpose in life as well, in the consciousness of his own limitations and preferences, and with equal skill and determination.

We must not overlook the fact that Willie had become a journalist in the strictest sense of the word by virtue of his Daily Bible Readings output: he wrote a *journal* specifically destined for daily use (even as some of his Youth Committee and Boys' Brigade handbooks had also contained reading schedules for daily use). Moreover, he was, as we have seen, a great admirer of the profession of journalism, a member (as he had noted to Robin Stirling) of the National Institute of Journalists, and a former editor, perhaps himself becoming the most notable exponent of its arts (religiously, of course) in Scotland during the '50s and '60s, writing for several quite distinct constituencies. Nearly thirty of his books were simply permanent collections of his (often unrevised!) journal articles, which were typically written under intense pressures and not infrequently completed on the eve or even the day of (not to say the day after) his deadline.

When I edited *Men and Affairs,* it seemed natural to select as the first example his review of a writer, John Buchan, who had already set the pace for Willie with an amazing literary record of producing not only a multitude of books, but countless contributions to periodical literature. Significantly, we may add, Buchan was also a man whose maternal influence was of tremendous and lifelong significance. I might well have chosen instead of Willie's article on Buchan one of the earliest of his book reviews, published under the heading "Mr Porritt, Journalist," in which Willie states that "the first lesson that a journalist must learn is to be interesting."[111] While Mr. Porritt's name is no longer common property, and his services to *The Christian World* are all but forgotten, his autobiography clearly interested and influenced Willie—another forgotten link in the

474

great chain of influences. And, as if to emphasize a point Willie made in his very first published article at Renfrew, he noted that this "rich book . . . is written by a man with the secret of happiness . . . a man who would not change his *home*, . . . his *parents*, . . . his *life*." Happy, contented man!

By the beginning of 1955 Willie's journalism had reached its maturity, and from that time his popularity increased by leaps and bounds. We have already seen that his work was by this time greatly appreciated in the form of reviews, articles, expositions, and not least in his books. At this point, after an already promising working relationship had been established on a small scale between Willie and Shaun Herron, the editor of *The British Weekly*, this influential Irishman risked his own reputation and his paper's circulation by giving Willie a complete page of his own. (*The Expository Times* had already done so in 1950, you will recall, but that was restricted to reviews aimed at a more limited readership that shared closely Willie's professional interests as minister-lecturer.) Herron was not to be disappointed; the "William Barclay Page for Preachers and Teachers" rapidly became one of the most popular features of the paper, many of its readers following the habit of those of *The Expository Times* by turning to his page first—and occasionally to his pages, as from time to time he ran over his allocation of space.

Herron advertised the new feature in December 1954, hailing it as "unique" in the history of Christian journalism: "So far as we know, or have been able to discover, no preacher's or teacher's feature quite like this one appears in print in any Christian journal anywhere in the world."[112] It was to remain such until the journal itself, by a series of vicissitudes beyond Willie's control, came under different management and with a very different theological attitude and generosity than his own, helped to freeze the theological world into two irreconcilable hemispheres—the "conservative" and the "liberal." But while he wrote, what a feast he offered his readers! He was careful to fulfill the first lesson of all good journalism, providing articles full of vital human interest, at once engaging and exciting, and sometimes not a little provocative. Robertson Nicoll had formerly spoken of the age limit for journalists as being "not much past fifty," but by December 1957 Willie had himself reached that venerable age not only without showing signs of any decrease in his powers, but with accelerating acclaim and influence.

"What an inspiration William Barclay's page is," wrote one enthusiastic reader from Essex early in the page's life.[113] And the front page of the March 3 issue was predominantly occupied with admiring comments of the same sort; commented Professor James Stewart of Edinburgh,

> To Bible students everywhere William Barclay's is one of the most familiar and honoured of names . . . such a prince of expositors . . . a man possessed by the Gospel and passionately eager to share it. Everything from his pen is characterised by freshness and lucidity, vivid illustration and telling phrase, accurate scholarship and spiritual insight . . . this distinguished and well loved scholar-evangelist.

And Victor Murray, a noted conservative, himself the recipient of a complimentary review by Willie in 1953, spoke of the importance of "edification . . . the building up of men in the faith," adding that "William Barclay's page performs this service, and *we are grateful.*" Wrote Charles Duthie, Principal of the Scottish Congregational College and shortly to be a journalist-colleague of Willie's, "What insight, what diversity, what maturity, what devotion and, above all, what labour goes into this page." As if to underline their own appreciation, the editor and proprietors of the paper issued some of his features in a special publicity brochure reprinting in full Willie's articles of January 6, 13, and 20, now a collector's item of "Barclayana."

The compliments were sometimes interspersed with criticism, as when S. W. Murray of Belfast objected to Willie's review of E. K. Simpson's book *The Pastoral Epistles*[114] on the grounds that it was too negative—though, as we may see from Willie's high recommendation of it in his Daily Bible Readings commentary, this was not the case. T. J. Foinette of Plymouth took him to task for (characteristically) criticizing Harold Roberts' book as being "inhuman."[115] And fellow countryman John Tait of Inverness toward the end of the year pedantically found fault with Willie's use of the word *sadistic* (Tait was unconvinced that the epithet as applied to Antiochus Epiphanes was really due to the emperor's misdirected sexual frustration of instinct).[116] But by far the greater number of letters were of pure praise. Sometimes they were somewhat partial, as when they praised him for his use of Wesley's *Notes on the New Testament,* for example.[117] At other times they were expressions of gratitude from fellow ministers, such as, "[the page] enlivens my thinking, and also my preaching. . . . Long may it continue."[118] And there were requests for reprinting in permanent (i.e., book) form. In August the paper again collated several of the pages and offered them as an inducement to subscription, challenging its readers to study its "consistently high level." Commented one enthusiastic reader in January 1956, "the *British Weekly* has never been better"—because of Willie's contributions.

Willie's publications in 1955 included his four commentaries in the Daily Bible Readings series (two volumes on John and one each on Romans and Hebrews), his book on the miracles of the Bible, his *New Testament Workbook,* and his six booklets on *The Christian Way.* His exposition of the Draft Catechism continued in *The Scottish Sunday School Teacher,* as did his "Entre Nous" column in *The Expository Times.* A similar breadth of outlook was maintained in this page for preachers and teachers, though many "ordinary" people were avid readers. Curiously, few of the compliments came from his professional colleagues, something he was to take sad note of on several occasions in the future to some of his former students; alas, even spiritual matters feel the touch of the green-eyed monster. Willie was discovering anew and contending the importance of the layman long before J. A. T. Robinson and others fought publicly for his rights in the leadership of the church.

But apart from his prodigious authorship of books, he was also making a most significant journalistic effort, and his main thrust in that regard was made, as we have seen, in his page in *The British Weekly.* The page included a column entitled "Obiter Visa" and three other sections—on word studies, biblical exposition, and prayer—features that together catered to a large variety of tastes and needs.

1. The title of his column, "Obiter Visa," means roughly, "incidental insight." That he would choose a Latin phrase is, as in the case of his *Expository Times* column, "Entre Nous" (French for "between ourselves"), something of a curiosity, since he was elsewhere so keenly critical of inaccessible jargon; perhaps it merely indicates that he still had a few blind spots to overcome. In any case, the title is pregnant with meaning for this Highlander's son, to whom a "picture" was such an important element of thought and communication. As Johnston Ross said to S. F. Collier of the Methodist Central Hall, Manchester, "I can *see.* You know a Celt cannot think."[119] *Visa* is a form of the Latin verb *videre*, "to see," and is properly interpreted "view" or "sight" or "prospect"—but all Willie's viewings were in reality *insights.* Like his beloved parables, they were essentially "earthly stories with heavenly meanings," a definition that even Bultmann accepted though he transposed it into a "more theological" if less comprehensible key. ("Myths," he wrote in his *Jesus Christ and Mythology,* "give worldly objectivity to that which is unworldly.")

The "Obiter Visa" pieces might be termed the Barclay equivalent of Luther's Table Talk, the only sustained example of such we have from him, though it was never small-minded, uncareful, or demeaning of others. It is in this weekly budget of small talk that his parables-of-life usage finds mature expression, after the manner of the One who found inspiration and illustration in the birds of the air, the smallest seed known to man, the hairs of one's head, and many other such things. Indeed, as his appeals to friends of the time testify, his problem was to find enough apposite examples to turn into lessons, his heavy writing schedule binding him all too closely to desk and typewriter. In this work as in no other of Willie's, Kate was able to help, she who loved so much the chitchat and banter of friends' conversation.

In this series of causeries he addressed virtually every aspect of human society and behavior, much of it in autobiographical terms. In them William Barclay encountered life, sometimes life in the raw, and his buoyant response to it was one of humility, openness, gratitude, and firm resolve. We learn of his prejudices, his foibles, his pleasures, and his preferences. We learn of his home life, his traveling, his work, and his associates. We even learn of his love of animals, of his pets Rusty and Sammy, who must be two of the best known pets of the century! And we learn of his appreciation of goodness and beauty and his preference, if they can be held in polarity with each other, for beauty over truth. We see him ever finding beauty in the spurned thing, fellowship in the disavowed, and reality in what to others was but meaninglessness. It is pure blindness not to recognize in this attitude Another who also sought the lost and was crucified for so doing. Like Brother Lawrence of old, or Rabbie Burns of more recent memory, Willie not infrequently found in the world of common, despised things the very presence of the Almighty and the All-loving. Even academically

477

he had turned from the classical to the "common," from the beauties of Homer to the *koiné* of unknown clerks and householders. He spoke of high things, too, to be sure; not a few of these pieces were taken up with books or ideas or advancements of one kind or the other. We might also say they were a running, if unconscious, commentary on Philippians 4:8, a text on which his own evangelical constituency has all too often turned its back.

2. Another section of the page commenced, or rather continued, his word-book articles, which ran on into September 1956, and continued to unfold new riches to unsuspecting readers. The "trick" (if I may use his own word to describe his method)[120] of such exposition he had learned from such linguistic masters as A. T. Pierson of YMCA fame, though Willie's practice here went beyond that of Pierson and was founded on more enlightened scholarship (thanks to the archaeologist's spade) and a more outgoing message.

3. Biblical exposition was ever his best-loved occupation, and so it is not surprising that the early "Preachers' Commentary" of June and July 1951, in which he had expounded Philippians, should now flower into more sustained exposition. The first passages selected were his favorite Letters to the Seven Churches, of Revelation 1–3; they, too, later found their way into book form (in 1957). These were followed, in April, with a long series of articles (forty-eight in all) on "Life in Palestine in Jesus' Time," which described the historical and political backgrounds of the Gospels as well as the religious and social ones.

4. The final section, though smaller, was of inestimable value both in Willie's own life and in his work. It would be wrong to call this the devotional aspect, for a devotional element ran through all his work at all times: to work was to worship. But prayer was a compelling factor in his life, and there were very few issues that did not offer one or another sort of prayer to his readers. It began most typically with "Prayers for People," in which virtually the entire range of human experience was included (at least, from the male viewpoint!). The persistent requests that these prayers be collected into a book, as well as the phenomenal sales that followed when they eventually were published, show what a timely blessing this section was to many. It is given to very few to frame the prayers of people the world over, covering all age groups, but it was given to William Barclay, and their use continues still. There was nothing Cranmerian about his prayers, though they are beautifully balanced and written. They are nearer Michel Quoist than Cranmer in their subject and language. I nearly wrote "secularity" instead of "language," for the atmosphere they breathe is not the religiously institutionalized one of the great Reformer but that of a modern, liberated, humane follower of Jesus, of one who loves God, enjoys life, and ever seeks to fulfill his commands—not least in gathering others into that same state of happiness that he enjoys. It would not be too much to say that these prayers were themselves a new art form, a sort of open-verse poetry of the religious life.

By these things did he become the hugely influential figure of the 1950s and 1960s, truly "a man sent from God." Indeed, his influence and confidence were such that in April 1955, in reviewing C. S. Lewis at the launch of the now world-famous Fontana Paperbacks (which, like SCM paperbacks, sought to meet the challenge of mass production and mass markets so much a feature of postwar developments and itself a sign of the common man's claim for himself and his family), Willie called on publishers throughout the land to discover new authors who could write as Lewis did, "for everyman."[121] He himself was leading the way, journalistically and through the resultant books, and so it is not surprising to find him quietly conducting, throughout the mid 1950s, a Christian Journalists meeting in Glasgow, which included the late Peter Mitchell, who finally went out to New Zealand (at Willie's recommendation) to take over the editorship of *The Presbyterian Magazine*. By such means did his influence spread, and all of it was done in a fine spirit of humility and forebearance; as Mrs. Mitchell has stated of her late husband's mentor, he was "the most loveable, human man of God I ever had the privilege to meet."[122]

To refer to such exploits as his "battery hen years" is in one clear sense wholly misleading: he was not entrapped, as the subjects of that industry are, in a limiting, lightless, and undesirable condition (even if his fellow sufferers were sometimes driven to a similar internal feuding and opposing claims in the pecking order!). He was still essentially able to range free, and although his timetable necessitated some seclusion (usually after dark), he was most active up and down the length of the land, everywhere producing heartening and edifying results in his labors, some of which were to have effects for decades and some of which influence us still.

On 15 June 1954 he appeared in the pulpit of Manchester's prestigious Central Hall, scene of so many pulpit orations throughout its illustrious history, not least of which was that of A. S. Peake. Willie has not left us his reflections on this initial experience, but the register briefly records the visit; his name appears alongside such modern princes of the pulpit as W. E. Sangster, Nels Ferré, Donald Soper, Bryan Green, Leslie Weatherhead, Leonard Small, and Howard Williams, to name but a few. The service commenced at 12:45 P.M. and finished at 1:40 P.M., and Willie preached on part of one of his favorite texts: "every tongue [will] confess that Jesus Christ is Lord, to the glory of God the Father" (Philippians 2:11, RSV). Thus he admirably commenced a special ministry that was to last for fifteen years, broken only in 1957 and 1963 when "more important duties"— those of his students—forbade his absence from Glasgow. His regular midday services became an institution, a significant part of his overall ministry (as did the later series of services he delivered to the Newcastle YMCA and the Bloomsbury Central Baptist Church). It is appropriate to emphasize here that he always recorded the length of his Central Hall services, for it demonstrates an aspect of his punctilious mind that we encountered earlier. He was one of the few visiting speakers to record his finishing time to the nearest minute (e.g., on 14 June 1960 it was 1.32 P.M., on 6 September 1966 it was 1.27 P.M., and so on). He was aware that busy working people often made a special effort to get to such services, and he was totally conscientious in his use of their time as well as of his own; he never ran overtime at such gatherings, and he never outstayed his welcome—a very useful habit for the television lecturer he was to become.

It is interesting to note that of the fifteen occasional addresses he delivered at Central Hall, six were based on Matthew, three on Philippians, and only one directly on an Old Testament text. It would be foolish to make too much of this, but it is mildly suggestive of the focus of his interests over seventeen years when left completely free to choose his own themes, suggestive perhaps of both his preferences and his theology. Such Pelagianism as he had, we might venture, was decidedly Matthean. Another interesting feature of his performance in the pulpit was his immediate commencement: once in the pulpit, there was no dilly-dallying, no toying with his paperwork—which in any case amounted on such occasions to only two sheets, one for his prayer(s) and the other containing the merest headings of his address. (See pages 482–83 for a facsimile of one such note.) Nor was any place given in the pulpit to his own prayerful preparation of mind and spirit: he firmly believed that should be done elsewhere. It could almost be said that he commenced too quickly, his harsh voice booming out in supplication of the divine presence and blessing, resonant in fast, strong sentences, though whatever concentration on himself this produced in the newcomer to his style was quickly banished in the sheer reality of spiritual conviction. Worship of and gratitude to God were simple yet profound, as to a Father-God and friend, reverent yet trusting. Confession was never absent, and was always plain and specific, following Luther's admonitions. And his intercessions were very moving, both wide and narrow in their purport, social and individualistic. And so the congregation was propelled toward the sermon, which was announced in clear, almost strident tones; he always broke the text into neat parts, each punctuated with clear exposition and illustration, always totally demanding in their call to new or renewed discipleship. And thence to the concluding hymn, the congregation rising rapturously to its carefully chosen lines, whether of praise or commitment.

The late summer of 1954 was a busy time for the Barclays in another sense. After having lived for eight years in the home at 87 Vardor Road—an unprepossessing terraced house of the '30s, as we saw—they now moved to the slightly larger and much more conveniently situated one on Berridale Avenue, Clarkston. The move was made entirely to please Kate, for, unlike Compton Mackenzie and many other writers, Willie had no need to be constantly moving to new households in order to keep his mind and his creativity fresh. The springs of Willie's motivation were different, being spiritual, inspired by his close walk with God, in which he was ever surprised by new truths, or new aspects of old truths, and new causes of wonder (another Barclay keyword) and worship. His method, like his material, was naturally very different from that of the novelists, being firmly anchored to the biblical text, but similar too, for through that text he and his readers endlessly traveled the biblical and classical lands of Europe and the Near East, and elsewhere. Gifted with Celtic imagination and a richly stored memory, he had no such need for travel and change. His traveling, while excessive by most people's standards, was essentially functional, though he did find refreshment in breaking his journeys in both isolated and historic places of interest (York, Manchester, Birmingham, Lincoln, Peterborough, and at various places between or around them), always in private hotels, and increasingly at his own expense.

Another aspect of his work at this time also served to extend his influence into new spheres, with definite and encouraging recollections of past opportunities: I. D. Neil, C.B., C.B.E., Warden of the Training Centre and Depot of the Royal Army Chaplains Department at Bagshot, invited him to address a Senior Officers Course on Christian Information and Leadership. In many ways this completed the circle opened in 1939, when Willie, rebuffed by the clergy of his locality for his ardent pacifist views, nevertheless led the civilian support for the forces in that same area, which led in turn to his part-time chaplaincy of the Royal Air Force at Renfrew and much else besides.

The senior officers present at this course (of the rank of Colonel and above) were thirty in number, and represented the cream of the army's traditions and leadership. They were busy, thorough, and practical men whose own well-disciplined principles of efficiency were not unlike those of the unmilitary and peaceable Willie. Mr. Neil comments,

> He stood to lecture almost tentatively, being on—what was to him—unfamiliar ground. "I want to talk to you about the Beatitudes," he said, and I as Warden held my breath and said my prayers! Within a sentence or two all anxiety had gone and, like all officers present, I was sitting on the edge of my chair in interest and eagerness. He lectured twice that morning, and during the afternoon, which was normally set aside as a free period until tea-time. I was asked by two quite unlikely looking officers if it would be fair to ask "old man Barclay if he would lecture again" during the free period of the afternoon.[123]

This must be ranked one of the most authentic portraits of Willie at that time: his tentative manner before such company (he was ever susceptible to high authority—a throwback to the repressive molding influence of his father—though never defeated by it) was reinforced by a natural humility. His daring in selecting so unlikely a passage for war-experienced men recalls that of John the Baptist, though, like John, he presented a messsage challenging the men to adopt more ethical behavior, not pacifism. His complete mastery of his material was so patent that it not only silenced the anxieties of his kindly host but captured the minds and wills of those decorated officers, even to the point of inducing a readiness to sacrifice their leisure hours! The reference to "old man Barclay" was also appropriate in capturing Willie's worn appearance, though he was (at forty-seven) actually younger than some of the trim and fit individuals he was addressing.

It is not unknown for some academics to lord their knowledge over their hearers, albeit unconsciously. There was nothing of that in Willie's makeup. The same serving, gentle spirit with which he welcomed his returning servicemen home from the war and with which he welcomed similar men to his college

Transcript of a prayer of William Barclay

O God our Father,
in whose presence all joys are
doubly dear, make us on
this day of our gladness,
conscious of your presence
here.

And so let your spirit
be in our hearts

   that we may be
remembering all your
blessings of the past and all
the love both human and
divine which has
brought us to this present
hour,

   that we may find the
strength and grace to
meet the challenge of
the present,

   that we may know
the hope and certainty
that the best is yet
to be.

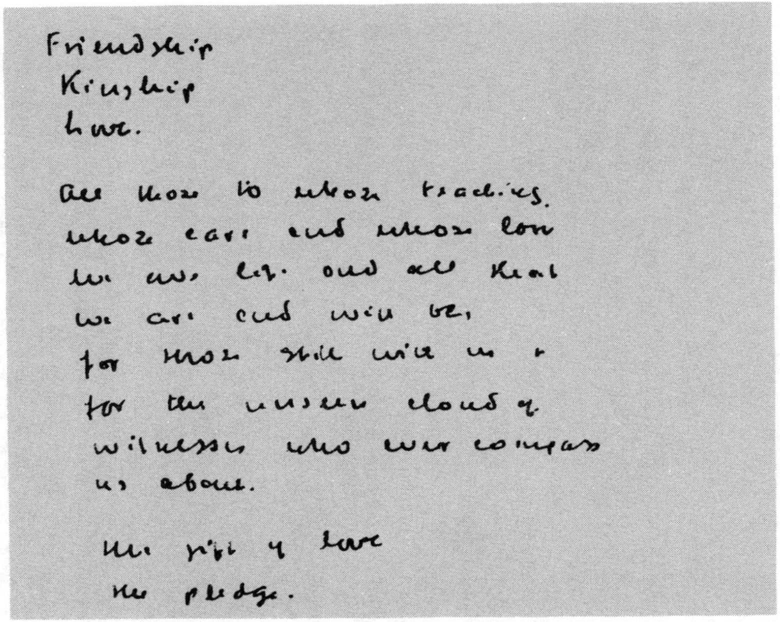

Friendship
Kinship
Love

All those to whose teaching,
whose care and whose love
we [owe life] and all that
we are and will be,
for those still with us &
for the unseen cloud of
witnesses who ever compass
us about,

the gift of love
we pledge.

A facsimile reproduction and transcription of some of Willie's notes for a prayer (above) and a sermon (below)

The Barclay home on Berridale Avenue

courses from 1946 onward was also displayed here. He was ever the slave of Christ, the servant of his fellow men. Mr. Neil illustrates his attitude by way of recalling an incident that occurred on a later visit to Bagshot, due to an administrative error. The house in which visiting lecturers stayed for these courses was some distance from the railway station, and so a staff car was sent to collect them. To the Warden's dismay, he found Willie on this occasion entering the premises on foot, having walked, carrying his own bag, from the station. (We should remember that Willie, though he traveled light, always took several of his books and his typewriter with him, so his case was heavy.) We need have no concern over his ability to do so. However prematurely aged he may have looked, he was actually as strong as an ox, as his fearsome work schedule demonstrates. He turned aside the apology offered by Mr. Neil, who was later able to say, "I honestly believe that at that moment I was the only one to feel distressed." As usual, Willie took no offense at having been overlooked, not even presuming that they should feel obliged to provide transportation for him at the end of his long journey. As the Warden commented, "his graciousness and Christian humility enriched his every visit."

There is yet another element in this story that reflects one of the reasons for his success on such occasions: as with many of his congregations (e.g., at Manchester Central Hall), there were powerful and distinguished individuals present, and they willingly sat at his feet to learn from him—though he would always insist they were learning *with* him. Said the Warden of this experience,

> We all learnt from him without ever feeling even that we were being advised. . . . He entered into discussion with learned and unlearned, and with those who had "the certainty of ignorance," making each feel that their contributions mattered to the discussion, and always being eagerly anxious never to cloud the faith or Christian understanding of any with perplexities or questionings they were not mature enough to handle. His real joy was to see the relationship of simple faith between any individual and his/her Saviour.

This is by no means to say that Willie encouraged a simplistic faith or easy "believism," however; his contendings against shut minds is evidence enough of that, and his reading and reviewing lists are full of difficult and challenging things—philosophically, religiously, and biblically. Rather, he avoided *unnecessary* complication, as is evident in another example related by Mr. Neil, of a Conference of Assistant Chaplains General (who had been gathered chiefly from the Far East). On this occasion Willie had been invited to conduct the Quiet Day of Devotion, which was preceded by a brilliant theologian giving an after-dinner lecture on "The Trends of Modern Theology," an occasion when "everyone felt the strain" of the subject dealt with, including the hapless lecturer himself. Willie was incapable of inflicting such treatment on his listeners, knowing better the needs of humanity and the arts of communication. He spoke of his concern the next morning at the foot of the grand staircase. "Those busy and devoted people," he remarked characteristically, "have come to be warmed and strengthened in their task, and not to be puzzled." Theologians may well complain about this attitude—their work is important, and Willie would certainly want to emphasize that the implications and frontiers of knowledge must be hard-pressed, and faith's validity and logic must be subjected to ruthless self-criticism—but this was not his way, nor did he judge this to be the right time for it. And any misuse of such work (in his view it was essentially private, internal, and self-judgmental, the church's introspective obligation) received his censure. To be warmed and strengthened was much more important, on this and similar occasions, than being strained or puzzled.

A confirming illustration of Willie's attitude toward theological complications can be seen in an event that occurred some years later, when a member of the Senior Officers group, a retired general, required somebody to talk to a house group of industrial managers on matters of faith and belief. The call again fell on Willie, who was found willing to travel from Glasgow to Reigate for the small group. He did so, moreover, in the knowledge that the outlook of the organizers in religious matters was of a fundamentalist disposition, and not at all sympathetic to his broader purview. His audience, disgusted at an unsuccessful previous attempt by another expert, became eager and spellbound in listening to him as he delicately trod around the minefields of faith and truth that lay before them. Here was no self-appointed iconoclast working against sincere belief and disbelief, but a servant of the word and of those he served by it. They recognized him as such despite their differences.

The same spirit typified his work among young men, a party of whom was found at one of the Bagshot conferences on a training program for prospective chaplains. Every shade of churchmanship was represented, though Anglicans predominated. On this occasion partisanship was sadly obtrusive, and arguments and counterarguments raged in the working sessions, at meal times, and in the free periods. It was still rankling at the end of the course, for which a Quiet Day had been arranged. Willie was expressly approached to undertake the difficult task of instituting peace and reverence. "The result was dramatic," Mr. Neil reported. "Gone were the arguments which tore people apart, and in their place were discussions and studies around the deep truths of scripture binding together those who had been at variance." If his was the aura of saintliness in those days, it was because it was also the aura of peacemaking, "blessed" in the truest sense, but never achieved at the expense of his humanity, his dynamic, or his humor.

Not that he forebore to declare his own theological persuasion. He was a plain speaker in both senses of the phrase. In one of his *British Weekly* causeries he refers to his pointed refusal to participate in a communion service (a service, as it happened, at Bagshot) because his and others' baptism and ordination were not recognized by the Anglicans present.[124] (It had been but recently that his own church had removed all such barriers in its laws.) His indignation and public condemnation were well warmed; the minority party was delighted to have such a doughty defender, though he was careful not to embarrass his hosts.

Mr. Neil once visited one of the "very senior officers," leaving a few books for the sick man to help while away his hours of somewhat impatient suffering. On his next visit Neil was challenged about his underhanded slipping in a "holy" book (it was one of the Daily Bible Readings volumes). But, confessed the surprised officer, "It told me that I had never studied my Bible as a grown man," to which he added the resolution of determined study henceforth. Just how widespread Willie's influence was becoming may be judged from this and other incidents of the time: he attended his second meeting of the directors of the National Bible Society of Scotland in July; he wrote "Christ, the Hope of the World" for *The British Weekly* (a preparatory article for the World Council of Churches' Evanston Assembly); he went on to dedicate new church halls at Craighall in Edinburgh; a little while after this he celebrated the twenty-fifth anniversary of the Reunion of 1929 (and Churchill's eightieth birthday!); and he preached at the Barony Church, Glasgow, in the "Tell Scotland" campaign in November. In this the year that Roger Bannister broke the four-minute mile, Willie in his own sphere was also setting new records. Little wonder he began to miss some important faculty meetings at university!

In the winter of 1954 there opened up to him another opportunity for service closely parallel to that of Manchester's Central Hall: he was invited to be the special guest speaker at the annual Presbyterian rally at Newcastle, which was held in its great city hall—a prestigious invitation indeed, at which such southern Presbyterians as T. W. Manson (Peake's successor—via C. H. Dodd—at Manchester, and Moderator of the General Assembly of the Presbyterian Church of England) were distinguished invitees. Willie arrived in desperate wintry conditions to find that over two thousand had also braved the deep snows to hear him (some had traveled over thirty miles to do so), and for forty-five minutes he discharged his duty to the grateful admiration of his newfound friends. Comments of the impact he made soon reached the ears of the Council of the Newcastle YMCA and, as we shall see, an exactly parallel ministry to that at Manchester Central Hall was soon under way.

Amid much controversy, the rock 'n' roll era was ushered in in 1955. (It reached its height in 1959, when we shall find Willie expressing enjoyment of its music.) Some regarded it as lewd; others failed to recognize it as music at all. It was the age when the "square" members of society were ridiculed by the "in crowd," and vice versa. In all truth, compared with later developments, there was very little to justify the reaction to it; many of its chief critics were middle-aged, bespectacled men, showing the weight of their years in more ways than one. Stars such as Bill Haley look as harmless as city gents in the light of more recent styles, and were certainly more altruistic. It was also the era when black music (both blues and gospel) became highly fashionable, with such characters as Ray Charles, Little Richard, Fats Domino, and Chuck Berry hitting the headlines. Deeply indebted to this music, and the greatest exponent of it, was the "King of Rock," Elvis Presley. Once again we see foundations being laid for the seething '60s, as the self-indulgent songs of the repressed were transmuted into the socially conscious protest songs of the later figures of Bob Dylan, Julie Felix, Joan Baez, and others. In the catalogue of their concerns, the scourge of racism was overtaken by the scourge of modern warfare; Willie was a staunch opponent of all such brutality and inequality.

It was an unhappy period for British politics, with Bevan "eructating bitterness" in the Labour Party, soon to lurch to the right, as the younger, more donnish element asserted itself in favor of the new technocrats and their skills, and Winston Churchill's premiership began to show signs of its imminent discomfiture. These were still the days of cheap money, but the finances of the nation were in persistent trouble, which fed industrial unrest despite unemployment being at its lowest since the war. Harold Macmillan's fourth volume of biography (covering 1956–59, though the description of it is of wider application) was titled *Riding the Storm,* and such was the experience of those years for many.

There was much excitement religiously, itself another symptom of the general dynamic then at work, as postwar want gave way to an age that had "never had it so good." Arguments still proliferated over the Billy Graham campaigns, though the public had moved beyond the "should we welcome him?" point; the campaigns had taken place, and even the skeptical had to admit that good work had been done. Willie, as ever, was more than welcoming, his participation in the "Tell Scotland" campaign despite the literary pressures he felt are evidence of that; if he wrote sparingly of the evangelist, it was at least a positive view he presented. Well over a million people had attended the meetings, and nearly twenty-eight thousand professed faith (over sixty percent of these—almost seventeen thousand—had no prior church connections, a factor Willie could not but greet with admiration and respect as the burden of the unchurched masses fell increasingly upon him). Some cavil at Dr. Graham's theology, some at his sermon structures, some at the expense of the campaign (though it came to less than fifteen pence per head of those who attended), and some at his salary, but the spiritual reality was plain and outlived the critics. "All London Is Talking about Billy Graham" declared one headline,[125] and while the response was different north of the border, his influence was clearly felt, and his methods continued. It was not long before Willie became indirectly involved in the work of the Billy Graham organization, largely through his old friend Merricks Arnot, whose work in audio/visual-aid techniques was recognized by the American organization. As a result of this, Willie was invited to write the script for one of their films, but withdrew at embarrassingly short notice from the involvement, ostensibly because of the pressure of other work.

The World Council of Churches Assembly met at Evanston, Illinois, and the papers were full of reports and "post-Evanston" conferences in Edinburgh, Glasgow, and elsewhere. John Leith has seen 1955 as a turning point in theology, marking "the end of the dominant influence associated with Karl Barth and the emergence of many new theological interests." He has noted that since then theology has been, in Schubert Ogden's phrase, "plagued by lust for novelty and narcissistic delight in being original," which has resulted in faddism. But whatever we may make of Willie's own theology, it is clear that he was not in the least impressed by the stream of fads that now emerged, provoking articles and reviews and filling the letters-to-the-editor columns of many papers and journals. Leith's view is that these movements (extending over two decades and more) of civil rights, the Jesus movement, black theology, secular theology, and theologies of hope, politics, peace, women's rights, and play—*thematic* theologies, significantly—marked the resurrection of Schleiermacher (who was himself eclipsed by Barth in the 1930s). These movements included some really weighty matters, such as the renewed quest for the historical Jesus, the nature of "God-talk" (theological language), the death of God (or of our ideas of God), and the post–Vatican II renaissance in Roman Catholicism—siren songs, all of them, to fundamentalists and the more narrowly defined type of evangelicals who per-sisted in proclaiming the basic, simple truths of the gospel story, as did Willie himself, though not in their limiting language and manner. A total eclipse of the sun had taken place on 30 June 1954, but many evangelicals looked on such theological innovations and explorations as attempts to eclipse the "sun of righteousness" himself. Willie was changing too. His sudden withdrawal from involvement with the Billy Graham organization clearly involved more than merely the pressures he felt, for he went on to accept even more burdensome tasks.

Between these opposing forces, the voice of moderation, of reconciliation, was faintly heard. Perhaps no single author was more influential here than the celebrated lay theologian C. S. Lewis (after the manner of T. R. Glover of a previous generation, who likewise did sterling work of an apologetic nature). He brought an attitude of cool common sense to the heated agitation of the period, having a remarkable facility for being able to find just the right word for be-wildered, seeking modern man. Interestingly enough, there are remarkable parallels between Lewis and Willie as well as differences; it may be that their mutual influence for good was grounded in these very points: neither stood too close to denominational allegiance, still less ecclesiastical bureaucracy; both had sharp things to say about the role of the clergy in society; both rejected doctrinal and liturgical "fidgets"; and both maintained a strong commitment to long-substantiated articles of faith.

The times called for new methods, new emphases, a recognition of the new postwar spirit that had leveled society so much, in order to supply a new moral force—intellectually, rather than just by authoritative proclamation. A new opportunity thus arose, and Willie, in the midst of his arduous writing schedule, was ready to step in to fill the gap, though not suddenly nor yet easily.

CHAPTER FIFTEEN

The Crucible of Suffering

Opportunity, Travel, and Fame Multiply

In the preceding chapter we took brief note of the fact that Kate was able to help Willie in his preparation of the "Obiter Visa" column on his page in *The British Weekly*. She was in fact better able to help him in many ways by this time (1956), having finally recovered enough from the exhaustions of their work at Renfrew Trinity to begin enjoying Willie's hard-won prestige and popularity. One who noted Kate's contribution to that hard-won success was Ian Grant, who sold and serviced Willie's cars (he was now beginning to trade them in more often as literary royalties eased the family's straitened finances); as Grant put it, Kate was "a real gem, and the living proof of the saying that 'behind every great man there is a great lady.'" Free now from the confinements entailed by parish obligations and small children as well as the pecuniary disadvantage entailed by the ministry, Kate was coming into her own as a domestic secretary and public relations aide to her husband, becoming once more in her own right *une femme du monde*. The health problems that had plagued her since the war years had mostly disappeared—with one significant exception, to which Willie referred in a letter to Braidwood, stating that her health had "not been good," and that in fact her condition was "very crippling."[1] Acute fibrositis was the problem, making both her arms "pretty well helpless." A long course of therapeutic massage had little effect, but electrical treatments eventually ameliorated her "insuperable problems."

Kate was able to take delight not only in Willie's successes, but those of her children as well. Ronnie had commenced university in October 1952, reading modern languages in the Honours School with all the promise his father had shown thirty years before. He was a tall, fair, athletic young man, highly articulate, worldly-wise, and independent. Kate and Willie were naturally delighted and proud. In October 1955, having fully justified their expectations in his examinations, he set out to spend a year at Romorantin, near Orléans in France, as *assistant d'anglais,* teaching English and British customs to the higher classes of its Lycée. In doing so he befriended Roger Aussourd, who in turn was

490

befriended by Willie; thus the latter's genius for friendship and kindliness was extended to the continent of Europe—though it showed that his facility in the French language was no longer at top form! On the basis of Ronnie's experiences at Romorantin, Willie hazarded to tell Braidwood that "he certainly will not teach." (In this he was soon proved to be quite mistaken: Ronnie went on to be not merely a teacher, but a distinguished teacher of teachers at Jordanhill College—the very place Willie had but nine years previously thought he might very possibly find meaningful work for himself.)

Barbara, too, was now at university, reading the subject her father had been captivated by in his own arts course and planning to follow her brother in a teaching career. At the beginning all three of them traveled from Clarkston together by car, an experience that delighted Willie and filled Kate with that special form of pride common to all caring, hopeful mothers. As the picture of them together on page 396 shows, they were a relaxed, united, happy family; the special relationship between Barbara and Kate was one many were to comment on especially. Perhaps Barbara, a consummate sympathizer like her father, understood the loneliness her mother felt despite the wide circle of family and friends; perhaps she realized something of the void in her mother's life that had been caused by her husband's total commitment to his work and calling. Not that Kate spoke often of this, or bemoaned her lot; she did not need to do so, thanks to the mature intuition of her daughter, ever attentive to her mother's feelings and moods—and that despite the fact that she was already "going steady" with Billy Regan, her Irish boyfriend, whom, Willie confided to Braidwood, "if present indications are to be relied upon, she will marry." Like all fathers, Willie had a very special place in his heart for his daughter, perhaps not least because she shared his mother's lovely temperament as well as her name. They certainly had more in common than just their love of Eng. Lit. and their masterful human sympathy. Saturday afternoons would sometimes find them sharing an interest at Hampden Park together, watching the Queen's Park Rangers matches (presumably when his beloved Motherwell United F. C. was not playing at home).

And Willie was still feeling "indestructible," enjoying a level of health and vitality astonishing for someone with his crushing work load, not to mention his smoking and eating habits, in both of which he exercised little restraint, though we should not charge him from our hindsight position for the irresponsibility such excesses now attract. Those were the days of scarcely five hours of sleep per night, of long hours of hard mental concentration, interrupted by insistent telephone calls (in June 1955 he actually confessed to *hating* these interruptions,[2] such were the pressures on him), visits, lectures, sermons, travel, and very heavy correspondence. At the very time he complained of the interruptions, having been deeply involved in various training schemes for the Boys' Brigade in Glasgow, he paid his first visit to Billy Regan's homeland—not to check up on his future son-in-law, but to participate in meetings associated with the General Assembly of the Presbyterian Church of Ireland, such as the annual ministers conference at Portrush. He was "thrilled to be there," he wrote.[3] At the Youth

Night Rally he spoke to over two thousand young people, holding them "spell-bound." He described it as "a wonderful meeting"; and "it was a still greater joy to enjoy the gracious hospitality" of Ronnie Craig's family and Belfast home. Fearful flier that he was, he found even the flight home "just perfect." He had also spoken at the General Assembly of the Presbyterian Church itself, following which the Moderator, the Very Reverend J. C. Breakey, wrote to him, "If ever you can find time to come back again, we shall all be in our seats waiting for you."[4] Little did any of them anticipate that he would be back all too soon, under very different circumstances, against his will, and with a breaking heart.

In July 1955 he attended his third (and final) meeting with the Board of Directors of the National Bible Society of Scotland. The next month found him in Eastbourne, Sussex, the Special Summer Preacher at the famous Presbyterian conference at Kirn, held at the Abbey Hill Hotel, arriving with "L-plates" on his car, as Ronnie was then learning to drive. June Macfarlane was a former member of Renfrew Old Church, and so had personal reasons for attending this

Barbara Barclay: idealization of "the beautiful and the good"

492

conference. She found Willie standing there with his jacket torn from the top of the pocket to the seam, but tied together with enormous stitches, fully half an inch across. "How did you do that?" she asked. "Oh!" he replied, "that happened in one of my usual hurrying episodes. I caught it on the handle of my car door, but I didn't think it was noticeable, as I had sewn it up." He was, Mrs. Macfarlane reports, "A handless creature in domestic things, indeed!"⁵ In October another notable event took place at his old church in Motherwell, when he was called on to unveil a window in memory of Thomas Marshall, who had died in 1953. (Willie didn't allow even this to be his last expression of appreciation for the old minister—the only one under whom he worshiped; in 1967 he dedicated his book *The Lord's Supper* to "Thomas Marshall . . . who prepared me for my first Communion.")

"An exceptional year" for visits to the south, 1956 might well have seen Willie make his exit from the British Isles altogether. Duke University of Durham, North Carolina, offered him the New Testament Chair, but he declined, ostensibly on the grounds of his lack of adventurous spirit. "I don't think I'll ever be anywhere else but Glasgow," he told Braidwood, adding that "at forty-eight I don't feel able to make such a drastic change." He confessed that he often wished he was back at Trinity Church, for he missed being at the center of such a lively community. He even confessed to some disenchantment with his students, the universities having fallen on "evil days." The students were too easy-minded, he thought; they merely wanted a degree "to sell," and had no real understanding of the joy of learning for learning's sake.⁶ Moreover, he missed "the more intelligent" conversations of his Firewatchers, one night of which he found more interesting than a complete term of university teaching! By this time he was Senior Lecturer at the University, in charge of its Department of Hellenistic Greek and responsible for a heavy schedule of New Testament lectures at all levels. Thanks to Macgregor's indifferent health, he had all the academic responsibilities—if not the status—he needed. A move to another house, and the familial disruption it would involve, now held no temptation for him. One suspects that he (and even more Kate) had no desire for the very different life-style American society entailed, for although he admired many individual Americans, he frequently found opportunity to suspect and criticize American attitudes, as did many Britons at that time.

In March he journeyed to Bagshot again, this time to lead one of the chaplains' training courses. A. C. Dow, one of Willie's college companions in the early '30s, was also present. Twenty or so officers took the course, all "Major Generals and above,"⁷ and once again Willie "kept them thrilled for two long talks on the Beatitudes." He was interrupted by a phone call from Kate at 8:45 one morning during his stay there, and was "shattered" by the news she gave. At first he did not understand what she was saying, his mind no doubt being full of his imminent lecture. He did realize, however, that it must be important: the time of the telephone call "seemed to me to indicate either extreme extravagance or extreme emergency. . . . I did not think my wife would be extravagant so I went to the telephone expecting death and disaster—so DD will always stand for Death and Disaster to me!"[8] In writing to Braidwood, he reminded his friend of "my wife's notorious inability to understand any official document, and her well known ability to misunderstand all such documents." But the reality of the message finally dawned on him: the University of Edinburgh "had a rush of blood to the head, and made me a Doctor of Divinity."[9] It was a complete and total shock; as he confessed to Braidwood, "I did not in my wildest dreams think that I would ever wear Edinburgh's scarlet and purple." Congratulations soon poured in to him from former church members, Sunday School teachers, fellow lecturers and churchmen, readers of his books and articles, and many others. To A. C. Dow, who humbly asked whether he now had to call him "Doctor or Willie," he emphasized that it would make no difference; "I shall still be Willie to my friends."

His successor to the editorship of *The Scottish Sunday School Teacher,* Mrs. Murray, soon heralded the good news under the headline "A Well-Deserved Honour."[10] She wrote, "this magazine [rejoices] almost as if *it* were receiving a DD," significantly drawing special attention not to his having been editor of their magazine, nor to his Senior Lesson Notes (despite the fact that they were still being used by various bodies overseas, in Athens and Nigeria, for example), nor even to his occasional articles, but to his "Suggestions for Worship." They knew their man, and were keen to assert his real power even at this time of academic recognition. The Executive of the Scottish Sunday School Union resolved "to record our pleasure in learning that the degree of DD was to be conferred [upon him and] agree to convey to Mr Barclay our warm congratulations on *this well-deserved honour.*"[11] It was an appropriate time for this to happen, since Willie had only just conveyed to the Executive at the Annual General Meeting his regrets that he could no longer serve him formally (this was the meeting, open to all teachers who could attend, at which he had delivered his final and very well received address "which dealt with the fundamentals of all good Sunday School teaching."[12]

Such tributes were gathered together in a special meeting with delegates from Trinity Church, Renfrew, and Trinity College, at which Professor Mauchline, Mrs. Murray, Andrew McCosh, and Willie's old college friend Stanley Munro presented him with his doctoral robes at his old Renfrew church. A letter from a delighted reader in *The British Weekly,* noting that Willie's D.D. had been given at the same time as Father Trevor Huddleston (whose book *Nought for Your Comfort* was now making great waves) obtained his from Aberdeen University, congratulated the respective universities not only for their "common sense" but also for the paper's supporting of two such illustrious figures in the modern church[13]—a

Page opposite: *William Barclay, D.D.* Above: *Willie in his doctoral robes.* Below: *The document announcing his honor.*

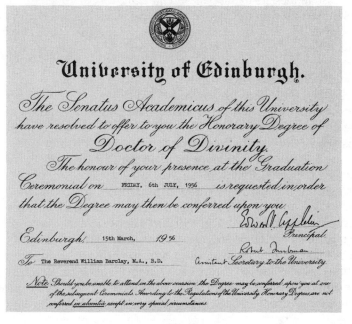

University of Edinburgh.

The Senatus Academicus of this University
have resolved to offer to you the Honorary Degree of
Doctor of Divinity.
The honour of your presence at the Graduation
Ceremonial on   FRIDAY, 6th JULY, 1956   is requested in order
that the Degree may then be conferred upon you.

Edward V. Appleton
Principal.

Edinburgh,   15th March,   19 56

Robert Inkman
Assistant Secretary to the University.

To   The Reverend William Barclay, M.A., B.D.

Note Should you be unable to attend on the above occasion the Degree may be conferred upon you at one
of the subsequent Ceremonials. According to the Regulations of the University Honorary Degrees are not
conferred in absentia except in very special circumstances.

juxtaposition that must have delighted the ever-practical Willie. The Faculty of Theology at Glasgow also "recorded its congratulations . . . on the intimation of the degree."[14]

In April Willie was again found in England, this time as the guest speaker at the Easter Conference of the Presbyterian Church of England Fellowship of Youth at Limpsfield in Surrey. It was an experience he found particularly exhilarating, and he afterward wrote it up as an "Obiter Visa" piece under the title "The Gift of Laughter."[15] Two weeks later he took part in a week-long teaching mission at Rutherglen, Glasgow, speaking on the Lord's Prayer on behalf of the "Tell Scotland" campaign. This was followed a week later by another refresher course for chaplains in Germany, his first return to that country since 1932. It was in 1956 that Bultmann's *Primitive Christianity in its Contemporary Setting* was published in an English translation, but there is no record of Willie's seeking to reestablish the relationship he had with his former (if but briefly) professor. He crossed the Channel to Germany by BEA, again recording the "thrill" he got from it, though also adding that he undertook the flight with "a certain trepidation." This trip was also made the subject of one of his occasional pieces, not least because he slept in a bed Field Marshal (later Lord) Montgomery himself had occupied.[16]

On June 10 he and Kate took off for their summer holidays after the most gratifying and successful year since leaving Renfrew, well pleased with themselves. They had decided to go on tour of the Highlands together. Barbara was virtually independent, as was Ronnie, who was now working part-time for the recently established Church of Scotland Mobile Bookshop, his own father's books being not the least requested of his stock. *Life and Work* reported in August that Ronnie's initial tour with the mobile library had taken him on almost exactly the same route as his parents were now taking: along the Great North Road to Inverness, Thurso, and Wick, and back via Inverness, the Moray Coast, Angus, and Perthshire, even including a visit to lovely Dunkeld, from which his maternal great-grandfather hailed. For Willie it was an appropriate choice, returning there for the very first time since his youth. We can imagine how full his mind must have been as the scenes of his upbringing and childhood holidays came before him: the breathtaking drive along the A 82 on the shores of Loch Lomond, the gorgeous scenery of the southern Grampians through Ardlui (they by-passed Lochgoilhead, Willie not then knowing of his family's earlier roots at the head of Loch Goil), Crianlarich, Tyndrum, and on to Glen Coe—site of the most infamous slaughter in Scottish history, awe-inspiring in its silence and the might of its towering peaks. And on to Fort William itself, past the former military square standing in front of his maternal grandfather's house and the seat of his mother's upbringing, down the High Street, where his father first worked as a youthful apprentice to the dour Colonel McLeish, and onward to the nigh deserted harbor front. From this they looked across Loch Linnhe to Loch Eil, beyond which was Corpach and that sacred spot where lay the mortal remains of his parents, now united in death as they had been in life. A private man like Willie does not make

public his thoughts of such a pilgrimage, but a man of his temperament, gratitude, and sentimentality was bound to have deep and moving recollections. We
may visualize him figuratively laying on their fine tombstones the proud scarlet
and purple of Edinburgh University, so recently won. "I thank God on every
remembrance of my mother," he wrote in *Testament of Faith*,[17] and this must
have been especially his feeling on this long overdue visit.

Along Loch Eil they passed toward Mallaig. Undoubtedly, Willie took this
beautiful scenic route deliberately, with its twists and turns, rises and falls, past
the tall column to Prince Charlie at Glenfinnan, which must have reminded
them both of the joyous years at "the Cradle of the Stuarts" in Royal Renfrew
Town. They would have known full well that they had to return the same way, for
the quaint fishing port of Mallaig stands on a peninsula. And so back they came,
doubly reminding themselves of so much that is fine in Scottish landscape,
history, and culture, all of it so near to Willie's own heart. Thence along Loch
Lochy and through the Great Glen they went, on to the banks of Loch Ness
(apparently without seeing anything except its calm waters and woody hillsides),
and on to Inverness. From Inverness they traveled through the Black Isle to
Dingwall, and thence through the fine countryside of Ross and Cromarty to that
of Sutherland and Caithness, Willie's original home county, the scene of his
birth and the formative years of his life. Having spent some time at Thurso
(without being tempted to go on to John O'Groats—beginnings more than ends
were Willie's style), they returned southeastward to Wick, his hometown. It was
the first time in forty-five years he had walked its streets, but he remembered it
well! As he told his *British Weekly* readers in an article entitled "The Unobliter-
ated Pictures," he recognized it "immediately and without hesitation": High
Street, the former bank where his father first flexed his managerial muscle, the
nearby riverside walks and park, the harbor—it all came back to him, as if he
were still there in August 1912. And yet so much had changed. . . .

Arriving home (via Aberdeen), he found a letter awaiting him from his
friend by correspondence for nearly twenty years, Rita Snowden, who had written
to inform him that she was dedicating her latest book *I Believe in the Dawn*
(1958) to him. The dedication reads

> To my friend Doctor William Barclay,
> one of the blessed who give without remembering,
> and receive without forgetting.

Commented the manager of a London bookshop to Miss Snowden, warmly
shaking her by the hand (as opposed to shaking her hand), "Any writer who can
set a dedication in the front of a book as you have done in your new book, to our
dear friend William Barclay, can always find a welcome here."[18] Willie, of course,
was delighted with the news—"thrilled" was his own word—adding, "I honestly
think it is the biggest honour that anyone has ever suggested conferring upon
me."[19]

July 6 was the date when the D.D. was actually presented to him, in the presence of His Royal Highness the Duke of Edinburgh and the cream of Auld Reekies' citizenry and the whole University, a prestigious and moving occasion for both Willie and Kate. Here follows the Laureation Address:

Your Royal Highness and Chancellor,
In the name and by the authority of the Senatus Academicus, I have the honour to make the following presentation for the Degree of Doctor of Divinity:

The Reverend WILLIAM BARCLAY, M.A., B.D.,
Lecturer in New Testament, University of Glasgow.

In proposing Mr Barclay's name we are desirous of honouring one who has proved himself a highly skilled lecturer and teacher in our sister University of the West. He has so far spent virtually the whole of his life in the West of Scotland but perhaps, as a result of the link we are today establishing, he will now not be averse to let himself be blown upon by an occasional east wind. He was indeed born in Wick, but it was in Motherwell that he received his early education; and to that burgh his affections would still appear to be attached, for when I asked him some little time ago how he spent his leisure hours, his first reply was, "In watching football matches, and especially in agonising at those in which Motherwell is engaged." Proceeding afterwards to the neighbouring University, he graduated in 1929 with first-class honours in classics.

Having decided to enter the ministry of the Church of Scotland, he then went on to Trinity College, where he was the leading student of his year, won many prizes and was awarded the valuable Maxwell Forsyth Scholarship which enabled him, after completing his Bachelor of Divinity examinations, to spend a year [sic] of post-graduate study in the University of Marburg. For some thirteen years thereafter he carried on a notable ministry in Trinity Church, Renfrew, before being recalled in 1946 to the Faculty of Divinity in his old University, where he now also serves as lecturer in Hellenistic Greek within the Faculty of Arts.

Mr Barclay is, however, well known to a much wider public both as preacher and as expositor. There are not many divines in the Church of Scotland whose pulpit ministrations are so much in demand, and it is doubtful whether anybody else in our generation has been so assiduous in the preparation of manuals for the study of Holy Writ. Year after year he has been responsible for the New Testament section of the Syllabus prepared by the Joint Committee on Religious Education; he has written three hand-books for the Youth Committee of the Church of Scotland; he has published a volume of New Testament Studies for the Scottish Sunday School Union and five Bible Class Handbooks for the Boys' Brigade; he has been entrusted with the authorship of the New Testament volumes in the Daily Study Bible, of which some nine have already appeared; and recently he published also a most useful New Testament Word-Book. It is not surprising that one who has been so busy with his pen should be not only a member of the Institute of Journalists but also the Chairman of the Newspaper and Editorial Workers' Society, and since he has recently been appointed both to the Kerr and to the Croall Lectureships we may look forward to the appearance in due course of two further volumes more substantial than any he has yet given us. I venture to forecast, Your Royal Highness, that when that time comes, the University will rejoice that it had the prescience to add him to its list of Honorary graduates at so comparatively early a stage in his teaching career.

The prescience of Scotland's foremost university was not mistaken, though it remained the only university so to honor William Barclay, a surprising circumstance in the light of his services to ministerial training and the church generally, especially when one considers the normal traditions of universities toward their distinguished sons and alumni. The reference to Willie's chairmanship of the Newspaper and Editorial Workers' Society is unique, and attempts to pursue it have sadly not been fruitful.

Willie was not alone in these honors. The Principal of the now-extinct Yorkshire United Independent College, Hubert Cunliffe-Jones,[20] a former critic of Willie's, was similarly honored, as was Ronald Selby Wright, a great Chaplain to the Forces and himself a distinguished broadcaster and famed minister of the Kirk of Holyroodhouse and Edinburgh Castle. David H. C. Read, a former chaplain to the University and well-known writer and minister of Madison Avenue Presbyterian Church, New York, was also honored.

These were heady days indeed, during which his fame as a teacher and preacher spread by leaps and bounds, not least in Edinburgh itself, which now allowed its kindlier east winds to blow upon him. Thus he was found during July and August preaching every weekend in the capital, preferring to stay over Saturday and Sunday nights, which enabled him to meditate in one of his favorite spots: on the foreshore between Cramond and Granton, binoculars ever in hand, ever the observer of human life, ever turning what he saw into meaningful symbols of the higher life.

In the Storms of Life

The joy of the recent events was to continue into August for Willie and Kate, for news was now received that the Church of Scotland Publications Committee had decided on a second edition of his Daily Bible Readings. For this they put on new and more durable covers, by which decision "the little red commentaries" came formally into existence. They omitted the tipped-in reading schedules (though these continued to be available for domestic purchasers), the sequence of some of the volumes was reorganized, and the volumes that had run out of stock were brought back into circulation. The "great success" of the scheme had been a monthly caption in the advertising in *Life and Work* and other media outlets during the first half of the year; the continuity of the series was now well assured.

Barbara and Billy went off to share a holiday at Billy's parents' home at Moville, County Donegal, Eire. It was a time of great excitement and jollity for them too, for the holiday was to celebrate Mr. Regan's recent retirement, and their first summer in "Glenburnie," their new house. It was the holiday weekend for the locality. In Portstewart, Portrush, and Antrim (on the County Londonderry coast opposite) the annual pageants, dances, and fireworks displays were everywhere publicized; they were to be broadcast for the first time by the BBC. The Ulster Senior Grand Prix was to take place on the Dunrood Circuit, and a huge turnout was expected. A whole week of Carnival was advertised at Ballycastle. Excursions were arranged to cover the area—the chief holiday resorts of Ulster—when the populace would cheerfully respond to "the call of the seaside." One party alone included over six hundred people. Surprise Nights, Carnival Dances, and a floodlit Military Tattoo were also arranged. Ironically, in view of what was to happen, the Coleraine Picture Palace was advertising a film starring Mickey Rooney called *The Twinkle in God's Eye,* to be followed by one featuring Dirk Bogarde and Brigitte Bardot called *Doctor at Sea.* The churches and the Orange Order organized processions and special services; at the latter, "full regalia was to be worn," the advertisements always adding "God Save the Queen" to their ebullient presentations. And John Wesley White, an up-and-coming evangelist from Florida, was scheduled to lead a United Crusade under the sponsorship of the Youth for Christ movement. Of special interest was the presence of Billy Graham's cousin, Homer James, who was to sing solos accompanied by his wife, Iva; George Beverley Shea was also to appear. They were set to be interesting and lively holiday weeks.

Billy and Barbara were as excited as anyone, not least by news of Mr. Regan's purchase of a twelve-foot dinghy of new design, equipped with the latest buoyancy aids. He had been a keen sailor out in India, where he had worked as a teacher for the British Council for many years. Though from Strabane himself, he had retired to the commodious Glenburnie House, Ballybrack, on the edge of the Lough Foyle between Moville and the fishing port of Greencastle in order to indulge his passion for boating. The dinghy had only been collected on Thursday, August 8, following which Mr. Regan and some of his friends sailed it into Ballybrook. The next day the same party sailed eastward to Greencastle, testing its potential and getting used to the three sails: mainsail, reef, and jib. While the Regans senior were thus enjoying their new boat, Billy, Barbara, and Nicholas Wakelin (Nicholas, age twelve, was also staying with the Regans at Ballybrack; his own parents, for many years close friends of the Regans, were still working out at Lahore, Pakistan) enthusiastically entered the Swimming Gala at Portrush. All three of them hoped to do well in the long-distance swimming and lifesaving events at which they were well experienced—and so they did, on Friday, August 9, distinguishing themselves in their respective events and enjoying the publicity caused through their successes in the medal-winning competitions.

Thus excited, Barbara and Billy set off next morning to practice their own sailing skills on the new boat, again accompanied by Nicholas. From his shore-side garden near the loch—an open one, giving onto the north channel of the Irish Sea, some thirty miles from Port Ellen off the Sound of Jura, and less than forty miles off the Mull of Kintyre itself—Mr. Regan and his daughter watched them go, content in the knowledge of Billy's seamanship and the boat's excellent performance to date. It was the last time Billy and Barbara were seen alive.

The first Willie and Kate heard of the tragedy was in one of those telephone calls all parents dread. It came late in the afternoon of Saturday, August 10, just prior to Willie's leaving for Edinburgh, where he was to preach at the Palmerston

Scene of a tragedy. Above: *The spot at Moville from which Barbara and Billy set out.* Below: *The sands of Magilligan Point, where Barbara was eventually found.*

Place Church. As is usual in such missing-persons reports, nothing made sense except that the boat and its passengers were missing and that air and sea rescue operations had been launched. Willie, his diary full of commitments of various sorts, was in a fix. Kate, always fearing such news, suspected the worst and became inconsolable. Ronnie, over a thousand miles away in his small-town French school, was stupefied by the telegram received: "Barbara lost in boating accident. Come home soonest. Dad." He borrowed a friend's cycle and pedaled to the nearest telephone to place an international call, hoping to sort out the curious message that way. Shaken by the news, he returned immediately to Scotland.

As Willie later confessed to Leslie Mitton, then editor of *The Expository Times,* it was "a very distressing time";[21] it was made worse by the incessant telephone calls and messages of goodwill—and the fact that though the boat was soon recovered, there was no sign of the three occupants. Even more confusing, there was no water in the dinghy. Everything was as it should have been; even the cushions and fishing tackle were dry and in their assigned places.

Courageously, Willie preached as scheduled at Palmerston Place from a breaking heart, but with some hope for his daughter's recovery. *The Sunday Post* had informed the public of the tragedy in banner headlines, so Willie had the sympathy of his whole congregation to contend with as well as his own forebodings. He was notified of the recovery of the empty boat while he was still in Edinburgh. On Monday he flew out to Belfast to see if he could do anything to help the rescue efforts—and, such was his self-mastery and altruism, to comfort the Regans in their own sorrows. (The Wakelins were by now on a flight home from Pakistan, on compassionate leave.) The lonely, uneventful return was no less poignant for Willie than the outward journey; they could only watch and wait, quietly fearing the worst. Their fears were intensified by the onset of gale conditions that wreaked havoc in the area, overturning caravans with sixty-five-mile-per-hour winds, blowing a bread van into the sea, toppling trees, and bringing down cables and telephone wires. The Royal Navy vessel *Empire Demon* had to be diverted from the sea search when a Russian tug radioed for assistance; it had to be towed into Moville Bay, since the conditions were such that it was "impossible to bring it into Lough Foyle."[22] During all this it rained incessantly— an incredible six inches of rain in less than twenty-four hours.

Willie was pressed by a double sorrow: not only by the disappearance of his beautiful, gifted daughter, but by Kate's obviously imminent breakdown, a breakdown that was to affect her in every way—physically, mentally, and spiritually. The shock of the disappearance intensified through the suspense (cruelly lasting for three weeks) and deepened into profound grief, and then anger, as is often the way. There was anger over the Regans' and Billy's and Barbara's own willingness to let them sail off like that, anger over the boat's construction and their handling of it, anger over the rescue services' limitations, and, most of all, a pernicious anger at this apparent denial of God's wisdom and love, at his unwillingness to act. "It was a dark time," commented Willie sadly to friend Braidwood, adding, "if I stopped [working] I would never begin again."[23]

Work was his consolation now, as it had been at the time of his mother's suffering and death. To Charles Presho, one-time neighbor of the Barclays and later Executive Director of the Northern Ireland Auxiliary of the British and Foreign Bible Society, Willie confided that his daughter's loss would "either kill me or drive me to work twice as hard."[24] The next twenty-five year's output demonstrates his resolve to continue. As the old version says of Joseph's own heartbreaking experiences, "the iron entered his soul." Willie would never be quite the same man again.

He was stoically determined to keep going; it was what he needed to keep at bay the strain and anguish and offset the endless waiting. Toward the end of August, with the wretched business still unresolved, he was due to appear as Special Speaker at the British Council of Churches' Second National Conference of Christian Young People at Bristol. The organizers thoughtfully suggested he call it off, but he refused, only to find at the last minute that Kate was in no state to be left alone, and so a replacement had to be hurriedly found.[25] One engagement he did not break was the small King's Park Youth Fellowship, despite the organizers' seeking to relieve him of it. "Cyril," he said to the Fellowship's secretary, "if we who call ourselves Christians cannot keep going through times like these, who can?"[26] One anonymous writer of *The Scottish Sunday School Teacher* had noted in 1938 that "It is in adversity that men often show their real greatness." And Willie himself argued, in *Ambassador for Christ,* to select but one aspect of his beliefs regarding personal disaster, "there are basically two types of people: those who are mastered by circumstances, and those who are masters of their circumstances."[27] He was determined not to go under, but that determination could not lessen the sorrow.

His day at the University at this time normally commenced promptly at 8:20 A.M. He went there even in the vacation, as it afforded him the best atmosphere in which to work; his having his own key obviated any inconvenience to the staff. He worked at his desk till 11:00 A.M., when coffee was served. In term time he had lectures that lasted till 1:00 P.M., when he took lunch, returning to his lectures or desk at 2:00 P.M. and staying there till anywhere between 5:00 and 8:00 P.M. After his evening meal and a catnap, more often than not with Sammy his cat and Rusty his dog at his feet, he then worked till 11:00 P.M., when he took supper, often left for him by Kate, who preferred to turn in early. Three or four uninterrupted hours of work would follow, his typewriter clacking away noisily, Willie sitting in the window of their modest front room in full view of anyone who chanced to be out and about, a few feet from the street itself. Thus, by the time he himself turned in, he would have put in a fourteen-hour working day— sometimes more when he was particularly busy! Not infrequently the local night watchman would see him drive off into the city center to catch the first early post to London, to make (or just miss) his deadline.

During this time of particular sadness, he unsparingly burnt the midnight oil, and not a few of those who read this material felt the special anointing that characterized his work: the blessedness of the mourners comforted of God, whose happiness lay not in external, worldly things, but in quiet reliance on God and trust in his unfathomable ways. He drove himself relentlessly, studying, writing, proofreading, and answering a voluminous correspondence. Kate, with little else to do but attend to her small homestead and Willie's undemanding requirements, merely grieved yet more deeply. Willie was to comment ruefully much later that she never did accept her loss.[28] And he, the consummate pastor, knew well the outcome of such holding on, knew well the agony she continued to endure, and knew that this was not the way of peace or wholeness. He tells a moving story in one of his causeries of the little girl who was diagnosed as having an irremediable eye disease. Her minister, the great W. E. Sangster, strangely bade her not to allow the disease to take from her her sight: "Give it to God," he gently exhorted. Willie, too, was learning that painful lesson, learning it at the desk of life, which brooks no favor nor mitigates any hurt.

Their suspense was lifted toward the end of the third week after the disappearances when Nicholas's body was found by Bernard McKinney at Culdaff, twelve miles away on the bleak coast of County Donegal. Never was there a bleaker moment for all the distressed parents involved. It signaled the destruction of their thread-slender hopes; the grimmest of all human realities was obtruding itself on them. An inquest was arranged in which it was found that Nicholas had died of "asphyxia, due to drowning." A death by misadventure verdict was recorded, and his body was quietly laid to rest in Moville cemetery.

Almost a week later, on Friday, August 31, at 3:30 P.M., George Doherty of Aughill came across Billy's body off the Benone beach, which is situated on the north side of Magilligan Point, facing the Atlantic. He recovered it himself from the sea. Four hours later Barbara's body was found by Jane Quigley on the beach half a mile from where Billy's body had been recovered. And what an isolated, melancholy beach it is! Now a bird sanctuary, fenced off on the eastward side for a Ministry of Defence firing range, it faces the Atlantic swell from the furthest tip of a peninsula, populated only by young soldiers, a farmer or two, and a few migratory seabirds. The same sea that so cruelly snatched its victims now returned them close to their starting point, but with life-shattering consequences for the Barclays. The bodies of Barbara and Billy were taken to Roe Valley hospital, near Limavady, Antrim—united again, but in death.

Willie had the horrendous duty of identifying his daughter's body and making arrangements for its transportation to Scotland. This was followed a little later, after the Fatal Accident Enquiry (which recorded the same verdict as that for Nicholas), by the cremation at Woodside, Paisley. Willie escorted Kate to the service, his eyes streaming with tears, desperately holding on to Christian hope, which was now reduced to harshest reality for Willie and near meaninglessness for Kate. She wanted, she needed, her daughter *now*.

Willie's hope in the resurrection, in the afterlife, and the comforts of the gospel were never quashed by this experience; to the contrary, they were strengthened, just as they had been at the time of his mother's and father's deaths. As he said emphatically to Mrs. Rita Perry, his language taking on the image of the literary endeavors with which he found solace from his grief, "This is only the end of one chapter; it is *not* the end of the book."[29] We need to be quite certain about this, for he has often been slandered, sometimes with deliberation, as to his lack of belief in the afterlife. Ronnie Craig received one of the formal letters of gratitude for the condolences expressed (in all, over six hundred were sent out, which number necessitated the use of a printed form). This simply read:

> Reverend William and Mrs Barclay
> thank you most sincerely for your
> kind message of sympathy.

Opposite this desolate message, Willie, having thanked his friend for "your kind and comforting words," typed these words: "There is a comfort in coming to the end of the chapter, although we are very sure it is not the end of the book. . . . It is not easy to pick up threads and go on; but if we who are messengers of the gospel cannot go on, who can?" It will be noticed that his language to both Craig and Mrs. Perry is virtually identical; it is quite normal for those suffering from such personal trauma to have their language stereotyped in this way. Willie's was, but in faith.

The foregoing account of the tragedy has been largely drawn from Willie's own account of it to friends in various letters of this time and later. It has to be added, however, that it does not present quite the same picture as the local newspaper reports and the inquests themselves offer. Willie, of course, would not have had access to these, and would certainly not have been interested in the broader aspects, convulsed as his life then was. Had he known the details, the eventual effect of the tragedy on his theodicy might well have been different.

Even before the accident the signs were already evident to those living in the area that trouble was not far away. *The Coleraine Chronicle* had reported on August 4 that according to the Royal National Lifeboat Institution, "the busiest twenty-four hours in the history of the lifeboat service" occurred at the end of July; it was also the busiest month on record. On the evening of July 28/29 there were no fewer than forty lifeboat launchings, and over the whole month of July there were well over one hundred launchings (seventy-eight was the past highest figure, recorded as long ago as 1952). This increase was partly due to the growing popularity of yachting, but chiefly to the unusually choppy seas and inclement weather. On the very day Billy, Barbara, and Nicholas were lost, the Portrush Yacht Club postponed its Annual Regatta "because of a rough choppy sea."[30]

At the inquest Mr. Regan said his son was "a fairly experienced sailor," but it cannot be doubted that this was an exaggeration of the young man's skills, given the new boat, which even with its mainsail reefed would have tested any man on his first ride. He was emphatic that the boat was checked for seaworthiness and that he had "no worries" about his son following the same course he and his companions had taken the previous day. They had set off at 10:30 A.M. in good weather (though apparently without listening to the forecast), and Mr. Regan "immediately noticed" that the boat was running fast before the wind and tide, an ebb tide, toward the main channel at the neck of the Lough. He noted that the waters were "stormy" there, and became apprehensive. He turned aside to talk to his daughter "for two minutes," and on returning to observe the boat found that it had already gone out of sight. From their position on the shore at this point, that could only have meant that it had overturned or been dismasted.

It is certain that the boat was by this time in the open sea—that is, the Atlantic—though the newspaper reported it as having still been in the open Lough. (Mr. Regan had noted the boat's being opposite McKinney's Light, which is beyond the neck of the Lough on the leeward side, when he talked to his daughter.) The distance between Dunagree Point and Portrush is about eight miles, and the conditions must have presented a terrifying ordeal to the young people, two of whom were inexperienced. Mr. Regan stated that he was now distressed, only too well aware of the dangers, and so he ran to Philip Doherty's nearby cottage. Doherty, an experienced seaman, knew well the dangers this passage offered to untried hands (present-day seamen are emphatic that it is quite safe to knowledgeable sailors), and the two of them drove into nearby Greencastle to alert the Gardai (Eire's police force) and Mr. Polin, the Excise Officer on duty. He immediately telephoned the sea rescue services, while Regan and Polin bought a pair of binoculars and hired a motor launch to do their own bit.

A full-scale operation was soon under way that included the launching of the Portrush lifeboat, the naval tug *Empire Demon* (mentioned earlier), and a helicopter from the British Naval air station at Eglinton. One of the on-shore watchers, Patrick McKinney of Carnagarve, had seen the little brown boat (the color itself made even more difficult the searchers' job) getting into difficulties and had noted its being carried off-shore toward Magilligan Point on a strong southeasterly wind. It was going very fast (which suggests it was carrying far too much sail for the deteriorating conditions), and in no time at all it was on the far side of the deep channel, seaward bound.

The dinghy was soon reported drifting aimlessly by a passing aircraft; it was recovered after six hours by the expert lifeboatmen. Samuel Cunningham, coxswain, reported its being found in an upright condition six miles from Ballybrack on the open sea. There was no sign of the occupants, and so it was towed into Portrush for examination. The helicopter and Inoshowen shore watchers continued their melancholy search, but by nightfall hopes of finding them alive were fading fast, especially as the tide would soon be carrying all before it out into the Atlantic. The following day the search continued, but with considerably less hope and dispatch; the gale, now at its peak, was forcing attentions elsewhere. By the time the reporter began to write his next article on the affair, it was obviously going to be a tale of woe, and the headline "ULSTER'S BLACK SATURDAY" naturally evolved. This included stories of the three yachting deaths, the death of a world motorcycling ace, several fatal accidents, and a great deal of storm damage, not least to the farmers of the area. To these were added, but one week later, another three deaths by drowning off the Donegal coast at Portnoo, from which accident thirteen others were rescued. A few days later yet another man was drowned off Portnoo, and two men were lost in a fishing accident off nearby Roaninish Island two days after that. It was a black summer indeed.

There is no evidence to suggest that Willie made any attempt to walk the beaches of that cruel Atlantic sea that claimed his daughter's life, nor should we expect anything so morbid of him. He would never forget her, he could never forget her, and on more than one occasion he would allude to his consciousness of her presence, much as he did with regard to his own parents.[31] His gaze was ever forward, not backward, even as Sir Walter Scott's resolution was *cha till mi tuilleadh*—"I return [here] no more."[32] He well knew that time would fill the aching void, even if it could not replace the feelings of loss and despair. Kindness and good taste demand that we should draw the veil over the personal aspects of this arch-tragedy, as Dean Inge endeavored to do when in the memorial volume to his own daughter, also snatched prematurely from the domestic circle, he refrained from expressing the intimate, fatherly feelings except in some Latin verse.

The humanity of the experience is well captured in Burns's "Epitaph on the Poet's Daughter":

> Here lies a rose, a budding rose,
> Blasted before its bloom;
> Whose innocence did sweets disclose
> Beyond that flower's perfume.

> To those who for her loss are grieved,
> This consolation's given—
> She's from a world of woe relieved,
> And blooms, a rose in heaven.

Not different were the bard's "Verses Written under Violent Grief," which presents the reality behind the self-mastery:

> You think I'm glad; oh, I pay weel
> For a' the joy I borrow,
> In solitude—then, then I feel
> I canna to mysel' conceal
> My deeply ranklin' sorrow.

Henceforth the bonhomie of William Barclay was to be counterbalanced by a "deeply ranklin' sorrow." It was from this time that the phrase "heart-scalded" became more prominent in his writings—though it was offset by a commensurately greater Christian joy (which is not borrowed, but given) and hope.

We remarked earlier that a double misfortune came Willie's way—both Barbara's death, which he later referred to as "the accidental destruction of the beautiful and the good,"[33] and the traumatic effect the tragedy had on Kate his wife (the pain she felt at her beloved mother's death and more recently at her father's was nothing compared to what she felt in losing Barbara). For the next few months Willie's life was to be storm-clouded by these things, and for the rest of his life he would live in the shadow of that trauma as their thoughts would turn back, relentlessly causing them to wonder "what she would have been like."

If we discreetly lift a corner of the veil on this matter, it is only to understand Kate's—and Willie's—anguish, to see how it affected their lives and his work. It is one of the more distressing of the "warts" that call for comment—but not for intrusion. Three effects on Kate imposed themselves upon him: the mental, the physical, and the spiritual. Her health, never perfect, though better of late (save for the disabling fibrositis), now all but collapsed under the mental strain and anguish. The numbness of shock was soon replaced by anger and then by a whole range of nervous disorders that bordered on a complete breakdown. Basically high-strung to begin with, she responded to the new tensions with symptoms of neurasthenia, various neuralgias, eczema, and a persistent insomnia. A little after this a series of accidents began (the first was getting her hand caught in a train door in the early autumn) that were almost certainly psychological in origin, perhaps a form of self-punishment or a cry for help.[34] Her deep sympathies for and intuitions concerning other people, which had made her such an excellent minister's wife and surrogate mother of countless students, provoked in her the most painful vision of her daughter's death. In that death Kate lost her dearest companion.

Willie was all sympathy and concern, but he himself was disconsolate save in his ability to blot out the pain by increased work—and the absences entailed by such extra work only served to intensify Kate's self-preoccupation and loneliness. There was a two-way barrier between them now: Willie was unable to stem the tides of grief that were overwhelming his wife, and his natural withdrawal from such exposure thrust him into increased work. But he himself needed someone to talk to, and he especially needed the more receptive company of a strong woman for his own sorrow. As he stated on the telephone to Marie Campbell, who had looked after Barbara in her childhood and knew how close to her mother she had been, "I would have given my right arm to talk to you of it."[35] Sinclair Armstrong (the second of the three people Willie telephoned to break the news of Barbara's body being found) came round to visit them immediately, and preserves a telling picture of their distress: Willie was working in his study at his typewriter, his face wet with grief; Kate simply fell into Mr. Armstrong's arms, devoid of strength, reason, and hope.[36] As Mrs. Livingstone, Kate's sister recalled, she could only exclaim "My wee Barbara!" and murmur, characteristically, "I don't know how Barbara will get on in heaven without me."[37] She could not let go. All the signs were that Kate had given up the will to live. It was a throwback to her childhood days, at which time when she was taken ill she would turn her back on everyone and face the wall.

But the change in her religious life was the most marked, even though it did not change much outwardly. She still attended church (at Clarkston; Willie continued to go to Williamwood), but she confessed on more than one occasion to Mrs. Livingstone that she had lost her faith by the tragedy. She could not understand or believe in a god who let such things happen. The "stern voice of duty" was obeyed, but the inner realities of religion no longer possessed validity or meaning for her. She was utterly alone, and in that loneliness she was estranged still further from the living heart of Willie's own faith and life. The rejection was part of her refusal to accept her daughter's death, a bitter and embittering reaction that prohibited any possibility of God's love or consolation, a defiance of reality and an espousal of resentment. Pictures and photographs of Barbara now proliferated throughout the house, by which Kate sought her own consolation. These were later to disappear when Willie forbade all talk of Barbara. In response to the ban, Kate became cynical about people, about Willie's work, and at times about Willie himself; it was no longer a happy home for them. The effects of this tragic accident remained as a backdrop to his work for the rest of his life.

It was mentioned that Rita Snowden dedicated her book *I Believe in the Dawn* to Willie. In this series of daily meditations, there is one titled "They That Mourn." It was written specifically in response to Willie's losing Barbara and shows how positive his response was to their loss:

> For some days there has lain on my desk a thin blue air-letter from the friend to whom this book is dedicated. I haven't known how to answer it; not only because words are poor things, but because my heart has been numbed with sorrow by the tidings that slim letter brings. The Doctor writes of his family—"a boy of twenty-two who is reading for honours in modern languages, and who has been in the last two years, one year in France and one year in Germany," and of his daughter Barbara. "But our daughter Barbara, nineteen years old," he says, "was drowned in a yachting accident in Moville, in Eire, on 11th August. We do not know what happened and we will never know. Barbara always went with her friend Billy Regan to Moville to his home for the holidays. They lived in and on the water. The yacht was unsinkable; they swam like fishes; they knew all about boats; the yacht was found undamaged with even the cushions on the bottom of it. We think that the boat must have swung and that probably Barbara was knocked overboard, and that Billy lost his life trying to rescue her. We had the suspense of having to wait for three weeks until last Friday when Barbara's body was found. On Tuesday we had her funeral service. The service was a great relief. It marked the end of the chapter, but not as we who are Christian believe, the end of the book.
>
> "There remains nothing now but to go on. When all this happened I was occupying the pulpit of Palmerston Place in Edinburgh. I went back to the pulpit the next Sunday. I felt I had to. . . . If we who are the messengers of the glory of the Gospel cannot go on, who can go on? And the strange thing is that I never felt Barbara nearer. As I pile away at these beloved Greek words of mine I still feel that she is interested. And I will always thank God for a poem your book gave me—'Shall I wear mourning for my soldier dead?'

509

Shall I wear mourning for my soldier dead,
I—a believer? Give me red,
Or give me royal purple for the King
At whose high court my love is visiting
Dress me in green for growth, for life made new,
For skies his dear feet march, dress me in blue,
In white for his white soul; robe me in gold
For all the pride that his new rank shall hold.
In earth's dim gardens blooms no hue too bright
To dress me for my love who walks in light!"[38]

It was a triumphant song of faith!

The changes that Barbara's death brought had an influence that extended well beyond the Barclay household. Willie was now expositor of the Bible to tens of thousands, with a worldwide constituency to serve, and it is crucial to see that this responsibility weighed heavy on him. Since early childhood he had been mindful of the Priscilla Owen hymn that became the anthem of the Boys' Brigade, which asks in part,

Will your anchor hold in the storms of life,
When the clouds unfold their wings of strife?
When the strong tides lift, and the cables strain
Will your anchor drift, or firm remain?

Not long after their ordeal, the first volume of the Daily Bible Readings commentary on Matthew being safely consigned to the publishers, Willie found himself face to face with the passage dealing with the storm on the lake (Matt. 8:23–27). His exposition of these few verses—a sign of the importance he attached to the incident, perhaps bearing in mind Gossip's advice concerning the ubiquitous nature of sorrow—was extended over two days of meditations. In none of his comments does he obtrude a reference to the violence of wind and weather and waves that claimed his daughter; perhaps the memory of that "Black Saturday" was too painful for him, or perhaps he ignored its significance in his grief. He was brought face to face with the grim encounter of natural force versus human fragility. "In less than half an hour the placid sunshine had become a raging storm," he stated.[39] We should note, in refutation of those who say he denies the miraculous, that he specifically states that "in their moment of terror the disciples awoke him, *and the storm became a calm.*" As was his wont, he acknowledges the miracle, but swiftly—perhaps too swiftly—moves on to the present-day meaning behind the past event. Listen to his introduction to the second day's exposition:

In this story there is something very much more than the calming of a storm at sea. Suppose that Jesus did in actual physical fact still a raging storm on the sea of Gallilee . . . that would in truth be a very wonderful thing; but it would have very little to do with us. . . . If that is all the story means, we may well ask, "Why does he not do it *now*? Why does he allow those who love him nowadays to be drowned in the raging sea without intervening to save them?" *If we take the story simply as the stilling of a weather storm, it actually produces problems which for some of us break the heart.*[40]

The "suppose" here is rhetorical—from a man deeply and responsively trained in the schools of rhetoric of ancient Greece. Rhetoric is the art of using language to persuade other people; it is a technique, the goal of which is not merely to produce elegance and style, but—chiefly—forceful communication. And that is exactly what Willie is doing here, as he had done hundreds of times up and down the length and breadth of the land. He is not in fact writing strictly as an expositor, but as an advocate. In the old language, he is "preaching for a decision." And we must never forget that his central commitment was to make "intelligible" the good news of Jesus Christ, as one "haunted by the people outside the church."[41]

He has already dealt, somewhat peremptorily, with the physical (i.e., historical) aspect: "In less than half an hour the placid sunshine had become a raging storm. . . . The waves were so high that the boat was hidden. . . . The disciples awoke [Jesus], and the storm became a calm." In dealing with the parallel passage in Mark two years earlier, we find greater emphasis on the physical and the historical, greater description of the details—of lake and weather and Jesus' position in the boat; we find Willie emphasizing the command to the weather itself (in doing so he draws a significant parallel to his words to the demoniac), but the same awareness of the greater importance of its relevance is also present:

> We do this story far less than justice if we *merely* take it in a literalistic sense. If this describes *simply* a physical miracle in which an actual storm was stilled, it is a very wonderful story . . . but nonetheless it is something which happened once and which cannot happen again. *In that case it is quite external to us. But if we read it in a symbolic sense it is far more valuable.*[42]

He does not deny the actuality of the miracle. He does suggest that we would not take it "merely" in its physical sense alone. Preachers have always given this warning: Willie does so likewise, though with greater emphasis, increasing the thrust of the suggestion in order to illuminate its significance for the present as well as the past. "The meaning of this story is not that Jesus stopped a storm in Galilee; the meaning is that *wherever Jesus is the storms of life became a calm.* It means that in the presence of Jesus the most terrible tempest turns to peace."[43] Note the threefold emphasis on "meaning"; the emphasis is not on the original circumstance, but on the present-day reality. It is a great pity that James Martin, in revising the text, has lessened the force of his statement by removing (for stylistic purposes) two key phrases of emphasis, here italicized: "the lesson of this story, *the meaning of this story, the fact of this story,* is that when the storms of life shake our souls Jesus Christ is there; and in his presence the raging of the storm turns to the peace that no storm can ever take away."[44] We do the cause of truth no good, and still less do we aid the cause of love, by refusing to own the meaning that Willie puts on the passage, even if we wish his emphasis had not *appeared* to undermine the historical and factual element (as some have wrongly claimed it does).

And what are "the storms of life" to which he alludes, emphasizing that they can be overcome by Jesus' power, today? They are three in number: "the cold, bleak wind of sorrow," "the hot blast of passion," and "the storms of doubt"—in short, the afflictions of heart, body, and mind, all of which can be conquered by Jesus Christ. What Willie is claiming—out of fierce, unsmiling personal disaster— is total victory for those who company with Christ. Willie's anchor held, held right fast, and through it thousands have benefited and been comforted. As he later affirmed in his testament of faith, "if anything is true of [Jesus], it is that he is the Great Contemporary."[45]

I deal with his broadcasting in a later section, but we should mention one very unpleasant experience that came to him shortly after penning these words. He had been asked to appear on the early morning program *Lift Up Your Hearts*. On the final day, instead of talking, Willie allowed himself to be interviewed by David Winter, and thus his personal tragedy was given great publicity, as was the sustaining help of Jesus Christ which brought him through the ordeal. Following the completion of the broadcasts, over six hundred people wrote to him in appreciation of his talks, to whom he tirelessly replied individually. But one letter was of a very different sort, written out of malice and foul intent. Sadly, it came from Northern Ireland and bears all the hallmarks of that paganism that speaks before it thinks, whose intent is to injure and not heal. The astonishing thing about this letter is that Willie allowed its message of hate to get to him. Indeed, he carried it around in his pocket for a long time; it was as if he felt the need to don some kind of hair shirt. Kate discovered it still among his papers after his death. This is what it said:

> Dear Dr. Barclay,
>   I know now why God killed your daughter; it was to save her from being corrupted by your heresies. . . .[46]

We ignore the fact that hate corrupts far more than alleged heresies, and merely note Willie's wounded reply: "The day my daughter was lost at sea there was sorrow in the heart of God."[47] He was himself unmovable because he was

> Fastened to the Rock which cannot move,
> Grounded firm and deep in the Saviour's love.

If the tragedy confirmed his faith, made his hold on the hope of eternal life yet more resolute, and helped to clarify for him the *relevance* of his faith, as opposed to its "mere" facticity, it had other, more disturbing effects as well. It raised questions as to the human situation itself; it led him to ask deep questions about God's management of the world and about human life, questions that already tormented his wife almost to the point of derangement at times, questions that offered no easy solutions and that were especially grievous in light of their many years of hard work in God's cause, dark things that took Kate sadly along the road of skepticism and, at times, of despair itself.

We must remember that while Willie's world view was essentially theistic—he believed in a God personally involved in the affairs of men, and responsive to them—he was also aware of the vastness of the universe, of the microscopic size of man compared with the "worlds beyond worlds" outside. Man, for all his self-assumed importance, was but an infinitesimal speck of dust when compared to all this. Willie's theism never altered, but at times it was shadowed by a deistic strain, not least in a shift of emphasis on prayer, as we shall see. This shift became more marked through this calamitous experience, as did his emphasis on human responsibility and choice—and not only of human choice, for although he had no scientific training of any sort, Willie went on to propose—*against* evolutionary theories of chance development and mutation—his own theory of development, which rested on (divine) invitation and (human) response.[48] This, he stated, had been "an idea . . . in my mind" since his earliest encounter with evolutionary theories. There always was an element in him of stoical endurance to life's misfortunes: he saw the uselessness of combating the *impossible* (not to be mistaken for the *difficult* or *barely possible*). As early as 1933 we found him recommending his readers "to take life as you find it," to accept the inevitable, to enlarge their vision by a "sense of the possibility of impossibilities." Acceptance is the key, even when the outlook is dark and the purpose lost in apparent senselessness; all will be made plain one day. It is the human side of trust in God. The object of that trust was never in doubt.

Clearly the effects of Barbara's death extended beyond just Kate's experience of personal bereavement, poor health, and dispeace and Willie's changed perspective on God's providential ruling; it may well have changed their lives in terms of the direction it was now to take. We have already seen that Willie once wrote to Miss Snowden saying he was not sure what he was going to do after the Daily Bible Readings scheme was completed, but if there were any doubts as to the direction of his work when he commenced the series, there were none by the time the end was in sight. Even his one "unintelligible" essay in Christology had been shelved (though some of it would reappear, in vastly changed form, in his *British Weekly* articles, which found permanent expression in his trilogy on Jesus—*The Mind of Jesus* [1960], *Crucified and Crowned* [1961], and *Jesus as They Saw Him* [1962]). But the path away from strict scholarship was now well marked; he could not say no to that. His stock in Ireland had risen high, through his *Scottish Sunday School Teacher* lessons and articles, through his more recent Daily Bible Readings books, and not least through news of his personal loss and sorrow. He now came under pressure from Belfast to offer for the vacant Chair of New Testament at Queen's College, a position that earlier would have sorely tempted him. It necessitated no great distance in moving from his beloved west of Scotland (unlike the offers from Duke University and elsewhere), and was recommended by the fact that his son Ronnie was engaged to be married to a young lady from Coleraine. It was clear that Garth Macgregor would not be vacating his own Chair for many years, and Willie was over fifty years of age. Had the accident not occurred, Billy and Barbara might well have decided to settle themselves in Northern Ireland, or even Eire. But it was too painful a decision, and so the post was declined, as was every invitation—save one—to return to preach in that beautiful yet troubled land.

This one exception involved a minister's fraternal conference at Portrush. Willie agreed to give seven lectures on the Beatitudes. Robert Cobain, former secretary of the conferences, recalls Willie's voice ringing out about the blessedness of the poor in spirit, the mourners, the meek, those who hunger and thirst after righteousness, the merciful, the pure in heart, the peacemakers, and the persecuted. As he did so he was able to look out through the windows of the hotel, across Lough Foyle toward Moville, aware that in the waters off Magilligan Point Barbara and Billy lost their lives, and Kate and Willie their dreams.

The pressures under which he was lecturing showed even in the drawing room of the conference, which Willie took over between sessions in order to mark the huge pile of B.D. papers he had brought with him. The maid on one occasion took him a cup of tea, but was confused to have no response to her knocking at the door. She opened it and instead of finding him hard at it, found him recumbent, mouth open, fast asleep. "I'm sure," his friend Craig commented, "that all candidates passed"! Perhaps not. He had the ability to catnap and then return to his work with total recall of the work he had been reading. As some of the marked papers of his students show, he let pass little that was second-rate, misinformed, or irrelevant. Out of this Irish visit arose his six leaflets on "The Christian Way," which were produced for the youth of the Irish Church and still circulate today.[49]

Toward the Dawn, Anchor Holding

It is hard to resist the assumption that a new phase of Willie's life commenced in the mid '50s. He had by now completed his work on the Church of Scotland handbooks and had almost finished his long stint as author of the Boys' Brigade training books. The last reprint of his earlier *Scottish Sunday School Teacher Lesson Notes* had been circulated, and the International Bible Reading Association had reprinted its final piece of daily meditation from his pen. (In December 1956 the Executive of the Scottish Sunday School Union decided not to reprint *New Testament Studies;* other books were now appearing that eclipsed such temporary writing.) His Daily Bible Readings notes were nearing completion, and by August 1956—that fateful month in the Barclays' lives—he had acquired his first major advertisement on the cover of *Life and Work,* announcing the availability of both paperback and hardcover editions of the Daily Bible Readings, now retitled as the Daily Study Bible.[50] *Life and Work* reported that the astonishing success of the Daily Bible Readings project had prompted a worldwide scheme by the IBRA to stimulate scripture reading and study among missionaries and young churches.[51] *Light for Our Faith* accordingly appeared; its success was directly the result of Willie's own work, to which it was partly linked. At home his theological weight had been considerably increased by his service as one of the official commentators of the Draft Catechism (which Dryburgh and the Committee on Youth described as "a teaching instrument for instruction in the main doctrines of the Christian faith . . . to create an *intelligible* grasp of the main tenets of the Faith").[52] And of course his page in *The British Weekly* was widely hailed and appreciated for both its devotion and learning.

Largely through his work for *The British Weekly* and the appointment of London representatives for the marketing of the Daily Study Bible (C. Vernon & Sons, Ltd.), the center of his publishing was shifting from Scotland to London. He was now being published by Collins and SCM (Student Christian Movement) Press, and he was also regularly attending the Scottish Advisory Group of the Lutterworth Press of London. "William Barclay, D.D." was now a force on the religion scene, without the flamboyance of Billy Graham (or the string of would-be Grahams who followed their charismatic evangelist-leader) perhaps, but with a depth that many found irresistible. While some were giving themselves to the various "new wave" theologies, he kept industriously to his expositions, content to make plain the more basic points of biblical realism.

It was at this time that Nels Ferré gave a short series of lectures at Trinity College in criticism of the theology of Paul Tillich, one of the leading influences of the time. Moreover, and much more importantly for Willie, Ronald Gregor Smith came to the University as the new Professor of Divinity; he was to become, alongside Ian Henderson and others, a powerful influence on Willie's thinking.

On the wider front there was still much concern over the cold war situation (a visit to the West by Khrushchev and Bulganin merely exacerbated tensions), and the situation in the Middle East. The Suez Crisis erupted on the world in July 1956 (British troops had been withdrawn in June), when President Nasser of Egypt seized and nationalized the Canal. Prime Minister Eden, with the scalding memories of the Munich Agreement of 1939 still fresh in his mind, was staunchly against appeasement. Behind Nasser's bold step lay a dream of the leadership of a pan-Arabic movement aided by Soviet finance and arms, with the destruction of the state of Israel as a principal aim. Negotiations broke down, a British-French ultimatum was rejected, and on October 31 the troops went in. The military action flew in the face of American policy and thus "the Anglo-American Schism" commenced. Even Churchill's brief emergence from retirement did nothing to repair the situation (rather the opposite, as he backed the British-French-Israeli initiative). The cold winds now blew on Britain from both sides, unnerving many.

American influence was affecting Great Britain at a different level as well. In the wake of America's nuclear program there arose new concern about adequacy of education in the sciences (worse fears yet were soon to be sparked by the launch of the Russian Sputnik satellite). This new emphasis on the sciences sparked anew a fundamentalist reaction to the teaching of biological evolution, much as happened in the infamous Scopes trial of the 1920s. Evolution remained linked in the minds of many to a denial of God's creative sovereignty, which in turn was linked adversely to biblical criticism. The rift between conservatives and liberals deepened. In November 1956 it grew deeper still when *Christianity Today* was introduced; the liberal faction was as outraged by the positive marketing techniques the publishers of the periodical employed as by the "easy believism" they felt the magazine propagated. Concern over public morals increased as gambling reached an all-time high and in literature *Lady Chatterley's Lover* fomented strife. John Braine had yet to make his mark, but the complaints of Britain's "angry young men" against society were already being heard. On the cinema screens Hollywood extravagances featured voluptuous icons of the Marilyn Monroe/Brigitte Bardot variety. The number of weddings—and divorces—shot up. Professor McKenzie, one of the leading Christian writers on ethics of his day, produced the significant document *The Sexual, Marital and Family Relations of the English Woman,* as provocative of discussion in secular circles as the issue of the position of women in the church was in ecclesiastical circles. The greatest social catalyst of the century was thus already making its mark. Other changes were also occurring, not least in church life. Men in "advanced" years were now completing their late vocational training, and Willie, having himself trained some of them, now had the joy of preaching them in. He wrote of one such event in his "Obiter Visa" column, describing it as "an amazing experience."[53]

At this time John Baillie retired from New College, "full of years and honour"; the following year (1957) found him at the center of a controversy that rocked his church, when the so-called "Bishops' Report"—recommending the principle of "bishops-in-presbytery" as a step toward reunion—was published. South of the border it scarcely caused a ripple, but in the homeland of Knox and Melville mighty waves foamed and dashed in all directions. (The English grossly misunderstand Scottish antipathy to the idea of bishops, which stems from the political undertones the office carries. When the new church hymnal was published a decade later, the committee could not even then bring themselves to accord the title to such men as William Walsham How or Reginald Heber.) Andrew Herron regarded it as the most public furor of his lifetime, despite a recent World War, the pacifist debates, the nuclear threat, the breakdown of sexual mores and family relationships, and the unprecedented political and economic turmoil![54] Within a year the issue was dead, condemned as an unrealistic *faux pas* in the cause of church reunion.

The most conspicuous event of this autumn term of Trinity College was the centenary celebration which took place on October 3. The principal figures in this were naturally the Principal himself, John Mauchline, and the longest serving professor, Willie's chief, G. H. C. Macgregor, although Willie had a notable part to play as the conductor of the College Choir. Doubtless he found the civic reception and the commemoration dinner (sitting adjacent to the top table, next to Professor A. B. Miller and opposite John Macquarrie) a welcome relief from external and internal pressures. James Little recalls some of the choir concerts at this time as being not altogether restrained emotionally. He writes of Willie, "the tears . . . pouring down his face, and the choir's too for most of it."[55] *The British Weekly* also found good cause to celebrate, for its seventy-fifth anniversary took place in November. Willie was again given a foremost place, his page for preachers and teachers being in the view of many one of the best developments for years.

But there was hard work alongside such things, beyond even that of his writing and day-to-day learning. In this academic year he delivered the Kerr Lectures at Glasgow and the Croall Lectures at New College; it was the first time in their histories that they had been delivered by the same person in the same year. The former was published in 1959 as *Educational Ideals in the Ancient World,* a stiff and somewhat restricted study that garnered a rather disappointing response from both the public and the reviewers.[56] Nevertheless, its importance cannot lightly be dismissed. Willie envisaged it as serving a double purpose: (1) the first chapters provided exposition of educational ideals among the Jews, the Spartans, the Athenians, and the Romans (nearly two hundred pages of solid detail underpinned by no fewer than 631 footnotes and several appendices); and (2) it provided a sort of "threshold apologetic" for New Testament understanding and belief. Commented the author, "Before we can understand the reaction of the Jewish and Graeco-Roman world to that which Christianity brought to it, we must first understand what it brought to Christianity."[57]

Willie's view, however, as befitting a very serious thinker on the whole question of Christian education in the modern world, could not rest there, and so two further chapters are offered: "The Christian Attitudes to Pagan Culture" (pages 192–233, an important exposition of Willie's own world view as well as that of the Early Church) and "The Child in the Early Church" (pages 234–62, in which the experience and the problems of the previous twenty years of work are gathered together). The same painstaking attention to historical detail is reflected in these last two chapters, which offer nearly 230 citations covering a wide range of ecclesiastical writings and sources in both Greek and Latin, one of which corrects Adolf Harnack no less.[58] It is a tour de force of linguistic accomplishment, broad-based learning, and mature reflection, withal lightly and interestingly offered and practical. It is moving to see that this book is dedicated simply to "KBB" without comment, as if to emphasize that he had little to *say* to this the scarred love of his life, but much to offer: his love and gratitude and—would she accept it?—his work, which cost so much.

We have seen how often work well done led to yet more work and opportunity for Willie. From the occasional work he had been doing as Alternate to the General Secretary of the National Bible Society of Scotland, he now moved on to that of a fully delegated member ("Visitor") on one of the translation panels of the British and Foreign Bible Society. His first attendance at one of their meetings took place at Queen's College in Oxford (soon to become a sort of second preferred home to him) from the 20th to the 22nd of December 1956. The particular work he shared there could not have been more congenial, his place

517

being on the Greek-English New Testament Committee. The Committee was divided into two groups, group "A" being the translators (comprising G. D. and W. D. Reynolds, both of them staff members of the British and Foreign Bible Society), and group "B" being the revisers (comprising G. D. Kilpatrick, W. D. McHardy, Nigel Turner, and Willie). They were dealing with stage three of Matthew 12 and 13, and it was not long before the newcomer made his presence felt. (At Matt. 13:38, for example, he interjected his preference for "pots," rather than the already accepted "baskets," pointing out that fish were often kept alive during transportation to prolong freshness.) Thus it was that his expertise in background information conjoined with the linguistic skills they all possessed.

He was a popular member of this committee, though it was soon noticed that he was possessed of a certain restlessness concerning matters of organization and administration, and would often miss such meetings. Colleagues at those meetings he did attend would notice the sudden quiet as he simply switched off his hearing aid! This inevitably caused some concern to the Committee, which expected Willie to act in a liaison capacity between them and their northern colleagues. The problem was solved when a second delegate was found to take up the purely liaison work; thus it was that Neil Alexander joined Willie in the work. But in the "real work" of the committee, the business of translation, he was indefatigable, if somewhat distracting: his hearing aid would whistle and screech obtrusively, only partially helping him to follow the discussions; often enough he had to interrupt to ask for repetition. Ronnie Falconer preserves an amusing anecdote of this sort of thing, though from a different occasion. One of the ecclesiastical dignitaries was asked to say grace at a meal, which invitation was misheard by Willie, who obligingly jumped up and officiated before the said dignitary could move. Commented one of the quick-witted ministers nearby, "The hands are Esau's hands, but the voice is that of Jacob"!

Gwen Anderson and Kathleen Cann of the British and Foreign Bible Society also recall the quiet of the panel being interrupted by his somewhat noisy movements—of papers, books, chair, and feet—added to which would be his not always timely, and sometimes brusque, interjections into the discussions. "No, no, no! Haven't you considered. . . ?" he would ask, leaning sideways in his seat and wagging his finger in genteel menace, and off on another tack the members would go, in fast pursuit of the idea he had launched. His fidgeting was often in inverse proportion to his share in the argument. For all of that, however, he was a most respected member of their panels, never showing any sign of deep irritation over others' views and special pleading, and adding distinction to both the academic standards and their social life. To peruse the study notes that circulated after the translators' meetings is to be made aware that once again Willie was prepared to be the workhorse behind the scene.

Need for these Notes often arose out of disputes as to the meanings of words or clauses, and so extra notes were called for. Willie was ready to do his share—and more than his share—in this area. For example, the panel met in April 1957 at Trinity College, Glasgow, to discuss the third (penultimate) draft of

John 1:19–5:35. Discussion centered on the notoriously difficult problem of direct versus indirect speech in John—how to determine which were the *ipsissima verba* of Jesus and which were John's reflections on them. A note was required on this, and Willie was found willing to write it. Again, at John 4:5 Willie called attention to their translation of *polis* (the RSV interprets it as "city," which the translators favored); he was doubtful about this and asked what criteria were being used. Was size the only criterion? Some discussion followed, further information was felt necessary, and Willie increased his homework. (In his own translation of 1963 he used "town" rather than city, as he had done in his Daily Bible Readings commentary.) Likewise at John 4:9 the word *sunchrōntai* divided the panel: should it be translated "associate together" or "share vessels"? Willie promised yet another Note.

Many such examples of this work could be extracted from the minutes; sometimes the conversations centered on minute particles of speech, or even punctuation marks. It was crucial, foot-washing work, and Willie was careful to give his best and longest hours to it. He was never contentious over the final decision, though such "finality" must ever be temporary, according to our present knowledge, and often owning a disparity of viewpoint in a footnote or glossary.

One of Willie's quirks was his insistence that he stay by himself in the hotels of his own choice, usually high grade. It was something he inherited from his parents' Edwardian life-style. He would not tolerate second-rate standards in service or cleanliness, nor was he willing to lose his privacy—even if it were a matter of only four or five hours amid his overfull schedules and commitments. Despite his unconcern as to his clothing (which must not be overemphasized), he was never a slummer, and abominated slovenly attitudes. He could be devastating in his disapproval of ministers who did not dress properly for their work, even in their own studies, especially those daring to work in carpet slippers. And he was particular in his choice of restaurants or hotels for his family, favoring three-star (or better) standards. In a way, this love of fine dining helped to strengthen a friendship he struck up with Professor McHardy, which continued strong until Willie's death, for it was at its best over the dining table, when they would explore the delights of haute cuisine together. (One of their favorite haunts was the prestigious Randolph Hotel in the center of Oxford; another was the Carlton Hotel, Edinburgh.) They looked on themselves as the gourmets of the translation groups, though Willie's acumen for the fruit of the vine was never profound or extensive. He did develop a palate for good claret, but in the main he and his fellow Scot held loyal to the national tipple. It was not long before they became well-known to the manager, staff, and the local customers. On one occasion, McHardy asked Willie if he would like a glass of wine. "A *glass* of wine?" Willie asked, his voice conveying the deep feeling of drought that only ecclesiastical talk can produce. "Well, a bottle, then," his friend suggested. "Now you're talking," he said, passing on the order to the waitress. "And two straws, Sir?" she quipped, entering into the spirit of the exchange.[59] His only remuneration from the years of work on the panels was his expenses, but these were later restricted by the administrative heads of the British and Foreign Bible Society.

Professor McHardy recalls another amusing incident that took place at the Randolph, which was caused by Willie's habit of walking up and down his room when working through a problem (a habit not unknown to those who heard—and watched—him lecture). He was doing so very late one night, causing a loose board to creak, which produced an objection by one of the weary guests of the hotel. On hearing of the objection, Willie apologized and obligingly removed his hearing aid to still the noise, thence continuing his peripatetic activities unaware of the continuing problem, having made himself unapproachable to the staff!

We should not limit his contribution to the society's work to the assignments formally offered by the panels. He and McHardy regularly helped the Society in a wide variety of ways, and were careful to make themselves available for general advice and expert comment. The work of the Bible Society was an ongoing task, not only in producing a Greek text that took full cognizance of the rapidly developing scholarship of the postwar era (mainly linguistic, but also taking into account historical, topographical, archaeological, and many other factors), but also in offering aid to missionaries and indigenous workers in their own training, translating, and revising work. It is a great pity that no record of this occasional work has been kept; appeals for help and advice were simply posted on to Willie, who replied directly to the inquirer. We shall never know the real extent of these priceless labors of love, unsung and forgotten (as the central participant wished them to be), but they were not few. There were some who criticized him for extravagance over his meals, but these were never so extravagant as his expenditure of time, talent, and energy, which took place often late in the night as he grappled with the baffling problems of translating the Greek of the New Testament into this or that language or culture, always via a restricting English medium. And we should bear in mind that this not infrequently involved him in sensitizing himself to the language or culture from which the appeal emanated. He would never rest content merely to repeat material given to his students; he always bore its wider interpretation and application in mind.

Wilfred Bradnock, for many years Translations Secretary of the British and Foreign Bible Society, speaks of Willie's high reputation in missionary circles and among various national Christian leaders. Willie once drove him through Renfrew on their way to a meeting. They were talking of making the gospel comprehensible to the common man of whatever culture, and Willie said of his "cloth-capped congregation" that "it was there that I learned what the gospel was about."[60] Interestingly enough (and by this we have seen how he fed his imagination and tested his approach), he admitted that the Bible societies were well ahead of him in seeking to make the Bible and gospel *intelligible*. And he admitted being spurred on in his own pursuits to this end by the British and Foreign Bible Society textual Notes. From such experience came his understanding of theology as being essentially grammar. The aim of the translation panels was to root out "biblical English" (we may compare this with S. H. Hooke's "Basic English"),[61] which had a very definite effect on Willie's style by its insistence on an easy vocabulary, short sentences, avoidance of the passive voice, and a sturdy attempt to produce a clear sequence of ideas that "hinged" well with each other throughout the paragraph. Dr. Bradnock also noted (almost uniquely among Willie's former colleagues) "a keen nationalism" in Willie's comments that sympathized with that of overseas Christians in their own aspirations. (It has to be said that this "keen nationalism" never obtruded itself into his books; at most he occasionally cited some Scots words and usage to make certain linguistic points.)

Willie went on to make significant contributions in two other key areas that had beneficial results for biblical specialists and the general public respectively. The first followed his acceptance of a direct invitation from the British and Foreign Bible Society to help in the revision of The Translators' New Testament (T.T.N.T.), which was to serve as a basic tool for a worldwide constituency. The second commenced when he was invited by Professor William McHardy, Convenor of the Apocrypha Panel of the New English Bible, to join him and his panel members in their work, which by then had virtually ground to a halt. What attracted them to Willie was his well-known expertise in Hellenistic Greek, for while Willie was still not of professorial rank, he was nevertheless Head of Department in this subject at Glasgow University.

Willie brought new life and enthusiasm to the revisionary work, and the panel's superb results will continue to serve the cause for many years to come. But it was observed that he had some notable blind spots, not least on the Hebraic side, wherein important work was going ahead in the full glare of the media, thanks to the sensational finds at Khirbet Qumran. More basically, he had not kept up even the preparatory work of his Trinity College days, still less advanced it by study or research. Given his style of approach, essentially grammatico-linguistic and centering on a certain verbal dexterity, he was bound to be at a disadvantage concerning recent developments, notably the Dead Sea Scroll research. In fact he made virtually no use of it.[62] At one point he startled his colleagues by asserting a first-person plural understanding at Genesis 1:26— "us" (which favors an anachronistic doctrine of the trinity unacceptable to modern-day theologians)—as opposed to the more likely interpretation of the expression as a "plural of majesty."

He traveled light to those meetings, which is to say that he used a small hand-case for his personal effects though his boot could be full of textbooks, set-work, examination papers waiting to be marked, and proofs awaiting correction. He never went without his typewriter and a good supply of carbonized paper. For letterheads he frequently made use of the notepaper supplied by the hotel. Thus collectors of Barclayana have a most interesting array of color, type, and size in his correspondence, itself a helpful guide to his movements and life-style. Readers of The British Weekly articles will recall him mentioning doing his own washing when on tour, favoring drip-dry shirts from the first moment of their introduction, and proud of his newfound self-sufficiency! A certain absentmindedness about such things characterized his manner, and so a trail of forgotten shirts, gloves, umbrellas, and even his beloved binoculars marked his

The New English Bible Apocrypha Translation Panel. Professors C. H. Dodd and William McHardy sit second and third from the left, respectively.

progress throughout the land. It reminds one of Robertson Nicoll's droll comments concerning Henry Drummond, who seems to have made a principle of "natural selection" in dropping off his personal effects in order to make more room for his books; there is no evidence that Willie ever left a book behind.

One of the by-products of his visits to Oxford was admittance to the dining rights at Christ Church and an early invitation to take prayers for them, which highly gratified him. He made close friends of some of the Fellows, not least with Cuthbert Simpson, then the Dean. This male-centered ambiance was a special delight to him; he was never happier than when within its walls and atmosphere, where the conversation was strong and lively. Never was his understanding of "Christian manliness" so much at home. His conversation there, like that of C. S. Lewis, was by no means religious. Indeed, there was a salty, Rabelaisian quality about it that amazed some, delighted others, and offended the more sanctimonious, who failed to realize (or preferred to ignore) how close to the great Reformers Willie was in this. Indeed, it might be argued that Willie's was a more refined, more consciously "sanctified" usage than theirs. Willie's world, as we have seen so often, was much more integrated, more of a uni-verse than that of the modern affecters of piety, and he attacked in principle the suppression of the boldly human and mundane. One colleague overheard him discussing at high table the use and abuse of hotel toilets, sympathetically siding with the maids who were employed to maintain the comforts of their "superiors." Willie simply found such attitudes a blasphemy, a denial of men and women, and therefore a denial of religion itself.

Meeting his translation panel colleagues at the bar on one occasion prior to starting another session, he confessed that other pressures had kept him from the promised preparation. So there and then he excused himself from their company, found a small table in a corner of the bar, and worked unplugged from his hearing aid for half an hour, oblivious of the sounds—and strange looks—such uncommon behavior provoked. Life was one to him whether in the sacred learning of his Greek New Testament or the "secular" activities of the day-to-day; and all work was worship, ascribing worth to God. Like Boswell, his attitude toward sensuality was to accept and enjoy the natural—although, unlike Johnson's great biographer, he preserved high standards of personal morality and rectitude for himself. This meant that he could see and appreciate the folly and humor of humanity in a risqué story, and sometimes felt obliged to pass such stories on to his more heaven-minded students by way of "manly" counsel, as well as in frank enjoyment of the human condition. He could never understand, still less compromise with, behavior that hurt other people, whether by reducing their self-esteem or denying their rights as human beings. Such pharisaism, ever prevalent in ecclesiastical circles and seats of learning, where special temptations to snobbery and self-aggrandizement lie in wait, was much the greater violation of his ethic than were any personal frailty or misspent bodily functions.

We need to look more closely at this, for it is not the picture we might be prepared to envisage. For one thing, his upbringing was of a wholly different order. There was nothing in his home life that was not strictly in line of the highest, purest awareness of life and religious endeavor; indeed, there is much to suggest that any diminution of it would have been sternly repressed. The high view of life inculcated by Paul in Philippians 4:8 had been raised to an ethical principle, to which was linked the Victorian work ethic. But, unlike so many homes in Scotland, Willie's parents' home was not geared to simple—still less frugal—things. From this arose part of the dichotomy that is so much a feature of his mind and life: he was a man of two worlds, both of which were real and assertive. The word "repression" was used by his future son-in-law, an honors graduate in psychology, in characterizing Willie, though he was also at pains to emphasize that Willie was "one of the most relaxed and natural individuals I have met."[63] In the particular context in which that judgment was expressed—that of society's changing sexual mores—it was a very significant comment, but one that must not be overemphasized. In such a home as that of his parents, the merest look from his mother was sufficient to censure, though his father was not averse to repeated full-scale attacks on the dangers of unchecked "worldliness," sensuality, or insobriety.

There was another feature of Willie's character that was highlighted by his relationship with Oxford, which Neil Alexander has dealt with in almost painful detail, a matter that has surprised more than one of his former colleagues at Glasgow. I refer to Alexander's assertion that Willie "overvalued the attainment and experience he did *not* have and the type of man they might have made him, and was too impressed by them in others."[64] To be fair, Alexander—who did not know Willie as an academic colleague till he joined his staff (at Willie's behest) in 1964—was writing particularly of the experience that led to his being appointed Professor on Macgregor's death, to which we must return later; nevertheless, he does make statements that are not supported by other evidence from this stage of his career. In fact, all the evidence, all the recollections of those who did then know him, point away from Alexander's bold contention. To be sure, Willie was aware that he did not possess an "earned degree" of high order, and he did regret it (though even Alexander admits that he never spoke of such regret in his presence), but that mattered little in the light of his proud—if "shattering"—D.D. and the astonishing success of his books. Shoulder to shoulder with Oxford men who possessed multiple doctorates, he knew that his understanding of Greek could challenge theirs any day and felt no need to apologize for himself. Indeed, the recollections of those who saw him in action there provide no substantiation whatever for the contention that he felt "quite uneducated down there." He was in Oxford by December 1956, and from that time established himself as a man of immense erudition, clearly enjoying the prestige it brought. It is interesting to see how quickly his initials rose in the pecking order of the minutes of the meetings he attended, and that in the company of the very best of British biblical scholarship. By May 1960 he was taking the chair alongside such names as C. K. Barrett, R. S. Barbour, George Beasley-Murray, and T. F. Glasson. Mr. Alexander has made a point, but it is a mistake to posit such feelings of inferiority on Willie's part at this early period.

One final incident from this period is of interest here, for it is reflective of Willie's consummate acquaintance with Greek as well as his manner of working. Mr. Bradnock had asked (via Professor McHardy) if he could help Willie in any way. He was somewhat surprised at the response he got: Willie requested that he bind the Nestle–Schmöller *Novum Testamentum Graece* and *Hand-Konkordanz* into a single volume, to facilitate his "light" traveling. The two volumes had never been brought together before in this way, and doing so necessitated direct correspondence with the Stuttgart publishers that went on endlessly, as the binding of so large an amount of material proved to be extremely difficult. Henceforth this overlarge volume was to accompany Willie wherever he went, a *vade mecum* of extraordinary power that symbolized the purpose and axis of his life's work.

"There Remains Nothing Now but to Go On"

The year 1958 was in several ways quite spectacular. Prime Minister Anthony Eden resigned in January, and the premiership hopes of R. A. Butler (of 1944 Education Act fame, a highly competent Chancellor of the Exchequer and

Foreign Secretary) were dashed by Churchill, who found Harold Macmillan "more decisive," and so recommended him to the Queen. Macmillan had the forceful backing of Edward Heath, then Chief Whip, and with his appointment a new era in British politics began, the era of "managerial politics," to use Jo Grimond's phrase. In March the Treaty of Rome began to take effect, one year after it had been signed, heralding a new era in European political and economic life, from which was excluded, thanks to Gallic hauteur, the one country that had done more than any other to free Europe from political and economic tyranny. In May Britain exploded her first H-bomb; so dawned a period of threat, violence, and bellicose international competition. This move had been adumbrated when the White Paper on defense was approved at the Cabinet meeting of 4 April, inaugurating "the biggest change in military policy ever made in normal times."[65] Through this development arose the Campaign for Nuclear Disarmament, which was to become both the focal point for left-wing agitation in Britain for more than a decade and the spearhead for pacifism and passive resistance, which Willie himself was to advocate from time to time. The mushroom cloud hovered menacingly over the Western world, and people were afraid. In October the Russians successfully launched the first satellite into space, accentuating still further cold-war fears. It was looked on as the greatest military menace to date, as well as an astonishing technological breakthrough. It began to overturn deep-seated beliefs about man's place in the universe and the presumed inaccessibility of the planets, and it provided the impetus for a great uplift for scientific and technological training. Student interest in such subjects soared and ministerial attitudes and training came under inspection yet more deeply.

Willie, totally without experience in this area, but foreseeing the enormous importance of the developments and the opportunities they presented, sought of his friend Braidwood advice as to his son's future in industry. But, he reported, "to my utter astonishment he has decided to go to Jordanhill and to qualify as a teacher. He [always] swore he would never do anything like that. Maybe with the years he is learning prudence!"[66] It is a feature of the man that he never sought to impose his own ambitions or hopes on Ronnie, wisely content to let him make his own way in life. He was bemused at his son's independence and occasionally wrote in awed terms of it, admitting that he himself could never have so acted. "He goes off into the blue without a tremor," he stated as Ronnie returned to the Continent, adding, "I'm never quite clear how he finances himself!" There followed a very fetching account of Ronnie's habits, which differed markedly from Willie's own at Marburg in the early '30s. There is no suggestion of the dependency on a serving maid that Willie grew up with—and still had, thanks to Kate's tireless and painstaking care of his every need. He went on to tell Braidwood that

> he always takes a room, and does his own cooking and catering! He somehow manages to buy or hire a motorised push-bike and tours the country. He is just as at home on the continent as here. I strongly suspect that he makes his money by rescuing Americans who know no French or German!

Other matters obtruded themselves during this eventful year. The Wolfenden Report on homosexuallity was published toward the end of it, much to the horror of the ecclesiastical establishment, Willie included; at this time he responded with a firm condemnation, refusing (unlike his colleague J. G. Mackenzie of *The British Weekly*) to draw any distinction between the condition and the sin. Bob Kernohan has in a phrase encapsulated a very perceptive description of Willie's ethical attitudes (admittedly of a slightly later period): "A Puritan who enjoyed life."[67] Certainly he remained an unswerving advocate of the biblical ethic in a time of almost concerted attack on the normative teaching of the churches. Bertrand Russell, charismatic leader of the Campaign for Nuclear Disarmament and noted freethinker, was in the van of such attacks, soon to be aided by his philosophical confrère Alfred Ayer, whose penetrating questioning of religious language was to transform theological debate and training. It was during this time that *The News Chronicle* published a Gallup Poll on religion in Great Britain showing that while seventy-one percent of the population twenty years old or older believed Jesus to be the Son of God, a mere fourteen percent went to church. Institutionalized religion had been, even then, judged and found wanting. Such publications as John Allegro's reappraisal of Christian origins (far beyond the radicalism of Bishop Barnes) and Roderick Dunkerley's *Beyond the Gospels*, as well as the newly discovered *Gospel of Thomas*, caused much unrest and militated directly against the Bible-centered approach of Willie and others. The Billy Graham campaigns and Tell Scotland missions were making way for men of the stature of Tom Rees, who ran "Evangelistic Bible Rallies" around the country supported by Youth for Christ and many similar organizations. Moreover, some exotic and apparently more peaceable Eastern faiths rapidly drew large numbers of bored and disenchanted young people; even a High Court judge became a leading proponent of Buddhism in England.

In Scotland, *The British Weekly* was taken over by the Publications Department of the Church of Scotland. It was a daring move that undoubtedly saved the paper from a fate at least as bad as failure, though only temporarily. It is typical that although it was itself a true scion of the Scottish Free Church, it was ever reliant on southern support and management. But the committee structure of the church was never conducive to its prosperity, undermining the contribution that gifted editors such as Shaun Herron (who departed for a pastoral charge in Canada in October 1957) and Denis Duncan could make when left to themselves. Duncan actually took over in January 1958; before that Jack Stevenson had edited the paper, ably assisted by Glen Gibson of Scottish Television fame. But we must be fair. By definition the organs of a great national church must serve the objectives and aspirations of that church; the demands of good journalism, not to mention issues of interest to the general public, often lie in other directions. Unhappily, the move was seen by the Free Church as yet another opportunity to snipe, and so the bold venture was exposed to an unbecoming criticism characteristic of the spirit of those times. Queried *The Monthly Record,* with a singular lack of goodwill to the new managers, "Will it have the strength of conviction to raise it to worthwhile levels? Or will it fall into the hands of the Barthians to pour out its nebulosities for a year or two and then expire?"[68]

The use of the term "Barthians" is significant; it is indicative of a particular response to the theological scene, which was at that time more dominated by the magisterial efforts of the Swiss theologian than it is now. It was used as a term of general opprobrium by many who had never read Barth or, having done so uncarefully, failed to understand him. The emergence of open biblical studies and research among some evangelicals was as anathema to the ultraconservative faction as it was to Pius XII. The Free Church of Scotland was sadly resolute in condemning any man who appeared to express views not strictly within its own credal framework—regardless of the freedom the Reformers responsible for the new confessions enjoyed, and clearly oblivious of the reality of the original Reformers' positions in such matters!

An unhappy and very public example of evangelical witch-hunting had taken place a little earlier, in 1955. The Old Testament writer H. L. Ellison had written a paper on biblical inspiration that rocked the imagination of some conservatives and led to the dismissal from his academic post of one of the most gifted evangelicals of the time. In point of fact Mr. Ellison had done little more than remind his readers of what many of them already accepted as necessary for a true confrontation with the Word of God—that is, a personal encounter with it. F. F. Bruce, the recently appointed editor to *The Evangelical Quarterly* in which the offending essay had been published, soon to be widely heralded as the leading evangelical scholar in Europe, was also taken to task in no uncertain way. (Commented *The Monthly Record's* editor of the appointment of Bruce's predecessor to the editorship of the journal, "they took the wrong turning and called in a scholar who had scant sympathy with the aims and aspirations of its founders,"[69] an allegation that borders on fabrication.) It was a sad sign of the hysteria that had begun to penetrate their circles. Even W. E. Sangster was sharply criticized for associating with the "modernists" (another general term of opprobrium) and for being prepared to make concessions to their thinking. The divide between liberals and conservatives continued to widen.

This is of more than passing interest, for it is this attitude that quashed part of Willie's own sympathy with the evangelical cause. Though never a party man, as we have seen, his sympathies were as instinctively with the evangelicals as his doctrines were of their stock. It was remarked earlier that he was delighted at the emergence of an informed biblical awareness among evangelicals from the late '30s on, having trod that way himself. This is not to say that evangelicals of a previous generation were less informed or receptive to the changes taking place in biblical studies; many of them were, though the consolidation and communication of those studies to the general public was still in its infancy. Not a few were careful to receive the results tentatively, awaiting confirmation or rebuttal. Such a one was Graham Scroggie, a master of biblical exposition and a choice devotional speaker. Well loved at that citadel of evangelical experience the Keswick Convention, he nonetheless closely followed the course of biblical discovery and was ever grateful for the unfolding of "yet more truth." And there is a more than a suggestion that even WDB himself, despite his devotion to the teaching of the Scofield Reference Bible (a copy of which he received as a gift marking his retirement from Motherwell's Brotherhood meetings), was never simply dismissive of biblical scholarship per se (even as Moody and Drummond before him had not been). But when Willie heard of such personal attacks, and when he pondered on the simple fact that they were made by men who claimed to know the full truth, who instructed others on demonstrating it in their personal lives, he found a curious and wounding dislocation, not least at the point where God's love and generosity meet. He was, in fact, alienated by it.

In November 1957 he was himself subjected to an attack by the Free Church magazine following comments he wrote on how God becomes real to ordinary men and women in their daily lives. There was nothing exceptional about this expression of doctrine, which appeared in his *British Weekly* page for preachers and teachers, explicitly combining the theological with the mundane (à la Brother Lawrence). Willie only said what many others have frequently said—that we may find God in ourselves (i.e., in our own experiences), in the world (after Psalm 8:1, etc.), and in each other (fellowship, after all, being a dominically ordained element of Christian life). It is particularly unexceptional to find Willie saying this against the background of his own series of articles on the teaching of Jesus, which emphasized the revelatory aspects of our knowledge of God, especially as he had been producing no fewer than three books of New Testament exegesis each year for the past four years! Willie must have been puzzled (other readers were indignant) to read the charges now laid against him. Commented the editor, "he must have heard of the Scriptures . . . but apparently it has not yet occurred to him that one may discover and rediscover God in the revelations deposited and recorded in the Scriptures."[70] Such scurrility has no place in Christian circles, being neither truthful nor loving. It is this sort of thing that Willie reacted against and that checked—in the light of the welcoming friendship of those who did not hold "evangelical" doctrines—his fellowship with evangelicals. We should not be surprised over Willie's feeling that if this was the standard and measure of evangelicalism (and the long contentious years of his early life suggested that it was), then there was clearly more than a grain of truth on the other side. And so emotional factors were added to the intellectual arguments he heard from such gifted and impressive minds as Ronald Gregor Smith and Ian Henderson, his colleagues at Glasgow University. As Merricks Arnot has observed, the influence of Gregor Smith was now becoming a forceful factor in Willie's ever-responsive mental equipment; it served to consolidate some of the questionings that had formed in his mind during long years of study, reflection, and experience. He was facing up to the "decided questions" of his ordination charge in a new way, no longer preemptively—and not always consistently.

The year was significant of several other things for Willie too, things that were also to affect his thinking and writing. *The Daily Scottish Express* commented at the end of January on his "marathon speaking spree,"[71] which took place at the time of the annual Burns festivities. Willie not only spoke on "the immortal memory" twice on Burns Day (at Trinity College during the lunch hour, and at his beloved

Ring Mallet Club of Renfrew in the evening), but on other occasions as well, as, for example, at the St. Andrew's Club, Nottingham, on Saturday, January 26. (He preached at St. Andrew's Presbyterian Church on the following day, thus combining—without excesses—his secular and sacred roles.) The year that saw the publication of his commentaries on Romans and Hebrews, two great peaks of doctrinal exposition, also saw his reputation as a secular speaker heighten dramatically. That, too, was Willie's way.

Other lecturing and speaking continued as before. He returned to lecture at Bagshot at the end of January, and in March commenced an annual and vital contact with the Newcastle YMCA that was to remain intact for the next sixteen years. In May he was invited to stay at the London YMCA by his old friend Harry Stevenson, who had taken over as the organization's General Secretary, for he had not been finding it easy to obtain hotel accommodations to suit his particular life-style. He needed a regular base from which to work and at which his London publishers (now four in number) could find him. Sir William Collins was concerned that Willie might not have the comfort appropriate to such a well-known author, and generously offered to install him at the London Hilton. Willie, despite his appetite for comfortable appointments, nevertheless declined the invitation in order to stay within the ethos of his upbringing, the place of opportunity and service. The Board of Directors of the YMCA was glad to agree to Stevenson's proposal, and so a penthouse flat was made ready. From now on "Room 200" was Willie's in a special sense, a real prophet's chamber. It ideally suited him. It was a large room, with a bathroom en suite, and became virtually an extension of his Clarkston home and Trinity College room. Mr. Stevenson recalled that "a considerable part of his writing of books was done at the various vacation periods, viz. New Year, Easter and Summer."[72] It was from here that his regular contacts with Bloomsbury Central Baptist Church developed, it being situated round the corner from the Tottenham Court Road "Y." Willie was able to offer Dr. Howard Williams, its busy minister, pulpit supply that developed into regular appearances at its Watchnight services and on Sunday evenings, and occasional appearances in a series of midweek services.

The YMCA naturally benefited from having so gifted a speaker on hand, one who was ideally experienced to deal with the multiracial and multicredal constituency of its idealistic young members. Willie's Sunday evenings were frequently rounded off by speaking at its evening service in the lounge, at its midweek services in the chapel, and occasionally at their annual dinners. His daytime hours were taken up with various appointments and committee and editorial meetings. Around these Willie wove a tight web of remorseless activity: writing, reading, and personal contacts. When possible he would work in his room during the daytime, emerging only for meals, which he never prolonged. He made an occasional exception to this regimen to indulge in one of his favorite treats—taking his main meal at the Lyons' Corner House nearby, which in those days boasted a six-piece orchestra as well as good food and service. In the early evenings he could be seen chatting to various members of the coffee lounge, following up his talks in a personal way or offering friendship to some lonely soul passing through the capital. Harry Stevenson would call in to say good night about 11:00 P.M., and would frequently find Willie at the center of an animated group of young people, all arguing after the manner of his own Young People's Society of former days. Ever the Socratic gadfly, he would take care to move the discussions toward positive ends, never merely to undermine beliefs. Sometimes Mr. Stevenson would find him in his room at this late hour, still hard at it even after a strenuous day of meetings and work. He was greatly impressed by Willie's habit of working directly from his Greek New Testament on to his typewriter without other aids, notes, or whatever, his prodigious memory supplying all he needed by way of comment or notation. It was in this way he produced most of his new translation of the New Testament.

Desmond Jenkins recalls another facet of this curiously complex but totally committed man. Late some evenings Willie would cross the Tottenham Court Road and enter the red-light district of Soho, observing the still fast-moving circulation of people from all walks of life and many different countries, the gormandizing of the rich, and the sale of sex that was also abundantly present. His knowledge of the human situation apparently precluded any embarrassment at such displays. Sometimes he would turn the sexual advances of the prostitutes into opportunities of a more elevating kind, even as he did from time to time in Glasgow's city center. Such sorties sometimes lasted till 4:00 A.M., and it would be a weary man who found his way back to the "Y," only to rise and labor at eight the next morning as strenuously as ever.[73] He was not shocked by what he saw on the streets, even if he was disturbed by it, and he would return to his writing with added zest, to write yet more freshly of the unsullied goodness of the One who also delighted to be called the friend of publicans and sinners. Willie's way was not that of a false separation from evil; he could not condone in any respect a rejection of mankind, which he held to be an act—perhaps the supreme act—of unlove. On one occasion he preached at the Salvation Army center in Oxford Street (Regent's Hall) and was deeply moved on seeing an old down-and-out man stagger up to the penitent rail when the captain gave the altar call—so moved in fact that he had to retire to the side room and dry his eyes, true pastor, true man, that he was!

One aspect of his day whenever away from home was a telephone call to Kate. When in London he would always call promptly at 8:00 P.M. The telephone bills were in consequence enormous, but nothing would deter him from this daily link and the assurance it brought that all was well at home.

None of these activities disturbed him from his main business as trainer of young men and university lecturer, however. He never failed to take very seriously the duties attendant on these roles. In March he and the college principal, John Mauchline, were appointed by a special meeting of the theological faculty to discuss a new course in biblical studies. It was a crucial piece of work, to be presented to the Faculty of Arts as a qualifying course in its M.A. regulations—a notable addition to the development of biblical studies beyond theological training by which he "completed" his more secular ambitions in Religious Education of the late '40s. In this a course on world religions (i.e., Comparative Theology) was included for the first time. It was not the only innovation of the faculty that year. At the June meeting it was proposed that two things be added to the next year's routine. The first was a presessional (freshman's) conference, largely for intending ministers, but open to all the general members of faculty who wished to come. It soon became an important ice-breaking feature of life at Glasgow in which Willie played his own part, not least in "conscripting" new choir members. The second innovation was the introduction of a midterm "Quiet Day," the final arrangements for which were to be made by Willie and Professors Gregor Smith and Pitt-Watson. They took care to ensure that the devotional element was not eclipsed by new academic concerns in the faculty's life, since both elements were important aspects of the one training program.

Kate, meanwhile, was still feeling the effects of Barbara's loss; the memory was still a sharp and grievous part of both their lives. By April her fibrositis had become intolerable, severely limiting her arm movements and rendering her practically an invalid. Their spirits were raised by good news about Ronnie's honors degree, which enabled him to take a scholarship for a second period of study—and American rescue?—in Germany. But his imminent departure to the Continent raised problems in Willie's mind as to once more exposing Kate to loneliness and himself to charges of neglect. And so, at fifty years of age, they turned their minds to the possibility of restarting their family life again, by adoption. It was a bold and daring move; it would obviously give Kate "something to do," though taking into account Willie's professional life and crammed diary one wonders how he envisaged its working out. Writing to Braidwood a little later, he acknowledged that "there might have been trouble"—not least with Ronnie's feelings—but in the end things did work out admirably and the decision became "a complete success."[74]

One of his former parishioners was herself working at Quarrier Children's Homes, Bridge of Weir, at the time and became an important element in the arrangements that took place. Their hearts were stolen by Jane, who had been at the Home since soon after her birth in 1952, and was now in her sixth year. She was an engaging and attractive little girl whose vitality and innocence brought new life to a household long overshadowed by the tragic death. As Willie said to Leslie Mitton of the adoption (which was completed in the autumn of 1957), "it has made a very great difference to my wife. So far it has been an unqualified success."[75] And he commented to Mrs. Jane Braidwood, whose shared name he was keen to emphasize, "she is very pretty and very charming, and it has been a complete success." He was particularly pleased with the Home's open policy, which meant that from the very start Jane had been fully apprised of the facts; they had no cause to be concerned over having "to break the news over the adoption." A period of hospitalization followed her arrival at the Barclays, due to an ill-timed call for a tonsillectomy, but that only proved to be the final move in breaking down the barriers in their new-formed family. "She has done Mrs Barclay all the good in the world," Willie continued with pardonable exaggeration, adding that Kate had finally "put on some much needed weight; and for the first time for a long time she is sleeping without sleeping tablets."[76]

Willie and Kate were naturally concerned at Ronnie's reaction to his new sister, but found their concerns swept away in a mutual devotion the one to the other. Ronnie, in fact, spent more than a quarter of his sparse vacation earnings on a new tricycle for Jane, and all was well. "It may seem reckless to start all over again at fifty," confided Willie to another friend, "but it has worked." From now on Jane would have to suffer the embarrassment, as Barbara and Ronnie had before her, of being the subject of anecdotes of private life made exceedingly public by her "unfeeling father,"[77] though this time in print rather than the pulpit of Renfrew Trinity. And so the exploits of "Dumpling," as he nicknamed her, came before the general public: her love of Bimbo the monkey, her friendships, her love of dining out, her first steps in theologizing ("God must be dead," said she, annoyed at unanswered prayer, ten years in advance of the theologians),[78] her prayers, her schooling, and her early love of books. Willie was delighted by her unawareness of class or credal divisions; she brought to her home friends from a full complement of races, faiths, and social standings.

Kate, Willie, and Ronnie were not the only ones at Berridale Avenue to welcome Jane. There was also the question of one overweight, decidedly

A joyous new light in a time of darkness: Jane enters the family.

overpetted, near-human Staffordshire Bull terrier. Local residents were familiar with its taking Willie for a walk late at night—Willie's arm and chain at full stretch as it sped round the block, inspecting its landmarks, and staking out doggy-fashion its claims within its territory. Readers of *The British Weekly* were even more familiar with its skills, habits, and even its sins. At first sight it was a peculiar choice of dog for a minister to make, especially peculiar for a strong pacifist like Willie. A former fighting dog with a mean reputation for aggression, it had nevertheless stolen the Barclays' hearts with its wily ways and its skillful exploitation of their softheartedness. One of the delights of reading *The British Weekly* in those days was to take up the unfolding drama of Rusty, which commenced on 26 January 1956. He had "an unlimited capacity for doing the forbidden thing," as puppies do. Readers throughout the country were entranced at the marvelous descriptions Willie conveyed to them of it, and at how they were turned to good effect as parables of life. From now on his "velvet brown eyes," his "efforts to speak," his "extensive vocabulary," his "tempestuous affection" (a significant indication of his master's reserved temperament), his attachment to his rubber bone and one of Ronnie's old tennis shoes, and so much more would become a familiar feature of Willie's teaching page. Along with this went the normal activities of a happy home: walks on Willie's much-loved moorland at Bonnyton Moor or in Crow Wood, Jane's attempt to ride Rusty's back, the need of "an occasional thrashing" at which he would cry "like a baby." Willie had to admit—with more than a touch of shame, but tinged with pride redolent of his own sporting attitudes—that Rusty had abnormally aggressive attitudes toward the canine population of the area. This posed a problem to its owner: "Which end am I to believe," he once inquired—the ever-wagging tail end, or the ferocious snarls that emanated from his throat when he thought his territory was threatened? This too was translated into a parable of human reality.[79]

To his great credit, the dog took to shepherding Sammy the Siamese cat when he joined the Barclay household in early 1959. Its early "terrifying violent approaches" were soon turned into not merely the "armed neutrality" its owners had hoped for, but real affection. Sammy's activities, no less than Rusty's and Jane's, also became points of stimulus for Willie's devotional writings, and for his many readers, as they visualized his sleeping on the fridge, hiding in Jane's doll's house, escaping up the chimney, indulging his astonishing capacity for food, and maintaining his hard-won priority over Rusty at the shared eating bowl. All this came to an abrupt end in the spring of 1960, when Sammy suddenly died. "The best medical attention in the area" could not save him, Willie lamented. Once more the Barclay household was plunged into gloom, though the pall lifted quickly when Tiptoes scampered into their lives. He, too, was taken over by Rusty, whose fulsome fatherly treatment was almost too much for the three-week-old kitten.

These months began to see the scar-tissue of their great loss healing, and we find the three of them (Ronnie soon married) enjoying themselves in a wide

Above: *The new family on holiday.* Below left: *Willie and "one overweight, decidedly overpetted, near-human Staffordshire bull terrier."* Below right: *Ronnie, Kate, and Jane.*

range of activities and outings. Undoubtedly Willie made considerable efforts to amuse and please them both, even though he was now more in demand than ever. Thus we find them at restaurants, at Glasgow's busy airport (where Willie especially liked to stop for tea), at music concerts, art galleries, the cinema, the theater, and—a throwback to Willie's undergraduate days—at old-time music hall shows with such stars as Harry Lauder, Jimmy Edwards, Arthur Askey, Wyn Calvin, and many others. It was not long before Jane was introduced to the operatic delights of Gilbert and Sullivan, in Willie's view the best of all subjects in a young person's educational formation next to book learning. Jane apparently failed to share this view, for she burst into tears and vowed never to return. But her father was unmovable, and boldly canvassed the educational advantages the operas promoted as well as their rich humanity and joyful music. Swimming and the enjoyment of water (for example, in Llandudno's open-air lido) were not forgotten, despite the brutal reminders they gave to Willie and Kate. As Willie was ever ready to tell those overtaken by tragedy and sorrow, "life must go on." Manfully, he ensured that it did.

Terrified of the Microphone

Mention was made earlier of Willie's involvement in the *Lift Up Your Hearts* radio program. It was not his first broadcast, though he was by no means in the van, still less among the most popular, of the Church of Scotland religious broadcasters in the postwar years. Some of the big names of the time include George MacLeod ("the most uncompromising Christian of the century with the common touch"), Tom Allan, Ronnie Falconer, Stanley Pritchard, E. H. Robertson, Selby Wright, Leonard Small, and G. N. M. Collins. One might be led to suspect that Willie's prospects for similar success in broadcasting were not good, in light of A. B. Macaulay's warning about the effect his voice would have on his future, but Willie was about to overcome that handicap and proceed to a singular success.

To understand his attitude toward the wireless set (as we should call the device of those days), we would do well to remember that he could clearly recall the actual introduction of the device in his early years. Even yet he preserved a sense of the astonishment it had initially generated, and it was in part this wonder that made him reluctant to become involved in broadcasting. While ever working "forward," he was not always a pacesetter, nor was he even particularly progressive, and that in the country that produced the "father of broadcasting," John Reith.

His first broadcast was relayed on Sunday, 21 September 1949. It was the sixth talk in a series entitled "Charity Begins at Home." No record exists of what he said or of the effect it produced. We shall not be too wrong in supposing that the effect was not overwhelming, for he thenceforth remained off the air for over five years. During this time religious broadcasting made important strides forward, not least in Scotland where the "Radio Missions" of 1950 and 1952 attracted large numbers of listeners. Willie did not participate in either; it may well be that he was not wholly persuaded of the power of radio for religious ends, that he was concerned that it might seriously weaken parish structures and the already declining church-going habit. Ronnie Falconer, doyen of Scottish religious broadcasting in the '50s and '60s, explored these possibilities in an article entitled "The 'Why' of Radio Broadcasting" in 1949.[80] He found that there were, broadly speaking, three main varieties of religion in Britain at the time: that of the Protestant, which made a man stand on his feet; that of the Roman Catholic, which caused a man to go down on his knees; and that of the BBC, which allowed him to lounge at home in his armchair! To the extent that Willie shared that understanding, he was a marked opponent of the radio ministries; he was seeking to keep discipline in discipleship, not to dissipate it. There is another reason for Willie's noninvolvement. Falconer suggested that the chief objectives of "radio religion" were threefold: to challenge the careless, to recover the lapsed, and to strengthen the faithful. Willie's essential work at this period lay in different spheres—in the Sunday Schools and youth work and in ministerial training. It was only as his books and journalism became widely popular that he was looked on as a more general communicator, and that came but slowly.

Stanley Pritchard, Falconer's assistant, who had first met Willie at his Bruce Lectures in 1937 and thereafter stood in occasionally as pulpit supply for him at Renfrew, recalls that it was Willie's prayers that first achieved public acclaim in his early broadcasting. In point of fact, Mr. Pritchard did not find Willie a good broadcaster at all in the beginning. Quite apart from the problems of his guttural voice, thick accent, and very fast delivery, there was an essential problem in his style: he was too much the expansive lecturer, and he could not get his timing right. James Martin's gloss over this problem in *William Barclay: The Plain Uncommon Man*[81] reveals his unfamiliarity with Willie's early broadcasting background. *Testament of Faith* shows that he suffered from a loss of contact with his audience at the microphone—a thing of critical importance to an empathic speaker like Willie, who was always finely tuned to congregational atmosphere and response. Recalling a prebroadcast briefing, Willie was reminded of Pritchard saying to him, "There's a man in a house in a room reading the Sunday paper. *Stop him!*"[82] He began to work at this with no small success. Indeed, if WDB's household made him the man he became, and if Renfrew Trinity made him the minister he became, Stanley Pritchard and Ronnie Falconer (in that order) made him the broadcaster (and later the telecaster) he became.

This is not the place to expatiate on broadcasting arts and techniques, matters that in Willie's case came later anyway; but we may usefully bear in mind Lord Moran's recommendations to Winston Churchill in February 1950, when he spoke to him of the transformation in communications that radio was bringing about. Moran was speaking, of course, to a man of superlative gifts in this field, who had kept alive the aspirations and fighting spirit not merely of Great Britain, but of the free world itself. He nevertheless pointed out that broadcasting had *reduced* the power of the normal means of communication. He commented, with telling significance for Willie, that "argument had been replaced by little *word-*

pictures which humble folk would remember."[83] If Churchill was to reject learning the new techniques and retreat into his beloved House of Commons, Willie was not. He became a master of the "little word-pictures" to his own equally beloved "humble folk," after the manner of his already tried and trusted parables-of-life method. And how these were remembered! His powers of logical argument must not be minimized, even if it is true that he did not seek to hone the logician's tools. Nevertheless, by way of finely demonstrating the rhetorician's arts, he placed himself within the imagination of his listeners and spoke to their hearts and wills as well as their minds.

His second broadcast took place in September 1954, when he conducted the Light Programme's "People's Service"—significantly named, as was the program itself. He preached from Palmerston Place, Edinburgh, on the first four Sundays of the month, between 11:30 A.M. and 12:00 noon. As the basis of his little word-pictures he took the five Greek words that are in English versions translated as "sin." Falconer recalls how Willie commenced, uncharacteristically, with a complaint: English was too "poverty-stricken" to permit of exact translations on a word-for-word basis.[84] He made up the deficiency in quick, bold strokes, expounding and illustrating his themes and bringing to life before Greekless thousands the meaning and the message (ever-present partners in his preaching and teaching) of the words. As D. M. G. Stalker noted in reviewing *A New Testament Wordbook* (published after the broadcasts), three things happen to the reader when escorted by William Barclay through the Greek language:

> (1) he will be fascinated by the author's detective work—it is really difficult to lay the book down; (2) he will have learned, in a most easy way, an immense amount about the world into which Christ came, with the result that Gospels and Epistles have come alive in quite a new way . . . and (3) he will, almost unconsciously, have had his Christian faith greatly clarified and extended.[85]

A year later, on September 8, 15, 22, and 27, he broadcast his first midweek series, from the Glasgow studio of the BBC. This time he took one of his favorite subjects, the Beatitudes, and once again highly favorable responses were made, refuting the confident warnings of the experts (Falconer admitted that "certainly Willie Barclay would never have passed a BBC Audition test"),[86] and thereby adding to the already overworked writer-lecturer a huge correspondence as waves of letters cascaded onto his desk.

Little has been recorded of further broadcasts over the next two years. We know from Willie's own hand that he conducted a further week of talks for the *Lift Up Your Hearts* program shortly after Barbara's death (Falconer recollects that one such talk saved the life of a young woman on the verge of committing suicide),[87] but pressures of lectern, pulpit, and typewriter seem to have prevented much more involvement before January 1958, when he took on another "People's Service" series. This time the program format was different, for each of the four talks had a different location in Glasgow—High Carntyne, East and West Busby, and Claremont. But the response was the same, if not more enthusiastic. Mrs.

Braidwood heard one of these broadcasts in far-off Sussex, and wrote to say how glad she was to hear his voice and be reminded of their Renfrew days. In answer, Willie mentioned that he had left replying to their letter till last, so as to offer more news than was normal. Between the end of his series of broadcasts (on 26 January) and the time of writing (15 February) he had written "rather more than seven hundred letters"—over 240 a week, when he was in the midst of completing his series of "readings" on the New Testament. Most of them, he added, "had to be rather short."

An interesting light is thrown on the broadcaster in this four-page letter to the Braidwoods: "I'm still terrified of the microphone after all these years of facing it," he wrote. "The BBC say that twelve-and-a-half million people listen to the People's Service, and it is a fearful thought when you utter the first sentence into it." We should note that *courage* was a keyword in his vocabulary, and that his emphasis stemmed from his own experiences as well as his knowledge of human frailty and fear. Much has rightly been made of Willie's exuberant humanity, of the fact that he could be the natural center of any group, being a master of the varied arts of conversation, courtesy, and bonhomie. But his very ebullience was itself a sign of the essentially reserved temperament that lay beneath. In his autobiography he tells of the pastoral side of his ministry being "a terror and an agony." "I dreaded pastoral visitation," he confesses. Likewise, "to enter a pulpit has always been a literally terrifying experience. . . . I have always been haunted by the sheer dread of preaching."[88] The fears born of the immense responsibility of the pulpit were only magnified by the presence of a microphone or, worse, a camera and the vastly greater audiences they implied. Still he found courage to face them.

The man who endured the rigors of the pastoral office, who was prepared to stand in sacrificially to produce Sunday School lessons and teaching handbooks for both the Boys' Brigade and the youth of his church, and who then went on—"accidentally," but unswervingly—to expound the word of God for countless thousands of daily and weekly readers and preachers, was now found expending yet more resources in further avenues of service, despite the high cost. These, all of them examples of the major aspects of his life and work, illustrate the "not I, but Christ" commitment he had discovered in Royal Renfrew. There is more than one sort of martyrdom, and who can say that "living martyrdom" is not the finest example? Certainly, Willie took pains to defend the "royalty of Christianity" understood in terms of "white martyrdom." "To call a man a martyr," he said, "did not necessarily mean to say that he had died for the faith; it could mean that he had lived for it."[89] That, especially, was Willie's way.

CHAPTER SIXTEEN

Life at Its Peak

The Pendulum Years: Foundations Shaking

THE period from the late '50s to May 1963 was one of consolidation for Willie both personally and professionally. For the world it was a period of rapidly changing political situations, of international threats and dangers. The Middle East crisis had led to marked anti-American feelings in Great Britain, and there is more than a touch of evidence to show that Willie shared in it. This was to change strikingly later, but at this time we may note that despite his professional ambitions he was never seriously tempted by offers of lucrative chairs in the States. Britain was, moreover, now isolated from Europe, and the tag "Little Englander" was frequently applied to government foreign policy and many personal world views; it was no less true of thinking north of the border. To be sure, the nation enjoyed the prestige of the Commonwealth and a number of important colonies, and these gave it some clout in the world, but clear signs of a national loss of identity and purpose were already showing. This fed nationalist resentment in Wales and Scotland; home rule and nationalism once more became lively issues of political life and debate. In 1958 provision was made in Parliament for representation of the Church of Scotland in the House of Lords, a late corrective to southern ecclesiastical dominance. Further, industrial and racial unrest, aggravated by a *shortage* of labor, began to erupt into public demonstrations; a national bus strike took place in May and June, and Notting Hill exploded with vicious black/white confrontations in July and August. Inflation remained reasonable (between three and five percent), posing no fears for government or populace. A General Election took place in October 1959, returning the Conservative Party to power for its tenth consecutive year in office, which administration would continue for a further three and a half years.

Internationally, the fierce East–West conflict, dominated by the mutual suspicion and intransigence of the superpowers, continued to cast a long shadow over the whole globe. In the Antarctic, thirty nations signed a treaty, agreeing to preserve that continent's political and military neutrality, but this did nothing to thaw the icy animosity of the cold war. By October 1962 the Cuban Missile Crisis thrust itself upon an astonished world. In the end Khrushchev backed down in the face of John F. Kennedy's iron resolve, but it was a frighteningly near thing. The Kennedy cult and the dream that went with it disintegrated in the wake of his assassination in the autumn of 1963. Within five years yet more dreams were extinguished as more assassins' bullets felled both Martin Luther King, Jr., and Senator Robert Kennedy.

By the late '50s great material prosperity was beginning to replace the stark postwar conditions; already they were a fast-receding reality to the younger generation. The "swinging sixties" were imminent, significantly foreshadowed in the gaiety of newfound color and the extravagances of rock 'n' roll. The new decade brought a nihilistic outlook that was to characterize a significant proportion of young people and find its fruition in anarchistic groups of all sorts. The "swinging sixties" would change into the "seething sixties" soon enough. But in these early years of the decade, style and fashion and daring personal expression were more in evidence than criticism and social resentment. Norman Hartnell, Jean Simpson, and Andy Warhol were three typical, and highly influential, names of the period, behind whom lay the liberated life-style and disturbing philosophies of Jean-Paul Sartre, Simone de Beauvoir, Martin Heidegger, Karl Jaspers, and Georges Marcel. It is important to realize that such movements presented, essentially, *styles* of philosophizing and living rather than great architectonic systems. The vital medium was the novel or the play rather than the treatise, though the treatises were to follow. With French and German existentialism came Left Bank attitudes of personal liberty and political anarchy, often projected in song by such masters of communication as Juliette Greco, "the little Sparrow," and other members of the growing subculture. Drug use and abuse aroused national concern, as did such figures as Quentin Crisp, who outraged the conventions of both morality and fashion.

By 1962 the exaggerated hedonism of James Bond, to say nothing of his cheap view of human life, was devoured by a society hungry for it; *Dr. No* was met with an eager Yes! and *Goldfinger* eclipsed Christian Aid and Oxfam, which also strove for the public's attention at this time. The essential trait was change, and Bernard Levin, one of the most percipient journalists of the time, commented thus in his significantly titled book *The Pendulum Years*:

> Fashions changed and changed again, changed faster and still faster: fashion in politics, in political style, in causes, music, in pop-culture, in myth, in education, in beauty, in heroes and idols, in attitudes, in responses, in work, in love and friendships, in food, in newspapers, in entertainment. . . . What had once lasted a generation now lasted a year, what had lasted a year now lasted a month, a week, a day. There was a restlessness in the time that communicated itself everywhere and to everyone, that communicated itself to the very sounds in Britain's air, the stones beneath Britain's feet.[1]

If we are to understand William Barclay from this time on, this man whose motto and attitude was ever "forward, not backward," we must understand him in that light and against that background: not as drifting straw caught up and swept along by unseen winds, but as a man, humane and red-blooded, who constructively sought the word of God for his own generation, who positively heard, read, and pondered on the spirit of the age. After the manner of Ezekiel of old, he was not afraid to sit where his people sat. By birth an Edwardian and by upbringing a child of the twittering '20s whose own twitterings were partially suppressed and whose great natural abilities were molded and channeled, shaped, and redirected into the dream of his father and mother, he fulfilled that dream and then—perhaps to his own astonishment—found himself deeply captivated by it. Through it he became a man of deep religious experience and insight who gladly, tenaciously dedicated and rededicated his gifts in the service of God and who by 1959 had completed his greatest work but still sought a role, a deeper fulfillment. And we must never forget that all this he did with a sensitive understanding of the frailty of human life and endeavor that knew full well the pain of loneliness and personal infirmity and the scalding power of bereavement but was determined not to be conquered by it.

The era was characterized by protest as well as progress and change, and to the vocal demonstrations of the Campaign for Nuclear Disarmament marchers, middle-class, bearded, and arty, guitars swinging from their shoulders, was added a movement of considerable importance for the underprivileged, the victims of racism and the poor. The voices of Martin Luther King, Jr., Sally Trench, Julie Felix, Bob Dylan, and Mother Teresa (as much a passive protestor as the others were active) were soon to echo and reecho throughout society with a sound that would increase in power and penetration through confrontation and even riot in condemnation of the weapons of war unleashed in Vietnam. Unilateralism was briefly added to the Labour Party's creed, only to be high-handedly taken out of it by an enraged Hugh Gaitskell. Along with this ferment came an explosion of betting shops and casinos; "U" and "non-U" categories obtruded themselves on the scene, equally destructive of society and humanity, despite the attendant growth in social caring and welfare. Spy scandals rocked the establishment, and the Profumo Affair was a revelation to many of "how the other side lives."

It was an era of both "new morality" and "new theology," when national leaders and prominent ecclesiastics sought to be "modern" at all costs. The acids of reductionism ate away at social and moral values alike. Marshall McLuhan reflected the sadly widespread cynical attitude that neither idealism nor values counted for much: the media was the message. Something similar also took place in religion, and a large part of the process was directly attributable to evangelistic ends. The old, old story was sought in all its simplicity, but was simplified still further by those who carelessly exchanged thought for song, rationality for experience, truth for cliche. Willie saw a middle way, and not infrequently found himself rejected by both sides.

On the other hand a strong rejection of external authority took place in the name of individual integrity and self-expression, the most noticeable signal of which was the commencement of change in emphasis within the armed services

541

from mindless obedience toward teamwork. In religious education, as in education generally, the decreasing stress on obedience (still a keyword in Willie's ethical understanding) in favor of personal discovery and responsibility was inculcated. It all too easily disguised the fusion of a godless existentialism with the newly discovered experiential emphasis. The conservative, "fundamentalist" reaction sharpened.

We saw that Willie welcomed this revival in the early '50s, but by the mid to late '50s—and following the arguments generated by the Billy Graham campaigns and their fundamentalistic supporters—changes in his attitude began to appear. For example, in a review of Alexander Ross's *The Epistles of James and John* and Herman N. Ridderbos's *The Epistle of Paul to the Churches of Galatia,* he was critical of both the slovenly publishing (the spelling mistakes in particular) and the chronological framework that Ridderbos had proposed for Acts (he could not, for example, accept Ridderbos's contention that the journey of Acts 15 should be identified with Galatians 2).[2] Again, in reviewing a month later Basil Atkinson's *Pocket Commentary on the Bible,* Willie found it almost wholly unacceptable—it was "a most regrettable volume," on both scholarly and ethical grounds.[3] The last point is important, for it reminds us that Willie looked for something more than mere academic acceptability in the writings of others (even as he sought to provide it in his own): the whole man mattered and, by extension, all men mattered, which "universalism" was a regular feature of his books and articles. Atkinson, he suggested, was contemptuous of others' views, and nothing alienated Willie more than such contempt or personal demeaning. Despite the efforts of a minority, one of the very sad aspects of evangelicalism during this period was the readiness of these professing Christians to slight, ridicule, and reject their opponents. Defensiveness was weakening their spiritual power because it was by no means the sort inculcated by Christ and his apostles: they had forgotten the lesson of not hitting back. But it must not be thought that the conservative element was alone in its petty backbiting. Liberals were wont to hold the entire conservative camp in contempt, snidely assuming that no one could hold such views save through ignorance—nor did they hesitate to make such views public. Willie strove to rise above the small-mindedness of both groups. Evangelicals claimed to know and practice the full truth of the gospel; their lives were ostensibly fashioned by biblical precept. Willie knew that they could not claim one thing and practice something quite different. They were defeating their own cause—his cause. He delighted in the sound scholarship of such men as C. H. Dodd, A. M. Hunter, F. F. Bruce, and H. A. Guy (whose work he applauded for eschewing "fault-finding and searching for errors" in favor of "careful judgment").[4] With real regret he had to admit that by and large he found in those of a nonconservative persuasion greater courtesy, a humbler attitude, more reasonable argumentation, and frequently more attentive scholarship than was evident in the ranks of the evangelicals. It was one of the reasons he was himself becoming more alienated from the conservative viewpoint. Gradually the parting of the ways was becoming more decisive, more open, more complete.

It was at this time that Willie indicated his being influenced by Kermit Eby's high valuation of the individual, notably *vis-à-vis* scholarship's "desk-fodder" attitudes: "People are more important than footnotes," he would quote from the Welsh principal, adding emphatically, "no one knows that better than I do."[5] Where such behavior was evident, he was merciless in exposing it, though it never caused him to withhold praise whenever he thought it was due. He continued to look for a tripartite standard in the books he reviewed: they ought to be interesting ("the worst of all heresies is that a work of scholarship must be thought to be dull"),[6] they ought to contain informed and accurate statement, and they ought to have an elevating tone, both ethically and devotionally. Thus he highly commended John Bright's careful study of *The Kingdom of God* and characterized the *Prayers of Peter Marshall* as "a very precious book." Stauffer's *New Testament Theology* he found to be "a thrilling and illuminating book [that] comes like a new revelation,"[7] and he praised C. K. Barrett's classical commentary on John for being "singularly free from the waste of space consequent upon contradicting other people" (a hallmark of his own writing).

Willie was not, of course, alone in being aware of the changes taking place in conservative-evangelical circles, nor in looking upon them in a not wholly favorable light. Michael Ramsey, then Archbishop of York, also warned of their dangers. His article "The Menace of Fundamentalism"[8] is a lucid and penetrating unveiling of the weaknesses of the evangelical cause—in its attitude toward the Bible, in its blinkered fixation on a simple (i.e., simplistic) penal theory of atonement (the Inter-Varsity Fellowship position here was specifically mentioned), in an overstrong emphasis on "deciding for Christ" (which Ramsey felt ignored the problems and the mental processes of the action), and in an individualistic understanding of the Holy Spirit's activities that implicitly slighted his work in the councils and sacraments of the church (and, we might add, in the world at large). We should remind ourselves that both Methodists and Congregationalists, as well as other evangelical bodies such as the Baptists, the Brethren, and a whole variety of independent churches, did not consider themselves as "churches" at this point in time; that development came in the late '60s and '70s in response to the evolution of the ecumenical cause. Archbishop Ramsey's final point therefore cut in more than one direction, effectively so. But the immediate response was an avalanche of letters to the editor protesting, arguing, pronouncing, presuming, and condemning. Some who never went near an Anglican church asked if the Archbishop were a fit person to hold so high an office.

The debate was not less forceful in the pages of *Life and Work,* where it continued throughout the late '50s. In July 1959 J. I. Packer published his *Fundamentalism and the Word of God,* and other books soon joined it.[9] In September of 1960 a conference of evangelical churchmen met at Oxford to discuss the issues at hand and offered six proposals for reconstruction.[10] Tempestuous days! And in the tempest Willie, as was his wont, listened and learned and found his creed changing yet more in the direction of "iron rations." This process, too, was part of the spirit of the age—dialogue, not monologue—which accounts (with some significant exceptions) for the decline of preaching in the postwar years. Willie himself had participated in *The British Weekly's* "Christian Conversation" column, an open forum that lasted only two years. In this he not only dealt with matters of biblical exposition (e.g., the meaning of John 3:5 and Christ's descent into hell), but with such issues as "Religious Vocabulary and Usage," "The Task of Christology," and even an explanation of existentialism.[11]

But we must not overlook the continuing conservative element in Willie's thinking. Significantly, when the editor of *Life and Work* called attention to "the many signs in Scotland of a 'return to the Bible,' "[12] the first thing he mentioned was Willie's Daily Bible Readings commentaries. The position was never more plainly exhibited than in Willie's review of the first volume of Rudolf Bultmann's *Theology of the New Testament.*[13] He recognized that "the publication of any new work by Professor Rudolf Bultmann of Marburg is an event of the first theological magnitude." He defended his former professor's right to theologize and respected the homiletic orientation it manifested—and that at a time when Bultmann was under fire from the bishops of his own United Evangelical Lutheran Church. And yet he waded into Bultmann in the spirit of a crusader seeking to restore Jerusalem, noting "perverse thinking," which he described in a headline as "Theology without History." "Bultmann," Willie stated, "leaves very little historical fact in the New Testament at all." He nevertheless appreciated "the sheer consummate scholarship of this book," and, leaving aside a catalogue of rejected gospel events and doctrines, he applauded "its basic contention that the faith of a man must never be made dependent on the labours of the historian." This is highly significant, for only recently had Willie written similar things himself, yet had demonstrated his own attitude toward New Testament historicity in his Daily Bible Readings commentaries.

Willie rested his case for rejecting his old professor's views on the general historical trustworthiness of the New Testament. "If we have no historical knowledge of anything [Jesus] ever said or did, if all the stories of Him are legends and compositions," Willie wrote, "then we still do not know what God is like." And, "it is not true to say that faith is entirely independent of the historian, because without the guarantee of the historian there would be nothing to have faith in." He goes on to cite a fragment from Quadratus, one of the earliest Christian apologists, who worked against a ferocious Jewish and Roman attack on Christianity to show how plain "the works of our Saviour were." But in addition he asserted unequivocally that this Jesus was completely human even though the "human Jesus of Nazareth" was in fact "the Word become flesh": "It is the basic fact of Jesus' life that He came to show us what God is like." He lived among men "in order that men might have something to experience." Willie concluded his review by stating that "this is a book of first-rate importance which no New Testament student can afford not to read." There were at least three reasons for this recommendation: (1) Christology is the living heart of Bultmann's interest and work; (2) what Bultmann failed to do was nevertheless the whole point of theology and preaching, namely, to make Jesus Christ prominent and relevant;

and (3) there remained the historic need to hold together the doctrines of Jesus' full humanity and deity. As he had commented to his *British Weekly* readers earlier, "the great test of Christology is to maintain the fact that Jesus is both God and man. All Christological heresies spring from mistaken attempts to solve or oversimplify that problem."[14]

Kenneth Galbraith termed this period the "Age of Uncertainty," and such it was. But the uncertainty developed out of a positive effort to understand and utilize the changes taking place, rather than out of a mere failure of nerve. In mid 1959 there came a celebration of the four hundredth anniversary of the publication of the definitive edition of Calvin's *Institutes of the Christian Religion* and of the four hundred and fiftieth anniversary of Calvin's birth. It also marked the centenary of the publication of Darwin's *Origin of Species,* a less joyful note to many who appreciated the Reformer, though not to Willie, whose grasp of God's creatorial powers was both broader and stronger than those who limited themselves to a literal understanding of what was (to Willie's understanding) poetically expressed truth.

The following year the four hundredth anniversary of the Reformation in Scotland was celebrated in both national and local events, and Willie, a fervent and joyful heir of the Reformation and a practitioner of Reformed principles, played his own part. Neville Davidson pled for an assembly of divines to meet "to examine Christian doctrine in the light of present-day knowledge," but was rejected—too many favored looking back, rather than forward.[15] Willie celebrated the central emphasis of the Reformation by publishing the first volume of his trilogy on the doctrine of Christ, *The Mind of Jesus.* And if it did not so much explore and explain the mind (as opposed to the life) of Jesus, as some of his friends would have liked, it is still a notable presentation by one who was now fully immersed in New Testament studies—and sound in his appreciation of their foremost object. Moreover, he offered a personal confession:

> In this book I have not wished to argue, I have simply wished to set down the picture of Jesus as I see it, and to set out what he means to me. . . . I can only say . . . that in the Jesus of this book I have found the Jesus who is the Saviour of men and who is my Saviour. . . . This is what I believe, and this is how there came into my life the new relationship with God which is the very essence of the Christian faith and of the work of Jesus Christ.[16]

Originally published as a series of eighty-two articles in *The British Weekly* (through 1958/59) under the title "The New Testament Interpretation of Jesus," the material had, he conceded, "been so extensively rewritten that the book bears little relation to the original articles." It is unique of all his material in having been subjected to so careful a preparation, which care underlines the high importance he attached to the subject. It was not merely the *result* of ten years of hard work—not so much interrupted by as founded upon his commentary of the complete New Testament—as its justification, its consummation. He lived to explain and extol Jesus.

He explained to his readers that what he was seeking to accomplish in *The Mind of Jesus* was "to make it possible [for them] to understand the mind, the work, and the meaning of Jesus a little better." Further, he sought to restrict himself to the Synoptic Gospels for source material; only occasionally would he allow himself to use material outside of Matthew, Mark, and Luke (though in actual fact he allowed more of John's influence than he admitted). While agreeing with the critics that "we do not possess the material to write a biography of Jesus," he was nevertheless convinced that "in these three gospels we have material on which we can rely to reconstruct the basic events of Jesus' life, to understand his teaching, and at least to some extent to enter into his mind."[17] Interestingly enough, in light of his rejection of paradox in his Adoptionist essay a decade earlier, we now find him not only mentioning it as an element in the teaching of Jesus, but actually relying on it himself as an acceptable form of logical argumentation. This exposition of the "fourfold gospel" so loved of the early church is impeccably orthodox; in it he brilliantly summarizes the key incidents in the life of Jesus (following the Markan chronology), laying bare the real meaning of his life to those who would follow him today.

Life and Work and *The British Weekly* had both announced in 1962 that this material in its journalistic form was being provided free of charge to overseas workers as "a direct contribution to mission."[18] *The Church Times* advocated its teaching as "a fresh, reverent and realistic presentation," and *The Expository Times* cited it as "'theology' presented in personal and preachable form"—a somewhat lackluster endorsement perhaps, but one that at least identified Willie's métier and acknowledged his mastery in it. He was a long way from the urge he had felt in 1949 to write "unintelligibly." His methods and conclusions may have been very different from those of his old Marburg mentor, but their aims were identical; and who would dare say that Willie's were any less effective than those of the great theologian?

It was not different when the second volume of the trilogy appeared in 1961 under the title *Crucified and Crowned*—reminiscent of the old evangelical catch phrase "no crown without a cross" with which Willie had grown up. On publication, the Student Christian Movement publicized Willie as "probably the most popular expositor of the Bible now writing in Britain" and rightly saw this volume, which deals with the trial, crucifixion, resurrection, ascension, and Lordship of Jesus, as taking us to "the heart of the life of Jesus." What it did not highlight, and what its reviewers regrettably neglected, was how forceful Willie was in stressing that Jesus' life—and therefore his mind also—was *the* expression of God's love, the center, the foundation principle of the divine word and action. Never did Willie so positively affirm the love of God as when writing of the death and resurrection of Jesus, in which *God* reconciled the world to himself. He makes explicit mention of "Love" in titles of the first six chapters, which deal with the precursors to the crucifixion, and in the following six shows how it is exemplified "once and for all." The seventh chapter elucidates the meaning of the word *Lord*, which is the culmination of that expression of love: "The word 'Lord' became a one-word creed, a one-word expression of complete devotion, a one-word expression of reverence and adoration."[19] The love that prompted that action, of which it is the astounding expression and confirmation, is now the basis on which all subsequent activity and relationships take place: we love him because he first loved us.

Had he left the matter there, his stock might well have risen to new heights across the theological board, and his acclaim might have been joyfully recognized by all parties. But he did not do so; he went on to append a seven-page excursus addressing the question of *when* the Lordship of Christ took place. Of this there is among the orthodox little doubt; the answer is writ large throughout the New Testament. Willie obviously courted controversy by implicitly suggesting that the matter was still open to debate—and he went further still by raising the issue of what he called Jesus' "unique relationship with God," which naturally plunged him once more into the old Adoptionist debate, as he freely acknowledged: "This is in fact the foundation of what is known as adoptionist Christology" (186). This led in turn to a discussion of the Virgin Birth, from which he emerged to make a statement that did more to undermine his work even among those with deep sympathy with his viewpoint than any other he had made to date:

> I do not think that we are intended to take the Virgin Birth literally. . . . I think we are clearly intended to take the story of the Virgin Birth as a parabolic, symbolic, pictorial, metaphorical method of carrying the unique relationship with God back to the very birth of Jesus. . . . (191)

It was a turning point in his career. To critics who had long harbored suspicions concerning his orthodoxy, it mattered little that Willie was in no way compromising his belief in the essence of the doctrine of incarnation per se, in the "en-manning" of God, to use Nels Ferré's expression (which Willie applauded). Indeed, Willie stated clearly just a few sentences later that "in Jesus Christ we see the very essence and being of God in human flesh" (192). To the conservatives this confession was wholly eclipsed by that more spectacular reference to the Virgin Birth as "parabolic, symbolic, pictorial, metaphorical." What he had only hinted at before as he quite properly explored the problem in his explications of the Gospels of Matthew and Luke was now set down in "imperishable print." He had stated his case, he had crossed the line, he had avowed an Adoptionist Christology, and he had thereby parted company with the historic traditions of the Christian church. The orthodox were scandalized. The tag "heretic" was not long in surfacing, and it stuck. Henceforth he was a marked man. He could not satisfy the liberals because of his "conservatism," and he could not satisfy the conservatives because of his "liberalism." And yet, in spite of it all, his books continued to sell astonishingly well, and his general popularity rose still higher—though at a price, as we shall see.

Willie's position on the creeds was both negative and positive: a vein of what David Daiches called "antisyzygy"—an ability to feel and respect mutually excluding positions—ran through him. And he had long recognized this in himself. Truth for him was more symbolic than propositional, a thing of the heart as well as of the mind. He had long sought some resolution of this sort of paradox. It came to him unexpectedly in the summer of 1960, at the very time such matters were uppermost in his mind. His "blinding-flash of illumination" occurred as he pondered Bishop Barry's contention that the creeds are the expression of the faith of the church, not that of individuals.[20] He had found the key to mental anguish and credal confession! In reciting the great creeds of the church, the individual sides with the church in its affirmations, as it were, declares his commitment to it and to its Lord; but this does not involve the individual himself in a meticulous agreement with each clause. It is not a matter of one's saying "I believe . . . " but rather "*We* believe": it is a corporate, not a personal act. Such a position is not without its problems, both on the part of the individual, who is presumed to make an *ex animo* confession in reciting the church's doctrines, and on the part of the church, which insists on exacting such a recitation. Suffice it to say here that for Willie the distinction provided the illuminating, liberating mechanism for which he had sought. Such was his modesty (perhaps we should add his myopia) that the problem this posed regarding his being an authorized teacher and leader of the church never occurred to him. After the manner of the existentialists who not infrequently ignore unassimilated reality, he was free! Herein lay a matter of meaningful significance in his thinking concerning the transcendental nature of religious truth, especially truth about God: he never believed it possible for man to know the whole truth; what he could know was limited to the symbolic, the pictorial. As he once said to Ian Cameron of *The Scottish Daily Record,* "It's better that a man gets a grip of half a truth instead of being puzzled and bewildered."[21]

Willie drew together the divergent and convergent lines of thought about Jesus throughout the whole of the New Testament in the third volume of the trilogy, *Jesus as They Saw Him.* This work must surely have greatly taxed a budget of hours and minutes already being clamored for by all manner of duties and demands, for it is in many ways larger than the preceding two volumes—in scope, in depth, and, not insignificantly, in size. *The Mind of Jesus* had run to 190 pages and *Crucified and Crowned* to 192 pages, but *Jesus as They Saw Him* required 429 pages. (The American edition combined the first two volumes under the single title *The Mind of Jesus,* but even together they did not match the length of the third volume.) In many ways the first two books are prolegomena, preparatory statements on the life of Jesus largely drawn from the Synoptic Gospels (though not, as noted, exclusively so). The third is different in two ways: first, it uses the entire New Testament material thematically; and second, just because of this, it is more systematic, more theological. It was, in fact, Willie's foremost attempt at biblical theology (four years later he would try his hand at systematic theology in his exposition of the Apostles' Creed). Comprehensiveness was his aim, and in selecting "the titles and the interpretations of Jesus which we meet in the New Testament" (strangely, he omits *Teacher, Master,* and *Rabbi,* or *rabboni*), he remained faithful to his biblical base.

548

Expansion and Counterattack

We need to look more carefully at the background to Willie's great success, for he continued to pour himself out in service at every opportunity, content to let his written work make its own mark in its own way.

The Presbytery of Glasgow congratulated Willie and ten of his fellow students in February 1958 on the semijubilee of their ordination, and Willie wrote to friends of "a veritable spate of jubilee celebrations" he had to attend in consequence. To grieving Kate it was not all gaiety and joyfulness. Willie's responsibilities continued to multiply in all directions, in Bible translation work, in preaching engagements up and down the country, in publishing contacts and committee meetings (his trips to London were now on a regular monthly basis), and at university.

In March 1958 he was appointed to a subcommittee of the Faculty of Theology to arrange a better disposition of the timetable, and on March 14 he led—in the wake of a number of rehearsals—the annual college concert, conducting the choir with his usual élan. In May he was appointed College Representative (with G. H. C. Macgregor) on the Bruce Lectureship Trust; later that month he presided over the college's end-of-term communion service. (From late 1956 on he played a larger part in the faculty proceedings.) In November, as if in recognition of the haste—and perhaps the superficiality—of his early years as lecturer, he proposed a course of open lectures for former students, which idea was "held over for more mature consideration."[22] The following year he was appointed to a special subcommittee to deal with "the large and complex questions" of University/College relationships and their mutual future. The Adult Education lectures commenced in 1959, with 120 students enrolling for the Tuesday and Thursday sessions. The following year *The British Weekly* publicized the second part of the course under the headline "All Roads Lead to Trinity Again,"[23] and such was its appeal that it was raised to constitute a three-year training program (under the direction of Dr. John Macquarrie). Following this, Willie attended (on June 27) a prize-giving ceremony at Hillhead Academy, at which he found, still enjoying full vigor and delighting over the successes of his former pupil, James "Monkey Brand" Paterson, to whom Willie owed his "love of Greek which [gave] me my life-work."[24] Three days later he participated at a similar meeting at Dalziel High School itself, his first return—"duly clad in full panoply"[25] (i.e., Edinburgh's scarlet robes)—since his matriculation thirty-three years previously. He preached in heat wave conditions before a huge congregation at Eastbourne in August on "The Significance of Endings," his text being Matthew 26:58; as always, he pointed out that ends were merely new beginnings—forward, not backward.

April 1959 saw Willie indulging one of the sporting loves of his life but little recognized by those who had been closest to him, perhaps due to the unfavorable climatic conditions of the north, which nullified so much effort: he became a member of the Scottish Cricket Union, pledging himself to support them wherever he could. In June he wrote to Ronnie Craig expressing the hope of following the national team to Dublin, but it does not appear that he managed to do so. This love of the sport was to continue throughout his life (in the spring of 1972 he even contributed to *The Journal of the Cricket Society* a fascinating piece under the title "I remember").[26] His attitude toward the game is typical. He confessed to only mediocre ability, suggesting that his school had chosen him to be secretary only as "a reward for writing letters and fixing games"—a forgivable misrepresentation of the record. It was the gentlemanly aspect he cherished, and he was unable to resist turning it into a sermon:

> There is something about Cricket. You would never say "That isn't football" in the same way as you sometimes say "That isn't cricket." . . . The greatness of Cricket lies in the ability of the players to honour the foe. That is the spirit in which not only Cricket should be played, but life should be lived.

But that very month a health warning was delivered in the uncompromising form of a "burst blood vessel,"[27] by which his preaching was abruptly stopped for six months on doctor's orders—a fact (one of several) he omitted when he wrote of his sickness-free life in *Testament of Faith*.[28] He was more expansive in his "Obiter Visa" column, in which he recorded being confined to bed and even being sedated by his doctors. There is little doubt that this setback was the result of his compulsive work schedule, excessively increased in the wake of Barbara's death. In writing to Mr. Drake of the Newcastle YMCA, he said that he had been "knocked out" by the incident, which introduced some changes to his life-style and his work style. He now employed a secretary, which enabled him even in illness to keep up his weekly average of forty letters to correspondents.[29] His diet was forcibly changed. Gone (temporarily!) was the high living, the large meals supplemented by outrageous snacks of chocolate, biscuits, and a mind-boggling consumption of cheese—all of which he naively defended as necessary to sustain him in his health-defying work schedule. Gone, too, was the alcohol and the eighty or so cigarettes per day. In their place came chicken and sole, custards and black grapes, plus a favorite indulgence (smuggled in by Jane) of bread and butter and his favorite raspberry jam! This diet, too, was turned to good account (i.e., for religious ends), for he decided to expound the seven deadly sins, among which gluttony was heartily castigated. Notwithstanding this, he continued to preach his message of temperance in all things—not total abstinence—though he did concede that fasting had its good points, even if it was only to increase the enjoyment of food and drink to come.[30] Ochaye!

By August he was in full flight again, lecturing to the Welsh National Youth Conference at Aberystwyth; once more the giddy routine of conferences, committee meetings, and travel was resumed.

Willie began 1960 by giving three addresses at the RAF Chaplains Conference at Andover, presiding at an opening communion service at Trinity College, and becoming embroiled in a lively faculty discussion on his teaching of Christian

Ethics. As we have seen, he was by no means at an end of his New Testament work, but having concluded the taxing Daily Study Bible series, he began to turn toward ethical problems again. His line in ethics was to be restricted to biblical exposition in these early years, as in *Flesh and Spirit* (on Galatians 5), and *Turning to God* (on the subject of conversion) in 1962, and *The Plain Man Looks at the Beatitudes* in 1963; it was not till later that he produced the short work *Thou Shalt Not Kill* (1967) and *Ethics in a Permissive Society* and *The Old Law and the New Law* (1972). It would be interesting to know what were his secret thoughts about Gossip's old Chair—so much the earlier passion and hope of Willie's life. John Macquarrie eventually took over the job, and Willie waved a permanent goodbye to personal preferences and ambitions.

In March *The British Weekly* reported on his extraordinary fecundity in producing books.[31] So far thirty-three had been published and six more were in process of preparation; in the thirteen years since he had taken up his academic appointment, he had managed to write an average of three books per year. Kate, Jane, and Willie took a fortnight off in April, which is to say that while they stayed at the London YMCA, the ladies enjoyed the sights and London shopping and Willie continued his relentless routine of meetings, writing, and proofreading sessions. In June the Presbytery of Glasgow sought to draw him into its work, appointing him to a small team that was to lead a three-way conference of the British Sailors Society at Leith Sailors' Home. Of this nothing has been recorded, though we do find them being welcomed to the capital with a civic reception on June 23. It was the first professional contact Willie had had with the problems of seamanship, though he may well have been reminded of his birth in one of Scotland's great ports of the past. It was at this time that he attended his last meeting of the Society of New Testament Study. His immediate successor at Renfrew, Sydney Adamson, was interested to learn how the difficulties of such a multinational group were overcome. "Oh that was easy," said Willie airily. "We all spoke Latin."[32]

It was in August 1960 that Willie's association with Howard Williams and Bloomsbury Chapel got under way. It was a meeting of like minds: both men had been raised in the great pulpit traditions of the past and both were of evangelical stock, with a passion for spreading the gospel and a sharp awareness of the changing conditions and needs of modern society. In all Willie preached a dozen or so times at this focal point of Baptist influence, the one church in London "out of all its churches I would choose to worship in."[33] Doubtless the collaboration would have continued longer, but poor health was shortly to intervene and render further contact impossible, though we shall see that Dr. Williams could well claim to have literally saved Willie's life.

From Bloomsbury he went on to Buittle Holiday Centre in the late summer to conduct a series of meetings, and in the autumn delivered his fourth academic lectureship at the missionary training complex of the Selly Oak colleges. His introduction to Selly Oak came almost certainly via John Foster, formerly of Selly Oak, but now Professor of Ecclesiastical History at Glasgow. The Joseph Smith

One of Willie's favorite pulpits: Bloomsbury Central Baptist Church in London

Memorial Lecture is not widely known, being in memory of a relatively obscure biblical scholar (it was sponsored by the Churches of Christ, whose place of training was then Overdale College, at which Smith had labored), but it could boast of a proud succession of preachers and thinkers since its foundation in 1947—such men as John S. Whale, H. H. Rowley, H. H. Farmer, W. E. Sangster, and James S. Stewart. Willie's lecture, printed separately in 1960, but later expanded into his book *Fishers of Men* (1966), could not have been more appropriate. Its subtitle was "The Life and Work of the Evangelist," and Willie pungently expounded the commission, the message, and the task of the evangelist, concluding with a call to full and careful preparation—matters that were Willie's daily meat at Trinity College. In November he held special meetings for laymen under the auspices of the British and Foreign Bible Society at Eastbourne, lecturing on "A General Introduction to the New Testament."

A few months earlier Stanley Pritchard had given him his first full-length interview in the "This Is My Job" series, as noted earlier. It was a measure of the widespread acknowledgment of Willie's work that he was chosen to speak of "his unique work as a Theological Middleman."[34] The broadcast was so successful that it was repeated twice. Commented Willie at the beginning of the program,

"When any man is really happy in his work, it is almost always true that he did not choose his work, but his work chose him. That is certainly true of me."

It was toward the end of this year that Willie received from Cecil Northcott, Editorial Secretary of the Lutterworth Press, an invitation to participate in a project designed, as the general introduction to the series eventually put it, "to present in twenty-two volumes a total view of the Bible, and to present the purpose, plan and power of the Scriptures." Looking back on the previous fourteen years of Willie's life, it would be harder to find a more adequate description than this of all the work he had already completed. True, his actual contribution to Old Testament scholarship was slight (though we should be careful not to underrate his Daily Readings of 1948–1951), but anyone familiar with his method of exposition will know how the Old Testament feeds and underpins his exegesis both historically and religiously. It was axiomatic with him that the New Testament cannot be properly understood without the Old Testament, that the coming of Christ is but the fulfillment of what was long promised and expected, and that the calling, history, and meaning of the Jewish people constituted the divine preparation for ultimate reality in the experience of mankind. So he was more than ready to throw himself into an exposition of "a total view," even as he was full of enthusiasm to present "the purpose, plan and power of the Scriptures." Of his ability to do so there was not the slightest doubt.

He was informed that he was to have the opportunity to work in harness with Professor F. F. Bruce, the recently installed Professor of Biblical Criticism and Exegesis at the University of Manchester. As we have seen, Willie had for many years admired Bruce for his scholarship and clear expositions of the gospel. They had much in common, both being of Highland stock, raised in the single-minded evangelicalism of the early twentieth century, both trained in the Scottish tradition of the classics, and both deeply involved in their respective church-life traditions. (Bruce was technically a layman, but never was there a more closely involved layman or one more widely respected in all the Protestant denominations, not least in the federated system of ministerial training that A. S. Peake had founded at Manchester.) Moreover, both were widely traveled preachers and teachers, and both used their pens indefatigably. It has to be said that Bruce is by far the better stylist, the more penetrating scholar *qua* scholar, and not so ready to go out on a limb in argumentation. He might sympathize as readily as Willie with this or that theological or grammatical nicety, but he was more careful for the halt, the blind, and the weak in such matters. Willie had no qualms about trailing his coat—or even misrepresenting his case—in the cause of Socratic enlightenment. Both had long experience in Christian journalism,[35] and they were united in their desire to publicize a total view of the Bible, along with its purpose, plan, and power, a combination of "modern knowledge . . . together with all the evangelical zeal of sound biblical expression."

The aim of the series—described as "Bible Guides"—was to provide guidance concerning the main themes of the books (or groups of books) of the Bible rather than a detailed exposition of its text. It was to be done "free from the technicalities of Biblical scholarship but . . . soundly based on all the generally accepted conclusions of modern Bible research." Further, it was to be presented "in clear, simple, straightforward English," for which the coeditors were well noted. It was to be written for "non-theologically equipped readers," though the not dissimilar needs of teachers, preachers, educators, and expositors were not to be overlooked. The coeditors sought to provide "in a handy readable compass" a reflection of the "common biblical understanding which is acceptable to all types of Christian tradition and churchmanship," and so to offer a real "contribution to biblical knowledge and interpretation in the twentieth century," for which "a world-wide constituency" was envisaged.

Professor Bruce recalls that he and Willie each submitted a list of possible contributors to Northcott, who then amended the list according to his own preference, along with the suggestions of the Abingdon Press, which was to publish the volumes in the USA in conjunction with Lutterworth.[36] The resultant list—which does not, therefore, entirely reflect the editors' preferred choices—includes such notable scholars as B. W. Anderson, George Knight, William Neil, C. L. Mitton, E. Earle Ellis, G. E. Ladd, Donald Guthrie, George Beasley Murray, and, not least, Bruce and Willie. (We should note in passing how many of these would be labeled "conservative" writers by liberals.) Willie, ever working in top gear and never slow to make eight days' work of the 168 hours in any given week, was first off the mark with a volume entitled *The Making of the Bible* (he later wrote a volume on the Letter to the Hebrews). His colleague and editor from *The Expository Times,* C. L. Mitton, followed with a volume entitled *The Good News.* John Paterson and George Knight were also published at this time, offering *The Wisdom of Israel* and *Isaiah* respectively. Professor Bruce wrote on *Paul and His Converts* (which dealt with Thessalonians and the Corinthian correspondence).

Despite the criticisms of *The Monthly Record,* Bruce's editorship of *The Evangelical Quarterly* was highly respected; he had during his tenure with that publication added breadth and excellence to its fine tradition "in Defence of the Historic Christian Faith," and he had increased its circulation. Willie's writings had consistently been generously reviewed in its pages. For example, in January 1959, in considering Willie's *The Letters to the Seven Churches,* the anonymous reviewer spoke of being "never disappointed" by his work, and lauded his "unremitting toil." But the "unlikely yoke" of the foremost teacher of the Brethren with the "resiler" of the Church of Scotland was too much for some. *The British Weekly* greeted it as a "bold" move,[37] but Harold Lindsell in his one-man, one-line "defense" of scripture, *The Battle for the Bible,* was less kind:

> What is perhaps most distressing of all is that William Barclay and F F Bruce are listed as the editors of this commentary series. That their names should be attached to a vehicle through which Enslin [one of the contributors nominated by Abingdon Press, whom Lindsell took to task for daring to propose the view that Paul was not the writer of the pastoral epistles—"deception, fraud and plain lying" in Lindsell's view] can infect others, and send forth this type of pseudo-scholarship to the detriment of men's souls, is unfortunate.[38]

Laurence Porter of Birkenhead, writing for *The Evangelical Quarterly* under the watchful eye of his editor, was more positive, not to say welcoming, suggesting that Willie "must surely have strong claims to be considered the most prolific religious writer of his generation."[39] Willie's moving epilogue "The Final Test" was particularly appreciated, as it must be by any true follower of the Reformed tradition, with its dominant note of the centrality of Jesus.

This is not the place for a digression on Reformed faith and practice, but those brought up in the emasculated Puritan/Reformed tradition of England or New England, or the sometimes equally emasculated Reformed/Scottish Presbyterian tradition, might do well to reflect on the simple fact that when the younger Cop, the son of Erasmus's doctor, decided to make "a revolutionary speech" at his inauguration as Rector at the University of Paris in 1534, he wisely invoked the help of his friend Jean Calvin, a man who really knew that all truth is God's truth. As Mann Phillips says in his very fine book *Erasmus and the Northern Renaissance*, "the result was a neat dovetailing of the *Paraclesis* [of Erasmus] and Luther's doctrine of justification by faith, and the combination surprised nobody."[40] Willie was all too readily rejected by his theological confrères in the Reformed tradition. Perhaps the great Reformer's appreciation of the humanist Erasmus should act as a check on this facile condemnation and prevent the broad-minded attitudes of the Reformers from sinking into a new form of medieval scholasticism. In fact there are some significant parallels between Erasmus and Willie, not least in their mutual appreciation of fine writing, beauteous expression, and elegant style, as well as in the strong desire they both had to make such delights available to all. In addition they shared a certain suspicion of the power wielders of the establishment, and it is perhaps from this root that most of Willie's latent (political) liberalism grew, intertwining with his theological "liberalism": in all respects he held that the worth of the individual must not be minimized or denigrated. Further, both men drank deeply at the well of Greek philosophy—of the Stoics and the Epicureans, of Socrates, Aristotle, Plato, Plutarch, Cicero, and Seneca—and saw in this great movement of mind a preparation for Christ and his gospel for the human spirit, as much as Judaism was a preparation for the religious element. In neither did this interest in Greek philosophy damage their first and abiding love for the Bible itself; rather, they put their knowledge to use in exposition, elucidation, and illustration of scripture. Jean Calvin, fresh from his break with Rome and even then working at the first edition of his *Institutes,* was serving more than the younger Cop with his dovetailing of Luther's doctrine with that of Erasmus; he was offering a conjunction of thought that has largely been ignored by the evangelical wing of the church since, but that would doubtless be exceedingly fruitful if it were to be appropriated.

One final point we must note in this respect. Willie not only possessed an appreciation of the "humanist" perspective detailed above, but managed to bind it together with a view of the world, of nature, and of the fine flowerings of the human spirit—in art and science, in literature, architecture, and sculpture, in conversation, wit, and merriment, in church, music hall, and theater—in a way that consciously challenges the rejection of such things in the name of God. It was, we may remind ourselves, a proclamation of the imperative of Philippians 4:8—"whatsoever is true, honorable, just, pure, lovely, gracious; if there is any excellence, if there is anything worthy of praise, think about these things." At the very time that he occupied himself with such things, surely and wholeheartedly, he was serving his generation in a way that may be called unique: as biblical scholar and man of the world, as man of power and man of culture, as man of God and man of the people.

Further, if we analyze Calvin carefully, we find that his *Institutes* are essentially an exposition of the Decalogue, the Apostles' Creed, the Lord's Prayer, the sacraments, and church government. The first three are absolutely basic to Willie's whole viewpoint, the actual texts on which he built his own theology and by which he structured his own doctrines. Unlike Calvin, Willie did not begin to theologize until after he had come to detailed terms with the entire New Testament (as well as much of the Old). Had the great Reformer done so before he embarked on the *Institutes* (the final edition was not completed till 1559), his views on some matters might well have been different and—dare we say it?— even closer to Willie's. And if Willie never showed much interest in church government per se, if indeed he slowly changed his understanding of it (and the process was slow—from a humble serving of it at Renfrew through to a fearless questioning of some of its aspects in Glasgow and Edinburgh), he never gave up the apostolic truth it stood for—that all things must be done decently and in order, in fellowship, not "as by law established."

All these things run directly against the emphasis of modern-day proponents of a boiled-down Calvinism who, without the learning and great-soul attitudes of the Reformer, see everything through the disfiguring lens of their own reduced world view. They are no more than modern Pharisees, in whom even laughter itself becomes a thin-lipped smile rather than manly mirth. *The Monthly Record* spoke accurately, but not well, of the distinctiveness of the Reformed faith when it stated that "it is Protestant not Roman; reformed not Lutheran; evangelical not sacerdotal; Calvinist not Arminian; Federal not Dispensational."[41] Such fractiousness was decidedly not Willie's way; he was seeking to win the world for God not reject it, seeking to be positive not negative, inclusive not exclusive.

The Plain Man's Servant

Stanley Pritchard's interview with Willie of 1960—if we may allow it to stand *simpliciter,* allowing for his modesty and self-denigrating habits—demonstrated Willie's twofold understanding of his own work: "I began to see that I never could be a great technical scholar. . . . I began to be more and more conscious of the wide gap between . . . the work of theological experts and the man in the street. . . . The problem of communication began to be the problem which came first in my thoughts." It reminds one of Erasmus's own hopes, which also fathered—and this is what we claim for Willie's work—a great popular interest in the scriptures:

> I wish that all women might read the Gospel and the Epistles of Paul. I wish that they might be translated into all tongues of all people, so that not only the Scots and Irish, but also the Turk and the Saracen might read and understand. I wish the countryman might sing them at his plough, the weaver chant them at his loom, the traveller beguile with them the weariness of his journey.[42]

It was Willie's hope as well. Like Wesley, he now looked on the world as his parish. And he worked accordingly.

The present century has been called the century of the ordinary man. Never has he been so much at the center of society's interests; never have so many of his number been able to play their part, seek the truth, or speak their minds so publicly. The era has produced innumerable guides, introductions, exposes, and the like in conjunction with a level of research beyond precedent. Sidney Webb once asked Beatrice Potter, "How can John Stuart Mill fear that life will become uninteresting? To play on these millions of minds, to watch them slowly respond to an unseen stimulus, to guide their aspirations, often without their knowledge, all this whether higher capacities or humble, is a big endless game of chess, of ever extravagant excitement."[43] To be sure, Willie's approach was to be more serious, motivated by service and not self-interest, but it was to revel equally in the diversity of humankind and the sheer challenge of the declining popularity of religion. Said Wesley, "I desire plain truth for plain people," and a century and a half later D. S. Cairns saw the need for the theologian to preach the gospel in relation to "plain human needs, if he is to be a good theologian at all."[44] Samuel Mucklebacket (a pseudonym of the journalist-writer James Lumsden) expressed the need perfectly at the end of the last century when he wrote, "Mind, I want nane o' yer lang, interminable, wearisome yarns. Brek the shell o' yer tale affhand, and hand me the kernel precise an' concise as the yowk o' an hen's egg."[45] And a young contemporary of Lumsden, destined to become a great journalist himself and a setter of trends in the art of popularization, W. R. Nicoll, stated that "It is a great mistake for Westcott to think he has nothing to learn from Spurgeon. . . . The fact is that the Spurgeonic type of preaching is the only kind that moves democracy."[46] As H. R. Lottmann says in his brilliant biography *Albert Camus,* "it is sometimes advantageous to art to descend from its ivory tower, and believe that the sense of beauty is inseparable from a certain sense of humanity."[47] Such characters as the Radio Doctor in medicine, Alan Gemmell in horticulture, Patrick Moore in astrology, Robert Mackenzie in politics, Bill Thomas in law, and Mortimer Wheeler in archaeology were all to engage in such work. And, of course, Willie also set his hand to it, in the things that matter most.

Already Willie had begun his extraordinary popularizing work in daily Bible readings for all ages, in instruction manuals for young people, and in the more technical discussions—which were to increase in numbers rapidly through the next nine years—of the textual and translation panels of the British and Foreign

Bible Society and the NEB committees, a process that was to culminate in his own translation of the entire New Testament (this being the second and definitive aspect of such translation work, the first having already been printed in his *Daily Study Bible*)—and most notably in his *British Weekly* articles since 1953, which laid the foundation of that which was to follow. Now another venture was afoot, through the good offices of Lady Collins, wife of the international publisher, who took a strong personal interest in developing the religious book side of her husband's business.

The first the public heard of this was through the advertising of *The Plain Man's Book of Prayers,* a slim paperback volume of some 120 pages. Characteristically, the book includes not only Willie's selection of Bible readings for the thirty days around which the book is built (plus special prayers for four Sundays, festival days, and special occasions in the home—ever the focal point of Willie's religious fervor), but a specially compiled list of Bible readings by William Somerville for a complete year. In a long, fourteen-page introductory essay, Willie outlines his understanding of prayer as a natural activity of man that requires certain techniques if it is to be fully understood and enjoyed. The basic fact of all prayer, Willie asserts, is that "God is even more ready to listen than we are to speak to Him, and even more ready to give than we are to ask." He lays down (and illustrates) certain "laws of prayer":

1. We must be honest in prayer
2. We must be very definite in prayer
3. There can be no real prayer without self-examination
4. God cannot grant a selfish request
5. God always knows best
6. God will not do for us that which we can do for ourselves
7. Prayer moves within the natural laws which govern life

A great deal of Willie's theology is encapsulated in these seven "laws," which significantly contain only two negatives: Willie's viewpoint was always positive, ever seeing the stars, ever thrusting toward the possible. Following this he outlines the "five great divisions of prayer": invocation, confession, thanksgiving, petition, and intercession, adding that inasmuch as prayer is a *natural* activity of man, "there is no special language in which to pray." "God is not looking for perfect English style or even for perfect grammar. . . . All that God wants is that we should speak to Him."

There is nothing precious about Willie's prayers, in keeping with his usual style and approach. He acclaims the writings of such men as Hallesby, Peter Marshall, and even Andrew Murray, the "patron saint" of the Keswick movement. But there is nevertheless a wider vista, a more human touch, in Willie's prayers: he is deeply in sympathy with human weakness, never "above" it, as is the Great High Priest himself. The prayers significantly appear in the form of free verse. It is as if he were finding in the prayers an outlet for the sort of literary expression he suppressed by altering his course from English Literature. Like Burns's poetry, they encompass life.

He specifically rules out the necessity of using biblical or prayer-book language, of using *Thee* and *Thou* in reference to God, for instance (though in point of fact he himself does so throughout the book and never felt the need to have it revised). His understanding of prayer here is essentially private; the book was after all designed for home use, and familial aspects are not neglected. And we should note that external things such as posture do not figure, much less aids, mechanical or otherwise. "God," he says in reaching the core of his understanding of prayer, "is our friend. . . . Our friendship with God should be a daily and a constant thing"—as it was for the writer himself. But even this is not the end of the matter, and so he comes to "the most important thing of all":

> Prayer is not a monologue in which we do all the talking; prayer is listening even more than it is talking. The highest form of prayer is silence when we wait on God and listen to God. . . . Prayer is a way of offering ourselves to God in order that He should be able to make use of us. . . . We linger in His presence for His peace and prayer to flow over us and around us; we lean back in His everlasting arms and feel the serenity of perfect security in Him.[48]

If anyone wants to know why this book became Willie's all-time best-seller (by the time he was "knocked out" again, in 1969, it had gone through eleven reprints and sold in excess of three hundred thousand copies), the answer surely lies in the profundity of these three statements of prayer's deepest reality, aspects of Willie's deepest, most personal experience. For all his industry of study, for all his extrovert activity, he was essentially a man of the secret place, a man who walked with God. His world of silence, imposed by the childhood illness that damaged his hearing, cloistered him like a mobile sanctuary, making solitude an ever-present experience from which he emerged to work and write, to teach and preach.

The response of the public as well as the reviewers was one of intense admiration and gratitude, as it had been when these prayers were originally published in *The British Weekly*. The "plain man" label, so important in Willie's career, had made a notable breakthrough. But it is a mistake to credit Willie with this title. He had explicitly welcomed the concept of "plainness" when he reviewed Williams's translation of the New Testament, *A New Testament in Plain English*, in February 1953 (this translation rested on the Interim Report on Vocabulary Selection of 1936), in which Willie praised the Authorized Version's prose fulsomely: "no plainer English . . . pure Anglo-Saxon." Three years after this William Neil had published his book *The Plain Man Looks at the Bible*, which, meeting the appetite of people at the time for such things, enjoyed great success. In the preface to this work, Neil specifically addressed the problem of technical religious language in communication, pointing out how he had sought to replace it with "ordinary language" that was free from jargon and unnecessary technicalities.

But even William Neil was not pioneering the use of the "plain man" designation with his book's title. Before him stood a long line of distinguished writers who were all concerned with the same problem—the plain man's under-standing, needs, and hopes. (It ought to be noted that in American usage the phrase "the plain man" has some negative connotations foreign to British usage: accordingly, Willie's American publishers substituted the word *everyman* for *plainman:* the title became *Everyman's Book of Prayers,* and so on—a phrase that happily coincides with the biblical "whosoever," which in turn admirably suits Willie's evangelical predisposition.) Leslie Weatherhead, for instance, a man who certainly influenced Willie directly in his early period, not least with his "iron rations" doctrine and the relatively new application of psychology to pastoral studies, published *A Plain Man Looks at the Cross* in 1945. And four years before this Lindsay Martin had published *A Plain Man's Life of Christ,* which Willie, a loyal Religious Book Club member, found useful in working among the troops at Renfrew. It was this book that Sydney Cave commended for "its happy combina-tion of true scholarship and simplicity . . . its mellow wisdom and freedom from mere pedantry. . . . It is written with knowledge and insight . . . with reverence and imagination."[49] Of special interest to us is Martin's view that the picture of Jesus presented by the Synoptic Gospels, as opposed to the more mystical comprehension of John, is precisely the one the plain, wayfaring man awaits. He does not want explanation, Martin argues, so much as description; he does not want interpretation so much as the actual events.

And before Martin there was Alec Vidler, "theological midwife," as he called himself, to thousands, who had published his own *Plain Man's Guide to Christian-ity* in 1936 in response to countless requests after the delivery of his addresses to the young men and women of Cambridge. Vidler's style is always lucid and memorable, presenting a middle way between Catholic and evangelical doctrine (though he was a staunch liberal Catholic himself). We may note that the "plain man" approach arose out of a liberal ethos, in which churchmanship was closely anchored to life and parish serving—in the tradition of Charles Gore, Bishop Headlam, and Father Joe. Significantly, one of the most influential publishers of this type of theology has been A. R. Mowbrays of Oxford, which produced the earliest "plain man" title ever published—B. W. Randolph's *The Plain Man's Book of Religion* (1919). In all truth Randolph, the former Canon of Ely, had a somewhat different emphasis from his successors, as we should expect from a middle-class Victorian. He does not bother to define his intent or explain his approach in any way, and his attitude is much more propositional than that of his followers, almost catechetical in fact. But at least the attempt was made and the trend was established, in the very year Willie dedicated himself in far-off Fort William to the work of the ministry. When Mowbrays published Willie's autobiography in 1975 as a genuine "testament of faith," the full circle was drawn.[50] And of course there was the posthumously published volume of A. S. Peake's causeries, *Plain Thoughts on Great Subjects.* It was Peake's conviction that his first duty was "to make the assured results of religious scholarship plain to the man in the street." Twentieth-century popularization really began with A. S. Peake—Willie's great example.

Willie did not lamely follow popularizing predecessors, but, as ever, thought the problem through himself, eliminating the technical (and pietistic) jargon, increasing the emphasis on God's Fatherhood and Jesus' elder-brotherly love (chief aspects of the liberal inheritance), 'shortening the sentences, boiling the language down from polysyllabic to monosyllabic words wherever possible (though this strategy should not be overstressed, for he continued to enjoy his educative role enormously), and above all reintroducing a narrative emphasis while heightening the interest of the story with verbal pictures drawn with bold strokes and a Churchillian sense of color. To this cause he rendered his great scholarship and his powers of research (as illustrated in his *Educational Ideals in the Ancient World*) subservient. Like Paul of old, he was ready to be counted a fool for Christ's sake.

And so commenced a distinguished sequence of books drawn from his journalistic activity in *The British Weekly* and all reflective of its style and approach. In 1962 *More Prayers for the Plain Man* appeared, "written in the same way, and . . . intended to be used in the same way, as the first volume"[51]— although, he added, "there are certain differences": the prayers are slightly longer (as became prayers for his now experienced readers!), he provides prayers for a period of forty days rather than thirty, and there is a greater recognition of "special occasion" prayers and, indeed, of differing moods and feelings. By no means least among Willie's offerings are his "Prayers for Different Occupations" (he provides an intriguing list of thirty-six jobs, paid and voluntary) and "A Prayer for Animals." By this time he has replaced the *Thee* and *Thou* of his upbringing with the more popular *you* and *your;* in doing so he was well in advance of his contemporaries in both public and ministerial training contexts. "Life would be very different," Willie asserted, "if each one of us could take the whole of life to the whole of God"; it was something he himself did unfailingly.

Once again he included in addition to his explanatory foreword an essay on prayer. This essay, entitled "When We Pray," develops an essential aspect of Willie's approach to religion and theology, namely, his determination not to overturn man's humanity or make of it a spurious, pretentious existence divorced from God and his work in Christ. The ghetto syndrome of pietistic evangelicalism, a rejection of the world and even of one's own physicality, is always a temptation to ardent souls aware of the sullying potential of the bodily and secular aspects of man's existence. Willie, like Paul, was not only conscious of the impossibility of avoiding such things, but was intent on asserting their reality—and winning them for Christ. It is a deep and penetrating aspect of his understanding of the incarnation, wherein he joins William Temple in perceiving a sacramental universe, in which the numinous—the disquieting experience of Someone Other, greater and more powerful than man—complements his experience of God's fatherly care. Following the Reformation, it was Blaise Pascal who first sought to harness the natural order and stress the duality of man's nature—*ni ange ni bête*—as Erasmus had in his own way beforehand. It is an emphasis that men ignore only at their peril, as succeeding generations have shown.

God could never be for Willie the aloof God of the Deists, the far-off God of those who understood him merely as the Wholly Other, still less "the ground of being," "the ultimate reality" of Paul Tillich and the philosopher-theologians. When David Edwards gave Willie an advance copy of *Honest to God,* Willie said that he agreed with much of it, despite the fact that he would never have written such things himself: what he welcomed was the "new stirring in English [and Scottish!] Christianity," a new spirit of adventure for Christ, a determination to return to the roots of the gospel. God is, in fact, our Father, our Friend—and, says Willie, using the words of Dr. Johnson, "a man should keep his friendships in good repair." And so in his prefatory essay he presents seven pages of exhortation to prayer in this light: ceaseless and regular prayer, universal, all-consuming prayer, in hope and with trust, for strength to bear and not flee life's difficulties, friendly and unselfish prayer—the sort of prayer that made William Barclay the man he was.

His third "plain man" book was very different. Appearing in 1963, *The Plain Man Looks at the Beatitudes* put into printed form the sermons and lectures of many years, from the earliest Renfrew days to more recent work at the University of Glasgow. As with his book on the parables of Jesus, the material originated in quite varied constituencies, and was honed further by being printed serially in *The Preacher's Quarterly* during 1961.

We have noted repeatedly Willie's close concern with behavior and ethics. This is his first book on the subject, though it is characteristically attached to a biblical pattern and text (just as he had conversely found a place for the ethical in all his previous books that dealt principally with scripture). Just how strongly he felt about the subject may be seen in his reference to the Beatitudes as "the essence of the essence of the Christian way of life . . . the very essence of what [Jesus] came to say."[52] The section of Matthew in which the Beatitudes are found he describes as "the central document of the Christian faith." We should note that his is a quite deliberate reemphasis of Reformed doctrine, in which the attitude "all is of God" predominates. It is this emphasis that earned him—unfairly in my view—his "Pelagian" reputation; he was never closer to Denney. And he was boldly assertive of the Spirit's help and stimulus. He does not quarrel with Reformed tradition in its emphasis on good conduct, but he does part company with those who view it as a secondary, reflexive aspect of Christian faith. His call to discipleship demanded discipline and commitment and lacked the "mysticism" of his evangelical roots, which sought provision for the good life by the indwelling Spirit of Christ alone. Moreover, he emphasized that this call to discipleship was itself *good news,* hence his translation of *makarios* ("blessed") as "O the bliss of . . ."—a bliss that was "nothing less than the blessedness of God . . . the bliss of the life of God."

There is something very profound here and it is frequently misunderstood; its elucidation requires more space than is presently available. Suffice it to say that Willie does not overthrow the New Testament and Reformed doctrines of new birth, regeneration, or justification by faith—a fact that can be verified from his commentaries on John, Romans, and other sources of the doctrines. It is untruthful to argue that he does. The very year he so boldly stated his case for this "paramount emphasis" on conduct was the year in which he published *Turning to God: A Study of Conversion in the Book of Acts and Today.*

We should note that he commences his study of conversion with an exposition of the classic text 2 Corinthians 5:17, so totally assertive of new life in Christ, and that he goes on by way of preface to quote from J. C. Pollock's *Moody without Sankey*.[53] But whereas traditional evangelicalism (save for the Wesleyan tradition) has been content to see in the decision-making process a work exclusive to God, Willie was equally emphatic in contending that it is a work that also involves man's freedom, willingness, and obedience. The *cooperative* view that we see propounded in his doctrine of inspiration thus reemerges in a quite different context but one that nevertheless has this link: behind both situations—revelation and renewed relationships—God, ever sovereign, ever taking the initiative, cannot act except when man is willing to meet that act with due response; in other words (and Willie felt this very strongly), he remains deliberately in touch with a fundamental aspect of morality, namely, that moral acts are worthless unless they are voluntary expressions of man's will. This is all too easily overlooked by some who seek to emphasize divine grace and goodness. The gentle renewal of man's shattered conscience and will is no less a sign of the grace of God than the stunning re-creation of a Damascus Road experience; and we cannot omit that for such as the young ruler, to whom even Jesus felt attracted, the injunction was one of social application, not merely spiritual renewal.

Willie takes that fundamental principle one step further when he argues (implicitly, as far as I can trace) that the expression of that act of free will itself empowers further reform and new life. In other words, he has not rejected God's sovereign, gracious acts (indeed, he praises them repeatedly and emphatically in his books and sermons), but he takes their operation back one step, to the enlightenment of mind and conscience, to the point at which God says "I will if . . . ," to which the disciple must respond—joyfully or reluctantly—"yes"! And Willie owns this as the work of the Holy Spirit: "The man whose heart has been cleansed in Jesus and by the Spirit of God . . . will be given nothing less than the vision of God."[54]

In many ways this book on the Beatitudes could be said to be a climax in the life and teaching of William Barclay, but it stands only at the commencement of the "plain man" series. In the following year (1964) he published *The Plain Man Looks at the Lord's Prayer*, another collection of his articles in *The Preacher's Quarterly*. Once again he supplied a long introductory discussion of the nature of prayer, in which Jewish forms and formality provide the springboard to his own personal and homely insights. Central to this work is Willie's emphasis on Jesus' new designation of God as *Abba*, "Daddy"—not that Willie advocated our use of the term—elsewhere a usage he deprecated as "bizarre"—but he did teach that our attitude should take note of God's fatherly love and care, that our actions be found worthy of the word. In *The British Weekly* he defended—in response to the heaps of letters that came in—this "modern" attitude (it was, after all, just this attitude that led to Jesus' being crucified at the hands of the outraged Pharisees and priests) on the grounds that religion must be up-to-date in speech, since clinging to archaisms is exclusivist behavior, self-indulgent and selfish, the very antithesis of Christianity's inner meaning and reality.[55] Willie's emphasis encouraged an outgoing activity, not an introverted, self-serving mentality: "And so, when we have prayed the Lord's Prayer, we rise from our knees *and go out.*" He who had little time for what he dismissed in Glover's phrase as a "balcony mind" must necessarily apply the language of an activist, a participator.

He went on to produce yet more "plain man" books—on the Apostles' Creed (in 1967) and on ethics (in 1973), to which we shall return. But it must be noted that he also wrote other books of the same genre and with the same objective that did not carry that designation in the title. Indeed, from 1962 to his death in 1978, his pen was busy almost exclusively with the "plain man" theme. Such titles as *Many Witnesses, One Lord, The All-Sufficient Christ, Prayers for the Christian Year, A New People's Life of Jesus, Fishers of Men, Seen in the Passing,* and *Prayers for Help and Healing,* to name only those that appeared before 1968, all belong to this category. As the editor of *The British Weekly* said of him, "He is known far and wide, indeed all round the world now, for his exposition of Scripture. It is a great service he is rendering."

Professing the Faith through Difficulties

The '60s were already beginning to shift and seethe, and Willie was caught up in the atmosphere of change. It was about this time that the theory of continental drift was being recognized in geophysics; it was an appropriate symbol for what was going on in the religious sphere as well, though some felt more cataclysmic language was called for. As far back as 1948 Paul Tillich had published his influential book *The Shaking of the Foundations,* the aftershocks of which were now being felt more clearly. The foundations were shaking in several key areas, not only in intellectual issues of existence and meaning, but also in industry, medicine, psychology, and sociology. And things began to change politically too. Hugh Gaitskell died, and Harold Wilson became Leader of the Labour Party, quickly achieving great popularity, largely for stressing the importance of the new technology and the management systems necessary for "the new society." A golden age of science was forecast, and "technological man" emerged. The consequent need for more scientists and technicians, the need for better training in new and enlarged universities and technical colleges, and the need to modernize industry and acclimate society to such changes, were having a great influence on academic life, ministerial training included, and so they inevitably began to influence Willie directly. Modern men were needed for modern society, modern ministers for modern needs.

Just how much change was taking place may well have been brought home to Willie by his recollection that 1964 actually marked the centenary of his father's birth. It was also the year in which Willie, had he chosen to serve in the armed forces after the tradition of so many of his fellow Highlanders, would have started enjoying retirement. No such thought had entered his head, of course; he had soldiered on in another, greater cause, still serving under his chief, G. H. C. Macgregor, to whom, as "a man of prayer," he dedicated his book *The Plain Man*

Looks at the Lord's Prayer. As if to emphasize the passage of time, Rebecca—who had joined the Barclays at Motherwell as a young girl and who had since become the respected Head of Domestic Affairs (i.e., house matron) in a large Glasgow hospital—announced her own retirement. She was the elder sister Willie never had, and this was sobering news. Work was now almost his exclusive preoccupation. "I happen to be practically completely deaf," he wrote in his "Obiter Visa" column. "I can sleep anywhere, work anywhere, and shut myself off in boring committee meetings."[56] He did all three at "lovely St. Andrews," at a summer conference for day-school teachers, enjoying any amount of good talk, some excursions to local beauty spots, and "fun in plenty," all the while "learning about the Bible, the Christian faith." They were "one hundred and eighty learners together, of all ages, from all over the world."[57] He admitted he was "no good about the house," confessing that this was "not because I am handless and cannot do things [a comment he was later forced to contradict in his auto-biography, as we saw] but I just don't do them—I am so busy." However, at this time he did make use of the fruits of modern technology by learning the art of house painting (their kitchen) with the newly introduced nondrip paint. "Technique is everything," he commented, turning even that experience into a lesson of life.[58] Domesticated or not, he was not prevented from proudly greeting his first granddaughter, Jill, in the autumn of that year, although the joy of the event was tempered by her poor health, which gave them all several weeks of anxious waiting and caring. His lot was to suffer, even at this joyous point.

Writing, lecturing, preaching, more writing, attending committee meetings of various sorts, marking essays and papers, and yet more writing—even on Saturday evenings after speaking at rallies and conferences—was his merciless routine. He was a special favorite at conferences and house parties, where his humanity could express itself at least as clearly as his divinity. For example, in April he met with sixty other ministers at Glasgow to rally for nuclear dis-armament, at which time he delivered a speech entitled "The Church's Choice—Faith or Obliteration?" It was a stinging attack on the madness of nuclear arms, with Willie posing the choice between so-called prudence (the counterattack principle) or "risking everything on the adventure of being *fully* Christian."[59] As before the war, it was either/or: full-blooded Christianity or a pale shadow of it. And any campaign that called for nuclear disarmament, Willie declared, was foredoomed to failure without an equal campaign for the revitali-zation of the church and the full commitment of its members. Their aim was to form a new world; it could only be done on *spiritual*—not social, still less political—principles. In November he attended his second conference on the same theme, concluding it with an all-night vigil at the Cenotaph. Here also his speech caused a furor, and *The British Weekly* took up his blunt comment that "you can't defend a Christian civilization by war."[60] He was reasserting the antiwar principles of 1939 even more publicly, and receiving a more concerted rejoinder. He was now regarded as a dangerous influence, linked in some people's minds with such left-wing figures as Bertrand Russell, Michael Foot, and

Willie in a typical lecturing stance. The worn cover of the preaching case given him by his mother is just visible on the lectern. [Photo courtesy of the BBC]

Donald Soper. In presenting his case, Willie was typically pugnacious: "Can you imagine Jesus pulling the switch that will set off the Bomb?" he demanded. "Great Britain showed the way to Democracy; perhaps now she should show the way to Theocracy."

At a less provocative but no less enthusiastic gathering at Scarborough in mid June, he was the main speaker and chaplain at the sixty-fourth Annual Conference of Secretaries of the YMCA. There were five hundred of them present. He lectured on the general subject of "God and His Church" to their great delight—and to Willie's also, as he once more discovered his roots and the invigorating fellowship of his youth. On the third day he daringly spoke on the subject of the YMCA in the '60s, roundly reminding the secretaries of their organization's original spiritual motives and objectives. The impact was such that he was invited to return the following year, 1962, and again in 1974, thus creating a precedent. No one before this had been given three invitations to speak at their conferences; a fourth was to follow.

At the end of June he attended the Baptist Lay Preachers and Pastors Conference at Oxford, thus regaining direct contact with another group who had encouraged his early efforts at Motherwell nearly forty years previously. The weather was stifling hot, but this did not prevent Willie from entrancing his audience with masterly outlines of the gospel as seen through the eyes of Paul, John, and the unknown writer of Hebrews. As usual, these sessions were followed by question-and-answer sessions, where Willie was in his element, answering knotty questions with his own brand of humor and audacity. The secretary of the association, John Hough, was on one occasion somewhat disconcerted to find him off-duty, dressed only in his vest and trousers, but still typing away as if his life depended on finishing his script. They went together to Blackwells, the booksellers, and once again Mr. Hough was surprised—this time at the huge quantity of books Willie bought, and the commensurate invoice he got for them.[61]

In July he was main speaker at the fourth lay preachers' conference of the Presbyterian Church in England (now part of the United Reformed Church) at Cambridge. Thus he visited, within the space of four weeks, the two most prestigious university towns for two major denominations. Here again he treated of the differing slants of the New Testament writers, speaking on the theme "The Gospel and the New Testament: Many Ways to God," a very Barclayan emphasis. He reiterated the often-quoted lines "there are as many ways to the stars as there are men to climb them," which he unfailingly geared to Christ himself.

It was a time of opportunity, and two new opportunities presented themselves on his return from holidays in the south (via Broadstairs, where he was delighted to stay in the hotel where Dickens had written much of *Nicholas Nickleby*). The attitude in which he approached the winter's work was summed up in one of his causeries entitled "Fire."[62] Said he, "I am never tired of pleading for sermons which teach, but I am equally aware that light without heat is largely ineffective." He appealed for both light and heat, to the fundamentalist and liberal respectively. His first new opportunity was heralded in headlines in *The British Weekly*: "All Roads Lead to Trinity Again. Lay Training Course Resumes." Willie was to be indirectly involved in this third and final year of lay training, offering "some extra Talks on the Bible on Tuesdays during both terms."[63]

Adult Christian Education—the sort A. S. Peake had pioneered at Manchester over fifty years previously (it was already a renowned center of secular Adult Education)—was also the point of another series of lectures Willie undertook in November and December, in which he broke new ground in a splendid way. This second opportunity involved a series of broadcast talks in the tradition of C. H. Dodd and C. S. Lewis that appears to have grown out of his Trinity College lectures and was in fact recorded at Trinity College. It was arranged in cooperation with the General Assembly of the Church of Scotland and was scheduled to be broadcast on Sunday evenings, in the Scottish Home Service. There were to be five talks: "Why Read the Bible?" "What Do We Mean When We Say That the Bible Is the Word of God?" "Bringing the Dictionary to the Bible," "Bringing History to the Bible," and, by way of summation, "Finding the Faith in the Bible."

It made such an impression on Ronnie Falconer that he became determined to convert Willie into a television personality, although Willie had already rejected such invitations several times—twice a year in fact over the past few years.[64] Clearly better means of persuasion were called for. It was Kate who had the key, who knew the location of Willie's Achilles' heel, and she shot her arrow with consummate feminine skill: she called him a coward! She knew full well that nothing was more likely to precipitate his acceptance of the challenge than that affront to his manliness. And so he wrote to Falconer, and the arrangements were put under way. He made one request, that some of his students be with him for the recording, which took place in the old Springfield Road studios in Glasgow, the former buildings of the Black Cat Cinema. "Many a person will have a pleased feeling when a black cat crosses his path," he had written in 1955.[65] He was not superstitious himself, but he did have a very pleased feeling once the terror had subsided and the event was over!

So much was he pleased in fact that he declared this work (including radio broadcasting) to be "the most important thing I have done."[66] Part of the reason for his enthusiasm was that he counted himself among those "who have always been haunted by the people outside"[67]—as his work at Renfrew, in the open air, among the soldiers, and the unchurched youth of the Boys' Brigade and the YMCA testifies—and the mass media gave him a better opportunity to reach out to them. (In this sense it could be inferred that his universitiy teaching had doubly checked his real career, by diverting him from his ambitions to teach practical theology and by diverting him toward an academic role.) He gives his one-sentence advice to would-be broadcasters and televisers—"Never underrate your audience"—but immediately feels the need to expand the thought into a complete paragraph:

> Nothing less than the best will do. The person who is going to listen does not want pleasant little talks or souped up children's sermons. He wants to know what the Bible is saying, and what religion is all about. The broadcaster must speak as a thinking man to thinking men.[68]

It was in 1962 that technology took a leap forward as Telstar relayed the first trans-Atlantic television pictures to Great Britain. Willie's breakthrough was on a lesser scale, but a breakthrough it nonetheless was. For the next eight years, as Falconer has recorded, he dominated the Scottish, Australian, and New Zealand television screens in religious matters.[69] His series on the Beatitudes was shown no fewer than three times in each state in Australia; the talks were recognized by the Supervisor of Religious Broadcasts as "the best things we had ever put on." The Australians were faring better than the English audiences, whose viewing was restricted to stereotypes of approach and accent despite a breakthrough in radio broadcasting. Falconer reminds his readers that the eight broadcasts were "all centred upon the New Testament."[70]

It was not an unqualified success, however, this first venture into television work. "The viewers loved Barclay," Falconer tells us, "but the students merely

irritated them. 'Get rid of them' was the common demand." And so the format
changed; Willie alone remained in the studio, and ordinary people responded to
the questions he raised. This change was well received, but still the viewers
"demanded Barclay on his own, with a free rein to get on with his job."[71] So back
to Trinity College the broadcast team went, and Willie began addressing his
audience "in full flight"—in his chalky-white gown, blackboard at his elbow,
walking up and down and every now and then turning a page of his script over,
as if he were reading it. This format defied all the rules—he was a talking head
delivering a monologue with a Clydeside accent (as many supposed it to be) and
a harsh, guttural voice, talking fast, and technically too! Even so, Willie did for
religion at zero-cost what Bronowsky later did for evolution and Clark for civilization at enormous cost, with teams of researchers, writers, programmers, and
the like. Willie did it by himself, "the great master" of his art, as Falconer
accurately described him.

The great majority of the audience for these broadcasts was composed of
"the ordinary man and his wife . . . , [who] is socially, industrially, and politically,
very much more important in this last quarter of the twentieth century. . . . The
future of our country," Falconer suggests, "is in his hands." And it was this

The great communicator faces the camera [Photo courtesy of the BBC]

ordinary man that Willie reached. He worked hard to do so; he refined his craft. The experience of the "plain man" books—an ongoing experience, to be sure—was still with him, ever haunting him. "A broadcaster . . . must always work hard to hold attention," he stated. "He should always remember that he is at the mercy of a switch. . . . It is his job to ensure that the viewer or listener does not use it." Several years later he was even moved to predict (overturning a previous conviction) "that the future of religion lies with broadcasting. . . . A Church of the air is not an impossible dream."[72]

The last prediction, of course, was heresy. It outraged some of his ministerial colleagues who were out of touch (as were many of their congregations) with what was being done. They were then enjoying the "hymn sandwich" together in sparsely filled pews and churches, hard-pressed by financial needs and shrinking congregations, talking to the converted about how to win the absentees to their rigid modes and forms. Their vision was blocked by the system, which drained their resources and kept the churches in chains. It has to be said that Willie himself did not yet in the early '60s have the perspective he later developed. Having watched a television service in a friend's house (at that time they had no set of their own), he declared that "no broadcast or television service can ever be a substitute for a service in church,"[73] citing the need for personal involvement in a congregation, the importance of direct preaching, and the benefits of the spirit of camaraderie that congregational worship fosters—which he favorably compared with that of a football crowd! But his mind was ever flexible, ever open to the need to rethink, especially on matters of pure strategy.

The seeds were there, and if Willie was slow to recognize the dangers (from the establishment point of view), his colleagues were not. They sought to frustrate his attempts to reach the "unchurched masses" that were haunting him. As Falconer has noted, the views of his fellow ministers "were hostile, on the whole." Falconer himself was attacked for letting loose "this sentimentalist, this wishy-washy liberal" on the air waves; and, he concedes,

> it was ever thus. . . . His brethren were ungenerous and derogatory. Call it professional jealousy or what you will, this was one of the hardest facts I had to stomach in my work. . . . It took five years of brilliant communication before parish ministers at last recognized that he was an immense ally to their cause.[74]

Here was no small problem. By and large, Willie's colleagues tended to look upon "this ministry business" as *their* cause. Willie did not so regard it, and was therefore open in his attitudes, flexible in his methods, and willing to be used in whichever way the winds of the Spirit blew. And he suffered over "the envy which provides the mud that failure throws at success." "I never knew what hatred was," he admitted in his autobiography, "until I began to teach."[75] It was not only the fundamentalists or the conservatives who railed at him. He found the silence of his fellow academics hardest to bear; after all, they were the more enlightened ones. On more than one occasion he commented that the only people not to speak of his broadcasting or writing were his colleagues at the

University. Twice in 1961 he had written on the subject of criticism,[76] but now he was beginning to feel its full force himself. It was not till the '70s that he began to hit back, very gently and with not a little sadness, and only in order to defend his teaching, not himself. Beyond the criticism, beyond the ecstasy of the media men, lay "the real people," to whom Willie directed his words, as if personally. His broadcasting involved him in a further huge correspondence and brought home to him the startling realities beyond the hubbub: a widowed lady, a homesick girl, a broken man, a defeated youth—and so much more.

The routine of daily travel to university now had to be modified to include escorting Jane, who had recently commenced at the prestigious Park School "amidst tears and lamentations." His work at the University still mattered greatly to him, training his young men for "a learning ministry," a process in which both lecturer and student learned together. He was quick to say that "teaching has always been a joy," although he admitted it was "no easy task"; the sheer diversity of his students' aptitudes and talents posed great problems. He tells us, quite apart from the concern he admitted to in Pritchard's interview in 1960, that such work presents two opposite dangers—that of being "too detailed, too academic, too arid," and that of painting "with too big a brush"; he had sought to find "the happy medium between too much and too little."[77] (The range of abilities possessed by incoming students had begun to widen recently, to the point that a Licentiate in Theology award for nondegree students had to be introduced.) And there was another difficulty he encountered: it was becoming harder to find a balance between the task of providing information and the task of stimulating—even compelling—his students to think. The responsibilities were increasingly heavy upon him, due to Macgregor's failing health.

We should not lose sight in all this of Willie's other interests, which he continued to pursue undaunted, nor of the historical setting in which he worked. Generally, it was a time of great dynamism, when the fruits of modern technology—in the home, at school, and at the place of work—were reaching everyone, not least through television (still black and white, of course). This dynamism was seen in religious circles, too, though the divisions among Christian people, despite all the talk about ecumenicity, were all too obvious. In Willie's own Church of Scotland there was great concern over the question of baptism. The General Assembly received and debated a report on the divisive subject at its Assembly in May. It was but one controversy among many, including issues of the relevance of the Westminster Confession of Faith, the role of women in the church, and, not least, the divinity of Christ and the infallibility of the scriptures. In 1962 The New Bible Dictionary was published—"a landmark in the development of evangelical scholarship," according to Laurence Porter[78]—with which came of age the Tyndale Press and, it may be claimed, conservative scholarship.

In all of this Willie was found to be a lively participant. His series on the Apostles' Creed began to make waves, thanks to an advertising campaign that outdid even those for his books. He enjoyed his access to growing constituencies—in *The British Weekly*, in his books, in lectures and conference involvements—and the chance to stimulate people to think adventurously. Miss McCulloch, one of his part-time students in the sparsely attended Hellenistic Greek classes, deeply impressed him by her adventurous mind, which stimulated him to comment that "Some people's minds are tight shut at twenty, and other people's minds are wide open at seventy. . . . If you want to keep alive, keep learning."[79] Another aspect of his thinking that found expression at this time was his universalism, to which he was by now committed. Harry Stevenson recalls "a warm discussion" at the London "Y" lasting well into the early hours, in which Willie propounded and defended his position.[80] (His beliefs in this matter received formal expression in *Testament of Faith*.[81] At the center of the issue was Willie's doctrine of the unconquerable love of God, ever the fulcrum of his theology, to which we will shortly return.)

Two unrelated events especially delighted him during that year. First, he baptized the son of his friend Charles Miller, for which he was presented with a fine bedroom clock. "One of the shaming calculations," he wrote, turning even this into a sermon, "was to calculate how much time we waste."[82] The second event involved the centenary celebration of his old church at Renfrew, which included the publication of *A History of Trinity Church, Renfrew: 1862-1962*. Willie's contributions to the volume (edited by A. M. Ferguson, who had happily rejoined its congregation after Willie's departure) were a greeting and, as became a famous former pastor, a profile.

Meanwhile his peripatetic ministries proceeded on behalf of the British and Foreign Bible Society, the New English Bible Apocrypha panel, and the editorial panel of the International Bible Reading Association, as well as in innumerable conferences and preaching engagements. His participation in one such conference, for the YMCA at Skegness, where he spoke on "Communicating the Gospel," was a huge success, and more invitations from all over the country flooded in.

In October of 1962 G. H. C. Macgregor took seriously ill, leaving Willie to cope alone in the Department of New Testament in addition to shouldering his responsibilities in the Department of Hellenistic Greek (part of the Faculty of Arts).[83] So began what he called his "worst year to date."[84] Macgregor had gone down with asthma, bronchitis, and heart failure, but his assistant had to soldier on, delivering sixteen hours of lectures (which included five hours of new lecture material). And as if that weren't burden enough, Willie was now encumbered with an increasing uncertainty of his being appointed to the professorship, something hitherto regarded as a matter of course.

As if to symbolize the changes and highlight the speed at which they were taking place, his "Obiter Visa" column was replaced by "Seen in the Passing": he would no longer provide a reflective gaze on human life, but something more like a glance—a snapshot rather than a portrait. It was all part of the "new look" that had been prepared by *The British Weekly*, but it was a pointed indication of the pressures being placed on Willie himself. The very first piece could not have been more appropriate—"Faithful in Little Things" (which featured Basil Oliver, a former factotum at the London "Y"). To the majority of people Willie was still the same man, but a closer study would have revealed clear indications of subtle changes taking place under those pressures: he began to exhibit a tendency to impatience (quite out of character), a greater sense of world-weariness, a marked increase in his enjoyment of alcohol (which he now "needed"), a slight falling away from the high-mindedness he had hitherto shown (and a concomitant increase in earthiness), and his smoking became nonstop.

These changes did not happen overnight, of course. From the early '20s, for instance, when his Dalziel High School "fan club" had stolen cigarettes from their fathers for him, the smoke of which he blew up the Bank House chimney, his smoking habit had been growing. And Willie had no qualms about it, despite his father's fierce opposition. After all, the great C. H. Spurgeon himself was a heavy smoker, as were many others among his father's heroes. WDB's views were otherwise; he agreed with the Reverend Doctor Gillan of Inchinnan, a pioneer in the penny bank scheme at Glasgow in the mid nineteenth century, who regarded it as a form of debauchery. Not so Willie; he had become possessed of the habit long before medical science commenced its vigorous campaign against it. (As recently as 1953, the President of the British Medical Association had stated that the connection between lung cancer and smoking was "not proven," though he was aware of pulmonary complications in smokers long before that.) Willie simply enjoyed his smoking, and he loved to give cigarettes to others, too—to students, to Mr. Lewis (the janitor at Trinity College), and others. He was a convivial as well as a private smoker. The pleasures of tobacco relaxed him and increased his creative powers and his concentration even as it gripped him more and more in its tyrannical powers.

There is another problem that cropped up at this time that was likewise significant in its effects on Willie. Jane began to resent Ronnie's children, or rather, she began to resent the very natural affection their grandparents gave to them. Jill, now three, frequently stayed with the Barclays, both because it pleased them to have her and because Ronnie's wife had recently given birth to their second daughter, Karen, and she welcomed the relief. Amid the fuss over the young visitor, Jane felt neglected, not least when Jill and Rusty took to each other, and played endlessly together. Soon Jill was proudly brushing her little sister's hair, an attention Willie feared came perilously close to battery.[85] Jill never stopped talking, as Willie noted in one of his occasional pieces.[86] She was called *ba' heid* (bald head) by her grandfather; to Jane's surprise she returned the compliment without admonition. Simply put, Jane began to feel that she was no longer the center of attention in the little family, and she took it hard. To make matters worse, she was finding her schoolwork difficult—and Willie wrote even of that, mentioning that she would gain fewer prizes, that she was never in the top ten, but that she was at least good with her hands. She could not help but be aware that she had been a "replacement" for Barbara, no matter how careful the

573

Barclays were to show her affection. Frequently left to support her adoptive mother in her grief and alternating moods of sorrow, anger, and despair, she now felt painfully isolated. There was something tragic about this; they were all caught in a web of tangled emotions and conflicting loyalties. Given a pound note for her birthday, she went out and bought perfume for Kate and cigarettes for Willie. She loved them and needed their love; she needed to be reminded constantly of it, and yet Willie brushed aside her attempts to explain how things really were when he was away from home—those long hours, and days, of absence. So she rebelled, and there were scenes.

Willie knew that not all was well, but perhaps he was unsure how to handle such things, given the delicacy of both Kate's state of mind, and Jane's. As it was, he was occasionally a little hard, sentimentalist though he was. "A parent's duty," he wrote at the end of May 1962, "is to teach a child to live for himself, and the sooner the better."[87] Jane had little choice but to learn this lesson as he once more buried himself in work, unable to prevent the pressures piling up on him. He was increasingly worried. He confessed in May 1963 that "there is an odd unfairness in life. The busier a man becomes, the more work he undertakes to do, the more he needs the help and support of his wife, the less time he has to give to her."[88] Notwithstanding this, or perhaps because of it, he launched a "League of Volunteers of Comfort" through a correspondence with Allan Young (then of Troon). The organization was a sort of Alcoholics Anonymous for the bereft and sorrowing—and it provided another pressure on Willie. He took one small step toward reducing these pressures when he took to using a dictating machine to help in answering his voluminous correspondence—though he still insisted on typing all the "highly personal" letters himself.

Stanley Pritchard noticed another change: Willie's enjoyment of the publicity and prestige he was given became more noticeable; to some extent he seemed to be getting dependent upon it. This change affected Kate as well. She became less sympathetic to the weaknesses and follies of others in consquence; apparently plenty was breeding insensitivity. And by now Willie was a rich man, keeping as much as £50,000—to the horror of his bank manager—in his current account. Urged to make more profitable use of it through investments, he turned the suggestion brusquely aside. "What is the point of doing that, when so much is claimed by the government in tax?" he demanded. And so, to Kate's alarm, he sought to "invest" it in other ways—by helping needy (and not so needy) students, by giving it to charitable causes, by lavishly entertaining at the college and at Royal Automobile Club of Scotland, and by spending it at hotels of all descriptions with better than three-star ratings. He took to waiving travel expenses as well as some royalties and other fees proper to his services.

In early 1963 he commenced a new series in *Life and Work*, a column called "Dr Barclay Takes Up Your Point," which dealt mainly with a whole range of New Testament problems (e.g., the fourfold gospel, chronology, Jesus of history, resurrection), some theological problems (e.g., the doctrine of the trinity, the nature of Judas's evil, the existence of angels), and some practical issues (e.g., the relevance to youth of Jesus' teaching). His secular engagements, such as his speaking at the Burns Suppers, were also extended. On February 22 he celebrated the thirtieth anniversary of his ordination; his ministry was now almost equally divided between pastoral work and academic training. Four days later he delivered the Alex Wood Memorial Lecture, choosing to speak on "Christian Discipline in Society Today" at New College. Lack of space prevents a detailed account of this, but the event did mark Willie's formal reestablishment of an involvement in practical affairs—his primary interest—even as it recalled the contributions Professor Wood, a distinguished Presbyterian and scientist and the former chairman of Dick Sheppard's Peace Pledge Union, had made to society. The lecture was delivered under the auspices of the Fellowship of Reconciliation (Willie's chief, G. H. C. Macgregor, was one of its international leaders), and so Willie did touch on the topic of pacifism; the real issues with which he grappled, however, involved the deeper questions of public law and morality that were then troubling society. His viewpoint and orientation were staunchly biblical, and reconciliation—to God and men—was his fundamental principle: "The Christian ethic is impossible without the Christian dynamic, and the Christian dynamic is Christ."[89]

A. S. Peake would have warmed to that thesis, ever keen as he was to preserve Christ's supremacy and centrality, ever underscoring it as the unique basis for practical living and fruitful service. And Willie was now himself linked publicly with Peake by virtue of his delivering the eighth A. S. Peake Memorial Lecture, following such fine predecessors as Norman Snaith, T. W. Manson, H. H. Rowley, and John Wilkinson. They represented Old Testament, New Testament, ecclesiastical history, and practical training (interests, all of them, as much of Peake as of Willie himself) in addition to representing differing emphases in the church universal, for whose unity Peake had striven so long. None of these things moved Willie so much as another facet of Peake's work, however. As Willie noted in the published edition of his Peake lectures,

> Great scholar though he was in his own right, he gloried in the title of theological middle-man; and he mediated to us and to many more the results of the best theological scholarship in an intelligible and digestible form. . . . He was the possession not of one Church, but of all the Churches.[90]

In keeping with Peake's evangelical nexus (he "gave us a view of the Bible which satisfied both the mind and the heart," said Willie) and recent evangelical campaigns, Willie chose as his subject the doctrine of conversion as it is developed in the book of Acts. But the Alex Wood Lecture had whetted his appetite, and so he decided not merely to lecture on what "the word once meant," but to seek to discover "what it *now* must mean," pointedly adding that "one of the strangest phenomena of the present-day situation is that it is rather outside than inside the Church that conversion is expected to happen."[91]

To his general public he confessed that he was behind in his work,[92] as he was in his correspondence, and he also had to beg pardon of some of his publishers for his delays (e.g., of Paul Meacham of The Westminster Press in America, who handle the American edition of the Daily Study Bible).[93] Apologizing to Miss McCulloch for delays in replying to her letter, he said he was having to write between sessions of an NEB Apocrypha translation panel, after which he was going on directly to a panel of The Translators' New Testament at Oxford, then on to an Easter Conference, then back to Newcastle for the YMCA midday service, and then back to London to fulfill various publishing and preaching engagements.[94] His second TV series took place at this time, four programs on the parables of Jesus, three of which were to be "straight talks" and the fourth a culminating question-and-answer session. Studio A—the largest outside London—was required. Reactions to this series, noted his producer, "were even more lyrical than for Series I."[95] He was cheered by "Scotland's epic victory over England at Wembley," in which it had been scientifically proven that the Scots made more noise than the English! To this Willie attributed the victory, neatly turning the fact into a heartfelt sermon, "Let's Try Encouragment."[96] Whatever his problems, he was determined not to allow them to distract him from his main work.

Professor at Last

The encouragement he desperately needed during the time of "this protracted ordeal," as Neil Alexander has described the selection process for the professorship,[97] was nearing its end. Alexander recalled its being "agonisingly slow and incredibly painful" to Willie, a time in which he saw him "distraught" as never before. The announcements of the vacancy had been circulated in February 1963. By the 27th Willie had returned his application to the Secretary of the University Court. The job description stated that

> The Professor will be a member of the Senatus Academicus and of the Faculty of Divinity. He will be responsible to the University Court for the teaching and examining work in New Testament language and literature, as well as for the direction of advanced students and research. . . . The appointment is a whole-time appointment, the Professor undertaking to accept outside paid work only with the prior consent of the University Court. . . .

Three testimonials were required; Willie obtained four! Professors G. D. Kilpatrick, W. D. McHardy, Matthew Black, and A. M. Hunter wrote on his behalf. G. H. C. Macgregor's name is notably absent, and it was widely rumored (Falconer told John Birkbeck that Macgregor had actually admitted it to him)[98] that Willie's chief of so many years, whose departmental work had been supported so loyally by Willie, had refused to recommend him for the post. This would have been a considerable blow to Willie, worsened by the criticism Macgregor made of his written work. Alongside his testimonials, Willie listed his education, his degrees, his previous and present positions, his external lectureships (Edinburgh, St. Andrews, Aberdeen, and Leeds), his occasional lectureships, his membership on various translation panels and in various societies for Old and New Testament study, and twenty-nine of the thirty-seven of his books so far published. (He omitted the devotional handbooks he had written for the Boys' Brigade and the Church of Scotland, the books on prayer, and the new ones then being printed, such as *Turning to God* and *The All-Sufficient Christ;* he also chose not to list the "plain man" books.)

By May 28, *The Scotsman* and *The Glasgow Herald* were announcing the appointment: Willie was at last successful in his application. Three months is not such a long time for deliberation over an appointment to so prestigious a chair, and in any case Macgregor was not due to retire until the end of September. The University Court had to allow an interval to elapse so that would-be applicants might apply. They then had to collate the information, check it, apply for references, assess them, and adjudicate on the outcome. It would have been unbecoming merely to rubber-stamp Willie's appointment even if they had wished to do so. Did Willie really expect them to do this?

We have to take into account Alexander's recollection of the process, one that Bob Kernohan once remarked was not necessarily free from his own experiences and disappointments. It does seem clear that this period was a time of marked anguish to Willie, who was no stranger to sorrow, criticism, or discomfiture. And yet we might well ask why this particular anguish? Perhaps the first element of importance in assessing the matter is the simple fact that he had been hoping for such an appointment for twenty-five years. His professors, A. A. Bowman, W. M. Macgregor, W. D. Niven, J. E. M'Fadyen, A. B. Macaulay, and A. J. Gossip had all encouraged him in such academic ambitions (and who knows that WDB had not nurtured them, both before and after their positive influence at university). Some of these men had actually aided him in applying for such posts before the war. Since then, and for at least seven years, he had listened to a number of overtures from this or that college or university around the world, all tempting him away from his beloved Glasgow. Secondly, the Free Church tradition, which still coursed in Willie's blood despite his thirty-four years of work for the Church of Scotland—in his view, the best expression of Reformed faith in Scotland—looked on a professorship as more than merely an academic distinction. Its incumbents were not only teaching elders *par excellence;* their excellence lay in character, experience, and wisdom as well as in "soulless things." Thirdly, a part of the historical tradition of Glasgow was its high regard for the close link between town and gown. (*The Glasgow Herald* was shortly to make much of this, taking note of the civic work as well as the academic excellence of Denney and Moffatt.)[99] And lastly, Willie was now on a world platform, in the eyes of not a few who had already subjected him to barbed criticism. Any humiliation now would be sore pain indeed, totally undeserved in his view.

Alexander adduces other aspects of Willie's mindset that are no less important than these general things. "What rankled, I am sure," he wrote, "was the discounting of his universally-acclaimed seventeen-year teaching record in the department as the Professor's right-hand man." Given the inside information that Willie supplied through his letters (alas! none has come down to us directly from Macgregor himself), we can see that this was a record of unsurpassed loyalty and industry. For long periods during these seventeen years he not only assisted in the department; he *was* the department. Whenever wanderlust or sickness or official business took his chief away, there was Willie, who never accepted an invitation that clashed with his primary work, his students' needs. He attended to those needs assiduously, beyond the call of duty, at university and in his own home—with gifts of books and money, show tickets, and even gratis holidays when he felt they were required. To have doubt cast on that record was doubly wounding—of his sense of ethical responsibility as well as his academic integrity. Willie would never have said this, but we might feel that it was his chief's record that might better have come under review (though of course Willie had to share whatever criticism was voiced for the department's recent record). We shall shortly see that when he was finally appointed to the Professorship, he quickly introduced many changes, some sweeping, which shows that he had held his silence on matters of some interest to him for long years.

Alexander also lists some of what the University Court held as arguments against selecting Willie: his occasionally controversial theological views, his questionable academic fitness, the general belittling of his books, and—a formidable doublet—his alleged lack of a philosophical bent and of the power to grow mentally. We might also note that the anti-academic aspects of his 1960 interview with Pritchard, thrice broadcast, did not endear him to the fraternity of pure scholarship.

As to academic fitness, his first in the classics—"the blue ribband of a university career"—and his distinction in his B.D. (which was tantamount to a first in this subject, classes not then being awarded in divinity) were equal to a double first. To have satisfactorily delivered the Bruce, the Kerr, and the Croall Lectureships, to say nothing of the international recognition of his work on the NEB and Diglott translation panels, surely must dispel doubt as to his fitness academically. His theological views were certainly castigated by some, but they at least had the virtue of being clearly expounded and (Willie believed) well defended.

If some academics belittled his books, they did not do so publicly, except by omission; the sheer scale of his influence silenced many would-be detractors. True, he had not produced many of the sort that budding Ph.D.'s love (Alexander suggested *Malchus's Ear: The Case for the Left* and *The Beast: Was He a She?*), but few could doubt the academic excellence of *Educational Ideals in the Ancient World,* or the minutiae Willie excavated in presenting it (it contained almost 900 footnotes in 262 pages; 6 appendices; and a bibliography of 89 general works, 15 dictionaries and encyclopedias, and 4 universally recognized translations of classical authors). And as for his more popular works, even given the devotional parameters of the Daily Study Bible, a seventeen-volume, four-thousand-page introduction to the New Testament with its own translation from the Greek could not be gainsaid; neither could his *New Testament Word-book, The Mind of Paul, Flesh and Spirit,* or his three-volume Christology (which he significantly described to the University authorities in his application for the Chair as "The Life of Jesus in three parts"). Over all these things towered his Edinburgh D.D., which had preceded the offer of a Professorship at Queen's University, Belfast, by only a matter of months.

I leave aside the suggestion that he had no philosophical bent, both because his record and his work in Hellenistic Greek (thought as well as language, not to mention *Educational Ideals,* in which he had detailed the educational philosophies of Sparta, Athens, and Rome, as well as the very different Greek understanding of Judaism) simply disprove this. And did not the 1937 recommendation of A. B. Macaulay, who had sought to interest Willie in the work of systematic theology, also substantiate his claims? And certainly we must refute Alexander's astonishing declaration that "he lacked the *power* (or perhaps only failed to take the opportunity) to *grow.* . . . He leaves no evidence of having grown over his long years of academic life."[100] Such a statement could only have been written by one who has not studied his academic life, who has ignored his writings; it is pure denigration and highly irresponsible. Anyone who compares Willie's pretentiously titled *New Testament Studies* (eighty-two pages of disconnected themes and uncoordinated theses that died an early death even at the hands of Sunday School teachers throughout Scotland) with his monumental two-volume work *The Gospels and Acts* (a 640-page introduction to just over half the New Testament, published on his retirement) cannot fail to see the definite growth in the power, perception, and eloquence of Willie's scholarship over the span of his academic career.

Let us be clear here as to one thing: I do not say that Willie gave evidence of consummate academic distinction. I do not pretend that he did not have his blind spots and preferences (indeed, I shall later suggest that in his departmental work he might well have better developed his potential as the guardian of academic skills and competence); but on the other hand it is a travesty to say that Willie did not develop, grow, or change. To say that "he got nothing useful out of [modern methods of biblical criticism] for himself nor anything he felt the urge, or competence, to communicate or condemn" is simply patently false. And to refer to him as "William Barclay, putative scholar" is to descend into wholly unwarranted sarcasm.[101]

Mr. Alexander makes two unfortunate mistakes when he asserts that Willie "never significantly altered" the theology and biblical criticism he had come to hold by 1946 "to assimilate the measure of truth within such trends as Neo-Orthodoxy, Biblical Theology, Form-Criticism and Redaction Criticism." In the first place, he overlooks the simple fact that by 1946 some of these things were already old hat (not to Alexander, of course, who was then finishing his studies—which he concluded under Willie himself at Glasgow between 1946 and 1948); Neo-Orthodoxy and Biblical Theology had had their heyday in the '30s, as had Form Criticism. This is not to say that much useful work was not done on them during the '40s (though indeed work in that decade was largely stultified by the war and its effects), '50s, and early '60s, but it does cast doubt on the assumption that Willie—with his well-earned reputation for progressiveness and his marvelously stocked personal library—failed to come to terms with these "new" disciplines at the commencement of his university career. And we must not lose sight of the simple fact that when Willie began his theological studies, Form Criticism, "the child of disappointment" (i.e., of source criticism) according to that redoubtable critic Vincent Taylor, was already enjoying its tenth year of influence and of critical assault (if not actual undermining) in its own right by such scholars as Dodd, Manson, and Taylor himself. Redaction Criticism was in a different situation, for it only began in the late '50s with Conzelmann's *Theology of St. Luke* and Marxsen's *Mark the Evangelist;* even Stephen Neill, who describes Conzelmann's book in his survey of New Testament criticism (1964), fails to identify the new discipline by name.[102] Willie, when he revised *The First Three Gospels,* did pay express attention to it, emphasizing the point that as a catalyst it was useful (i.e., analytically), but as a critique of history, and still more of theology, it had overreached itself.[103]

In sum, Mr. Alexander's declamations on this matter are too subjective by far. We should not forget that Willie, unlike Mr. Alexander, chose to go to the source of these new movements after completing his own theological studies—to Marburg, where, however short and undocumented his stay, he did sit at the feet of Bultmann and von Soden, though never becoming one of their disciples. The war certainly delayed and eclipsed much in New Testament scholarship, but it is preposterous to suggest that such schools of New Testament criticism as Alexander lists began in 1946, or that Willie only became aware of them later. The fact of the matter is that when he was appointed Lecturer he had already rejected much of them as the only (still less the best) tools for understanding the New Testament. He recognized, as does John Leith, an observant assessor of theological trends, that "by the 1950's it was apparent that the Barthian theological movement [i.e., of Biblical Theology] had lost much of its vigor."[104]

Alexander makes his second mistake when he assumes that Willie had "liberal" attitudes during his student days, going so far as to say that "in 1974 he was still a liberal, however much he protested he was now a fundamentalist!"[105] The simple fact of the matter is that he has stood Willie's theological history on its head. He ignores the patent fact that Willie was a fundamentalist of fundamentalists in 1925, when he became an undergraduate. As he affirmed in 1975, "At that time I was so conservative in my attitude to Scripture that the removal of a comma seemed to me to be nothing short of sin." Moreover, Willie expressly acknowledged the changes he had undergone as the result of critical study when he said that "for me scholarship and discovery made the Bible a far greater book than ever it had been before"[106]—statements that Alexander chooses to ignore. Willie's early conservatism is also borne out by fundamentalist adherents such as John Laird (who could even publish Willie's mistaken recollection that he actually founded the C.S.F. at Glasgow!). Indeed, even the vilifying criticism that

Willie received from conservatives later in his career is more understandable in the light of their former appreciation of his work for the Scottish Sunday School Union and the like, all of which was very conservative and orthodox.

In any case, Alexander's talk of Willie's "apparent stagnation" is both unjust and untrue. To the contrary, the facts bespeak his having yielded to the influence of critical scholarship (and, according to Macaulay, his having exceeded every other student's record to date therein); he adopted it and went on to wrestle with the problems it posed for evangelical faith throughout his ministerial and academic life. His attitude toward the parables and the miracles shows how much he "gained" from liberal interpretation, behind which rests a carefully disguised appreciation—not acceptance—of critical, even form-critical, methods. His conservative leanings are plain for all to see (certainly they were recognized by the liberal scholars, who were equally scathing in their criticisms), not least in his emphasis on Christ himself. Never was Willie nearer to the heart of the Reformed tradition than when, concluding his 1961 introduction to the Bible, he affirmed as the ultimate test, "the touchstone," Luther's one test: "Does a book speak of Christ?" That which impels toward Christ (*was Christum treibet*) was ever Willie's test, too, affirmed most emphatically in his 1975 testament of living faith.

Time and again he bears witness to the new understanding the "liberal" attitudes and viewpoints gave to him; and his continual justification of the usefulness of doubt shows that he supposed they might have an equal value for others. But to call him a liberal at all is in one sense to empty the word of its deepest meaning, for the inner reality of liberalism is the assertion that man can attain to religious truth and reality by himself, of his own efforts, without humbling himself before the Word of God.[107] Willie's doctrine was anything but that. He ever placed a strong emphasis on sin, repentance, conversion, and above all on God's re-creating activity; but he also stressed (sometimes at the apparent expense of the foregoing) man's responsibility. Here was inculcated a *reciprocal* relationship (to use a word that lies at the center of his ethical understanding), a *cooperative* relationship (to use a word that lies at the center of his biblical and theological awareness). His so-called liberalism was a broadening of the old Harnackian emphases on the biblical teaching of the Fatherhood of God and the brotherhood of man, to which Willie linked the infinite value of the individual he learned from Jesus. It was, moreover, grounded in his "neo-orthodox" belief that the higher criticism was an essential tool in the understanding of scripture (but only a tool—not the revelation itself). As a tool, Willie applied it; but he never allowed its more doubtful obfuscations to detract from the reality of God's self-revelation. So, in 1974 it was not just a matter of Willie's being "still a liberal," but of his becoming one publicly, even of his appearing to enjoy the consternation among former allies it caused, as we shall see. To say that such disciplines as Alexander mentions "never entered into the essential William Barclay" is to be as incautious and hyperbolic as he accuses Willie himself of being. Herein is a clue as to why Willie was ceaselessly criticized by the conservatives (and not merely criticized indeed, but rejected), why he was condemned by *The Monthly Record* (as early as 1953) as being "a resiler of the faith." There was at work the converse of Madame de Staël's tenet that "To understand everything makes one very indulgent": those who did not understand Willie were prone to be censorious. And of course it is also true that Willie frequently abetted the misunderstanding by leading with his chin.

Sadly, some at least of this censoriousness would appear to have been shared by some members of the University Court. Some did suspect his doctrine; some did question his commitment to the academic cause *qua* meticulous scholarship; and some did choose to deal selectively with his record and work. It would even appear that the rightfully proud tradition of bridging town and gown was thereby ignored, despite Willie's huge contributions in the religious field. Doubtless some also resented his evangelical sympathies, his white-hot spiritual applications, and his occasionally incautious comments regarding the establishment and democratic freedom. It is curious that Mr. Alexander does not even consider these political aspects. On the whole I imagine they drew considerably more antipathy to Willie than any of his theologically "liberal" pronouncements; all the signs were that he was being drawn increasingly into this area, and some (Kate included) feared an "incident," an indiscretion.

Whatever the reality of the private deliberations of the University Court, there were leaks about their concern over his appointment, and Mr. Alexander has served us well in describing in such dramatic terms the effect they had on Willie. (Alexander does acknowledge that Willie was "a scholar of the highest quality, in two of the most fundamental aspects of New Testament scholarship"— linguistics and background knowledge—and thereby added a rich vein of comment to the tapestry of his life that many have found thoroughly authentic.) Privacy is never total. Gossipmongers were bound to extract (or invent) this or that detail. The tragedy here is that such things appear to have been leaked even to the students themselves. James Little, one of their number, knew of these rumors and understood that some of them stemmed from Willie's "recognised deficiency in Systematic Theology."[108] It was, after all, a Chair of *Divinity* and Biblical Criticism. But if "Divinity" be interpreted in a biblical sense, as opposed to systematic, dogmatic, or historical theology, it would seem that his more biblical-theological writings would also be downgraded. We must leave the criticism of such books as *The Mind of Paul,* his trilogy on Jesus (whether judged as "life" or "mind"), and *The Promise of the Spirit* for treatment elsewhere. Suffice it to say that not a few were glad to own these books as real divinity even if they do not break new ground, but rather leave some of the interminable (and unanswerable!) questions unanswered.

There were warts, and it is only fair to look at these now, even as the Senate had to in judging his technical competence for the post advertised. We have seen that this post was one of joint responsibility—divinity and biblical criticism. In neither discipline had Willie produced a work of high technical merit; nor could

582

he offer much evidence of "technical" research (on Malchus's ear or anything else). It has to be said that the New Testament department had not for some time made a name for itself in the way of scholarship except by living off the massive capital of Bruce, Denney, and Moffatt, and that Willie has to take some responsibility for that, along with his chief. The level of postgraduate work was low compared to that of other universities, and there was no sign yet of a possible increase. Macgregor himself, the author of a fine commentary on John's gospel (published as far back as 1928), had done little since that, for all his "ambassadorial" wanderings, and his recent books had all been written in harness with other scholars, such as A. Q. Morton, T. P. Ferris, and A. C. Purdy. There is more than one explanation of the criticism he made of Willie in 1959 that was recorded by Alexander in 1981. He may well have felt pressured by Willie's ceaseless productivity and increasing popularity. His latest involvement with A. Q. Morton, on the computerized analysis of Greek writings, had only produced low whistles in the academic camp, and was very far from proving itself as a valid method, let alone producing a convincing result. (Willie himself was unconvinced.) Moreover, for all Willie's respect for scholarship, the selectors must have been aware of his caveats against the wrong sort of scholarship, warnings that are so easily misconstrued. A new image for the department would have been a very great temptation to the selectors, who had before them some candidates who were unexceptionably authoritative in strict academic terms.

Even linguistically Willie was not on wholly convincing ground. Alexander contends that he possessed "impeccable linguistics," but that is only partly true. It is true insofar as knowledge of Hellenistic Greek goes, for in this he was brilliant—there were few scholars to match his sensitivity to the language, his broad knowledge, and his immense powers of instant recall—but even here there were gaps. For example, the *Hermetica,* edited by Nock and Festugière in 1945, were very influential in Asia Minor in the first century, but are mentioned only three times in the Daily Study Bible and not once in the *The Gospels and Acts.* And, as we have noted, in Hebrew Willie fell down, never having taken beyond the undergraduate level his interest in that subject. It has always been an imperatively important background subject for a deep understanding of the New Testament; following the Dead Sea Scroll discoveries of the late '40s and their wide publication in the '50s, familiarity with Hebrew was even more crucial. A double dimension is here involved, for not only does the top-ranking scholar (and that is what a professorship is all about) need to be aware of the classical Hebrew dimension, but the related and subtle Aramaic overtones are of consummate importance, as the work of such scholars as Torrey and later (more effectively) Black demonstrates. Willie himself gave lip service to this in his work, conceding (albeit erroneously) that the relationship of Aramaic to Hebrew was similar to that between modern English and Anglo-Saxon.[109] For a New Testament scholar the want of Aramaic is a formidable deficit. It simply means that one is not *au fait* with the language Jesus and his disciples ordinarily spoke. Moreover, one cannot be at home with the literature that diasporic Judaism customarily used, the language of the Targums, nor even that in which Josephus—of classic importance to the period—wrote some of his books (e.g., *The Wars of the Jews*). The Jews took Aramaic seriously despite their veneration of Hebrew, even if some of their leaders believed that angels could not understand it! Jesus had both; Willie had neither.

Another matter also worried the selectors. Willie was a most outgoing and friendly individual. Some regarded his close friendship with his students and his involvement in their affairs as a potential problem. Among his junior colleagues he was also markedly friendly and deferential. Here, again, some saw problems. At the same time, in terms of the general academic body he was an individualist, a loner, and this also posed problems. His record on committees was not exceptional; indeed, he appeared to air too readily his low opinion of such work ("a body of people who keep minutes, but waste hours"). Further, he was not famed for attendance at, or contributions to, the specialist societies connected with his academic work. He did not appear to be listening too intently to what his colleagues were saying. (Clearly he was an individualist partly through his disability, of course.) And we should not underestimate the fact that in the Kennedy era a clean-cut, youthful dynamism was *the* mark of leadership—the sort of image Ian Henderson promoted, clear-thinking and dashing as he was. For all Willie's youthfulness of spirit, it was not only senior army officers who addressed him in his early fifties as "old man Barclay."

Lastly, his attitude toward his job also inspired doubts in some minds. Not a few thought that he was in love with teaching rather than his subject, that his subject was merely the vehicle of his teaching, rather than vice versa. Some looked on him as a sort of theological Marshall McLuhan. Stanley Pritchard's comment about his growing enjoyment of the publicity hints at this, as do comments from other quarters. If Henry Drummond could be labeled a dilettante, why not Willie Barclay? And some openly thought he was making too much money from his high-profile role as popularizer of their hard-won, slowly developed ideas. Neil Alexander latches on to his worrisome ability to be passionately in favor of something one moment and against it the next, of his inability to see things as a whole, to keep things in balance. In this Alexander is both right and wrong; but in any case Willie was never feckless nor unprincipled. (Alexander's view of him stems from the latter part of Willie's life, when real medical problems, which eventually forced his early retirement, were asserting themselves. It is unquestionable that his tendency toward vacillation of this sort increased as his illnesses worsened.) Willie believed in the essential *poikilotēs* nature of truth as well as grace—its "many sidedness"—but it did not favorably impress everyone when he would stress one side exclusively on one occasion and another side exclusively on another occasion. They expected him to make of the universe a more complete whole than he ever could himself. He was especially aware, with Faber, that "The love of God is broader / Than the measure of man's mind." He was content at times to have loose ends flapping round his world view and, worse, his doctrines. He was also keenly aware that the ancients were not necessarily less intelligent than their twentieth-century successors and that they were just as conscious of mystery, contradictoriness, and paradox as we are today.

By the end of May the pressures were being reflected even in his devotional pieces for *The British Weekly*. In a piece entitled "The Truth about Ourselves," he said "I believe . . . that everyone requires a compliment now and again."[110] He got his that very week—the appointment he had yearned for. The decision of the University Court was eventually made, and by the end of May the press—without abounding enthusiasm, it must be admitted—welcomed him as the new professor. At fifty-six he had realized his dream at last; the waiting, the disappointments, the frustrations were over. It remains an open question whether he ever got over the threatened rejection of his application.

One of the first letters of congratulation that he received came from his old tutor at DHS, Jimmy Paterson, now in retirement. "You lit the fire," Willie replied, unconsciously answering the criticism of Alexander mentioned above and at the same time declaring the nature of the enthusiasm that burned within him. (This linguistic approach is of critical importance to Willie's understanding of theology, to which we must return; but we may pause to recall a comment he made two months previously in reviewing J. H. Moulton's fine book *A Grammar of New Testament Greek,* the third volume of which—by Nigel Turner—was, significantly, on syntax: "There is a sense in which grammarians and lexicographers are the most important scholars of all."[111] There is a real sense in which his work was geared to this conviction, providing prolegomena to doctrinal considerations for teachers and preachers.) Willie wrote to tell his former school friend Walter Henderson that "One of the very first letters which came to me was from Jimmy Paterson. I felt that it should have been I who was writing to thank him. We owe him a lot, those of us who took classics." Another letter he received at the time, from his old Glasgow colleague Charles Miller, enclosed a cartoon his friend had drawn of Willie struggling up a mountainside—a significant representation of his long, arduous haul to its fulfillment (a reproduction appears on page 586). Commented Willie, perhaps a little sardonically, "[it is] quite easily the most sensible and attractive message that I have so far received." On top of these personal messages, he received one from the presbytery at Paisley that greatly cheered him; the prophet was being honored in his own county.

"JM"—Martin?—welcomed him to the faculty of theology in *The College Courant,* not quite accurately stating that "his academic distinction is recognized by his colleagues and wondered at by his students," but happily making the point that, "it is good that Dr. Barclay has now been appointed to be head of department in which he has given manifold and distinguished service for many years."[112] As we saw earlier, *The Glasgow Herald* also welcomed "his ripe fruits of scholarship," which he brought "to the service of ordinary people, and thus continues a tradition that has long been established in Glasgow."[113] That tradition—of Denney and Moffatt—he had every intention of advancing, though not at the expense of his students. He had written to his old teacher virtually the day after hearing of

THE FULFILLMENT

Greetings from fraternal colleague Charles Miller on the occasion of Willie's appointment to his professorship

his appointment to say that "at the present moment I am in process of realising the added responsibility this lays upon me." He began as quickly as that, and old ideas and attitudes were swept away with all the dispatch of the proverbial new broom.

There is a world of difference between the introduction to the department's courses in *The University Calendar* for 1964/65 and those of its predecessors. Its layout bears all the hallmarks of Willie's mind and hand: the aims and objects are lucidly stated, the paragraphs are shorter and more direct, the subsections betoken an underlying structure (ever Willie's expositional strength), and the choices of subject are broadened and modernized. For the first time such subjects as Form Criticism and Gnosticism are offered explicitly. Further, "new" textbooks are listed—Guthrie on general introduction, Redlich on form criticism, C. S. C. Williams's revision of Souter's work on the canon, Grant on the Synoptic problem, Kenyon on the text, Cranfield on Mark—to which we may add such names as Bultmann, Dodd, A. M. Hunter, W. D. Davies, and H. J. Schoeps, to name but a few modern commentators now given precedence. In all, twenty-four new names were introduced to the lists of textbooks. It is a direct rebuttal of the absurd charge that "he got nothing out of" such things himself that "he felt the urge, or

586

competence, to communicate or condemn." Willie all but declared that the years of traditional approach were over.

Another example of his progressive work lay in his revisions of the "New Testament Exegetical Exercise," a copy of which was given to every student to be fulfilled in his second year and handed in before the end of February. Willie heightened its standards; he meant to make "good workmen" of them. It provided a complete quarto page of instructions, broken neatly into a sevenfold scheme, with two additional riders covering the basic material to be consulted. The students were to provide the following seven items:

1. A fully transcribed Greek text of a designated passage, with notes as to significant readings
2. A brief introduction to the context of the passage and to the book in which it is found
3. A concise commentary of the passage
4. The student's own paraphrase of the passage
5. An essay on the central theme or doctrine of not fewer than 6,000 words (i.e., fifteen full pages)
6. A sermon based either on the whole passage or its central text
7. A bibliography of consulted material

He was interested in producing not only good workmen, but workmen who need not be ashamed. He meant to continue as he had started.

CHAPTER SEVENTEEN

The Crest of the Wave

Riding High, Fu' Healthy

Fʀᴏᴍ this point on the pattern of Willie's life was set in two directions: the primary responsibilities of running his department on the one hand, and his *parerga* of translation panels, writing, lecturing, and preaching on the other. For six years after his appointment, he undertook his duties with breathtaking enthusiasm and drive, as if he were trying to restore the years eaten—if not by locusts, then at least by enforced professional delay and frustration. This pattern was broken at the end of 1969 by the traumatic breakdown of his health, a total breakdown, after which his doctor gave him a specific period before death would claim him. Thenceforth he was a man literally under sentence of death. The first six-year period of professorship was therefore the penultimate period of his life, and it was lived and worked on the crest of a wave, with consummate dedication and a commensurate joy: he was fulfilled.

But it is necessary to bear in mind that the man who now fulfilled his long-awaited destiny was not quite the same man that had abandoned himself to his role earlier. The changes mentioned earlier were developing still, and the troubled waters of his professorial appointment added a new note of sobriety. It reminds one of what W. R. Nicoll said of Ian Maclaren (John Watson) at a time when Willie only knew encouragement and success: "He could face contradiction and opposition, but not the steady environment of antagonism." Willie did in fact have to face it, and the ordeal told on him, however much he pretended otherwise, as we shall see. The ubiquitous calls in his writings to the "manly" virtues of courage, perseverance, patience, and the like sounded now ever more loudly—because he himself was living them. Alas, his newfound status was all the stimulus some needed to turn yet more tightly the thumbscrew of personal criticism.

Nor was Willie untouched by grief of the more mundane sort. Professor Pitt-Watson had died at the beginning of the year (he was succeeded by Murdo Macdonald, whose pulpit ministry in Glasgow was epoch-making), and G. H. C. Macgregor, the man Willie respected for being "so much the mystic and the scholar," whom he came to love deeply as the years went by, died in July, before the *festschrift* volume Willie and Hugh Anderson were preparing for him was ready. *The New Testament in Historical and Contemporary Perspective* became a memorial volume. Happily he lived long enough to learn of the honorary D.D. his university was to bestow upon him. Whether the postmortem technician noticed Willie's name engraved on his worn-out heart as Macgregor had said he would[1] we shall never know, but the feelings between the two men were clearly mutual and profound, despite their differences. From now on Willie would carry the department publicly, not privately. Of particular sadness to Willie was the news of Andrew McCosh's resignation from the Saint Andrew Press, which ended fourteen years of imaginative publishing and advertising as well as a personal friendship for Willie. With it went the announcement of McCosh's appointment as Manager of Stirling Tract Enterprises, a name that conjures up reminiscences of Henry Drummond and his activities of a previous generation. Not that they rated highly in Willie's attitudes at that time, even though he eagerly greeted "a notable blurring of the lines between liberals and fundamentalists in the last fifteen years"[2]—though that assessment is open to challenge on other grounds. The move brought back memories of old and happy times to Willie, when he and Shaun Herron and Ronald Gregor Smith spent lively weekends together celebrating the muscular Christianity to which each in his very different way ascribed. Almost the last act that McCosh presided over was the introduction of the famous Goodwill Scheme, by which Church of Scotland ministers in India and Africa (and by extension elsewhere) were enabled to buy the Daily Study Bible at cost. Willie, deeply troubled about the money he was obtaining from his books, was glad to waive all royalties, even as Saint Andrew Press was supposed to waive all profits.[3]

This was a year of momentous change, at the end of which the assassination of President Kennedy dashed the dreams and idealism of many. Commented Willie, "like most other people I have a personal sense of loss at the death of this man whom I never saw in the flesh."[4] Regardless of his somewhat starry-eyed advocacy of the rapprochement between liberals and fundamentalists (he would have been nearer the mark had he used the phrase "conservative evangelicals," though even this is not a completely adequate description), he began to do battle for a more outgoing, ongoing religious determination. In September he wrote two pieces for his column "Seen in the Passing" that sum up his attitude at that time concisely.[5] The first carried a challenge to those whose faith was centered in a Protestant creed: "the main thing which clearly matters is not theology but personality." He expressed his revulsion at Orange Day marches and parades, with their un-Christlike bravado and negative witness. He drew a sharp distinction between such antics and the work of Stephen Colwell, prophet of the social gospel, whose faith was nothing like that of the Orange Order—"a Creed without charity, theology without humanity, protestantism without Christianity." The thumbscrews tightened yet more. His second piece provided a powerful rejection of what the law in one of its more asinine moods declared to be "acts of

God"—blasphemously so, to Willie's way of thinking. Willie's God was of a different order, One who loved and forgave, welcomed and made new. Winning men for God and, by the restatement of old doctrines, winning God for men, now heightened as his twin concerns.

With such denouncements came more mundane criticisms, for these were already the "seething sixties," and Willie was glad to call into question clerical collars, the use of the title "reverend," the use of tokens (slightingly called "tickets of admission" by Willie), the absurdity of elders wearing pin-striped suits at Communion, and the overall clerical disposition to dress in a color more suitable to a wake than to a celebration of joy. Willie's gadfly impulse was now strengthened by a newfound authority in his post, and he discharged volley after volley of discomfiting rounds, pricking, questioning, probing, daring his readers to think and believe. The challenge of his ordination address rang in his ears and now received a positive, if disconcerting, fulfillment—decisiveness asserted!

In August Willie reached another high point in his career when he went to lecture at St. Anne's College, Oxford, at a vacation-term Bible study conference. There were to be four main courses plus miscellaneous lectures. The other two lecturers were C. H. Dodd and C. K. Barrett of Durham, whose expertise did not belie their devotion or their practical wisdom. Holidays were taken after this, and once more the academic year resumed, with all its challenges to Willie's absorbed allegiance.

And so a full year drew to its close, with Willie and Kate going off to their "presidential suite" at the London "Y," strong and glad in the assurance of being once again at the center of things. Their mood might be summed up in the words of Keir Hardie, penned while Willie was yet a boy, settling down with his parents at Motherwell, though now applicable to him in his maturity:

> Dear Comrade, if you flatter so,
> You'll make an old man vaunty:
> I'm six and fifty years, 'tis true
> And much have had to daunt me.

> But what of that? My life's been blest,
> With health and faith abiding;
> I've never sought the rich man's smile
> I've never shirked a hiding.

> I've tried to do my duty to
> My conscience and my neighbour,
> Regardless of the gain or loss
> Involved in the endeavour.

Hardie went on to praise his happy home, his loving wife, and his beloved Independent Labour Party "fu' healthy." Willie could do so, too, and if his political convictions were not of the party type, at least they were full and healthy. It was not a bad way to end the year.

Yet More Views, Method, and Purpose

Karl Barth declared his deep concern at the state of theology in 1964, calling the situation "a theological Vanity Fayre." The problem was that the Bultmannians and the Tillichians had shaken deeply, in the wake of German cultural disintegration, the theological foundations. To this general theological ferment the disciples of Bonhoeffer had added their own brand of unorthodoxy in his name by declaring themselves in favor of "religionless Christianity," which to some people sounded like unsweetened sugar or nonalcoholic whisky—a contradiction in terms. To others desperately concerned to bridge the world of the Bible and that of modern man, it was a profound challenge to rethink their beliefs in more "intelligible" forms. Commented the great Swiss theologian himself, his eye on the British scene, "and poor Bishop Robinson in his *Honest to God* . . . has drawn off the froth from all this to put it on the market as the ultimate wisdom. . . . The theology of this bishop [is] wretchedly flat-footed." That is somewhat hard on Dr. Robinson, who had only the best motives and intentions in writing that controversial book. (Few people knew, for example, that he was donating the royalties of his book—which had sold over a quarter of a million copies within six months—to charitable causes.) He was extraordinarily like Barth himself in 1919, who likened his own experience on publishing *Römerbrief* to that of a man who loses his balance in a darkened belltower and, clutching a rope to steady himself, hears the bell tolling out above his head. By the time the critics had finished with him, the "poor bishop" must have felt as if the bell were actually tolling in his head, so great and protracted was the cacophony of vituperation.

Willie, while he expressed sympathy with *Honest to God*, was somewhat bemused by all the bother about it; he who thought in pictures—some of them the very pictures Dr. Robinson wanted to dispose of—found it difficult to handle coils of wire that appeared not only to be knotted with razor barbs but carrying a stiff electric charge. In any case, he continued to sweep clean his department, and added to his oeuvre in the twelve months of office since his appointment to the professorship more than half a dozen books, three of them on prayer.

It was not all devotion and piety, however. It was at this time that Dr. C. L. Mitton took over the editorship of *The Expository Times* from the Hastings family, and Willie expressed the secularity he felt—admittedly a highly "religious" secularity—by asking Dr. Mitton for permission to review only secular books on his page in that prestigious journal. Willie's reading had always been broad; he now made it ostensibly "secular" in a determined attempt to see God's activity at work in society, an extension of the groundwork of natural theology, which had curiously gone into decline by this time. He also became more and more involved in secular organizations such as Tenovus, a number of housing schemes, and almost anything that showed nonprofit, unbureaucratized social concern. Early in the year, in an article entitled "Actions Not Words,"[6] he called into question the effectiveness of institutionalized (or established) religion, as became a liberal leader of the '60s. The church offices were full of reports, schemes, and plans, he said, but what of it? They were just words. Willie was concerned—concerned about the work, the effects, the cost, and above all about the people. Another man, with a less virile faith, might well have slipped into cynicism. Instead, Willie wrote a piece on growing old gracefully, himself expressing the secrets of so doing, by developing a still greater sense of proportion, an increasing serenity, an enlarging tolerance, a broadened sense of humor, a widening knowledge, and—it was never absent—"the ability to care."[7] He cared ceaselessly and admired such individuals as Kagawa of Japan, one of his heroes, who gave themselves over to caring work. He declared that "Christians must be the foremost fighters in war against want," and later wrote to Alistair Rennie, a successor of Thomas Marshall at Willie's church at Motherwell, to say "I admire people like you who work on the frontiers." It was not that he had lost sight of his evangelical roots—he certainly had not—but he was well in advance of many evangelicals in expressing the practical obligations of new standards, as well as new life in Christ. Still, he was fulsome in his praise of not a little that now emanated from the fundamentalist camp, as, for example, in welcoming Billy Graham's autobiography, of which he wrote that it would be "difficult to find a better summary of salvation."[8]

His third series of television lectures—they were just that, Ronnie Falconer having given up trying to compress him into another man's mold—were now broadcast from Trinity College under the title "A People's Life of Jesus." They ran for six consecutive Sundays from mid March to end April. The title was taken from Pat Smythe's best-seller, and the lectures were published (in 1965) as *A New People's Life of Jesus* (*Jesus for the Everyman* in the United States). It was now "Professor Barclay" that brought out things new and old from his vast erudition—appalling the new theologians with his "archaic" attitudes, crossing swords with the new moralists with his adherence to biblical morality, and upsetting the fundamentalists with his "modernism." Whether he danced or mourned, wept or laughed, they criticized. He simply pressed on, knowing that "the man in the street," who would often postpone his visit to his "local" to listen to him, thought and prayed as a result. (We should bear in mind that it is "the ordinary man and his wife," not the "religious," who constituted the 6:15 P.M. audience for his broadcasts.)

Willie had to put up with busy recording sessions, sometimes delivering two lectures in one evening or delivering the same lecture twice if faults developed. In any case, every lecture had a full rehearsal, with Willie and the technical people running through the entire script in private—not that the second run always followed the first exactly! His script, always meticulously prepared well in advance, was never of very great use to the recording engineers. His son Ronnie remembers being in the outside broadcast van on one such occasion. Willie's first few sentences were word-perfect, but then off on a tangent he soared, drawing out this nuance and illustrating it with that fact. "He's back on page four," cried one perspiring engineer, only to find that he was by then off on another tangent, producing facts and figures and felicitous comment like a conjurer produces rabbits. "Back to page seven," murmured another, once more perplexed as a new period approached its climax and Willie, relaxed and confident, rose with it. They looked anxiously at the studio clock—a minute to go, and Willie was still airborne. Then to their relief they found him reproducing exactly the final words of the script as he touched down with the precision of a computerized flight. On one such occasion the power lines failed them, and they had to ask him to repeat his lecture from the beginning. He did so without complaint, but it was not the same lecture that appeared the second time around! The introduction and the conclusion were the same, but the middle sections had changed: tangential inspiration, the listing of the spirit, had taken over. Another colleague has written of a different broadcasting experience that arose when Willie was asked point-blank to give in three minutes his thoughts on the meaning of death. He thought for a while, listed a few points on a scrap of paper, adjusted his hearing aid, and commenced. Exactly two minutes and fifty-seven seconds later he terminated his mini-address. It was perfect, and perfectly suitable to his hearers' needs.

If any other man had chosen to work on Willie's scale—had been found *able* to work on his scale—would the results have been very different? Could they have been better? Like can only be compared with like, in this as in other things. You cannot compare *The Master's Men* with Macquarrie's *Existentialist Theology,* or even *The All-Sufficient Christ* with Barrett on the Gospel of John. Willie took his students through to B.D. level, but he took them on to being potentially good ministers of the gospel too. And at the same time he bridged directly the gulf between academic and practical theology, between town and gown. Others did likewise—for example, the doyen of New Testament scholarship Charles Harold Dodd. He wrote both a brilliant popular introduction to the Gospels (the result of his own postwar broadcasting) *About the Gospels* and the successful volume *The Bible and its Background* (also taken from his broadcast talks). It would be a brave man who would dare claim that these were essentially "better" books academically than Willie's *The Making of the Bible,* say, or his *Introducing the Bible.* And it is incontestable that Willie's books of this kind sold in vastly greater quantities than did those of C. H. Dodd. Or take Alan Richardson's *Preface to Bible Study,* or T. W. Manson's *The Beginning of the Gospel,* or any of the material of this sort at this time. It is not possible to say that comparable works by Willie were inferior in content, style, or pitch; they were simply different, bearing his hallmark (part of which was his capacity to interest and provoke, gadfly fashion). Comparisons are odious, and the *odium theologicum* is particularly vile, as the sad history of the divided church demonstrates. All these scholars made unique contributions; Willie's special contributions were directed to the children and young people of his church, to their aspiring—if ignorant—parents, and to the unchurched masses, and affected them all deeply.

Willie felt sorry for the academic who lived in the straitened world of his own discipline, a world rendered ever narrower as specialization screwed home its necessary but relentless threads. As early as 1933 he recalled the story told by C. L. Hodgson of the Oxford mathematician whose attenuated world dissolved into cynicism, provoking in history, said Willie, "a sort of sardonic laughter." Karl Barth, it will be remembered, never allowed himself too serious a self-assessment. He pictured the angels joking at his approach, as he pushed his great and learned tomes before him in a wheelbarrow. Willie had a similar tendency toward self-deprecation. He did not reject academic excellence, as many of his reviews (laudatory and critical) show. In 1956, for example, he wrote to Braidwood of "the sheer joy of learning for its own sake."[9] Five years later he wrote to Douglas Millard, his would-be publisher, stating that true scholarship should be "real and wide *but unobtrusive*.[10] Ten years later, to the same publisher, he complained of one scholar's faults in failing to list his sources adequately: "I want to know more," he said[11]—not that he himself did not know the sources; he was simply speaking on behalf of his fellow readers, whose opportunities were diminished by the book's deficiencies.

No one has better summed up his position than his former editor, C. L. Mitton, who wrote in a letter of sympathy to Kate at Willie's death of what he counted to be his "scholarship in the service of Christ and his Church, rather than scholarship for its own sake."[12] And we should note the words of F. F. Bruce written on the same occasion: "His concern for careful scholarly study of the New Testament went alongside his concern to communicate its message."[13] He was a practical academic working in an applied science to whom some of his "pure" colleagues gave no more prestige than others give to technical-college tutors. They would have been well advised to note what Willie said about 1 Timothy 6:3–5, his practical eye seizing the reality:

> There is a kind of Christianity which is more concerned with argument than life. To be a member of a discussion circle or a Bible study group and spend enjoyable hours in talk about doctrines does not necessarily make a Christian. J S Whale in his book *Christian Doctrine* has certain scathing things to say about this pleasant intellectualism. . . . Subtle argumentation and glib theological statements do not make a Christian. That kind of thing may well be nothing other than a mode of escape from the challenge of Christian living.[14]

He was not knocking scholarship: note his adjectives—*enjoyable, pleasant,* and so on. Willie genuinely found enjoyment in such things, but he knew full well that one could spend one's life in such pleasant occupation and yet miss the greater reality. He also knew the danger signaled in Lord Moran's comment that "in Science the sterile worker soon loses caste. . . . We have no patience with empty vessels."[15] Willie would have agreed with him that to *add* to knowledge was the essence of "the creative mind," but that to fall short in its fulfillment was "to be bundled unceremoniously into the second category."

That is what actually happened with Willie. But he was unrepentant, even if he was hurt by it. Alexander's descriptions of Willie's doubts concerning his scholarship, which, he says, "dogged him throughout his career," and of his tendency to overvalue the attainments and experiences of well-known academics,[16] ought surely to be seen in this light and gauged for the overstatements they manifestly are. Willie's former colleague admits that Willie never once spoke in concern about his lack of a Ph.D., that certain passport to academic recognition; nor has any other scholar reported observing such a concern on his part in the multitude of letters I have received and interviews I have been given, although many did say that they had frequently noted a sense of caution, possibly of insecurity, in his demeanor. Perhaps these good men, immensely valuable to the church and to their disciplines, felt the penetration of the point John Watson made in the introduction to his biography of Gypsy Smith (under whose influence Willie grew up), when he wrote,

> Lord, we were so busy studying deep theological questions, arguing about the validity of critical enquiries as to the dates of the books of the Bible, preaching and hearing eloquent discourses, comforting and edifying one another, that we had to leave the Christless masses alone. . . .

Willie could not do that. Nothing illustrates the point so bluntly as Falconer's account of a meeting he had with the BBC hierarchy of the day. "The only people that matter for you," one southern manager informed the religious producers, "are the people who read *The Sunday Times* and *The Observer*." Falconer's comment that inasmuch as Christ died for all men a broader audience should be envisaged provoked "a furious riposte," and Willie's program was rejected.[17] That is how and why Willie's ministry came to be outlawed in southern Britain despite its phenomenal success in Scotland, Australia, New Zealand, and elsewhere. ("The Sermon of the Mount" series was later televised in England on Tuesday evenings, but only well after 11:00 P.M.!)

In the long run Willie's efforts to reach the man in the street were not seriously impeded by such small-minded attempts to obstruct him in that endeavor. He was, as we have seen, a superlative communicator throughout his career. As Robin Barbour put it, "No man of the present generation in the English-speaking world has done more to bring the Bible to the people than Professor William Barclay."[18] And, as the editors of his *festschrift* stated, "he has had an impact quite unique in our day. Indeed, to find a parallel in Scottish Church history, we would have to go back to Henry Drummond."[19] In reviewing that volume, Professor Rupp wrote of Willie as "an impressive and endearing modern Christian, the last perhaps of the great popularisers in our time, of biblical learning."[20] Surely he was all of these things (though we would hope that he will not prove to be the last of the great popularizers of biblical learning!), but what are the roots of his considerable success? Let us once more consider not the ingredients of his work, but the methods he employed in expressing them.

We would do well to begin where Willie began, by exploring that first most substantial influence upon him, on his mind and character, on his sense of vocation, on his determination in that calling, and on his early understanding of what constitutes good communication. I refer, of course, to his father, WDB, whose magnetic effect on his contemporaries took him to the top of his own profession and into a vital and successful lay ministry that was itself heavily influenced by the enigmatic, heavily criticized Henry Drummond. WDB was never more impressive than when he gave his very popular lantern lectures, often drawing audiences of over a thousand men. In his use of pictures to facilitate the delivery of his message we can see a highly significant parallel to the method eventually developed so successfully by his son. Willie used word pictures rather than actual photographic slides, and yet we can see in his method of presentation—short bursts of compelling description—a clear resemblance to the slide show format.

And so we can see why Willie always placed so much emphasis on the pictorial mind, why he never tired of saying he thought in pictures. But his enthusiasm for this method was not only linked to his own experience in the past; it reflected a perceptive understanding of contemporary needs. In using word pictures to good effect he was moving forward, not backward—coming to terms with a generation that had exchanged a fascination with the audible for a fascination with the visible, a generation that would rather look than listen. This emphasis was not altogether new, of course. We might recall Alexander Whyte's biographer commenting that Whyte's use of language relied on "visual images." Willie's did too. In the early days, writing for his Senior Sunday Schools, he very often recommended the use of Elsie Anne Wood's brilliant artwork in illustration of the main theme. The illustration naturally remained secondary to the central point, and yet in a sense it made the point, as is the case in the parabolic teaching of Jesus, to which Willie owed a tremendous debt, in method as in matter. He *visualized* (the word has a particularly apposite meaning when connected with Willie's thought-processes) his plot, his story, even his doctrine. He explained and expounded them in terms of little pictures, each carrying the matter one stage further, though not necessarily in a strictly logical progression. A chemist has to resort to a word picture of sorts to convey the idea of a bond between elements joined in chemical compound, even if it is so simple a one as the notation H_2O designating the union of hydrogen and oxygen in the elementary compound water. A biologist would have to go to great lengths to convey some idea of the extremely complex compound DNA, perhaps picturing its various component compounds as so many "lollipops" interacting with each other. The point is that whereas logicians ask for linear argument, chemists and biologists may find the need to present reality differently, pictorially. Willie knew that spiritual reality was nearer life than logic, that the various components of life cannot always all be comprehended as consisting in a strictly "logical" relationship to one another. Ofttimes a *description,* a picture, discloses a superior understanding of that reality. Sometimes the reality is simple, but sometimes it is fearfully complex, and so it is with the reality of God, of Jesus, of the truth—the *revealed* truth, Willie would remind us—of the gospel story.

Let us take an actual example of his writing from this time. It is an interesting example, because it reflects a central ambition of his life (which may well have been stimulated by Dr. Macaulay): to write effectively on Christology. We saw how he first attempted to do it "unintelligibly," that is, as a theological discipline; now he comes to it with all the experience of fourteen years of university lecturing, having written thirty or so books and having preached continually around the country. He is astonishingly evergreen in his approach; "the old, old story" is displayed in such telling freshness that the work became a best-seller, and that as a trilogy on the mind of Jesus!

Listen to what this deft communicator says of his method: "In this book I have not wished to argue; I have simply wished to set down the picture of Jesus as I see it."[21] And so he starts, the first frame (or paragraph) establishing "the beginning of the great discovery—why Jesus was born." The second frame, entirely unrelated to the first, jumps to the Passover festival of the Jews, set off against the background of festivals in Judaism. Frame three follows with a description of the preparations required for the festival and its meaning in history. Then in frame four comes the link with frame one—how Jesus came to understand the Why through his own mental preparation for the Passover. Frame five paints a description of the caravan journey to Jerusalem, emphasized by frame six, and frame seven conveys Jerusalem's splendor itself. Frame eight cuts away to the sacrifice of the Passover lambs, a highly dramatic picture of blood and sacrifice. Frame nine extends this yet more dramatically, and frame ten increases the drama with statistical detail of the slaughter that took place. Frame eleven brings us to the tension this bloodletting caused in the mind of Jesus with a pictorial representation of a conscience stricken by doubt as to this destruction of life clashing with Jesus' knowledge of God as Father. End of Scene 1. Willie has painted a brilliant picture of the background to the question of why Jesus was born. A whole series of subordinate pictures on Jewish festivals, history, sacrifice, and topography was used. "Argument" is entirely absent; logicality does not really come into it, at least as judged by the schoolmen.

Let us be clear about one thing in all this: that Willie's writing is accessible to nonscholarly readers by no means implies that it is unscholarly. His work is in fact underpinned by a voracious reading and an exhaustive study of scholarship at its best and most modern. He had perused the careful arguments and counterarguments that appeared in New Testament Studies and Old Testament Studies and many other similar journals, selecting what he with his computer-like brain wished and rejecting what he found unacceptable; he had been doing this for years. But he knew that sterile arguments were not the stuff that satisfied hungry souls, stimulated uninterested minds, gave hope to the forlorn and defeated, or strengthened those laid low by life's cruel twists. He was more intent on the picture of Jesus, which he knew was able to do those things. As he said in the preface to The Mind of Jesus, "this is what I believe, and this is how there came into my life the new relationship with God."[22] The inner reality rather than the external framework was what inspired his approach and his exposition. The framework is important—the "form" of the Gospel narratives must be explored— but we have before us a group of documents (the Gospels) that tell us of the reality of Jesus *as they stand.* Merely focusing on how they got to that state was in Willie's view as foolish and as clumsy, in artistic terms, as concentrating wholly on the artist's techniques and ignoring the picture itself. Willie was too much a pragmatist (an existentialist even!) to be waylaid by mere history or mere redactional techniques.

As Professor he had a duty to explore and explain those technical matters, and in class he did so fully and conscientiously. The fact that he was skeptical of some of their results is entirely another matter. He knew what needed to be made known and discussed, and he wrote of it from time to time (for example, in his collective 250 pages of introduction in his Daily Study Bible and more than 600 pages of introduction in *The Gospels and Acts*). But he also knew that in the end his students and readers needed *food,* not explanations or theories of nutrition; they wanted *life,* not descriptions of physiological processes. Only the person of Jesus could satisfy that demand—and that Willie sought to supply through his moving and trustworthy pictures. If others wished to spend their lives making and painting frames, so be it; he would paint pictures, and even pictures of pictures if need be.

The Pace Increases

The new year, 1964, opened with a certain air of contention evident. The demythologizers were trying to demythologize the New Testament, and the unconvinced were trying to demythologize them. Bishop Robinson had chosen to set his work in a posture of honesty, and his critics, piqued at its implications, thought it fair to reply in like fashion. In November, Dr. Robinson came to the fore again when he launched his campaign in favor of "a genuine lay-theology" of the church.[23] The Church of Scotland remained in the throes of ongoing arguments about baptism, Sunday observance (an issue that inspired a pamphleteering war), and the doctrine of the divinity of Christ. They also hotly debated the position of women in the church, coming out in favor of their admittance to the eldership, but finding themselves divided as to their eligibility for the ministry. Never had the gaps between "liberal" and "conservative" been wider, both adjectives now degenerating into terms of abuse rather than of meaningful description. Personal criticism was hurled at Willie by Captain Anderson, who strangely accused him of denying the new birth.[24] The '60s seethed yet more. "Radical chic" became a popular phrase used to describe the trendier dilettante activists (mainly middle-class), urgent in their support of various left-wing causes from Marxism on the one hand to "Christian socialism" on the other. In this latter category fell a whole series of good causes, such as the recently founded Amnesty International, Oxfam, Christian Aid, and many more. The writings of F. D. Maurice became popular again, and Alec Vidler boldly led in the cause of "participation." Willie never became a radical chic theologian himself, although he did express himself increasingly on behalf of such causes.

By this time Jane was into the teenybopper stage. It was the time of the youth-quakers, when everything traditional went by the board, self-expression predominated, and the only standards or relationships that mattered were the "existential" ones of the moment. War was anathema; the flower people heralded an era of peace. Much to her parents' embarrassment, Jane began to declare her sympathies for the hippie cause, though Willie took this with remarkable detachment and understanding—not with mere parental forebearance, but with an understanding of genuine youthful self-seeking. Willie himself sought that reality, if at times somewhat tongue-in-cheek. He was soon announcing that he had gone to see the Beatles, calling it a pilgrimage![25] In making this anouncement, he also made it clear that he did not go merely for Jane's sake, but because he wanted to. It was a social phenomenon of significance; he needed to see what drew the crowds, what excited and held them—this at fifty-eight years of age. He described the group as master-craftsmen—significantly, ordinary people who did things extraordinarily well, who were happy in their work, and by whom the church stood judged for its "petrified and fossilised orthodoxy."

In time, Willie's departmental pressures were partly relieved by the arrival of "much needed help" in the person of Neil Alexander.[26] He described the period from March 1963 to March 1964 as his "worst year of pressure yet." A month later he wrote regarding a manuscript sent for assessment that "I am thoroughly ashamed to have kept the book so long," explaining that he was still having to lecture fifteen hours each week and having to prepare four (sometimes five) hours of new lecture material on top of this. The manuscript in question, which he did eventually get around to, was Tenney's work on the resurrection, which Willie described as "ultra-conservative." That faction, he brusquely commented, "would hail it; it is no use to anyone else. If you want to go on that line, publish it; if not, leave it alone." He dashed off the letter of evaluation at The Queen's Hotel, Birmingham, as he zigzagged around the country, squeezing work into every spare minute of his time away from Glasgow.

In 1964 he had books published by three different publishers—Collins, SCM Press, and Westminster Press in the USA. He was also working for at least three more publishers and was at the same time committed to translate for Collins and Harper of America the entire New Testament. One of these publishers was James Clarke & Company of Cambridge, whose editor Douglas Millard pressed him remorselessly as a reader and assessor of manuscripts, as an author (Millard wanted a book of prayers for ministers, à la John Baillie), and as a potential editor for a series of foreign translations of theological works.

It was in November 1961 that he and Millard first met, in London, after a YMCA midweek meeting. Even then Willie confessed to "getting behind with everything"; he was soon enough apologizing yet again for being late in assessing another writer's manuscript. This manuscript was also conservative in its approach, but he nevertheless recommended it for publication—even enthusiastically—as "a very useful and attractive volume." The three-year gap between his letters to Millard is an indication of Willie's attitude against conservative (which is not to say evangelical) scholarship that was beginning to take place, as we have seen, in the mid '50s already. Despite the increasing pressures, we find him advocating to Millard the need for a good book on Pentecostalism and committing himself to become foreign translations editor for the Cambridge company. It was a considerable commitment for him to make, not only because of his already impossibly busy schedule, but because his German was not very good at all; he would have to rely on what others believed translatable. He expressly recommended the recently published survey of New Testament interpretation by Stephen Neill as a reliable source for titles that would be worthy of translation into English.

The file of correspondence between Willie and Millard concerning this project contains over three dozen letters, short and long, praising and carping, excusing and explaining, and generally reflecting the predicament of a man who had taken on too much work—work for which he could not claim real expertise. The work he did for the Cambridge publisher was valuable—of that there can be no doubt—though how he found the time to do it is a mystery. Willie was expected to read and assess, to travel, to attend to the basic bibliographical research, and all the while to hold up his end of their at times strained relationship over eleven years. Millard gave him lunch from time to time at his club, the National Liberal Club in Whitehall, which must have reawakened Willie's undergraduate convictions and perhaps literary recollections of W. R. Nicoll and his generation. Millard even called on him to explain things quite unconnected with manuscripts or publishing, such as, on one occasion, the objectives and history of the Drew Lectureship at New College, London. Willie did so without demur, and sadly with very few recorded words of thanks either. At times it was Willie that was kept waiting for information, as delays produced postponement and manuscripts piled up. In many ways this relationship and work is a good example of Willie's application of his expressed belief that it is better to do work imperfectly than not to do it at all. Like Paul Tillich, he always felt "the whip of anxiety about unfinished work," even if it was volunteer work, beyond the call of duty.

David Adams remembers seeing him working till 2:00 A.M. at a Lay Preachers' Conference in Oxford and then finding him still up and at it at 6:00 A.M. the next morning. And Professor G. B. Caird recalls a typical comment from him, made at this same conference following a dinner they shared: said Willie, "I'd be worn out if I had more than five hours of sleep!"[27] When his old friend Merricks Arnot wanted to contact him urgently, Kate suggested he telephone at 2 A.M.—that was the best time to be sure of reaching him! Commented Karl Barth in similar conditions, "I amble like a drunken man back and forth between desk, dinner-table and bed, travelling every kilometre with my eye on the next."

The delays and the misgivings Millard developed over the years eventually told on them both. Willie turned down Manton's *German Grammar for Theological Students*—he had actually gotten his son to read and report on it, despite the fact that Ronnie had no theological training (although he was a very accomplished German and French student)—and Millard was somewhat chagrined to find

Inter-Varsity Press taking it up and doing quite well with it. Willie recommended Dibelius's great work on form criticism, which the Cambridge publisher expedited only to find that the Americans had already commissioned the translation and published it. A book by a Church of Scotland minister, also recommended by Willie, sold very slowly—and Willie was asked what was to be done. The Library of Theological Translations series did eventually see the light of day (but only just); following the publication of volumes by Wrede and Dibelius it fizzled out, as did Willie's relationship with Millard.

This was by no means characteristic of his relationship with his other publishers, however. Willie enjoyed the closest of relationships with Andrew McCosh, as he did with several of the senior members of the Church of Scotland Publications Committee, with the International Bible Reading Association, with Ronnie Gregor Smith and then David L. Edwards of the SCM Press, and with Lady Collins. He saw his work for all of them as a function chiefly of service. Virtually all his books at this time were based on his journalistic work for *The British Weekly*. His contacts with his editors—Jack Stevenson, Shaun Herron, Denis Duncan, Ann Hastings, C. L. Mitton, and Bob Kernohan—were no less friendly. David Edwards has recorded his own recollections of this in the preface to *Testament of Faith:*

> For some years I was one of William Barclay's publishers and his name stood at the top of our authors' royalties. During those years I never discussed with him either publicity or money. He would sign any contract sent to him without a quibble over its financial terms, *provided only that he thought the book proposed might be useful.* [28]

Other publishers echoed the same sentiments. He was not conceited about his work; indeed, he held it in low esteem in comparison with work done by others, and was happy to allow editors whatever freedom they demanded in copyediting. Listen to his almost casual words to Paul Meacham regarding *The All-Sufficient Christ,* the only one of his books to have been commissioned by an American publisher: "Here, then, is the book. I hope that it is what you want. You need not refer to me about the adjusting of any words or phrases necessary for American purposes. I give you *carte blanche* to adjust as you like." [29] As Tim Honeyman has noted, he gave evidence of the same attitude when it came to translating his books into a wide variety of foreign languages. [30] Accuracy was important, but idiomatic expression had to be preserved: he was writing for the man in the street, whether in Japan or South America, Denmark or Malaya, Arabia or Korea, France or Germany.

But we must not understand Dr. Edwards's words as implying that Willie was foolish in respect to money or royalties. He had reason to be concerned, because the interests of others were involved: he often gave the proceeds from sales away, as in the case of several of his titles originally published for the Youth Committee of the Church of Scotland (which enjoys to this day the fruits of his industry) and in the case of his daily readings books, in token of his gratitude to

The British Weekly's last editor, Denis Duncan. He said of an overseas translation royalty, agreeing that its terms should be kept to the barest minimum, that "it will not be a big royalty, nor would anyone wish to make money out of the Japanese Church."[31] He even overlooked the breach of the agreement he made with the Church of Scotland in the matter of the Goodwill Scheme (originally supposed to be a strictly nonprofit venture, the agreement was broken when a second edition was produced). Not once did he bemoan or seek to increase the miserly four percent royalty he received on all overseas sales of the books written for his own church, which went a long way to subsidize the work of the Saint Andrew Press. But again, when others would suffer as a result of such niggardly treatment, he was quick to act, as for example in early 1968, when the Saint Andrew Press was seeking the rights to publish *The King and the Kingdom* from the Boys' Brigade. They offered two and a half percent on sales up to ten thousand copies, and three percent over that. Representatives of the Boys' Brigade were not amused. The General Secretary wrote a sarcastic "£106!" in the margin of his copy, and asked Willie if that was fair. Willie was not amused either; he refused to sign the proposed agreement, and correspondence developed. Commented Willie to the General Secretary,

> The Saint Andrew Press proposes to take fifty percent of these [American] royalties . . . and this will mean that the S.A.P., who have done nothing whatever to earn the money, will receive more than I, the author, and you, the owners of the copyright; which, as Euclid said, is ridiculous.[32]

Eventually the matter was settled (though whether the settlement in fact adequately served the interests of the Boys' Brigade is something of a moot point, even though a substantial increase was extracted). Henceforth the royalty check was to be shared by Willie and the Boys' Brigade. Commented Willie typically to its General Secretary, on hearing of its eventual arrival, "Just do as you wish about the cheque." Euclid had been satisfied; the money itself was a matter of no consequence to him.

During 1964 he continued to remodel his departmental work. A significant change took place in the autumn, when a presessional conference (at Troon) was introduced, the object of which was to break the ice with freshmen about to commence their ministerial studies—and, from Willie's personal point of view, to enroll members for his beloved choir, which he was leading for his seventeenth year.

The choir was serious business with him; it provided both a relaxation from the hard academic work of the college and an extra focal point of interest and publicity. The college held prayers each day for students and staff (in addition to the prelecture prayers offered), and Willie used to pray on Fridays for his students' work on the weekend (to which some students would murmur "and for those who will preach Willie's words"!) in addition to holding a terminal communion service, at which all were expected to be present. But the Choir was one of the outward-bound activities of the college, and the only one in which the

Above: *Willie with the Trinity College Choir.* Below: *At Troon, the Professor surrounded by his students, disguised as a* maître de choeur!

student body participated as a group. Its concerts had two important objectives: to raise cash for the college and to "recruit" likely young men (and later, young women) for the ministry. John Barclay Burns thinks they may well have put more people off the ministry than they attracted, but no one can deny the publicity the concerts attracted or the stimulus they gave to church work around the country. This year they had been on tour visiting for the first time the northeast of Scotland, traveling and singing (and joking) through Forres, Elgin, Aberlour, Lossiemouth, and Hopeman. In addition to the "entertainment" they provided, the members preached in many churches, conducted a broadcast service from High Street Church, Elgin, and held a youth rally there. Willie himself was extremely popular (his TV series on the parables of Jesus, "Stories Jesus Told," had just been broadcast, receiving terrific acclaim); he based himself at the Station Hotel, Inverness, from which he supervised his students' daytime work in schools and on industrial estates, working at his typewriter the meanwhile.

But the pace was having its effect. He wrote to Tom Strang of the Boys' Brigade that "doing a TV period [sic] always leaves me completely exhausted. As a means of communication I think it takes more out of the communicator than anything else."[33] He had revisited Bagshot prior to this, gone on to British and Foreign Bible Society translation meetings in London, returned to college duties for a month, and then gone away to Oxford to work with the NEB Apocrypha translation panel. On his way back from Oxford he preached at Newcastle, went on to a conference of Baptist ministers at Scarborough, and then returned to London to preach at the reopening service at Bloomsbury Baptist Church. Little wonder he enjoyed his holiday in the summer, from which he produced such occasional pieces as "The Necessary Exhaustion,"[34] and a piece of self-instruction entitled "Delegate That Work."[35] This holiday was notable in that he was able to enjoy "a lot of golf," which led to his being laid off after he sustained an injury to his arm (the result of unaccustomed exercise). Kate rebuked him for it, saying that it was a punishment for his pride in supposing he could do so much. His doctor demurred; he thought it a matter of conceit.

Willie *was* pleased with his work rate—of that there can be no doubt—but it was for him a bounden duty, not a prideful exercise. In him the Protestant work ethic (we may note how later he lists "work" among his beliefs, as part of his creed)[36] reached its apogee. It was a major inheritance from WDB, his father. He described his attitude to a young Methodist minister by the name of "Raymond" in an open letter in *The British Weekly* in April 1965, under the title "How I Get My Work Done."[37] There were nine ingredients to his success, the first four of which he called "rules":

1. He would always begin early, leaving home at 8:00 A.M. each day and starting work at 8:30.
2. He would keep going, seizing every opportunity to work even if time were short.
3. He would keep to schedule, not stopping to wait for inspiration.
4. He would do the work he was paid to do. ("This," he comments, perhaps wryly, "involves learning to say 'No.'")
5. He would employ every labor-saving device he could. As an example, he mentions his use of a dictating machine and secretary, which enabled him to get through an average of "forty or fifty letters a week."
6. He would tolerate no distractions. His deafness, he admits, provided him with the perfect protection.
7. He could keep going on five hours of sleep a night.
8. He was able to take short catnaps whenever he needed them.
9. He was blessed with a helpful wife. "Without her to look after me and put up with me," he said, "I could not do my work at all."

There can be no denying that last statement. A few months later he stated that "all the material demands of life are removed from my shoulders," and he went on to cite the old proverb that "a doting wife makes a helpless husband."[38] Not that Kate's doting was absolute—she was too shrewd for that. And she would freely speak her mind, though with little effect on Willie. He recognized her need for an outlet. As he said in another connection, "Far better to explode than live in a domestic refrigerator for days on end."[39] Kate traveled little at this time, preferring the familiar things of Glasgow and the quiet comfort of their Cathcart home, content with her husband and Jane and Ronnie and his family nearby. She was happy, once more enjoying good health.

Their grandson Michael had been born at the beginning of 1964—an event that provoked his elder sister, with an eye on her portly grandfather, to ask if he was not expecting a baby, too—a remark that made Willie take seriously his physical shape and made him determined to cut down on his high sugar intake (despite the fact that he believed it gave him energy). He even considered taking Rusty for a walk twice a day. Rusty himself was now a pudgy ten-year-old, and was almost as averse as his master to exercise. Such domestic concerns and interests are close to the heart of the essential William Barclay: a man who loved his family and his dog. Therein are reflected his essential humility and candidness, his sense of fun. And of course his home was a wellspring of anecdotes that he could so naturally incorporate into sermons, into parables-of-life. "There is no surgery," said he who hated doctors and hospitals and feared their devices, "like the gentle surgery of love." What a brilliant, penetrating, memorable phrase that is! Compared with the butchery of criticism, so slighting and denouncing, so full of sarcasm and snobbery, how majestic, how creative and healing is such a sentiment! And he was a master surgeon himself in applying it. Perhaps it should have been his epitaph, he who admired the right sort of gentleness and set kindness on a throne as the king of virtues. In him the meek were indeed inheriting the earth. It was based on his own privileged experience, into which suffering and death had obtruded their icy fingers on several occasions, without causing defeat. As he had urged in August, following a delightful Summer School Conference during which he was thrilled to stand arm-in-arm with Bishop Oji of Nigeria, "The greatest heroism of all is to keep going."[40] He kept going because he loved.

The pace did not lessen. From holiday he had gone on to summer school, where he lectured on "The Making and Meaning of Mark's Gospel." From summer school he went to Blackpool—ostensibly as a treat for Jane, though Willie enjoyed as much as she did the boisterous vulgarity of the Lancashire resort. Then it was down to London (where he bought some shoes in his favorite Charing Cross Road boutique—it was the age of boutiques), on to Oxford for another Lay Preachers Conference, thence to Skegness for the YMCA conference, and then to a triennial International Conference in the south of England at which he led the Bible studies. Returning north for the new academic year, he participated in the centenary celebrations of Brandon Parish Church at Motherwell, the scene of so many good memories for him. He was now the first choice in the minds of many when consideration was being given to conference, summer school, or retreat speakers. He served as the main attraction at the Centenary Social meeting, and at the start of the year he proposed the toast to the Immortal Memory at his publisher's Burns Supper, quoting from "The Vision":

> Preserve the dignity of Man,
> with soul erect
> And trust the Universal Plan
> will all protect

At this festive function he declared himself in full voice, holding his listeners spellbound with his recitation of the changes that had taken place during the last hundred years in society generally and in their locality specifically. He was at this time reviewing the biography of General Booth of the Salvation Army for *The Expository Times*,[41] and so was happily reminded of Booth's disturbing master-piece of 1890, *In Darkest England;* we can be sure he did not fail to remind his audience that the second part of the title of that book, so often ignored, is *And the Way Out*. At the end of the year he renewed contact with Renfrew Trinity by sending a tape-recorded message to Elizabeth Maddock, who had just concluded her forty-fifth year of Sunday School teaching.

Social concern and evangelical enthusiasm jointly charged this tireless and diligent worker. They were the twin pillars of his theology in its external mode, and he strengthened and reinforced them daily by his work and witness. No doubt the visit to the scene of his youth and the memories of childhood promises and of his father's preaching caused him to reflect on his own position and attitudes. He was both excited and anxious over the gathering pace of the ecumenical movement, the positive changes taking place in the Roman Catholic Church, and a growing social awareness among evangelicals. In 1962 the Evan-gelical Alliance, feeling (and perhaps *fearing*) the weight and growing influence of the World Council of Churches, had issued a statement on current issues that triggered much discussion—and contention. In this it had listed "certain essential doctrines on which no compromise is possible," a list with which Willie himself concurred very largely. (They were presently enjoying even more publicity, as the first National Evangelical Conference got under way.)

As the informal teacher to tens of thousands around the world, with a weekly responsibility to aid teachers and preachers of all descriptions by way of a journal committed to extend the social awareness as well as the devotional depth of its readers, Willie was bound to comment on such things. He did so at the beginning of October in a piece entitled "All One Body We," in which he characteristically criticized the tendency toward exclusiveness exhibited by the conservative faction. He declared, "I have all my life been grieved that the word 'evangelical' should have been annexed as their private property by people who think in a certain way. An evangelical is by definition a man of the Gospel."[42] May God save us, he continued, from evangelicals who put up barriers to worshiping God. It was bound to have irritated and angered those of their number who preferred personalities to principles, and criticism to affirmation.

In November he was delighted to be invited to address a group of Rangers and Rovers footballers. Fifty-four were present, and Willie once again witnessed to his virile faith, in which sport and honor—and even an "honest Rabelaisian vulgarity"—had their proper place. Someone spoke of the priggishness of some Christians, which led Willie to expatiate publicly on those who are "a bad debt to Christianity."[43] He was far from writing them off, but some conservative believers were again alienated by his rugged condemnation. Not that his pen was wielded exclusively against the conservatives. In early December he very cleverly wrote of the work of the radical critics in a piece entitled "On Reading the Bible," in which he castigated those radical critics who delight in finding a discrepancy because they can then use it "either to prove that the people who wrote the Bible are untrustworthy, inaccurate or unreliable, or that the story never happened at all, and that it is no more than a blundering fiction."[44] He concluded the piece by giving expression to one of his main emphases in biblical understanding: "Only the Spirit through whom men wrote the Bible can help us to understand and interpret the Bible. What the Spirit said, the Spirit can expound."

The British Weekly heralded a unique event in December with the headline "The Astonishing Dr Barclay": they were anticipating the imminent sale of the millionth copy of the Daily Study Bible—and that just in the United Kingdom! In America, which only took up the series in 1958, half a million copies had already been sold; foreign translations were now well under way in Chinese and Spanish as well, and other translations (e.g., in Norwegian) were already in hand. Commented Denis Duncan, ever the loyal protagonist,

> For years now he has served the whole Christian mission to the world by a fantastic contribution to Christian Education. His books now numbering nearly fifty publications run into huge quantities. His *BW* page for years has been unique in religious journalism. His appearances in pulpits and conferences all over the British Isles are hailed with admiration. His TV appearances as a teacher of the Bible have been acclaimed as the first of that kind ever produced. . . . What an achievement![45]

The language, while extravagant, is surely apposite. As the editor said elsewhere, yet more superlatively, his ministry is "the most outstanding personal ministry of print the world has ever seen." Willie, Kate, and Jane, following a much-appreciated interview with Glen Gibson of Scottish Television appropriately entitled "Life Begins on Sunday," quietly slipped away from Glasgow and the ensuing hullabaloo to their London hideaway, Kate and Jane to shop and Willie, as usual, to work (although he did find time to visit the "Sunday Night at the Palladium" show, upon which he reflected on the importance of fellowship).[46]

The presentation of the millionth copy of the Daily Study Bible was actually made to Kate on January 13, after their return to Glasgow. It coincided, happily, with the opening of a new religious bookshop in Edinburgh, part of the front offices of the Church of Scotland's headquarters having been set aside for the purpose. It was not the only plaudit he received at this time, for in the issue of *The British Weekly* that coincided with the presentation he was named the seventh of the ten most important people of his day.[47]

Of more consequence to Willie was his appointment as Dean of Faculty in his university, which necessarily increased his workload and stretched him beyond his limits. Former colleagues have been at pains to stress how business-like was his work in this area, a very important facet of his all-around personality. He was not only the committed (if not always the meticulous) scholar, not only the conscientious teacher and pastor, the head of family and immensely human man who delighted in young people, pets, and every strength and foible of mankind; he was also a conscientious manager of his department's—and now his faculty's—business. Neil Alexander nobly defends Willie against those who criticized him for his performance in this area: "They completely underrated his powers as manager of departmental affairs," he notes: "the actual distribution and discharge of teaching and examining duties and of administrative and pastoral obligations towards individual students: and his management of *us*, his junior and subordinate colleagues"—now three in number—Ainslie McIntyre, John Riches, and Alexander himself.[48] As Professor Allan Galloway, Principal of Trinity College, has noted, "He ran a tidy and happy University department. He did his tour of duty as Dean of the Faculty with flair, panache and evident enjoyment."[49] Alexander has further commented on Willie's primary commitment to his duties; he made it a point never to make any appointment that would clash with his lectures or any departmental business. This needs to be underlined; it recalls the practice he followed when minister at Renfrew: First things first, and faithfulness in little things. Galloway also underscores this faithfulness, stating that "this massive public involvement never tempted him to give short measure to the affairs of scholarship. . . . He never stinted his availability to his students."

History and the Gospel: Willie States His Case

Apart from his contributions to *The British Weekly*, there was an obvious drop in the amount of material Willie was producing for publication by 1966, clearly the result of pressures exerted by his increased duties as Dean. And, in addition to his university work, he was now also deeply committed to the painstaking work of translating the New Testament, the first volume of which—covering the Gospels and Acts—was to be completed in 1967. It would appear that he now regarded this translation as his chief work among his *parerga;* the whole project consumed over six years of his life, comparable only to the work invested in his Daily Study Bible. *The First Three Gospels* was his most scholarly work to date apart from his *Educational Ideals in the Ancient World;* unlike any other of his earlier books, it was written specifically for students, though he hoped that "laymen [would] be able to read it with profit." As ever with his books, it went out with the prayer that its readers might "gain a clearer knowledge of Jesus himself." He was glad to own his debts, "which are many"—not least to J. Ainslie McIntyre for help in correcting the proofs. What lay behind this book, like so many of his books, was his lecture-room notes, which succeeding generations of students had received. If *Educational Ideals* represents his New Testament bequest, *The Plain Man Looks at the Apostles' Creed,* published a year later, represents his theological bequest, to date, at least.

The Gospels were ever the real center of his faith and theology. Already he had written an eighty-two page book (*New Testament Studies*) introducing them, and for the Daily Study Bible Series he had written seventy-four pages of further introduction and well over two thousand pages of commentary. In addition to this, most of his handbooks either centered on the Gospels or contained large sections devoted to them, and there were also his two volumes on the parables and miracles of Jesus. Towering over all this was his three-volume "Christology," which was essentially a two-volume life of Jesus, with an additional volume on the forty-one titles used in reference to him throughout the New Testament.

The centrality of Jesus, to use the old evangelical phrase, was a tenet of substantial concern to William Barclay, and his work and witness must be judged in that light. But now, at the very peak of his career, he set out the scientific base, as it were, for his attitudes and convictions. Commented Michael Green, the evangelical scholar, "I have read no better book by Dr Barclay than this." It quickly sold out, and plans were drawn up to reproduce it in a properly extended form, as becomes a *chef d'oeuvre*. But, said his publishers regretfully, "various mishaps caused considerable delays." Indeed, it was not for ten years—until 1976—that it found its true fulfillment and status. It was no longer one volume, but two; no longer 317 pages long, but now a massive 644, with the additional study of John's Gospel and the second part of Luke's work (Acts) complementing the earlier purview.

The first edition was dedicated

> to the Memory of my chief
> G H C Macgregor
> who taught me many things
> but from whom above all I learned
> that scholarship and devotion
> can walk hand in hand

Willie did not claim anything new for his book, but he did believe its comprehensiveness would be useful, not least because he had dealt at length with such issues as the priority of Matthew, the calendrical theory of Mark, and "the all-important question of historicity." Comprehensive it certainly was, if by that one means "having the power of comprehending much." It is an astonishingly well-integrated mosaic of viewpoints as to the origins and nature of the Synoptic Gospels and the most pointed expression of Willie's phenomenal mind. In it he builds a substantial picture not only of the structure of the Gospels themselves, but of the constructive (and destructive) attempts made by scholars over two centuries to explain their present condition. Nearly everyone of repute in this field, from C. A. Abbott to Theodor Zahn, is cited; direct quotations abound in every chapter and on virtually every page, from Roman Catholics to "Plymouth Brethren," from Lutherans and Calvinists to Anglicans, Baptists, Congregationalists, Deists, Evangelicals, Fundamentalists, Greek Orthodox, and others. Astonishingly, he omits C. H. Dodd from his bibliography of sixty-eight general commentators and eight-one works of introduction (as he does in listing the thirty-three commentaries he had found most useful in preparing the work), although he does acknowledge Dodd's importance and contribution in a reference to *According to the Scriptures*.[50] The books cited (his footnotes number over three hundred) cover a period from 1890 to 1965, excluding ancient works such as those of the Church Fathers. Interestingly, he cites a number of literary (or quasi-literary) figures from the past by way of preface: W. E. Gladstone, Erasmus, Dora Greenwell, John Ruskin, and John Cairns. Such citations indicate that his interest in the Gospels is traceable to his youth, not least to the influence of WDB and, behind him, W. R. Nicoll (who highly rated Dora Greenwell, for example).

There are essentially five sections, covering nine chapters:

I. The Nature of the Gospels
II. The Initial Stage (i.e., the gospel before the Gospels)
III. Form Criticism Assessed (a sort of extended footnote to Section Two)
IV. The Pedigree of the Gospels:
    Chapter 4: "The Priority of Mark"
    Chapter 5: "The Hypothesis of Q"
    Chapter 6: "The Special Material of Matthew and Luke"
V. The Individual Gospels Explained
    Chapter 7: "Mark"
    Chapter 8: "Matthew"
    Chapter 9: "Luke"

Nothing demonstrates Willie's understanding of the Gospels better than this structure: only one section is given over to higher criticism per se, and that a mere six-page assessment of form criticism. Mr. Alexander might feel that this provides additional evidence to support his criticism of Willie on this point, and indeed it has to be admitted that Willie does choose a somewhat indirect approach to the subject—assessing form criticism by surveying Cardinal Bea's assessment—but the book's second chapter, "The Initial Stage," itself provides a masterly study of the practice of form criticism, in which Willie shows his knowledge and ability to survey and weigh intricate detail. (Significantly, the number of quotations from ancient literature and sources in this chapter nearly equals the number of quotations from modern sources: thirty-one to forty, respectively). All this is simply to say that Willie does in fact give adequate expression to the results of modern biblical criticism and their usefulness— repeatedly, throughout the whole book. Criticism to Willie bore the same relationship to right understanding of the Gospels, and to theology beyond it, as do anatomy and physiology to medicine: it was the indispensable prerequisite, the groundwork, but no more than that. And when it overreached itself, as form criticism tends to do in making historical judgments on literary-critical grounds, he issued a clear caveat. Typically, Willie never lost sight of the goal of criticism, which is to understand the Gospels as they have to come to us, as we have them today, and not in some tentative, theoretical preexistent form of which manuscript evidence supplies little confirmation; it was a principle he had first espoused in 1945, when he published the brief (and immature) New Testament Studies. Willie was never closer to Karl Barth's understanding of doctrine in the church than here. The Gospels—"the most important books in the world"—were the possession of the church; it was imperative to understand what they were saying, as well as how they were saying it, and that within the tradition of the church.[51]

This brings us back to "the all-important question," the question of the historicity of the Gospels. Much criticism of Willie could have been avoided had those who commented on his work understood this basic concern of his. The fundamentalists, many of whom rather simplistically dismiss the problem as not being serious, resting on an easy believism that pretends that no such difficulties exist—attacked him for making too much of the issue. The radicals—who tend to lose sight of the goal of their studies, becoming transfixed by an equally easy skepticism instead of pressing on to the spiritual realities—attacked him for being so positive, for not simply remaining equivocal about everything that was in the least problematical. Willie took the middle course, which after all was the straightest path to his destination: he addressed the difficulties, but made straight for the goal. And once again, he came under fire from both sides.

Behind this historical concern lay Willie's convictions concerning the over-arching reality of God, his understanding of God and his world, which ever powered his thinking and his acting: he could not separate the two—he would not. One of the curious (some might say unforgivable) deficiencies of his book is his omission of the *Entmythologisierung* controversy—the "demythologizing" debate that had created havoc in the '50s and '60s (not least in reaction to *Honest to God*), producing a library of monologues, discussions, and learned treatises. Willie's colleague Ian Henderson had produced a notable introduction to the essential features of the debate as early as 1952,[52] and throughout his university career Willie worked in its wake. And yet he omits it here! There are two reasons for this, in my view: first, he believed it was not immediately relevant to a straightforward introduction to the gospel, and in any case it had already been treated satisfactorily by the mainstream of British biblical scholarship (not excepting authoritative argument from men such as R. H. Lightfoot, whose work actually antedated the movement); and second, there is a little to be said for Alexander's opinion that its reality had not yet reached him, that it had not really penetrated into his mind. This is the truth behind Alexander's glib comment (which also omits any reference to the demythologizing debate) that Willie's "biblical criticism . . . never significantly altered to assimilate the measure of truth within such trends as Neo-Orthodoxy, Biblical Theology, Form-Criticism and Redaction Criticism."[53] He misses the mark in suggesting that this failure to assimilate such "truth" was the result of mental stagnation on Willie's part; the truth is that Willie had weighed the evidence and decided that history mattered, that the Gospels recorded historical events even as they also, simultaneously, promulgated theological truths. The "measure of truth" in the *Entmythologisierung* movement had been safeguarded by other means, as witness his emphasis (an embattled emphasis, we might say) on an "existential" understanding of the storm on the lake. Here, on the crest of a wave personally and professionally, he was not forgetting the lesson of the trough, even though it found expression before personal disaster overtook him: "the last thing in my mind is to make the miracles smaller, or to explain them away. What I want to do is to make them far greater, by trying to show that they are happening yet. God is everywhere active, if we had only eyes to see."[54]

If we had only eyes to see! Behind the sheer clumsiness of that expression (omitted in the revised edition of 1975, in which he nevertheless searched for other ways to reaffirm his twofold aim, "to explain the Miracles, not explain them away" and "to present Jesus as someone, not who *did* things, but who *does* things") lies a vibrant faith and profound theological awareness: "As I see it, there was not one specially miraculous age, but we are living in a miraculous world, because it is God's world." That was how he saw it in 1955. Eleven years later, his case having been further developed through a dozen intervening books, he quotes Adolf Harnack to express his belief that "the gospel as Jesus proclaimed it has to do with the Father only, and not with the Son." It is the action of *God,* Willie continued (significantly, though hardly less contentiously), that we see in Jesus Christ; a hero cult of Jesus is not Christianity.[55] There is not space here to go into the thought processes that led to this statement, which are traceable in his writings even though some facile commentators have chosen to ignore them. Still less do we have space to trace the developments from this to his later views (e.g., those of his revised and expanded edition of 1976, and the sometimes quite different views expressed almost contemporaneously with it in *Testament of Faith,* which led directly from his Adoptionist Christology).

Lying at the back of Willie's historical emphasis was his awareness of the central importance of the activity of God in the world, among men. Deny that, he says, and you deny God. Let the gospel realities evaporate into a thin mist of myth and fable and legend (no matter how carefully you may wish to define and refine those terms) and the God-man encounter itself will break down. The historicity of Jesus and his deeds is bound up with the incarnation itself. Not once does Willie allow the doctrine of the incarnation to be watered down, no matter how disconcertingly equivocal he appears to be in his interpretation of the deity of Jesus.

If we are to see more than a mere introduction to gospel criticism in his *First Three Gospels,* it is this—that it was his determined objective to wrest the Gospels from the hands of their traducers, to ensure that this "flight from history" (a phrase that repeatedly finds expression in this book) is arrested and reversed, exposed for the falsehood it really is. Not that Willie would have expressed it like that, nor that those who engage in such work should be thereby belittled. Willie welcomed their work, their methods, their erudition and powers of analysis and criticism. He may not have—he did not—agree with much of it, but he never denied its validity or the right, the duty, of free and full-scale enquiry; indeed, he gladly owned the positive results it provided. He owned that a certain "embroidery" of narrative had taken place (that is, a form of redaction!), that progress or development among the Gospel writers was clearly evident, and that it was necessary to expose and explain this if the truth were to be secured and clarified. But he also held that the "truth of the gospel" cannot be separated from "the truth about the gospels."

The world that Willie loved, in which he saw God's hand ever at work, was the same world in which these things had taken place. History was important because humanity was important—the "enmanning of God" was its proof. That is what it was all about. He was a man of—and for—the people *par excellence,* and a man of the world to boot.

PART FOUR

The Conclusion

Contemplating the next volume?

CHAPTER EIGHTEEN

His Highest Honor, His Lowest Point

An Undeviating Commitment

It was not only wrongheaded criticism of the New Testament against which Willie contended. The general spirit in which he worked was one of criticism, self-questioning, putting things—even the most "sacred" things—to the test. The essence of real education, he was to say in fond recollection of John M'Fadyen (who had introduced him to the questioning mind of Adams Brown) was for the teacher to be "an animated question mark."[1] The decade was seething with doubt, but the seething was essentially constructive, reforming. Seething is a culinary term, and the whole painful process was sustained in order that satisfying fare might be offered. Professor William Barclay, D.D., wore the Socratic mantle well, as became a man who walked—and drove, and talked, and played—with God. So it is that we find him, for example, asking in April 1955 if the church was just a place for old folk these days,[2] speaking of "colorless Christianity" in June,[3] and wondering in September if it might not be worthwhile to close popular downtown churches temporarily, making people attend their own parish churches, and then reopen them for the real, often underprivileged people who actually lived there.[4] The next month he was advocating rechanneling men's natural fighting instincts into socially acceptable endeavors such as a war against poverty and injustice,[5] and criticizing the judgmental attitudes of the pious in refusing donations from "questionable sources," pointing out that Jesus allowed himself to be anointed by a prostitute.[6] In December he was found reminding his readers that the Kingdom of God belongs to the childlike, not the "adults," and was clearly prepared to be counted a fool in so saying.[7] In February 1966 he was at it again, remorselessly applying the disturbing reality of first-century Christianity to twentieth-century smugness by recounting some of the perceptions that "nonreligious" people have of the religious as being sourly disapproving, unable to enjoy themselves roundly, and tongue-tied in the face of those outside the church. It was not a waste of time, Willie boldly enjoined (à la Wesley), to read newspapers, see films, watch television, or participate in sports.[8] He took stick for this "worldliness," and later admitted to it as such in confession-like tones.[9] But this should not lead us to believe that he failed to deplore the real worldliness of the selfishness and self-seeking of men, their tendency to compromise, do deals, bend the truth; expediency was not part of *his* language. "In a very real sense I love the world and all that is in it," he remarked, placing himself at the center of things in ways that some of his critics could not even guess at.

In April 1966 another series of his television lectures was broadcast, his subject being the nature of the church—its worship, its proclamation, and its apostles. As usual in his final week he was subjected to questioning, placed in the witness box and interrogated about his life, his beliefs, and his faith. Kate, for all her interest in Willie's work and his students (which James Gilfillan, himself one of those students, reported on in *Life and Work* in August of this year),[10] was not much pleased by this sort of breast baring, much less by the criticism and abuse it tended to evoke. Raised in her father's sober and dignified parish, in which "duty" rather than the abandonment of real love was of the essence, she looked on this involvement in the same way all such have looked on "enthusiasm": she felt not so much unamused as degraded. The cynicism that had grown in her following Barbara's death now found fresh expression in private criticism. Had Willie not done enough in the discharge of his convictions? Was he trying to kill himself with yet more work, more commissions, more seemingly impossible promises? Was not all this publicity going to his head? How could he think his views were so correct when so many silently smiled at him, at them? Concern led to embarrassment, and embarrassment became humiliation. Her attitude was not one of hatred, but of love—of feeling left out, left behind. It was a development that was to disrupt their life together, to bring the most terrible of all sufferings to Willie and to Kate his loving wife.

One thing haunted Kate, as it haunted the minds of not a few at this time, as Willie more and more declared himself in favor of the underprivileged, the underdog, the drop-out, and the hippie. In his Alex Wood lectures of 1963 (published under the title *Christian Discipline in Society Today*) he had even called into question the judicial system of Great Britain. He was speaking in Scotland, where the system is different from the rest of Great Britain, but this made no difference to the point he was making: "If the principles laid down here are correct, then the whole system of justice in this country is wrong and unchristian."[11] Kate may well have remembered the fracas of 1939, when Willie made his appeal for pacifism over the heads of government to the people directly. It was disturbing, revolutionary-sounding nonsense to her way of thinking, and she knew she was not alone in thinking so. And Willie agreed! But he knew his Tennyson ("the civic slander and the slight") too well to worry about such things. He acknowledged Kate's help in writing his occasional pieces ("I need a critic," he said, "in case I say something silly")[12] and later said of her, "my wife is my sternest critic."[13] Nevertheless there came a time when being misunderstood did wound and worry him.

In early March he produced another disturbing sally, this time asking if the church had not taken a wrong turn when it went into its own buildings, thereby extinguishing its true light. Better, Willie urged, to have churches more like homes than ecclesiastical institutions.[14] He never felt guilty about rocking established positions; indeed, he felt it his business to do so! He also battled against irrelevancies by writing on "the things which matter."[15] He found it incredible that so much energy was being directed by his church (and, by extension, other churches) to mere money raising, when the alarming drop in participation in churches, Sunday schools, and youth work continued apace. In 1976 he would be found writing to one of his former students lamenting the loss of over a quarter of a million members from the Church of Scotland in a single decade.[16] Urgent relevant action was called for. The church was not being true to its real character and its basic calling, he felt. In June he admitted he was going to be controversial: in a piece entitled "Systematizing the Grace of God" he denied the validity of ordination at the hands of bishops and superintendents![17] Such human regulations he could not dare accept; it was a blasphemous dictation to God of how he should act. (Earlier, he had inveighed against the standardization of the conversion experience, another bête noire of his, in speaking on his oft-repeated theme of "many ways to the stars," when he contrasted appositely the conversions of Saul Kane and C. S. Lewis.) It was not only bishops and evangelicals who came under fire from him. In a provocative piece entitled "Intellectual Suicide" he assessed the attitude of his ministerial colleagues toward their *essential* function as teaching elders, complaining that they had forfeited the right of being "the best educated ministry in the world." His concern had been provoked by a refresher course for ministers that he had helped to organize; 820 personal invitations had been posted, garnering a miserable fifty-two enrollments, of which only forty-eight actually showed up.

In all this Willie was quite unlike the man of yesteryear, who was evergreen in his positive attitudes, patient to the extreme, nonjudgmental, tolerant, positive, and encouraging. A new mood was taking over—perhaps a result of his sense that he had only grudgingly been given his professorship, perhaps the result of his feeling left out of some scholarly circles and even some circles of influence in the committees of his church. Certainly incipient poor health was also a factor, though not yet one he consciously recognized. Another cause, surely, was his crushing work load, for despite the extra help provided by his departmental assistants, he was unbearably hard-pressed, not least by his publishers. In the autumn of 1966 *The British Weekly* inaugurated a new page for teachers and preachers, which to that point Willie had been handling superbly alone. Following the renewed emphasis on lay ministry, and in preparation for still further developments, the page took the new heading "School for Laymen." Alongside Willie, such writers as Charles Duthie and Edwin Robinson were to appear regularly, with other experts (such as G. A. F. Knight) taking up occasional series. Willie himself commenced the new feature with a series called "William Barclay on New Testament Theology." Despite an introduction on October 6, it was necessary to explain the scheme still further on October 27 and again on

November 3. The change was not an uncritical success, and by November 17 the paper was publishing letters to the editor complaining that the new series was too heavy, too theological. The word was "keep it simple." Willie owed his success, they said, to the fact that he had "a ready ear for the layman"—a significant comment to make of a stone-deaf man whose mental strength lay in thinking in pictures! James Martin made the point in another regard when he said, "I have never known anyone who matched his faculty for understanding questions. . . . Times without number he got to the heart of . . . a question better than the questioner himself understood it."[18] And so 1966 wore on. Willie writing and lecturing, traveling, speaking, and broadcasting, all the while ensuring a smooth and efficient running of his department, and of the faculty itself.

In the autumn of each year one of the most prestigious committees of the church, the Nomination Committee for the Moderator, meets to decide who shall be Moderator of the General Assembly for the year following. The committee is made up of about fifty senior individuals, ministers and lay people, who are appointed by the Synods for the purpose. Included among them are the ex-Moderators. Anyone may nominate, and the committee by tradition makes the result of their deliberations a unanimous vote. The post itself is for one year only. Ostensibly the duty of the Moderator is to oversee the affairs of the General Assembly, but the position also entails a broad range of invitations to represent the church the length and breadth of Scotland and beyond. By tradition, at least one official visit is arranged to an overseas mission or area of special interest, and there are several more official visits to civic and ecumenical gatherings of all sorts. It is the highest public office in the church, though curtailed within the presbyterian system of church government. As such it is widely regarded as the acme of all service for the church, whether pastoral or academic. When the Nominations Committee made its choice for 1967, to echo the words of Acts, the lot fell on Willie.

To the committee's consternation, and in breach of all tradition, Willie refused the honor. *The Scottish Daily Express* said what many churchmen wanted to say when it published a plea for Willie to reconsider his decision: "THINK AGAIN, PROFESSOR BARCLAY" it thundered in headlines.[19] It spoke of the disappointment, the confusion, and the dismay his rejection of the invitation had caused. It reminded him of the high esteem in which he was held— "universally respected as a good and wise man," admired for his simplicity and respected for his humility. It portrayed him as a wonderful teacher who had inpressed "thousands" of students and ordinary people with his powers and ability, and it spoke of the "millions" who had been taught and illuminated through his writings. No one doubted he would be "an outstandingly successful Moderator," a man to match the occasion on which Queen Elizabeth the Queen Mother would be serving as High Commissioner. (This latter statement was quite incorrect: Her Majesty the Queen Mother has never so acted, though Her Majesty Queen Elizabeth did appear in person in the Assembly of 1969.)

"Please think again, Professor," *The British Weekly* pleaded, adding its voice to the others, reminding him of the consideration due the committee for nominating him "unanimously," to the "thousands of people in the Kirk who regard you as an ideal choice," and not least to the man who would be "appointed as the second (at least) choice for the job" (who did in fact later come to be called, unkindly, "the substitute Moderator").[20] It concluded by lecturing him on the need to balance service against what the newspaper portrayed as his undue modesty: "Modesty is indeed a virtue. But it ceases to be beneficial when it keeps such a man out of the Kirk's most senior office." The piece is highly reflective of what others were thinking. To say that his refusal had a stunning effect is to risk understatement. Once surprise and confusion were overcome, the church had to get on with its business. A first-class replacement was found in the person of Roy Sanderson, though it was not till December that *Life and Work,* which had rigorously observed the protocol, made his acceptance known in a "Stop Press" announcement. A great silence, almost of complicity, fell over the incident; those who have since written of Willie have been almost unanimous in choosing to pretend it never happened. Commented *Life and Work,* in a later article entitled "Subject for Speculation," "There has been considerable speculation as to who declined to stand as Moderator of the General Assembly. . . . It is not for *Life and Work* to guess, and Dr Barclay has rightly avoided being drawn into comment."

But it is important that we look into the reasons Willie had for refusing to accept the honor of what presumably would have marked the high point in his career as a loyal servant of his national church, if for no other reason than that the refusal was an apparent contradiction of his service attitudes and commitments to date. No one can deny that he would have been a brilliant incumbent of the Moderator's Chair. His record to that point had ideally suited him to put the church on the map advantageously during his year in office, enhancing the already high prestige in which the Church of Scotland was held around the world. Few doubted that he would have fulfilled the hopes of T. W. Manson of the Presbyterian Church of England, who said on his own nomination to that office that "what the Presbyterian Church needs is not a Moderator, but an Accelerator." Willie's daughter Jane might complain of her father's habit of driving at twenty-eight miles per hour in the center of the road, but Willie would have conducted the affairs of the Assembly with aplomb, at a brisk pace, and would have added flavor and distinction to a great line of Moderators in the united church stretching back to John White himself.

Life and Work was quite wrong in stating that Willie avoided commenting on the matter (unless it merely meant that he had refused to comment to his own church's paper): by December he had commented to a number of people, and in fact had agreed to be interviewed about it on television by David Steel, then a newspaper and television journalist. As a son of the manse himself, a lawyer by training, and a former member of Murdo Macdonald's great St. George's West Church, Glasgow, Steel was in a position to understand what many were feeling and to probe for the truth. The interview took place at the end of

December, but viewers south of the border had to wait until January 5, when *The British Weekly* reproduced an edited script. In this interview (in which Willie interestingly stated that his call to the ministry took place when he was fifteen, not twelve), he answered Steel's blunt question of why he had refused by saying, "It would be impossible for the head of a University Department to be away for a year. I have an obligation to the American research students [there were seventeen of them] who have paid to study under me. I am afraid that, in any case, I haven't got the figure for the traditional moderatorial dress!"[21] These are two of the reasons he regularly gave, and gave quite sincerely. Although the humor was meant to be diversionary, he did in fact criticize and even scoff at the seventeenth-century costume the Moderator was expected to wear, and he had deep feelings against it. To former church member of Renfrew Trinity Anne Dunderdale (née Evans) he once "did a prance of himself in the outfit . . . and wondered how long he would survive the mincing gait [it] necessitated"—a performance she found "hysterically funny."[22] His personal shape had nothing to do with it; it was the *image* it presented that he strongly objected to. His son Ronnie is emphatic on this: had his father consented to wear the costume, he would have overthrown a principle of long standing; he could not have done so in good faith.

Willie had a similar genuine concern over forsaking his general and advanced students. We shall shortly see that criticisms were made of his super-intendence of the research students' work, which he took very seriously. Every day from 2:00 P.M. to 4:15 P.M. he attended to this task specifically. We have seen that it was his practice to refuse any invitation that might have interfered with any of his teaching responsibilities. Others called to the Moderatorship had not taken such care for their regular work. Many of them looked on the position as a higher calling than their academic duties and sought a leave of absence to fulfill it. Since White's moderatorship in 1929/30, no fewer than ten academics had served their church in this way, two of them—Professors Main and Pitt-Watson—coming from Glasgow itself. We need have no doubt that the universities themselves appreciated the honor, in which they properly shared. But Willie was not merely the head of his department, but Dean of Faculty as well, and he clearly felt that that was his overriding duty.

Do these reasons represent the whole truth? Did he really reject the invitation on the principled basis of old-fashioned clothing and present responsibilities? We cannot doubt that he possessed the moral courage to have refused the ceremonial dress had he so chosen. And he had on occasion excused himself from certain obligations in deference to yet more compelling duties: he stopped writing for the Boys' Brigade, for instance, when greater opportunities to write came his way, and we shall soon see him refusing to appear on television (the only man to have done so, in Falconer's experience) because he thought it right. Why could not the higher give way to the lower in this case?

We are bound to look upon his regular explanations, then, as something of a diversion, despite the grain of truth within them. Let us recall our

In his office, ready to see students: duty first!

man. He was of virile Free-Church extraction, still possessed of the beliefs, attitudes, and spirit that made "Free Churchmanship" the force it had been. He was irregular—some would say irresponsible—in the matter of his attendance at presbytery, a "sin" of which he was quite unrepentant. (As Bob Kernohan has suggested, "Barclay was probably a better Christian and a better Protestant . . . than he was a Presbyterian in the purely literal sense.")[23] He was an individualist, not a committee man, ever defending the propriety of the individual asserting his freedom,[24] applauding those who dared to break the mold; in fact he was actually anti-committee, declaring them on more than one occasion to be the *cause* of decline in preaching and sound pastoral work.[25] If it is saying too much to call him antiestablishment, it is certainly not too much to say that he was not averse to attacking the establishment viewpoint, be it in matters of the safety of the realm, the practice of the judiciary, or whatever; and, indeed, he would appear not a little antiestablishment when he vigorously defended the ordinary man caught up in an administrative or procedural web. He was a fearless proponent of church unity, but for the most part opposed to the ecumenical movement insofar as it attempted to engineer such unity "from above." All his viewpoints centered on his being a man of the grass roots, not of the leadership, still less of the manipulators.

The oligarchic constitution of the church worried Willie, as he was frank to say in the Steel interview when the interviewer carefully turned him back from his diversion to the real issue:

621

STEEL: You have criticised the church for moving in what you call "an atmosphere of antiquity" and you have attacked "archaic language, architecture and clerical dress"—even the Moderator's eighteenth-century
court dress. But, by changing these, wouldn't you be divesting the
church of its dignity?

WB (bluntly): It is not dignity but dynamism that the church needs. I would take
away the dog-collar and the robes and have the minister in ordinary
clothes. The church should be a family.

Nothing expresses Willie's view of the church or his role in it better than that
statement. He was affronted by artificial barriers, class structures, social discrimination, backstairs intrigue, the compromise of committees, and the pressures of
peer groups. Nothing thrilled him more than when the Queen or the Duke of
Edinburgh broke through those barriers—"royal service" he called it. In this
interview he also reiterated his view of the familial nature of the church in
stronger terms, at the expense of the church/state relationship (which he nowhere
defends), by emphasizing the need for laughter and joy in church life, by
objecting to Communion Cards ("tickets of admission" to the Lord's Supper),
and by asserting the need for greater lay involvement in the leadership of the
church. Nowhere does he suggest that he accepts the meetings of presbyteries
and synods as "courts" of the church. That was not Willie's understanding of
koinōnia, fellowship.

Behind all this, there is a still deeper conviction, to which he draws attention
when he tells Mr. Steel that his favorite disciple was Peter. He was not actually
asked why, but he supplied the answer all the same: "because he was reckless
and uninhibited." Now, Willie was a stern critic of recklessness at times, especially
evangelical recklessness, so what does he mean here? It is surely an admittance
of and a demand for spiritual freedom. He would not be tied down to a certain
way of life any more than to a propositionally defined belief. He genuinely
believed that his ministry to the plain man could not afford to be linked publicly
to an ecclesiatical system so divorced from his chosen constituency. Lord Morley
once said that "the opinion of Parliament is the opinion of yesterday; the opinion
of the judges that of the day before yesterday." In matters of state this is necessarily
so, advantageously so: it is dangerous to legislate too quickly, to ignore precedent,
long deliberation, and public opinion. But Willie held it a false analogy to
suggest that ecclesiastical bodies were similar to democratic governing bodies;
church committees, after all, are notoriously oligarchic and bureaucratic. Did not
Andrew Herron himself explain that a Moderator, by definition, is "a mechanical
contrivance to regulate and control the flow of gas"?

Five years later, answering another question about his refusal to accept the
nomination, Willie stated, "I just could not see myself in that job . . . nor could I
run the General Assembly. . . . One must be honest with oneself and know one's
limitations."[26] What matters most, in matters of church, he contended, is that its
leaders be Spirit-sensitive, Spirit-directed, and Spirit-prompted. And Willie had
little faith in committees (or courts) to safeguard this. A few years later, when the

dust had settled, he was interviewed by his friend Jack House for the "Monday Interview" in *The Evening Times*. Asked why he had declined the nomination, Willie said with great directness, "I felt that I was totally unfitted for that kind of duty. I've never been a member of the Establishment. It's not for me."[27] It was, then, an action dictated by principle. He would be an Accelerator in his own way, "recklessly" when necessary; he could not be a Moderator.

Kate's reaction to all this has not been left on record. One of her proud family recollections was of her father walking behind Dr. Mitchell on the Union Walk of 1929 as his moderatorial chaplain. Willie's honor would of course have been so much the greater, and she would doubtless have delighted in taking up the role of Moderator's wife, loved the official car, the Edinburgh flat, the ceremonial functions. She would surely have made a fine consort and helped him in fulfilling its duties. She may well have felt he was taking his role too seriously and not taking his corporate duty seriously enough. Nevertheless, though she may well have been disappointed by Willie's decision, she probably recognized along with Ronnie how impossible it would have been for him to accept.

Once Willie had made his decision, he put it behind himself and began to devote himself with yet greater resolve and fervor. But others were not so quick to forget. An undercurrent of disapproval remained. In "The School for Laymen" page of *The British Weekly* he was explicitly criticized for being "unnecessarily confusing"[28]—an unusual criticism for him—and his plan to provide an introduction to the Psalms was shortly dispensed with. (He was to return to the project when he attempted to produce a Daily Study Bible commentary on the Old Testament in retirement, but he was once again criticized for his work there.) Quiller Couch used to say that public speaking should be repetitive to the point of tedium, and public writing terse to the point of obscurity. Willie was now all but reversing that advice. His speaking was in many respects repetitive, but scarcely to the point of tedium, as he began to inject new—and often disturbing, sometimes outrageous—elements. He was becoming known for baiting opponents, and it was not always certain when he was being ironic and when he was being serious. He was becoming reckless. His writing, notably his journalistic writing, was by no means terse, and obscurity in any case was anathema to him. From the middle of 1967 his "Seen in the Passing" causeries in *The British Weekly* became noticeably more prolix and began to lose the "Vintage Barclay" sparkle; the wine had become a little fusty. Details of his domestic life became much less prominent. Rusty was gone, Jane was now a self-conscious teenager "coming on sixteen," the grandchildren were now an everyday part of their grandparents' lives, and Kate had again begun to fall victim to migraine attacks. (She and Jane had spent part of the summer with Kate's sister, but only a temporary respite was found.) At sixty, Willie now preferred to keep his home life private, a world of seclusion despite the frequent visits of his students and others. His causeries had became more formal and less spontaneous, less spicy. Anecdotes of home life were replaced by anecdotes of his college work; he began speaking of the busiest day in the college year,[29] patterns of ministry,[30] and any number of references to the religious and theological problems of the time.[31]

Some of the familiar landmarks, both physical and personal, were disappearing. The man who had always "looked forward" and worked accordingly was now quite definitely looking back. He once remarked that when one began looking back it was a sure indication that one was getting old. It was in this year that meetings of the Old Dalzielians commenced, of which Willie has written in *Testament of Faith*.[32] Not every school could produce such a distinguished array of talent, covering so wide a field of human endeavor and success as medicine, law, education, industry, banking, and the church. In September 1968 he attended the memorial service for Andrew McCosh (significantly held in the chapel of the Glasgow YMCA), where he deeply mourned the loss of his "closest friend for the last thirty years."[33] He was reminded of the great comfort and strength McCosh had supplied at the time of Barbara's loss, of the genuine concern that had highlighted by contrast the superficiality of other friendships of the sort that always gather around men of distinction and substance. Kate had long been sensitive to the hypocrisy of such fair-weather friends, at times exasperated to the point of anger at Willie's apparent inability to see them for what they were. He simply sought to follow the advice of Dr. Johnson and keep what friendships he had in good repair. It has to be said that he was not an entirely happy man (that itself was a marked indication of change from former days), as some of his photographs—and especially the artists' impressions—show.[34]

Willie lost another friend and colleague at this time when Ronnie Gregor Smith, Willie's former publisher at SCM Press (and later at the Department of

Dalziel High School reunion—men only! [Photo courtesy of *The Scottish Daily Express*]

Publications of the Church of Scotland, which then published *The British Weekly*), died. At first glance, Smith does not seem to be the sort of person to whom Willie would have deep attachments. He was highly intellectual, with great theological depth and considerable involvement in radical Continental theology—a theologians's theologian. But his widow, Käthe, states that their friendship was nonetheless strong; perhaps it had the special virtue of complementarity. In any case another ally had disappeared, adding yet more work to the already overburdened Dean of Faculty and his colleagues. The strain proved too much for Ainslie McIntyre, who now fell ill himself.

Furthermore, some of Willie's views were also the subject of change and concern. *The Lord's Supper* had been published a little earlier, in which he had simply sought "to examine the history of the sacrament." Reviewing it, Kenneth Grayston bluntly stated that "he is out of touch with modern discussion and present needs."[35] Even the normally adulatory *New Zealand Messenger* declared it in headlines to be "Not the Best Barclay,"[36] and *The Church of Ireland Gazette* commenced its own survey of the book by saying that it was "a disappointing book on an important subject." One man who did enjoy it was the principal of the Scottish Baptist College, R. E. O. White, who wrote to say so. Apparently encouraged, Willie wrote back to White to say that having explored and aired his views on the one sacrament he was now ready to tackle the other—the doctrine of infant baptism, which he admitted had long troubled him.[37] It would be interesting to know who deterred him from this project; presumably it was the same sort of individual who warned Bob Kernohan "against ever giving him a platform for his views on the Old Testament and insisted: 'Don't on any account let him give you a series on the Atonement.'"[38]

"William Barclay's Finest Hour" is a tribute written by Denis Duncan that appeared in October of that same year vaunting Willie's incredible record of industry and success with journalistic freedom.[39] It was manifestly untrue for him to say in it that "for over a quarter of a century William Barclay has written every week in *British Weekly*"; editors often have to be their own publicists and the result is usually exaggeration. But Duncan was right in describing his work as "phenomenal" and "extraordinary," and he could scarcely avoid using such phrases as "this dedicated writing machine" and the like. Nor did he neglect to point out the additional weight of his university work and its guelling responsibilities. He, too, had noticed the difference in Willie: "There was a time when it looked as if his appointment as Dean had been the straw that broke the man. The sense of burden came briefly through. But briefly it was." The physical aspect of this burden was to restart him slimming—"with very considerable success" (he managed to lose two and a half stone [thirty-five pounds] in three months).[40] But caused by a *straw*? Some straw, this "welter of administrative work associated with the modern university"! Some of his nonofficial correspondence has latterly come to light that shows with what carefulness he sought to safeguard the University's standards and his students' interests at all levels. Some students needed special attention, and they got it—not from an interview with a friendly Dean remorselessly applying the regulations, sifting the academic wheat from the chaff, but from a father figure, interested, concerned (too concerned, said some colleagues, and too soft), himself volunteering to go the extra mile, urging them on to make one final effort, easing their anxieties with calming words, gifts of books, and, in at least two cases, fully paid holidays to secure adequate recovery from illness.

And *briefly?* The record shows that this was an inaccurate description, despite Willie's valiant attempts to do the impossible. He was no longer the man he had been, for all his attempts to refute the predictions that "it couldn't be done" and to reply with a chuckle. Alas, his chuckle became a grimace from effort and sheer strain, which Kate at least recognized. And he was frank in his reply to James Gilfillan's question as to whether he did not regret having left the parish ministry: "Yes, many times. . . . There was personal contact with people, it was one of the happiest times of my life. At university things are different. . . ."[41] As his interviewer stated, "it is when he says this that one realises that the parish ministry remains his first love, and that not even the university has supplanted it in his affections." If he had secured the Chair of Practical Theology, which would have kept him more closely related to parish and ministry matters, it might have been different. Perhaps not. Willie never seemed to come to terms with the speed at which students come and go—a sure mark of his essential shyness. He needed time to build deep relationships; he needed deep relationships; he felt these changes keenly.

The purpose of Mr. Duncan's tribute was to greet Willie's first volume of New Testament translation. "Yes—his greatest hour. . . . Words fail to describe the importance of this achievement. It must be William Barclay's finest hour. . . . This particular event marks the reaching of a mark. And New Testament work can never be the same again." That it was the culmination of all that had gone before cannot be doubted; Willie himself referred to it as "my own biggest news."[42] But even his greatest admirers—and they were legion—did not really expect it to transform New Testament work. Influence it a little, perhaps; overturn this or that detail, probably; greatly facilitate the plain man's reading of the Gospels and Acts, certainly; but no more than that in the wake of the "translation fever" that had gripped the academic and the general Bible market since the end of the war. For one thing it was a paraphrase, a sentence-for-sentence rendering of the original (in some places, even a paragraph-for-paragraph rendering), not a word-for-word translation, and such cannot, by definition, be a wholly reliable tool. For example, when Willie used the phrase "a normal day's pay" for a denarius, he economically provided a bit of useful information (it is a good illustration of what Duncan calls Willie's "interpretative genius"—it is brilliantly immediate in its effect), but he simply did not provide a pure translation.

We ought to take note of the fact that it was never Willie's aim to make a pure translation of the text of the New Testament (even supposing such a thing to be possible). In doing this work (he had been at it for six years now, to the exclusion of other work and activities) he had two aims in view: "The first was to

626

Willie at work on his translation of the New Testament

try to make the New Testament intelligible to the man who is not a technical scholar. . . . The second was to try to make a translation which did not need a commentary to explain it."[43] That is no easy challenge when one is dealing with a two-thousand-year-old text from a Mideastern, if not actually Oriental, culture. And to seek to do it without further aids being necessary (which is quite unlike the objective of his first translation in the Daily Study Bible) took him necessarily into paraphrase, and further, into doctrinal interpretation itself. The New Testament does "speak for itself," but to try to facilitate that—Willie's explicit goal—is to risk objection at many different points.

He had long experienced these objections on the translation panels of the NEB Apocrypha and the Diglot—the "Translator's Translation" of the British and Foreign Bible Society (which was published virtually simultaneously with his own translation). Many and many a time (to use one of Willie's own favorite locutions) he had fenced with his colleagues over this or that particle, nuance, word, or phrase. Often he had gone away to write a complete screed on some point at issue (e.g., on *polis,* "town"; on *angeion,* "vessel"; on the actual speech— the *ipsissima verba*—of Jesus in the Gospel of John, and the Johannine practice of direct quotation; on *sunchrontai,* "associate"; on *paraklētos,* "helper"). And often

627

he had been overruled by the Chairman, aware of a majority of dissenting voices being raised against Willie's viewpoint. In sum, Willie was acutely aware of the deficiencies under which any one man labors in such work. He noted Luther's criticism of Jerome's great work, the Latin Vulgate translation (significantly from *vulgus*, "the common people") for its having lost the promise that "where two or three are gathered together in my name, there am I in the midst." He also noted that this did not prevent Luther making his own translation; any more than the disagreements he had encountered would prevent him from doing so. But if his work lost the depth brought by the fellowship of a translation panel, there can be no doubting that it carefully preserves the sense of thrill, of immediacy, of urgent reality that characterized all Willie's writings. And readers are further aided by the inclusion of very short introductions—one to all of the Gospels collectively, and one to each of the gospels individually. Even the arrangement of his material is significantly interpretative. Further scholarly apparatus was kept to the barest minimum; there are a mere twenty-six footnotes, all of them explaining textual difficulties regarding omissions of phrases, sentences, or even verses from the best manuscript evidence. In this the popularizer was nearly overtaken by the scholar (properly so), though the occasions are few. Most notable of these is the story of the woman taken in adultery in John 8:1–11. It is entirely in character that Willie retains this in the body of his text (the RSV, like some other modern versions, relegates it to a footnote), though Willie does indent the passage. Here the heart has overtaken the head, for manuscript evidence in its favor is very weak; but the heart of the gospel—the forgiving love of God—is contained in that incident, and Willie could do no other than give it the full honor of inclusion.

We have seen that when Willie published his books of prayers, he could not refrain from writing long introductions on the nature of prayer. Here he does something similar, adding a forty-five-page appendix entitled "On Translating the New Testament" (it was properly omitted in the paperback editions). It is full of good things, and full of acknowledged debts, too. It contains more footnotes in its first twelve pages than are contained in the whole of the preceding 306 pages! But space forbids any further explanation of his thinking here.

And so there appeared William Barclay, translator. Even with only half the work actually done, it was a magnificent achievement. As Professor Bruce of English Bible fame commented, "he never exercised his gift to better purpose." He was releasing the dynamite he knew the church needed, the only sort he felt able to give; that, for William Barclay, was the highest honor.

The End of an Era, the Beginning of the End

The death of Karl Barth became public knowledge in mid December, signaling the end of an epoch in modern theology. Willie had worked in very different pastures from Barth, but the two of them had much in common despite some obvious differences in theological emphases and expression. The event was scarcely noticed by struggling Willie, who confided to his readers that he disregarded overseas news—a habit he denigrated.[44]

It was the end of an era in this sense, too, that he was to receive for the first time a national honor. Bringing, as it were, the foregoing years to a happy conclusion, it was the perfect complement to the academic honor conferred on him by Edinburgh University and the honor conferred on him when he was made a Freeman of the Borough of Motherwell and Wishaw. In the New Year's Honors List of 1969, he was made a Commander of the [Order of the] British Empire (CBE). Delight ran throughout Scotland, the United Kingdom, and indeed throughout the world. Almost twenty years of unique service—in books and journals, on radio and television—was at last recognized, as was his unfailing work for his university. The letters once more poured in, necessitating his second circularized letter:

Dear _____

I must begin by apologising for sending a duplicated letter to you, but so many people have been kind enough to write to me that this is the only way I can answer them.

All my thanks for your very gracious letter. It is good of you to write as you do, and I appreciate it very much indeed. I can assure you that I get as much

Willie and Kate, holding the Commander of the British Empire Medal (1969)
[Photo courtesy of *The Glasgow Herald*]

629

pleasure out of the good wishes of my friends as I do out of this totally unexpected honour itself.

Again, all thanks and every good wish,

Ever yours, William Barclay

In the haste to get the letter out, it was put on the ordinary letterheads of the University—not on those of either the department or faculty, which he normally used. Further, he forgot to add "C.B.E., D.D." after his name.

One of his letters of congratulation came from John Ferguson, then of Hampton, Virginia, the author of a superb book on suffering from which Willie had benefited himself. Another came from his old friend from down under, Rita Snowden, to whom Willie replied with a personal letter rather than the circular- ized form, in typical style: "The nicest thing about this is that it was completely unexpected, and the most pleasant thing of all has been the letters it has brought from many friends."[45]

He celebrated in various ways, but chiefly in two that gave special pleasure to this man who so loved his family and friends. The announcement was made when he was in London with Kate and Jane, "when we are really and truly and completely on holiday,"[46] so they seized the opportunity to indulge in a whole series of visits to various theaters—without being altogether scrupulous in their choices! "When I go to the theatre," Willie explained, "I want to laugh." He reminded his readers of the restorative effects of full laughter—not a thin smile or chuckle, but "good, broad vulgarity . . . an earthy Rabelaisian humour," which he found (pointedly at this time) "a healing thing." He and Kate also had a celebration meal in Edinburgh with their friends of many years standing Cyril and Gladys Rose. They chose to do so appropriately at the North British Hotel, and Willie was in a specially patriotic mood—as the Roses' daughter commented, "all he could celebrate with was haggis!"[47]

He needed the healing, as did Kate, for the difficult period of Jane's adoles- cence was now upon them. She was not averse to indulging in bold assertions of individuality—in clothing, hairstyle, and habits. Kate became highly anxious; her migraines got worse, and by the middle of the year Willie was writing to friends of deeper health problems. Her feeling a "bit wobbly" in August 1969[48] was a prelude to actual hospitalization by May 1970. Thus commenced a period of general and particular health disorders that make incredible reading—and not only "disorders," but accidents and reactions that sound more like cries for help than superficial incidents.

And Willie was also feeling the pressure, not so much from his daughter and Kate—he had developed methods for defusing potentially explosive domes- tic situations and cooling down the perennial conflicts between the generations— but from his work, not least his *parerga,* his "extracurricular" activities, and the ever-pressing demands of Douglas Millard of James Clarke & Company of Cam- bridge, who sent manuscripts, follow-up letters, and even telegrams in order to speed up the reading, assessment, and advisory work of his beleaguered friend. The more important work on the Library of Theological Translations had ground to a halt because of delays in the translation of Wrede's *The Messianic Secret*.[49] This pressure remained high right into the summer, letters overtaking him while he was on lecturing tours, his sabbatical, and even holidays. And his letters of apology in response proliferated as well—not only to Millard for uncompleted work, but also to such bodies as the Royal Philosophical Society of Glasgow (of which Willie was a Council Member) and the Scottish Hellenic Society (of which he was an Executive Committee member and in which he took much personal pleasure, although he was slowly forced by want of time to relinquish his involvement in it). Of greater significance was his decision not to undertake preaching invitations of any sort, as he explained to W. G. Morrice of Motherwell, sadly refusing the opportunity to return to his old stomping ground:

> I have almost given up week-end work during this term time. This is for two reasons: I want to attend the University Chapel as a worshipper (and as an example!) and even more I have discovered that the Bible is right and that it is not possible to work a 7-day week and remain efficient. When I preach on Sunday I come back to work still tired on Monday. . . . I have to keep Sundays free except on rather rare occasions.[50]

We should note that he made the decision to reduce the number of his preaching engagements even before he was laid low with the medical crisis that soon effectively removed his choice in the matter (the crisis being of sufficient severity to lead one journalist to publish his obituary prematurely); the fact of the matter is that for some time he had been slowing down and—most unheard of—declining some of the requests that he accept yet more work. Part of his problem was that he could not face up to the implications of his progressive decline in health.

He did not turn down all the requests he received; he did, for instance, commit himself to academic lectureships, one of which he eagerly anticipated in the middle of March—the D. Owen Evans Memorial Lectures at the Prifysgol Cymru, the University College of Wales, Aberystwyth. The subject of these lectures, to which he now directed his attention, was "Education in the Early Church and Its Greek and Jewish Background." They were virtually a recapitulation of his Kerr lectures of ten years previous, yet another indication of strain and enfeebled powers. He complicated the arrangements somewhat by immediately reserving a room in the best hotel in the area in order to safeguard his privacy, a reservation he had to cancel a few days later when he heard from the University's Vice Chancellor of the institution's well-meaning intention to organize his visit with dinners and introductions. Willie wrote to tell the Vice Chancellor that he intended to prolong his stay there "to try to get caught up with some work" that he was taking with him, but that nevertheless he would be "more than delighted to be at the dinner-party on the Wednesday."[51] He also found time and energy to give the James Reid Memorial Lecture, and thereby commenced some early preparation for the Baird Lectures he was to give the following year. And he had to make time for the College Choir's Easter Tour, which entailed a particularly heavy week-long program of concerts, meals, and worship in churches, retirement homes, the Hawick Town Hall, and various other sites.

After this considerable flurry of activity, he arrived back to "the task of clearing a mountain of correspondence,"[52] as usual. Despite the pressures, he was still available to undertake the planning, with his son and daughter-in-law, of his grandchildren's education, which he was arranging at his own expense. Nor was he prevented from continuing his involvement in difficult matters of biblical interpretation of a personal sort with correspondents. He wrote, for example, to Dr. Cummings of Gourock on one of his favorite Greek words— *splagchnistheis,* "compassion"—at Mark 1:40. And he continued to write to former students overseas in the United States, and to find time for Americans on holiday who merely wanted to shake him by the hand and have him sign their copies of his books.

Further contacts from Douglas Millard elicited the information that, now relieved of his Deanship (it had been a three-year term of office), Willie would be taking his first sabbatical *term* (not year!) after twenty-two years of university teaching. It was not Willie's way to let on that he was not feeling well, but Kate did this for him (without his knowledge) when she wrote to the General Secretary of the Newcastle YMCA, which Willie had promised to address in April on his way back from Wales! He made the journey directly after his Aberystwyth lectures, unconcerned at traveling the 250-odd miles of tortuous roads for the sake of a single midday fellowship meeting. It had always been that way. It was in the spring of 1969 that he delivered his penultimate series of television lectures, as spellbinding as the first and, if possible, even more influential. But the strain was telling.

It came to the notice of Ronnie Falconer (who has recounted part of the story) that the minister of Lochgoilhead Parish Church was involved in highly interesting renovation and expansion work; they decided to make a film of it.[53] The sequence opened with the steamer arriving at the Jetty, once presumed to be Barclay's Jetty (see page 11 herein; it was almost certainly the very same spot where Willie's great-grandfather had arrived over a century and a half before). During the filming, a "most hostile . . . retired naval officer," who had upset Falconer by his right-wing views, took Willie to one side and asked if he knew about his family's connections in Lochgoilhead—about the Jetty and the tombstones. Willie did not, of course, but he was informed about them by Mr. and Mrs. MacDougall, a most charming and hospitable (and far from hostile) couple. Following this, Harry Thomson, the minister of the church being filmed, sent Willie some photographs of the Jetty taken by the MacDougalls. Commented Willie, "I must come and see this for myself." But he never did. Instead, he went south with his choir, touring the borders, "Steel country," unhappily finding the life of its churches and presbytery "dead,"[54] very much in need of his "accelerating" work.

Very little information is available regarding his sabbatical term in Oxford. He told John Ferguson that he intended to use the time to write a book about

Willie and Kate at his beloved Oxford

baptism, the quiet of the Oxford colleges being "a release from telephones and the real chance to get some work done,"[55] but the book was never written, and one suspects that he worked instead on catching up on his translation work, doing his occasional writing, and cat-napping more than he cared to admit. His pattern of sleeping had changed by now, and in two or three of the interviews he gave around this time he spoke of going to bed at 11:00 P.M. for an hour and then getting up for a further two hours' work. It was another sign of his reduced physical stamina, though at sixty-two he still slept relatively few hours. By now his prestige had overflowed into Roman Catholic circles; they warmed to his open attitudes, if not his actual doctrine. Not least in this cordial receptivity was Lady Collins, whose remarkable influence opened doors normally tight shut to Glaswegian Protestants, of which Willie remained, however untypically, one. Indeed, a small number of Catholics had actually been through his department, and it is clear that he was helping to bridge the divide between the camps in the west of Scotland. And in the east, too, for on his return he accepted an invitation to meet with Bernard Haering in a specially arranged seminar at Churches' House, Edinburgh, to discuss modern problems, ecumenical and ethical. Alas, his physical condition dulled his performance there, much to the discomfiture of the Protestants, who found their champion being routed on ground not quite his own.

From this somewhat unhappy encounter he went to Nottingham to be the main Bible Study speaker (lecturing on the parables of Jesus) at a World Council

633

meeting of the YMCA by which he made his entry into the international sphere of the movement. It was an important meeting, at which over seven hundred members from sixty-two countries attended. Willie was in his element again, on familiar ground and talking to youth and youth-oriented workers. The secularizing trend of the period had partly alienated him from such normal church involvements as preaching and church services. At his own church, Williamwood, he and its minister, Colin Campbell, held evening meetings more after the manner of Paul at the School of Tyrannus than of the typical Presbyterian evening service. They called in secular experts to speak about their jobs, throwing the whole thing open afterward for discussion in order to relate it to the Christian ethic and task today. They were immensely successful, regularly attracting very full "congregations."[56] His preferences were now cast more than ever in such quasi-religious directions as these meetings, and similar ones for secularized youth work such as the YMCA. Following the Nottingham congress, Frederick Franklin of Sweden recalled Willie's "large audience, spellbound with the simplicity of his language, his colourful descriptions of the situations, questions, problems of our present time" as well as his ability to provoke laughter even in his Bible studies.[57] In the *World Communiqué,* the Alliance commented that they had shared with Willie "a spiritual and educational, never-to-be-forgotten experience. . . . To walk with this great teacher . . . was a privilege and a highlight of the Fifth World Council."

Holiday in 1969 was more a matter of convalescence than enjoyment because of Willie's apparent exhaustion and Kate's indispositions. Willie made all the arrangements: a room with twin beds and bath for Kate and himself, a single room for Jane (just home from her first taste of Continental life in France), and accommodations for Ronnie (now teaching at Jordanhill College, to his father's delight) and his family. They returned home in time for Willie to treat Kate to the gift of her first car, a Rover 2000. After having rushed into things somewhat, he found that he had made a mistake in registering it in Kate's name (it ruled out his insuring it on his own insurance policy, thus increasing the premium). Much correspondence and wrangling took place before it was eventually settled, but when it finally was, Kate was delighted and Willie took off again to host the first American Summer School studies at St. Andrews. This developed into an annual institution, and gave a large number of Americans (mainly ministers with their wives) the chance of meeting the man behind the books. By this time Willie was well past the anti-American prejudice he had felt during the war years; indeed, he had come to admire intensely the openness, the warm hospitality, and the sheer sense of efficiency and professionalism they generated. It was very like his own. He also admired their wide-eyed delight in the things of the old country and (perhaps recognizing something of himself in this) their alleged naivety. Moreover, he had a special appreciation for their readiness to enjoy a hearty laugh over a wee dram.

After St. Andrews Willie moved on almost immediately to the East Neuk of Fife to be main speaker at their Bible Week, drawing crowds of between 650 and

800 each evening. Early October found him even harder pressed than hitherto, and functioning without the reserves of energy, either physical or, more importantly, mental, that he was used to. He had to decline more invitations and struggle to keep up with the demands of the department, his translation work, his *British Weekly* articles, and much else besides. A matter of deep regret to him was his having to say that he could not address the Scottish Hellenic Society on the subject of "The Influence of Greece on Early Christian Thinking," which would have brought full circle his Bruce Lectures of 1936. One task he did not decline, however, cost him many hours of work (for which he was paid fifteen guineas) and brought him into indirect contact with F. F. Bruce again: he agreed to serve as external examiner for the Degree of Doctor in Philosophy for the University of Melbourne. It was the seventh such task he had accepted at this time, in addition to all of which he had to prepare for his Reid Memorial Lectures at Cambridge, the St. Giles's Lectures in Edinburgh, and—most prestigious of all—the Baird Lectures for 1970.

In all this, matters of great moment were clearly troubling him. Secularism had made enormous inroads into society, and "secular Christianity" had received a great impetus from the writings of Harvey Cox and Paul van Buren, though as a modern force it goes back to George Holyoake of Birmingham, who died a year before Willie's birth, in 1906. In Christian terms the progenitor of the postwar movement was Dietrich Bonhoeffer, martyred at the hands of the Nazis in 1945. Despite Holyoake's having spent a year in London in the '30s, there does not appear to be a direct link between his ideas (which were given substantive form in the writings of his contemporary Charles Bradlaugh)—or those of any of the English secularists—and Bonhoeffer. But the spirit at large was secular, and "religionless Christianity" was but one notable expression of it. Willie picked out "three driving forces" that characterized Bonhoeffer's life: his sense of destiny, his "supreme" standing as a man of faith, and, most importantly, his "conviction of the right." Willie quoted Bonhoeffer approvingly: "If we claim to be Christians, there is no room for expediency."[58]

Willie's orientation had indeed become increasingly secular, but in a sense only somewhat superficially. So far as it affected him personally, he was still himself a man of faith, claiming the whole of life for God and expressing himself in traditional modes, if not precisely traditional terms and phrasing. Where his secularity really shows through is in his increasing alienation from ecclesiastic influence and control—from the church establishment, if you will—an alienation that surfaces in a painful letter he wrote to his former graduate student Keith Snow of Canajoharie, who likewise felt the challenge of secular society, and saw more opportunity to take it up outside the church as a teacher than within it as a minister. Commented Willie, "I entirely agree with you. If I were starting out all over again—unfortunately at sixty-two this is impossible—I would go either for Religious Education in a Secondary School or I would go for teaching Biblical Studies as an Arts subject in a purely secular University."[59] Ronnie's recent appointment to Jordanhill undoubtedly reawakened former hopes and ambitions

635

in Willie; and thoughts of such men as Professor Bruce—one of the foremost incumbents of such a chair at a secular university—could only have made the opportunities all the more tempting. Willie found increasingly painful the powerful shadow of church authority (and we must remember that in Scotland this was then a harder reality of life, dominantly so as men of the caliber of Tom Torrance sought to strengthen the relationship between church and state, aided by leaders in local and national government and the law). Willie was arguing for a broader and clearer understanding of the lordship of Christ, a cosmic lordship, but he found unconvincing and unjustified any suggestion that the church, any church of the deeply divided body of Christ, presented the real form of theocratic rule. Accordingly, while he was fulfilling his ministry in what was virtually a church chair, his eyes were elsewhere—as was his heart.

So a long and busy term drew to its close, with Willie thankfully looking forward to his return to the London "Y" (for the second time since the summer), to the relaxation he found there in the unfettered atmosphere of its halls and opportunities. He did not realize that his lifestyle, and indeed his whole life, was about to be convulsed yet again. Before leaving he found time to pen one of his pastoral letters to Mrs. Annie Farrow, a widow of a Church of Scotland minister who lost his life after he received what was said to have been a corrupted transfusion of blood. As the heartbroken widow sought to fight her way back to normality, she was stunned to encounter a vast insensitivity among her husband's presbyterial colleagues; it was for her "a shattering experience." Hearing of this unconscionable behavior, Willie was confirmed yet further in his growing alienation: the system was not fulfilling its role. "I think it may help you," he wrote to Mrs. Farrow, "that other people are remembering you and wishing you well"; and apparently without being aware of the fearful indictment he was making, he went on to say, "This is the way of the world."

Year of Crisis, Year of Change

Willie waited twenty-seven years to get his professorship. Within six years of obtaining it, he knew it could not last, that his days—according to the best medical opinion available—were numbered, and that he must retire early from his work. It was the last shattering blow of a lifetime not infrequently marked by disappointment and suffering.

Willie and Kate arrived at the London "Y" on December 27, having driven from Glasgow after the family festivities. He had contracted over Christmas a very heavy cold but had refused to listen to suggestions to see his doctor, as was his way. By the time he took to his bed in London early that evening, he was causing Kate real anxiety, which she confided to Willie's friend Howard Williams. He came in to see Willie the next morning, and countermanded Willie's request not to bother the doctor. One was immediately called, and hospitalization was ordered; the Williamses took Kate under their care. "I shall never forget your kindness," Kate wrote to Dr. Williams long afterward.[60] His action literally saved Willie's life, for it was not just influenza he was suffering from, but pneumonia.

Said Lord Moran of another famous patient, "When a man approaching his seventieth year gets pneumonia, it is, broadly speaking, the heart and not the lungs that decide the issue."[61] Willie was as yet only sixty-two, but he was an old sixty-two physically, and Moran's prognosis proved to be true in his case. Heart problems developed, and Willie was placed on the danger list. At one stage his life was despaired of. Dr. Williams was not the only good friend Kate had in those disturbing days; Lady Collins also heard of the emergency, and quickly took matters in hand. Willie was transferred from the ordinary hospital to the highly acclaimed London Clinic, whose staff were instructed to spare no expense in safeguarding his life and comfort. He who had denied himself the comforts of the London Hilton was now in extremity given a comfort he could not afford to do without.

The Christian world caught its breath at the news, and Kate was deluged by a formidable correspondence from around the globe. Her anxiety turned to despair, and at times to annoyance, at the intolerable burden placed on her. Some have criticized Kate's manner at this and at other times, feeling she lacked the warmth and generosity that characterized Willie. It is scarcely a fair criticism. Their neighbors, their congregation at Renfrew, and countless hundreds of students bear witness to her friendliness, her unstinting service, and her total commitment to the sacrifice that Willie's dedication demanded. Behind his life stood a loving and loyal lady of royal proportions who combated fatigue, poor health, and the wounding criticism to which he was relentlessly exposed, quite apart from the tragedy and grief of their unforgettable loss. With her high-strung disposition and moral fiber formed of the refined upbringing of her talented parents in Dundonald, it is not surprising that at times she sharply reacted to unthoughtfulness, rudeness, and occasional viciousnes. She knew the cost from the inside and had to view it through the powerful lenses of reduced companionship and home life, long periods of absence (regularly from 8:00 A.M. to 6:00 or 7:00 P.M. if not later), and the responsibility for attending to the upkeep of house and garden and their mutual relationships herself. The dream of a lifetime, that at the end there would be a comfortable retirement, was in one painful weekend reduced to a chimera.

Friends were appalled at his present condition. His old *British Weekly* friend Charles Duthie popped in to see him and "found him looking really feeble, I must say."[62] Moran has noted, with typical medical understatement, that "A man feels pretty rotten . . . when he fibrillates during pneumonia."[63] Willie was so ill that Ronnie flew from Glasgow to be near his father, with Kate and Jane. The press soon brought news of his condition to the attention of its readers. "Bible Man Barclay Is Ordered to Rest" read the headlines of one report by Vincent Donnelly, who added the detail that Willie had been incoherent during the course of his pneumonia and cardiac arrest.[64] Elton Trueblood, in his "Plain Speech" column in *Quaker Life*, actually published Willie's obituary. (Later, this gave Willie great amusement, not least in being able to share Mark Twain's own experience and write of such premature reports being "greatly exaggerated.")[65]

The official diagnosis stated that he was suffering from pneumonia and a weakened heart; privately his doctors appended a formidable prognosis: he could not expect more than another eight years of life. Even that was tentative, based on the assumption that he would follow to the letter strong medical advice concerning his habits of work and leisure. What Willie had long dreaded was now made painfully plain: he was on the verge of being invalided, a thought he could not tolerate. So the great fight began, with greatly impoverished resources and in the face of a complication the medical tests had discovered that made the future even more problematical and helps to explain some of the curious things in his life and even in his writings: he was suffering from Parkinson's Disease, for which medical science could offer very little treatment, and no cure. It is a progressive disorder of the central nervous system making grim indeed the outlook. Eight years in that light was more a sentence than a reprieve, especially to one of Willie's nature. Surgery aimed at ameliorating the victim's plight was at this time in its infancy, and with Willie's heart condition it would have been out of the question for him anyway. The new synthetic antispasmodic drugs were not yet available; a daily dose of Stramomium was virtually all that could be offered, and that had only a palliative effect.

Parkinsonism entails a disturbance of the motor function of the brain and is characterized by an enfeeblement of the emotions and voluntary movements. Muscular rigidity and tremor often become apparent, as does the "Parkinson face"—staring eyes, muscular torpor, infrequent blinking, a tendency to salivation, and sometimes problems of mastication. Moreover, the movement of the short joints and ligaments (notably of the hands) is progressively retarded, and a certain clumsiness obtains, as does micrographia. A shuffling and festinating gait—a *marche à petits pas*—may be detectable (due to spinal rigidity), and the sufferer demonstrates restlessness ("cannot get comfortable") whether in bed, sitting, or standing. It is virtually certain that Willie suffered from the arteriosclerotic form of the disease, which produces many of the aforementioned symptoms and also some mental deterioration, with a tendency to profound depression. Unhappily, the synthetic antispasmodic drugs that were eventually made available to him had two unfortunate side effects, both of which rose to cloud his last days and precipitate his demise. One of these, the tendency to confusion, was to be very marked at times. Soon enough these symptoms would be plain, his looks, stance, gait, powers of argumentation, and physical dexterity all bearing witness to the encroachment of the disease. Alas, the majority were unable to detect them as such, and he became the butt of ignorant criticism and sometimes of jocular comment and even abuse. He was about to experience for himself the reality of the oft-quoted words of the Orphic mysteries, *sōma sēma*—"the body is a tomb." It was the final blow to one who had placed so high a value on physical well-being. But Willie was not the man to complain; indeed, he sought to ignore his condition until pressed by it into open statement. Against increasing odds he sought to continue as before.

All engagements were cancelled for three months (these included his St. Giles's Holy Week Lectures), and his work load was subjected to drastic pruning: one third, no less, he was ordered to shed; his work henceforth had to center in Glasgow; no extramural engagements were to be undertaken, and no weekend work was permitted. In actual fact he took off four months,[66] after which, following a short convalescence of ten days at Troon, he immediately commenced writing and reading again, but under Kate's strict supervision. "At the moment," he wrote to Braidwood at the end of January, before he left for Troon, "I am being very obedient; Kate sees to it that I am!" As she would increasingly, though not without some artful resistance.

Not till the middle of November 1970 did he have any articles published in *The British Weekly,* and even then, his return was not complete; his indisposition necessitated a progressively diminished presence in the great paper. But that he wrote less voluminously does not mean that his name ceased to feature in it. In January of 1970, for instance, there was a report on a much-publicized extramural lecture that Willie had delivered late in 1969, expressing the view that single as well as married women should be given the contraceptive pill.[67] Today this suggestion would be taken for granted, but in the boisterous aftermath of Pope Paul VI's *Humanae Vitae* encyclical, this was daring comment, especially from such a well-known leader of the Church of Scotland. And, predictably, his views (which he always maintained were published out of context) did not go without a challenge—nor, indeed, without a howl of indignation. Willie's subsequent explanation was that unmarried women could not be prevented from engaging in sexual intercourse, and so they ought to be given the pill to prevent the greater evil of unwanted children. It was not a prescription for free love; as usual, his deepest concern lay with the possible casualties. Nevertheless, it was "capitulation to permissiveness" according to one enraged reader,[68] who must have been shaken to the core when the General Assembly of the Church of Scotland itself confirmed such a line by stating its own unwillingness to deny "to the unmarried promiscuous women the pill."

Willie now had to observe this debate, and others, from the sidelines of his own study. He soon heard even more disquieting news about the mutual rejection of the unity proposals between his own church and the Congregational Church, the failure of the periodical *The New Christian* (edited by his friend Harold Williams), the ongoing argument about the Virgin Birth which Duthie himself had triggered, and the extraordinary attack on Christian origins perpetrated in John Allegro's *The Sacred Mushroom and the Cross* (which one reviewer called "an academic practical joke").[69] On the positive side of things there was the welcome appearance of "Black Theology," with its deep involvement in theological and political reality, and also news of the success of Andrew Cruikshank's recorded readings of Willie's translation of the New Testament and the "translation" of his books into Braille—for which, Willie insisted, there would be no charge. The republication of some of his earliest work (antedating *Ambassador for Christ*) by the Saint Andrew Press was now undertaken. This whole period, though late in his career, marked a renewed interest in Willie's works within his own church, thanks largely to the efforts of James Martin. Some time later two new series of articles by Willie appeared in *Life and Work,* entitled "The Men, the Meaning, and the Message of the Books" and "Religion and Life" (a series on ethics). Such work brought full circle his efforts at the commencement of his career, precipitated to some extent by Jack Stevenson and the Youth Committee.

While Willie was glad to see his early books being made available to a broader public, it is doubtful that he was well advised to cooperate without a clear understanding of the intent of the venture. Especially questionable was his agreement to allow republication without his own personal revision, even though that was out of the question. We have already seen that a marked decline in his productivity had taken place, of which the present crisis was the fruit, not the root cause. With the prospect of a rigidly curtailed future and increasingly limited time and energy, he was unable himself to do what was required. This is not to say that revisions ought not to have been made. But in the revisions that were made, the nature of the original work was not always respected (e.g., such aspects as the intended audience—typically young people—and the fact that most of the books were linked to a calendrical framework, that space was rigidly curtailed, and that a devotional objective was a prime requirement). I leave aside the question of stylistic changes, which were meant as improvements, but which altered the highly characteristic "spoken" style of Willie to a pseudo-literary style that, because it was not presented with a commensurate attention to academic detail (still less *recent* academic detail), brought on its author increased criticism.

It is by no means certain that Willie was an enthusiastic participant in the reissue of his books. The project made good sense from the point of view of the Saint Andrew Press, but had it not decided to reproduce them, Willie would never have considered the matter. Over the years he had largely lost interest in these works particularly.[70] And it has to be said that there is more than a little evidence pointing to his disenchantment with the Saint Andrew Press itself following the resignation of his friend Andrew McCosh. He was aware of the recommendations made by Gregor Smith that the Press be converted from an external arm of the church into a modern company organized along commercial lines, oriented toward the marketplace and not to internal considerations— recommendations that still awaited fulfillment. As it was, the Press was not very imaginative in marketing his books, and in building up the list (so important for the healthy sale of backlist publications) it was very remiss. As an arm of the church, it was doubtless fulfilling part of its responsibilities, but Willie, in light of the vigor and market penetration of mainline publishers such as the SCM Press, Collins, and the Lutterworth Press, could not help but be aware of its limitations. To Bill Christman he presently wrote, having already informed him that he was sending his manuscript to Lady Collins, that "There is of course the St. Andrew

Press but if we could get a national publisher to take the manuscript it would obviously be far better."[71] To his successor at Renfrew Trinity he shortly wrote, "I am sorry to appear disloyal but I would really regard the St. Andrew Press as a last refuge."[72] And to Bill Scott of Word Books of America he confided that he did not know what the Press was up to with regard to his cassette tapes; he simply had not been informed.[73]

This was not the only publishing house to try his patience by any means, and we should bear in mind that the Publications Department of his church was his first love; it is a very human failing to hit hardest the ones we love. Douglas Millard ignored Willie's state of health at this time of crisis, and piled on yet more pressure in order to promote the threatened Library of Theological Translations. He said he had made of this a New Year resolution. Terribly unfeeling were the words he sent on Willie's shaky emergence from hospital: "I hope you keep well and Mrs Barclay is flourishing." Said Willie in reply, "I have been and am still a bit under the weather," adding that the complications he was still experiencing were "not serious, quite controllable, but making it necessary to take things a bit easier"![74] And yet there were clear evidences of the fact that he was not so well in this letter—he got the date wrong, made an unusual grammatical error, and produced several strikeovers as well as the statement "I hope to go off to Troon tomorrow for a week or ten days torecup erate [sic]." Meanwhile, Mrs. M. Gow (his secretary) and Kate sought to ward off other pressures—from learned societies, academic sponsorships, bothersome but needy students, and innumerable well-wishers.

By mid March Willie was back at work in his department, against medical advice, seeking to reduce the correspondence that had built up in the intervening time. He was still far from well, but his sense of humor was unimpaired. To Robert Brown, a former student seeking a postgraduate position at Duke University, he wrote, "I told them all kinds of things about you, some of them factual and some of them a matter of opinion. And since my opinion of you is quite high it could be there was some non-factual material as well. They even know that you are good golfer now. . . ."[75] His ardor for life and enjoyment also showed through, as well as some pride in his determination. "I have not smoked a cigarette since Christmas Day," he boasted. "Fortunately, there are other pleasures which the doctors have not forbidden!" Another highly typical reflection found expression in March, when he received a letter signed by the "5th and 6th Form scripture groups" of the Southport High School for Girls. It enclosed a get-well message, a note of appreciation for his "commentaries and records which have proved very useful in our 'O' level and 'A' level studies," and—of all things—a Book Token. Willie was greatly moved. Such a tribute counted higher with him than any of the plaudits offered by the learned or mighty: his message was getting through; he was achieving his aim. This compensated for all the criticisms and the snubs others offered, and comforted him over his declining powers. Said he in grateful reply, "I am happy to say that I am better now except that I have taken so many pills that I practically rattle when I walk! I am most

641

grateful to you all for your kind thought and I can assure you that I appreciate it very much indeed."[76] He added, proud father that he was, "my own daughter is sitting what we call Highers in English, History, Biology and French next month." To Roger Harris of Rutland, Vermont, he expressed similar feelings, stating "the greatest satisfaction that comes to me is when I find out, usually by letter, that I have been able, through my books or writings, to help some person whom I do not know at all in some time of trouble or distress. I find this far more uplifting than any academic achievement."[77]

Three days later he disclosed the most momentous decision he had made in over forty years when he intimated his early retirement to an old friend, Alec Hamilton:

Dear Alec,
    Herewith the Translation with every good wish. I envy you [an uncharacteristic expression] being able from very soon to do exactly what you like. I hope it won't be very long before I have the same privilege.

The dream of a lifetime was being prematurely extinguished.

But, incorrigibly, by this date Willie was also informing a number of people that the doctor had given him "a clean bill of health"![78] To Mrs. Marion Carmichael, an old friend from Dalziel High School, he mentioned his imminent departure for Inverness with the College Choir. He had been expressly forbidden to conduct it, but he claimed "the doctors tell me that if I can only learn to say 'no' I can live to be 100." And if pigs had wings, they could fly! He did temper his optimism by adding "I doubt if anyone would want to live to 100 spending their time saying 'No.'" He would rather burn out than rust out, as his family and friends well knew. He was exhorted by former student John Burns to "look after yourself. There are some of us who can't manage without you."[79]

To Leslie Goskirk of Sutherland, who had heard the choir at Inverness, Willie wrote that he was gratified that its standards were being upheld, "but I don't think the first tenors are just as good as they were in your day."[80] And he mentioned that he was already planning to take the choir to Cullen, Keith, and Banff (this latter the scene of an earlier visit), that he already had "a great desire to get my hands on the Choir!" On this visit John Campbell took hold of him and danced with him in the middle of the main street at Portsoy during a march through the town, such was Willie's irrepressibility of spirit. On his return he wrote to the Secretary of the Royal Philosophical Society of Glasgow, correcting the misinformation his secretary had supplied, to the effect that he was no longer able to lecture.[81] He recognized that "her first instinct, [was] to protect me," but he wanted it known that he would be able to lecture for them in the next session. "I am not really barred from lecturing, only from preaching—for which I am devoutly grateful," he explained. He did try to follow the rules in some things. Word Books of Texas now appears frequently in his correspondence, and while he could not bring himself to say "no," he was at least able to say "not yet" with some consistency (though he was just as consistently pressured to reverse his decision). In the hard world of publishing—even religious publishing—they could not take "no" for an answer. And they did not, to Kate's rising anxiety and indignation. It was under such circumstances that another letter arrived from Millard of Cambridge:

> Do you think we ought to have an index to the Wrede translation? Nothing appears to have been done about this and the question only occurred to one when on the point of returning the page proofs. . . . Sorry to trouble you, just let me know at your convenience.

Willie intended to, but after a month another letter appeared asking him if he had yet thought about the index. The reply was not recorded; perhaps it was telephoned for speed. In any event, the book appeared without its index. It did include a General Editor's foreword in which Willie himself sowed the seeds of the series' demise (unrecognized by the publisher) when he stated that "the purpose of this series in not to translate new and recent works, but rather the classical theological books which have not been translated." The real market lay elsewhere.

He was checked out by the doctor on April 14 and commenced work (officially) that same day. He had been sternly warned that he should confine himself to university work only, and he doubtless agreed to do just that—except perhaps for this and that, and doubtless something else additionally. . . . Kate was coming to terms, albeit reluctantly, with the fact that her man would never stop of his own volition. It had all been too much for her, and she soon needed to be hospitalized herself "for a general checkup." She was subsequently in and out of hospital for two months due to a stomach disorder and chronic depression. She had in fact been ill since February (as Willie confided to Howard Williams),[82] undoubtedly because of the anguish of nearly losing him; scarcely a month would go by without some disorder or other manifesting itself. The thumb-screws turned tighter on them both.

Willie denied the suggestions made by some that he was on the verge of retiring. He wrote to Miss Brenda McGilliard, rather bluntly stating "it is not true," and added, "In actual technical fact I can go on for another eight years. I have no intention of going on as long as that but I do hope to be here to welcome you when you come to the Faculty."[83] The remainder of the term was filled with lecturing, corresponding, and attending to various administration functions; at the same time, he was watching his weight, limiting himself to restricted exercise, and resting between periods of work as never before. These were the days when he began to picture heaven as a place without stairs—not least, surely, as he trudged up the steep staircase that led to his room in one of the twin towers of Trinity College.

CHAPTER NINETEEN

Anchor Firm Remaining

Situation Ethics—or Situation Vacant?

By the early '70s, great changes were taking place at *The British Weekly.* A new management team had taken over, incorporating the journal into the Christian Weekly News Group, and providing it with a new managing editor in the person of John Capon. (Across the top of Capon's first letter Willie had written "Keep this for name," but by December it had been misplaced and he was found writing to his new boss "Dear Editor," a symbolic alienation as we shall see.)[1]

Capon was not due to commence as editor till early October of 1970, but early planning was required. He had intimated his hope that Willie would recommence his former work for the paper, and this wish was relayed to Willie via the retiring editor, Denis Duncan. Commented Willie, clearly torn between common sense and deep conviction, "Just give me a little more time and I will, but I am not ready to start yet and when I do start I think that I will have a scheme to offer you."[2] He regretted the changeover. "No one could possibly have done more to keep the thing alive than you have done," he wrote to his colleague. And he intimated his willingness to let Duncan make a Day Book of his occasional pieces after the manner of Rita Snowden's *Seen in the Passing.* But to Duncan's proposal to write his biography, Willie was adamant in his opposition, and gave his reasons:

> I would not be terribly keen on having a biography of myself written. I am not just dead yet. . . . If I am spared to do so I think I can still do something yet. I always remember a quotation from Johnston Jeffrey. He quotes the saying of a man to whom it was suggested that his biography should be written while he was yet alive . . . "I would rather not. I have seen two many men fall on the last lap of the race."[3]

From that position, despite a number of approaches, Willie never waivered.

In the same letter to Duncan he declined a preaching engagement for the London Welsh Congregational Union, but declared his intention to participate in two conferences in June. One of these was the Summer School of Theology for

644

Ministers, at St. Andrews; the other was a Chaplains Conference, at which the serious problem of ministerial shortages was discussed. To one of his students Willie ebulliently commented, "this is bad for the Air Force and bad for the Church of Scotland. If they do not get Church of Scotland Chaplains the jobs will go to Methodists. I have nothing against Methodists but I prefer a first-division team when we can get it!" He was in a similar mood when he wrote to the Assistant Superintendent of Fabric at the University, reminding him that he had written previously about the condition of the private road outside the faculty building. He wrote the day before he went off on holiday, stating, "It has now become almost impossible to bring a car into the Terrace with any safety. . . . I really do think that something should be done." The holes were duly filled. Willie rarely allowed practical things to go by untended; he even found time to attend committee meetings of the Hutchenstown and Gorbals Youth and Community Association (of which he was a nonactive member) a few months after it had opened.

July saw him in action at his beloved Summer Institute of Theology for Americans (at St. Andrews). There were 166 participants that year, and while Kate convalesced at her sister's home at Dundonald, Willie thrived among the open-hearted, open-minded men of the New World. "Very enjoyable" it was too, Willie informed Howard Williams, optimistically adding, "I myself have more or less recovered. . . . I am pretty normal again. . . ."[4] It was only a partial view. His successor, Professor Best, recalls one of his party on one occasion finding Willie sound asleep in the lounge. "Gee, what a worker that man is," he observed, not realizing that a tot or two of John Barleycorn is a powerful help to a postlunch catnap in a man whose health has been ravaged! He was, despite this, still larger than life, and if not now indefatigable, at least very determined to keep going, and just as sure in his statements. Typically, now that Williams's duties for *The New Christian* had ceased, Willie was offering encouragement and advice, acting as literary go-between by prizing open publishing doors for him, which effort produced a delighted response from Lady Collins.

He spent his holidays at Elie again, with Kate and Ronnie and his wife and their three children, at the Marine Hotel of which they had grown so fond—but without Jane, whose independence now found new forms of expression. Alas, the weather was very poor. Willie wrote to a former student, Allan Macpherson, complaining that in a fortnight there had only been one reasonable day— "probably the worst weather I have ever spent a holiday in."[5]

But he did manage to enjoy a rest of sorts, and by mid September was once more pitching himself into extramural activities. He attended the Scottish Sunday School Union Conference at Largs on September 12, experiencing a much-appreciated reengagement of former ties, speaking (*not* preaching!) twice on the same day. In the morning he spoke on "The Bible in Christian Teaching," affirming his belief in the Bible's priority, authority, and relevance; the address was listened to "with rapt attention." In the afternoon he gave "another sparkling address," this time on "The Bible and Ourselves," stressing the importance of regular Bible reading, especially in a modern translation. Since he had laid down the editorship of their journal over twenty years earlier, his teaching on such fundamentals had changed very little, if at all, even though he was now Professor Barclay, C.B.E., D.D., Honorary President of the Glasgow YMCA, Honorary Vice President of the Boys' Brigade, and world-reputed author and broadcaster. To them, servants one and all in the great work of Christian education, he was merely an elder brother, a much appreciated teacher and friend; that was how he liked it, true *koinōnia*.

In a similar vein, and as compensation for having to say No to their request that he preach, he wrote a message of good will to the Tynemouth Corps of the Salvation Army:

> I have heard from Corps Sergeant-Major Flack that you are having a Bible Weekend on 5th and 6th December. Nothing could be more useful for the ordinary person today. There is no problem in life but which the Bible does not supply, if not an answer, at least the way to find an answer. If we are in sorrow, there is comfort; if we are in temptation, there is strength; if we are in ignorance, there is wisdom.
>
> The Bible doctrines of love and fellowship have never yet been worked out in life. As G. K. Chesterton said long ago, "Christianity has not been tried and found wanting; it has been found difficult and has not been tried."
>
> Apart from anything else, both in the Old and the New Testament[s], the Bible has stories to stimulate the mind and to stir the heart. . . . May your weekend be for many a time of rediscovery of the Bible and rediscovery of the Grace of God.[6]

From the jaws of death he had clearly emerged to make yet more clear and persistent the biblical roots of his faith, ever the origin and nature of his message, and the direction of his life. But there was tension, too, behind such a statement, for he could not forget the inexplicable attitude (to his way of thinking) of the Salvation Army toward Major Fred Brown. He knew him personally, had preached for him on occasion, and used his space in *The Expository Times* to review sympathetically his book *Secular Evangelism*. The book had by no means been influential in a catalytic sense on Willie's thinking, but its publication did enable him to express himself in favor of the "new evangelism," in the wake of the "new theology" and the "new morality." It is important to see where Willie stood on such things, especially in the light of his message to the good people of Tynemouth. He underscored four emphases he found in Major Brown:

> 1. He was "compelled even in reluctance to seek a new way and a new language" in order to establish contact with modern man and speak intelligibly to him. He noted the major's experience that "more unhappiness [was] caused by prayer and its problems than by drunkenness and adultery."
>
> 2. He saw no future for traditional evangelical theology. In stating this, Willie made it plain that it was in its *expression*—in its *language*—that it was at fault. Orthodoxy was obsolete because it found no place for "something new and adventurous," as well as because it failed to convey meaning adequately.
>
> 3. Young people count, and their unique understanding of serving and of

caring is important: "they are not interested in talking about what to believe; what matters to them is how to live." Nevertheless, they were "intensely interested in the historic Jesus," and they notably "display the Christian virtues in a supreme way without the transcendent." This is not to say that he was against "the beyond," however; prayer and worship, he said, "make us sensitive to it . . . [but] in our midst."

4. What is needed is "real involvement," a latching on to the new crusading spirit of youth against the evils of modern society, a humanizing of our understanding of it.

Brown had a lot more to say than this, as had Willie himself (and at root, less radically), but this review shows the hub of his concern and how he was seeking to face up to the difficult questions being asked. Where he found an insuperable difficulty was in expressing loyalty to the Bible itself while at the same time seeking that new way and language. The former tended to overthrow the latter; this was the core of Willie's problems, the heart of his antisyzygy.

The good start he made in the autumn was clouded by a short and anxious note received from Millard, who had just discovered that Scribners, the American publishers, had already published in translation Dibelius's *From Tradition to Gospel* five years earlier (Clarke's translation was presently being printed). Did Willie know this? "If you have any further information or comments," Millard insisted, "please let me know." Willie was not the sort of man to get rattled by such things, and so he simply said he did not know anything about the American edition! In point of fact, the translation had been made from the second edition of the German work in 1934. Millard had clearly done his homework as poorly as Willie had. "I don't think we need worry too much," Willie concluded, not intending to worry at all. Thus began a hectic academic year in which he also had to see to a new series of "Seen in the Passing" articles for *The British Weekly* and two further lectures. These lectures showed that the biblical interest everywhere else apparent was forged of a hard concentration on the practical issues of life, and that although much work remained based upon the Bible, it was tending to displace exposition for current issues. The first of these lectures, delivered on October 7 under the auspices of the Royal Philosophical Society of Glasgow and the chairmanship of Willie's friend Professor William Fletcher, was on "situation ethics," a phrase made popular—some would say notorious—by Professor J. Fletcher of Philadelphia, whose book of that title had been published in 1966. It was more or less a rehearsal of some of the views Willie was to propound in his Baird Lectures.

The invitation to this highly prestigious lectureship had come to Willie over eighteen months earlier, delighting him as much by the honor it conveyed as by the opportunity it afforded him to express himself on practical issues of society. The lectures had been delivered continuously for ninety-seven years (every fourth year) by a series of distinguished scholars. Willie's own professor W. M. Macgregor had published his own Baird Lectures on Paul's letter to the Galatians under the provocative title *Christian Freedom*. But Willie, as ever, and despite his recent indisposition, was about to break new ground. For it was proposed that instead of delivering them in the relative privacy of a university classroom, he should do so on television. Willie's preferred title was "The Christian Ethic in the Twentieth Century," but it was clear that a more popular title would have to be found. So, two days after proposing it, he suggested instead "The New Testament Way of Life in the Twentieth Century." "Way of Life" was certainly better than "Ethic," but Willie's biblical blind spot had misled him. Ronnie Falconer was having none of that! And so they settled on "Jesus Today: The Christian Ethic in the Twentieth Century," to be advertised simply as "Jesus Today," and abbreviated in its published form (a considerably revised and expanded version) to *Ethics in a Permissive Society.* The first lecture was televised on November 15 and the remaining five followed in quick succession.

The titles of the lectures were as follows: "The Cradle of the Christian Ethic (the Old Testament)," "The Ethics of Jesus," "Situation Ethics," "Work," "The Christian and the Community," and "Person-to-Person Ethics." It will be noted that these are very representative of the mood of the period, and confirm to some extent the wisdom Willie had seen in Major Brown's insights. On publication, he added new material on the ethics of Paul and the Christian view of pleasure and money. Because not a few felt that he was somewhat traditional, somewhat unimaginative in his preparation (and some reviewers expressed this rather forcefully), it should be noted that he prepared for his lectures not only by reading very widely (he provided a list of no fewer than eighty titles "which have been specially helpful to me in the preparation of these lectures") but also, and essentially, by reading "the New Testament and most of the Old afresh to come to a *scriptural* understanding of the Christian ethic."[7] Those who talk of Willie's radicalism should note this, for such radicalism as he possessed was shaped by a biblical dimension, and not infrequently even by biblical imagery. Stanley Pritchard called him "a hard man" ethically, thereby providing a rare insight into one who was by nature quintessentially sympathetic and kind. While ever pastorally sensitive to human need, and especially to the sorrowing and defeated, he was not, as we have seen, a compromiser in matters of principle, as his firm jaw and thin lips suggest.

Little wonder Kate protested when she found that he had smuggled a suitcase full of books into his car (so heavy that she could not lift it) for their holiday together! He devoured everything in sight in order to be adequately primed for his job, from Selby-Bigge's *British Moralists* of 1897, to the 1970 Oxford Paperback edition of D. J. Allan's *The Philosophy of Aristotle,* just released. And every form of ethical theory had been traversed (partly through Philippa Foot's brilliant *Theories of Ethics*), from the ancient divines and lay thinkers of Israel, Greece, and Rome, via Jesus, Paul, and Kant, to the recently published work of Marx, Bonhoeffer, van Buren, and Galbraith, and the report of the British Council of Churches *Sex and Morality,* which had caused such an outcry. The excessively codified complex of Jewish morality *and* the amorphous intuitionism of modern-day existentialists, the high-brow contemplation of a Gifford Lecturer *and* the low-brow good sense of Bishop Barry: Willie sought out, surveyed, and pondered it all, and only then propounded his own well-considered conclusions. His express intent (and at times his speed was indeed express) was more "to open avenues for further thought than to offer any solutions."[8]

And yet, however much he toiled at firing the minds and the imaginations of his viewers, he whose purview could not be anything other than biblical in its final analysis concluded the historic occasion by saying pointedly, "It may be that what the church needs to get the people back is not compromise, but a message of uncompromising purity" (215).

That, especially, was Willie's way. It reminds one of Kierkegaard's definition of purity: "Purity of heart is to will one thing." To love God is to live purely, and such love—directed to God and man—is the fulfilling of the law. To Willie it was not a question of law *or* love, but love *and* law, though never woodenly interpreted. This was nowhere more apparent than in his treatment of Joseph Fletcher's doctrine of "situation ethics," the argumentation and application of which were more vigorously laid out in his book *Moral Responsibility* (1967). Willie's description of its essence, a masterly summary in ten pages (his third Baird Lecture amplified), is a typical example of how Willie "popularized." It is faithful to Fletcher's views, but not restricted to Fletcher's material; throughout the summary Willie weaves his own ideas, elucidating and expanding Fletcher's and adding his own illustrations. It was his ability to do this that confused his students (and others) as to where Willie himself stood. He could, and did, present arguments and suggestions in such a way as to cause his listeners to believe they were his own convictions, only to present later—with equal force— the opposite view. This is not genuine Caledonian antisyzygy, though there is much of that in Willie; it is simply an educational instrument, finely honed, and worked with precision. He takes what subject matter is available to him (fundamentalist and radical, right and left), listens to it intently, describes it with care, and even enters into the spirit of the ofttimes mutually exclusive arguments it offers; he then turns back on it for assessment, picking out positive insights for later application, but not unusually delivering an actual rejection of the view under discussion, usually gently. This he does here: situation ethics, with its posture of total freedom, largely reliant on abnormal situations as examples, misunderstanding the nature of law itself because it misunderstands the nature of good and evil themselves, resting on a too optimistic view of the effectiveness of psychological aids (a view Fletcher picked up from his American background, in which such a view was generalized, to the exclusion by and large of Old World presumptions of man's fallen nature), he found to be quite simply, though crucially, ignorant of the grace of God. Willie found in Fletcher's viewpoint not situation ethics, but situation vacant; it was unworkable, it could not deliver given the nature of man and demands of God. Willie saw that if man had total freedom and full moral responsibility, such a system *might* work; but, having observed present reality throughout a deeply involved, widely experienced life, he staunchly declared that ethically "man has not yet come of age" (81). By that declaration he destroyed the one foundation on which much in modern ethics, and in theology itself, rested.

Soon enough (in 1975), as we shall see, Archbishop Coggan of Canterbury was heard to murmur "this is a new William Barclay" on hearing Willie address himself to the subject of justification by faith before a largely conservative audience. It was not an exact observation. Willie's doctrine in 1975 was essentially the same as it was in 1925, when he staunchly defended the punctuation marks in the Authorized Version, and in 1932, when he committed himself *ex animo* to the standards of his church at ordination, and in 1939, when he presented a "Faith for the Times," and in 1955, when he expounded the Draft Catechism, and in 1967, when he expounded the Apostles' Creed. Throughout these years he rested on the divine revelation of the scriptures exclusively. His beliefs rested on two pillars: first, the Ten Commandments (to which he now recalled Fletcher's readers—"Let us return to the ten commandments" [76]), and second, "the good news of Jesus Christ," which was his plain-language equivalent for "the grace of God." It was never otherwise. True, he took up this and that doctrine, called one or another of its aspects into question, posed alternate explanations, even overturned traditional concepts in an effort to make the underlying reality—God's love for men in Jesus Christ—relevant and meaningful. The Socratic gadfly was never rendered more irritating than when he fell into the hands of a journalist in need of a headline, especially a journalist who had not done his homework! By such provocations he stirred theological talk and religious need and kept the church in the fore. But his doctrine remained basically scriptural, fundamentally evangelical—to some disappointingly conservative, to others outrageously liberal. But in matters ethical, he was on the whole unexceptionably traditional.

It was a wise and clever decision to televise the lectures; apart from the predictable wail of denigrators, it was widely recognized as a brilliant and persuasive performance. He had done what few men had done: he had made true goodness attractive (and that, to Willie, was the essence of holiness). In consequence, his work load increased dramatically. As he mentioned to William Braidwood, a "hail of correspondence" descended upon him.[9] Once more the midnight oil was consumed. Ronnie Falconer tells of one occasion on which he tried to call Willie only to find his telephone perpetually engaged. "Willie," he complained when he finally got through, "you've been on the 'phone all morning!" "Well, it's your fault," growled his friend. "When I'm doing a television series, I have to spend two mornings and two evenings a week, 'phoning folk with pastoral problems, as well as both writing and seeing them."[10] That was singleness of mind; that was William Barclay's concept of loving God and serving man. As he explained in one of his last pieces in *The British Weekly* that year, "Sweat is the price of all things."[11]

In the Shadow of Retirement, a Dream Realized

The year closed unusually, with Willie still in Glasgow. Arrangements had been made for Kate and him to occupy the "presidential suite" at the London "Y," but fears of his recent overwork, of the possibility of a recurrence far from home of last year's disaster, and awareness of Kate's poor health, conspired to keep them local. He regretted it, not only because he missed the rich fellowship of the YMCA and that of nearby Bloomsbury Central Baptist Church, but because he found it too cold for comfort in the west of Scotland.[12] He was cheered by signs of his own return to better physical well-being, however, and Kate, thanks to the discovery and correction of her serious vitamin deficiency, soon showed signs of some improvements as well. But even those little victories could not soften the growing realization that he no longer had the same powers, no longer exerted quite the same influence. In his beloved *British Weekly* that fact was now evident in virtually every issue. Since the takeover, the journal had been enlarged, had an improved lay-out, and was more "newsy," having cast round more widely for items. Theologically it was changing, too. The proud standard-bearer of Christian radicalism was now being sedately driven along the smooth road of evangelical credalism. And Willie was being displaced, despite John Capon's expressed pleasure at (and gratitude for) his contributions. Already his pieces had been placed below Charles Duthie's feature on the center page, and "Seen in the Passing" was being flagged in smaller type—a thing unthinkable in former days, when at least one wag thought *BW* ought to be known as WB.[13] And Willie was himself missing what Samuel Johnson called "the anxious employment of a periodical writer," not that he brought to his task "an attention dissipated, a memory embarrassed, an imagination overwhelmed, a mind distracted with anxieties," even if his body was by now "languishing with disease."

His feature was to continue for another year. There would be flashes of the old master from time to time, but two cannot walk together unless they be agreed, and in any case Willie's day was clearly over. A sad piece found expression on 2 April 1971, when he published "When Everything's Gone." Rediscovering an old crutch, he expatiated on the importance of accepting what happened, drawing on the example of the misfortunes of Carlyle and Scott, "who found their only comfort in work," itself almost a signed piece of autobiography. As the magazine stressed more and more the divine initiative and the grace of God, so Willie seemed to stress still harder human responsibility and self-wrought opportunity; the gulf widened, more cries of "Pelagian!" were heard, not least from Martyn Lloyd-Jones, doyen of traditional Calvinism south of the border,[14] who recognized in Willie an evangelical siren, but who suspected that his "radicalism" made him "the most dangerous man in Christendom." And so the newly won readership found his approach less convincing than the old. At times he tried pure evangelism; at times he proposed a variety of approaches; at times he provided simple confession.[15] He wrote of life in the round; his readers more and more wanted comment on the way that was narrow and the path that was straight. He spoke to the ordinary man; an increasing number of his readers regarded themselves as special. He called for involvement; they preferred exclusiveness, even embattlement. He offered insights from the world around them; they wanted biblical and doctrinal exposition. He was for the world, claiming it for God; they were against it, seeking to wrest it from their subconscious clutches. He sought to act as a disturber; they wanted peace. His contributions sizzled, fizzled, and finally expired in June 1972. Commented his old editor, Denis Duncan, his work was "one of the most extraordinary pieces of output in religious journalism." But at the end many of his readers simply did not understand what lay behind that remark.

But in other respects, the flame still burned. In March 1971 he and his famous choir drew nearly eight hundred people to listen to their songs and hymns in the Fisherman's Hall, Buckie. He also made a visit to Walsall in Staffordshire, his address on the Bible being delayed by a small bird trapped in the sanctuary of the church. Willie emerged from the vestry, and within a few minutes the frightened creature had flown on to his shoulder. To the astonishment of all present, not least the Reverend C. E. Norwood, he quietly walked to the door and the bird few off into freedom.[16] Of such tales saints are made! He was kept hard at work in his department, finding fresh encouragement in "a good First Year, intelligent and lively."[17] In March, at the Final Year Dinner, he was asked to respond to the toast to the alma mater. He did so, wistfully recalling that thirty-two of his sixty-four years had been spent within its walls. The occasion was made especially sad for him as John Mauchline, "full of years and honour," took leave of them as Professor, though he was to continue as Principal. The following year also saw a good enrollment of first-year students, though Willie bemoaned the lack of Greek scholars among them. He had consented to a first degree in divinity without Greek and Hebrew, but he never believed it could produce true biblical understanding or excellence. He was now doing all the first-year work himself, struggling with the revised curriculum he had done so much to introduce, which gravely complicated life for everyone (not least himself, who had no fewer than twenty different examination papers to prepare). John Riches was now his junior assistant in the department and Neil Alexander continued as his Senior Lecturer. The former brought with him a good knowledge on German theology, "which we do not really possess," Willie admitted.

His mind was now made up to retire at the end of the next academic session (in September 1974). "I flourish," he commented to Bill Telford, "but grow shorter in breath."[18] Kate's health fluctuated, too, more so than Willie's, which proceeded on an even keel suitable for the low tidal flow on which he now floated. During 1972 Kate became even thinner, and three times found herself in hospital. She did improve, at least in spirit, toward the summer, only to break her hip at the end of the year in a fall. A few days later, at the beginning of 1973, it was discovered she had cracked her pelvis as well; an allergy to pain-killing drugs gave rise to disturbed nights and fretful days. A few weeks later another crack was discovered by X-ray; three months later she cracked another rib in falling heavily on the stairs; and in September she broke a finger. Then, as if by way of final indignity, they found their wee house in Clarkston the subject of a Compulsory Purchase Order because of road widening in the area. This, along with her recurrent migraines, made life "unpleasant for her"—and for Willie too, we may surmise, though he seldom complained. Perhaps saddest of all, he had to dispose of more than a thousand books—there were lucky students and fellow ministers about at that time!—and exchange a seven-room house for one with but four, in deference to Kate's decreasing energy.

Willie's health rapidly became more frail as well. He developed a tendency to take cold quickly, which often developed into "influenza"—a camouflage word he typically used for his irreversible condition and his permanently weakened heart and lungs. By early 1974 he was virtually disabled, each morning needing forty minutes to dress, and then only with much pain and discomfort.[19] Moreover, he had now become absent-minded (he always did have a tendency to lose gloves, lighters, binoculars, and other personal effects), and Kate was increasingly anxious over his tendency to leave doors open, fires burning, and lights—and even the cooker—switched on.[20] In fact, she was forced to alter her own sleep habits, now staying up late (even to listen to Scottish Television's *Late Call* programs) to ensure that they were safe in bed. When she did go first, she usually had to get up and check things before being able to sleep.

It was not just their own home and health that caused concern. Trinity College, which had written such a glorious history for itself for more than a century, was finally being closed down. Willie, still managing to look forward, judged its closure as being "long overdue," inasmuch as it had long been divorced from the main life of the University.[21] Involvement was now Willie's watchword: in industry, education, politics, trade unions—in every aspect of life. Nevertheless, he still cherished a fatherly concern for the old building, which evoked such happy memories of so many years. He knew that there would be "many and many a committee meeting before it is all settled." And indeed, such meetings continued long after his death.

For months now all external engagements had been rigorously refused on doctor's orders, but in spring 1973, he went on tour with the College Choir. This time their outreach was based on Ayrshire, and they visited such well-known watering places as Ayr, Troon, Prestwick, Girvan, and Dundonald. During the week they sang to six thousand people, half of them children at school, a magnificent witness and challenge to youthful faith from youthful faith.

The "American Institute" was not forgotten. It had developed into "an amazing business,"[22] no fewer than 346 applications having been turned down (enrollment was deliberately restricted to 180 to ensure "personal contacts and fellowship"). It lasted for three weeks, the members listening to Hugh Anderson and John McIntyre in the first week, Jim Blackie and Robert Davidson in the second, and Ian Muirhead and Willie in the third. Commented Willie, it was "a really wonderful experience to work with these Americans." But he also confessed that he was no longer feeling efficient, and suspected that he "ought to go while the going is good." Doubtless echoes of Lady Macbeth's "Stand not upon the order of your going, but go" now reverberated through his mind.

His final year, 1974, saw the completion of the full circle opened in 1947. The department had its largest enrollment since that year, with fifty-four students registering for the courses (fifteen being young females from England attending by virtue of the new Universities Central Council on Admissions regulations). In a curious and unexpected way, he now found himself teaching RE to intending secular teachers, the fulfillment of a long-deferred dream. Recalling if but briefly these feelings of the past, he said that "teaching the first year [was] an exciting proposition." Despite this, he spoke of "the odd sensation of doing things for the last time,"[23] necessarily a deflating experience. He was, after all, exchanging Compline for Complan, activity for rest, public for private life; he was finally "putting his toys away." And even his indomitable hopefulness was overshadowed by one certain fact: soon for Kate and himself the waters cold would chill their latest breath. It was, however, an inevitability for which he felt fully prepared: "It should be a joyous occasion," he affirmed.[24]

News of his retirement broke in March 1974, and both Kate and he must have been gratified by the coverage given to the event. It was, indeed, world news. *The Scottish Daily Express* spoke of his "forthright Christian views,"[25] and *The Daily Express* mentioned "the controversy [that] has always dogged his steps."[26] Commented Charles Gillies of *The Glasgow Herald,* "Professor William Barclay has strived throughout his career to be an ordinary man, and has succeeded so brilliantly as to have become an extraordinary one."[27] The New Zealand Presbyterian church magazine *The Outlook* spoke highly of "the prowling, growling television personality," calling attention to Willie's gleeful comment "I've never been a member of the establishment," which enabled him to work and speak freely.[28]

And so the day Willie "got finished up"[29] finally dawned. It saw him repaying, as it were, one or two old debts. He averred that he still worked a twelve-hour day (perhaps more playfully than realistically, as was his way). He spoke as Principal Lecturer at the Association of Secretaries of the YMCA, whose conference took place from June 8 to 13; he gave three lectures based on his Baird Lecture material—the ethics of personal relationships, of community, and of international affairs. And he paid his last respects to New College by giving a final course of lectures there. Following this he and Kate spent a quieter summer than usual. He could not forego his visit to the American Institute, at which over two hundred attended.

On returning from their holiday at Stranraer, Willie found waiting for him a most welcome letter. It was from the Principal and Vice Chancellor of the University of Strathclyde, Sir Samuel Curran, with whom Willie had shared the honor of being made a Freeman of Motherwell and Wishaw some seven years earlier. Thanks to the good offices of Professor William Fletcher (whose subject was biology, though Willie knew him better as the President of the Royal Philosophical Society of Glasgow), Willie received his second professorial appointment, this time a visiting professorship, of which there were thirty at Strathclyde, in the Department of Biology. It was tenable for a period of up to five years, renewable annually, and it made of Willie a fully accredited member of the staff while he held the appointment.

It was an appointment of some genius—and some boldness, considering acrid academic comments from elsewhere. But the University knew what it was about, and knew the importance of keeping the doors open to all knowledge, not just the high specialization for which it was known. Willie was there not so much to lecture as to share his knowledge and experience in an attitude of cross-fertilization. Commented the Principal,

> He was supposed to work mainly in this seminar fashion, and certainly it was hoped that he would encourage a mutual interest in the wide variety of disciplines found in universities. We did not want to see him as a theologian, but rather as someone who was very widely informed and very willing to talk with experts in a considerable range of expert disciplines.[30]

In expressing his "very real pleasure" in accepting the appointment, Willie reminded Sir Samuel of "how often and how publicly I have said that if I were younger I would have loved to have had an association with the virility of Strathclyde; and now in my old age the dream is realised."[31] It is yet another aspect of his essentially open and forward-looking stance, of his being all things to all men, of his owning that all truth is God's truth.

This was by no means the only opportunity that bolstered his spirits as the fateful day of actual retirement dawned. For years people had been asking him (his publishers included) if he was going to do for the Old Testament what he had done for the New. And his commitment to biblical unity—to a divine plan in scripture, to an unfolding purpose of God centered on Israel in history—challenged him to take the Old Testament more seriously than he had heretofore. The Daily Study Bible itself is full of references to the Old Testament, and it is heavy in its emphasis on the purposes of God. He could not resist the challenge. As early as 1964 he had spoken to Desmond Jenkins of his determination to undertake such work, but Jenkins had extracted a promise from Willie that he would not touch it till he retired, a promise of which he was reminded by letter in June 1974. Similarly, on 4 January 1972 Willie had written to Floyd Thatcher of Texas, informing his would-be publisher that he was already "committed to Collins for work on the Old Testament to match the New Testament Daily Study Bible." And in June 1972 he had informed one of his former students, Alton McEachern, that when he retired in 1974 he was going to "Collins the publishers to do nothing but write for them; in particular to do a Daily Study Bible on the Old Testament." His original publisher, the Saint Andrew Press, was not pleased by Willie's new desire to be published more professionally, as it were on the open market, with all the expertise available to those who had managed some of his most successful books to date. According to Tim Honeyman, the American publishers of the Daily Study Bible were so displeased that they "patented" his title, thus making it impossible for Willie to produce his work under that title in the USA.[32]

At sixty-three he was now within sight of starting that great new venture, and looked forward (how else?) to publishing three volumes every two years, commencing with Psalms and Genesis. It was no pipe dream even though he recognized his limitations, both academically and physically. To Bill Telford, another former student, he confided with typical exaggeration, "I know nothing about the Old Testament."[33] Some of his friends who *were* experts in the field, not least Professor McHardy of Oxford, did not hesitate to agree with him on this. Of the demands it would make on him, of his inability to fulfill them completely, he was quite candid. As he said to a reporter from *The Glasgow Herald,* "It will be a Schubertian situation. . . . I'll be dead before it is finished."[34] But he saw the need, he believed no one was fulfilling that need adequately, and he knew he had something to offer. As he had provocatively said in one of his "Seen in the Passing" pieces about an ill-played production of *The Gondoliers,* "If it's worth doing . . . it's worth doing badly!"[35]

An office and a job at his publishers, a visiting professorship at a university of opportunity—it was a fine outlook for his retirement. And he was going out in style. Two celebrations were arranged to mark the occasion. The first took place on September 24 at the University of Glasgow, presided over by its Principal and Vice Chancellor, Sir Charles Wilson. Commendatory speeches were made by Sir William Gray, Lord Provost of Glasgow, and by two ministerial colleagues, Johnston McKay of Greenock and James Miller of Peterhead (who were engaged in editing a volume of essays in his honor), and Willie made suitable reply. The second celebration was more informal, named by James Martin (its chairman) as "The Plain Man's Tribute to William Barclay."[36] It took place at Wellington Church, Glasgow, on November 8, and was a more personal tribute, with "addresses" by Robert Brown of Garthamlock, Robert Watson of the Motherwell Football Club, Archie Maynard of Greenock, Ian Chapman of Collins, Ronald Falconer (recently retired from the BBC), Robert Martin of Princeton (USA), and Stanley Munro representing "the rest of the world"! Willie replied, speaking for himself and for Kate, to whom a special presentation was appropriately made. He was presented with a check on behalf of *The Bush,* the Presbytery of Glasgow's magazine, "representing the people of Glasgow."[37] One of the lighter moments occurred when the sixty ministers present were organized into an impromptu choir. Spirits were too high for serious singing, but over the hubbub Willie made the comment "You were aye good at singing, but not so good at listening!" What distinguished him from others was his own ability to listen. The evening closed with the singing of Martin Rinkart's hymn, "Now Thank We All Our God." That, too, was Willie's way.

Willie celebrated his retirement in his own way—by publishing a book, a revised and much expanded version of his introduction to the Synoptic Gospels of 1966. (With characteristic modesty, he placed it on a list of "odds and ends" he was clearing up!) Indeed, it was virtually a new work, not by reason of his wholesale revision so much as his extensive supplementation. He found he had little to add to the work on the Synoptics except in one important instance, which dealt with the question of redaction criticism. In point of fact, Willie did not approve of the term itself (which had been coined by Marxsen in 1956, but not made familiar to English readers till 1969). He ignored R. H. Lightfoot's 1935 "anticipation" of redaction criticism,[38] relying more on Haenchen, who in 1966 used the term "composition criticism," which was plainer and more accurate. Willie wrote to Bill Telford stating that when he wrote *The First Three Gospels* in 1966, "redaction criticsm had not fully emerged." He acknowledged that redaction critics were "on to something," more or less accepting the validity of their hypotheses concerning Matthew and Luke (that these Gospels rested on Mark and Q) but he rejected their handling of Mark—"a very different thing . . . for what Mark redacted does not exist." On the whole he applauded the approach as "an exceedingly useful tool, and a very valuable means of gospel interpretation,"[39] although inasmuch as he clearly regarded its conclusions (especially with regard to Mark) as purely speculative, it did not influence the picture of Jesus he had previously painted. He also added twenty-five pages on "The Development of Gospel Criticism"; this did not have to do with the general development of the discipline since his first edition, as one might have expected, but with the emergence of something he regarded as much more important and fruitful: historiography, the science of history-writing, which had not been dealt with sufficiently in the earlier book.

But the real enhancement, one that many considered to be long overdue, was his addition of Acts and the Gospel of John to the earlier work, which produced a second volume of some 340 pages. Curiously, whereas Willie had followed the chronological (not the canonical) order of the books in the first volume, he did the opposite in the second volume, placing John before Acts. This unfortunately disrupted the very relationship between Luke and Acts he wished to demonstrate—a clear illustration of his diminished condition. For all that, however, he managed to produce an exceedingly competent survey of the position to date. If we take both volumes together they provide us with literally the largest introduction to their subject matter available in English. It was his final word on the subject, the culmination of twenty-six years of academic work in the field.

Willie gave several interviews after his retirement but he took special pleasure in one he gave to Arthur Montford on the Radio Clyde program *Meeting Place* (a sort of Scottish version of *Desert Island Discs*). It was a human and sensible interview that kept to the main outline of Willie's life and special interests, program construction and presentation at its best. It was full of good things, sometimes humorous, sometimes spicy, sometimes exaggerated. It projected Willie at his best, too, relaxing and chatting, provoking and amusing, all against a background of his favorite music: Highland pipes opened the interview and were followed by excerpts from the overture to Tchaikovsky's *Romeo and Juliet,* Kenneth McKellar singing "All the Things You Are," Ravel's *Bolero,* the Beatles singing "Yesterday," Gilbert and Sullivan's "Savoy" opera *Iolanthe,* Russ Conway playing "Misty," and, finally, the slow movement from Dvořák's *New World Symphony.*

The choice of music for such a program is necessarily of the shop window variety. The guest has to choose music to illustrate his character and personality,

Willie at home, celebrating his retirement by continuing to work [Photo by kind permission of Archie Maynard]

not just to amuse himself, and this choice did exactly that for Willie. The high-minded enjoyment of Tchaikovsky, Ravel, and Dvořák was carefully balanced with McKeller, Conway, and the Beatles—three choices highly typical of the people Willie sought to serve in his work. Willie confessed that he chose Tchaikovsky because it was possible to listen to his music with his feelings rather than his mind, a very Barclayan attitude. The Gilbert and Sullivan selection was personal, of course, as were all the choices, but in choosing this piece Willie was making an almost political statement, as he was in choosing to be introduced by the pipe music of the Highlands.

The interview outlined his life in its characteristic shape, though some details do not find substantiation from other sources—his suggestion that he was Scottish School-boy Champion, for instance, or that he spent a full academic year in Germany, or the strange comment that the BBC "soon lost hope of me." Among the more interesting things he mentioned was the fact that he had indeed coveted Gossip's Chair of Practical Theology in 1947—"the department which teaches people how to preach, how to do things, how to be ministers. . . . But," he added wistfully, "I was turned down for it." He spoke of his and Kate's "blissful happiness" at Renfrew Trinity, and the large Sunday School of which he had baptized every member. Speaking on communication he urged the need to talk of serious things, but to avoid big words. He voiced his rejection of "the normal pattern" of church services (the "hymn sandwich") and his belief that it was pure selfishness on the part of church members that prevented changes that might induce unchurched people to attend services. He was certain that the Church of Scotland was destined to become much smaller. He was equally certain that none of his books could be called great or would last. In closing, he made two final points. They related to "the kick" he was getting out of concentrating on the Old Testament after nearly thirty years of involvement with the New. He admitted knowing very little about it, but was now finding it "as interesting as the New." The second point involved his philosophy of life. He commenced by discussing his earlier "threshold evangelism" approach, and went on to link it to his literary preoccupation and his ethical perspective. At the same time, he expressed his view of providence and theodicy. The whole discussion reflected a struggle for coherence. Because of its importance, I print it in full, grateful for Radio Clyde's permission to do so.

> I have a philosophy of life. Three things. I start with a practical thing. The first is, quite definitely I would say, that the only thing in life that matters is *work*. If I couldn't work, I would want to be taken away. And I think this is true. Suppose you're in sorrow, suppose you're in worry, suppose you've got anxiety problems, suppose you've got this or that. If you can lose yourself in work, this I think is *the* important thing. In other words, I think that work is at one and the same time a stimulus and an anaesthetic. And it can get you through most things.
>
> The other thing. The less practical thing. The more definitely religious thing, is that I think man is entirely to blame for almost everything that happens to him. We are to blame for whatever happens to ourselves. We may not be ourselves to blame, it may be our fathers who are to blame, it may be our fathers' fathers. You get, for instance, people who say, "Why does God allow an aircraft disaster?" God didn't allow it. Nobody is sorrier about it than God. It's due to some human error nine times out of ten.
>
> So I would say, "I believe in work." I believe that you've got to take the consequences of what we do. But the third thing is that I also believe, very strongly, that if we do work, and we do take the consequences of what we do, we do get help. You're not left to do it alone. This, I would say, is where God comes in.

That is not a statement of belief—it was never intended to be such—and does not pretend to be a doctrinal statement. But it is an indication of his approach, a pointer toward belief. It offers a basis for hope, it opens the door, as he intended it should.

A Testament of Faith

It may seem strange to attend at this point to his "autobiography," published in 1975, but it has close links with his "philosophy of life," and it relates closely to his preretirement period in two ways: first, he was commissioned to write it and he fulfilled that commission (in part) at this time; second and more importantly, the conditions that brought about his early retirement and the realization that his ministry was thereby curtailed created the need to write in a *testamentary* way. Without these inducements it is doubtful that he would ever have consented to write an autobiography—for the same reasons he had set his face against anyone writing his biography while he was still alive. But thanks to the creative publishing of Richard Mulkern, then Managing Editor of A. R. Mowbrays of Oxford (and perhaps thanks to the fact that it was from his beloved Oxford that the idea emanated), Willie found congenial the invitation he had received in June 1971 to write on "What I believe." Part of his reply is worth producing.

> I am sadly aware . . . that I am no theologian. I mean this. I know what I can do! I am a good linguist and a good student of New Testament background and history, but I fall down very badly on the theological side and on what Tillich used to call "conceptualisation." It may be that like Miles Coverdale when he started to translate the New Testament . . . I should take this as a sign that I should do it because, as I said, since no one else will do it this poor creature must try.[40]

His essential humility comes through strongly here, as does his deference and his frankness. He knew well the injunction to "know thyself," and he also knew well the need—and where need lay unfulfilled, it was his way to do what others ignored. It was an attitude of life as characteristic as his accent, as typical as his waggish sense of humor. Not that others had really ignored doing this; they had simply ignored doing it in Willie's way. Just a year earlier (in 1970) David T. Niles had produced his own *Testament of Faith,* which may well have spurred Willie into action, not least because of Niles's creed.

As we follow the development of Willie's book, we clearly see his evolving concern for the project; but perhaps more importantly, we see how Willie himself acted in a turbulent period of his life, when the storms of life and the strong tides buffeted. He knew full well the severity of his health breakdown, he could count off the eight years leased to him, he was daily reminded of his (and Kate's) deterioration—and yet he never complained. So far as he could, he simply ignored it and went on, anchor steadfast and sure, "grounded firm and deep" in that to which he witnessed most strongly—the love of God in Jesus Christ.

He informed Mulkern that he was saddened by the tendency of many scholars to "continue to give us works which would be entitled WHAT I DON'T BELIEVE rather than WHAT I DO BELIEVE." Despite a tough schedule (of administration and lecturing—not of writing, which had sharply declined since his crisis of December 1969), he promised to start it "towards the end of the year" and hoped to complete it within eighteen months. That schedule in itself shows how drastically Willie's attitudes had changed. If we except his translation of the New Testament, the fruit of nearly seven years' work, he had not written any books since *Communicating the Gospel* in 1968, when clear signs of poor health and chronic fatigue were evident, nor would he do so until *Ethics in a Permissive Society* (published in 1972). Moreover, he would finish only three more (*Introducing the Bible, The Plain Man's Guide to Ethics,* and *By What*

Authority between 1972 and 1975, when Mowbrays published *Testament of Faith.* That is perhaps not a bad production rate for most men, but for Willie it represents a considerable reduction; he was no longer the man he had been, despite all his protestations to the contrary. And he knew it. It was time, therefore, to put on record his personal testament of faith; his days were numbered.

He was aware that what he had to say would create a reaction, despite the generally favorable reception that had been given to his book *The Plain Man Looks at the Apostles' Creed* (1967). "It would be very simple," Willie continued to Mulkern, "and in my case the philosophers and the theologians would smile, if not laugh, but it would be interesting to see what I do believe. I have often wondered and this might be the chance to find out." (It will be noted that this was only the second time he had contemplated writing a book not for others so much as for himself: exploration continued yet.) But it had to be a confession of faith as well as a testament of faith. Whereas he had earlier made statements (e.g., the "philosophy of life" he described to Montford) that were outgoing, for the benefit of others, this one was to be introspective, a self-examination. In the light of Willie's statement that none of his books would last, we might recall William Robertson Nicoll's view that the enduring part of literature is autobiography.

Was Willie about to write a classic? Reviewing Robert Graves's *But Still It Goes On* at the outset of his academic career, Willie had said that "a good autobiography is a transcript of life."[41] Insofar as this book became autobiographical, we shall need to judge it by the standard that he himself laid down, although we might also keep in mind Graham Greene's observation in *A Sort of Life* that while autobiography may be relied on to contain fewer errors of fact than a biography, it is "of necessity even more selective; it begins later and it ends prematurely. . . . Any conclusion must be arbitrary."[42] This is certainly the case with Willie's work, particularly as autobiography was not itself the real aim, but a mere by-product of the exercise. Said Willie to his publisher some six months later, gradually changing his ground:

> I have thought quite a lot about the TESTAMENT OF FAITH . . . but the thing that did strike me most of all has been that unless it contains some passages of autobiography it will not really explain such faith as I have. I think it must be partly a personal story and partly a personal testament.[43]

Mulkern pressed him to offer an outline of the manuscript, which request elicited this revealing comment: "It will not be easy for me to supply an outline because I am afraid I have a bad habit of writing books without making an outline except in a most brief way. I find that a book writes itself or it doesn't write it at all," adding (by way of reassurance), "but there will be some kind of outline, no doubt." Not only in writing books, but in preaching and even some lecturing, Willie was wont to produce a postcard-size piece of paper on which were written his headings; from such faultless surveys his expositions and addresses emerged. I remember Tim Honeyman telling me that this was how he produced his teaching cassettes, which have helped so many. They were not only faultlessly spoken but also minute-perfect in their timing.

Mulkern kept the pressure on. Twelve months after his original invitation, Willie was promising "to have the book ready for the autumn delivery to you."[44] This same promise carried two further points of interest from this period. First, an expected visit by Willie to Oxford "had to be cancelled because so many of our staff went off on their own concerns that I was about the only person left of seniority on the premises"; the conscientious attitude that had tied him to the department as Junior Lecturer in Macgregor's wanderlust days now clearly did so at the end of his days as well, when he was the senior member of the staff. Second, he wrote of having done "a good deal of thinking about [the manuscript] and making a good deal of notes on it and I think it will write itself fairly quickly when I do sit down to write." Later, at the beginning of September (when he was acting as manuscript assessor for Mowbrays), he wrote to promise that he would start writing that month—three months ahead of schedule.

Alas, it was not to be. An opportunity to appear on the radio program "Thought for the Day" intervened, and "produced a vast correspondence." He also had to record ten broadcasts for Australia and six for America, as well as keep his academic work in order and finish the already overdue revision of *The First Three Gospels* for John Bowden. "I shall definitely hope to get at least something done before the end of the year," he promised yet later.[45] Hope was all he managed, however, the work remained unwritten. By March Willie was thanking Mulkern for being "unbelievably patient" and denying that he considered his reminders to be "nagging." "I am meaning to start and I should hope to deliver by early September," he concluded.[46] A gentle reminder of this promise in mid June provoked the confession that he was troubled over "what to put in and what to leave out": the principle of selectivity propounded by Greene had caught up with him. Moreover, "it is very difficult to separate what one believes and why one believes it and what experiences and life brought it all about." This needs to be taken seriously. Many reviewers have commented on the inadequacy of *Testament of Faith,* have chastised its author for omitting this or that aspect, have been scandalized that more (usually personal) details were not provided. It cannot be claimed that that book is pleasing in all aspects, still less does it have a sound architectonic structure, with each and every element adding to the strength and proportion of the whole. But we need to see it for what it was meant to be—not autobiography, but an expression of faith; not theology, but a practical world view centered on God and his self-revelation in Christ; not a creed, but a simple and positive description of "what I believe" in the light of such publications as John Robinson's *But That I Don't Believe!* Willie's aim was pastoral; his views were personal. "However," he affirmed, ever ready to supply encouragement, "I do assure you things are on the way and the typing has started."[47] He expressed the hope that he could deliver his manuscript "by the end of July or August."

Writing a fortnight later from his beloved Summer Institute at St. Andrews, he said, "I am actually writing the book at the moment and having some pleasure in doing it." The pleasure was short-lived; within another fortnight a further serious breakdown of health took place, requiring hospitalization and intensive care. His old enemy pneumonia had struck again; once more his life was threatened. His secretary, Mrs. Alexander, dourly stated that "his convalescence will be of unpredictable duration."[48] The response to this from the public was so great that a circular letter had to be prepared to inform inquirers of the serious nature of the indisposition, to assure them that he was making some progress, but to indicate that it would be "some weeks before he is fully recovered." Willie's concern for his Oxford publisher was such that the same day the circular letter was produced (August) he got his secretary to assure Mulkern personally that the matter was still very much in mind, and that he would produce his manuscript "about a month later than he had originally planned." He also apologized for the inconvenience he had caused. Slowly he recovered, found his strength, and recommenced his work; but his testament was elbowed out by inescapable duties and assorted pressures. One of these, from Malcolm Mackay of Australia, went on for several months and brought Willie directly into contact with the problems of international politics. Commented Willie (in a broader context, but indicative of his personal attitudes), "If love has to sacrifice, the sacrificing has to be made";[49] it was costing him dearly, this love.

Toward the end of January 1974 Willie received another overture, from Claude Frazier of North Carolina, asking him if he would be willing "to share your personal faith with the reading public?" Willie's reply was blunt, but revealing:

> I am not, at least at present, willing to contribute to the kind of book which you have in mind. The title of the book doesn't appeal to me. NOTABLE THEOLO-GIANS AND THEIR FAITH seems to me to indicate that he who would contribute to it must have what we Scots call "a good conceit of himself"! . . . I have already undertaken to write *a book* of witness. . . .[50]

The principle of selectivity was thereby further strengthened, and the nature and motivation for his *Testament of Faith* expressed with crystal clarity. Writing about himself was "unavoidable," a "necessity,"[51] for beliefs were inseparable from life. He was not, however, proposing to be self-indulgent; he was *witnessing*.

Valentine's Day was a very good one for Richard Mulkern that year, for that was the day he received the first three chapters—sixty-eight pages when printed—of the long-awaited book: "This for Remembrance" (an account of his indebtedness to family and teachers), "Self-Portrait" (a description of his physical and intellectual characteristics), and, finally, what it was all about, "I Believe." The first chapter filled eighteen printed pages, the second fifteen, and the third thirty-five; a careful balance between life and belief was thus achieved. The last remaining chapter, he informed his publisher, would demonstrate how that belief was expressed in his work, the work that was in fact his life. He apologized again for the delay caused by his poor health and now accentuated by his being compelled, in his last year at university, "to write lectures for an Honours student who is taking a course which was never taken before and which we never expected anyone to take." It is so typical that this man, at this time of life, should be found willing to stand in and make the unexpected provision of special lectures for a single student. They were conscientiously written, too! To many, the temptation to take shortcuts, to speak off the cuff, would have been irresistible. That was not Willie's way. "The result is," he continued, "if you want a commentary on *Wisdom* I could supply it almost overnight but it has stopped other things." So Mulkern was asked to wait "ten days or a fortnight"; and Willie hoped he approved of the material he had sent so far.[52]

In point of fact it was over two and a half months before the final chapter came, and even then it was incomplete—a page "for summing up" was still unwritten. During this time his "bronchitis" (an umbrella term he used for a complex of quite serious ills, from heart disease to a deterioration of his brain that made dressing a nightmare) got worse. Willie's invitation to Mulkern to come to see him was turned by Kate into an embarrassing rebuff, and Mulkern's experience with authors' wives was dramatically broadened. The "one page" summing up was delayed yet further, but it eventually turned up as a fifth chapter (of fifteen pages), which repeated not a little of the third chapter, "I believe." On May 15 Willie wrote triumphantly, if wearily, "At last the end has been reached." For him who thought it a sin to cease looking for more experience and knowledge, that was some statement. But it was appropriate to his "testament" of faith, his final expression of what he "most surely believed."[53] He acknowledged that he had not "re-read the thing as a whole," and that he was conscious of some repetitiousness. He gave Mulkern carte blanche to make "whatever alterations you want in it," explaining, "I have no pride as far as that is concerned." He also confessed to another bad literary habit of his—"of completely losing interest in a book once it was written." And, perhaps a little guilty at the delays, not to speak of Kate's earlier indignation, he finished by saying, "Don't forget that meal together when you come north."[54] Therein lay the seal of friendship.

But it was not quite the end. One of his former subeditors from the SCM Press was asked to edit it, and Miss Downham catalogued a whole list of problems: it was not ready for the printers; it was not "a literary production"; it was "entirely personal to William Barclay" (though she had tried to "pull some of the sentences together"); there was a plethora of semicolons (a strong indication of incomplete thought); there was "no consistent method with regard to quotations"; there were "no references, no footnotes." She concluded regretfully that "one cannot make [of] it too neat a thing."

It had been an emotional experience for Willie, painfully recording his memories of loved ones, of former, happier, carefree times; the harsh (though not brutalizing) experiences of life; the wounding criticisms made against him, fairly, unfairly, and sometimes treacherously; the successes and the joys. Perhaps only Kate knew how much this labor cost him, how often during its long gestation she had helped to wash and dress and feed him. Willie knew his debts here, as heretofore: "I said that Kate did not read my books. I hope that she will read this one, for I want her to know, and I want everyone to know, that without her life for me would be impossible."[55]

The cost to them both showed in other ways. Mulkern's assistant, John Stockdale, telephoned to ask if there was a list of Willie's writings that could be appended. He was told that Willie could not remember what he had written since 1972, and that he did not think it was necessary to include this. An internal memo reported his telephoned comment: "If people don't know I write books they haven't been reading much"! The author questionnaire remained un-answered, and Willie had to promise to find a picture of himself for publicity purposes. (He eventually obtained one from the BBC.) In June he was sent the preface David Edwards had written for the book, which Willie found "embarrass-ingly kind." He could not return it immediately; Kate must see it first! The proofs arrived on October 5, and within five days were on their way back to Mowbrays. "It is a grim test of a book to read it over in correcting proofs," Willie reflected, again adding that David Edwards's preface was "much too complimentary."[56] It has to be said that his speed was gained at the cost of accuracy, for several curious mistakes found their way into the first edition.

Further delays were caused in the organization of the publicity when Kate spilled a pan of burning fat over her feet, an accident from which her recovery was painful and slow. It was during this time that Willie, despite his own disabilities, became cook and housekeeper, clumsy as his movements now were. An advance copy of the cover produced a rare protest from him. Thanks to faulty workmanship at the printers, the cover gave Willie a completely bald head. "Horrible," declared the aggrieved author; "I admit to being no oil painting, but I am not a Prussian Colonel."

The book is worth reviewing here, for it shows as nothing else does where Willie now stood. Paul's letter to the Romans has long been regarded as his chief work. It would be foolish to make much of a parallel between that great standard of doctrine (the least conditioned by momentary situations of Paul's occasional writings) and this personal confession of Willie's, and yet both do have this one central attribute: they are both testamentary in character. Of Romans Willie had written, "It is as if Paul was writing his theological last will and testament, as if into Romans he was distilling the very essence of his faith and belief."[57] In the original edition of his Daily Study Bible Willie was even more emphatic, saying that Paul "was distilling the very essence of the last word of his faith and belief"; it is strange that Martin should have so completely missed the emphasis in his revision. Willie said of his own "last word" that "at my age I ought to know where I stand. . . . it is time to put the toys away and to see just where I stand. It is a good time to look back across life and to ask what the things are by which I have lived."[58]

As noted earlier, Willie presents two formulations of those "things which I have most surely believed" in Testament of Faith, one in Chapter 3 of the work ("I Believe") and one in Chapter 5 ("Testament of Faith"), which he added later.

Below I list the essential points of these largely overlapping formulations—side by side for clarity of comparison.

"I Believe"	"Testament of Faith"
1. God (37–41)	1. God (106–7)
2. The world: God the Creator (41–42)	2. The world (109–11)
3. The love of God (43–45)	3. God cares (107)
4. Prayer (46–48)[59]	
5. Jesus (48–53)	4. Jesus (107–9)
	5. The Holy Spirit (109)
6. Life after death (54–65)	6. Work (111–12)
7. Home, marriage, and family (65–68)	7. Love, marriage, home, and family (115–17)
	8. The church (117–21)[60]

These are not traditional outlines of doctrine; their very format challenges us to take seriously his intention as well as his viewpoint.

For years scholars and theologians, churchmen and teachers of religion have been speaking of the need to *restate* the faith in a way acceptable to modern man. The creeds of Chalcedon and Nicaea, and even the so-called Apostles' Creed itself, were products of the first to fourth centuries, and each admirably suited the needs of its generation. Likewise, the confessions of the Reformation (and, we may add, of the Counter-Reformation) were all expressions of the life and thought of the sixteenth and seventeenth centuries. For our changed situation, in the wake of scientific, industrial, and social revolutions, the need was clamant to express the faith consonant with our fresh understanding and knowledge. The challenge to do this was, you will recall, thrown down to Willie at his induction at Renfrew Trinity. It is curious, then, that when he rose to the challenge and attempted such a restatement, many insisted upon judging it as if it were a commentary on a traditional model.

Willie was not alone in his attempt. We have already seen that he was deeply involved in explaining and publicizing one or two of them, perhaps with Macaulay's ordination injunction still ringing in his subconscious. Indeed, in one sense it was his life's work to attend to such things. The devotional and doctrinal obsessions of his father produced in Willie—very much an aware child of the Edwardian age, of the "twittering twenties"—a fascination (in the sense of the Latin original, *fascinans*, "an allurement") that he could not resist, a lifelong struggle to understand anew and to restate. Enough has been said already to show that he lived his life on two levels: one, the outward fulfillment of his appointments, both pastoral and academic; and two, the lifelong struggle with the problems of belief, the search for new ways of exploring and expressing it. In *Testament of Faith* he hints at this long struggle in various ways. He describes himself as being at heart a "natural believer": "in the deepest part of me there is a certainty which nothing can touch."[61] Throughout his life he continually called attention to the dangers of the shut mind, and just as frequently he counseled the *moral* duty of preserving an open, adventurous mind. "To think," he said, "is a necessity of the Christian Life."[62] We can get a sense of the frustration and concern he felt when we hear him saying "There seem to be two different and even contradictory sides to me. One half of me will doubt everyone and everything; but somehow there is something deeper."[63] And we may also note that this statement, expressive of both his intellectual tension and his mental fatigue, is not really finished. The "other half," the "something deeper" not made explicit, came to light in his affirming and "protesting" the faith—in sermons, articles, and books, on radio and on television. But what the meticulous and perceptive A. B. Macaulay saw in Willie in 1932 when he sought to win him for Systematic Theology was another side—that of an intelligent man of faith who was prepared to realign his faith with classical, economic, and human realities, a man who reflected the spirit of modern mankind in its hopefulness and in its determination to capture and enjoy the world's resources, a man who could dare believe in the pertinence of faith for mankind, a man whose beliefs were not so emotionally forfeit as to exclude new light and new emphases, a man who looked forward, but who was nonetheless conscious of the past and determined to safeguard its abiding realities. It had been a long, hard road.

Throughout these years we see the "two different and even contradictory sides" at work—posing questions, exciting exploration, probing doubt, and yet always preaching a positive message, compelling decision, urging discipleship, and alarmed, indignant even, that belief should be limited to any particular historical perspective or viewpoint, anxious that the knowledge of God should not be artificially limited to one small island of experience, one historically or culturally limited expression. Long before J. B. Phillips made the phrase popular, Willie was warning his readers and listeners that "your God is too small."

Many refused to hear Willie's message—the scholars because he was not expressing himself academically, the pillars of society (the steadfast and the stuckfast) because he dared say things that undermined the status quo, the radicals because he was not rejecting enough, and the fundamentalists because he appeared to reject too much. And yet tens of thousands from all over the world heard him gladly and came back for more, again and again. The story of one occasion on which he ran out of cigarettes in Dumbarton on Clydeside on his way to deliver a lecture to a learned society will serve to demonstrate the sort of popular acceptance he found. He did not frequent public houses (though he did often suggest that ministers would be better parish men if they did!), but on this occasion he hurried into one to purchase his favorite brand of cigarettes.

He asked for fags and the voice did the trick. He was "yon fella Barclay on the telly," and the pub erupted around him with good-natured banter, and questions galore. All about the Kirk and how unlike Jesus she was; the bonhommie tinged with that friendly aggression which is the hallmark of the Scottish working-class on his home territory. When Willie was finally able to tear himself away, they lined up, insisted on shaking hands with him and, as he related in his characteristic way, "Paid for my cigarettes, forbye!"[64]

He was accorded so warm a reception quite simply, unnervingly simply, because he did what Jesus did (he who was also hounded by the theologians, the establishment, the revolutionaries, and the timidly conservative): he met his public where they were and, consummate communicator that he was, worked from the known to the unknown, using their symbols, their language.

Acknowledgement of his "simple-mindedness" is a confessional theme that runs strongly throughout *Testament of Faith;* in one sense it constitutes the book's supporting mechanism. In learned works of theology the supporting mechanism (or controlling principle—call it what you will) is typically introduced, defined, clarified, logically developed, and shown against the background of cultural, communal, or competing ideals or experiences. That was not Willie's way. When he came to declare his belief, his first substantive comment was, "I have already said that I am a simple-minded person. I have neither a philosophical nor a theological mind. For that reason I need to think in pictures."[65] He supplies a graphic illustration of the difference between conceptualized and concrete thinking (the difference between "God is an omnipotent being" and "Thou art my Rock") and characteristically adds, "But granted that I must think in that way, I still must think." He then presents an outline of the development of his thinking—the dual formulations of his theology mentioned previously. (For the sake of comprehensiveness and simplicity, I will dovetail the two accounts as I believe he himself would have united them had he been well.) He gives us pictures of God, his world, and his love—his caring; of talking with God (prayer); of Jesus and the Holy Spirit; of our work, our nature, and life after death; of the home, love, marriage, and family; and—finally—of the church.

Now that is a structure, a pattern of belief, that even a child can follow: its elements, its "categories," are drawn from life; it starts from the world of experience. In putting God first, Willie was merely reflecting what every opinion poll on religion has ever showed—that man does have a deep sense of God, of ultimate reality (to use the words of the philosophers and theologians Willie himself disdained). He then moves on to the world itself, and to his own theory of evolution; whatever we may think of his somewhat controversial opinions in this matter, they at least have the merit of once more starting where modern man starts: in the world of his knowledge and experience, a world television has brilliantly expanded and exploited in sitting rooms up and down the length of the land. (We might note in passing that he stressed this link between God and the world in his exposition of the Apostles' Creed as well, citing the influence of C. H. Dodd in the development of his perception that "the way in which Jesus uses the natural processes of the world in his parables makes it quite clear that he too believed that there is a kinship between the world and God.")[66] This leads him into a discussion of the relationship between God and the world, which for the average man is lived out in a cloud of deep (frequently irrelevant) mystery.

Willie understood that the average man struggles with the relationship of God and the world most profoundly at the point of pain, of loss and bereavement, and so he was bold in dealing with the issue in this context, unlike his fellow theologians, who felt that such an approach risks savaging belief "by a thousand qualifications" as medicine and science propel faith backward through the problems. Willie knew it was most important to treat the things his readers felt most strongly about—their bewilderment or anger, for instance, at the thought that a powerful, caring God could permit such pain in his world. The average man *wants* to believe in God, Willie believed, but he is repelled from doing so by the evidence of a pain-racked world and—it needs to be said—sometimes by the incomprehensible language of those who do believe, but explain it in such ways as merely to darken the reality, who wrap it up in a life-style that demands suit and tie, clean fingernails, and an appreciation of centuries-old hymns and music. He is thus made to feel uncomfortable in body and mind by the imposition of something totally unlike the familiar experiences of his home, his work, and his favorite leisure-time activities. If Willie was ever a radical, it was only in this sense, that he came to realize that the church had erected a vast barrier of class and unbelief between those it sought to serve—its people and its God. If Willie was ever possessed of prophetic fury, it was when he protested against this barrier in the manner of Amos, Isaiah, Micah, and—supremely—of Jesus himself. God loves, God cares, Willie testified, and so we may pray, as pray we must—but not "religiously," not according to ordinance, be it of Crown, Parliament, or General Assembly. "Real prayer," he explained, "is simply being in the presence of God."[67] It stems naturally from the realization of God, his love, and his caring—and of his world.

For all his "antiestablishment" sentiments, Willie was a great admirer of, and worker for, the Church of Scotland—not the Church of the careerists, the manipulators of this or that committee, the seekers-after-power, but the Church of the people, ably led by ministers and elders of compassion, conviction, learning, and experience. This was the Church his grandfather's generation thought they had lost, and which they sought to regain first in the Disruption, then with the establishment of the United Free Church of Scotland in 1900, and, climactically, in 1929 in the Union itself. Willie mentioned nothing of this in his autobiography, and yet it was an integral part of him; the Union was, after all, formed at the time he himself was formed, and he was a privileged member of the first generation of "united" ministers in training.

But even given this, Willie the Presbyterian was more "religionless" than Bonhoeffer the Lutheran, and in no aspect more than in prayer. It has never been sufficiently emphasized that Willie wrote more books on prayer, of prayers, than on any other single subject. Even his Christological concentration gives way to this feature of his thinking. He did not write prayers for church services; he wrote them for individuals, for the praying man (and woman!), the plain man (and woman!)—at home, at work, at school, at play, in sickness, and in health. Whenever man becomes aware of God, of the world, of himself, he prays. Willie supplied not just verbal forms for prayer, but emotional directives. He, a man of constant prayer (albeit rarely on his knees), simply supplied as it were a guided tour in the house of prayer, which to him was the day-to-day reality of life. Away with the alienating mystery, the superficial fencing off of so-called holy things! "Be still, and know that I am God" was Willie's message.

If his prayer life arose out of daily reality, so in one important sense did his understanding of Jesus, the next element in his "creed" (*creed*, from the Latin *credo*, "I believe"—but belief understood not as dogma, but as action, commitment). Note how integral a part of his belief is this most characteristic, most central affirmation; "For me Jesus is the centre and the soul of the whole matter."[68] It takes him straight to John 1:14, which was ever his favorite text, "the most important single text in the Bible."[69] He continues, drawing the core of the matter out into the open, away from linguistic and Greek philosophy (which he ever handled with ease and elegance):

> And what is the *logos?* The *logos* is the mind of God, interpenetrating the universe and making sense of it. . . . Why is H_2O always water? In other words, what makes the universe a cosmos and not a chaos? The answer is the Logos, the mind of God. It is the Logos, the mind of God, which puts order into the universe and reason into the mind of man.[70]

In so saying Willie has linked his experiential world view to the historic Jesus (a fundamental of all his writing and teaching) and has given credence and substance to what he elsewhere declared to be John's "real contribution to Christian thought." Declares he, "the truth in John's thought is so modern that the conventional thought of the church has not assimilated it or caught up with it even yet."[71]

Willie made his declaration about the modernity of John's thought at about the same time he wrote *Testament of Faith*, but the conviction had long been part of his considered opinion. Note this statement, for instance, published twenty years previously, in July 1955:

> The first chapter of the Fourth Gospel is one of the greatest adventures of religious thought ever achieved by the mind of man. . . .
> Greek thought knew all about the *Logos*; it saw in the *Logos* the creating and the guiding and the directing power of God which made the universe and which keeps the universe going. . . .
> So John went out to Jews and Greeks to tell them that in Jesus Christ this creating, illuminating, controlling, sustaining mind of God had come to earth. He came to tell them that men need no longer guess and grope; all they had to do was to look at Jesus and see the Mind of God.[72]

And he expressed this even ten years earlier than that, in his prentice years at Renfrew, when he wrote his very first book in 1945:

> As Greek thought developed, the idea of God became very spiritualised. It became so spiritualised that there came a time when they could not conceive of God the spirit having any contact with the material world at all. . . . They thought of God as having an intermediary or an instrument or a principle through which He acted on the material universe and on men. That principle was *The Word* or the *Logos*. . . . The Word was that principle of reason which guided and directed the

world.... It is the power by which they came to know God.... *This doctrine keeps us in remembrance that though in history Jesus the Son of God emerged and lived at a definite time, nevertheless He existed before the beginning of time and will exist until after the end of time, that God is eternally three in one, and one in three.*[73]

Let us briefly note two essential things. First, Willie never shared in the revulsion for the material world that has adversely influenced Christianity (evangelicalism not excluded) far more than is realized.[74] The Jewish faith exalted in the gifts of God in creation—in his provision of good things to be enjoyed with thanksgiving, whether of food or drink, of health or home, of hard work or joyous exercise, of mental enjoyment or bodily pleasure. In becoming teacher to the plain man, Willie became an apostle of the common things, uniting (scandalously, to some sensibilities) not only Solomon and Paul, Isaiah and John, but Jesus and the more principled aspects of Rabbie Burns and even of the Beatles themselves, as in their very different way they sang of such things. Second, despite his protestations about simple-mindedness (we should note that he does not deny the need for abstract thought), Willie was authoritatively conversant on an issue that has intrigued some of the best minds in the history of Christian thought. Even the great predecessors in his chair, A. B. Bruce, James Denney, and James Moffatt, failed to produce meaningful expositions of this doctrine, the doctrine of the "cosmic Christ." Willie not only produced it in this popular autobiographical work, but found there a doctrine of God, of the world, and of Jesus that integrated all three; and he managed to formulate therefrom a plea for a broad and "natural" understanding that kept the universe united. The doctrine is but John's equivalent to the early church's one-sentence creed "Jesus Christ is Lord"—Lord of heaven and earth, of man and beast, of life and death. It is the profoundest possible understanding of Christian faith, and Willie expressed it simply and cogently.

All other aspects of his belief are mere commentary on these two. Not least among the subordinate tenets was his high claim for the dignity of man, of which his daily work and his home life were the finest expressions. Little wonder that his doctrine of the church comes last! Not that he ever denigrated it; he simply kept it where it was always intended to be—not at the peak of society, but humbly subservient; not lording it over men, but washing their feet. Said Willie, abruptly bringing his comments on the church (as well as his testament of faith) to a close, "And so to the end—and if I were to begin life over again, I would choose exactly the same service."[75]

CHAPTER TWENTY

The Evening-Time of Life

A New Job and a New Direction

Not surprisingly, when *Testament of Faith,* the capstone of Willie's public profession of faith, was finally published, some critics did smile, some laughed, some scoffed, and some simply yawned. "Barclay?" mused one, "isn't he the fellow who could tell you what Jesus had for breakfast?" As David Edwards dryly observed, he probably could. For all the criticisms he received (and at this time of weakness, they outweighed the encouragements he got from his colleagues), he could still claim to have been a thorough workman. Alexander Whyte had learned the secret of living with criticism—and of portraying its nature—long ago, and expressed it thus: "I will be impervious to the shafts of envy and malice even though they be tipped with the poison of pseudo-friendship." Nearer our own day, Albert Camus has noted that "There are more things to admire than scorn." And Churchill neatly turned the whole business on its head when he commented that the venom of a man's enemies is the measure of his strength. When applied to Willie, that puts him in a very strong position indeed!

And he was strong, seemingly impervious, in the sense that when he had studied a problem (and by the time he left Renfrew there were few problems he had not encountered) and come to what he believed was an adequate answer, he saw no need to keep "unmaking his bed." He was in many ways an open-minded man, but his mind was not open at both ends. And he did in fact settle on some very definite beliefs about God and the world, beliefs that were formed of his parents' evangelicalism, re-formed through strenuous mental concentration over eight years of university preparation, and fashioned as it were in iron during his parish ministry. There he tempered them in the fire of life's unsparing circumstance; there he saw they were able to withstand the ferocity of human mortality and failure. What refashioning had to be done before his students at university was not balked at. Some people's minds are like elastic: having been stretched by external forces, they spring back virtually to their original condition; other minds are like plasticine: once stretched, they are thinner, often too fragile for further manipulation; Willie's was vital and ever responsive. He never became insensitive to the things that stimulate growth; he remained alive—too much alive, some said—to the problems and doubts people have about Christian doctrine and ethics. The core of his faith remained unaltered: "Jesus Christ is Lord" echoed through his heart and mind during the whole of his ministry as it has echoed through the centuries. After all, he had seen enough of intellectual and practical life to know where he stood. His own record was one of incontrovertible success. He looked on the record of radicals and liberals and pondered their empty churches and declining college traditions; he looked on the record of fundamentalists and conservatives and pondered their failure to reach the mass of people, pondered the lack of grass-roots contact in many of their "successful churches"; he recalled the hours of private conversations he had passed with countless representatives of both camps, and he knew the secret of life: "The others we know about," he asserted; "Jesus we know. The others we remember: Jesus we experience."[1]

Apart from that firm foundation very little else mattered much, be it the technical arguments for the existence of God, the question of his governance of the world, the problems of human and social evolution, or the latest documentary (or nondocumentary) theory of gospel or Pauline criticism. Like W. R. Nicoll of old, his reading—and it was enormous, voracious, always instantly available to his remarkable memory—was "an account of his soul's adventures among books." He adventured still, at sixty as at six.

It is not really correct to say, as has Neil Alexander, that he was impervious to the wounds inflicted by fellow academics.[2] He often laughed them off, and he never mentioned them to his family, but they hurt nevertheless. And the very fact that he knew they hurt Kate, who had long struggled against despair and the cynicism that followed Barbara's death, vastly exacerbated the pain. No man with as high a view of work as Willie possessed could have been anything other than distressed by such a response. This in part explains why he was such a commendatory critic himself. A book or a manuscript may have been wrongheaded or full of the blemishes of carelessness, but Willie would find something to praise. W. H. Clement made an apposite point in recalling an occasion during the '50s on which Willie, some other ministers, and the youth of one of his many house conferences attended a local church service and suffered through an indifferent sermon. Afterward, over coffee, Willie was asked what he thought of the sermon, and he replied, silencing the unvoiced criticism, "Son, ye niver ask one minister whit he thinks o' anither minister's sermon!"[3]

On Willie's retirement his former student Angus Stewart wrote to thank him for his Daily Study Bible (he wrote that he had "waded through Westcott, Temple, Tasker and Morris" only to find "exactly what I wanted in your own work, and I am profoundly grateful").[4] Willie replied by return post, though Stewart had asked him not to bother. "Of course I must answer it!" he exclaimed. "A letter like yours makes a lot of things worthwhile, and that a former student should have so written is a very precious thing to me." And when Linda Harris sent him a clutch of reviews, he was grateful, despite the brickbats contained in some of them: "They are very encouraging. I have read them with pleasure and must pray to be delivered from pride!"[5] Where his views had raised real problems, he was willing to enter into serious and sometimes protracted correspondence, as he did with Miss Moira Grego of Garvald and Fred Bailey of Somerset and Mrs. Agnes Innes of New Zealand.

These were days in which every least task was a significant undertaking; his larger efforts, such as his lectures on ethics at Strathclyde and his Old Testament work at Collins, entailed the most appalling difficulties. To W. J. G. Macdonald, interim moderator of North Morningside church, who had appealed to him for pulpit supply, Willie confided, "I can hardly get across the road now." Breathlessness was now chronic, and the intermittent bouts of "bronchitis" with which he was stricken had become an irreversible emphysema. Willie did not need reminding that he had now lived five of the eight years promised in 1969. Every day was a new challenge and a new struggle; every day was a *memento mori*. Kate, too, felt the distress of deteriorating health, combatting sciatica and other maladies with a continuous intake of pills of all descriptions. By early 1975 she was once more hospitalized, and Willie again had to shift for himself, attending to his work as well as the extra traveling necessary to visit her. Despite all this, between September 3 and 13 he maintained a phenomenal correspondence (over forty letters have been preserved from this period, covering a wide variety of queries, appeals, congratulations, and invitations).

October 1 was a memorable day, for it was then that he began his fourth phase, as resident author for Collins in his new office, with Mrs. Hamilton as his new secretary. It was the day after he "got finished up" at the University: not even one day of holiday was considered. He went in at the deep end, as he had done when he moved from Trinity Church to Trinity College. In point of fact there were still a number of things left over "from what you may call my previous existence," as he put it[6]—mainly letters and personal undertakings. "I hope to really get cracking on the Old Testament next week." He was delighted with the commercial atmosphere, the first he had sampled in his entire career, and he spoke to everyone of their kindness and generosity. Within six weeks he was immersed in the Psalms. "Very interesting," he commented to David Anderson, another former student. But he acknowledged that his work was "comparatively slow because I have to start from scratch."[7] To Rita Snowden he wrote, "This is a new world to me—both Collins and the Old Testament— and I am finding it very interesting indeed."[8] A familiar Barclay note sounds in this letter: "I am settled down . . . and working as hard as I am able to"—but, truth to tell, it was a formidable, uphill battle. To Bryden Maben he said, also indicating his difficulties, "in about two years something should happen."[9] By now his handwriting had noticeably deteriorated, doubtless due to the ever-worsening Parkinsonism. It was now an evident reality that affected even his typing ability. The sense of having completed his course began to predominate. Such phrases as "end of the chapter" and "end of the book" now found regular expression. He was saddened by the fact that he no longer heard news of his old Faculty, though letters from former students continued to come—requests for advice and references and the like.

Had he restricted himself to Strathclyde and Collins, it would have been enough, but Willie could not do so, especially when a request came from an old friend like Aubrey Smith of the International Bible Reading Association whom Willie himself owned as being responsible for his popular writing career (gallantly redirected by Smith to Jack Stevenson). Now General Editor of the National Christian Education Council and the IBRA, Willie had written in 1971 his *Introducing the Bible* for him. It was a very serviceable handbook and was well received on both sides of the Atlantic, the material being made available in both book and cassette form. Commented one ecstatic reader, "he rolled back the stone from the tomb of my ignorance, allowing me to ascend to the threshold of Christian understanding." So a second book was planned, on the nature of God, the actual title to be decided later.

Mr. Smith admitted that this book was "a long time coming"; even when it came it presented almost insurmountable problems for publishing. It presents yet another indication that the aftermath of the crisis of 1969/70 was very grave. The material, Willie acknowledged, was "cobbled together"; it did not read well, and the development of his themes was neither smooth nor satisfying. Some doubted his sequential unfolding of the idea of God (from polytheism through henotheism to monotheism). Willie had reached the point Dean Inge reached in 1937, when he felt that his "hand had lost its cunning." By early 1975 Willie was offering to rewrite the material for Smith, adding ominously, "I'll do my best. I fear that I will have to be back to the old days of the night-shift!"[10] *The Character of God* is Willie's shortest book (at sixty-four pages), and is curiously reliant on H. E. Fosdick.

The subject itself was problematical for Willie. All his ministerial life he had emphasized the loving-kindness of God, the linchpin (rightly or wrongly) of his beliefs. In 1961 he had written how our lives would be changed if "each one of us could take the whole of life to the whole of God."[11] It is beyond question that he himself strove to take "the whole of life" to God—that may well be considered to be one of his most characteristic and important contributions—but it seems clearly open to debate whether the God he took it to was in fact "the whole of God," at least as that phrase is understood by theologians, especially the conservative theologians of his upbringing (such as Richard Charnock and James Orr). God in his plenitude is wanting here. In the more theological language of James Denney, whom Willie himself quotes on more than one occasion, he confessed that it is never right to isolate one attribute of God, and he went ahead and did so, endlessly highlighting God's love to the exclusion of other considerations. When he came to write of the nature of God, he fell back on "historical" development rather than theological statement. His theme naturally comes alive at the point where he understands it best: "there does come a radical alteration in the New Testament's attitude. . . . God is, so to speak, christianized. . . . God was seen to be Christlike."[12] This is a shorthand and rather crude way of putting it, but it is exactly representative of Willie's thinking, in which the point he wants to stress eclipses all others.

We cannot spend too much time on this tendency of Willie toward "over-balanced" argument, although we might let a comment he made in an interview on 18 April 1975 stand as a perplexing paradigm of this approach. Denis Duncan, his interviewer, had reminded Willie of the influence of highland evangelicalism, which stresses the sovereignty of God, on him personally. "What does that have to do with our praying?" he asked. "I'm afraid I don't think much of the sovereignty of God," Willie replied, with total unconcern as to the implications of such hyperbole. "I think almost altogether of the Fatherhood of God. . . . I don't think of God as King so much as I think of God as Father. I'm not thinking so much of the control of God as I'm thinking of the love of God and the arrangement of my life and the enabling of me to lead life as it is."[13] In fairness, one has to remember two things—Willie's poor state of health when he made the statement and the off-the-cuff nature of the interview (which was concluded by the rectifying statement that in prayer one must remember two things: "you are praying to someone who loves you, and . . . you are praying to someone whose love is *almighty*"). Nevertheless, it is true that Willie used love to interpret the other attributes of God, whereas traditional theology has always sought to understand them separately, though in harness with each other.

On 24 April 1975 Kate wrote a distressing letter to their mutual friend William Braidwood:

Dear Bill,
I simply do not know what to do!
My husband is in the Victoria Infirmary in a side-ward with an oxygen mask and heavily doped. I have been so worried about him for weeks, as his breathing was getting so laboured. And what a struggle he was having walking, dressing, etc. etc.!
If you knew him the way I do, you would know he never admits to being ill, and I had to take the law into my own hands and phone our doctor. When he came, he sent for a specialist, and within an hour an ambulance arrived and he was in the Victoria.
I see him every night for about fifteen minutes, but he is so doped I can't bother him with anything. . . .

Pneumonia had struck again, and Kate—herself unwell, presently dependent upon a walking stick, and inundated with "so many letters that my mind is more or less a blank by now"—once more feared the worst. To Aubrey Smith she confessed that even when she did visit him, accompanied by Ronnie (the only other visitor allowed), he "sometimes [did] not seem to know us." On rare days of lucidity, he expressed anxiety over delaying his work, and even asked for his typewriter to be brought into hospital! It was of course out of the question on several grounds; his Parkinsonism now made even holding a newspaper a wearying struggle, and Kate doubted his ability even to be able to read. A little later she commented to Howard Williams, "I do thank you so much for your letter—which is more than I can say for the majority of the letters I am trying to cope with."[14] She was having to cope virtually alone—Mrs. Hamilton, Willie's secretary at Collins, also played her part—but since Mrs. Hamilton was new to Willie's work her help was limited, and the bulk of the burden remained on Kate's shoulders. "I am so worried I can't concentrate," she declared to Williams. And the worry was intensified by a specialist's pronouncement that she would "just have to make up her mind to the fact that Bill was the type who would die in harness." But "what comfort is that to me?" she wondered. Yet again, circularized letters were prepared for his well-wishers, and for some who were plaguing him for information readily available from any reference library.

The precipitating factor for this further bout of illness was an event of some prestige in Edinburgh organized by The Upper Room, an American evangelical organization which produced a devotional reader of extraordinary influence and range.[15] Each year it organized a citation honoring an individual for his contribution to Christian literature. Such figures as John Mott, Ralph Cushman, John Mackay, Helen Kim, Billy Graham, and Elton Trueblood had been recipients. This year tradition was broken and two men were chosen—old colleagues and former competitors for the same university chair James Stuart Stewart and William Barclay.

The event took place on April 18 at the famous Assembly Rooms, 480 people gathering to fête the two incomparable Scots. The meeting was presided over by John Birkbeck, editor of the British Isles edition of the organization's publication *The Upper Room* and successor to Andrew McCosh at Stirling Tract Enterprises. The special guests included the Archbishop of Canterbury Donald Coggan and Cardinal Gordon J. Gray as well as Bailie John Gray of Edinburgh, Neville Davidson (on behalf of the Moderator of the General Assembly of the Church of Scotland), and the President of the Baptist Union of Scotland, James Taylor, to name but a few. The World Editor of *The Upper Room*, Wilson O. Weldon, read a loyal message to the Queen and Her Majesty's gracious reply; he also spoke on the importance of communication today. Willie's musical enjoyment was not neglected, as the Salvation Army Singers provided some lighter relief. The meal featured a full selection of Caledonian delights, commencing with Solway Prawns and Orcadian Sauce, followed (appropriately, some critics would say) by Poacher's Broth, which was followed by Sirloin of Angus Beef, Ayrshire Potatoes, and Lothian Beans. This was topped off by Edinburgh Fog—the gastronomic variety, not the meteorological. The fog did not permeate the speeches, however, which were bright and witty. According to John Birkbeck's newsletter, "the company represented every credal colour in the rainbow of God's witness in Britain," and "both recipients . . . spoke with heart-stirring happiness and gratitude." They were not the only recipients, for both the wives were given monetary gifts in just recognition of their share in their husbands' work.

Alas, others also marked the occasion. In typical style and mood, the followers of Jack Glass, a former Glasgow Paisleyite of the lesser ilk, protested against

The Upper Room

Citation

William Barclay

Native son of Wick, Scotland.

Early master of New Testament studies and teacher of preachers.

A prolific and disciplined writer with insight and power on the meaning of prayer.

Translator of the New Testament and expositor of relevant Biblical applications.

One who appreciates music and trains and directs student choirs.

A lover of persons, whose focus is upon interpretations vividly and strikingly stated.

Effective and versatile communicator of the scriptures.

Faithful disciple of Jesus Christ and untiring witness of His love for all the world.

Presented in Edinburgh, Scotland
April 18, 1975
THE UPPER ROOM, Nashville, Tennessee

Wilson O. Weldon
Editor

Above: *The Upper Room citation, presented to the "native son of Wick . . . faithful disciple of Jesus Christ and untiring witness of His love for all the world." Below: The presentation of the citation. Shown are (from left to right) Archbishop (now Lord) Coggan, John Birkbeck, Willie, James Stewart, and Wilson O. Weldon.*

678

Willie with banners and consummate ill will. But the spiritual violence was more disconcerting than the physical contact. Word of their rowdy intentions had caught the ear of the police, who supplied escorts and even plainclothes detectives (said to have been the worst-dressed individuals present). The police concern led to at least one inadvertently humorous incident that epitomized the characters of the men to be celebrated. Professor Stewart arrived in his own car and sought to park it nearby. "I'm sorry sir," said a young constable, "but these spaces are reserved for the VIPs." Without a word, the Very Reverend Professor James S. Stewart, D.D., former Moderator of the General Assembly, took his car off and parked elsewhere.

In addition to being privately interviewed, Willie also spoke publicly, declaring his understanding of the doctrine of justification by faith in unambiguous terms—a rare occasion on which his essentially Reformed beliefs found clear-cut expression. It was this declaration that caused Archbishop Coggan to comment, "This is a new William Barclay." The event elicited less worthy responses as well. Mr. Glass, in his private publication *The Scottish Protestant View,* wrote of the "ceremony . . . to honor one of Scotland's most evil apostates. False Professor William Barclay." It is sad to have to dignify such scurrilous insult with inclusion in these pages, but it is necessary that some indication be given of the sort of abuse that both Willie and Kate were made to suffer during these years of illness and vulnerability—if only to explain the undercurrent of defensiveness in *Testament of Faith* that some readers have found puzzling.

Glass's uncalled-for attack was merely one in a long campaign of cruel character assassination—a campaign doubly cruel in light of Willie's physical condition, for although he could have shrugged the barbs off easily enough had he enjoyed full health, they stung him to the quick in his weakened state. And the barbs were tipped with the poison of ill will (Glass had refused Willie's handshake) and were delivered with exaggeration and outright misinformation. In Glass's diatribe, the 480 guests attending the "ceremony" (the word *ceremony* itself carrying connotations of old contentions) became a throng of two thousand; the modest servant of Christ became "the apostate . . . a crafty emissary of hell . . . not a communicator of the gospel, but a contaminator of the gospel"; and Willie's teachings became his "blasphemies," his "errors." Seven years later, in 1982, Glass's two-page "refutation" was still being circulated via the Free Presbyterian Bookroom to anyone who cared to mention Willie's name.

The celebration took an immediate toll as well. Kate was quick to see that the exertion was costing Willie dearly. "I don't know how he managed to get through that citation," she wrote to Williams. In fact he nearly failed to do so; only sheer willpower kept him going amid the clatter and the noise, his mind straining for clarity, his head spinning with headache and fever, his body aquiver with aches, pains, and threatening spasms. And so few even noticed! Two weeks later, Kate was still watching anxiously as her husband, in the hands of the medical experts he both feared and admired, fought for his life. In one of his periods of lucidity, he mentioned to Kate that the specialist had forbidden him to take on any outside work during the coming summer, and that he had replied that that was nonsense! He was *determined* to go to his American Institute for the first three weeks of July. Kate grew yet more apprehensive, fearing what this would do to him. "The Americans are the worst and most demanding," she said, knowing well that kindness and veneration can kill as quickly as their opposites. "I know I can't stop Bill altogether," she sighed. "He loves every aspect of his work. . . . If only he would content himself with his new subject, the Daily Bible Studies of the Old Testament . . . but I know he won't."

By June 3 he was up and at it again, assuring Doubleday, his would-be private publisher, that he was "newly back at work" and that he hoped to complete the promised volume of prayers "very soon." In fact, he was now strictly limited to half days of work, a disappointing allotment that Willie simply had to accept. He had so much still to do! To his publisher at Oxford he wrote accepting another commission, this time to undertake a six-month stint with the parish magazine published by Mowbrays. And he was delighted to receive news of the publication of the American edition of his *Testament of Faith* (he had forgotten Eerdmans had undertaken it). "I now consider my orthodoxy indisputably guaranteed," he commented, adding ruefully, "I am not sure whether I am thrilled or discouraged!"

"Growing old!" he exclaimed to an interviewer some months later. "You only grow old if you have nothing to do."[16] Readers of *Seen in the Passing* and *Through the Year with William Barclay* will remember that he defines old age as the point at which one begins to look backward instead of forward, when one lives in memory rather in hope. Virtually at death's door at the age of sixty-eight, he was once more looking ahead, to new work and new opportunities. Accordingly he laid aside his Daily Study Bible work and wrote "a series of helps for study" for Collins's new edition of the Revised Standard Version of the Bible, which also served to introduce him to Old Testament criticism.

During his illness, Willie had received an unusual letter from Allan Bowers, then of Wolverhampton. It concerned a "Desert Islands Books" evening organized by the minister of his congregation. Bowers wanted to know what eight books Willie would take to a desert island with him if those were the only ones he could have. His response shows how entertainingly he could enter into the spirit of such a thing even yet, despite his serious condition. It also serves to throw light on some of his past and present attitudes toward knowledge and books. He divided his selection into two parts—two necessary books, and six interesting ones:

1. A dictionary; not an ordinary dictionary but a dictionary like the *Readers' Digest Encyclopaedia* . . . which has sections on Music and Art and Food and Science—all kinds of things
2. *The Guinness Book of Records*
3. Boswell's *Life of Johnson*
4. Gibbon's *Decline and Fall of the Roman Empire*
5. Plato's *Republic* [He commented that he had never read this and the two foregoing titles right through, an astonishing admission for one whose own writings sparkle with quotations from such classical authors.]

6. The *Oxford Dictionary of Quotations*
7. A handbook on astronomy ["I have always wanted to know something about astronomy and don't know anything," he wrote, "and a desert island seems to offer unlimited opportunities."]
8. An omnibus volume of detective stories

With this list, he concluded, equanimity would be achieved.

Later that summer 206 Americans gathered at St. Andrews. "They are extraordinary people but they are instinctively and characteristically kind, so kind that they can almost kill you with kindness," Willie commented. He was now taking nine different pills a day, and still tended to "rattle when I walk." To some he mentioned taking on further tasks once he was over the present indisposition! But Kate and he both knew that his condition was irreversible. The eight years given to him in 1969 seemed very short indeed now; Kate's burden grew heavier. Following the Institute, he and Kate went off together to Arbroath in their new Vauxhall Magnum 1800 Automatic, every facility and every aid helping to safeguard his frail health. He was by this time admitting that even "half a day's work is plenty."[17] To the Braidwoods he commented that Kate had "developed an addiction to Arbroath"; the Seaforth Hotel supplied all they needed by way of service and comfort. Willie was pleased, too, for he was near Robert Glover, one of his favorite former ministerial students, who was qualified both in music and in theology; their meals together gave Willie great pleasure.

October saw the commencement of his Strathclyde lectures on Professional Ethics. There gathered to hear him no fewer than 240 students of production engineering, of which, astonishingly, "rather more than half were Japanese, Chinese and Malaysians."[18] Considering Willie's clear-cut biblicism, one wonders at the politeness of these Shinto and Buddhist adherents in listening imperturbably to Scotland's foremost religious communicator. What an opportunity Willie now seized! (Some of these lectures were later published in *Life and Work* under the title "Religion and Life.")

One of the interesting changes that Willie underwent at this time involved his speaking out more often on political issues. Perhaps it was the result of his being able to reflect on such things for the first time in his career, in the unprecedented extra hours of leisure at home. (He could now often be found resting in his chair, a handkerchief neatly folding under his chin in protection of his clothing—uncontrolled salivation being one of the troublesome symptoms of his Parkinsonism.) And yet the interest was not new to him; speaking of the Old Testament prophets under the significant, if anachronistic, heading "Communicating the Gospel in the Prophets," he had said in 1967 that "they believed that the man of God must be interested and involved in the political situation. If history is the arena in which the will of God is being worked out, then clearly the man of God must be involved in its events."[19] He had long been committed to this principle, and now free from the normal ministerial stance of nonalignment, he could declare his views more forthrightly. So it was that he commented on the action taken by university lecturers in withholding examination results to bring pressure on the authorities for increased pay. It "hurts the wrong people," he exclaimed.[20] To Senator Norman Paterson of Canada he commented on the Common Market debate, and reflected his gladness that Britain was still a member.[21] He did not think too highly of Mr. (now Lord) Wilson's political manipulations, finding it especially distasteful that trade union "approval" was necessary for some decisions. He was not against unions per se ("they have done a terrific job," he acknowledged), but he could no more acclaim their use of brute force than anyone else's, whether the purpose be judicial, national, disciplinary, or capitalist. Willie was against allowing price rises in basic commodities, which caused inflation, he asserted (falling back on the economic studies of more than forty-five years previous!) To Fred Bailey of the Salvation Army, himself involved in local politics, Willie said he was "flattered that you should call me a socialist." Overturning the convictions of his youth and of his parents, he went on to say that "I would indeed call myself a socialist, but I would be very far from being a supporter of the Labour Party."[22] He spoke out on Devolution ("something I do not really believe the Scottish people desire"), Princess Margaret's marriage difficulties, and the sad lack of "a Churchillian voice today."[23] He also commented on the Queen's jubilee celebrations,[24] the Watergate scandal, and even nudism ("nothing wrong with nudism itself. . . . I am sure a beach set apart for nudism and for nudists would very soon become a very commonly accepted thing").[25] His correspondence with Malcolm Mackay on international issues continued from time to time, and allowed him an appreciated opening therein.

Sad to recall, another succession of mishaps now came to the beleaguered Barclays. Toward the end of the year Willie wrote to Braidwood of Kate, perhaps a little impatiently. "She has cracked everything," he wrote. "You name it, she has had it," and he went on to describe the migraine headaches she had been suffering from continually.[26] In February 1976 he came down with influenza again, which threatened a further outbreak of "bronchitis." And Kate, as if in sympathy, came down with what Willie described as nettle rash, but which clearly was some form of neurological disorder.

Their spirits were somewhat lifted by the presentation to Willie of a *festschrift* volume, *Biblical Studies in Honour of William Barclay.* Whatever was said about Willie, as Richard Holloway said in reviewing the volume, "he is an unignorable part of the contemporary religious landscape."[27] The work was edited by Johnston McKay and James Miller, both former students of Willie's, themselves engaged in pastoral work, at Glasgow and Peterhead, respectively, and it contained essays by such well-known scholars as Robin Barbour, Robert Davidson, Hugh Anderson, George B. Caird, Charles Scobie, Neil Alexander, Ernest Best, Matthew Black, A. M. Hunter, William Neil, J. C. O'Neill, George Johnston, and W. D. McHardy—a representative array of academic talent, many of them with ministries that overlapped Willie's own, either in Scotland or further afield. Each of the traditional Scottish universities was represented, Glasgow three times (appropriately), Oxford twice, and Cambridge and Nottingham once each. A trans-Atlantic influence is reflected in pieces from Scobie of Sackville, and Johnston of McGill University, both of Canada.

Mr. McKay has related that Willie expressly wished that the book might be written for the plain man, against tradition, though the search for authors who could successfully have addressed such an audience would have been a "fruitless attempt" in the editor's estimation.[28] I am not so sure; the emergence of able scholarly communicators in the areas of lay theology and "young church" theology would surely seem to challenge that assumption. And in any case, Willie would surely have welcomed even a "fruitless attempt" rather than merely have himself set in the very mold from which he had struggled to distance himself over so many years. But the gesture was good, and the individual essays—on biblical introduction (three), Old Testament (two), New Testament (six), and general doctrinal matters (two—of politics and Christology)—are an apposite indication of at least some of his foremost concerns. The first full bibliography of Willie's writings concluded the volume, naming seventy-two separate publications, plus his "Christian Way" pamphlets of 1962 and his Alex Wood Memorial Lecture of 1963, "Christian Discipline in Society Today." The contributions were prefaced by two quite different essays, "A Personal Appreciation" by Johnston McKay (which includes the statement that Willie was influenced by Henry Drummond's thought and method) and "Barclay the Broadcaster" by Ronnie Falconer.[29]

In one of only four comments directly made about Willie in this volume, J. C. O'Neill happily states that "Professor William Barclay . . . has done more than most New Testament scholars to keep open the traffic between scholars who argue—who must argue—about words, and ordinary Christians who simply want to help to pray and live." Willie would have asked no higher accolade than that. Had that been made the text or the objective of the *festschrift*, it would have been an impressive monument to the man who strived so carefully, so tirelessly, to be "a theological middleman." We ought not to criticize the editors, still less the contributors, for failing to do so, however, as some reviewers chose to do. In one sense, you cannot have a *festschrift* volume without learned articles. And we must not overlook the simple fact that their very presence was a compliment to him, a long overdue acknowledgement by the academic world of its somewhat unorthodox, if not eccentric, Glasgow colleague. And even if it were "caviare for the general, rather than porridge for the many," to use Gordon Rupp's waggish comment,[30] even generals require feeding, and few would sniff at caviare.

In March, a traumatic event shook Kate and Willie, when a mentally disturbed youth with a yen for starting fires found their garage door open (no doubt left so by Willie) and a handy can of paraffin lying within. The result was an explosive conflagration that destroyed the garage and all its contents (including their car), and threatened the adjacent house itself. The *Scottish Daily Express* created a sensation with the front-page headline "Fire Bomb Attack on Barclay." *The Glasgow Herald* announced a "Fire Bomb Attack on TV Professor's House," and *The Scottish Daily Record* declared "Fire-bomb Inferno." As is usual in such situations, reporters found different accounts of what happened. Alistair Campbell had Willie looking for an incendiary device and "pulled clear by a neighbour with only seconds to spare." *The Scotsman,* with becoming eastern sangfroid, had him discovered in bed with Kate, both of whom were ill at the time, adding the comment that a neighbor later prevented him from entering the garage to save his car. Reflection and good police work soon established the real story, and Willie and Kate were eventually left in peace to recover from the ordeal, not only struggling from their normal afflictions, but now from delayed shock to boot. The incident made waves, and once more Willie's correspondence mounted. To his old friend in New Zealand Rita Snowden, he wrote without any real sign of having been greatly disturbed by the ordeal, his mind ever dwelling on practical aspects:

> It is not a question of repair, it is a question of replacement. Fortunately, there is the insurance, but it is a nuisance being without my own car. They got the boy, and I hope that he is put in some place where he will receive the treatment and the guidance that he obviously so much requires.[31]

The following month saw Willie in the news again, though not by his own doing. The editor at *Life and Work* at this time, Robert Kernohan, had reflected on the concern that a number of Church of Scotland ministers felt at the Vatican proposal to canonize the Jesuit martyr John Ogilvie, which action they thought might impair the ecumenical movement. It was a thin reason, but the issue had to be faced and Kernohan was at liberty if not duty-bound to express the concern. He did so with a flourish, and a storm blew up. Cardinal Gray replied, pointing out that the editor had "misunderstood the real nature of ecumenism" (a broad hint that many radical ecumenists prefer to ignore even yet). And the Moderator of the General Assembly obliquely reprimanded Kernohan by saying "If they believe so, why all the fuss?" Archbishop Winning tried to calm the troubled waters, but Willie, for all his friendship with Roman Catholics and his interest in Christian unity, found the attempt unacceptable. He gallantly supported Kernohan, denying that the ecumenical cause would be retarded by the proposal, and stating,

> I do not see that shutting your eyes to these things will do the cause any good. There comes a time when you can be too cautious and you have got to open eyes and say these things—and that is what Bob Kernohan has done. In the Protestant Church there is only one line to be taken on Roman Catholic canonisation . . . and that is the hard line.[32]

He might be down, but he was certainly not out.

Willie's indomitability was demonstrated by yet more projects with which he preoccupied himself, meantime allowing his work on the Old Testament to be retarded yet further. A year previously he had promised Mulkern of Mowbrays a book on New Testament background (the subject of one of his unpublished *British Weekly* series), but this project had been transmuted into the even more interesting one of writing a sequel to *Testament of Faith* to be entitled *Why I Believe* (the title originally proposed for *Testament of Faith,* it will be recalled, was *What I Believe*). Readers of *Communicating the Gospel* will remember that Willie stressed a fivefold approach to the communication of the biblical message: literary, linguistic, historical, psychological, and devotional. In *Why I Believe* it was clearly Willie's aim to explore the psychological aspects of his own work, but, regrettably, he was unable to do so. To David Anderson, then of Ontario, he admitted that such matters were proving to be "much harder to write about" than merely setting down "what I believe."[33]

Perhaps because his thoughts were on authorial problems rather than his driving, Willie blackened a hitherto blameless driving record at this time by taking "a very blind corner" too widely at Montrose, which involved him in "an argument with a lorry." The accident led to an appearance before the magistrate, an order to sit a driving test (after forty-five years or more of driving experience), a fine of five pounds, and a mortifying endorsement. He informed Charles Miller, an Advanced Institute of Motoring enthusiast and the Church of Scotland's spokesman on road safety, of all this and was suitably repentant.[34]

Happier news was soon in the offing, however, as Willie received a new opportunity for work from Collins related to Franco Zeffirelli's film *Jesus of Nazareth,* which had recently caused a sensation, proving to Willie's way of thinking that if only the right approach was found, public interest in matters religious could be gained and heightened. It was a visual extension of his "threshold evangelism" approach. The film, produced by Vincenzo Labella, had used a galaxy of "superstars"—Laurence Olivier, Robert Powell, Cyril Cuzack, Peter Ustinov, Michael York, Christopher Plummer, Anne Bancroft, and Claudia Cardinale, to name but a few. It was presented by Sir Lew Grade, and had eaten up over twelve million pounds sterling in production costs. Collins had purchased publication rights to the script, written by Anthony Burgess and Susso Cecchi d' Amico with additional material by Zeffirelli himself, and Willie was asked to rework the material, using his own expertise to clarify and safeguard the integrity of the narrative. The text was to be enhanced by some of the best color plates ever produced for a religious book, drawn from the library of over five thousand photographs that had been taken during filming. It was a wonderful, unique opportunity, and once again, Willie could not say "No." One of the reasons for his decision to accept the task—it was scarcely a struggle, so keen was he to try new methods—was that "there are fewer and fewer people who read, and more and more who learn, by looking at pictures"; it was "an opportunity to be seized."

There was to be no attempt at sensationalism. The story was to be told in all its natural simplicity in order that it might "send viewers back to the gospels themselves . . . [which] they will read with a new intelligence and a new vividness after seeing the film": the perfect *raison d'être* for "threshold evangelism." "I did no more than change the script into narrative form," Willie modestly stated in the book's introduction. And he was given only two months to complete it! As Lady Collins has recalled, the request came in one of her many telephone calls to him, which began, "Help, Willie, please help." His answer was immediate: "Right you are, I'll get down to it at once."[35] The work appeared in full-color splendor in 1977, almost three hundred pages of superb narrative and illustration, which represented the cream of his life's work. It was published simultaneously in a Fontana paperback edition of 126 pages, and many fewer photographs.

The publication of the Collins book virtually coincided with that of another book Willie had been asked to do for the Roman Catholic publishers Darton, Longman and Todd. A more modest volume, it was a pioneering attempt to produce a life of Jesus in strip-cartoon form, a project for which Willie was subjected to a certain amount of criticism. Nevertheless, he contended that "the picture-gate is the only gate into so many people's lives." (It is not inappropriate to recall that it was in part thanks to his enthusiasm and recommendation that the very successful *Gospel According to Peanuts,* a similar project, had been published.) Kate was none too happy about this new venture, not so much because of the format (though she did not share Willie's enthusiasm for that either), but because of the additional strain the added work placed on him. The family now openly talked of his "death wish," not being able to comprehend his determination to keep working in any other way than as an intention to die in harness. Kate simply found it too much, an act of unreason. And when she saw the proofs, her despair was almost absolute. She tried every means at her disposal to get him to object to what she judged to be the denigrating likeness that the artist had produced of her husband. Almost every page includes a frame picturing Willie as narrator of the story (it was a clever piece of strategy to proceed in this manner, but was subject to misunderstanding). Nearly 120 such frames are interspersed throughout in the book, sometimes as many as four per page, picturing him in a variety of poses—at his desk, lectern, and blackboard, standing, sitting, writing, pointing, and more often than not merely as a "talking head" with an uncharacteristically downcast, almost bitter mouth and wooden posture. This was not Kate's man; but Willie would not take any action.

I myself added to the pressures under which Willie now worked. As Marketing Manager of Inter-Varsity Press, I was preparing a large sales campaign for the Tyndale New Testament Commentaries. I knew he recommended the series to students and friends, and so I asked him if he would be willing to supply a promotional blurb. By return of post came the reply: "It is a pleasure to say something." He provided us with a first-rate recommendation for the sales brochure. "If this is too short and you want more, let me know and I will adjust it," he added. No adjustment was needed. He knew too much about communication to err on either side; it was perfect. Some conservative souls sighed "treachery," others murmured "an enemy hath done this," and my boss pontificated on "an error of judgment"; we sold a lot of commentaries.

By this time he was, to use his own phrase, "boiling up for Christmas," when the whole family gathered in their home and the holiday spirit was both liberal and liquid. The winter was very severe, the coldest in several years, and was to test Kate and Willie severely. They both came down with "influenza" again in the new year, 1977, at the very time Collins decided to move their offices from Cathedral Street in the city center to Bishopbriggs. More excitement, more disruption—and less output! They moved in mid February, and it took Willie a week to settle down.[36] Bill Telford obtained his doctorate, winning an appointment to Willie's old love, Mansfield College at Oxford. "All kinds of congratulations!" wrote the old warrior, adding, "Perhaps I will manage another term there . . . and I can sit at your feet and listen to you lecturing."[37] It was a very typical and gracious tribute to his former student.

Willie's recent publications generated a number of problems for his readers, who were surprised at this or that statement, and through these months he kept up a lively and in some instances extended correspondence with some of them. Space forbids any further expression of his views here, but among the key subjects featured in this correspondence were the issue of the deity of Jesus (with a Roman Catholic teacher from near Haddington), arguments about the sonship of Christ with Fred Bailey, a strong defense of the resurrection, and some interesting questions on the nature of the human soul (with T. E. W. Townsend, a retired Congregationalist minister), some good-natured discussion of his now explicit universalism (with Frank Bersch of Virginia), and some debate concerning Paul's "Jewish qualifications" (with Anthony Jenkins of London). It was during these months that he found time for luncheons with Malcolm Mackay, over which they mused on the global significance of Jesus among other things. He enjoyed other invigorating discussions as well, although both physical and mental deterioration was now manifest.

Kate and Willie celebrated forty-three years of marriage at the beginning of July. Together they hobbled into a newly opened restaurant in Cathcart, just around the corner from their home, Willie now almost prevented from walking by a fierce ulceration of his leg, and Kate disabled by rheumatism in the ankles. The long, cold winter had given way to a long, wet spring, and they were desperate for respite, warmth, and physical comfort. They got none of this, and had to cancel their planned return to Arbroath, Willie suffering from arthritis in his leg and Kate from the same in her hips. All they could manage was a few short drives together to places such as Ayr, Troon, and Prestwick. But misadventure befell them even there, Kate taking too much sun one day, getting sunburn that developed into painful dermatitis. Willie's prayer, "for one who is old and dependent," written in 1967, is poignantly apropos to this period in their lives. It is contained in a prayer for "the evening-time of life":

> O God,
> I have come to the stage
>   when I can no longer work,
>   and when I can no longer even look after myself.
>   I am not ill;
>   I am just old . . .

You have left me here still.
Help me to accept life as it is;
and help me to live in the evening-time of life
with cheerfulness and with serenity,
and without complaint. . . .[38]

Thoroughly Placed in the Geriatric Category

"Thoroughly . . . in the geriatric category" was where Willie placed himself in a
letter to an old correspondent, Percy Strachan, in a moment of particular weakness and gloom.[39] The winter of 1976/77 had been too great a test; the old
buoyancy had gone. Just how ill he was may be seen from the facsimile below of
a letter written during the summer to Fred Bailey. Coordination was slipping
away, confusion erupted, and Willie was deeply depressed. Despite this, he
grimly held on in a posture of faith, and he could say, "I still manage to get out to
work every day."[40] A fortnight later he wrote to Mrs. Innes a letter that gives

Facsimile reproduction of a letter from Willie to Fred Bailey, dated 8 July 1977

688

ample evidence of his decline in its lamentably poor typing—and even that, he apologized, was "more legi[b]le th[a]n my hand-writing would be." It is clear that he scarcely had the strength to work the keyboard even when lucid thought did come for him. Still, he found time to warn Bill Telford, who was about to take up his Oxford Fellowship, of the many other attractions he would find in the famed university town, especially those of the summer term's theatrical shows in the college gardens—shades perhaps of Marburg in 1932, and his own summer term at Oxford in 1969! "There is nowhere in the world like Oxford," he was to say later.[41]

But the work did go on, despite mourning at the premature death of one of his former students, Finlayson Niven, taken away by a double coronary. On August 9 Willie wrote to Brydon Maben again, to encourage him in his broadcasting work and to commiserate with him at the lack of interest his fellow ministers paid his first attempt at it. "It was exactly the same in my own case," he commented. "Even when I was broadcasting quite a lot, not one of my colleagues ever said that they had heard or seen me on the air. Students did, but colleagues never." His cheerless existence received a further jolt at the end of the month when news came of the death of John Kidd, his former session clerk at Renfrew Trinity. "I never knew a man whom I admired more. . . . He was the straightest man I ever met," Willie said to Kidd's daughter Catriona. "Remember me to Joe"—one of the POW boys Willie had waited for before taking up his academic post—"and give him my sympathy," he concluded.[42]

"I am sorry I am not going to be on anywhere in 1978," he remarked in a letter to James Baldwin of Minnesota, declining yet another invitation. He no longer had the breath even for lecturing now, let alone preaching, which he said he had not done "for seven or eight years." He was still "spending me time writing, mainly a DSB on the Old Testament," but predicted that it would be a good two years before it would be completed; it is clear that his powers had all but deserted him. By now his handwriting and his signature were so miniscule that they were almost unreadable. He admitted to David Anderson that he "found the Psalms difficult to write about. . . . After you have written about one or two of them you find yourself repeating yourself over and over again."[43] Nevertheless, he also wrote "I shall I think at the same time try to keep Genesis going. I think it will be more interesting from the point of view of writing to write about Genesis." The future tense is very significant. He could not yet admit it, at least not all in one go, but he had come to the fulfillment of his own words of 1952:

> The Christian test is not, "What did you get out of life?" but, "What did you put into life?" George Bernard Shaw put it this way, "I am of the opinion that my life belongs to the whole community. And so long as I live it is my privilege to do for it whatever I can. I want to be thoroughly used up when I die. . . ."[44]

No one could argue that Willie, with his marvelously rich record of work and achievement, was not "thoroughly used up."

Once again he found himself hampered by the weather. Writing on

November 1, he said, "we have had pretty bad weather so far this winter." The cold, the wind, and the rain all conspired to make life difficult for both Kate and Willie. His varicosed ankle was particularly troublesome, but "I was never kept off work in Collins in spite of it all."[45] To Fred Bailey he confessed that after driving for half an hour, "I have just got to stop."[46] Fortunately, Collins was only a thirty-minute drive away! He arrived there exhausted. He still took his lunch at the Royal Scottish Automobile Club from time to time, keeping his friendships in good repair, regaling fellow diners with anecdotes, throwing off spicy comment about political leaders, trends, and events. But he was now a shadow of his former self and only raised himself with difficulty—and subsequent lassitude. A letter to the Braidwoods at the end of November from Kate revealed that he was now totally dependent on her for domestic things, and totally dependent on Mrs. Hamilton, his secretary at Collins, for business matters. "Bill has not now the strength to type," Kate wrote. "Ask him how he is and he'll say, 'A bit breathless.' Ask *me*, and I'll say 'practically an invalid.'"[47]

Looking forward (as ever) to Christmas, he affirmed that "Christianity ought to leave a man happy and contented." And despite everything, even despite a pervading sense of weakness, Willie remained essentially a happy and contented man. He looked forward immensely to the "usual Christmas parties when we assemble the family." He who had enjoyed so much being at the center of things at Renfrew now found a like enjoyment in the midst of a much reduced circle at nearby Cathcart, wholly in character: "I believe in the family: I believe in the home," he had asserted earlier.[48] "Home," he had testified, revealing for once the essential reserve of his personality, "is the only place in the world where it is possible to relax."[49] There were thirteen of them in all: Kate and Willie, Ronnie and Mildred and their three children, Jane and her husband Rab, and their in-laws. "It will be quite a party," he concluded, adding that the early snow made it all feel "quite like Christmas."

In early December he found himself "called to the duty of remembering my friends" (in letters typed by his secretary now, to be sure), again writing to the Braidwoods. He mentioned that the only ones of "the old gang" he saw were Archie and Margaret Maynard, with whom he and Kate continued to have dinner once a month. He wistfully recalled the fire-watching conversations of long ago; they "would have been interesting just now," he reflected. He was writing on his seventieth birthday, "which is a real milestone, because the years that are left are what they call the borrowed years."[50] He did not feel he was "past working altogether," but he recognized that he was now working much more slowly—and perhaps even better than hitherto. To Charles Miller he wrote in glowing terms of his pride in his family, especially of his grandchildren. The eldest had just returned from a six-month stint in Germany and was making plans to do a year in France. Her sister planned to follow her example. "It is great to see how Europeanised those young people became," he said.[51] Another voice from the past came through a letter from Motherwell, from his old tennis club secretary and church organist, James Fearon, now retired to Glenrothes in Fife. "There are

"*I believe in the family: I believe in the home.*" Above left: *A devoted grandfather.* Above right: *Willie and Kate with Ronnie's family and friends Archie and Margaret Maynard.* Below: *A rare family photograph with some of Kate's sisters and Mrs. Livingstone's husband (now deceased).*

not so very many young people left who knew my father well," Willie replied gratefully.[52]

And so Christmas, with its promise of a new year, came and went. But it was unlike any other Christmas for the Barclays, owing to Willie's declining powers. The Directors at Collins had been very aware of this, as was Willie himself, though he nevertheless had every intention of soldiering on. But it was clear that the Old Testament Daily Study Bible could not now reach its desired end, and the open-plan conditions of a modern office suite were not helpful in the discharge of his correspondence, so they tactfully suggested that the arrangement be brought to an end. It marked not merely the close of the year for Willie, but the closing of the last door to "usefulness" too. For the second—and final—time he had to "put the toys away." He took it manfully, owning its rightness, but with great sadness too. He knew he could not work at home, but he had nowhere else to go. His one remaining dream evaporated in the cold and wintry December air.

And so 1977 passed into 1978, perhaps bringing with it an awareness that the dismal forecast of his doctors in 1969 was even now passing into reality. Alas, there were to be no Burns celebrations for him this year. "To walk any distance," he informed Frank Bersch, was now "an impossibility," and yet "it has never kept me from getting to work and that is always something to be thankful for"[53]—gratitude finding expression, as ever, come what may. To his old schoolmate Willie Barclay of Troon, who had earlier written to say how much he enjoyed *Testament of Faith,* especially the reminder it gave him of shared undergraduate days together, Willie also mentioned his difficulties of walking and breathing, and expressed similar gratitude for being able to keep working, albeit at home.

His secretary, Mrs. Hamilton, now traveled across Glasgow to him, having at Kate's insistence reduced the four days per week that Willie had requested to three. (He would have asked for five, but medical attention was necessary on Wednesdays, and to this he acquiesced.) And so they gallantly if feebly pressed on into the bleak January. Thursday, January 19, commenced as usual, though Willie was noticeably showing signs of increased discomfort, and his attitude toward his work likewise indicated that some change had occurred within him. Of this he said not a word; Mrs. Hamilton needed none. He bade her goodby at the end of the session and then for the very first time stood at the window and waved to her as she drove off. She knew it was the end. He was not saying goodby to his secretary merely, but to his work—and to life, which was his work.

That very evening his health deteriorated sharply, and his doctor was summoned. Within an hour he was admitted to Mearnskirk Hospital, his condition being described as "serious." They knew it was going to be a hard fight, wrestling against his emphysema, his weakened heart, and the effects of his Parkinsonism as well as the results of long years of drugs prescribed to palliate its effects. On January 21 Kate found him propped up in bed holding a letter from his old school friend Walter Henderson. Willie was very moved. Henderson had written to encourage his friend, referring to the fact that the presentation copy of *The*

Vale! Task completed [Photo courtesy of *The Motherwell Times*]

New Testament Wordbook Willie had given to Jimmy Paterson had been on display at his school's recent prize-giving. Memories of Motherwell, of his parents, of Dalziel High School, of that famous tower room where he and Paterson had explored the *Iliad* together and listened to "the surge and thunder of the Odyssey," all came running back. Doubtless he recalled the happy days at Renfrew, the delights he and Kate shared in its work, in the birth and development of Ronnie and Barbara, their life during the war years when there was so much danger, so much excitement, so much opportunity, and of his strange postwar life, when he had been fêted and condemned, hailed and criticized. It had been a life of great happiness, and yet throughout it a black thread of pain and sorrow had been finely woven. And now he was no longer "useful"; only life as an invalid, mere existence, lay ahead. He no longer had anything to live for.

He died in his sleep at 1:00 A.M., Monday, 24 January 1978. Commented his son to one reporter, "The end was very peaceful"[54]—peaceful, as became a man of peace. His eight-year lease was at an end. Those who still read his *British Weekly* pieces, as gathered together by Denis Duncan, were reminded of his singleness of mind that very day, as they awoke to his words in *Through the Year with William Barclay*: "It is true that a man will never become outstandingly good at anything unless that thing is his ruling passion. There must be something of which he can say, 'For me to live is this.'" This is how William Barclay lived; it was not different when he died.

This is what he wrote in the book he delighted to own as his literary firstborn, writing of Paul:

> But in spite of everything there is no defeat. . . . He has come to the end like a fighter, weary but undefeated; like an athlete, exhausted but triumphant; like a standard-bearer, battered but with his standard still intact.[55]

It was exactly as he said in his testament of *faith*:

> When I die, I should like to slip out of the room without fuss—for what matters is not what I am leaving, but where I am going.[56]

Appendices

APPENDIX I
TRINITY CHURCH SERMON TITLES

An asterisk indicates the commencement of a new series; a dagger indicates a possible series.

1933

3/5	Coming down from the Mount
	That Which Costs Me Nothing
3/19	The Childlike Faith [Baptism]
	The Invincible Allies
3/26	A Pure Religion?
	What Is Christianity? ⎱ [Foreword
4/2	What Is the Gospel? ⎰ Movement]
	What is Happiness?
4/9	The Exultant Faith
	Giving Up the Second Best
	for the Best
4/16	The Most Dramatic Moment
	in History [Easter]
4/23	A Leader of Men
	This Only
4/30	Knit Hearts
	A Vice or a Virtue?
5/7	Strong as Iron Bands
	When You Least Expect It
5/14	Witnessing for Christ
	The Saviour's Claim
5/21	The Moment on the Mount
	The Man Who Stopped Helping
5/28	The Accusing Finger
	The Trifles That Matter
6/4	The Gateways to Heaven [Baptism]
	The Uncertain Trumpet
6/18	An Everlasting
	Question [Elders' Ordination]
8/6	The Sunless Stretch
8/13	The Honesty of Jesus [Baptism]
	Thou Shalt Not Forget

8/20	Comfort in Grey Days
	Onwards, Not Backwards
8/27	The Secret of Waiting
9/3	The Everlasting Choice
	What Is Jesus to You?
9/17	The Garden of God ⎱ [Harvest
	God's World ⎰ Festival]
9/24	Why Did You Come to Church?
	The Sin of Being a Spectator
10/1	How God Loved and Gave
10/8	The Only Way
	A Prophet's Bewildered [Sankey
	Question Night]
10/15	The Greatest Affirmation
	The Seven Churches of Asia,*
	1: Ephesus, the Last Enthusiasm
10/22	A Changed Man†
	The Seven Churches of Asia,
	2: Smyrna, Faithful unto Death
10/29	Man's Needs and God's Grace
	The Man to Whom Jesus Had
	Nothing to Say
11/5	The Man Who Crucified
	Jesus [Baptism]
11/12	The Seven Churches of Asia,
	3: Pergamum, Holding Up Christ's
	Standard in Satan's Country
11/19	Studies in the Life of Jesus,
	1: Baptism, the Decisive Stand
	The Seven Churches of Asia,
	4: Thyatira, a Good Thing
	Gone Wrong

695

2/17	He Whose Heart Is True	8/25	The Lord of Death
2/24	Men of the Bible,	9/1	The Good Shepherd
	8: The Man Whose Lips Are Clean		Our Most Popular Sins, 2
	The Ultimate Triumph	9/15	Something More
3/3	He Whose Friendship Is True		The One Just Man
3/17	The Idol of Comfort	9/22	The Garden of the Soul ⎱ [Harvest
	Men of the Bible,		The Greater Blessedness ⎰ Festival]
	9: The Man Who Was a Politician	10/6	Truth Will Out
3/31	God's Curse on Inaction		Unanswered Prayer
	Men of the Bible,	10/13	The Peak of Practice
	10: The Man of the Flaming Heart		The Story of Some Favourite Hymns,
4/7	The First Step of the Last Journey		1: "Lead Kindly Light"*
4/14	A Deliberate Challenge ⎱	10/20	Lessons from Some Famous Books,
4/21	The Victorious Christ ⎰ [Easter]		1: Walpole's Fortitudes*
	Death and the Angels	10/27	All-weather Christianity
5/9	The Inescapable God	11/3	The Everlasting Gospel
	Men of the Bible,		The Difference
	11: The Man Who Was a Traitor	11/10	Your Responsibility
5/19	The Secret of Victory		Lessons from Some Famous Books,
5/26	Difficulties, and How to Face Them		2: Masefield's The Everlasting Mercy
	Christianity and . . . , 1: Citizenship*	11/17	The Guest Without a Garment
6/2	The Hearer's Duty	12/15	Personal Religion
	Christianity and . . . , 2: Industry		The Story of Some Favourite Hymns,
6/23	Christianity and . . . , 3: War		2: "Rock of Ages"
6/30	Lost and Found	12/29	When We Come to the End
	Christianity and . . . , 4: You		Lessons from Some Famous Books,
8/18	The Comprehensive Claim of Christ		3: Jerome's The Passing
	Our Most Popular Sins, 1*		of the Third Floor Back

1936

1/5	Let Us Go on	4/12	A Compelling Question
	The Man Who Was Saved		If Not
	by His Friends	4/19	Where Punishment Begins
1/12	Proud of It		What's in a Name?
	On Seeing Things Through	5/3	Dead Religion [Baptism]
1/19	Revolution		The Conflict of Christ
	The Story of Some Favourite Hymns,	5/10	God and Our Sorrow
	3: "Jesus, Lover of My Soul"		When Jesus Was Angry*
1/26	Memorial Service to His Majesty	5/17	Only the Best Is Good Enough
	the King		The Pity of Jesus
	Lessons from Some Famous Books,	5/31	The Temple and the Kitchen
	5: Kipling [No title]		Jesus and Fear
2/2	Where to Start	6/7	Jesus and Tears
2/23	Storm and Sleep	6/21	If the Worst Comes to the Worst
3/1	What Think Ye?		Jesus and Joy
	Lessons from Some Famous Books,		The Supreme Emotion of Jesus
	6: Browning's Pippa Passes	7/5	Inalienable Rights
3/15	Our Own Doorstep		Something to Make Life Easier
	The Story of Some Favourite Hymns,	7/12	God and Man
	4: "When I Survey		A Dead-weight or an Inspiration?
	the Wondrous Cross"	9/6	The Home-coming
3/22	Sight-seeing		[Reopening of Trinity Church]
	The Spirit Which Cannot Be Beaten	9/20	The Acid Test
3/29	Crowns		On Jumping over Walls
	Shut Out	9/27	The Penalty of the Truth
4/5	If All Wishes Come True		Out of the Frying Pan, into the Fire

10/4	Enjoying Life	[Harvest		The Story of Some Favourite Hymns,	
	Nature and God	Festival]		6: "God Moves	
10/11	Is There Such a Thing as Chance			in a Mysterious Way"	
	in the World?		11/22	The Day of Reckoning	
10/18	The Text That Made History			Speed	
	The Story of Some Favourite Hymns,		11/29	Talking with God	
	5: "O Love That Wilt Not Let			Our Country and Our Saint	
	Me Go"			[St. Andrew's Day]	
10/25	Sure and Certain		12/6	The Light That Will Not Fail	
	Values	[Sankey Night]		The Sharpest Sin of All	
11/1	Freedom and Fetters		12/20	After the Cross	
11/8	For Their Sake	[Armistice-		When They Called Jesus "King"	
	The Haunting Question	day]	12/27	Laughter and Tears	
11/15	Unto the End				

1937

1/3	Whither?		6/6	When the Dawn Breaks	
	The Pattern			The Religion of All Free Men	
1/10	The Fence and the Danger Spot			[Orange Order]	
	Did the Miracles of Jesus		6/13	On Taking Things Easy	
	Really Happen?			[Communion]	
1/24	When Things Go Wrong		6/20	On Wanting What You Have Not Got	
	Robert Burns: The Glory and		6/27	The Secret of Sir James Barrie	
	the Shame		7/4	The Mistake of Leaving Things	
2/7	Royal Poverty* [The Beatitudes]			to Others	
	*The Birth of D. L. Moody:			On Being Greedy	
	Centenary Celebrations		7/11	The Deadliest of Deadly Sins	
	[Sankey Night]		9/19	The Lost Star	
2/14	The Happy Mourner			Is It Peace or Is It War?	
	D. L. Moody: A Man Sent from God			['Peace Sunday']	
2/28	The Might of the Meek†		9/26	The Way of Faith	
3/7	The Hunger Which Is Blessed			On Talking Too Much	
	The Man Who Brought Christ		10/17	Darkness and Light	
	to Scotland [St. Columba]		10/24	Order out of Chaos	
3/21	The Meriting of Mercy		10/31	Able for Anything	
3/28	The Abiding Presence	[Easter]	11/7	The Wasted Years	
	Your Life in a Sentence		11/21	God and the Clock	
4/4	The Victory of Peace			One-way Traffic	
	Darkness and Light		11/28	God's World and Man's Mistakes	
4/11	The Victory of Purity			The Meaning of Patriotism	
	Burden-bearers			[St. Andrew's Day]	
4/18	A Hard-won Blessing		12/5	On Putting the Blame on Others	
4/25	The Man Who Made Good			How We Got Our Bible	
	The Scot Who Never Found			[A lantern lecture]	
	the Faith of Any Man		12/19	The Sudden Discovery	
5/9	God Save Our King!			The Impossiblitiy of Being	
	Caesar and God	[Coronation		Self-centred [Sankey Night]	
5/16	Loyalty	of George VI]	12/26	The Gifts That Men	
	The Essence of a King			Have Never Taken	
5/23	The Unconquerable Hope				
	On Being Bored with Life*				

1938

1/2	The Impossibility of Living		1/23	Things to Forget	
	in the Present		2/6	In His Steps	
	On Making Things Too Easy		2/13	The Mark of God	
1/16	Lessons from Negro Spirituals,			Lessons from Negro Spirituals,	
	1* [No title]			2: "'Tis Me, O Lord"	

2/27	The Ideal of the Church		A Man and Himself
	The National Covenant	9/4	The Characteristics of Faith
3/6	Reliability		On Considering One Another
	John Wesley: The Apostle of England	9/25	The Hand That Guided
3/20	The End of Fear		The Little Things of Life
	The Meaning and the Method	10/2	Nature and God ⎫ [Harvest
	of Conversion [Sankey Night]		The Art of Giving ⎭ Festival]
3/27	Christianity and Results	10/9	What Is the Use of Church?
4/3	Love's Way of Giving		John Bunyan: ⎫
	The Pessimist		The Man Who Wrote ⎬ [Recall to
4/10	Defiance		a Classic in Gaol ⎭ Religion]
	Without the Vision	10/16	Where There Is No Sign
4/17	The Living Christ		What God Is Like
	Live Here and Hereafter	10/23	The Wisdom of Facing Things
5/15	"Thy Foot He'll Never Let Slide"		The Villain of the Peace
	Lights in a Dark Place	10/30	Where to Begin
5/22	Cities out of Ruins		Who Was Jesus?
	The Willing Slave	11/6	Lest We Forget [Remembrance
5/29	The Perfect Sacrifice		Their Works Do Follow Them Day]
	The Pilgrim	11/13	The Privilege of the Church Member
6/5	The Indelible Past		Lessons from Some Famous Books:
	All Things in Trust		*The Bridge of San Luis Rey*
6/19	Ambassadors for Christ	11/20	What Part Does Chance Play in Life?
6/26	The Highest Command of All	11/27	The Happy Ending
8/7	Without Respect of Persons		The Man Who Judged Jesus
	Life Must Go On	12/4	In the Hands of God
8/14	In the Presence of the Master	12/11	At the Touch of the Cross
	The Necessity of Enemies		[Communion]
8/21	On Giving Direction to Life	12/18	The Duty of the Church Member
8/28	The Welcome of Jesus		On Thinking the Worst
		12/25	The Gift of God

1939

1/1	The Needs of the Unknown Way		On Remaking Things
	A Man Who Made Good	4/30	Four Kinds of Things
1/8	The Necessity of Being Different		The Peril of the Fringe
1/15	Living the Good News	5/7	A Christian and War
	Time Enough, but Not to Spare	5/14	Salvation and Life
1/29	Beyond a Doubt		Why Do Men Suffer?
2/5	Publishing the Good News	5/21	The Necessity of Decision
	The Legacy of Jesus		Does God Answer Prayer?
2/19	In Memory of the Late A. M. Ferguson	6/4	The Simplicities of Life
	[Memorial]		The Might of Meekness
	The Causes of Desertion	6/18	The Greatest Victory
2/26	The Limits of Temptation	6/25	The Warning of Jesus
	The Causes of Fear	8/6	The Final Proof
3/5	Things Never to Be Abandoned		God and Our Weakness
	The Traitor	8/13	On Looking Back
3/19	How To Look at Things		The Creed of Courage
	[Woman's Guild]	8/20	The Audience
3/26	The Uses of the Past		The Paradox of Humility
	The Values That Cannot Be Replaced	8/27	In the Day's Work
4/2	A Courageous Gesture	9/3	On Rising Above Things
4/9	The Easter Faith ⎫		[A sermon interrupted
	After Death ⎭ [Easter]		by the declaration of war]
4/16	In Perplexity		In Suspense
	The Highest Praise	9/17	Seeking a Way
4/23	The Danger of Delay		The Things a Man Must Meet

Trouble: Past, Present and Future

2/16	Hindering God's Purposes	
	The Fascination of Work	
2/23	With Head Up	
3/2	Values Human and Divine	
	The Negative Life	
3/16	When a Master Wields the Weapon	
	On Taking Second Place	
3/30	The Havoc of Thoughtlessness	
4/6	The Desire to Give	
4/13	The Risen Lord ⎱ [Easter]	
	The Eternal Question ⎰	
4/20	The Limitation of Life	
	The Right Place	
4/27	There Is Nothing	
	That Does Not Matter	
	When We Understand	
5/4	Life on the Retreat	
5/11	Transmitting the Voice	
	The Energies of Life	
5/18	Short Notice	
	Speaking to You	
5/25	How Not to Give Your Life	
	The Wrong Way Round	
6/1	Things God Only Can Do	
	The Uses of Prayer	
6/15	Is the World Getting Better or Worse?	
6/22	A Trouble Shared	
	What a Word of Praise Can Do	
6/29	Only a Beginning	
7/13	Wondering	
7/27	An Audience of One	

Is It Wise to Be Different?

8/10	The Uses of Humility
	With Mind Made Up
8/17	Life and Glory
	The Dangerousness of Living
9/7	The Past and the Spirit ⎱ [National
	Does the Right Day of Prayer]
	Always Prevail? ⎰
9/21	The Saving Shock
	The Right and Wrong Ways of Living
9/28	The Power to Comfort
	When Silence Speaks
10/5	When There Is Nothing
	to Do but Wait
	The Sense of the Possible
10/12	Tremendous Trifles
10/19	When Things Go Wrong
	Three Rules for Life
10/26	Used to It
	The Fear of Failure
11/2	On Settling the Differences
	The Art of Admiration
11/9	A Glorious Company ⎱ [Remem-
	The Sorest Wand of All ⎰ brance Day]
11/16	The Slippery Places of Life
11/23	Things Which Hurt Our Witness*
	The Three Stages in Failure
12/7	The Witness of the Church
	The Witness of the Individual
12/21	The Necessity for God
	On Looking Back
	On Coming to the End

1942

1/11	The Virtue of Being Disturbed	
	The Spirit and the Task	
	[Dedication Service]	
1/18	Unto the End	
	Restraints	
1/25	Truths We Forget	
	The Church with Which	
	Burns Quarrelled	
2/8	On Getting to Know God Better	
	The Signs of a Snob	
2/15	Does God Care?	
	On Going On	
2/29	To Be or Not to Be	
	Does Religion Pay?	
3/15	For the Sake of Principle	
	What God Makes of Us	

[From March 22 to May 10 Willie had a leave of absence from his pulpit duties.]

5/17	When Responsibilities Are Heavy
	To Keep Us Right
5/31	When Knowledge Is Power
	When Jesus Visits a Home
6/7	The Supreme Value of Life

6/21	On Seeing Life as a Whole
6/28	Never Too Late
7/12	Against the Will
7/19	For Those in Peril on the Sea
	The Christian at Home*
7/26	Failure and Success
	The Christian in the State
8/2	The Compensation of Life
	The Christian in the Church
8/16	God and This Life
8/23	On Selling One's Soul
8/30	Like Lights in a Dark Place
9/6	Clutching at God
	You Can Never Tell
9/20	The Nameless Ones
	By Accident and by Design
9/27	On Thanking God for What We Have
	In the Presence of the Master
10/4	The Mind of God ⎱ [Harvest
	The Joy of Living ⎰ Festival]
10/11	Ready for Either
10/18	On Going a Little Further
	What Will Heaven Be Like?

701

1943

1944

2/20	When Life Seems Not Worth Living
	Second Thoughts Are Best
2/27	The Second Chance and
	the Last Chance
2/27	The Towering Rock
	Fate or Freewill?
3/19	Eye, Heart and Hand
	The Thrill of Being Trusted
3/26	The Workings of Providence
	On Dealing with the Situation
4/2	The First Challenge and
	the Final Claim of Jesus
	The Something Lacked
4/9	The Meaning of Easter } [Easter]
	The Eternal Question
4/23	Ambassadors of Christ
	[Ordination of elders]
4/30	Duty at All Costs and at All Times
	Our Faith and Our Heritage
	[Reformation Sunday]
5/7	The Blessing of Those Who
	Are up against It
	Fires and Icebergs
5/14	The Boundaries of Prayer
	The Limits of Forgiveness
5/21	Officers, NCOs and Privates
	[Empire Youth Service]
	A Child's Reason for Choosing
	a President
5/28	The Understanding Heart
6/18	The Necessity of Encouragement
	The Hardest Thing to Understand
6/25	On Making Up Our Minds
	The Wide Arms of Christianity
7/9	For Those in Peril on the Sea
	The Undying Fire

7/16	The Unmoved Heart
	Our Contribution to Life
7/23	Christ and the Christian
	The Disgrace of Inaction
7/30	The Development of the Christian
	God and the Individual
8/6	The Sources of Certainty
	Consecration and Life
9/3	Towards the [National Day
	Sunrise of Prayer]
	The Long View
9/17	So Few [Battle of Britain Sunday]
9/24	What Is Religion?
	The Lights Go Up
10/1	The Inherent Goodness
	of Human Nature
10/8	God and His Word
	Man's Work and God's Grace
10/15	The Time for Action
	Men of Destiny,* 1: Churchill
10/22	Past, Present and Future
10/29	The Glorious Privilege
	of Being Independent
11/5	The Ultimate Test
11/12	Emergency Religion
	What Should You Say to an Atheist?
11/19	The Gift of Life
	Men of Destiny, 2: Roosevelt
11/26	The Foundation Stone of the Protes-
	tant Faith
	Talking to an Agnostic
12/3	We Never Know What We Are Doing
12/17	The Titles of the Christian
	Men of Destiny, 3: Stalin
12/24	The Gift of God
12/31	On Coming to the End

1945

1/7	On the Way
	The Religion of Scotland
1/14	The Foundations of Courage
	God and Our Intentions
1/21	Man's Complaint and
	God's Response
	The First Sermon
	in the Christian Church
1/28	Men of Destiny, 4: Smuts
2/4	Chosen by God
	What the Church Ought to Be
2/11	The Greatest Age in History
	The World's Demand for Proof
2/18	On Coming to Terms
	with the Inevitable
	A Signature Test
2/25	Men of Destiny, 5: Chiang Kai Shek
3/4	Tests Which a Religion Must Satisfy
3/18	The Accent of Certainty
	[Sankey Night]

3/25	The Challenge of Christ
	Miracles Still Happen
4/1	The Easter Faith
	This Life and the Life } [Easter]
	Everlasting
4/8	The Spiritual Glow
	It's Hard to Be a Christian
4/15	Why Be Good?
4/22	The Work of the Red Cross
4/29	Glory to God
	The Power of Faith
5/6	The Power of Words
	The Three Judgements
5/13	Thanks Be to God
	The New Day
5/20	Cities from Ruins
	The Gifts Which All Can Give
5/27	Our Share in the Task
6/3	God's Direction to His People

1946

7/28	The Grace of God		10/27	The Eyes of Jesus
	What Is Your Religion to You?			The Essentials of Belief,
9/1	Struggling along the Way			6: I Believe in the Church
	The Essentials of Belief,*		11/3	Broken Barriers
	1: I Believe in God			The Essentials of Belief,
9/15	Defender of the Faith			7: The Christian View of Man
	The Essentials of Belief,		11/10	For Their Sake [Remembrance Day]
	2: I Believe in the Lord Jesus Christ			The Essentials of Belief,
9/22	The Christian Fellowship			8: The Life Everlasting
	The Essentials of Belief,		11/24	In the Midst of the Years
	3: The Assurance That My Sins			The Essentials of Belief, 9: Sin
	Are Forgiven		12/1	The Settled Life
10/6	The Essentials of Belief,			The Essentials of Belief,
	4: He Rose Again			10: The Forgiveness of Sins
10/13	The Wonder	[Harvest	12/15	The Downward Path
	of Created Things	Festival]		"Thy Foot He'll Not Let Slide"
	God and the World		12/22	The Meaning of Christmas
10/20	The Source of Power		12/29	The Lesson of Life
	The Essentials of Belief,			Farewell!
	5: The Work of the Spirit			

APPENDIX II
A STATISTICAL REVIEW OF WILLIE'S PASTORAL CHARGE

Year	Communicants	Elders	SS [1]	BC [2]	Christian Liberality [3]	MM [4]	Stipend
1933	1,074	28	284	108	£1,587	427	£450
1934	1,094	30	230	112	1,566	490	450
1935	1,095	28	257	143	1,524	490	450
1936	1,109	29	265	148	1,518	480	450
1937	1,138	30	270	130	1,836	500	450
1938	1,200	31	270	117	1,689	540	500
1939	1,224	30	230	102	1,576	540	500
1940	1,265	34	246	120	1,730	540	500
1941	1,291	32	206	135	1,726	540	500
1942	1,340	32	245	188	1,806	540	500
1943	1,380	32	270	147	1,720	550	500
1944	1,400	40	350	95[5]	1,852	655	600
1945	1,418	40	396	88[5]	?	655	600

1. Number of enrolled Sunday School members, not just attenders
2. Number of Bible Class members
3. Free-will offerings total for the year
4. Membership figure, excluding occasional attenders
5. These figures exclude those who attended the highly popular Young People's Society, members of which ranged from young teenagers to retired persons.

APPENDIX III
SCOTTISH SUNDAY SCHOOL UNION
CORRESPONDENCE COURSES

Session	Topic
1945/46	The Parables of Jesus
1946/47	The Life of Christ
1947/48	The Study of the Gospels
1948/49	The Expansion of Christianity in the Acts of the Apostles

APPENDIX IV
SCOTTISH SUNDAY SCHOOL UNION SENIOR LESSON NOTES

1948

THEME: LIFE AT ITS BEST, 1

(i) Jesus, the Pioneer of Life

1/4	Jesus' New Way of Life	Luke 4:16–21
1/11	New Life for an Outcast	Matt. 9:9–17
1/18	New Life for the Samaritan Woman	John 4:4–30, 39–42
1/25	New Life for the Self-satisfied	John 3:1–17
2/1	New Life for the Son of Thunder	Mark 3:17; Luke 9:49–56
2/8	New Life Offered and Refused	Mark 10:17–20

(ii) Followers of Jesus

2/15	Dying for the New Way: Stephen	Acts 6:8–15
2/22	Dying for the New Way: Patrick Hamilton	
2/29	Breaking the Barriers	Acts 11:1–18
3/7	Liberating the Slaves: W. Wilberforce	
3/14	Into Regions Beyond	Rom. 15:15–33
3/21	Review Lesson	
3/28	Easter	Luke 24:13–35

THEME: POWER TO LIVE ARIGHT, 1

4/4	Through Home and Friends	Deut. 6:1–9
4/11	Through Sunday School	Prov. 3:13–19
4/18	Through Public Worship	Neh. 8:1–12
4/25	Through Reading the Bible	Ps. 1; Acts 8:26–35
5/2	Through Private Prayer	Luke 6:12–13; 9:18–20, 28
5/9	Through Serving Others	Matt. 25:31–46
5/16	Whitsunday Review	Acts 2:1–11
5/23	Missionary: James Chalmers of New Guinea	

THEME: THE FOUR GOSPELS, 1: An Introduction

6/6	Mark	Mark 1:1; 14:51–52
6/13	Matthew	Matt. 2:11–23
6/20	Luke	Luke 1:1–4
6/27	John	John 20:30–31; 2:24–25

THEME: THE PARABLES OF JESUS, 1

9/5	The Seed and the Soil	Matt. 13:1–9
9/12	Mustard Seed and Leaven	Matt. 13:31–39
9/19	Treasure and the Pearl	Matt. 13:44–46
9/26	Loving Father	Luke 15:11–24

THEME: THE WORLD IN WHICH WE LIVE

10/3	In the Beginning, God	Gen. 1
10/10	God, the Bountiful Giver	Ps. 65
10/17	Man's Disobedience	Gen. 3:1–13
10/24	God's Saving Love	Luke 19:1–10
10/31	God's Controlling Power	Matt. 21:33–41

THEME: THE CHRISTIAN FELLOWSHIP, 1

11/7	What Is the Church?	1 Cor. 12:8–27
11/14	How the Churches Live	Acts 2:1–11

707

11/21	The Purpose of the Church	Acts 2:41–47
11/28	Missionary: Grenfell of Labrador	
12/5	Missionary: James Evans	
12/12	The Church and Myself	John 6:1–14
12/19	Jesus: Son of God and Son of Man	Matt. 16:13–16
12/26	Christmas Worship	

1949

THEME: LIFE AT ITS BEST, 2: JESUS AND LIFE

1/2	His Faith in God	Mark 4:35–41
1/9	"According to Your Faith"	Matt. 9:27–31
1/16	Jesus at Prayer	Luke 5:16–17; 6:12–13; 9:28–29
1/23	"Wait upon the Lord"	Ps. 63:1–8
1/30	His Compassion	Matt. 9:35–36; 14:13–21
2/6	"Inasmuch"	Matt. 25:31–46
2/13	His Courage	Luke 13:31–33; Matt. 21:12–13
2/20	"Be of Good Courage"	Matt. 10:16–22; Acts 4:13–21
2/27	His Forgiving Spirit	Mark 16:7; Luke 23:34
3/6	"Seventy Times Seven"	Matt. 18:21–35
3/13	His Friendliness	Mark 10:13–16; John 4:4–9, 27
3/20	A New Commandment	Acts 9:10–28
3/27	His Cross	Matt. 26:51–54; 27:39–44
4/3	Our Cross	Matt. 9:9; 27:1–5
4/10	Review Lesson	
4/17	Easter	Matt. 28:1–10
4/24	Missionary: Africa—a College Set on a Hill	
5/1	Missionary: Africa—through a College Gateway	

THEME: POWER TO LIVE ARIGHT, 2

5/8	James: Conquest of the Tongue	James 3
5/15	John: Conquest of the Temper	1 John 4:7–21
5/22	Peter: Conquest of Fear	1 Pet. 4:12–19
5/29	Paul: Conquest of Hatred	1 Cor. 13
6/5	Whitsunday	Acts 2:1–11
6/12	Paul, 1: Conquest of Pain	2 Cor. 12:1–11
6/19	Paul, 2: Conquest of Captivity	Phil. 1:1–14
6/26	Paul, 3: Conquest of Final Victory	2 Tim. 4:6–18

THEME: GOD THE CREATOR

7/3	Day and Night	Gen. 1:1–5, 14–18
7/10	Growing Things	Gen. 1:6–12
7/17	Living Creatures	Gen. 1:20–25
7/24	Man—"in His Own Image"	Gen. 1:26–31
7/31	Through Men—Work in the World Today	

THEME: JESUS OUR FRIEND

8/7	Friends at Bethany	Luke 10:38–42
8/14	Washing the Disciples' Feet	John 13:3–17
8/21	The Great Friend Rejected	John 18:28–40; 19:16–18
8/28	Restored to His Friends	John 20:1–18

THEME: THE WORLD IN WHICH WE LIVE

9/4	"Who Hath Created These Things?"	Isa. 40:26–31
9/11	"What Is Man?"	Ps. 8; Rom. 7:15–25
9/18	"The Lord Will Provide"	Ps. 104:10–28

9/25	"The Lord Reigneth"	Ps. 96
10/2	Jesus and the World	Matt. 6:24–34; 5:44–45

THEME: THE LIFE OF JESUS ACCORDING TO ST. LUKE, 1

10/9	Introduction: The Beloved Physician	Luke 1:1–4; Acts 1:1; Col. 4:14
10/16	The Early Years: Growth in Wisdom and Stature	Luke 2:15–16, 21–22, 23, 40–52
10/23	Beginning His Ministry: "My Beloved Son"	Luke 3:1–21
10/30	Beginning His Ministry: "Him Only Shalt Thou Serve"	Luke 4:1–13
11/6	Ministry in Galilee: "As His Custom Was"	Luke 4:14–30
11/13	Ministry in Galilee: "That They Might Find an Accusation"	Luke 5:36–39; 6:6–12
11/20	Ministry in Galilee: "Follow Me"	Luke 6:12–16; 18:18–23
11/27	Missionary: Contrasts in Kenya, 1	
12/4	Missionary: Contrasts in Kenya, 2	
12/11	Ministry in Galilee: "So Great Faith"	Luke 7:1–10
12/18	Ministry in Galilee: "Not Dead But Sleepeth"	Luke 8:41–42, 49–56
12/25	Ministry in Galilee: "Glory to God in the Highest"	Luke 2:1–20

1950

1/1	Ministry in Galilee: "Sent Forth"	Luke 9:1–6, 10; 10:1–5, 17–20
1/8	His Teaching: The Kingdom of God	Luke 13:18–21
1/15	His Teaching: Prayer	Luke 11:5–13; 18:1–8
1/22	His Teaching: "Go, and Do Thou Likewise"	Luke 10:25–37
1/29	His Teaching: Lost and Found	Luke 15:11–32
2/5	His Teaching: "Into the Highways and Hedges"	Luke 14:12–24
2/12	The Turning Point: "The Christ Is God"	Luke 9:18–20, 28–36
2/19	The Last Journey: "Steadfastly, towards Jerusalem"	Luke 9:51–62
2/26	The Last Journey: "Have Mercy upon Me"	Luke 18:31–43
3/5	The Last Journey: "Blessed Be the King That Cometh"	Luke 19:28–40, 45–48
3/12	The Last Week: "The Stone Which the Builders Rejected"	Luke 20:17
3/19	The Last Week: "When the Hour Was Come"	Luke 22:7–20, 39–46
3/26	The Last Week: "What Evil Hath He Done?"	Luke 22:66–71; 23:13–25
4/2	The Last Week: "There They Crucified Him"	Luke 23:33–47
4/9	Easter: The Lord Is Risen!	Luke 24:13–25
4/16	Missionary: Ichang, China, 1	
4/23	Missionary: Ichang, China, 2	

THEME: THE CHRISTIAN FELLOWSHIP, 2

4/30	At Ephesus	Acts 20:28–35
5/7	At Pergamum	Rev. 2:12–17
5/14	At Sardis	Rev. 3:1–6
5/21	At Rome	Rom. 15:20–24; Acts 28:11–16
5/28	Whitsunday	Luke 3:4–6

THEME: THE WORSHIP OF GOD

6/4	Praising God	Ps. 100
6/11	Speaking to God	Ps. 25:1–10
6/18	Hearing God's Word	Ps. 19:7–14
6/25	Bringing Gifts to God	Ex. 35:4–5, 20–22

THEME: FAITHFUL SERVANTS OF GOD

7/2	Abraham: Obedience	Gen. 12:1–9
7/9	Elijah, 1: Courage	1 Kings 18:1–18
7/16	Elijah, 2: Justice	1 Kings 21:1–8, 17–20
7/23	Ruth: Loyalty	Ruth 1:1–19a
7/30	Elisha: Faith	2 Kings 6:8–18

1951

THEME: THE CHURCH OF GOD

5/20	The Church's Faith	John 20:19–29
5/27	The Church's Fellowship: Forgiveness	Acts 9:26–31
6/3	The Church's Fellowship: Service	2 Tim. 1:16–18
6/10	The Church's Mission: Preaching	Acts 17:16–34
6/17	The Church's Mission: Teaching	Acts 8:26–40
6/24	The Church's Mission: Healing	Acts 16:11–18

THEME: THE LORD'S PRAYER

7/1	Our Father in Heaven	Luke 15:11–32
	Thy Kingdom Come	Mark 1:14; Matt. 13:44–46
7/15	Our Daily Bread	Matt. 6:25–34
7/22	Forgive Us Our Debts	Matt. 18:23–35
7/29	Lead Us Not into Temptation	John 22:31–34. 54–62

THEME: THE APOSTLE PAUL

8/5	A Young Man's Enthusiasm	Phil. 3:4–6; Acts 7:58–8:3
8/12	A New Master	Acts 22:3–21
8/19	A Momentous Journey	Acts 15:40; 16:15
8/26	A Purpose Fulfilled	Rom. 1:8–15; Acts 25:10–12

THEME: THE FOUR GOSPELS, 2

9/2	The Gospel before the Gospels	Luke 1:1–14
9/9	Mark	Mark 1:1; 14:51–52
9/16	Matthew	Matt. 2:11–23
9/23	Luke	Luke 1:1–4
9/30	John	John 20:30–31; 21:24–25

THEME: GOD MAKES HIMSELF KNOWN

10/7	Through Conscience	Gen. 3
10/14	Through Judgment	Gen. 6:5–22
10/21	Through Mercy	Gen. 9:1, 5–17
10/28	Through Testing	Gen. 22:1–14
11/4	Through a Cry for Justice	Ex. 2:23–3:10
11/11	Through a Great Deliverance	Ex. 14:10–31
11/18	Through a Covenant	Ex. 24:3–8
11/25	Missionary to the Jews	
12/2	Missionary to Arabs	
12/9	Through Worship	Ex. 29:42–46
12/16	Through the Promised Messiah	Deut. 18:15–18; John 1:29; Mark 1:9–11
12/23	Christmas Carol Service	Luke 2:1–20
12/30	"All Nations Shall Come"	Matt. 2:1–12

1952

THEME: WE WOULD SEE JESUS

1/6	In His Home	Luke 2:39–52
1/13	At the Carpenter's Bench	Mark 6:1–6
1/20	In the Wilderness	Matt. 4:1–11
1/27	In the Synagogue	Luke 4:14–37
2/3	With the Crowds	Mark 2:1–2; 3:7–12; Matt. 9:35–38
2/10	Among His Critics	Mark 2:18–28
2/17	In a Foreign Country	Mark 7:24–37

2/24	Missionary: India	
3/2	Missionary: Pakistan	
3/9	Among His Friends	Luke 10:38–42; Matt. 21:17
3/16	In Jerusalem	Luke 19:41–48
3/23	In Gethsemane	Matt. 26:36–56
3/30	On Trial	Matt. 26:57–68
4/6	On the Cross	Matt. 27:33–50
4/13	Easter	Matt. 28:1–10

THEME: YE SHALL BE WITNESSES

4/20	Peter before the Multitudes	Acts 2:29–41
4/27	Peter before the Council	Acts 5:17–32
5/4	Peter before the Gentiles	Acts 11:1–18
5/11	Paul at Damascus	Acts 9:1–22
5/18	Paul at Lystra	Acts 14:8–22
5/25	Paul in Prison	Acts 23:11; Phil. 1:12–14
6/1	Whitsunday	Acts 2:1–18

THEME: THE CHRISTIAN FELLOWSHIP

6/8	At Thessalonica	1 Thess. 3
6/15	At Colossae	Philem.
6/22	At Corinth	1 Cor. 13
6/29	At Philippi	Phil. 4

THEME: JESUS SHOWS WHAT GOD IS LIKE

7/6	By Feeding the Hungry	John 6:1–13
7/13	By Caring for Those in Danger	Mark 4:35–41
7/20	By Healing a Leper	Luke 5:12–15
7/27	By Giving Sight to the Blind	Luke 18:35–43
8/3	By Befriending the Despised	Luke 19:1–10

THEME: THE PARABLES OF JESUS, 2

8/10	The Seeds and the Soil	Matt. 13:1–9
8/17	The Mustard Seed and Leaven	Matt. 13:31–33
8/24	The Treasure and the Pearl	Matt. 13:44–46
8/31	The Loving Father	Luke 15:11–24

APPENDIX V
SHORT TALKS FOR CAMPERS

1. As Good as I Found It
2. Why Camp Prayers?
3. Our Appointment with God
4. A Man Short
5. How to Be Happy
6. Time Is Short
7. On Coming to the End
8. The Hard Way
9. The Magpie's Nest
10. Pullers and Sooners
11. He Did It with Odds and Ends
12. In Defence of Weakness
13. A Postage Stamp
14. On Knowing How to Do It
15. Showing Your Colours
16. More Than One Thing at a Time
17. An Ounce of Mind
18. Lights of the World
19. Four Kinds of Boats
20. Three Kinds of Motor Cars
21. The Upward Look
22. Difficulties Are Made to Be Overcome
23. Only the Sunny Hours
24. Two Kinds of Walls
25. The Hardest Worked Word

APPENDIX VI
MANCHESTER CENTRAL HALL MIDDAY SERVICES

Date		Text	Finishing Time[1]
1954:	June 15	Phil. 2:11	1:40
1955:	June 28	Matt. 13:33	1:35
1956:	July 17	Matt. 5:6	1:30
1957:	——		
1958:	June 10	Matt. 26:58	1:35
1959:	June 30	Phil. 2:4; Col. 4:15; 2 Tim. 4:10	1:35
1960:	June 14	Gen. 15:12; Ps. 18:11; John 9:5	1:32
1961:	Sept. 5[2]	Matt. 13:31	1:35
1962:	Sept. 4	John 14:6	1:30
1963:	——		
1964:	Sept. 8	Col. 1:28	1:30
1965:	Sept. 21	Matt. 4:1–11	1:33
1966:	Sept. 6	Isa. 6:8	1:27
1967:	Sept. 5[3]	Phil. 4:7	1:30
1968:	Sept. 3	Acts 14:16	1:30
1969:	Sept. 2	Matt. 20:1–16	1:25

1. All services commenced punctually at 12:45 P.M.
2. He changed from a spring to an autumn date in 1961 because he found that his absence from the University in the late spring threatened to interfere with his greater work load at that time.
3. He actually entered the date as the 8th, but that was incorrect.

APPENDIX VII
BLOOMSBURY CENTRAL BAPTIST CHURCH SERVICES
(An incomplete record)

1960:	March	"The Beatitudes"
	Aug.	Sunday sermon
1961:	Aug. 19	
	Aug. 26	
1963:	Apr. 7	"A Plea for the Forward Look" (Haggai 2:9)
	Aug. 18	
	Aug. 25	
1964:	Apr. 25	Reopening address
1967:	?	Tuesday lunchtime addresses
1968:	Dec. 31	"Student Unrest"
1969:	Aug. 31	
	Dec. 9	"The Christian Ethic in the New Testament and the Twentieth Century"
	Dec. 30	
1975:	Aug. 29	

APPENDIX VIII
NEWCASTLE YMCA MEETINGS

1957: March 28
1958: March 18
1959: Canceled for health reasons
1960: April 5
1961: March 28
1962: March 27
1963: March 26

1964: March 24
1965: March 30
1966: March 22
1967: March 21
1968: March 19
1969: March 25

Bibliography

AUTHOR'S NOTE: This list of Willie's publications is necessarily incomplete, largely because of the reluctance of British publishers to supply bibliographic information—a curious mentality that mistakes such cooperation for an invasion of confidentiality.

Abbreviations used herein:

BW	*The British Weekly*
CoS	The Church of Scotland
DBR	Daily Bible Readings
DSB	The Daily Study Bible
ExpT	*The Expository Times*
IBRA	The International Bible Reading Association
L&W	*Life and Work*
NSSU	The National Sunday School Union
RP	*The Renfrew Press*
SPQ	*The Scottish Primary Quarterly*
SSSU	The Scottish Sunday School Union
SSST	*The Scottish Sunday School Teacher*

Titles preceded by an asterisk are collections of Willie's journalistic pieces in their final form.

1923–1925

During this period as a member of the Editorial Committee at Dalziel High School, Willie made several contributions to *The Dalzielian,* anonymously. The following pieces appeared with his initials:

"Ave Atque Vale" [poem]. June 1924, 15.

"Regret" [poem]. December 1924, 15.

"From Catullus" [poem]. June 1925, 11.

"On Taking Tea" [essay]. June 1925, 11.

1933

"On the Secret of Happiness: Taking Life as We Find It." *RP,* June 2.

"The Art of Forgetting: Never Worry about Past Ills." *RP,* November 3.

1934

"Negro Spirituals: Beautiful Songs and Poems." *RP,* April 13

"The Christmas Service" [joint lesson]. *SSST,* December 23, 351–54.

"The Hope of the World" [junior lesson]. *SSST*, December 30, 355–57.

1935

"The Immortal Memory." *RP*, February 1.

"Man, Plus an Idea: Possibilities and Impossibilities." *RP*, February 12.

"A Venerable Old Lady" [obituary]. *RP*, February 15.

"An Excuse in Thanksgiving" [a report]. *RP*, March 19.

"Pacifism: The Only Way." *RP*, November 5.

1938

"Church and State in the Apologists." *ExpT*, 49:360–62.

1939

"Religion in Contemporary Fiction" [review article]. *ExpT*, 51:76–79.

"A Calm Spirit in Troubled Days." *RP*, November 10.

1940

"The Annual Address." *SSST*, May, 138–40.

"The Faith of a Christian." A series of eight articles in *SSST*: "I Believe in God," 8–9; "I Believe in Jesus Christ," 34–35; "I Believe in the Holy Spirit," 71–72; "I Believe in the Christian Hope," 98–99; "I Believe in the Holy Scriptures," 130–31; "I Believe in the Church," 164–65; "The Life of a Christian as an Individual," 199–200; "The Life of a Christian as a Member of a Community," 218–19.

1945

New Testament Studies. SSSU. Pp. 82.

"Open Letter to All Sunday School Teachers." *SSST*, September, 166–67.

New Testament Syllabus, First Year: *Religious Education for Secondary Day Schools.* Department of Education, the Scottish office.

REVIEWS

The Spiritual Nature of Sunday School Teaching, by G. Johnston Jeffrey. *SSST*, September, 168.

1946

"Fearfulness" [sermon]. *ExpT*, 57:102–3.

"Modern Autobiography" [review article]. *ExpT*, 57:301–4.

REVIEWS

The Art of Teaching, by Leslie Duncan. *SSST*, January, 3.

1947

New Testament Syllabus, Second Year: *Religious Education for Secondary Day Schools.* Department of Education, the Scottish office.

"God with Us" [sermon on John 1:14]. *ExpT*, 59:48–49.

"Poetry" [review article]. *ExpT*, 59:55–56.

"Worship and the Child." *ExpT,* 59:67–69.

"Temptation" [sermon on Psalm 121:3]. *ExpT,* 59:129–30.

1948

Daily Bible Studies: The Foundation of the Christian Faith (the Gospel according to Saint Luke). CoS Publications Committee, October–December.
  Also published by the NSSU, January–March, 1949.

"Beginning Again." A series of eight articles on the Gospel of Mark in *L&W:* January, 9; February, 25; March, 41; April, 57; May, 77; June, 93; July, 129; August, 147.

"The World's Most Beautiful Book." A series of three articles on the Gospel of Luke in *L&W:* "Introduction to Luke's Gospel," September, 172; "Characteristics of the Gospel," October, 187; "The Universal Gospel," November, 207.

"A Jesuit Poet" [review article of the work of Gerard Manley Hopkins]. *ExpT,* 59:167–68.

"Mr. Perrot, Journalist" [review article]. *ExpT,* 59:251–52.

"The Destined Unity" [sermon of Colossians 1:28]. *ExpT,* 59:333–34.

REVIEWS

What Life Has Taught Me, by J. Marchment. *ExpT,* 59:279–80.

The Theology of Dostoevsky, by L. A. Zander. *ExpT,* 60:27–28.

The Way, by E. Stanley Jones. *ExpT,* 60:38.

The Englishman's Religion, ed. Ashley Sampson. *ExpT,* 60:55–56.

Teaching the Old Testament in the Sunday School, by C. Burnet; and *The Book of Common Order. SSST,* December, 345–46.

1949

"Easter Meditation," in *Life and Work Daily Bible Studies.* CoS Publications Committee, April.
  Also published by the NSSU, April.

"Ephesians and Philippians," in *Life and Work Daily Bible Studies.* CoS Publications Committee, July.
  Also published by the NSSU, July.

"1 and 2 Corinthians," in *Life and Work Daily Bible Studies.* CoS Publications Committee, October–November.
  Also published by the NSSU, October–November.

New Testament Syllabus, Third Year: *Religious Education in Secondary Day Schools.* Department of Education, the Scottish office.

"Ascension Faith" [selections from *Life and Work Daily Bible Studies*]. *L&W,* 83.

"Modern Translations of the New Testament" [review article]. *SPQ,* February, 4.

"Patience" [sermon on Romans 5:3–4 and 1 Thessalonians 1:3]. *ExpT,* 60:106–7.

"Palm Sunday" [sermon]. *ExpT,* 60:164–65.

"Prophet and Craftsman: The Preacher's Task and Technique." *ExpT,* 61:13–14.

"The Way of Joy" [sermon on John 16:22]. *ExpT,* 61:53–54.

REVIEWS

The Gospel According to Saint Mark, by A. M. Hunter. *SSST,* April, 110.

Poetry and Prayer, by Edward Shillito. *ExpT,* 60:140.

The Cost of Discipleship, by Dietrich Bonhoeffer. *ExpT*, 60:148–49.

A Man's Job, by J. T. Inskip. *ExpT*, 60:260.

T. S. Strong, by P. R. Anson. *ExpT*, 60:300.

Bishop Grundtvig, by E. L. Allen. *ExpT*, 60:323–24.

Neville Stuart Talbot, by F. H. Brabant. *ExpT*, 60:356.

Concerning the Faith in Christ, by J. Howat. *ExpT*, 61:9.

Mr. Buchan, Writer, by A. C. Turner. *ExpT*, 61:32.

1950

Notes on Daily Bible Readings. CoS Publications Committee, January–June.

The Sword. IBRA, January–March.

Daily Readings for Children: The Last Days of Jesus. CoS Publications Committee, April–June.

God's Plan for Man. Boys' Brigade. Pp. viii + 109.

"The Company Bible Class." *The Boys' Brigade Gazette*, December, 29.

"Thoughts from the Daily Bible Readings." *L&W*, January, 13.

"Sympathy" [sermon on Hebrews 4:15]. *ExpT*, 61:310–11.

REVIEWS

Poetry and Personal Responsibility, by G. Evans. *ExpT*, 61:127–28.

The Cross in the Cup, by H. Forbes. *ExpT*, 61:192.

Epitome of the Divine Institutes, by Lactantius. Ed. and Trans. by E. H. Blakeney. *ExpT*, 61:196–97.

Booker T. Washington, by Basil Mathews. *ExpT*, 61:223–24.

Bright is the Shaken Torch, by A. A. Cowan. *ExpT*, 61:235–36.

The Brightening Cloud and Other Poems, by Frances Beleroy. *ExpT*, 61:256.

The City of God: Augustine's Philosophy, by J. H. S. Burleigh. *ExpT*, 61:297–98.

The Greatness of the Soul [and] The Teacher, by St. Augustine. Trans. Joseph M. Collevan. *ExpT*, 61:328–29.

The Ministry of the Word, by R. E. McIntyre. *ExpT*, 61:351.

The Life of Saint Anthony, by R. T. Meyer. *ExpT*, 61:315–16.

From Constantine to Julian, by H. Lietzmann. *ExpT*, 62:11.

Foredawn, by Nicodemus. *ExpT*, 61:384.

Song of Self and God, by A. T. Cadoux. *ExpT*, 62:32.

Christ in Catastrophe: An Inward Record, by Emil Fuchs. *ExpT*, 62:63.

1951

One Lord, One Faith, One Life. Boys' Brigade. Pp. xii + 144.
   Rev. ed. by Martin Strang, 1958.

Ambassador for Christ: The Life and Teaching of Paul. CoS Publications Committee. Pp. 171.
   Rev. ed. by Saint Andrew Press, 1974 (with "Questions for Discussion" by James Martin), pp. 187; U.S. ed. by Judson Press; trans. into Spanish, Norwegian.

"The Lord's Prayer" and "The Sermon on the Mount," in *Life and Work Daily Bible Studies*. CoS Publications Committee, January–February, June.

"James Grieg—an Obituary." *SSST*, January 4.
   Also published in *SPQ*, February 1952, 3.

"Prayer" [sermon]. *ExpT*, 62:213–15.

REVIEWS

Concordance of the Bible in the Moffatt Translation, by W. J. Grant. *ExpT*, 62:104–5.

Private Views of a Public Man, by E. R. Richards. *ExpT*, 62:127–28.

The Assumption of Our Lady and Catholic Theology, by R. Winch and V. Bennett. *ExpT*, 62:134–35.

Saint Augustine and the Donatist Controversy, by G. Grimshaw Willis. *ExpT*, 62:136–37.

Poems by Father Andrew, ed. H. Collett. *ExpT*, 62:159–60.

The History of the Salvation Army, vol. 2, by R. Sandall. *ExpT*, 62:192.

Saint Gregory the Great, trans. H. Davis. *ExpT*, 62:234.

The Preparation of Sermons, by A. W. Blackwood. *ExpT*, 62:255–56.

The Coming-of-Age of Christianity, ed. J. Marchant. *ExpT*, 62:263.

No Faith of My Own, by J. V. Langmead Casserley. *ExpT*, 62:288.

The Shorter Oxford Bible, ed. G. W. Briggs. *ExpT*, 62:297.

The Gospel in the Hymns, by A. E. Bailey. *ExpT*, 62:320.

Philip Doddridge: 1702-1751, by G. F. Nuttall. *ExpT*, 62:328.

The Approach to Preaching, by W. E. Sangster. *ExpT*, 62:351–52.

The Letters of Saint Athanasius, trans. C. R. B. Shapland. *ExpT*, 62:360.

A South India Diary, by Lesslie Newbigin. *ExpT*, 62:383–84.

The Fall of Jerusalem and the Christian Church, by S. G. F. Brandon. *ExpT*, 63:42.

Teaching Scripture: A Book on Method, by M. Avery. *ExpT*, 63:64.

If Any Man Minister, by E. D. Jarvis. *ExpT*, 63:95.

1952

And Jesus Said: A Handbook on the Parables of Jesus. CoS Publications Committee. Pp. 215.
   Reprinted by Saint Andrew Press, 1970, 1971 (twice), and 1972; rev. ed. by Saint Andrew Press (ed. James Martin), 1975, pp. 223; U.S. ed. by Westminster Press.

God's Men, God's Church and God's Life. Boys' Brigade. Pp. ix + 159.

Notes on Daily Bible Readings. IBRA, January–June.

"Ezra," "Nehemiah," "Joshua," "Judges," "Proverbs," and "The Christian Hope (Apocalypse)," in *Life and Work Daily Bible Readings*. CoS Publications' Committee, February, April/May, August, November.

Camp Prayers and Services, Boys' Brigade. Pp. 113.
   Rev. ed. by Boys' Brigade, 1958; reprinted 1959, 1965.

"Preacher's Commentary." A series of six articles in *BW*: "I Thank My God" [on Phil. 1], June 5; "The Mind of Christ" [on Phil. 2:1–11], June 12; "The Saved Life" [on Phil. 2:12–18], June 19; "The Citizens of Heaven" [on Phil. 3], June 26; "Entreaties and Commands" [on Phil. 4:1–7], July 3; "The Heart of Paul" [on Phil. 4:8–23], July 10.

"The Religious Education of the Child" [preface to a series on teaching religious education]. *ExpT*, 63:259.

"The Problem of Living Together" [sermon on Romans 12:8]. *ExpT*, 63:280.

REVIEWS

The Book of Unveiling, by M. R. Newbolt. *BW,* July 10, 2.

The Authorship of the Fourth Gospel, by H. P. V. Nunn. *BW,* July 24, 2.

The Lord's Supper in the New Testament, by A. G. B. Higgins. *BW*, August 21, 2.

New Testament Literature, by T. Henshaw. *BW,* October 8, 2.

Epistle to the Ephesians, by C. L. Mitton. *BW,* October 23, 2.

After the Apostles, by J. Foster. *ExpT,* 63:128.

Switch on the News, by J. G. Williams. *ExpT,* 63:159.

Florence Allshorn and the Story of St Julian's, by J. H. Oldham. *ExpT,* 62:196.

Treatises on Marriage and Remarriage, by Tertullian, trans W. P. Le Saint. *ExpT,* 63:237–38.

The Modern Rival of the Christian Faith, by G. Harkness. *ExpT,* 63:291–92.

The Communication of the Gospel, by D. H. C. Read. *ExpT,* 63:324.

The Beatitudes, by H. Martin. *ExpT,* 63:330–31.

Faith and Education, by G. A. Buttrick. *ExpT,* 63:387–88.

The Study of the Gospels, by H. A. Guy. *ExpT,* 64:10.

The Patristic Doctrine of Redemption, by H. E. W. Turner. *ExpT,* 64:73.

Freedom and Authority in Education, by G. H. Bantock. *ExpT,* 64:96.

The Revised Standard Version of the Bible. *L&W,* December, 271.

1953

DBR: The Acts of the Apostles. CoS Publications Committee, January–April. Pp. x + 213 + map.
  Reprinted (as *DSB: The Acts of the Apostles*) by Saint Andrew Press, 1955, 1957, 1958, 1960, 1961, 1962, 1964, 1966, 1972, 1973; rev. ed. by Saint Andrew Press (ed. James Martin), 1975; U.S. ed. by Westminster Press; Braille ed., 1975; trans. into Chinese, German, Japanese, Korean, Spanish, Norwegian.

The King and the Kingdom. Boys' Brigade. Pp. x + 210.
  Reprinted 1960; rev. ed. by Saint Andrew Press (ed. James Martin), 1969, pp. 211; U.S. ed. by Westminster Press; trans. into German.

DBR: The Gospel of Luke. CoS Publications Committee, September 1953–January 1954. Pp. xvi + 314.
  Reprinted (as *DSB: The Gospel of Luke*) by Saint Andrew Press, 1956 (twice), 1957, 1958 (twice), 1960, 1961, 1962, 1964, 1965, 1967, 1971; rev. ed. by Saint Andrew Press (ed. James Martin), 1975; U.S. ed. by Westminster Press; trans. into Chinese, German, Japanese, Korean, Spanish.

"Preacher's Commentary: Studies in the Miracles." A series of seventeen articles appearing weekly in *BW* from March 19 to July 16. No individual titles. (Being still firmly anchored to the biblical text, Willie simply used a portion of the text as heading.) The passages studied are, in order of appearance, John 2:1–11; Luke 5:1–11; Mark 7:31–37; Mark 5:1–20; John 6:1–14; John 9:1–38; Mark 4:37–41; Mark 2:1–12; Matthew 17:14–21; Luke 18:35–43; Luke 7:11–15; Luke 4:38–39; John 5:1–9; Luke 8:43–48; Luke 17:11–19; Matthew 17:24–27; Mark 4:22–23, 35–43.

"Preacher's Concordance: First Series." A series of articles appearing weekly in *BW* from July 23 to December 31. The following words, addressed in the articles, are, in order of appearance, *kurios; pistis; metanoia; hamartia, parabasis, papaptomia, anousia, opheileia; ptochos; dikaioun; hagios; eleemon; epieikes; praus; arrabon; leitourgia; koinonia, koinonein, koinonos; teleios; epistates; charis; mathetes; katartizein; eritheia; kerussein; apostolos; archegos.*

"Then Opening Their Treasures, They Offered Him Gifts." *BW,* December 3, 3.

REVIEWS

The New Testament in Plain English, trans. Charles Kingsley Williams. *L&W*, February, 44.

The Formation of the New Testament, by H. F. D. Sparks, and *According to the Scriptures*, by C. H. Dodd. *BW*, March 19.

The Theology of the New Testament, vol. 1, by R. Bultmann. *BW*, September 17.

How to Know Your Bible, by A. V. Murray. *ExpT*, 64:127–28.

Design for Life, by A. M. Hunter. *ExpT*, 64:201.

"Aids to Teachers." Reviews of *The Education of Souls*, by J. R. Lumb; *What the Church Teaches*, by A. W. F. Blunt; *What is Man?* (N.A.S.U. publications); *Jesus and His Teaching*, by N. J. Bull; and *Concise Bible Guides*, by E. H. Hayes. *ExpT*, 64:224.

A Faith to Proclaim, by J. S. Stewart. *ExpT*, 64:256.

The Call of All Nations, by St. Prosper of Aquitane. Trans. P. de Letter. *ExpT*, 64:262–63.

Mere Christianity, by C. S. Lewis. *ExpT*, 64:320.

1954

DBR: Galatians, 1 & 2 Thessalonians, 1 & 2 Corinthians. CoS Publications Committee, May–August. Pp. xviii + 403.

This volume proved unwieldy in this form, and so was reissued as three separate volumes—*DBR: Galatians, DBR: 1 & 2 Thessalonians*, and *DBR: 1 & 2 Corinthians*—all in 1954. The three-volume format also proved unsatisfactory, however, and so the commentary of Galatians was reissued in a volume with Ephesians in 1958 (q.v.) and the commentary on 1 & 2 Thessalonians was reissued in a volume with Philippians and Colossians in 1960 (q.v.); *DBR: 1 & 2 Corinthians* remained a separate volume.

DBR: The Gospel of Mark. CoS Publications Committee, September–December. Pp. xxi + 390.

Reprinted (as *DSB: The Gospel of Mark*) by Saint Andrew Press, 1956, 1957, 1958, 1960, 1961, 1962, 1964, 1965, 1969; rev. ed. by Saint Andrew Press (ed. James Martin), 1975; U.S. ed. by Westminster Press; trans. into German, Japanese, Korean, Spanish, Bahasa (Indonesian), Chinese.

God's Law, God's Servants, and God's Men. Boys' Brigade. Pp. viii + 169.

"Preacher's Concordance: First Series." A Continuation of the *BW* series begun in 1953, the group of fifty articles appearing weekly from January 7 to December 30. The words treated in the articles include *kopos, kopian; hupomone; exaleiphein; makrothumia; parousia; diatheke; charisma; mesites; pleonexia; soteria, sozein; euaggelion; lutron, lutroun, apolutrosis; logos; aselgeia; hupokrisis, hupokrites; autarkes, autarkeia; eilikrines, elikreneia; katharos; apoblepein, aphoran; atenizein; elpis, elpizein; eleutheros, eleutheria, eleutheroun; phobos; dikaiosune; harmartia, hamartanein; prosagein, prosagoge; apechein; poroun, porosis; skandalon, skandalizein.*

"Towards Easter." A series of four articles in *BW*: "Premonitions," March 6; "The Crimes of Christ," April 1; "There They Crucified Him," April 8; "The Risen Lord," April 15.

"Christ, the Hope of the World: A Preparation for Evanston." *BW*, August 5, 8.

"A Draft Catechism for Use in Sunday Schools." A series of articles in *SSST*. Appearing in 1954 were "Questions 1–5: Teaching about Man," October, 269–71; "Questions 6–9: Teaching about God," November, 309; "Questions 10–11: Teaching about Sin and the Holy Spirit," December, 342.

REVIEWS

"Explaining the New Testament." Review of *The Vision and Mission of Jesus*, by A. H. Curtiss; *The New Testament: An Historical and Analytical Survey*, by M. Tenney; *2 Corinthians*, by R. P. C. Hanson; and *A New Testament Commentary*, by R. A. Knox. *BW*, October 7.

"A Jew or a Jew." Review of *The Parting of the Ways: Judaism and the Rise of Christianity*, by R. Cohen. *BW*, October 21.

"Saint Paul for Today." Review of *Interpreting Paul's Gospel*, by A. M. Hunter. *BW*, November 4.

"Helps to Understanding." Reviews of *Aspects of Progressive Jewish Thought*, by L. Baeck; *An Approach to the New Testament*, by G. P. Lewis; and *The Christology of the Later Fathers*, by E. R. Hardy. *BW*, November 11.

"The Age of Full-Scale Commentaries Has Returned." Reviews of *The Pastoral Epistles*, by E. K. Simpson; *The Acts of the Apostles*, by F. F. Bruce; *Notes on the Hebrew Text of 1 Kings 17-19, 21-22*, by N. H. Snaith; and *He Walked in the Light*, by Lord Gorrell. *BW*, November 25.

"Helps (and Gifts) for Student and Preacher." Reviews of *The Parables of Jesus*, by J. Jeremias; *1 Corinthians*, by F. W. Grosheide; *Life in Christ*, by T. Preiss; *The Mission and Achievement of Jesus*, by R. H. Fuller; *Studies in the Book of Lamentations*, by N. K. Gottwald; and *Appointment with God*, by J. B. Phillips. *BW*, December 2.

The Lord's Prayer and the Beatitudes, by Saint Gregory of Nyssa. Trans. H. C. Graef. *ExpT*, 66:40-44.

Back to the Bible, by H. C. G. Herklots. *ExpT*, 66:64.

The Eyelids of the Dawn, by J. C. Winslow. *ExpT*, 66:95-96.

1955

DBR: *The Gospel of John*, vol. 1: *Chapters 1-7*. CoS Publications Committee. Pp. xxxix + 267 (a leaflet providing a system of readings was tipped in).
Reprinted (as DSB: *The Gospel of John*, vol. 1) by Saint Andrew Press, 1956, 1965, 1969, 1972; rev. ed. by Saint Andrew Press (ed. James Martin), 1975; U.S. ed. by Westminster Press; trans. in Chinese, German, Japanese, Korean, Bahasa (Indonesian), Norwegian.

DBR: *The Gospel of John*, vol. 2: *Chapters 8-21*. CoS Publications Committee. Pp. 338.
Reprinted (as DSB: *The Gospel of John*, vol. 2) by Saint Andrew Press, 1956, 1964, 1972; rev. ed. by Saint Andrew Press (ed. James Martin), 1975; U.S. ed. by Westminster Press; trans. into Chinese, German, Japanese, Korean, Spanish, Bahasa (Indonesian), Norwegian.

DBR: *The Letter to the Romans*. CoS Publications Committee. Pp. xxxi + 244.
Reprinted (as DSB: *The Letter to the Romans*) by Saint Andrew Press, 1957, 1966, 1968, 1969, 1971, 1972; rev. ed. by Saint Andrew Press (ed. James Martin), 1975; U.S. ed. by Westminster Press; trans. into Chinese, German, Hindu, Japanese, Korean, Spanish, Bahasa (Indonesian), Norwegian.

DBR: *The Epistle to the Hebrews*. CoS Publications Committee. Pp. xxi + 231.
Reprinted (as DSB: *The Epistle to the Hebrews*) by Saint Andrew Press, 1957, 1958, 1959, 1962, 1963, 1966, 1971; rev. ed. by Saint Andrew Press (ed. James Martin), 1975; U.S. ed. by Westminster Press; trans. into Chinese, German, Japanese, Korean, Spanish.

And He Had Compassion on Them: A Handbook on the Miracles of the Bible. CoS Youth Committee. Pp. 292.
Reprinted by Saint Andrew Press, 1956; rev. ed. (as *And He Had Compassion*) by Saint Andrew Press (ed. James Martin), 1975, pp. 272; reprinted in a special Boys' Brigade ed.; U.S. ed. by Judson Press.

A New Testament Wordbook. SCM Press. Pp. 128.
Largely an outgrowth of the BW word studies of 1953-54, this volume treats the following words: *aggareuein; apechein; apoblepein, aphoran, atenizein; arrabōn; aselgeia; charisma; diathēkē; eilikrinēs; ekklēsia; epieikēs; eritheia; euaggelion; exaleiphein; hamartia, hamartanein; hupogrammos; hupokrisis, hupokritēs; hupomonē; kalein, klētos, klēsis; katartizein; katharos; koinōnia, koinōnein; koinōnos; leitourgia; lutron, lutroun, apolutrōsis; makrothumia; mesitēs; paidagōgos; parousia; phobos; pleonexia; pōroun, pōrōsis; praus, praotēs; prosagein, prosagōgē; proslambanesthai; ptōchos; skandalon, skandalizein; sōtēria, sōzein; xenos, parapidēmos, paroikos.*
Reprinted by SCM Press, 1956 (twice), 1959; reissued with additional material as *New Testament Words* in 1964 (q.v.).

"The Christian Way," nos. 1-6. A series of six pamphlets on the Christian life; reprinted in *Turning to God* in 1978 (q.v.).

"A Draft Catechism for Use in Sunday Schools." A continuation of the series begun in *SSST* in 1954. Appearing in 1955 were "Questions 12–16: Teaching about Sin and Salvation, Part 1," January, 5–7; "Questions 17–19: Teaching about Sin and Salvation, Part 2," February, 48–49; "Question 20: Teaching about the Church, Part 1," February, 49; "Questions 21–22: Teaching about the Church, Part 2," March, 81–82; "Questions 23–26: Teaching about the Means of Grace, Part 1," October, 272–74; "Questions 27–30: Teaching about the Means of Grace, Part 2," November, 315–16; "Questions 31–32: Teaching about the Means of Grace, Part 3," December, 345.

"The William Barclay Page for Preachers and Teachers." A unique example of religious journalism that appeared in *BW* from 6 January 1955 to September 1961. At the outset the page included the following columns:

1. "Obiter Visa." A miscellany of essays on topical events, books, and autobiographical anecdotes presented in Table Talk fashion, which ran until January 1972.

2. "Word Book." A series of expositions of Greek words, including *kalein, klētos, klēsis; hupogrammos; paidagōgos; parakoē, parabasis; aggareuō; bebēlos, bebēloun; xenos, parepidemos; paroikos; agapē, agapan; paraklētos; merimna, merimnan; akolouthein; splagchnizesthai; sophia, phronesis, sunesis; epitagē; paraggelia, paraggellein; entugchanein, enteuxis; kataggellein; semnos, semnotēs*.

3. "Letters to the Seven Churches." A series of fourteen pieces on Revelation 2–3 that appeared from January 6 to April 7.

4. "Life in Palestine in the Time of Jesus." A series of forty-eight articles on the background of the gospel story that appeared from 14 April 1955 to 8 March 1956. The 1955 pieces addressed the following topics: Home, Marriage, Birth and Education of Children; Synagogue Worship; The Law of the Scribes, the Pharisees, and the Sadducees; The Sanhedrin; The Temple and Its Worship; The Priesthood; Jewish Feasts of Passover, Pentecost, Tabernacles, Dedication, Purim, and the Day of Atonement; The Family Circle; The Land of Palestine; and Galilee.

5. "Prayers for People." A series of prayers that appeared throughout 1955.

"Something for Everyone" [review article]. *BW*, February 10.

"Variety of Teaching Aids for Sunday School Teachers" [review article]. *ExpT*, 66:149–50.

"Gleanings from the Daily Bible Readings" [selected by Margaret Bain]. *SSST*, August, 231.

"The Truth and Its Communication" [review article]. *BW*, August 18.

"Ammunition for the Preacher" [review article]. *BW*, October 13.

"Contrast in Saints" [review article]. *BW*, November 10.

"There It Is: Use It" [review article]. *BW*, December 1.

REVIEWS

The Pure in Heart, by W. E. Sangster. *ExpT*, 66:105.

The Rediscovery of the Bible, by W. Neill. *ExpT*, 66:149–50.

The God in You, by K. Eby. *ExpT*, 66:159–60.

Social Life of the Early Christians, by J. G. Davies. *ExpT*, 66:168.

Smoke on the Mountain, by J. Davidson. *ExpT*, 66:191–92.

Saint Anselm and His Critics, by J. McIntyre. *ExpT*, 66:201.

Appointment with God, by J. B. Phillips. *ExpT*, 66:201–2.

Selections from the Psalms, by Father Andrew. *ExpT*, 66:232–33.

Evangelical Non-conformists and Higher Criticism in the Nineteenth Century, by W. D. Glover. *ExpT*, 66:256.

The Authentic New Testament, ed. and trans. H. J. Schonfield. *ExpT*, 66:264–65.

William Roby, by W. B. Robinson. *ExpT*, 66:266.

Mr Pepys and Non-conformity, by A. G. Matthews. *ExpT*, 66:288.

God in His World, by C. E. Duthie. *ExpT,* 66:320.

Prayers and Exhortations, by Origen; and *A Commentary on the Apostles' Creed,* by J. N. D. Kelly. *ExpT,* 66:332.

The Old Testament in the Secondary School, by H. F. Mathews. *ExpT,* 66:364–65.

Belief and Unbelief since 1850, by H. G. Wood. *ExpT,* 66:384.

The Acts of the Pagan Martyrs, ed. H. A. Musurillo. *BW,* January 6.

Life in Christ, by G. B. Verity. *BW,* March 10.

"For Saints, Sinners and Scholars." Reviews of *Isaiah,* by E. J. Young; *Brunner's Concept of Revelation,* by H. Jewett; and *The Great Prayer: Concerning the Canon of the Mass,* by H. W. Ross. *BW,* March 17.

"Two Notable New Testament Books." Reviews of *The Epistles of James and John,* by Alexander Ross; and *The Epistle of Paul to the Churches of Galatia,* by H. N. Ridderbos. *BW,* March 24.

"On Commentaries." Reviews of *Selections from John Wesley's Notes on the New Testament,* ed. John Lawson; and *The Pocket Commentary on the Bible. BW,* April 28.

"On Commentaries." Review of *Esther, Song of Solomon,* by G. A. F. Knight. *BW,* May 5.

Early Christianity: The Purpose of Acts, and Other Papers, by B. S. Easton; ed. F. C. Grant. *BW,* May 5.

"On Commentaries." Review of *The Annotated Bible: Ezekiel. BW,* May 12.

The Primacy of Preaching, by A. Cowan. *BW,* June 9.

The Teachers' Commentary, ed. Hugh Martin. *BW,* June 23.

The Eucharistic Words of Jesus, by J. Jeremias. *BW,* September 29.

The Cross in the Old Testament, by H. Wheeler Robinson. *BW,* October 20.

There also appeared a number of reviews in issues of *BW* in a series of articles under the heading "Barclay on Books" that appeared on March 31; April 7, 14, and 21; May 19 and 26; June 2, 9, 23, and 30; July 7, 14, 21, and 28; August 4 and 25; and September 1. On December 8 a similar column appeared under the heading "William Barclay on Books."

1956

DBR: The Gospel of Matthew, vol. 1: *Chapters 1–7.* CoS Publications Committee.
Reissued in a different form by Saint Andrew Press in 1958 (q.v.).

DBR: The Epistle to the Ephesians. CoS Publications Committee. Pp. xxiii + 136.
Reissued in a volume with commentary on Philemon (as *DSB: Timothy, Titus and Philemon*) by Saint Andrew Press, 1960 (q.v.).

"A Draft Catechism for Use in Sunday School." A continuation of the 1954–55 *SSST* series. Appearing in 1956 were "Questions 33–37: Teaching about the Means of Grace, Part 4," January, 4–6; "Questions 38–39: Teaching about the Means of Grace, Part 5," February, 43–44; "Questions 61–62: Teaching about the Kingdom of God," February, 44–45; "Questions 63–66: Teaching about the Future, Part 1," March, 73–75; "Questions 67–68: Teaching about the Future, Part 2," April, 107–8.

"God and This World" [sermon]. *ExpT,* 68:86–88.

"Quiet Time for Busy Men." *SCIO News,* October.

"The William Barclay Page for Preachers and Teachers." Appearing in *BW* throughout the year, the page included the following columns:
  1. "Obiter Visa."
  2. "Word Book." The words expounded in 1956 include *eusebeia; epaggelia, epaggellesthai; alazōn, alazoneia; huperēphania, huperēphanos; hubris, hubrizein, hubristēs; aiōnios; penthein; kalos; katallassein; mataios; poikilos; energeia, energein, energēma, energēs.*

3. "Life in Palestine in the Time of Jesus." A conclusion of the series begun in 1955; topics addressed in 1956 include the Plain of Esdraelon, Samaria, and Judaea; and How the Romans Came to Palestine.

4. "The Mind of Saint Paul." A series of thirty-seven pieces running from March 15 to November 22.

5. "The Master's Men." The first five installments of a twenty-five-part series that began on November 29 and ran well into 1957.

6. "Prayers for People." Nineteen additional columns continuing the series begun in 1955, running through September 6.

7. "Prayers for the Pulpit." A new series of twenty-one installments providing prayers specifically for church use, beginning September 13 and continuing in 1957.

REVIEWS

Many Things in Parables, by R. S. Wallace. BW, January 5.

"The Preacher as Teacher." Reviews of *What is Spiritual Healing?* by Douglas Webster; *The Church and Spiritual Healing*, by Harry Hutchison; and *Epistle to the Philippians and Colossians*, by W. E. Vine. BW, April 19.

The Formation of the Pauline Corpus of Letters, by C. L. Mitton. BW, April 19.

"The Preacher as Teacher." Review of *The Stylistic Criteria and Analysis of the Pentateuch*, by W. J. Martin. BW, April 26.

From One Language to Another: The Principles and Problems of Biblical Translation, by W. Schwarz. ExpT, 68:63–64.

God Comes Four Times, by A. C. Craig. ExpT, 68:75.

Father Potter of Peckham, by G. Potter. ExpT, 68:96.

Strength to Live with God, by Nels Ferré. ExpT, 68:255–56.

A Greek-English Lexicon of the New Testament and Other Early Christian Literature, trans. and adaptation of Walter Bauer's *Griechisch-Deutsches Wörterbuch zu den Schriften des Neuen Testaments und der übrigen urchristlichen Literatur*, 4th rev. ed., by W. F. Arndt and F. W. Gingrich. ExpT, 68:262–63.

The Modern Pilgrim, by William Purcell. ExpT, 68:287–88.

The Box and the Puppets, by H. Micklem. ExpT, 68:319–20.

Poetry and God: Mastery and Mercy, by P. M. Martin. ExpT, 68:351–52.

A Paraphrase of Saint Mark and *In My Father's House*, by R. Tatlock; and *Living with God*, by E. W. Trueman Dicken. ExpT, 68:364.

The Small Woman, by A. Burgess. ExpT, 68:383–84.

Conversation with God, by H. A. Hamilton. ExpT, 69:31–32.

The Living of These Days, by H. E. Fosdick. ExpT, 69:63–64.

The Gospels, by F. C. Grant. ExpT, 69:74–75.

Inherit the Promises, by P. Parker. ExpT, 69:96.

1957

DBR: *The Gospel of Matthew*, vol. 2: *Chapters 8-13*. CoS Publications Committee. Pp. 218.
Reissued in a different form by Saint Andrew Press in 1958 (q.v.).

DBR: *The Gospel of Matthew*, vol. 3: *Chapters 14-28*. CoS Publications Committee. Pp. 315.
Reissued in a different form by Saint Andrew Press in 1958 (q.v.).

Letter to the Seven Churches. SCM Press. Pp. 128.
Reprinted by SCM Press, 1958; rev. ed. by SCM Press, 1969.

"The William Barclay Page for Preachers and Teachers." Appearing in *BW* throughout the year, the page included the following four columns:

1. "Obiter Visa."

2. "The Master's Men." The remaining twenty installments of the series begun in 1956, running through May 16.

3. "The Mind of the Master." A series of thirty articles on the mind of Jesus that began on May 23 and ran to the end of 1957.

4. "Prayers for the Pulpit." An additional fifty-two installments of the series begun in 1956.

"This for Remembrance." *ExpT*, 69:26.

"The Personal Relationships of the Christian" [parts 1–2 of 4]. *The Preacher's Quarterly*, September, 196–201; December, 295–300, 307.

"Books: Cheap Wealth" [review article]. *BW*, October 10.

"Books: Interpreters of the Scriptures" [review article]. *BW*, October 17.

"For the Students of the Bible" [review article]. *BW*, October 24.

REVIEWS

A Tale of Old Raasay, by A. A. Macdiarmid. *L&W*, October, 210.

Jesus and His People, by P. S. Minear; and *Did Jesus Rise from the Dead?* by J. Martin. *ExpT*, 69:107.

Where the Saints Have Trod, by D. W. Lambert. *ExpT*, 69:127–28.

Premanand: The Autobiography of the Rev. Premanand Aneth Nath Sen. *ExpT*, 69:160.

A Teacher's Commentary on the Gospel of Saint Matthew, by R. Glover. *ExpT*, 69:171.

Reading and Preaching with Understanding, by F. C. Grant. *ExpT*, 69:192.

The Riches of His Grace, by R. Menzies. *ExpT*, 69:202.

Missing Diary, by R. Siefried. *ExpT*, 69:224.

"Understanding the Bible." Reviews of *Amos, Hosea and Micaiah*, by N. H. Snaith; *The Epistles of Paul to the Thessalonians*, by Leon Morris; *An Analysis of the Gospel of Mark*, by Harold St. John; and *A Paraphrase of Ephesians*, by S. C. C. Carpenter. *BW*, March 21.

"Sound Assistance." Reviews of *The Epistle of James*, by E. C. Blackman; and *St Paul's Epistle to the Thessalonians*, by W. Neil. *BW*, October 31.

"Gathering up the Fragments." Reviews of *Beyond the Gospels*, by Robert Dunkerley; and *The Epistle to the Romans*, by C. K. Barrett. *BW*, November 7.

"For the New Testament Student." Reviews of *A Commentary on the Acts of the Apostles*, by C. S. C. Williams; *A Teacher's Commentary on the Gospel of Mark*, by Richard Glover; and *Studies in the Fourth Gospel*, by F. L. Cross. *BW*, November 21.

1958

*The Mind of Saint Paul. Collins. Pp. 256.

A collection of articles of the same title run in 1956 issues of *BW*, plus additional chapters on sin and the church in the thinking of Paul.

Reissued in a paperback edition by Fontana in 1965, pp. 192; reprinted by Fontana, 1969, 1970, 1971, 1972.

More New Testament Words. SCM Press.

Reissued with additional material as *New Testament Words* in 1964 (q.v.). This volume treats the following words: *agapē, agapan; aiōnios; akolouthein; alazōn, alazoneia; elpis, elpizein; energeia, energein, energēma, energēs; enteugchanein, enteuxis; epaggelia, epaggellesthai; epitagē; eusebeia; hubris, hubrizein, hubristēs; huperēphania, huperēphanos; kalos; kataggellein; katallassein; logos; merimna, merimnan; paraggelia, paraggellein; parakletos; penthein; poikilos; semnos, semnotēs; sophia, phronēsis, sunesis; splagchnizesthai*.

DBR: The Epistles of James and Peter. CoS Publications Committee. Pp. xvii + 415.

Reprinted (as *DSB: The Letters of James and Peter*) by Saint Andrew Press, 1960, 1965, 1968, 1972; rev. ed. by Saint Andrew Press (ed. James Martin); trans. into Chinese, German, Japanese, Korean, Spanish, Bahasa (Indonesian).

DBR: The Epistles of John and Jude. CoS Publications Committee. Pp. xiii + 245.

Reprinted (as *DSB: The Letters of John and Jude*) by Saint Andrew Press, 1960, 1965, 1970; rev. ed. by Saint Andrew Press (ed. James Martin), 1976; U.S. ed. by Westminster Press; trans. into Chinese, German, Japanese, Korean, Spanish, Bahasa (Indonesian).

DSB: The Gospel of Matthew, vol. 1: *Chapters 1–10.* Saint Andrew Press. Pp. xii + 417.

Reprinted by Saint Andrew Press, 1961, 1965, 1969; rev. ed. by Saint Andrew Press (ed. James Martin), 1975; U.S. ed. by Westminster Press; trans. into German, Japanese, Korean, Spanish.

"The William Barclay Page for Preachers and Teachers." Appearing in *BW* throughout the year, the page included the following columns:

1. "Obiter Visa." Thirty-five installments throughout the year.

2. "The Mind of the Master." Thirty additional articles in the series begun in 1957.

3. "New Testament Interpretations of Jesus." A new series on the titles given to Jesus by New Testament witnesses, beginning on October 30 and running into 1959.

4. "Prayers for the Pulpit." A continuation of the series begun in previous years, running throughout 1958.

"For One Alone." *ExpT,* 69:118.

"Paul's Certainties: Our Security in God." *ExpT,* 69:324.

"Aid to New Testament Study" [review article]. *BW,* January 2.

"Moments with the Saints" [review article]. *BW,* January 9.

"Existentialism." *BW,* February 4.

"The Personal Relationships of the Christian" [parts 3–4 of 4]. *The Preacher's Quarterly,* March, 10–15; June, 108–13, 123.

"A Commentary for Laymen" [review article]. *BW,* March 6.

"New Testament Commentaries" [review article]. *BW,* October 23.

"The Blessed Life: Studies in the Beatitudes" [part 1 of 7]. *The Preacher's Quarterly,* December, 291–96.

REVIEWS

"Christology." Review of *The Person of Christ in New Testament Teaching,* by Vincent Taylor. *BW,* March 6.

The Way of the Cross, by W. Manson. *BW,* October 16.

Archibald of the Arctic, by A. L. Fleming. *ExpT,* 70:128.

Five Minutes to Twelve, by W. B. J. Martin. *ExpT,* 70:159–60.

The Gospel from the Mount, by J. W. Bowman and R. W. Tapp. *ExpT,* 70:172.

Onward Christian Soldier, by W. E. Purcell. *ExpT,* 70:191–92.

The Life of Edward Woods, by O. Tomkins. *ExpT,* 70:224.

An Architect Preaches, by H. H. Kent. *ExpT,* 70:234–35.

Through Gates of Splendour, by E. Elliott. *ExpT,* 70:255–56.

With Paul in Greece, by R. S. Kinsey. *ExpT,* 70:266–67.

Man's Estimate of Man, by E. H. Robertson. *ExpT,* 70:287–88.

Preaching the Cross, by J. C. Fenton. *ExpT,* 70:297.

727

Beyond the Gospels, by R. Dunkerley. *ExpT*, 70:318–19.

Power in Prayer, by W. E. Sangster. *ExpT*, 70:352.

The Book of Revelation, by T. Kepler. *ExpT*, 70:364–65.

The Late Herods, by S. Perowne. *ExpT*, 70:383–84.

1959

DBR: Philippians, Colossians and Philemon. CoS Publications Committee. Pp. xi + 228.
Reissued in a different form by Saint Andrew Press in 1960 (q.v.).

DBR: The Revelation of John, vol. 1: *Chapters 1–5.* CoS Publications Committee. Pp. xxxix + 207.
Reprinted (as *DSB: The Revelation of John*, vol. 1: *Chapters 1–5*) by Saint Andrew Press, 1959; reissued in a different form by Saint Andrew Press in 1971 (q.v.).

DBR: The Revelation of John, vol. 2: *Chapters 6–13.* CoS Publications Committee. Pp. 133.
Reissued in a different form by Saint Andrew Press in 1959 (see below).

DBR: The Revelation of John, vol. 3: *Chapters 14–22.* CoS Publications Committee. Pp. 164.
Reissued in a different form by Saint Andrew Press in 1959 (see below).

DSB: The Revelation of John, vol. 2: *Chapters 6–22.* Saint Andrew Press. Pp. 297.
Reissued in a different form by Saint Andrew Press in 1971 (q.v.).

Educational Ideas in the Ancient World: The Kerr Lectures for 1957. Collins. Pp. 288.
A survey of educational aims and methods among the Jews, Spartans, Athenians, and Romans, with additional chapters addressing the Christian attitude toward pagan culture and the child in the early church.
U.S. ed. (as *Train up a Child*) by Westminster Press, 1959.

The Plain Man's Book of Prayers. Collins. Pp. 128.
This, Willie's all-time best-selling single title, comprises a preparatory chapter ("Ourselves and Prayer"), three sections of prayers ("Prayers for Thirty Days," "Prayers for Four Sundays," and "Prayers for Festival Days"), an offering of "Special Prayers for the Home," and a Bible reading plan (by W. C. Somerville) for the complete year.
Reprinted by Collins sixteen times between 1959 and 1972.

*The Master's Men. SCM Press. Pp. 125.
A collection of articles of the same run in 1956–57 issues of *BW* that deal with the twelve apostles.

"The William Barclay Page for Preachers and Teachers." Appearing in *BW* throughout the year, the page included the following columns:

1. "Obiter Visa." This column now began to incorporate occasional series, such as one on the seven deadly sins that began on March 26, and one on Scottish family mottos that began on October 1.

2. "New Testament Interpretations of Jesus." A continuation of the series begun in 1958, running weekly throughout 1959.

3. "Great Words on the Old Testament." A seventeen-part series.

4. "Prayers for the Pulpit." Seven more articles concluding the long-running series on February 12.

5. "Morning and Evening Prayers for Everyday." A new series of prayers begun on November 12 and running into 1960.

"Words That Intrigue." *The Bible Translator*, January, 5–17.
An excerpt from *A New Testament Wordbook* (1955) including treatments of *aggareuein; apechein; exaleiphein; koinōnia, koinōnein, koinōnos; lutron, lutroun, apolutrōsis.*

"The Sermon of the Mount." *BW,* January 22.

"Exposition of John 3:5, 'of water.'" *BW,* February 5.

"Religious Vocabulary and Usage." *BW,* February 19.

"Christ's Descent into Hell." *BW,* February 26.

"The Blessed Life: Studies in the Beatitudes" [parts 2–5 of 7]. *The Preacher's Quarterly,* March, 12–17; June, 101–7; September, 199–206; December, 288–97.

"The Task of Christology." *BW,* May 7.

"Recommended Books on the Parables" [review article]. *BW,* July 7.

REVIEWS

"The Best Book on the Atonement." Review of *The Atonement,* by David Smith. *BW,* February 5.

The Secret Sayings of Jesus: The Gnostic Gospel of Thomas, by R. M. Grant and D. N. Freedman. Trans. of the Gospel of Thomas by W. R. Schoedel. *BW,* November 26.

"Book of the Year." Review of *Christ and the Christian,* by Nels Ferré. *BW,* November 17.

The Gospel of God, by H. Kelly. *ExpT,* 71:32.

Sermons Preached in a University Church, by G. A. Buttrick. *ExpT,* 71:64.

1960

DSB: Timothy, Titus and Philemon. Saint Andrew Press. Pp. xv + 324.
   Reprinted by Saint Andrew Press, 1965; U.S. ed. by Westminster Press; Braille ed., 1966; trans. into German, Japanese, Korean, Spanish.

DSB: Philippians, Colossians and Thessalonians. Saint Andrew Press. Pp. xiv + 253.
   Reprinted by Saint Andrew Press, 1966; rev. ed. by Saint Andrew Press (ed. James Martin), 1976; U.S. ed. by Westminster Press; trans. into German, Japanese, Korean, Spanish.

The Mind of Jesus. SCM Press. Pp. 190.
   U.S. ed. by Harper and Row, 1961.

The Promise of the Spirit. Epworth Press. Pp. 120.

"Fishers of Men: The Life and Work of the Evangelist." Berean Press. Pp. 19.
   Reprinted as Chapter 1 of *Fishers of Men* by Epworth Press in 1966 (q.v.).

"The William Barclay Page for Preachers and Teachers." Appearing in *BW* throughout the year, the page included the following columns:
   1. "Obiter Visa." Fifty-two installments throughout the year.
   2. "New Testament Interpretation of Jesus." An additional thirty-nine articles in the series begun in 1958–59, running through October 6.
   3. "The Mind of John." Twelve installments of a new series begun on October 13 and running into 1961.
   4. "Morning and Evening Prayers for Everyone." A series of forty-seven articles running throughout the year.

"Hellenistic Thought in New Testament Times." A series of fourteen articles in *ExpT* appearing in 1960 and 1961. The following articles appeared in 1960: "The New Emphasis, Part 1," 71:207–9; "The New Emphasis, Part 2," 71:246–48; "The New Emphasis, Part 3," 71:280–84; "The Sceptics," 71:297–301; "The Cynics," 71:371–75; "Cyrenaics," 72:29–31; "Epicureans, Part 1," 72:78–81.

"Tools for Teachers" [review article]. *ExpT,* 71:136–37.

"Saint Bernard of Clairvaux" [review article]. *ExpT,* 71:256.

"Laymen's Bible Commentaries" [review article]. *ExpT,* 71:265.

"The Blessed Life: Studies in the Beatitudes" [parts 6–7 of 7]. *The Preacher's Quarterly,* March, 14–20; June, 112–21.

"Among the New Commentaries" [review article]. *BW,* April 14.

"The Nag Hammadi Discoveries" [review article]. *BW,* June 2.

"Another Life of Jesus" [review article]. *BW,* June 16.

REVIEWS

A Treasury of Christian Verse, ed. Hugh Martin. *ExpT,* 71:128.

The Undying Fire, by Dewi Morgan. *ExpT,* 71:160.

Cyril Foster Garbett, by C. Smyth. *ExpT,* 71:192.

A Great Gospel for a Great Day, by D. L. Edwards. *ExpT,* 71:224.

The Lord's Prayer, by W. R. Matthews. *ExpT,* 71:236–37.

Plain Mr Knox, by E. Whitley. *ExpT,* 71:288.

Letters from the Early Church, by R. Lloyd. *ExpT,* 71:303.

He Heard from God, by E. K. Crossley. *ExpT,* 71:320.

Tyndale Commentaries: Epistle of Paul to the Philippians, by R. P. Martin. *ExpT,* 71:334–35.

No Pious Person, by H. Kelly. *ExpT,* 71:352.

Patrology, by B. Altaner. *ExpT,* 71:363.

Know Your Faith, by Nels Ferré. *ExpT,* 71:384.

Historicity of the Fourth Gospel, by A. G. B. Higgins. *ExpT,* 72:9.

Men of Unity, by S. Neill. *ExpT,* 72:32.

Prayers of the Reformers, by C. Manschreck. *ExpT,* 72:43–44.

Point of Glad Return, by L. Webb. *ExpT,* 72:64.

The Study of Divinity, by D. Nineham. *ExpT,* 72:73.

The Glorious Company, by F. G. Gill. *ExpT,* 72:96.

The Amplified New Testament, trans. Frances E. Siewert. *BW,* April 14.

1961

Crucified and Crowned. SCM Press. Pp. 192.

   U.S. ed. by Abingdon Press.

The Making of the Bible. Bible Guides, no. 1. Lutterworth Press. Pp. 96.

   U.S. ed. by Abingdon Press.

"God and His Church." In the Sixty-fourth Annual Report of the Association of Secretaries of YMCAs in Great Britain and Ireland, 26–65.

   A collection of four addresses ("God the Father," "God the Son," "God the Holy Spirit," and "The Church of God") delivered at the Association's 1960 conference at Skegness.

Foreword to *Brief and to the Point: Suggestions for Preachers,* by A. C. Dalton. J. Clarke and Co.

"The William Barclay Page for Preachers and Teachers." Appearing in *BW* throughout the year, the page included the following columns:

   1. "Obiter Visa." Fifty-two installments throughout the year.

   2. "The Mind of John." A continuation of the series begun in 1960, with thirty-eight additional installments concluding on September 28.

   3. "The Making and Meaning of the Gospels." Thirteen articles in a new series begun on October 5 and running into 1962.

   4. "Morning and Evening Prayers for Everyday." The final six installments of the series begun in 1959.

   5. "For Clubs and Fellowships." A new series of prayers, running into 1962.

"Hellenistic Thought in New Testament Times." A continuation of the *ExpT* series begun in 1960, including the following articles: "Epicureans, Part 2," 72:101–4; "Epicureans, Part 3," 72:146–49; "Stoics, Part 1," 72:164–66; "Stoics, Part 2," 72:200–3; "Stoics, Part 3," 72:227–30; "Stoics, Part 4," 72:258–61; "Stoics, Part 5," 72:291–94.

"To Help Bible Study" [review article]. *BW*, February 16.

"Abreast of Modern Scholarship" [review article]. *BW*, February 23.

"Studies in the Lord's Prayer" [parts 1–3 of 12]. *The Preacher's Quarterly*, June, 155–60; September, 247–52; December, 270–76.

"The Open Book" [review article]. *BW*, March 16.

REVIEWS

Between the Testaments, by D. S. Russell. *ExpT*, 72:109–10.

This World and Beyond, by R. Bultmann. *ExpT*, 72:128.

The Bible Word Book, by R. Bridge and L. A. Weigle. *ExpT*, 72:138–39.

Persecution in the Early Church, by H. B. Workman. *ExpT*, 72:159–60.

The Novelists and the Passion Story, by F. W. Dillistone. *ExpT*, 72:173–74.

Dean Inge, by Adam Fox. *ExpT*, 72:192.

Kagawa of Japan, by C. J. Davey. *ExpT*, 72:224.

The English Bible: A History of Translations, by F. F. Bruce. *ExpT*, 72:230–31.

A Christian in Eastern Europe, by J. Hamel. *ExpT*, 72:256.

The Layman's Bible Commentary, ed. B. H. Kelly. *ExpT*, 72:313–14.

William Carey, by J. B. Middlebrook. *ExpT*, 72:320.

The Word of God and Fundamentalism, ed. G. Hebert. *ExpT*, 72:327.

They Wrote the Hymns, by H. Martin. *ExpT*, 72:352.

My Spiritual Pilgrimage, by E. K. Evans. *ExpT*, 72:384.

The Stranger of Galilee, by R. E. O. White. *ExpT*, 73:13.

The Map of Clay, by J. Clemo. *ExpT*, 73:32.

The Ark of God, by D. Stewart. *ExpT*, 73:64.

The Greatness of God, by H. E. Fosdick. *ExpT*, 73:73–74.

Dangerous Delusions, by K. N. Ross; and *The Challenge of the Sects*, by H. Davies. *ExpT*, 73:96.

1962

Flesh and Spirit: An Examination of Galatians 5:19–23. SCM Press. Pp. 127.
  Reprinted by Saint Andrew Press, 1978.

*Jesus as They Saw Him: New Testament Interpretations of Jesus. SCM Press. Pp. 429.
  A collection of articles run under the series title "New Testament Interpretations of Jesus" on "The William Barclay Page for Preachers and Teachers" in *BW* in 1958 and 1959.
  U.S. ed. by Eerdmans, 1962.

More Prayers for the Plain Man. Collins-Fontana. Pp. 160.
  Reprinted by Collins, 1963, 1965, 1966, 1968.

Prayers for Young People. Collins. Pp. 95.
  Reprinted by Collins, 1963.

Foreword in *2 Corinthians*, by H. C. G. Moule. Pickering & Iglis, Ltd.

"Communicating the Gospel." In the Sixty-fifth Annual Report of the Association of Secretaries of YMCAs in Great Britain and Ireland, 13–56.

A collection of four addresses ("The People We Teach," "The Faith We Teach," "The Methods of Our Teaching," and "The Aim of Our Teaching") delivered at the Association's 1961 conference.

"A Message from the Rev. Dr. William Barclay, Former Minister." In *A History of Trinity Church, Renfrew: 1862-1962,* by A. M. Ferguson, 2-3. Privately published. .

"The William Barclay Page for Preachers and Teachers." Appearing in *BW* throughout the year, the page included the following columns:

1. "Obiter Visa." Forty-six installments concluding on November 29.

2. "Seen in the Passing." A new title for the "Obiter Visa" column. Four articles appeared under the new title in 1962, commencing with the December 6 issue.

3. "For Clubs and Fellowships." A continuation of the devotional series begun in 1961, with forty-four installments appearing from January 4 to September 27.

4. "Prayers for the Christian Year." A new series begun on November 22, running into 1963; six pieces appeared in 1962.

5. "The Making and Meaning of the Gospels." A continuation of the series begun in 1961, with twenty-eight installments appearing from January 4 to July 19.

6. "The Making and Meaning of Acts." A new series of ten articles appearing from July 16 to September 27.

7. "I Believe." A new series of articles introducing and expounding the Apostles' Creed, begun on October 4 and running into 1964; thirteen installments appeared in 1962.

"Studies in the Lord's Prayer" [parts 4-7 of 12]. *The Preacher's Quarterly,* March, 31-37; June, 134-40; September, 199-204; December, 294-99.

"Christian Education for the Layman: A New Testament Bibliography" [review article]. *BW,* March 15.

"Tyndale Commentaries" [review article]. *ExpT,* 73:369.

REVIEWS

A Greek-English Lexicon of the New Testament and Other Early Christian Literature, trans. and adaptation of Walter Bauer's *Griechisch-Deutsches Wörterbuch zu den Schriften des Neuen Testaments und der übrigen urchristlichen Literatur,* 4th rev. ed., by W. F. Arndt and F. W. Gingrich. *New Testament Studies,* 9 (1962):70-72.

The Bible in Germany, by E. H. Robertson. *ExpT,* 73:128.

The Preacher's Portrait, by J. R. W. Stott. *ExpT,* 73:160.

Teenage Religion, by H. Loukes. *ExpT,* 73:192.

The New Year of Grace, by V. Gollancz. *ExpT,* 73:224.

Preaching and Pastoral Evangelism, by R. Menzies. *ExpT,* 73:255.

A Faith for This One World, by L. Newbigin. *ExpT,* 73:287.

Doctor Sangster, by P. Sangster. *ExpT,* 73:320.

Woodbine Willie, by W. E. Purcell. *ExpT,* 73:351.

Elizabeth Fry, by J. Kent. *ExpT,* 73:383.

The Troubling of the City, by R. Lloyd. *ExpT,* 74:32.

1963

Turning to God: A Study of Conversion in the Book of Acts and Today. The Peake Memorial Lectures, no. 8. Epworth Press. Pp. 103.

U.S. ed. by Westminster Press, 1964.

Reissued in a different form by Saint Andrew Press in 1978 (q.v.).

*The Plain Man Looks at the Beatitudes. Collins–Fontana. Pp. 124.

A collection of articles that appeared in The Preacher's Quarterly from December 1958 to June 1960 under the title "The Blessed Life: Studies in the Beatitudes."

Reprinted by Collins eight times through April 1976; reissued in a Fount paperback edition, March 1977, with a tenth impression in 1978.

Many Witnesses, One Lord: A Study in the Diversity of the New Testament. SCM Press, Pp. 128.

*Epilogues and Prayers. Collins–Fontana. Pp. 224.

The All-Sufficient Christ: Studies in Paul's Letter to the Colossians. Westminster Press. Pp. 142.

British ed. by SCM Press.

Christian Discipline in Society Today: The Alex Wood Memorial Lectures for 1963. The Fellowship of Reconciliation. Pp. 42.

"The William Barclay Page for Preachers and Teachers." Appearing in BW throughout the year, the page included the following columns:

1. "Seen in the Passing." Fifty-two installments throughout the year.

2. "Prayers for the Christian Year." A continuation of the series begun in 1962 with forty-nine pieces appearing throughout the year.

3. "I Believe." A continuation of the series begun in 1962 with fifty-two pieces appearing throughout the year.

"Dr Barclay Makes His Point." L&W, February, 47. Correspondence on the dating of New Testament documents and the question of why we have four Gospels.

"Computers and the Bible" [review article]. BW, January 10.

"The Computer and the New Testament" [review article]. BW, November 14.

"Studies in the Lord's Prayer" [parts 8–11 of 12]. The Preacher's Quarterly, March, 35–40; June, 122–29; September, 230–37; December, 276–85.

"Dr Barclay Takes up Your Point." A series of eight articles in L&W presenting correspondence on the following topics: the connection between historic events and present-day faith, 124; the relation between the resurrection appearances of Jesus and present-day faith, 142; the trinity, 174; angels, 238; God's "needing" the sin of Judas, 279; the relevance of the teaching of Jesus for today's youth, 301; the relevance of the teaching of Jesus regarding the end of the world for the present day, 332; the nature of the preparation for the coming of Christ in the intertestamental period, 367.

REVIEWS

A Grammar of New Testament Greek: The Syntax, rev. ed. by J. H. Moulton. BW, March 21.

Historical Introduction to the New Testament, by F. C. Grant. New Testament Abstracts, 8:762.

The New Hastings Dictionary of the Bible, ed. James Hastings. ExpT, 74:198–200.

A Man to Be Reckoned With, by Werner Hühne. ExpT, 74:128.

Prophets of Palestine, by E. F. F. Bishop. ExpT, 74:160.

Courage to Change, by June Bingham. ExpT, 74:192.

Men of Fire: Torchbearers of the Gospel, by Walter Russell Bowie. ExpT, 74:224.

The Eternal Dimension, by Stephen Neill. ExpT, 74:256.

Objections to Christian Belief, ed. A. R. Vidler. ExpT, 74:288.

Moody without Sankey: A New Biographical Portrait, by J. C. Pollock. ExpT, 74:320.

Tower Hill, 12.30, by Donald Soper. ExpT, 74:352.

F. M. Dostoevsky: His Image of Man, by M. T. Šajković. ExpT, 74:384.

Sons of the Prophet: Leaders in Protestantism from Princeton Seminary, ed. Hugh T. Kerr. ExpT, 75:32.

John Flynn: Apostle to the Inland, by W. Scott McPheat. *ExpT*, 75:64.

The Minister's Vocation, by John Kennedy. *ExpT*, 75:96.

1964

*The Plain Man Looks at the Lord's Prayer. Collins–Fontana. Pp. 128.

A collection of articles that appeared in *The Preacher's Quarterly* from June 1961 to March 1964 under the title "Studies in the Lord's Prayer."

*Prayers for the Christian Year. SCM Press. Pp. 176.

A collection of pieces run under the same title on the "William Barclay Page for Preachers and Teachers" in *BW* from 22 November 1962 to 7 May 1964.

U.S. ed. by Harper and Row, 1965.

New Testament Words. SCM Press. Pp. 288.

A reprint of *A New Testament Wordbook* (1955) and *More New Testament Words* (1958) together in one volume.

"The William Barclay Page for Preachers and Teachers." Appearing in *BW* throughout the year, the page included the following columns:

1. "Seen in the Passing." Fifty-four installments throughout the year.

2. "Prayers for the Christian Year." A conclusion of the series begun in 1962–63, with an additional nineteen pieces running through May 7.

3. "I Believe." A conclusion of the series begun in 1962–63, with an additional thirty-two pieces running through July 30.

4. "New Testament Names [sometimes "Titles"] for the Christian." A new series begun on May 14 and running into 1965; thirty-five pieces appeared in 1964.

5. "Christian Ethics: The Life of the Christian." A new series begun on August 6 and running into 1965; twenty-two pieces appeared in 1964.

"Questions and Answers with Professor William Barclay." A continuation of the series in *L&W* begun (as "Dr Barclay Takes up Your Point") in 1963, presenting correspondence on the following topics: the discrepancies among lists of the apostles, the background of the twelve disciples, the characteristics of their leadership, and the postbiblical traditions concerning the apostles, 12; the Aramaic dialect spoken by Jesus, 55; the meaning of John 3:1–8, 87; the scriptural basis for diversity in denominational practice, 119; the sevenfold gifts of the Holy Spirit and their manifestation in Jesus' life, 170; the evidence for infant baptism in the New Testament, 203; the place of women in Paul's teaching and the present day, 252–53; the possibility of moral progress in the afterlife, 368; the meaning of 1 Corinthians 11:27, 411; the historical facts concerning the birth of Jesus and the purpose of the doctrine of the virgin birth, 449.

"Studies in the Lord's Prayer" [part 12 of 12]. *The Preacher's Quarterly*, March, 133–43.

REVIEWS

God, Sex and War, ed. D. M Mackinnon. *ExpT*, 75:127–28.

African Saint: The Story of Apolo Kivebulaya, by Anne Luck. *ExpT*, 75:160.

The Faith of Robert Browning, by Hugh Martin. *ExpT*, 75:192.

The Chavasse Twins, by Selwyn Gummer. *ExpT*, 75:224.

The History of the Salvation Army, by A. R. Wiggins. *ExpT*, 75:256.

The Minister's Prayer Book, by John W. Doberstein. *ExpT*, 75:288.

The Caring Church, by Peter Smith. *ExpT*, 75:320.

The Four Lives of Elsbeth Rosenfeld, by E. Rosenfeld. *ExpT*, 75:352.

Parson's Pitch, by David Sheppard. *ExpT*, 75:384.

Mary Baker Eddy, by Norman Beasley. *ExpT*, 76:40.

Ernest Renan: A Critical Biography, by H. W. Wardman. *ExpT*, 76:72.

Markings, by Dag Hammarskjöld. *ExpT*, 76:104.

1965

A New People's Life of Jesus. SCM Press. Pp. 96.

In the Fullness of Time. Boys' Brigade. Pp. x + 118.

The Epistle to the Hebrews. Bible Guides, no. 20. Lutterworth Press. Pp. 96.
    U.S. ed. by Abingdon Press.

"The New Testament and the Papyri." In *The New Testament in Historical and Contemporary Perspective: A Memorial Volume In Honour of G. H. C. Macgregor.* Ed. William Barclay and Hugh Anderson. 57–81.

"Divinity: An Introduction to the Faculty." In *The Glasgow University Student Handbook, 1965–66.* 34–35.

"The William Barclay Page for Preachers and Teachers." Appearing in *BW* throughout the year, the page included the following columns:
    1. "Seen in the Passing." Fifty-two installments throughout the year.
    2. "Christian Ethics: The Life of the Christian." Fifty-two installments throughout the year.
    3. "New Testament Titles for the Christian." The concluding two sections of the series begun in 1964.
    4. "The Gifts of the Spirit and the Men of the Spirit." A new series begun on January 21 and concluded on April 22.
    5. "Prayers for Health and Healing." A new series begun on April 29 and running into 1966.

"Questions and Answers with Professor William Barclay." A continuation of the *L&W* series begun in 1963–64, with nine pieces presenting correspondence on the following topics: the behavior of work mates, the reading of the Bible in church, and our attitude toward immoral people, January, 30; the cities of refuge, the oldest manuscript of the New Testament, and our attitude toward examination cheats, February, 14; the meaning of John 10:33–36 and of Hebrews 4:15, March, 27; historicity in the Gospel of John, April, 18; the case for abridging the Bible, May, 32; the use of the word *faith* in the New Testament, June, 28; methods for teaching the New Testament in schools, October, 13; how Paul could prove his Roman citizenship, and the meaning of the Holy Spirit to a Jew of the pre-Christian era, November, 16; the question of whether Jesus was one of "the quiet of the land," December, 36.

"The Life and Message of the Early Church" [parts 1–2 of 6]. *The Preacher's Quarterly*, September, 187–96; December, 246–61.

REVIEWS

The Faber Book of Aphorisms, ed. W. H. Auden and Louis Kronenberger. *ExpT*, 76:136.

Come out the Wilderness, by Bruce Kenrick. *ExpT*, 76:168.

They Looked at the Cross, by E. L. Wenger. *ExpT*, 76:200.

Charles Wesley: The First Methodist, by Frederick C. Gill. *ExpT*, 76:232.

Josiah Stamp, Public Servant: The Life of the First Baron Stamp of Shortlands, by J. Harry Jones. *ExpT*, 76:264.

The Seeds of Peace, by Dewi Morgan. *ExpT*, 76:296.

Teilhard de Chardin: A Biographical Study, by Claude Cuénot. *ExpT*, 76:328.

In the Service of the Lord, by Otto Dibelius. *ExpT*, 76:360.

The Geeta: Gospel of the Lord Shri Krishna, trans. Shri Purohit Swami. *ExpT*, 76:392.

The General Next to God, by Richard Collier. *ExpT*, 77:32.

People Matter More Than Things, by George Burton. *ExpT,* 77:64.

Canon Peter Green: A Biography of a Great Parish Priest, by H. E. Sheen. *ExpT,* 77:96.

1966

*The First Three Gospels. SCM Press. Pp. 317.

Based on a series of articles that ran under the title "The Making and Meaning of the Gospels" on "The William Barclay Page for Preachers and Teachers" in *BW* from 5 October 1961 to 19 July 1962.

U.S. ed. by Westminster Press.

Fishers of Men. Epworth Press. Pp. 113.

A volume including the essay "Fishers of Men: The Life and Work of the Evangelist" (published by Berean Press in 1960), a lecture delivered to the Lay Preachers of the Congregational Union of England and Wales, a lecture delivered to the Religious Booksellers Group of the Booksellers Association, and an essay on preaching that originally appeared in *ExpT,* 61:13–14.

U.S. ed. by Westminster Press.

The Old Law and the New Law. Boys' Brigade. Pp. viii + 123.

Reprinted by Saint Andrew Press, 1972; U.S. ed. by Westminster Press.

*The Plain Man Looks at the Apostles' Creed. Collins–Fontana. Pp. 384.

Based on a series of articles that ran under the title "I Believe" on "The William Barclay Page for Preachers and Teachers" in *BW* from 4 October 1962 to 30 July 1964.

Reprinted by Collins, 1969, 1971, 1972.

*Seen in the Passing. Ed. Rita Snowden. Collins. Pp. 158.

A selection of articles run under the same title on "The William Barclay Page for Preachers and Teachers" in *BW* from 6 December 1962 to 29 September 1966.

Reprinted as a Fount paperback edition under the title *In the Hands of God,* 1977.

Foreword to *Did Jesus Rise from the Dead?* by James Martin. Saint Andrew Press.

"The William Barclay Page for Preachers and Teachers." Appearing in *BW* for thirty-nine weeks, from January 6 to its conclusion on September 29, the page included the following columns:

1. "Seen in the Passing." Thirty-nine pieces.
2. "Christian Ethics: The Life of the Christian." Thirty-nine pieces.
3. "Prayers for Health and Healing." Thirty-nine pieces.

"Aids to Understanding" [review article]. *BW,* 27 January.

"The Life and Message of the Early Church" [parts 3–6 of 6]. *The Preacher's Quarterly,* March, 4–10; June, 81–88; September, 155–63; December, 248–56.

"The Bible Society's Greek New Testament" [review article]. *BW,* May 12.

"School for Laymen." A new feature in *BW,* introduced on October 6 in place of "The William Barclay Page for Preachers and Teachers." The following columns appeared:

1. "Prayers for Public Worship." Four pieces.
2. "Studies in the Psalms." Three pieces.
3. "New Testament Characters." Three pieces.
4. "The Teaching of the New Testament." Two pieces.

REVIEWS

Joseph Priestly, Adventurer in Science and Champion of Truth, by F. W. Gibbs. *ExpT,* 77:128.

The Forgotten People, by Norman S. Power. *ExpT,* 77:160.

Shaw in His Time, by Ivor Brown. *ExpT,* 77:192.

As at the Beginning, by Michael Harper. *ExpT,* 77:224.

Light on C S Lewis, by Jocelyn Gibbs. *ExpT*, 77:256.

Richard Baxter, by Geoffrey E. Nuttall. *ExpT*, 77:288.

Billy Graham, by John Pollock. *ExpT*, 77:320.

Opportunity My Ally, by Lewis L. L. Cameron. *ExpT*, 77:352.

Children in Need, by Anthony Denney. *ExpT*, 77:384.

What I Believe, ed. George Unwin. *ExpT*, 78:32.

The Healing of Persons, by Paul Tournier. *ExpT*, 78:64.

Urban Churches in Britain, by K. A. Busia. *ExpT*, 78:96.

1967

The Lord's Supper. SCM Press. Pp. 128.

God's Man. Boys' Brigade. Pp. 86.

"Thou Shalt Not Kill." The Fellowship of Reconciliation. Pp. 24.

"The School for Laymen." This *BW* feature appeared most weeks throughout the year with the following columns alternating with one another (and sometimes failing to appear at all):

1. "Prayers for Public Worship." A continuation of the series begun in 1966, with an additional twenty installments appearing throughout the year.

2. "Studies in the Psalms." A continuation of the series begun in 1966, with five more installments concluding on April 20.

3. "New Testament Characters." A continuation of the series begun in 1966, with four more installments, concluding on March 30.

4. "The Teaching of the New Testament." A continuation of the series begun in 1966, with thirteen more installments, concluding on August 31.

5. "Prayers for the Pulpit." One piece only.

6. "Seen in the Passing." A reintroduction of the column from "The William Barclay Page for Preachers and Teachers," with eight pieces appearing from September 7 to the end of the year.

REVIEWS

Frazer of Tain, by John T. Carson. *ExpT*, 78:128.

The End of the Roman World, by Stewart Perowne. *ExpT*, 78:160.

I Knew Dietrich Bonhoeffer, by W. D. Zimmerman and R. Gregor Smith. *ExpT*, 78:192.

Shaw on Religion, by Warren Sylvester Smith. *ExpT*, 78:224.

The God I Want, ed. James Mitchell. *ExpT*, 78:256.

Alison Cairns and Her Family, by Lyn Irvine. *ExpT*, 78:288.

The Churches and the Labour Movement, by Stephen Mayor. *ExpT*, 78:320.

Makers of Our Heritage, by Marcus L. Loane. *ExpT*, 78:352.

Herbert G Wood: A Memoir of His Life and Thought, by Richenda C. Scott. *ExpT*, 78:384.

Augustine of Hippo, by Peter Brown. *ExpT*, 79:32.

Faith on Fleet Street, by Dewi Morgan. *ExpT*, 79:64.

Youth to the Rescue, by Lawrence Bailey. *ExpT*, 79:96.

1968

Communicating the Gospel. Drummond Press. Pp. xii + 106.

A transcript of the first Laird Lecture delivered at Stirling University, plus an additional chapter, "The Gospel in Tradition" (72–106), a lecture delivered separately to an audience of both Protestants and Roman Catholics under the auspices of the University's Extramural Department.

Reprinted by Saint Andrew Press, 1979; U.S. ed. (as *Meditations on Communicating the Gospel*) by The Upper Room, 1971 (q.v.).

Prayers for Help and Healing. Collins–Fontana. Pp. 124.
  Reprinted by Collins, 1969, 1970, 1971, 1972, 1973, 1974.

Living and Learning. Boys' Brigade. Pp. vi + 106.

The New Testament, vol. 1: *The Gospels and the Acts of the Apostles.* Collins. Pp. 352.
  An original translation, with an appendix, "On Translating the New Testament" (308–52).

[With others.] *The Bible and History: Scriptures in Their Secular Setting.* Ed. William Barclay. Lutterworth Press. Pp. 370.
  U.S. ed. by Abingdon Press, 1969.

"A Letter to You Both." National Bible Society of Scotland. Pp. 4.
  A leaflet designed to be distributed with Bibles presented at weddings, containing a daily Bible readings plan.

"Memorial Tribute to Andrew McCosh." *BW,* June 19.

"Seen in the Passing." A series of twenty-six pieces appearing biweekly in *BW* throughout the year.

"Prayers for Public Worship." A series of twenty-six pieces appearing biweekly in *BW* throughout the year.

REVIEWS

Spurgeon: Heir of the Puritans, by Ernest W. Bacon. *ExpT,* 79:128.

Thomas Becket, by Richard Winston. *ExpT,* 79:160.

Readings from Pope John, ed. Vincent A. Yzermans. *ExpT,* 79:192.

Richard Wilton: A Forgotten Victorian, by Mary Blamire Young. *ExpT,* 79:224.

A Question of Conscience, by Charles Davies. *ExpT,* 79:255.

The Essence of T H Huxley, by Cyril Bibby. *ExpT,* 79:288.

John Evelyn Esquire: An American Layman of the Seventeenth Century, by Florence Higham. *ExpT,* 79:320.

Poems from Hospital, by Jean and Howard Sergeant. *ExpT,* 79:352.

Journeys in Belief, by Bernard Dixon. *ExpT,* 79:384.

Words of Comfort, by Cecil Pawson. *ExpT,* 80:32.

Race: A Christian Symposium, ed. Clifford S. Hill and David Matthews. *ExpT,* 80:64.

Markings, by Dag Hammarskjöld. *ExpT,* 80:96.

1969

The New Testament, vol. 2: *The Letters and Revelation.* Collins. Pp. 350.

Foreword to *Seeing Jesus Today,* by John Bishop. James Ltd.

"The Three Tenses of Advent." *The Oscope,* December 3, 2–6.

"Seen in the Passing." Thirty-seven pieces in *BW* throughout the year.

"Prayers for Public Worship." Fifteen pieces in *BW* throughout the year.

REVIEWS

My Call to Preach, by C. A. Joyce. *ExpT,* 80:128.

Personal Evangelism, by Cecil Pawson. *ExpT,* 80:160.

Sir Halley Stewart, by David Newton. *ExpT*, 80:192.

Dialogue in Medicine and Theology, ed. Dale White. *ExpT*, 80:224.

Collected Poems, by Gilbert Thomas. *ExpT*, 80:256.

Nathan Söderblöm: His Life and Work, by Bengt Sundkler. *ExpT*, 80:288.

The Church and the New Generation, by Charles E. Mowry. *ExpT*, 80:320.

Many Voices: The Autobiography of a Medium, by Eileen J. Garrett. *ExpT*, 80:352.

Once Caught: No Escape, by Norman Grubb. *ExpT*, 80:384.

The New Testament and Criticism, by George Eldon Ladd. *ExpT*, 81:32.

William Tyndale, by C. H. Williams. *ExpT*, 81:64.

An Introduction to Pastoral Counselling, by Kathleen Heasman. *ExpT*, 81:96.

1970

God's Young Church. Ed. James Martin. Saint Andrew Press. Pp. 120.

>A selection of pieces that had previously appeared in *God's Men, God's Church and God's Life* (1952) and *God's Law, God's Servants, and God's Men* (1954).

>Reprinted by Boy's Brigade, 1971–72; U.S. ed. by Westminster Press; trans. into Japanese.

"A Comparison of Paul's Missionary Preaching and His Preaching to the Church." In *Apostolic History and the Gospel: New Testament Essays Presented to F. F. Bruce*. Ed. W. Ward Gasque and Ralph P. Martin. Paternoster Press. 165–75.

[With others.] *To God in Prayer*. Ed. F. G. Doubleday. Bagster. Pp. 102.

>Sixteen prayers on various themes.

Foreword to *Reason to Believe*, by Harry Dean. Salvationist Publishing and Supplies.

"Seen in the Passing." Thirteen pieces in *BW* (three appearing in January and ten appearing from October 16 to the end of the year).

"Prayers for Public Services." *The Clergy Review* 55 (June 1970):434–39.

REVIEWS

Patterns of Ministry: Theological Education in a Changing World, by Steven G. Mackie. *ExpT*, 81:128.

John Bunyan, by Richard L. Greaves. *ExpT*, 81:160.

The Church in Experiment: Studies in Congregational Structures and Functional Mission, by Rudiger Reitz. *ExpT*, 81:256.

Luther: An Introduction to His Thought, by Gerhard Ebeling. *ExpT*, 81:288.

Dag Hammarskjöld's White Book: An Analysis of Markings, by Gustaf Aulén. *ExpT*, 81:320.

Scotland's Greatest Athlete, by D. P. Thomson. *ExpT*, 81:352.

The Image of Man in C S Lewis, by William Luther White. *ExpT*, 81:384.

Martin Luther, by E. G. Rupp, et al. *ExpT*, 82:32.

Secular Evangelism, by Fred Brown. *ExpT*, 82:64.

George Whitfield: The Life and Times of the Great Evangelist of the Eighteenth-Century Revival, by Arnold Dallimore. *ExpT*, 82:96.

1971

DSB: The Revelation of John. Saint Andrew Press. Pp. xvi + 297.

>Rev. ed. by Saint Andrew Press (ed. James Martin), 1976; U.S. ed. by Westminster Press; trans. into Chinese, German, Hindu, Japanese, Korean, Spanish.

Ethics in a Permissive Society. Collins–Fontana. Pp. 222.
>A revised and expanded version of the 1971 Baird Lectures.
>Reprinted by Collins, 1971, 1972 (three times).

Meditation on Communicating the Gospel. The Upper Room. Pp. 64.
>An edition of *Communicating the Gospel* (1968) omitting the final chapter of that earlier edition.

*Through the Year with William Barclay: Devotional Readings for Every Day. Ed. Denis Duncan. Hodder and Stoughton. Pp. 316.
>A collection of articles that originally appeared in *BW.*
>Reprinted in a paperback edition by Hodder and Stoughton, 1977.

"The Men, the Meaning, the Message of the Books." A new series in *L&W* begun in October and running into 1972–73. Appearing in 1971 were the following: "Six Honest Serving Men," October, 13–14; "Matthew: The Bridge Between," November, 8–9; "Mark: The Men of Galilee," December, 8–9.

"Seen in the Passing." Nineteen pieces in *BW* throughout the year. An additional twenty-six pieces in the same style appeared throughout the year without the "Seen in the Passing" designation.

"Did Jesus Really Exist?" [review article]. *L&W,* April, 15–16.

REVIEWS

Thomas Coke: Apostle of Methodism, by John Vickers. *ExpT,* 82:128.

Religion in Communist China, by Richard C. Bush. *ExpT,* 82:160.

Thomas Becket, by David Knowles. *ExpT,* 82:192.

Martin Luther King, by Kenneth Slack. *ExpT,* 82:256.

The Mushroom and the Bride, by John H. Jacques; and *A Christian View of the Mushroom Myth,* by John C. King. *ExpT,* 82:288.

I Know It Was the Place's Fault, by Des Wilson. *ExpT,* 82:320.

Arthur Samuel Peake, by John T. Wilkinson. *ExpT,* 82:352.

The Liberated Zone, by John Pairman Brown. *ExpT,* 82:384.

Born to Rebel, by Benjamin E. Mays. *ExpT,* 83:32.

Arminius: A Study in the Dutch Reformation, by Carl Bangs. *ExpT,* 83:64.

Elysion, Ancient Greek and Roman Beliefs concerning Life after Death, by W. F. Jackson Knight. *ExpT,* 83:96.

1972

Introducing the Bible. IBRA. Pp. 155.

Introduction to *Late and Early,* by James Dow. Saint Andrew Press.

"I Remember." *Journal of the Cricket Society,* Spring 1972, 23–24.

"The Men, the Meaning, the Message of the Books." A continuation of the *L&W* series begun in 1971. Appearing in 1972 were the following: "Luke: Friend of the Friendless," January, 8–9; "John: The Mind of God in Human Form," February, 8–9; "Acts: The Message of the Church," March, 8–9; "Romans: Faith Alone," April, 6–7; "1 Corinthians: The Pastor and His Problems," May, 6–7, 32; "2 Corinthians: Strife and Reconciliation," June, 6–7; "Galatians: Christian," July, 4–5; "Ephesians: The Function of the Church," August, 4–5; "Philippians: The Letter of Joy," September, 8–9; "Colossians: The All-sufficient Christ," October, 8–9; "Thessalonians: The Importance of the Present," November, 8–9; "Philemon: Slave and Brother," December, 8–9.

"Seen in the Passing." Two pieces in *BW.* An additional eight pieces in the same style appeared without the "Seen in the Passing" designation.

REVIEWS

George Bell, by Kenneth Slack. ExpT, 83:128.

Sybil Casson Thorndike, by Elizabeth Sprigge. ExpT, 83:160.

Robert Newton Flew, by Gordon S. Wakefield. ExpT, 83:192.

The Autobiography of Howard Spring. ExpT, 83:224.

The Mystery and the Magic of the Occult, by John Stevens Kerr. ExpT, 83:256.

Socialism in Britain from the Industrial Revolution to the Present Day, by T. L. Jarman. ExpT, 83:288.

The Pentecostals, by Walter J. Hollenweger. ExpT, 83:320.

John Wesley: A Theological Biography, by Martin Schmidt. ExpT, 83:352.

The Faber Book of Religious Verse, ed. Helen Gardner. ExpT, 83:384.

The Puritan Pleasure of the Detective Story, by Erik Routley. ExpT, 84:32.

Healers of the Mind, by Paul E. Johnson. ExpT, 84:64.

The Elaborate Funeral: Man, Doom and God, by Gavin Reid. ExpT, 84:96.

1973

*The Plain Man's Guide to Ethics. Collins–Fontana. Pp. 205.

> An exposition of the Ten Commandments based on articles that appeared in BW from 6 August 1964 to 29 September 1966.

> Reprinted in a Fount paperback edition, 1977, 1979.

Every Day with William Barclay: Devotional Readings for Every Day. Ed. Denis Duncan. Hodder and Stoughton. Pp. 285.

Marching Orders: Daily Readings for Young People. Ed. Denis Duncan. Hodder and Stoughton. Pp. 192.

> An abridged version of *Through the Year with William Barclay: Devotional Readings for Every Day* (1971).

Jesus Christ for Today. Methodist Home Mission. Pp. 22.

> A collection of seven studies in the Gospel of Luke.

> Reprinted in a "Special Emergency Edition" and various other editions in other countries; trans. in Spanish by Robert Escamilla, 1977.

Preface in *The Bible Readers' Reference Book*, by Donald M. McFarlan. Blackie & Son Ltd.

"Somersaulting Freeman." In *The Centenary Brochure of the Motherwell Cricket Club, 1873–1973*, 30–31.

"The Men, the Meaning, the Message of the Books." A conclusion of the *L&W* series begun in October 1971. Appearing in 1973 were the following: "Timothy and Titus: The Letters of the Church," January, 8–9; "Hebrews: Let Us Draw Near," February, 6–7; "James: Practical Christianity," March, 6–7; "1 Peter: The Obligations of Grace," April, 8–9; "2 Peter and Jude: Threats to the Church," May, 8–9; "1 John: The Tests of Faith and Life," June, 6–7; "2 and 3 John: The Conflict of Ministries," July, 20–21; "Revelation: Visions of the End," August, 20–21.

REVIEWS

The Expectation of the Poor: The Church and the Third World, by B. N. Y. Vaughan. ExpT, 84:128.

The Common Bible. L&W, February, 8–9.

Portrait of Soper, by William Purcell. ExpT, 84:160.

Rose Macaulay, by Constance Baubington Smith. ExpT, 84:192.

Lewis and Sybil, by John Casson. ExpT, 84:224.

Francis of Assisi, by John Holland Smith. ExpT, 84:256.

Personal Living: An Introduction to Paul Tournier, by Monroe Peaston. ExpT, 84:288.

Memoirs, by W. A. Visser 't Hooft. *ExpT,* 84:320.

Hand to the Plough, by Cecil Pawson. *ExpT,* 84:352.

1974

By What Authority? Darton, Longman and Todd. Pp. 221.

Marching On: Daily Readings for Younger People. Ed. Denis Duncan. Hodder and Stoughton. Pp. 223.
  U.S. ed. by Westminster Press.

"The Christian Ethic." In the Seventy-seventh Annual Report of the Association of Secretaries of YMCAs in Great Britain and Ireland.
  A collection of three addresses ("The Ethics of Personal Relationships," "The Ethics of the Working Life," and "International Ethics") delivered at the Association's 1973 conference.

"New Wine in Old Wine-skins: Law in the Old Testament." *ExpT,* 86:68–72.

REVIEWS

The Grain of Wheat: An Autobiography, by Frank Longford. *ExpT,* 86:32.

The Sun is High, by Rita Snowden. *ExpT,* 86:64.

Marie Curie, by Robert Reid. *ExpT,* 86:96.

1975

Testament of Faith. A. R. Mowbray. Pp. xii + 124.
  Reprinted by Mowbray, 1975; paperback edition by Mowbray, 1977; U.S. ed. (as *William Barclay: A Spiritual Autobiography*) by Eerdmans; cassette recording for the blind by Calibre of Aylebury.

Foreword in *No Better Than I Should Be,* by J. L. Dow. Hutchison.

Foreword in *Personal Evangelism,* 2d ed., by Cecil Pawson. Saint Andrew Press.

"Religion and Life." A new series in *L&W* begun in January and running into 1976. Appearing in 1975 were the following: "Doctor and Patient," January, 12–13; "The Unborn Child," February, 28–29; "The Ethics of Death," March, 16–17; "The Ethics of Gambling," April, 22–23; "The Ethics of Education," May, 23–24; "The Ethics of Politics," September, 12–13; "The Ethics of Journalism," October, 26–27; "The Ethics of Industry," November, 22–23; "The Ethics of the Law," December, 29–30.

"The Hastings' Tradition." *ExpT,* 86:288.

"Building Faith into Life." *The Upper Room Daily Devotional Guide,* March/April, 46.

REVIEWS

Crowded Canvas, by Max Warren. *ExpT,* 86:128.

Times to Remember, by Rose Fitzgerald Kennedy. *ExpT,* 86:160.

Modern Man Looks at Evolution, by W. W. Fletcher. *ExpT,* 86:192.

The Joy of the Snow, by Elizabeth Goudge. *ExpT,* 86:224.

Turn on the Fountains, by Betty Massingham. *ExpT,* 86:256.

Charles Raven: Naturalist, Historian, Theologian, by F. W. Dillistone. *ExpT,* 86:388.

The Beast and the Monk: A Life of Charles Kingsley, by Susan Chitty. *ExpT,* 87:32.

The Gulag Archipelago, by Alexander Solzhenitsyn. *ExpT,* 87:64.

Trotsky: An Appreciation of His Life, by Joel Carmichael. *ExpT,* 87:96.

1976

The Gospel and Acts, vol. 1: *The First Three Gospels*. SCM Press. Pp. 303.

A revised and expanded version of *The First Three Gospels* published by SCM Press in 1966 (q.v.).

U.S. ed. by Westminster Press.

The Gospels and Acts, vol. 2: *The Fourth Gospel, the Acts of the Apostles*. SCM Press. Pp. 341.

U.S. ed. by Westminster Press.

The New Testament: A New Translation. Collins. Pp. 576.

A new edition of the two-volume translation of the New Testament published by Collins in 1968 and 1969 (q.v.), with some reordering of the sequence of the books, and without the essay "On Translating the New Testament."

*The Men, the Meaning, the Message of the Books. Saint Andrew Press. Pp. 149.

A collection of articles that appeared under the same title in *L&W* from October 1971 to August 1973.

U.S. ed. (as *The Men, the Meaning, the Message of the New Testament Books: A Series of New Testament Studies*) by Westminster Press; trans. into Indonesian.

"Religion and Life." A conclusion to the *L&W* series begun in 1975. Appearing in 1976 was the final installment, "Man and the Beasts," January, 9–10.

"Tribute to C. L. Mitton." *ExpT*, 88:64.

REVIEWS

C S Lewis: A Biography, by Roger Lancelyn Green and Walter Hooper. *ExpT*, 87:128.

India: The Speeches and Reminiscences of Indira Gandhi, Prime Minister. *ExpT*, 87:160.

The Door Wherein I Went, by Lord Hailsham. *ExpT*, 87:192.

Thomas Merton, Monk: A Monastic Tribute, by Patrick Hart. *ExpT*, 87:224.

Washington: The Indispensable Man, by James Thomas Flexner. *ExpT*, 87:256.

Watch How You Go, by Martin Sullivan. *ExpT*, 87:288.

A Biography of Aldous Huxley, by Sybille Bedford. *ExpT*, 87:320.

Robespierre, by George Rude. *ExpT*, 87:352.

Daily Readings from F W Boreham, ed. Frank Chambers. *ExpT*, 87:384.

Albert Schweitzer: A Comprehensive Biography, by James Brabazon. *ExpT*, 88:32.

Encounter with Martin Buber, by Aubrey Hodes. *ExpT*, 88:64.

Mother Teresa: Her People and Her Work, by Desmond Doig. *ExpT*, 88:96.

1977

Jesus of Nazareth. Collins. Pp. 285.

A rewritten version of the script of the film of the same title by Anthony Burgess, Suso Cecchio d'Amico, and Franco Zeffirelli, including quotations from Barclay's own translation of the New Testament.

Reprinted in a paperback edition by Fountain Books, pp. 128.

*More Prayers for Young People. Collins–Fontana. Pp. 160.

The Character of God. Robert Denholm Press. Pp. 64.

[With Iain Reid.] *A Life of Christ*. Darton, Longman and Todd. Pp. 95.

Japanese ed. by Shinkyo Shuppansha, 1970.

Men and Affairs. Ed. Clive L. Rawlins. A. R. Mowbray. Pp. ix + 149.
   A selection of book reviews from *ExpT*.

Foreword to *Message, Media and Mission*, by Ronald Falconer. Saint Andrew Press.

Foreword to *We Joy in God*. Society for Promoting Christian Knowledge.

REVIEWS

The Good News Bible. *ExpT*, 88:128.

The Way the Wind Blows, by Lord Home. *ExpT*, 88:160.

No Continuing City, by Frederick Coutts. *ExpT*, 88:192.

Karl Barth, by Eberhard Busch. *ExpT*, 88:224.

Dick Sheppard, by Carolyn Scott. *ExpT*, 88:256.

Paul Tillich: His Life and Thought, by Wilhelm and Marion Pauck. *ExpT*, 88:288.

Born Again, by Charles W. Colson. *ExpT*, 88:320.

First Love: A Journey, by Leslie Paul. *ExpT*, 88:352.

Cornish Bishop, by Alan Dustan and John S. Peart-Binns. *ExpT*, 88:384.

Michel Quoist, by Neville Cryer. *ExpT*, 89:32.

J R R Tolkien, by Humphrey Carpenter. *ExpT*, 89:64.

Part of My Life, by A. J. Ayer. *ExpT*, 89:96.

POSTHUMOUS PUBLICATIONS

1978

Turning to God: A Study of Conversion in the Book of Acts and Today. Saint Andrew Press. Pp. 104.
   A revised version of the 1963 edition by Epworth Press containing an additional chapter on the converted life drawn from the 1955 booklet "The Christian Way."
   U.S. ed. by Baker Book House.

REVIEWS

Charles Simeon of Cambridge, by Hugh Evan Hopkins. *ExpT*, 89:128.

C H Dodd: Interpreter of the New Testament, by F. W. Dillistone. *ExpT*, 89:160.

Teilhard, by Ellen Lukas. *ExpT*, 89:192.

Audacity to Believe, by Sheila Cassidy. *ExpT*, 89:224.

1979

Great Themes of the New Testament. Ed. Cyril Rodd. T. & T. Clark. Pp. 116.
   A collection of essays from *ExpT*.
   U.S. ed. by Westminster Press, 1980.

1980

Arguing about Christianity: Seven Discussions between William Barclay and Iain Reid. Saint Andrew Press. Pp. 70.
   With a foreword by Ronnie Barclay.

The Lord Is My Shepherd: Expositions of Selected Psalms. Collins. Pp. 153.
   With an introduction by Allan Galloway.

MISCELLANEA

1933–46 Biannual pastoral letter in the Renfrew Trinity church magazine and forewords to the church's annual reports.

1945 "Scotland for Christ" [unpublished series of plays for young people].

1945–49 Correspondence course for SSSU (see Appendix III).

1947–52 SSSU Senior Lesson Notes (see Appendix IV).

1949 "New Testament Christology" (see pp. 375–83).

1950 "The Place of the Bible in Christian Belief" [unpublished paper].

1960 General introduction to the Approach to the New Testament.

1961–66 Coeditor (with F. F. Bruce) of the twenty-two-volume Bible Guides series for Lutterworth Press.

1962 *The Beatitudes.* Christian Recordings, Ltd. A long-playing phonograph record of Willie's exposition of the Beatitudes and the Lord's Prayer.

1965 Coeditor (with Hugh Anderson) of *The New Testament in Historical and Contemporary Perspective: A Memorial Volume in Honour of G. H. C. Macgregor.* Blackwell. Pp. viii + 280.

1971 "A Prayer for Old People."

1973 "A Faithful Servant."

1976 Introductory material in Collins's RSV Study Bible.

N.d. *The Christian and His Prayers.* Saint Andrew Press.

N.d. "The Place of the Bible in Christian Belief."

N.d. *Basic Christianity* [parts 1 and 2]. Saint Andrew Press. Reissued in 1976 by Abingdon Press under the title *Study Guide: New Testament Studies* as an eight-page pamphlet and a cassette tape containing the following lectures: "Romans 12: Belonging to the New Age," "John 1:1–18: The Prologue to John's Gospel," and "Revelation 13: The Playground of the Eccentrics."

Notes

In citing works in the notes, I have generally used short titles. For works frequently cited, I have used the following abbreviations:

BW	*The British Weekly*
DBR	Daily Bible Readings
DSB	*The Daily Study Bible*
ExpT	*The Expository Times*
GH	*The Glasgow Herald*
GUM	*The Glasgow University Magazine*
L&W	*Life and Work*
MT	*The Motherwell Times*
RP	*The Renfrew Press*
SPQ	*The Scottish Primary Quarterly*
SSST	*The Scottish Sunday School Teacher*
SSSU	The Scottish Sunday School Union
ToF	*Testament of Faith*

PREFACE

1. Freud, in a letter to Arnold Zweig, May 1936; quoted by Klaus Bolker in his definitive biography *Brecht* (1976; ET, 1979).

2. Willie, in a letter to Alton McEachern, 16 March 1973.

3. Willie, in a letter to Claude A. Frazier, 18 September 1973.

4. Lockhart in *Archbishop Lang,* v. We might recall Alexander Whyte's very similar comment about Bishop Butler, that "Butler has no biography. Butler's books are his whole biography" (R. F. Barbour, *Life of Alexander Whyte,* 1). William Robertson Nicoll showed greater perception when he said, "Before we do justice to a great teacher we must trace his spiritual ancestry" (T. H. Darlow, *W. R. Nicoll,* 199); he went on to say, "No biography can record the best portion of a good man's life—his little, nameless, unremembered acts of kindness and love" (426–27).

5. See *DSB: Galatians and Ephesians,* 184, for Cromwell's Ironsides fighting with Bible and sword in hand. Nor should it be forgotten that "the greatest preacher of the nineteenth century," Charles Haddon Spurgeon, who was a great favorite of the Barclay family, wrote a highly popular book entitled *The Bible and the Newspaper.*

6. Simone de Beauvoir, *Force of Circumstance,* vii.

7. G. A. Smith, *Henry Drummond,* 249. Professor Smith laid down his own rules of writing biography when he specified his four aims: "to trace the influences which moulded him, the growth of his character, the development of his opinions, and give a record of the actual work that he did and of the movements he . . . enforced" (13). This has been my own approach as well,

whenever the data permitted, but the development of his opinions—understood as critique rather than description—must be left to another book.

8. *Through the Year with William Barclay,* ed. Denis Duncan, 71.

9. In Who's Who he listed *arguing* as one of his hobbies: it was at once a declaration of his enjoyment and an intimation of his Caledonian antisyzygy—his ability to allow opposites to jostle more or less harmoniously in his mind—for he was essentially a man of peace, and consistently enjoined toleration and peaceful coexistence.

CHAPTER ONE

1. See page 5 of *Testament of Faith* (hereafter abbreviated *ToF*); this volume was published in America under the title *William Barclay: A Spiritual Autobiography* by the William B. Eerdmans Publishing Company.

2. McLeod, *Reminiscences of a Highland Parish,* 67.

3. The name McLeish has variants such as MacLish, Makleis, and so on. It is a shortened form of MacGill' loasa, "son of the servant of Jesus," and was connected with the clan Macpherson ("Mac a Phearsein" means "son of the parson," and many descendants and members of the clan were sons of the clergy). In 1613, one Malleis McColleis of North Perthshire was fined for reset by the clan Gregor.

4. Mackenzie, *One Hundred Years in the Highlands,* 41.

5. According to Joseph Mitchell, in *Reminiscences of My Life in the Highlands,* 1:183.

6. Facts taken from the 1881 census returns.

7. Noted by I. M. Mackintosh in a letter to the author, 18 February 1980.

8. See Cecil Woodham Smith's *Florence Nightingale* (1950), 238.

9. Smith, 575–76.

10. *ToF,* 5. A vigorous prose stylist who regularly employed double, triple, and at times even quadruple adjectives, Willie heaped six atop one another on only this one occasion anywhere in his voluminous writings; it emphasizes the profound degree of his regard for his mother.

11. *ToF,* 5. In any case, Fort William was a town, not a village! (There were 1,856 people living there in 1891, sixty-five percent of whom spoke Gaelic!)

12. See George Hay's booklet *The Church of the Three Holy Brothers* (1957). Ronald Falconer produced a television program on Lochgoilhead that he describes fully in his book *Message, Media and Mission* (which includes a foreword by Willie); see especially 60–63.

13. Mackenzie, 37; W. M. Stewart, *Keir Hardie,* 213.

14. Mitchell, 1:169, 198, 210.

15. Comments Walter Cameron (in *The Burgh of Fort William, 1875-1975,* 17), in tones that doubtless reflect Daniel McLeish's attitude toward the Barclays, "Middle Street and Low Street occupied the space between the Imperial Hotel and the north wall of the High Street buildings. The streets were very narrow, and there was a long line of narrow old buildings between the two streets or lanes. Among them were shops, dwellings, a blacksmith's forge and a house occupied by ten paupers and two children. Many of the houses . . . were quite good, but some were overcrowded and poor." McLeish would not have ignored the simple fact that one had to go *down* from High Street to Low Street!

CHAPTER TWO

1. G. F. Barbour, *The Life of Alexander Whyte,* 20.

2. Barbour, 32.

3. Checkland, *Scottish Banking: A History, 1695-1932,* 491–92.

4. A phrase made popular in the first chapter of Ian Maclaren's best-selling book *Beside the Bonnie Briar Bush.* The work carries the following lines as a frontispiece: "There grows a bonnie briar bush in our kail-yard, and white are the blossoms on't in our kail-yard." It is this book that gave rise to the so-called "Kailyard School" of Scottish writers: Maclaren (John Watson of Liverpool), Samuel Crockett of Penicuik, Annie S. Swan (Mrs. Burnet Smith), and, most notable of all, James M. Barrie. (An interesting connection existed between Mrs. Swan and A. S. Peake in Christina Hartley, of whom Peake wrote the official biography; see *Letters of Annie S. Swan,* 223.)

5. Checkland, 491.

6. Rae, *The Country Banker* (1885; rev. by E. Sykes, 1936), 199.

7. Checkland, 492. Thus, even on promotion, McLeish the lawyer would have been little impressed by WDB's prospects.

8. Riddell, *Adventures of an Obscure Victorian,* 178.

9. Barbour, 230.

10. Barbour, 377.

11. G. A. Smith, *Henry Drummond,* 115.

12. Quoted by F. F. Bruce in a letter to the author, 30 November 1981.

13. Smith, 298.

14. Professor Stalker reported well of Drummond's essay of 1873, in which the younger man adversely contrasted the science-oriented training of medical students with that of the theological (Smith, 50).

15. Smith, 340. On more than one occasion Willie stayed at hotels used by Drummond.

16. Smith, 132.

17. See J. T. Wilkinson, *Arthur Samuel Peake,* 195. C. Howard Hopkins, in his biography *John R. Mott, 1865-1955* (1979), suggests that the gulf was *widened* by the publication of *The Fundamentals,* 416.

18. Information supplied by Eric D. Hood, Publicity Director of the Bank of Scotland in a letter to the author, 12 December 1979.

19. Rees, *The British Isles: A Regional Geography.*

20. D. Omaid, *The Caithness Book,* xv.

21. May, *Paulus,* 72.

22. Barrie, quoted in Pawson's *Hand to the Plough,* 9.

23. Guttery, quoted by Pawson, 9.

24. Willie's writings are full of unacknowledged dependencies of this sort. Some have criticized him for an exaggerated usage of quotations, but he could scarcely help himself in this regard: to think of a subject, an incident, was to recall virtually without effort quotations, anecdotes, and the like, with which his mind naturally teemed.

25. *ToF,* 2, 4–6.

26. From minutes dated 11 December 1906. Italics mine.

27. D. S. Cairns, *Autobiography,* 126.

28. T. H. Darlow, *W. R. Nicoll,* 44.

29. W. R. Nicoll, *My Father,* 39.

30. According to minutes dated 26 February 1907.

31. *ToF,* 2.

32. Nicoll, 201.

33. He was also brought into regular contact with Browning through the lectures of A. J. Gossip, who quoted the poet ceaselessly. In 1975 Willie remarked, "there never was an examination into which I did not succeed in inserting quotations from Browning" (*ExpT,* 86 [1975]: 288)—a psychologically alert, if not calculating, attitude! (It was in this piece that he offered the information that his first review in the *Expository Times* appeared in 1933, in which he dealt with Browning's poetry. I have not been able to corroborate that comment from either the journal itself or the papers its publishers kindly placed at my disposal at the National Library of Scotland.) Willie's response to the poet was both admiring and critical—"deliberate awkwardness" was how he characterized it on one occasion (*ExpT,* 61 [1950]: 256—an essay reproduced in part in *Men and Affairs,* 27).

34. G. N. M. Collins, *Heritage of Our Fathers,* 93.

35. *Letters of Principal James Denney to His Family and Friends,* ed. W. R. Nicoll, 110.

36. Barbour, 431–33.

37. Smith, 462–63.

38. *ToF,* 3.

39. Georgeson, quoted in *The John O'Groats Journal,* 6 September 1912.

CHAPTER THREE

1. *ToF,* 6.

2. According to C. W. Hill, *Edwardian Scotland,* 43.

3. "A hoarse voice and a red face." In *The Journal of Laryngology and Otology*, October 1964.

4. "This Noisy Age," *BW*, 1 March 1962; reprinted in *Seen in the Passing* (subsequently entitled *In the Hands of God*), ed. Rita Snowden, 54-56.

5. *Through the Year with William Barclay*, ed. Denis Duncan, 41-42.

6. *ToF*, 3.

7. Smith, *John Buchan*, 43.

8. The amusing incident is recounted by R. J. Campbell in his autobiography, *A Spiritual Pilgrimage* (1916), 156.

9. *The Motherwell Times* gave no fewer than three full columns to reporting the sinking, 19 April 1912.

10. Winston Churchill, who influenced Willie by both his manly courage and his literary accomplishments, showed a profounder understanding of this disaster when he remarked, "All my world was very angry that the government should have allowed a bridge like this to tumble down" (*My Early Life*, 15). Willie was to espouse such a "secularist" view himself as an essential part of his theodicy.

11. *ToF*, 3.

12. See James B. Johnson's *Place Names of Scotland* (1934). This is the standard explanation, though Johnson notes that there may have been a connection via the Old English *woel*, indicating the genitive case—that is, "of the mother." In either case, the principal reference is to the Blessed Virgin of Catholic tradition.

13. According to G. F. Barbour in *The Life of Alexander Whyte*, 518.

14. According to Augustus Muir in *John White*, 166.

15. Muir, 466-71. This actually contains both the Articles as passed by Parliament and a first draft made by John White along with the "Proposals of the Minority." It was White's sterling contribution to reunion that caused the General Assembly of 1914 to be dubbed "White's Assembly" by *The British Weekly* (see Muir, 170).

16. Muir, 556.

17. *Letters of Principal James Denney to His Family and Friends*, 87.

18. Drummond, *The Greatest Thing in the World* (1904), 61.

19. *MT*, 30 October 1914.

20. *ToF*, 3: "At what age did you discover that your father was fallible?"

21. *ToF*, 3; Willie reflects in this denial the historical fact that lay preachers per se were not formally recognized as they are now. Barr, for example, writing as late as 1934 (in his book *The United Church of Scotland*) does not even refer to their existence. The true preaching of the Word, to use a phrase of technical evangelical importance (in line with the great Scottish tradition of a liberally educated ministry), is properly fulfilled by its accredited ministers—despite Barr's contrary statements (see page 31) on the true apostolic succession!

22. *MT*, 15 January 1915. *Dreich* is one of those lovely onomatopoeic Scottish expressions; it means "dull, miserable, discomfiting."

23. A typical Barclayan attitude. In emulating WDB, Willie raised it to the level of a principle in his work.

24. Mrs. Swan's household undoubtedly fared better than most in any case, not least because she and her husband were able to offer the military governor the comfort of their home (see Swan's *My Life*, 144).

25. "Captain Kidd," a.k.a. John Gilkinson.

26. *ToF*, 6.

27. We should not overlook the fact that Willie, in hindsight, recognized that above everything else it was "that whole life of community" (*ToF*, 7) that most impressed him. This is an admission of consummate importance: the single child, the loner ever wishful of company, looks back—to school, university, church, faculty—for their pleasures and enjoyments. It is an integral part of the Barclayan antisyzygy (see the Preface, n.9).

28. As reported in *MT*, 26 June 1914.

29. *MT*, 24 December 1915.

30. *ToF*, 6.

31. *MT*, 23 March 1917.

32. *ToF*, 8. Words—"the poor boy's arsenal," according to Saul Bellow—had gripped Alexander Whyte, from whom WDB gained his own passion. G. F. Barbour refers meaningfully to

Whyte's method of "penetrating to the bed-rock of the author's meaning or to 'the visual image' behind the words he used" (in *The Life of Alexander Whyte*, 331). "Meaning" and "visual image" are of supreme importance here. "I am not a theologian," declared Willie to Canon Wallace Bird of the Guild of Health; "I am a dictionary." The subtitle of Willie's *New Testament Words* might be *A Companion to the Daily Study Bible*, such is its significance for him—the *only* book which he himself suggested (to Shaun Herron of *The British Weekly*). Never were Sir Edwyn Hoskyns' words better fulfilled: "Bury yourself in a dictionary and come up in the presence of God." But to raise this point of words and meanings is to divulge the fact that Willie never shared the dramatic step forward of the twentieth century to that perception of language in which words no longer possess (in Bertrand Russell's phrase) the "transparency of language." For Willie, language retained the surface (superficial) connotation it had possessed hitherto: a thing *is* what it is called, and vice versa. He saw little or no problem in the relationships among language, meaning, and truth; the problems of linguists and philosophers of language left him cold. This is one of the reasons he maintained the importance of feeling and located belief in the area of the spirit (see *ToF*, 28–29) rather than of the mind. But oversimplification of his attitude is dangerous; a more extended consideration of it must be left to another occasion.

33. T. H. Darlow, *W. R. Nicoll*, 284.

34. G. F. Barbour, *The Life of Alexander Whyte*, 3.

35. *MT*, 29 May 1925.

36. *SSST*, 22 October 1933, 279. I have grave doubts as to whether Willie was in fact the author of this piece.

37. Colville, *The Churchillians*, 111.

38. Barbour, 38.

39. According to the author of a retrospective review of his schoolwork appearing in *MT*, 13 June 1924.

40. *MT*, 2 July 1920.

41. Rev. Mackintosh was buried near the McLeish grave at Fort William, Proverbs 10:7 being inscribed on his tombstone (in Gaelic): "The memory of the righteous is a blessing." His parishioners ensured the continuity of his memory by naming the church after him: the John Mackintosh Memorial Church, which overlooks the High Street.

42. *MT*, 25 November 1921.

43. *MT*, 13 May 1921.

44. Connor promised he could produce twenty thousand supporters in the streets if need be (*MT*, 22 July 1921).

45. *BW*, 4 August 1955.

46. Black, in a letter to the author, 17 May 1982.

47. *ToF*, 9.

48. See *C. S. Lewis: A Biography*, by R. L. Green and Walter Hooper (1974), 40ff. Cf. *Surprised by Joy*, 127ff.

49. *The Dalzielian*, June 1925, 4.

50. *The Dalzielian*, December 1924, 3.

51. See *MT*, 31 August 1921.

52. *The Dalzielian*, June 1924, 4.

53. Black, in a letter to the author, 12 August 1982.

54. The incident is described in *BW*, 12 October 1961; Willie treats *kalos* and *agathos* fully in *New Testament Words*, 152ff.

55. Begbie, quoted by Clyde Binfield in *George Williams and the YMCA*, 5. In his magisterial book *John R. Mott, 1865-1955: A Biography*, C. Howard Hopkins quotes Morse as saying that Mott was "the lineal descendant of Henry Drummond" (214).

56. *BW*, 16 June 1960.

57. That is to say, unity in diversity, *not* in uniformity.

58. *Oxford Dictionary of the Christian Church*, s.v. "YMCA."

59. G. A. Smith, *Henry Drummond*, 455. The Boys' Brigade had been founded in 1883 by William Smith of Caithness, who was known to WDB (thus accounting for his special interest in the group). Several similar groups had preceded it, however—not least among which was the Anglesea Boys' Brigade, as has been emphasized by the highly reputed missionary doctor, much loved by the Barclays, Sir Wilfred Grenfell (see his book *A Labrador Doctor*, 51).

60. Barclay, *God's Men, God's Church, and God's Life* (1952/53), 1.

61. See A. L. Drummond and J. Bulloch's *The Church in Late Victorian Scotland: 1874-1900*, 239–40.

62. Lumsden, in a letter to the author, 11 February 1980. When William McWhinney died in April 1980, *The Motherwell Times* referred to these individuals as members of "the famous Barclay Dozen." Walter Henderson later organized reunion meetings for them. Willie's comment in *ToF* (7) implies that they had met continuously over the years, but apart from an abortive attempt in 1926, they did not begin to do so till 1969.

63. *ToF,* 22.

64. *ToF,* 7.

65. Letter from Willie to Ferguson, 27 May 1971.

66. Eng. Lit., "the delight of a life-time" (which did not fail to include modern fiction, a daily diet of which he took "religiously") had been displaced as his favorite subject by Greek, thanks to "Monkey Brand" Paterson (*ToF,* 9). Willie used to remark that he was the best-read theologian of the worst possible literature, another thing he had in common with A. S. Peake.

67. Galloway, Introduction in *The Lord Is My Shepherd,* by William Barclay, 10.

68. *ToF,* 20.

69. Galloway, 10.

70. According to Mr. Henderson, the first recipient of the prize; he states that WDB informed him "with a smile" of his reason for delaying its implementation at its presentation (in a letter to the author, 20 January 1982).

71. *MT,* 21 August 1925.

CHAPTER FOUR

1. In this and the following sections I follow Frank W. Provan's essay "A Historical Sketch of the University," in *The Five Hundred-Year Book of the University of Glasgow,* 3–9.

2. In *ToF* (page 12) he writes of his bad handwriting on one occasion necessitating his reading it to his professor; but Macaulay, he acknowledges, was overfastidious.

3. Taken from Phillimore's obituary in *The Glasgow University Magazine* of 1926/27, 89. Some of his poetic pieces have been preserved in *University Verses, 1910-27.* His "Ballads of Bricks without Straw" therein (110–11) splendidly makes fun of *The Glasgow University Magazine* (and perhaps some of his academic colleagues), but also highlights its great influence:

> Blow, Triton, if upon the rocks thou find
> Themes to be trite on, blow thy wreathed horn!
> Alas, He'll try't on us with screeds outworn,
> In vain he whets his wits with many a gem
> Of purest Razorine . . . Black Monday morn . . .
> You really can't refuse the G.U.M.

4. Three hundred voices of one of the oldest *Scottish* universities singing "Ye Mariners of *England*"! Preposterous, but true. The song was originally written by J. W. Callcott of London, a leading exponent of the "glee tradition" (which suited the young Barclay's style ideally). The song that was sung by the proud Glaswegians was not Callcott's original, however, but a rewritten version by Alexander Campbell of Perthshire—the original home of Daniel McLeish. Campbell, a former pupil and close friend of Sir Walter Scott, went on to render great service to the Gaelic by collecting Old Gaelic songs from around northwest Scotland (an area in which the mature McLeish served a similar purpose by collecting Gaelic stories, as we have seen). Their interrelated activities constitute a good example of the sorts of movements that undergird the whole of Scottish history and the history of the Barclay family in particular.

5. *ToF,* 10.

6. Raleigh, quoted by "J. S. P." in *GUM* (1926/27), 89.

7. *ToF,* 11.

8. Willie, in the Trinity church magazine, January 1934 (i.e., just ten months after he had been inducted there); Willie quotes Davies ten times in the Daily Study Bible.

9. Dixon was not Professor of English and Rhetoric as Willie suggests in *ToF* (page 10).

10. A. L. Drummond and J. Bulloch, *The Church in Late Victorian Scotland: 1874-1900,* 220.

11. Keats, quoted in Dixon's *Tragedy,* 22.

12. *ToF,* 6. Willie goes on to say, with great poignancy, that "Nothing was ever the same when she was not there to tell it to."

13. Heron, *Record Apart* (1974), 136.

14. The apt phrase appears in the obituary of A. A. Bowman in *The College Courant,* 1948/49. Dorothy Emmet, in Ironmonger's fine biography of William Temple, states that "his zest for *synthesis* was reinforced by his gift for clarity of exposition and rotundity of statement" (522); she links this synthesizing zeal to the *Logos* of Christianity. We shall see that Willie was also to put exceptional emphasis on the *logos* doctrine (partly a result of his "secular" work on Greek authors). His writings were similarly "rotund" at a different level.

15. See *ToF,* 4.

16. Gallacher, *Revolt on the Clyde* (1936). Gallacher was actually in prison at the time. A whole decade was overpowered by this struggle in the west.

17. *ToF,* 5.

18. *MT,* 5 July 1929.

19. *DSB: The Gospel of Matthew,* 1: 109 (Matt. 5:9).

20. *YMCA Report: 1961,* 44.

21. Whyte, quoted in G. F. Barbour's *Alexander Whyte,* 382.

22. T. H. Darlow, *W. R. Nicoll,* 83–84.

23. Knight, *What Next?* (1980), 20.

24. CSF minutes of 17 February 1927. Italics theirs. The assumption of difficulty in *their* speakers working with others is fallacious. Few objected to doing so; most simply sought to serve the gospel and their fellow men in a spirit of humility and self-sacrifice wherever they could.

25. *GUM* (1928/29), 243.

26. I am grateful to Professor F. F. Bruce for this information regarding the matter (letter to the author, 15 December 1979); corroboration can be found in John Laing's autobiography, *No Mere Chance,* 26–27.

27. *ToF,* 96.

28. In his *Commentary on the Bible* (1919). Peake had himself contributed the commentary on Isaiah, in preparation for the volume on the prophet he was preparing for the International Critical Commentary series—sadly, a volume he never completed.

29. Black, in a letter to the author, 12 August 1982.

30. Willie, *God's Plan for Men,* 38.

31. Hardie, quoted by W. M. Stewart in *Keir Hardie,* 130; he goes on to extend this to the doctrine of nationalization, of which Willie had little to say.

32. It should be remembered that Hardie's socialism arose directly out of his Evangelical Union involvements, as his friend Frank Smith's endeavors arose out of his Salvation Army work (see Stewart, 111). It is not often remembered that Hardie, even when a busy M.P., found time to give of his energies to various SA centers.

33. See Potter's *Victorian Courtship,* 96.

34. Potter, 41.

35. Cairns, *Autobiography,* 171.

36. Marshall, quoted in Potter's *Victorian Courtship,* 61.

37. Watson, quoted in W. R. Nicoll's *Life of Ian MacLaren,* 276.

38. *BW,* 5 May 1960.

39. Martin, "Barclay's Humanity and Humility," in *William Barclay: The Plain Uncommon Man,* ed. R. D. Kernohan, 50–69. It was originally published in the American magazine *Our Church,* July 1979. Curiously, he discusses Willie's humanity in three short paragraphs, ignoring any sort of temporal or developmental perspective.

CHAPTER FIVE

1. *ToF,* 11.

2. *ToF,* 4.

3. *ToF,* 3.

4. Bruce, in a letter to the author, 15 December 1979.

5. C. Howard Hopkins, *John R. Mott, 1865-1955* (1979). David Cairns warned the American movement against the danger of sinking "from a religious to a moral, philanthropic and humanitarian level" (*Autobiography,* 416)—precisely the opposite way!

6. "Experience" is much emphasized by Leith (see *An Introduction to Reformed Theology*, 126–27) and receives a similar emphasis from Willie.

7. *ToF*, 12.

8. *ToF*, 13.

9. *ToF*, 14.

10. *ToF*, 13.

11. *ToF*, 13.

12. Cairns, *Autobiography*, 198.

13. See *ToF*, 10.

14. Dow, *No Better than I Should Be* (1975), 117–18.

15. Arnot, in an interview with the author, 18 March 1980.

16. *ToF*, 6. In fact, two "notes" are hereafter sounded: one of comfort, which Willie ever extolled as an indispensable element of any sermon worthy of the name; and the second of the nature of reality, the bleak human condition, and its influence on understanding God's "ordering" of life, which is bound up with the "laws of nature," and so on.

17. From Charles Lamb's "On the Death of His Mother."

CHAPTER SIX

1. *RP*, 13 January 1933.

2. Burleigh, *The Minister's Manual* (1947), 58.

3. According to figures produced by the local Labour Exchange and recorded in the town council's minutes.

4. Stevenson, in an interview with the author, 30 December 1979.

5. See Willie's *Ethics in a Permissive Society*, 99; see also *Through the Year with William Barclay*, ed. Denis Duncan, 42.

6. Kernohan, *Scotland's Life and Work*, 137.

7. On the other hand, Willie also described Macgregor as "a difficult character . . . a saturnine character . . . a man of terrible silences" (*ToF*, 13).

8. Willie, "The WPB," in *Seen in the Passing*, ed. Rita Snowden (1966), 83–84.

9. Cox, *The Principles and Practices of the Church of Scotland* (1976), 56.

10. *RP*, 26 May 1933.

11. *RP*, 23 June 1933.

CHAPTER SEVEN

1. Bowers, in a letter to the author, 11 March 1980.

2. The following information is taken from a letter from Mrs. Livingstone (née Gillespie) to the author, 6 October 1980 and subsequent conversations. I am particularly grateful to her for access to some excellent articles she wrote on her family history for the Dundonald church magazine.

3. According to S. Simpson in his *Traditions of the Covenanters*, 396.

4. See MacVicar's *Salt in My Porridge*, 10, 60–61, and subsequent volumes of reminiscences.

5. Arnot in a letter to the author, 18 March 1980, and subsequent conversation.

6. Willie, "Life's Greatest Blessing," *BW*, 16 December 1965. In *ToF* he adds, "She is no weakling as a critic. . . . My wife has all our married life kept me from pride. . . . She has all the qualities which I do not possess" (15–16).

7. Houston, in communication with the author (through the good offices of his minister, the former being unwell at the time of writing).

8. Information taken from the minutes of Trinity College for 11 October 1929.

9. *ToF*, 117. Willie shared the belief of this myth only as a "vivid pictorial form"—that is to say, illustratively, not essentially. The pictorial element, as opposed to the power of abstract reasoning ("I cannot think in abstractions at all; I think in pictures" [*ToF*, 27]), was predominant throughout the whole body of his theology, in which he sought to communicate more a poetic form of reality than its essence.

10. Dow, in a letter to the author, 12 February 1980.

11. Doyle, in a letter to the author, 13 February 1980.

12. Smith, in a letter to the author, 18 February 1980, and subsequent conversation.

13. *ToF,* 31. Elsewhere he blamed committee meetings for the downgrading of preaching he had witnessed.

14. Charles Raven, *A Wanderer's Way,* 81. The whole chapter "An Office in Liverpool" is a brilliant and moving description of the impact the "plainness" of Liverpool made on that "spoiled child of fortune," as he described himself—a characterization suggesting that his upbringing was not greatly different from Willie's; Willie actually met Raven at Liverpool in 1930, when he attended a Student Christian Movement conference there.

15. *RP,* 13 October 1933.

16. Books such as *Letters to the Seven Churches* (1957), *The Plain Man Looks at the Beatitudes* (1963), and *The Plain Man Looks at the Lord's Prayer* (1964), all of which were first published serially in *The British Weekly.*

17. Willie, *Letters to the Seven Churches,* 53.

18. *ToF,* 27–28: "I tend to run away from things, and to avoid all unpleasantness. . . . I have often . . . failed to intervene."

19. *RP,* 3 November 1933.

20. *BOC,* 1936.

21. Willie, in *The History of Renfrew Trinity Church: 1862-1962,* ed. A. M. Ferguson.

22. *BW,* 10 February 1966.

23. *ToF,* 69. He goes on to say that it was a feeling of *responsibility* that weighed on his mind; *duty* was ever an essential feature of his ethical consciousness.

24. *RP,* 19 January 1934.

25. *ToF,* 17.

26. See *ExpT,* 73 (1962): 383.

27. *ToF,* 16.

28. "Ministerial Miniature," *RP,* 7 December 1934. Gossip emphasized the risk the church took in accepting a minister "without assistantship experience." Willie contradicts that point when he refers to his student assistantship under Duncan Blair—"a mystic, who could walk in realms which to the rest of us were shut" (*Fishers of Men,* 111–12).

29. Lees, in a conversation with the author, 8 February 1980.

CHAPTER EIGHT

1. See the February 1935 issue.

2. Grey, in a letter to the author, 3 March 1980.

3. Braidwood, in a letter to the author, 13 February 1980.

4. Mechie, *Trinity College, Glasgow: The Centenary Volume, 1856-1956,* 33.

5. From the minutes of 27 February 1935; the title *Moderator* was commonly used in reference to the minister to underscore his role as a *primus inter pares* in the session.

6. *RP,* 29 March 1935.

7. See the June 1935 issue.

8. *MT,* 10 May 1935.

9. *GH,* 9 May 1935.

10. *ToF,* 2.

11. There were also some savings, and a modest amount of cash. Willie acted as executor of his father's estate, and was the sole beneficiary.

12. *ToF,* 4.

13. Willie, in *The Lord's Supper,* 112.

14. See *BW,* 6 January 1955.

15. See the June 1935 issue. Willie was no newcomer to the "elite society" of the east; he took holidays there (at North Berwick and Longniddry, the latter well-known by railway enthusiasts of the time) with his parents, and was to return there with his own children quite soon.

16. Julian, in a letter to the author, 21 February 1980.

17. See the session minutes for 23 June 1935.

18. Borthwick, in a letter to the author, 14 February 1980.

19. By "MD" in *RP,* 7 May 1937.

20. *RP,* 28 January 1938.
21. *RP,* 30 December 1938.
22. See *RP,* 17 February 1939.
23. See *RP,* 10 March 1939.

CHAPTER NINE

1. *ToF,* 96.
2. *ToF,* 79. It was the fifth of eleven points (!) in Willie's "certain conclusions about preaching."
3. "When I asked what book, he said, 'Need you ask? There is but one'" (J. G. Lockhart, *The Life of Sir Walter Scott,* 5: 423).
4. On this point, see my essay "Barclay's Biblicality: Mode and Method," in *William Barclay: Plain Uncommon Man,* ed. R. D. Kernohan, 76–99.
5. *ToF,* 23.
6. See Falconer's *Message, Media and Mission,* 101.
7. Mackenzie, in a letter to the author, 31 August 1981.
8. *ToF,* 96. The first independently recorded preaching that Willie did was actually at the Baptist Church in Motherwell, on 17 June 1927.
9. *RP,* 25 January 1935.
10. See *RP,* 12 April 1935.
11. *RP,* 20 November 1936.
12. See *RP,* 15 October 1937.
13. This attitude was considerably more characteristic of the Free Church than of the Church of Scotland itself, notwithstanding Barr's bold involvement in mainline politics. Willie became much more politically aware and involved in the 1960s, as we shall see, but throughout his career the real world of action attracted him more than a simple "theoretical" understanding of ethics and conduct.
14. *RP,* 5 November 1937.
15. His emphasis on *usefulness* and *uselessness* stemmed from his work ethic, and his related principle of efficiency/economy: it was not enough to *be;* one had to *do*—that is, make a contribution, realize an opportunity, attain a goal. "It is again and again New Testament teaching that *uselessness invites disaster*" (*DSB: The Gospel of Matthew,* 2: 183; italics his). Significantly, Willie stresses that it is action that can "justify the simple fact of [man's] existence."
16. *RP,* 5 November 1937. Twenty-six years later, in *Christian Discipline in Society Today,* he reaffirmed this central pillar of his personal faith: it was the reason for his being a minister of the gospel (see especially page 41).
17. According to J. Maxwell Blair, in his editorial prefacing the series (*SSST,* January 1940, 1).
18. That Willie should have been chosen to occupy Mackintosh's place shows that A. B. Macaulay was not alone in perceiving that, apart from particular linguistic skills, his natural bent lay in communicating doctrine, especially practical doctrine. We shall see that he struggled against involvement in primary biblical studies for just this reason.
19. According to Laurence Porter, *The Evangelical Quarterly,* 34 (July 1962): 172.
20. "What Jesus says, God says. Jesus reveals to man the illimitable, the unconquerable, the literally infinite love of God" (*ToF,* 51).
21. He unequivocally stated that "God is eternally Father, Son and Holy Spirit" (*DSB: Acts,* 12). In later life he moved away from a full asseveration of this doctrine, accepting the modalism of Sabellius as "half-true" and boldly asserting that the doctrine of the trinity was "a transcript of experience" (in a letter to Moira Grego, 22 September 1975). I shall deal more fully with this matter elsewhere.

CHAPTER TEN

1. *RP,* 22 September 1939.
2. *RP,* 10 November 1939.
3. *RP,* 27 October 1939.

4. *RP,* 24 November 1939.
5. See the December 1939 issue of the church magazine.
6. *RP,* 22 December 1939.
7. George VI, quoted in Alan Moorhead's *Churchill: A Pictorial Biography.*
8. *RP,* 2 February 1940.
9. According to Smith, in a letter to the author, 13 February 1980, and subsequent conversation.
10. February 1940 issue of the church magazine.
11. *RP,* 23 February 1940.
12. In the issue of 8 March 1940.
13. See the SSSU's commemorative booklet *One Hundred and Fifty Years of the Sunday School: 1797-1947,* 15.
14. See the executive minutes for 18 March 1940.
15. *SSST* (1940), 138–40.
16. *Through the Year with William Barclay,* ed. Denis Duncan, 96.
17. *The Memoirs of Field Marshall Montgomery* (1958), 251. What Drummond did for Christianity via the categories of "natural law" Willie was wont to do for exhortation using the terminology and attitudes of war—pacifist that he was!
18. See the August 1940 issue. *The Scottish Primary Quarterly* was a sister publication to *SSST.*
19. Colville, *The Churchillians,* 53.
20. According to the church magazine of June 1940.
21. In *RP,* 23 August 1940.
22. *RP,* 23 August 1940.
23. See Lord Moran's *Churchill,* 74.
24. According to the September 1940 issue of Trinity's church magazine.
25. As reported in *RP,* 15 November 1940.
26. The author is E. W. Wilcox.
27. According to Mrs. Wilson, in a letter to the author, 18 February 1980.
28. In *RP,* 19 September 1941.
29. *RP,* 10 October 1941.
30. From the September 1941 issue.
31. From the December 1941 issue of the church magazine.
32. Churchill, quoted by Moran, 26.
33. See the session minutes for 6 March 1942.
34. Moran, 38.
35. *RP,* 13 November 1942.
36. According to Mrs. J. Macfarlane, in a letter to the author, 14 February 1980.
37. Willie, in a letter to Braidwood, 11 October 1943.
38. *RP,* 26 November 1943.
39. *RP,* 10 December 1943.
40. See the session minutes of 4 February 1942.
41. See the session minutes of 3 May 1944.
42. See the session minutes of 31 May 1944.
43. See *ToF,* 71.
44. Moran, 130.
45. Willie, in a letter to Braidwood, 1 January 1945.
46. Swan, *My Life,* 270–71.
47. *RP,* 26 January 1945.
48. See Colville, 39.
49. See Moran, 251.
50. Willie, in a letter to Braidwood, 22 July 1945.
51. Willie, in a letter to Braidwood, 15 July 1945.
52. Willie, in a letter to Braidwood, 22 July 1945.

CHAPTER ELEVEN

1. White, quoted by Augustus Muir in *John White,* 348.
2. Davidson, quoted in *RP,* 13 November 1942.

3. See *RP,* 24 December 1943.

4. *BW,* 10 March 1944.

5. See *RP,* 23 April 1944.

6. King, in *SSST,* July 1943, 122.

7. *SSST,* August 1943, 138.

8. In the minutes of the Presbytery of Paisley for 26 October 1943.

9. According to the minutes of the Presbytery of Paisley for 5 May 1944.

10. Willie, in a letter to Braidwood, 1 January 1945.

11. Blair, *SSST,* May 1945, 1.

12. Willie, in a letter to Braidwood, 15 July 1945, written immediately on his return from Aberdeen—his tenth letter that evening.

13. See J. W. D. Smith's *Religious and Secular Education,* 1.

14. *SSST,* September 1945, 166.

15. Willie, in a letter to Braidwood, 15 July 1945.

16. Inge, quoted in Adam Fox's *Dean Inge,* 70.

17. Willie, in a letter to Braidwood, 15 July 1945.

18. Willie, in a letter to Braidwood, 24 December 1945.

19. Trinity session minutes, 12 December 1945.

20. Trinity session minutes, 3 April 1946.

21. Willie, in a letter to Braidwood, 23 June 1946.

22. Graham, in an interview with the author, May 1982.

23. Willie, in a letter to Braidwood, 23 June 1946.

24. Willie, in a letter to Braidwood, 11 April 1946.

25. Willie, *God's Law, God's Servants, and God's Men* (1954), 96.

26. According to the archive of Glasgow University 49.8.756 (1944).

27. Willie, in the December 1946 issue of the Trinity church magazine.

28. *RP,* 3 January 1947.

CHAPTER TWELVE

1. See A. L. Drummond and J. Bulloch's *The Church in Late Victorian Scotland: 1874–1900,* 195.

2. See Augustus Muir's *John White,* 71.

3. Willie, in a letter to Edwin W. Stock, Jr., 28 August 1946.

4. Willie, in a letter to Braidwood, 11 November 1946.

5. Willie, in a letter to Braidwood, January 1947.

6. *ToF,* 16.

7. Willie, in a letter to Rita Snowden, 22 June 1956.

8. Willie, in a letter to Braidwood, 11 November 1946.

9. Muir, *John White,* 392.

10. Muir, 394.

11. Muir, 396.

12. Muir, 396–97.

13. Willie, in a letter to Braidwood, January 1947.

14. Willie, in a letter to Braidwood, 9 April 1956.

15. Willie, in a letter to Braidwood, 1 January 1949.

16. Willie, *God's Law, God's Service, and God's Men* (1954), 78.

17. Neil Alexander, "Portrait of a Scholar and Colleague," in *William Barclay: The Plain Uncommon Man,* ed. R. D. Kernohan, 100–115.

18. Galloway, in a conversation with the author, 9 December 1980.

19. See Gasque's *Sir William M. Ramsay: Archeologist and New Testament Scholar* (1966). Gasque significantly uncovers "the real heart of Sir William Ramsay" (60) when he directs his reader's attention to a sermon Ramsay preached at the Moody Bible Institute, Chicago, which reminds us of other things he had in common with Willie beyond a refreshing eclecticism and tolerance. Professor Bruce took pains to observe that though Ramsay was a Glaswegian by birth, all his academic work took place at Aberdeen (in a letter to the author, 11 December 1982). Shades of the old rivalry here!

20. See the *Dictionary of National Biography, 1933-1940,* s.v. "Ramsay, William M."

21. *Educational Ideals in the Ancient World,* 78.

22. Macgregor, *Persons and Ideals* (1939), 41–48.

23. In a letter to the author, 14 February 1980.

24. Burns, in a letter to the author, 22 February 1980.

25. *BW,* 25 August 1960; reprinted in *Seen in the Passing,* ed. Rita Snowden, 130–31.

26. *ToF,* 100. It is Kennedy to whom Willie refers here, though he does not mention him by name.

27. See F. W. Dillistone's biography *Charles Raven,* 284ff. Dillistone notes that Raven owed "an incalculable debt" to the great Scottish divines of the early twentieth century, as well as to earlier figures such as Thomas Erskine and Henry Drummond (who motivated him to explore the natural sciences).

28. See *The New Testament in Historical and Contemporary Perspective* (ed. Barclay and Anderson), viii.

29. *ToF,* 14.

30. *ToF,* 24. It is relevant to note here that this willingness to be directed by others is specifically linked to his feeling that he had a second-class mind, and that this is best expressed through his gift for popularizing—"the only claim I can make" (25). It is not a view his professors would have confirmed.

31. *New Testament in Historical and Contemporary Perspective,* vii.

32. See *Trinity College, Glasgow: The Centenary Volume, 1856-1956,* 45.

33. See the minutes of Trinity College, Glasgow, 12 December 1947.

34. See *BW,* 5 September 1963; reprinted in *Seen in the Passing,* 31–34.

35. *ToF,* 29.

36. *DSB: The Gospel of Mark.*

37. *DSB: The Letters of James and Peter.* Italics mine.

38. Baxter, in a letter to Kate Barclay, 25 January 1978. Willie himself used the phrase at this time to emphasize his lowly estate.

39. Cardus, *Autobiography,* 83.

40. Martin, "Barclay's Humanity and Humility," in *William Barclay: The Plain Uncommon Man,* 66.

41. Alexander, in *William Barclay: The Plain Uncommon Man,* 109.

42. See John T. Wilkinson's *Arthur Samuel Peake: A Biography,* 74. We might note in passing that Peake, who stood for "the unison of scholarship and evangelism" (57), was himself greatly influenced by Drummond (23–24), not least in his manner of illustration: "wonderfully fertile . . . well-nigh perfect." It is surely significant that Willie, whose theology was genuinely mimetic, should have these two as his spiritual forebears.

43. *ToF,* 82.

44. See my essay "Barclay's Biblicality: Mode and Method," in *William Barclay: The Plain Uncommon Man,* 82.

45. *ToF,* 97. Professor Bruce records the incident when the (Brethren) missionary Alec Clifford returned home from service in Argentina and spoke to Martyn Lloyd-Jones. He mentioned that the two authors from whom he got most help in his work were Willie and F. F. Bruce. "Barclay!" exclaimed the defender of the faith of Westminster Chapel. "Barclay's an enemy of the faith!"

46. Macgregor, 20.

47. *This Is My Job,* no. 7, 19 July 1960.

48. Ibid. Italics mine.

49. The New Testament was published in 1941; the whole Bible appeared in 1948.

50. *The English Bible,* 185.

51. *The Church of Scotland Handbook* (1933), 78, vow 3.

52. In 1977, against the tide of general religious opinion, Willie was to assert that "what is wanted is not a new language but a new method" (*A Life of Christ,* Foreword).

53. That being the seventeen-volume Daily Study Bible.

54. Strachan was a graduate of Aberdeen University, where he had studied with Charles Duthie, William Duff Hardy, and F. F. Bruce—all of them fellow travelers with Willie. Strachan's friendship is especially interesting, for he was the great-grandson of General Booth, founder of the Salvation Army. Another link with Willie consists in the fact that the present bishop of Manchester (scene of his great-grandfather's upbringing and early life) is the Very Reverend Stanley Booth-Clibborn, Strachan's first cousin.

55. Strachan, in a letter to the author, 8 January 1980.

56. Bearing in mind his willingness to be directed by others, we should not forget that Willie was a man inspired with a great sense of *duty*; his work, both in its range and in its persistence, stemmed from this sense of obligation, as did his ethical understanding. It is not irrelevant to recall here that one of his favorite Gilbert and Sullivan operas, *The Pirates of Penzance,* has as its subtitle "The Slave of Duty"! Willie himself sometimes displayed the characteristics of "the very model of a modern Major-General"! (shades of Colonel Daniel McLeish?)

57. In May 1948.

58. Miss I. Myers, in a letter to the author, 10 February 1980. Willie informed her that his favorite hymn was "Work, for the Night Is Coming," adding typically that he would rather burn out than rust out.

59. In an editorial comment in *SSST,* January 1948.

60. *SSST,* September 1945, 166. "None has been more willing than he to further the work of Christian education through the Sunday School," Mr. Mills explained.

61. *SSST,* February 1947, 42.

62. Hubery introduced his methods in *The Experiential Approach to Christian Education* in 1960; since then he has produced a series of books, the most relevant in this context being *The Teaching Methods of Jesus* (1970).

63. Willie, in *SSST,* September 1945, 166.

64. The report of the Deliverance is dated 10 October 1948.

65. See the minutes of the SSSU Lessons Panel, 15–17 April 1947.

66. See *BW,* 10 April 1947.

67. *God's Plan for Men,* 84.

68. See *SSST,* April 1949, 103.

69. George Mills thanked Willie publicly in a fulsome piece entitled "Our Editor" (*SSST,* September 1949, 251). He enumerated the services Willie had rendered "that have enriched Sunday School work throughout Scotland" and disclosed the concern of his friends that Willie's physical powers should be impaired by his eager willingness to "give himself so ungrudgingly to others." To this Willie replied in an article entitled "Hail and Farewell" (as he had on leaving Dalziel High School), expressing regret at leaving such influential and interesting work, thanking everyone (not least his printers, McCorquodale & Company, whom he was shortly to meet under another hat), and wishing God's blessing on them all and their work.

70. In point of fact, he became a co-opted member of the Executive Board of the SSSU shortly after resigning this post, and he remained an active member in that capacity till 1955. Once again the General Assembly received a Deliverance from its Youth Committee acknowledging "Mr. Barclay's services to the religious instruction of youth," which it found "too numerous to mention." His successor, Mrs. McMurray, recorded the gratitude of the SSSU in her editorial (of June 1955, 176) on behalf of "teachers of senior classes all over Scotland and far beyond." She felt that they would "feel that they had lost 'a guide, philosopher and friend' whom it was an inspiration to meet each week." She highlighted four aspects of his work especially: the provision he made each month of "a wealth of scholarship," and his gift for memorable illustration, which "revealed the wideness of his interests, his understanding of human nature, his prodigious memory"; but, she continued, "the notes have been more than scholarly, more than comprehensive, they have been the result of spiritual insight. They have dealt in worthy fashion with the deep things of our faith." Finally, she noticed the practicality of his notes and work, reminding her readers of one of his favorite illustrations—of the telephone operator who says "Trying to connect you" and then effaces himself. "A magnificent and costly contribution," she concluded.

71. *ToF,* 111.

72. *BW,* 28 September 1961; reprinted in *Through the Year with William Barclay,* ed. Denis Duncan, 82.

CHAPTER THIRTEEN

1. *BW,* 4 July 1976.

2. See Augustus Muir's *John White,* 420.

3. Muir, 421.

4. Stephen Neill, *Men of Unity,* 90.

5. Neill, 148. The full history of the ecumenical movement is well recorded in the magisterial two-volume work *History of the Ecumenical Movement,* by Neill and R. Rouse. Willie played

virtually no part in this movement, remaining to the end quite unconvinced of the value of efforts to unify elements of diversity he believed to be advantageous to the church. Nevertheless, he was always conscious of it in the background of his work, and he did seek to advance the ecumenical spirit in nonadministrative and nondirectional ways. Reconciliation was always important to him, as were tolerance, mutual understanding, and a spiritual laissez-faire attitude.

6. For example, on freedom he asserts apropos Galatians 5:13 that "we are free, but our freedom loves its neighbour as itself" (see *DSB: Galatians and Ephesians*); and he baldly denounces apartheid in *DSB: The Gospel of John*, 1: 159. He was never prouder (despite being humbled) than when he stood in John Knox's pulpit in St. Andrews with Bishop Agwu Oji of Nigeria (see *BW*, 5 August 1965).

7. See Eberhard Busch's *Karl Barth*, 347.

8. David Edwards has brilliantly described the changes taking place in religious thinking in its broader aspects in his book *Religion and Change* (1969), which concentrates on the question of secularization.

9. See the Trinity College, Glasgow, faculty minutes for 14 April 1947.

10. See *The Witness*, May 1975, 167–68.

11. Willie, in a letter to Braidwood, 1 January 1949. Willie actually informed his friend that it was Oxford University that did him the honor of election, but this was incorrect; it was in fact the SNTS itself that elected him (along with F. F. Bruce), though it did then meet at Oxford (from 1948 to 1951). Willie referred to it as an "August [sic] body [that] meets every September in Oxford."

12. Mitton, in a letter to the author, 15 December 1979.

13. This is a notable Reformed emphasis, stemming from Luther's "What is theology but grammar applied to the text?" It is his unwillingness to go beyond this that must account for his frequent disavowal of being a theologian to students and friends alike. In this sense his theology is best described as prosthenic.

14. Davidson, *A Commentary on the Book of Job*, v–vi. This was one of the volumes Willie studied under "Johnny" M'Fadyen in 1930.

15. A. S. Peake, *A Guide to Bible Study*, 39.

16. A. L. Drummond and J. Bulloch, *The Church in Late Victorian Scotland: 1874-1900*, 274.

17. *ExpT*, 68 (1957): 262–63, and *New Testament Studies*, 9 (1962): 70–72.

18. Willie, in a letter to Clarence Finlayson, confirmed in a postcard to the author, 30 April 1980. On Willie's death, the Consul General of Greece, His Excellency George Tombazis, wrote a personal note to Kate, in the course of which he said, "There are few indeed who can portray Greek thought in the English language with clarity, and in this field he excelled" (30 January 1978).

19. Allan Galloway, *The College Courant* (1974), 30.

20. Willie, in a letter to Brenda McGilliard, 5 May 1970.

21. Willie, in a letter to Braidwood, 1 January 1949.

22. *BW*, 4 August 1950.

23. *ToF*, 13.

24. Lees, in a letter to the author, 16 January 1980.

25. *The College Courant* (1974), 20–21.

26. Published in 1977 by A. R. Mowbrays and Westminster Press. Explanatory comments were added by William Purcell of Worcester against the wishes of the editor.

27. *The Journal of the College of Preachers*, November 1979, 53.

28. *The Officer*, September 1978.

29. We should not forget, though Willie would not express it so, that *Angst*—anxiety, dread—is at the very center of the philosophical preoccupation. I know of no direct references to Kierkegaard in his writings, but Willie was no stranger to the existential anxiety of which the Dane wrote so pervasively (as witness his references to fear in times of war and cold war). Similarly, there are very few references to Tillich from his pen, but he was aware of and extolled the need for a Christianized concept of "the courage to be."

30. Hobbes, quoted by Willie (without attribution) in *DSB: The Gospel of Luke*, 66. Stevenson's "glorious morning face" was directly linked to his "great task of happiness," a task Willie was glad to make his own—hence the title of his very first article, "The Secret of Happiness." The happiness motif runs large throughout his writings. Nevertheless, he was aware of the instability of happiness, of its being subjected to chance (see *DSB: The Gospel of Matthew*, 1: 89, where the link is

specifically made). Simone de Beauvoir has observed that the ability to be happy is frequently linked to the satisfaction (or otherwise) of infantile desires: those who have satisfied desires have a higher and more natural aptitude, whereas those who have not satisfied their desires find their later happiness in more abstract things (see *The Prime of Life*, 27). Willie disowned the abstract and the purely theoretical and found great happiness in the commonplace thing—surely an indication of his parents' devotion to him?

31. *ExpT*, 57 (1946): 301–4. See Appendix II for a detailed list of contributions.

32. *ExpT*, 59 (1947), 67–69.

33. *SPQ*, February 1949, 4.

34. *ExpT*, 61 (1950): 310–11.

35. In an article that militated against "pious clap-trap"; see *BW*, 10 June 1965.

36. *ExpT*, 63 (1952): 259ff. The following year he wrote a review article on recent books on this theme, "Aids to Teachers," which appeared in *ExpT*, 64 (1953): 224.

37. *ExpT*, 61 (1950): 127.

38. *ExpT*, 61 (1950): 384.

39. *ExpT*, 62 (1951): 127.

40. *ToF*, 28: "very much a natural believer." This needs to be explored, which I hope to do elsewhere, for the burden of belief hung heavy on him at times, and was all too easily disguised by facile statement for one cause or another. Unresolved tensions clearly existed, often appearing through his love of argument or plain self-contradiction. He set himself to explain the enigma of faith, but his own faith (even to himself) was an enigma: "there seem to be two different and even contradictory sides to me," he admitted. We should not, however, read too much of this into his earlier period, for while it was certainly present, the formal espousal of his doctrines was clearly orthodox, even conservative. As I maintained in *William Barclay: The Plain Uncommon Man*, "his faith was decisively evangelical, and that in a way no self-respecting liberal would wish to be paired with" (90). In October 1968, when writing to the President of the Royal Philosophical Society of Glasgow, W. W. Fletcher, Willie went so far as to say "consistency is the least of all virtues"!

41. *ExpT*, 62 (1951): 192.

42. In November 1970 Lieutenant Colonel Harry Dean of the Editorial and Literary Department of the Salvation Army's international headquarters wrote to Willie to thank him for "the two blows you have struck on behalf of our mutual friend, Fred Brown." He went on to say how "very much appreciated by those who remain in the Army" Willie's comments were, and assured him "of our conviction that what you have done has proved useful already." In reply, Willie spoke of his being "very distressed" about Brown's dismissal and of his view that in taking the action, the Army, "which I so much admire, has made a very real mistake." I gave permanent record to the more important of his "two blows" in *Men and Affairs*, 145–46.

43. In a review in *ExpT*, 62 (1951): 288.

44. See his review of Newbigin's *South India Diary* in *ExpT*, 62 (1951): 383–84.

45. See Willie's review in *ExpT*, 63 (1952): 291–92.

46. *ExpT*, 63 (1952): 387–88.

47. See *ToF*, 96.

48. *L&W*, January 1948, 3–4.

49. R. D. Kernohan, *Scotland's Life and Work*, 165.

50. According to Smith, in a letter to the author, 17 December 1979.

51. *SSST*, October 1949.

52. *L&W*, February 1948, 25.

53. *L&W*, May 1948, 41.

54. *L&W*, September 1948, 147.

55. *BW*, 13 December 1945.

56. Smith, in a letter to the author, 17 December 1979.

57. In a radio interview with Stanley Pritchard, *This Is My Job*, no. 7, 19 July 1960.

58. Willie, in a letter to Braidwood, 1 January 1949.

59. Perry, in a letter to the author, 10 February 1980.

60. This was the only instance of such a departure, of which I was informed by William Barclay of Troon. In the light of his later writings about sin (e.g., "*Hamartia* and *Hamartanein*: The Failure Which Is Sin," in *A New Testament Wordbook*, 48–53) and in light of its effects on people (see Ronald Falconer's essay "Barclay as Broadcaster," in *William Barclay: The Plain Uncommon Man*, ed. R. D. Kernohan, 120), this comment does not bear examination.

61. So says G. A. Smith in his biography *Henry Drummond*, 142.

62. The phrase is Luther's.

63. Reported by William Barclay of Troon, in an interview with the author, 2 March 1980.

64. *The Shorter Catechism: Answers to Questions*, 2.

65. *God's Law, God's Servants, and God's Men* (1954), 152.

66. In his essay "A Late and Vital Friendship," in *William Barclay: The Plain Uncommon Man*, Malcolm Mackay records Willie's instant rejoinder to this text, which highlights the Fatherhood of God (149).

67. See Vogel's *The Iron Rations of a Christian* (1941), a book significantly written out of the German church struggle of 1937.

68. It will be noted that the spelling of Adoptionism is followed here consistently. Willie made no distinction between Adoptionism and Adoptianism, a matter of some significance. Adoptionism was that view championed by Adolf Harnack; it originated in the doctrine of the Ebionites and came into Greek theology via Theodotus and the Antiochene theologians (Paul of Samosata, Theodore of Mopsuestia, etc.). Adoptianism, strictly speaking, originated in Spain in the eighth century through the writings of Elipandus and Felix. Some contact between the two strains was made through Nestorianism (itself a derivation of Antiochene traditions), some aspects of which were highly congenial to Moorish ideology.

69. *God's Plan for Men*, 21.

70. *RP*, 12 April 1935.

71. *ExpT*, 71 (1960): 189–90.

72. For example, he makes the assertion twice on page 52. Moreover, there are at least half a dozen uses of paradox throughout the book (69, 92–93, 118, 120, 130); on page 96 he asserts the importance of "the logical dilemma" in the teaching of Jesus.

73. In the second volume of his 1969 translation of the New Testament, *The Letters and the Revelation*.

74. See, for example, Hoole's edition of *The Shepherd of Hermas*, xx–xxi.

75. *BW*, 18 August 1955.

CHAPTER FOURTEEN

1. Churchill, quoted in Lord Moran's *Churchill*, 337.

2. Cf. Ronald Falconer's description of Willie as "the most brilliant 'common-man's' communicator of our generation" (in *Message, Media and Mission*, 101).

3. Gilmore, in a letter to the author, 14 February 1980.

4. Rutland, in a letter to Kate, 28 January 1978.

5. According to Willie, in a letter to Braidwood, 1 January 1949.

6. Young, in a letter to the author, 11 February 1982.

7. The letter is dated 30 September 1952.

8. *Trinity College, Glasgow: The Centenary Volume, 1856-1956*.

9. Willie, in a letter to McCulloch, 25 September 1962. Willie was greatly impressed by Miss McCulloch's adventurous retirement attitude and wrote one of his "Seen in the Passing" pieces about her: "Some people's minds are tight shut at twenty, and other people's minds are wide open at seventy. . . . If you want to stay alive, keep learning" (*BW*, 15 November 1962).

10. "This is the first book I ever wrote," Willie states in the foreword to the revised edition of *Ambassador for Christ* (1974).

11. *SSST*, September 1951, 238.

12. *Ambassador for Christ* (rev. ed.), 92. Subsequent references to the revised edition will be made parenthetically in the text.

13. Cf. page 55 in the revised edition and page 51 in the 1951 edition.

14. See Adam Philip's *Thomas Chalmers*, 99. Scotland had good reason to back off from what Lord Grimond has recently called "the pall of uniformity" (*Memoirs*, 246), though even the redoubtable Chalmers was willing to persevere "to 'incorporation' afterwards" (98).

15. The 1951 edition reads "Christianity is the most important thing in the world"; the editor, James Martin, is responsible for the change.

16. From the foreword to the first edition (1952). A revised edition appearing in 1970 introduced some general changes worthy of note. For instance, in adding chapter numbers, the

editor, James Martin (following Willie), has overlooked the fact that Chapter 1 is in fact the Introduction, not the first chapter (see page 94, where readers are directed to the now nonexistent Introduction); in addition, Chapter 28 and Chapter 29 have been combined with Chapter 27, whereas in the 1952 edition they were separate chapters dealing with separate parables, albeit less expansively.

17. *And Jesus Said* (rev. ed.), 22. Subsequent references to the revised edition will be made parenthetically in the text.

18. The phrase is highly reminiscent of Drummond's *Spiritual Law in the Natural World.* Italics mine.

19. In *One Lord, One Faith, One Life* (1951), 88–89. He gave two definitions, in fact; the foregoing was primary, and the second was derived from the Latin *sacramentum,* "an oath of loyalty."

20. Indeed, it has been wholly secularized, rendered religionless—but still highly religious! See Willie's treatment of John 6:1–13, item "b," in *DSB: The Gospel of John,* vol. 1.

21. *L&W,* February 1971, 33 (review of the revised edition); *ExpT,* 64 (1953/54): 44.

22. *SSST,* October 1952, 295.

23. Cardus, *Autobiography,* 214.

24. The passage occurs in this version in the 1952 edition only (137); in the revised edition, the phrase "after entering the world Himself in the person of Jesus" is curiously omitted (144).

25. *Living and Learning* (1968), vi. Sir William Smith took his style of "Christian manliness" from such figures as Norman Macleod, who commented, "If ever 'muscular Christianity' was taught to the rising generation, the Highland manse of these days was its gymnasium" (*Reminiscences of a Highland Parish,* 38).

26. *God's Plan for Men,* vi.

27. According to John MacNaughton, in a letter to the author, 9 March 1980.

28. *ToF,* 24.

29. See G. A. Smith's *Henry Drummond,* 81.

30. *God's Law, God's Servants, and God's Men,* 55–56.

31. Ibid., 89.

32. Chalmers, quoted by Willie in *And Jesus Said,* 124.

33. *One Lord, One Faith, One Life,* 1. Subsequent references to this volume will be made parenthetically in the text.

34. *God's Men, God's Church, and God's Life,* 1. Subsequent references to this volume will be made parenthetically in the text.

35. *DBR: 1 & 2 Corinthians* (1954), in the commentary on 1 Cor. 9:19–23.

36. Donald MacLeod, *Memoir of Norman MacLeod,* 301. We might well note that MacLeod's early ministry took place in the Highlands at the time of the great revivals. His espousal of literature in the cause of the gospel may well have been directly influential on WDB.

37. *The King and the Kingdom,* v. Subsequent references to this volume will be made parenthetically in the text.

38. *God's Law, God's Servants, and God's Men* (1954), viii.

39. In the introduction to the full edition (1958), 1.

40. *The Boys' Brigade Gazette,* December 1950, 29.

41. *ToF,* 25.

42. Willie, in a letter to Braidwood, 1 January 1945.

43. *DBR: The Acts of the Apostles* (1953), iii. Subsequent references to this volume will be made parenthetically in the text.

44. The volume, a collaborative effort of Macgregor and T. P. Ferris, was published in 1954 in The Interpreter's Bible series.

45. *ToF,* 2. Soutar actually made the acknowledgment within the context of his overall view of life, not of any academic accomplishment.

46. In *The Gospels and Acts* (1976), he describes it as one of the most exciting and most essential books in the world (2: 227).

47. In *The Gospels and Acts,* having surveyed the main lines of historical criticism concerning Acts, he held to his basic tenet of its historical trustworthiness. He did yield, however, to the possibility of Lukan fallibility: "the writer of Acts was personally acquainted with Paul, and . . . loved him even when he did not understand him" (2: 281).

48. See *L&W,* August 1953.

49. See *ExpT,* 62 (1950): 63.

50. *L&W,* September 1952, 188.

51. From the foreword, dated November 1952.

52. *BW,* 19 March 1953, 2.

53. *BW,* 5 June 1952, 10.

54. Furness, in a letter to the author, 14 May 1980.

55. *SSST,* November 1954, 309–10. The movement of his thinking in later days will be toward a diminution of the first part and a heightening of the second, as I hope to demonstrate elsewhere.

56. *SSST,* October 1954, 269ff.

57. *SSST,* November 1954, 309

58. *SSST,* December 1954, 342.

59. *SSST,* January 1955, 5–6.

60. *SSST,* February 1955, 48–49.

61. The basis of his "secularity" is clearly seen in this definition of worship. It constitutes the obverse of his view of a sacramental universe. He presents whichever side of the coin is most useful, according to need, but his view was never strictly secularist: he never denied God or spiritual realities.

62. *SSST,* October 1955, 272–74.

63. *SSST,* October 1955, 273.

64. *SSST,* November 1955, 315–16. In *DSB: Romans* he baldly states that baptism in the early church was by total immersion (208).

65. *SSST,* December 1955, 345.

66. *DBR: The Gospel of Luke* (1953), v.

67. Moran, *Churchill,* 347.

68. William Braidwood, in a letter to the author, 28 February 1980.

69. According to N. Warman, in a letter to Kate Barclay, 27 January 1978.

70. *DBR: The Gospel of Luke* (1953), 10.

71. *DBR: Galatians, 1 & 2 Thessalonians, 1 & 2 Corinthians* (1954), vii.

72. R. D. Kernohan selected Willie's article on the Gospel of Mark from *Life and Work* (January 1948), "a piece," he says, "which is of historical and biographical importance," as one of just four pieces to convey something of the range and clarity of style of his writing (see *William Barclay: The Plain Uncommon Man,* 31–34).

73. *DBR: The Gospel of Mark* (1954), xii.

74. These articles were eventually collected and published in book form under the title *The Mind of Saint Paul* in 1958.

75. *DBR: The Letter to the Romans* (1955), ix. Subsequent references to this volume will be made parenthetically in the text.

76. *ToF,* 13.

77. *DBR: The Gospel of John,* 2 vols. (1955), 1: vii. Subsequent references to this volume will be made parenthetically in the text.

78. *ToF,* 6. It was the last thing she gave him, undoubtedly knowing she was dying—hence its sentimental value. Alas, it was destroyed in the clearing-out at his death.

79. Those who criticize his doctrine of the Holy Spirit ought to reflect on this emphasis, which persists throughout the volume—for example, "It is the essential meaning of the words [of Jesus]; that is the guidance of the Holy Spirit" (1: 229). Martin once more weakens Willie's emphasis in his later edition of this passage, by deleting the word *meaning,* which stands in parallel to the inner significance.

80. It is the *institution* of the Last Supper that is missing, of course. Willie ignores this point and omits the "sacramental" aspect of the event described in John 13:1–2, though he makes space for a double entendre regarding baptism in his commentary on John 13:8.

81. It did resurface from time to time, not least when he declared that "a church of the air"—that is, a radio- or television-oriented church life—was "not an impossible dream" (*ToF,* 5).

82. *DBR: The Epistle to the Hebrews* (1955), viii. Subsequent references to this volume will be made parenthetically in the text.

83. *ToF,* 14.

84. *DBR: The Epistle to the Ephesians* (1956), xi. This overthrows what he said about Luke, of course, but no matter! Subsequent references to this volume will be made parenthetically in the text.

85. The passage is somewhat changed in the revised edition (1975), in which see page 66.

86. *DBR: Timothy, Titus* (1956), vii. Subsequent references to this volume will be made parenthetically in the text.

87. Not for the first time does Willie without defensiveness draw out meanings that many Protestants feel give too much weight to Roman Catholic interpretations.

88. See *Memoir of Norman MacLeod,* 182–83.

89. *DBR: The Gospel of Matthew,* 3 vols. (1956), 1: ix.

90. In *The Old Law and the New Law,* 2d ed. (1972), 49. To be strictly accurate, he says "this new law is to be found specially in the Sermon on the Mount" (1st ed. [1966], 51). Curiously, I have not been able to trace any reference to this in the DSB, though it was clearly a subject of close interest to him and his ethical system.

91. *DBR: Philippians, Colossians & Philemon* (1959), 3. Subsequent references to this volume will be made parenthetically in the text.

92. Little, in a letter to the author, 19 December 1980.

93. *DBR: The Epistles of James and Peter* (1958), ix. Subsequent references to this volume will be made parenthetically in the text.

94. *DBR: The Epistles of John and Jude* (1968), ix. Subsequent references to this volume will be made parenthetically in the text.

95. *DBR: The Revelation of John,* 3 vols. (1959), 1: vii. Subsequent references to this volume will be made parenthetically in the text.

96. He is actually quoting Carrington, who rated Revelation "greater than Stevenson or Coleridge or Bach."

97. See *DSB: The Gospel of Matthew,* 2 vols. (1958), 1: 7 and 2: 300ff.

98. *L&W,* January 1956, 3.

99. *BW,* 5 April 1956.

100. *L&W,* October 1956, 273. A complimentary report was made to the General Assembly of 1953 (see *Reports to the General Assembly* [1953], 436) in which the first volume was held to have been "most favourably received." By 1961 reference was being made to their serving "in a preeminent degree one of the primary functions of the Church's mission—the serious, devout and informed study of the Word of God" (see *Reports to the General Assembly* [1961], 526ff.).

101. *L&W,* February 1957.

102. *L&W,* 1957, 195.

103. Willie, in a letter to Rita Snowden, 22 June 1956.

104. Willie, in a letter to Mitton, 1 November 1957.

105. Willie, in a letter to Stirling, 2 March 1958. The resultant article was printed in *MT,* 28 March 1958.

106. Knight, in an obituary for Willie in *The Outlook,* March 1978; italics his.

107. See *GH,* 15 December 1959.

108. Martin offered no explanation for the nature of his revisionary work in the DSB volumes; Willie himself pointed out in the new General Introduction that it had been done "entirely" by him. At the time of revision, the bookselling trade was informed that it was being done for typographical reasons, the original plates being no longer capable of more reprints. It is obvious, however, that much more was involved. In *William Barclay: The Plain Uncommon Man* Martin refers to "a whole crop of little grammatical loosenesses and other infelicities" that he had to put right (52). That doesn't account for a reduction of nearly six hundred pages in the entire text, which was clearly subjected to some vigorous pruning of Willie's phrasing, not least in his homiletical style of tautology. Some of the more important matters, such as his much-desired revision of the Acts and Ephesians commentaries, were not attended to at all. Sad to say, the standards of the revision, not least in producing greater consistency (e.g., of proper names) and in careful correction of the proofs, are not of the highest order. Martin's implication that Willie never read anything he wrote (in *William Barclay: The Plain Uncommon Man,* 52) is not wholly reliable, as we shall see.

109. Dixon, *The Human Situation,* 11.

110. Dixon, 12.

111. *ExpT,* 59 (1948), 251–52.

112. *BW,* 30 December 1954.

113. *BW,* 3 February 1955.

114. *BW,* 6 January 1955.

115. *BW,* 30 June 1955.
116. *BW,* 11 November 1955.
117. *BW,* 12 May 1955.
118. *BW,* 19 May 1955.
119. Ross, quoted by David Daniell in *The Interpreter's House: A Critical Assessment of the Work of John Buchan* (1976), 10. As he put it earlier, "The perfect performance comes when the deep experience meets the perfect technique" (78). Willie was a master because he had both.
120. *ToF,* 100.
121. *BW,* 28 April 1955.
122. Mitchell, in a letter to the author, 16 February 1980.
123. Neil, in a letter to the author, 23 February 1980.
124. In *BW* of 16 March 1961 he pointedly asks the question of whether it is indeed the *Lord's* table, and states that "fencing" of any sort is "humiliating." Elsewhere he gives vent to his "lifelong" concern about Communion cards—"tickets of admission" he calls them (*BW,* 29 November 1962). "Ecclesiasticism," he remarked later, "is worshipping systems even more than worshipping Jesus Christ" (*BW,* 22 August 1963). Writing to Mrs. Mary Flynn (on 4 December 1972), he shared with her his delight in being "associated with" a Roman Catholic mass, and a few months later he expressed his pleasure to Frank Price of Brisbane, Australia, that his prayers were used at the end of the masses there and that some of his books were required reading in some Roman Catholic schools.
125. *BW,* 1 April 1954.

CHAPTER FIFTEEN

1. Willie, in a letter to William Braidwood, 7 April 1956.
2. See *BW,* 16 June 1955.
3. Willie, in a letter to Ronnie Craig, 12 June 1955.
4. As reported to the author in a letter from E. P. Gardner of Ballymena, 21 August 1980.
5. Macfarlane, in a letter to the author, 14 February 1980. Willie refers to his ineptitude in matters domestic in *ToF,* 16, but that was written at a time of particular physical deterioration, as we shall see. Sewing he may well have left unmastered—such an "unmanly" exercise!—but in this the ever-ready-to-please Kate swiftly came to his aid.
6. So said Willie, in a letter to Braidwood, 7 April 1956.
7. A. C. Dow, in a letter to the author, 12 February 1980.
8. Willie, in a letter to Rita Snowden, 22 June 1956.
9. Willie, in a letter to Allan Galloway, 6 September 1974.
10. *SSST,* May 1956, 138.
11. From the minutes of the SSSU for 14 May 1956.
12. From the minutes of the SSSU for 26 February 1955. The fundamentals referred to include the following four tenets: (1) God is active in history; (2) because ours is a living God, we can know him and love him *today;* (3) all our work must be done as unto Christ himself, our Lord and Master; and (4) the child's experience in Sunday School must be made an integral part of the fuller life of the church, although this goal of inclusiveness ought not to go so far as to urge the admittance of children to Communion, still less to propose that they be allowed, à l'Américaine, to serve the elements. (Willie develops this latter point in a letter to David T. Anderson dated 9 December 1975.)
13. *BW,* 12 April 1956.
14. From the minutes of the University of Glasgow Faculty of Theology for 30 April 1956.
15. *BW,* 24 May 1956.
16. The piece is reprinted in *Through the Year with William Barclay,* 79.
17. *ToF,* 6.
18. According to Snowden, in a letter to the author, 14 February 1980.
19. Willie, in a letter to Snowden, 22 June 1956.
20. The College later united with its Lancashire counterpart to form the Northern Congregational College, which was partly integrated into the Faculty of Theology at Manchester University. Cunliffe-Jones was Associate Principal of the NCC till his appointment as Professor of History and Doctrine in 1966.

21. Willie, in a letter to Mitton, 1 November 1957.

22. According to *The Coleraine Chronicle,* 18 August 1956.

23. Willie, in a letter to Braidwood, 15 February 1958.

24. As related by Presho in a letter to the author, 9 February 1980.

25. According to John Hough in a letter to the author, 3 January 1980. Hough's information was confirmed by the Dean of Liverpool Cathedral, Edward Patey, in a letter to the author, 29 January 1980.

26. So wrote Cyril Rose to Kate in a letter dated 27 January 1978. The information was conveyed to the author by Mrs. Rita Perry in a letter, 10 February 1980.

27. *Ambassador for Christ,* 134.

28. According to M. R. S. Thornton, in a letter to the author of April 1980.

29. Willie, quoted by Perry in a letter to the author, 29 February 1980.

30. According to *The Coleraine Chronicle,* 18 August 1956.

31. See *The Lord's Supper,* 112. To several of his friends he mentioned feeling Barbara's presence after her tragic death.

32. John G. Lockhart, *The Life of Sir Walter Scott* (1957), 627.

33. *ToF,* 46.

34. Willie and Kate's friends of over forty years Archie and Margaret Maynard have agreed with this understanding of much of Kate's consequent troubles (in an interview with the author of 7 June 1980), as have Ronnie and Jane, separately. Kate's sister, Mrs. Livingstone, has also concurred, not least concerning the effects of the tragedy on Kate's faith.

35. According to Campbell, in a letter to the author, 3 March 1980.

36. According to Livingstone, in a letter to the author, 1 August 1980, and in a subsequent interview.

37. According to Mrs. Livingstone, in a letter to the author, 2 March 1980, and in a subsequent interview.

38. *I Believe in the Dawn* (1958), 56–57. The book, with its touching dedication and essay, clearly meant much to Willie, for he conveyed a copy of it to the Braidwoods, which copy was kindly loaned to the author in 1979.

39. *DSB: The Gospel of Matthew,* 1: 317. (In the original three-volume version this appeared in volume 2.)

40. *DSB: Matthew,* 1: 318; italics mine.

41. See *ToF,* 102.

42. *DSB: The Gospel of Mark,* 114–17.

43. *DSB: The Gospel of Matthew,* 1: 318.

44. *DBR: The Gospel of Matthew,* 2: 28.

45. *ToF,* 92.

46. *ToF,* 45.

47. *ToF,* 46.

48. See *ToF,* 40–41.

49. The author gave them permanent form when he reprinted them in *Turning to God* (1978), 104–26. They provide a useful description of "the turned life," which may be called a "potted theology" for the newborn in Christ.

50. The Daily Study Bible title was actually used as far back as April 1954, but with no firm commitment or consistency.

51. See *L&W,* December 1957, 295.

52. The Draft Catechism, 6–7.

53. *BW,* 29 November 1956.

54. See Heron's *Record Apart,* 52.

55. Little, in a letter to the author, 16 December 1980.

56. Professor Bruce informs me that when Willie applied in 1959 for the Chair at Sheffield that Bruce was vacating, the adverse response to this book from the Professors of Greek, Latin, and Ancient History (all of whom were on the appointing committee) actually decided them against him. Had he been successful, his life would doubtless have been very different, for he would have been placed in the secular teaching context he at times so much coveted.

57. *Educational Ideals in the Ancient World,* 9.

58. *Educational Ideals,* 211 n. 92.

59. According to McHardy, in an interview with the author, 8 March 1980.

60. According to Bradnock, in an interview with the author, 6 March 1980.

61. See *The New Testament in Basic English* (1941), 5–6, for a brief explanation.

62. The Dead Sea Scrolls are not once referred to in DSB, and only once in an *L&W* article of a later date. He made countless references to other Jewish works and sects of the time, not least concerning the rabbinic literature (always citing them from English translations). In May 1972 one of his students, Robin Watt, was engaged in what Willie called "an interesting and quite important PhD": basic work on the Qumran *Manual III,* 13–IV, 14 and related documents, seeking to determine a Hebrew origin. But Willie offered no guidance on the student's confrontation of de Jonge's arguments, or on those of Becker, still less his own viewpoint (see his letter to Watt, 22 May 1972). On 5 September 1974 he wrote to John Bowden of SCM Press *vis-à-vis* important parallels (if not connections) between the Gospel of John and the scrolls, saying "Here I am on ground that I know very little about."

63. Rab Wright, in an interview with the author, 29 May 1981.

64. Alexander, in "Portrait of a Scholar and Colleague," in *William Barclay: The Plain Uncommon Man,* ed. R. D. Kernohan, 101.

65. According to Harold Macmillan, in *Riding the Storm,* 263.

66. Willie, in a letter to Braidwood, 15 February 1958.

67. See *William Barclay: The Plain Uncommon Man,* 43. While it is perceptive concerning one part of Willie's mind, however, it does ignore the Rabelaisian side of his character that so greatly puzzled some of his students, who were reduced to whispering *les mots chargés* when I interviewed them. It should not be overlooked that Rabelais has long enjoyed a sympathetic acceptance among the Scots, not least among the Glaswegians. Medical doctor, humanist, writer, priest, and humorist, he strikes a deep chord in the Caledonian mentality to which Willie heartily responded. The University of Glasgow library has a very fine collection of his early writings—perhaps the finest in Britain. There is much about the man of the world–cum–Benedictine monk that appealed to Willie: renaissance man devoted to God, comic, and male chauvinist to boot!

68. *The Monthly Record,* September 1957, 179. One man's nebulosity is, of course, another man's profundity.

69. *The Monthly Record,* September 1955, 178–79.

70. *The Monthly Record,* November 1957, 219.

71. *The Daily Express,* 22 January 1957.

72. Smith, in a letter to the author, 1 January 1980.

73. According to Jenkins, in letters to the author of 17, 20, and 25 February 1980.

74. Willie, in a letter to Braidwood, 15 February 1958.

75. Willie, in a letter to Mitton, 1 November 1957.

76. Willie, in a letter to Braidwood, 15 February 1958.

77. Braidwood's phrase, in a letter to Willie, 25 April 1956.

78. Jane, quoted by Willie in *BW,* 17 October 1957.

79. *BW,* 6 March 1957.

80. Falconer, in *L&W,* May 1949.

81. Martin, "Barclay's Humanity and Humility," in *William Barclay: The Plain Uncommon Man,* 50–69.

82. *ToF,* 104.

83. Moran, *Churchill,* 337.

84. See Falconer's *The Kilt beneath My Cassock,* 175. Incidentally, Falconer mistakes the sources of these broadcasts in his account, stating that they originated from Glasgow rather than the capital.

85. Stalker, in *L&W,* April 1956, 103.

86. Falconer, *The Kilt beneath My Cassock,* 176.

87. Ibid.

88. *ToF,* 69–74.

89. Nevertheless, he generally used the term *martyrdom* solely to denote a literal death for the faith. In each of the twelve places the word is used in the DSB it had this meaning, nowhere more plainly than in his commentary on Revelation 20:4–5: "*Martyrs* were those who actually died for their faith, *confessors* were those who suffered everything short of death."

CHAPTER SIXTEEN

1. Levin, *The Pendulum Years* (1970), 9.

2. *BW,* 24 March 1955.

3. *BW,* 28 April 1955.
4. *BW,* 7 July 1955.
5. *BW,* 16 June 1955.
6. *BW,* 30 June 1955.
7. *BW,* 18 September 1955. We can see in Willie's comments on Stauffer's book another angle on his ever-fresh delight in learning, an almost youthful response to old things newly stated, or new things pungently expressed.
8. *BW,* 9 February 1956. F. F. Bruce rightly calls attention (in private correspondence) to Lord Ramsey's "intemperate and unbalanced . . . lumping together [of] fundamentalists and evangelicals," but we should not forget that in the late '50s the two groups were not so sharply distinguished. Men like Bruce were, as it were, pioneering in evangelical scholarship, over which their more conservative brethren snorted, "neo-orthodoxy."
9. Packer's work was a response to G. Hebert's *Fundamentalism and the Word of God,* which was the opening shot in the vigorous debate specifically on Christian fundamentalism that continues still (as it does in other world faiths).
10. Reported and outlined in *The Evangelical Quarterly,* 33 (October 1961): 193ff.
11. See his articles in *BW* of 5, 19, and 26 February 1959 and 7 May 1959. His exploration of existentialism came in an article that appeared in the 4 February 1958 issue. In this latter there is more than meets the eye. Willie drank deeply of the spirit of the age, a task no would-be communicator can afford to overlook. In doing so he was clearly influenced by existentialism—not, it must be emphasized, formally, but as an individual who took seriously his own existence as well as that of others (always under God, which separated him from atheistic existentialism). We should bear in mind that he preferred French to German generally, and his existentialism was therefore not surprisingly of the French sort, even tinged with its tendency toward defiance of the establishment at times. Willie's was an involvement in one sense similar to Sartre's, inasmuch as it was expressed more in aesthetic than systematic terms: imagination rather than logic predominated; it came to light in stories (and plays) rather than through direct philosophical formulation. Sartre was a far greater and purer existentialist than Willie, but Willie shared Sartre's commitment to the language of visual imagery, which both found self-sufficient, despite the protests of their academic confreres.
12. *L&W,* December 1958, 295.
13. *BW,* 17 September 1953.
14. In "Christian Conversation," *BW,* 5 July 1959. This is a complete *volte face* from his unpublished "false start" of ten years earlier. The opposites were not so much jostling as ejecting each other!
15. See G. N. M. Collins's *Heritage of Our Fathers,* 2d ed. (1976), 158.
16. *The Mind of Jesus,* ix.
17. Ibid.
18. See *BW,* 26 July 1962.
19. *Crucified and Crowned,* 181. Cf. page 180: "nothing less than the creed of the early Church"—the ultimate in iron rations, as it is of theological expression itself; in this sense the word *became* is of some importance. Subsequent references to *Crucified and Crowned* will be made parenthetically in the text.
20. He related the details of the epiphany in an "Obiter Visa" piece (*BW,* 18 August 1960). It is altogether appropriate that he should have expressed this conviction not in formal teaching, but in one of his causeries—not in exposition of a doctrine, but in practical exhortation.
21. Willie, quoted by Cameron in an obituary notice in *The Daily Record,* 25 January 1978.
22. According to the faculty minutes for 2 November 1956.
23. *BW,* 5 October 1961.
24. *ToF,* 9.
25. Willie, in a letter to James K. Scobbie (rector of Dalziel High School at this time), 7 June 1958.
26. *Journal of the Cricket Society,* Spring 1972, 24–25.
27. That is how Willie described the problem in a letter to Ronnie Craig, 4 April 1959.
28. *ToF,* 20.
29. A statistic he mentioned in a letter to Drake, 2 July 1959.
30. *BW,* 23 April 1959.
31. *BW,* 17 March 1960.

32. According to Adamson, in an interview with the author, 22 January 1980.

33. Willie, in *BW*, 30 August 1962. It was a surprisingly public admission, one that risked the charge of insensitivity.

34. Pritchard used the phrase in the introduction to the interview. I am grateful to him for the loan of his transcript.

35. They began virtually together, although Bruce's journalistic career began within a Christian context, whereas Willie's was secular. Bruce's most persistent contribution took place in the "Answers to Questions" column of *The Harvester*, which, like Willie's "Entre Nous" and "Men and Affairs" pieces, were collected and reprinted in book form in 1972, a project in which I had the honor of playing a small part.

36. Bruce, in a letter to the author, 15 December 1979.

37. *BW*, 19 January 1961.

38. Lindsell, *Battle for the Bible*, 156.

39. Porter, rev. of *The Letters to the Young Churches*, by William Barclay, in *The Evangelical Quarterly*, 33 (1961): 245.

40. Phillips, *Erasmus and the Northern Renaissance*, 85.

41. *The Monthly Record*, December 1955, 235–36.

42. Erasmus, quoted by Phillips, 79.

43. Webb, quoted by Potter in *A Victorian Courtship*, 97.

44. Cairns, *An Autobiography*, 159.

45. Lumsden, in *Lays and Letters of Linton* (1889), 177.

46. Nicoll, quoted by T. H. Darlow in *W. R. Nicoll*, 73.

47. Lottman, *Albert Camus*, 96.

48. *The Plain Man's Book of Prayers* (1959), 21.

49. Cave, in the Preface to *A Plain Man's Life of Christ*, by Lindsay Martin, 9.

50. On the matter of the whole "plain man" tradition, we might also note that Weatherhead had links with A. S. Peake—primarily as a fellow Methodist, but also through involvement in pastoral work in Manchester. Following the death of Peake in 1929, his son Leslie published the aptly named collection of Peake's causeries *Plain Thoughts on Great Subjects*. That title had originally been suggested to Peake by the editor of *The Sunday Strand* when he was considering reprinting those of Peake's articles that had appeared in his journal; when that volume of reprints was eventually published (in 1908), it became a best-seller (see Wilkinson's *Arthur Samuel Peake*, 117 n.2). It was Peake's undying conviction that his first duty was "to make the assured results of religious scholarship plain to the man in the street." Twentieth-century popularization of religious scholarship really began with A. S. Peake, Willie's great example.

51. *More Prayers for the Plain Man*, 7.

52. *The Plain Man Looks at the Beatitudes*, 7.

53. *Plain Man Looks at the Beatitudes*, 9.

54. *Plain Man Looks at the Beatitudes*, 81.

55. *BW*, 15 February 1962. Former parish minister that he was, Willie regularly criticized congregations for "selfish" attitudes, expressed in such things as formalized worship, language, and practices that set apart church members and alienated the "unchurched masses," who did not understand, like, or appreciate their religiosity.

56. *BW*, 26 October 1960.

57. *BW*, 25 August 1960.

58. *BW*, 8 September 1960.

59. From a report in *GH*, 25 April 1961.

60. *BW*, 30 November 1961.

61. Hough, in a letter to the author, 3 January 1980.

62. *BW*, 25 September 1961.

63. *BW*, 5 October 1961.

64. See Falconer's "Barclay as Broadcaster," in *William Barclay: The Plain Uncommon Man*, ed. R. D. Kernohan, 118.

65. *DBR: The Gospel of John*, 1: 160.

66. *ToF*, 101. Elsewhere, Falconer quotes Willie as having said, "If it had not been for religious broadcasting, Scotland would have become more pagan than she already is" (*The Kilt beneath My Cassock*, 240).

67. *ToF*, 102.

68. *ToF,* 104–5.

69. See *The Kilt beneath My Cassock,* 96, and *William Barclay: The Plain Uncommon Man,* 122–25.

70. In *Message, Media and Mission,* 55.

71. *Message, Media and Mission,* 56.

72. *ToF,* 104–5.

73. *BW,* 27 October 1960.

74. Falconer, *The Kilt beneath My Cassock,* 176, 179.

75. *ToF,* 95.

76. In *BW,* 12 and 20 April 1961.

77. *ToF,* 100.

78. *The Evangelical Quarterly,* 34 (July 1962): 174.

79. *BW,* 15 November 1962.

80. Stevenson, in a letter to the author, 1 January 1980.

81. *ToF,* 58ff. From this there developed some interesting correspondence between Willie and Frank L. Bersch of Virginia, which I hope to publish elsewhere.

82. *BW,* 9 August 1982.

83. According to a letter he sent to Miss McCulloch on 25 September 1962, one of his classes met three afternoons a week and was set to study Milligan's *Selections from the Greek Papyri,* Pseudo-Longinus's *On the Sublime, The Didache,* "and maybe some other things." In addition he was offering "the most popular of all my courses . . . a complete survey of early and late Greek philosophy and the Mystery Religions."

84. In a letter to Douglas Millard of James Clarke & Co., Ltd., of Cambridge, 21 March 1964.

85. *BW,* 28 December 1961.

86. *BW,* 9 November 1961.

87. *BW,* 31 May 1962.

88. *BW,* 2 May 1963. In *ToF* he quotes William Neil to the effect that "True marriage is beautifully described as an unselfconscious relationship, where a man and a woman find that they have become part of each other, almost as if they became a joint personality" (116). This is to some extent a convenient rationalization of his life's work—his neglect of Kate at times—and a romanticization of it, too. It is a perennial problem of ministerial life; as Willie declared, "I am astonished that the work of the ministry does not destroy ministers' marriages" (*ToF,* 16).

89. *Christian Discipline in Society Today,* 42.

90. Willie, *Turning to God: A Study of Conversion in the Book of Acts and Today,* 42.

91. *Turning to God,* 8.

92. See *BW,* 11 April 1963.

93. Letter to Meacham, 29 March 1963.

94. Letter to McCulloch, 14 March 1963.

95. Falconer, *The Kilt beneath My Cassock,* 177.

96. See *BW,* 18 April 1963.

97. Alexander, "Portrait of a Scholar and Colleague," in *William Barclay: The Plain Uncommon Man,* 102.

98. Birkbeck confirmed this contention in a private conversation with the author, 8 October 1982.

99. See *GH,* 28 May 1963.

100. Alexander, in *William Barclay: The Plain Uncommon Man,* 103–4.

101. Alexander, 104.

102. See Neill's *Interpretation of the New Testament: 1861-1961,* 264ff.

103. In a letter to Bill Telford of 4 October 1974, Willie notes that the subject "had not yet fully emerged" when the first edition of his book was prepared. He confirms that his sources for the new discipline included Marxsen, Conzelmann, and Rohde (i.e., *Rediscovering the Teaching of the Evangelists* [translation of *Die Redaktionsgeschichtliche Methode*], 1968).

104. Leith, *An Introduction to the Reformed Tradition* (1977), 122.

105. Alexander, in *William Barclay: The Plain Uncommon Man,* 104.

106. *ToF,* 96.

107. For more on this, see my essay alongside Alexander's in *William Barclay: The Plain Uncommon Man,* 76–99, especially page 90.

108. Little, in a letter to the author, 16 December 1980.
109. See *DSB: The Gospel of John,* 1: 29.
110. *BW,* 23 May 1963.
111. *BW,* 21 March 1963.
112. *The College Courant* (1963/64), 57–58.
113. *GH,* 28 May 1963.

CHAPTER SEVENTEEN

1. *ToF,* 14.
2. *BW,* 22 August 1963.
3. Such was their promise reported in *L&W,* December 1963, 353.
4. He made the statement in a *BW* piece under the strange heading "The Twilight of the Church" (28 November 1963).
5. They were entitled "This Wins Men for Christ" (*BW,* 19 September 1963) and "This Was No Act of God" (*BW,* 3 October 1963).
6. *BW,* 16 January 1964.
7. *BW,* 23 January 1964.
8. *BW,* 18 June 1964.
9. Willie, in a letter to Braidwood, 7 April 1956.
10. Willie, in a letter to Millard, 11 November 1961.
11. Willie, in a letter to Millard, 29 March 1971.
12. Mitton, in a letter to Kate, 27 January 1978.
13. Bruce, in a letter to Kate, 31 January 1978.
14. *DSB: Timothy, Titus and Philemon,* 127.
15. Moran, *Churchill,* 112.
16. See Alexander's essay "Portrait of a Scholar and Colleague," in *William Barclay: The Plain Uncommon Man,* ed. R. D. Kernohan, especially 100–101.
17. "Barclay the Broadcaster," in *Biblical Studies in Honour of William Barclay,* 24.
18. "Barclay the Broadcaster," 28.
19. "Barclay the Broadcaster," 12–13.
20. Rupp, rev. of *Biblical Studies in Honour of William Barclay, The Guardian,* 3 March 1976.
21. *The Mind of Jesus,* ix.
22. *The Mind of Jesus,* x.
23. See *BW,* 26 November 1964 through 17 December 1964. This was a much more positive contribution (not least to the Anglican Church) than others of his reforming interests. Curiously (in light of his overall approach), Dr. Robinson has maintained a conservative view on matters relating to the discipline of New Testament study. In 1976 (too late for Willie to be significantly affected) he published *Redating the New Testament,* which all but overturns the mainstream position on New Testament chronology. In point of fact, Dr. Robinson justly noted "a remarkable degree of consensus" had been achieved between the radical and the conservative critics by 1950, although the gap had widened on other more basically theological issues.
24. *L&W,* June 1964, 194. Anderson was an elder of the Church of Scotland in the Highland tradition.
25. *BW,* 21 January 1965. Perhaps, strictly speaking, in the etymological sense he was: *pilgrim* derives from *peregrinus,* "foreigner," or "stranger," though his interest was essentially an extension of his love of the music hall and Gilbert and Sullivan.
26. "Much needed" according to Willie, in a letter to Douglas Millard, 21 March 1964.
27. Willie, quoted by Baird in a letter to the author, 26 February 1980.
28. *ToF,* ix. Italics mine. Edwards also notes that Willie claimed "to be lazy when there [was] no deadline to meet" (viii). I hope sufficient has been written to disprove any such claim, though what Willie meant to refer to was presumably not any lack of activity on his part, but the sort of pestering introspection that never allowed him to be satisfied with his own work, that always sought to improve it. Alexander's insolent phrase "putative scholar" is therefore applicable, if not apposite, but a comment Willie made concerning W. E. Sangster provides a more appropriate portrait of Willie himself than does Alexander's lame characterization: "Sangster might have done

772

more had he not been such a tornado of energy, rushing from town to town and from continent to continent to preach" (*Men and Affairs,* 17).

29. Willie, in a letter to Meacham, 29 March 1963.

30. See Honeyman's essay "Communicating across the World," in *William Barclay: The Plain Uncommon Man,* 120–31, especially 131.

31. Willie, in a letter to Ian G. Neilson, 6 February 1967.

32. Willie, in a letter to Neilson, 23 March 1968.

33. Willie, in a letter to Strang, 18 March 1964. He was incorrect in suggesting that the Boys' Brigade was to own the copyright; it was renewed in his own name.

34. *BW,* 13 August 1964.

35. *BW,* 10 September 1964.

36. *ToF,* 111–12. This comes in his second outline of belief (see page 666 herein), and is a new element in it. It significantly appears between his discussion of his understanding of the world and his understanding of man (both of which, he implies, are extensions of the nature of God). "God needs men," he affirmed in explanation of the relationship among men, work, and the world—a crucial Barclayan emphasis.

37. *BW,* 29 April 1965.

38. *BW,* 16 December 1965.

39. *BW,* 30 December 1965.

40. See *BW,* 12 August 1965.

41. That is, *The General next to God,* by Richard Collier, which he reviewed in *ExpT,* 77 (October 1965): 32.

42. *BW,* 7 October 1965.

43. *BW,* 25 November 1965.

44. *BW,* 9 December 1965.

45. *BW,* 2 December 1965.

46. See *BW,* 20 January 1966.

47. See *BW,* 13 January 1966.

48. Alexander, in *William Barclay: The Plain Uncommon Man,* 111.

49. Galloway, in *The Lord Is My Shepherd,* 18.

50. See *The First Three Gospels* (1966), 202.

51. This sometimes led him to "un-Reformed" viewpoints, but such "sectarianism" meant little to Willie if it offered a more convincing explanation; and indeed, his broader, more essentially inclusive Christian purview made his work more acceptable to Roman Catholics as well as to the officers of the Salvation Army, to members of the "Plymouth Brethren" as well as to those of the Greek Orthodox Church.

52. The work was *Myth in the New Testament.*

53. Alexander, in *William Barclay: The Plain Uncommon Man,* 104.

54. *And He Had Compassion,* 6. The last phrase is a good example of his bent for "natural theology," which shapes his view of the world—of creation, evolution, history, and so on. For more on this, see pages 666ff. herein regarding his testament of faith, and also *The Lord Is My Shepherd,* 130–53.

55. See *The First Three Gospels,* 29.

CHAPTER EIGHTEEN

1. *BW,* 17 February 1966.

2. *BW,* 22 April 1965.

3. *BW,* 24 June 1965.

4. *BW,* 30 September 1965.

5. *BW,* 14 October 1965.

6. *BW,* 21 October 1965.

7. *BW,* 30 December 1965.

8. *BW,* 10 February 1966.

9. See *ToF,* 30–32. Not a little of his attitude owes itself to a reaction to WDB's unworldliness, which ever challenged Willie, perhaps unconsciously, leading to one aspect of his antisyzygy and

accounting for his conservative views regarding such matters as money, homosexuality, divorce, and the work ethic.

10. *L&W,* August 1966, 10.

11. *Christian Discipline in Society Today,* 26.

12. *BW,* 16 December 1965.

13. *ToF,* 16.

14. *BW,* 28 April 1966. This was in the van of the house-church movement, which gathered particular force in the '70s.

15. *BW,* 31 March 1966.

16. Willie, in a letter to David Anderson, 8 October 1976.

17. *BW,* 2 June 1966.

18. Martin, "Barclay's Humanity and Humility," in *William Barclay: The Plain Uncommon Man,* ed. R. D. Kernohan, 55.

19. *The Scottish Daily Express,* October 1966.

20. *BW,* 18 May 1967.

21. *BW,* 5 January 1967.

22. Dunderdale, in a letter to the author, 16 February 1980.

23. Kernohan, in *William Barclay: The Plain Uncommon Man,* 25.

24. In a letter to M. Grego of 17 October 1975, Willie states that committees "are not more reliable than an individual." He frequently had salty things to say of his own church's headquarters. To one student who prefers to remain anonymous, he admitted he had "no idea of what they are up to at 121"; to Stanley Abel of Glasgow, on the verge of his retirement in 1974, Willie denied any responsibility for it: "I have had little or nothing to do with the Administrative side of the Church." To Donald Macdonald of Inverness, an engineering Gold Medalist of outstanding experience whose application for late entrance to the ministry had run into trouble, Willie wrote in 1970, "I have to say, to my disgust and my shame, that this is what you must expect from the Church of Scotland offices. If you can get past their barriers, it is a true sign that you do have a call to the ministry!" And later that year he wrote to Ian McIntosh of Texas, who wanted to transfer his ministerial allegiance from the Congregational Church to the Church of Scotland: "I am perfectly willing to write a testimonial to get you into heaven, let alone the Church of Scotland, but believe me there is a difference!"

25. See *Through the Year with William Barclay,* 28.

26. Willie, in response to a question from Emile Coia, in *Scots Field,* August 1972.

27. *The Evening Times,* 5 March 1976.

28. *BW,* 13 April 1967.

29. *BW,* 18 January 1968.

30. *BW,* March 1968.

31. For example, in *BW* of 11 April, 20 June, and 12 September 1968.

32. *ToF,* 7.

33. See *BW,* 19 September 1968. Unfortunately I have been unable to locate any more direct information concerning this friendship.

34. Of the many portraits available, all except Juliet Pannett's (see frontispiece) portray Willie with a downcast mouth.

35. *The Methodist Recorder,* 18 July 1968.

36. *The New Zealand Messenger,* 23 May 1968.

37. Willie, in a letter to White, 1 November 1968.

38. Kernohan, *Willilam Barclay: The Plain Uncommon Man,* 28.

39. *BW,* 17 October 1968.

40. *BW,* 17 July 1968.

41. Duncan, in *The Scots Magazine,* 94 (October 1970).

42. Willie, in a letter to Charles Miller, 12 August 1968.

43. *The New Testament,* vol. 1, *The Gospels and the Acts of the Apostles,* 5.

44. See *BW,* 19 December 1968.

45. Willie, in a letter to Snowden, 11 April 1969.

46. *BW,* 30 January 1969.

47. Miss Rose, in a letter to the author, 29 April 1980.

48. That was how Willie described her condition in a letter to David Wright, 25 August 1969.

49. "And when at last the translator sent his work in, it wasn't very well done, as reviewers

were quick to point out," commented F. F. Bruce (in a letter to the author, 11 December 1982). The book's weakness was a sure sign of Willie's faulty German, as well as a suggestion of some half-heartedness on his part regarding the whole working relationship with Millard.

50. Willie, in a letter to Morrice, 21 February 1969.

51. Willie, in a letter to Vice Chancellor Thomas Parry, 14 February 1969.

52. So he wrote in a letter to Professor Davies, 27 March 1969.

53. See Falconer's account in *Biblical Studies: Essays in Honour of William Barclay,* 60ff.

54. So Willie described it in a letter to Charles Miller, 12 August 1968.

55. Willie, in a letter to Ferguson, 11 March 1969.

56. Stanley Pritchard properly has pointed out that this was a natural extension of Willie's wartime canteen work, in which Pritchard, who preceded Campbell at Williamwood, had helped.

57. Franklin, in a letter to the author, 15 March 1980.

58. Bonhoeffer, quoted by Willie in *Men and Affairs,* 39.

59. Willie, in a letter to Snow, 7 November 1969.

60. Kate, in a letter to Williams, 4 May 1975.

61. Moran, *Churchill,* 88.

62. Duthie, in a letter to Kate, 11 October 1971.

63. Moran, *Churchill,* 151.

64. Donnelly, in *The Evening News,* 8 January 1970.

65. See *BW,* both the 5 and the 12 February 1970 issues.

66. So Willie informed Bill Scott of Texas, in a letter, 8 December 1970.

67. *BW,* 1 January 1970.

68. See *BW,* 4 June 1970.

69. *BW,* 28 May 1970.

70. In fact he once stated, "I have a bad habit of completely losing interest in a book once it is written" (in a letter to Richard Mulkern, 15 May 1974).

71. Willie, in a letter to Christman, 27 April 1970. When I took over as Publishing Manager of the Saint Andrew Press in 1978, I found a note concerning the Christman manuscript in a closed correspondence file. We published his manuscript that same year as *The Christman File* to resounding approval; Willie's earlier comments were a valuable aid in marketing the book.

72. Willie, in a letter to Sinclair Armstrong, 28 September 1973.

73. In a letter to Scott, 10 October 1973.

74. Willie, in a letter to Millard, 4 February 1970.

75. Willie, in a letter to Brown, 20 March 1970.

76. Willie, in a letter to the Southport High School for Girls, 23 March 1970.

77. Willie, in a letter to Harris, 23 March 1970.

78. As, for instance, in a letter to Millard, 26 March 1970, and one to R. O. Black, 1 April 1970.

79. Burns, in a letter to Willie, 1 April 1970.

80. Willie, in a letter to Goskirk, 20 April 1970.

81. Willie, in a letter to the Secretary of the Royal Philosophical Society of Glasgow, 21 April 1970.

82. In a letter dated 27 July 1970.

83. Willie, in a letter to McGillard, 5 May 1970.

CHAPTER NINETEEN

1. In fairness, it has to be said that the new editor encouraged Willie to stay with the paper (although he must have been conscious of the fact that had he failed to do so, it is likely that several other old-timers would have resigned at once in sympathy). Willie himself felt alienated; and he was far from well.

2. Willie, in a letter to Duncan, 17 June 1970.

3. Willie, in a letter to Duncan, 30 July 1970.

4. Willie, in a letter to Williams, 27 July 1970.

5. Willie, in a letter to Macpherson, 26 August 1970.

6. Willie in a letter to Sergeant-Major Flack, 20 October 1970.

7. According to Falconer in his essay "Barclay as Broadcaster," in *William Barclay: The Plain Uncommon Man*, ed. R. D. Kernohan, 125.

8. *Ethics in a Permissive Society*, 10. Subsequent references to this volume will be made parenthetically in the text.

9. In a letter dated 30 December 1976.

10. Falconer, in *Biblical Studies: Essays in Honour of William Barclay*, 26.

11. *BW*, 26 November 1970.

12. So he said in a letter to Leslie Avery, 5 January 1971.

13. That being Eric P. Gardiner, who included the *bon mot* in a letter to the author, 21 February 1980.

14. I emphasize that it was from the ranks of *traditional* (i.e., English) Calvinism that Willie received complaints. He did not live to see the published fruit of R. T. Kendall's doctoral researches, *Calvin and English Calvinism* (1979), which argues that the Puritan tradition developed from Beza, not Calvin. Scotland to a large extent shared its "Westminster" theology, of course, but has been more open to a wider range of influences at times. Willie's theology, once it had emerged from his father's incubus, was *instinctively* broader, deeper, more inclusive, more truly that of a renaissance man—as was John Calvin's at certain points.

15. See *BW* of 21 May, 2 July, and 8 October 1971, respectively.

16. According to Norwood in a letter to the author, 14 February 1972.

17. Willie, in a letter to Bill Telford, 14 February 1972.

18. Willie, in a letter to Telford, 22 December 1972.

19. So he reported in a letter to Harry Smith, 31 May 1974.

20. So Willie reported in an interview with Charles Gillies of *GH*, 8 March 1974.

21. So he wrote in a letter to Telford, 22 December 1973.

22. So Willie described it in a letter to Telford, 17 July 1973.

23. *ToF*, 1.

24. *GH*, 8 March 1974.

25. *The Scottish Daily Express*, 8 March 1974.

26. *The Daily Express*, 9 March 1974.

27. *GH*, 8 March 1974.

28. *The Outlook*, July 1974.

29. As he put it in a letter to Telford, 4 October 1974.

30. Curran, in a letter to the author, 18 February 1980.

31. Willie, in a letter to Curran, 23 August 1974.

32. Honeyman, in a private conversation with the author, January 1978. (Shortly after this I commissioned Dr. John Gibson of New College, Edinburgh, to proceed with the quite different *Daily Study Bible: Old Testament*.)

33. Willie, in a letter to Telford, 13 October 1975.

34. *GH*, 8 March 1974.

35. *BW*, 3 July 1969.

36. For another account of this event, see Martin's essay "Barclay's Humanity and Humility," in *William Barclay: The Plain Uncommon Man*, 63–65. Archie Maynard kindly loaned me a tape recording of the whole proceedings, from which this account is taken.

37. Willie used the money to establish the Barclay Lectureship in Communication of the Christian Gospel, although the gift was insufficient to fund the lectureship fully and had to be supplemented by the proceeds from a Barclay Testimonial Fund organized by Stanley Munro and sponsored by Ronald Falconer and others. By August 1975 £1453 had been raised (£282 of which—virtually one fifth—had come from Australia), and in 1978 the Saint Andrew Press contributed £2500. The first lecturer was the highly acclaimed author Bishop David Sheppard of Liverpool, himself a man of extraordinary sympathies for ordinary people.

38. That being Lightfoot's *History and Interpretation* (1935). Norman Perrin makes much of this anticipation in his excellent introduction, *What Is Redaction Criticism?* (see especially page 21 therein).

39. *The Gospels and Acts* (1976), 1: 278.

40. Willie, in a letter to Mulkern, 18 June 1971.

41. *ExpT*, 57 (1946): 301–4.

42. Greene, *A Sort of Life*, 9.

43. Willie, in a letter to Mulkern, 3 January 1972.

44. Willie, in a letter to Mulkern, 22 June 1972.

45. Willie, in a letter to Mulkern, 28 November 1972.

46. Willie, in a letter to Mulkern, 9 March 1973.

47. Willie, in a letter to Mulkern, 21 June 1973.

48. Alexander, in a letter to Mulkern, 23 July 1973.

49. Willie, quoted by Malcolm Mackay in his essay "A Late and Vital Friendship," in *William Barclay: The Plain Uncommon Man,* 145.

50. Willie, in a letter to Frazier, 30 January 1974.

51. *ToF,* 2.

52. Willie, in a letter to Mulkern, 12 February 1974.

53. *ToF,* 106.

54. Willie, in a letter to Mulkern, 15 May 1974.

55. *ToF,* 18.

56. Willie, in a letter to Mulkern, 10 October 1974.

57. *DSB: Romans,* 2d ed., 1.

58. *ToF,* 1.

59. It is very curious that this element of prayer—"without which [he] could not live"—should be omitted from the second formulation, but such was his mental state.

60. Omission of this point in the earlier formulation serves to emphasize the changes in Willie's views concerning the church and the encroachment of radicalism in those views, as is indicated by his preparedness to conceive of such things as a "Church of the air." But the church remained!

61. *ToF,* 29.

62. *ToF,* 35.

63. *ToF,* 28–29.

64. Ronnie Falconer provides this account of the incident in *The Kilt beneath the Cassock,* 179.

65. *ToF,* 34–35.

66. *The Plain Man Looks at the Apostles' Creed,* 27.

67. *ToF,* 47.

68. *ToF,* 48.

69. *ExpT,* 59 (1947): 48–49.

70. *ToF,* 49.

71. *The Gospels and Acts,* 2: 223–24.

72. *DSB: The Gospel of John,* 2d ed., 1: 26, 36–37.

73. *New Testament Studies,* 15–16. Italics his.

74. Although Oriental in origin, the denigration of the physical had permeated some aspects of Greek thought that Willie tended to overemphasize. Willie's own doctrine of man is not beyond criticism in its own right, however, resting as it does on a crude tripartite understanding rather than the biblical concept of man as a psychophysical unity.

75. *ToF,* 121.

CHAPTER TWENTY

1. *ToF,* 109.

2. See Alexander's essay "Portrait of a Scholar and Colleague," in *William Barclay: The Plain Uncommon Man,* ed. R. D. Kernohan, 114. Alexander writes specifically here of Willie's being unperturbed by such criticisms as that he had engaged in "some glaring logical fallacy," but however well he rode out these criticisms it is nonetheless the case that he did feel their cutting edge. He lived for his work, and to be criticized for it was to be criticized very personally—hence his emotional reaction to the appointing procedure for his professorship, which his former colleague has so vividly described. Professor Bruce concurs: "the disparagement he suffered from some fellow-academics was more wounding" (in a letter to the author, 11 December 1982).

3. Clement, in a letter to the author, 25 February 1980. Willie frequently volunteered such information about those preachers he *admired,* however—such as Gossip and Jeffrey.

4. Stewart, in a letter to Willie, 4 September 1974.

5. Willie, in a letter to Harris, 8 September 1975.

6. Willie, in a letter to William Telford, 4 October 1974.
7. Willie, in a letter to Anderson, 25 November 1974.
8. Willie, in a letter to Snowden, 16 December 1974.
9. Willie, in a letter to Maben, 4 February 1975.
10. Willie, in a letter to Smith, 16 February 1975.
11. *More Prayers for the Plain Man,* 7.
12. *The Character of God,* 23ff.
13. Willie, in an interview reprinted in *The Upper Room* (1975), 9. We should beware of stereotyping "Highland evangelicalism" as Duncan would appear to do here. Willie's weak reply undoubtedly resulted from his Parkinsonism, which was affecting him significantly at this time. We should bear in mind that his earlier understanding stood much closer to that of P. Carnegie Simpson: "the genius of true Highland religion—devout towards God, tender towards Christ, sensitive towards sin, wistful towards the unseen" (*The Life of Principal Rainy,* 1: 452) than did this latter-day exaggeration.
14. Kate, in a letter to Williams, 4 May 1975.
15. It was by 1975 circulating over half a billion copies of this reader in more than forty languages. Willie's one and only contribution to it appeared on 8 April 1975—a characteristic piece urging social awareness.
16. Willie, in an interview in *The Sunday Post,* 4 January 1976.
17. Willie, in a letter to Doubleday, 4 August 1975.
18. According to Willie, in a letter to Braidwood, 24 October 1975.
19. *Communicating the Gospel,* 12.
20. Willie, in a letter to Telford, 3 June 1975.
21. Willie, in a letter to Paterson, 11 June 1975.
22. Willie, in a letter to Bailey, 18 September 1975.
23. Willie, in letters to Paterson of 22 December 1975 and 17 and 18 March 1976.
24. Willie, in a letter to Anderson, 13 May 1977.
25. Willie, in a letter to Bailey, 11 October 1977.
26. Willie, in a letter to Braidwood, 24 October 1975.
27. *Christian Weekly Newspapers,* 27 February 1976.
28. See McKay's essay "Barclay among the Scholars," in *William Barclay: The Plain Uncommon Man,* 75.
29. Falconer's essay also appears in slightly altered forms in both his autobiography, *The Kilt beneath My Cassock* (as Chapter 16, "William Barclay: Man for the Common Man"), and in *William Barclay: The Plain Uncommon Man* (as Chapter 8, "Barclay as Broadcaster").
30. In *The Guardian,* 3 March 1976.
31. Willie, in a letter to Snowden, 4 March 1976.
32. In *GH,* 24 April 1976.
33. Willie, in a letter to Anderson, 10 June 1975.
34. In a letter dated 30 December 1976.
35. Willie, quoted in an obituary in *The Bookseller,* 4 February 1978.
36. So Willie reported in a letter to Harry Stevenson, 24 January 1977.
37. Willie, in a letter to Telford, 5 April 1977.
38. *Prayers for Help and Healing,* 57.
39. Willie, in a letter to Strachan, 25 October 1977.
40. Willie, in a letter to Fred Bailey, 8 July 1977.
41. In a letter in Telford, 20 December 1977.
42. Willie, in a letter to Catriona Kidd, 29 August 1977.
43. Willie, in a letter to Anderson, 4 October 1977.
44. *And Jesus Said,* 122.
45. Willie, in a letter to Mrs. Innes, 1 November 1977.
46. Willie, in a letter to Bailey, 14 November 1977.
47. Kate, in a letter to the Braidwoods, 30 November 1977.
48. *ToF,* 115.
49. *ToF,* 67.
50. Willie, in a letter to the Braidwoods, 5 December 1977.
51. Willie, in a letter to Miller, 15 December 1977.

52. Willie, in a letter to Fearon, 20 December 1977.
53. Willie, in a letter to Bersch, 12 January 1978.
54. Ronnie, quoted in *The Glasgow Evening News,* 24 January 1978.
55. *Ambassador for Christ,* 140.
56. *ToF,* 65.

Index of Personal Names

Subject Index